GRANITE CITY PUBLIC LIBRARY
0 00 04 0117741 5
D0081035

5th Edition

THE PRESS AND AMERICA

An Interpretive History of the Mass Media

EDWIN EMERY

Professor of Journalism and Mass Communication
University of Minnesota

MICHAEL EMERY

Professor of Journalism
California State University, Northridge

Discarded
By The
Mile Regional Library District

85-4232

Prentice-Hall, Inc., Englewood Cliffs, New Jersey 07632

Library of Congress Cataloging in Publication Data

Emery, Edwin.
The press and America.

Includes bibliographies and index.
1. Press—United States. 2. American newspapers.
I. Emery, Michael C. II. Title.
PN4855.E6 1984 071'.3 83-26852
ISBN 0-13-697988-2

Editorial/production supervision
and interior design: Virginia McCarthy
Cover design: Ben Santora
Page layout: Gail Collis
Manufacturing buyer: Harry P. Baisley

© 1984, 1978, 1972, 1962, 1954 by Prentice-Hall, Inc.,
Englewood Cliffs, New Jersey 07632

All rights reserved. No part of this book may be
reproduced, in any form or by any means,
without permission in writing from the publisher.

Printed in the United States of America

10 9 8 7 6 5 4 3 2 1

ISBN 0-13-697988-2

Prentice-Hall International, Inc., *London*
Prentice-Hall of Australia Pty. Limited, *Sydney*
Editora Prentice-Hall do Brasil, Ltda., *Rio de Janeiro*
Prentice-Hall Canada Inc., *Toronto*
Prentice-Hall of India Private Limited, *New Delhi*
Prentice-Hall of Japan, Inc., *Tokyo*
Prentice-Hall of Southeast Asia Pte. Ltd., *Singapore*
Whitehall Books Limited, *Wellington, New Zealand*

071.3
EME

Contents

Foreword

Journalism history is the story of humanity's long struggle to communicate with each other—to dig out and interpret news and to offer intelligent opinion and entertaining thoughts in the marketplace of ideas. Part of the story has as its theme the continuing efforts by men and women to break down the barriers that have been erected to prevent the flow of information and ideas, upon which public opinion is so largely dependent. Another aspect of the story is concerned with the means, or media, by which essential news, opinion, and other desired information reached the public, from the days of the handwritten "newes letter" to the printed page, radio, and television. Just as important to this story are the heroes and villains, as well as the bit actors, who made the world of communication what it is today. Finally, all of this becomes truly meaningful when the development of America's journalistic tradition is related to the progress of its people.

The title, *The Press and America,* was conceived in 1949, when the newspaper industry was dominant, there was only a smattering of interest in the history of radio, and television was in its infancy. There have been many changes in media roles and communications technologies since then, as demonstrated by the extensive revisions of this book through five editions. For reasons of tradition and continuity, our title remains the same, reflecting as always the emphasis placed upon the correlation of journalism history with political, social, economic, and cultural trends. The same interpretation is offered when dealing with other media industries and the emerging technologies. In this interaction, the media have had their influence upon the course taken by the United States. Conversely, the conditions and influences present in each historical era have cumulatively determined the shape and character of the media. Within this framework emerges the special story of the men and women of journalism and of the institutions and traditions they created. Thus, the story ranges from newspaper editor James Franklin to television reporter Dan Rather; from newspaper publisher Mary Katherine Goddard to Katharine Graham; from opinion-molder Horace Greeley to Edward R. Murrow; from radical publicist Sam Adams to I.F. Stone; from talented writer Tom Paine to Tom Wolfe.

In the opening pages there is a greatly expanded treatment of the ancient roots of communications history. This leads to the traditional account of European beginnings and English influences and also to the first of several new sections relating the Spanish contribution to American journalism. When discussing the long time-span ending with the Civil War, the primary concern is with an exposition of the principles upon which the American Fourth Estate was founded.

The entire second half of the book has been rewritten and reorganized to continue the story—decade by decade—and to include extensive examinations of media other than newspapers: magazines, book publishing, advertising, public relations, photojournalism's documentaries, newsreels, motion pictures, radio, and television. Thus in the 1920s, the stories of radio's David Sarnoff and Amos 'n' Andy, of Hollywood's David Wark Griffith and Charlie Chaplin, of the newspapers' Adolph Ochs and the *New York Daily News,* of the *Reader's Digest* and the *New Yorker,* and of the rise of advertising agencies and public relations counsels become interrelated. With words and pictures the book surveys landmark events in communications history, probing significant issues, personalities, and media organizations, all the while tracing how major events in American history were covered by reporters, editors, and broadcasters and how other writers, advertisers, and advocates influenced American life.

The electronic media have been given broadened emphasis in this edition, reflecting the impact of first radio and then television on news and politics, but also the entertainment area. A hard look is given to television's performance during the Vietnam War and the Watergate era and to its controversial social role from the 1960s to the 1980s. There is expanded coverage of women journalists, minorities, alternative journalism, investigative reporting, and media law. Closing chapters review in detail the character and impact of the "new technology" for print and electronic media, the economic power of major media organizations, the internationalizing of both media impact and media technologies, and pressures from the Third World for changes in the international news flow. Chapter bibliographies have been expanded and updated. Many illustrations have been added, reflecting in particular the substantial changes and expanded coverage of this edition.

ACKNOWLEDGMENTS

Thanks are due to many persons who have aided in this venture during four decades. For this edition, criticisms and suggestions for change were elicited from Professors William H. Taft of the University of Missouri, Sam Kuczun of the University of Colorado, Ted C. Smythe of California State University, Fullerton, Maurine Beasley of the University of Maryland, and Calder M. Pickett of the University of Kansas. Making information available generously were journalism professors Félix Gutiérrez of the University of Southern California, Betty Winfield of Washington State University, and Nancy Roberts of the University of Minnesota. Of great assistance was research compiled by Professor Emeritus Robert W. Desmond of the University of California and research findings organized and edited for *Journalism History* by Professor Tom Reilly, California State University, Northridge. Others whose research or comments were of special aid included journalism professors David Nord, Indiana; Marion Marzolf, Michigan; Paul Peterson, Ohio State; Sharon and James Murphy, Southern Illinois; Warren Francke, Nebraska at Omaha; and Robert Drechsel, Wisconsin. Our special thanks go to Steve Dalphin, journalism/mass communication editor, and Virginia McCarthy, production editor, of Prentice-Hall, Inc.

The debts for aid with earlier editions can be acknowledged here only in part. A very substantial acknowledgment is due Henry Ladd Smith, then at Wisconsin, co-author of the first edition, particularly for the graceful writing in the early chapters. Co-author Michael Emery began his association with the book during the third edition revision. Manuscript critics have been Professors Ralph D. Casey, Minnesota; Frederick B. Marbut, Pennsylvania State; Kenneth E. Olson and Richard A. Schwarzlose, Northwestern; William H.

Taft, Missouri; and Bruce H. Westley, Kentucky. Professor Harold L. Nelson of Wisconsin has given many suggestions for text revisions, particularly in the colonial period, and gave invaluable assistance during the preparation of the original index. Journalism bibliographers upon whom we have most depended are Warren C. Price, Oregon; Calder M. Pickett, Kansas; Eleanor Blum, Illinois; and Christopher H. Sterling, editor of *Communication Booknotes,* George Washington University.

Mention must be made of past aid by journalism professors Ralph O. Nafziger and William A. Hachten, Wisconsin; Quintus C. Wilson, Northern Illinois; Roland E. Wolseley, Syracuse; Paul Jess, Kansas; Henry G. La Brie, III, Boston; John D. Stevens, Michigan; William E. Ames, Washington; Donald L. Shaw, North Carolina; Randall L. Murray, California Polytechnic, San Luis Obispo; Ralph E. Kliesch, Ohio; Joseph P. McKerns, Southern Illinois; Harvey Saalberg, Angelo State; Robert V. Hudson, Michigan State; Richard B. Kielbowicz, Iowa State; and R. Smith Schuneman, Raymond B. Nixon, Edwin H. Ford, J. Edward Gerald, and Donald M. Gillmor, Minnesota. We also wish to thank the many others whose comments have aided and encouraged us. To Mary M. Emery and Suzanne Steiner Emery, we express appreciation for assistance and patient support.

Finally, we acknowledge our debt to the many scholars and writers whose contributions to media history are listed in the footnotes and bibliographies.

EDWIN EMERY
MICHAEL EMERY
December 1983

The first edition of *The Press and America* won the coveted Sigma Delta Chi national research award, the highest in the field of journalism.

Edwin Emery, Ph.D., is Professor of Journalism and Mass Communication at the University of Minnesota. He has been president of the Association for Education in Journalism and editor of its research journal, *Journalism Quarterly.* Author or editor of ten books, Professor Emery also won the Sigma Delta Chi national award for his *History of the American Newspaper Publishers Association,* the AEJ Bleyer award for historical research, and a Guggenheim Fellowship. He is a former United Press bureau manager.

Michael Emery, Ph.D., is Professor of Journalism at California State University, Northridge. He is coeditor of *Readings in Mass Communication,* which won a Kappa Tau Alpha special research award, and of *America's Front Page News, 1690–1970.* He has been associate editor of *Journalism History,* chair of the West Coast Journalism Historians Conference, and consultant to the Newspapers in America exhibit at Chicago's Museum of Science and Industry. He was a United Press International correspondent.

The Daily Courant.

Wednesday, March 11. 1702.

From the Harlem Courant, Dated March 18. N. S.

Naples, Feb. 22.

ON Wednesday last, our New Viceroy, the Duke of Escalona, arriv'd here with a Squadron of the Galleys of Sicily. He made his Entrance drest in a French habit; and to give us the greater Hopes of the King's coming hither, went to Lodge in one of the little Palaces, leaving the Royal one for his Majesty. The Marquis of Grigni is also arriv'd here with a Regiment of French.

Rome, Feb. 25. In a Military Congregation of State that was held here, it was Resolv'd to draw a Line from Ascoli to the Borders of the Ecclesiastical State, thereby to hinder the Incursions of the Transalpine Troops. Orders are sent to Civita Vecchia to fit out the Galleys, and to strengthen the Garrison of that Place. Signior Casali is made Governor of Perugia. The Marquis del Vasto, and the Prince de Caserta continue still in the Imperial Embassador's Palace; where his Excellency has a Guard of 50 Men every Night in Arms. The King of Portugal has desir'd the Arch-Bishoprick of Lisbon, vacant by the Death of Cardinal Sousa, for the Infante his second Son, who is about 11 Years old.

Vienna, Mar. 4. Orders are sent to the 4 Regiments of Foot, the 2 of Cuirassiers, and to that of Dragoons, which are broke up from Hungary, and are on their way to Italy, and which consist of about 14 or 15000 Men, to hasten their March thither with all Expedition. The 6 new Regiments of Hussars that are now raising, are in so great a forwardness, that they will be compleat, and in a Condition to march by the middle of May. Prince Lewis of Baden has written to Court, to excuse himself from coming thither, his Presence being so very necessary, and so much desir'd on the Upper-Rhine.

Francfort, Mar. 12. The Marquiss d' Uxelles is come to Strasburg, and is to draw together a Body of some Regiments of Horse and Foot from the Garisons of Alsace; but will not lessen those of Strasburg and Landau, which are already very weak. On the other hand, the Troops of His Imperial Majesty, and his Allies, are going to form a Body near Germeshein in the Palatinate, of which Place, as well as of the Lines at Spires, Prince Lewis of Baden is expected to take a View, in three or four days. The English and Dutch Ministers, the Count of Frise, and the Baron Vander Meer; and likewise the Imperial Envoy Count Lowenstein, are gone to Nordlingen, and it is hop'd that in a short time we shall hear from thence of some favourable Resolutions for the Security of the Empire.

Liege, Mar. 14. The French have taken the Cannon de Longie, who was Secretary to the Dean de Mean, out of our Castle, where he has been for some time a Prisoner, and have deliver'd him to the Provost of Maubeuge, who has carry'd him from hence, but we do not know whither.

Paris, Mar. 13. Our Letters from Italy say, That most of our Reinforcements were Landed there; that the Imperial and Ecclesiastical Troops seem to live very peaceably with one another in the Country of Parma, and that the Duke of Vendome, as he was visiting several Posts, was within 100 Paces of falling into the Hands of the Germans. The Duke of Chartres, the Prince of Conti, and several other Princes of the Blood, are to make the Campaign in Flanders under the Duke of Burgundy; and the Duke of Maine is to Command upon the Rhine.

From the Amsterdam Courant, Dated Mar. 18.

Rome, Feb. 25. We are taking here all possible Precautions for the Security of the Ecclesiastical State in this present Conjuncture, and have desir'd to raise 3000 Men in the Cantons of Switzerland. The Pope has appointed the Duke of Berwick to be his Lieutenant-General, and he is to Command 6000 Men on the Frontiers of Naples: He has also settled upon him a Pension of 6000 Crowns a year during Life.

From the Paris Gazette, Dated Mar. 18. 1702.

Naples, Febr. 17. 600 French Soldiers are arrived here, and are expected to be follow'd by 3400 more. A Courier that came hither on the 14th. has brought Letters by which we are assur'd that the King of Spain designs to be here towards the end of March; and accordingly Orders are given to make the necessary Preparations against his Arrival. The two Troops of Horse that were Commanded to the Abruzzo are posted at Pescara with a Body of Spanish Foot, and others in the Fort of Montorio.

Paris, March. 18. We have Advice from Toulon of the 5th instant, that the Wind having long stood favourable, 22000 Men were already sail'd for Italy, that 2500 more were Embarking, and that by the 15th it was hoped they might all get thither. The Count d' Estrees arriv'd there on the Third instant, and set all hands at work to fit out the Squadron of 9 Men of War and some Fregats, that are appointed to carry the King of Spain to Naples. His Catholick Majesty will go on Board the *Thunderer*, of 110 Guns.

We have Advice by an Express from Rome of the 18th of February, That notwithstanding the pressing Instances of the Imperial Embassadour, the Pope had Condemn'd the Marquis del Vasto to lose his Head and his Estate to be confiscated, for not appearing to Answer the Charge against him of Publickly Scandalizing Cardinal Janson.

ADVERTISEMENT.

IT will be found from the Foreign Prints, which from time to time, as Occasion offers, will be mention'd in this Paper, that the Author has taken Care to be duly furnish'd with all that comes from Abroad in any Language. And for an Assurance that he will not, under Pretence of having Private Intelligence, impose any Additions of feign'd Circumstances to an Action, but give his Extracts fairly and Impartially; at the beginning of each Article he will quote the Foreign Paper from whence 'tis taken, that the Publick, seeing from what Country a piece of News comes with the Allowance of that Government, may be better able to Judge of the Credibility and Fairness of the Relation: Nor will he take upon him to give any Comments or Conjectures of his own, but will relate only Matter of Fact, supposing other People to have Sense enough to make Reflections for themselves.

This Courant (as the Title shews) will be Publish'd Daily: being design'd to give all the Material News as soon as every Post arrives: and is confin'd to half the Compass, to save the Publick at least half the Impertinences, of ordinary News-Papers.

LONDON. Sold by *E. Mallet*, next Door to the *King's-Arms* Tavern at *Fleet-Bridge*.

Facsimile of the first daily newspaper in the English language.

1

The Heritage of the American Press

Give me but the liberty of the press and I will give to the minister a venal House of Peers . . . and servile House of Commons . . . I will give him all the power that place can confer upon him to purchase up submission and overawe resistance—And yet, armed with liberty of the press . . . I will attack the mighty fabric he has reared . . . and bury it amidst the ruins of the abuses it was meant to shelter.

—Richard Brinsley Sheridan

The modern press system is the gift of no one nation. It is only the current stage in the evolution of communications efforts, spanning all continents and at least 10,000 years. A series of developments in printing and writing, beginning in the Middle East and Asia, slowly spreading to Europe and finally to America, led to today's marvelous linkage of reporting talent, computers, high-speed color presses, and satellites. Each historic breakthrough was motivated by the need to keep track of trading records, communicate to far-flung empires, spread religious ideas, or leave behind artistic records of accomplishments. The story of American journalism would not be complete without tracing a number of these notable achievements.

THE DEVELOPMENT OF PRINTING

The first systematic attempt to collect and distribute information was *Acta Diurna,* the hand-lettered "daily gazette" posted regularly in the Roman Forum between 59 B.C. and A.D. 222. Prepared by *actuarii,* the earliest known news writers, the reports told of both senate votes and popular events. These were in turn copied by scribes and carried throughout the empire. This enlightened program, enjoyed by Romans who learned of government decrees, legal notices, and even the latest gladiatorial results, had been preceded by many attempts to make the storage and distribution of information convenient. Around 3500 B.C. the Sumerians of the Middle East devised a system of preserving records by inscribing signs and symbols in wet clay tablets using cylinder seals and then baking them in the sun. They also devised a cuneiform system of writing, using bones to mark signs in wet clay. Stamp seals, engraved objects used to denote ownership, had been common 1000 years earlier. Pictographs or ideographs—drawings of animals, commonly recognized objects, and humans—were popular in the Mediterranean area, China, India, what is now Mexico, and Egypt, where they became known as hieroglyphs. There is evidence that a system of movable type was devised in Asia Minor prior to 1700 B.C., the date of a flat clay disk found in Crete. The disk contained forty-five different signs that had been carved on individual pieces of type and then pressed onto the clay.

Elaborate carvings in stone and wood became common in the eastern Mediterranean around 1500 B.C., roughly the same time that the Phoenicians, successful traders and bankers for 1000 years, introduced symbols for sounds and created an alphabet. Colored fluids were used to outline the "letters" of the alphabet and to produce the pictographs. Around 500 B.C. the Egyptians used reeds found along the Nile River to make papyrus. Scribes using brushes or quills could then "write" their hieroglyphics and sheets of papyrus could be joined to make a scroll. For several hundred years the scroll collections were housed at the centers of learning. Whereas the clay and stone tablets were heavy and difficult to store or carry any distance, the papyrus sheets and scrolls allowed information to be shared easily.

Vellum was used as another writing surface beginning about A.D. 100. The parchment, made from animal skins, was used in the Greek and Roman empires for special manuscripts or scrolls. At this same time the Chinese invented a smooth, white paper from wood pulp and fibres and also discovered a way to transfer an ideograph from stone to paper after inking the surface. These "rubbings" were joined together to produce beautifully colored scrolls.

Wang Chieh published what is considered the world's oldest preserved book from wood blocks in A.D. 868. Large blocks could be carved so that one sheet of paper, printed on both sides, could be folded into thirty-two pages of booksize. Feng Tao printed the Confucian classics between 932 and 953 and in about 1045 the artisan Pi Sheng was inspired to devise a set of movable clay carvings—a sort of earthenware "type"—that could be reused. This process was also used in Persia and Egypt. Wood-block printing was introduced to Europe when Marco Polo returned from China in 1295. It is difficult to establish Chinese influence, but block printing became popular in Europe during the fourteenth and fifteenth centuries. Its most striking use came in the production of illustrated books. Meanwhile, in Asia, the innovations continued; movable type cast in copper or bronze was used in Korea in 1241.

Johann Gutenberg of Mainz and Strasbourg is credited with introducing printing from movable type in Europe. Beginning about 1450, with the help of his partner Johann Fust, Gutenberg used a mixture of lead and other metals to cast individual letters in reverse and high relief. Apparently he did not realize this was being done in China. After printing several books, he began to reproduce the Bible in 1456. However, unable to pay his loans to Fust, Gutenberg lost his shop the following year and Fust finished the printing of the Bible in 1460.

William Caxton imported the first printing press into England in 1476 and by 1490 at least one printing press was operating in every major European city.

EARLY WRITINGS

The longest continuing information program on record was in China, where, beginning about A.D. 750, the imperial court published semiannual reports on the condition of the people, in addition to monthly bulletins and calendars. Known as *Tching-pao,* these bulletins were printed weekly beginning around 1360; by 1830 they had become daily publications. Known later as the *Peking Gazette,* the reports lasted until the end of the empire in 1911. Another publication for provincial governors appeared in about 950 and also lasted until 1911.

The preservation of history was a goal of writers from the earliest of times. In the opening pages of his monumental five-volume history of world news reporting, the press historian Dr. Robert W. Desmond suggests that the first writers were performing functions "akin to those performed later by literary men and by journalists of the printed media. They were writing of their own times and people; they were gathering and recording information. . . ."[1] Desmond included here the Greek epic poet Homer and his *Illiad* and *Odyssey,* the "father of history" Herodotus, who traveled throughout the Middle East, and Demosthenes of Athens, who often wrote speeches for others and was something of a public relations expert. Confucius dealt with his times and contemporaries in China, Thucydides wrote eight volumes on the history of the war between Athens and Sparta, Julius Caesar reported the Roman wars in his *Commentaries,* and Plutarch turned out numerous "profiles" of prominent leaders. The reports on the life of Jesus Christ, the *New Testament,* and the letters of the traveling Paul have influenced untold millions. Copies of the *Acta Diurna* were kept for the public in a special building, just as scrolls were preserved in many lands.

Marco Polo's detailed, hand-written accounts of his two trips to China, totaling 33 years, were recopied and distributed for more than 250 years. Finally *The Travels of Marco Polo* was one of the first books to appear in Europe, in 1559. A history of the entire world was written by Mongol historian Rashid al-Din in the early fourteenth century. At least three volumes appeared in Arabic, dealing with the conquests of Genghis Khan, the prophet Muhammad, the history of China, the history of India including the life of Buddha, Old Testament history, and reflections on other peoples whom Mongols encountered during their thirteenth century invasions. A lavishly illustrated partial manuscript of the second volume was sold in London for $2 million in 1980, after having been lost for nearly 500 years.[2]

THE SPANISH INFLUENCE IN AMERICAN JOURNALISM

The oldest known preserved report of a current event describes a 1541 storm and earthquake in Guatemala. Written by a notary public named Juan Rodríquez, the eight-page booklet was printed in Mexico City by Juan Pablos, an Italian who was the representative in New Spain of Juan Cromberger, the owner

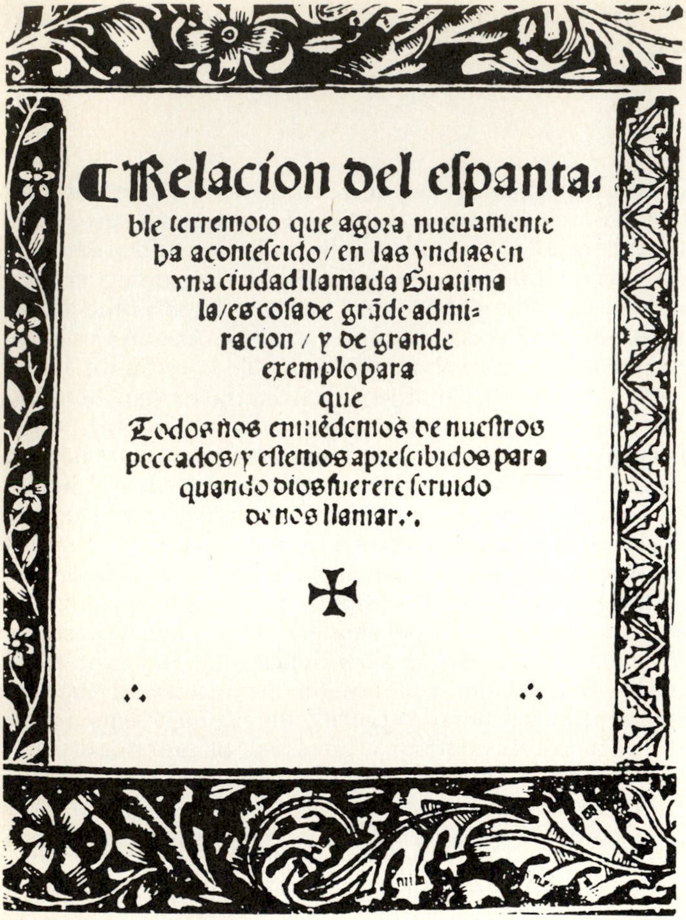

Relacion del espanta-
ble terremoto que agora nueuamente
ha acontescido / en las yndias en
vna ciudad llamada Guatima
la / es cosa de grãde admi-
racion / y de grande
exemplo para
que
Todos nos enmẽdemos de nuestros
peccados / y estemos apercibidos para
quando dios fuere seruido
de nos llamar.

Oldest known preserved news report, printed in 1541 in Mexico City.
Journalism History

of a well-known Seville printing house. Entering the world of the highly developed Aztecs, Incas, and Mayans, the Spanish brought the first press to the Americas in 1534. Bishop Juan de Zumárraga delivered the press to Mexico City, and Esteban Martín was said to have done the first printing. But surviving examples are of Pablos' work, dating from 1539 when he, pressman Gil Barbero, and a black slave turned out their first pages.[3] A translation of the "headline" on the cover sheet of the storm report of 1541 reads:

> Report of the Terrifying Earthquake Which Has Reoccurred In the Indies in a City Called Guatemala.
>
> It is an event of great astonishment and great example so that we all repent from our sins and so that we will be ready when God call us.
>
> Summary of what happened in Guatemala:

This first printing was of high quality. Elaborate woodcuts and ornate borders and initial letters were used almost from the beginning.

A second center for printing in the Americas was Lima, where a press was established in 1583. The first printer there was Antonio Ricardo, who printed a catechism in Indian languages the following year. Much of the early work was the bilingual printing of religious materials, many of them colorfully decorated. By 1600 at least 174 books, possibly more, had been published. Primitive newssheets called *hojas volantes* (flying pages or bulletins) or *noticias, relaciones, sucesos, relatos* also appeared in Spain. Some were printed in the Americas in the late sixteenth century; one, printed by Ricardo in Lima in 1594, was preserved. It gave an account of the capture of the English pirate "John of Aquines," son of John Hawkins, off the coast of Peru.[4]

Although the development of a regular periodical press was delayed in the Americas by Spanish censorship and the high cost of printing news for a small group of literate persons, publications of approximately monthly frequency began to appear in Lima in 1618. These *noticiarios* reflected the excitement over European news, and some of them were copies of European newssheets. Scholars have not determined that any real periodicals came into being during the seventeenth century, although a *Gaceta de Mexico* was published irregularly in 1667 and four volumes of *Mercurio Volante* were published by Carlos de Siguenzay Gongora in 1693, detailing the military campaigns in Mexico. It appears that the first regular periodical was Mexico's *Gaceta de Mexico,* which began carrying both local and foreign news in 1722. It was published monthly by a church official, Juan Ignacio Castorena Ursua y Goyeneche, who included items from California, Manila, Havana, Guatemala, Acapulco, and other cities of New Spain. In his first issue Castorena asked governors and church officials in other cities to send him items "worthy of the public light and for good example."[5] Castorena's paper lasted 6 months because he was transferred, but it was revived in 1728 and lasted until about 1739. The second periodical appeared in Guatemala in 1729, *Gazeta de Goatemala,* and the third in Lima, *Gaceta de Lima* in 1744. Although all three publications were short-lived, they provided the foundation for the strong Spanish-language press of the future.

EUROPEAN NEWS REPORTING

The oldest known and preserved copies of a titled, regularly published newssheet were produced in Germany in 1609, but the existing copies do not indicate the city of publication, the printer, or the publisher. From an analysis of paper, type, printing technique, political content, and religious coloring, experts deduced that the site of this earliest known newspaper had to be in northern Germany. According to Dr. Ralph O. Nafziger, who made a lengthy study of the evidence produced by German researchers, the 1609 *Aviso* appeared in Wolfenbüttel rather than in nearby Bremen as was thought earlier. This was a weekly publication, as were the *Relation* of Strasbourg and the *Avisa Relation oder Zeitung* of Augsburg. Both of these publications also date from 1609.[6]

Between 1610 and 1661, titled newssheets appeared in Switzerland, England, Spain, Austria, Belgium, Holland, Sweden, Italy, Poland, and elsewhere.

Amsterdam printers issued untitled *corantos* for readers in both Holland and England as early as 1603. From around 1620 to 1631 a French version was sent to Paris. This ended when the first titled weekly appeared in Paris in that year. Desmond's research indicates that European printers produced untitled, small "flysheets" from wood blocks as early as 1415. These sheets, printed on one side only, were sold to the public in the Germanic states and Central Europe. Reportedly an account of the Battle of Agincourt in 1415 and a letter from Christopher Columbus in 1493 were published.[7] Newsletters were also common, the most famous being the Fugger newsletters from the Fugger banking house in Augsburg. Between 1568 and 1604 a general readership learned of such historic events as the execution of Mary Queen of Scots, the defeat of the Spanish Armada, and early voyages of Sir Francis Drake. A court newspaper begun in Stockholm in 1645 still appears and is the world's oldest known continuously published newspaper.[8] A German newspaper begun in 1616, the *Frankfurter Oberpostamtzeitung* (renamed the *Postzeitung*), later became the first daily newspaper in the world.[9] It continued until 1866, when it merged with the famed *Frankfurter Zeitung.* Minute-by-minute reports of the English Parliament were published daily for four consecutive weeks in 1660 by Oliver Williams in his *Perfect Diurnal,* a small booklet.

THE PRESS DEVELOPS IN ENGLAND

The point to all this is that England had no special claim as the home of the modern press, even though it advanced beyond all other countries journalistically. In England, as in other lands, news was exchanged long before there was even the most primitive form of newspaper. One of the great attractions at the country fairs of the Middle Ages was the opportunity to exchange gossip and information. Country folk and gentry traveled annually to Bartholomew, Donnybrook, or Stourbridge as much to swap news as to buy yearly supplies of staples. Newspapers did not create news; news created newspapers.

It has been said that a true newspaper must meet the following qualifications:

> (1) it must be published at least once a week; (2) it must be produced by mechanical means (to distinguish it from the handwritten "newes letters"); (3) it must be available to anyone willing to pay the price, regardless of class or special interests; (4) it must print anything of interest to a general public, as contrasted with some of the religious and business publications; (5) it must have an appeal to a public of ordinary literary skill; (6) it must be timely, or at least relatively so in light of technical development; and (7) it must have stability.[10]

To produce a publication of this type, there was some incentive for gathering and processing information of interest to the general public—news. News thereupon became a commodity, like food or merchandise, produced for profit to meet a demand. Up to about 1500, the world *Tydings* usually described reports of current events. The word *news* was coined to differentiate between the casual dissemination of information and the deliberate attempt to gather and process the latest intelligence.

It is significant that the newspaper first flourished in areas where authority was weak, as in Germany, which at that time was divided into a patchwork of small principalities; or where rulers were more tolerant, as in the low countries. This explains why the development of the press lagged in England. True, William Caxton set up the first press in England in 1476, but nearly two centuries elapsed before the country had a genuine newspaper.

Caxton learned about printing on the continent, where it had been a craft since the middle of the fifteenth century. He had been governor of a chartered association of "adventurers," or merchants interested in foreign enterprise. Caxton was a learned man, the author and translator of several volumes, and a collector of fine books. He believed that it was his mission to bring the culture of the continent to his compatriots. His king, Edward IV, encouraged these ideas. Edward had just come to power, following a long civil war that had split the country. Not until 1471 was he safely in control of his government.[11] At once he began to repair the ravages of the internal conflict. Edward was responsible for progress in law, industry, and culture. It was under such circumstances that Caxton set up his tiny press "at the Sign of the Red Pale" in the almonry of the abbey at Westminster in 1476.[12]

THE TUDOR REIGN: LICENSING

The Battle of Bosworth Field in 1485 brought a new dynasty into being. Henry Tudor, the victor, ended the long feud between the royal houses of York and Lancaster, thereby bringing the country back to the stability it so desperately needed. A Lancastrian by blood and a Yorkist by marriage, Henry emerged from the Wars of the Roses, as the civil strife was called, with powers that were eventually to make the Tudors as nearly absolute in power as English monarchs could be. The nobility, which had previously restrained the powers of the English kings, was decimated by the long years of fighting. The Tudor monarchs took full advantage of the situation. Most of them were brilliant and able administrators. Under Tudor leadership England experienced a golden age. It was not, however, conducive to the progress of the press.

Caxton enjoyed relative freedom from royal interference, mostly because he never tried to test his status. Printing was not a social force for about 50 years after its establishment in England. Under the Tudors, however, the press became a matter of kingly concern, for that strong dynasty was noted for its attempts to grasp all possible power. Henry VIII started the control of the press in 1529 with a list of prohibited books. His purpose was to set up a bulwark against the rising tide of Protestantism. The first licensing system under government control was established a year later, and by a proclamation on Christmas day 1534, Henry VIII required printers to have royal permission before setting up shop. Thus the concept of "prior restraint" became law.

During this period the powers of the Privy Council were also increased, at the expense of Parliament and the older courts but to the advantage of the crown. The Council supervised the administration of laws, regulated trade, kept an eye on the courts, and controlled the press. Beginning in 1542 the records of the Council show a continuous report of proceedings against individuals for "unfitting worddes," seditious utterances, and the like. As early as 1540 the Council made arrests for the printing of street ballads about political matters. The proclamation (ordinance) was the tool employed by the king or his Council to give legality and force to the regulation of the press. By later standards there was no legality to such royal ordinances, but they were enforced as law by the strong Tudors.[13]

Despite these repressive measures, a kind of literary black market supplied the forbidden information and entertainment. We know, for example, that Henry VIII was angered in the thirty-sixth year of his reign by accounts of a battle in Scotland. The news was peddled by London "broadsheet" vendors (a broadsheet was a paper printed specifically to describe a certain event). The king's complaint was not so much that the reports were false but that the news had been printed without his permission. Apparently, even the absolute powers of the king could not throttle the press, but the climate was not healthy for the steady growth of journalism.

THE STATIONERS COMPANY

One way to control an industry is to make it a monopoly and then to hold the directors of it responsible for abuses. The Tudors did that with the printing industry in 1557 when Queen Mary established the Stationers Company. This organization had existed since 1357 as a society of court and text writers, to which the "limners," or illustrators, were admitted after 1404. By 1500 the printers had also been admitted, but by Mary's time the word "stationer" was applied to the publishers and dealers in books, as distinct from the printers.[14] The Stationers Company was a kind of printing trust, and it made it easier for authorities to run down rebel printers not members of the elite group or sanctioned by it. Queen Elizabeth supplemented this control by her "Injunctions," which gave the religious hierarchy a measure of control over printing. Until the upheavals of the midseventeenth century the Stationers Company exerted powerful controls over the press. In 1576, for example, the Stationers adopted an order for weekly searches of London printing houses (where almost all printing was concentrated). Pairs of searchers reported on work in progress, the number of orders on hand, identity of customers, number of employees, and wages paid. This constituted an effective check on extensive bootleg printing.

THE STAR CHAMBER

The infamous Star Chamber court, originally set up to protect the public but later the symbol of repression, was another barrier to free expression during the long period preceding the appearance of the English newspaper. By edicts of the Privy Council in 1566 and the Star Chamber in 1586, the pattern of restrictions for the next hundred years was outlined. Severe penalties were prescribed for printers foolish enough to defy the authorities. Strange as it may seem, there were printers willing to run that risk. One was William Carter, who was hanged for printing pamphlets favorable to the Catholic cause. Arrested and tortured in 1580, Carter was executed in 1584.[15] Puritan rebels against the Established

Church included Hugh Singleton, Robert Waldegrave, John Stroud, and John Hodgkins. The attack on the monopoly control was led by John Wolfe, Roger Ward, William Holmes, and John Charlewood. Waldegrave was the printer of the first "Martin Marprelate" tracts, the Puritan arguments published surreptitiously against the Established Church. Hodgkins carried on when Waldegrave was hounded from the country.

The Tudor control of the press was said to be in the interest of public safety. From Henry VIII to Elizabeth I, the Crown acted on the principle that peace demanded the suppression of unwarranted dissent. On the whole the Tudors were able, and even brilliant, administrators. Sensitive to public opinion, they understood their people so well that they knew just how far to push their arbitrary rule. Ruthless and erratic as they were at times, their subjects admired them (with some exceptions, of course). Under the Tudors the country had developed great national pride. The Tudors "had the feel" of the country and more often than not were interested in the general welfare. Resistance to them was negligible, therefore, at least from the journalistic standpoint.

THE STUARTS AND TURMOIL

The upheaval came when a new dynasty came to power. James I (who was James VI of Scotland) was sincere and well-meaning, but he was never in tune with the times, or with his subjects. He was the son of the unfortunate Mary Queen of Scots, whose life had been marked by scandal and violence. As the son of Mary, James was early suspected of "Papist" sympathies in a day when that was religious jargon for treason. It was also his misfortune to succeed one of England's great rulers, Elizabeth I—"Good Queen Bess." He suffered badly in comparison with that astute and able monarch. Under the Stuarts, beginning with James, the opposing factions formed battle lines. That the press thrives in such a climate, if restraints break down, perhaps partially explains the rapid development of journalism during the seventeenth century.

During the early part of that century news became of great importance to the English people. The religious disputes, the rise of England as a maritime power, the struggles between king and Parliament, and the changing social conditions made the public more interested in events beyond its local sphere. The balladeers and broadsheet vendors could not meet the demand. Prose pamphlets were much more effective, as evidenced by the success of the Marprelate tracts, but such publications were not regular enough. The newsletter writers, or "intelligencers" as the publishers of hand-written sheets were called, were capable journalists, but the average person could not afford their products.[16] The time was ripe for a new type of publication.

FIRST ENGLISH CORANTOS

In the summer of 1621, nearly a century and a half after Caxton introduced printing to England, the very rudimentary prototypes of the modern newspaper appeared on the streets of London. These primitive newssheets were called *corantos.* They lacked the regularity that is necessary for a true newspaper, and they were too specialized in content, but they did fulfill a need.

In 1620 the English were interested in continental developments. The popular Princess Elizabeth had married Frederick, Elector of the Palatinate, in 1613. He was a Protestant, highly favored by nonconformists both on the Continent and in England. When he decided to accept the crown of Bohemia against the wishes of the Holy Roman Emperor, he precipitated the Thirty Years' War.

Printers in the Netherlands were quick to capitalize on this interest. At least twenty-five English-language corantos reporting war news were produced, nearly all in Amsterdam, by George Veseler and Broer Jonson. These single sheets, now in the British Museum, were dated December 2, 1620, to September 18, 1621. Nathaniel Butter, a bookseller, was the English distributor. Sales were so brisk that in the summer of 1621 Butter decided to do the publishing himself, pirating his news from Dutch newssheets. Thomas Archer, a printer, was probably his partner. Copies of their sheets printed in the summer of 1621 have not survived. Six similar corantos,[17] dated September 24 to October 22, have. But by that time printer Archer had run afoul of the law.

When Frederick, the newly elected king of Bohemia, led his forces to defeat in revolt against the Hapsburgs at a battle near Prague, English sentiment favored intercession by James I for his son-in-law. James could not make up his mind, however. The corantos were critical of his foreign policy, and in retaliation the king cracked down on the editors, using the old rules of the Tudors. In December, 1620, and again in July, 1621, the king issued proclamations against "the great liberty of discourse concerning matters of state." He followed this up with an order suppressing corantos, but apparently some of the printers flouted his orders, for there is a record of the Stationers Company calling up Archer for a hearing in August. He was imprisoned.

Then Nicholas Bourne entered the picture. He was a respected printer, and it is possible that Butter teamed up with him because of his prestige. Their first coranto was authorized in September, 1621, and undoubtedly bore the legend "Published With Authority" at the top of the page, as did later issues. The earliest surviving coranto of this press is dated May 23, 1622. Archer, now out of prison, was the printer. Butter was probably the editor and Bourne was the publisher, or responsible promoter. The paper was printed on one side only, and the sheet was somewhat smaller than a page of modern typewriter paper.

It was not until 1624 that the corantos began to be identified by name, thus supplying something of the continuity required of a true newspaper. The earliest known coranto published by title was *The Continuation of Our Weekly Newes,* from the office of Bourne and Butter. Because this title appeared on at least twenty-three consecutive issues, the offering marks another step in the development of the newspaper.

The earliest corantos printed nothing but foreign news. The first domestic reports can be traced back to the publication by the Westminster clerks of Parliamentary proceedings dated about 1628. Out of these accounts developed the *diurnalls*, or daily reports of local events. The *diurnalls* flourished during the struggle between king and Parliament, when it was safe to comment on local news because neither side was strong enough to take punitive measures and when both factions were seeking public support. Many of the restrictions on the press were modified by the Long Parliament, and after 1640 *diurnalls* appeared by the score. The oldest known paper of this type is John Thomas' *Diurnall Occurrences,* which first appeared November 29, 1641.

MILTON'S *AREOPAGITICA*

The interim of the first decade of the revolution beginning in 1640 was a period of great development for the press. The Long Parliament abolished the dreaded Star Chamber in 1641. Voices began to be raised in favor of a greater freedom of expression. On November 24, 1644, the poet John Milton published his famous *Areopagitica,* probably the best known of the great pleas for a free press.[18] Milton spoke eloquently for the right of discussion and declared that

> . . . though all the winds of doctrine were let loose to play upon the earth, so truth be in the field, we do injuriously by licensing and prohibiting to misdoubt her strength. Let her [truth] and falsehood grapple; who ever knew truth put to the worse, in a free and open encounter?[19]

Milton gave the most perfect expression to the idea of a free press, but just as courageous and articulate were such journalistic heroes as William Walwyn, who argued for liberty of the press following his studies on religious toleration; Henry Robinson, who based his theory of a free press on economic principles and free enterprise; Richard Overton, the Tom Paine of his day, who expanded his Separatist views on religion into principles of democracy; and John Lilburne, who did more than any of his compatriots to make them conscious of their right of discussion.[20] As a matter of fact, Milton had very little effect in bringing about any improvement. His words were not widely disseminated at the time. The ideas expressed in *Areopagitica* were picked up nearly 100 years later by people all over the world, notably in America, struggling to obtain even greater freedom than they already enjoyed.

With the execution of Charles I in 1649 and the rise of the Commonwealth under Oliver Cromwell, the press again fell upon evil days. Cromwell's "Roundheads" had taken over the royal prerogatives, which had at times so restricted Puritan writers and publishers, but the new regime was no more tolerant of the press than the Crown had been. Cromwell permitted only administration organs to be published, such as *Mercurius Politicus,* censored by the great Milton, *A Perfect Diurnall,* also controlled for a time through Milton, and later the *Publick Intelligencer* (1655). All unauthorized publications were treated roughly. Marchamont Nedham was Cromwell's leading editor.

The mercury and intelligencer followed the coranto and diurnall as publications in the progression of English news reporting. Carrying a wide range of information, their pages were numbered consecutively, week by week, for the life of the publication. There were similar innovations on the Continent. In England most printers had broken away from the booklet form by the 1660s.

The restoration of Charles II in 1660 resulted in the establishment of an exclusive patent, or monopoly, system under Henry Muddiman and Roger

L'Estrange. For a time the ancient, hand-written newsletters were the only means of disseminating information with any degree of freedom. Printed newspapers could be liquidated by confiscating presses, whereas newsletters could be produced as long as scribes could find a hideaway or were willing to defy authorities. During this period ultimate control was divided between the Crown and Parliament. Regulations and restrictions were fewer, but they were clearly stated and enforcement was effective under the Surveyor of the Press.

Under Charles, a new era of journalism was ushered in with the publication of the *Oxford Gazette* in 1665. Edited by Muddiman while the royal court was fleeing from the London plague, it was, strictly speaking, the first periodical to meet all the qualifications of a true newspaper. It was printed twice a week, by royal authority. After twenty-three issues, the publication became the *London Gazette,* when the court moved back to the capital. It continued to be published through the twentieth century as the official court organ.

LICENSING ENDS

The old licensing powers appeared to be crumbling as the Restoration period drew to a close. This was not through choice of the authorities but was more likely a result of the growing tendency for class and political alignments. In 1679 Parliament allowed the Licensing Act of 1662 to lapse. It was revived from time to time, but with the increasing tension between the Crown and Parliament, each side sought to protect its own spokespeople. The so-called Regulation of Printing, or Licensing, Act expired in 1694, not because authorities were convinced of the injustice of licensing, but because licensing was politically unsound. From 1694 to the passage of the first Stamp Act of 1712, the only controls were the laws of treason and seditious libel and regulations against reporting proceedings of Parliament. Prior restraint had ended.

One last victim under Charles was Benjamin Harris, a brash and somewhat reckless journalist. Harris was convicted of violating the king's laws. He was fined and pilloried. Unable to pay the fine, he spent 2 years in prison. When his office was again raided in 1686, Harris fled to Bristol with his family and took passage for America. He appears again soon in these pages as the publisher of one of the first newspapers in America.

After the Revolution of 1688, which brought a change in the monarchical institution, journalists were accorded considerable freedom. William and Mary were rulers by right of public opinion, and they had the common sense not to antagonize printers and publishers, who were factors in the development of public opinion. There are no serious persecutions in their reign. By 1694 the old Licensing Act died of senility and neglect. With the rise of the two-party system during the reign of William and Mary, it was difficult to maintain licensing. Without the decisive action of the old monarchs, it was impossible to continue such an archaic system. The attack on the Act in Commons centered around the commercial unfairness of the monopoly system, the restrictions on the printing industry, the tendency of suspected violators to use bribery, and the inadequacy of censorship. But as Macaulay declared in his *History of England,* "on the great question of principle, on the question whether the liberty of unlicensed printing be, on the whole, a blessing or a curse to society, not a word is said."[21]

RISE OF A MIDDLE CLASS

Journalistic progress was speeded up by the development of the party system of government. It is significant that parties emerged at the very time that the newspaper began to be a force in the political and social affairs of a people interested more and more in government. The corantos were printed during the death throes of an outworn social system. England was moving steadily from feudalism, whose economic manifestation was production for use, to capitalism, translated economically into production for profit. The change brought social strains as power was grasped by one class at the expense of another.

A new type of citizen began to emerge, the commercial person—the trader, the merchant, and (later) the manufacturer. A great middle class was arising. Standing between the producer and the consumer, it profited from the processing and distributing of goods. In so doing, it helped to raise living standards to the highest level. And the wealth accumulated during this process was inevitably translated into power. The emerging middle class could win recognition and influence only by acquiring some of the feudal privileges and powers of the traditional classes.

Three groups struggled for power. One was largely Anglican in religion, Tory in politics, and aristocratic as a class. The second was likely to be Presbyterian, Whig, and middle class. The third was made up of religious dissenters, radicals, and people of more lowly station. All three classes produced newspapers and journalists; perhaps inevitably the Whig middle class would provide the capital and the printing equipment for writers and editors emerging from the working class, dissenters or radicals though they might be.

EIGHTEENTH-CENTURY JOURNALISM

The popularity of the newspaper was so great that publishers were encouraged to print daily issues. On March 11, 1702, the *Daily Courant* appeared on the streets of London. It was the first daily newspaper printed in the English language. It was produced and "sold by E. Mallet," and authorities differ on the sex of the founder—Elizabeth or Edward? Whichever, the initial venture lasted only a few days.

The real hero of the *Daily Courant* was Samuel Buckley, who revived the daily and made it into a remarkable newspaper. Buckley insisted on a standard of journalism quite unheard of at the time.[22] It was a *news* paper, not a rumor mill. Buckley insisted upon reporting factual news, rather than opinion. He was impartial in his publication of these facts. He was careful to dateline the articles, ". . . that the Publick, seeing from what Country a piece of News comes with the Allowance of that Government, may be better able to Judge of the Credibility and Fairness of the Relation. . . ."[23] He practiced what he preached. Although

Buckley was a Whig, he did not manipulate news of that party to its favor, even when the Whigs were engaged in a desperate struggle for power. Printing on a single sheet of paper, with the reverse largely devoted to profitable advertising, except on exceptional news days, he had little opportunity for experimentation in makeup. Occasionally, however, Buckley used maps and tabulated figures to clarify his reports. Much of the advertising was spurious by modern standards, but Buckley made money from it. Undoubtedly this revenue made possible his excellent coverage of foreign news.

The high literary quality of eighteenth-century journalism is indicated by the "essay papers," read by students on both sides of the Atlantic even today. The *Tatler* (1709 to 1711) and the *Spectator* (1711 to 1712, 1714) were the products of, first, Richard Steele and then of Steele and Joseph Addison. Printed on one side of a sheet and selling for a penny, this type of paper was enormously popular. The *Spectator* was issued daily and at one time reached 60,000 readers, its promoters boasted. Moreover, its literary form was widely imitated, even in America.

The greatest English journalist of the period was Daniel Defoe, who edited *Mist's Journal* from 1717 through 1720. Steele probably got the idea for his *Tatler* series from reading Defoe's brilliant offerings in earlier papers. Some authorities go so far as to hold that Defoe was the founder of the modern editorial. He discussed all manner of topics in a most charming and persuasive style. He, too, was widely copied by American journalists. But Defoe, like all other editors, was always in danger of arrest for seditious libel, especially for reporting news of Parliament. Newsletter writers like John Dyer, the Tory adherent, smuggled hand-written reports to select readers.

CATO'S LETTERS

In the great controversy between the Tories and the Whigs, Dean Swift wrote some of his greatest satire while he was editing the *Examiner* (1710). The conflict brought out other great writers whose ideas were conveyed to the masses mostly through the newspapers. Influential both in England and America were the so-called "Cato Letters," written by John Trenchard and Thomas Gordon over the pen name "Cato." The series appeared between 1720 and 1723 in the *London Journal,* later called the *British Journal.*[24] In convincing, readable form they discussed theories of liberty, representative government, and freedom of expression. In 1724 this series was collected and published in four volumes. Copies were in great demand in the colonies, where the first stirrings of revolution were beginning to be felt. Through American newspapers and pamphlets, the influence of "Cato" can be seen right up to the signing of the Declaration of Independence.

Such progress came at great cost, however. Although party conflict raised the voices of free expression, a reactionary government in control was able to force new restrictions. In 1712 the Tories succeeded in imposing a tax on newspapers and advertisements. These "taxes on knowledge" tended to curb the press by economic sanction. Even worse, they kept the price of papers high, so that the masses did not have ready access to such publications—which was certainly one of the intentions of the authorities. Advertisement taxes and the stamp tax on newssheets were not fully removed for another 140 years. The British newspaper, as a result, was low in circulation and small in size until the 1850s. Thanks to the satire of Dr. Samuel Johnson and the courage of newspaper publisher John Wilkes, whose jailing for sedition in the 1760s aroused widespread public reaction, the ban on reporting proceedings of the Commons was dropped in 1771. But threat of trial for seditious libel still hung over those who defied authority.

It is clear from a study of this period that modern journalists can learn much from the experiences of the past. The progress of press freedom shows that the press belongs to those who rule. If power is concentrated in the hands of a monarch, or an elite group, there is no need for the public to receive information and ideas pertaining to political or social matters. Indeed, providing the public with intelligence (news) may actually constitute a threat to national security and stability, and hence the press must be confined strictly to entertainment or innocuous comment under such a system. On the other hand, if the public participates in government, it must have access to information in direct ratio to its place in the political scheme.

Another lesson to be learned from this period is that the more secure a government is, the less it fears undermining, and the more freedom it accords its press. This is true right up to the present moment. During and after wars, when political leaders and their followers are apprehensive about national safety, liberty of speech and press are in danger of restrictions. Henry VIII's insecurity after his establishment of the English church resulted in strict enforcement of press regulations. Elizabeth cracked down on the press when her claim to the throne was in some doubt. On the other hand, the stability of the government from the end of the seventeenth century was accompanied by press freedom such as the world had never before seen. As Siebert says, "It is axiomatic that government does not exert itself in its own protection unless it is attacked, or believes itself to be seriously threatened."[25]

In the next chapter we see the process carried over to America, where the concept of a free press was eventually to prevail as it had in no other country. The philosophy providing the stimulus for this progress developed from the English, however, and the American debt to English press traditions is incalculable.

NOTES

1. Robert W. Desmond, *The Information Process: World News Reporting to the Twentieth Century* (Iowa City: University of Iowa Press, 1978), p. 14. This first volume of a planned five-volume series offers a most detailed explanation of ancient communication methods that led to the development of printing. A brief account appears in John Hohenberg's *Free Press/Free People: The Best Cause* (New York: Columbia University Press, 1971). As could be expected, there are some discrepancies in these and other accounts of the "firsts" in printing and newspaper history. See also Karlen Mooradian, "The Dawn of Printing," *Journalism Monographs*, 23, May 1972.

2. Paul Lunde, "A History of the World," *Aramco World Magazine*, 32 (January–February 1981), 3. This article is accompanied by full-page photographs of the manuscript.

3. For the most authoritative treatment of Spanish contributions to journalism in America, see the

"Spanish Language Media Issue" of *Journalism History,* IV (Summer 1977), edited by Félix Gutiérrez, and *Journalism History,* VI (Autumn 1979), including "Newspapers and Newspaper Prototypes in Spanish America, 1541–1750," by Al Hester and "The 1541 Earthquake: Dawn of Latin American Journalism," by Félix Gutiérrez and Ernesto Ballesteros. The cover of the eight-page pamphlet is reproduced and a full translation of the 1541 news report is included. The Spanish contribution was discussed by Isaiah Thomas in the opening pages of his 1810 *History of Printing in America,* but that section was excised from the 1874 edition. In his *American Journalism,* Frank Luther Mott made footnote reference (p. 6, 1941 edition) to the 1541 *newssheet* and to *relaciones* in the Spanish colonies, but he also said "no regularly published newspaper on the continent antedated the earliest Boston papers." There is some question whether the first news account was printed in 1541 or 1542, but the majority of Latino historians favor the 1541 date. So does Desmond, *The Information Process,* p. 37.

4. See Félix Gutiérrez' tracing of the roots of news recording and book publishing, *Journalism History,* IV (Autumn 1979), 79, and Al Hester's description of the *relaciones,* including the 1594 Lima publication, p. 76 of that issue.

5. Hester, *Journalism History,* p. 77.

6. Desmond, *The Information Process,* p. 32.

7. No evidence exists that any of these copies were preserved, so there is some doubt about these news accounts. Hohenberg, *Free Press/Free People,* p. 13, claims that the first newssheet was printed in Augsburg in 1505.

8. Folke Dahl, ed., *The Birth of the European Press* (Stockholm: The Royal Library, 1960), summarizes much of this research. Dahl found local news emphasized in a Viennese paper of 1629—an unusual development. The oldest known Swedish paper was printed at Strängnäs in 1624.

9. Desmond, *The Information Process,* p. 33, offers no date for this newspaper. Mott, *American Journalism,* p. 116 (1941 edition), says that the *Leipzig Zeitung* (under an earlier title) was a daily for several years beginning in 1660 but that the first successful German daily was the Augsburg *Ordinari-Zeitung,* begun in 1718.

10. Eric W. Allen, "International Origins of the Newspapers: The Establishment of Periodicity in Print," *Journalism Quarterly,* VII (December 1930), 314, quoting from Otto Groth, *Ein System der Zeitungskunde* (Journalisik) (Mannheim: J. Bensheimer, 1928), Volume 1, pp. 21 ff.

11. Relatively speaking, that is. The wars continued after his death in 1483, when his heir was pushed aside by Richard of Gloucester. Gloucester was ultimately defeated by young Henry Tudor at Bosworth Field. There was a period under Edward IV when England was peaceful, however, and it is to this time that the text refers.

12. It is not absolutely established where Caxton set up his press, but the consensus is that it was in the abbey. In 1660, Richard Atkyns, a Stuart supporter, tried to prove that the first press was established by royal grant in 1468. Atkyns was trying to show precedent for royal control of printing. Caxton apparently began printing on his own initiative and without sanction. Most authorities on the subject now agree that there is no validity to the Atkyns claims. See Fredrick Seaton Siebert, *Freedom of the Press in England, 1476–1776* (Urbana: University of Illinois Press, 1952), pp. 22–24.

13. Siebert, *Freedom of the Press in England,* Chapter 1, describes the situation admirably.

14. Ibid., Chapter 3, contains a detailed discussion of the Stationers Company. Siebert has found that some of these dates have been incorrectly reported.

15. Carter's was the only execution of this type under the Tudors, however.

16. As Siebert points out, the first real English reporters were the "intelligencers" John Chamberlain, John Pory, William Locke, and the Reverends Larkin and Mead.

17. These six corantos, bearing only the initials "N.B." as publisher, have perplexed English historians. They were probably issued by Nicholas Bourne (discussed next), but they could have been a continuation of Nathaniel Butter's summer series. The account here of the first London corantos is based upon Siebert, who found evidence in records and correspondence going beyond that offered by the surviving corantos. See also Matthias A. Shaaber, *Some Forerunners of the Newspaper in England, 1476–1622* (Philadelphia: University of Pennsylvania Press, 1929), pp. 314–18. The accounts of Desmond, *The Information Process,* p. 33, and Hohenberg, *Free Press/Free People,* p. 21, offer different names for the first titled coranto, but the Siebert account was based on an observation of the preserved copies.

18. Milton's ideas and even some of his phrases had already been expressed by Peter Wentworth, who made a speech in Parliament in 1571 on freedom of discussion. Milton's Parliament speech, later published as *Areopagitica,* arose out of his difficulties with the Stationers Company after Milton published a series of licensed and unlicensed pamphlets on divorce.

19. Quoted from Rufus Wilmot Griswold, ed., *The Prose Works of John Milton,* Volume I (Philadelphia: J. W. Moore, 1856), p. 189. Milton's glory is dimmed somewhat by the fact that he himself was serving as licenser and censor only 7 years later.

20. The Separatists, one of many dissenting sects, were strong believers in the separation of church and

state. The Lilburne thesis was that the English had a birthright in speaking out fearlessly on all measures and that restrictions were a usurpation of power.

21. Siebert, *Freedom of the Press in England,* p. 262, from T. B. Macaulay, *History of England* (London: J. M. Dent and Sons, Ltd., 1906), Volume III, p. 328.

22. An excellent description of the paper is given by Marvin Rosenberg, "The Rise of England's First Daily Newspaper," *Journalism Quarterly,* XXX (Winter 1953), 3–14.

23. Ibid., p. 4.

24. The first series appeared in the *Independent Whig* between January 20, 1720, and January 4, 1721. Much of the text in the fifty-three essays was concerned with religious liberty. After the financial crash known as the "South Sea Bubble," the authors wrote 144 more letters on the responsibilities of government in protecting citizens. These appeared in the *London Journal* and the succeeding *British Journal* between November 12, 1720, and December 7, 1723.

25. Siebert, *Freedom of the Press in England,* p. 10. For a scholarly proof of Siebert's proposition ("The area of freedom contracts and the enforcement of restraints increases as the stresses on the stability of the government and of the structure of society increase"), see Donald L. Shaw and Stephen W. Brauer, "Press Freedom and War Constraints: Case Testing Siebert's Proposition II," *Journalism Quarterly,* XLVI (Summer 1969), 243, an analysis of the threats against a North Carolina Civil War editor.

ANNOTATED BIBLIOGRAPHY

Bibliographies

Indispensable references for students of the history of American journalism are Warren C. Price, *The Literature of Journalism: An Annotated Bibliography* (Minneapolis: University of Minnesota Press, 1959), which has 3147 entries, and Warren C. Price and Calder M. Pickett, *An Annotated Journalism Bibliography 1958–1968* (Minneapolis: University of Minnesota Press, 1970), which has 2172 entries including some from pre-1958. Entries are particularly full in the areas of general journalism histories, specialized and individual histories, biographies, and narratives of journalists at work. Other sections cover press appraisals, press law, international communication, magazines, radio and television, public opinion and propaganda, communication theory, techniques of journalism, journalism education, periodicals of the press, bibliographies, and directories. British and Canadian journalism is well covered. The best single volume of bibliography for mass communication, and one which updates the Price-Pickett work in history by a decade, is Eleanor Blum, *Basic Books in the Mass Media,* 2nd ed. (Urbana: University of Illinois Press, 1980). It covers the fields previously listed. M. Gilbert Dunn and Douglas W. Cooper, "A Guide to Mass Communication Sources," *Journalism Monographs,* 74 (November 1981), describes indexes, union lists, catalogs, directories, and some major collections for print and broadcast media. Current annotated bibliography is reported in *Communication Booknotes,* edited by Christopher H. Sterling, and published monthly by the Center for Telecommunication Studies, George Washington University, Washington, D.C.

The earliest annual directory of U.S. periodicals was *George P. Rowell & Co.'s American Newspaper Directory* (1869), superseded by *N. W. Ayer & Son's American Newspaper Annual* (1880), later titled the *Directory of Newspapers & Periodicals.* Standard U.S. source is *Editor & Publisher International Year Book* (1921), which also includes international listings. From London, *Benn's Press Directory* (1846) has separate *United Kingdom* and *International* volumes annually. The *Willings Press Guide* (1874) is international in scope, focusing on Britain.

For listings of American newspaper files, Clarence S. Brigham's *History and Bibliography of American Newspapers, 1690–1820* (Worcester, Mass.: American Antiquarian Society, 1947) is the guide to surviving early newsprint (updated and corrected in the April 1961 *Proceedings* of the Society and a 1962 edition; the Society published chronological tables to accompany Brigham in 1972). Winifred Gregory's *American Newspapers, 1821–1936: A Union List of Files Available in the United States and Canada* (New York: Wilson, 1936) has diminished usefulness since libraries began to discard their more recent bound volumes in favor of microfilm. The Library of Congress publishes *Newspapers on*

Microfilm, updating periodically, listing microfilm holdings of libraries newspaper by newspaper.

The largest single newspaper collection for the entire period of American history is at the Library of Congress; the largest for the colonial period, at the American Antiquarian Society. Ranking high in overall strength are the libraries of the Wisconsin State Historical Society and Harvard University; the Bancroft Library of the University of California is famous for its western collections as well. Strong in importance for their regions are the New York Historical Society, New York Public Library, Chicago Historical Society, University of Chicago, Pennsylvania Historical Society, and Boston Public Library. Noteworthy for general collections are the University of Missouri, University of Minnesota, Yale University, University of Washington, and UCLA. The two major museum exhibits are Newspapers in America, at the Museum of Science and Industry in Chicago, and the Smithsonian's Hall of News Reporting in Washington, D.C.

Two major bibliographies for the study of American history are *A Guide to the Study of the United States of America* (Washington: Library of Congress, 1960) and the *Harvard Guide to American History* (Cambridge, Mass.: Harvard University Press, 1974). The former, although less voluminous, carries extensive annotations lacking in the latter.

Discussions of historical method are found in Michael Kammen, ed., *The Past before Us: Historical Writing in the United States* (Ithaca, N.Y.: Cornell University Press, 1980), a book of twenty essays planned by the American Historical Association; John Higham and Paul K. Conkin, *New Directions in American Intellectual History* (Baltimore: Johns Hopkins University Press, 1979); and Barbara Tuchman, *Practicing History* (New York: Knopf, 1981), which discusses her views on the writing of history and the role of history in society. Richard E. Beringer, *Historical Analysis* (New York: Wiley, 1978), explores nineteen approaches to historical study; James West Davidson and Mark Hamilton Lytle examine historical method in terms of debatable episodes in *After the Fact: The Art of Historical Detection* (New York: Knopf, 1982); and quantification techniques are discussed in Robert P. Swierenga, *Quantification in American History* (New York: Atheneum, 1970), and Roderick Floud, *An Introduction to Quantitative Method for Historians* (Princeton, N.J.: Princeton University Press, 1973). A special issue of *Reviews in American History* (Volume 10, No. 4, December 1982) is entitled "The Promise of American History: Progress and Prospects" and contains twenty essays. What history books do not say about the nation's past conventions is the theme of Frances FitzGerald, *America Revised* (New York: Vintage, 1979).

For well-balanced discussions of recent trends in American historiography—involving the progressive, consensus, and New Left schools—see Richard Hofstadter, *The Progressive Historians: Turner, Beard, Parrington* (New York: Knopf, 1968), by a onetime consensus advocate; John Higham, *Writing American History* (Bloomington: Indiana University Press, 1970), by a critic of the newer schools; and C. Vann Woodward, ed., *The Comparative Approach in American History* (New York: Basic Books, 1968). Bibliographies in this volume identify leading exponents of these various approaches to American history.

For historiography in journalism and mass communication, the best single volume is John D. Stevens and Hazel Dicken Garcia, *Communication History* (Beverly Hills: Sage, 1980). Two chapters on historiography by David Paul Nord, Harold L. Nelson, and Mary Ann Yodelis Smith are found in Guido H. Stempel, III, and Bruce H. Westley, eds., *Research Methods in Mass Communication* (Englewood Cliffs, N.J.: Prentice-Hall, 1981). An older study is Ronald T. Farrar and John D. Stevens, eds., *Mass Media and the National Experience* (New York: Harper & Row, 1971), which discusses research techniques and subject areas. A good discussion linking newspaper history and public affairs is William H. Taft's *Newspapers as Tools for Historians* (Columbia, Mo.: Lucas Brothers, 1970).

Books

BLAGDEN, CYPRIAN, *The Stationers Company.* London: Allen & Unwin, 1960. A scholarly account of licensing and control of printing.

BLEYER, WILLARD GROSVENOR, *Main Currents in the History of American Journalism.* Boston: Houghton Mifflin, 1927. Chapter 1 is a good description of early English journalism, to about 1750.

BOND, DONOVAN H., and W. REYNOLDS

McLeod, eds., *Newsletters to Newspapers: Eighteenth-Century Journalism.* Morgantown, W.Va.: West Virginia University, 1977. Symposium papers covering England and the colonies.

Bond, Richmond P., *The Tatler: The Making of a Literary Journal.* Cambridge, Mass.: Harvard University Press, 1971. Addison and Steele's London paper.

Carter, Thomas F., *The Invention of Printing in China and its Spread Westward,* rev. by L. Carrington Goodrich. New York: Ronald Press, 1955. The standard source.

Clyde, William M., *The Struggle for the Freedom of the Press from Caxton to Cromwell.* New York: Oxford University Press, 1934. This excellent study is now largely superseded by Siebert (see later reference).

Cranfield, G. A., *The Press and Society: From Caxton to Northcliffe.* London: Longman, 1978. A British overview. See Cranfield, *The Development of the Provincial Newspaper, 1700–1760* (London: Oxford University Press, 1962), research-based.

Dahl, Folke, ed., *The Birth of the European Press.* Stockholm: The Royal Library, 1960. A thirty-six-page brochure cataloging an exhibition of early papers from the library's famous collection.

Desmond, Robert W., *The Information Process: World News Reporting to the Twentieth Century.* Iowa City, Iowa: University of Iowa Press, 1978. A scholarly, comprehensive survey integrating worldwide data from the invention of alphabets to 1900. It is the first of a five-volume series including *Windows on the World: World News Reporting 1900–1920* (1980) and *Crisis and Conflict: World News Reporting between Two Wars 1920–1940* (1982). The series won two national research prizes.

Eisenstein, Elizabeth L., *The Printing Press as an Agent of Change.* Cambridge, Eng.: Cambridge University Press, 1980. A depth analysis of communications and cultural change in early modern Europe (to the seventeenth century).

Ford, Edwin H., and Edwin Emery, eds., *Highlights in the History of the American Press: A Book of Readings.* Minneapolis: University of Minnesota Press, 1954. Selected articles from magazines; the first four discuss sixteenth-century ballads, journalism of the Civil War (1640) period, the eighteenth-century British press, and Daniel Defoe.

Frank, Joseph, *The Beginnings of the English Newspaper.* Cambridge, Mass.: Harvard University Press, 1961. Carries the story through the Restoration of 1660. See also Frank, *Cromwell's Press Agent: A Critical Biography of Marchamont Nedham, 1620–1678* (Washington, D.C.: University Press of America, 1980); readable, scholarly.

Hart, Jim Allee, *Views on the News: The Developing Editorial Syndrome, 1500–1800.* Carbondale: Southern Illinois University Press, 1970. An overview of the origins of the newspaper editorial and development of the opinion-giving function.

Hogben, Lancelot, *From Cave Painting to Comic Strip: A Kaleidoscope of Human Communication.* New York: Chanticleer Press, 1949. Illustrated chronological development of communication systems and technology.

Hutt, Allen, *The Changing Newspaper: Typographic Trends in Britain and America, 1622–1972.* London: Gordon Fraser, 1973. A standard work.

Koss, Stephen, *The Rise and Fall of the Political Press in Britain: The Nineteenth Century.* Chapel Hill: University of North Carolina Press, 1981. By a noted historian who has projected a second volume.

Kunzle, David, *The Early Comic Strip: Narrative Strips and Picture Stories in the European Broadsheet from c. 1450 to 1825.* Berkeley: University of California Press, 1973. A 471-page study, with artistic analysis.

Lee, Alan J., *The Origins of the Popular Press in England.* Totowa, N.J.: Rowman and Littlefield, 1976. Highly interpretive, broadly Marxian approach to the press of second half of the nineteenth century.

McMurtrie, Douglas C., *The Book: The Story of Printing and Bookmaking.* New York: Oxford University Press, 1943. Tells the Gutenberg story, and traces the spread of printing in Europe and the New World.

Moore, John Robert, *Daniel Defoe: Citizen of the Modern World.* Chicago: University of Chicago Press, 1958. Defoe's ideas and role in early press development.

Moran, James, *Printing Presses: History and Development from the Fifteenth Century to Modern Times.* Berkeley: University of California Press, 1973. Detailed and illustrated.

MORISON, STANLEY, *The English Newspaper: Some Account of the Physical Development of Journals Printed in London between 1622 and the Present Day.* Cambridge, Eng.: Cambridge University Press, 1932. One of the recognized histories in its field, well illustrated.

PAINTER, GEORGE D., *William Caxton.* New York: George Putnam, 1977. England's first printer and the times in which he lived. See also Edmund Childs, *William Caxton: A Portrait in a Background.* New York: St. Martin's Press, 1976.

PEI, MARIO, *The Story of Language.* Philadelphia: Lippincott, 1965. Readable overview of the concept of language.

SHAABER, MATTHIAS A., *Some Forerunners of the Newspaper in England, 1476–1622.* Philadelphia: University of Pennsylvania Press, 1929. Authoritative, detailed.

SIEBERT, FREDRICK SEATON, *Freedom of the Press in England, 1476–1776.* Urbana: University of Illinois Press, 1952. The outstanding study of the subject. Corrects many inaccuracies of older histories.

SMITH, ANTHONY, *The Newspaper: An International History.* London: Thames and Hudson, 1979. Races over 400 years, drawing the story together in 192 pages and with 111 illustrations. See also Smith, *The British Press Since the War* (Totowa, N.J.: Rowan and Littlefield, 1974), beginning in 1945.

STEINBERG, S. H., *Five Hundred Years of Printing.* Baltimore: Penguin, 1974. A brief account of the history of printing, emphasizing the relationships of technical developments and ideas.

STRAUSS, VICTOR, *The Printing Industry.* New York: R. R. Bowker, 1967. A history of printing from Gutenberg to computers.

The Tatler and The Spectator. London: G. A. Aitken, ed., 1898–99. The complete file of the famous Addison and Steele literary papers.

VON KLARWILL, VICTOR, ed., *The Fugger News Letters,* first series. New York: G. P. Putnam's Sons, 1924. Second series, 1926. An interesting study of the content of news before the days of newspapers.

WERKMEISTER, LUCYLE, *The London Daily Press, 1772–1792.* Lincoln: University of Nebraska Press, 1963. Only detailed history of late eighteenth-century press.

WILLIAMS, FRANCIS, *Dangerous Estate: The Anatomy of Newspapers.* New York: Macmillan, 1958. History of the British press since 1702 with emphasis on the press as a social institution.

Periodicals and Monographs

ALLEN, ERIC W., "International Origins of the Newspapers: The Establishment of Periodicity in Print," *Journalism Quarterly,* VII (December 1930), 307. Discusses qualifications of the true newspaper.

BAKER, HARRY T., "Early English Journalism," *Sewanee Review,* XXV (October 1917), 396. A detailed account which highlights Nathaniel Butter and Sir Roger L'Estrange.

BLEYER, WILLARD G., "The Beginnings of English Journalism," *Journalism Quarterly,* VIII (September 1931), 317. A study of foreign news in early English corantos, showing ties with the continent.

FACKLER, MARK, and CLIFFORD G. CHRISTIANS, "John Milton's Place in Journalism History: Champion or Turncoat?" *Journalism Quarterly,* LVII (Winter 1980), 563. Milton is judged a champion for his *Areopagitica.*

GIFFARD, C. A., "Ancient Rome's Daily Gazette," *Journalism History,* II (Winter 1975), 106. Begun in 59 B.C. by Julius Caesar, known as *Acta Diurna.*

GUTIÉRREZ, FÉLIX, and ERNESTO BALLESTEROS, "The 1541 Earthquake: Dawn of Latin American Journalism," *Journalism History,* VI (Autumn 1979), 78.

HESTER, AL, "Newspapers and Newspaper Prototypes in Spanish America, 1541–1750," *Journalism History,* VI (Autumn 1979), 73. Best sources.

LOWENTHAL, LEO, and MARJORIE FISKE, "Reaction to Mass Media Growth in 18th-Century England," *Journalism Quarterly,* XXXIII (Fall 1956), 442. Discusses how literary tastes were lowered by mass consumption.

MOORADIAN, KARLEN, "The Dawn of Printing," *Journalism Monographs,* 23 (May 1972). First steps of printing—stamp and cylinder seals—found in Mesopotamia and Crete; movable type in Crete dates 3000 years before use in China.

ROSENBERG, MARVIN, "The Rise of England's First Daily Newspaper," *Journalism Quarterly,* XXX (Winter 1953), 3. An excellent description of the *Courant.*

SYMPOSIUM, HENRY G. LA BRIE III, ed., "History in the Journalism Curriculum," *Journalism History,* VIII (Autumn–Winter 1981–82). See also a symposium, "Seeking New Paths in Research," with essays by Garth S. Jowett, Richard A. Schwarzlose, John E. Erickson, Marion Marzolf, and David H. Weaver, in *Journalism History,* II (Summer 1975), and Fred F. Endres, "Philosophies, Practices and Problems in Teaching Journalism History," *Journalism History,* V (Spring 1978), 1.

WILSON, C. EDWARD, "The *First* First Daily Newspaper in English," *Journalism Quarterly,* LVIII (Summer 1981), 286. Oliver Williams published *A Perfect Diurnal or the Dayly Proceedings in Parliament* for four weeks in 1660.

Numb. 1.

PUBLICK OCCURRENCES

Both *FORREIGN* and *DOMESTICK*.

Boſton, Thurſday *Sept.* 25*th.* 1690.

IT is deſigned, that the Countrey ſhall be furniſhed once a moneth (or if any Glut of Occurrences *happen, oftener,) with an Account of ſuch conſiderable things as have arrived unto our Notice.*

In order hereunto, the Publiſher will take what pains he can to obtain a Faithful Relation *of all ſuch things; and will particularly make himſelf beholden to ſuch Perſons in* Boſton *whom he knows to have been for their own uſe the diligent Obſervers of ſuch matters.*

That which is herein propoſed, is, Firſt, *That* Memorable Occurrents *of* Divine Providence *may not be neglected or forgotten, as they too often are.* Secondly, *That people every where may better underſtand the Circumſtances of Publique Affairs both abroad and at home; which may not only direct their* Thoughts *at all times, but at ſome times alſo to aſſiſt their* Buſineſſes *and* Negotiations.

Thirdly, *That ſome thing may be done towards the* Curing, *or at leaſt the* Charming *of that* Spirit of Lying, *which prevails amongſt us, wherefore nothing ſhall be entered, but what we have reaſon to believe is true, repairing to the beſt fountains for our Information. And when there appears* any material miſtake *in any thing that is collected, it ſhall be* corrected *in the next.*

Moreover, the Publiſher of theſe Occurrences *is willing to engage, that whereas, there are many* Falſe Reports, *maliciouſly made, and ſpread among us, if any well-minded perſon will be at the pains to trace any ſuch* falſe Report *ſo far as to find out and Convict the* Firſt Raiſer *of it, he will in this Paper (unleſs juſt Advice be given to the contrary) expoſe the Name of ſuch perſon, as* A malicious Raiſer of a falſe Report. *It is ſuppos'd that none will diſlike this Propoſal, but ſuch as intend to be guilty of ſo villanous a Crime.*

THE Chriſtianized *Indians* in ſome parts of *Plimouth*, have newly appointed a day of Thanksgiving to God for his Mercy in ſupplying their extream and pinching Neceſſities under their late want of Corn, & for His giving them now a proſpect of a very *Comfortable Harveſt*. Their Example may be worth Mentioning.

'Tis obſerved by the Husbandmen, that altho' the With-draw of ſo great a ſtrength from them, as what is in the Forces lately gone for *Canada*, made them think it eſtimated impoſſible for them to get well through the Affairs of their Husbandry at this time of the year, yet the ſeaſon has been ſo unuſually favourable that they ſca ce find any want of the many hundreds of hands, that are gone from them; which is looked upon as a Merciful Providence

While the barbarous *Indians* were lurking about *Chelmsford*, there were miſſing about the beginning of this month a couple of Children belonging to a man of that Town, one of them aged about eleven the other aged about nine years, both of them ſuppoſed to be fallen into the hands of the *Indians*.

A very *Tragical Accident* happened at *Water-Town*, the beginning of this Month an *Old man*, that was of ſomewhat a Silent and Moroſe Temper, but one that had long Enjoyed the reputation of a *Sober* and a *Pious Man*, having newly buried his Wife, The Devil took advantage of the Melancholly which he thereupon fell into, his Wives diſcretion and induſtry had long been the ſupport of his Family, and he ſeemed hurried with an impertinent fear that he ſhould now come to want before he dyed, though he had very careful friends to look after him who kept a ſtrict eye upon him, leaſt he ſhould do himſelf any harm. But one evening eſcaping from them into the Cow-houſe, they there quickly followed him found him *hanging by a Rope*, which they had uſed to tye their *Calves* withal, he was dead with his feet near touching the Ground.

Epidemical *Fevers* and *Agues* grow very common, in ſome parts of the Country, whereof, tho' many dye not, yet they are ſorely unfitted for their imployments; but in ſome parts a more *malignant Fever* ſeems to prevail in ſuch ſort that it uſually goes thro' a Family where it comes, and proves *Mortal* unto many.

The *Small-pox* which has been raging in *Boſton*, after a manner very Extraordinary is now very much abated. It is thought that far more have been ſick of it then were viſited with it, when it raged ſo much twelve years ago, nevertheleſs it has not been ſo Mortal, The number of them that have

BY THE

GOVERNOUR & COUNCIL

WHEREAS *ſome have lately preſumed to Print and Diſperſe a Pamphlet, Entituled,* Publick Occurrences, both Forreign and Domeſtick: Boſton, Thurſday, *Septemb.* 25*th.* 1690. *Without the leaſt Privity or Countenance of Authority.*

The Governour and Council having had the peruſal of the ſaid Pamphlet, and finding that therein is contained Reflections of a very high nature: As alſo ſundry doubtful and uncertain Reports, do hereby manifeſt and declare their high Reſentment and Diſallowance of ſaid Pamphlet, and Order that the ſame be Suppreſſed and called in; ſtrickly forbidding any perſon or perſons for the future to Set forth any thing in Print without Licence firſt obtained from thoſe that are or ſhall be appointed by the Government to grant the ſame.

By Order of the Governour & Council.

Iſaac Addington, Secr.

Boſton, September 29*th.* 1690.

The first effort at a colonial newspaper, and the order banning it.

2

The Birth of the American Newspaper

The way to get at the nature of an institution, as of anything else that is alive, is to see how it has grown.[1]
—A. G. Keller

New England was the birthplace of the American newspaper, but it was not until 1704, or 84 years after the establishment of the first successful colony in that area, that a publication meeting all the qualifications of a true newspaper appeared. Printers were available from the very beginning. William Brewster and Edward Winslow, two of the "elders," or leaders, of the Pilgrims who came to Plymouth in December, 1620, were printers. They had published religious tracts for the Separatists, the more radical offshoot of English Protestantism, and they had lived for a time near George Veseler, who was printing the first English coranto in the Netherlands while the Pilgrims were on the way to the New World in the *Mayflower.* Despite this background, the Plymouth colony existed for nearly a century before it enjoyed a newspaper or popular periodical.

Ten years after the arrival of the Pilgrims, another group of religious exiles settled around Boston, a day's sail to the north of Plymouth. This Massachusetts Bay Colony, as it was then known, was to be the cradle of American journalism. Many of its members were prosperous. The educational level was high, and some of the settlers were respected scholars. Unlike the Plymouth settlement, which grew slowly, the Massachusetts Bay Colony increased rapidly in population and area of influence. From the beginning it had a high degree of self-government. The charter of the organization had been brought to America, where it served as a kind of constitution beyond the tampering of jealous officials in the home government. In effect the colony had a form of autonomy, or at least of participating home rule, that was to be of great significance in the political development of New England.

THE NEW ENGLAND ENVIRONMENT

Massachusetts Bay colonists were concerned about the education of their children. Having enjoyed educational advantages themselves, they wished to pass on the heritage to succeeding generations. Six years after the founding of the settlement, they established Harvard College (1636). The larger towns had "grammar schools," which prepared boys for Harvard. As part of this educational process, the authorities established the first press in the English colonies in Cambridge in 1638. Its function was to produce the religious texts needed in school and college: the first book was the *Bay Psalm Book* of 1640. Other presses were set up not long after. Later, these presses printed cultural material, including the first history of the colony and some poetry.

It was this interest in education and cultural dissemination that made Boston famous as the intellectual capital of the New World. Here were all the ingredients for the development of a newspaper—high literacy, interest in community matters, self-government, prosperity, and cultural leadership—yet no successful newspaper appeared until the fourth generation.

There was good reason for the lag. At first, the wilderness absorbed the energies of the colonists. Any demand for news was satisfied well enough by the English papers, which arrived on every ship from home. The colonists had few ties with other communities in the New World. Years after they arrived, the settlers were still oriented toward the homeland, not toward their neighbors.

So there was no demand for the type of news that had fostered early newspapers in Europe. Nor was there any visible means of supporting a popular press. There was little to sell and little to advertise. Yet during this period the area was producing a breed of citizen that was to expand the frontiers of social and political freedom in America, aided by an aggressive and powerful press. It took time, that is all.

The New Englander was a product of glaciation, rugged climate, and Calvinism. Glaciers had scored the country into a land of narrow valleys, swiftly flowing streams, and thin soil. The endless field stone fences of New England are evidences of the toil involved in scratching a living from such a land. It was difficult for one family to care for many backbreaking acres, and so the individual farms tended to be small. The narrow valleys and the small farms brought people closer together. This suited the New Englanders, who preferred to live in towns where they could attend church and the meetinghouse. In the South, where broad rivers drained the wide savannahs, people lived more spaciously. It is significant that here the gatherings were more in the nature of social events. Southerners met to enjoy themselves; New Englanders met to improve themselves—and others.

It was fortunate for later generations of Americans that the New England settlers had great appreciation for property, especially in the form of land. Land had been the symbol of prestige and standing in England. The decline of feudalism and the emergence of the capitalist class brought many dispossessed British farmers to America. Driven from the land by the manor lord who had turned from subsistence farming to wool raising and required much less help, sick of the stinking slums that were the only refuge of the dispossessed, and unwanted, large numbers of these ex-plowmen fled to America. The country needed them, and that alone is enough to start strong loyalties. In America they could not only work the land they loved, but they could also acquire property, the mark of a superior person.[2]

The New England woman was another significant factor in the development of the region. Women came over with the original settlers. They reared large families, and the group kept its identity. In South America and to some extent in French Canada, colonists tended to be absorbed by the native populations, because Europeans in those regions did not generally bring women along with them. The New England pioneer preserved the traditions of an old race and the characteristics of a great culture. This solidarity was even more secure in New England than in other American colonies because of the rejection of Negro slavery there. In the South, slavery was to be disruptive of homogeneity in years to come. New Englanders were saved from the curse of slavery not just because they were opposed to the system, but also because it was uneconomical.

COMMERCE: FORERUNNER OF THE PRESS

The commercial stimulation that encourages the development of a popular press was brought to New England in a curious way. Because farming paid such a small return on the energy invested in it, the New England Yankee turned to fishing as an easier way of earning a living. Surrounding waters teemed with fish. Soon Yankees were the main suppliers of fish to the Mediterranean basin, where a combination of religions and diet provided a ready market. The South might just as well have developed a fishing industry, but plantation life was more satisfactory to the southerner than spending cold weeks in pitching vessels on the Grand Banks fishing grounds.

Fishing made New Englanders into great seafarers. Soon they were building their own vessels, designed for special purposes and superior to anything under sail up to then. The forests provided the raw materials for a thriving industry. The region abounded in excellent harbors. Shipbuilding and ocean commerce stimulated the growth of lumbering, wood manufacture, and other small industries, for which there was abundant water power. As a result, a class of shrewd, tough, independent businesspeople began to win renown for New England. Many of them became wealthy and were ready to help support a publication that could advertise wares and spread pertinent information.

For a time the coffeehouses had sufficed as a news medium, in the same way that the market places and fairs had served Europe in previous centuries. Here people of congenial interests met to exchange gossip and useful information. Buyers, as well as retailers, were interested in the arrival and departure of ships. Businesspeople were curious about conditions in areas largely ignored by the British papers. Commerce along the American coast was slowly increasing, for example, and there was a thriving trade with the West Indies. What was being done to disperse local pirates? Was it true that a new postal system was about to be established by His Majesty's Government? Finally, as rivalry spurred trade in the growing communities, merchants discovered that they could move their goods to the local customers faster if they printed notices, or advertisements, in publications read by their customers. The emphasis on this aspect of journalism is indicated by the number of early newspapers with the word "Advertiser" in the name plate. The development of commerce, then, had an important bearing on the establishment of the first newspaper, and all the early publications appeared in commercial centers.

Commerce and Calvinism, the religion of the Yankee, fitted well together. The New Englander was usually a believer in the doctrine of John Calvin, the sixteenth-century reformer who had set up a theocratic government in Geneva. The essence of Calvinism is "predestination." The Calvinist believed that the world and its people followed a plan of God. An individual's salvation or damnation was thus already predetermined according to this pattern. Prosperity was a sign that God had looked upon an individual with favor. Successful businesspeople could think of themselves as having passed through the eye of the needle into the circle of the elect. So, of course, good Calvinists tried to look prosperous to show the world that they had been marked by God for salvation.

THE SOUTHERN AND MIDDLE COLONIES

The New England "Puritan" made many important contributions to the culture and society that were to prepare the way for the American experiment in self-rule and eventual independence. Other areas fortunately infused some of the more human qualities into the product, however. The South, for example, was in strong contrast to New England. Life was easier and more relaxed on the wide plantations. The general viewpoint remained agrarian rather than commercial. Communications develop slowly in such a society. Although Virginia, the "Old Dominion," was settled 13 years before the Pilgrims landed at Plymouth, it lagged far behind in press progress. But the South contributed great ideas and spokespeople, essential to the development of democracy, with which the press was to be so closely integrated. The graciousness of the South was a fortunate leavening for the tough-mindedness of the Yankee, when the time came for the colonies to cooperate.

The South could even teach a few lessons on democracy in the earliest days of colonization. The New England Puritan was not noted for tolerance. Intellectual misfits, such as Anne Hutchinson, the first great American feminist, and Roger Williams, were driven into exile by the intransigent theocrats of Massachusetts because their ideas were unacceptable to the leaders. It took a little while for Americans to learn the lesson that it takes ideas to keep democracy dynamic—that is, adjustable to changing conditions. The institutions of the South were not necessarily more democratic, but the areas of intolerance were different. At least the Southerner appeared to have a more human outlook on life.

The Middle Atlantic, or "bread," colonies helped to fuse the regional characteristics of the colonies. Philadelphia and New York were the great commercial centers. In this respect the middle colonies resembled the New England of Boston, Salem, and Providence in this first century of colonial history. But the inhabitants tended to live more spaciously, like the Southerner. Young Ben Franklin, hiding out in Philadelphia, found it to be as bustling as Boston but more congenial to his inquisitive nature. And it is significant that Philadelphia was the second American city to support a successful newspaper.

The middle colonies attracted settlers of various national and religious backgrounds. Along the Delaware river the Swedes had established communities dating from the early seventeenth century. In 1621 the Dutch West India Company established New Netherland colony, later to be renamed "New York" by its English conquerors. Later many other groups moved into the area. Parts of Pennsylvania became almost as Germanic as the cities in the Palatinate whence the "Pennsylvania Dutch" (Deutsch) had come. The region also absorbed religious expatriates, such as Catholics, Lutherans, Quakers, and Dutch Reformers.

By the end of the seventeenth century there were about 250,000 inhabitants of European extraction in the American colonies. Massachusetts had grown from about 100 in 1620 to 45,000 by 1700. Virginia had a white population of about 50,000. Maryland was next, with 20,000. The others were much smaller but were growing fast. A few families had accumulated respectable fortunes by this time, but the general income level was relatively low.

POLITICAL UNREST

The colonies reflected the religious and political troubles of Europe. Many Americans had emigrated because of differences in beliefs, and they brought their problems with them. The restoration of Charles II after the revolution of 1640 was a period of political reaction. Once again the king exerted his old powers—or tried to. James II, who succeeded Charles, should have learned that it was dangerous to flout the good will of his subjects, but James was even more unpopular than this predecessors. Under James, revolt seethed. The unrest was reflected in the colonies.

In 1664 the British vanquished the Dutch and took as one of the spoils of war the New Netherland colony. In the next few years the king tried to strengthen his power in England. It is not surprising that the same process was apparent in the colonies. The General Court of Massachusetts, for example, passed the first formal act restricting the press in 1662. The only printing plant in the colony at the time was the one at Harvard, consisting of two presses, but the authorities were taking no chances with possible subversive literature, and the law provided for rigorous censorship.[3]

One of the governors sent out to the colonies about this time was Sir Edmund Andros. He first took over the seat of government in New York in 1674. It was Andros' understanding that his commission gave him jurisdiction over the area between the Delaware and Connecticut rivers. This was interpreted by colonial leaders as proof that the Crown wished to establish a more effective control of this area by means of centralization of authority. The charters of the New England colonies were declared invalid, and Andros believed he had a mandate to take over this region, too. By 1686 he was in control of most of the populated and prosperous colonies.

Two years later (1688) Parliament deposed James II in the "Glorious Revolution." The crown was then offered jointly to his eldest daughter, Mary, and her husband, William of Orange. William and Mary were wise rulers. Aware of the circumstances under which they had been offered the crowns, they tended to be conciliatory. The counterpart of these events in America was the revolt against royal authority in the guise of Andros. He was sent back to England in 1689 for trial.[4]

BENJAMIN HARRIS, PRINTER

It was at this very time that an ex-London bookseller and publisher decided to offer a periodical that the ordinary person could afford and could understand. Boston then had a population of nearly 7000 and was the largest city in America. It offered sufficient sales potential for the type of publication the promoter had in mind. Cultural and literacy levels were sufficient to warrant the financial risk. There was a demand by the commercial interests for such an organ, and they could offer the essential support. The situation was made to order for a newspaper, and the man of the hour was at hand, although he never did quite achieve the honor of producing the first American newspaper.

The hero of this episode was the exiled printer, Benjamin Harris, who was last seen fleeing from the law. Harris arrived in Boston in 1686. Already he had had considerable experience in the London publishing business. Unfortunately, Harris was a troublemaker, and shortly after he had started his London newspaper in 1679, he was arrested for having seditious literature in his possession. He was sentenced to the pillory, which was erected in front of his own office. Friends kept passersby from throwing refuse at the prisoner, but they could not help him pay the stiff fine imposed, and Harris had to go to jail. From his cell he continued to edit his paper. In 1686 his shop was again raided. Officers seized a quantity of pamphlets connecting Harris with subversive organizations, and a warrant was issued for his arrest. Warned of the danger, Harris fled with his family to America. In the fall of 1686 he opened a combined coffee and book shop in Boston at the corner of State and Washington Streets.

The shop was a favorite meeting place for some of Boston's most interesting citizens. Judge Sewall, chronicler of his times and a former publisher, was a regular customer. Most of the local wits and writers made the shop their headquarters. The progressive views of the proprietor are indicated by the fact that his was the only coffee shop in the city where respectable women were welcome.

Harris was a shrewd businessperson. He succeeded against formidable opposition. There were seven booksellers in the neighborhood when Harris set up shop. He sat down and wrote a spelling book that was a best seller in the country for many years. He published books for a distinguished clientele and thus acquired a respect and prestige that some of his rivals lacked. He was not a printer at this time, but rather the promoter of literary works. The downfall of Andros gave Harris the opportunity to go back to his first love, the publication of a newspaper.

PUBLICK OCCURRENCES, 1690

On September 25, 1690, the printing shop of R. Pierce issued a four-page newspaper. It was printed on only three sides. The fourth page was blank so the reader could add his or her own news items before passing it on. The pages measured only 6 inches $\times$ $10\frac{1}{4}$ inches. There was very little attempt at makeup. This was Harris' *Publick Occurrences, Both Foreign and Domestick,* called by some authorities the first American newspaper. It might very well have been, except that it was banned after the first issue, and one of the qualifications of a newspaper is periodicity, or continuity. If continuity is ignored, a publication printed the year before might just as logically be called the first American newspaper. This was *The Present State of the New-English Affairs,* printed in 1689 as a report from the Reverend Increase Mather to Governor Broadstreet of Massachusetts. The Reverend Mr. Mather was representing the colony in London, and the publication was designed to let the public know what progress had been made in colonial problems. This was certainly news and was printed as such. There are even earlier examples of broadsheets and reprints of big news events. The characteristic that set *Publick Occurrences* apart was that, unlike the others, it looked like a newspaper, it read like a newspaper, and it was intended as a permanent news organ.[5] Harris was a good reporter for his time. His style was concise—"punchy," the modern editor would call it. The paper included both foreign and local news—another distinction from earlier news publications. Indeed, his "occurrences" covered a multitude of interests. Thus, we find at the bottom of the outside column on page one:

> The *Small-pox* which has been raging in *Boston,* after a manner very Extraordinary is now very much abated. It is thought that far more have been sick of it than were visited with it, when it raged so much twelve years ago, nevertheless it has not been so Mortal. The number of them that have dyed in *Boston* by this last Visitation is about three hundred and twenty, which is not perhaps half so many as fell by the former. . . .[6]

Harris knew what would interest his readers. He included intelligent comment, but he knew that most of his readers would be attracted more by appeals to basic emotions and by reference to familiar persons and places. Conflict and fear were two such emotions emphasized in his paper. The pattern has been used successfully right up to today, which is not to say that this is the *only* means for winning subscribers.

Harris got into trouble with the local authorities, not because he printed libels, but because he printed the truth as he saw it. He had also violated licensing restrictions first imposed in 1662. One of Harris' items reported that Indian allies of the "English Colonies & Provinces of the West" had forced an army under General Winthrop to postpone an attack on the French. The Indians, Harris wrote, had failed to provide "canoo's" for the transportation of the forces into enemy territory. War chiefs had explained that their warriors were too weakened from smallpox to fulfill their commitments, and that was probably true. They were not too weak to make individual raids, however. From one of these raids, Harris reported, they "brought home several *Prisoners,* whom they used in a manner too barbarous for any English to approve." The journalist referred to these Indian allies as "miserable savages, in whom we have too much confided."

All these remarks could be taken as criticism of colonial policy, which at that moment was concerned with winning, not alienating, Indian neighbors. Harris was also accused of bad taste. He had spiced up his paper by reporting that the French king had been taking immoral liberties with the prince's wife, for which reason the prince had revolted. Judge Sewall wrote in his diary that the Puritan clergy was scandalized by this account in a publication reaching the Boston public.

It was the Massachusetts licensing act that ended Harris' career as an American newspaper publisher, however. How he expected to get around that restriction is not at all clear. Harris eventually returned to England, where he faded out of the scene as the penurious vendor of quack medicines.

Not for another 14 years was there a newspaper in the American colonies, and when one did appear, it operated alone for 15 years. The example of *Publick Occurrences* may have warned away any journalistic promoters during this interim. When the next newspapers did appear, they were inclined to be stodgy and dull, partly because the publishers lacked Harris' color and boldness and partly because all news had to be "safe" to pass the licensers. All of the successful Boston publishers in the next 30 years were careful to notify their publics that they printed "by authority." More important, they had the protection of an important office, for the journalists who followed immediately after Harris were all postmasters.

In Europe there had been a long tradition of affiliation between the postal service and journalism. Many of the early continental newspapers had been published by postmasters. There was good reason for this. Postmasters were especially interested in disseminating information. That was their principal business. They had access to most of the intelligence available to the community. They broke the seals of official pouches and delivered important dispatches.

Postmasters then, as today, heard much of the local gossip. They were "in the know." And in colonial times, as in modern times, the postmaster was likely to be an important political figure. That was how he usually earned his office.

But such advantages do not necessarily produce good newspapers. Softness and safety never beget great journalism—then or now. Newspapers have progressed farthest in times of strife. Yet the early postmaster-publishers contributed much to American journalism. At least they understood that the main problem was survival, which is more than could be said of Harris. It was the ability to adjust to conditions that enabled a postmaster to produce the first genuine newspaper in America. And if he lagged 14 years behind Harris, the fault was not all his. Until 1692 there had been no official postal service in the colonies. In that year the British government authorized an intercolonial mail system—an indication that the respective colonies were beginning to take note of each other.

JOHN CAMPBELL'S *NEWS-LETTER,* 1704

One of the postmasters appointed by the Crown for the new intercolonial service was John Campbell, who took over the Boston post office in 1700. From the very beginning Campbell made use of the postal service to supply information to special correspondents in other colonies. He issued this intelligence in the form of a newsletter—the primitive, hand-written report that had been the common medium of communication in Europe before the invention of printing. Most of the information sent out by Campbell was concerned with commercial and governmental matters. Boston was the most important city in the colonies then, and the postmasters' information was therefore highly pertinent all along the Atlantic seaboard. Meetings, proclamations, complaints, legal notices, actions in court, available cargo space, and the arrivals of Very Important Persons provided the grist for Campbell's news mill. There was such a demand for his newsletter that Campbell began to look around for some way of relieving the pressure upon his time and energy. He got his brother, Duncan, to help, but even together they could not supply the demand for news: They just could not write longhand fast enough. Shrewdly, the Scottish Campbell decided there must be an easier way to earn a living. He set out one afternoon to make a call on Bartholomew Green, one of the few printers in the area. That day the two struck a bargain.

On the morning of April 24, 1704, Green's shop on Newbury Street printed the first genuine American newspaper. It was called the *Boston News-Letter,* an appropriate title since it was merely a continuation of the publication the Campbells had been producing since 1700. The *News-Letter* was printed on both sides of a sheet just a little larger than the dimensions of Harris' paper—that is, slightly larger than a sheet of typewriter paper.

The news in the first issue was not very startling. The publisher-editor-postmaster had simply clipped the incoming London newspapers, already weeks old, and had inserted the items as foreign exchanges. Since he did not have

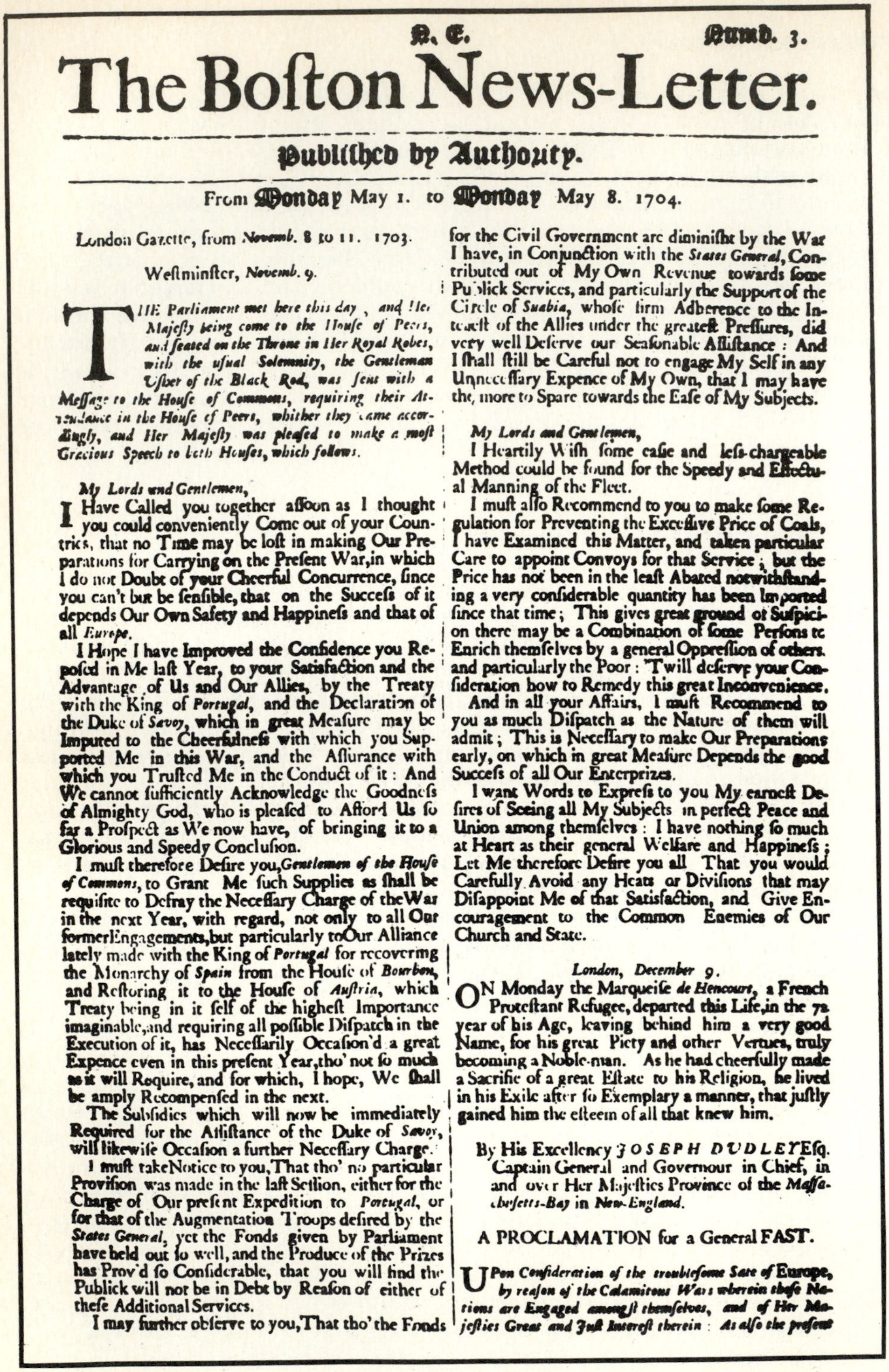

N. E. **Numb. 3.**

The Boston News-Letter.

Published by Authority.

From Monday May 1. to Monday May 8. 1704.

London Gazette, from *Novemb.* 8 to 11. 1703.

Westminster, *Novemb.* 9.

T*HE Parliament met here this day, and Her Majesty being come to the House of Peers, and seated on the Throne in Her Royal Robes, with the usual Solemnity, the Gentleman Usher of the Black Rod, was sent with a Message to the House of Commons, requiring their Attendance in the House of Peers, whither they came accordingly, and Her Majesty was pleased to make a most Gracious Speech to both Houses, which follows.*

My Lords and Gentlemen,

I Have Called you together assoon as I thought you could conveniently Come out of your Countries, that no Time may be lost in making Our Preparations for Carrying on the Present War, in which I do not Doubt of your Cheerful Concurrence, since you can't but be sensible, that on the Success of it depends Our Own Safety and Happiness and that of all *Europe*.

I Hope I have Improved the Confidence you Reposed in Me last Year, to your Satisfaction and the Advantage of Us and Our Allies, by the Treaty with the King of *Portugal*, and the Declaration of the Duke of *Savoy*, which in great Measure may be Imputed to the Cheerfulness with which you Supported Me in this War, and the Assurance with which you Trusted Me in the Conduct of it: And We cannot sufficiently Acknowledge the Goodness of Almighty God, who is pleased to Afford Us so far a Prospect as We now have, of bringing it to a Glorious and Speedy Conclusion.

I must therefore Desire you, *Gentlemen of the House of Commons*, to Grant Me such Supplies as shall be requisite to Defray the Necessary Charge of the War in the next Year, with regard, not only to all Our former Engagements, but particularly to Our Alliance lately made with the King of *Portugal* for recovering the Monarchy of *Spain* from the House of *Bourbon*, and Restoring it to the House of *Austria*, which Treaty being in it self of the highest Importance imaginable, and requiring all possible Dispatch in the Execution of it, has Necessarily Occasion'd a great Expence even in this present Year, tho' not so much as it will Require, and for which, I hope, We shall be amply Recompensed in the next.

The Subsidies which will now be immediately Required for the Assistance of the Duke of *Savoy*, will likewise Occasion a further Necessary Charge.

I must take Notice to you, That tho' no particular Provision was made in the last Session, either for the Charge of Our present Expedition to *Portugal*, or for that of the Augmentation Troops desired by the *States General*, yet the Fonds given by Parliament have held out so well, and the Produce of the Prizes has Prov'd so Considerable, that you will find the Publick will not be in Debt by Reason of either of these Additional Services.

I may further observe to you, That tho' the Fonds for the Civil Government are diminisht by the War I have, in Conjunction with the *States General*, Contributed out of My Own Revenue towards some Publick Services, and particularly the Support of the Circle of *Suabia*, whose firm Adherence to the Interest of the Allies under the greatest Pressures, did very well Deserve our Seasonable Assistance: And I shall still be Careful not to engage My Self in any Unnecessary Expence of My Own, that I may have the more to Spare towards the Ease of My Subjects.

My Lords and Gentlemen,

I Heartily Wish some easie and less-chargeable Method could be found for the Speedy and Effectual Manning of the Fleet.

I must also Recommend to you to make some Regulation for Preventing the Excessive Price of Coals, I have Examined this Matter, and taken particular Care to appoint Convoys for that Service; but the Price has not been in the least Abated notwithstanding a very considerable quantity has been Imported since that time; This gives great ground of Suspicion there may be a Combination of some Persons to Enrich themselves by a general Oppression of others, and particularly the Poor: 'Twill deserve your Consideration how to Remedy this great Inconvenience.

And in all your Affairs, I must Recommend to you as much Dispatch as the Nature of them will admit; This is Necessary to make Our Preparations early, on which in great Measure Depends the good Success of all Our Enterprizes.

I want Words to Express to you My earnest Desires of Seeing all My Subjects in perfect Peace and Union among themselves: I have nothing so much at Heart as their general Welfare and Happiness; Let Me therefore Desire you all That you would Carefully Avoid any Heats or Divisions that may Disappoint Me of that Satisfaction, and Give Encouragement to the Common Enemies of Our Church and State.

London, December 9.

ON Monday the Marqueise *de Hencourt*, a French Protestant Refugee, departed this Life, in the 72 year of his Age, leaving behind him a very good Name, for his great Piety and other Vertues, truly becoming a Noble-man. As he had cheerfully made a Sacrifice of a great Estate to his Religion, he lived in his Exile after so Exemplary a manner, that justly gained him the esteem of all that knew him.

By His Excellency JOSEPH DUDLEY Esq. Captain General and Governour in Chief, in and over Her Majesties Province of the *Massachusetts-Bay* in *New-England*.

A PROCLAMATION for a General FAST.

U*Pon Consideration of the troublesome Sate of Europe, by reason of the Calamitous Wars wherein these Nations are Engaged amongst themselves, and of Her Majesties Great and Just Interest therein: As also the present*

The first successful newspaper to be printed in North America, by John Campbell.

space for all the European dispatches, he put aside excess information for future use. As a result, some of his news was months old before it reached the readers. On the other hand, local news was fairly timely. It was terse, but surprisingly informative. For example:

> Boston, April 18. Arrived Capt. Sill from Jamaica, about four Weeks Passage, says, they continue there very sickly.
>
> Mr. Nathaniel Oliver, a principal Merchant of this place dyed April 15 & was decently inter'd. April 18, Aetatis 53. . . .
>
> The 20 the R'd Mr. Pemberton Preached an Excellent Sermon on 1 Thes. 4:11. "And do your own business"; Exhorting all Ranks & Degrees of Persons to do their own work, in order to a REFORMATION; which His Excellency has ordered to be printed.
>
> The 21 His Excellency Dissolved the Gen. Assembly. . . .[7]

But it was savorless journalism, after Harris' reports on bloodthirsty savages and lustful kings. Campbell cleared all the copy with the governor, or with his secretary. That made his paper libel-proof, censor-proof, and well-nigh reader-proof. Though we have noted that it was the only newspaper in the colonies for 15 years, Campbell never had enough subscribers to make his venture profitable. The first advertisement in an American newspaper was concerned with this problem of circulation. It was what the trade would call a "blind ad," or piece of promotion. Campbell discovered, as many another editor-publisher was to find out later, that the public is never willing to pay the full price for the information it must have to exert its rights. The postmaster was frantic on several occasions because so many subscribers were in arrears. His circulation seldom exceeded 300. Twice Campbell was saved from bankruptcy by a government subsidy. The paper was valuable for the publication of official notices, which could be reproduced cheaper in the *News-Letter* than by private printing. Despite this support, at one critical period the publisher had to suspend publication for 8 months for lack of funds.

Even Campbell's embryonic journal contributed to the traditions of an honorable craft. Campbell had a strong sense of responsibility to his public, proved by his determination to print the news in spite of public apathy and financial distress. It was also evidenced by his sincere policy of printing "for a Publick Good, to give a true Account of all Foreign & Domestick Occurrences, and to prevent a great many false reports of the same"—a policy still respected by honest publishers.

Despite his clumsiness at news gathering and news writing, Campbell tried his best to be fair and accurate. In one issue he apologized for misplacing a comma in a preceding number, although this was only a drop in the sea of other errors. An uninspired minor bureaucrat in an unpopular administration, he still had the good editor's sense of decency and kindness for his fellow citizens. Of a suicide involving a poor woman, he wrote that "he hoped the Inserting of such an awful Providence here may not be offensive, but rather a Warning to all others to watch against the Wiles of our Grand Adversary." He obviously regretted having to print the account of a prisoner's whipping, but the culprit had cheated the public by selling tar mixed with dirt. The news, Campbell explained sadly, "is here only Inserted to be a caveat to others, of doing the like, least a worse thing befal them." Clearly, Campbell deserves better of history.

Unimpressive as it was, the *Boston News-Letter* was like the Biblical mustard seed. From it stemmed the mighty American Fourth Estate, a force no one could ignore.

NOTES

1. Keller was famous as a great teacher and lecturer on sociology at Yale University in the early twentieth century.

2. True, the farm colonist might have settled in other areas, but New England had its share, along with its middle-class émigrés.

3. One of the best discussions of this period is found in Clyde A. Duniway, *The Development of Freedom of the Press in Massachusetts* (New York: Longmans, Green & Company, 1906).

4. He was never tried. Indeed, he was soon returned to favor and came back to America as governor of Virginia.

5. Even on this count it would fail to qualify technically as a newspaper, according to the criteria listed on page 6, because Harris intended to issue the paper only once a month, unless an "unusual glut of occurrences" made greater frequency of publication practicable.

6. From a facsimile filed in the London Public Office (1845), as reprinted in Willard G. Bleyer, *Main Currents in the History of American Journalism* (Boston: Houghton Mifflin, 1927), p. 45.

7. From a facsimile in the Wisconsin State Historical Society Library.

ANNOTATED BIBLIOGRAPHY

Books

For the general reader the most useful books from among histories of American journalism earlier than this volume are those by Mott, Bleyer, A. M. Lee, and Payne, listed in the following bibliography. The earliest attempt at a general account was that by Isaiah Thomas in 1810 (see bibliography for Chapter 3). Next were those by Frederic Hudson in 1873 and by S. N. D. North in 1884 (see bibliographies for Chapters 11 and 15, respectively). These three books remain of special use to journalism historians. Other general histories have been those by James Melvin Lee, *History of American Journalism* (Boston: Houghton Mifflin, 1917); Robert W. Jones, *Journalism in the United States* (New York: Dutton, 1947); Edith M. Bartow, *News and These United States* (New York: Funk & Wagnalls, 1952); John W. Tebbel, *The Compact History of the American Newspaper* (New York: Hawthorn, 1963), a readable but quick survey of high points; Sidney Kobre, *Development of American Journalism* (Dubuque, Iowa: Wm. C. Brown Company, 1969), a compiling of earlier works that adds details about many regional papers; Robert A. Rutland, *The Newsmongers* (New York: Dial Press, 1973), a readable popular supplement to basic journalism history books; John W. Tebbel, *The Media in America* (New York: Thomas Y. Crowell, 1974), a popular account emphasizing the nineteenth century; and George N. Gordon, *The Communications Revolution* (New York: Hastings House, 1977), an uneven account lacking a framework of interpretation. For analysis of the subject, see Chapter 1 of Stevens and Dicken Garcia, *Communication History;* the annotations in Price, *The Literature of Journalism,* pp. 3–7; and Allan Nevins, "American Journalism and its Historical Treatment," *Journalism Quarterly,* XXXVI (Fall 1959), 411. For documentary sources, see the following citation for Pickett.

For historical accounts of the roles of women in United States journalism, see the following citations for Marion Marzolf and for Madelon Schilpp and Sharon Murphy, and others in bibliographies for succeeding chapters, especially 6, 11, 16, 18, and 25. Extensive unannotated bibliographies were published in two issues of *Journalism History* devoted to women in journalism: Marion Marzolf, Ramona R. Rush, and Darlene Stern, eds., "The Literature of Women in Journalism History," *Journalism History,* I (Winter 1974), 117; and a supplement edited by Marzolf, *Journalism History,* III (Winter 1976), 116. For documentary sources, see the following citation for Beasley and Silver.

Especially recommended for background reading in American history are the interpretive histories by the Beards and Boorstin and the studies of American thought and society by Curti, Furnas, Parrington, and Williams, listed in the following bibliography. Other excellent general histories include James MacGregor Burns, *The Vineyard of Liberty,* Volume 1 of *The American Experiment* (New York: Knopf, 1981); John M. Blum, et al., *The National Experience,* 4th ed. (Boston: D. C. Heath, 1977); John A. Garraty, *The American Nation,* 4th ed. (New York: Harper & Row, 1979); Thomas A. Bailey and David M. Kennedy, *The American Pageant,* 6th ed. (Boston: D.C. Heath, 1979); Bernard Bailyn, et al., *The Great Republic* (Boston: Little, Brown, 1977); Samuel Eliot Morison and Henry Steele Commager, *A Concise History of the American Republic* (New York: Oxford University Press, 1977); and Richard Hofstadter, William Miller, and Daniel Aaron, *The United States: The History of a Republic* (Englewood Cliffs, N.J.: Prentice-Hall, 1972).

BEARD, CHARLES A., AND MARY R. BEARD, *The Rise of American Civilization.* New York: Macmillan, 1930. A provocative history of the United States, with much socioeconomic and intellectual detail woven into a general narrative. Brilliantly presents a progressive history theme of economic class conflict. Even though the images of conflict for the Constitutional Convention and Jacksonian era proved to be overdrawn, the Beards' accounts of revolutionary aspects of 1776 and the Civil War, and of racial, ethnic, and religious conflict, stand tests.

BEASLEY, MAURINE, AND SHEILA SILVER, *Women in Media: A Documentary Source Book.* Washington, D.C.: Women's Institute for Freedom of the Press, 1977. Thirty documents from Mary Katherine Goddard to *Ms.* magazine.

BLEYER, WILLARD GROSVENOR, *Main Currents in the History of American Journalism.* Boston: Houghton Mifflin, 1927. One of the standard histories of journalism—reliable and detailed. Places emphasis on leading editors after the 1830s.

BOORSTIN, DANIEL J., *The Americans: The Colonial Experience.* New York: Random House, 1958. A major voice of the consensus school of historians, stressing "togetherness" and continuity rather than conflict. The first of three volumes that feature group-action themes and minimize the impact of individuals' ideas. Thus Sam Adams is a "local hero," Andrew Jackson is a Western "booster," and Alexander Hamilton is ignored. To put Boorstin's imaginative thematic essays into perspective, the reader needs the background of a conventional narrative.

CHANNING, EDWARD, *History of the United States,* Volume II. New York: Macmillan, 1927. A learned and readable summary of events and forces significant in colonial social and political development.

CURTI, MERLE, *The Growth of American Thought,* 3rd ed. New York: Harper & Row, 1964. One of the most scholarly studies of the American social and literary heritage by a Pulitzer Prize historian. See also Curti, *Human Nature in American Thought* (Madison: University of Wisconsin Press, 1980).

DUNIWAY, CLYDE A., *The Development of Freedom of the Press in Massachusetts.* New York: Longmans, Green & Company, 1906. A detailed and invaluable contribution to the history of early American journalism.

EMERY, MICHAEL C., R. SMITH SCHUNEMAN, AND EDWIN EMERY, eds., *America's Front Page News 1690–1970.* New York: Doubleday, 1971. Some 300 newspaper pages reproduced to trace main themes of United States political history, wars, popular movements, triumphs, and tragedies. See also Edwin Emery, *The Story of America as Reported by Its Newspapers 1690–1965* (New York: Simon & Schuster, 1965).

FURNAS, J. C., *The Americans: A Social History of the United States, 1587–1914.* New York: G. P. Putnam's Sons, 1971. A fresh approach, consensus-oriented.

Kammen, Michael, *People of Paradox: An Inquiry Concerning the Origins of American Civilization.* New York: Oxford University Press, 1972. Won 1973 Pulitzer Prize.

Lee, Alfred McClung, *The Daily Newspaper in America.* New York: Macmillan, 1937. A topical history with a sociological approach, especially useful for its discussions of economic factors.

Marzolf, Marion, *Up from the Footnote: A History of Women Journalists.* New York: Hastings House, 1977. A study from colonial days to the present. See also Marzolf, "The Woman Journalist: Colonial Printer to City Desk," *Journalism History,* I–II (Winter 1974–Spring 1975), a two-part article.

Miller, Perry, *The New England Mind: The Seventeenth Century.* New York: Macmillan, 1939; and *The New England Mind: From Colony to Province.* Cambridge, Mass.: Harvard University Press, 1953. The first volume, covering to 1660, is a readable interpretation of the Puritan character. The second volume discusses society and thought to 1730.

Mott, Frank Luther, *American Journalism.* New York: Macmillan, 1941, rev. eds. 1950, 1962. The most detailed general reference book by an outstanding scholar of American journalism. The revisions add sections for the 1940s and 1950s.

Nettels, Curtis P., *The Roots of American Civilization.* New York: Appleton-Century-Crofts, 1938. Study of economic factors leading to colonial self-development and conflict with Britain.

Paneth, Donald, *The Encyclopedia of American Journalism.* New York: Facts on File, 1983. Has 1000 entries covering print and electronic media and film, plus bibliographies.

Parrington, Vernon Louis, *Main Currents in American Thought,* Volume I, "The Colonial Mind." New York: Harcourt Brace Jovanovich, 1927. A Pulitzer Prize winning study of the social, economic, and political backgrounds of American literature, in three volumes, which ranks as a classic of the progressive historians.

Payne, George H., *History of Journalism in the United States.* New York: Appleton-Century-Crofts, 1920. An old history, but accurate and detailed, particularly useful for the period up to 1800.

Pickett, Calder M., *Voices of the Past: Key Documents in the History of American Journalism.* Columbus, Ohio: Grid Publishing, 1977. A storehouse of first-hand materials.

Poulson, Barry Warren, *Economic History of the United States.* New York: Macmillan, 1981. Uses an institutional framework.

Schilpp, Madelon Golden, and Sharon M. Murphy, *Great Women of the Press.* Carbondale: Southern Illinois Press, 1983. Eighteen working journalists from colonial era to present are portrayed.

Tebbel, John W., *A History of Book Publishing in the United States,* Volumes 1–4. New York: Bowker, 1972, 1975, 1978, 1981. Volume 1 covers 1630–1865; Volume 2, 1865–1919; Volume 3, 1920–1940; Volume 4, 1940–1980. The standard authority.

Wertenbaker, Thomas Jefferson, *The Founding of American Civilization: The Middle Colonies.* New York: Scribner's, 1938. Describes contributions of the region to the cultural development of the country.

Williams, William Appleman, *The Contours of American History.* Cleveland: World Publishing, 1961. A ground-breaking reinterpretation of moral, social, and economic development since colonial times, in New Left outlook by a major spokesperson.

Wish, Harvey, *Society and Thought in Early America.* New York: Longmans, Green & Company, 1950. An excellent background study of the period under discussion. First of a two-volume work (Volume 2, New York: McKay, 1962).

Wright, Louis B., *The Cultural Life of the American Colonies, 1607–1763.* New York: Harper & Row, 1957. A study focusing on the aristocracies of the plantations and the trade centers.

Periodicals and Monographs

"The First American Newspaper and the 'New England Primer,' " *Bookman,* LXXVI (January 1933), 103. A brief account of the life of Benjamin Harris.

Kobre, Sidney, "The First American Newspaper: A Product of Environment," *Journalism Quarterly,* XVII (December 1940), 335. Social and economic factors leading to the founding of the press.

PARKES, H. B., "New England in the Seventeen-Thirties," *New England Quarterly,* III (July 1930), 397. A valuable appraisal of the Puritan traditions, which also discusses the effect of British essay papers.

SHAABER, MATTHIAS A., "Forerunners of the Newspaper in America," *Journalism Quarterly,* XI (December 1934), 339. Describes predecessors of *Publick Occurrences.* Reprinted in Ford and Emery, *Highlights in the History of the American Press.*

THORN, WILLIAM J., "Hudson's History of Journalism Criticized by his Contemporaries," *Journalism Quarterly* LVII (Spring 1980), 99. *Herald*'s managing editor was suspect.

[No 58

THE New-England Courant.

From MONDAY September 3. to MONDAY September 10. 1722.

Quod est in corde sobrii, est in ore ebrii.

To the Author of the New-England Courant.

[No XII.

SIR,

IT is no unprofitable tho' unpleasant Pursuit, diligently to inspect and consider the Manners & Conversation of Men, who, insensible of the greatest Enjoyments of humane Life, abandon themselves to Vice from a false Notion of *Pleasure* and *good Fellowship*. A true and natural Representation of any Enormity, is often the best Argument against it and Means of removing it, when the most severe Reprehensions alone, are found ineffectual.

I WOULD in this Letter improve the little Observation I have made on the Vice of *Drunkeness*, the better to reclaim the *good Fellows* who usually pay the Devotions of the Evening to *Bacchus*.

I DOUBT not but *moderate Drinking* has been improv'd for the Diffusion of Knowledge among the ingenious Part of Mankind, who want the Talent of a ready Utterance, in order to discover the Conceptions of their Minds in an entertaining and intelligible Manner. 'Tis true, drinking does not *improve* our Faculties, but it enables us to *use* them; and therefore I conclude, that much Study and Experience, and a little Liquor, are of absolute Necessity for some Tempers, in order to make them accomplish'd Orators. *Dic. Ponder* discovers an excellent Judgment when he is inspir'd with a Glass or two of *Claret*, but he passes for a Fool among those of small Observation, who never saw him the better for Drink. And here it will not be improper to observe, That the moderate Use of Liquor, and a well plac'd and well regulated Anger, often produce this same Effect; and some who cannot ordinarily talk but in broken Sentences and false Grammar, do in the Heat of Passion express themselves with as much Eloquence as Warmth. Hence it it is that my own Sex are generally the most eloquent, because the most passionate. "It has been said in the Praise of some Men, "(says an ingenious Author,) that they could talk "whole Hours together upon any thing; but it "must be owned to the Honour of the other Sex, "that there are many among them who can talk "whole Hours together upon Nothing. I have "known a Woman branch out into a long extempore Dissertation on the Edging of a Petticoat, and "chide her Servant for breaking a China Cup, in all "the Figures of Rhetorick."

BUT after all it must be consider'd, that no Pleasure can give Satisfaction or prove advantageous to a *reasonable Mind*, which is not attended with the *Restraints of Reason*. Enjoyment is not to be found by Excess in any sensual Gratification; but on the contrary, the immoderate Cravings of the Voluptuary, are always succeeded with Loathing and a palled Appetite. What Pleasure can the Drunkard have in the Reflection, that, while in his Cups, he retain'd only the Shape of a Man, and acted the Part of a Beast; or that from reasonable Discourse a few Minutes before, he descended to Impertinence and Nonsense?

I CANNOT pretend to account for the different Effects of Liquor on Persons of different Dispositions, who are guilty of Excess in the Use of it. 'Tis strange to see Men of a regular Conversation become rakish and profane when intoxicated with Drink, and yet more surprizing to observe, that some who appear to be the most profligate Wretches when sober, become mighty religious in their Cups, and will then, and at no other Time address their Maker, but when they are destitute of Reason, and actually affronting him. Some shrink in the Wetting, and others swell to such an unusual Bulk in their Imaginations, that they can in an Instant understand all Arts and Sciences, by the liberal Education of a little vivifying *Punch*, or a sufficient Quantity of other exhilerating Liquor.

AND as the Effects of Liquor are various, so are the Characters given to its Devourers. It argues some Shame in the Drunkards themselves, in that they have invented numberless Words and Phrases to cover their Folly, whose proper Significations are harmless, or have no Signification at all. They are seldom known to be *drunk*, tho they are very often *boozey, cogey, tipsey, fox'd, merry, mellow, fuddl'd, groatable, Confoundedly cut, See two Moons*, are *Among the Philistines, In a very good Humour, See the Sun*, or, *The Sun has shone upon them*; they *Clip the King's English*, are *Almost froze, Feavourish, In their Altitudes, Pretty well enter'd*, &c. In short, every Day produces some new Word or Phrase which might be added to the Vocabulary of the *Tiplers*: But I have chose to mention these few, because if at any Time a Man of Sobriety and Temperance happens to *cut himself confoundedly*, or is *almost froze*, or *feavourish*, or accidentally *sees the Sun*, &c. he may escape the Imputation of being *drunk*, when his Misfortune comes to be related.

I am SIR,
Your Humble Servant,

SILENCE DOGOOD.

FOREIGN AFFAIRS.

Berlin, May 8. Twelve Prussian Batallions are sent to Mecklenburg, but for what Reason is not known. 'Tis said, the Emperor, suspecting the Designs of the Czar, will secure all the Domains of the Duke of Mecklenburg. His Prussian Majesty, to promote the intended Union of the Reformed and Lutherans in his Dominions, has charged the Ministers of those two Communions, not to make the least mention in the Pulpits of the religious Differences about some abstruser Points, particularly the Doctrine of Predestination, and to forbear all contumelious Expressions against one another.

Hamburg, May 8. The Imperial Court has order'd the Circles of Lower Saxony, to keep in Rea-

Ben Franklin's "Silence Dogood" essay on drunkenness.

3

The Press Wins a Beachhead

They that can give up essential liberty to obtain a little temporary safety deserve neither liberty nor safety.

—Benjamin Franklin

Colonial readers had a choice of newspapers for the first time after December 21, 1719, when Campbell fell from political favor. William Brooker won the appointment as postmaster. He was encouraged by his sponsors to continue publication of a semiofficial newspaper. Campbell refused to relinquish the *News-Letter,* however, so Brooker had to start a new publication. And so, after 15 years of monopoly, the pioneer American newspaper faced "opposition." The new rival was the *Boston Gazette.*

Competition did not noticeably improve either the semiofficial *Gazette* or the free-enterprise *News-Letter.* The *Gazette* started out as an imitator, and a stodgy one at that. Except for a market page, it offered nothing that Campbell had not given his readers. Brooker had one great advantage, however. As postmaster, he could distribute his publication at lower cost.

Five successive postmasters continued the *Gazette* until 1741, when it was merged with another rival that had appeared in the meantime: the *New England Weekly Journal.* The merger was only noteworthy as the first such transaction in the history of American journalism, since these early newspapers were all rather dull. Campbell, Brooker, and their successors, as minor bureaucrats, were careful not to offend officials upon whom they were dependent for privileges and subsidies. Every issue of the papers was approved by a government representative before publication, even though formal licensing laws had lapsed before 1700 in England. The line "published by authority" also provided an aura of credibility to the contents at a time when it was difficult for the printer to indicate the sources of his news and verify the reliability of specific items.

THE *NEW ENGLAND COURANT,* 1721

This safe policy was brought to an abrupt end in 1721 with the establishment of the *New England Courant.* This vigorous little sheet was published by James Franklin, elder brother of the more famous Benjamin, but a notable American in his own right. James had been printer of the *Gazette* when Brooker was postmaster. When the publisher lost his appointment and the *Gazette* passed on to the succeeding postmaster, the paper was printed in another shop. Franklin was irked by this turn of events, and when a group of leading citizens opposed to the governing group encouraged him to start another paper, he agreed to the proposal.

The spirit of rebellion was manifest in the *Courant* from the start. Although it lasted only 5 years, it exerted a great influence upon the American press. It was a fresh breeze in the stale journalistic atmosphere of Boston. The *Courant* was the first American newspaper to supply readers with what they liked and needed, rather than with information controlled by self-interested officials. Its style was bold and its literary quality high. James Franklin had one of the best libraries in the city. He was also familiar with the best of the London literary publications. Here was a publisher who knew how to interest readers. He lightened his pages by poking fun at rivals. His personality sketches appealed to local interests.

James Franklin was also the first to use a device that was almost an essential of the newspaper at a much later date. This was the "crusade" type of journalism, involving an editorial campaign planned to produce results by presenting news in dramatic form. A crusading editor is not content with the mere reporting of events but knows how to generate stories of interest to the public. Franklin was an expert in the use of this device.

James Franklin was much more than just a tough and independent newspaper owner. The *Courant* also filled a great literary vacuum. Literature of a high standard for popular consumption was rare in colonial America in the first quarter of the eighteenth century. Now and then a peddler sold a copy of some such classic as Hakluyt's *Voyages,* but most of the available reading of that day was heavily larded with moral lessons and religious doctrine. James Franklin was a cultured man, for his day and society, and while learning the printing trade in England he had enjoyed the essay papers that were then so popular.

Franklin, and many editors who followed him, offered a starved reading public something new in literary fare. Most of the *Spectator* and *Guardian* essays were reprinted in colonial newspapers. Addison and Steele were introduced to hundreds of Americans through such papers as the *Courant.* Such writers were imitated in the colonies, and some of this local material was very good. The young Benjamin Franklin, apprenticed to his brother James at an early age, secretly authored such essays for publication in his brother's newspaper. Indeed, Ben Franklin's "Silence Dogood" essays rank as about the best of the American imitations, even though he was just 16 when he wrote them.

The literature in the *Courant* was witty, pertinent, and even brilliant at times. But after the appearance of the *Courant* the colonial press also offered more solid cultural contributions. Daniel Defoe's great book, *Robinson Crusoe,* was printed serially in many colonial papers as fast as installments could be pirated from abroad. Not every reader could discern the significance of Defoe's work, which expressed in the novel form his criticism of the existing social structure. Those who missed the social message could still enjoy the excellent narrative, and indeed it is still read for this purpose alone, as any youth can testify. In thus broadcasting the new literature, the American newspaper made another contribution to the culture of a new society.

JAMES FRANKLIN, REBEL

But the most important contribution of James Franklin was his unshackling of the American press from the licenser. All previous publishers had bowed to official pressures to print "by authority" despite the end of actual licensing.[1] Franklin printed his paper not "by authority" but in spite of it. He thus helped establish the tradition of editorial independence, without which no press can be called free. Nor was Franklin cautious in the use of this new power. The pompous and restrictive religious and political leaders of the community were the particular targets of his editorial shafts.

The restrictive authorities were both spiritual and temporal. Censorship was supervised by government officials, of course, but the influence of the church leaders was nearly as great, if less direct. Puritan thought dominated the region, and the hierarchy was directed by two brilliant and strong-willed clergymen, Increase Mather and his son, Cotton. Many citizens of the region secretly detested the stern discipline imposed by the Mathers and their followers, but few dared challenge the dominant theocrats. This situation changed when Franklin began to publish the *Courant.*

A man of James Franklin's intellectual independence was certain to be irked by the type of restraint imposed by the Mathers. Franklin began his attack at once. One wishes that he might have selected some other issue to contest with the Mathers, however, because in this case he actually obstructed medical progress.

The issue was smallpox inoculation. The disease took an enormous toll of life in those days; an epidemic which began in Boston in May, 1721, claimed 844 lives by the following March. Cotton Mather was aware of experiments in which blood from recovered smallpox patients had been injected into the bodies of other persons. He encouraged Boston's doctors to try this, and in June Dr. Zabdiel Boylston inoculated his own young son and two slaves. There was a popular outcry, supported by the *News-Letter.* The *Gazette* published the letters of the proinoculation forces, including the Mather camp.

Thus the issue of inoculation had become political and social, as well as medical. Coming into the arena in August with his *Courant,* for a time James Franklin used the inoculation quarrel as a means of attacking the Mathers. What he did in his first issue was to launch a front-page attack on Boylston and the Puritan ministers who were supporting inoculation. The *Courant* was both witty and vindictive in its crusadelike news and comments. The rebels against Increase and Cotton Mather gathered around Franklin, contributing articles and spurring public attention for the new paper. The insufferable Mathers[2] discovered the tide of public opinion was strong against them. They defended themselves in vain in the *Gazette.* Eventually the tide turned in their favor; inoculation began to prove its worth in both England and Boston. Even Franklin came to report favorable news items about inoculation as the issue waned.[3]

But when the spunky journalist turned around and fired a fusillade at the administration, the authorities believed it was time to swat this gadfly. Franklin accused the government of ineffective defense against pirates in the vicinity. Called before the Council in 1722 on a charge of contempt, Franklin was as outspoken as he had been in the columns of his paper. For such impertinence the editor-publisher was thrown into jail.

BENJAMIN FRANKLIN, APPRENTICE

James showed not the slightest remorse for his rude appraisal of the administration, and jail had no effect upon him in this way. Once free, he stepped up his criticism of authorities—both religious and political. By the end of the year both factions agreed on one thing, at least: James Franklin was too troublesome to be allowed in the community without restriction. At this point the General Court declared that "James Franklin be strictly forbidden . . . to print or publish the *New-England Courant* or any Pamphlet or paper of the like Nature, Except it be first Supervised, by the Secretary of this Province."[4] This, of course, was a reaffirmation of the old licensing power.

James evaded the order by making his brother, Ben, the official publisher of the paper. No such restriction had been imposed upon the younger Franklin. But in carrying out this evasion, James eventually lost the services of his essential brother. James ostensibly canceled Ben's apprenticeship in order to name the boy publisher. At the same time, he made Ben sign secret articles of reapprenticeship. This was the chance Ben had been awaiting. True, the secret articles were binding, and under the law James could return his brother if Ben tried to run away. But if James did so, he would thereby acknowledge that he had flouted the Court's order. Young Ben was clever enough to size up the situation. The next time we meet him is as a printer in his own right in Philadelphia.

The *Courant* declined in popularity and influence after that. Five and a half years after he had established the paper, James abandoned it. Later he accepted the position of government printer for Rhode Island. At Newport, in 1732, he founded the *Rhode Island Gazette,* first newspaper in that colony. It survived only a short time, and James never did achieve his former eminence in journalism.[5] If he did nothing else but establish the principle in America of printing "without authority," James Franklin would deserve a high place in America's journalistic hall of fame. He had accomplished much more, however. He had shown that when a newspaper is aggressive and readable in serving the public cause, it will elicit support sufficient to protect it from powerful foes.

PHILADELPHIA'S JOURNALISM BEGINS

The second largest city in the colonies at this time was Philadelphia. Two years after the founding of that city in 1683, William Bradford set up the first printing press in the colony. At first he printed only pamphlets and religious tracts for Quaker patrons, but because he had the only press in the region, he was also useful to the administration. Soon he was devoting much of his time to the printing of government documents. Unfortunately, he quarreled with his Quaker superiors, and in 1693 he moved his printing shop to New York, where many years later, in 1725, he established the first newspaper in that city. We meet him again in the next chapter.

William Bradford's son, Andrew, published the first newspaper in Philadelphia. It was also the first newspaper outside Boston. His *American Weekly Mercury* first appeared on December 22, 1719, the day after Brooker published the first issue of the *Gazette,* Boston's first rival to the *News-Letter.* The *Mercury* was another postmaster paper, but it was little more outspoken than the usual safe, semiofficial publications of that type that were to appear in the next two decades. On occasion the *Mercury* criticized the administration. It defended James Franklin when the Boston journalist was jailed by angry authorities. It printed the controversial "Cato Letters," which had first appeared in London as arguments for civil and religious liberties. But Bradford was overshadowed in Philadelphia by the greatest printer-journalist of the period.

BENJAMIN FRANKLIN'S *PENNSYLVANIA GAZETTE*

He was Benjamin Franklin, who arrived almost penniless in the City of Brotherly Love after running away from his apprenticeship to his brother James. Within 5 years he was a successful and prosperous citizen of the town. Ben Franklin's whole career was one of success, color, and usefulness. There has never been another American quite like him. He was "the complete man," like DaVinci, Michelangelo, or Roger Bacon. First of all a printer and journalist, he was also an inventor, scientist, politician, diplomat, pioneer sociologist, business leader, educator, and world citizen.

Franklin took over the management of the *Pennsylvania Gazette* in October, 1729, from its founder, Samuel Keimer. Keimer had employed Franklin when he first arrived in Philadelphia, but Ben outgrew that role after traveling to London to learn printing and engraving from England's best. With a friend, Hugh Meredith, he opened his own shop in the spring of 1728 and planned a paper to rival Andrew Bradford's *Mercury.* Keimer, learning of Franklin's project, issued the *Pennsylvania Gazette* in December, 1728. It attracted some readership until a new feature began to appear in the rival *Mercury.* A series of clever essays in the

Addison and Steele style soon brought delighted patrons to Bradford's shop for copies of the *Mercury*. The series came to be known as the "Busy-Body Papers." The anonymous author was actually Benjamin Franklin, and his most frequent target of satire was none other than Samuel Keimer. With his sales down to fewer than 100 copies, Keimer gave up the struggle. On October 2, 1729, Ben Franklin took over as publisher.

Franklin had little difficulty winning public acceptance, and with this acceptance came a volume of profitable advertising. In addition to being a readable paper, his was a bold one. Franklin's experience in Boston, plus his innate common sense, kept him from getting into serious trouble with the authorities. But he took a stand on issues, just the same. Men have many opinions, he explained to his readers, and printers publish these opinions as part of their business.

"They are educated in the belief," he added, "that when men differ in opinion, both sides ought equally to have the advantage of being heard by the public; and that when truth and error have fair play, the former is always an overmatch for the latter [shades of Milton and his *Areopagitica*]. . . . If all printers were determined not to print anything till they were sure it would offend nobody," said he, "there would be very little printed."[6]

With Keimer out of the way, Andrew Bradford remained Franklin's only serious rival. He had what amounted to a government subsidy through his contract for official printing. Franklin met that challenge by writing up an important legislative address, which he then sent to every member of the Assembly at his own expense. The same report appeared in the *Mercury,* but the *Gazette* story was so much better that Franklin made a great impression on the lawmakers. He continued this reporting, and within a year had won away the government printing contract.

He now bought out his partner, Meredith, with money loaned to him by influential businesspeople he had cultivated in his short career in Philadelphia. Thus, at the age of 24, he was the sole proprietor of the best newspaper in the American colonies. It soon had the largest circulation, most pages, highest advertising revenue, most literate columns, and liveliest comment of any paper in the area. By the time he retired from publishing 18 years later, Franklin had made a fortune in a business that usually offered a bare subsistence to its promoters.

Franklin excelled as a printer, engraver, and type founder. He is regarded as a patron saint not only of printers but also of the advertising world, in recognition of his own advertising copywriting and business skill. Franklin's shop made 60 percent of its money on the *Gazette* and 40 percent on other printing, including the fabulously successful *Poor Richard's Almanack* begun in 1732. Franklin also tried to issue a magazine in 1741, as did his rival Bradford, but both failed. It was Franklin, too, who helped establish the first foreign-language paper at Germantown, near Philadelphia. When he retired from the active management of the *Gazette* at 42, he busied himself helping young men set up newspapers in other colonies. He became deputy postmaster general for the colonies and employed postriders to carry newspapers between colonies. His role as diplomat and statesman lay ahead.

But Franklin's greatest contribution to American journalism was that he made it respectable. Campbell, Brooker, the Bradfords, and Keimer were dull fellows, on the whole. Some, like Campbell, lived and died in their communities without achieving more than casual recognition. James Franklin was too tactless to win the respect of "solid" citizens. Most of the printer-journalists had trouble meeting expenses, as their frequent pleas to delinquent subscribers indicate. Franklin showed that a good journalist and businessperson could make money in the publishing field. That was, and is, an effective way of making any business respectable. When intelligent and industrious youths saw the possibilities of journalism, as developed by the grand old man of the press, they began to turn more often to this calling. Getting this improved type of personnel into the craft was the best possible tonic for American journalism.

PAPERS IN OTHER COLONIES

After 1725, newspapers sprouted all over the colonies. In Boston, Samuel Kneeland established the *New England Weekly Journal* on March 20, 1727. It is worth a mention because it was the first newspaper to have correspondents in nearby communities whose duty it was to send in pertinent information about the neighborhood, a practice still followed by newspaper publishers. Another important Boston paper was the *Weekly Rehearsal,* founded in 1731 by Jeremy Gridley, a lawyer. A year later Gridley turned over the publication to Thomas Fleet, James Franklin's old printer. A few years later Fleet changed the name of the paper to the *Evening Post.* Under Fleet, the *Evening Post* became the best and most popular paper in Boston. It lasted until Revolutionary War times. Gridley went on to become editor of Boston's *American Magazine* (1743 to 1746).

Maryland was the fourth colony to have a newspaper.* William Parks, a former English editor, set up the *Maryland Gazette* at Annapolis in 1727. His paper reflected good taste, literary skill, and pride in the craft he had learned so well under the best English masters. Later, in 1736, Parks founded the *Virginia Gazette,* the first newspaper in Virginia, at Williamsburg. That little shop has been restored and is now one of the interesting exhibits at the old colonial capital. Because it tells us what the printing business must have been like in colonial days, it might be worth a moment to look into this quaint building.

THE ENGLISH COMMON PRESS

The office is on the ground floor of a small brick building. In the center stands the English Common Press, which was shipped over in pieces from London, for no presses were to be had in America until Isaac Doolittle of Connecticut began

*The other colonies were Massachusetts, Pennsylvania, and New York. Other firsts in their respective colonies were the *Rhode Island Gazette* and *South Carolina Gazette,* 1732; *North Carolina Gazette,* 1751; *Connecticut Gazette,* 1755; *New Hampshire Gazette,* 1756; *Georgia Gazette,* 1763; *New Jersey Gazette,* 1777; *Vermont Gazette,* 1780; and *Delaware Gazette,* 1785. James Parker, one of Ben Franklin's protégés, founded the Connecticut paper. Another of Franklin's "boys" established the South Carolina paper, although there is some doubt as to which one of two has the more valid claim.

turning them out in 1769. Close at hand are the accessories: the imposing stones, upon which the type is gathered; the "horse" and "bank" tables, from which the paper is fed to the press; the wetting trough, for the preparation of the paper; an ink grinding stand; and the matrix punches, made in England by William Caslon himself, for cutting the beautiful type that bears his name. The press stands 7 feet high and weighs about 1500 pounds. It is firmly braced to the floor and ceiling by heavy oak beams to ensure rigidity when heavy pressure is applied to the type forms.

From this clumsy apparatus colonial printers such as the Bradfords, Greens, Sowers, Parks, and Franklins produced letterpress work of the highest quality.* There was much bad printing during this period too, but that was often the fault of poor work quality and worn equipment. There is abundant proof that the colonial printing press was capable of turning out superb work, under the supervision of a skilled printer. The printer had to know his business, however. A single impression, or "token," required thirteen distinct operations. Two expert craftspeople and an apprentice might turn out about 200 tokens an hour.

Let us watch the colonial printer working. The bed of the press is rolled out by means of a wheel and pulley arrangement. The type, all set by hand, is locked tight in the form and is placed on the bed. A young apprentice, or "devil," applies the homemade ink to the type, using a doeskin dauber on a stick for this purpose. The paper is then moistened in a trough so that it will take a better impression. It is placed carefully over the type. The bed is rolled back under the press. The "platen," or upper pressure plate, is then pressed against the type by means of a screw or lever device. The platen is released; the bed is wheeled out; the sheet is hung on a wire to dry before it is ready for its second "run" for the reverse side.

*There were two great Bradford printing families. William Bradford was founder of the Pennsylvania line and was a pioneer printer in Philadelphia and New York. His son, Andrew, established the first newspaper in Philadelphia. William Bradford, III was the famous soldier-editor of the Revolution and publisher of the *Pennsylvania Journal* in Philadelphia. His son, Thomas, succeeded him as editor, John Bradford, no relative of the Pennsylvania clan, was a surveyor who founded the first paper in Kentucky, at Lexington. His brother Fielding was also active in journalism. James, another member of this branch, founded the first newspaper in Louisiana and may have been the first American war correspondent, according to Mott, *American Journalism,* p. 196. The Greens were prominent in New England. Bartholomew and Samuel were pioneers in the Boston-Cambridge area, the former as printer of the first successful newspaper in America. From Samuel Green of Cambridge descended a long line of printer-journalists. Timothy, Jr. founded the New London, Connecticut, *Summary* in 1758. His son, Timothy, III, changed the name to the *Gazette* after Timothy, Jr.'s death. Samuel and Thomas founded the first paper in New Haven in 1767. Thomas, the brother of Timothy, III, founded the *Connecticut* (now *Hartford*) *Courant* in 1764. Timothy, IV was cofounder of the first Vermont paper. The fourth printing family were the Sowers, Germans who settled near Philadelphia. First in the printing dynasty was Christopher, who, with the encouragement of Benjamin Franklin, established one of the earliest foreign-language newspapers, the Germantown *Zeitung.* A mechanical genius, Christopher constructed his own press and made his own ink and paper. His sons carried on the business, but Christopher, III was a Tory during the Revolution and his journalistic career was ruined by the American victory. The Franklin influence in Massachusetts, Rhode Island, and Pennsylvania has been described.

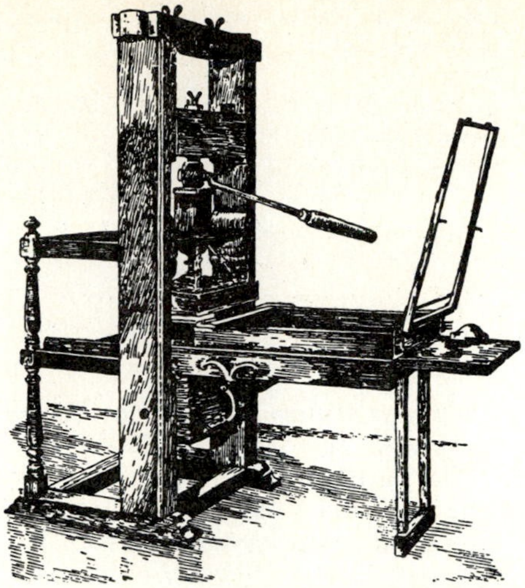

Drawing of a colonial wooden hand press.

The usual colonial paper consisted of four pages, often about 10 by 15 inches in dimension. The paper was rough foolscap. There were no headlines, as we know them, until after 1750, and even then they were uncommon. The only illustrations were the colophons, or printers' trademarks, on the title page, and an occasional woodcut to embellish an advertisement. The Greens and Sowers made their own paper, but most paper was imported from England. It was made of rags and was of surprising durability, despite its mottled appearance. With this primitive equipment printer-journalists not only produced fine graphic art, but they also had at hand implements that were soon to make the press truly a Fourth Estate.

NOTES

1. This thesis is emphasized by Daniel Boorstin in *The Americans: The Colonial Experience* (New York: Random House, 1958). Boorstin considered the early printer as a "government man" acceptable to the ruling group in his colony (p. 335).

2. The Mathers were insufferable in the sense that their righteousness made them too sure of themselves, but this does not detract from their important place in colonial history. Increase was licenser of the press after 1674, in addition to being the leading minister of the dominant Puritans. He was president of Harvard and was a respected agent of Massachusetts in London. Cotton opposed the arrogant Sir Edward Andros, ousted from New England after the Revolution of 1688. The Mathers were prolific writers of considerable merit. They were also outstanding historians. In later life they became more tolerant. In all, they contributed much to the development of their community.

3. Professor C. Edward Wilson of the University of Western Ontario offered some differing interpretations of this episode in "The Boston Inoculation Controversy: A Revisionist Interpretation," *Journalism History* VII (Spring 1980), 16. It was not until 1796 that Dr. Edward Jenner developed the safer smallpox vaccination using the milder cowpox virus.

4. As quoted in Frank Luther Mott, *American Journalism* (New York: Macmillan, 1950), p. 20. Colonial writing style called for use of many hyphens, such as

in New-England, which are not used here for reasons of simplicity in identifying newspapers.

5. James' widow, two daughters, and a son carried on the printing business in Newport. In 1758, James, Jr., with the help of his rich uncle Benjamin, established the *Newport Mercury*, which survived until 1934. Its name was then retained in a small weekly edition of the *Newport News*.

6. As quoted in Carl Van Doren, *Benjamin Franklin* (New York: Viking, 1938), p. 100.

ANNOTATED BIBLIOGRAPHY

Books

BOWEN, CATHERINE D., *The Most Dangerous Man in America: Scenes from the Life of Benjamin Franklin.* Boston: Little, Brown, 1974. See also Ronald W. Clark, *Benjamin Franklin* (New York: Random House, 1983). Best recent biographies.

BRIGHAM, CLARENCE S., *History and Bibliography of American Newspapers, 1690–1820,* 2 vols. Worcester, Mass.: American Antiquarian Society, 1947. Gives brief descriptions of all newspapers up to 1820. An indispensable tool of the colonial press historian.

———, *Journals and Journeymen.* Philadelphia: University of Pennsylvania Press, 1950. Fifteen essays on the colonial press; one particularly interesting one on advertising.

Cambridge History of American Literature, I. New York: G. P. Putnam's Sons, 1917–21. Volume I of this four-volume work discusses Franklin (pp. 90–110) and colonial newspapers and magazines (pp. 111–23).

COOK, ELIZABETH C., *Literary Influences in Colonial Newspapers, 1704–1750.* New York: Columbia University Press, 1912. Describes the role of the press in supplying the craving for popular literature.

DE ARMOND, ANNA JANNEY, *Andrew Bradford: Colonial Journalist.* Newark, Del.: University of Delaware Press, 1949. Well documented.

FRANKLIN, BENJAMIN, *The Autobiography of Benjamin Franklin,* edited by Leonard W. Labaree. New Haven: Yale University Press, 1964. A new text, restored to Franklin's original.

KOBRE, SIDNEY, *The Development of the Colonial Newspaper.* Pittsburgh: The Colonial Press, 1944. A short, but classic, study of the integration of political, social, and economic forces in the development of the American press.

The Papers of Benjamin Franklin, Volume I. New Haven: Yale University Press, 1959. Covers the period to 1734, including "Silence Dogood" and "Busy-Body" letters. Extensive introduction by editor Leonard W. Labaree.

THOMAS, ISAIAH, *History of Printing in America,* 2 vols. Worcester, Mass.: Isaiah Thomas, Jr. (first printing), 1810; Albany, N.Y.: Joel Munsell, 1874. The standard authority on colonial journalism; contains biographies of printers and accounts of newspapers in all colonies and in some states after independence.

VAN DOREN, CARL, *Benjamin Franklin.* New York: Viking, 1938. The most readable account of a great printer-journalist by a prize-winning biographer.

WROTH, LAWRENCE C., *The Colonial Printer.* Portland, Me.: Southworth-Anthoensen Press, 1938. An excellent study of the printing craft.

Periodicals and Monographs

FOGEL, HOWARD H., "Colonial Theocracy and a Secular Press," *Journalism Quarterly,* XXXVII (Autumn 1960), 525. A study of how the colonial press won its freedom from interference by religious authorities.

FORD, EDWIN H., "Colonial Pamphleteers," *Journalism Quarterly,* XIII (March 1936), 24. A scholarly discussion of the journalistic contributions of such colonial leaders as Increase and Cotton Mather and Samuel Sewall. Reprinted in Ford and Emery, *Highlights in the History of the American Press.*

HUDSON, ROBERT V., "The English Roots of Benjamin Franklin's Journalism," *Journalism*

History, III (Autumn 1976), 76. Influence of British essayists.

KING, MARION REYNOLDS, "One Link in the First Newspaper Chain, the South Carolina Gazette," *Journalism Quarterly,* IX (September 1932), 257. Describes the arrangement by which Franklin financed his apprentices.

LIPPER, MARK, "Comic Caricatures in Early American Newspapers as Representations of the National Character." Ph.D. thesis, Southern Illinois University, 1973. Concludes they were primarily vehicles for satire.

MOTT, FRANK LUTHER, "What Is the Oldest U.S. Newspaper?" *Journalism Quarterly,* XL (Winter 1963), 95. Title goes to *Hartford Courant,* founded as the weekly *Connecticut Courant* in 1764 and a daily since 1837.

STEFFENS, PETE, "Franklin's Early Attack on Racism," *Journalism History,* V (Spring 1978), 8. Ben wrote a 1764 essay against a massacre of Indians.

WILSON, C. EDWARD, "The Boston Inoculation Controversy: A Revisionist Interpretation," *Journalism History,* VII (Spring 1980), 16. Detailed research in newspaper files and documents.

THE

The Pennsylvania GAZETTE.

Containing the freshest Advices Foreign and Domestick.

From July 24. to July 31. 1735.

TO BE SOLD,

At the House of the Widow Richardson in Front-Street, near the North-East Corner of Market-Street.

A LIKELY Negroe Wench about 16 or 18 Years old. single and double refin'd Loaf-Sugar, Barbadoes white and muscovado Sugar. Also Choice Barbadoes Limes in Barrels at reasonable Rates.

Just Imported from London and Bristol,

And to be SOLD by JOHN INGLIS, at his Store below the Draw-Bridge, in Front-Street, Philadelphia:

BRoad-Cloths, Kerseys and Plains, Ruggs, Blankets, Oznabrigs, Checks, London Shalloons, Tammies, Calimancoes, seven eighths and yard wide Garlix, Men and Womens worsted Stockings, Men and Womens Shammy Gloves, Pinns, Baladine Silk, silk Laces, fashionable Fans, Paduasoys, Ribbons, silk Ferrits, Gartering, Caddis, Buttons and Mohair, cotton Romals, linnen Handerchiefs, Chiloes, Mens worsted Caps, Bunts, fine Bed-Ticks made up in Suits, India Taffities, Damasks and Persians, six quarter Muslins, Suits of super fine Broad-Cloth, with Lining and Trimmings, London double refin'd Sugar, Bird, Pidgeon, Duck, Goose and Swan Shot, Bar Lead, 8, 10 and 20 penny Nails, Window Glass, Patterns of Chintz for Beds, sarsnet Handkerchiefs, Bristol quart Bottles; and sundry other Goods, for ready Money, or the usual Credit.

WHereas George Carter, a thick short Man, with light bushy Hair, about 40 Years old, born in White Parish, six Miles from New-Sarum, in Wiltshire, by Trade a Baker, went on board a Ship at Bristol, bound to Pensilvania, about the Year 1722: These are to desire the said George Carter (if living) to return to his native Country, or to give Notice where he lives to John Atkinson, at the White Lyon Tavern, on Cornhil, London, or to Israel Pemberton, jun. of Philadelphia, who can inform him of something considerable to his Advantage: If he be deceas'd, Information is desir'd when and where he died. And if any of his Children be living they may have the same Advantage, by applying as aforesaid.

TO BE SOLD,

BY James Oswald in Front-Street, at the House of Mr. Joseph Turner, and by William Wallace, at the Upper-End of Second-Street, Sugar Bakers, Choice double refin'd LOAF-SUGAR at Eighteen-pence the Pound, single refin'd, Sugar Candy, Mollasses, &c. at seasonable Prices.

RUN away from the Subscriber, the 4th Day of November last, a Servant Woman, aged about 28 Years, fair Hair'd, wants some of her Teeth before, a little deafish, named Susannah Wells, born near Biddeford, in England: She had on when she went away, a Callico Gown, with red Flowers, blue Stockings, with Clocks, new Shoes, a quilted Petticoat, Plat Hat. Whoever secures said Servant, and delivers her to said Subscriber at Wilmington, or to Robert Dixson in Philadelphia, shall have Twenty-five Shillings Reward, and reasonable Charges paid by Robert Dixon, or Thomas Downing.

Philad. December 4. 1740.

N. B. It's believed the said Servant was carried from New-Castle in the Ship commanded by Capt. Lawrence Dent, now lying at Philadelphia.

Just Published.

POOR Richard's ALMANACKS, for the Year 1741. Also, Jerman's Almanacks, and Pocket and Sheet Almanacks. Printed and Sold by B. Franklin.

ALL Persons are hereby desired to take Notice, That the Bills of Credit of the Province of Pennsylvania, bearing Date any time before the Year 1739, are by an Act of Assembly of the said Province, made in the Year aforesaid, declared to be null and void, since the tenth Day of the Month called August last past: And that the same should be no longer the current Bills of the said Province. Therefore all Persons who are possessed of any of the said Bills, are desired forthwith to bring them in to the General Loan-Office of the said Province at Philadelphia, where Attendance will be given to Exchange them for New-Bills. J. KINSEY.

RUN away from the Subscriber the 3d Inst. a Servant Man named Thomas Wenn, by trade a Barber, appears by his looks to be at least 40 Years old, but pretends he is not 30, middle Stature, well set, sore ey'd, and near sighted: Had on when he went away, a small Hat but good, a small black Wig, but may have taken another of some other colour, a kersey Coat almost new of a mixt colour redish and white, lin'd through with a red half thick or serge, large flat metal Buttons, old white dimity Jacket, a pair of stout buckskin Breeches almost new with brass Buttons, a pair of new thick mill'd Stockings of a bluish colour, Shoes about half worn. Whoever secures the said Servant so that he may be had again, shall have if twenty Miles off this City Twenty Shillings, if thirty, thirty Shilings, and if forty, forty Shillings Reward, paid by

Philad. January 5. 1740. William Crosthwaite.

TO BE SOLD

By ELIZABETH COMBS, at her House over the Draw-Bridge,

ALL kinds of white and check Linnens, Dimities, Callimancoes, Frises, Hankerchiefs, Cotton Gowns, sortable Shot, Sail Cloth, and several other Goods, for ready Money or short Credit.

For SOUTH-CAROLINA directly,

The Ship Loyal-Judith, LOVELL PAYNTER, Commander,

WILL Sail when the Weather permits. For Freight or Passage agree with the said Master on board the said Ship, now lying at Mr. Samuel Austin's Wharff; or with Benjamin Shoemaker, Merchant, in High-Street Philadelphia.

Just Imported,

A Parcel of likely Negro Men, Women, and Children: As also, choice London double and single refin'd, clay'd and Muscovado SUGARS, and GINGER; to be sold by Joseph Marks at the Corner of Walnut and Second-Street, Philadelphia.

Just Imported,

And to be Sold very reasonably by Peter Turner, at his Store over against the Post-Office in Market-Street, Philadelphia;

A Large Sortment of Kerseys, napt and fine Drab Kerseys, Broad-Cloths, London Shalloons, Embos'd Flannens, Womens Shoes and Cloggs, Hat Lineings, fine Gulic and Hingham Holland, Seven-eights Garlix, Callicoes, Writing Paper, crimson, blue and green harateens for Beds, fine half Ell crimson, blue and green worsted Damasks, 3, 4, 8 penny Nails, London Steel, Scythe, Wool-Cards, Shot and Lead, fine and coarse Bolting Cloths, Hungary Water, fine Green Tea, fine lacked Sconces, ell wide Persians, black and coloured Taffitys, with sundry other Goods.

PHILADELPHIA: Printed by B. FRANKLIN, POST-MASTER, at the NEW PRINTING-OFFICE, near the Market. Price 10 s. a Year.

The *Pennsylvania Gazette* advertises sales of Negroes, *Poor Richard's Almanack.*

4

Rise of the Fourth Estate

The question before the court . . . is not [just] the cause of the poor printer. . . . No! It may in its consequence affect every freeman . . . on the main of America. It is the best cause; it is the cause of Liberty . . . the liberty both of exposing and opposing arbitrary power . . . by speaking and writing Truth.

—Andrew Hamilton's defense in the Zenger trial

In the second quarter of the eighteenth century the newspaper became a force to be feared by arrogant administrators. True, the infant newspaper mortality rate was high, usually as a result of financial malnutrition. For example, more than half of the 2120 newspapers established between 1690 and 1820 expired before they were 2 years old.[1] Only thirty-four lasted a generation. Nevertheless, by 1750 most literate Americans had access to some journal of information. In that year there were fourteen weekly newspapers in the six most populous colonies, and soon afterward, there was a rapid increase in such publications, as we see in the next chapter.

The product was better, too. Semiweekly and even triweekly newspapers, which had first appeared even earlier, were available after the mideighteenth century. Circulation was rising. A few publishers had won fame and fortune in the business. Rapid increase in population, better transportation and communication facilities, and rising political tensions partly explain the growth of the press. Many colonials had become prosperous and were looking around for ways of investing capital. Ports, such as New York, began to achieve world importance. About a third of the ships in the British merchant fleet were launched by New England shipwrights. There were 360 whalers operating from American ports. There were skillful artisans in the towns. The famous "Pennsylvania Rifle," one of the great weapons of the time, was a product of such craftspeople, for example. Despite the restrictions of the home country, manufacture of finished articles continued to furnish employment for many hands. In one year alone during this period New Englanders shipped out 13,000 pairs of shoes.[2]

The press was useful to the ambitious trader and merchant. Advertising was the cheapest way to move goods offered for sale by the rising commercial class. Business intercourse between the colonies increased, and accordingly there was need for information only American journalists could provide quickly and cheaply.

Better roads led to better communications. Early editor-postmasters had a double reason for improving roads. Benjamin Franklin, who reversed the process by being appointed postmaster *after* taking up journalism, was named as deputy postmaster of all the colonies, along with William Hunter of Virginia, another printer-journalist. When Franklin took office in 1753, it required 6 weeks to bring the posts from Boston to Philadelphia by land, and there was a mail pickup only fortnightly. Franklin, who took over most of the postal responsibility because of Hunter's ill health, cut the travel time in half and established weekly service.

There was also improvement in education, always a factor in developing publics favorable to the newspaper. Many parents could now afford to send their children to school, and seminaries and academies were available in the urban centers. Colleges in many colonies produced not only teachers and ministers, effective foes of illiteracy, but also writers and political leaders.

The great technical advances in printing were far in the future, but better type was available during this period. About 1720 William Caslon began modifying Nicolas Jenson's fifteenth-century type into a more readable form. Caslon type was adopted by American printers soon after, and it is still popular. The best standard press was the invention of Willem Janszon Blaeu, a Dutch craftsman of the seventeenth century. Not until around 1800, when Adam Ramage and the Earl of Stanhope came out with the iron press, was there any great improvement in this essential equipment.

THE FIRST ADVERTISING MESSAGES

The development of commerce led to progress in the advertising field. Advertising and printing had been closely associated almost from the beginning. William Caxton, who set up the first press in England, issued a broadside advertising his service (religious) book, *The Pyes of Salisbury Use,* in 1480. Number 62 of the *London Gazette,* the first complete newspaper in the English language, included an announcement of a special advertising supplement in June, 1666. An interesting use of advertising is shown in Number 94 of the same paper. After the great fire of London in the fall of 1666 the paper opened its columns to those seeking word of missing loved ones. There were also advertisements concerning salvaged furniture, addresses of scattered families, and houses offering shelter to the homeless.

Presbrey calls John Houghton the father of modern advertising.[3] Houghton was an apothecary; merchant of coffee, tea, and chocolate; book critic; Fellow of the Royal Society; and publisher. In 1692 he established a newspaper for commercial readers. This prototype of the *Wall Street Journal* was the first newspaper to emphasize the role of advertising. Houghton had an appreciation of advertising ethics in an age when the margin between quackery and professional knowledge was narrower than it is today. He was willing to advertise almost any product, but he would not give his seventeenth-century "seal of approval" to statements he believed to be dangerously dishonest. That advertising was a topic for debate and criticism 200 years ago, as it is today, is implied by a comment of the famous pundit, Dr. Samuel Johnson, in the *Idler* of January 20, 1758:

> . . . Advertisements are now so numerous that they are very negligently perused, and it is therefore become necessary to gain attention by magnificence of promises and by eloquence sometimes sublime and sometimes pathetick. Promise—large promise—is the soul of advertising. . . . The trade of advertising is now so near perfection that it is not easy to propose any improvement.[4]

The advertisers could teach the journalists some important lessons on the subject of reader response. For example, the advertisers quickly discovered that their messages must be simply stated to reach the most people. It took the news writers a long time to learn this lesson. Advertisers also understood the value of attractive presentation. They led the way in experimentation with type, illustrations, makeup, and legibility. The press owes much to these practical psychologists and graphics artists.

RISING POLITICAL TENSION

The greatest stimulus to the development of the American press of this period was the rising political tension that was to culminate in the War of Independence. The press had an essential role in the drama about to unfold. The newspaper thrives on controversy, provided it is able to take part in the discussions with any degree of freedom. The great development of the press during the first half of the eighteenth century was its victory over the forces that would have restricted that liberty. This victory made the press the most powerful weapon of the American revolutionaries. Almost forgotten today are the battles and sacrifices by which this concept won general acceptance.

In 1692, before the first successful newspaper had yet been born in America, a Philadelphia printer boldly stated one of the cardinal principles of a free press. He was William Bradford, founder of a remarkable printing dynasty. Bradford had to placate both a jealous government and a sensitive Quaker hierarchy when he set up his little shop. Every now and then he was threatened by one or the other because of ideas expressed in pamphlets he turned out at regular intervals. Arrested in 1692 for a minor infraction, Bradford declared he was tired of such interference and notified the authorities he was taking his press to a more congenial community. Officials were alarmed by this threat, for they depended upon Bradford for the dissemination of governmental, religious, and commercial information. The General Assembly therefore quashed the charge and induced Bradford to remain by granting him a yearly retainer of 40 pounds and all the printing he could handle by himself.

Because of the disposition of this case, Bradford's defense was not widely known, but it is worth mentioning here because it brought up an issue that was hotly debated a generation later. The printer had insisted that the jury in such cases was responsible for judging both the *law* and the *fact*. Courts at the time had held that when seditious libel (criticism of government) was charged, it was the duty of the jury only to establish the authorship of the statement. This was a point of *fact*. It was up to the judges to determine whether the statement was punishable. This was a point of *law*. Bradford objected to this. Some 40 years later, the issue that Bradford had successfully pressed in 1692 was to become a principal point in the trial of John Peter Zenger.

THE ZENGER CASE: BACKGROUND

The most celebrated case involving freedom of the press was the Zenger trial of 1734 to 1735. It has been much overrated for its effect on legal reform, and it settled nothing because of the dubious circumstances under which it was conducted. Its inspirational impact, however, was tremendous.

At this point we meet again William Bradford, late of Philadelphia. The senior Bradford had moved to New York when he was offered the position of government printer there. As a subsidized businessman, Bradford printed nothing that would antagonize his patrons. On November 8, 1725, he printed the first newspaper in the colony: the *New York Gazette*. Of course it favored the administration on all issues. Like many an editor who followed, Bradford rebelled when persecuted, as in Philadelphia, but conformed when offered special privileges and inducements by the same group he might have fought under different circumstances.

By 1733, New York was experiencing a mild revolution. A group of wealthy merchants and landowners insisted upon a greater share of control in the colony's affairs. But it had no way of communicating its ideas. Bradford had the only newspaper, and he was firmly committed to the royal faction. However, Bradford's former apprentice and partner had opened his own print shop. He was John Peter Zenger, an immigrant from the German Palatinate who had been apprenticed at the age of 13. In the fall of 1733, a delegation of the commercial faction asked Zenger if he would be willing to edit a paper that would be a medium for expressing their news and views.

The situation that prompted this request was complex. The colonial governor died in 1731, and it was 13 months before his replacement, Sir William Cosby, arrived from London. Rip Van Dam, member of the governor's council for 30 years and a colonial Dutch leader, served as acting governor. Cosby demanded half the fees Van Dam had collected for his services; Van Dam refused. Money cases were to be heard in regular courts, but Cosby moved his case to a court of chancery that he controlled. In the ensuing struggle, Chief Justice Lewis Morris sided with Van Dam and was removed by the governor. Van Dam and Morris now sought to have Cosby recalled by London. The antiadministration forces had other grievances close to their pocketbooks: Cosby was accused of demanding one-third of the sale of all public lands sold under his jurisdiction; there was suspected illegal acquisition of land around what is now Utica; and Cosby was seeking to juggle the council membership so that it would approve his new chief justice, young James Delancey.[5]

The leaders of the antiadministration forces were articulate and able citizens. They included men like Van Dam; Justice Morris; James Alexander, a member of the council and also surveyor general for the colonies of New York and New Jersey; and William Smith, noted for his *History of the Colony of New York from Its Founding to 1762* and a well-known public figure at the time of the trial. They, and other important citizens, were interested in having Zenger start a newspaper that would express their views.

The first issue of Zenger's *New York Weekly Journal* appeared on November 5, 1733. From the very first day, the *Journal* clashed with the administration. Bradford at the *Gazette* was no match for Zenger and the brains behind his venture. The main voice was that of lawyer Alexander, who with his friends had successfully put up Lewis Morris for an Assembly seat in a by-election. The first *Journal* issue reported Morris' election despite what was called harassments of voters over their qualifications. On December 3, a story appeared in Zenger's paper attacking Governor Cosby for permitting French warships to spy on lower bay defenses. In the same issue, an irate New Jersey settler (who wrote very much like Alexander) denounced the colonial bureaucracy for incompetence, referring to the Van Dam–Morris controversy.

The public enjoyed this show, and Zenger had to run off extra copies to satisfy customers. The governor was not so enthusiastic about such journalistic enterprise. Charging Zenger with "Scandalous, Virulent and Seditious Reflections upon the Government," Cosby ordered his hand-picked chief justice, Delancey, to obtain an indictment against the brash editor. But the grand jury refused to return a true bill. The Assembly likewise balked at filing any charges. Finally, a selected group of the governor's council agreed to start an action against Zenger. On a Sunday afternoon, November 17, 1734, Zenger was arrested on a charge of "raising sedition."

ZENGER'S TRIAL, 1735

The trial did not begin until August 4, 1735. Richard Bradley, Cosby's attorney general, filed an "information" that held Zenger in jail. The *Journal* continued to appear, with Zenger's wife, Anna, running the shop and Alexander filling the editor's role. When Alexander and Smith disputed the validity of the prosecution, they were disbarred. John Chambers, appointed to the case, asked for a postponement until August. The Zenger defense then prevailed on an 80-year-old Philadelphia lawyer, famed for his courtroom presence, to risk traveling to New York for the trial. He was Andrew Hamilton. With him, the stage was set for a drama.

Chambers made a plea to Justice Delancey, then Hamilton arose, his white hair falling to his shoulders. His first words were a bombshell: "I cannot think it proper to deny the Publication of a Complaint which I think is the right of every free born Subject to make," he declared, "and therefore I'll save Mr. Attorney the trouble of examining his Witness to that point; and I do confess (for my Client) that he both printed and published the two Papers set forth in the Information. I do hope in so doing he has committed no Crime."

Bradley, delighted at this apparent easy victory, said that since publication of the offending articles had been admitted by the defense, there was nothing more for the jury to do but bring in a verdict of guilty. To this Hamilton replied calmly, but firmly: "Not so, neither, Mr. Attorney. There are two Sides to that Bargain. I hope it is not our bare printing or publishing a Paper that will make it a Libel. You will have something more to do before you make my client a libeller. For the words themselves must be libelous—that is, *False, Malicious, and Seditious*—or else we are not guilty."

Bradley approached the bench and renewed his arguments. One by one Hamilton demolished them. He went back to the Magna Carta and to the abolishing of the Star Chamber to prove that the concept he was upholding—freedom to express justifiable truth—had long been accepted in the older courts and that colonial New York was behind the times. His arguments were worded in decisive language, but his manner was so courtly, and his voice so mild, that the fascinated crowd listened as though hypnotized. When the spectators began to cheer during a lull, however, the prosecution objected to Hamilton's statements, and when Hamilton insisted that "the *Falsehood* makes the *Scandal,* and both the *Libel,*" and then offered to "prove these very Papers that are called Libel to be *True,*" Justice Delancey remonstrated.

"You cannot be admitted, Mr. Hamilton," said the judge sternly, "to give the Truth of a Libel in evidence . . . The Court is of the Opinion you ought not to be permitted to prove the Facts in the Papers," and he cited a long list of supporting authorities.

"These are Star Chamber Cases," answered Hamilton patiently, "and I was in hopes that Practice had been dead with that Court."

Angered by this veiled criticism of his legal knowledge, the youthful Delancey cried out angrily: "The Court have delivered their Opinion, and we expect you will use us with good Manners. You are not permitted to argue against this Court."

ANDREW HAMILTON'S GREAT PLEA

Hamilton paused a moment. He looked at the jury, then at the audience, and then at Zenger, like a great actor sensing the mood of his public. Then he turned to the judge and bowed courteously.

"I thank you," he replied without a trace of rancor. Then, turning his back upon the bench, he acknowledged the jury with a courtly flourish. He spoke to the jurors directly, in a voice loud enough to carry to all parts of the room.

"Then it is to you, Gentlemen, we must now appeal for Witnesses to the Truth of the Facts we have offered, and are denied the Liberty to prove. . . ."

Hamilton was talking as though Delancey were not even in the room. He exhorted the jury to act like free people and to follow their own consciences, without fear of official reprisals, as guaranteed under the English system of law. He ended:

> . . . old and weak as I am, I should think it my Duty if required, to go to the utmost Part of the Land, where my Service could be of any Use in assisting to quench the Flame of Prosecutions upon Informations, set on Foot by the Government, to deprive a People of the Right of Remonstrating (and complaining too), of the arbitrary Attempts of Men in Power. *Men who injure and oppress the People under their Administration provoke them to cry out and complain; and then make that very Complaint the Foundation for new Oppressions and Prosecutions.*

> . . . But to conclude; the Question before the Court and you Gentlemen of the Jury, is not of small nor private Concern. It is not the Cause of the poor Printer, nor of *New York* alone, which you are now trying; No! It may in its Consequence affect every Freeman that lives under a British Government on the main of *America.* It is the best Cause. It is the Cause of Liberty; and I make no Doubt but your upright Conduct, this Day, will not only entitle you to the Love and Esteem of your Fellow-Citizens; but every Man who prefers Freedom to a Life of slavery will bless and honour You, as Men who have baffled the Attempt of Tyranny; and by an impartial and uncorrupt Verdict, have laid a Noble Foundation for securing to ourselves, our Posterity and our Neighbors, That, to which Nature and the Laws of our Country have given us a Right—the Liberty—both of exposing and opposing arbitrary Power (in these Parts of the World, at least) by speaking and writing—Truth."

On that note, Hamilton won his case. The jury returned a verdict of "not guilty," and Zenger was freed. He has now become a hero of American journalism. Less known, but equally heroic, was Andrew Hamilton, who argued the cause of liberty so ably.

THE ZENGER TRIAL ANALYZED

But there are some negative aspects of the Zenger case. The verdict had no effect on libel law for more than half a century. Pennsylvania was the first state to recognize the principles of truth as a defense and the right of the jury to decide both the law and the fact, by including them in its 1790 constitution. New York accepted them in 1805. It was 1792 in England before Fox's Libel Act gave the jury power of decision, and it was 1843 before Lord Campbell's Act recognized truth as a defense.

It is very possible that expediency, rather than principle, guided the authorities after trial. They admitted no new legal precedent in the Zenger case. It is quite probable that Zenger would have been rearrested for his very next offense, except for circumstances. Governor Cosby was cautious for a time after the trial ended, because Justice Morris was in England arguing for Cosby's dismissal, and the governor had no wish to achieve any further notoriety for himself. Then he fell desperately ill during the winter of 1735 to 1736 and died the following March. Had he lived, he might not have accepted defeat so easily.

Again, all the reports of the trial are one-sided. The only complete account of the trial is in Zenger's own newspaper. The Crown never did issue a report giving its side of the verdict. Since the accused had good reason to paint the picture in black and white, the Crown arguments and principles have been largely ignored. O'Callaghan's *Documents Relative to the Colonial History of New York* (Albany, 1849, V) include statements of Governor Cosby to the Lords of Trade, and they are the nearest thing to a presentation of the other side of the argument.

Justice Delancey, who has always been portrayed as an arrogant judge, showed great restraint in refusing to set aside the verdict and in not overruling Hamilton. He might even have had the old lawyer arrested for his contempt of the bench. The British government in this case, as in many others including the Stamp Act of 1765, did not use its powers to curb opinion, but backed down in the face of overwhelming public dissatisfaction.

This is an important point. The courts as much as the press guard the freedom so jealously maintained by a democratic people. To flout the law for the sake of expediency in a press case is a dangerous precedent. When defendants are acquitted because of political feelings, rather than because of a calm appraisal of the known law, that is a threat to a system that is every bit as important to our freedom as the liberty of the press.

Justice Delancey appears somewhat ridiculous today in his opinion that truth could not be offered as a defense in this type of libel action. The fact is, he had considerable precedent to back him up, because the principle recognized by the courts of that day was "the greater the truth, the greater the libel." The logic behind this doctrine was this: Public accusations, or criticisms of those in authority, might upset the entire community and cause a serious breach of the public peace. In Zenger's case, popular opinion was behind him, but this did not sway colonial writers on the subject of seditious libel. Almost all of them agreed that government could be libeled and that to do so was properly to be considered a crime. And many responsible citizens agreed with them. The threat of punishment—under the common law of seditious libel or under the power of a legislature to punish for contempt—for those who criticized officials remained strong until the close of the eighteenth century when the struggle over the Sedition Act of 1798 brought the issue to a climax.[6]

These negative aspects of the case are counteracted by the inspirational contributions of Zenger and Hamilton and the psychological effects of the trial. For the trial did enunciate a principle—even if it did not establish legal precedent—and this principle is vital to our libertarian philosophy today in matters of free speech and press. The right to criticize officials is one of the main pillars of press freedom.[7] Psychologically, the Zenger trial advanced this goal, for after 1735 no other colonial court trial of a printer for seditious libel has come to light. Some printers were found to be in contempt by their own colonial legislatures or governors' councils, but none was tried by the Crown.[8] Popular opinion had proved its power. The Zenger case thus merits its place in history as a forerunner of what was to follow.

NOTES

1. Clarence S. Brigham, *History and Bibliography of American Newspapers, 1690–1820* (Worcester, Mass.: American Antiquarian Society, 1947), p. xii (Introduction).

2. These aspects of development are admirably presented in Sidney Kobre, "The Revolutionary Colonial Press—A Social Interpretation," *Journalism Quarterly*, XX (September 1943), 193–97.

3. Frank Presbrey, *The History and Development of Advertising* (Garden City, N.Y.: Doubleday, 1929), p. 56.

4. Ibid., p. 70.

5. Warren C. Price, "Reflections on the Trial of John Peter Zenger," *Journalism Quarterly*, XXXII (Spring 1955), 161, provides many new data on the Zenger case and points to the land-grabbing episode as one reason why public opinion swung to the Zenger-Morris side so heavily. "Cosby Manor" at Utica, 20 miles by 10 miles in extent, was an example of the governor's greed.

6. Leonard W. Levy, *Legacy of Suppression* (Cambridge, Mass.: Harvard University Press, 1960), develops this thesis of colonial adherence to the concept of seditious libel except as it could be turned against one's own faction. Levy traces this attitude as prevailing as late as the 1790s.

7. The others are: (1) the right to publish without official license, established in America by James Franklin; and (2) the right to report matters of public interest, which was not widely recognized until well into the nineteenth century and is still contested by reluctant public officials.

8. Harold L. Nelson, "Seditious Libel in Colonial America," *American Journal of Legal History, III* (April 1959), 160–72.

ANNOTATED BIBLIOGRAPHY

Books

ADAMS, JAMES TRUSLOW, *Provincial Society, 1690–1763,* A History of American Life. Volume III. New York: Macmillan, 1927. This series was the first large-scale attempt at social history and remains highly usable.

ALEXANDER, JAMES, *A Brief Narrative of the Case and Trial of John Peter Zenger, Printer of the New York "Weekly Journal,"* ed. Stanley N. Katz. Cambridge, Mass.: Harvard University Press, 1963. Scholarly reprint with annotations of document by Zenger's lawyer.

BRIDENBAUGH, CARL, *Cities in the Wilderness: The First Century of Urban Life in America, 1625–1742* and *Cities in Revolt: Urban Life in America, 1743–1776.* New York: Knopf, 1955. Cities studied are Boston, Newport, New York, Philadelphia, and Charleston.

BURANELLI, VINCENT, ed., *The Trial of Peter Zenger.* New York: New York University Press, 1957. Reprint of the text of the trial, with biographical information about participants and an analysis of its meaning.

DUNIWAY, CLYDE A., *The Development of Freedom of the Press in Massachusetts.* New York: Longmans, Green & Company, 1906. An early and scholarly study.

LEVY, LEONARD W., ed., *Freedom of the Press from Zenger to Jefferson.* Indianapolis: Bobbs-Merrill, 1966. A collection of documents tracing theories of freedom of the press from the Zenger trial to the Jeffersonian period and the rise of libertarianism.

———, *Legacy of Suppression.* Cambridge, Mass.: Harvard University Press, 1960. A prize-winning study of the English and colonial roots of freedom of expression that documents a thesis that only a narrow concept of such freedom was held before 1800.

MACCRAKEN, HENRY NOBLE, *Prologue to Independence: The Trials of James Alexander, 1715–1756.* New York: Heineman, 1964. The lawyer who edited Zenger's paper.

MOTT, FRANK L., ed., *The Case and Tryal of John Peter Zenger.* Columbia, Mo.: Press of the Crippled Turtle, 1954. An exact reprint of Zenger's original pamphlet.

OSGOOD, HERBERT L., *The American Colonies in the Eighteenth Century,* Volume II. New York: Columbia University Press, 1924. Pages 443–82 give the political background for the Zenger trial, examining the Cosby administration.

OULD, HARMON, ed., *Freedom of Expression.* London: Hutchinson International Authors, Ltd., 1945. A memoriam on the tercentenary of Milton's *Areopagitica.* Contributors are important British and foreign writers, journalists, and lawyers.

PRESBREY, FRANK, *The History and Development of Advertising.* Garden City: Doubleday, 1929. The best-known and most complete history of advertising. Especially useful because of its numerous illustrations.

SCHUYLER, LIVINGSTON R., *The Liberty of the Press in the American Colonies before the Revolutionary War.* New York: Thomas Whittaker, 1905. A short history of an important period in press development.

SHERIDAN, EUGENE R., *Lewis Morris 1671–1746: A Study in Early American Politics.* Syracuse, N.Y.: Syracuse University Press, 1981. Morris defended the interests of landed aristocracies in New Jersey and New York.

WOOD, JAMES PLAYSTED, *The Story of Advertising.* New York: Ronald Press, 1958. Less extensive but more readable than Presbrey.

Periodicals and Monographs

COVERT, CATHY, " 'Passion Is Ye Prevailing Motive': the Feud Behind the Zenger Case," *Journalism Quarterly,* L (Spring 1973), 3. Zenger was the printer of James Alexander's ideas.

KOBRE, SIDNEY, "The Revolutionary Colonial Press—A Social Interpretation," *Journalism Quarterly,* XX (September 1943), 193. A digest of a more detailed study by the same author. Especially useful for its background information.

NELSON, HAROLD L., "Seditious Libel in Colonial America," *American Journal of Legal History,* III (April 1959), 160. Establishes thesis that after the Zenger trial, printers were disciplined by legislatures or governors' councils rather than by trial courts. The colonial assembly became the major force in limiting press freedom. Exhaustive study by legal scholar.

PRICE, WARREN C., "Reflections on the Trial of John Peter Zenger," *Journalism Quarterly,* XXXII (Spring 1955), 161.

STEINER, BERNARD C., "Andrew Hamilton and John Peter Zenger," *Pennsylvania Magazine,* XX (Summer 1896), 405. Hamilton is as much a hero of this period as is Zenger.

Thursday, October 31, 1765. THE NUMB. 1195.

PENNSYLVANIA JOURNAL; AND WEEKLY ADVERTISER.

EXPIRING: In Hopes of a Resurrection to LIFE again.

I AM sorry to be obliged to acquaint my Readers, that as The STAMP-ACT, is fear'd to be obligatory upon us after the *First of November* ensuing, (the *fatal To-morrow*) the Publisher of this Paper unable to bear the Burthen, has thought it expedient to STOP a while, in order to deliberate, whether any Methods can be found to elude the Chains forged for us, and escape the insupportable Slavery; which it is hoped, from the just Representations now made against that Act, may be effected. Mean while, I must earnestly Request every Individual of my Subscribers, many of whom have been long behind Hand, that they would immediately Discharge their respective Arrears, that I may be able, not only to support myself during the Interval, but be better prepared to proceed again with this Paper, whenever an opening for that Purpose appears, which I hope will be soon. WILLIAM BRADFORD.

Remember, O my friends! the Laws, the Rights,
The generous plan of power deliver'd down,
From age to age, by your renown'd forefathers,
O let it never perish in your hands!
But piously transmit it to your children.
Do thou, great Liberty, inspire our souls,
And make our lives in thy possession happy;
Or our deaths glorious in thy defence. ADDISON's Cato.

LIBERTY is one of the greatest Blessings, which human beings can possibly enjoy. When we are deprived of this earthly happiness, we are fettered with the Chains of inimical servitude. Nations, who are born for the mutual support of each other, should preserve a steady attachment to the welfare and happiness of that nation with whom they are united, that their mutual alliance of friendship might be sincere and permanent. When this union is separated by the illegal encroachments on that Liberty, which is the Soul of Commerce, and the support of Life, it degenerates into implacable Enmity, which in time grows inveterate, and finally recoils upon those who have been the means of its unhappy dissolution. *The Liberty of the Press* has very justly been esteemed one of the main Pillars of the Liberty of the People. While this is maintained, the first Steps to Oppression are detected, and the Attention of the People seasonably awakened. When this is suppressed, the Suspicion of the People, and their Ruin may admit of so sudden a transition, as renders the Success of the first impracticable, and the Miseries attending the latter unavoidable. So dangerous is this to lawless Power, that the farthest approaches to it are resolutely opposed, or rigorously punished. So essential is this to Freedom, Property, and Happiness, that the most plausible Attempts to curtail it even in the smallest Degree, have always been most strenuously opposed by the virtuous, free, and unbiassed Patriots. It is the Priviledge of Britons to speak Truth with impunity, and even to fear no Danger from speculative Errors whether in Religion or Politicks. The want of attending to this has produced needless Enquiries, and unjustifiable Censures, of what is true in Fact or no more than bare [illegible] Speculation.—But how unhappily is it to be debarr'd from this last Relief in a dangerous and sickly State! How melancholy to pine and die while no kind Physician is allowed to explore the Cause, or prescribe the Cure of our manifold Disorders? The love of Life, and absence of Pain in some Distempers, is a fatal symptom of the desperate Circumstances of the Patient.

And in all political Disorders the more contented we are under them, so much the worse are they, and so much the worse are we for them. It is a very happy Circumstance attending public Virtue and public Spirit, that the more it is vilified, the more illustrious it always appears. No Falshood formed against it can prosper, for it at once detects and confutes the darkest and most inveterate Calumny. But although public Virtue cannot be affected by the Indulgence of the most unlimited Freedom of speaking or writing, yet Oppression and Tyranny as it derives all its Influence from its Secrecy, may be extremely benefited by the Reverse. For this reason, in Countries subjected to the insatiable Demands of Power and Avarice, the first Attempts to inspire People with a just Sense of their Condition, are commonly nipt in the Bud. It is of the last Importance to the Views of designing Men to shut up the most successful and universal Channel of Information from the People, when they are forming such Schemes as need only to be known in order to be Opposed. Besides the Deprivation of our whole Liberty may be justified on the same Principles as the Deprivation of any individual Part, such as the Liberty of the Press undoubtedly is.

How amiable is the Enjoyment of Liberty! But how detestable are the Bonds of Servitude! 'Tis therefore sincerely to be hoped, that the old *New-England* Spirit so exemplarily free in former Times, will never condescend in Submission to new and unwarrantable Restrictions.

A Day, an Hour of virtuous Liberty,
Is worth a whole Eternity in Bondage.

May we all as loyal Subjects, and free born Britons exert our utmost to preserve the Rights and Liberties of our Country, in a Manner that shall add Honour to our Endeavours; that future Posterity may reap the Benefit, and bless the Hands which were the Instruments of procuring it....

That Glory then, the brightest Crown of Praise,
Which every Lover of his Country's Wealth,
And every Patron of Mankind deserves,
Will gracefully adorn such Patriot's-Deeds,
And leave behind an Honour that will last
With Praise immortal to the End of Time.

Thursday last arrived here the ship Philadelphia Packet, Capt. Budden, from London, by whom we have the following advices.

ROME, *July* 20.

THE harvest in this country hath not proved so good as we hoped. This event hath engaged the congregation established for inspecting into the supplies of provisions for this capital, to seek all possible means to prevent a fresh scarcity.

St James's, August 17. The king has been pleased to appoint the most honourable the Marquis of Rockingham to be lord lieutenant of the west-ridings of the county of York, and of the city of York, and county of the same city; and also Custos Rotulorum of the north and west ridings in the said county of York and of the city of York, and county of the same city; and Ainsty, otherwise Aynstry, of York.

The king has been pleased to appoint the right hon. William Earl of Dartmouth, Soam Jenyns, Edward Eliot, John York, George Rice, John Roberts, Jeremiah Dyson, and William Fitzherbert, Esqrs; to be commissioners of trade, and for inspecting and improving his majesty's plantations in America, and elsewhere.

The king has been pleased to grant unto the right hon Richard Viscount How, the office of treasurer of his Majesty's navy.

St James's, August 27. By the last letters from Col Desmarets, his majesty's commissary at Dunkirk, we are assured, that orders were given by the French ministry, for immediately setting about the demolition of the Jettees, which are the support of the harbour of Dunkirk.

Warsaw, August 1. The tribunal of Great Poland, held at Posnania, has granted permission to the Lutherans at Lobsens to open their church, which has been shut near twenty years, to provide a minister, and to perform divine service in public.

Corunna, July 27. The detachment of one hundred men destined for Louisiana, are on the march for Ferrol, where they are to embark on board the Unicorn frigate with a governor, two capuchin friars, a commissionary at war, and some civil officers.

Cadiz, July 23. Letters brought by the last post from Gibralter say, the report before spread, that the Algerines have killed their Dey, and declared war against all the European powers except England and France, proves not true.

LONDON.

August 17. On Thursday at the king's arms tavern in Cornhill, an elegant entertainment was given by the committee of North-American merchants to Richard Glover, and Charles Garth, Esqrs; when those gentlemen received the thanks of that body, for their endeavours to prevent the soldiery from being billeted upon the private houses of their fellow-subjects in America.

Part of a letter from an officer in the East-India service, dated from the Arcatur camp, January 8, 1765.

"In my last I acquainted you that we did at last reduce Madure. The army has since conquered the Arcatur country for the Nabob, of 100,000l. revenue a year. We are now under orders to attack another chief, or polygor contiguous to this country; both chiefs have mutually maintained an independency of the Nabob till now; merely on account of the impenetrable woods they are possessed of. You certainly have heard before of the memorable battle Major Munro gained at Bengal over Suja Dowla, one of the most formidable powers of India: The consequence of this battle gives the company the command of trade in the greatest part of the Mogul's dominions; and, without exaggeration, the East-India company at present may be brought in comparison with Alexander the Great, whose command, from the river Indus to the river Ganges, was not so much respected as their's."

It is said the new m.....y, taking into consideration the present deplorable situation of the Canadians, have determined to take up all the Canada bills at par, with interest to the present time; and afterwards to demand, in the most spirited terms, *immediate* and *full* payment of France, under pain of all the consequences that can result from a refusal.

The new lords of trade and plantations will hold a board on Monday next, for the first time, at the Cockpit Whitehall.

We hear the rent rolls of the several proprietary estates in America, obtained by former grants under the crown are ordered to be made out, as also an estimate of the annual produce of their land tax, in order to introduce a more equitable form of levying his majesty's revenues in that part of the world.

They write from Gibralter, that English officers and seamen are engaging both there and at Minorca by foreign agents, to serve on board his Sardinian majesty's ships of war in the Mediterranean.

August 20. The right honourable the Earl Cornwallis, lieutenant colonel to the 24 regiment of foot, is appointed one of his majesty's aids de camp, with the rank of colonel of foot in the army.

We are informed, that a gentleman lately very popular in this country, is soon to reside at Lousanne, in Switzerland, where he intends publishing his friend Mr. Churchill's poems, with explanatory notes; and we are likewise informed, that he has an intention of publishing, at the same place, a history of England wrote by himself.

By a vessel arrived at Guernsey from Belleisle there is advice, that the French are erecting several batteries at Sandy Bay, on the south east of the island, and in the great road where the descent was made in the late war by the seamen and troops under Admiral Keppel and General Hodgson.

Aug. 23 We hear lord Viscount Spencer is shortly to be created an earl.

All thoughts of any farther changes are said to be entirely laid aside.

It is reported, that a person of high rank, on being lately offered a great employment, refused it, saying, "that he could not possibly accept of it, consistently with the love he bore to the British nation, which would ever be the object of his care and attention."

Monday some dispatches said to be of importance, were received here from Holland, but the subject has not yet transpired.

Private letters from Paris mention that the true reason

An Emblem of the Effects of the STAMP.

O! the fatal STAMP.

Adieu, Adieu to the LIBERTY of the PRESS.

Facsimile of the famed "Tombstone Edition" protesting the 1765 Stamp Act.

5
The Seeds of Revolution

The United Voice of all His Majesty's* free *and* loyal *Subjects in America—Liberty and Property, and no Stamps.

—Motto of various colonial newspapers

Many believe today that the American Revolution was strictly a struggle by freedom-loving people for independence from a tyrannical British king. Actually, the reasons for the Revolution were much more complex. The clash of debtor and creditor was a factor. The weakness of British policy, inept leadership, and overemphasis of the mercantile system (by which Europeans exploited colonies) were all involved in the dispute. Colonists resented restraints on American development of commerce and industry. They complained that their frontier was being denied to them after the hard-won victory over the French, which they had expected to open up vast new areas to expansion. Refusal of the British to grant home rule was another point of dispute.

But these are not sufficient *reasons* for the war. All of these disputes might have been settled peaceably, some historians say. Other British colonies had similar grievances at the time, yet they did not have to resort to war. Nor can it be held that the issue was confined to Britain and its colonies. In other parts of the world the same issues were being raised. France and South America were soon to be embroiled in revolution, indicating that the War of Independence was a regional manifestation of world unrest.

Many students of the period maintain that the war was unnecessary. American shippers might quarrel over British denial of certain markets, but they knew that the British navy made it possible for them to sail the high seas with reasonable safety from seizure. Certainly the little Atlantic seaboard communities in America could not have provided such essential protection—not by themselves, at least. Merchants resented the trade restrictions, but they knew full well that they also enjoyed great benefits through monopolies and bounties that only a great trading nation, such as Great Britain, could make possible. Frontier settlers might curse such measures as the Quebec Act, which limited westward expansion, but the same complainants were aware that Britain provided the roads by which the frontier was developed and tamed. They knew, also, that British troops garrisoning forts up and down the colonies were the main bulwarks against Indian retaliation.

CAUSES OF THE REVOLUTION

How, then, did the American colonies find themselves at war with the homeland in 1775? Perhaps it can be explained that the war was as much a class struggle—a domestic rebellion, even—as it was a struggle for political separation. The fight for freedom was both internal and external, if we see it as a class conflict. This class struggle was directed by an able and articulate group of "agitators"—one of the best proofs, indeed, of the nature of the conflict. It is even possible that there might have been no shooting war, had it not been for these class leaders. Sam Adams was a typical leader of this movement. He was a spokesperson for a class insisting upon a greater share of control. Having aroused his public, he proceeded to win his goals. For that reason, it is pertinent to study this period in terms of public opinion and through the eyes of those who manipulated public support leading to war.

It is significant that the Stamp Act of 1765 alienated two very influential groups: the lawyers and the journalists. The new law placed a heavy duty on paper used in publishing newspapers. There was also a heavy tax on all legal documents. Thus, the lawyer, who swayed people by the spoken word, and the journalist, who had an even wider influence through the written word, were both turned against those who favored the unpopular act.

Yet one can scarcely blame the British for proposing some such law. After the Seven Years' War, which saw the British triumphant over the French in North America and India, Great Britain emerged as a great empire—one of the greatest of all time. On the other hand, victory found the British nearly bankrupt. Some way had to be found to pay the cost of defending the wide frontiers. Since the Americans had gained so much from the victory over the French, they should be willing to pay a small share of the defense costs, the politicians in London insisted.

The colonists were indeed willing to offer help—in their own fashions. Colonial legislatures were ready to raise levies, but they did not raise enough, and they did not exert themselves enough to turn over such funds when needed. Since the legislatures controlled the colonial purse strings, not much could be done when levies were in arrears. Empire leaders believed the solution was the imposition of special taxes that could be collected more effectively for this purpose. The Stamp Act was one such attempt. The British themselves paid such a tax. George Grenville, sponsor of the hated measure, pointed out that even Massachusetts had imposed a similar tax in 1755. A little later New York did the same.

The colonists replied that the local stamp acts were imposed by the people paying the tax. As Sam Adams brought out in his resolutions of 1765, the colonies had no direct representation in Parliament. He recognized that this would be impracticable, considering the distance apart of the two areas. That was why he insisted that the colonies be given home rule under a common king.[1] But that was no solution to the immediate problem.

The opposition of the editors took many forms. Some suspended publication. Some publications appeared without title or masthead, which technically took them out of the newspaper classification. A few appeared without the required stamp but with the notice that none could be procured, which may have been true since mobs prevented the sale of stamps in every colony. Several publications satirized the event. On the day before the tax was to be enforced, the *Pennsylvania Journal and Weekly Advertiser* appeared with heavy black column margins, or "turned rules," the traditional symbol of journalistic mourning but this time in the shape of a tombstone.

The Stamp Act agitation was actually only an episode in a long conflict between Great Britain and its colonies. The British were leading exponents of the "mercantile system." Under this program, colonies were to be developed for raw materials and again as markets for finished products. Essential to the system was a favorable balance of trade for Great Britain, meaning that the value of exports must exceed that of imports. This policy was fostered by whatever party gained control. That was why the British Government had imposed restrictions on trade, industry, and finances in the colonies beginning in 1651. Scarcity of money in the colonies became a serious matter, for example, but the refusal of British creditors to ease the debt burden embittered many a colonial.[2] An Act of 1751, specifically, denied the printing of paper money secured by land, which would have made money less dear. Sam Adams, often called "The Father of the Revolution," never forgot that his father had been ruined by these restrictive laws and that he had thereby been cheated of his patrimony.

The colonists did not make violent objection, however, until after the victory over the French. Smuggling went on openly, engaged in by respected citizens as a legitimate way around measures believed to be unsound by local consensus. But after 1763, the British began to enforce old laws and to impose new ones. A royal proclamation closed all the frontier west of the mountains to settlement and expansion, thereby raising land values in the older areas. Smuggling was reduced by an effective amendment to an old law of 1733. Currency restrictions were tightened. Commodities never before taxed were now enumerated. And just to rub it in, the home government asserted the right of Parliament to make all laws for the colonies.

The reaction to the trend is seen in the colonial attempts to present their grievances peaceably at first and then by more direct action when this policy failed. The Stamp Act Congress, which succeeded in bringing about the repeal of the hated law, showed the colonies what could be accomplished by united, decisive action. Granted all this, one must still conclude that economics were only a factor in the coming revolution. For ideas were stirring people, too. Indeed, it can be said that the revolution was completed by 1775, if ideas are the criteria, in which case the war was only the means of defending them against those who could not subscribe to the new thought.

Here is where the press of the time played such an important part. The literature of the Revolution appeared in newspapers and pamphlets (often reprints of weekly journals) which expressed the passions and arguments of the revolutionaries. As Beard has said:

> . . . Unlike France of the Old Regime, provincial America did not produce, long before the struggle commenced, great treatises such as the *Encyclopedia* or the ringing calls for revolt such as Rousseau's *Social Contract.*
>
> The reasons were not difficult to find: the colonists already had textbooks of revolution in the writings of Englishmen who defended and justified the proceedings of the seventeenth century—above all, John Locke's writings, wherein was set forth the right of citizens to overthrow governments that took their money or their property without their consent. . . . All that editors and publicists had to do was to paraphrase, decorate, and repeat. . . .[3]

The conflicting ideas as the Revolution progressed can be followed conveniently by studying the products of three journalists who represented their respective classes or groups. They were James Rivington, the Tory spokesperson; John Dickinson, "the penman of the Revolution," representing the Whig philosophy; and Samuel Adams, the evangelist of democracy and leader of the "agitators" or Radicals.

JAMES RIVINGTON, VOICE OF THE TORIES

We are likely to think of the American Tories as traitors because of their refusal to bear arms against their king in the War of Independence. Actually, it was the Tories who remained loyal to their country when others rebelled. Only defeat in war made the Tories traitors. Readers of Kenneth Roberts' historical novel, *Oliver Wiswell,* can understand that there were many sincere and honest Americans who believed in the Tory cause in the middle of the eighteenth century. About 20 percent were Tories in 1776.

The goal of the Tories, apparently, was to retain the basic structure of colonial society. They wished to continue governing by right of property, heredity, position, and tradition—which would appear to be the attributes of a nobility. This seems a strange and distasteful desideratum, by democratic standards, but it had its persuasive proponents. Such a one was Rivington.

"Jemmy" Rivington came to the colonies in 1762, after he had lost his fortune at the race track—not the last newspaperperson to suffer in this way, it might be added. Despite this preoccupation with the sport of kings, Rivington was a credit to journalism and to his class. One can hardly blame him for his Tory views. For generations his family had been official publishers of religious books for the Church of England—the Established Church, and therefore the one that had the most general appeal to most good Tories. King and Bishop represented authority, by which order could be maintained most effectively, the Tory argued. Thus, an attack on the authority of the state was also a threat to the authority of the church, people like Rivington insisted, and the history of

John Dickinson, the Colonial Whig.
Pennsylvania Magazine of History and Biography

James Rivington, leading Tory editor.
Magazine of American History

Samuel Adams, the Radical propagandist.
Bettmann Archive

Isaiah Thomas, Patriot editor.
C. K. Shipman and American Antiquarian Society

revolution has shown that this is indeed the usual consequence. It was the duty of all citizens, therefore, to help the forces of law and order against anarchistic elements.

Rivington was influential in America and could do much for the Tory cause. He was proprietor of the first chain of bookstores in America, with branches in Boston, New York, and Philadelphia. He had been so successful in this venture that he decided to publish a newspaper. In 1773, on the eve of the revolt in the colonies, he founded *Rivington's New York Gazetteer or the Connecticut, New Jersey, Hudson's River and Quebec Weekly Advertiser,* a local paper, despite its impressive, regional title. The paper was well edited and skillfully printed. It was also very profitable, as shown by the fact that it averaged about 55 percent advertising.

Rivington merited respect for his venture because he was willing to discuss both sides of political questions—an objectivity that was not the standard in his era. Such objectivity was just what the "Patriot" rivals resented, however. They were not interested in fair and accurate reports. That was no way to fight for a cause, they believed, and so we find Rivington complaining in his issue of April 20, 1775:

> The Printer is bold to affirm that his press has been open to publication from ALL PARTIES. . . . He has considered his press in the light of a public office, to which every man has a right to have recourse. But the moment he ventured to publish sentiments which were opposed to the dangerous views and designs of certain demagogues, he found himself held up as an enemy of his country.

Rivington's complaint was a common one for Tories in the decade preceding outbreak of war. Power was slipping away from the English authorities into the hands of the colonial assemblies. In their eyes, criticism of the Crown was no longer seditious libel. But criticism of the assemblies, or of the Patriot cause, might well be seditious or contemptuous. Freedom of expression meant largely freedom for your side—and the Tory was on the losing side.

The troubles of the Tory printers came largely from public pressures generated by such Radical "agitators" as Sam Adams rather than from official actions. An organized campaign of threats and economic coercion was reinforced at times by mob action against printers who were not all-out for the Radical cause. The Tories, or Loyalists, were nearly all hounded out of business; those who tried to be neutral were either forced into the Radical camp or into suspension.[4]

In Boston, for example, the well-organized Radical group used threats to persuade some reluctant printers to use their propaganda and to mute Tory voices. When John Mein's stoutly Tory *Chronicle* refused to cower, but instead attacked the Radical leaders, Mein was hanged in effigy, attacked on the street, and finally mobbed. He had to flee to England, and his paper was suspended in 1770. Thomas Fleet's *Evening Post* which tried to print both sides of the argument, closed down in 1775, as did the Tory *Post-Boy.* The last Tory voice, the *News-Letter,* died early in 1776. In Philadelphia, Patriot William Goddard was roughed up for publishing pro-Crown materials in his *Pennsylvania Chronicle.* Rivington thus could complain about the experiences of others, as well as his own, in opposing the Radical-generated tide of public opinion.

After Lexington and Concord, Rivington ceased to be objective. During the war he was as partisan as his Patriot rivals. His wartime paper, renamed the *Royal Gazette,* reeked with unfounded charges against American leaders. He appeared to relish vicious rumors that might harm the rebels—but this was in time of war, whose first casualty is objectivity. And he had little reason to feel charitable toward his political and social enemies. He had been burned in effigy by mobs for expressing his views. Twice his shop had been raided, the type destroyed on one occasion. He had been forced to sign a humiliating public apology for merely voicing his opinions. He had even been driven back to England in 1776, to return as king's printer in 1777. When, in 1781, the news of Yorktown reached the *Royal Gazette,* Rivington became conciliatory. He objectively reported the scene in which General Washington bade farewell to his officers in New York City, after the British had departed. But the Radicals, led by Isaac Sears, were unrelenting; the same mob that had burned him out in 1775 came back New Year's Eve 1783 to close him down. Rivington did not leave with other Tories; he died in New York in 1802.

JOHN DICKINSON, THE WHIG PHILOSOPHER

Advocates for other groups disputed Tory views—some mildly, and some violently. The American Tory was opposed by a rising capitalist faction—it could not as yet be called a party—often referred to as the Colonial Whigs. An articulate Whig was John Dickinson of Pennsylvania, sometimes called "The Penman of the Revolution."

Although not a publisher or printer, Dickinson deserves to be ranked with the great journalists of the period. By newspaper and pamphlet he spread the gospel of his political faith. The gist of his philosophy appeared in a series of articles entitled "Letters from a Farmer in Pennsylvania." The first such letter was printed in the *Pennsylvania Chronicle* in 1767. Eleven others followed on into 1768. They were widely reprinted up and down the seaboard.

Two 1767 events had alarmed Dickinson: the imposition of the Townshend Acts as direct taxes by Parliament, and the suspension of the New York Assembly for not granting tax money to the governor. The Colonial Whigs, to be safe in their properties, had to control taxes in their own assembly, argued Dickinson. This emphasis upon property was the hallmark of sound government.

Dickinson had no wish to bring on a war for independence, but he, more than any other writer except Sam Adams, prepared public opinion for the Revolution, since he stated basic principles that Colonial Whigs came to feel they must defend. Ironically, this mild Quaker became the author of the *Declaration of Rights of the Stamp Act Congress* and two *Petitions to the King* and coauthor of the Articles of Confederation.

Dickinson was as contemptuous of rabble-rousers as were Rivington and the rest of the Tories, for the Whigs had rather narrow ideas of liberty. The great battle cry of the Whigs, for example, was "no taxation without representation," which is strictly an economic aspect of the struggle. The Whigs had no great interest in the rise of the common person. They had only the vaguest of ideas regarding the "natural-rights" philosophy of social reform, for they thought more in terms of property than of human rights. Yet they, too, were fighting for a principle, and in the conflict they brought liberties to others less able to fight on fair terms. The curious twist to all this was that the worst enemies of the American Whigs were their counterparts in England. The British Whigs imposed commercial restrictions that were considered harmful to American business interests. The Americans argued that if British businesspeople in control of the government both at home and abroad could impose taxes arbitrarily without colonial representation, then American business rivals could be driven into oblivion.

When the Revolution had to be defended by arms, the American Whigs had to choose between loyalty to the Crown, which provided the law and order they so prized, or loyalty to the local government, which held the promise of the unrestricted enterprise they coveted. The dilemma forced the Whigs into becoming either Loyalists or Patriots during the shooting war, for there was by that time no place for compromisers. Dickinson himself had to make this choice. He could not bring himself to stand for outright independence from his beloved homeland, and he refused to sign the Declaration of Independence. But he carried a musket in defense of his home.

Dickinson was influential because he was respected by the propertied class—a group generally regarded as hardheaded, practical, and unemotional. Once convinced, the businessperson could do more than anyone else in swinging neighbors in favor of a cause. For neighbors reasoned that if a "sound" businessperson believed in proposed changes, there must be good reason for this attitude. Dickinson reached this group by articles geared to their interests. His letters were brilliant, convincing, and readable. They were widely printed. All but three of the newspapers of the period carried the complete series by the "Pennsylvania Farmer." Ideas expressed in these contributions were reflected in the press for weeks, and even for years.

SAMUEL ADAMS, THE RADICAL PROPAGANDIST

The weakest group at the beginning of the struggle, and the most important at the end of the conflict, was the so-called "Radical" or "Patriot"—words not at all synonymous at a later date. The Tory had great interest in hereditary rights; the Whig was preoccupied with economic issues; but the Radical carried on into a very different field. The Radicals were the only ones seriously interested in social change. They might have been overcome, as they had been in England, however, had it not been for the very effective leadership in America. Probably the best example of the Radical leader was Samuel Adams, one of the most prolific journalists of his time.

As a propagandist, Adams was without peer. He understood that to win the inevitable conflict, he and his cohorts must achieve five main objectives. They must justify the course they advocated. They must advertise the advantages of victory. They must arouse the masses—the real shock troops—by instilling hatred of enemies. They must neutralize any logical and reasonable arguments proposed by the opposition. And finally, they must phrase all the issues in black and white, so that the purposes might be clear even to the common laborer. Adams was able to do all this, and his principal tool was the colonial newspaper.

Adams believed that the American colonies were justified in repudiating the home country because Parliament continued to ignore basic rights. It was the British who broke the contract, he argued, and hence the obligations of the colonials no longer applied. (The theory of the law of contracts was, and still is, that violation by one party releases all other contractors from obligations.) Adams made it appear as though his class and party fought for the traditional rights, now ignored by the British Parliament. Technically, then, it was the British who were in revolt—the colonists were the people maintaining the traditional ways.

Sam Adams was not the only propagandist of the revolution, but he was the greatest of them all. He was truly the "master of the puppets," as his enemies dubbed him. He was perfectly fitted for the role. Adams had turned away from the ministry, from law, and from teaching, although he was familiar with all these professions. As a young Radical, Adams met regularly with the Caucus Club, founded by his father and other aggressive Boston spirits. The club sponsored a newspaper, the *Independent Advertiser,* and in 1748, at the age of 26, Sam Adams became editor of that publication. Later, he was a regular contributor to the *Boston Gazette and Country Journal,* descendant of the second newspaper published in the colonies.

Adams made a strike for liberty in May, 1764, when he was appointed one of a committee of five to instruct his town's representative to the legislature. Included was a denial of Parliament's right to impose Grenville's hated Stamp Act. A final paragraph of the document also suggested a union of all the colonies for the most effective expression of grievances.[5] These instructions were printed by the *Gazette,* and since this paper was closely followed as the mouthpiece of the "Patriot" element, the stirring message was broadcast up and down the seaboard.

EDES AND GILL'S *BOSTON GAZETTE*

At once Adams was recognized as leader of a small but vociferous group. Two of this band were Benjamin Edes and John Gill, boyhood friends and now proprietors of the *Gazette.* By the end of 1764 the newspaper was the nerve center of the Boston Radicals. Many famous Americans wrote for the paper, especially after the passage of the obnoxious Townshend Acts of 1767, which levied new duties on colonial imports, but none was more effective than Sam Adams.

He was more than a writer; he was an expert news gatherer. His Committees of Correspondence, organized in 1772, kept him alert to every movement and sentiment throughout the colonies. His agents "covered" every important meeting as ably as modern reporters gather information for the press services today. In a remarkably short time all such news reached Adams' local committee, which then processed it for effective dissemination where such information was needed. This primitive news service was highly efficient, yet no one in the colonies had thought of such a device until Adams came along.

He was just as successful at instilling his enthusiasm for the cause into the hearts of useful helpers. Since a person's greatness can be measured by the caliber of his or her associates, we must assume that Adams was a great man indeed. Cousin John, who later became second president of the United States, sometimes disappointed Sam, as in John's defense of the British soldiers involved in the "Boston Massacre," but on the whole the two respected each other, as indicated by the fact that Sam used his influence in John's behalf even while the two argued. They were both honest men. John was useful in enlisting the more dignified members of the community, especially the legal fraternity, disdainful of Sam's noisier methods.

Another associate was Josiah Quincy, who understood what some organizers now refer to as "solidarity." Quincy argued that to think justly was not enough; citizens must also think *alike* before there could be a united force of public opinion strong enough to make warriors of the cause invincible. Still another great coworker was Joseph Warren, the charming and kindly physician, who spoke with great logic for the Patriot cause. Warren insisted upon taking direct action when the shooting began. He lost his life as a high-ranking officer in the first pitched battle of the war at Breed's (Bunker) Hill. James Otis was the spellbinder of the group—one of the great orators of his day. The British feared Otis most of all, because of his persuasive powers.

THE SONS OF LIBERTY

The Boston Radicals who gathered about Sam Adams at the *Gazette* office were the core of the revolutionary movement. But they needed a way to win the support of other colonies for the hard line they were developing in Massachusetts toward the British. This was supplied by the Sons of Liberty, whose chapters sprang into being during the spontaneous popular uprising over the Stamp Act of 1765. Adams, printer Benjamin Edes, and engraver Paul Revere were among the key Boston members, from the *Gazette* group. Other printers rated as strong activists in the Sons of Liberty propaganda network were fellow Bostonian Isaiah Thomas of the *Massachusetts Spy;* John Holt of the *New York Journal;* Peter Timothy of Charleston's *South Carolina Gazette;* William Goddard of Philadelphia's *Pennsylvania Chronicle* and Baltimore's *Maryland Journal;* and Solomon Southwick of the *Newport Mercury.* William Bradford, III was a Sons of Liberty officer in Philadelphia but did not fully commit his *Pennsylvania Journal* to the Radical line.

The Townshend Acts of 1767 permitted the Radicals to develop their Non-Importation Agreements, which bound merchants not to import British goods and citizens not to use them. Dickinson's letters had given support to the Boston group, and James Otis and Joseph Warren made bitter attacks on Governor Francis Bernard in the *Gazette.* Bernard played into their hands by persuading London to send two additional regiments of redcoats to Boston to ensure his control. The Boston press and public greeted these troops with indignation and hostility.

Adams and the Sons of Liberty decided to cash in with an intensive campaign of intercolonial propaganda communications that has been called "the most sustained effort to spread ideas through news items that was made in the entire twenty years (1763–83)."[6] This was the "Journal of Occurrences" of 1768 to 1769, which began with the arrival of the new British troops and ended when Governor Bernard was replaced by Thomas Hutchinson.

The still unidentified authors of the "Journal of Occurrences," working under Adams' direction, compiled a record of alleged events involving the British troops and sent it to John Holt to publish in his *New York Journal.* Other papers from New England to Georgia picked up items. The writers chronicled misdeeds of the British troops in garrisoned Boston, ranging from insults and indignities to assault and attempted rape. Since the events were reported in the Boston papers approximately 2 months after Holt printed the "Journal of Occurrences" in New York, rather than concurrently, researchers have concluded that Tory complaints of falseness were probably justified. What the "Journal of Occurrences" did was foster the public feeling that an occupying military force treated people badly and that London was thus punishing Patriots in Boston.

John Holt was the major conduit for this activity of the Sons of Liberty and the most important Radical printer outside Boston. He worked with Franklin's associate James Parker before launching his *New York Journal* in late 1766 as a Whig paper. He became increasingly activist as events occurred that fed the Sons of Liberty movement: the "Boston Massacre" of 1770; the Tea Act of 1773, which precipitated the Boston Tea Party in December; the passage of the Intolerable Acts and closing of the port of Boston in 1774 in retaliation. Holt ran stories from the Boston papers, funneling the Radical arguments to Timothy in Charleston, Goddard in Baltimore, and others.

This helped keep intercolonial support for the hard line the Boston Radicals were proposing. When tempers flared in Massachusetts in September, 1774, Joseph Warren wrote the Suffolk Resolves, which were carried by Paul Revere on horseback to Philadelphia. There the Continental Congress, barely organized, adopted them at the urging of Sam Adams. The action pledged support for the Massachusetts rebels who soon were to be facing British rifles. Not everyone who voted that day realized what Adams had accomplished.

ADAMS' KEY ROLE

Sam Adams could sense victory in 1774. Behind him lay 20 years of propagandizing, organizing, and using every device to foward his aims. Day after day Adams had pressed his foes through newspaper and through pamphlet. He emphasized the need for a realignment of class power. Tory doctrine, which was made to sound so noble by newspaper editors such as Rivington, was only window dressing, said Adams. It could fool only the gullible. He appealed to the self-interest of every type of American, shifting his style with his quill. At least twenty-five pen names have been recognized as in his hand. Late at night passersby looked up at the lighted window of the Adams home, and they knew the veteran revolutionary was still at work, writing a piece for the *Gazette,* perhaps, making it hot for the Tories. His neighbors could not help but be impressed. Many of his loyal followers may not have known just what all the furor was about, but they knew that Adams spoke for them, and they were certain that "whatever the old man wanted" must be all right.

Granted all this, is a public writer justified in smearing people's characters, even for a cause? The question is pertinent right up to modern times. Adams believed that his technique was essential to victory. For years the laborer and clerk had shown inordinate deference to aristocratic "superiors." This attitude was less marked in America than in England, but the attitude had to be completely changed if the masses were to make the big push for liberty and popular sovereignty. For if one class were to be treated with special deference, then the words and ideas of these "superior" persons would have weight all out of proportion to merit and numbers. Somehow, Adams had to whittle the aristocrat down to size. Until the common person was raised and the aristocrat was brought down to a common level, the majority of workers was clearly at a disadvantage. Adams knew how to find the soft spots in the Tory shell.

The ways of the idol wrecker may not be pretty. Governor Hutchinson was correct when he called Adams an assassin of reputations. The governor knew whereof he spoke, for the last British administrator was a favorite target for the caustic rebel journalist. In the end, Hutchinson, who traced his ancestry back to the illustrious and independent Anne (first outstanding woman in American public life), was forced to leave his native land for England. No wonder Hutchinson was so bitter. But Adams was playing a desperate game. His smear attacks were one way of helping to bring down the odds.

The "Master of the Puppets" did his work well. No one had more to do with the outcome than Adams. On the morning of April 19, 1775, the "shot heard 'round the world" was fired at the battle of Lexington and Concord. From then on, the country was in arms, fighting for the ultimate victory that Adams had helped to engineer.

NOTES

1. "Resolutions of the House of Representatives of Massachusetts, October 29, 1765," in Harry R. Warfel, Ralph H. Gabriel, and Stanley Williams, eds., *The American Mind* (New York: American Book, 1937), p. 138.

2. Curtis P. Nettels, "The Money Supply of the American Colonies Before 1720," *University of Wisconsin Studies* No. 20 (1934), pp. 279–83.

3. Charles A. and Mary R. Beard, *The Rise of American Civilization,* Volume I (New York: Macmillan, 1930), p. 187.

4. See Arthur M. Schlesinger, *Prelude to Independence: The Newspaper War on Britain, 1764–1776* (New York: Knopf, 1958), for the story of the use of the press by the Radical propagandists.

5. William V. Wells, *The Life and Public Services of Samuel Adams,* Volume I (Boston: Little, Brown, 1865), p. 48.

6. Philip Davidson, *Propaganda and the American Revolution 1763–1783* (Chapel Hill: University of North Carolina Press, 1941), quoted from the Norton Library edition (New York, 1973), p. 237.

ANNOTATED BIBLIOGRAPHY

Books

BAILYN, BERNARD, *The Ordeal of Thomas Hutchinson.* Cambridge, Mass.: Harvard University Press, 1974. Sam Adams' conservative victim.

———, *The Ideological Origins of the American Revolution.* Cambridge, Mass.: Harvard University Press, 1967. A structured study, utilizing the Harvard Library pamphlet collection, that exhibits feeling for the radical nature of the Revolution. See also Bailyn, *Origins of American Politics* (Cambridge, Mass.: Harvard University Press, 1968).

BECKER, CARL L., *The Eve of the Revolution.* New Haven: Yale University Press, 1918. An excellent one-volume summary of this period by an eminent authority.

BEER, GEORGE L., *British Colonial Policy.* New York: Macmillan, 1907. Presents the British point of view in a way that may not be familiar to the reader.

BOWEN, CATHERINE D., *John Adams and the American Revolution.* New York: Little, Brown, 1950. Follows the school of historical writing that allows the author to describe the feelings of her subjects.

CALHOON, ROBERT M., *The Loyalists in Revolutionary America, 1760–1781.* New York: Harcourt Brace Jovanovich, 1973. Traces the Loyalists' enunciation of principles, search for accommodation, and final appeal to doctrine.

COMMAGER, HENRY STEELE, *The Empire of Reason.* New York: Anchor Press/Doubleday, 1977. The roots of the American Revolution are traced to the imagination and formulation of the Enlightenment of the Old World.

DAVIDSON, PHILIP, *Propaganda and the American Revolution.* Chapel Hill: University of North Carolina Press, 1941. Reveals the tremendous impact of pamphlets, broadsides, newspapers, and books in conditioning the public to rebellion.

FLOWER, MILTON E., *John Dickinson, Conservative Revolutionary.* Charlottesville: University Press of Virginia, 1983. Examines pattern of his political and private life.

GIPSON, LAWRENCE H., *The Coming of the Revolution, 1763–1775.* New York: Harper & Row, 1954. Stresses colonial resistance to more efficient English administration. Part of the New American Nation series.

GREENE, EVARTS B., *The Revolutionary Generation, 1763–1790.* A History of American Life, Volume IV. New York: Macmillan, 1943. Source for social history.

MIDDLEKAUFF, ROBERT, *The Glorious Cause: The American Revolution, 1763–1789.* New York: Oxford University Press, 1982. The first volume of the new Oxford History of the United States.

MILLER, JOHN C., *Sam Adams: Pioneer in Propaganda.* Boston: Little, Brown, 1936. A "debunking" treatment of Adams; sometimes vague, but useful. See also Miller, *Origins of the American Revolution* (Boston: Little, Brown, 1943).

MINER, WARD L., *William Goddard, Newspaperman.* Durham, N.C.: Duke University Press, 1962. Detailed study; also covers his mother and sister.

MORGAN, EDMUND S., AND HELEN M. MORGAN, *The Stamp Act Crisis.* Chapel Hill: University of North Carolina Press, 1953. A scholarly study of the 1765 crisis as a "prologue to revolution."

ROSSITER, CLINTON, *The Political Thought of the American Revolution.* New York: Harcourt Brace Jovanovich, 1963. Written with consensus theory approach, emphasizing unity and continuity in U.S. experience.

SCHLESINGER, ARTHUR M., *Prelude to Independence: The Newspaper War on Britain, 1764–1776.* New York: Knopf, 1958. An excellent detailed study of the role of the newspaper in promoting revolution, and a history of the press for the period.

WALETT, FRANCIS G., *Patriots, Loyalists, and Printers.* Worcester, Mass.: American Antiquarian Society, 1976. Bicentennial booklet containing many reprints. See also Walett, *Massachusetts Newspapers and the Revolutionary Crisis, 1763–1776* (Boston: Massachusetts Bicentennial Commission, 1974).

WOOD, GORDON S., *The Creation of the American Republic, 1776–1787.* Chapel Hill: University of North Carolina Press, 1969. An analysis of political and social thought and the institutions shaping it.

Periodicals and Monographs

CULLEN, MAURICE R., JR., "Benjamin Edes: Scourge of Tories," *Journalism Quarterly,* LI (Summer 1974), 213. Traces Edes' life and role in Sons of Liberty.

———, "The Boston Gazette: A Community Newspaper," *Journalism Quarterly,* XXXVI (Spring 1959), 204. Tells how the *Gazette* reflected Boston life in the 1760s and 1770s.

"The Father of the Revolution," *Harper's New Monthly Magazine,* LIII (July 1876), 185. A good summary of the influence of Adams.

HIXSON, RICHARD F., "Literature for Trying Times: Some Pamphlet Writers and the Revolution," *Journalism History,* III (Spring 1976), 7. A survey.

LAWSON, JOHN L., "The 'Remarkable Mystery' of James Rivington, 'Spy,'" *Journalism Quarterly,* XXXV (Summer 1958), 317. Disposes of myth that Rivington was a secret spy for George Washington.

SCHLESINGER, ARTHUR M., "The Colonial Newspaper and the Stamp Act," *New England Quarterly,* VIII (March 1935), 63. An outstanding Harvard historian describes the influence of the newspaper medium.

TEETER, DWIGHT L., "'King, Sears, the Mob and Freedom of the Press in New York, 1765–76,'" *Journalism Quarterly,* XLI (Autumn 1964), 539. The mob, disrespectful of freedom of ideas, drove James Rivington out of business.

YODELIS, MARY ANN, "Who Paid the Piper? Publishing Economics in Boston, 1763–1775," *Journalism Monographs,* 38 (February 1975). Based on Ph.D. thesis, University of Wisconsin, 1971. See also Yodelis, "Courts, Counting House and Streets: Attempts at Press Control, 1763–1775," *Journalism History,* I (Spring 1974), 11, and "Advertising in the Boston Press," *Journalism History,* III (Summer 1976), 40. Depth studies by colonial journalism scholar.

Facsimile from *Pennsylvania Gazette,* 1754.

THURSDAY MAY 25, 1775. [Nº 110.]

RIVINGTON's NEW-YORK GAZETTEER

Connecticut, Hudſon's River, New-Jerſey and Quebec WEEKLY ADVERTISER

PRINTED at his OPEN and UNINFLUENCED PRESS fronting HANOVER SQUARE.

Aſſize of BREAD,—*Flour at 16s. per cwt.*

A wheaten Loaf of the fineſt Flour, to weigh 1 lb. 13 oz. for 4 coppers.

Publiſhed the 3d of April, 1775.

HIGH WATER at NEW YORK, this Week.

Thurſday	57 min. after 6	Monday	50 min. after 9
Friday	45 min. after 7	Tueſday	27 min. after 10
Saturday	33 min. after 8	Wedneſday	59 min. after 10
Sunday	10 min. after 9		

PRICE CURRENT, in NEW YORK.

Wheat, per Buſhel,	6s. 4d.	Muſcovado Sugar,	50 to 60s.	Fine Salt 3s. 6d. Coarſe do. 2s. 0d.
Flour,	16s. 0d.	Single refined do.,	1s. 2d.	Indian Corn, per Buſhel, 3s. to 3s. 6d.
Brown Bread,	14s. 0d.	Molaſſes,	2s. 0d.	Bills of Exchange, £165
Weſt India Rum,	3s. 4d.	Beef, per Barrel,	45s. 0d.	Do. at Philadelphia, 155
New-England do.	2s. 6d.	Pork,	60 to 65s.	Do. at Boſton,

PHILADELPHIA, MAY 13.

AFFIDAVITS and depoſitions relative to the commencement of the late hoſtilities in the province of Maſſachuſetts-Bay; continued from our laſt:

Lexington, April 25, 1775.

JOHN PARKER, of lawful age, and commander of the militia in Lexington, do teſtify and declare, that on the 19th inſtant, in the morning, about one of the clock, being informed that there was a number of regular officers riding up and down the road, ſtopping and inſulting people as they paſſed the road; and alſo was informed that a number of regular troops were on their march from Boſton, in order to take the province ſtores at Concord; ordered our militia to meet on the common in ſaid Lexington, to conſult what to do, and concluded not to be diſcovered, nor meddle or make with ſaid regular troops (if they ſhould approach) unleſs they ſhould inſult or moleſt us, and upon their ſudden approach I immediately ordered our militia to diſperſe and not to fire; immediately ſaid troops made their appearance and ruſhed furiouſly, fired upon and killed eight of our party, without receiving any provocation therefor from us.

JOHN PARKER.

We, Nathaniel Clarkhurſt, Jonas Parker, John Munroe, junr., John Winſhip, Solomon Pierce, John Murray, Abnez Meeds, John Bridge, junr., Ebenezer Bowman, William Munroe, 3d, Micah Hager, Samuel Sanderſon, Samuel Haſtings, and John Brown, of Lexington, in the county of Middleſex, and colony of Maſſachuſetts-Bay, in New England; and all of lawful age, do teſtify and ſay, that on the morning of the nineteenth of April inſt. about one or two o'clock, being informed that a number of regular officers had been riding up and down the road the evening and night preceding, and that ſome of the inhabitants as they were paſſing had been inſulted by the officers, and ſtopped by them; and being alſo informed that the regular troops were on their march from Boſton, in order (as it was ſaid) to take the colony ſtores there depoſited at Concord! We met on the parade of our company in this town; after the company had collected, we were ordered by Captain John Parker (who commanded us) to diſperſe for the preſent, and be ready to attend the beat of the drum; and accordingly the company went into houſes near the place of parade. We further teſtify and ſay, that about five o'clock in the morning we attended the beat of our drum and were formed on the parade—we were faced towards the regulars then marching up to us, and ſome of our company were coming to the parade with their backs towards the troops; and others on the parade began to diſperſe when the regulars fired on the company, before a gun was fired by any of our company on them; they killed eight of our company, and wounded ſeveral, and continued the fire until we had all made our eſcape.

Signed by each of the above Depoſers.

NEW-JERSEY, MAY 16.—

SPEECH of his Excellency WILLIAM FRANKLIN, Eſq., Captain General, Governor and Commander in Chief, in and over the Province of NEW-JERSEY, and Territories thereon depending in America, Chancellor and Vice Admiral of the ſame, &c.

To the GENERAL ASSEMBLY of the ſaid Province, Convened at Burlington.

Gentlemen of the Council, and Gentlemen of the General Aſſembly.

THE ſole occaſion of my calling you together at this time is to lay before you a reſolution of the Houſe of Commons wiſely and humanely calculated to open a door to the reſtoration of that harmony between Great-Britain and her American colonies on which their mutual welfare and happineſs ſo greatly depend.

This reſolution, having already appeared in the public papers, and a great variety of interpretations put upon it, moſtly according to the different views and diſpoſitions by which men are actuated and ſcarcely any having ſeen it in its proper light, I think I cannot at this juncture better anſwer the gracious purpoſes of his Majeſty, nor do my country more eſſential ſervice than to lay before you as full an explanation of the occaſion, purport and intent of it as is in my power. By this means you, and the good people you repreſent, will be enabled to judge for yourſelves how far you ought or ought not to acquieſce with the plan it contains, and what ſteps it will be prudent for you to take on this very important occaſion.

You will ſee in the King's anſwer to the joint addreſs of both Houſes of Parliament on the 7th of February, how much attention his Majeſty was graciouſly pleaſed to give to the aſſurance held out in that addreſs, of the readineſs of Parliament to afford every juſt and reaſonable indulgence to the colonies whenever they ſhould make a proper application on the ground of any real grievance they might have to complain of. This addreſs was accordingly ſoon followed by the reſolution of the Houſe of Commons now laid before you. A circumſtance which afforded his Majeſty great ſatisfaction, as it gave room to hope for a happy effect, and would, at all events, ever remain an evidence of their juſtice and moderation and manifeſt the temper which has accompanied their deliberations upon that queſtion which has been the ſource of ſo much diſquiet to the King's ſubjects in America.

His Majeſty, ardently wiſhing to ſee a reconciliation of the unhappy differences by every means through which it may be obtained without prejudice to the juſt authority of Parliament, which his Majeſty will never ſuffer to be violated, has approved the reſolution of his faithful Commons, and has commanded it to be tranſmitted to the governors of his colonies, not doubting that this happy diſpoſition to comply with every juſt and reaſonable wiſh of the King's ſubjects in America will meet with ſuch a return of duty and affection on their part as will lead to a happy iſſue of the preſent diſpute, and to a re-eſtabliſhment of the public tranquility on thoſe grounds of equity, juſtice and moderation which this reſolution holds forth.

What has given the King the greater ſatiſfaction in this reſolution, and the greater confidence in the good effects of it, is his having ſeen that, amidſt all the in-

James Rivington balances a colonial account of the battle of Lexington with a speech by Tory William Franklin, Ben's son.

THE

Maſſachuſetts Spy

Or, Thomas's Boſton Journal.

"Do THOU Great LIBERTY inſpire our Souls—And make our Lives in THY Poſſeſſion happy—Or, our Deaths glorious in THY juſt Defence."

VOL. IV.) THURSDAY, JULY 7, 1774. (NUMB. 179.

JOIN OR DIE

NC V M P NJ NY NE

WORCESTER, MAY 3.

AMERICANS! forever bear in mind the BATTLE of LEXINGTON!—where Britiſh Troops, unmoleſted and unprovoked, wantonly, and in a moſt inhuman manner fired upon and killed a number of our countrymen, then robbed them of their proviſions, ranſacked, plundered and burnt their houſes! nor could the tears of defenceleſs women, ſome of whom were in the pains of childbirth, the cries of helpleſs babes, nor the prayers of old age, confined to beds of ſickneſs, appeaſe their thirſt for blood!—or divert them from their DESIGN of MURDER and ROBBERY!

The particulars of this alarming event will, we are credibly informed be ſoon publiſhed by authority, as a Committee of the Provincial Congreſs have been appointed to make ſpecial enquiry, and to take the depoſitions, on oath, of ſuch as are knowing to the matter. In the mean time, to ſatisfy the expectation of our readers, we have collected from thoſe whoſe veracity is unqueſtioned the following account, viz.

A few days before the battle, the Grenadier and Light-Infantry companies were all drafted from the ſeveral regiments in Boſton; and put under the command of an officer, and it was obſerved that moſt of the tranſports and other boats were put together, and fitted for immediate ſervice. This manœuvre gave riſe to a ſuſpicion that ſome formidable expedition was intended by the ſoldiery, but what or where the inhabitants could not determine—however, the town watches in Boſton, Charleſtown, Cambridge, &c. were ordered to look well to the landing-places. About 10 o'clock on the night of the 18th of April, the troops in Boſton were diſcovered to be on the move in a very ſecret manner, and it was found they were embarking in boats (which they privately brought to the place in the evening) at the bottom of the Common; expreſſes ſat off immediately to alarm the country, that they might be on their guard. When the expreſſes got about a mile beyond Lexington, they were ſtopped by about fourteen officers on horſeback, who came out of Boſton in the afternoon of that day, and were ſeen lurking in bye-places in the country till after dark. One of the expreſſes immediately fled, and was purſued two miles by an officer, who when he had got up with him preſented a piſtol, and told him he was a dead man if he did not ſtop, but he rode on until he came up to a houſe, when ſtopping of a ſudden his horſe threw him off; having the preſence of mind to hollow to the people in the houſe, "*Turn out! Turn out! I have got one of them!*" the officer immediately retreated as faſt as he had purſued: The other expreſs after paſſing through a ſtrict examination, by ſome means got clear. The body of the troops in the mean time, under the command of Lieut. Colonel Smith had croſſed the river, and landed at Phipp's Farm: They immediately to the number of 1000 proceeded to Lexington, 6 miles below Concord, with great ſilence: A company of militia, of about 80 men, muſtered near the meeting-houſe; the troops came in ſight of them juſt before ſun-riſe; the militia upon ſeeing the troops began to diſperſe; the troops then ſat out upon the run, hallooing and huzzaing, and coming within a few rods of them, the commanding officer accoſted the militia in words to this effect, "*Diſperſe you damn'd rebels!—damn you diſperſe!*" Upon which the troops again huzzaed, and immediately one or two officers diſcharged their piſtols, which were inſtantaneouſly followed by the firing of four or five of the ſoldiers, and then there ſeemed to be a general diſcharge from the whole body; It is to be noticed they fired upon our people as they were diſperſing, agreable to their command, and that we did not even return the fire: Eight of our men were killed and nine wounded;— The troops then laughed, and damned the Yankees, and ſaid they could not bear the ſmell of gun-powder. A little after this the troops renewed their march to Concord, where, when they arrived, they divided into parties, and went directly to ſeveral places where the province ſtores were depoſited. Each party was ſuppoſed to have a tory pilot. One party went into the goal yard, and ſpiked up and otherways damaged two cannon belonging to the province, and broke and ſat fire to the carriages—They then entered a ſtore and rolled out about an 100 barrels of flour, which they unheaded, and emptied about 40 into the river; at the ſame time others were entering houſes and ſhops, and unheading barrels, cheſts, &c. the property of private perſons; ſome took poſſeſſion of the town-houſe, to which they ſet fire, but was extinguiſhed by our people without much hurt. Another party of the troops went and took poſſeſſion of the North-bridge. About 150 provincials who muſtered upon the alarm, coming towards the bridge, the troops fired upon them without ceremony, and killed two upon the ſpot!———(Thus did the troops of Britain's king fire FIRST at two ſeveral times upon his loyal American ſubjects, and put a period to ten lives before one gun was fired upon them.)—Our people THEN returned the fire, and obliged the troops to retreat, who were ſoon joined by their other parties, but finding they were ſtill purſued, the whole body retreated back to Lexington, both provincials and troops firing as they went. During this time an expreſs from the troops was ſent to General Gage, who thereupon ſent out a reinforcement of above 1400 men, under the command of Earl Piercy, with two field pieces. Upon the arrival of this reinforcement at Lexington, juſt as the retreating party had got there, they made a ſtand, picked up their dead and took all the carriages they could find and put their wounded thereon; others of them to their eternal diſgrace be it ſpoken, were robbing and ſetting houſes on fire, and diſcharging their cannon at the meeting-houſe. Whilſt this was tranſacting a few of our men at Menotomy, a few miles diſtant, attacked a party of twelve of the enemy, (carrying ſtores and proviſions to the troops) killed one of them, and took poſſeſſion of their arms, ſtores, proviſions, &c. without any loſs on our ſide. The enemy having halted above an hour at Lexington, found it neceſſary to make a ſecond retreat, carrying with them many of their dead and wounded. They continued their retreat from Lexington to Charleſtown with great precipitation; our people continued the purſuit, firing till they got to Charleſtown Neck, (which they reached a little after ſun-ſet) over which the enemy paſſed, proceeded up Bunker's Hill, and the next day went into Boſton under the protection of the Somerſet man of war of 64 guns.

A young man, unarmed, who was taken priſoner by the enemy, and made to aſſiſt in carrying off their wounded, ſays, that he ſaw a barber who lives in Boſton, thought to be one Warden, with the troops, and that he heard them ſay, he was one of their pilots; he likewiſe ſaw the ſaid barber fire twice upon our people, and heard Earl Piercy order the troops to fire the houſes: He alſo informs, that ſeveral officers were among the wounded who were carried to Boſton, were our informant was diſmiſſed. They took two of our men priſoners in battle who are now confined in barracks.

Immediately upon the return of the troops to Boſton, all communication to and from the town was ſtopped by Gen. Gage. The provincials who flew to the aſſiſtance of their diſtreſſed countrymen, are poſted in Cambridge, Charleſtown, Roxbury, Watertown, &c. and have placed guards on Roxbury neck within gun-ſhot of the enemy; guards are alſo placed every where in view of the town to obſerve the motion of the King's troops: The Council of War, and the different Committees of Safety and Supplies ſet at Cambridge, and the Provincial Congreſs at Watertown. The troops in Boſton are fortifing the place on all ſides, and a frigate of war is ſtationed up Cambridge river, and a ſixty-four gun ſhip between Boſton and Charleſtown.

Deacon Joſeph Loring's houſe and barn, Mrs. Mulliken's houſe and ſhop, and Mr. Joſhua Bond's houſe and ſhop, in Lexington were all conſumed. They alſo ſet fire to ſeveral other houſes, but our people extinguiſhed the flames. They pillaged almoſt every houſe they paſſed by, breaking and deſtroying doors, windows, glaſſes, &c. and carrying off cloathing and other valuable effects. It appeared to be their deſign to burn and deſtroy all before them; and nothing but our vigorous purſuit prevented their infernal purpoſes from being put in execution. But the ſavage barbarity exerciſed upon the bodies of our unfortunate brethren who fell, is almoſt incredible: Not content with ſhooting down the unarmed, aged and infirm, they diſregarded the cries of the wounded, killing them without mercy, and mangling their bodies in the moſt ſhocking manner.

We have the pleaſure to ſay, that notwithſtanding the higheſt provocations given by the enemy, not one inſtance of cruelty, that we have heard of, was committed by our Militia; but, liſtening to the merciful dictates of the Chriſtian religion, they "breathed higher ſentiments of humanity."

Isaiah Thomas arouses hatred in his famed *Massachusetts Spy*.

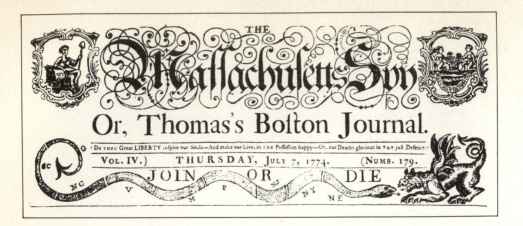

6

The Press and Revolution

Should the liberty of the press be once destroyed, farewell the remainder of our invaluable rights and privileges! We may next expect padlocks on our lips, fetters on our legs, and only our hands at liberty to slave for our worse than EGYPTIAN TASK-MASTERS, OR—FIGHT OUR WAY TO CONSTITUTIONAL FREE-DOM.

—Isaiah Thomas

Printers, publishers, and editors were important influences in preparing the public for revolution and in maintaining the fighting spirit during the War of Independence. Edes and Gill, mentioned in the previous chapter as proprietors of the Radical *Boston Gazette,* were examples of the patriot-journalist. William Bradford, III, grandson of the founder of a famous printing dynasty, wielded both the pen and the sword during the war. His *Pennsylvania Journal* was faithful to the Patriot ideology. But the greatest journalist of the period was Isaiah Thomas, one of the important pioneers of the American Fourth Estate.

ISAIAH THOMAS, PATRIOT EDITOR

Thomas began his career, as an apprentice printer, when he was only 6. He had to help support his widowed mother and therefore missed the advantages of formal education. Later, he became a great scholar, owner of one of the finest private libraries in the country, first president of the learned Antiquarian Society, and historian of the colonial press.

Thomas once wrote that he owed his education to the type case over which he worked so long as a lad. He learned to spell from setting type. He broadened his knowledge by studying galley proof. Zechariah Fowle, Thomas' master, was an inconsiderate employer who turned over much of the actual operation of the shop to his apprentice without appropriate recognition of the young man's worth. The resentful Thomas ran away to Halifax. In 1766, at the age of 17, Thomas was aroused by the agitation over the Stamp Act. He was so outspoken in his views that his new master had to discharge him. After a time as an itinerant printer's helper, Thomas returned to Boston in 1770. Fowle welcomed his runaway apprentice and offered to take him into partnership. Together they founded the *Massachusetts Spy,* a newspaper that lived until 1904.

THE *MASSACHUSETTS SPY,* 1770

Thomas soon bought out his shiftless partner. Under his proprietorship the *Spy* became one of the most successful newspapers in the colonies. It was nominally nonpartisan, but it followed the Whig philosophy for the most part in its early days. Thomas tried to be fair, however. A line under the name plate advertised that the *Spy* was "A Weekly Political and Commercial Paper—Open to All Parties, but *influenced* by None." Until hostilities began this was a successful formula, for at 21 the handsome publisher owned a paper exceeded only by Rivington's in circulation and bulk.

Thomas began to shift his Whig doctrine as it became apparent that conciliationists like Dickinson were ineffective. Eventually he had to make the choice all Whigs had to make—to remain loyal, or to side with the Radicals. Thomas chose the latter course. Soon he was the acknowledged spokesperson for the Independence group in his area. When British troops arrived in Boston to enforce laws formerly flouted by the colonials, Thomas became a leader of the underground movement. It was they who flashed the signal light from the steeple of Old North Church warning the Minutemen couriers of the impending British raid on Lexington and Concord.[1]

The next day Thomas was an eyewitness of the first battle in the War of Independence. If he did not hear "the shot heard 'round the world," he at least understood its significance. His report of the encounter remains today as the most notable war reporting of that conflict. He would have been the first to deny that his "story" of the fight was objective. By that time he was committed to the use of his press as an instrument of war, and his report is therefore highly colored with propaganda favorable to his compatriots. Even so, his word picture of the event was probably accurate in its main theme, and there is so much color and vigor in his writing that the account deserves mention here. According to Thomas' report:

> About ten o'clock on the night of the eighteenth of April, the troops in Boston were discovered to be on the move in a very secret manner, and it was found they were embarking in boats (which they privately brought to the place in the evening) at the bottom of the Common; expresses set off immediately to alarm the country, that they might be on their guard. When the expresses got about a mile beyond Lexington, they were stopped by about fourteen officers on horseback, who came out of Boston in the afternoon of that day, and were seen lurking in by-places in the country till after dark. One of the expresses immediately fled [this was probably Dr. Samuel Prescott], and was pursued two miles by an officer, who, when he had got up with him presented a pistol, and told him he was a dead man if he did not stop, but he rode on till he came up to a house, when stopping of a sudden his horse threw him off, having the presence of mind to halloo [the rider, of course, not the horse] to the people in the house,

> "Turn out. Turn out. I have got one of them."
> The officer immediately retreated and fled as fast as he had pursued. The other express [Paul Revere], after passing through a strict examination, by some means got clear.
> The body of troops in the meantime, under the command of Lieutenant Colonel Smith, had crossed the river and landed at Phipp's Farm. They immediately, to the number of 1000, proceeded to Lexington, about six miles below Concord, with great silence. A company of militia, of about eighty men, mustered near the meeting house; the troops came in sight of them just before sunrise. The militia, upon seeing the troops, began to disperse. The troops then set out upon the run, hallooing and hussaing, and coming within a few rods of them, the commanding officer accosted the militia, in words to this effect,
> "Disperse, you damn'd rebels—Damn you, disperse."
> Upon which the troops again hussaed and immediately one or two officers discharged their pistols, which were instantaneously followed by the firing of four or five of the soldiers; and then there seemed to be a general discharge from the whole body. Eight of our men were killed and nine wounded. . . .[2]

The war was hard on Patriot editors and publishers. They had committed themselves to the cause so wholeheartedly that it was impossible to stay in business under British occupation. Both the *Gazette* and the *Spy* printing plants had to be smuggled out of Boston, if these two Patriot organs were to continue beating the drums for the American cause. The *Gazette* was moved at night across the Charles River to Watertown, where it was published until the British were forced out of Boston in 1776. Thomas had his press sent by trusted employees to Worcester on the eve of the Lexington battle, and he made that city his permanent home thereafter.

Once firmly established in Worcester, Thomas again began to thrive as a journalist and publisher. By the time his fellow Patriots emerged from war triumphant, he was the leading publisher of his day. Seven presses and 150 employees kept his shop in Worcester humming. Under his imprint appeared more than 400 books on law, medicine, agriculture, and science. He was the first American to publish Blackstone's *Commentaries,* a Greek grammar, printed music, and a novel by a native author: William Hill Brown's *Power of Sympathy.* The first American dictionary, by William Perry, was brought out by Thomas and sold 50,000 copies. Later Thomas also published Perry's speller, with sales of various editions totaling 300,000 copies. Among his hundred children's books were the first American versions of *Mother Goose* and *Little Goody Two-Shoes.* Thomas had something for everyone. When he retired from business in 1802, he wrote his two-volume *History of Printing in America* (1810), a classic, and founded the American Antiquarian Society, whose Worcester building today houses the leading collection of colonial printing.

TOM PAINE, THE RADICAL WRITER

Thomas did much to *prepare* the public for the conflict. Another effective journalist of the war was a penniless and somewhat disreputable stranger to these shores.[3] He was Tom Paine, the Thetford Quaker, who arrived on the eve of the war. He was then 37 years old, and his life up to that point had been anything but inspiring. His mother, whom he disliked, belonged to the Established Church. Apparently there was philosophical friction between parents and son from the beginning. After an unsuccessful attempt to work in the corset-making business, young Tom Paine was appointed an exciseman. He was soon accused of incompetency and neglect of duty. Reinstated, he was discharged again for what we would now call "unionization." He had been chosen by the excisemen of his district to represent them in their agitation for higher pay, and it was partly because of his failure as an agitator that he left his homeland.

By a fortunate coincidence, he met Benjamin Franklin, then at the height of his career as our spokesperson in Europe. Franklin, a shrewd judge of character, saw enough in Paine to write a letter of recommendation. Paine was advised to go to America, where Franklin's son-in-law, Richard Bache, would offer helpful advice. Paine arrived in Philadelphia sick in mind and body. He later said that the very air of America was his tonic. With every breath of freedom he grew stronger. He spoke wonderingly of being able to sit in the same coffeehouses with the "gentry." Paine's first contributions were to Robert Aitken's *Pennsylvania Magazine,* one of several such periodical ventures that flowered and withered during this period. Aitken's magazine was one of the better ones. It did not survive, but Paine wrote for it long enough to establish a reputation as a stimulating commentator. Already he was arguing against the institution of Negro slavery and British arrogance and in favor of universal suffrage and education.

Paine's fame as a writer was achieved by means of a pamphlet copied by many of the colonial newspapers of 1776. This was *Common Sense,* which helped to bring the lukewarm Patriots into the revolutionary movement. *Common Sense* appeared in January, 1776, just a little more than a year after the arrival of the uncouth English immigrant. Its popularity was instantaneous and amazing. More than 120,000 copies were sold in the first 3 months. "I challenge the warmest advocate for reconciliation to show a single advantage that this continent can reap by being connected with Great Britain," he wrote. This challenge was hurled at the Dickinsonian Whigs, who shuddered at the word "independence," and they replied in the local newspapers with condemnation of this upstart. In a matter of weeks, however, Paine's views in *Common Sense* were known to virtually every literate American, and it is significant that only 6 months later, the Declaration of Independence committed the former colonies to this doctrine.

THE DECLARATION OF INDEPENDENCE

Congress declared the colonies independent of Great Britain on July 2, 1776, approving the motion offered on June 7 by Richard Henry Lee of Virginia and seconded by John Adams of Massachusetts. Benjamin Towne added this one-line insert in his triweekly *Pennsylvania Evening Post* as he went to press that day: "This day the CONTINENTAL CONGRESS declared the UNITED COLONIES FREE and INDEPENDENT STATES."[4] On July 4, Congress asked John Dunlap, the printer of the *Pennsylvania Packet or The General Advertiser,* to print broadsides of the document that had been penned by Thomas Jefferson and edited by Franklin and Adams. In fact, on the 4th, Jefferson and Franklin worked in the printing room with Dunlap, helping him correct typographical errors. Towne carried the full text on July 6, Dunlap on July 8, and by the end of the month at least twenty-nine papers had carried the glorious news.[5]

The next task of Congress was to mobilize world opinion against the British. Despite censorship in many countries, it was impossible to keep the news of this shocking announcement from spreading. The *London Chronicle* and the *Daily Advertiser* in London carried accounts on August 17 and 2 weeks later King George III made more news by denouncing the "daring and desperate" colonists before the House of Lords. The news was welcomed in oppressed lands such as Ireland and India, but kept secret or ignored in authoritarian countries such as Spain, the German states, and Russia. The greatest impact was in France, where the Declaration and state constitutions were printed as part of a propaganda campaign against the British.

Indeed, from the French Revolution of 1789 to Ho Chi Minh's 1945 revolt in Indo-China, the words of the Declaration were copied in recognition of this dramatic, creative challenge to Old World practices. Being ushered in was a revolutionary age that swept the Western world. The printer-journalists who spread the word in 1776 were making a contribution of permanent value to humanity.

PAINE'S *CRISIS* PAPERS

After fighting broke out later in 1776, the rebels found themselves in a difficult situation. The ideology of the conflict was still vague to the tattered troops. Companies were breaking up fast. The British cut the Americans to pieces at Amboy, where Tom Paine fought as a volunteer. Making his way to Washington's headquarters at Fort Lee, Paine saw the defeated Americans licking their wounds, preparatory to withdrawing to the Delaware River line. His curious status as a foreigner, which was neither that of an officer nor of an enlisted man, gave him access to both groups and he talked with all types of Americans as he walked along the wintry roads. Actually the season was unusually mild, but for the ill-clad troops the nightly bivouac brought only misery. At this crucial moment Paine wrote his first *Crisis* paper.

Whether or not he wrote it at Washington's direction, by candlelight on a drum head, is inconsequential. There is no doubt, however, that it was written from the heart and under pressure. There was nothing new in what Paine said, but like a poet, he expressed what others could only feel. His work was rough, but that made it all the more appealing to the common people for whom it was written. The foot-slogging militiamen understood that one of their own was speaking.

And who can overestimate the power of words in arousing the will to fight? Down through history hopeless wars and battles have been won when words have doubled the force of arms. So it was with Paine's *Crisis.* His style had a kind of Biblical resonance and rhythm. Like Winston Churchill's "We shall fight them on the beaches" speech of World War II, the words rallied weary people by that

The *American* CRISIS.
NUMBER I.
By the Author of COMMON SENSE.
Will be publiſhed in a Hand-Bill this evening.

Advertisement for first *Crisis* paper in the *Pennsylvania Packet.*

most potent of spiritual tonics: dedication to a cause. Paine's words have lived through the generations. In the bleak days of World War II, when there were no victories to report, the conquered peoples, despairing of freedom, listened with kindling hope as these words, written December 19, 1776, came through the ether to their secret radio receivers:

> These are the times that try men's souls. The summer soldier and the sunshine patriot will, in this crisis, shrink from the service of his country; but he that stands it NOW, deserves the love and thanks of man and woman. Tyranny, like hell, is not easily conquered; yet we have this consolation with us, that the harder the conflict the more glorious the triumph. What we obtain too cheap, we esteem too lightly—Tis dearness only that gives every thing its value. Heaven knows how to put a proper price upon its goods; and it would be strange indeed if so celestial an article as FREEDOM should not be highly rated.

The first *Crisis* paper exceeded *Common Sense* in popularity. Printed first in John Dunlap's *Pennsylvania Packet* on December 27, the clarion call was echoed from Patriot newspapers throughout the colonies. Washington had the *Crisis* papers read to his numb troops as the words emerged fresh from Paine's pen. It is significant that the week after Paine made his first plea to the dejected, they turned on the foe and won a needed victory at Trenton.

Other *Crisis* papers appeared as the need demanded. More than any other writer of the war, Paine caught the significance of the American Revolution. While others presented political and economic arguments, Paine advocated social revolt as well. But his adopted country rejected him for his radicalism. The author of the *Rights of Man* and *Age of Reason,* a participant in both the American and French revolutions, Paine died ignored in 1809. His tombstone lists as his most important contribution to democracy his pamphlet *Common Sense.*

THE REVOLUTIONARY PRESS

Only twenty of the thirty-five newspapers being published at the beginning of the war survived. Considering the vicissitudes of the times, that was not a bad record. Many would have disappeared had there been no war. And thirty-five new papers were established during the 6 years of fighting. Enough of these survived to bring the total number of papers at the end of the war up to the prewar figure. All were weeklies, and most of them were Patriot in sentiment.

Revolutionary newspapers went into about 40,000 homes, but each issue had a larger number of readers per copy than would be true in modern times. Every word was read, even to the small "liners" and advertisements. Such enterprise is impressive. On the other hand, any student of the times becomes aware very soon of the primitive communications facilities of the period. It took 6 weeks for the account of Lexington and Concord to reach Savannah. Often the reporting of war events was the most haphazard type. "The Hartford Post tells us," Hugh Gaine, the turncoat Patriot editor wrote in the February 2, 1778, issue of his *New York Gazette and Mercury,* "That he saw a Gentleman in Springfield, who informed him that he (the Gentleman) saw a letter from an Officer in Gen. Howe's Army to another in Gen. Burgoyne's, giving him to understand, war was declared on the sides of France and Spain against the MIGHTY Kingdom of Britain." The news had actually come from a Boston paper already a month old, and the story was not true in any case.[6] Some of the news was high in reporting quality, however. Often it was printed verbatim, which added to its charm and authenticity. That was how the details of the battle of Yorktown reached the office of the *Freeman's Journal* in Philadelphia:

> BE IT REMEMBERED
>
> That on the 17th day of October, 1781, Lieut. Gen. Charles Earl Cornwallis, with about 5,000 British troops, surrendered themselves prisoners of war to His Excellency, Gen. George Washington, Commander-in-Chief of the allied forces of France and America. LAUS DEO.[7]

That was all the paper had to tell of the greatest, and final, victory of the war. The account should have been authentic, because the reporter was none other than General Washington. The editor had printed verbatim the dispatch sent out by the general.

If such momentous events were sparsely handled, so was the run of local and colonial news. Close students of colonial newspapers have found only a little local news throughout the eighteenth century. It was largely political, and in times of crisis, military. Pious obituaries, sermons, fires, murders, suicides, epidemics, and the weather were other topics. Considerable attention was paid to local court proceedings, recent research has found, but usually in summary fashion. However, in the 1730s the *Boston News-Letter* ran reports of trials that included descriptions of the reactions of the accused in court.[8] It was another 100 years before detailed crime and court reporting appeared regularly in newspapers; as in England the colonials bought specially produced pamphlets to get such human interest. They fared little better in the available selection of foreign items; in the 1760s two-thirds of that space went to governmental and military news, only 15 percent to human-interest items (one-third of that crime and justice). Three-fourths of the foreign news came from England. Furthermore, for most items the time lapse between an event and colonial publication was between 6 and 11 weeks.[9]

A serious problem was the shortage of printing supplies. For the most part, paper, ink, and type had come from Europe before the war. Not until 1769 was an American press sold commercially. American paper mills could not begin to supply the demand for stock. Paper at that time was made of linen, and cloth of any kind was scarce, especially in wartime. That was why Washington did not consider it beneath his dignity to issue a plea, asking Patriot women to save all available material that might be converted into printing paper, which shows how important the Commander-in-Chief considered the press to be. In this connection, it is interesting to note that he contributed his prestige to encourage the founding, by the Quaker printer Isaac Collins, of the *New Jersey Gazette,* which for a time served as a kind of army newspaper.

An example of journalistic prosperity in wartime was the *Connecticut Courant.* By 1781 it had the then amazing circulation of 8000 subscribers for each issue. It was full of advertising. Few London papers could boast of such success. The *Courant* printed on paper from its own mill. It was one of the best-printed papers in America. On the other hand, Patriot John Holt had to leave his *New York Journal's* printing equipment behind in New York when the British came in 1776. He settled down in Kingston, but was routed again by British troops. He finally reestablished the *Journal* in Poughkeepsie, and returned to New York in 1783—only to die the following year a worn-out man.

COLONIAL WOMEN PRINTERS

Recent research has shown that women played significant roles in the story of early journalism. Many of the seventeen known colonial women newspaper printers took up and carried on the trade after the death of their printer husbands, a common colonial practice. Two notable exceptions were Sarah and Mary Katherine Goddard, respectively the mother and eldest sister of printer William Goddard.[10]

The Goddards lived in Providence, Rhode Island, when the widowed Sarah apprenticed William to James Parker in 1755. William came back in 1762 and with his mother and Mary Katherine founded a print shop and the *Providence Gazette.* William soon disappeared to follow up connections his work for Parker had given him in New York and Philadelphia, and he founded the *Pennsylvania Chronicle* in 1767. Sarah and Mary Katherine put the nearly defunct *Gazette* back in order and also offered Providence a print shop, bookstore, and post office. Their paper was staunchly Whig. The *Gazette* and *Chronicle* were quick to carry the twelve letters of John Dickinson, for example, and Sarah advised William not to include abusive pieces "against the *Farmer,* who deserves so well of his country."[11] Sarah possessed a keen sense of political timing, calling the Dickinson letters ". . . the completest pieces ever wrote on the subject in America."[12]

Sarah's and Mary Katherine's success in Providence was interrupted when William called on them for help with his *Pennsylvania Chronicle,* in the wake of difficulties caused by his erratic and quarrelsome conduct. Both went to work in the Philadelphia shop in late 1768; Sarah died 2 years later. Mary Katherine

Mary Katherine Goddard.
John Carter Brown Library

managed the print shop and made it one of the largest in the colonies by 1774. Again, William's wanderlust brought a change. He had founded the *Maryland Journal* in Baltimore in 1773 and needed his sister to manage it while he worked to establish a colonial postal system independent of British control. So Mary Katherine directed the *Maryland Journal* and its print shop for the next 10 years. Returning it to William after a quarrel, she ran her bookstore until 1802. She was called "a woman of extraordinary judgment, energy, nerve, and strong, good sense." Isaiah Thomas, the colonial press historian, found she met his exacting standards as an "expert and correct compositor."

So did Elizabeth Timothy of South Carolina and two daughters of James Franklin. Mrs. Timothy was the first colonial woman newspaper publisher, for the *South Carolina Gazette* (1738 to 1746), and mother of Sons of Liberty hero Peter Timothy. Anne Franklin and her daughters took over her husband James' printshop in Rhode Island in 1735, and Mrs. Franklin, her son's *Newport Mercury* (1762 to 1763). Margaret Draper, the last printer of the *Boston News-Letter* (1774 to 1776), did battle against the Radicals and left with the British. From Dinah Nuthead, the first woman printer (Maryland, 1696), to the present, women did and continue to do their jobs.*

*The other colonial women printers: Anna Catherine Zenger, *New York Journal,* 1746–48; Cornelia Bradford, *American Weekly Mercury,* Philadelphia, 1742–52; Anne Green, *Maryland Gazette,* 1767–75; Clementina Rind, *Virginia Gazette,* 1773–74; Mary Crouch, *Charleston Gazette,* 1778–80, and *Salem Gazette,* 1781; Hannah Watson, *Connecticut Courant,* 1778–79; Elizabeth Boden, *South Carolina Weekly Advertiser,* 1783; Ann Timothy, *Gazette of South Carolina,* 1783–92; and Elizabeth Holt, *New York Journal,* 1784–85. (Widows of John Peter Zenger, Andrew Bradford, Peter Timothy, John Holt.)

NOTES

1. Rider Paul Revere was an influential member of the Patriot group and made engravings for their publications. A major mission of the riders was to warn Samuel Adams and John Hancock that General Gage had ordered their arrests.

2. *Massachusetts Spy,* May 3, 1775. This appeared on the inside (page 3) of the paper under a Worcester dateline. After moving to Worcester, Thomas described his paper in a page-one skyline as "THE MASSACHUSETTS SPY, or American ORACLE of Liberty."

3. Paine is usually identified as a writer or political philosopher. In this book the journalist is defined as one who acts as the transmission belt carrying ideas, information, and inspiration to the general public, which is dependent on such resources for rational opinion. This was Paine's prime function during the American Revolution. His work for Aitken on the *Pennsylvania Magazine,* often ignored in sketches about him, also qualifies him for consideration as a journalist, in the broad sense.

4. *Pennsylvania Evening Post,* July 2, 1776.

5. Dunlap was also the first to print the Constitution and Washington's Farewell Address. Journalism historian Frederic Farrar examined many of these early newspapers and displayed them around the United States.

6. Frank Luther Mott, *American Journalism,* rev. ed. (New York: Macmillan, 1962), p. 100.

7. From *America Goes to Press,* by Laurence Greene, copyright 1936, used by special permission of the publishers, Bobbs-Merrill.

8. Robert E. Dreschel, *Newsmaking in the Trial Courts* (New York: Longman, 1982), pp. 35 ff.

9. Al Hester, Susan Parker Hume, and Christopher Bickers, "Foreign News in Colonial North American Newspapers, 1764–1775," *Journalism Quarterly,* LVII (Spring 1980), 18. Newspapers sampled were the *Boston Gazette, Maryland Gazette,* and *Pennsylvania Gazette.*

10. Marion Marzolf, "The Woman Journalist: Colonial Printer to City Desk," *Journalism History,* I (Winter 1974), 100. See bibliographies for Chapter 2 and this chapter.

11. Letter from Sarah Goddard to William, early 1768, quoted by Susan Henry in "Sarah Goddard, Gentlewoman Printer," *Journalism Quarterly,* LVII (Spring 1980), 28.

12. Ibid.

ANNOTATED BIBLIOGRAPHY

Books

ALDRIDGE, ALFRED O., *Man of Reason: The Life of Thomas Paine.* Philadelphia: Lippincott, 1959. The best study of Paine since Moncure D. Conway's two-volume *Life of Thomas Paine* (London: Putnam's, 1892). See also Mary A. Best, *Thomas Paine* (New York: Harcourt Brace Jovanovich, 1927).

CHANNING, EDWARD, *History of the United States,* Volume III. New York: Macmillan, 1927. The high literary quality and thoughtful comments make this volume particularly useful as background reading of the period.

COMMAGER, HENRY STEELE, ed., *Documents of American History.* New York: Appleton-Century-Crofts, 1934; Hawthorn Books, 1969. Contains writings of Dickinson, the Adamses, Madison, Jefferson, and so on. Very useful in checking the original sources.

DEMETER, RICHARD I., *Primer, Presses, and Composing Sticks: Women Printers of the Colonial Period.* Hicksville, N.Y.: Exposition Press, 1979. Incomplete 155-page study of nine women printers.

DRECHSEL, ROBERT E., *Newsmaking in the Trial Courts.* New York: Longman, 1982. Includes an historical review chapter on court reporting in the eighteenth and nineteenth centuries, based on literature review and substantial content analysis of leading U.S. papers. Based on Ph.D. thesis, University of Minnesota, 1980.

EAST, ROBERT, *Business Enterprise in the American Revolutionary Era.* New York: Columbia University Press, 1938. A scholarly review of the capitalistic development during this period.

FONER, ERIC, *Tom Paine and Revolutionary America.* New York: Oxford University Press, 1976. Places Paine in the American setting as a radical contributing to a new society.

GREENE, LAURENCE, *America Goes to Press.* Indianapolis: Bobbs-Merrill, 1936. Goes to source materials to describe how the news of important events reached the people through the press.

HIXSON, RICHARD F., *Isaac Collins: A Quaker Printer in 18th Century America.* New Brunswick, N.J.: Rutgers University Press, 1968. The scholarly biography of a Patriot printer-editor.

HUDAK, LEONA M., *Early American Women Printers and Publishers, 1639–1820.* Metuchen, N.J.: Scarecrow Press, 1978. Brief biographies of twenty-five women printers and library collection listings.

JENSEN, MERRILL, *Founding of the New Nation: A History of the American Revolution.* New York: Oxford University Press, 1968. A major study.

JONES, MICHAEL WYNN, *Cartoon History of the American Revolution.* New York: G. P. Putnam's Sons, 1975. Both an illustrated history of the period and a collection of drawings.

LORENZ, ALFRED L., *Hugh Gaine: A Colonial Printer-Editor's Odyssey to Loyalism.* Carbondale: Southern Illinois University Press, 1972. Business conservatism led to Gaine's moderate politics. His "turncoat" *New York Gazette and Mercury* did not survive.

MARBLE, ANNIE R., *From 'Prentice to Patron—The Life Story of Isaiah Thomas.* New York: Appleton-Century-Crofts, 1935. The standard biography.

MONTROSS, LYNN, *Rag, Tag and Bobtail.* New York: Harper & Row, 1952. Demonstrates that the people's army and government operated remarkably effectively.

PAINE, THOMAS, *The Life and Major Writings of Thomas Paine,* ed. Philip S. Foner, New York: Citadel Press, 1961. Annotated texts of Paine's major works.

SMITH, PAGE, *A New Age Now Begins: A People's History of the American Revolution.* New York: McGraw-Hill, 1976. A two-volume narrative of the revolutionary era. Newspapers were used extensively to provide precise details for its 1900 pages.

SNYDER, LOUIS L., and RICHARD B. MORRIS, eds., *A Treasury of Great Reporting.* New York: Simon & Schuster, 1962. This book contains excerpts from outstanding journalistic writings between colonial times and post-World War II.

TREVELYAN, SIR GEORGE OTTO, *The American Revolution,* Part III. New York: Longmans, Green & Company, 1907. The epoch viewed from the standpoint of a great British historian.

Van Tyne, Claude H., *The War of Independence: American Phase.* Boston: Houghton Mifflin, 1929. Volume two of a study by a leading authority.

Periodicals and Monographs

Garcia, Hazel Dicken, "Of Punctilios among the Fair Sex: Colonial American Magazines, 1741–1776," *Journalism History,* III (Summer 1976), 48. The bulk of material printed about or for women came from men.

Henry, Susan, "Colonial Woman Printer as Prototype: Toward a Model for the Study of Minorities," *Journalism History,* III (Summer 1976), 20. Argues for the use of social, biographical, economic, and local history sources.

———, "Notes toward the Liberation of Journalism History: A Study of Five Women Printers in Colonial America," Ph.D. thesis, Syracuse University, 1976. The five are Ann Franklin, Sarah Goddard, Margaret Draper, Hannah Watson, and Mary Crouch. See also Henry, "Sarah Goddard, Gentlewoman Printer," *Journalism Quarterly,* LVII (Spring 1980), 23.

Hester, Al, Susan Parker Hume, and Christopher Bickers, "Foreign News in Colonial North American Newspapers, 1764–1775," *Journalism Quarterly,* LVII (Spring 1980), 18. Content analysis of three leading papers.

Hooper, Leonard J., "Women Printers in Colonial Times," *Journalism Educator,* XXIX (April 1974), 24. A factual survey. See also Susan Henry, "Margaret Draper: Colonial Printer Who Challenged the Patriots," *Journalism History,* I (Winter 1974), 141; and Norma Schneider, "Clementina Rind: 'Editor, Mother, Wife,'" *Journalism History,* I (Winter 1974), 137, for sketches of Massachusetts and Virginia women printers.

Jensen, Merrill, "The American People and the American Revolution," *Journal of American History,* LVI (June 1970), 5. Excellent example of newspaper, pamphlet, broadside use.

Mott, Frank Luther, "The Newspaper Coverage of Lexington and Concord," *New England Quarterly,* XVII (December 1944), 489. A day-by-day analysis of how the news was spread. Reprinted in Ford and Emery, *Highlights in the History of the American Press.*

Parker, Peter J., "The Philadelphia Printer: A Study of an 18th Century Businessman," *Business History Review,* XL (Spring 1966), 24. The colonial artisan becomes a fledgling capitalist.

Steirer, William F., Jr., "A Study in Prudence: Philadelphia's 'Revolutionary' Journalists," *Journalism History,* III (Spring 1976), 16. The journalists shied away from social and political issues. Uses stand on slavery as basis for judgment.

Teeter, Dwight L., "A Legacy of Expression: Philadelphia Newspapers and Congress during the War for Independence, 1775–1783," Ph.D. thesis, University of Wisconsin, 1966. A perceptive and scholarly study; the existence of contending factions enabled the press to freely criticize. See also Teeter, "Press Freedom and the Public Printing: Pennsylvania, 1775–1783," *Journalism Quarterly,* XLV (Autumn 1968), 445.

"Tom Paine's First Appearance in America," *Atlantic Monthly,* IV (November 1859), 565. Describes Paine's propaganda activities and journalistic contributions. Reprinted in Ford and Emery, *Highlights in the History of the American Press.*

Yodelis, Mary Ann, "The Press in Wartime: Portable and Penurious," *Journalism History,* III (Spring 1976), 2. Apparently subscriptions and advertising paid for newspaper printing costs, with profits coming from other printing. General and religious customers, rather than government and political patrons, were major sources of that income.

Philip Freneau

Benjamin Russell

William Cobbett

Philip Freneau, as an Anti-Federalist editor, helped stimulate the "Second Revolution" that put Thomas Jefferson into the White House. Benjamin Russell, editor of the *Columbian Centinel,* was a pillar of the Federalist party and a noted journalist of his time. William Cobbett, better known as "Peter Porcupine," came from Britain to become a rabid Federalist editor who perhaps has never been exceeded in the art of invective. (Magazine of American History)

7

The Press and the Second Revolution

Men who distrust the people and the future may overwhelm us with their learning, but they do not impress us with their wisdom—thank God

—Gerald Johnson

During the war the Tory had disappeared as a political factor in America, but two other groups now struggled for control of the government. One of the elements was conservative in tone. It consisted, for the most part, of citizens engaged in commerce, banking, manufacturing, and property management. Generally, this group was more interested in preserving and extending its economic advantages than in risking social experiments. The other element was largely made up of the agrarian, small-farmer class, increasingly strengthened by the city wage earners, or "mechanics," as they were called then, but with a significant leavening of intellectuals and political philosophers interested in social reform.

At the end of the American Revolution, the people of the United States had a choice to make. They might continue to experiment with social change, endorsing the ideas that had been their battle cries. Or they might consolidate strength by making right of property the fundamental consideration. Or they might work out some arrangement completely satisfactory to neither but warranting mutual support. The record of the Confederation gave the conservatives hope that public opinion might be swung to their side. The opportunity was the proposal to draft a new national charter.

State legislatures sent the delegates to the Constitutional Convention at Philadelphia, and state assemblies were dominated by the property group. This was because the big commercial centers were strongholds of the conservatives, where land ownership and voting qualifications disfranchised many "mechanics," or laborers. It was therefore the citizens of means and community standing who brought about the fundamental change in government under the Constitution. They succeeded in placing financial power in the hands of a strong, central government and otherwise protecting the position of property against attacks within individual states. But they could not have their way entirely. They could not have obtained acceptance of the new charter by the people unless the authors had made concessions. The document they produced is a marvel of balanced forces.

THE BILL OF RIGHTS AND PRESS FREEDOM

One of the concessions offered by the conservatives was the Bill of Rights. Offered as the first ten amendments, these articles have since been considered part of the Constitution in the sense that they were the price paid by the authors for the liberal consent that made the document practicable. The first article of the Bill of Rights is of special interest to journalists. It provides that "Congress shall make no law respecting an establishment of religion, or prohibiting the free exercise thereof; or abridging the freedom of speech, or of the press; or the right of the people peaceably to assemble, and to petition the Government for a redress of grievances." This is the cornerstone of our press liberty, but there is evidence that the authors of the Constitution spent little time discussing this issue. Madison's careful minutes of the convention show only casual and infrequent mention of the press.

But there was long precedent for the protection that finally was provided the press. British Common Law, as used in the various states, provided great freedom of expression for the times, even though it still recognized seditious libel laws. The same basic principles were stated in the Declaration of Rights written by John Dickinson when the First Continental Congress convened in 1774. Nine of the thirteen states had already provided such constitutional protection by 1787. The Virginia Bill of Rights, of 1776, stated: "That freedom of the press is one of the great bulwarks of liberty, and can never be restrained but by despotick governments. . . ." Article XVI of the Massachusetts Bill of Rights, of 1780, expressed similar sentiments, and other states used variations of this theme to establish the principle.[1]

This probably explains why the authors of the new national charter ignored the press issue. They assumed that full protection was already granted under the states. Charles Pinckney of South Carolina did present a draft of a constitution with a clause similar to the one eventually adopted, but apparently little attention was paid to his suggestion at that time.

It was soon clear, however, that the Constitution could not possibly succeed without concessions to public sentiment. Delegates from Massachusetts reported that it would be impossible to win ratification of the Constitution in that state without a clause concerning freedom of expression. Virginia could not muster enough votes for ratification until Governor Edmund Randolph called upon the framers to add the Bill of Rights. A constitutional committee was appointed to draft such a bill. The resolution was a modification of the Virginia document. Delegates were then told to return to their respective states and to use all influence available in mustering support for ratification of the main document on the promise that the Rights clauses would be included in the charter. It was on this understanding that New York finally approved the Constitution, but even so, it was not an easy victory for the Federalists.

Because of promises given, the Bill of Rights was an important issue in the first session of Congress. Madison headed the committee charged with drafting the amendments. When his first draft was read out of committee, it stated: ". . . no state shall violate the equal rights of conscience or of freedom of speech. . . ." The select committee to which the report was referred added ". . . or of the press." Modified by House and Senate, the clause became the first amendment, as ratified in 1791.

It should be noted that freedom of the press is part of our fundamental law, regardless of how it came to be included. In Great Britain, Parliament provides the protection granted by our Constitution, and presumably, Parliament could also take away that right. In the United States, such freedom could not be restricted legally without submitting the question to Constitutional amendment. Neither the president nor Congress could abridge freedom of the press without running into resistance from the courts. In Great Britain, the courts have no such check. Furthermore, the specific mention of press freedom in our Constitution *in addition* to our recognition of the common law on the subject, upon which the British have depended as a safeguard, showed that liberty of the press was more advanced on this side of the Atlantic in 1791 than it was in the freest state in Europe.

THE FEDERALIST SERIES

Curiously, the press, which had to be protected as a concession to the public sentiment, was the most effective weapon of the conservatives in winning support for the charter they grudgingly admitted was the best document they could obtain in favor of their interests. The best exposition of the conservative doctrine was a series of articles that first appeared in the semiweekly *New York Independent Journal* from October, 1787, to April, 1788. Reprinted throughout the country and later published in pamphlet and (with six new essays) book form, these articles are known collectively as *The Federalist.*

They were written for mass consumption, and they were so effective that they gave their name to the party that was actually nationalist in doctrine, rather than federalist. The Federalists, as they came to be known during the publication of the eighty-five offerings, won their fight with this journalistic effort. Written hastily, much as daily editorials were written later on, these are still read, not only as revealing political studies but also as good literature. Alexander Hamilton wrote the largest number of *Federalist* articles over the pen name "Publius." James Madison is believed to have written twenty-nine, some of which are the best in the series. John Jay, a noted New York state political leader, probably wrote a half dozen. In clear, concise style, *The Federalist* explained the philosophy of the Constitutional party. The gist of this doctrine is described in the tenth, supposedly written by Madison. Madison stood somewhere between the two opposing leaders. He disapproved of Hamilton's financial and autocratic ideas, but he veered from his mentor, Jefferson, in sponsoring a stronger national government. Madison had attended all the meetings of the constitutional committee and had engineered many of the modifications in the document. Said he, in describing the form of government prescribed by the framers of the national charter: ". . . justice must prevail [even] over a majority" to prevent the whims of an unstable public from wrecking the ship of state. This control would be accomplished through a republican form of government, offering protection to the masses, without direct control by them, as under the true "democratic" system.

ALEXANDER HAMILTON, LEADER OF THE FEDERALISTS

The Federalist firmly established Alexander Hamilton as leader of the party that took the title of the series as its label. He saw himself as the St. George of the anarchist dragon, fostered, he felt, by the radicalism and disorganization of the liberals. "We should be rescued from democracy," Hamilton insisted, and he looked forward to a restoration of an aristocracy, according to at least one of his biographers.[2] It has been suggested that Hamilton's respect for the aristocracy, and his continual seeking of recognition by those who valued heredity most highly, may have depended on the uncertainty of his paternity. Why was he a Patriot in the Revolution, instead of a Tory then? Born and reared to young manhood in the British West Indies, Hamilton became an American not so much out of hatred for the British social and political structure as out of contempt for British corruption and mismanagement.

That is why he fought for home rule, and there can be no doubt that he had strong feelings on the subject before the cause of revolution was generally endorsed. His war record was excellent. General Washington, who recognized Hamilton's virtues and who understood the youngster's faults (he was 18 at the time of Lexington and Concord), had a hard time keeping the fiery Patriot out of battle and behind the ledgers, where he was much more useful.

This was the man who led the Federalists. One cannot speak of him without indicating bias, one way or the other. In his day he was one of the most respected and reviled men in government. He had little knowledge of social forces. Never having lived the life of toil, he tended to dismiss the problems of the working people. He was quick to see that a government of fine phrases and glittering shibboleths was certain to be ineffective. He believed that the way to make government work was to let those with special interests in it control it, since they had most to lose by inept rule. Let those qualified take command, insisted Hamilton, who always imagined himself as the ideal soldier, ruling by command rather than by consultation.

Hamilton believed it his duty to establish the credit of the country by drastic financial measures, regardless of the luckless victims of an inadequate monetary system. He had no compassion for popular leaders such as Daniel Shays, the Massachusetts war veteran who led a hopeless revolt in 1786 against a taxation and hard money policy that threatened the very livelihood, to say nothing of the freedoms, of the small farmer. Hamilton saw the danger in such uprisings of the common people, and that was one reason he wished to rush through the Constitution, which he correctly predicted would solve many problems. But he would have taken care of the Shayses by force, rather than by placating the aggrieved. He admired military efficiency. Yet his life was to prove his genius not as a soldier but as a writer and political thinker. As Bowers says:

> He was a natural journalist and pamphleteer—one of the fathers of the American editorial. His perspicacity, penetration, powers of condensation, and clarity of expression were those of a premier editorial writer. These same qualities made him a pamphleteer without peer. That he would have shone with equal luster in the reportorial room of a modern paper is shown in his description of the hurricane and in his letter to Laurens picturing vividly the closing hours of Major Andre. From the moment he created a sensation with "A Farmer Refuted" in his eighteenth year, until in the closing months of his life he was meeting Coleman surreptitiously in the night to dictate vigorous editorials for the New York *Evening Post* he had established, he recognized his power. No man ever complained more bitterly of the attacks of the press; none ever used the press more liberally and relentlessly to attack . . . Nowhere in the literature of invective is there anything more vitriolic than the attack on a war speculator and profiteer, under the signature of "Publius." . . . But usually he appealed to reason, and then he was at his best. . . . It will be impossible to comprehend the genius of Hamilton, his domination of his party, and his power, despite his unpopularity with the masses, without a foreknowledge of his force with the pen. It was his scepter and his sword.[3]

That was how the biographer, Bowers, answered those who underestimated Hamilton's journalistic role. This was the man who led the forces working for the ratification of the Constitution. Curiously, Hamilton did not like the document. It was a "shilly-shally thing of milk and water which could not last and was good only as a step to something better," he once said.[4] Although the Constitution was supposedly the product of the conservatives, it was all too liberal for an admirer of aristocracy, such as Hamilton. He sponsored it, however, by facing what he believed to be the facts. The document offered a means of drawing together the types of persons Hamilton believed should control government. And although he disapproved of its populist concessions, he was shrewd enough to see that such compromise was essential, if any protection of property was to be imposed. When, on a summer day, he drifted slowly down the Hudson River on the New York packet and thereupon decided to subordinate his personal preferences in writing the first of *The Federalist* papers, he reached the height of his greatness. Had he accomplished nothing else in his lifetime, his services as a journalist that day would have justified his niche in the memory of fellow citizens.

THE FEDERALIST EDITORS: FENNO, WEBSTER, COBBETT, RUSSELL

The outstanding Federalist newspaper in the lush days of the party was the *Gazette of the United States.* Sponsored and supported by Hamilton, it was edited by John Fenno, who issued the first edition at the national capital, then in New York, April 15, 1789. With Fenno, who had been a school teacher, we are already beginning to see the development of the specialized journalist. Most of the previous editors and publishers had come up through the print shop. Fenno established his reputation as a journalist without benefit of mechanical apprenticeship. Soon his paper was the acknowledged mouthpiece of the Federalist party and it moved with the government when Philadelphia became the national capital in 1791.

Another powerful Federalist voice was that of Noah Webster, remembered for his dictionary but a man of many parts. Lawyer, pioneer weatherman, translator, historian, economist, and scientific farmer, Webster was recognized in his day as a great editor. He started out as a lawyer and teacher. He was fascinated by words. His avocation resulted in a three-part *Grammatical Institute of the English Language.* The first part, the speller, appeared in 1784 and enjoyed a phenomenal sale—eventually 60 million copies were sold (not all within the author's lifetime, of course). Webster came back to New York in 1793 to edit the daily *Minerva* and the semiweekly *Herald* (after 1797 the *Commercial Advertiser* and *Spectator,* respectively), as a supporter of Hamilton.

Webster was an articulate and intelligent interpreter of the Federalist program. He defended President Washington against the smear tactics of such editors as Freneau and Bache and stood firm for the party against opposition attacks. Webster was no mere party hack, however. He resented what he called the "betrayal" of President Adams by Hamilton, the circumstances of which are described later. At any rate, the *Minerva* was an important organ in the Federalist attempt to regain control. Eventually Webster tired of politics, however, and returned to his old love: linguistics. He is remembered now for his dictionary, which appeared in preliminary form in 1803 and as a great contribution to lexicography in 1828.

Another great Federalist editor was William Cobbett, who was never an American at all but who offered severe criticism of the (Jeffersonian) Republicans and defended the Federalists between 1794 and 1800. Cobbett became a refugee in this country after exposing graft and corruption in the British army. He first showed his writing abilities in an attack on Joseph Priestley, whose scientific views were curiously related to his political views, which were leftist. Encouraged by the success of his writing and sponsored by friends of the Federalist party, Cobbett gave up his modest tutoring position in 1797 to edit *Porcupine's Gazette and Daily Advertiser* in Philadelphia. He timed its appearance with the inauguration of John Adams.

In the short span of 3 years, Cobbett made a name for himself throughout the new country. He made no pretense of objectivity. His purpose was to expose his enemies, and his weapon was his vitriolic pen. Few editors in history have surpassed the British exile in sustained vituperation. His general theme was alliance with Britain, war against France, and perdition for Republicans. Tom Paine was his special target, and his biography of the Revolution's penman was all the more readable because Cobbett never let himself be restrained by the facts. In short, he had a marvelous time lampooning his enemies and their ideas. His pseudonym, "Peter Porcupine," appeared regularly after he "told off" a magazine editor in a pamphlet entitled *A Kick for a Bite.* A reviewer of the piece likened Cobbett to a porcupine, a creature with bristles erect against those who sought to manhandle it. That was just the creature Cobbett fancied himself as being, and he gloried in the name.

The oldest Federalist paper was Major Benjamin Russell's *Massachusetts* (later *Columbian*) *Centinel,* published in Boston. Russell fought at Lexington as a lad of 13. He learned the printing trade under Isaiah Thomas and after serving his time as a journeyman founded his paper in 1784. His first big crusade was his attempt to push his state toward ratification of the Constitution. That put him in the forefront of the forces that eventually rallied under the Federalist banner. Russell was pro-British, anti-French, an advocate of an American nobility, and later a hater of Jefferson. His paper followed the Federalist line 100 percent, but in addition, it had excellent news coverage, and it enjoyed great prosperity.

THE FRENCH REVOLUTION

With such journalistic big guns trained upon their hapless opponents, the Federalists rapidly consolidated their power. Had it not been for the French Revolution, they might have annihilated the ideas for which many an American had fought. As Colonel Thomas W. Higginson wrote in his voluminous notes of the period, the French Revolution "drew a red hot plow share through the history of America."[5] Whereas America had triggered the French upheaval after its own fight for freedom, the French were now repaying in kind—and just in time. The French influence stopped the American monarchists in their tracks. It destroyed the last hope of the aristocrats and it changed the trend toward realliance with the British. It also provided the literature and philosophy needed as ammunition against the skillful journalistic batteries defending the Federalist citadel. All that was needed was a great leader. As usual in such emergencies, a great one emerged.

THOMAS JEFFERSON, ANTI-FEDERALIST

He was Thomas Jefferson, then Secretary of State in Washington's cabinet. Jefferson was the antithesis of his colleague, Hamilton, both in temperament and in ideology. The American yeoman, rather than the commercial person, was Jefferson's ideal of the sovereign citizen. He was convinced that no other people of the world were so well off as the independent, rural landowners of the United States. Having seen the wretchedness of European cities, he was all the more certain that the benefits of the American yeoman must be maintained. It should be pointed out, however, that Jefferson did not stand as tribune for all the groups made up of the common people. He distrusted the proletariat—the workers in the cities. The slum was his measurement of a sick society.

It is commonly believed that Jefferson was an idealist, as opposed to Hamilton, the hardfisted realist. Actually, an argument could be presented to show that just the reverse was true. If we assume that a realist is one who would make the best of the situation facing him or her, and the idealist is the proponent of things as they should be, then Jefferson emerges more and more as the realist. Jefferson and Hamilton lived before the age of great industrial development in this country. Jefferson based his political philosophy on an existing agrarian economy. He faced conditions as they were and sought to make the best of them. Under the preceding definition, that would make him a realist. Hamilton did everything he could to gear America for a capitalist, industrial future. He was so far ahead of his time that we can only conclude that he was an idealist.

The two clashed on every point. For Jefferson's purposes, a decentralized, states'-rights government was sufficient. Since credit, commerce, and manufacturing were subordinate matters, Jefferson would have been content with no more government than was necessary to preserve internal order. Hamilton stood for exactly the opposite. Thus, the Federalist leader insisted upon a *responsible* government—one that could protect property and aid commerce—whereas Jefferson was much more interested in a *responsive* government and was more concerned with the current needs of the people than with security.

The two champions inevitably clashed openly, as they had privately since their appointments as cabinet officers. The issue came to a head in 1791. Jefferson returned from a tour through New England with Madison to find himself the center of controversy. The two had already been mentioned in the *Maryland Journal* as potential Anti-Federalist leaders. At this point, Edmund Burke in England had launched an attack upon those who defended the French Revolution. Paine had replied in his brilliant defense of democracy, *Rights of Man.* The Federalists saw to it that Burke's charges were widely reprinted in America. Paine's reply was slow in coming. Jefferson had obtained a copy from Madison, however, and it elated him; here was the answer to the Federalist gospel. He encouraged the American publication of Paine's book. Unfortunately, Jefferson had to return the only copy of the *Rights of Man* before he had finished it, so that it could be set up in type. To save time, he sent it directly to the printer, and he enclosed a note explaining the reason for the delay: "I am extremely pleased to find it will be reprinted here," he wrote, "and that something is at length to be publicly said against the political heresies which have sprung up among us. I have no doubt our citizens will rally a second time round the standard of *Common Sense.*"

Jefferson maintained that he was surprised when he discovered the printer had used this note as a preface to the book. The general reader could only assume that the Secretary of State meant that the "political heresies" applied to such leaders as Vice President John Adams, whose tedious "Discourses of Davilla" were being accepted as holy writ by Federalists as the essays appeared serially in John Fenno's *Gazette of the United States.* This was, of course, a serious breach of official family etiquette. Cabinet members were not supposed to bicker publicly. As a result, a storm of abuse broke over Jefferson. His friends rose to defend him. Another result was that thousands rushed to buy copies of the Paine book. Thus, the political battle was joined, and Jefferson found himself thrust into the van as leader. He accepted the responsibility.

PHILIP FRENEAU, JEFFERSON'S EDITOR

Philip Freneau, who helped to start the second internal revolution, was a lifelong rebel. It is significant that he was of Huguenot extraction; the Huguenots had suffered for generations in the cause of religious freedom. Freneau was graduated from Princeton in 1771. At that time the college was a hotbed for sedition. Among the students who gathered in the room Freneau shared with James Madison were such "Radicals" as Harry Lee, Aaron Burr, and William Bradford, later a member of Washington's cabinet. Freneau was the most zealous Patriot of the lot. Long before the Revolution he was writing newspaper contributions and fierce poems on liberty. After Lexington and Concord, he took an active part in the conflict—a rather pathetic little man, pitting his feeble efforts uselessly, as it turned out, against the enemy. In disgust, he took to the sea in one of his father's ships.

He was in Bermuda when news arrived of the Declaration of Independence. Here was Revolution he could understand. Freneau hurried home to take an active part in the movement. With Letters of Marque (license for a civilian to wage war) from the Continental Congress, he put his available resources into a privateer, a vessel he called the *Aurora.* The ship had to strike its colors in the first battle, and Freneau spent weary weeks in the notorious British prison hulks anchored in New York harbor—an experience that left him physically shattered and made him an even more implacable hater of the British. At length he was exchanged. Returning to New York sick and penniless, he turned to his last resource: his pen. Freneau's poem, "The Prison Ship," whipped apathetic Patriots into renewed efforts against the enemy. His account of the exploits of John Paul Jones instilled pride into a dejected nation.

By the end of the war he had given his health, his fortune, and all his soul to the cause of liberty. As he saw it, the sacrifice had been in vain. He charged his old leaders—Washington included—with failure to carry out the promises of 1776. He saw Jeffersonian Republicanism as a movement to carry on the original drives of the Revolution over the opposition of the Federalists.

It was Madison, Freneau's classmate, who brought the little rebel to Jefferson's attention. Madison had told the Anti-Federalist leader that Freneau was just the man to engage in journalistic jousting with such champions as Fenno or Russell. Jefferson was always considerate of the ideas of Madison, who was like a son to the master of Monticello. He offered Freneau a small subsidy as State Department translator if he would found an Anti-Federalist paper. It was not money that lured Freneau to the capital at Philadelphia, however. He saw himself as a journalistic crusader.

FRENEAU VS. FENNO: VITUPERATIVE PARTISANSHIP

And so it was that Freneau became editor of the *National Gazette* in 1791. The early editions were mild enough, but there were hints of what was to come. Fenno, his rival, would never have tolerated a phrase like "public opinion sets the bounds to every government, and is the real sovereign of every free one."[6] The four short columns of comment on page one of the *National Gazette* looked innocuous in those first few months, but while Fenno was ridiculing the right of plain citizens to complain against government officials, Freneau was telling his readers that "perpetual jealousy of the government" was necessary against "the machinations of ambition," and he warned that "where that jealousy does not exist in a reasonable degree, the saddle is soon prepared for the back of the people."[7]

Then one day Freneau discharged both barrels at Hamilton over the injustices of debt funding. He used the pen name "Brutus" that day, and at once the Federalist leader discovered he had a journalistic foe worthy of his steel. Day by day Freneau sent succeeding volleys after the first one, and his brashness encouraged other articulate voices to sound the call to battle stations. Even the less gifted Anti-Federalist editors could arouse readers now, by picking up *National Gazette* "exchanges." The alarm of the Federalists was indicated by the torrent of abuse flowing from their editorial pens, but this, too, Freneau could return in double measure.

Freneau was so nettlesome that Hamilton made the mistake of joining in the fray personally, writing an unsigned article for Fenno's paper saying that an employee of the government should not be criticizing its policies. Freneau replied that the small stipend paid him in Jefferson's state department did not muzzle him. Hamilton's identity as a writer being already revealed, he now accused Jefferson of being the real author of the *National Gazette's* vilifications. The quarrel between the two cabinet officers had to be refereed by President Washington, but he found the breach beyond repair. Indeed, Washington was dismayed by "that rascal Freneau," as he called him, when he wrote such items as: "The first magistrate of a country . . . seldom knows the real state of the nation, particularly if he be buoyed up by official importance to think it beneath his dignity to mix occasionally with the people." Freneau considered Washington a fair target because in the editor's opinion the old general had lent his name as "front man" for Federalism.

In the end, it was neither the opposition nor the government that defeated Freneau. The *National Gazette* simply died of financial malnutrition. There were no "angels" to come to the rescue, as there had been for Fenno under Hamilton's sponsorship. Jefferson could offer some help, but when he left the cabinet in 1793, Freneau had virtually no financial support. When yellow fever drove his workers out of the city, Freneau closed the office. He never reopened it. The paper had lasted only 2 years, but it is doubtful if any other publication accomplished so much in that time. The end of the paper was just about the end of Freneau as a journalist, too. He tried his hand for a time in New Jersey and New York, but eventually he returned to the sea. Later, he was rediscovered as a poet.

BACHE AND THE *AURORA*

One of the leading journalists who carried the torch of Anti-Federalism dropped by Freneau was Benjamin Franklin Bache, the grandson of Benjamin Franklin. Bache was just 21 in 1790 when he founded the *Philadelphia General Advertiser,* better known as the *Aurora* (the name appeared in small print around the name plate). Bache was a mercurical young man—impetuous, brilliant, and often intemperate in expression. He was influenced by the style of Freneau, and his paper was even more violently partisan than the *National Gazette* had been. Too often he was downright vicious.

Not that the Federalists did not give him cause for his editorial mudslinging. He had seen the statue of his grandfather—one of the great men of the country—desecrated by hoodlums inspired to acts of vandalism by those opposed to the principles so ably enunciated by "Poor Richard" in Franklin's famous *Almanac.* Brought up in France and Switzerland by his doting grandfather, young Bache was sympathetic to the French cause from the beginning of his journalistic career. That put him in opposition to President Washington when the old war hero backed the anti-French party headed by Hamilton and others. Like Freneau, Bache resorted to personal attack in his campaign to wreck the Federalist party. He even tried to besmirch the character of "The Father of His Country."

"If ever a nation was debauched by a man, the American nation has been debauched by Washington," he wrote in the December 23, 1796, issue of the *Aurora.*

Federalists wrecked the *Aurora* office and beat the editor in retaliation. Fenno caned Bache in the street and Cobbett wrote of him in *Porcupine's Gazette:*

> This atrocious wretch (worthy descendant of old Ben) knows that all men of any understanding put him down as an abandoned liar, as a tool and a hireling, . . . He is an ill-looking devil. His eyes never get above your knees. He is of a sallow complexion, hollow-cheeked, dead eyed, and has a *toute ensemble,* just like that of a fellow who has been about a week or ten days in a gibbet.[8]

Some historians have called this period the "Dark Ages of Journalism," because of the scurrility of the press. This was a transition period, however, and perhaps violent partisanship, as reflected in the press, was a means of expending some of the venom stored up against the British after the war.[9] Adding to the tension was the war between Great Britain and revolutionary France. It was not easy for Americans to take the advice of Washington, who warned against entangling foreign alliances in the last hours of his administration.[10] The new nation had little to gain by taking sides, but unfortunately, the war was forced on the attentions of Americans by the belligerents.

The French and the British were about equally callous regarding American foreign policy. The "paper" blockades imposed by Napoleon violated international precedent, and American shipping interests were infuriated by unlawful seizure of their vessels by the French. But the British were annoying, too. They had fallen back on the "Rule of 1756," which forbade neutrals from trading in wartime with nations not ordinarly regular customers. This made sense to the British, for it was clear to them that otherwise the enemy could supply itself through adjoining neutral countries, despite the blockade. However, the enforcement of this rule threatened the development of American commerce.

THE ISSUE OF FRANCE

But the Federalists saw evil only in France. They were repelled by the excesses of the French Revolution and by the success of Napoleon. Since the Federalists were in firm control of the government, they could manipulate foreign policy to favor the British. The Anti-Federalists argued that America had the duty of siding with France in the name of Rochambeau, Lafayette, and DeGrasse, who had come from France to help us win our war with Britain. Federalists answered that our promises of assistance to France in time of trouble had been made to a government since overthrown by a regime to which we had no binding ties. The fact is, the Federalists and Anti-Federalists were in conflict over the issue not because of persuasive logic but because of partisan bitterness.

Both sides found ammunition for their cause in the European issue. There was, for example, the case of "Citizen" Edmond Charles Genêt, minister to the

United States from the French Republic. Genêt arrived in Charleston in the spring of 1793. Had he arrived in Boston he might have been sent home packing, but the South was Anti-Federalist territory, and on Genêt's month-long trip north, it was roses, roses all the way. By that time he was so certain he had public opinion behind him that when President Washington brushed off suggestions that the French be allowed to use American ports for refitting damaged war vessels. Genêt went right ahead with his plans. Washington was correct in slapping down such a presumptuous guest of the country, and the people, as a whole, approved. The Federalists used the incident to discredit their pro-French opponents.

Even more embarrassing to the Anti-Federalists was the so-called "XYZ Affair," in which it appeared that the unscrupulous French foreign minister, Talleyrand, had informed our diplomats that he would receive them as accredited ministers only after they had paid him a bribe. It was very difficult to defend pro-French sentiment in the face of such raw insults to national pride.

On the other hand, the Anti-Federalists were collecting a few rocks to throw at their enemies, too. Genêt's mistake hurt the Anti-Federalist cause in one way, but it did show how many Americans were opposed to Federalist policy. Many a timid Republican was thus encouraged to enlist in Jefferson's party. The treaty signed by John Jay in 1794 was also used against the Federalists. "Jay's Treaty" was an attempt to get the British to meet agreements negotiated during the Treaty of Paris, which ended the War of Independence. It did get the British out of the frontier forts that they had promised to evacuate, but nothing was settled about impressment of American seamen, which irritated many Americans, especially those doomed to the harsh life of the British Navy.

Partisan feeling was running high when John Adams took the oath of office as the second president of the United States, after the election of 1796. With the Federalists in firm control, the administration began to prepare for war with France. Congress dutifully authorized an army of 35,000, which was a larger force than Washington had ever had at his disposal during the Revolution. Two new superfrigates, the *United States* and the *Constitution,* were laid down as part of the war program. To pay for these items Congress levied a tax that fell particularly heavily on the small landowner, who was least interested in foreign wars.

The result was a political and journalistic battle that passed all the bounds of decency. Even during the Revolution, when Tory and Patriot clawed at each other, there had never been such a caterwaul. Bache and Fenno carried their personal feud beyond the pages of their papers by engaging in a street brawl. "Peter Porcupine" (William Cobbett) brought invective to finest flower by attacking well-known Anti-Federalists, living and dead. It should be noted that the bulk of the party press was basically conventional and contributed to the orderly development of the political party system.

THE ALIEN AND SEDITION ACTS OF 1798

This was the situation when the administration tried to throttle such violent opposition in the summer of 1798. In June and July of that year, Congress passed the Alien and Sedition Acts. One was a law aimed at troublesome foreigners living in the country; the other concerned the muzzling of irritating editors.

There were then about 25,000 aliens in the United States. Many of them were refugees from stern authorities in their homelands, and they therefore tended to be on the side of the Jeffersonians, who believed in as little government as possible. Others were poor, or at least propertyless, and again such persons were more likely to gravitate into the ranks of the Anti-Federalists. Groups such as the Irish immigrants were by tradition opposed to the British and so could not possibly see any good in the Hamiltonian policy of British appeasement. There were also many intellectuals in this category. Dr. Joseph Priestley, the discoverer of oxygen and seven other gases, was a British expatriate noted for his leftist views. The Du Ponts, at that time aggressive backers of liberalism, brought French ideas into the platform of the Anti-Federalists. And there was Albert Gallatin, destined to be a great secretary of the treasury under Jefferson, who was already making a name for himself in Pennsylvania, despite his difficulty in adjusting to a country so different from his native Switzerland. Men like these were almost certain to be opposed to the administration. The Alien Act, it was hoped, would reduce the ranks of these threatening foreigners.

One provision of the law was an extension of the naturalization period from 5 to 14 years. Another clause empowered the president to deport aliens judged by him to be subversive (a power Adams did not actually employ). Some foreign-born Americans, such as John Burk, publisher of the Anti-Federalist *Time Piece* in New York, went underground until the trouble blew over. Anyone could see that the alien section applied only to enemies of the administration. William Cobbett was not only a foreigner who held Americans in contempt, but he was also becoming obnoxious, even to some Federalist leaders, as the editor of a paper that attacked Vice President Jefferson in almost every issue. But the Sedition Act did not protect the office of vice president against false criticism.

The Sedition Act was an obvious attempt to control the journalistic spokespeople of the Anti-Federalists. It declared: "That if any person shall write, print, utter, or publish . . . any false, scandalous and malicious writing . . . against the government of the United States, or either house of the Congress . . . or the said President . . . or to excite against them the hatred of the good people of the United States . . . or to resist or oppose, or defeat any such law . . . shall be punished by a fine not exceeding two thousand dollars, and by imprisonment not exceeding two years."[11] The laws were to stand for two years.

One of the cornerstones of press freedom is the right to express criticism of government and its administrators freely. The Alien and Sedition laws reversed a process that had made America the envy of the oppressed. And yet there were important contributions in the laws. Nor have the repressive features been properly appraised in many accounts of the period. The original bill called for a declaration of war with France. The clauses that followed imposed penalties on all who gave any aid or comfort to this enemy. At the last minute, the war declaration was defeated by a narrow margin, but the following clauses concerning aliens and the press were allowed to stand. That was why all pro-French sentiment was so ruthlessly attacked by the administration.

And in some ways the Sedition Act can be called a milestone on the road to freedom of the press. The law did not forbid criticism of the government. It only attempted to curb malicious and false statements published to defame officials. And it provided a pair of safeguards: Truth could be offered as a defense, and the jury could determine both the law and the fact. This was the twin argument made by Andrew Hamilton in the John Peter Zenger trial. Now it was enacted into the law of 1798.[12]

At first glance the Sedition Act may appear to merit support. But experience has shown us time and again that the party in power will inevitably abuse such controls in the interest of expediency. It was so in 1798. Even Alexander Hamilton, the founder of the Federalist party, was apprehensive of the measure. The ailing and retired General Washington rose from his bed to warn against the abuses he foresaw. President Adams, an honest man despite his political ineptitude, did what he could to modify the bill. Unfortunately, the leaders who had made the Federalist party dominant in all branches of government no longer had the power to impede the machine they had set in motion. Extremists had taken over control, and they were intent on revenge for all the indignities heaped upon them by opposition editors.

Fearful for their personal safety, Jefferson and his friends gathered at Monticello and planned the Virginia and Kentucky Resolutions, affirming the right of states to nullify federal actions. Missing in 1798 was the far better safety valve of "judicial review," or the right of the United States Supreme Court to declare a legislative act unconstitutional. Not until 1803 did John Marshall establish that court function in *Marbury v. Madison.* Having taken the only available course, Jefferson then sat back to await the next step.

SEDITION ACT PROSECUTIONS

The Adams administration played right into his hands. The Federalists abused the new laws so openly that for a time freedom of the press was seriously threatened in America. It was far from being the "reign of terror" charged by the opposition, but the record is not one of which Americans can be proud. Timothy Pickering, the secretary of state, spent half his time reading Anti-Federalist papers so that he could ferret out violators of the law.

One of the victims of the Sedition Act was Matthew Lyon of Vermont. Born in Ireland, Lyon had landed in America as an indentured servant. He had worked his way up to a position of respect and prestige in his community and was the representative to Congress from his state. Lyon was one of the famous "Green Mountain Boys" in the War of Independence. Cashiered from the army for an act that should have earned him a medal, he was later reinstated and promoted to the rank of colonel.

One afternoon in the House of Representatives, Roger Griswold, a leading Federalist from that citadel of Federalism, Connecticut, made insulting remarks about Lyon's war record. The Vermonter ignored Griswold at first, but when his colleague grasped his coat and repeated the insult, Lyon replied in the uncouth but effective manner of the frontier—he spat in Griswold's eye. The next day Griswold walked up to Lyon's desk in the House and began beating him with a cane. Lyon grabbed a handy pair of fire tongs and beat back his adversary. The Federalists tried to expel Lyon from the House but failed to muster the needed two-thirds vote.

The Sedition Act was used to settle scores with such persons. The crime charged against Lyon under the Act was the publication of a letter to an editor accusing President Adams of "ridiculous pomp, foolish adulation, and selfish avarice." For such remarks, Lyon was hailed before a Federalist judge, who sentenced the defendant to 4 months in jail and a fine of $1000. The vindictiveness of the judge was indicated by the fact that although the trial was held in Rutland, Vermont, where there was a passable jail, Lyon was condemned to a filthy cell at Vergennes, some 40 miles distant. Thousands of local citizens signed a petition requesting parole for the prisoner. It was ignored. When editor Anthony Haswell printed an advertisement in his *Vermont Gazette* announcing a lottery to raise money for paying the fine, he, too, was hustled off to jail for abetting a "criminal."

The Federalists should have heeded the warning, for the public reaction to such injustice was positive and immediate. Lyon was jailed in October, 1798, convicted by what he called a packed jury of political opponents. In December he was reelected to the House by a two-to-one vote over his closest opponent. Freed in February, 1799, after money had flowed in to pay his fine, the Vermonter returned in triumph to the capital at Philadelphia. At one time the procession behind his carriage was 12 miles long. In 1801 he was to play a crucial role in making Jefferson president.*

Other editors had also felt the lash of the Federalist masters. James Callender, who edited the *Richmond Examiner,* was one. For criticizing the president, Callender was brought to trial. He probably deserved what he got, for he was an unprincipled political opportunist. The Federalists were not attacking him on principle, however, but on technicalities, and his case is just as significant as if he were a man of high character. Callender was defended by William Wirt, the South's leading lawyer and man of letters. The judge was Samuel Chase, who had said before he had even arrived in Virginia that he was going to give the Anti-Federalists a lesson. Just as predicted, Callender was found guilty. He was sentenced to 9 months in jail.

A Connecticut editor was imprisoned because he criticized the Army and the military policies of Congress. A New York editor wrote an uncomplimentary article about the president and was promptly jailed. Then the general public began to see through the hypocrisy of the repressive laws. It was noticed that whereas the slightest criticism of President Adams resulted in penalties, violent abuse of Anti-Federalist officials passed unpunished. Bache, for example, was indicted for criticism of Adams and others, while Fenno, who was just as violent, went unscathed.

The persecutions under the Alien and Sedition Acts have sometimes been described as insignificant. In all, there were fourteen indictments under the Sedition Act. Eleven trials resulted, with ten convictions. During the same time

*The 1800 election brought out a flaw in the political machinery. Jefferson was clearly the popular choice for president, but he and his running mate, Aaron Burr, both received seventy-three electoral votes under the indirect system of election. This threw the election into the House of Representatives, with sixteen states having one vote each. The Federalists, despite Hamilton's opposition, voted for Burr. For thirty-five ballots Jefferson had eight states, one short of a majority. Burr had six and two state delegations were split. One was Vermont. On the final ballot the Federalist from Vermont abstained, thus allowing Lyon to cast the decisive vote. Lyon had not run again in 1800, but he was to serve in the House from 1803 to 1811 as the representative from Kentucky.

span there were at least five other convictions for seditious libel under the provisions of British Common Law in state or federal courts. Eight of the convictions involved newspapers.[13] Whatever the numbers, the uproar over the prosecutions was enough to make it clear that the states had erred during the Revolution in enacting laws perpetuating the concept of seditious libel. What caught a Tory then caught a Republican now. There were a few more seditious libel cases after 1800 but the example of the Sedition Act proved conclusive. People saw that the test of tyranny is not necessarily the number of prosecutions but the number of men and women restrained from speaking freely because of fear.

THE END OF THE BATTLE

By 1800 the battle was over. Fenno and Bache both died in the terrible yellow-fever epidemic that scourged Philadelphia in the summer of 1798, while Bache was still under indictment. Freneau, driven out by the fever, never reestablished his *Gazette.* Cobbett had left the country, following a libel suit that forced him into bankruptcy.

On the whole, the press improved after the oustanding character assassins were silenced in one way or the other. The widow Bache married her husband's assistant, William Duane, whose wife had died of the fever. Duane made a decent publication of the *Aurora.* The *Aurora* continued to back Jefferson and his party, but it was much more reasonable in tone under Duane. He was as courageous as Freneau, without Freneau's shrillness and bad taste. He was as colorful in his writing as Cobbett, but without Cobbett's recklessness. Duane suffered for the cause, along with other Anti-Federalists: He was beaten by hoodlums. He was also arrested under the Sedition Act.

The party battle in the House over the Sedition Act continued after the close 44–41 passage vote in 1798. Attempts were made to amend or repeal it in 1799 and again in 1800. In February, 1801, a Federalist effort to extend it 2 more years was defeated 53–49, with six Federalists from the South deserting the party to join all forty-seven supporters of the new President Jefferson. The law expired March 3, 1801, under its own terms and was the last federal sedition law until the wartime of 1917. Jefferson promptly pardoned all those in jail and canceled remaining trials.[14]

The removal of the national capital from Philadelphia to Washington ended an epoch and began a new one. There had been a complete change in party and administration control, too. In the election year of 1800, Federalists were dominant in the House, the Senate, the presidency, the cabinet, the courts, the churches, business, and education. Up to four-fifths of the newspapers opposed Jefferson and his party. Yet Jefferson won.

As the historian Arthur M. Schlesinger, Jr., has written: "When a party starts out by deceiving the people, it is likely to finish by deceiving itself."[15] Since there is good evidence that this statement is true, the press, as demonstrated in this chapter, is more essential than ever in its role of disclosing party deceptions, for without such disclosures the vast majority of the public would not remain free long. Unfortunately, men had to suffer before this was generally understood—men like Lyon, Bache, Duane, and Thomas Adams of the *Boston Independent Chronicle.* Adams and his brother, Abijah, refused to be intimidated by their Federalist persecutors, although prison and worse confronted them. Sick and near death, they answered their detractors in double-space, double-measure Caslon bold type: "The Chronicle is destined to persecution. . . . It will stand or fall with the liberties of America, and nothing shall silence its clarion but the extinction of every principle which leads to the achievement of our independence."[16]

NOTES

1. Henry Steele Commager, ed., *Documents of American History* (New York: Appleton-Century-Crofts, 1934), p. 104, Article XII, and p. 109, Article XVI.

2. Claude G. Bowers, *Jefferson and Hamilton* (Boston: Houghton Mifflin, 1925), p. 31.

3. Ibid., p. 26. Bowers, it should be pointed out, is a respecter, but no admirer, of Hamilton.

4. As quoted in Wilfred E. Binkley, *American Political Parties: Their Natural History* (New York: Knopf, 1943), p. 32.

5. Quoted from Vernon L. Parrington, *Main Currents in American Thought,* I (New York: Harcourt Brace Jovanovich, 1927), p. 321.

6. *National Gazette,* December 19, 1791.

7. *National Gazette,* February 9, 1792.

8. *Porcupine's Gazette,* November 16, 1797.

9. See, for example, B. E. Martin, "Transition Period of the American Press," *Magazine of American History,* XVII (April 1887), 273–94.

10. It is a remarkable that all during these critical years all roads to safety eventually led right back to Washington. He was not a political genius, but he appeared to know instinctively the policies that would offer the greatest security to the nation he had saved in wartime.

11. *U.S. Statutes at Large,* "The Sedition Act," I, Sec. 2, p. 596.

12. The key votes in the House of Representatives on the Sedition Act were almost entirely on party lines. There were forty-seven Federalists, thirty-nine Anti-Federalists. The bill passed 44–41, with forty-three Federalist votes. Six Federalists joined in the modifications involving truth as a defense. The jury provision, however, was backed by all thirty-nine Anti-Federalists and twenty-eight Federalists. See John D. Stevens, "Constitutional History of the 1798 Sedition Law," *Journalism Quarterly,* XLIII (Summer 1966), 247.

13. James M. Smith, *Freedom's Fetters: The Alien and Sedition Laws and American Civil Liberties* (Ithaca, N.Y.: Cornell University Press, 1956), verifies fourteen indictments under the Sedition Act. Other totals are from Mott, *American Journalism* (New York: Macmillan, 1950), p. 149.

14. Stevens, "Constitutional History," p. 254.

15. *The Age of Jackson* (Boston: Little, Brown, 1945), p. 282.

16. Thomas Adams was the first important editor to be indicted under the Sedition Act. Before he could be tried, he was indicted under the common law for criticizing the Massachusetts legislature. He was too sick to stand trial, but his brother, Abijah, was convicted and jailed for a month, although he too was ailing. The defiant Thomas, faced with both federal and state sedition trials, sold the *Chronicle* in May, 1799, 2 weeks before he died.

ANNOTATED BIBLIOGRAPHY

Books

AUSTIN, ALEINE, *Matthew Lyon: "New Man" of the Democratic Revolution, 1749–1822.* University Park, Pa.: Pennsylvania State University Press, 1981. Definitive.

AXELRAD, JACOB, *Philip Freneau: Champion of Democracy.* Austin: University of Texas Press, 1967. Carefully researched biography.

BAILEY, THOMAS A., *A Diplomatic History of the American People.* Englewood Cliffs, N.J.: Prentice-Hall, 1980. Tenth edition of a leading work on foreign policy.

BINKLEY, WILFRED E., *American Political Parties: Their Natural History.* New York: Knopf, 1963. A clear and thoughtful study of the topic. The chapters on the early party era are good background reading.

BOORSTIN, DANIEL, *The Americans: The National Experience.* New York: Random House, 1965. Consensus history; traces social history to the Civil War, minimizing political conflicts, clashes of ideas.

BOWERS, CLAUDE G., *Jefferson and Hamilton.* Boston: Houghton Mifflin, 1925. This book is particularly interesting to the student of journalism because the author draws heavily on newspaper sources for much of his documentation. Strongly Anti-Federalist.

COBBETT, WILLIAM, *Selections.* Oxford: Clarendon Press, 1923. These excerpts from the journalist's detailed *Works* demonstrate the style and content of Cobbett's best contributions.

FAŸ, BERNARD, *The Two Franklins.* Boston: Little, Brown, 1933. A contrast between Benjamin Franklin and his grandson, Benjamin Franklin Bache.

HARTZ, LOUIS, *The Liberal Tradition in America.* New York: Harcourt Brace Jovanovich, 1955. An interpretation of political thought since the Revolution; leading effort to generalize the idea of an American consensus—a liberal community which developed no proletariat but a victorious middle class.

JENSEN, MERRILL, *The New Nation.* New York: Knopf, 1950. A brilliant refutation of the dreary picture of the confederation period, as painted by such classic historians as John Fiske.

KROUT, JOHN ALLEN, AND DIXON RYAN FOX, *The Completion of Independence, 1790–1830, A History of American Life,* Volume V. New York: Macmillan, 1944. Social history.

LEARY, LEWIS, *That Rascal Freneau.* New Brunswick, N.J.: Rutgers University Press, 1941. The standard "life" of the Anti-Federalist editor.

LEVY, LEONARD W., ed., *Freedom of the Press from Zenger to Jefferson.* Indianapolis: Bobbs-Merrill, 1966. Contains documents and essays related to the Sedition Act, the rise of a Libertarian outlook toward the press, and Jefferson's philosophy.

LIPSET, SEYMOUR, *The First New Nation: The United States in Historical and Comparative Perspective.* New York: Basic Books, 1963. Application of the comparative approach to U.S. history.

MCMASTER, JOHN BACH, *A History of the People of the United States from the Revolution to the Civil War* (8 vols.). New York: Appleton-Century-Crofts, 1883–1913. McMaster is chosen from among some of the best historians who wrote of this period, because he depended on newspaper sources to bring out the flavor and the temper of the times.

MILLER, JOHN C., *Crisis in Freedom: The Alien and Sedition Acts.* Boston: Little, Brown, 1951. A relatively brief account of passage of the laws and details of the trials. See also Miller, *Alexander Hamilton: Portrait in Paradox* (New York: Harper & Row, 1959), and *The Federalist Era* (Harper & Row, 1960).

NEVINS, ALLAN, *American Press Opinion, Washington to Coolidge.* Boston: Heath, 1928. An excellent selection of the partisan editorials of the period.

OSBORNE, JOHN W., *William Cobbett: His Thought and His Times.* New Brunswick, N.J.: Rutgers University Press, 1966. Biography of the Federalist editor of *Porcupine's Gazette.*

POLLARD, JAMES E., *The Presidents and the Press.* New York: Macmillan, 1947. The attitude of the Chief Executive regarding the press is an indicator of journalistic prestige and power, decade by decade.

RUTLAND, ROBERT ALLEN, *The Birth of the Bill of Rights, 1776–1791.* Chapel Hill: University of North Carolina Press, 1955. A documented study. See also Rutland, *The Ordeal of the Constitution* (Norman: University of Oklahoma Press, 1966).

SCHACHNER, NATHAN, *Alexander Hamilton.* New York: Appleton-Century-Crofts, 1946. A middle-of-the-road interpretation.

SCUDDER, H. E., *Noah Webster.* Boston: Houghton Mifflin, 1882. An adequate, concise biography of a versatile and interesting personality, who, among his other accomplishments, was a noted journalist.

SISSON, DANIEL, *The American Revolution of 1800.* New York: Knopf, 1974. Scholarly.

SMITH, JAMES M., *Freedom's Fetters: The Alien and Sedition Laws and American Civil Liberties.* Ithaca, N.Y.: Cornell University Press, 1956. Detailed and documented analysis of the laws and court cases.

STEWART, DONALD H., *The Opposition Press of the Federalist Period.* Albany: State University of New York Press, 1969. A scholarly study of the partisan press with much new detail.

VAN DOREN, CARL, ed., *The Federalist.* New York: Heritage Press, 1945. An annotated edition of the famous series of political editorials.

Periodicals and Monographs

BALDASTY, GERALD J., "Toward an Understanding of the First Amendment: Boston Newspapers, 1782–1791," *Journalism History,* III (Spring 1976), 25. Revises Levy by focusing on common law of defamation rather than seditious libel.

BOSTON, RAY, "The Impact of 'Foreign Liars' on the American Press (1790–1800)," *Journalism Quarterly,* L (Winter 1973), 722. Political refugees from Britain spearheaded press attack on Federalists.

"Cobbett," *Fraser's Magazine,* XII (August 1835), 207. A personality sketch that brings out the journalist's wit and pugnacity.

COLL, GARY, "Noah Webster: Journalist, 1783–1803," Ph.D. thesis, Southern Illinois University, 1971. Assesses his contributions to both form and content of the newspaper and magazine.

DOWLING, RUTH N., "William Cobbett, His Trials and Tribulations as an Alien Journalist, 1794–1800," Ph.D. thesis, Southern Illinois University, 1972. Seven libel charges, some unfairly made, prompted Cobbett to leave for England.

GOLDSMITH, ADOLPH O., "The Roaring Lyon of Vermont," *Journalism Quarterly,* XXXIX (Spring 1962), 179. The stormy career of congressman Lyon, who was reelected while in jail for Sedition Act conviction.

GROTTA, GERALD L., "Phillip Freneau's Crusade for Open Sessions of the U.S. Senate," *Journalism Quarterly,* XLVIII (Winter 1971), 667. The editor wins out.

KNUDSON, JERRY W., "Political Journalism in the Age of Jefferson," *Journalism History,* I (Spring 1974), 20. Summarizes Knudson's Ph.D. thesis, University of Virginia, 1974. Jefferson faced criticism of a predominantly Federalist press.

LIST, KAREN K., "William Cobbett in Philadelphia, 1794–1799," *Journalism History,* V (Autumn 1978), 80. From List, "The Role of William Cobbett in Philadelphia's Party Press 1794–1799," Ph.D. thesis, University of Wisconsin, 1980, condensed in *Journalism Monographs,* 82 (May 1983).

PADOVER, SAUL K., "Wave of the Past," *New Republic,* CXVI (April 21, 1947), 14. A concise description of the effect of the Alien and Sedition laws on the Federalist defeat of 1800.

PRINCE, CARL E., "The Federalist Party and Creation of a Court Press, 1789–1801," *Journalism Quarterly,* LIII (Summer 1976), 238. Political rivalries and favors account for transformation of the press system.

REITZEL, WILLIAM, "William Cobbett and Philadelphia Journalism," *Pennsylvania Magazine,* LIX (July 1935), 223. An excellent interpretation of the journalist. Reprinted in Ford and Emery, *Highlights in the History of the American Press.*

SLOAN, WILLIAM DAVID, "The Party Press: The Newspaper Role in National Politics, 1789–1816," Ph.D. thesis, University of Texas, 1981. Finds party press played a constructive role in U.S. political development. See *Journalism History,* IX (Spring 1982), 18, for article.

STEVENS, JOHN D., "Congressional History of the 1798 Sedition Law," *Journalism Quarterly,* XLIII (Summer 1966), 247. A detailed report of the partisan battle in the House, with analysis of votes.

"William Cobbett," *Littell's Living Age,* XLI (Spring 1854), 61. A short but surprisingly complete biographical sketch, with an interesting section on Cobbett's career in America.

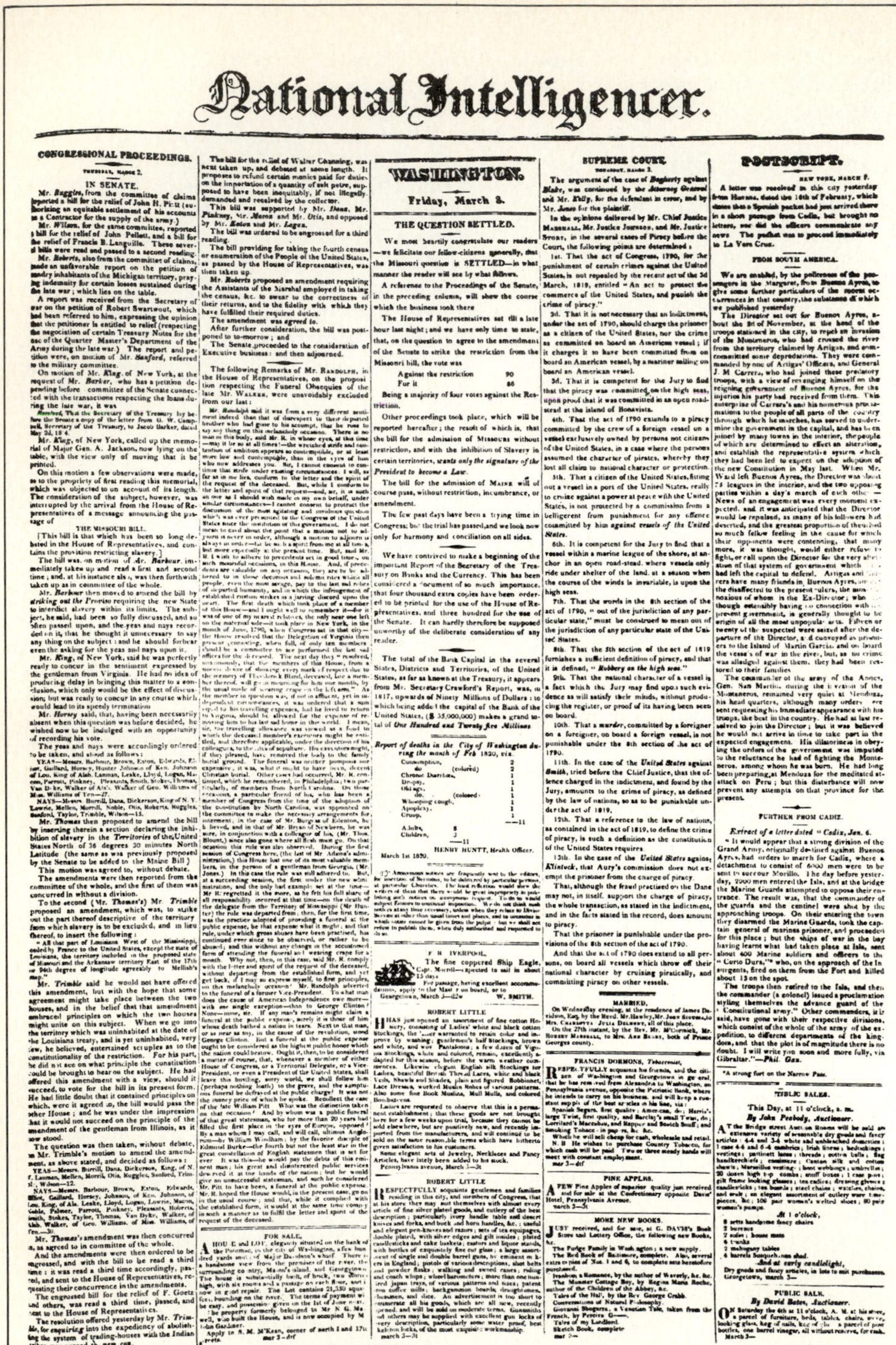

National Intelligencer.

CONGRESSIONAL PROCEEDINGS.

IN SENATE.

THE MISSOURI BILL.

WASHINGTON.

Friday, March 3.

THE QUESTION SETTLED.

We most heartily congratulate our readers —we felicitate our fellow-citizens generally, that the Missouri question is SETTLED—in what manner the reader will see by what follows.

A reference to the Proceedings of the Senate, in the preceding column, will shew the course which the business took there.

The House of Representatives sat till a late hour last night; and we have only time to state, that, on the question to agree to the amendment of the Senate to strike the restriction from the Missouri bill, the vote was

Against the restriction	90
For it	86

Being a majority of four votes against the Restriction.

SUPREME COURT.

POSTSCRIPT.

FROM SOUTH AMERICA.

FURTHER FROM CADIZ.

PUBLIC SALES.

PUBLIC SALE.

The *National Intelligencer* reports the passage of the 1820 Missouri Compromise.

8

The Press and the Expanding Nation

I have lent myself willingly as the subject of a great experiment . . . to demonstrate the falsehood of the pretext that freedom of the press is incompatible with orderly government.

—Jefferson to Seymour

Jefferson's victory in 1800 made his party subject to the same type of attack that had so recently been launched against the Federalists while they were in power. The Jeffersonian "republicans" had gained control of the administration, but the President estimated that up to three-fifths of the editors continued to support Federalist policies. In some areas Federalist newspapers outnumbered their political rivals by as much as five to one. The rank-and-file voters were not impressed by this "one-party" press, apparently, for they continued to return to office a long succession of candidates representing the Republican party (as the Anti-Federalists became known before eventually adopting the name Democratic party).

The disparity between public and editorial opinion in the periods of Jefferson and Jackson, and since the administration of Franklin D. Roosevelt, has concerned students of our press. They point to the occasions when overwhelming popular mandates coincided with preponderant press opposition to the popular cause, and critics sometimes wonder if the American press is the power the journalists say it is. This history indicates that the power of the press is not in its persuasion by opinion, but in its dissemination of information and its arousal of interest in important issues hitherto submerged in public apathy.

THE *NEW YORK EVENING POST,* 1801

One of the important Federalist organs was founded by Alexander Hamilton a year after the defeat of his party in 1800. The Federalist leader believed that a reputable party paper was needed more than ever to stem the tide of Republican popularity. The result was the *New York Evening Post,* destined to become the city's oldest newspaper. Hamilton chose William Coleman as the first editor. That Coleman was a lawyer and former court reporter again indicates the trend of journalism since the days when the printer-editor was the rule. He was an able editor, but while "The General," as Hamilton liked to be called, was around, it was plain to all that Coleman was subordinate in the office.

Coleman was, nonetheless, a writer of some literary pretensions. He could express his convictions in a slashing style that often cut down wavering opposition within and without the party. He had also had great personal charm and courage. Eventually, Coleman broke with Hamilton because of his loyalty to Aaron Burr,[1] but in the founding days of the *Post,* Coleman did not make an editorial move without consulting his sponsor. It is significant that Coleman was a shorthand expert, and that was one reason he had been selected by Hamilton. Late at night Coleman could have been seen in the empty streets hurrying to the home of the Federalists' great leader to take dictation for the next days' editorials. These editorials needed no reworking: They were the work of Hamilton at his journalistic best. Picked up by Federalist editors around the country, they exerted an important party influence.

The victorious party in 1800 needed opposition, as does any party in power. Jefferson had committed himself frequently as a believer in press freedom. His party had fought against the Alien and Sedition Acts in accordance with this doctrine. He had sponsored and encouraged the Virginia and Kentucky Resolutions as attacks on press restrictions by the Federalists. He had helped Freneau and Thomas Ritchie establish newspapers to help stem the tide of Federalist dominance.[2] Now, after the party victory, he found himself accused of press restrictions by the Federalists. This is a pattern commonly found in the history of American journalism—the reversal of free-expression policies once a group wins power.

JEFFERSON'S VIEW OF THE PRESS

Jefferson appears to have been sincere in his defense of a free press. Even when the press humiliated him, he defended its freedom. Wrote Jefferson to his friend Carrington in 1787:

> I am persuaded that the good sense of the people will always be found to be the best army. They may be led astray for a moment, but will soon correct themselves. The people are the only censors of their governors; and even their errors will tend to keep these to the true principles of their institution. To punish these errors too severely would be to suppress the only safeguard of the public liberty. The way to prevent these irregular interpositions of the people, is to give them full information of their affairs through the channel of the public papers, and to contrive that those papers should penetrate the whole mass of the people. The basis of our government being the opinion of the people, the very first object should be to keep that

> right; and were it left to me to decide whether we should have a government without newspapers, or newspapers without a government, I should not hesitate a moment to prefer the latter.

This part of Jefferson's letter to Carrington is widely quoted. It is bandied about particularly when press moguls fear various degrees of restrictions or inconvenience from any quarter. But the second part of Jefferson's letter is not so well known, though it is a qualification essential to the preceding statement. The great statesman went on to say:

> But I should mean that every man should receive those papers, and be capable of reading them.

Later, when the Federalist editors had made life miserable for him, he wrote in exasperation to a friend:

> The newspapers of our country by their abandoned spirit of falsehood, have more effectually destroyed the utility of the press than all the shackles devised by Bonaparte.[3]

But that was in 1813, when Jefferson was very tired. His more considered views of the vicious opposition press are better summed up in the following 1802 letter:

> They [Federalists] fill their newspapers with falsehoods, calumnies, and audacities. . . . We are going fairly through the experiment of whether freedom of discussion, unaided by coercion, is not sufficient for the propagation and protection of truth, and for the maintenance of an administration pure and upright in its actions and views. No one ought to feel under this experiment, more than myself. Nero wished all the necks of Rome united in one, that he might sever them at a blow. So our ex-federalists, wishing to have a single representative of all the objects of their hatred, honor me with that post and exhibit against me such atrocities as no nation has ever before heard or endured. I shall protect them in the right of lying and calumniating, and still go on to merit the continuance of it, by pursuing steadily my object of proving that a people, easy in their circumstances as ours are, are capable of conducting themselves under a government founded not in the fears and follies of man, but on his reason, on the predominance of his social over his dissocial passions, so free as to restrain him in no moral right, and so firm as to protect him from every moral wrong, which shall leave him, in short, in possession of all his natural rights.[4]

But although Jefferson's views on the press were well known to his followers, and although he wielded strong control over his party, he could not keep his subordinates from trying to impose restrictions on opposition editors, now that the Jeffersonians were in power.

An example of this vindictiveness was the prosecution of Joseph Dennie for remarks deemed by Republican party leaders to be seditious. Dennie, a grandson of Bartholomew Green, Jr., onetime printer of the *Boston News-Letter,* was one of the ablest editors of his day. His *Farmer's Weekly Museum,* published at Walpole, New Hampshire, was so popular that it achieved national recognition. Later, Dennie took over the editorial direction of the *Port Folio,* an outspoken Federalist magazine published in Philadelphia. Shortly after Jefferson moved into the unfinished White House, Dennie wrote a series of editorials pointing out the weaknesses of popular rule. Although he did not attack the American government specifically, he made it clear that he believed democracy to be futile. These remarks were declared by government officials to be seditious, and the editor was indicted on that charge. After all that Jefferson had written about the press as a rightful censor of its government, the administration action appeared to be highly hypocritical. The jury must have thought so, too, for after a brilliant defense by Joseph Hopkinson, composer of the Patriot song, "Hail, Columbia," Dennie was acquitted.

THE CROSWELL SEDITIOUS LIBEL CASE

The most celebrated case involving the press during this period was prosecuted under a state law, as recommended by the President. The defendant was Harry Croswell, editor of a Federalist paper at Hudson, New York. Croswell called his little weekly *The Wasp,* and it was an appropriate name. It was so vicious and annoying that respectable Federalists disdained it. *The Wasp* stung political opponents in every column. One day Croswell printed an "exchange" from the *New York Evening Post,* Hamilton's personal mouthpiece. The article reported that Jefferson had paid James Callender, the Richmond editor, to spread the word that George Washington had been a robber, traitor, and perjurer, and that other Federalist leaders were equally reprehensible. This was a serious charge against Jefferson and the dignity of his office. *The Wasp,* rather than the *Post,* was prosecuted because Croswell's paper was the type of scandal sheet Jefferson had in mind when he suggested smoking out the worst of the Federalist editors under state law.

Croswell was indicted in 1804. He was found guilty, but appealed the case. When the trial was called, a titan arose to argue for the defense. He was Alexander Hamilton, Jefferson's arch rival. The four judges listened with obvious respect as the brilliant pleader stated a principle as applicable today as it was in 1804. The press, Hamilton argued, had "the right to publish with impunity truth, with good motives, for justifiable ends, though reflecting on Government, Magistracy, or individuals." Since the "good motives" and "justifiable ends" would have to be disproved by the complainant, Hamilton was essentially saying that truth, and truth alone, was a defense in a libel action. In his arguments against the need for a Bill of Rights covering press freedom, Hamilton had not appeared as very sympathetic to the cause of liberty of written expression. But when he stood up at the Croswell trial and insisted upon the "right" of submitting truth as a full defense, Hamilton won his place alongside the great fighters for press freedom.

It so happened that Hamilton lost the case, because the four judges were evenly divided in their opinions. The New York state laws still adhered to the old policy, "the greater the truth, the greater the libel." Truth had been recognized as a defense in the Sedition Act, but the law had lapsed 4 years before, and the precedent had not been accepted in the courts. Hamilton also insisted on the right of a jury to determine both the law and the fact. Both issues had been raised in the Zenger case, but only in Pennsylvania had they been recognized in law (in 1790).

The significance of the Croswell trial can be seen in legislation immediately following Hamilton's plea. Even before the judges had handed down the verdict, a bill was introduced in the New York Legislature providing that truth thereafter was to be admitted in defense. The same bill gave the jury the right to determine both the law and the fact. By 1805, these principles had become law in New York—70 years after Zenger's trial. Soon other states followed suit and the shadow of the British Common Law of seditious libel was lifted. In 1812 the Supreme Court held that the federal government could not prosecute under the old law.

The great pioneer in press freedom did not live to see his eventual triumph; ironically, it was another libel episode that brought about Hamilton's violent death. A remark attributed to Hamilton that appeared in an Albany newspaper while the Croswell case was being tried angered New York's second most imposing political figure—Aaron Burr. By this time Burr's prestige was slipping, which probably made him especially sensitive to insults, real or imagined. He challenged Hamilton to a duel. Hamilton might have declined with no great blackening of his honor, but he accepted the gage. On July 11, 1804, his seconds rowed him across the Hudson River to the grassy bank near Weehawken where his son had been killed in a duel several months before. Burr was an expert marksman, and in the exchange of shots he wounded Hamilton so critically that the great leader died the next day.

GROWTH OF THE PRESS: FIRST DAILIES

The first daily newspaper in America was established by Benjamin Towne in Philadelphia in 1783. His *Pennsylvania Evening Post* was as characterless as its publisher. Towne was a Patriot in 1776 and was one of the first to print the Declaration of Independence for the public. Later, he became a Tory. After the surrender he confessed his sins and resumed a partial state of grace in his community. However, this shoddy little daily lasted only 17 months.

It was succeeded by a very good daily, the *Pennsylvania Packet and Daily Advertiser,* published by the partnership of John Dunlap and David C. Claypoole. Like the *Pennsylvania Evening Post* owned by Towne, the *Packet* was originally a weekly publication that had been founded by Dunlap in 1771. Switching from triweekly to daily status in 1784, the Dunlap and Claypoole venture was successful from the beginning. The first American daily in a foreign language was the *Courrier Français,* published in Philadelphia between 1794 and 1798, one of several short-lived French papers that appeared while American loyalties were divided between France and England.

By 1800, most big American ports and commercial centers were supporting daily papers: Philadelphia had six; New York, five; Baltimore, three; and Charleston, two. But for some curious reason Boston, the home of the American newspaper, had no daily paper at this time. Many of these publications had been forced into the daily field to meet the competition of the coffeehouses, where the London papers were available and where news was freely exchanged. The American journalists met the challenge by issuing first semiweekly, then triweekly, and finally daily editions.

Philadelphia even had an all-day newspaper for a time. It was the *New*

World, published by Samuel Harrison Smith in morning and evening editions. It was not successful, but it indicated the growing interest in fresh news presentation. Of 512 papers being printed in 1820, twenty-four were dailies, sixty-six were semiweeklies or triweeklies, and 422 were weeklies. They were still generally slanted toward the more prosperous citizens, for the price was more than the average person could afford. Circulations were not impressive, either, by present standards: A circulation of 1500 was considered adequate in all but the largest centers.

In the hinterlands the press was also booming. The number of newspapers beyond the urban fringe increased sixfold during this period.[5] Advertising helped to support this newspaper boom, because although most families tended to buy their supplies in wholesale lots for seasonal storage, there was already some development of the retail trade that was to sustain the press in later years. The development of the postal system also accounted for some of this expansion. By postal acts of 1782 and 1792, educational and informational matter could be mailed at very low rates.

THE PRESS MOVES WESTWARD

The expansion of the press reflected the spirit of the country. It had taken 150 years to settle the seaboard colonies, and on the basis of the past record, it should have taken another 200 years to push the frontier to the Mississippi River. But once the Appalachian Mountains were conquered, the lands to the west were rapidly taken up. In 1803 Jefferson, who had always opposed national imperialism, had a chance to purchase the vast Louisiana territory, and the bargain was too good to turn down out of principle. When this domain was added to the United States as a vast territory for exploitation, settlers poured in from the East. The lust for western lands is indicated by the numerous petitions for statehood during this period: Between 1790 and 1820, nine new states joined the Union.

The waterways were the highways into these frontier regions. Along the Ohio, the Kanawha, and the Cumberland, tiny communities began to appear that would some day become teeming cities. By present standards they were mere hamlets, but each served a wide trading area. They were thus far more important as markets and social centers than their populations alone indicate. If they were county seats, with courts, law-enforcing agencies, and land offices, they were even more important. And usually among the first to set up shop in such communities were the frontier printer-editors. They were the enthusiastic promoters of the villages that they were certain would one day rival London. They were leading businesspeople. But most of all they were the people who more than anyone else, knit the communities into organizations that could begin to bring civilization to the remote areas.

The first newspaper in this new West was John Scull's venture of 1786, the *Pittsburgh Gazette,* which is still thriving as the *Post-Gazette.* A year later, John Bradford, who bore a name well known in the printing industry although he was only indirectly related to the famous Philadelphia publishing family, set up his shop in Lexington, Kentucky. His *Kentucky Gazette* might have been the first paper in the West, had his equipment not been wrecked in transit the year before the establishment of the Pittsburgh enterprise. By 1800, twenty-one newspapers had been started west of the mountains. The Ohio River was the most important artery of commerce in this early period, but there were also important settlements, and newspapers, along the Wabash and lesser streams, such as the Muskingum, Scioto, Maumee, and Cuyahoga.

Advertising was rarely adequate to support the news business, but fortunately there needed to be some means of publishing legal information in this new area, and that was often sufficient inducement to start up a paper. Elihu Stout, for example, poled himself up the Wabash with his press to found the *Indiana Gazette* at Vincennes in 1804. He had been induced to give up his business in Frankfort, Kentucky, on the promise that he would be awarded the territorial legal printing contract—enough of a stake for him to establish a paper.

The northern route to the frontier was along the Mohawk valley, straight across New York state from the Hudson River. This was the route of the Erie Canal, which was soon to make New York City the largest metropolis in the land, but even before that, it was an important highway. At the end of the valley, the Great Lakes served as transportation and communication routes between the vast wilderness and the East. Detroit, one of the outer bastions of the frontier then, had a newspaper, the *Gazette,* by 1817. Soon other communities in the area could boast the same. A Congressional Act of 1814 provided that all federal laws must be printed in two (later, three) newspapers in each state and territory. This was a logical way of letting electors know what their representatives were doing, but it also encouraged the founding of pioneer papers in communities not quite ready to support such ventures.[6]

The first New Orleans paper, begun in 1794, was the *Moniteur de la Louisiane,* a four-page edition for the French population living under Spanish control. It lasted until 1814. The first Spanish-language newspaper in the United States was *El Misisipí,* printed in 1808 in New Orleans, the city linking the new nation with Spanish-speaking countries. *El Misisipí* was published for 2 years in Spanish and English. Texas' first paper, *La Gaceta,* appeared in 1813. These early Spanish-language papers reported the war between Spain and its colonies and the divisions between groups seeking power. A few years later, in 1828, the Cherokee Nation founded the first Indian newspaper, the *Cherokee Phoenix,* in Georgia. Editor Elias Boudinot printed four pages, partly in English and partly in Cherokee, using an eighty-six-character alphabet devised by Sequoyah. Boudinot, a Cherokee school teacher, published Cherokee laws, spelling lessons, news, and his own observations, twenty of which were reprinted in *Niles' Weekly Register.* Boudinot resigned in 1832 and the paper finally died in 1834. It was followed by the *Cherokee Advocate* in 1843.[7]

THE FRONTIER NEWSPAPER

The flimsy little weeklies of the isolated villages and booming river towns had much to do with the crystallization of public opinion that made the West a new factor in American politics. What were they like, these newspapers that exerted such influence in the West? On the whole, they were small, hand-set, scrubby publications. It is apparent that there was no place on them for large staffs, regular correspondents, or columnists furnishing opinions for readers too busy to form their own. There was plenty of opinion, of course, but most of it was contributed by readers. Usually there was a column or two of local news, sometimes printed as scattered items without benefit of headlines. There might be half a column of exchanges, or news gleaned from other newspapers arrived by the last post. The remaining material, exclusive of the notices, or advertisements, was very likely submitted by readers. Every subscriber who could wield a pen sooner or later appeared in the columns. All the aggrieved wrote out their pet complaints for the pages of the local mercury. Even government officials participated in this exchange, not always openly, true, but with sufficient identity to warrant spirited replies. Often this material was strident and in bad taste. "Straight news" tended toward distortion, flamboyance, and vindictiveness. But whatever its faults, it was a robust, colorful press. The great French observer, de Tocqueville, described the institution at a somewhat later period, but his remarks then were pertinent to this decade. He was impressed by the virility of the American press even while repelled by its provincialism. Western crudeness shocked him, but he was amazed at the success of the democratic experiment, and he conceded that the press had been an important implement in this development. De Tocqueville found a close relationship between the press and its public, fostered, no doubt, by the active participation of readers in the local journalistic effort. The public appeared to respect the Fourth Estate, he reported, and this was manifest in the great freedom accorded the institution.

By the end of the first decade of the nineteenth century, the Western press was lusty and influential. Editors and politicians who understood their constituencies saw that the region had its special problems. They tended to side with the Jeffersonians on the rights of the common people, but their dependence on the federal government to defend their sparse settlements against the Indian threat made them favor strong, centralized administration.

THE INFLUENCE OF THE FRONTIER

The new states also turned to the federal government for the development of transportation, so essential to their growth and prosperity. Again, the great land companies, organized to promote colonization at a profit, were dependent on the national administrations rather than on the territorial or parent-state politicians. There was a tendency, then, for the Westerners to demand local and statewide autonomy to work out their destinies; they visualized government as a kind of public-service corporation, not as a dispenser of privileges for the wealthy and powerful. Under the Northwest Ordinances, land was set aside to be sold for educational revenue. Suffrage was likely to be broader than in the more settled regions; property might be a voting requisite, but it was easy to acquire.

The West had a profound influence on the development of the new nation. The importance of that influence has been disputed since Professor Frederick Jackson Turner suggested that the frontier was a political and social laboratory that had produced a distinctive American character.[8] Turner pointed out that the men and women who moved across the mountains usually accepted the perils and discomforts of pioneer life because they were dissatisfied with the older community life.[9] When people suffer and face dangers together, they tend to act together, regardless of past customs, privileges, or attitudes. They blame those in control for failing to consider their problems. When they become strong enough politically and economically, they tend to force the older society to adopt their ideas. Thus, the Turner school maintains, the frontier has been responsible for much of the social and political experimentation that helped to distinguish the American character and organization.

"Historians have debated so long and hard whether the frontier thesis is profoundly valuable or fundamentally misleading that there has been a danger of losing sight of the paradox that it can be both," writes historian Richard Hofstadter, adding that Turner's sharpest critics have rarely failed to concede the core of merit to his thesis: the obvious influence of the frontier on American life.[10] Critics have most often quarreled with Turner's views concerning the effects of the frontier on democracy and individualism and its role as a "safety valve" for Eastern discontent. Of the Turner themes, the supposed role of the West in forcing democratization in the East proved most vulnerable. Turner's vagueness in defining the term *individualism* has led to unresolved debates in that area. As Daniel Boorstin points out, because of the danger, "Westward-moving pioneers everywhere found group travel and group living normal," and thus became what he calls Joiners and Organizers.[11]

THE WAR OF 1812

The War of 1812 serves as an example of how the frontier had come to influence American thought and politics. This disgraceful conflict reflects little on either of the belligerents. We do not like to be reminded of General William Hull's abject surrender to an inferior British and Indian force at Detroit or the burning of our national capitol. There were heroic episodes, too, such as Commodore Oliver Hazard Perry's useless naval victory on Lake Erie;[12] the courageous, but futile, sea battles of American naval vessels and privateersmen against the world's greatest sea power; and General Andrew Jackson's victory at New Orleans, 2 weeks after the peace had been signed at Ghent.[13] But for better or for worse, the force of public opinion in the West was largely responsible for that war.

Generations of Americans believed that the War of 1812 resulted from American resentment over British abuses of free transit on the high seas and the "impressment," or forcible return, of former British naval ratings by methods insulting to our national pride. If these were major causes for war, then New England should have been preponderantly in favor of the conflict. The big shipping interests were centered in that area, and the commercial interests there suffered most from British naval arrogance. The fact is, New Englanders emphatically voiced disapproval of the war. It was the West that forced military action. Western newspapers offer the evidence on this point.

In 1810 the Indians went on the warpath under the great leader and statesman, Tecumseh, and his brother, Teuskwatawa, "The Prophet." Frontier settlers discovered that the Indians were killing Americans with weapons supplied by the British through Canada. The leaders of the West who were in favor of war to settle the dispute became known as the "War Hawks." They were not interested in the plight of the seafarers, or the Napoleonic blockades, or the shipping embargoes imposed by the United States to boycott the arrogant Europeans at such great sacrifice to the commercial interests. It is significant that Henry Clay, perhaps the most vehement of the War Hawks, was elected speaker of the House by the Western bloc.

And poor Madison, best known for his constructive contributions to the American experiment, found himself in the role of a war president, thanks to the pressure of Western public opinion. Clay controlled enough votes by 1812 to swing the election against Madison, if that great American did not go along with the War Hawks. Madison's opponent, Governor DeWitt Clinton of New York, was opposed to war, so the issue was clear in 1812. It was Madison and war, or Clinton and peace. Thus, it is easy to read the influence of the West by examining the records. The electoral vote of the Northeast, where the shipping and commercial leaders were important, was unanimous for Clinton and peace. Madison, who was presented to the voters as protector of the shipping interests, received not a single vote from the electors of New England. But the electoral vote of the West was unanimous for Madison and war. The Middle and Southern states were more evenly divided, but there was enough war sentiment in those areas to endorse the Western stand and, from then on, it was "Mr. Madison's War."

As in most wars, the press suffered to some extent in the 1812 period. The most notorious attempt to muzzle an editor was in Baltimore, a shipping center with a strong faction opposed to administration war policies. Especially critical of the President was the *Federal Republican,* published by Jacob Wagner and Alexander Hanson. Some of their statements, made while an enemy was threatening our shores, no doubt merited censorship, but editors and contributors of the paper were charged by the opposition as traitors, although two of the protectors were Generals James Lingan and "Light Horse Harry" Lee, heroes of the War of Independence. When the mob descended on the office, the defenders held out until the irate citizens set up a cannon to blow the building down. At this point cooler heads negotiated a truce, including safe conduct of the besieged to the jail for protection. After the mob destroyed the press and building, its leaders ordered an assault on the jail. Some of the prisoners escaped, but nine were beaten and thrown to the mob. General Lingan was killed; General Lee was maimed for life.

The Federalists, discredited by their Hartford Convention plot, which encouraged New England states to secede from the Union instead of joining the war effort, failed to field a presidential candidate against James Monroe in 1816. On the surface, the country seemed to enjoy peace and prosperity. There was a kind of political truce while the forces realigned themselves: "the era of good feeling," Major Benjamin Russell of the *Columbian Centinel* in Boston called it.[14]

GOVERNMENT REPORTING: THE *NATIONAL INTELLIGENCER*

The most important press development at this time was in government reporting. The right to report meetings of interest to the general public is one of the tests of a free press, by the English-American concept. Reporters had access to the national House of Representatives from April 8, 1789, 2 days after it was established. For a time the Senate was more secretive, since it excluded not only reporters but also members of the House from its debates. By December 9, 1795, the Senate had completed a gallery for reporters, however. When the capital was transferred from New York to Philadelphia, the gallery was too far from the rostrum for the reporters to hear clearly, but on January 2, 1802, the Senate (by then in Washington) voted the reporters access to the floor. There was some squabbling between reporters and the House over arrangements. In Philadelphia, reporters were assigned "four seats on the window sill," and in Washington, after some agitation, they won the right to report the debates.[15]

One of the most effective reports of government was provided by the *National Intelligencer,* an outstanding newspaper of the period. Its founder was Samuel Harrison Smith, who was only 28 when Jefferson induced him to give up a promising publishing venture in Philadelphia to start a newspaper in the new capital in Washington. Jefferson was head of the learned American Philosophical Society of Philadelphia (founded by Franklin), and Smith had been secretary of the organization. Jefferson was much impressed with the young man. The *National Intelligencer* soon became the semiofficial organ of the administration, but it served papers of all factions outside Washington with its remarkably objective reporting of Congressional debates.

Smith retired from the paper in 1810, but his work was carried on ably by the partners who succeeded him, Joseph Gales, Jr., and William W. Seaton. One reported proceedings in the House, while the other covered the Senate. Both were experts in a recently perfected shorthand technique, and they were able to offer complete, accurate reports of the debates. Gales and Seaton made the *National Intelligencer* a daily when they assumed control (it had been a triweekly since its founding in 1800).

A patronage system for publishing the acts and journals of the Congress was vital to the development of the *National Intelligencer* and its rivals in the capital. Under this system the House, Senate, and other agencies selected their own printers. John Fenno had held a Senate contract from the Federalists before 1800 and the *National Intelligencer* the House contract for 1801 to 1805. Then printing firms got the work on low bids until Congress decided to give the business to the hardworking newspaper reporters covering the debates and providing the country's press with the only immediately available accounts. Gales and Seaton held the Senate contract for 1819 to 1826 and the House award for 1819 to 1829. As political fortunes tilted to the Democrats, Duff Green's *United States Telegraph* won the contracts in voting battles on the floor, later sharing them with Francis P. Blair's *Washington Globe.* Congress ended the patronage plan for newspapers in 1846 and established the Government Printing Office in 1860. During 26 years of patronage, the *National Intelligencer* had $1 million in contracts, the *Washington Globe* had $500,000, and the *United States Telegraph* had some $400,000. The system provided financial support for at least two, sometimes three, high-quality capital papers.[16]

Gales and Seaton earned another $650,000 for printing the *Annals of Congress* (1789–1824) and the *American State Papers* series. They began the *Register of Debates* in 1824, which was superseded by the *Congressional Globe* in 1834, which was in turn replaced by the official *Congressional Record* in 1873. The

National Intelligencer was the voice of the Whig party and briefly became the administration paper when the Whigs elected Harrison in 1840 and Fillmore became President in 1850. Daniel Webster, a close friend of Gales and Seaton, was Secretary of State in both administrations. The Whig party collapse, and the death of Gales in 1860, reduced the once-great *National Intelligencer* to a minor role, but it survived until the close of the Civil War.

MAGAZINES GAIN A FOOTHOLD

But the *National Intelligencer* was not typical of the press of the "era of good feeling." Few other newspapers won historical recognition at this time. On the other hand, there was an interesting development in the magazine field during the period. Efforts to publish magazines had been made occasionally since 1741, when Benjamin Franklin was thwarted in his plans by Andrew Bradford, who published the first periodical 3 days before Franklin's magazine appeared.

Five magazines were established in the revolutionary period. By that time there was some indication that the magazine might one day be self-supporting. It was the *Pennsylvania Magazine,* published in Philadelphia by Robert Aitken, that offered the American public its first taste of Tom Paine. This periodical was well edited, and it was full of interesting political information, literary contributions of good quality, and discussions of important issues. Eventually it failed, but it showed that the magazine had possibilities.

An interesting publication started in the period of the party press was the *Farmer's Weekly Museum,* printed at Walpole, on the New Hampshire side of the Connecticut River. Founded by Isaiah Thomas, who retained his interest in it, it gained its greatest fame under the same Joseph Dennie who later got into trouble for his attacks on democracy printed in the *Port Folio* during Jefferson's first administration. Dennie was so witty, critical, and readable that his paper was in demand all over the nation. It was actually a forerunner of the news magazine.

Other magazines that were available at the end of the eighteenth century are now valuable sources of information for the historian. The *Columbian Magazine,* founded in 1786, was elaborately illustrated (with copperplate engravings), and thus pointed the way to the picture magazine. According to Frank Luther Mott, the leading authority on magazine history in this country, Mathew Carey's *American Museum,* founded a year later, was the best-edited periodical of its day. It has been a mine of information on political, social, and economic history for students of the period. Some issues ran to more than 100 pages.

The war with Britain ended in 1815, but magazines of that period continued to present views both favorable and unfavorable to the British. One of the anti-British publications was the *North American Review,* founded in 1815 under the auspices of the Anthology Club of Boston. It became a quarterly after 3 years as a bimonthly magazine and was published until 1914. After its first few years it became closely associated with Harvard. Jared Sparks and Edward Everett, foremost scholars of the day, were regular contributors. Although circulation was small, the magazine was read by thoughtful men and women who wielded influence in their communities.

NILES' WEEKLY REGISTER

Mott estimates that several hundred quarterly, monthly, and weekly magazines were printed at one time or another in the first third of the nineteenth century. Most of them have long since been forgotten. One that deserves special mention, however, was *Niles' Weekly Register.* Edited by Hezekiah Niles, a printer with common sense, integrity, and a flare for concise reporting on current trends, the *Register* is known to every historian of the period. Although it was published in Baltimore, it was read in every state in the Union. The *Register* was the early nineteenth-century equivalent of the modern news magazine. At first Niles' publication, started in 1811, contained a minimum of opinion. Most of the material was a weekly roundup of speeches, important documents, and statements of leaders everywhere concerning current problems. Niles was an objective journalist. He was conservative in his views but he was also honest in his evaluation of events. Thus, both sides of a controversy found space in the *Register,* and the material was indexed for ready reference, much to the delight of the later researchers. Its files were so important to historians that the entire publication has been reprinted, issue by issue, for libraries all over the world needing authoritative chronicles of the first half of the nineteenth century (to 1849). Probably no day passes without some researcher's digging into the information supplied with so much care and responsibility by Hezekiah Niles, a journalist who deserves the honorable recognition of his craft.

NOTES

1. Coleman was a great admirer of Burr and remained loyal to him even after Burr killed Hamilton in a duel in 1804. By that time the editor of the *Post* was expressing himself independently.

2. In 1804 President Jefferson helped Thomas Ritchie found the *Richmond Enquirer,* soon the most influential paper in Virginia. Ritchie was political boss of his state; his views were, therefore, of significance throughout the South and were widely reprinted there.

3. From the *Letters,* quoted from Saul K. Padover, *Thomas Jefferson on Democracy* (New York: Penguin, 1939), pp. 92–93. Copyright 1939, D. Appleton-Century Company, Inc.

4. To Volney, 1802. New York Public Library, Manuscript II, 199, in Padover, *Jefferson,* p. 95.

5. Most of the newspaper figures and comments in this section are based on Clarence S. Brigham, *History and Bibliography of American Newspapers, 1690–1820,* 2 volumes (Worcester, Mass.: American Antiquarian Society, 1947).

6. Regulations such as this and the law requiring publication at state cost of letters uncalled for at the post office were also a means of rewarding proadministration editors. As administrations changed, political rivals found ready-made organs of expression.

7. Sharon M. Murphy and James E. Murphy, *Let My People Know: American Indian Journalism* (Norman: University of Oklahoma Press, 1981), pp. 20–31.

8. The Turner theory, first suggested by the Wisconsin historian in 1893 and elaborated by him and an entire school of historians, is explained in Turner, *The Significance of Sections in American History* (New York: Holt, Rinehart & Winston, 1933), in Walter Prescott Webb, *The Great Plains* (Boston: Ginn, 1931), and with a modified updating in Ray Billington, *America's Frontier Heritage* (New York: Holt, Rinehart & Winston, 1967). It is opposed in Henry Nash Smith, *The Virgin Land* (Cambridge, Mass.: Harvard University Press, 1950), by Fred A. Shannon in "Critiques of Research in the Social Sciences," *Social Science Research Council Bulletin,* No. 46 (New York: The Council, 1940), and by Louis M. Hacker in "Sections or Classes," *Nation,* CXXXVII (July 26, 1933), 108. For two well-balanced discussions of Turner's influence on American historiography, see Richard Hofstadter, *The Progressive Historians: Turner, Beard, Parrington* (New York: Knopf, 1968) and John Higham, *Writing American History* (Bloomington: Indiana University

Press, 1970). For a biography, see Ray A. Billington, *Frederick Jackson Turner* (New York: Oxford University Press, 1973).

9. Studies have shown that by no means were all of the pioneers of this type. It took some capital to head West; otherwise the slums would have been the reservoirs of the frontier society, which they were not. But dissatisfaction can take many forms, and, in general, the statement would appear to be true.

10. Hofstadter, *The Progressive Historians,* p. 119.

11. Daniel J. Boorstin, *The Americans: The National Experience* (New York: Vintage Books, 1965), p. 54.

12. This was a useless victory, because the armies to be supplied by the Great Lakes route, such as Hull's command, were ineffective by the time Commodore Perry cleared the enemy from the lake.

13. The treaty was signed December 24, 1814. Jackson won his remarkable victory January 8, 1815. News of the battle reached Washington January 28; news of the treaty reached New York by ship February 11. As a result, many Americans believed that Jackson's victory had much to do with the successful negotiatons.

14. This is just one of Russell's many colorful phrases, which were widely quoted. Another had its birth in 1812, when a man named Gerry was governor. The Republican legislature of Massachusetts had divided a political district into a weird shape in order to gain voting power. According to one account, Gilbert Stuart called Russell's attention to the new district's resemblance to a salamander. "Better say a Gerrymander!" replied the Federalist editor, although in truth the governor had had no part in the original "gerrymandering."

15. See Elizabeth Gregory McPherson, "Reporting the Debates of Congress," *Quarterly Journal of Speech,* XXVIII (April 1942), 141–48.

16. William E. Ames, "Federal Patronage and the Washington, D.C. Press," *Journalism Quarterly,* XLIX (Spring 1972), 22.

ANNOTATED BIBLIOGRAPHY

Books

ADAMS, HENRY, *History of the United States of America During the Administration of Thomas Jefferson.* New York: A. & C. Boni, 1930. The first two volumes of Adams' brilliant history; the next two cover Madison. Adams' first six chapters magnificently portray the United States of 1800. The nine-volume work first appeared in 1889 to 1891.

AMES, WILLIAM E., *A History of tbe National Intelligencer.* Chapel Hill: University of North Carolina Press, 1972. Intensive use of files, other documentary materials; covers Smith, Gales, Seaton, other editors of the outstanding paper. See also Ames, "Samuel Harrison Smith Founds the *National Intelligencer,*" *Journalism Quarterly,* XLII (Summer 1965), 389, and "Federal Patronage and the Washington, D.C. Press," *Journalism Quarterly,* XLIX (Spring 1972), 22.

BARTLETT, RICHARD A., *The New Country: A Social History of the American Frontier, 1776–1890.* New York: Oxford Press, 1974. Most recent work.

BOWERS, CLAUDE G., *Jefferson in Power.* Boston: Houghton Mifflin, 1936. A continuation of the author's *Jefferson and Hamilton.* Bowers uses newspaper sources heavily.

FORD, WORTHINGTON C., *Jefferson and the Newspaper, 1785–1830.* New York: Columbia University Press, 1936. Gives examples of how Jefferson regarded journalists.

LUXON, NORVAL NEIL, *Niles' Weekly Register.* Baton Rouge: Louisiana State University Press, 1947. This doctoral dissertation contains the best information on this influential publication.

MALONE, DUMAS, *Jefferson and His Time,* 5 volumes. Boston: Little, Brown, 1962–75. Volume three, *Jefferson and the Ordeal of Liberty,* is followed by two on his presidential terms.

MOTT, FRANK LUTHER, *History of American Magazines, 1741–1850.* New York: Macmillan, 1930. Volume one of a series by the outstanding authority on the subject. The author won a Pulitzer award for his study.

———, *Jefferson and the Press.* Baton Rouge: Louisiana State University Press, 1943. An excellent monograph.

NELSON, HAROLD L., ed., *Freedom of the Press from Hamilton to the Warren Court.* Indianapolis: Bobbs-Merrill, 1967. A collection of documents, cases, essays, with a lucid introduction by the editor summarizing press freedom trends since 1800.

PADOVER, SAUL K., *Thomas Jefferson on Democracy.* New York: Penguin, 1939. Excerpts from his letters and speeches. One section is concerned with the press.

PERDUE, THEDA, ed., *Cherokee Editor: The Writings of Elias Boudinot.* Knoxville: University of Tennessee Press, 1983. First American Indian editor.

PETERSON, MERRILL D., *Thomas Jefferson and the New Nation.* New York: Oxford University Press, 1970. Biography by a leading Jeffersonian scholar covering his entire life.

POLLARD, JAMES E., *The Presidents and the Press.* New York: Macmillan, 1947. Describes relationships of Jefferson, Madison, and Monroe with the press during this period.

SMITH, CULVER H., *The Press, Politics and Patronage.* Athens, Ga.: University of Georgia Press, 1977. A detailed account for 1789 to 1875.

William Winston Seaton. Boston: James R. Osgood and Company, 1871. The biography of the great Washington editor of the *National Intelligencer,* with notes of family and friends.

WOOD, JAMES PLAYSTED, *Magazines in the United States.* New York: Ronald Press, 1956. A study of the influence of magazines on American society.

Periodicals and Monographs

AVERY, DONALD R., "The Newspaper on the Eve of the War of 1812: Changes in Content Patterns, 1808–1812," Ph.D. thesis, Northern Illinois University, 1982. Content analysis of a 10 percent sample of 1810 newspapers showed foreign news declining, domestic news increasing, and one-half of space advertising.

CLARK, CARLISLE, "The Old Corner Printing House," *Granite Monthly,* XXX (August 1901), describes the *Farmer's Weekly Museum,* started by Isaiah Thomas.

GARCIA, HAZEL DICKEN, "Communication in the Migration to Kentucky, 1789–1792," Ph.D. thesis, University of Wisconsin, 1977. An examination of all aspects.

GARRISON, BRUCE L., "Robert Walsh's *American Review:* America's First Quarterly," *Journalism History,* VIII (Spring 1981), 14. Published during 1811 to 1812.

GLICKSBERG, CHARLES, "Bryant and the United States Review," *New England Quarterly,* VII (December 1934), 687. Describes early nineteenth-century periodicals.

LEE, ALFRED, MCCLUNG, "Dunlap and Claypoole: Printers and News-Merchants of the Revolution," *Journalism Quarterly,* XI (June 1934), 160. The story of the men who founded the first successful American daily.

LUEBKE, BARBARA F., "Elias Boudinot, Cherokee Editor: The Father of American Indian Journalism," Ph.D. thesis, University of Missouri, 1981.

LYLE, CORNELIUS R., II, "New Hampshire's *Sentinel:* The Editorial Life of John Prentiss, 1799–1846," Ph.D. thesis, Northwestern University, 1972. The story of a weekly editor, first a Federalist, then a Whig.

MARTIN, BENJAMIN ELLIS, "Transition Period of the American Press—Leading Editors in This Century," *Magazine of American History,* XVII(April 1887), 273. Describes battles between Federalist and Republican journalists. Includes interesting facsimile examples.

MURPHY, LAWRENCE W., "John Dunlap's 'Packet' and Its Competitors," *Journalism Quarterly,* XXVIII (Winter 1951), 58. The story of a struggle for survival.

PLASTERER, NICHOLAS N., "The Croswell Case: Paradox of History," *Journalism Quarterly,* XLIV(Spring 1967), 125. Argues that Croswell deserves more attention than Zenger.

RILEY, SAM G., "The Cherokee Phoenix: The Short Unhappy Life of the First American Indian Newspaper," *Journalism Quarterly,* LIII (Winter 1976), 666. The 1834 *Phoenix* succumbed to tribal problems, white harassment.

TEETER, DWIGHT L., JR., "John Dunlap: The Political Economy of a Printer's Success," *Journalism Quarterly,* LII (Spring 1975), 3. Making of a fortune by the publisher of the *Pennsylvania Packet.*

ZIMMER, ROXANNE M., "The Urban Daily Press: Baltimore, 1797–1816," Ph.D. thesis, University of Iowa, 1982. News emphasis was on shipping, trade; little local news, much advertising.

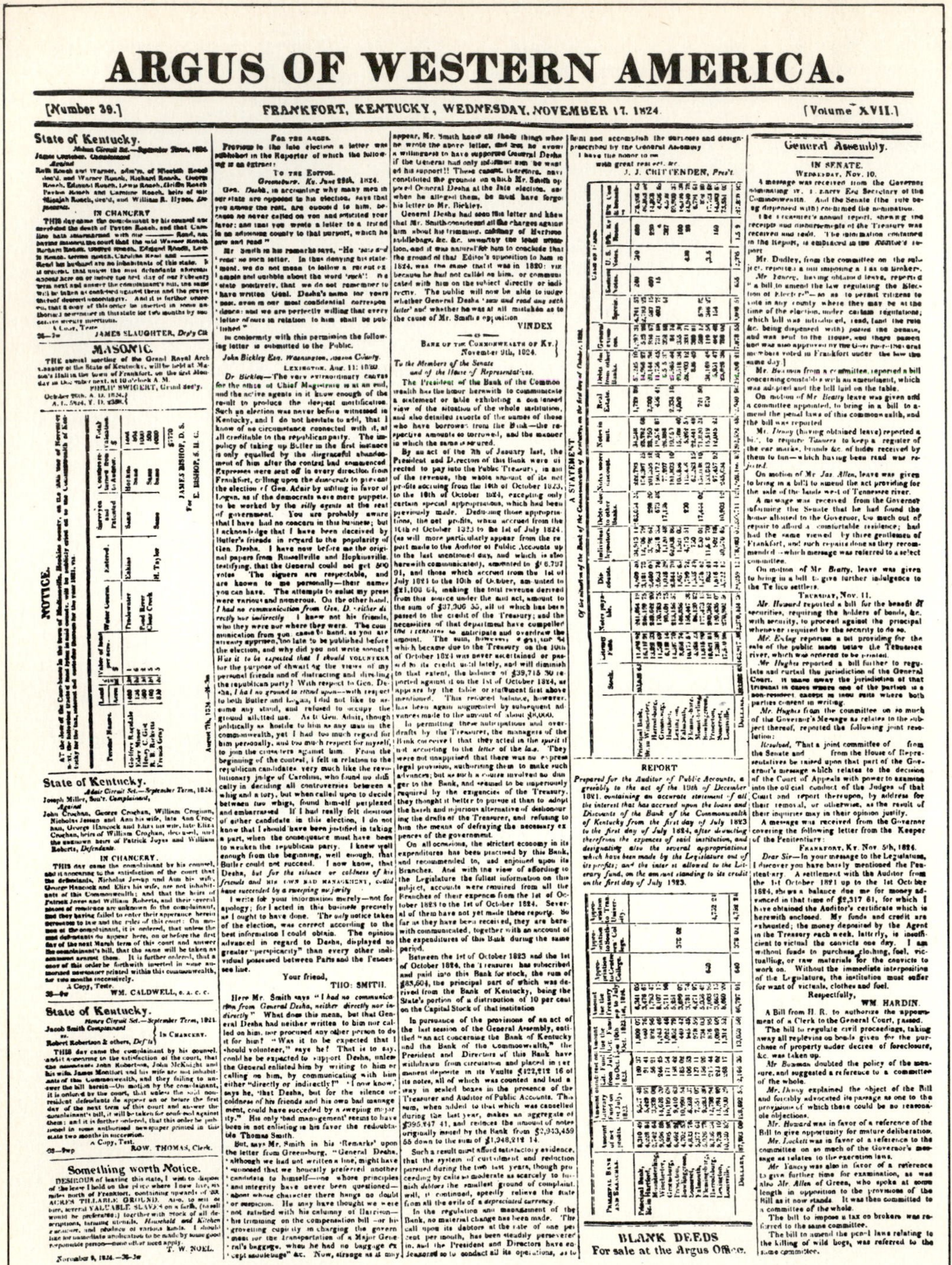

ARGUS OF WESTERN AMERICA.

[Number 39.] FRANKFORT, KENTUCKY, WEDNESDAY, NOVEMBER 17, 1824. [Volume XVII.]

State of Kentucky.

IN CHANCERY

JAMES SLAUGHTER, Dep'y Clk

MASONIC.

NOTICE.

State of Kentucky.

IN CHANCERY.

WM. CALDWELL, c. a. c. c.

State of Kentucky.

ROW. THOMAS, Clerk.

Something worth Notice.

T. W. NOEL.

FOR THE ARGUS.

TO THE EDITOR.

Your friend,

THO: SMITH.

VINDEX

BANK OF THE COMMONWEALTH OF KY. November 9th, 1824.

J. J. CRITTENDEN, Pres't.

A STATEMENT

REPORT

BLANK DEEDS

For sale at the Argus Office.

General Assembly.

IN SENATE.

WM HARDIN.

This pro-Jackson frontier paper was edited by Amos Kendall and Francis P. Blair.

9

Coonskin Democracy and the Press

A country, like an individual, has dignity and power only in proportion as it is self-informed.

—William Ellery Channing

America in the 1820s was still largely rural, but industry was beginning to exert the influence that was to be so profoundly felt by society in the near future. All the new states followed the Vermont pattern in providing suffrage for all white males. After 1810, state after state in the East dropped restrictive voting qualifications, though not always peaceably. The enfranchisement of the common man was to bring about what amounted to a bloodless revolution, but in the 1820s the so-called "common man" was not yet fully aware of the new power he had won. Until 1828, federal administration of government was still largely by "gentlemen," like Madison, Monroe, and John Quincy Adams. Yet it was in this period that the pressures for popular sovereignty began to be exerted, and the press played an important role in this drama.

AN EXPANSION OF THE PRINTED WORD

Indeed the press was counted on more and more to supply the information, inspiration, agitation, and education of a society often unable to keep up with its need for schools. Newspapers, books, and magazines increased so fast in this period that presses could not meet the craving for such material. There were 375 printing offices in 1810. By 1825 there were three times as many. Between

1820 and 1830, publication of books alone increased 10 percent and still did not supply the need, for Americans continued to buy 70 percent of their books from European publishers. Despite this literary dependence on the Old World, Americans were offering every encouragement to journalist promoters. It is significant that by 1820 more than 50,000 titles, including books, magazines, and newspapers, were listed as American. Sale of such products increased by more than a million dollars in the decade beginning in 1820, when publications grossed about $2.5 million.[1]

True, much of this American material was extremely shallow and provincial. The *Port Folio,* one of the most literate of the magazines, rarely exceeded 2000 subscribers. The authoritative *North American Review* had a normal circulation of about 3000 copies. The biggest New York newspapers printed up to 4000 copies an issue, but printing 1500 to 2500 was much more common. Only in the religious field was circulation impressive. The Methodist *Christian Journal and Advocate,* for example, had about 25,000 subscribers by its own estimate in 1826. But although circulations were small, popular publications were reaching more and more citizens, and their numbers increased yearly.

Unfortunately, most ordinary citizens could not afford to pay $5 or $10 a year in advance for such publications. The prevailing wage scale gave many workers only about $8 a week, which put virtually all magazines, and most newspapers, out of their reach. Even so, enough circulation reached the common people to give the United States the highest per capita newspaper readership in the world. In 1826, newspaper circulation in America exceeded that of Great Britain by more than 3 million readers annually. In 1810 there were 376 newspapers in the United States. By 1828, at the time of Jackson's election, there were nearly 900 (mainly weeklies). Nevertheless, what the nation needed was a newspaper press that could reach deeper into the population—first to the middle class, then to the workers.

In many communities, newspapers were the only literature available for the bulk of the citizenry. They served as the main educational device until other cultural institutions could take up the slack caused by rapid migrations. European visitors often did not realize the obstacles to cultural progress in such a new land. They sometimes failed to see that the United States was at a stage at which rudimentary education fulfilled the needs of much of the population. What had Americans, other than Franklin, contributed to science, literature, the arts, or philosophy, Reverend Sydney Smith asked rhetorically, in an article from the *Edinburgh Review* reprinted in an American newspaper? Actually, the United States was beginning to fill this vacuum. In the field of letters the country could offer Washington Irving, James Fenimore Cooper, William Cullen Bryant, Margaret Fuller, Nathaniel Hawthorne, and Ralph Waldo Emerson, all of whom would soon be recognized, even in Europe.

JOHN MARSHALL'S COURT DECISIONS

The trend toward a more enlightened age was noticeable by the end of the 1820s. By that time there were forty-nine colleges in the United States. The increase in endowed institutions of learning was appreciable after the decision of the Supreme Court in the Dartmouth College case of 1819. Until then, the trend had been toward state control of such educational establishments. The apathy of philanthropists in supporting universities is therefore understandable. In the Dartmouth College case the court held that a state had no right to change contracts, specifically, to make a private institution into a state university. Potential patrons of endowed education had hesitated to make donations to educational institutions threatened by state control.

The Dartmouth College decision was one of a series by which Chief Justice John Marshall guided the Supreme Court in establishing a philosophy of government. Two famous decisions, *McCulloch v. Maryland* (1819) and *Gibbons v. Ogden* (1824), asserted the supremacy of the national government over the states. Other decisions limited the states from restricting the rights of property holders. Such decisions were indicative of the general attitude regarding the superiority of private controls. This was the heyday of unrestricted enterprise. The attitude on this subject is also reflected in the philosophies of Justice Joseph Story of Massachusetts, author of *Commentaries on the Constitution,* and of James (Chancellor) Kent of New York, who wrote *Commentaries on American Law.* The two eminent and influential jurists interpreted laws so as to make them fit the needs of an increasingly commercial nation. They had no sympathy for an extension of government regulation that might curb the individual businessperson, but they were willing to let the government come to the help of the commercial interests when such aid was convenient.

This was what Senator Thomas Hart Benton of Missouri had in mind when he argued at the end of the decade that the "East," the symbol of business and banking, saw to it that Western demands for the homestead laws were obstructed in order to maintain a cheap labor supply for the Eastern businesspeople. Another instance of this philosophy in action was the passage of the tariff of 1828—the "tariff of abominations"—which protected the business promoter at the expense of other interests.

AMERICA OF THE 1820S

But this turn to the right had brought social and political strains. As the businesspeople assumed more dominant places in federal control, and as they began to exert their influence to their own advantages, there was an equal and opposite reaction. It is significant that labor unions and a labor press emerged about this time. The cries of anguish over the "tariff of abominations," especially in the agrarian areas, were a prelude to the battle cries of the War Between the States. And yet, curiously, American writers had little to say about the forces shaping the destiny of our country at this time. We can learn more by reading the reports of foreign observers who visited our shores during the first 30 years of the century.

Many, such as Basil Hall and Mrs. Frances Trollope, were devastating in their contempt for American culture and materialism. Others, such as Harriet Martineau, a trained journalist with an understanding heart, saw through the American veneer. In between were reporters, such as Charles Dickens, who were generally severe but reasonably accurate.[2] They were appalled, for the most part, by American provincialism, unmindful that the American was preoccupied with hacking a nation from a wilderness. This complete absorption in the development of our own resources had resulted in a strong nationalism obnoxious to the foreign observer. Earlier visitors had confined their observations to the more sophisticated East, but the European reporters of the 1820s to 1830s were more interested in the Western regions. They were disgusted by the boastfulness, smugness, superior attitudes, and ill-mannered ignorance of the type of American about to step into control of the government. Most of these observers carried home great disdain for the American concept of popular rule. One who did not was the French observer, Alexis de Tocqueville, whose *Democracy in America* reflects his observations of 1831 to 1832. In 1980 the journalist Richard Reeves retraced de Tocqueville's journey and discovered the same basic values that had made America attractive so many years before. Another early admirer was Sandor Farkas, an Hungarian intellectual who compiled *Journey in North America* following his 1831 visit. In Europe, governments acted and thought for the people; in America, Farkas noted human associations:

> In Europe it is considered something of a magic solution that America so quickly raised the national level of enlightenment. That magic at work in America is the printing of newspapers. For instance, stagecoaches regularly carry newspapers, whose delivery in the wilderness delighted and surprised me. No matter how remote from civilization or poor the settler may be, he reads the newspaper. As the stagecoach approaches a clearing in the wilderness, it sounds a horn and then the driver reaches under the seat box and tosses newspapers by the roadside. The scene repeats itself all day: tossing newspapers at roadside settlements (sometimes only a lonely log cabin).[3]

The full consequence of the Industrial Revolution in America was not apparent until a later date, but the trend was already started in the 1820s. The opening of the Erie Canal in 1825 was to make New York truly the "Empire State" and its metropolis one of the world's great commercial centers. In 1830, only about 7 percent of the people lived in cities, but the influence of industry was manifested by the obsession of political leaders with such problems as tariffs and the recognition of the working man's vote.

On the whole, the new class emerging out of the industrial revolution was at first inarticulate. The so-called "common man" appeared to be unaware of his new power. But as early as 1820 there was the beginning of populist revolt in Massachusetts, where workers were insisting upon a greater voice in government. New York experienced the same thing in 1821. In Rhode Island, where the worker was less successful at first, pressure built up into actual violence (Dorr's Rebellion), although the denouement dragged out into a later period. The issue was the rights of property versus the rights of the individual. The mechanics, as the urban workers were called at that time, resented exploitation by what they believed to be a privileged class. They resented being paid in wildcat banknotes that sometimes depreciated to less than half of their contracted wages. It is significant that in 1829 about 75,000 people were jailed for debt. More than half of these victims owed less than $20. Conditions of labor, especially for women and children, brought out a long line of social reformers who insisted on protective legislation.

Slowly the common man began to realize his power at the polls. In 1824, only six states still chose presidential electors through the legislators, heretofore the frequent tools of the property group. By 1832, only South Carolina maintained this system, and it was in that year that the party convention took at least some of the power away from "King Caucus"—the selection of candidates by a secret conclave of political leaders.

THE JACKSONIAN REVOLUTION

By 1824 a realignment in American politics was well underway. A financial panic in 1819 had brought distress to speculators and debtors in the South and West, where the Bank of the United States became a great absentee landlord through foreclosures. Those affected saw politics as a way out, if they could get relief laws and new public land and tariff policies and make war on the older money interests of the East, typified by the national bank. But presidential politics were fragmented in 1824, and party lines were blurred. Andrew Jackson, military hero and Westerner, led in the small popular vote and had the largest electoral total, but not a majority. John Quincy Adams, typifying the Federalist elitist tradition, ran a strong second. Henry Clay threw his support to Adams in the balloting in the House of Representatives; when Adams named Clay as Secretary of State, Jackson labeled it a "deal" and began campaigning as a Democrat for 1828.

In his strongholds in the South and West, Jackson appeared to be one of their kind: a militant nationalist who could handle the Indian, a natural enemy of the older Eastern money power, and a champion of egalitarianism, particularly a symbol of equal access to office. As Richard Hofstadter puts it, "So far as he can be said to have had a popular mandate, it was to be different from what the people imagined Adams had been and to give expression to their unformulated wishes and aspirations."[4] Like all victors in political revolutions, Jackson was bound to disappoint some of the groups who supported him. The growing support for the Jacksonian Democratic party in the East included many of the workers and immigrants, but it also counted some of the skilled workers and small and large traders and merchants who were more immediate beneficiaries of the democratization of politics. Shifting trends in transportation and manufacturing had also created a democratization of business; the new entrepreneurs and capitalists were sometimes alienated by the older money power and its symbolic political strength in Federalism and Adams. The unfortunate Adams was painted as an intellectual snob, aristocrat, and defender of the old order—images that won votes both West and East for Jackson.

But Jackson clearly began as the candidate of the South and West; only later did the Jacksonian Democrats make a temporary inroad in the East. In 1828 Jackson won 56 percent of the popular vote and defeated Adams 178 to 83 in the electoral college. But Jackson won only Pennsylvania and New York in the East, while Adams won only Maryland and Delaware in the South and West. In 1832 Jackson added Maine, New Hampshire, and New Jersey to his Eastern total while holding onto 54 percent of the popular vote against a weak Whig candidate Henry Clay, who carried only his home state of Kentucky in the West. Martin Van Buren, Jackson's astute political manager from the East, won all that area except Massachusetts and New Jersey as the 1836 Democratic candidate against three Whig rivals. But when the Whigs united behind a Western military hero, William Henry Harrison, in 1840, against a depression-plagued Van Buren, the Jacksonian party coalition was shattered. Van Buren held onto only New Hampshire and Illinois in the East and West and five Southern states. In 1844 and 1852 respectively, Polk and Pierce won the East as Democrats but against extremely weak Whig opponents.

The Whigs had three problems to face, Louis Hartz points out: the absence of an aristocracy to fight, the absence of an aristocracy with whom to ally, and the absence of a mob to denounce (although they tried this when Jackson's Western friends trod White House floors in muddy boots). The capitalist Whiggery of Hamilton was frightened of democracy, and the democratic tradition of Jackson was therefore able to destroy it, thereby seeming to deny its faith in capitalism. In reality, Hartz believes, Jacksonian democracy promoted a democratic-based capitalism and the Jacksonian revolution was a middle-class revolution insofar as political impact was concerned.[5]

Amos Kendall, the West's contribution to the Jacksonian leadership, saw the conflict differently. He described it as a fight between the "producing" classes of farmers, laborers, and skilled workers and the "nonproducing" capitalists and landlords. Although outnumbered, this nonproducing class remained dominant through control of banks, education, most of the churches, and the bulk or the press. Thus, Kendall pointed out, "those who produce all the wealth are themselves left poor."[6] This was "radical" thinking, well to the left of that of Van Buren, the East's leader in the Jackson camp.

The Whig party was just as far to the right in its thinking. The sanctity of property was explained very comfortably by the ultra-Whig *American Quarterly Review,* published in Philadelphia, which reported just after the end of the decade: "The lowest orders of society ordinarily mean the poorest—and the highest the richest. Sensual excess, want of intelligence, and moral debasement distinguish the former—knowledge, intellectual superiority, and refined, social and domestic affections the latter." As the Pulitzer Prize historian of this period remarks: "Property, in [Whig] reflexes, became almost identified with character." Nicholas Biddle, who as head of the powerful Second Bank of the United States, believed he was the leader of a class too strong for any attempted restraint by the Jacksonians, smugly summed up the opposition Democrats as a party made up of "men with no property to assess and no character to lose."[7]

The pompous Biddle was utterly astounded when, in the summer of 1832, Jackson vetoed a bill for rechartering the Bank of the United States. "Biddled, diddled, and undone," Charles Gordon Greene of the *Boston Post* wrote of Jackson's veto. In his veto message Jackson paid respects to the farmers, mechanics, and laborers who were seeking protection against governmental injustices, but he also declared that government should provide equal protection for both high and low, rich and poor—something with which the new entrepreneurs could agree. Unfortunately for Jackson and his party, the destruction of Biddle's bank opened the door to poor fiscal policies, wildcat banking, and inflation. By 1837 both rich and poor were victims of a "panic" of major proportions. Van Buren, rather than Old Hickory, caught the blame. But, all told, Jackson deserves having his name attached to an "era" of political reform, expanded economic opportunity, better schools, a growing literature, and a popular press. Its keynote was faith in the common people.

FIRST LABOR PAPERS

A direct result of the Industrial Revolution and the growing need for recognition of a new type of citizen was the development of the labor press. A depression during the icy winter of 1828 to 1829 and the rising cost of living fostered the beginning of a long-overdue labor revolt. The appearance of the first labor paper in 1827—the *Journeyman Mechanic's Advocate* of Philadelphia—was a clear signal that laborers intended to fight for their advantages, as property owners had long fought for theirs. The first labor paper lasted only a year. The times were too difficult for workers to provide sufficient support. It was a significant "first," however, for in conjunction with the success of the populists at the polls in 1828, the attempt of labor to express itself was prophetic. Two months before Jackson's election, the first workers' party was organized. It was sponsored by the Mechanic's Union of Trade Associations. In the same year the *Mechanic's Free Press* was established as the first successful labor newspaper. Until the depression of 1837 killed it, the *Free Press* had an average weekly circulation of around 1500—very good for a period when even the biggest New York dailies rarely exceeded 4000.

In many ways, the early labor papers were superior to modern labor organs. Their functions were primarily to counteract prejudices against working people, to supply labor information that the commercial press ignored, and to offer inspiration to the dispirited. The *Free Press* actually had much less propaganda and biased reporting than would be found in the typical modern labor paper. It offered thoughtful articles on pertinent legislation. The reports were concise, reasonably factual for the time, and well written.

This agitation led to the organization of the first national labor association: the National Trades Union, founded in 1834. A strong supporter of the labor-organization movement was the *Working Man's Advocate,* founded in New York in 1829 by George H. Evans, an English printer. Another important publication supporting labor's cause (along with other social issues) was the *Free Enquirer,* edited in New York by the charming and talented Frances "Fanny" Wright. Fanny Wright, who came to the United States from Scotland in 1818, became a power in the New Harmony utopian experiment conducted by Robert Dale Owen. She had helped put out the *New Harmony Gazette,* published in New York from 1829 as the *Free Enquirer.* Among Fanny Wright's many admirers was a young carpenter who was a great believer in democracy, and whose poems in *Leaves of Grass* were to sing of the people. The poet was Walt Whitman, himself a journalist and a printer in Brooklyn.

Most of the standard newspapers had scant regard for this labor movement, but one or two helped the cause. William Cullen Bryant, the poet and editor of the *New York Evening Post,* pleaded the case of the working people. The stand of the *Post* indicated how far it had veered since its establishment by the founder of Federalism, Alexander Hamilton. Bryant had been employed in 1825 by Coleman, the militant Federalist editor of the paper. Four years later Bryant was in full charge of the *Post,* and remained with the paper, except for a few lapses, for half a century. Under Bryant, the *Post* cast off much of its Federalist tradition. On many issues the paper sided with the Jacksonian Democrats. Thus, denouncing what it believed to be an unjust verdict against a "criminal conspiracy" (strike) by the Society of Journeyman Tailors, the *Post* said:

> They were condemned because they determined not to work for the wages offered them. . . If this is not SLAVERY, we have forgotten its definition. Strike the right of associating for the sale of labour from the privileges of a freeman, and you may as well at once bind him to a master.[8]

William Leggett, part owner of the *Post* and interim editor after Bryant went abroad in 1834, was even more prolabor than was Bryant. He was so outspoken, indeed, that the more temperate Bryant had to cool him down on occasion. Later, as we see, the cause of the working people was taken up by another famous editor, Horace Greeley. There were magazines, too, fighting for labor during this period. One was the *Democratic Review,* edited by the fiery John L. O'Sullivan. Despite these editorial champions of the underprivileged, however, the press in general took a dim view of the labor movement.

KENDALL AND BLAIR: THE *WASHINGTON GLOBE*

As obnoxious to the Whigs as the labor organization was the "Kitchen Cabinet" of the President. Some of the most influential members of this inner circle were journalists. Duff Green, the editor of the party paper in Washington, was one of the cronies until his endorsement of Calhoun lost him Jackson's support. Isaac Hill, the crippled, rebellious, and vituperative New Hampshire editor, was another intimate of the President. The two important powers behind the party, however, were Amos Kendall and Francis Preston Blair.

Amos Kendall was the most important member of the group. Reared on a New England farm, he was too frail for such rugged work. He had a passion for scholarship, and his family recognized this bent. After he was graduated from Dartmouth College, Kendall headed for the frontier, where opportunities were better for inexperienced lawyers. He hung out his shingle in Kentucky.

As a lawyer, Kendall easily turned his energies to politics. He was a protégé of a regional political chieftain, Colonel Richard M. Johnson, who insisted that the erudite New Englander take over the editorship of the Democratic party organ. The newspaper was the *Argus of Western America,* published in Frankfort. Kendall made it the party voice of the entire region. His position was achieved not without great risk, politically as well as physically. For a time he carried a pistol and a bowie knife for protection against those he had scorched in his *Argus* articles. An able, honest, and articulate journalist, his fame as a party spokesperson eventually came to the attention of the party's supreme commander, General Jackson. Kendall fought courageously for the debtor's relief system that split Kentucky wide open during Adams' administration. After the voters of Kentucky were cheated of their victory in the "Relief War," Kendall put all his energies into the election of Jackson and came to Washington.

Perhaps their physical ills gave them a common bond. The President was old and full of the miseries. Kendall was something of a hypochondriac, but he had always been frail, so perhaps his attitude was justified. At any rate, there was a strong bond between the two men. Jackson was not a polished writer, and he was happy to have Kendall edit his important statements. Time and again Kendall took down the dictation of the wan warrior. Jackson would lie on a faded sofa beneath the portrait of his beloved Rachel, while Kendall skillfully interpreted his chief's rough ideas and put them into presentable form. Jackson spoke forcefully, but there was too much of the Western uncouthness in his diction. Kendall would smooth away the crudeness and read back the paragraph to the President. Perhaps they would have to try again, but eventually the old general would nod approval. Kendall was often surprised at the effectiveness of the speeches when they appeared in print.

When Jackson first moved into the White House, the administration organ in Washington was the *United States Telegraph,* founded in 1826.[9] Duff Green was editor of the paper. He had worked hard to elect Jackson, but his other hero was John C. Calhoun, Jackson's party rival. The split in loyalty cost Green the support of the President. The Jacksonian faction decided to make Francis P. Blair Green's successor. Blair had taken over the editorship of the *Argus* after Kendall went to Washington. He had proved to be a very able journalist, but he had to be cleared of $40,000 in debts before he could accept the Washington proposal.

Blair's paper, the *Washington Globe,* appeared at the end of 1830. By that time Jackson and Blair were on the best of terms. "Give it to Bla-ar," the President used to say when he had a particularly trenchant statement requiring journalistic finesse. From Blair's pencil, on scraps of paper held on his knee, came the fighting editorials that helped to knit the party even closer. In 1832, John C. Rives became Blair's assistant. Rives, a shaggy giant, quite in contrast to his colorless associates, also came to enjoy the confidences of the inner guard.

But Kendall was the most important of them all. As one of Jackson's rivals put it, Kendall was ". . . the President's *thinking* machine, and his *writing* machine—ay, and his *lying* machine. . . . He was chief overseer, chief reporter, amanuensis, scribe, accountant general, man of all work—nothing was well done without the aid of his diabolical genius."[10] And ex-President Adams, not given to exaggeration, once stated of Van Buren and Jackson, "Both . . . have been for twelve years the tool of Amos Kendall, the ruling mind of their dominion." Kendall became postmaster general in 1835.

INVENTIONS FOR A PEOPLE'S PRESS

But where were the publications for the masses? Surely all this democratic ferment must have had its consequences in developing a newspaper the person in the street could afford and enjoy. As a matter of fact, the same forces that brought about the emergence of the common people also accounted for the establishment of a people's press. The industrial revolution, which resulted in less expensive goods, also made it possible to produce less expensive paper. All the social pressures mentioned in the preceding pages shared in making possible the newspaper for the masses. There was a vast, untapped public tempting the promoter, if only the product could be made attractive. And by 1833, technical progress had reached the point at which this was possible.

In 1822, Peter Smith, connected with R. Hoe & Company, printing-press makers, invented a hand press with a much faster lever action than had been available to that time. Five years later Samuel Rust of New York put out the Washington hand press, which is still seen in some offices. It had many automatic devices: a platen raised and lowered by springs; an ingenious toggle device for quick impressions; a faster-moving bed; and later, automatic ink rollers.

The next step was to harness power to the press. This came with the Age of Steam, and at once inventors set themselves to the problem. Daniel Treadwell of Boston had partial success in 1822. A steam book press was developed by Isaac Adams of Boston in 1830 and was popular for many years, but it was a European who perfected the process for speedy power printing. He was Friedrich Koenig of Saxony, who after many delays produced the first of his presses in London in 1811. Koenig's press had a movable bed that carried the type back and forth to be inked after each impression. Paper was fed into the top of a cylinder. Three years later Koenig invented a two-cylinder press that printed both sides of the paper—the so-called "perfecting press." Late in 1814 the *Times* of London was the first to use this press for newspaper work. The paper proudly stated that it

An American adaptation of Koenig's power press.

R. Hoe & Co., Inc.

could outstrip all rivals by printing papers at the unbelievable rate of 1100 an hour.

In 1830 David Napier of England perfected the Koenig steam press and tripled the speed of printing. America's R. Hoe & Company, which was to become a byword in newspaper plants, chose the Napier press as the prototype of a new product for American printers. The new Hoe was actually a great improvement over the Napier, and it was able to produce 4000 double impressions an hour. Such technical progress was essential to the production of an inexpensive paper that the masses could afford to buy.

By 1833 all the ingredients were available for the establishment of such a venture. It was possible to print a paper that would sell for 1 cent, in contrast to the 6 cents charged by the average commercial dailies. To a worker, 6 cents was the equivalent of a quarter-pound of bacon or a pint of local whiskey. In England, Henry Hetherington had published two periodicals for the masses. He failed, not because of the price he charged but because he was caught evading the so-called "taxes on knowledge," which kept the price of British newspapers out of the reach of the common people, as intended. John Wight, the Bow Street police reporter, had also demonstrated by 1820 the type of news that would make the presses for the masses successful.

In 1829, Seba Smith founded a daily paper at Portland, Maine, that was smaller than a standard newspaper but cheaper by half than the usual daily. It cost $4 a year, payable in advance. A year later, Lynde M. Walter, a Boston brahmin, bought an existing paper and made it into the daily *Transcript,* also offered at $4 a year. More popular because it offered spicier items, perhaps, was the *Boston Morning Post,* founded as a $4-a-year daily by Charles G. Greene in 1831. Two years later Captain John S. Sleeper founded the *Boston Mercantile Journal,* offered at the same price. All were successful, but they were sold by subscription, which took them out of the reach of the usual worker, who could not pay a lump sum in advance.

In Philadelphia, Dr. Christopher Columbus Conwell established a penny paper, *The Cent,* in 1830. Although interesting as a forerunner of the press for the masses, it survived such a short time that it is of little significance to the present summary. A serious and nearly successful attempt to put out a genuine penny paper for the masses, to be sold by the issue and not entirely by subscription, was made by Horace Greeley in partnership with Dr. H. D. Shepard, a dentist, in January, 1833. This was the *New York Morning Post.* A violent snowstorm kept so many citizens indoors the first few days of this paper's appearance that the promoters had to give up the venture.

The time was ripe for a successful penny paper, however. Indeed, the next attempt to produce a penny paper was to bring such a significant change to American journalism as to warrant the description "revolutionary."

NOTES

1. Merle Curti, *The Growth of American Thought* (New York: Harper & Row, 1943), p. 215.

2. See Godfrey T. Vique, "Six Months in America"; Thomas Hamilton, "Men and Manners in America"; Harriet Martineau, "Society in America"; reprinted in Allan Nevins, ed., *American Social History* (New York: Holt, Rinehart & Winston, 1923).

3. Translation by Arpad Kadarkay, *Los Angeles Times,*

May 31, 1976, Part 2, p. 7. The original was not published in English.

4. Richard Hofstadter, *The American Political Tradition* (New York: Vintage Books, 1948), p. 55.

5. Louis Hartz, *The Liberal Tradition in America* (New York: Harcourt Brace Jovanovich, 1955), p. 89.

6. Arthur M. Schlesinger, Jr., *The Age of Jackson* (Boston: Little, Brown, 1945), p. 306.

7. All quotes in this paragraph from ibid., p. 14.

8. *New York Evening Post,* June 13, 1836.

9. The *electric* telegraph had not been invented at that time. The name probably derived from the semaphore signal.

10. Schlesinger, *The Age of Jackson,* p. 73.

ANNOTATED BIBLIOGRAPHY

Books

BROOKS, VAN WYCK, *The World of Washington Irving.* New York: Dutton, 1944. An interpretation of the period through the literary contributions of American writers.

BROWN, CHARLES H., *William Cullen Bryant.* New York: Scribner's, 1971. A comprehensive study of the editor of the *New York Evening Post.*

Cambridge History of American Literature, II. New York: G. P. Putnam's Sons, 1917–21. Pages 160–75 describe magazines during 1783–1850; pages 176–95 describe the general newspaper picture from 1775 to 1860. Book publishing is surveyed in Volume 4 (pp. 533–53).

FISH, CARL RUSSELL, *The Rise of the Common Man, 1830–1850, A History of American Life,* Volume VI. New York: Macmillan, 1927. Social history.

FORSYTH, DAVID P., *The Business Press in America, 1760–1865.* Philadelphia: Chilton, 1964. A prize-winning history of business journalism.

GABRIEL, RALPH H., *The Course of American Democratic Thought.* New York: Ronald Press, 1956. Intellectual history since 1815.

SCHLESINGER, ARTHUR M., JR., *The Age of Jackson,* Boston: Little, Brown, 1945. A penetrating study of the political background by a Pulitzer Prize winner. Includes a chapter on the press. See also Glyndon G. Van Deusen, *The Jacksonian Era* (New York: Harper & Row, 1959) and Edward Pessen, *Jacksonian America* (New York: Dorsey, 1969), whose revisionist study counters Schlesinger.

TOCQUEVILLE, ALEXIS DE, *Democracy in America.* New York: Doubleday, 1969. Editions have been appearing since 1835 of this famous French observer's study of American democracy and its effect on the social system. For a 1980s version, see Richard Reeves, *American Journey: Traveling with Tocqueville in Search of "Democracy in America"* (New York: Simon & Schuster, 1982).

TYLER, ALICE FELT, *Freedom's Ferment: Phases of American Social History to 1860.* Minneapolis: University of Minnesota Press, 1944. Emphasizes the effects of religious and reform movements.

WELTER, RUSH, *The Mind of America, 1820–1860.* New York: Columbia University Press, 1975. Emphasis is on commonly shared attitudes. See also Russel B. Nye, *Society and Culture in the United States, 1830–1860* (New York: Harper & Row-Torch, 1974).

Periodicals and Monographs

BALDASTY, GERALD J., "The Political Press in the Second American Party System: The 1832 Election," Ph.D. thesis, University of Washington, 1978. See also Baldasty, "The Boston Press and Politics in Jacksonian America," *Journalism History,* VII (Autumn-Winter 1980), 104. Editors were major leaders of the parties.

HAGE, GEORGE S., "Anti-Intellectualism in Press Comment: 1828 and 1952," *Journalism Quarterly,* XXXVI (Fall 1959), 439. Comparison of newspaper content in two presidential elections. A full study is in Hage's Ph.D. dissertation, "Anti-Intellectualism in Newspaper Comment in the Elections of 1828 and 1952," University of Minnesota, 1957.

MELTON, BAXTER F., JR., "Amos Kendall in Kentucky, 1814–1829," Ph.D. thesis, Southern Illinois University, 1977. Pre-Washington years.

MILLER, ALAN R., "America's First Political Satirist: Seba Smith of Maine," *Journalism Quarterly,* XLVII (Autumn 1970), 488. The creator of Major Jack Downing at the *Portland Courier.*

SINGLETARY, MICHAEL W., "The New Editorial Voice for Andrew Jackson: Happenstance or Plan?" *Journalism Quarterly,* LIII (Winter 1976), 672. Discussion of Blair.

SMITH, WILLIAM E., "Francis P. Blair, Pen-Executive of Andrew Jackson," *Mississippi Valley Historical Review* XVII (March 1931), 459. A vivid portrait of the *Washington Globe* and its editor. Reprinted in Ford and Emery, *Highlights in the History of the American Press.*

James Gordon Bennett of the *New York Herald.*

Bettmann Archive

Horace Greeley of the *New York Tribune.*

Harper's Weekly

10

A Press for the Masses

But the world does move, and its motive power under God is the fearless thought and speech of those who dare to be in advance of their time—who are sneered at and shunned through their days of struggle as lunatics, dreamers, impracticables, and visionaries; men of crotchets, vagaries, and isms. They are the masts and sails of the ship to which conservatism answers as ballast. The ballast is important—at times indispensable—but it would be of no account if the ship were not bound to go ahead.

—Horace Greeley

Whenever a mass of people has been neglected too long by the established organs of communication, agencies have eventually been devised to supply that want. Invariably this press of the masses is greeted with scorn by the sophisticated reader because the content of such a press is likely to be elemental and emotional. Such scorn is not always deserved. Just as the child ordinarily starts reading with Mother Goose and fairy stories before graduating to more serious study, so the public first reached by a new agency is likely to prefer what the critics like to call *sensationalism,* which is the emphasis on emotion for its own sake. This pattern can be seen in the periods when the most noteworthy developments in popular journalism were apparent. In 1620, 1833, the 1890s, or 1920, this tapping of a new, much-neglected public started with a wave of sensationalism.

The phenomenon is clearly exhibited in the period of the 1830s and 1840s covered by this chapter, for it was in 1833 that the first successful penny newspaper tapped a reservoir of readers collectively designated "the common people." The first offerings of this poor people's newspaper tended to be highly sensational. This was only a developmental phase, however. Very quickly the penny newspapers began to attract readers from other social and economic brackets. And the common people, as their literacy skills improved, also demanded a better product. Within a decade after the appearance of the first penny paper, the press of the common people included respectable publications that offered significant information and leadership.

Before the appearance of the penny papers, publishers charged from $6 to $10 a year in advance for a newspaper subscription. That was more than most skilled workers earned in a week, and in any case, people of limited means could not pay that much in a lump sum. The standard newspapers were usually edited for people of means, and that partially accounted for the preponderance of conservatism in the press. It was also a factor in keeping circulations small, although mechanical limitations certainly had a similar effect. In 1833 the largest dailies in New York were the morning *Courier and Enquirer,* published by the colorful and irascible Colonel James Watson Webb, and the *Journal of Commerce,* founded by Arthur Tappan in 1827 but soon taken over by Gerard Hallock and David Hale.[1] The largest afternoon paper was William Cullen Bryant's *Post.* These and the other eight city papers sold for 6 cents a copy, and most of them were distributed by subscription, rather than by the street sale that was to characterize the penny press.

DAY'S *NEW YORK SUN,* 1833

Jounalism began a new epoch on September 3, 1833, with the appearance of a strange little newspaper, the *New York Sun* ("It Shines for ALL"). Its founder was Benjamin H. Day, who arrived in New York as a lad of 20 after an apprenticeship on Massachusetts' excellent *Springfield Republican.* That was in 1831. For 2 years Day operated a printing shop without much success; there were financial disturbances, and in 1832 a plague further cut into the city's prosperity. In desperation, Day decided to publish a paper in an effort to take up some of the slack in his declining job-printing business. He had watched the early attempts to establish penny papers in Boston, Philadelphia, and New York, and it appeared to him that such a publication would be successful if it could be sold and financed on a per-issue basis. He discussed the proposal with two friends, Arunah S. Abell and William M. Swain. They warned him against the undertaking, a bit of advice they had to eat sometime later when they founded their own successful penny papers in Philadelphia and Baltimore. Day went ahead with his plans anyway.

The appearance of the *Sun* that September day did not give the impression that it would soon outshine all rivals in circulation.[2] It was printed on four pages, each about two-thirds the area of the modern tabloid page. The front page was three columns wide and devoid of any display devices. Emphasis was on local happenings and news of violence. Most of the material was trivial, flippant—but highly readable. Most important, it was inexpensive. Within 6 months the *Sun* had a circulation of around 8000, nearly twice that of its nearest rival.

The reporting of George Wisner accounted for some of this success. Remembering the popularity of the Bow Street police-station news in the London forerunners of the penny press, Day hired Wisner, a Bow Street veteran, to write for the *Sun.* He was an instant success. Wisner received $4 a week for covering the courts, plus a share of the profits of the paper. Within a year he had become coowner of the paper.

"Human-interest" news was a specialty of the *Sun.* Here is a sample of the *Sun* technique taken from a typical issue after the paper was firmly established:

> Some six years ago a young gentleman, the oldest son of a distinguished baronet in England, after completing his course in education, returned home to pay his respects to his parents, and to participate in the pleasures of their social circle.[3]

The account goes on to describe how the handsome youth fell in love with a girl his father had adopted as a ward. Eventually the couple ran off together because such marriages were forbidden, and the scion was disinherited by the angry baron. On the death of the father, however, the son was declared heir to the title. A younger son tried to wrest the estate by charging his elder brother with incest. This part of the story fills all of the *Sun*'s first page for that day. No names are used. It could have been complete fabrication, except that the word "recent" is used to give a news flavor to the piece. The fate of the heir is never determined, although the account is embellished:

> . . . And while our hero was unsuspiciously reposing on the soft bosom of his bride, a brother's hand, impelled by a brother's hate, was uplifted with fratricidal fierceness for destruction.

A half column on the following page headed "Shocking Accident" described how a 19-year-old New Hampshire youth had been buried alive in a well cave-in. This had been picked out of the exchanges, apparently because of the twist to the story. It seems the poor chap was to have been wed the following week, which was the type of tear-jerker the *Sun* editors loved. There was humor of a sort mixed up in all this rubbish. Under a standing head, "Police Office—Yesterday," there was an item about the night watch being called to foil a desperate jail break, only to find that a pet squirrel in a cage was the source of the suspicious riot sounds. A Negro woman before the police magistrate made a whimsical remark based on the confusion of the words "prosecute" and "prostitute." All good, rich fare for the sensation-hungry *Sun* reader.

The only concession to the commercial interests of the community in this typical issue was a column of shipping news on the third page. Obviously, the paper was not printed for the property class. And yet anyone could see that the paper was bringing in plenty of advertising revenue. The back page was solid advertising, and about half the third page was devoted to classified notices, including "Want Ads." Even page one contained advertising, such as the ad about Robert Hoe and Son, the printing-press maker at 29 Gold Street, who had just installed a new cylinder press for the *Sun* that was the fastest in the city: 1500 complete papers an hour.

A PENNY PRESS FOR THE COMMON PEOPLE

We have suggested that the appearance of the penny press and the rise of the common people in the Jacksonian democracy were closely integrated. Sociologist Michael Schudson gives support, saying the penny press emerged in response to the needs of what he calls a "democratic market society" created by the growth of mass democracy, a market place ideology, and an urban society. The new papers "were spokesmen for egalitarianism ideals in politics, economic life, and social life through their organization of sales, their solicitation of advertising, their emphasis on news, their catering to large audiences, and their decreasing concern with the editorial," he sums up—all trends documented in detail in these pages. In his essay Schudson analyzes in depth, but rejects, three theories, each basing the reason for appearance of the penny press on a single primary cause: technological innovation, the spread of literacy (both contributing causes), or a natural evolution of press growth.[4]

Politics for the laboring class which was beginning to win recognition in the Jacksonian era had some of the flaws corresponding to the faults of the factory system. Too often majority rule encouraged the spoils system, bossism, and mediocrity in government. And too often the early penny papers lowered standards. The *Sun*, for example, was ready to sacrifice truth if that would bring in more customers. The fact is, the paper nearly trebled in circulation in 1835 when one of its reporters, a descendant of John Locke, the political philosopher, wrote a series of articles purporting to describe life on the moon. The so-called "moon hoax" of Richard Adams Locke may not have increased public confidence in the paper, but readers did not appear to resent the journalistic trick that had been played on them.

And yet there was much that was revealed as good in the sunrise of this new journalism. Workers had already won the right to vote. The penny papers could reach out to them with something other than the erudite opinions comprising the main fare of the orthodox press. The newly recognized public was more interested in *news* than in *views*. The penny papers concentrated on supplying this type of intelligence in readable form. The *Sun* and its galaxy of imitators proved that news was a valuable commodity, if delivered in a sprightly manner.

Another person began to take a special interest in the newspaper for the masses. This was the advertiser, who was impressed by the amazing circulations of the new medium. Putting an ad in every publication bought by small splinter groups was expensive and ineffective sales promotion. The large circulations of the penny papers now made it feasible to publicize articles for sale that formerly would not have warranted advertising expense. The first advertising agency man, Volney B. Palmer, who opened shop in 1849 as a liaison between the papers and businesspeople, soon had offices in several cities.

On the other hand, advertising revenue made it possible for editors and publishers to expand and to experiment with new methods of news gathering. Since advertising flowed to the circulation leaders, and since news appeared to be the most popular type of literature, publishers began to invest heavily in various devices for improving news coverage. The full scope of this development is described in the next chapter, but the relation between advertising and the penny press deserves mention at this point. As publishers began to understand the technique of obtaining mass circulations, they had to have better presses. Moses Y. Beach, Ben Day's brother-in-law, who took over the *Sun* in 1837, used part of his profits to buy a new steam-driven Hoe cylinder press capable of producing 4000 papers an hour. It was the most advanced printing equipment of its day.

The penny papers also brought changes in distribution methods. Commercial and standard newspapers had been sold on a subscription basis. Workers not only could not pay large sums in advance, but many also moved around too much to subscribe regularly. There were times when the workers could not read at all because of their jobs, or because of their poverty. The penny papers reached such readers by depending primarily on street sales, under the so-called "London Plan." Vendors bought the papers from the publisher at the rate of 100 copies for 67 cents, to be sold for 1 cent each. This put a premium on individual initiative, as indicated by the shrill cries of the vendors on street corners. The distribution system also inevitably changed the appearance of the paper, as editors tried to lure readers from rival publications through the use of better makeup and more readable type.

The raw product of the press was also changed by the newspaper of the masses. When the *views*paper became a *news*paper, the style of the writer also changed. Editors were less interested in opinion and were more concerned with reporting straight news. This was less a development toward objectivity than it was a shift away from political partisanship.

BENNETT'S *NEW YORK HERALD,* 1835

One of the most successful promoters of a newspaper cutting through the partisanship of the times was James Gordon Bennett.[5] Bennett was strictly a reporter and editor, in contrast to the printer-publishers who have figured so prominently in this history. He had gained valuable experience as a Washington correspondent, which was to stand him in good stead when he began to develop national news as a commodity. As editor for Colonel James Watson Webb, he had engineered the 1829 merger of the *Courier* and the *Enquirer*, to make it the largest newspaper in New York. Twice he had tried to found a paper of his own, but without success. The newspaper he produced on the morning of May 6, 1835, changed this picture.

Bennett was 40 years old, disillusioned, and deep in debt when he founded the *New York Morning Herald.* His capital was only $500; he also had some credit from his printers. His office was a cellar in the basement of a building at 20 Wall Street. Equipment consisted of a desk made from a plank spanning two dry-goods boxes, a secondhand chair, and a box for files. His entire staff consisted of himself. On this basis Bennett built one of the most profitable newspaper properties of his time.

There was a month's delay after the first appearance of the *Herald,* but from June, 1835, the paper boomed. The *Herald* was an imitator of the *Sun* in using sensational material, but Bennett added many tricks of his own. When it came to crime reporting the *Herald* knew no equal. The issue of June 4, 1836, a year after regular publication of the paper, showed the typical *Herald* treatment of such news. The whole front page, unrelieved by headlines, was devoted to the Robinson-Jewett case. This involved the murder of a prostitute in a brothel by a notorious man-about-town, and Bennett gave the sordid murder all the resources of his paper. He stirred up so much interest in the case that the court could not continue hearing testimony when the defendant was up for trial. The tone of *Herald* reporting is indicated by this "precede" to the main story of the trial and the disturbances in the court room:

> The major—the sheriff, all endeavored to restore order—all in vain. A terrible rain storm raged out doors—a mob storm indoors. The Judges and the Officers left the hall. Robinson was carried out of court, and the Public Authorities were trying to clear the hall of the mob, when this extra went to press.
>
> Why is not the militia called?
>
> We give the additional testimony up to the latest hour. . . . The mystery of the bloody drama increases—increases—increases.[6]

The "extra" feature of this news coverage (an "extra" is a special edition) was typical of Bennett's aggressive style of journalism. Soon this type of news treatment gave way to an increasing interest in more significant news. Bennett himself had no qualms about using violent news, for he was certain his paper was getting better every day. He got out of the penny-paper category in the summer of 1836 and defended his policy by stating that his readers were getting more for their money—the new price was 2 cents—than they could get anywhere else.

Year by year the *Herald* branched out into other fields of journalism. The paper appealed to the business class by developing the best financial section of any standard journal. Bennett, a former teacher of economics, wrote what he called the "money page." He had had experience in such reporting, and he took a special interest in this phase of journalism. When administrative duties at last forced him to give up this work, he saw to it that his best staff were assigned to the Wall Street run. In the meantime, he was offering more serious background material than his rivals on the *Sun*. His editorial comment was seldom profound, but it was decisive, reasoned, and informative. The *Herald* led the pack in hounding news from all areas—local, foreign, and national, as we see in the next chapter. Bennett built up an interesting "letters" column, in which readers could comment on the paper as well as on events. He helped develop the critical review column and society news. Long before other editors recognized the appeal of the subject, Bennett was offering sports news. Thus it was all along. The great contribution of the *Herald* was as an innovator and perfecter.

This aggressive policy paid big dividends. The *Herald* was full of advertising and was on its way to circulation leadership. It had 20,000 readers in 1836 and would be the world's largest daily, at 77,000, by 1860. Such success for a disliked rival brought a movement to boycott the *Herald*. The attack by Bennett's critics was started in May, 1840, by Park Benjamin of the *New York Signal*. Colonel James Watson Webb, Bennett's onetime employer, joined in the fray (he once administered a caning to the editor of the *Herald*), and soon all the opposition papers joined the "moral war" against the upstart journalist. Bennett was accused of blasphemy (he had carried his saucy style into the coverage of religious news) and some of the leading clergy used their influence to make the boycott effective. Advertisers who feared to offend the moral experts withdrew

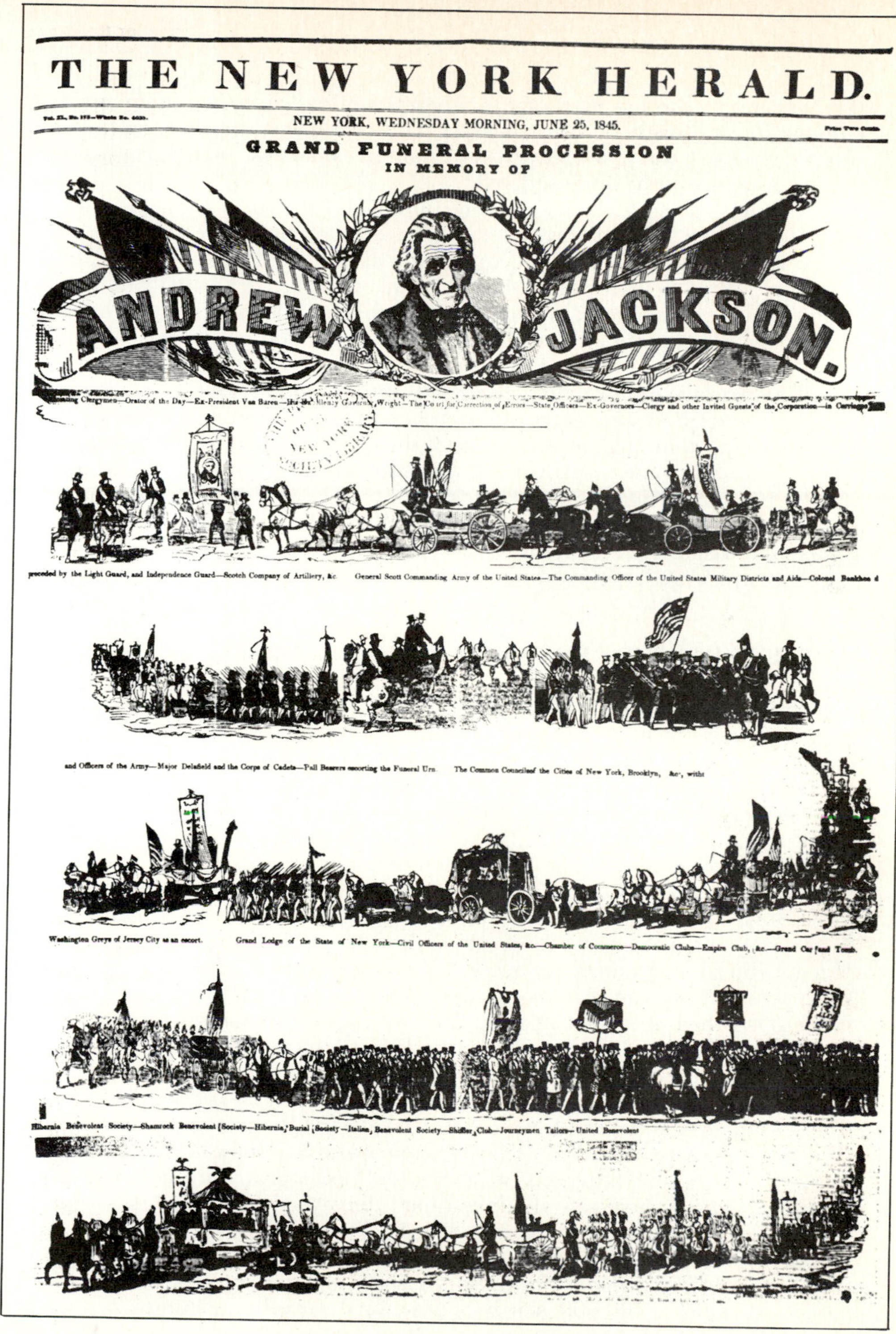

THE NEW YORK HERALD.

NEW YORK, WEDNESDAY MORNING, JUNE 25, 1845.

Price Two Cents.

GRAND FUNERAL PROCESSION
IN MEMORY OF

ANDREW JACKSON.

Officiating Clergymen—Orator of the Day—Ex-President Van Buren—His Excellency Governor Wright—The Court for Correction of Errors—State Officers—Ex-Governors—Clergy and other Invited Guests of the Corporation—in Carriages

preceded by the Light Guard, and Independence Guard—Scotch Company of Artillery, &c. General Scott Commanding Army of the United States—The Commanding Officer of the United States Military Districts and Aids—Colonel Bankhead

and Officers of the Army—Major Delafield and the Corps of Cadets—Pall Bearers escorting the Funeral Urn. The Common Councils of the Cities of New York, Brooklyn, &c., with the

Washington Greys of Jersey City as an escort. Grand Lodge of the State of New York—Civil Officers of the United States, &c.—Chamber of Commerce—Democratic Clubs—Empire Club, &c.—Grand Car and Tomb.

Hibernia Benevolent Society—Shamrock Benevolent Society—Hibernia Burial Society—Italian Benevolent Society—Shiffler Club—Journeymen Tailors—United Benevolent

One of Bennett's most famous front pages, using 1845 woodcuts.

their accounts. There is no doubt that Bennett offended decent members of the community with his bad taste, quackery, and sensationalism, but the real cause of the moral war was resentment over Bennett's amazing success. He had made his rivals appear stuffy and outdated.

Bennett solved the problem confronting the *Herald* in characteristic manner. He sent his best reporters out to cover the church beats, including all religious meetings of any consequence. A man of little religious feeling, he had the news sense to understand that here was another neglected public worth cultivating. He also toned down some of the obvious charlatanism that had made the *Herald* the symbol of publicized wickedness. The result was victory for Bennett.

Bennett put some needed ingredients into American journalism. He added spice and enterprise and aggressive news coverage. He proved that a publisher devoted to the continual improvement of the product could expect rich rewards. It cost a large fortune to provide all the machinery and personnel that put the *Herald* ahead of its rivals, but the investment paid huge dividends. Bennett left a valuable property to his son, and he died a rich man. But the *Herald* was remembered not so much for *what* it said as for *how* it said it. Bennett's contributions were largely technical.

PENNY-PRESS EXPANSION: PHILADELPHIA, BALTIMORE

Other publishers spread the gospel of penny-press journalism to other cities. Benjamin Day's printer friends, William M. Swain and Arunah S. Abell, saw the *Sun* thrive despite the pessimistic advice they had offered, but they fully admitted their errors when they founded the *Philadelphia Public Ledger* in March, 1836, with Azariah H. Simmons as partner. Philadelphia had already been introduced to penny-press journalism by Dr. Christopher Columbus Conwell, who had experimented unsuccessfully with a penny paper, *The Cent,* in 1830. In 1835 William L. Drane founded the *Daily Transcript* and was operating successfully when the three partners founded the *Public Ledger.* But the new paper was soon to become one of the great American dailies. It was a cleaned-up version of the *Herald*—full of sensational news but without the extreme bad taste of the New York paper. It was an effective policy. Within 2 years after its founding, the *Public Ledger* had absorbed its rival, the *Transcript,* and was printing more than 20,000 copies a day. Like the *Herald,* the *Public Ledger* made full use of the most modern technical and news-coverage developments.

Swain was the dominant figure on the *Public Ledger,* and after an interval, Abell decided to strike out for himself. He selected Baltimore as a likely city. It was second only to New York as a trade center and was then third in population. At first, Swain and Simmons were not enthusiastic about the undertaking. Eventually they underwrote the investment, but Abell promoted the Baltimore publication pretty much by himself. The *Baltimore Sun* first rose May 17, 1837. Its appearance coincided with a depression that had already closed the banks. The first issue of the paper played up the story of a city council meeting the day before, at which $100,000 worth of fractional currency ("shinplasters") was authorized to meet the financial crisis. This was scarcely the appropriate time to found a new paper, it would seem, but the *Sun* prospered, like its New York namesake, and appeared to be safely established at the end of the first year, with a circulation of 12,000. Like its Philadelphia affiliate, the *Sun* was always noted for its enterprise and technical progress. It was a pioneer in the development of telegraph news. Both the Baltimore and Philadelphia penny papers worked with the *New York Herald* in exchanging the latest news. The arrangement accounted for numerous scoops, especially during the Mexican war. But the *Baltimore Sun* made a contribution of its own. It developed the Washington bureau of correspondence in its first year of operation. Soon other papers came to value the Baltimore publication for complete and accurate coverage of national news. Government officials also began to follow the paper closely for trends in political development.

The success of the penny-paper pioneers encouraged other publishers to follow the pattern; thirty-five penny papers were started in New York in the 1830s. All but the *Sun* and *Herald* succumbed, but in other cities the promoters fared better. By 1840, the four largest American cities had penny papers. Most of them had similar news policies: much local news, great attention to human-interest stories, and a fat budget for entertainment material. But more and more significant news was creeping into the columns, and the penny papers led in aggressive news gathering.

GREELEY'S *NEW YORK TRIBUNE,* 1841

The maturing of the press for the masses was best indicated by the newspaper founded at the very beginning of the fifth decade of the century. The paper was the *New York Tribune,* and its founder was Horace Greeley, soon to become one of the most influential editors in the history of American journalism. More books have been written about Greeley than about any other American of the period, except Lincoln.

Horace Greeley was like a character from a Dickens novel—so real that he appeared to be a caricature. He had the angularity of the Vermonter (which he was), a stiff, homespun personality, coupled with the shyness that makes the New England breed so difficult for others to understand. His inconsistencies were legendary. A professed Whig (the party opposed to popular rule), he worked all his life to bring a greater share of material and political benefits to the common people. A leader of the group standing for a continuance of the status quo, he was one of the most "radical" persons of his age. At a time when the democratic process was under great stress, Greeley "put his faith in the unshackled mind."

He saw the ample resources of the United States, and he was certain that every American could enjoy the abundant life, if only simple justice could be made to prevail. He believed in what he called "beneficent capitalism." The practical application of this theory was the American System, sponsored by Henry Clay. Clay was Greeley's great hero. Until death ended the career of the Great Compromiser, Greeley devoted a column of his paper to discussions of current issues under the standing headline, "Henry Clay." Greeley, like Clay, honestly believed that if the proceeds of the protective tariff could be used to develop markets for the farmers, all the workers of the country would be prosperous. Because Greeley advocated the high tariff, he was sometimes suspected by the masses of opposing their interests. Because he had scant regard for agrarian dominance in an age of expanding industrialism, he was accused by the farmer of hypocrisy. Because he believed in the organization of unions to prevent exploitation by the privileged, he was frequently attacked by the property interests.

Actually, his idea was to direct the forces of capitalism so that industry, labor, and agriculture could complement each other in improving the common lot. The day Greeley had in mind was one in which opportunity, work, and education would be available to all. Women would be paid at the same rate as men, for similar services, and would have equal civil rights. Temperance would prevail in all things. Labor would be well organized for its own protection. Capital would reap the benefits of a prosperous community, but would feel responsible for better living standards. Slavery and imprisonment for debt would be abolished. John R. Commons, the great authority on the labor movement, called the *Tribune* "the first and only great vehicle this country has known for the ideas and experiments of constructive democracy."[7]

The man who proposed these revolutionary ideas was hardly messianic in appearance. He looked as though he had stepped out of a modern comic strip. He walked with a shambling, uncertain gait, as though he were feeling his way in the dark. His usual garb was a light-gray "duster," or gown, which he had purchased from an immigrant for $3 and wore winter and summer over his ill-fitting, nondescript suits. His guileless, baby-blue eyes were set in a moonlike face fringed with wispy whiskers sprouting out of his collar like reeds around a mossy stone. A high-pitched, whiny voice added nothing to this unimpressive ensemble. Yet this was the man who was to capture the loyalties of newspaper readers as few editors have in the history of American journalism.

Greeley began his career at the age of 15 as an apprentice to a printer whose business soon failed. Greeley traveled around New York state as a tramp printer for 5 years, reading voraciously all the while. When he arrived in New York City in 1831 he had just $10 to his name. After part-time work as a compositor, he finally landed a permanent position on the *Evening Post.*

Soon he and a partner, Francis Story, set up a shop of their own. They printed a small weekly on contract, but the main revenue was from lottery advertising, a circumstance his foes and rivals never let him forget later on. The attempt of the partners to found a penny paper in the winter of 1833 has already been described. In 1834, Greeley founded the *New Yorker,* a stimulating and well-edited publication mainly devoted to literary fare. While publishing this paper he wrote editorials for the *Daily Whig* and had entire charge of a political paper published in Albany by the Whig party leaders. For 6 months during the presidential campaign of 1840 Greeley edited and published a campaign paper, the *Log Cabin*. He was an experienced journalist, therefore, when he announced in the *Log Cabin* that beginning April 10, 1841, he would publish a daily penny paper, the *New York Tribune.*

His political activities had made Greeley one of the New York Whig triumvirate, which included state party boss Thurlow Weed, the Albany journalist, and Governor William H. Seward. Now was the time to found a newspaper that could carry the Whig message to the common people. It is significant that the *Tribune* appeared just a month after President William Henry Harrison's inauguration following the Whig victory of 1840. Greeley must have been aware that the climate was right for his undertaking. His influence in state and federal political circles must certainly have been a factor in the establishment of the paper. It should be pointed out, too, that Henry Clay, Greeley's hero, expected to be a key figure in the new administration and was confident that the American System, also promoted by Greeley, would be pushed through at once. But the President died a month after his inauguration, and many ambitions were thereby cut short. Not Greeley's, however.[8]

With $1000 of borrowed money and about that much money of his own, plus a mortgage on his shop—a total capitalization of not more than $3000—Greeley issued the first *New York Tribune* as a penny paper. It was not much to look at. Its four pages were five columns wide and about the dimensions of a modern tabloid. The printing was good, however, and so was the content, apparently. At least it attracted readers, for Greeley boasted of a circulation in excess of 11,000 after the second month. This was about one-fourth the print order of the *Herald,* the most popular paper in America, but it was enough to establish the *Tribune* firmly. Greeley was a good editor but a poor manager. He himself never shared in the fortune that his paper was to make for others. Indeed, the paper might have failed had not the very able Thomas McElrath purchased a half interest for $2000; the paper at that time was losing money. At the end of the second year the price was raised to 2 cents (weekly subscribers paid 1½ cents an issue) and the *Tribune* began to make money.

The *Tribune* always trailed both the *Sun* and the *Herald* in daily circulation, but part of its great reputation was to rest on its weekly edition, which was a phenomenal success. It first appeared September 2, 1841. Offered at $2 a year or $1 a year when "clubs" of twenty members bought it (which was very common) the weekly *Tribune* largely established Greeley's reputation as the greatest editor of his day. It was said to have been read in the Midwestern states' areas "next to the Bible."

The early issues of Greeley's *Tribune* offer no clue as to his greatness. The three pages of fine print describing the details of the President's funeral contain none of the stimulation and challenge for which Greeley was to become famous. And yet the very first issue indicates the significance of the *New York Tribune.* It sold for 1 cent, in competition with the other penny papers, and therefore was plainly intended for mass readership. But instead of pandering to emotionalism, the entire issue was devoted to serious discussion and reportage. The *Tribune* could offer its public murder stories just as sensational as those of its rivals, but that type of journalism was not the hallmark of the paper. Greeley had the curious faith that the masses could be attracted by reason as well as by emotionalism. He did not insult the common people by trying to "write down" to them. There is nothing that can raise the dignity of the scorned more effectively than honest recognition, and this appeal undoubtedly was a factor in the *Tribune*'s success.

GREELEY'S ROLE IN OPINION LEADERSHIP AND SOCIAL CHANGE

Admittedly, much of the *Tribune*'s later content was rational only in the broad sense. Any crackpot social philosopher could express him- or herself in the paper, if he or she wrote forcefully. The common criticism of Greeley, indeed, was that he was utterly irrational. But some of his "idealism" was founded on sound reasoning. He saw that Jeffersonian ideas, based on an agrarian society, were not applicable to a nation fast becoming an industrial power. He also realized the dangers of unrestricted industrialism. The slums of Europe warned of that. Allowing selfish business interests and rugged individualism to dominate American society could only lead to anarchy, Greeley reasoned. The duty of the statesperson, as Greeley understood it, was to reduce social friction between classes and economic interests. That could be done only when the state had strong regulatory powers.

So Greeley groped for the way out. Lacking formal education, he knew little about social and political philosophers. He preferred to learn by experimentation. That is why he allowed Albert Brisbane the use of his columns. Brisbane was the American prophet of Fourierism, a scheme for curing the ills of capitalism by a form of collective living he called *associationism.* Greeley and Brisbane were both visitors to Brook Farm, an 1840s communitarian experiment in the socialist mold of Charles Fourier. There Greeley met his later staff members Charles Dana and George Ripley. In the 1850s the *Tribune* spent many pages explaining Socialism, and Greeley himself debated the issue publicly with brilliant opponents, including Henry Raymond of the *New York Times.* For a decade one of the London correspondents Dana hired for the *Tribune* was Karl Marx, cofounder of Communism. Greeley also fought steadily for agrarian reforms, including the Homestead Bill which offered land in the West that immigrants could afford to develop. All this completely violated Whig doctrine, and yet Greeley was one of the leaders of the party. No wonder his critics were confused.

But it should be clear that Greeley did not endorse all the opinions ventilated in the *Tribune.* He was aware that most of the suggestions were impractical. But he was also aware that America was still groping toward a goal and that it would have to continue experimenting if democracy were to be kept dynamic. His readers appeared to understand. They saw that Greeley was intent on producing a better world—and a better press. If his experiments were ineffectual, they were no more so than those of a scientist who keeps working with test tubes to find solutions.

Despite all criticism, Greeley was read by all types of persons. Whether he wrote on politics, farming, labor, education, the horror of debt, the rights of women, temperance, marriage, the frontier, or slavery, all classes of society took note of the *Tribune.* He upbraided a nation for its whiskey consumption—and the liquor-loving public kept right on reading the *Tribune.* He denounced the tobacco smokers and chewers—they, too, remained regular readers.

Why should such persons, many of whom resented all this "radicalism," not only have tolerated the paper but also have supported it loyally? There was no doubt of its success. It was full of advertising—its front page was usually solid with commercial notices—universally read, and highly respectable. The weekly edition had more readers than any other publication of the period. Many of its 200,000 subscribers were farmers in the Middle West, who had no sympathy with many of Greeley's ideas on industrial society. The daily lagged behind the *Sun* and the *Herald,* but the circulation was always sufficiently high. Was it popular because the reader trusted the sincerity of its editor?

The secret of Greeley's popularity was his consciousness of responsibility to the reader. His flights into socialistic fancy were erratic and irresponsible, perhaps, but the average reader appeared to understand that the motives were sincere. That was why the farmers, who often disagreed violently with Greeley's views, read the "Try-bune," as they usually called it, "next to the Bible." How could anyone doubt the sincerity of a man who advocated a fairer distribution of wealth and who lived up to his advice by giving away to his employees all but a few shares of the gold mine he had made out of the *Tribune?* He changed the press of the masses from the vulgar level of sensationalism to a promoter of culture and stimulating ideas, and made it pay dividends. His protégés also raised the standards of the Fourth Estate. For many years Charles A. Dana, who appears again in these pages later, was Greeley's assistant, and much of the early success of the *Tribune* has been ascribed to Dana. Henry J. Raymond, soon to establish the *New York Times,* started out under Greeley. Margaret Fuller, one of the truly great literary figures of the period, wrote regularly for the *Tribune.* Carl Schurz, John Hay, Whitelaw Reid, Henry James, William Dean Howells, George Ripley, and Richard Hildreth, all of whom made names for themselves in various fields of literature, journalism, and history, served under "Uncle Horace."

The identification of Greeley with his paper is brought out by an anecdote told by Joseph Bishop in his *Notes,* written after Bishop had left the editorship of the *Post.* The editor was in Vermont a year or so after Greeley's death in 1872 and made some remark about an article that had recently appeared in the *Tribune.* "Does the Try-bune still print?" asked a farmer in the audience. "Why, I thought Greeley was dead."[9]

RAYMOND'S *NEW YORK TIMES,* 1851

A thesis was advanced at the beginning of this chapter that when a new public is first tapped by the mass media, the appeal is invariably on an emotional plane. The result is a "sensational" vehicle of communication. Readers of the *Sun* first bought it primarily for its police reports. Many of these readers matured with the years, however, for as time went on, cheap papers competing successfully with the *Sun* offered more nourishing fare. Greeley proved that a publisher could reach the masses without resorting to sensationalism. Even the *Sun* and the *Herald* offered more substantial material as time went on. They had to, to keep up with the increasing skills of their readers. Eventually, such papers left the semiliterate public behind, and another wave of sensational papers had to be established (as in the 1890s) to take up the slack. The completion of this cycle is exemplified by Henry J. Raymond of the *New York Times.*

From early boyhood, Raymond showed promise as a thinker, and he was graduated from the University of Vermont in 1840 with the highest honors. "Like most of his honors," one of his biographers has said, "they cost more than they were worth."[10] His studies almost ruined his health, and the habit of overwork established in college may have contributed to his early death.

As a college student, Raymond contributed to Greeley's *New Yorker,* which the youth admired greatly. After a visit to the New York editor, Raymond became Greeley's chief assistant in 1841, the year the *Tribune* was founded. George Jones was a colleague in the business office of the *Tribune.* Together they planned to put out the "ideal daily." Neither had sufficient money, however, for already it was impossible to establish a New York paper with $500 and a few packing-box desks, as Bennett had.

Raymond and Greeley were naturally incompatible. The younger man could never appreciate the erratic mental behavior of his employer, and soon Raymond left to work for Colonel James Watson Webb on the *Courier and Enquirer.* During this interim he established a reputation as an orator and budding politician. He was elected to the State Assembly in 1849 and became speaker in 1851. At this point he broke with Webb on the Free Soil Party issue. He took a position as an editor of *Harper's New Monthly Magazine* (established in June, 1850), where he remained until 1856 as part-time editor.

It was in 1851 that Raymond and Jones realized their old ambition of publishing a New York newspaper of their own. The first issue of the *New York Daily Times* appeared September 18, 1851. It sold for 1 cent, and thus showed its intention of being a paper for the masses, but it eschewed the sensationalism of the *Sun* and *Herald,* and the whimsy of the *Tribune,* as described in the policy expressed the first day: " . . . we do not mean to write as if we were in a passion [a slap at Greeley, who was regularly the butt of Raymond's jibes]—unless that shall really be the case; and we shall make it a point to get into a passion as rarely as possible."[11] One of the *Times'* strong points was the interpreting of foreign news. Raymond sought to excel in reporting European events.

Raymond soon established a reputation as a reasonable and objective editor. Actually, compromise, rather than objectivity, was Raymond's chief characteristic. "The great temporizer," Maverick, one of his biographers, called the *Times* editor, adding that this quality ruined him as a politician and eventually as a leader.[12] He appealed to readers who liked the *Herald*'s aggressiveness but resented its bad taste, who admired the *Tribune* but suspected Greeley's fanaticism, or who had confidence in the solidness of the *Courier and Enquirer* but were bored by its pompousness.

From the very beginning Raymond used every opportunity to plague his old mentor, Greeley. By 1852 Raymond was up to his neck in politics, despite the promise he had made to his partner after Jones warned that politics and editorships did not mix. At that time the prohibition of liquor was a big issue. It was one of Greeley's pet subjects, and he expected to be elected governor of New York because of his editorial stand on temperance. But Thurlow Weed, the Albany editor who controlled the state convention that year, needed an upstate man to hold the party together on the dry issue. That meant that the lieutenant governor had to be a big city "wet" in order to hold the party together on other issues. Weed selected Raymond, rather than his old teammate, Greeley. As Greeley once said of the episode: " . . . no other name could have been . . . so bitterly humbling to me."[13]

Indeed, from this time on, Raymond was as much a politician as he was an editor. As we see, the *Times* editor became a power in Republican circles. Greeley was to see his rival badly mauled in the postwar political arena, but in the 1850s Raymond rode the crest of the wave. Within 2 years after the founding of the *Times,* even Greeley admitted that it outsold the *Tribune* within the city limits. Raymond left a reputation as one of the great journalists of the century.

Raymond's contribution was the development of reasonable decency in public reporting. There was a minimum of personal invective in the *Times.* It seldom presented issues in the black and white patterns favored by Greeley. It was invariably fair in tone, if not in content, and no rival equaled it in developing the technique of careful reporting. It substituted accuracy for wishful thinking, even when Raymond was deep in politics. Curiously, Raymond, who was addicted to politics, stood for a strangely objective nonpartisanship in his paper. It was as though the man had two completely different personalities.

THURLOW WEED, PARTY BOSS

Two other journalists of the period deserve passing mention. One was Thurlow Weed, better known as a political boss, and the other was Samuel Bowles III.

Thurlow Weed began a career of influence as an apprentice printer in upstate New York. For a time (1808 to 1817) he worked as a journeyman, became interested in politics as a follower of DeWitt Clinton, and worked on the *Rochester Telegraph.* By 1825 he had become a political power. He purchased the *Telegraph* that year and used it to promote his candidates. Weed had strong anti-Masonic principles in a day when Masonry was a burning political issue. The Anti-Masonic party raised funds to establish a paper at Albany, and Weed was made editor while he was still serving as a leader in the Assembly. The *Evening Journal* appeared in February, 1830, and under Weed it became virtually the official organ of the Whigs. Weed was given much of the credit for electing William H. Seward governor in 1838, and the two, plus Greeley, were instrumental in putting Harrison into the White House in 1840.

Weed was the typical party boss. It was said that Seward had the principles and Weed had the votes. Greeley was the sounding board for new ideas. The big boss was Weed, however. He had the knack of making all acquaintances believe he was a special friend. The secret of his popularity was that he sincerely liked people—all kinds of people. During his heyday he was one of the important Americans of the period, and his paper was therefore influential.

Weed's power waned after Seward's defeat in 1842. He recouped his political fortunes somewhat when he backed General Zachary Taylor for president in 1848 and sent Seward to the Senate. The Whigs were doomed by 1850, however, and Weed went to Europe defeated and dejected. He accepted the new Republican party reluctantly, but was unsuccessful in promoting Seward within it. From then on, Weed's fortunes declined. He gave up the editorship of his paper in 1863. He tried to make a comeback as a journalist in 1867 by taking over the editorship of the *New York Commercial Advertiser,* but he had to give up the position because of poor health. He died in retirement in 1882.

BOWLES AND THE *SPRINGFIELD REPUBLICAN*

Another outstanding paper at this time was Massachusetts' *Springfield Republican.* Its founder was Samuel Bowles, II, although his son, Samuel Bowles, III, is more important to this history. The father was reared in Connecticut, where the family had been driven by depression. He was apprenticed to a printer at the age of 15, after the first Samuel Bowles, a grocer, died and bequeathed to the boy his entire worldly possessions—a Bible and a watch. Bowles grew up as a poor boy, but from an early age he was interested in cultural development, as evidenced by the literary club he established.

His first regular job was with the *New Haven Register.* In 1819 he joined with John Francis of Wethersfield as a partner in the *Hartford Times,* a weekly that soon failed under the adverse conditions of the time. He and his wife and family loaded their household possessions and the *Times* press on a flatboat and poled up the Connecticut River to Springfield, Massachusetts. There, a group of Anti-Federalists helped him relocate as a publisher. First copies of the *Springfield Republican* appeared September 8, 1824. It was a weekly, and its 250 subscribers paid $2 a year for it. Bowles ran the paper by himself; it grew slowly, but outlasted five rivals, and by 1840 Bowles had established a reputation as a reliable publisher. By that time Springfield was beginning to boom as a railroad center, and circulation was up to 1200. The original publisher died in 1851, but by that time the paper was largely the product of the son.

Samuel Bowles, III made the most of the excellent opportunities presented to him by his father, and it was the son who established the national reputation of the *Republican.* It was he who argued his father into "going daily" in March, 1844 (it was an evening paper then but became morning a year later). Bowles made the paper successful by skillful organization of regional correspondence, so that every little community in the upper Connecticut Valley had reason to take the paper. Young Bowles was educated for the role he was to take in journalism. As a boy he shared his room with his father's three apprentices. He grew up in the back shop. He delivered papers and personally knew all the local subscribers and their interests. At 18 he was ready to assume his place as a peer in the Fourth Estate. It was at this time that he persuaded his father to let him try a daily. It was hard going at first. He worked as much as 40 hours at a stretch without sleep. His health began to fail. The paper almost foundered financially. But in the end, Bowles produced one of the great newspapers of the nineteenth century.

Partly responsible for the success of the paper were William B. Calhoun, who wrote many of the editorials credited by readers to Bowles; Josiah Gilbert Holland, a fluent and articulate writer; and George Ashmun, a friend of Abraham Lincoln and a noted politician. But the main emphasis of the *Republican* was news, and Bowles made that his special department.

He took over full control after the death of his father in 1851 (Holland had an interest in the paper but not enough to control it). Actually, it is not until the late 1850s and the 1860s that the *Republican* exerted its greatest influence, so that this discussion must be reserved for a later chapter. But the foundations of success were laid in the period covered in this section. Bowles was a sponsor of the new Republican party. By 1860 his weekly edition was a national institution, with a circulation of about 12,000, but with a reputation throughout the country exceeded only by that of the *Tribune.* The daily hovered around 6000, but that, too, was good for a provincial paper.

The reporters and editors of the *Republican* were craftspeople, proud of their product, and absorbed in their work. Young men from all over the United States tried to get on the *Republican* staff. A tour with the Springfield paper was a kind of advanced degree in journalism. A "*Republican* man" was welcome on the biggest papers in the country.

NOTES

1. The paper had strong religious undertones, but it was aggressive in its news policies and business coverage. We refer to it again in a later discussion on the development of cooperative news gathering.

2. By 1837 the *Sun* was printing 30,000 copies a day, which was more than the total of all New York daily newspapers combined when it had first appeared.

3. *New York Sun,* January 3, 1835.

4. Michael Schudson, *Discovering the News* (New York: Basic Books, 1978), pp. 12–60.

5. It would be ridiculous to maintain that the penny press avoided partisanship. Papers like the *Herald* took up issues every day, and often fought for them as violently as in the old partisan-press days. But that was not the purpose of these papers, as it had been when papers reflected factions and parties. The newspaper was a little more impersonal than the viewspaper but the development of objectivity had barely started, and the goal had not been reached more than 100 years later. All such progress must be measured relatively.

6. *New York Herald,* June 4, 1836 (*Morning* was dropped from the nameplate in 1835).

7. John R. Commons, "Horace Greeley and the Working Class Origins of the Republican Party," *Political Science Quarterly,* XXIV (September 1909), 472.

8. Harrison's running mate, John Tyler of Virginia, proved as President to be more Southern than Whig and vetoed Clay's pet bills. In the 1844 presidential year the Whigs ditched Tyler for Clay, but Democrat James K. Polk won.

9. H. L. Stoddard, *Horace Greeley* (New York: G. P. Putnam's Sons, 1946), p. 322.

10. *Dictionary of American Biography,* XV, p. 408.

11. Willard G. Bleyer, *Main Currents in the History of American Journalism* (Boston: Houghton Mifflin, 1927), p. 240.

12. Augustus Maverick, *Henry J. Raymond and the New York Press* (Hartford: A.S. Hale and Company, 1870), p. 170.

13. Letter to Governor Seward, dated New York, November 11, 1854, in Thurlow Weed Barnes and Harriet Weed, eds., *Life of Thurlow Weed,* Volume II (Boston: Houghton Mifflin, 1884), p. 280.

ANNOTATED BIBLIOGRAPHY

Books

BARNES, THURLOW WEED, and HARRIET WEED, eds., *Life of Thurlow Weed,* 2 volumes. Boston: Houghton Mifflin, 1883–84. The first volume is the politician's autobiography, edited by his daughter, Harriet. The second volume comprises the memoirs, documents, and letters compiled by Weed's grandson.

BIGELOW, JOHN, *Retrospections of an Active Life,*

IV. New York: The Baker and Taylor Company, 1909–13. The journalistic field of the period described by a well-known *Post* executive.

BROWN, FRANCIS, *Raymond of the Times.* New York: Norton, 1951. A first-rate biography of a great editor.

CARLSON, OLIVER, *The Man Who Made News.* New York: Duell, Sloan & Pearce, 1942. The best biography of James Gordon Bennett, Sr.

CROUTHAMEL, JAMES L., *James Watson Webb, A Biography.* Middletown, Conn.: Wesleyan University Press, 1969. Carefully documented study of a leader in news gathering.

DAVIS, ELMER, *History of the New York Times, 1851–1921.* New York: The New York Times Company, 1921. Valuable for the early period of the great newspaper.

GREELEY, HORACE, *Recollections of a Busy Life.* New York: J. B. Ford and Company, 1868. The editor's own version of his career.

HALE, WILLIAM H., *Horace Greeley: Voice of the People.* New York: Harper & Row, 1950. A good modern biography.

HOOKER, RICHARD, *The Story of an Independent Newspaper: One Hundred Years of the Springfield Republican, 1824–1924.* New York: Macmillan, 1924.

ISELY, JETER ALLEN, *Horace Greeley and the Republican Party, 1853–1861.* Princeton: Princeton University Press, 1947. An examination of Greeley's writings for the eight years.

MAVERICK, AUGUSTUS, *Henry J. Raymond and the New York Press.* Hartford: A. S. Hale and Company, 1870. An outstanding authority, this book contains many valuable documents.

MERRIAM, GEORGE S., *Life and Times of Samuel Bowles.* New York: Appleton-Century-Crofts, 1885. More complete than the Hooker study just listed, and full of interesting letters and documents.

O'BRIEN, FRANK M., *The Story of The Sun.* New York: George H. Doran Company, 1918. Revised ed., New York: Appleton-Century-Crofts, 1928. The standard history of the first successful penny newspaper.

PARRINGTON, VERNON L., *Main Currents in American Thought,* Volume II. New York: Harcourt Brace Jovanovich, 1927. Greeley, Margaret Fuller, and Bryant are discussed.

PARTON, JAMES, *Life of Horace Greeley.* New York: Mason Brothers, 1855. The standard reference, written by a contemporary.

SCHILLER, DAN, *Objectivity and the News: The Public and the Rise of Commercial Journalism.* Philadelphia: University of Pennsylvania Press, 1981. Links rise of objectivity with 1830s penny press; makes detailed content analysis of the *National Police Gazette* (1845).

SCHUDSON, MICHAEL, *Discovering the News: A Social History of American Newspapers.* New York: Basic Books, 1978. Five essays dealing with the penny press, reportorial trends, and objectivity in a sociological framework.

SPENCER, DONALD M. *Louis Kossuth and Young America.* Columbia: University of Missouri Press,1977. How the Hungarian patriot interacted with U.S. audiences, 1851 to 1852. Raymond's *Times* played up Kossuth's visit to New York City; so did Greeley.

STODDARD, HENRY L., *Horace Greeley: Printer, Editor, Crusader.* New York: G.P. Putnam's Sons, 1946. Not as deep as some of the other biographies of the editor, but much more human, readable, and convincing than the earlier studies.

VAN DEUSEN, GLYNDON GARLOCK, *Horace Greeley: Nineteenth Century Crusader.* Philadelphia: University of Pennsylvania Press, 1953. This is the best, and most detailed, of the Greeley biographies. The same author is the biographer of Thurlow Weed and Henry Clay, who were so closely associated with Greeley.

Periodicals and Monographs

ABBOTT, LYMAN, "Reminiscences," *Outlook,* CVI (April 25, 1914), 897. Sidelights on Raymond's brush with the courts on a contempt citation.

BORDEN, MORTON, "Some Notes on Horace Greeley, Charles Dana and Karl Marx," *Journalism Quarterly,* XXXIV (Fall 1957), 457. It was Dana who kept Marx on the *Tribune*'s payroll. See also Summer 1959 issue for texts of five letters from Dana to Marx (p. 314).

BRADFORD, GAMALIEL, "Samuel Bowles," *Atlantic Monthly,* CXVI (October 1915), 487. An excellent character study. Reprinted in Ford and Emery, *Highlights in the History of the American Press.*

BROWN, JUNIUS HENRI, "Horace Greeley," *Harper's New Monthly Magazine* XLVI (April

1873), 734. Describes Greeley's idiosyncrasies.

COLEMAN, ALBERT E., "New and Authentic History of the Herald of the Bennetts," *Editor & Publisher,* LVI–LVIII (March 29, 1924, to June 13, 1925).

COMMONS, JOHN R., "Horace Greeley and the Working Class Origins of the Republican Party," *Political Science Quarterly,* XXIV (September 1909), 468. A significant article by a great authority and writer on American Labor.

EBERHARD, WALLACE B., "Mr. Bennett covers a Murder Trial," *Journalism Quarterly,* XLVII (Autumn 1970), 457. The 1830 trial of a sea captain, covered for the *Courier and Enquirer* in a style foreshadowing his *Herald* days.

HERBERT, WILLIAM, "Jackson, the Bank, and the Press," Ph.D. thesis, University of Missouri, 1975. Newspapers overlooked changing economics in debate on the Second Bank of the United States.

HOLLAND, DONALD R., "Volney B. Palmer (1799–1864): The Nation's First Advertising Agency Man," *Journalism Monographs,* 44 (May 1976). Palmer began offering his services to businesspeople to reach newspapers in 1842, had agency by 1849.

MELLOW, JAMES R., "Brook Farm: An American Utopia," *Dialogue,* Vol. 13, No. 1 (1980), 44. Examines that literary-oriented communal experiment.

NILSSON, NILS G., "The Origin of the Interview," *Journalism Quarterly,* XLVIII (Winter 1971), 707. Police and court reporting of 1830s were the progenitors of the interview.

PEEBLES, PAUL, "James Gordon Bennett's Scintillations", *Galaxy,* XIV (August 1872), 258. A revealing and rewarding study of the editor. Reprinted in Ford and Emery, *Highlights in the History of the American Press.*

"Personal Reminiscences of Horace Greeley," *Bookman,* XIII (April 1901), 126. Sympathetic and readable anecdotes.

SAALBERG, HARVEY, "Bennett and Greeley, Professional Rivals, Had Much in Common," *Journalism Quarterly,* XLIX (Autumn 1972), 538. Pioneers in developing news and editorial leadership are reviewed on hundredth anniversary of deaths.

"Sketches of the Life and Labors of Horace Greeley," *National Quarterly Review,* XXVI (December 1872), 153. Strong posthumous defense of the editor's character.

SLOAN, WM. DAVID, "George W. Wisner, Michigan Editor and Politician," *Journalism History,* VI (Winter 1979–80), 113. See also p. 112, James Stanford Bradshaw, "George W. Wisner and the *New York Sun.*" Two studies of the *Sun*'s police reporter.

TAYLOR, SALLY, "Marx and Greeley on Slavery and Labor," *Journalism History,* VI (Winter 1979–80), 103. Marx was a *Tribune* correspondent.

"The Herald—Onward," *Democratic Review,* XXXI (November 1852), 409. A favorable appraisal of a maligned newspaper.

TURNBULL, GEORGE, "Some Notes on the History of the Interview," *Journalism Quarterly,* XIII (September 1936), 272. An authority on journalism history holds that Greeley was the founder of the modern interview.

CALIFORNIAN.

SAN FRANCISCO, AUGUST 14, 1848.

The "Californian" again appears before its patrons this morning, as it will continue to do occasionally in these "golden times," during the temporary suspension of business. As soon as a re-action takes place, and business resumes its wonted channels, and our thoroughfares again wear their usual business-like and bustling appearance, we will issue the paper regularly, as heretofore.

To Correspondents. — "Soldado" is inadmissible. Reason why—we do not wish to conflict in any manner with military proceedings, especially during the absence of the proprietors.

"One of the People" is crowded out to make room for the Peace intelligence.

Our Sonoma friend "O'C" we hope will continue his favors.

All correspondents should be aware when writing for this paper, that they are responsible, and if public or private character should, inadvertently on our part, get maliciously assailed in its columns, and it should become requisite, their names will be freely given; otherwise we preserve them as an inviolable secret.

For the matter which appears as editorial, during the absence of the legitimate editor, Benjamin Franklin Foster is solely responsible.

GLORIOUS NEWS.

RATIFICATION OF THE TREATY OF PEACE.

END OF THE WAR.

We have received by a Courier from Monterey, bringing dispatches for the military department here, the glorious intelligence of the ratification of the treaty of peace made between the United States and Mexico, as amended and ratified by the Senate of the United States.

There is now no longer a doubt about the treaty being concluded. We get the news officially. The mail left Col. Burton, at La Paz, on the 27th June, and reached Monterey on the 6th inst.

We have not the exact terms of the treaty, but the most important points are as follows: the boundary is to commence at the mouth of the Rio Grande, up that river to the parallel of latitude which will strike the bend of the Gila, down that river to its junction with the Rio Colorado, and with that to the parallel which will strike the Pacific one league south of San Diago.

It is said that in consideration of this cession of territory by Mexico, that the United States pay their own expenses of the war, pay Mexico in cash fifteen millions of dollars, and assume the payment of the claims of the citizens of the United States against the Mexican government to the amount of three millions of dollars.

We have no disposition to speculate upon the terms of this treaty, as to its general bearing upon the two nations, nor have we the means of forming a proper judgment, but of one thing we feel satisfied: that the citizens of all the territory acquired by the United States, will be greatly benefited by the change, and so far as California is concerned, she will be elevated in the scale of human advancement beyond all possible calculation. Half a century has passed away since the first settlement of California, and although the mountains and the plains were covered with cattle and horses, yet the lands remained almost entirely uncultivated, the inexhaustible and unparalleled mineral wealth lay untouched in the bowels of the earth. The Indians made their houses literally of gold, without knowing that it was more valuable than other yellow dirt. The whole commerce [illegible] half a dozen [illegible] and received in payment a few hides and some tallow. Our towns (for cities we had none,) consisted of a few adobe houses, built with very little regard to arrangement, regularity, elegance or convenience: with no other public improvement than the churches and missions. Not a road in the territory except such as nature in her exceeding bounty, had made for us. All the beautiful locations on the great bay of San Francisco left unoccupied, showing no other signs of life than the herds of cattle and wild game which occupy its shores.

But a change has already come over the land. Two years have elapsed since the "stars and stripes" have been unfurled in this highly favored portion of the globe, and the settlers, though protected only by a military occupancy, have built large commercial houses, towns and villages, in every direction, increased our commerce, discovered and are rapidly working the gold mines, at least five hundred per cent. richer than has ever been known in the world. Discovered mercury or quicksilver, silver, iron, lead and copper, all of which mines are extraordinary rich. They have located farms over a great portion of the territory, and were rapidly bringing the land into active cultivation. All these things have been done in two years of comparative peace, and the hope of being protected by the free institutions of the United States. What then are our hopes and prospects, under a permanent peace, equal rights, fair competition, and perfect protection in the right of property? The prospective view is grand, beyond all possible calculation. The immagination is lost in wonder, when we attempt to look forward and judge of the future by the past.

THE GOLD MINE.

A few months ago we were in the habit of speaking of the agricultural resources and the commercial qualities of California, as being the source of her greatest wealth, and although now they are not inferior to any portions of the world, the soil constitutes but a small part of her wealth, all interests having been absorbed in the working of the mines.

The present number of the "Californian" is intended for circulation abroad as well as at home, and will, by giving a minute and general view of the all absorbing topic, the gold mine, be found useful to persons to send to their distant friends. The information which we shall give, has been gathered from actual observation, and from persons who have been engaged at the mines, and from the most authentic sources, as it is desirable that the facts be correctly known through other countries, and especially through the United States.

Some time in the spring, Messrs. Marshall and Bennet, in opening a ditch for a tail race for a saw-mill, which had been built on the American Fork of the Sacramento, found some gold, which the current had collected in the bottom of the race, which, after being examined, was found to be very pure. It soon began to attract attention, and some persons discovered the gold in the river below and for some distance above, in large quantities, so much so that persons who only gave credit to one third of what was said about it left their homes and went to work in the mines. It was the work of but a few weeks, to bring almost the entire populotion of the territory together to pick up the precious metal. The result has been, that in less than four months, a total revolution has been effected in the prospects and the fate o Alta California. Then, the capital was n the hands of a few individuals engaged in trade and speculation, now labor has got the upper hands of capital, and the laboring men hold the great mass of the wealth of the country—the gold.

There are now about four thousand white persons, besides a number of Indians engaged at the mines, and from the fact, that no capital is required, they are working in companies on equal shares or alone with their basket. In one part of the mine called the "dry diggins," no other implements are necessary than an ordinary sheath knife, to pick the gold from the rocks. In other parts, where the gold is washed out, the machinery is very simple, being an ordinary trough made of plank, round on the bottom, about ten feet long and two feet wide at the top, with a riddle or seive at one end to catch the larger gravel, and three or four small bars across the bottom, about half an inch high to keep the gold from going out with the dirt and water at the lower end. This machine is set upon rockers, which gives a half rotary motion to the water and dirt inside. But far the largest number use nothing but a large tin pan or an Indian basket, into which they place the dirt and shake it until the gold gets to the bottom and the dirt is carried over the side in the shape of muddy water. It is necessary in some cases, to have a crowbar, pick and shovel, but a great deal is taken up with large horns, shapen spoon fashion at the large end.

From the fact that no capital is necessary, a fair competition in labor without the influence of capital, men who were only able to procure one month's provisions, have now thousands of dollars of the precious metal. The laboring class have now become the capitalists of the country.

As to the richness of the mine, were we to set down half the truth, it would be looked upon in other countries as a "Sinbad" story, or the history of "Aladin's Lamp," which required that its possessor should but wish, and his wishes should be accomplished. Many persons have collected in one day, of the finest grade gold, from three to eight hundred dollars, and for many days together averaged from 75 to $150. Although this is not universal, yet the general average is so well settled, that when a man with his pan or basket does not easily gather 30 to 40 dollars in a day, he moves to another place, so that taking the general average, including the time spent in moving from place to place and in looking for better "diggins," we are of the opinion that we may safely set down an ounce of pure gold or $16 per day to the man. Suppose there are 4000 persons at work, they will add to the aggregate wealth of the territory about 4000 ounces, or about 60,000 dollars a day.

The value of the gold, like all things else, is regulated by the demand. Four months ago, flour was sold in the market for four dollars per hundred, now sixteen; beef cattle six, now thirty; ready made clothing, grocer's and other good have not risen in the same proportion, but are at least double their original cost. If we make bread and meat the standard by which to determine the value of the gold, then it is only worth one fourth of what it is elsewhere. But if gold and silver be the standard, then the bread and meat is worth four times what it was. But the relative value of the grain gold, compared with gold and silver coin, can only be changed by the action of government, for, however abundant the gold may be, it must produce its relative value in coin, and while a five dollar gold piece will be received in the treasury as five dollars, so long must an ounce of gold be worth *sixteen dollars*.

As to the future hopes of California, her course is onward, with a rapidity which will astonish the world. Her unparalleled gold mines, silver mines, iron ore and lead, with the best climate in the world, and the richest soil, will make it the garden spot of creation.

We call the attention of our readers to the Proclamation of Gov. Mason, on first page.

Laws.—Governor Mason has had printed both in the English and Spanish languages, a code of laws for the better government of the territory of California—the preservation of order, and the protection of the rights of the inhabitants, during the military occupancy of the country by the U. S. forces.

Appointment.—His Excellency Governor Mason has appointed Charles V. Gillespie, to be Notary Public in and for the district of San Francisco.

We acknowledge, with pleasure, our indebtedness for news, to several citizen gentlemen and military officers, all of whom will please accept our humble thanks.

The second Alcalde of the district of San Francisco, Dr. Leavenworth, we understand, will remain for the present in the discharge of the duties of his office.

ILLUMINATION MEETING.

At a large and respectable meeting of the citizens of this town, held at the City Hotel on Thursday evening at 8 o'clock, for the purpose of making suitable arrangements to celebrate the glorious news of peace having been made between the United States and Mexico, the following gentlemen were elected officers, viz:

His Honor Judge Hyde was called upon to preside.

W. D. M. Howard, Esq., Lieut T. J. Roach, Capt. S. E. Woodworth, and E. H. Harrison, Esq., were then elected Vice Presidents, and Jas. C. Leighton, Esq., Secretary.

The Chairman briefly stated the object of the meeting, after which the following resolutions were proposed:

Resolved, That in consequence of the arrival of the glorious news of a permanent peace between the United States and Mexico, that the citizens of San Francisco give a general illumination on Friday evening, Aug. 11, at 8 o'clock.

Resolved, That all the citizens of the town be called upon to lend their hearty co-operation in throwing light upon this patriotic movement.

Resolved, That the masters of the vessels in the harbor be requested to hoist their colors at sunrise and make every other demonstration of joy that may be possible to aid in making a suitable response to the same on shore.

Resolved, That a Committee of six be appointed to carry these resolutions into effect.

The following gentlemen were appointed as the Committee:

Robt Semple, Esq. of Benecia; Capt S Peny; Wm H Davis, Esq; Jas C Ward, Esq; C V Gillespie, Esq; Robt A Parker, Esq.

Wm M Smith, Esq. being called upon to address the meeting, stated that he was about leaving town to make an excursion to the "Gold Regions," and regretted that he would not be able to join with us in celebrating so glorious an event; still he would, he said, spread the news far and wide.

Dr Semple was then called upon to address the meeting, when he arose and said that he had not expected to be called upon for a speech, but upon an occasion like the present, he did not feel himself at liberty to decline. It was an event in which California was more interested and more benefited than any other portion of the United States or of Mexico. Whatever may be the terms of the treaty, it was enough for us to know that Upper California was left in the U. States. Give us equal privileges with citizens of that glorious Republic, and the industry, enterprise and intelligence of the "universal Yankee Nation" will soon develope the invaluable mineral wealth of this beautiful country to an extent hitherto unparallelled in the known world. Let us have peace with all Nations and ten years would make us one of the richest States in the Union. Every man here was directly interested in this question, and he asserted that the desire for peace on any terms which might be agreed on was unanimous in California. He thanked Providence that his feet were again finally in the U. States and that the "Star Spangled Banner" should continue to wave o'er this, his adopted land. Loud cheering.

Lt. Roach, of the New York Volunteers, was then called on for the patriotic song (by F Key,) of the "Star Spangled Banner"—which was sung by several gentlemen in chorus with great warmth of feeling.

Dr Leavenworth, Alcalde of San Francisco, was then called upon, and after making a few *peaceable* remarks, sat down amidst tremendous applause.

Ex-Gov Boggs of Sonoma was then called upon, and addressed the meeting in his usual happy style.

The meeting then adjourned,

Agreeably to the resolutions, on Friday the 11th, the ships in the harbor hoisted their flags and fired salutes, the merchants closed their doors, and citizens and soldiers one and all entered into the spirit of universal rejoicing. In the course of the day several gentlemen formed a cavalcade and passed through our principal streets in handsome order under the command of Lieut. Gilbert. In the evening, the Californian office, the hotels, and almost every dwelling house in town was brilliantly illuminated, some of them beautifully. Tar barrels were brought into requisition and bonfires blazed in every part of the town. A number of ladies and gentlemen promenaded the streets in social parties, while others followed the bent of their own inclinations, and the whole town presented one universal scene of rejoicing. Some were so much rejoiced with the news of peace that they first made war upon brandy, then upon each other, that they might have the pleasure of making a treaty of peace in which they alone were personally interested.

The *Californian*, the first state paper, reports on the Gold Rush and the Mexican War.

11

The Race for News

Journalism is literature in a hurry. . . .

—Matthew Arnold

The pioneers of the penny press probably did not realize what a profound change they were to bring about in American journalism. As the historian-journalist Gerald W. Johnson once pointed out, editors like Day, Bennett, Greeley, and Abell lived in a period of great change—change so profound that by comparison the modifications after the War of Independence were slight.[1] Many institutions were drastically altered after 1830, but none more than the press.

Three factors control the development of a newspaper. They are: (1) the reading public; (2) the system of communications; and (3) improvements in production. In the second quarter of the nineteenth century, all three factors exerted great influence on the press. The public was more discerning as it acquired a greater literacy skill and as more and more publications of various types were offered. The system of communications was developed beyond the wildest dreams of its promoters. The steam press, the beginning of automatic printing, and the perfection of paper making also helped to change the character of the press. The pioneers of the penny press thus found themselves engaged in a game, all the rules of which had been canceled, even though the new regulations were still in the process of being formulated. As Johnson says, "To survive, it was necessary to guess what the new rules would be, and to guess correctly most of the time. Conditions demanded alert and supple intelligence, backed by sturdy common sense; for policies whose necessity is as plain as day now were then wrapped in obscurity."[2]

The race for news reflected American zeal in promoting technological progress. The communications revolution described in this chapter evolved out of this expansionism. Its effect on the press has been measured in a study of news gathering from 1820 to 1860 undertaken at the University of North Carolina. The study's findings showed that the average number of stories of news events published in dailies within a week's time of occurrence increased from 45 percent to 76 percent during the period. Stories taking more than a month's time to appear dropped from 28 percent to 8 percent of the total. Increased ability to use telegraphic news would further decrease the lag. Part of this improvement in time lag was due to an increased number—from 32 percent to 55 percent—of news items actively gathered by reporters, editors, or correspondents of the sampled papers.[3] This meant a big drop in clipped items, contributions, and other general fare.

FIRST WASHINGTON REPORTERS

One of the first news sources to be tapped methodically was Congress. The beginning of a Washington press corps can be traced to the establishment by Nathaniel Carter of a capital service for his paper, the *New York Statesman,* in December, 1822. Carter's paper used the phrase "Washington Correspondence" from then until 1824. Next on the scene, when Congress convened in December, 1827, were three correspondents: James Gordon Bennett of the *New York Enquirer;* Joseph I. Buckingham, of the *Boston Courier;* and Samuel L. Knapp, of the *Charleston Courier.* These three inaugurated what has been continuous press coverage of Congress ever since. Buckingham left after the session; Knapp stayed into the 1830s. Bennett later became the correspondent of the *Courier and Enquirer* and the most famous of the early Washington press corps.[4]

Eliab Kingman, who was the first long-term Washington correspondent, ran a stringer service for various clients, including the *Journal of Commerce,* from 1830 to 1861. Matthew L. Davis worked from 1832 to 1840 for the *Times* of London and the *Courier and Enquirer* (who called him "The Spy in Washington"). James and Erastus Brooks, founders of the *New York Express,* reported in the 1830s.

Washington's first important woman journalist was Anne Royall, an unconventional but competent writer and editor who at age 61, in 1831, founded a four-page paper, *Paul Pry.* From 1836 to 1854 Royall printed *The Huntress,* which stood for Jacksonian principles, free public education, free speech, and justice to immigrants and Indians. Holding the honor of being the first woman to sit in a congressional press gallery was Jane Grey Swisshelm, editor of the antislavery *Saturday Visitor* in Pittsburgh. Swisshelm came to Washington to send her columns to Horace Greeley's *New York Tribune,* at $5 a week. On April 17, 1850, she sat in the Senate press gallery, but then decided not to return. Nationally known as a crusader and feminist, she became a Minnesota editor in 1857, escaping an unhappy marriage and seeking quiet. But her combative style led a mob to sack her press and throw the type into the river. Undaunted, she made her *St. Cloud*

Margaret Fuller (*left*) and Jane Grey Swisshelm, leading women journalists.

Democrat a voice of the newly founded Republican Party, a fierce opponent of slavery, and a shrill advocate of women's rights.[5] Ranking ahead of these women journalists was Cornelia Walter, who became the first woman editor of a major daily when she ran the family-owned *Boston Transcript* from 1842 to 1847.

Margaret Fuller of *Dial* fame came to Washington while she was a *New York Tribune* staff member, from 1844 to 1846. She had become editor of *The Dial*, a journal of transcendental philosophy sponsored by Ralph Waldo Emerson, in 1840 at age 30. Known in Boston for her intellectual leadership, literary skill, and feminist interests, she attracted Greeley, who asked her to write literary reviews and profiles. In 1846 she became the first U.S. woman foreign correspondent, and she wrote for the *Tribune* from Britain, France, and Italy. She settled in Rome, adopted Socialist thinking, married an Italian revolutionary who fathered her child, and covered the 1848 political upheavals for Greeley. En route home in 1850 to pursue her writing about the role of American women, Fuller died with her husband and child in a shipwreck off the Eastern coast.

By 1860 the Senate listed twenty-three correspondents, the House fifty-one. Lawrence A. Gobright became the Associated Press agent after 1853. Ben:Perley Poore of the *Boston Journal* arrived in 1854 for a 33-year career. John Nugent, *New York Herald*, and James W. Simonton, *New York Times*, had pre-Civil War brushes with Congress. Noah Brooks, of the *Sacramento Union*, and Samuel Wilkeson, *New York Tribune*, were among leaders of the wartime press corps.

FOREIGN NEWS

Foreign news, taken from European papers, had always been presented in American newspapers. But not until 1811 was there much concern about offering foreign news reports while they were still fresh. At that time British naval vessels were searching American ships at sea for British deserters. War was imminent, and every message from Europe told of new threats to American commerce. To satisfy the craving of his customers for such information, Samuel Gilbert had provided a reading room in his seven-story Exchange Coffee House, which dominated the Boston waterfront as the tallest building in America. The reading room was typical in that it supplied available foreign newspapers, as was the custom of coffeehouses. Gilbert's special contribution was a Marine News Book, which offered much more current and local intelligence for the edification of his merchant and shipping office clientele. When the preparation of the news books began to take too much time, Gilbert hired an assistant to carry on this work. On November 20, 1811, he announced in the *Columbian Centinel* that young Samuel Topliff, Jr., would henceforth be in charge of the "Marine and General News Books." Topliff began to meet incoming ships in his rowboat, so that he could return sooner with important news. This was the first systematic attempt in this country to gather foreign news. Later, Topliff hired correspondents in Europe to prepare the dispatches he received from incoming ship captains.

Other cities perfected similar services. The *Charleston Courier* was first in America with news of the peace with Great Britain in 1814, its ship-news reporter having learned of the event only 7 weeks after its occurrence. By 1828 New York had taken the lead in such news gathering. The most enterprising news merchant in the fast-growing city was David Hale, manager of the *Journal of Commerce,* published by Arthur Tappan. The paper was the newest of the ten dailies then being published in New York. Hale soon found that the older publications had combined to run him out of business. They had established a service for obtaining news from incoming ships, and they used rough tactics to keep Hale's boats from threatening the monopoly. In desperation, Hale purchased a fast sloop, which met the European packets as they were trimmed off Sandy Hook for the run up the bay. He was able to return with news hours before the merchantmen hove into view from Battery Place.

Not long after this Hale and his partner, Gerard Hallock, purchased the *Journal of Commerce* and made it into the most aggressive of the six-penny papers. Like the penny-press editors, the partners understood the value of news as a commodity. They sometimes put out extras when there were important stories to offer the public. They made the front page the show window, as in modern newspaper practice. But above all, they promoted any system that would speed the gathering and dissemination of news. It was Hale and Hallock who inaugurated the pony-express service between Washington and New York. The *Courier and Enquirer* offered stiff competition, but until Bennett came along and outperformed the partners, Hale and Hallock led the New York pack in sniffing out the news.

PONIES, PIGEONS, TRAINS, STEAMBOATS

Bennett was, of course, not content with anything short of the best in news gathering. When Daniel Craig began using carrier pigeons to fly news reports from distant points, Bennett subscribed to the service and even provided his own pigeons. When the steamship, the railroad, and the magnetic telegraph superseded sailing ships, ponies, and pigeons, Bennett was quick to use the new means of communication, but so were his competitors.

The United States government had a hand in developing the rapid processing of news during this period. Following the lead of the newspaper people, Postmaster General Amos Kendall established regular pony-express service between Philadelphia and New York, taking over a route from the *Courier and Enquirer* in 1835.[6] By 1836 this express service had been extended across the main routes, cutting the travel time between New York and New Orleans to less than 7 days. Express riders did not carry the full newspapers but rather proof sheets of important stories. These "slips," as they were called, preceded the regular papers by as much as a week on such long routes as the New Orleans system. The arrangement enabled newspapers around the country to work out cooperative exchange systems for beating rivals to big news.

In the 1830s and 1840s, railroads gradually began to replace the pony expresses. From 23 miles of track in 1830, construction completed up to 9000 miles by 1850. The railroad was a great boon to the newspapers. It not only provided fast distribution but also served as a communications agency. In May, 1837, the *Baltimore Sun* rushed President Van Buren's message from Washington in less than 2 hours by way of the Baltimore & Ohio Railroad. Previously, Abell and his associates would have had to wait until the following morning to obtain such news from the Washington papers.

In 1841, Bennett, Swain (*Philadelphia Public Ledger*), and Abell (*Baltimore Sun*) together hired a special locomotive to carry President Harrison's inaugural address from Washington to Baltimore, Philadelphia, and New York. The *Baltimore Sun* was able to put out an early afternoon extra covering the noonday speech. Proofs of the speech were mailed to the paper's exchanges, which thereby scored a 24-hour scoop over rivals.

The steamship also contributed to the development of fast news gathering. Travel across the Atlantic was reduced from weeks to days. In 1845, when the Oregon question brought a threat of war with England, leading papers cooperated in meeting fast ships at Halifax, the first port of call for the Atlantic steamers. Horses brought the news across the Nova Scotia peninsula to the Bay of Fundy, where a fast steamer relayed the information to Portland, Maine. A railroad train brought the news to Washington less than 50 hours after it had been received in Halifax.

NEWS BY TELEGRAPH

But the biggest boost in speedy transmission of news was given by the telegraph. On May 24, 1844, Samuel F. B. Morse sat at a table in the old Supreme Court chamber in Washington and tapped out a message in code. His assistant in Baltimore decoded the sounds. The message: "What hath God wrought?" Later that same afternoon, Morse sent the first telegraphic message published in a newspaper, the *Baltimore Patriot:* "One o'clock—There has just been made a motion in the House to go into committee of the whole on the Oregon question. Rejected—ayes, 79; nays, 86." This was one of the significant reports of the century—not because of the intrinsic news value, but because it portended a whole new system of communication.

Swain, the Philadelphia publisher, was one of the incorporators of the Magnetic Telegraph Company, which promoted Morse's invention. Abell, in Baltimore, used the columns of his paper to demand the help of Congress in subsidizing the inventor's work. He also helped finance the Washington-Baltimore test of the new device. But for some strange reason, the *Baltimore Sun* gave very little space to one of the big stories of the nineteenth century. The Monday paper relegated the first telegraphic news dispatch to the second page, under local news, headed "Magnetic Telegraph." Eleven lines told the story of the experiment that was to do so much for communication throughout the world.

Newspapers were quick to make use of the new invention, however. In May, 1846, President Polk's message to Congress calling for war with Mexico was telegraphed to Baltimore for the exclusive use of the *Sun.* Bennett became famous for his use of the invention to help him outperform his rivals.

The telegraph also stimulated the growth of small-town dailies. It was high time; unchecked, the metropolitan papers might soon have dominated the field, as they did in Great Britain. In Illinois, where city dailies from St. Louis, Cincinnati, and other big publishing centers had absorbed more and more of the circulation, thirty daily newspapers were founded during the decade following the start of telegraphic news service. The ability to get the same news as big city rivals was stimulating and pointed to cooperative news. For example, when the wire from Albany reached Utica early in January, 1846, the *Daily Gazette* there received its first telegraphic bulletins. The news was so fresh, and the transmission so novel, that the editor devoted about a column to the dispatches. To share the costs, the publisher at Utica and other upstate papers organized themselves by March, 1846, into what became the New York State Associated Press. Nineteen papers were in this first wire service by August and news agents were employed in Albany and New York City.[7] The telegraph line linked Albany and Buffalo by July, and New York City in September. Similar lines were stretching into the interior of the country and to other papers.

GENESIS OF THE ASSOCIATED PRESS

Development of a large-scale wire service to serve all these far-flung publications and to meet the needs of the big New York newspapers now seemed a logical step. Many persons had their eyes on the business, including Dr. Alexander Jones, a physician turned reporter, Daniel Craig, the pigeon expert, and various promoters of telegraph services. But the enterprising New York City dailies proved able to control the situation.

Frederic Hudson, the *Herald's* managing editor who later wrote a history of journalism, credits Hale of the *Journal of Commerce* with breaking the ice by calling Bennett, whom he despised, and suggesting that the rivals pool their news-gathering resources for the reporting of the Mexican War in 1846.[8] Nothing resulted on war coverage. But recent exhaustive research has established that the *New York Herald* and the *Tribune* began running identical telegraphic dispatches from Washington on May 7, 1846. These identical routine news stories continued on an almost daily basis.[9] The groundwork was being laid.

Supposedly the publishers of the leading New York papers met in the *Sun* offices in May, 1848, and reached an agreement. No record was kept, but later accounts named as those present Bennett and Hudson of the *Herald;* Colonel Webb and his assistant, Henry Raymond, of the *Courier and Enquirer;* Greeley of the *Tribune;* Beach of the *Sun;* Erastus and James Brooks of the *Express;* and Hale and Hallock of the *Journal of Commerce.* On May 13, 1848, Raymond was writing to the telegraph agent in Boston, telling him that those six papers wished "to procure foreign news by telegraph from Boston in common"—including both news arriving by steamships that docked in Boston before proceeding to New York and news relayed from Halifax. A week later Raymond was agreeing to a contract on behalf of the "Associated Press," providing for a payment of $100 for 3000 words of telegraphic news and stating that the news would also be forwarded to newspapers in Philadelphia and Baltimore.[10]

There is no documentary evidence of a formal organization in 1848, however, and the best precise date for the legal founding of the predecessor organization that grew into the modern Associated Press is January 11, 1849. A copy of the agreement signed that day, forming the Harbor News Association among the six previously named New York dailies, was found in 1967 in the file of Henry J. Raymond papers in the manuscript division of the New York Public Library. Its previously unknown details provided that the six partners would operate two boats to gather news in New York harbor from incoming ships, would share the costs, would sell news to papers outside New York City, and would set up membership rules.[11] In 1851, apparently because the selling of news by telegraph was becoming more important, the group signed a new agreement as the Telegraphic and General News Association.

The name "Associated Press" did not come into general use until the 1860s, but the New York City group was the forerunner of that modern-day press association. Dr. Alexander Jones became superintendent of the service and was succeeded in 1851 by Daniel Craig. That year the *Times* became the seventh newspaper member of the combine. In 1856 the group tightened its organization by adopting what was called the "Regulations of the General News Association of the City of New York."[12] Soon called the New York Associated Press, the group established a firm grip on cooperative telegraphic news reporting, and sold its service to outsiders.

THE MEXICAN WAR NEWS

The Mexican War provided the nation's press with an excellent opportunity to demonstrate news enterprise. It became the first foreign war to be covered extensively by American correspondents, and the papers made expensive, elaborate arrangements to have their reports carried back to the United States. By combining the abilities of the pony express, steamers, railroads, and the fledgling telegraph, the press established a 2000-mile communications link that repeatedly beat military couriers and the United States mails with the news from the front lines.

So effective was the express system devised by the press that an exasperated President Polk learned of the American victory at Vera Cruz via a telegram from publisher Abell of the *Baltimore Sun.*[13] Such enterprise boosted newspaper circulations. One Boston writer observed: "If our troops do but make as vigourous a charge upon the enemy as newsboys do upon the public with their extras the victory will be ours without a doubt."[14]

The purpose of the war, however, left a number of editors perplexed. Even though they reported the American victories with a mixture of pride, jingoism, and business sense, some also worried about the moral consequences of the conflict. To Horace Greeley it was a war "in which Heaven must take part against us."[15] James Gordon Bennett, meanwhile, was an adamant supporter of the conflict, arguing, "We are on the verge of vast and unknown changes in the destiny of nations."[16]

The penny-press leaders threw their editorial support behind the war and at the same time established the New York to New Orleans express system to deliver the news from the battle zones. The express system "is a creature of modern times," Bennett explained to his readers, "and is characteristic of the American people."[17] If not characteristic of the people, the system clearly was characteristic of the American press in the 1840s. Led by the New York morning dailies, a number of papers participated, including the *Philadelphia North American* and *Public Ledger,* the energetic *Baltimore Sun,* the *Charleston Courier,* and the *New Orleans Picayune.* During the final 6 months of the war these papers pooled their efforts to operate the delivery system on a daily basis.

The New Orleans press, closest to the war zones, led the coverage of the conflict.[18] Because newspapers of the day depended heavily on news from their "exchanges"—free copies they received of other newspapers—the reporting by the New Orleans correspondents with the armies was widely reprinted throughout the United States. One of the innovative New Orleans papers was *La Patria,* the nation's first Spanish-language daily. The *Baltimore Sun* and other leading dailies relied on letters from *La Patria*'s correspondents and on translations of Spanish-language papers in Mexico and Latin America.[19]

The star reporter of the Mexican War was George Wilkins Kendall, editor-publisher of the *New Orleans Picayune.* Kendall covered all the major battles from Monterrey to Chapultepec and gave accurate accounts of the military strategy involved. At least ten other "special correspondents" followed Kendall into the field: Christopher Mason Haile, Francis A. Lumsden, Daniel Scully, Charles Callahan, and John E. Durivage of the *Picayune;* James L. Freaner and George Tobin of the *New Orleans Delta;* John Peoples for the *Delta, Bee,* and *Crescent;* William C. Tobey ("John of York") of the *Philadelphia North American;* and John Warland of the *Boston Atlas.* Haile, a West Point dropout, matched Kendall's reporting ability and added the innovation of providing readers with detailed lists of battle casualties. Freaner and Peoples, former New Orleans printers, became accomplished writers and gained national reputations under their respective pseudonyms of "Mustang" and "Chaparral." Freaner capped his successful career as any army correspondent by personally delivering the peace treaty from Mexico City to Washington in a then-record 17 days.

In addition to the special correspondents, papers received reports from "occasional correspondents," usually former printers or reporters who initially joined the army as volunteers and later had time to write to the editors at home on an informal basis. Enterprising American printers also followed in the wake of the occupation forces and established "war newspapers." Before the fighting ended the Americans established twenty-five such publications in Mexican territory, including two dailies in Mexico City. Serving both the troops at the front and the public at home, these papers became important sources of news about the war.

The reports from the correspondents at the front often supported America's involvement in the war and the idea of Manifest Destiny. They also empathized with the plight of the invading American forces, which were isolated in the interior of Mexico; reflected attitudes of distrust and bias against the Mexicans; and promoted and reinforced the popular war-hero images of generals Zachary Taylor and Winfield Scott. Taylor, benefiting from a wave of favorable newspaper publicity resulting from his battlefield exploits, captured the White House in 1848.

A quixotic chapter in the war was provided by the colorful publisher of the *New York Sun,* Moses Yale Beach. Accompanied by Jane McManus Storms, an editorial writer for his paper, Beach went to Mexico City in 1847 on a secret peace mission for the American government. The effort failed and Beach, suspected of assisting antiwar forces in Mexico, barely escaped capture by Santa Anna. Storms, a strong advocate of Manifest Destiny, wrote commentaries about the war to the *Sun* and *New York Tribune* from Havana, Vera Cruz, and the Mexican capital under her pseudonym "Montgomery."[20]

PRESSES FOR MASS CIRCULATION

This brings us to the final factor in developing the press. Mass circulation, and all the changes it brought about, could not have been accomplished unless papers could be produced cheaply, quickly, and in general bulk. This problem had to be solved by the technical expert, especially the builder of printing presses.

The improvement in presses and the need for fast printing are indicated by the experience of the *Philadelphia Public Ledger.* It was founded in 1836 as a penny paper dependent on circulation for success, but its printing equipment consisted of the usual hand press, seen in a majority of newspaper shops. In 6 months the paper acquired a circulation of nearly 8000, and it was no longer possible to meet the demands of the public with the cumbersome Clymer press. Swain therefore installed the finest equipment obtainable at the time—a Napier single-cylinder press powered by steam. A year later the publisher had to order another press, this time a double-cylinder machine.

The first cylinder presses merely rolled back and forth over the flat typebed—like some of the proof presses seen in printing shops today. Speed could be doubled by using two cylinders at a time. But even these presses were not fast enough to keep up to the circulations developed by the penny papers. The problem was solved for the time by Richard Hoe's type-revolving press, first

This ingenious Hoe type-revolving press of 1855 printed 20,000 sheets an hour.

installed in the *Public Ledger* shop in 1846. Hoe substituted horizontal cylinders for the flat beds. Countersunk in these cylinders were curved iron beds, one for each page in the paper. Type matter was locked in these beds by an ingenious system of wedge-shaped rules to keep the type from flying out as the cylinders revolved at high speed. In 1849 *The New York Herald* installed one of these "lightning" presses with six cylinders capable of printing 12,000 impressions an hour. By the outbreak of the Civil War it was possible for an enterprising publisher to print up to 20,000 impressions an hour.

The type-revolving press speeded up the processing of news, but it also imposed limitations on the use of multiple-column makeup. These limitations were overcome by the development of stereotype plates. James Dellagana, a London printer, produced curved, solid plates by making an impression of the type forms in a soft mold, curving this mold to fit the cylinder, and then pouring hot lead onto the mold or "matrix" to make a type-plate. Stereotyping made possible duplicate pages for duplicate presses, bigger headlines, and advertising display devices. Bennett used five duplicate presses during the Civil War.

NEWSPAPERS MOVE WEST

The small-city newspapers changed much less radically than did their big-city rivals, but even in the hinterland the press was experiencing the impact of the communications revolution. The telegraph lines reached Portland, Maine, by 1846, Charleston in the South the next year, as well as St. Louis in the Middle West, and were extended to Chicago and Milwaukee in 1848. Pony expresses continued to operate beyond the ends of the lines—notably the overland pony express from St. Joseph, Missouri, to Sacramento, California, which opened in 1860 and continued until the telegraph reached the Pacific in October, 1861, with 50,000 miles of wires.

Newspapers in the interior did the best they could. Though local news was a leading commodity, they scrambled to get the Washington and foreign news from proof slips, exchange papers, and meager telegrams. Cincinnati and St. Louis, particularly, were major publishing centers and both had several daily newspapers by the 1850s. The leaders in Cincinnati were the *Gazette,* founded in 1815 as a weekly and transformed into a daily in 1827, and the *Commercial,* begun in 1843. St. Louis had as its top dailies the *Missouri Republican,* founded as the *Gazette* in 1808, and the *Missouri Democrat* in 1852. Secondhand presses, printing equipment, ink, and paper moved out from these centers to smaller towns as the newspaper followed the lines of settlement.

Population was booming in the Great Lakes area, where Chicago and Milwaukee became prominent. Chicago's first paper was the *Weekly Democrat,* begun in 1833 and made into a daily in 1840. The *Chicago Tribune* appeared in 1847, and after its purchase by Joseph Medill and his partners in 1855, it became the leading daily. It absorbed the *Weekly Democrat* in 1861. Milwaukee's initial weekly was the *Advertiser,* which was founded in 1836 and lived to become the *Wisconsin News.* The *Milwaukee Sentinel,* started in 1837, became the city's first daily in 1844. The transformation from weekly to daily publication was repeated elsewhere; the *Minnesota Pioneer* of 1849, the state's first paper, became a daily in 1854 and had several competitors in St. Paul.

The establishment of rival papers as mouthpieces for political groups accounted for some of the growth. Some of the Western papers were founded as means of promoting settlement and sale of lands; one such was the *Oregon Spectator,* begun in Oregon City in 1846 as the first Pacific Coast publication. Others were missionary papers, like the first publications in Kansas and the Oklahoma region. Army posts also contributed papers. The weeklies typically carried a good deal of literary material, in addition to local news. The dailies, too, attempted to satisfy the hunger for reading matter as well as news. The *Alta California,* which began in San Francisco in 1849 and became the city's first daily in 1850, later achieved fame for publishing the writings of Bret Harte and Samuel Clemens, better known as Mark Twain. Nevada's *Territorial Enterprise,* founded in 1858, boasted Mark Twain as city editor in the early 1860s.

Efforts to publish newspapers for the large Spanish-speaking population in the Southwestern states and California began in 1834 when *El Crepúsculo de la Libertad* was printed in Santa Fé. More than 100 periodicals existed at one time or another between 1846 and 1900. But following the American conquest of the Mexican territories the journalistic work appeared first as Spanish-language sections of English-language newspapers. The *Californian* in Monterey (1846), the *California Star* in San Francisco (1846), the *Santa Fé Republican* (1847), and the *Los Angeles Star* (1851) were subsidized to print legal notices in Spanish. Within a few years there were numerous separate Spanish-language papers from Texas to California.[21]

The push into the far West and into the mining country produced other early newspapers: the *Oregonian* in Portland (1850); the *Sacramento Union* (1851); the *San Francisco Bulletin* (1855) and *San Francisco Call* (1856); the Mormon Church's *Deseret News* in Salt Lake City (1850); and the *Rocky Mountain News* in the Denver mining area (1859). Easterners who flocked to the California gold fields and to the Nevada and Colorado mining towns wanted more news that the local papers offered, however. New York papers, particularly the *Herald* and the *Tribune,* issued California editions that were sent by steamer around the Horn, or by overland stage. Papers in other Eastern cities soon followed suit. For wherever an American went in the expanding nation, he or she wanted the news that an aggressive press corps was providing.

NOTES

1. Gerald W. Johnson, et al., *The Sunpapers of Baltimore* (New York: Knopf, 1937), p. 50.

2. Ibid., p. 51.

3. The North Carolina-based study, directed by Donald Lewis Shaw with the assistance of Mary E. Junck and David Pace, was reported by Professor Shaw in an unpublished paper presented at the 1981 Association for Education in Journalism (AEJ) convention, and was condensed in "At the Crossroads: Change and Continuity in American Press News, 1820–1860," *Journalism History,* VIII (Summer 1981), 38. The extensive sampling study covered sources of news items, topics of stories, locations of news events, and time lag in publishing. Papers presented to the AEJ in 1976 by David H. Weaver, "U.S. Newspaper Content from 1820 to 1860: A Mirror of the Times?" and by Gerald J. Baldasty, "The South Carolina Press and National News, 1807–47," reflect similar interest. In a random sample study of North Carolina-collected data, Weaver found that papers in all sections of the country emphasized general community, general political, and intellectual and cultural news; paid attention to economic news and science and technology, but little to education; and gave little emphasis to the conflict issues of slavery, abolition, expansionism, and sectional differences, except in the Lower South. The sample, of course, could not measure news play at exact moments of major sectional conflict events. Baldasty found that the South Carolina press depended heavily on the Washington press, particularly the *National Intelligencer,* through the 1830s, then reflected more diversity as technological change occurred. Baldasty's paper was later published (see the Bibliography for this chapter).

4. Frederick B. Marbut, *News from the Capital: The Story of Washington Reporting* (Carbondale: Southern Illinois University Press, 1971), pp. 29–37.

5. Maurine Beasley, *The First Women Washington Correspondents* (Washington, D.C.: GW Washington Studies, No. 4, 1976), pp. 3–9.

6. The *Courier and Enquirer* had found the cost of maintaining a pony route too great. But the *Journal of Commerce* continued its private express, and extended it to Washington to gain a day over rival New York papers depending on the government's Philadelphia-New York express. Other papers were showing similar news enterprise, particularly those in Boston, the *Providence Journal* and the *Charleston Courier.*

7. Richard A. Schwarzlose, "The Nation's First Wire Service: Evidence Supporting a Footnote," *Journalism Quarterly,* LVII (Winter 1980), 555.

8. Frederic Hudson, *Journalism in the United States* (New York: Harper & Row, 1873), pp. 366–67. Oliver Gramling, in *AP: The Story of News* (New York: Farrar, Straus & Giroux, 1940), presents a dramatic account of the beginnings of the Associated Press, but the historical basis for the details he relates has never been established.

9. Richard A. Schwarzlose, "Early Telegraphic News Dispatches: Forerunner of the AP," *Journalism Quarterly,* LI (Winter 1974), 595. The *Courier and Enquirer,* also studied, ran the identical story on July 7.

10. Victor Rosewater, *History of Cooperative News-Gathering in the United States* (New York: Appleton-Century-Crofts, 1930), pp. 64–66.

11. The document was uncovered by Richard A. Schwarzlose, a leading researcher in the history and operations of the press associations. See Schwarzlose, "Harbor News Association: The Formal Origin of the AP," *Journalism Quarterly,* XLV (Summer 1968), 253, in which he reviews all the evidence concerning the genesis of the AP.

12. Reprinted in Rosewater, *History of Cooperative News-Gathering,* pp. 381–88.

13. *Baltimore Sun,* April 12, 1847.

14. *New York Herald,* May 15, 1846.

15. *New York Tribune,* May 12, 1846.

16. *New York Herald,* May 12, 1846.

17. *New York Herald,* February 26, 1846.

18. The best known of these New Orleans papers were the *Picayune, Delta, Crescent, Tropic, Commercial Times,* and the *Bee.*

19. Tom Reilly, "A Spanish-Language Voice of Dissent in Antebellum New Orleans," *Louisiana History,* XXIII (Fall 1982), 327. The paper, founded in 1845, appeared under three names before it was destroyed by a mob on August 21, 1851 after criticizing the Cuban filibustering expedition. As *La Patria,* it was a daily from the fall of 1847 to early 1848.

20. *New York Sun,* January 20, April 15, 19, 1847. For a detailed study see Thomas W. Reilly, "American Reporters and the Mexican War, 1846–1848," Ph.D. thesis, University of Minnesota, 1975.

21. For a full description of these early Spanish-language papers, see the special issue of *Journalism History* IV (Summer 1977), edited by Félix Gutiérrez.

ANNOTATED BIBLIOGRAPHY

Books

BAUER, K. JACK, *The Mexican War: 1846–48.* New York: Macmillan, 1974. Good military account.

BLANCHARD, PAULA, *Margaret Fuller: From Transcendentalism to Revolution.* New York: Delacorte, 1978. Readable biography.

CHEVIGNY, BELL GALE, *The Woman and the Myth: Margaret Fuller's Life and Writings.* Old Westbury, N.Y.: Feminist Press, 1976. Biography of this famed intellectual leader of the 1840s.

COPELAND, FAYETTE, *Kendall of the Picayune.* Norman: University of Oklahoma Press, 1943. An interesting account of the life and times of a pioneer New Orleans editor and Mexican War correspondent.

DABNEY, THOMAS E., *One Hundred Great Years.* Baton Rouge: Louisiana State University Press, 1944. The centennial history of the *New Orleans Times-Picayune.*

GRAMLING, OLIVER, *AP: The Story of News.* New York: Farrar, Straus & Giroux, 1940. A colorful account of the rise of the AP. The content cannot always be substantiated by document and evidence, however.

GREELEY, HORACE, *Overland Journey from New York to San Francisco in the Summer of 1859,* edited with notes by Charles T. Duncan. New York: Knopf, 1963. Valuable biographical material as well as Greeley's view of the West.

HAGE, GEORGE S., *Newspapers on the Minnesota Frontier, 1849–1860.* St. Paul: Minnesota Historical Society, 1967. What frontier journalism was like. Carefully researched and well written.

HARLOW, ALVIN F., *Old Wires and New Waves: The History of the Telegraph, Telephone, and Wireless.* New York: Appleton-Century-Crofts, 1936. First half of the book covers the pre-Civil War period.

HOE, ROBERT, *Short History of the Printing Press.* New York: R. Hoe & Company, 1902. Obviously a promotional venture, but valuable in describing presses.

HUDSON, FREDERIC, *Journalism in the United States, 1690–1872.* New York: Harper & Row, 1873. One of the oldest journalism histories, but especially useful in the description of the midnineteenth-century period because the author knew many of the persons he discusses.

JOHNSON, GERALD, et al., *The Sunpapers of Baltimore.* New York: Knopf, 1937. An excellent case history of the penny press outside New York.

MARBUT, FREDERICK B., *News from the Capital: The Story of Washington Reporting.* Carbondale: Southern Illinois University Press, 1971. History of reporting, both print and broadcast, by a longtime student of the Washington press corps.

MCLAWS, MONTE BURR, *Spokesman for the Kingdom: Early Mormon Journalism and the Deseret News, 1830–1898.* Provo, Utah: Brigham Young University Press, 1977. Scholarly study.

MCMURTRIE, DOUGLAS C., and ALBERT H. ALLEN, *Early Printing in Colorado.* Denver: Hirschfeld Press, 1935. McMurtrie also wrote articles for *Journalism Quarterly* and other periodicals, about the journalism of other Western states.

ROSEWATER, VICTOR, *History of Cooperative News-Gathering in the United States.* New York: Appleton-Century-Crofts, 1930. Standard source for origins.

SWISSHELM, JANE GREY, *Half a Century.* Chicago: Jansen, McClurg and Co., 1880. Autobiography of first woman Washington correspondent, a crusader.

Periodicals and Monographs

BALDASTY, GERALD J., "The Charleston, South Carolina, Press and National News, 1808–

47," *Journalism Quarterly,* LV (Autumn 1978), 519. The *National Intelligencer* was major source.

BEASLEY, MAURINE, *The First Women Washington Correspondents.* Washington: GW Washington Studies, No. 4, 1976. Report on seven nineteenth-century newswomen. See also Beasley, "Pens and Petticoats: Early Women Washington Correspondents," *Journalism History,* I (Winter 1974), 112, and "The Curious Case of Anne Royall," *Journalism History,* III (Winter 1976), 98.

CARTER, JOHN D., *The San Francisco Bulletin, 1855–1865,* Ph.D. thesis, University of California, 1941. A study of the beginnings of Pacific Coast journalism.

CLOUD, BARBARA L., "Start the Presses: The Birth of Journalism in Washington Territory," Ph.D. thesis, University of Washington, 1979. Covers 1852 to 1882; young printers seeking profits were founders rather than editors with political motives.

DYER, CAROLYN S., "The Business History of the Antebellum Wisconsin Newspaper, 1833–1860," Ph.D. thesis, University of Wisconsin, 1978. Study of concentration of ownership and diversity of views.

ENDRES, KATHLEEN, "Jane Grey Swisshelm: 19th-Century Journalist and Feminist," *Journalism History,* II (Winter 1975), 128. Early Washington correspondent.

FIREBAUGH, DOROTHY GILE, "The Sacramento Union: Voice of California 1851–75," *Journalism Quarterly,* XXX (Summer 1953), 321. The story of a dominant paper.

"Frontier Press Issue," *Journalism History,* VII (Summer 1980), edited by Thomas H. Heuterman and Jerilyn S. McIntyre. Contains articles by Carolyn S. Dyer, Hazel Dicken Garcia, Barbara L. Cloud, Roy A. Atwood, Fred F. Endres.

HALL, MARK W., "1831–49: The Pioneer Period for Newspapers in California," *Journalism Quarterly,* XLIX (Winter 1972), 648. Mexican War brought Yanks.

"Journalism of the West," *Journal of the West,* 19 (April 1980). Articles by William H. Lyons and Thomas H. Heuterman.

KIELBOWICZ, RICHARD B., "News in the Mails, 1690–1863: The Technology, Policy and Politics of a Communication Channel," Ph.D. thesis, University of Minnesota, 1983. A depth study illuminating effects of postal distribution of periodicals on the media, reading public, and society.

LORENZ, ALFRED L., " 'Out of Sorts and Out of Cash': Problems of Publishing in Wisconsin Territory, 1833–1848," *Journalism History,* III (Summer 1976), 34. See also Lorenz, "Hamilton Reed: An Editor's Trials on the Wisconsin Frontier," *Journalism Quarterly,* LIII (Autumn 1976), 417.

MARBUT, FREDERICK B., "Early Washington Correspondents: Some Neglected Pioneers," *Journalism Quarterly,* XXV (December 1948), 369. See also Marbut, "The United States Senate and the Press, 1838–41," *Journalism Quarterly,* XXVIII (Summer 1951), 342.

MCINTYRE, JERILYN, "Communication on a Western Frontier—Some Questions About Context," *Journalism History,* III (Summer 1976), 53. News-use patterns.

NELSON, ANNA KASTEN, "Mission to Mexico—Moses Y. Beach, Secret Agent." *The New York State Historical Society Quarterly,* LIX (July 1975), 227.

NELSON, JACK A., "The Pioneer Press of the Great Basin," Ph.D. thesis, University of Missouri, 1971. Nevada and Utah editors lacked news ethics.

PICKETT, CALDER M., "Technology and the New York Press in the 19th Century," *Journalism Quarterly,* XXXVII (Summer 1960), 398. Based on "Six New York Newspapers and Their Response to Technology in the 19th Century," Ph.D. thesis, University of Minnesota, 1959.

REILLY, THOMAS W., "American Reporters and the Mexican War, 1846–1848," Ph.D. thesis, University of Minnesota, 1975. Coverage of war was extensive and reinforced the American belief in Manifest Destiny. Much new material presented interestingly.

———, "Newspaper Suppression During the Mexican War," *Journalism Quarterly,* LIV (Summer 1977), 262.

———, "A Spanish-Language Voice of Dissent in Antebellum New Orleans," *Louisiana History,* XXIII (Fall 1982), 325.

SCHWARZLOSE, RICHARD A., "Early Telegraphic News Dispatches: Forerunner of the AP," *Journalism Quarterly,* LI (Winter 1974), 595. Pinpoints AP birth.

———, "Harbor News Association: Formal Origin of the AP," *Journalism Quarterly,* XLV (Summer 1968), 253. This document discloses that the legal date of the AP predecessor's founding is January 11, 1849.

———, "The Nation's First Wire Service: Evidence Supporting a Footnote," *Journalism Quarterly,* LVII (Winter 1980), 555. The New York State Associated Press is nominated.

Shaw, Donald Lewis, "At the Crossroads: Change and Continuity in American Press News, 1820–1860," *Journalism History,* VIII (Summer 1981), 38–53. Detailed report on major flow of the news research project.

Weigle, Clifford F., "San Francisco Journalism, 1847–1851," *Journalism Quarterly,* XIV (June 1937), 151. The beginnings of a colorful journalistic tradition.

FREEDOM'S JOURNAL.

"RIGHTEOUSNESS EXALTETH A NATION."

CORNISH & RUSSWURM, Editors & Proprietors. | NEW-YORK, FRIDAY, MARCH 16, 1827. | VOL. I. NO. 1.

TO OUR PATRONS.

IN presenting our first number to our Patrons, we feel all the diffidence of persons entering upon a new and untried line of business. But a moment's reflection upon the noble objects, which we have in view by the publication of this Journal; the expediency of its appearance at this time, when so many schemes are in action concerning our people—encourage us to come boldly before an enlightened publick. For we believe, that a paper devoted to the dissemination of useful knowledge among our brethren, and to their moral and religious improvement, must meet with the cordial approbation of every friend to humanity.

The peculiarities of this Journal, render it important that we should advertise to the world the motives by whic we are actuated, and the objects which we contemplate.

We wish to plead our own cause. Too long have others spoken for us. Too long has the publick been deceived by misrepresentations, in things which concern us dearly, though in the estimation of some mere trifles; for though there are many in society who exercise towards us benevolent feelings; still (with sorrow we confess it) there are others who make it their business to enlarge upon the least trifle, which tends to the discredit of any person of colour; and pronounce anathemas and denounce our whole body for the misconduct of this guilty one. We are aware that there are many instances of vice among us, but we avow that it is because no one has taught its subjects to be virtuous: many instances of poverty, because no sufficient efforts accommodated to minds contracted by slavery, and deprived of early education have been made, to teach them how to husband their hard earnings, and to secure to themselves comforts.

Education being an object of the highest importance to the welfare of society, we shall endeavour to present just and adequate views of it, and to urge upon our brethren the necessity and expediency of training their children, while young, to habits of industry, and thus forming them for becoming useful members of society. It is surely time that we should awake from this lethargy of years, and make a concentrated effort for the education of our youth. We form a spoke in the human wheel, and it is necessary that we should understand our pendence on the different parts, and theirs on us, in order to perform our part with propriety.

Though not desirous of dictating, we shall feel it our incumbent duty to dwell occasionally upon the general principles and rules of economy. The world has grown too enlightened, to estimate any man's character by his personal appearance. Though all men acknowledge the excellency of Franklin's maxims, yet comparatively few practise upon them. We may deplore when it is too late, the neglect of these self-evident truths, but it avails little to mourn. Ours will be the task of admonishing our brethren on these points.

The civil rights of a people being of the greatest value, it shall ever be our duty to vindicate our brethren, when oppressed, and to lay the case before the publick. We shall also urge upon our brethren, (who are qualified by the laws of the different states,) the expediency of using their elective franchise; and of making an independent use of the same. We wish them not to become the tools of party.

And as much time is frequently lost, and wrong principles instilled, by the perusal of works of trivial importance, we shall consider it a part of our duty to recommend to our young readers, such authors as will not only enlarge their stock of useful knowledge, but such as will also serve to stimulate them to higher attainments in science.

We trust also, that through the columns of the FREEDOM'S JOURNAL, many practical pieces, having for their bases, the improvement of our brethren, will be presented to them, from the pens of many of our respected friends, who have kindly promised their assistance.

It is our earnest wish to make our Journal a medium of intercourse between our brethren in the different states of this great confederacy: that through its columns an expression of our sentiments, on many interesting subjects which concern us, may be offered to the publick: that plans which apparently are beneficial may be candidly discussed and properly weighed; if worthy, receive our cordial approbation; if not, our marked disapprobation.

Useful knowledge of every kind, and every thing that relates to Africa, shall find a ready admission into our columns; and as that vast continent becomes daily more known, we trust that many things will come to light, proving that the natives of it are neither so ignorant nor stupid as they have generally been supposed to be.

And while these important subjects shall occupy the columns of the FREEDOM'S JOURNAL, we would not be unmindful of our brethren who are still in the iron fetters of bondage. They are our kindred by all the ties of nature; and though but little can be effected by us, still let our sympathies be poured forth, and our prayers in their behalf, ascend to Him who is able to succour them.

From the press and the pulpit we have suffered much by being incorrectly represented. Men, whom we equally love and admire have not hesitated to represent us disadvantageously, without becoming personally acquainted with the true state of things, nor discerning between virtue and vice among us. The virtuous part of our people feel themselves sorely aggrieved under the existing state of things—they are not appreciated.

Our vices and our degradation are ever arrayed against us, but our virtues are passed by unnoticed. And what is still more lamentable, our friends, to whom we concede all the principles of humanity and religion, from these very causes seem to have fallen into the current of popular feeling and are imperceptibly floating on the stream—actually living in the practice of prejudice, while they abjure it in theory, and feel it not in their hearts. Is it not very desirable that such should know more of our actual condition, and of our efforts and feelings, that in forming or advocating plans for our amelioration, they may do it more understandingly? In the spirit of candor and humility we intend by a simple representation of facts to lay our case before the publick, with a view to arrest the progress of prejudice, and to shield ourselves against the consequent evils. We wish to conciliate all and to irritate none, yet we must be firm and unwavering in our principles, and persevering in our efforts.

If ignorance, poverty and degradation have hitherto been our unhappy lot; has the Eternal decree gone forth, that our race alone, are to remain in this state, while knowledge and civilization are shedding their enlivening rays over the rest of the human family? The recent travels of Denham and Clapperton in the interior of Africa, and the interesting narrative which they have published; the establishment of the republic of Hayti after years of sanguinary warfare; its subsequent progress in all the arts of civilization; and the advancement of liberal ideas in South America, where despotism has given place to free governments, and where many of our brethren now fill important civil and military stations, prove the contrary.

The interesting fact that there are FIVE HUNDRED THOUSAND free persons of colour, one half of whom might peruse, and the whole be benefitted by the publication of the Journal; that no publication, as yet, has been devoted exclusively to their improvement—that many selections from approved standard authors, which are within the reach of few, may occasionally be made—and more important still, that this large body of our citizens have no public channel—all serve to prove the real necessity, at present, for the appearance of the FREEDOM'S JOURNAL.

It shall ever be our desire so to conduct the editorial department of our paper as to give offence to none of our patrons; as nothing is farther from us than to make it the advocate of any partial views, either in politics or religion. What few days we can number, have been devoted to the improvement of our brethren; and it is our earnest wish that the remainder may be spent in the same delightful service.

In conclusion, whatever concerns us as a people, will ever find a ready admission into the FREEDOM'S JOURNAL, interwoven with all the principal news of the day.

And while every thing in our power shall be performed to support the chracter of our Journal, we would respectfully invite our numerous friends to assist by their communications, and our coloured brethren to strengthen our hands by their subscriptions, as our labour is one of common cause, and worthy of their consideration and support. And we do most earnestly solicit the latter, that if at any time we should seem to be zealous, or too pointed in the inculcation of any important lesson, they will remember, that they are equally interested in the cause in which we are engaged, and attribute our zeal to the peculiarities of our situation, and our earnest engagedness in their well-being.

THE EDITORS.

From the Liverpool Mercury.

MEMOIRS OF CAPT. PAUL CUFFEE.

"On the first of the present month of August, 1811, a vessel arrived at Liverpool, with a cargo from Sierra Leone; the owner, master, mate, and whole crew of which are free blacks. The master, who is also owner, is the son of an American slave, and is said to be very well skilled both in trade and navigation, as well as to be of a very pious and moral character. It must have been a strange and an animating spectacle to see this free and enlightened African, entering as an independent trader with his black crew into that port, which was so lately the *nidus* of the slave trade.—*Edinburgh Review for August*, 1811.

We are happy in having an opportunity of confirming the above account, and at the same time of laying before our readers an authentic memoir of Capt. *Paul Cuffee*, the master and owner of the vessel above alluded to, who sailed from this port on the 20th ult. with a licence from the British Government, to prosecute his intended voyage to Sierra Leone.—The father of Paul Cuffee was a native of Africa,—whence he was brought as a slave into Massachusetts. He was there purchased by a person named Slocum, and remained in slavery a very considerable portion of his life. He was named Cuffee, but as it is usual in those parts, took the name of Slocum, as expressing to whom he belonged. Like many of his countrymen he possessed a mind far superior to his condition; although he was diligent in the business of his master, and faithful to his interest, yet by great industry and economy he was enabled to purchase his personal liberty. At the time the remains of several Indian tribes, who originally possessed the right of soil, resided in Massachusetts. Cuffee became acquainted with a woman descended from one of those tribes, named Ruth Moses, and married her. He continued in habits of industry and frugality, and soon afterwards purchased a farm of 100 acres at the point in Massachusetts.

Cuffee and Ruth had a family of ten children. The three eldest sons, David, Jonathan, and John, are farmers in the neighborhood of West Point; filling respectable situations in society, and endowed with good intellectual capacities. They are all married, and have families to whom they are giving good educations. Of six daughters four are respectably married, while two remain single. Paul was born on the Island of Cutterhumpker, one of the Elizabeth Islands, near New-Bedford, in the year 1759—when he was about fourteen years of age, his father died, leaving a considerable property in land, but which being at that time unproductive, afforded but little provision for his numerous family, and thus the care of supporting his mother and sisters devolved upon his brothers and himself. At this time Paul conceived that commerce furnished to industry more ample rewards than agriculture, and he was conscious that he possessed qualities which under proper culture, would enable him to pursue commercial employments with prospects of success—he therefore entered at the age of sixteen, as a common hand on board of a vessel destined to the bay of Mexico, on a whaling voyage. His second voyage was to the West Indies, but on his third he was captured by a British ship during the American war, about the year 1776—after three month detention as a prisoner, at New-York, he was permitted to return home to Westport, where owing to the unfortunate continuance of hostilities he spent about two years in his agricultural pursuits. During this interval Paul and his brother John Cuffee, were called on by the collector of the district, in which they resided, for the payment of a personal tax. It appeared to them, that by the laws and constitution of Massachusetts, taxation and the whole rights of citizenship were united. If the laws demanded of them the payment of the personal taxes, the same laws must necessarily and constitutionally invest them with the right of representing and being represented in the state legislature. But they had never been considered as entitled to the privilege of voting at elections, nor of being elected to places of trust and honor. Under these circumstances they refused payment of the demands. The collector resorted to the force of the laws, and after many delays and detentions, Paul and his brohter deemed it most prudent to silence them by paying the demands; but they resolved, if it were possible to obtain the rights which they believed to be connected with taxation. They presented a respectful petition to the state legislature. From some individuals it met with a warm, and almost indignant opposition. A considerable majority was, however, favorable to their object. They perceived the propriety and justice of the petition, and with an honorable magnanimity, in defiance of the prejudice of the times, they passed a law rendering all free persons of color liable to taxation, according to the established ratio, for white men, and granting them all the privileges, belonging to the other citizens. This was a day equally honorable to the petitioners and the legislature—a day which ought to be gratefully remembered by every person of color, within the boundaries of Massachusetts, and the names of John and Paul Cuffee, should always be united with its recollection.

To be Continued.

COMMON SCHOOLS IN NEW-YORK.—It appears from the report of the Superintendent of Common Schools in the state of New-York, presented last week to the House of Assembly, that of the 723 towns and wards in the State, 721 have made returns according to law: That in these towns there are 8114 school districts, and of course the same number of schools; from 7544 of which returns have been received: That 341 new school dis-

Vol. 1, No. 1 of the Black Press in America: "Too long have others spoken for us."

12

The Press and the Rise of Sectionalism

He who opposes the public liberty overthrows his own.
—William Lloyd Garrison

The Jacksonian era brought out clearly the increasing absorption in America with sectional differences. The beginning of the "irrepressible conflict," as one historian has called the War Between the States, can be traced back to colonial times.[1] The petitions to the King long before 1776; the arguments over the Constitution at the Philadelphia convention; the drafting of the Kentucky and Virginia Resolutions after the Alien and Sedition Acts were passed; and the debates over the tariff of 1828 are some of the evidences of the fault line along which the country would one day split. By 1848, people were no longer voting by party but by section.

Up to about 1820 there was no great Southern unit with the regional cohesion that was apparent a decade later. The South was actually more torn apart by dissension than any other section up to 1820. The upland communities had fought against the tidewater elite in the Revolution, largely as a result of social strains. Large areas of the South had more in common with the West. And the blacks added another source of social friction.

There is a tendency to think of the South as turning away from American traditions when it seceded in 1861. But it was the North—meaning the industrial Northeast—not the South, that developed a different way of life after 1820.

Generally speaking, the South was about the same in 1861 as it had been in 1761. On the eve of the War Between the States, the South retained the impress of the eighteenth century. Life centered in the plantation, and so commercial cities did not assume the importance they had in the Northeast. Lacking such centers, the South had only a small middle class and virtually no white proletariat. But it abounded in great orators, great political leaders, and great writers. British cotton and tobacco buyers took the South's main crops, and the Southerner bought as well as sold abroad.

From this environment came a governing group with a high sense of honor and morals. Family and land counted for more than money in the South, because money was not as essential to the agrarian as it was to the Northern capitalist and wage earner. Money was the sign of success in the North. Land was the criterion in the South. But land values declined in the South some time after 1800, as the staple crops exhausted the soil. Little was known of soil fertilization then, and so immigrants moved to fresh land, thereby reducing the demand for, and consequently the value of, the older lands. Since there was no profit to be made in land speculation, trade, or industry, the capitalist tended to leave the agrarian in full control. The South thus had reason to fear for its future. The industrial North was growing much faster than the South. Population pressure would inevitably give the North political dominance. Already the "tariff of abominations" of 1828 had disclosed what the North would impose upon the South if given free rein.

Both sections turned to the West as an ally, when it became clear that the frontier region would determine the outcome of the conflict. The West was agrarian, like the South. It also suffered from high tariffs. Westerners had natural antipathies to the industrial North. They resented the Northern sabotage of every legislative attempt to ease the debt of the farmer and to open up free lands. On the other hand, Westerners were not as dependent on world markets as were Southerners. Westerners were interested in reaching local or regional markets. Their problem was to get their produce to these markets cheaply and easily, and here they found an ally in the Northern capitalists. Roads, canals, steamboat subsidies, and railroads were the prices paid by the North for the temporary allegiance of the West against the South.

Westerners also demanded the opening up of the frontier to homesteaders. Both the North and South were opposed to this. Southerners feared that the opening of new lands would lead to a preponderance of free states, which would add to the overwhelming weight against the South. Northerners, on the other hand, tended to block westward expansion because it depressed property values in their section and because free land kept wages higher than they would otherwise have been, or else reduced the reservoir of cheap labor in the industrial areas. The point here is that Western victory on this issue was a kind of bribe paid by the North for the support of the West. One evidence of this was the Homestead Act, passed on the eve of the war after years of Northern objection. Once the West had committed itself, the South had only two choices. It could admit defeat and modify its way of life to suit the North, or it could cast off from an alien system and go its own way—secede.

So far, nothing has been said about slavery as a main cause of the Civil War. If slavery had been such an important issue, time alone would have solved the problem. For slavery was already doomed. World opinion was against it. Already it had proved itself to be uneconomical in the upper tier of slave states. By 1860 these states were unloading surplus slave labor as fast as planters in the deep South could absorb it. The capitalist of the North had demonstrated that it was less expensive to pay a man only while he was useful than to support him as a slave throughout the unproductive years of his life.

Slavery was not a primary cause of the conflict, but it became important as the means for joining the battle, and here the journalist played a big role. There would probably have been sectional strife with or without slavery. But slavery, like the religious double talk of two centuries earlier, was the basket in which all the differences of peoples, regions, and ideologies could be carried. The slavery shibboleth was the rallying standard for all the various belligerents. It was the simplification of complex problems and summed up the attitudes of those who had to do the dying in battle.

It is unfortunate that slavery had to be the issue on which the concept of the American union had to be tested. When the South seceded, it did so on the principle that the minority had the right to protect itself from the tyranny of a majority. Slavery lifted the doctrines of North and South onto a plane that made them more discernible to the average citizen. Few would be willing to die for economic principles. But slavery could supply the hate transference that could make a John Brown, for example, die for such a cause at Harper's Ferry in 1859. To Ralph Waldo Emerson, "Old Ossawatomie" Brown had "made the gallows glorious like the cross." And Walt Whitman, poet and sometime journalist, wrote of Brown's execution:

> I would sing how an old man, with white hair, mounted the scaffold in Virginia, (I was at hand, silent I stood with teeth shut close, I watch'd, I stood very near you old man when cool and indifferent, but trembling with age and your unheal'd wounds, you mounted the scaffold. . .)[2]

This indicates what the slavery issue meant to people of lofty sentiment. It took some time to sweep the masses into the movement, but eventually the people of the North and South made slavery a fighting issue, and the press was effective in bringing this about. Advocates of the campaigns against slavery were known as "abolitionists." An outstanding abolitionist editor was William Lloyd Garrison, who makes an excellent case study of how the press became such an important factor in the struggle.

GARRISON AND THE *LIBERATOR*

Garrison was born in Newburyport, Massachusetts, of English and Irish stock. His father was a drunkard who abused his family, and Garrison must have been influenced by these circumstances when he took up the temperance issue while still a youth. He was a jack-of-all-trades until he became a printer. That appeared to be his proper niche. Like Benjamin Russell and Isaiah Thomas, Garrison received most of his education at the type case. It was an education that made him literate rather than learned.

He was in his 20s when he met Benjamin Lundy, the gentle Quaker who had started out as a temperance missionary but who had since carried this reforming zeal over into the antislavery movement. It is significant that Quakers had been important in the successful antislavery movement in Great Britain. At any rate, Garrison became one of Lundy's recruits. Soon Garrison had been satisfactorily persecuted—an essential step in the progress of any effective zealot. He emerged from 7 months in jail a confirmed abolitionist, and with that supreme gift: a cause so absorbing that life itself is not too great a price for it. He moved to Boston, and on January 1, 1831, he issued the first copy of the *Liberator* there.

It was not very impressive, this voice of the abolitionist. Garrison said in 1837 that his publication had never exceeded 3000 subscribers. Much of the time it hovered around 1500, and about one-fourth of the circulation was in black areas, where the readers were either disfranchised or had little political influence. The editor was always losing entire blocks of readers because of his tactless scorn of men, institutions, or traditions sacred to certain publics. And yet this was part of the medium that was to rouse the North to battle.

Garrison had one weapon, his press, but it was to make him invincible. Through this press he spread his creed far and wide, until the abolitionist movement began to work on the minds of the apathetic. He reached such persons with words like these:

> He who opposes the public liberty overthrows his own. . . . There is no safety where there is no strength; no strength without Union; no Union without justice; no justice where faith and truth are wanting. The right to be free is a truth planted in the hearts of men. . . .[3]

This describes Garrison, a man of courage and determination, imbued with righteousness, narrow and fanatical. What he said was bad for business. Most of the country was prosperous at this time. When people are comfortable, conscience is often half asleep. Garrison jerked consciences awake—always an unpopular move. Even the religious leaders resented the man, particularly his self-righteousness. One member of the clergy complained that abolitionists like Garrison did not do their work like "Christian gentlemen." To which Garrison replied:

> These are your men of "caution" and "prudence" and "judiciousness." Sir, I have learned to hate those words. Whenever we attempt to imitate our Great Exemplar, and press the truth of God in all its plainness upon the conscience, why, we are imprudent; because, forsooth, a great excitement will ensue. Sir, slavery will not be overthrown without excitement—a most tremendous excitement.[4]

Garrison caused the most violent public reaction since Tom Paine drew his red-hot plowshare through American history. Amos Kendall, himself a great journalist and a leader of Jacksonian democracy, believed that Garrison should be gagged. As Postmaster General Kendall allowed abolitionist papers to be rifled from the official mail sacks by Southern "committees" charged with that task.[5] The state of Massachusetts was ready to forbid the export of the *Liberator,* and in many states, distributors of the paper were intimidated without redress.

ABOLITIONISTS AND "FIRE-EATERS"

James G. Birney, one of the more reasonable abolitionists, was mobbed when he began printing his paper, the *Philanthropist,* in Cincinnati. Note that this was a city in a Northern, not a Southern, state. From that day on, Birney began to devote his energy to fighting for a free press along with fighting for freeing the slaves. The abolitionists saw very clearly that the slavery issue would sooner or later affect all the freedoms in both the North and the South. One of the most stirring messages on this subject, "Free Speech and Free Inquiry," appears in the April 2, 1847, issue of the *Liberator.*

At least one abolitionist died for this cause. He was Elijah Lovejoy, editor of the *St. Louis Observer,* a strident abolitionist weekly founded in 1835. A mass meeting of irate citizens resulted in a resolution informing Lovejoy that free expression as guaranteed in the Bill of Rights did not extend to editors such as Lovejoy who threatened the peace of the community. Lovejoy replied that public resolutions could not fetter an editor.

As an act of good faith, however, Lovejoy moved his press across the river to Alton, Illinois. His office was at once wrecked by a mob. He appealed nationally for support and received enough help to set up another press. This was also demolished. Again he appealed for assistance, and again there was a quick and positive response. The climax came in 1837 while he was setting up his third press in Alton. A group of citizens decided that the Lovejoy nuisance should be abated. They called a mass meeting to devise plans. Lovejoy refused to be intimidated and boldly attended the meeting to present his side. He promised to suspend publication if his readers requested him to, but he declared he would not be ruled by mob hysteria. He said he would return to his office and would defend his right to publish with his life, if need be. When the mob marched down the street after the meeting, it was motivated not by the desire to destroy a press but to destroy a man who refused to renounce his right to think and to express himself. Lovejoy was killed by the mob.

The Southern counterpart of the abolitionist was the "fire-eater." Outstanding fire-eaters were William Lowndes Yancey, Edmund Ruffin, and Robert Barnwell Rhett. Yancey was one of the great orators of his era. It was Yancey who led the South from the Democratic convention of 1860. Ruffin was an agricultural writer who introduced marl as a fertilizer to restore exhausted tobacco land. He was a tireless and indomitable Southern patriot. When more timid souls hesitated to fire upon Fort Sumter in 1861, it was Ruffin who snatched the lanyard of the nearest cannon and sent the first ball screaming its message of war. And it was Ruffin who committed suicide rather than take the

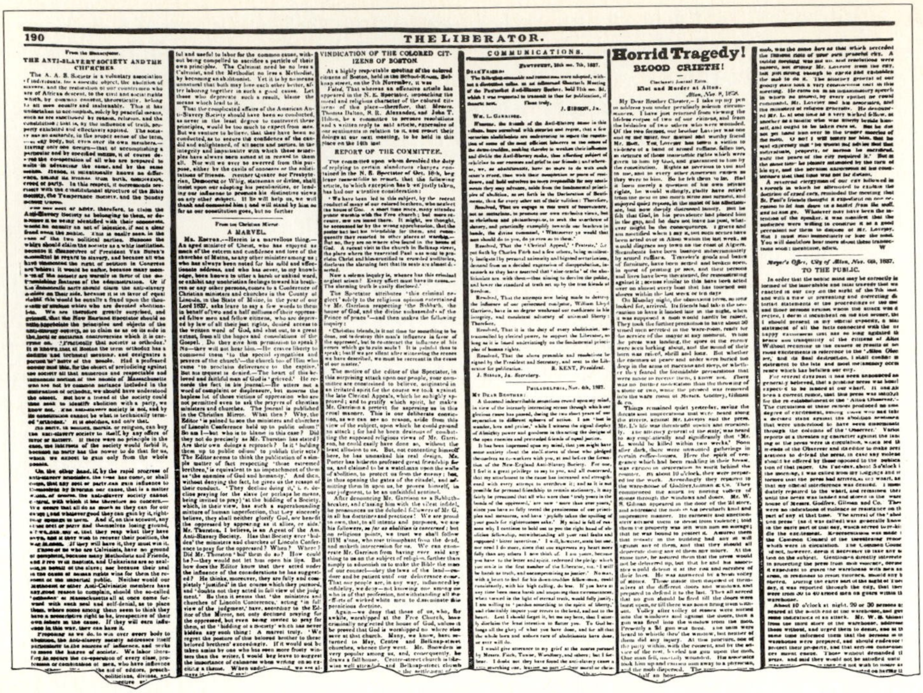

190 THE LIBERATOR.

THE ANTI-SLAVERY SOCIETY AND THE CHURCHES

A MARVEL.

VINDICATION OF THE COLORED CITIZENS OF BOSTON

REPORT OF THE COMMITTEE.

COMMUNICATIONS.

Horrid Tragedy!

BLOOD CRIETH!

TO THE PUBLIC.

Garrison's *Liberator* reports the murder of abolitionist Elijah Lovejoy.

oath of allegiance after Appomattox. But of all the fire-eaters, Rhett was most effective.

Rhett, sometimes called the "father of secession," was editor of the *Charleston Mercury,* which he made into one of the leading papers of the deep South. By 1832 he was declaring openly that the only safety for the South was for it to go its own way. No one paid much attention to Rhett at first. He was treated about as coldly in the South as Garrison had been in the North. But after such magnificent propaganda successes as *Uncle Tom's Cabin,* the South began to depend on its Rhetts, Yanceys, and Ruffins for justification. By 1848, Rhett was once again powerful politically. In 1851 he succeeded to the Senate seat of the great Calhoun.

Ironically, Rhett had no intention of involving his section in a war. He had aroused the South to fighting pitch, but he had assumed all along that the North would not dare fight. On the day Sumter was fired upon, Rhett was still reassuring readers of the *Mercury* that the South would secede peaceably. He should have known better. Lincoln's refusal to evacuate the fort peacefully was proof that this time the North meant business.

BLACK JOURNALISTS AS ABOLITIONISTS

Abolitionists like Garrison and fire-eaters like Rhett attracted both immediate and continuing attention because they represented the extremes of white America's reaction to black slavery, whose emotional clash eventually produced a civil war. Nothing the blacks could do or say for themselves seemed important to a society that viewed them as economic, political, and educational nonequals. In 1850 there were about a half-million free blacks in the American population, half of them in the North and half in the South. But in the South, state laws prohibited blacks from receiving any formal education, and chances to make decent incomes were few. In the North, state laws restricted black voting rights, and the uneven availability of public schools weighed quickly on children of disfranchised, poor, and illiterate blacks. There was a chance, however, to "get ahead," and some blacks succeeded. A handful of freed blacks won sufficient education to become writers, lawyers, physicians, and businesspeople in the era before the Civil War. To them, and to their friends in the white population, forty struggling black newspapers were addressed between 1827 and 1865.[6]

These were virtually all dedicated contributions to the antislavery, abolitionist movement. And as such, they rank high in the regard of today's students of the black experience in America. It should not be startling to discover that there were blacks who spoke out for themselves; what is startling is that they could succeed as well as they did in the face of poverty and illiteracy among most of their audience, as well as in the face of almost total rejection by a white society that ignored their existence.

Slavery was not abolished everywhere north of the Mason-Dixon line until 1804, and early leadership among slaves seeking their freedom is found in Massachusetts and Pennsylvania before 1800. By 1830 there were some fifty black antislavery societies, with the most active located in New York, Philadelphia, Boston, and New Haven. Black self-expression had long been centered in the folk songs and spirituals of the black slaves. Now a few freed slaves had become adept at oratory, at poetry, and at autobiographical writing that had produced moving accounts in book form of what it meant to live as a slave. Some freed slaves had seen their articles or letters published by white editors in the regular press; some had worked with Garrison and his *Liberator* group or the other white abolitionists. A particularly vicious attack on these black leaders by Mordecai M. Noah, editor of the *New York Enquirer,* is credited with spurring the founding of the first black-published newspaper in the United States.[7]

Freedom's Journal was its name and in its first issue on March 16, 1827, it printed this simple explanation of the venture: "We wish to plead our own cause. Too long have others spoken for us." Its editors were John B. Russwurm, the first black to graduate from a college in the United States (Bowdoin in 1826), and Reverend Samuel Cornish, a Presbyterian who edited three different weeklies in New York City in this period. A four-page paper, 10 inches by 15 inches in size, *Freedom's Journal* agitated ruthlessly against the inhumanity of slavery but also ran newsy items, sermons, poetry, and other literary fare. Russwurm left in 1828 to undertake a career as editor and government official in Liberia, and

Cornish continued the paper under the name *Rights of All.* The known file ceases in October, 1829.[8]

In 1829 David Walker issued his *Appeal* out of Boston, advocating violent measures to eliminate slavery, and George Moses Horton protested in Raleigh through the columns of his *Hope of Liberty.* During the racial turmoil in 1965 Walker's call for militant resistance was republished in paperback book form.

Another major effort at a black paper in New York City came in 1837 when Phillip A. Bell founded *The Weekly Advocate,* renamed 2 months later *The Colored American.* It appeared until 1842. Its first editor was Reverend Samuel Cornish and the publisher was a Canadian, Robert Sears of Toronto. Cornish and Bell retired from the paper in May, 1839, and Dr. Charles Bennet Ray became the guiding force of the spirited little paper. He made it not only an antislavery organ but also a "paper devoted primarily to the interests of the colored population, and . . . a first-rate family paper." Circulation reached 2000 in an area from Maine to Michigan.[9]

When the regular dailies in Pittsburgh refused to run contributions by blacks in 1843, Dr. Martin R. Delaney, first of his race to graduate from Harvard, founded *The Mystery.* William Wells Brown, the black writer and novelist of the period, described the physician as "decided and energetic in conversation, unadulterated in race, and proud of his complexion."[10] Delaney got in a libel suit but managed to keep his paper going until 1848 when it was purchased by the African Methodist Episcopal Church. It was renamed the *Christian Herald,* and then moved to Philadelphia in 1852 as the *Christian Recorder.* It was surviving in 1970 as oldest of the black religious weeklies.[11]

There were other notable efforts. One was the *Alienated American,* published from 1852 to 1856 in Cleveland by W. H. Day, a graduate of Oberlin College. Another was the *New Orleans Daily Creole,* an 1856 effort that was the first black-owned paper in the South and the first black daily. Bell, founder of the *Advocate* in New York, migrated to San Francisco and in 1865 began publishing *The Elevator,* which survived until 1889, an unusual feat for black papers. But the most famous of the pre-Civil War black papers were edited by the dynamic leader of the freed slaves and inspiration of his race, Frederick Douglass.

FREDERICK DOUGLASS, EDITOR

By the 1970s, Frederick Douglass had become a symbol of black achievement and inspiration—his home in Washington had become a national shrine, his autobiographical writings enjoyed fresh printings, his face was on a postage stamp, young black males spelled their names with a double "s" if they were named Douglas. All of which was merited, for this son of a black slave woman and a white man ran away from a Maryland plantation to make himself a leader of those of the black race who needed his skill at writing and oratory to assert their cause.

Born in 1817, he escaped slavery in 1838 and went to New England to work and gain additional education with the encouragement of William Lloyd

Frederick Douglass.
Bettmann Archive

Garrison, the abolitionist. He began to write for the newspapers and to speak as an eyewitness to the tragedy of the slavery system. In 1845 he went to England, where friends raised enough money to buy his freedom from his Maryland owner. Back in the United States and known for the first of his autobiographical books (*Narrative of the Life of Frederick Douglass*), he was named an editor of *The Ram's Horn.* The paper was started in January, 1847 by Willis A. Hodges as a black protest to such practices as that of the *New York Sun,* which had printed a letter from him and then sent him a bill for $15. Hodges' venture failed the next year but its columns carried this announcement in late 1847:

> PROSPECTUS for an antislavery paper; to be entitled *North Star.* Frederick Douglass proposes to publish in Rochester a weekly Anti-slavery paper, with the above title. The object of the *North Star* will be to Attack Slavery in all its forms and aspects: Advocate Universal Emancipation; exalt the standard of Public Morality; promote the Moral and Intellectual improvement of the COLORED PEOPLE; and hasten the day of FREEDOM to the Three Millions of our Enslaved Fellow Countrymen.[12]

Publication of *The North Star* began November 1, 1847. It quickly rose to a circulation of some 3000 and was both read in and received contributions from Europe and the West Indies as well as much of the United States. In addition to articles about slavery and blacks, *The North Star* carried a good cross section of national and world news. The masthead proclaimed: "Right is of no Sex—Truth is of no Color—God is the Father of us all, and we are all Brethren." Not everyone in Rochester thought so; just as the white abolitionists were terrorized, Douglass saw his house burned and his papers destroyed. But the spunky character of the paper and its literary quality were both so high that it survived financial difficulties and racial antagonism. Renamed *Frederick Douglass' Paper* in 1851 after a merger with a weaker sheet, the paper was symbolic of its editor's position as the recognized leader of the black population.

By mid-1860, with the issue of slavery clearly bringing the country to the verge of civil war, Douglass found the financial struggle too great and suspended his weekly. For the next 3 years he put out *Douglass' Monthly,* an abolitionist magazine aimed at a British audience, to aid the Northern war cause. In 1870 he became contributing editor of a Washington weekly, the *New Era,* that sought to aid the now-freed black people. The paper was no more popular than the cause; Douglass invested money in it, renamed it the *New National Era,* and became its fighting editor before admitting defeat (and a $10,000 loss) in 1875.[13] His second autobiographical effort, *My Bondage and My Freedom,* had appeared in 1855; now the final volume, *Life and Times of Frederick Douglass,* appeared in 1878. The remarkable ex-slave, skillful editor, polished orator, and inspirational fellow citizen died in 1895 at the age of 78.

THE NORTHERN PRESS AND THE SLAVERY ISSUE

The important standard papers of the day picked up the slavery issue presented to them by the black editors, the abolitionists, and the fire-eaters. By 1852 Horace Greeley's weekly *New York Tribune* had a circulation of more than 200,000, much of it in the crucial West. It was the acknowledged leader of those opposed to slavery. Greeley felt so strongly on the subject that he was willing to cast off the lifetime allegiances of the Whig to help organize a new party that brought Abraham Lincoln to the White House in 1860.

In January, 1861, Greeley published the first of his "stand firm" editorials—accepted by readers, at least, as Lincoln's own commandments. In February he called for unity against the South by a slogan in large type at the head of the editorial column: "NO COMPROMISE/NO CONCESSIONS TO TRAITORS/THE CONSTITUTION AS IT IS." When the first shot of the war was fired April 12, 1861, Greeley wrote: "Sumter is temporarily lost, but Freedom is saved! It is hard to lose Sumter, but in losing it we have gained a united people. Long live the Republic." He asked for patience when critics, including Raymond, offered unreasonable suggestions, but by summer, he, too, was demanding action. On June 26 appeared the memorable editorial: "The Nation's War Cry: 'Forward to Richmond! The Rebel Congress must not be allowed to meet there on July 20. By that date the place must be held by the National Army.' " This was repeated in subsequent issues. After all this pressure, Greeley had a heavy conscience following the rout of the Union Army at the first battle of Bull Run. Managing editor Charles A. Dana had been in charge of the paper while Greeley was traveling, and Fitz-Henry Warren, the *Tribune*'s Washington correspondent, had actually written the editorials.

All this time the "reasonableness" of Henry Raymond's *New York Times* had made the paper and its editor important journalistically and politically. When Greeley broke with Governor Seward and Thurlow Weed, Raymond largely succeeded as the mouthpiece of the old group. When the Whigs foundered on the free soil issue, Raymond threw in his lot with the new Republican party. He wrote the statement of principles at the Pittsburgh convention in 1856. It is noteworthy that he was lukewarm on abolitionism, however, until after Sumter. An early critic of Lincoln (possibly because his rival, Greeley, had helped nominate the rail-splitter) Raymond quickly adjusted to circumstance, as usual. Once the fighting began, Raymond was a staunch defender of the President.

Samuel Bowles III, who took over the *Springfield Republican* in 1851 after the death of his father, was faithful to the obsolete Whig party up to the eve of its death. He attacked the abolitionists at every opportunity, on the presumption that they were more interested in causing trouble than in solving problems. His concern over the growing quarrel between the two sections was shown in his approval of the Fugitive Slave law. He did not approve of slavery certainly, but neither did he approve of the agitation over it that might wreck the nation. His conversion came after passage of the Kansas-Nebraska bill in 1854, which junked the old compromises and once more opened up the question of slavery in the West.

The *New York Herald,* on the other hand, was mostly opposed to the abolitionist movement. It endorsed the Kansas-Nebraska Act, which the South looked upon as a victory for slavery. Bennett wrote on February 28, 1854: ". . . for twenty odd years, through good and evil report, the *New York Herald* has been the only Northern journal that has unfailingly vindicated the constitutional rights of the South." Naturally, the *Herald* was popular with Southern leaders, who quoted it often. The *Herald* was the most popular American newspaper in Great Britain, and because the British were inclined to favor the South, through the close relationship of their textile industry and the cotton growers, it was widely reprinted.

Although Bennett was an annoyance to Lincoln, and may have given readers of his editorials a false notion of the North's temper on the eve of the war, the *Herald*'s news columns offered clues to Lincoln's determination to protect federal laws. Virtually every detail about the Lincoln family was reported for the *Herald* and other New York Associated Press members by 25-year-old Henry Villard, the first person to cover a president-elect. Villard met with Lincoln in Springfield almost daily for 3 months and accompanied him on the long trip to Washington, as Lincoln changed from "a relatively unknown regional politician into a nationally known figure who commanded the public's interest and growing support."[14]

Under the guiding hand of William Cullen Bryant, the *New York Evening Post* continued to offer enlightened editorial leadership to its readers. It was Bryant who first put the more responsible elements of the standard press on the side of such people as James G. Birney, whose paper, the *Philanthropist,* was wrecked by antiabolitionists in Cincinnati. Birney had asked if freedom of the press were possible when slavery had to be protected from its critics. If freedom of expression were to be repudiated permanently by such measures as the Southern gag laws, could democracy continue to exist? he asked. Bryant picked up these arguments and made them respectable.

In the West, Joseph Medill's *Chicago Tribune* was a thunderer against slavery. Founded in 1847, the paper made rapid progress after Medill and five partners took it over in 1855. Medill was one of the Western leaders of the Republican party and was said to have suggested the name of the new political organization. The *Tribune* was an early supporter of Lincoln. Medill was largely responsible for the Lincoln boom. He enthusiastically followed the future president, reporting the speeches that are now history. Usually Medill followed his reports with a lively editorial on the subject. Lincoln often came to the *Tribune* office for conferences with the West's leading spokesperson. Medill's intimacy with Lincoln is indicated by the crude familiarity with which he conversed with the rising politician. "Dammit, Abe, git yore feet off my desk," Medill is said to have told the lanky backwoodsman on one occasion.

When Lincoln assumed office, faced with the virtually impossible task of preserving peace, the newspaper press that watched his every move was highly developed. The typical daily was likely to be drab, by modern standards, but the makeup and readability had improved since the advent of the first penny papers. The standard paper was six columns wide. Eight pages usually sufficed, although Raymond's *Times* often ran to ten pages. There were few pictures or graphic illustrations. Many of the penny papers actually sold for twice that by the end of the period, and the *Times* was up to three. Headlines were mostly confined by the column rules to one-column labels, and the great development in display headlines was still waiting on the war. Advertising was increasing steadily. Three of the eight pages of the conservative-looking weekly edition of the *Springfield Republican* were usually devoted to classified notices, and this was common throughout the country.

As a whole, the press was strong and prosperous. It was well that the publishing industry was so healthy, for it was about to be tested as it never had been before. The test began on the day Edmund Ruffin sent the first shot of the Civil War toward Fort Sumter: April 12, 1861.

NOTES

1. Arthur Charles Cole, *The Irrepressible Conflict* (New York: Macmillan, 1934). See also Avery Craven, *The Repressible Conflict* (Baton Rouge: Louisiana State University Press, 1939).

2. Both quotations are reprinted in Louis L. Snyder and Richard B. Morris, eds., *A Treasury of Great Reporting* (New York: Simon & Schuster, 1949), pp. 124–25.

3. Wendell Phillips Garrison and Francis Jackson Garrison, *William Lloyd Garrison: The Story of His Life Told by His Children,* Volume 1 (New York: Appleton-Century-Crofts, 1885), p. 200.

4. Vernon L. Parrington, *Main Currents in American Thought* (New York: Harcourt Brace Jovanovich, 1927), II, p. 356. Parrington's fascinating analysis of the abolitionist leader quotes many such statements by Garrison.

5. Kendall justified his action by holding that each issue of the *Liberator* reaching a Southern state was a criminal libel, that is, a threat to public peace. He tried to explain the situation in his annual report for 1835, when he asked Congress for an official banning of "obnoxious" literature in Southern states. This would have taken the responsibility out of the hands of the Postmaster General and indicates that Kendall knew that his past actions had been arbitrary. It is interesting to see the South's great leader, John C. Calhoun, challenge the constitutionality of Kendall's request. Calhoun's alternative was a recommendation for states with appropriate laws to ban such literature at the source.

6. Carter R. Bryan, "Negro Journalism in America Before Emancipation," *Journalism Monographs*, No. 12 (September 1969), 1, 30–33.

7. I. Garland Penn, *The Afro-American Press and Its Editors* (Springfield, Mass.: Wiley, 1891), p. 28.

8. Armistead S. Pride, *A Register and History of Negro Newspapers in the United States* (Ph.D. thesis, Northwestern University, 1950), p. 4.

9. Bryan, "Negro Journalism," pp. 11–14.

10. Ibid., p. 17.

11. Roland E. Wolseley, *The Black Press, U.S.A.* (Ames: Iowa State University Press, 1971), pp. 24–25.

12. As quoted in Bryan, "Negro Journalism," p. 19, from *The Ram's Horn,* November 5, 1847, p. 4.

13. Wolseley, *The Black Press,* pp. 22–23.

14. Tom Reilly, "Early Coverage of a President-Elect: Lincoln at Springfield, 1860," *Journalism Quarterly,* XLIX (Autumn 1972), 469–79. Also see "Lincoln-Douglas Debates of 1858 Forced New Role on the Press," *Journalism Quarterly,* LVI (Winter 1979), 734.

ANNOTATED BIBLIOGRAPHY

Books

COLE, ARTHUR CHARLES, *The Irrepressible Conflict,* A History of American Life, Volume VII. New York: Macmillan, 1934.

CRAVEN, AVERY, *The Repressible Conflict.* Baton Rouge: Louisiana State University Press, 1939. Both of these books present the debatable issues leading up to the war in a frame of reference still being investigated by historians.

DANN, MARTIN E., ed., *The Black Press: 1827–1890.* New York: G. P. Putnam's Sons, 1971. A collection of articles from black newspapers with theme of quest for national identity.

DETWEILER, FREDERICK G., *The Negro Press in the United States.* Chicago: University of Chicago Press, 1922. Quotes extensively from the papers.

DILLON, MERTON L., The *Abolitionists: The Growth of a Dissenting Minority,* DeKalb, Ill.: Northern Illinois University Press, 1974. Unravels abolitionist ideologies and strategies, places them in historical context.

———, *Elijah P. Lovejoy, Abolitionist Editor.* Urbana: University of Illinois Press, 1961. Used primary sources.

DOUGLASS, FREDERICK, *My Bondage and My Freedom.* Chicago: Johnson Publishing Company, 1970. Second of three autobiographical chronicles, originally published in 1855. Others: *Narrative of the Life of Frederick Douglass* (1845), *Life and Times of Frederick Douglass* (1878). Douglass lived from 1817 to 1895 as a slave, free man, politician, reformer, editor, and orator.

FONER, PHILIP S., *Frederick Douglass.* New York: Citadel Press, 1963. By the author of the outstanding four-volume *Life and Writings of Frederick Douglass.*

GARRISON, WENDELL PHILLIPS, AND FRANCIS J., *William Lloyd Garrison,* 4 volumes. New York: Appleton-Century-Crofts, 1885–89. The life story of the famous abolitionist, told by his children.

GARRISON, WILLIAM LLOYD, *Selections.* Boston: R. F. Wallcut, 1852. Excerpts from speeches and writings of the famous abolitionist.

GENOVESE, EUGENE D., *The Political Economy of Slavery.* New York: Pantheon, 1965. A New Left historian uses the comparative approach. See also *Roll, Jordan, Roll* (New

York: Pantheon, 1975), story of the world slaves made.

GILL, JOHN, *Tide without Turning: Elijah P. Lovejoy and Freedom of the Press.* Boston: Beacon Press, 1958. A well-documented biography.

ISELY, JETER ALLEN, *Horace Greeley and the Republican Party, 1853–1861.* Princeton: Princeton University Press, 1947. Analysis of Greeley's writings in the *New York Tribune* about slavery.

NEVINS, ALLAN, *The Evening Post: A Century of Journalism.* New York: Boni and Liveright, 1922. See especially Chapters 4, 5, 6, and 7.

NYE, RUSSEL B., *Fettered Freedom: Civil Liberties and the Slavery Controversy, 1830–1860.* East Lansing: Michigan State College Press, 1963. How the abolitionists finally won popular support.

PENN, I. GARLAND, *The Afro-American Press and Its Editors.* Springfield, Mass.: Wiley Company, 1891. The source book for the nineteenth-century black press.

POTTER, DAVID M., *The Impending Crisis, 1848–1861.* New York: Harper & Row, 1976. Political study; winner of 1977 Pulitzer Prize for history.

QUARLES, BENJAMIN, ed., *Frederick Douglass.* Englewood Cliffs, N.J.: Prentice-Hall, 1968. Black editor presented in own and peers' words.

THOMAS, JOHN L., *The Liberator: William Lloyd Garrison, a Biography.* Boston: Little, Brown, 1963. Excellent biography, but focuses on political activities.

WHITE, LAURA A., *Robert Barnwell Rhett.* New York: Appleton-Century-Crofts, 1931. Describes the southern "fire-eater" and his part in the slavery issue.

WOLSELEY, ROLAND E., *The Black Press, U.S.A.* Ames: Iowa State University Press, 1971. Chapter 2 deals with nineteenth-century black papers.

Periodicals and Monographs

BRYAN, CARTER R., "Negro Journalism in America Before Emancipation," *Journalism Monographs,* No. 12 (September 1969). Careful study of early black press.

CHU, JAMES C. Y., "Horace White: His Association with Abraham Lincoln, 1854–60," *Journalism Quarterly,* XLIX (Spring 1972), 51. Was reporter, adviser.

CULLEN, MAURICE R., JR., "William Gilmore Simms, Southern Journalist," *Journalism Quarterly,* XXXVIII (Summer 1961), 298. A South Carolina editor first opposes secession, then defies the invading Union army.

EATON, CLEMENT, "The Freedom of the Press in the Upper South," *Mississippi Valley Historical Review,* XVIII (March 1932), 479. A study of the muzzling of press freedom prior to the Civil War.

KENNEDY, FRONDE, "Russell's Magazine," *South Atlantic Quarterly,* XVIII (April 1919), 125. Analysis of the periodical published at Charleston, which argued the proslavery viewpoint.

MARTIN, ASA EARL, "Pioneer Anti-Slavery Press," *Mississippi Valley Historical Review,* II (March 1916), 509. Describes the *Philanthropist,* an early abolitionist paper.

PRIDE, ARMISTEAD S., "A Register and History of Negro Newspapers in the United States," Ph.D. thesis, Northwestern University, 1950. Most scholarly effort to identify black newspapers.

REILLY, THOMAS W., "Early Coverage of a President-Elect: Lincoln at Springfield 1860," *Journalism Quarterly,* XLIX (Autumn 1972), 469. Henry Villard reports for *The New York Herald.* Taken from "Henry Villard: Civil War Journalist," Master's thesis, University of Oregon, 1970. A discerning, carefully researched study of early news reporting.

———, "Lincoln-Douglas Debates of 1858 Forced New Role on the Press," *Journalism Quarterly,* LVI (Winter 1979), 734. Detailed analysis of the on-spot coverage.

SAALBERG, HARVEY, "Martyrs to the Press," *Editor & Publisher,* CIX (June 19, 1976), 7. First of a series of six articles on deaths of six United States news reporters.

STEWART, JAMES B., "Young Turks and Old Turkeys: Abolitionists, Historians, and Aging Processes," *Reviews in American History* (June 1983), 226. Discussion of recent book-length studies of abolitionism.

WINE, LIQUOR, AND CIGAR STORE.

Opposite Strother's Hotel, Pennsylvania Avenue.

RECEIVED, This Day, from Boston, per the schooner Alfred, a most choice and extensive selection of old and pure Wines and Liquors, to wit:

Old Cognac Brandy
Do Weesp Anchor Holland Gin } both in Wood, Demijohns, & Bottles
Do Jamaica Spirits
Do Irish Whiskey
Do London Particular Madeira Wine } both in Wood & bottles, and warranted to have been a voyage to India
Do Sherry
Do Teneriffe
Do Sicily
Do Pico
St. Estephe, St. Julian, and other Claret Wines
Old South Hampton Port in Bottles
Superior Hermitage Wine, in boxes of 25 bottles each
Sauterne and Burgundy Wine
J. C. Dinet, Ruin Art and J. H. G. Sparking Champaigne
Hibbert's best double Brown Stout, in quart and pint bottles
A few dozen very superior Old Arrack

Also, on hand, and for sale,
Choice old Rye Whiskey
Cabanas, Flint, Woodville, Zamora, Delpino, Deavernine, and Dosamycos Cigars, in wholes, halves, quarters, and eights of boxes, of the first quality.
Chewing Tobacco, &c.

dec 3—eotf WILLIAM COX.

BARGAINS AT THE NEW STORE.

WILLIAM W. WHITE & Co. have, in addition to their former stock, just received a new and seasonable supply of staple and fancy Dry Goods, which they are now opening at their cheap Cash Store, on the south side of Pennsylvania avenue, three doors east of the Centre Market, for which, if early application be made, they can be had cheap, wholesale or retail, or by the piece. Shop and tavern-keepers, heads of families, &c will find it to their interest to call and examine. The articles are such as

Cloths	Linens
Cassimeres	Hosiery
Cassinetts	Shirting
Venetian Carpeting	Cambric Muslins
Ingrain do	Mull do
Scotch do	Book do
Domestics	

Cashmere Shawls and Scarfs
Merino do do
Imitation do do
Super elegant French Chints
Figured black Silks
Do Mandarin Robes
Do Pekin do
Superfine black Bombazine
do Plaid do
Do Circassian Plaids
Ladies' party colored Hdkts.
Velvetine and Rob Roy do
Gentlemen's Military Cravats

And many other articles, comprising almost every other article in the dry good line.

dec 3—3t

REMEDY FOR THE PILES.

THE medicine now offered to the public is one which has been fully subjected to the infallible test of experience; and, in every instance where it has been fairly tried, it has been attended with the most complete success. In some of the cases, the patients have been laboring under this disease for years, and, during that period, had received the best medical advice, and had even undergone a painful surgical operation, without permanent advantage. It is not like those usually advertised and offered as an infallible cure for a long catalogue of diseases; but those afflicted with this complaint, for which alone it is recommended, may rely with confidence upon obtaining relief, even in its worst forms, in a short time, and they themselves are the best judges of the importance of such a remedy. Price 50 cents per box, with directions, signed by the proprietor. If the case is severe, and of long standing, more than one box may be necessary. Prepared and sold at James A. Austin's Drug and Chemical Store, No. 263, North 3d street, Philadelphia.

The proprietor has appointed Lewis Johnson, at the Snuff Store, corner of 12th street and Pennsylvania avenue, sole agent for the sale of this medicine, in Washington City.

dec 3—3teo

BUGGY FOR SALE.

A NEW complete Buggy Gig, with new good Harness, for sale, at JAMES SMITH'S Livery Stable.

dec 2—3t

STRAYED,

FROM the residence of the subscriber, in Frankfort, in September 1835, a red COW, horns bored, crop in one ear and a slit in the other. Any person finding said Cow, or giving such information that I may get her, will be liberally rewarded.

BATHSHEBA LONG.

March 6th, 1836.—7-3w.

IMPORTED HORSE SWISS,

WILL stand the present season at the Franklin association Race Course, 3½ miles East of Frankfort, on the Georgetown Road, and will be let to mares at $50 the season. His Pedigree and performance, and the performance of his Colts may be seen by reference to his Bills.

BEN. LUCKETT.

March 30th, 1836.—6.-10w.

Dr. J. O. T. HAWKINS,

WILL continue to practice his profession in the town of Frankfort, and its vicinity. His residence and office, is at the brick house of Mrs. Bryant, near the east end of the Market House, on Broad Way, where he solicits patronage and promises fidelity and attention to all who may employ him, and where he may be always found except when absent on professional business.

March 30th, 1836.—6-tf.

Mr. JOHN KERSEY.

YOU are hereby notified, that on the 10th day of June next, at the house of Edward Lewis, Esq. in the county of Green, I shall proceed to take the depositions of Freborn G. Grayham, William Hanks and others, to be read as evidence in the suit of myself against you, for a divorce now pending in the Green Circuit court in Chancery, and if all of said depositions be not taken on said day, I will continue from day to day, Sundays excepted, until all are taken, when and where if you choose, you can attend.

ELIZABETH KERSEY.

March 19th, 1836.—6-5w.

JAMES HENRY,

DOMESTIC DRY GOODS, COMMISSION MERCHANT, AND AGENT FOR THE SALE OF WOLCOTT'S STEUBENVILLE JEANS,

Wall Street, Louisville, Ky.

LIBERAL advances will be made on consignments of negro clothing, linsey and socks, all of which articles ought to be in this market by the middle of June. On hand and for sale—having just received 16 cases by steamer Wacausta—1000 pieces of Wolcott's Steubenville Jeans, which will be sold on liberal terms to responsible houses. Buyers will please to call and examine these goods.

JAMES HENRY,
Wall Street.

The following papers in Kentucky will publish the above advertisement, weekly, for 2 months, and charge Lou. Adv.—Gazette, Lexington; Enquirer, Covington; paper at Princeton; Argus, Frankfort; Gazette, Hopkinsville; Gazette, Greensburgh; Register, Elizabethtown, paper at Russellville; Citizen, Paris; paper at Richmond; Olive Branch, Danville; Whig, Mount Sterling; Monitor, Maysville; Sentinel, Georgetown; paper at Shelbyville; Gazette, Bowlinggreen.

March 3, 1836. —6-2m.

$100 Reward.

RANAWAY from the farm whereon Dr. Samuel B. Crockett resides, about the middle of July last, a negro man, named ISAAC. Said man is about 30 years of age, pleasant countenance, rather chunky built. He had on when he went away, a cassinet frock coat, linen pantaloons, and a white hat. The above reward of $100 DOLLARS, will be given for said Isaac, if taken out of the State, or FIFTY DOLLARS if taken in the State, and delivered to me, or secured, so that I get him.

JOHN M'KEE.

Franklin County, Dec. 9, 1835.-tf.

Advertisements from *National Intelligencer* (1823), *Argus of Western America* (1836).

HARPER'S WEEKLY.
A JOURNAL OF CIVILIZATION.

Vol. V.—No. 227.] NEW YORK, SATURDAY, MAY 4, 1861. [SINGLE COPIES SIX CENTS. $2 50 PER YEAR IN ADVANCE.

Entered according to Act of Congress, in the Year 1861, by Harper & Brothers, in the Clerk's Office of the District Court for the Southern District of New York.

THE HOUSE-TOPS IN CHARLESTON DURING THE BOMBARDMENT OF SUMTER.

A leading picture weekly depicts war's start.

13
The Irrepressible Conflict

Come with a sword or musket in your hand, prepared to share with us our fate in sunshine and storm . . . and I will welcome you as a brother and associate; but come as you now do, expecting me to ally the reputation and honor of my country and my fellow soldiers with you, as the representative of the press, which you yourself say makes so slight a difference between truth and falsehood, and my answer is, NEVER.

—General Sherman to Knox, of the *Herald*

The War Between the States affected all aspects of journalism. Reporting, editing, circulation, printing, advertising, and illustration were all modified during the conflict. Relations between press and government also changed during this period. One of the serious problems of the war was how to keep the public properly informed without giving aid and comfort to the enemy. This was the world's first modern rehearsal of mass warfare—involving both armies and civilians. It was one of the costliest wars, in terms of men and money, ever fought up to that period. And because large elements of the populations opposed the bloody strife on both sides of the lines, there was continuous and outspoken criticism of both administrations. The most usual medium for this expression was the newspaper.

In contrast with World War I and II, reporters in the War Between the States were much more irresponsible. But it should be pointed out that the communications lessons of 1861 to 65 were of invaluable assistance in working out later policies, for experience has shown that when a country with a free-press tradition mobilizes, leaders must adjust themselves to a dilemma.

A few voices still answered the roll call of the once-great legion of progress. Greeley did not change but he, too, was overwhelmed by the war. He lived to see all his illusions shattered on the rock of postwar public cynicism, but at least he stuck to his principles. His regard for humanity made Greeley abhor war. At one time he favored letting the South secede peacefully. But once the shooting began, Greeley concluded that the most humane course for the Unionists was to end the war quickly.

By the close of 1861, the *New York Tribune* was engaged in a campaign to free slaves in conquered areas. The President had already discussed the issue with his cabinet, and he had definite plans for accomplishing emancipation. The climax of the *Tribune* crusade was Greeley's famous "Prayer of Twenty Millions" editorial of August 20, 1862, which was a call for action on the slavery issue. Lincoln replied by a personal letter to Greeley, which he also gave to the *National Intelligencer* for publication on August 23. The letter included the paragraph familiar to students of the period:

> My paramount object in this struggle *is* to save the Union, and is *not* either to save or destroy Slavery. If I could save the Union without freeing *any* slave, I would do it; and if I could save it by freeing *all* the slaves, I would do it; and if I could do it by freeing some and leaving others alone, I would also do that.

Greeley wrote another open letter to the President urging more concern with the issue. When Lincoln announced his preliminary Emancipation Proclamation a month later, to be effective January 1, 1863, many readers of the *Tribune* assumed that "Uncle Horace" had done it again. "It is the beginning of the new life of the nation," Greeley exulted in his September 23 issue. The President and his cabinet had worked out the details without any help from the editor, but surely a man so sensitive to public feelings as Lincoln must have been aware of the popular pressure.

By the time of the election of 1864, Lincoln and Greeley appear to have tired of each other. "You complain of me—what have I done, or omitted to do, that has provoked the hostility of the *Tribune?*" asked the President.[1] But eventually Greeley swung around behind his old friend again. Of the seventeen New York daily newspapers, only five were solid supporters of the administration: the *Tribune,* the *Times,* the *Evening Post,* the *Sun,* and the *Commercial Advertiser.* Greeley did not hesitate to take unpopular stands when wartime passions made such outspokenness highly dangerous. When Greeley supported the President's draft call of 1863, the *Tribune* was stoned.

War was the golden age for Henry J. Raymond, who had made the *New York Times* one of the outstanding dailies of its time. The paper offered reasonable, penetrating, and thorough reportage. The feeling for objectivity on the part of *Times* writers is indicated by the four open letters Raymond wrote to Yancey, the Southern fire-eater. They were able and dispassionate antisecession arguments that showed an understanding of the Southern viewpoint. But on essential issues, the *Times* gave Lincoln strong support.

Raymond was an expert correspondent and writer, and his partner, George Jones, had wisely urged him to confine his energy to journalism rather than politics. The temptation was too great, however. By 1863, he was chairman of the Republican National Committee, one of the key political positions in the nation. He managed the 1864 campaign in which Lincoln and his "union" ticket partner, Andrew Johnson of Tennessee, defeated General George B. McClellan, the Democratic candidate, thanks to solid Union Army victories in the fall.

Henry J. Raymond.
Harper's Weekly

Raymond also wrote the party platform and was elected to the House of Representatives.

When Congress convened in 1865, it was assumed that Raymond represented the administration. He proved to be no match, however, for Thaddeus Stevens and other advocates of punishment for the South. Lincoln's assassination removed his party sponsor. He lost his national committee seat and declined to run for Congress again in 1866. He than bolted the party, ending his political career. "Shocking Cruelty to a Fugitive Slave," Greeley headlined the account of the episode in the *Tribune.* Later, Raymond and the *Times* returned to solid ground with the Republicans, but the paper's founder died of a cerebral hemorrhage in 1869 while waging an editorial fight against the infamous Tweed ring of political corruptionists that was looting the city treasury.

Bennett and his *Herald* caused the Lincoln administration considerable annoyance. The paper was politically independent, but it was definitely "soft" toward the South, where it had great influence. Because of its extensive news coverage, particularly of business and commerce, the *Herald* was the most popular American newspaper in Europe. The British government at this time was making friendly overtures to the South, which provided British mills with cotton in normal times. The attitude of the widely read *Herald* was therefore of concern to Lincoln and his cabinet, for it was important that European neutrals have a fair evaluation of the issues.

After the first battle of Bull Run, Bennett gave his full, but somewhat grudging, support to the Lincoln administration and the war. Even so, it was necessary from time to time for the President to "sweeten up"—as Lincoln put it—the aggressive editor of the *Herald.* "I write this to assure you that the Administration will not discriminate against the *Herald,* especially while it sustains us so generously . . . ," Lincoln wrote to Bennett after personally interceding for a *Herald* reporter who had been refused a pass to go down the Potomac river with a military detachment.[2] As a former pro-Southern newspaper, the *Herald* continued to attack specific issues of the Republican party, but its intentions were not subversive.

There were other instances in which *Herald* reporters tangled with authorities. Actually, the aggressiveness of the *Herald* could have caused it much more trouble, if military officials had exerted their authority. At any rate, the editorial tactics paid off, for the *Herald* climbed to a circulation of more than 100,000 soon after the beginning of the war. It was then the most popular newspaper in the United States.[3]

Few presidents suffered more from editorial abuse than Lincoln. Opposition editors and disappointed favor-seekers accused him in print of vicious deeds, which the patient President usually ignored. He was falsely accused of drawing his salary in gold bars, while his soldiers were paid in deflated greenbacks. He was charged with drunkenness while making crucial decisions, with granting pardons to secure votes, and with needless butchering of armies as a result of his lust for victories. Once he was accused of outright treason. Typical of his press detractors was the *La Crosse Democrat,* a Wisconsin weekly, which said of the draft: "Lincoln has called for 500,000 more victims."

Continuous and unlicensed criticism was voiced by political opponents. Democrats actually polled a larger vote than Republicans in 1860.[4] They were so split by sectional differences, however, that they could not agree on a candidate. The Republicans were aware that they had won by default.

Most northern Democrats were loyal during the war, although they tended to welcome peace overtures short of total victory for Lincoln's aims. There were some who served as a kind of fifth column for the South, however. They were called Copperheads, after the dangerous reptile that gives no warning of its attack. Some formed underground groups engaged in treasonable acts; others were vocal above-ground Copperheads.

Clement Laird Vallandigham, an Ohio editor and politician, was a well-known Copperhead. In 1847 he became coowner of the *Dayton Empire,* an antiabolitionist magazine, and won a seat in Congress in 1858. As secretary of the Democratic National Committee in 1860, he sought to avoid war. By 1863 he was one of the Copperheads arrested by order of General Ambrose E. Burnside. Sentenced to prison, he was banished behind the Confederate lines by Lincoln's order.

MILITARY CENSORSHIP IN THE NORTH

No war had ever been so fully and freely reported before. New York newspapers usually devoted at least a third of their space to war news. But sooner or later the press had to work out an understanding with military authorities in the interests of public security. There is no record in War Department files of military censorship prior to the Civil War, although there had been some censorship during the Mexican War. A system had to be developed by trial and error. As a result, both the press and the government made many mistakes in working out the problems, and criticism from all sides was often bitter. Yet many valuable lessons were learned in the Civil War about controls of communication agencies, which set the tone for wartime in this century.

The problem was aggravated by the fact that the American press had become so prosperous, aggressive, and independent in the years preceding the war that it was sensitive to any form of restriction. The telegraph and the railway posts were other factors to be considered. They made it possible to disseminate news much faster than before. The potential danger of information useful to the enemy was therefore all the greater. On the other hand, this was the first of the all-out wars involving civilian populations, and since public morale was now a much more important factor in prosecuting the war, the channels of information had to be kept open.[5]

There were three stages in the development of Civil War military censorship. The first period of fumbling began with the denial by the Post Office of messages sent to enemy areas. The high command in Washington began to realize that the enemy was obtaining valuable military intelligence through the free flow of information to the press and to persons in private life. Then, on July 8, 1861, General Winfield Scott, commander of the Union armies, issued an order, backed up by Secretary of War Simon Cameron, forbidding the telegraph companies from sending any information of a military nature. This was illegal, but it served the purpose until Congress gave the President such control in January, 1862.

The first drastic use of the telegraph censorship was after the first battle of Bull Run, July 21, 1861. Raymond, who had turned in a bulletin to the *Times* announcing a Union victory and was thereby put to shame by the reports of his rivals, maintained that his follow-up story had been blocked by the censors. The same thing happened to Lawrence A. Gobright of the New York Associated Press. Already it was clear that if the government had to restrict certain types of information, it was just as necessary to provide the news to which reporters were entitled.

Since honest journalists and military planners both recognized the problem, it was natural that they should try to work out some agreement. On August 2, 1861, General George B. McClellan, commanding the Army of the Potomac, called an historic press conference of Washington correspondents. Each of the delegates to the conference signed a document binding him to transmit no information of miltiary value to the enemy. On the other hand, the general agreed to use all his considerable influence to facilitate the gathering of news that was of interest to the public. The men who left the meeting that day congratulated themselves on the wisdom of the voluntary plan.

Unfortunately, the program was unsuccessful, not because of any serious flaw in the agreement but because of division of authority. The official censor was H. E. Thayer, who understood nothing about the problem. He was not under the supervision of the War Department but was under the direction of the Secretary of State. The jealousy of the War and State Departments resulted in a complete breakdown of the voluntary censorship plan less than 3 months after it was proposed: On October 22, Secretary of State Seward instructed Thayer to prohibit telegraphic dispatches from Washington that related to military *and civil* operations of the government. Since this violated the very spirit of the McClellan agreement, the press reverted to its old system of getting news as best it could.[6]

The second phase of censorship began when the censor was taken from the State Department and put under the direction of the Secretary of War, Edwin M. Stanton, who quickly brought order out of chaos. By an order of February 25, 1862, Stanton clarified the triple set of restrictions under which correspondents had been bound by voluntary, State Department, and War Department censorship. By the Stanton order, correspondents were to submit copy to provost marshals for approval before transmission, but it was understood that deletions would apply only to military matters. Now the reporters knew just about how far they could go in reporting battles, and the press was able to serve much more effectively.

General William T. Sherman also helped to clarify censorship rules. The general had been bedeviled by reporters, who were irked by his press relations. Sherman was certain much military failure could be blamed on information leaks. The issue came to a showdown after Thomas E. Knox, a correspondent for the *Herald,* transmitted information that clearly violated military regulations of censorship. Sherman had the reporter arrested and held as a spy. He had no intention of shooting the man, as he had every right to do, but he was convinced that this was a good test case. In the end, the President intervened, Knox got out of his predicament, and Sherman got what he wanted: the understanding that all correspondents must be *accredited,* or recognized, journalists and that they must be *acceptable* to commanders in the field. Thus was established a precedent followed ever since by military correspondents.

From 1864 to the end of the war, censorship entered its third and successful phase. General Sherman marched all the way to the sea in hostile country without once having his plans disclosed by the press. On the whole, the press was cooperating by the end of the war.

SUSPENSIONS OF NORTHERN NEWSPAPERS

In the main, the Northern press enjoyed great freedom throughout the war. The great power of the President after his suspension of habeas corpus was used sparingly. Most of the punitive actions were taken by military commanders. In June, 1863, the *Chicago Times* was suspended for 3 days by order of General Ambrose Burnside, commanding the Department of Ohio, which included the military districts in Illinois. This was one of the so-called "Burnside Decrees," based on the right of a commander to silence public expression of ideas and information deemed harmful to the military effort. The General appears to have had plenty of provocation for his action. Wilbur F. Storey, publisher of the *Chicago Times,* lacked both conscience and principle. He used the most violent language in attacking Lincoln after the Emancipation Proclamation was issued. He repeatedly ignored military warnings to stop fomenting Copperhead dissatisfaction in the area. Pushed beyond endurance by the anti-Federal sentiments of the *Times,* General Burnside ordered the newspaper padlocked. Lincoln's reaction was typical. He wished to back up his own general, and he knew Burnside had much to complain about, but the President also had definite ideas about freedom of expression. After 3 days he rescinded the military order.

Other newspapers ran afoul of the censor. One was the *New York World*, established in 1860 as a penny paper with religious overtones. At first the *World* was a supporter of the Lincoln administration. It lost money and continued to fail even after it absorbed the assets of the famous old *Courier and Enquirer*. Eventually it was taken over by Manton Marble, an able editor who increased circulation by espousing the cause of the "Peace Democrats." After the Emancipation Proclamation, the *World* was openly hostile to the administration. It became the focus of Copperhead infection in an area in which the war was already unpopular. In May, 1864, the military authorities had a chance to strike back.

The *World* and the *Journal of Commerce* published a forged presidential proclamation purporting to order another draft of 400,000 men. The document was actually the product of Joseph Howard, Jr., city editor of the *Brooklyn Eagle*, who had hoped to make a profit in the stock market by this hoax. Such a story in the tense metropolis was almost certain to cause bloodshed and probably death by rioting. Other editors refused to carry the story, after checking the facts, but the *World* and *Journal of Commerce* appeared with the article prominently displayed. General John A. Dix promptly suppressed them. After a lapse of 2 days, during which the editors were severely reprimanded, they were allowed to resume publication.

One of the most celebrated suspension cases outside New York was that of Samuel Medary, editor of the *Crisis* and of the *Ohio Statesman* in Columbus. The *Crisis* was a special organ of the Copperheads, and it supported C. L. Vallandigham, the Copperhead candidate for governor. In 1864 Medary was indicted by a federal grand jury as the spokesperson for a group then declared to be subversive. He was released from jail on bond furnished by the editor of the *Cincinnati Enquirer*, who wished to test the wartime freedom of the press. Medary died before the case was tried in court.

THE NORTH REPORTS THE WAR

Indeed, when it came to the reporting of military actions, Civil War correspondents, or "specials," as they were called then, enjoyed a freedom that would not be tolerated in modern times. Many of the battles were fought in remote areas, and the struggle to get back first-hand accounts was often heroic. Some of the best reporting in American journalism was offered to the public by the hundreds of correspondents during this test of a nation.

News reporters were everywhere. They roamed the South long after their detection might have resulted in their execution as spies. Some of them were famous already, including Raymond of the *Times*, who was at Bull Run, and William Howard Russell, the world-renowned British war correspondent fresh from his triumphs in the Crimea.

Some of the best war reporters earned their spurs after the conflict began, however. One of these was B. S. Osbon, a minister's son who had embarked on a life of seafaring and adventure. He was working for the *New York World* at $9 a week on that April morning in 1861 when the curtain went up on one of the great American tragedies. From the deck of a naval cutter, Osbon watched the bombardment of Fort Sumter. The lead of the story he sent back was a prototype of the news style developed during the war:

> CHARLESTON, APRIL 12—*The ball is opened. War is inaugurated.*
> The batteries of Sullivan's Island, Morris Island, and other points were opened on Fort Sumter at four o'clock this morning. Fort Sumter has returned the fire, and a brisk cannonading has been kept up.[7]

Later Osbon shipped back on the U.S.S. *Baltic,* carrying the exhausted Major Robert Anderson, commander of the fort's garrison. It was Osbon who disclosed in a published interview that a junior officer had raised the flag of surrender after Anderson had ordered the last round to be fired and further resistance appeared to be hopeless.

Not long after, Bennett hired Osbon to report for the *Herald* at $25 a week. He was on the quarterdeck with Admiral Farragut at the siege of New Orleans; he seemed to be wherever a good story was about to break.

But there were other stars, too. Albert D. Richardson of the *Tribune* sent reports from the deep South through the line by transmitting his stories in cipher by way of the New York banks. He watched the great battle of Fort Henry from a treetop observation post. He saw Island Number Ten at the Vicksburg approaches reduced to rubble as he stood with Commodore Foote on the hurricane deck of a Union ironclad. He ran the blockade of Vicksburg; was knocked from the deck by the shock of a cannon ball that nearly struck him; and was then picked up from the water and imprisoned by the Confederates. His escape through the lines was one of the exciting journalistic feats of the time.

George W. Smalley, later one of the pioneer foreign correspondents, first gained fame while covering the war for the *Tribune.* At the battle of Antietam, where he served as a dispatch rider for General Hooker, he lost two horses by gunfire. It was Smalley who first got the news of the battle to Washington, where Lincoln was anxiously waiting for some encouraging report before announcing his plans for emancipation.

Many of the correspondents wrote under pen names. There was "Agate," for example, who was actually Whitelaw Reid, the successor to Greeley on the *Tribune* in the early 1870s. He was already famous for his report on the battle of Shiloh when he sent a dispatch from Gettysburg. His story, datelined "Field of Battle, Near Gettysburg, July 2," took up fourteen of the forty-eight columns of the *Cincinnati Gazette.* It remains as a classic of Civil War reporting. Standing on Cemetery Hill, the point most exposed to rebel fire, Reid turned in an eyewitness account of the decisive battle, of which the following is an excerpt:

> Hancock was wounded; Gibbon succeeded to command—approved soldier, and ready for the crisis. As the tempest of fire approached its height, he walked along the line, and renewed his orders to the men to reserve their fire. The rebels—three lines deep—came steadily up. They were in pointblank range.
> At last the order came! From thrice six thousand guns there came a sheet of smoky flame, a crash of leaden death. The line literally melted away; but there came

THE NEW YORK HERALD

WHOLE NO. 10,451. NEW YORK, MONDAY, APRIL 10, 1865. PRICE FOUR CENTS.

THE END

SURRENDER

OF

LEE

AND HIS

WHOLE ARMY

TO

GRANT.

TERMS OF SURRENDER.

All Honor to Grant, Meade, Sheridan, Ord, Humphreys, Wright, Griffin, Parke, and their Brave Troops.

Highly Interesting Details of the Fighting Before the Surrender.

Ord Makes a Forced March of Thirty Miles a Day South of Lee's Line of Retreat.

Our Main Columns Follow Closely in the Enemy's Rear.

The Woods Filled with Rebel Stragglers and the Roads Strewn with Cannon, Caissons, Wagons, Ambulances, Muskets, Sabres, Knapsacks and Cartridge Boxes.

Announcement of the Capture of Richmond to the Troops.

INTENSE ENTHUSIASM.

Our Men Clamor to be Led Forward.

Sherman, with a Force of Union Cavalry, Reported Destroying the Railroad Between Danville and Greensboro.

JEFF. DAVIS AT DANVILLE, &c., &c., &c.

THE SURRENDER.

THANKS TO GRANT AND HIS ARMY.

NATIONAL SALUTE.

THE PREVIOUS FIGHTING.

CITY POINT.

THE PURSUIT.

THE TERMS.

THE FIFTH CORPS.

THE SECOND CORPS.

The *New York Herald,* leader in war correspondence, records the South's surrender.

> a second, resistless still. It had been our supreme effort—on the instant we were not equal to another.
>
> Up to the rifle pits, across them, over the barricades—the momentum of their charge, the mere machine strength of their combined action swept them on. Our thin line could fight, but it had not weight enough to oppose this momentum. It was pushed behind the guns. Right on came the rebels. They were upon the guns, were bayoneting the gunners, were waving their flags above our pieces.
>
> But they had penetrated to the fatal point. . . .[8]

In the Confederate camp near Hagerstown, Maryland, the reporter for the *Richmond Enquirer,* retreating with Lee's army, sent back this eloquent version of the same battle to soften the blow to the bereaved at home:

> Though many a Virginia home will mourn the loss of some noble spirit, yet at the name of Pickett's division and the battle of Gettysburg, how the eye will glisten and the blood course quicker, and the heart beat warm, as among its noble dead is recalled the name of some cherished one. They bore themselves worthy of their lineage and their state. Who would recall them from their bed of glory? Each sleeps in a hero's grave. . . .[9]

The *New York Herald,* true to its tradition, exceeded its rivals in aggressive war coverage. It had more than forty specials in the field at any given time. One of its foremost reporters was a young Bavarian immigrant, Henry Hilgard, who soon changed his name to Villard after his arrival in 1853. While learning the language, Villard edited the *Volksblatt,* a German paper published in Racine, Wisconsin. Later he covered the Lincoln-Douglas debates for the *Staats-Zeitung* of New York. His account of Lincoln's departure from Springfield for Washington, and of the long ride under increasing national tension, established Villard as one of the best correspondents of his day. He was only 25 when he began reporting the war for the *Herald.* He is best remembered for two great reporting "scoops." The first was his account of the first battle of Bull Run, the first accurate one to reach New York. The second exclusive account was his report of the battle of Fredericksburg.

THE SOUTH REPORTS THE WAR

Not much has been said about the Southern press up to this point, although it played an important part in the fortunes of the Confederacy. In many ways editorial reactions were the same in the North and South. Southern editors were highly critical of military strategy, and journalists such as Rhett, for example, attacked the Confederate administration just as violently as Lincoln was being attacked in the North. War aims were not as much an issue as they were in the North, however, nor was there anything quite corresponding to the Copperhead press.

Most of the news of the battles was supplied to Southern editors by the Press Association of the Confederate States of America, better known as "PA," which, appropriately enough, was just the reversed logotype of the biggest Northern news agency, the AP.[10] When the war began, the South had no system for preparing or transmitting news of public interest to replace the severed connection with the New York AP. An Augusta editor began sending out a brief daily summary by telegraph to a few papers willing to pay for the service, but this was never widely used. In 1862, the combined newspapers of Richmond tried to establish a more effective organization. Publishers realized that to meet the enormous expense of covering a war, they would have to work together. They also saw that in order to place correspondents where they were needed, they would have to pool resources. It was soon evident that the Richmond papers could not achieve these results by themselves.

Following a series of conferences, Joseph Clisby of the *Macon Telegraph* summoned the editor of every daily in the South to attend a meeting in Augusta on February 4, 1862. The Association of the Richmond Press had just been organized, and the plan was to expand the idea by organizing the PA. A board of directors hired a superintendent, J. S. Thrasher, "at a salary not to exceed $3,000," and the organization was ready to function.

The value of the association was at once apparent in the signing of contracts with telegraph agencies and the abolishing of onerous postal regulations. On May 15, 1863, the directors passed a resolution defending Thrasher for his stand against unwarranted military censorship.

On the whole, the PA served its clients well. When General P. G. T. Beauregard began to hold up dispatches, Thrasher called on him personally and told the general that the aim of the press association was to obtain accurate reports for the good of the public, consistent with military security. The general was impressed. He told Thrasher that the PA reporters "should have every facility for early access to intelligence compatible with the public interests," and he wrote letters to high military authorities recommending similar cooperation. Thrasher won the confidence of other leaders. In return, he instructed PA correspondents to send no opinions or comments on events—the procedure that had so irritated Northern commanders. They were warned to sift rumors and to offer no information that would aid the enemy. The objectivity of the PA stories has been regarded as constituting a "complete revolution" in journalistic writing.[11]

The superintendent, in return, was jealous of arrogant commanders who held up legitimate copy, and he used the power of his office to enforce cooperation from the military. Correspondents were ordered to send to the home office copies of dispatches unreasonably censored at the telegraph office. These reports were to include the name and rank of the responsible censor, and these documents were then used to pry greater concessions from those in higher authority.

The development of the PA was a big step in the progress of Southern journalism. The surviving forty-three daily papers in the South were all members. The editorial weight of this group was impressive. Dispatches were transmitted over the Military Telegraph Lines, the army system, at half rates. There was also a satisfactory arrangement with the private South-Western Telegraph Company. Newspapers that seldom had access to regular wire news budgets were now able to keep readers up to date on the war. Short, but complete, reports supplanted the rambling, confused accounts of prewar days. Reporters with the armies were paid $25 a week, which was good for that time, and the writing was of good quality. On the whole the PA gave a good account of itself until the crumbling Confederacy saw a collapse of restraints and organization. As in the Northern armies, reporters were sometimes ejected for releasing information believed useful to the enemy. But Thrasher appears to have perfected a great news-gathering agency. He offered relatively high objectivity. He kept the press as free as possible, considering the circumstances.

There were perhaps 800 newspapers being published in the eleven states of the Confederacy in 1861, of which about 10 percent were dailies. Hand presses were in use in most of these newspaper offices and circulations were small. The *Richmond Dispatch,* with 18,000 subscribers when war broke out, was outranked only by the largest New Orleans dailies. And as important as the Richmond papers were in the journalism of the Confederacy, the *Dispatch* had more readers than the *Enquirer, Whig,* and *Democrat* combined. The *Enquirer* was the organ of the Jefferson Davis administration until 1863 when the *Sentinel* was established for that purpose. Richmond also spawned a *Southern Illustrated News* in 1862 to fill the void left by the disappearance of *Harper's Weekly;* it soon had 20,000 readers.[12]

Southern publishers were harassed by a shortage of print paper; they were reduced eventually to printing single sheets, to printing extras on galley proof slips, even to printing on the back of old wallpaper. They also ran out of ink, type, and people to staff their shops. After 1863, when New Orleans fell, their cities were overrun by federal troops. Only about twenty of the dailies were still printing when Lee surrendered. But they had compiled a journalistic record of the Confederate arms, and had sent, all told, more than 100 correspondents to cover the Southern armies.

The historian of Civil War correspondents. J. Cutler Andrews, ranks two of these men as head and shoulders above the others.[13] One was Felix Gregory de Fontaine, who signed himself "Personne" in his dispatches to the *Charleston Courier.* The other was Peter W. Alexander, primarily identified with the *Savannah Republican,* but whose "P.W.A." signature was also found in the *Atlanta Confederacy,* the *Columbus Sun,* the *Mobile Advertiser,* the *Richmond Dispatch,* and the *Times* of London. Ranking behind them were such versatile war reporters as Samuel C. Reid, Jr., of the *New Orleans Picayune* and other papers; James B. Sener and William G. Shepardson of the *Richmond Dispatch;* Albert J. Street of the *Mobile Register;* John H. Linebaugh of the *Memphis Appeal;* and an unidentified "Shadow" who covered the Battle of Atlanta and who may have been Henry Watterson of future Louisville fame.

De Fontaine and Alexander crossed paths as "regulars" in the major campaigns; both were at Antietam in September, 1862, when Lee was repulsed in his invasion of the North, escaping a vastly superior McClellan. De Fontaine wrote a seven-column story of more than 8000 words about the campaign, in what Andrews calls his greatest story of the war. It appeared in the *Charleston Courier* first. At one point the young but war-weary correspondent described the scene in front of the Confederate center along a sunken road called "Bloody Lane":

> From twenty different standpoints great volumes of smoke were every instant leaping from the muzzles of angry guns. The air was filled with the white fantastic

> shapes that floated away from bursted shells. Men were leaping to and fro, loading, firing and handling the artillery, and now and then a hearty yell would reach the ear, amid the tumult, that spoke of death or disaster from some well aimed ball. Before us were the enemy. A regiment or two had crossed the river, and, running in squads from the woods along its banks, were trying to form a line. Suddenly a shell falls among them, and another and another, until thousands scatter like a swarm of flies, and disappear in the woods. A second time the effort is made, and there is a second failure. Then there is a diversion. The batteries of the Federals open afresh; their infantry try another point, and finally they succeed in effecting a lodgement on this side. Our troops, under D. H. Hill, meet them, and a fierce battle ensues in the centre. Backwards, forwards, surging and swaying like a ship in a storm, the various columns are seen in motion. It is a hot place for us, but is hotter still for the enemy. They are directly under our guns, and we mow them down like grass. The raw levies, sustained by the veterans, come up to the work well, and fight for a short time with an excitement incident to their novel experiences of a battle; but soon a portion of their line gives way in confusion. Their reserves come up, and endeavor to retrieve the fortunes of the day. Our centre, however, stands firm as adamant, and they fall back.[14]

This was at noon; by two o'clock Hill was out of men to defend the center—but McClellan failed to mount a breakthrough and settled for less than an overwhelming victory. More soldiers died in a single day at Antietam than in any other battle in American history: 23,000 in all.

Alexander was also at Antietam and composed his battle account for the *Mobile Advertiser* in the midst of the wounded and dying in an army hospital. "There is a smell of death in the air," he wrote, "and the laboring surgeons are literally covered from head to foot with the blood of the sufferers." It was Alexander who wrote the most penetrating Southern account of the Battle of Gettysburg, questioning Lee's wisdom in committing himself to full-scale assault the second day and wondering if Lee and his staff had not exhibited too much confidence in the ability of their troops to win against any odds. Most of the Southern press reprinted his story.[15]

ARTISTS AND PHOTOGRAPHERS: MATHEW BRADY

A small army of artists covered the war, describing the events in almost photo-like drawings that were printed by a laborious process of engraving by hand on a wooden block. Such woodcuts were not new, but they were used in newspapers much more regularly after 1861 to depict battle scenes and the likenesses of leading wartime figures. In another development, some of the metropolitan papers printed large maps to illustrate campaigns, thereby leading the way to new makeup no longer limited by column rules.[16] The *Herald* of September 12, 1863, is a good example of this technique. The paper was a little smaller than a modern standard daily and ran to eight pages, six columns wide. About a quarter of page one of this particular issue was devoted to a map accompanying a story on the Arkansas campaign. On page three a huge map of the Morris Island success in Charleston harbor filled all but two columns of the page from top to bottom.

Illustrations were also the touchstone for success in magazine publishing. Two forerunners of twentieth-century news and picture weeklies were *Frank Leslie's Illustrated Newspaper,* a sixteen-page 10 cent weekly founded in 1855, and *Harper's Weekly,* begun in 1857. Their superb artists' drawings for woodcuts brought the war visually to 100,000 or more subscribers. They also covered sports, crime, and disasters. *Harper's Monthly,* an 1850 entry from the same publishing house, achieved a record 200,000 circulation before the war by featuring woodcut illustrations along with its fiction in issues double the usual size. Hand-colored engravings of fashionable clothing for ladies and gentlemen were one of the secrets of *Godey's Lady's Book,* founded in 1830 by Louis Godey and edited from 1836 to 1877 by Sarah J. Hale. The illustrations and copious fiction and poetry brought a 150,000 circulation in the 1850s. Hale's famed contribution was "Mary Had a Little Lamb"; she also wrote or edited fifty books, promoted Thanksgiving as a national holiday, and discussed women's rights in *Godey's.* A rival in fashion illustration was *Peterson's Magazine,* begun in 1842 by Charles J. Peterson with Ann Stephens as associate editor and fiction writer. It exceeded *Godey's* in circulation during the war, indicating the growing recognition of women in the economic picture.

The most notable contribution to pictorial journalism in the 1860s was the photograph. One pioneer war photographer was a lovable Irishman, Mathew Brady. True, his photographs could not be used in newspapers of the time, since a practical method for transferring light and shade in the printing process was not perfected for another decade. But Brady was famous for his war pictures, and his photographic record of the conflict comes down to us as one of the finest examples of reporting.

Brady was everywhere during the war, apparently. He recorded on his clumsy plates the scene at Fort Sumter. His photographic interpretations of famous battles and war leaders could not be matched in mood and accuracy by the printed word. It is surprising how many of the great men of the period posed for Brady.[17]

Brady was born about 1823, either in Cork, Ireland, or more probably in upper New York State. As a youth he worked for A. T. Stewart, the pioneer New York department-store owner. Stewart took an interest in the bright lad. When Brady took up the study of photography, the wealthy merchant brought his protégé to the attention of Samuel F. B. Morse, famed as the inventor of the telegraph but equally interested in the science of optics. Morse made Brady his understudy. Together they worked with Professor J. W. Draper of New York University, who was to make the first instantaneous photographic exposure in America.[18] In 1839, Morse took Brady to Europe, where they met Louis Jacques Mandé Daguerre, inventor of the "daguerreotype," a photograph on metal. Other European pioneers included Joseph Nièpce of France and Fox Talbot of Britain.

Brady returned to America and set up a daguerreotype shop at the corner of Broadway and Fulton Street, opposite Barnum's museum. That was about 1842. Soon he was famed as a photographer of the great and the near-great.[19] Five years in a row he won the American Institute award for his contributions to photography. He was famous and prosperous.

But Brady was not satisfied with this success. The daguerreotype was too slow to be adaptable to anything but portrait work, and he sought a faster process. In 1855 he went to Scotland to learn about a new and faster "wet plate" developed by the scientist Scott-Archer. Brady returned with Alexander Gardner, Scott-Archer's associate, and they set up offices in Washington as semiofficial government photographers. When the war loomed, Brady gave up this lucrative business.

He persuaded his friends President Lincoln and Allan Pinkerton of the Secret Service to let him make a photographic record of the war with Gardner. They were permitted to go anywhere, protected by the Secret Service. Soon Brady's little black wagon, which was his portable dark room, was a familiar sight on the active fronts. He had an uncanny knack of knowing where the fighting would start. Soldiers dreaded the sight of Brady arriving on the scene, for they knew that soon thereafter the shooting would begin. He was often under sniper fire as he set up his camera at exposed vantage points. By the end of the war he had collected about 3500 photographs.

These pictures give us an entirely different impression than the usual reports of people and events. Although Brady's equipment was inferior to the simplest box cameras of three generations later, he produced amazing pictures. Somehow he was able to capture through his lens the hysteria, horror, and occasional glory of war.

WARTIME BRINGS TECHNICAL ADVANCES

War brought important technical changes to the press. Dependence on the telegraph led to modification in news writing, as correspondents tried to save tolls by striving to be more concise. One way to compress stories was to omit opinion and coloration. By modern standards, Civil War reporting was rambling and colored, but compared with the journalism of an earlier day it was much more readable. Some of the copy, such as that transmitted out of Washington by the New York Associated Press and out of Richmond by the Confederate Press Association, would not be much out of place in a modern newspaper.

The summary lead, which put the main feature of the story in the first paragraph, was developed during the war by reporters in the field who feared that their complete dispatches might not get through. Bennett once said that the cable, rather than the telegraph, was responsible for this, but the cable was not in successful operation until 1866, and the summary lead was fairly common by that time. Here, for example, is the way the *New York Times* started off one of its important front-page articles of April 16, 1865:

> WASHINGTON, Saturday, April 15—12 A.M. Andrew Johnson was sworn into office as President of the United States by Chief Justice Chase today, at eleven o'clock. . . .

Because vital news streamed from the telegraph by the hour, metropolitan papers began to bulletin the highlights, and soon the smallest papers were imitating this procedure. These bulletins led to the modern newspaper headline, which summarizes the story in a few lines.

Most of the newspapers continued to use the eight-page, six-column makeup carried over from before the war. By modern standards they were likely to be drab, with their small type, lack of pictures, and the dreadful uniformity of one-column makeup limitations. But the use of huge maps was breaking down the confines of the column rule, and the experimentation with headlines indicated the contrast with the page dress of only a decade earlier.

Presses had to be fast to keep up with other developments in journalism. On the Sunday following the fall of Fort Sumter, the *Herald* printed 135,000 newspapers—a record press run up to that date. In 1863, William Bullock brought out the web perfecting press, which printed both sides of a continuous roll of paper on a rotary press. Although it was not until 1871 that R. Hoe. & Company produced such presses as standard equipment, the stimulus of the war is nevertheless apparent.

It was indeed an exciting era that came to a close on the evening of April 14, 1865. Lawrence A. Gobright of the New York Associated Press was working late in his office. He had already sent out dispatches about President Lincoln's theater party, reporting that General Grant had declined an invitation to see the play, "Our American Cousin," in order to go to New Jersey with Mrs. Grant. The door burst open and an excited friend rushed in with news of the tragedy at Ford's Theater. Gobright quickly wrote out a bulletin before going to work on an extended account of the evening's development. No modern reporter could have broken the news more succinctly. The lead said:

> WASHINGTON, FRIDAY, APRIL 14, 1865—The President was shot in a theater tonight, and perhaps mortally wounded.

NOTES

1. For a discussion of the relations between Lincoln and the press, see James E. Pollard, *The Presidents and the Press* (New York: Macmillan, 1947), pp. 312–97.

2. Ibid., p. 360.

3. The *New York Times* climbed from 45,000 to about 75,000 in the same period. The daily *New York Tribune* trailed behind, but the weekly edition, largely responsible for Greeley's national reputation, reached more than 200,000. This was the largest circulation of any single American paper. The *New York Ledger* had almost twice that many subscribers, but it was not a newspaper, as its nameplate would indicate, but a weekly story periodical.

4. Lincoln had only 40 percent of the popular vote in 1860, and he won by only 400,000 votes in 1864, when none of the Southern Democrats had any voice in the elections. This was a serious consideration for Republican leaders contemplating the postwar political problem.

5. An outstanding study of this problem is Quintus Wilson, "A Study and Evaluation of the Military Censorship in the Civil War" (Master's thesis, University of Minnesota, 1945).

6. Ibid., p. 50.

7. Louis L. Snyder, and Richard B. Morris, eds., *A Treasury of Great Reporting* (New York: Simon & Schuster, 1949), p. 130.

8. Ibid., p. 146.

9. Ibid., p. 149.

10. This subject is presented in detail by Quintus C. Wilson, "The Confederate Press Association: A Pioneer News Agency," *Journalism Quarterly*, XXVI (June 1949), 160–66.

11. Ibid., p. 162.

12. J. Cutler Andrews, *The South Reports the Civil War* (Princeton: Princeton University Press, 1970), pp. 26–33.

13. Ibid., p. 50.

14. *Charleston Daily Courier*, September 29, 1862.

15. Andrews, *The South Reports the Civil War*, pp. 316–17.

16. It was not impossible to print spread headlines and large maps on the earlier type-revolving presses, but it was hazardous and inconvenient, because the column rules had to be locked tight to keep the metal

type from flying out as the presses revolved. It was accomplished now and then, however. Big maps were printed by the newspapers in the Mexican War period and after.

17. As must happen to all news photographers, Brady missed some great picture opportunities. He had his camera trained on President Lincoln at the time the immortal Gettysburg Address was delivered. Edward Everett, famous orator and the main speaker at the memorial, talked so long that Brady had to keep changing his plates, which had to be exposed while still wet with sensitizing solution. He was in the midst of removing a dried-out plate when the President arose to speak. The inspiring message was so short that Brady's assistant could not fetch a fresh plate from the portable dark room in time to photograph Lincoln before he bowed and retired. One of the great "news shots" of American history was thereby lost to posterity.

18. The word "instantaneous" had a much broader meaning then than now. It could mean anything up to several minutes.

19. This period is well described in Robert Taft, *Photography and the American Scene: A Social History, 1839–1889* (New York: Macmillan, 1938).

ANNOTATED BIBILOGRAPHY

Books

ANDREWS, J. CUTLER, *The North Reports the Civil War.* Pittsburgh: University of Pittsburgh Press, 1955. Most extensive (813 pages) of the histories of Civil War reporting, and thoroughly documented. Lists several hundred Northern reporters.

———, *The South Reports the Civil War.* Princeton: Princeton University Press, 1970. Like Andrews' *The North Reports the Civil War,* a prize-winning job of research and writing.

BUCKLAND, GAIL, *Fox Talbot and the Invention of Photography.* Boston: David R. Godine, 1980. Pioneer English photographer of 1830s–1840s; one-third illustrations.

CROZIER, EMMET, *Yankee Reporters,* 1861–65. New York: Oxford University Press, 1956. A readable account of correspondents' work.

FAHRNEY, RALPH RAY, *Horace Greeley and the Tribune in the Civil War.* Chicago: University of Chicago Press, 1929. Documented.

GOBRIGHT, LAWRENCE A., *Recollections of Men and Things at Washington during a Third of a Century.* Philadelphia: Claxton, Remsen, and Haffelfinger, 1869. By the AP correspondent.

HARPER, ROBERT S., *Lincoln and the Press.* New York: McGraw-Hill, 1951. Readable and detailed account of Lincoln's press relations after 1858; written from newspaper sources.

HORAN, JAMES D., *Mathew Brady: Historian with a Camera.* New York: Crown, 1955. A good biography, with 453 pictures.

KLEMENT, FRANK L., *The Copperheads in the Middle West.* Chicago: University of Chicago Press, 1960. Wilbur Storey, C. L. Vallandigham, and Samuel Medary are among those covered.

MATHEWS, JOSEPH J., *Reporting the Wars.* Minneapolis: University of Minnesota Press, 1957. History of war news reporting since the mid-eighteenth century. See also F. L. Bullard, *Famous War Correspondents* (Boston: Little, Brown, 1914).

MEREDITH, ROY, *Mr. Lincoln's Camera Man, Mathew S. Brady.* New York: Scribner's, 1946. A colorful account of the pioneer war photographer, with some of his best pictures.

Photographic History of the Civil War. New York: Review of Reviews Company, 1911 (10 volumes). A very complete collection of Brady's pictures, with explanatory material.

POLLARD, JAMES E., *The Presidents and the Press.* New York: Macmillan, 1947. The chapter on Lincoln and the press is very useful for those wishing to read a concise discussion.

REYNOLDS, DONALD E., *Editors Make War: Southern Newspapers in the Secession Crisis.* Nashville, Tenn.: Vanderbilt University Press, 1970. Research in the files proved that most Southern editors were in the forefront of the secession movement.

SALMON, LUCY B., *The Newspaper and Authority.* New York: Oxford University Press, 1923. The chapters on Civil War threats to a free press offer stimulating ideas on the subject.

SANDBURG, CARL, *Abraham Lincoln: The War Years.* New York: Harcourt Brace Jovanovich, 1939 (4 volumes). Contains excellent portraits of leading Civil War editors and newspapers.

SMITH, PAGE, *Trial by Fire: A People's History of the Civil War and Reconstruction.* New York: McGraw-Hill, 1982. Fifth volume of Smith's work.

SNYDER, LOUIS L., AND RICHARD B. MORRIS, eds., *A Treasury of Great Reporting.* New York: Simon & Schuster, 1962. Examples, with pertinent comment, of Civil War news stories.

STARR, LOUIS M., *Bohemian Brigade: Civil War Newsmen in Action.* New York: Knopf, 1954. One of the best studies; considers all aspects of the newspaper in wartime, including reporting, editing, censorship.

WEISBERGER, BERNARD A., *Reporters for the Union.* Boston: Little, Brown, 1953. Mainly a study of correspondents' political biases and criticisms of the military.

Periodicals and Monographs

BLACKMON, ROBERT E., "Noah Brooks: Reporter in the White House," *Journalism Quarterly,* XXXII (Summer 1955), 301. Brooks was the Washington correspondent of the *Sacramento Union* in wartime.

GOLDSMITH, ADOLPH O., "Reporting the Civil War: Union Army Press Relations," *Journalism Quarterly,* XXXIII (Fall 1956), 478. A good summary of the problem.

GUBACK, THOMAS H., "General Sherman's War on the Press," *Journalism Quarterly,* XXXVI (Spring 1959), 171. A well-done account, featuring Sherman's famous clash with the *New York Herald's* Knox.

JENSEN, OLIVER, "War Correspondent: 1864," *American Heritage,* 31 (August/September 1980), 48. Discusses James E. Taylor of *Frank Leslie's Illustrated Newspaper,* who left a manuscript memoir of his illustrator assignment.

PETERSON, DONALD CHRISTIAN, "Two Pioneer American Picture Magazines," Master's thesis, University of Wisconsin, 1953. A detailed study of *Harper's Weekly* and *Frank Leslie's Illustrated Newspaper.*

RANDALL, JAMES G., "The Newspaper Problem and Its Bearing Upon Military Secrecy During the Civil War," *American Historical Review,* XXIII (January 1918), 303. Long the main authority for a discussion of Civil War censorship, by a leading historian of the period.

WILSON, QUINTUS C., "A Study and Evaluation of the Military Censorship in the Civil War," Master's thesis, University of Minnesota, 1945. This is the most complete and best-documented study of the subject, and largely supersedes Randall's monograph.

———, "The Confederate Press Association: A Pioneer News Agency," *Journalism Quarterly,* XXVI (June 1949), 160. A digest of a chapter in Wilson's censorship study.

CHARLESTON

MERCURY

EXTRA:

Passed unanimously at 1.15 o'clock, P. M. December 20th, 1860.

AN ORDINANCE

To dissolve the Union between the State of South Carolina and other States united with her under the compact entitled "The Constitution of the United States of America."

We, the People of the State of South Carolina, in Convention assembled, do declare and ordain, and it is hereby declared and ordained,

That the Ordinance adopted by us in Convention, on the twenty-third day of May, in the year of our Lord one thousand seven hundred and eighty-eight, whereby the Constitution of the United States of America was ratified, and also, all Acts and parts of Acts of the General Assembly of this State, ratifying amendments of the said Constitution, are hereby repealed; and that the union now subsisting between South Carolina and other States, under the name of "The United States of America," is hereby dissolved.

THE

UNION

IS

DISSOLVED!

Original one-page sheet published by the *Charleston Mercury,* Dec. 20, 1860.

Charles A. Dana, the *New York Sun*.
Bettmann Archive

E. L. Godkin, the *Nation* and *Evening Post*.
New York Post

Harvey W. Scott, Portland's *Oregonian*.
The Oregonian

Henry Watterson, *Louisville Courier-Journal*.
Louisville Courier-Journal

14

The Press at a Watershed

. . . he was the last of those editors who wrote with the power of ownership.

—Arthur Krock, about Watterson

In many respects American history starts afresh at the close of the Civil War. This is not to deny the obvious fact that two and a half centuries of the American experience had produced fundamental guiding forces that would continue to influence the maturing of the nation's economy and the development of its political and social fabric. But great new forces were at work, and between 1865 and 1900 the United States was to pass through a revolution that affected every phase of the national scene. The forces were those of intensive industrialization, mechanization, and urbanization, which wrought with them sweeping social, cultural, and political changes. At some point between the Civil War and the turn of the century, the slow maturing process of virtually every aspect of American life was given powerful new impetus or redirection.

So it was with the nation's journalism. The great development of communication and of journalistic techniques that had come in the Jacksonian period of American growth was continuing through the war period. There was a popular press that had appealed to the human interests of its readers, utilized the new communication facilities to develop news enterprise, and sometimes developed editorial force. But the patterns that had emerged, the techniques that had been created, were drastically affected by an extensive new effort born of the impact of the new environment.

There was good reason for the development of new approaches to news reporting and editorial expression. The problems the United States faced in the years after the Civil War were heavy ones. The political leadership at hand was not equal to the tasks, and for a generation the talent exhibited in public life was far less than that shown in industry and business. There was no really great president between 1865 and the turn of the century, although Grover Cleveland won considerable recognition, primarily for his honesty and courage. But whatever the shortcomings in presidential leadership, the remainder of the political scene was far more depressing. The effort at political reconstruction of the South degenerated into an ugly battle between a vengeful Congress and an inept president; carpetbaggers and scalawags put in power in the South through arbitrary reconstruction policies gave way, in turn, to Southern home rule without participation by the blacks; scandals rocked the Grant administration and corruption permeated city governments; a "consistent rebellion" flared against economic maladjustments, money-supply inequities, and life-squeezing transportation and interest rates assessed against the farmer. In such a setting an independent-thinking editor devoted to presentation of the news was definitely encouraged.

A NEW GROUP OF EDITORS

Emphasizing this change is the passing from the scene of famous figures of the newspaper movement that had begun in the 1830s. Between 1869 and 1878, five leaders of the era of personal journalism died: Henry J. Raymond, founder of the *New York Times;* James Gordon Bennett, Sr., founder of the *New York Herald;* Horace Greeley, founder of the *New York Tribune;* Samuel Bowles, III, most famous of his name to edit the *Springfield Republican;* and William Cullen Bryant, for half a century editor of the *New York Evening Post.*

The newspaper builders who followed appeared not only in New York but also from coast to coast as the nation rushed to complete its geographical expansion and began in earnest to consolidate its economy. The new leaders were maturing and refining the processes and practices of their predecessors. Soon, sensing the opportunities presented by the changing environment in which they worked, some were to create what came to be known as the "new journalism."

Among those who replaced the departing leaders of journalism were some editors who represent a middle group, bridging the gap between the old and new: Charles A. Dana of the *New York Sun;* Edwin Lawrence Godkin of the *Nation* and *New York Evening Post;* Henry Watterson of the *Louisville Courier-Journal;* and Harvey W. Scott of the *Oregonian* in Portland. But even while these men and others like them were making their contributions to journalistic advancement as the leaders of a transitional period, representatives of the new order were appearing. For example, rising in the years between 1876 and 1887 were Melville E. Stone and the *Chicago Daily News;* Edward Wyllis Scripps and the *Cleveland Press;* Joseph Pulitzer and the *St. Louis Post-Dispatch* and *New York World;* William Rockhill Nelson and the *Kansas City Star;* and William Randolph Hearst and the *San Francisco Examiner.* These are among the most famous names of men and newspapers in American journalism, as we see later in detail, and their appearance with others of note in such a brief period testifies to the opportunity for journalistic advances that the revolution in American life afforded. By the time Hearst had invaded New York with his *Journal* to do battle with Pulitzer in the late 1890s—at a time when the careers of Dana and Godkin were closing—the transition from the older era to the new had been achieved. American journalism, like American history, is marked by what historian Henry Steele Commager calls "the watershed of the nineties," whose topography is as blurred as those of all watersheds, but whose grand outlines emerge clearly.[1]

POLITICAL AND FINANCIAL CRISES

Before we consider what the editors did, we should examine in more detail the political and socioeconomic situation in which they worked. The Republican party, which had elected Abraham Lincoln as its first president in 1860, found it necessary to run a Union ticket in 1864, pairing Lincoln with a Tennessee Democrat, Andrew Johnson. Even then, Lincoln polled only 400,000 more votes than the Democratic candidate, General George B. McClellan, with the South excluded from voting. In light of this, many Republicans viewed the immediate return of the South to full voting privileges with real alarm. They feared the result of accepting Lincoln's theory that since the Union was indissoluble, Southern states would automatically return to their former status when fighting ceased. Freed from this policy by Lincoln's death, Representative Thaddeus Stevens of Pennsylvania and Senator Charles Sumner of Massachusetts gave leadership to a group that maintained that the South had committed "state suicide" and should be considered as conquered territory. They and their followers, who came to dominate the postwar Congresses, were named the "radical Republicans."

In Andrew Johnson, the radical Republicans found an opponent who was made vulnerable by personality weaknesses that obscured his other qualities. When Southern states readmitted to the union by Johnson ignored black political rights, the radical Republicans moved to handle the South on their own terms. They passed a civil-rights bill; they submitted the fourteenth amendment to the Constitution for ratification; they passed, over Johnson's veto, the reconstruction acts that forced all Southern states to again seek reentry into the Union on radical-Republican terms; and they instituted military rule in the South. Northern carpetbaggers and Southern scalawags who took advantage of the unpreparedness of black voters for democratic responsibilities disrupted Southern life, and home rule was not fully restored until 1877. The contest between the radical Republicans and the President was climaxed by the impeachment of Johnson, who was saved from removal from office by a single vote in the Senate. Thereupon the Republican party turned to General Ulysses S. Grant as its candidate in 1868, and won the election easily.

Political reconstruction was thus a controversial problem, but financial reconstruction was even more so. Commodity prices in the North had doubled during the 5 years of war. Running of the printing presses to create legal tender paper money, dubbed "greenbacks," had driven coinage into hiding, intensifying the usual wartime inflationary trend. In 1866 Congress therefore voted to retire the greenbacks gradually over an 11-year period. The argument was advanced that retirement of the greenbacks, which constituted a part of the large federal debt, would deflate prices and increase the value of the dollar. Such action would be to the benefit of creditors and of wage earners whose incomes had not kept pace with prices. But farmers, who generally were debtors, would find money dearer and prices for their products lower. Opposition to retirement of the greenbacks from circulation began to develop in the Middle West agricultural areas and of course in the South, whose economy had been prostrated by the collapse of the Confederate currency and the ravages of war. Opponents of paper money forced final retirement of the greenbacks beginning in 1879, further intensifying the problem of an inadequate money supply for the rapidly expanding American economy. Currency supply was not the only complaint of the agricultural West and South. Farmers found interest rates on their borrowed money excessively high and impossible to pay in years of poor crops or low prices. They found that the railroads, which were extending their tracks across the country, were basing their rates on the axiom "charge all the traffic will bear."

By the early 1870s a depression was closing in on a country that had fought a costly and devastating war, that was plunged into a postwar expansion of capital investment at a faster rate than it was producing wealth, and that was still borrowing large amounts of money from European investors for its expansion. When the financial crash came in 1873, with declining prices for agricultural products, the farmers were certain that their lot was unbearable. A "consistent rebellion" began as the agricultural West and South sought economic redress. Currency reform, banking reform, regulation of railroad and grain-elevator rates, and lowering of interest charges were the major political issues. The Greenback party flourished as a result, to be followed by the rise of the Populists. The Patrons of Husbandry formed their Grange organizations that forced passage of state laws in the Middle West fixing maximum railroad rates, and in a famous decision (*Munn v. Illinois,* 1877) the United States Supreme Court upheld the doctrine that the railroads were subject to regulation in the public interest.[2]

GREELEY'S "MUGWUMP" PRESIDENTIAL RACE

In this troubled political and economic setting, the press found much significant news. And as the news principle gained ascendancy, the editorial columns showed definite signs of rebelling against unswerving loyalty to political parties and their beliefs. The way was eased by rebellion within the ranks of the political parties themselves and particularly by the emergence of a "liberal Republican" faction opposing the radical Republicans and their President, General Grant. Independence of editorial expression meant primarily the freedom to criticize the leaders and policies of the party the editor might normally support, but for some it also meant freedom to bolt the party and support a rival. Those who bolted were called "mugwumps" by their opponents.

The mugwumps of 1872 were led by a group of editors. The liberal Republicans, meeting in convention to find a suitable candidate to oppose Grant, included many editors, the most important of whom were Samuel Bowles of the *Springfield Republican,* Horace White of the *Chicago Tribune,* Murat Halstead of the *Cincinnati Commercial,* and Carl Schurz of the St. Louis *Westliche Post.* The convention ended with the selection of another famous editor, Horace Greeley, as the candidate. Greeley was also nominated by the Democrats, and thus an important segment of the Republican-aligned press found itself allied with pro-Democratic papers. But Greeley's bid for the presidency was ill-starred. Many liberals could not find their way clear to support the aging editor, and others commented cruelly on his eccentricities. Thus such critics of the Grant administration as the *New York Evening Post* and *New York Sun,* and the influential magazines *Harper's Weekly* and the *Nation,* shied away from the Greeley cause. And despite growing discontent with the radical Republicans' reconstruction policies, the administrative shortcomings of the Grant regime, and unsolved economic problems. Grant was reelected handily.

Even though the Greeley campaign had failed, the effect of the mugwump rebellion by such influential editors was a substantial gain in journalistic prestige. It added new proof that editors could shift their political positions and survive, and encouraged those newspapers that felt obliged to attack strong political groups.

SCANDALS IN GOVERNMENT

Scandals in government offer a tempting target for any editor, and the political ineptness and moral laxity that characterized the postwar years further stimulated newspapers and magazines to action. The most notorious example of corruption at the city level was in the operations of the Tweed Ring in New York City. Tammany boss William M. Tweed and his Democratic party cohorts, who milked the city of $200 million, had grown so bold and brazen by 1870 that they had listed a plasterer's pay at $50,000 a day for an entire month while constructing a courthouse. The Tweed Ring controlled some newspapers and frightened others into silence, but it met its masters in the *New York Times* and *Harper's Weekly.* The *Times,* published by George Jones and edited by Louis J. Jennings after the death of Raymond in 1869, obtained documentary proof of the Tweed Ring's thefts in 1871 and broke the astounding story. *Harper's Weekly,* ably edited by George William Curtis, provided a gallery for Thomas Nast, the great political cartoonist who used his pen and ink against Tweed in such devastating fashion that he was offered a bribe to halt his attacks. The answer was the driving of the Tweed Ring from power.[3]

The scandals that left the reputation of the Grant administration blackened were being hinted at before the 1872 presidential election, but it was not until the closing days of the campaign that the *New York Sun* publicized what became known as the Crédit Mobilier affair. When the evidence was developed fully after the election, it proved that promoters of the Union Pacific and Central Pacific railroads had developed a simple system for influencing legislators and others whose support was needed to obtain federal land grants for railroad construc-

Thomas Nast's famed Tammany Tiger cartoon in an 1871 *Harper's Weekly.*

tion. The railroad builders, operating under the name Crédit Mobilier of America, had sold stock to many public leaders, lending them the money to pay for the stock and then declaring such huge profits that the loans could be repaid in a single year. Exposure of what amounted to gifts from those seeking legislative favor ruined some politicians and cast suspicion on many more, including the prominent Republican leader James G. Blaine of Maine.

Other disclosures of weaknesses in the Grant administration came rapidly: the whiskey tax frauds in the Treasury Department, the bribing of the Secretary of War, W. W. Belknap, and the acceptance of improper gifts by Grant's private secretary. The dazed Grant was himself untouched by the scandals, but his party lost control of the House of Representatives to the Democrats in 1874, and politics became a seesaw affair. The country was entering a period of "dead center" government. For 16 of the next 22 years, control of the two houses of Congress and the presidency was split between the two major parties, so closely was the popular vote divided. Little political progress could be made in such a situation, and eventually the protective tariff became the principal issue of frustrated political aspirants who could not cope with the problems that were generating the "consistent rebellion" of the economically discontented West and South.

DANA AND THE *NEW YORK SUN*

Of the editors who worked in this turbulent postwar period, two in particular stand out as leaders. Their contributions are sharply different. In his years as editor of the *New York Sun* Charles A. Dana taught the journalism world new lessons in the art of news handling and writing. In his years as editor of the *Nation* and of the *New York Evening Post* Edwin Lawrence Godkin provided solid editorial-page leadership. With the deaths of the older New York leaders—Bennett, Greeley, Raymond, and Bryant—Dana and Godkin became the strong men who influenced the maturing of the older press.

In many respects Dana and his *Sun* represent the bridge between the older press and the new journalism that was to develop before the end of the century. A New Englander who had been attracted to the Brook Farm socialist experiment in the 1840s along with other intellectuals seeking the answer to the problems created by the industrial revolution, Dana had met Horace Greeley there. He joined Greeley's staff and became managing editor of the *Tribune* in 1849—the first American to hold such a position. When the Dana-Greeley association was broken in the early days of the Civil War as the aftermath of the *Tribune's* mistaken military predictions, Dana entered government service and emerged to struggle for a year as editor of a new Chicago paper, the *Daily Republican* (forerunner of the famous *Inter Ocean*). The newspaper venture was successful, but Dana wearied of Chicago. Returning to New York, he obtained sufficient backing to buy the *Sun,* the original penny newspaper. Its plant and 43,000 circulation were priced at $175,000 by Moses S. Beach, whose father had taken over Ben Day's paper. A career with Greeley on the *Tribune* already behind him, in 1868 Dana began a 29-year career as editor of the *Sun.*

Dana's audience consisted mainly of average New Yorkers: workers and small merchants. To them he addressed his first editorial in the *Sun,* which expressed his ideas on newspaper making. The *Sun,* he said, would present "a daily photograph of the whole world's doings in the most luminous and lively manner." Its staff would write simply and clearly as it tried to present that photograph of the life of the people of New York, as well as of the world's doings. The *Sun* would be low-priced and readable, yet it would use enterprise and money to be the best possible newspaper.

Dana insisted that the journalist must be interested in politics, economics, and government, but first of all in people. The average American, Dana knew, was hard at work, yet loved sentiment and fun and enjoyed stories reflecting a skillful touch of tenderness or wit. As one of the biographers of Dana and the *Sun* put it, Dana had "the indefinable newspaper instinct that knows when a tomcat on the steps of the City Hall is more important than a crisis in the Balkans."[4] By 1876 his circulation had tripled to 130,000.

Brilliant as the *Sun* was, however, it had serious weaknesses. Because Dana insisted on limiting its size to four pages, comprehensive coverage of significant news suffered. And the editorial page that could originate such ringing phrases as "No king, no clown, to rule this town!" to combat Tweed, and "Turn the rascals out!" to harass Grant, could also be so intellectually "smart" as to approach cynicism. Dana's fondness for wit and levity made for entertaining reading, but his cynical and sometimes perverse comments on public issues greatly weakened the character of his newspaper.

In its discussions of issues, the *Sun* became increasingly conservative, in contrast to Dana's earlier beliefs. The paper detested labor unions. It poked fun at civil-service reform advocates and others interested in good government, even though the *Sun* itself crusaded against misconduct in office. And it long advocated imperialistic schemes for the annexation of Canada, Cuba, and other neighboring areas.

GODKIN, THE *NATION*, AND THE *POST*

It remained for an English-born journalist to give the United States the vigorous and intelligent editorial leadership it needed in the postwar period. He was Edwin Lawrence Godkin, the founder of the magazine the *Nation* and successor to William Cullen Bryant as the driving spirit of the *New York Evening Post.*

Of Godkin, historian Allan Nevins has written: "Godkin showed at once a distinctive style, a refreshing penetration, and a skill in ironic analysis never before equalled in American journalism." And because this was so, philosopher William James could write: "To my generation his was certainly the towering influence in all thought concerning public affairs, and indirectly his influence has assuredly been more pervasive than that of any other writer of the generation, for he influenced other writers who never quoted him, and determined the whole current of discussion."[5] President Charles W. Eliot of Harvard University, President Daniel Coit Gilman of Johns Hopkins, James Russell Lowell, James Bryce, Charles Eliot Norton—the intellectual leaders of Godkin's generation—all publicly acknowledged the debt they owed to the pages of the *Nation.* Not, of course, that they always agreed with its editor's viewpoints.

Godkin had been a reporter and editorial writer for English newspapers and had written editorials for Henry J. Raymond's *New York Times* before deciding that the United States needed a high-grade weekly journal of opinion and literary criticism, similar to those in England. In 1865 he found the financial backing for the *Nation* and announced its aims.

The *Nation,* Godkin said, would discuss the political and economic questions of the day "with greater accuracy and moderation than are now to be found in the daily press." It would advocate "whatever in legislation or in manners seems likely to promote a more equal distribution of the fruits of progress and civilization." It would seek to better the conditions of the blacks. It would fix "public attention upon the political importance of education, and the dangers which a system like ours runs from the neglect of it in any portion of our territory." And it would print sound and impartial criticisms of books and works of art.[6]

Godkin was a mid-Victorian English liberal of the John Stuart Mill school of economic thought. Therefore, he believed that government should not intervene in economic matters. But unlike many of his time, he did believe that government should take action in social spheres. To a twentieth-century world that has used government as a regulatory force in both economic and social situations, Godkin thus appears at times to be reactionary and at other times liberal.

But in many areas, Godkin was in the forefront of progressive thought. He urged complete reconciliation with the South during the period of military rule; he was one of the earliest advocates of civil-service reform to end the spoils system; he believed in women's suffrage when it was an unpopular idea; he was a strong supporter of public education and the new land-grant universities; and, as mentioned previously, he wrote in behalf of the blacks. Above all, the *Nation* ceaselessly badgered politicians who were more interested in personal gain than in progressive improvement of government. Its influence ran far beyond its 10,000 circulation.

In 1881, Godkin moved onto a bigger but actually less influential journalistic stage. That year, Henry Villard, a Civil War correspondent who later won a fortune building railroads, purchased the *New York Evening Post,* and obtained a trio of outstanding editors for the newspaper. One was Horace White, who had edited the *Chicago Tribune* from 1866 to 1874, taking that newspaper into the liberal Republican camp for a brief period as he advocated tariff reduction, civil-service reform, and currency policies favorable to the farmers. A second was Carl Schurz, the former editor of the St. Louis *Westliche Post* who had become Secretary of the Interior in President Hayes' cabinet and who was a leading American liberal. The third was Godkin, who sold the *Nation* to Villard but continued to edit it as the weekly edition of the *Evening Post.* Within 2 years, Schurz and Godkin quarreled over Godkin's antilabor union views, and Schurz resigned, leaving Godkin in control of the *Evening Post* with White as his assistant.

With Godkin, the *Evening Post* and the *Nation* rose to new fame in the presidental election year of 1884. The contest lay between James G. Blaine, the Republican congressional leader from Maine, and Grover Cleveland, Democratic governor of New York. Godkin, declaring that Blaine was unacceptable because of the post-Civil War scandals, fought his election with all his editorial skill. As the campaign progressed, charges of immoral conduct were made against Cleveland, and emotionalism ran high. Some stalwart Republican newspapers in leading cities found themselves opposing Blaine in company with the usual dissenters: the *Evening Post,* the *New York Times,* the *Springfield Republican, Harper's Weekly,* and the *Nation.* Dana of the *Sun,* who would support neither major-party candidate, fastened on these papers the name "mugwump," indicating desertion of party regularity. The name applied particularly to the *Evening Post,* which had been Republican since the founding of the party in 1856.

The *Evening Post's* particular contribution was Godkin's famous "deadly parallel" column, in which he matched Blaine's campaign statements and congressional record against his personal associations with railroad builders and financiers. The campaign became exceedingly bitter, and it was evident that the New York State vote would decide the election. When Cleveland carried New York by 23,000 votes and became the first Democrat to win the presidency since the Civil War, many explanations were advanced. A Blaine supporter who had described the Democrats as a party of "rum, Romanism, and rebellion" received heavy blame, as did the antilabor *New York Tribune,* whose advocacy of Blaine was judged to be a handicap in the wooing of working men's votes. But Godkin asserted, with some justice, that the victory was proof of the creation of a group of independent voters who would put the public welfare ahead of party loyalty, as had the mugwump newspapers and magazines.

Godkin stood in the early 1880s as New York's leading editor primarily because of his great ability, but also because of the shortcomings of his contemporaries. After the death of Raymond, the *Times* was slowly going downhill and exhibited spirit and influence only sporadically. Dana's *Sun* was erratic, and the Bennetts' *Herald* had little editorial force. Greeley's *Tribune,* after the founding editor's death in 1872, switched position and became the voice for the dominant conservative wing of the Republican party. The *Tribune*'s new editor was a famous journalistic figure, Whitelaw Reid, but his editorial stand lacked the qualities of independence shown by an increasing number of editors. While Godkin was urging reconciliation with the South, the *Tribune* was waving the bloody shirt as late as 1880 to preserve Republican supremacy. Godkin was for tariff reform; the *Tribune,* for high tariffs and protection of the industrial interests of the expanding capitalism. Godkin long favored civil-service reform, which found favor with the Republican leadership only after the assassination of President James A. Garfield. And the *Tribune* more than matched Godkin's opposition to labor unions, fighting a printers' strike against itself for 15 years.[7] Still, the *Tribune*'s standards of news coverage and presentation were such that it was a formidable competitor for the readership of those whom the *Evening Post* called the "gentlemen and scholars."

Unfortunately, Godkin was not a newspaperman despite his editorial genius. He cared little for the news policies of the *Evening Post,* beyond his specialized interests. He disliked sentiment and color in the news, and he would have liked to have kept all news of crime and violence out the paper's columns. Whatever merit there was to his viewpoints, they put the *Evening Post* at a serious disadvantage in the competition for circulation, and the paper never attained the readership its editorial leadership deserved.

Godkin retired as editor of the *Evening Post* and the *Nation* in 1899. He died in 1902. When Henry Villard died in 1900, his son, Oswald Garrison Villard, became publisher and editorial leader of the two publications. They continued to be fighting liberal organs.[8]

HENRY WATTERSON AND THE *COURIER-JOURNAL*

Other strong editorial voices were raised outside New York during the period of Godkin's dominance. The most notable were those of Henry Watterson of the *Louisville Courier-Journal* and Harvey W. Scott of the *Oregonian* in Portland. Both enjoyed long careers that began at the close of the Civil War and continued until World War I, but both belong primarily in this transitional period of journalism history. Arthur Krock, an associate of Watterson on the *Courier-Journal* staff before becoming a *New York Times* fixture, offers one reason for setting Watterson apart from later editors: " . . . he was the last of those editors who wrote with the power of ownership."[9] The same was true of Scott. Other editors, like Godkin, exercised free rein because of their relationships to the owners of their papers, and they have continued to do so since, but admittedly with increasing difficulty as the newspaper became a corporate institution.

Watterson was editor of the *Courier-Journal* for 50 years, and his personality did much to make the newspaper one of the foremost in the country. He was a colorful representative of the era of personal journalism who loved to engage in editorial-page duels with other editors. One of his first foes was Dana, and he lived to banter with the editors of another journalistic generation in the twentieth century. He himself said that he belonged to the era of "the personal, one-man papers—rather blatant, but independent."[10]

Watterson had varied youthful ambitions: to be a great historian, a great dramatist, a great novelist, a great musician. He came no closer to those dreams than writing a rejected novel and serving as a music critic in New York, but his catholic interests served in time to make him a versatile and engaging writer of editorials. He was an editorial writer in Washington when the Civil War began, and he cast his lot with the South, editing a Tennessee newspaper named the *Rebel.* After stints on newspapers in Cincinnati, Atlanta, and Nashville, at the age of 28 Watterson found his lifetime work in Louisville.

There Walter N. Haldeman, editor of the *Courier,* was in the process of consolidating the *Journal* and the *Democrat* with his newspaper, and the editorship and part ownership of the new *Courier-Journal* went to Watterson. The year was 1868. Watterson, who despite his work for the Southern cause had believed secession to be wrong, raised his voice in behalf of reconciliation of the North and South and gave advice freely to both sections. He told the North that military rule should be relaxed, and he was listened to because he also had sympathy for the blacks. He told the South that Lincoln was a great man and that much of its misery had come about as a result of his assassination. And the South listened, because Watterson was a Southerner of good family, not a reforming Yankee. Soon the *Courier-Journal* editorial columns, and particularly its weekly edition, won a position as a leading voice of the new South.

HARVEY SCOTT AND THE *OREGONIAN*

In the Far West, another voice was raised by an editor whose intellectual powers and forceful writing brought him attention as the leading spokesperson of his area. He was Harvey W. Scott, who for 45 years edited the *Oregonian* in Portland. The *Oregonian,* founded in 1850 in a village near the junction of the Willamette and Columbia Rivers, grew with the community. Scott gave up a law career to become its editor in 1865, and in 1877 he and Henry L. Pittock became the owners.[11]

Like Godkin, Scott was scholarly and forceful in his expression of opinion, but like Godkin, too, he lacked Watterson's human touch. There was one major reason why Scott's editorials were widely read and quoted: He had the ability to grapple with complex problems that many an editor shied away from and to present new viewpoints originating in his own reasoning and analysis. His range of information seemed unlimited, and he used this resource as he thought an editor should, to guide public opinion in the public interest. The *Oregonian* was Republican by choice, but Scott wrote as an independent editor, taking his stand on the basis of his conception of the public good. An editor with Scott's abilities is rare in any peiod, and his fame spread from the home city in which he was a leading figure as the *Oregonian* won statewide circulation and its editorial voice became nationally recognized.

Dana, Godkin, Watterson, and Scott—particularly the latter two—lived through the enormous changes that were occurring in American life as the Industrial Revolution hit full stride. They were aware of change, and accepted it, but their journalistic roles were more of the older order than of the new. There were others among their contemporaries who might well be named, but these were the leaders and the symbols of a transitional era. They and their fellow workers contributed new strengths to American journalism as it approached the "watershed of the nineties."

NOTES

1. Henry Steele Commager, *The American Mind* (New Haven: Yale University Press, 1950), p. 41.

2. This is a brief summary of the farmers' problems, which are fully analyzed in such studies as John D. Hicks, *The Populist Revolt* (Minneapolis: University of Minnesota Press, 1931), and Solon J. Buck, *The Granger Movement* (Cambridge, Mass.: Harvard University Press, 1913).

3. Fuller details are given in Gustavus Myers, *The History of Tammany Hall* (New York: Boni and Liveright, 1917).

4. Frank M. O'Brien, *The Story of the Sun* (New York: George H. Doran Company, 1918), p. 231. New edition (Appleton-Century-Crofts, 1928), p. 151.

5. As quoted in Allan Nevins, *American Press Opinion* (New York: Heath, 1928), p. 299.

6. Godkin's full statement of purpose is found in Rollo Ogden, *Life and Letters of Edwin Lawrence Godkin*, I (New York: Macmillan, 1907), pp. 237–38.

7. As previously noted, the *New York Tribune*'s founder, Horace Greeley, had been the first president of New York City's Typographical Union No. 6, founded in 1850.

8. The younger Villard sold the *Evening Post* in 1918 but remained at the helm of the *Nation* until 1933.

9. Arthur Krock, ed., *The Editorials of Henry Watterson* (New York: Doran, 1923), p. 15.

10. Tom Wallace, "There Were Giants in Those Days," *Saturday Evening Post*, August 6, 1938 (reprinted in John E. Drewry, ed., *Post Biographies of Famous Journalists*).

11. The Scott and Pittock family heirs retained control of the *Oregonian* until 1950, when the 100-year-old paper was sold to Samuel I. Newhouse. See the *Oregonian*, December 11, 1950.

ANNOTATED BIBLIOGRAPHY

Books

BAEHR, HARRY W., JR., *The New York Tribune Since the Civil War.* New York: Dodd, Mead, 1936. One of the better histories of newspapers.

Casual Essays of The Sun. New York: R. G. Cooke, 1905. A collection of *Sun* editorials including "Dear Virginia."

DUNCAN, BINGHAM, *Whitelaw Reid: Journalist,*

Politician, Diplomat. Athens, Ga.: University of Georgia Press, 1975. A leading conservative voice at the *New York Tribune.*

FUESS, CLAUDE M., *Carl Schurz.* New York: Dodd, Mead, 1932. A biography of the famous liberal, whose own *Reminiscences* (1907) are rewarding reading.

HICKS, JOHN D., *The American Nation.* Boston: Houghton Mifflin, 1964. A standard text for American history since 1865.

JOSEPHSON, MATTHEW, *The Robber Barons.* New York: Harcourt Brace Jovanovich, 1934. A scathing description of the low state of public morality after the Civil War, focusing particularly on corruption in railroad building. *The Politicos* (1938) is a companion volume.

KELLER, MORTON, *The Art and Politics of Thomas Nast.* New York: Oxford University Press, 1968. A beautifully printed, illustrated, and researched story of the great cartoonist.

KROCK, ARTHUR, ed., *The Editorials of Henry Watterson.* New York: George H. Doran Company, 1923. Excellent preface.

LOGSDON, JOSEPH, *Horace White, Nineteenth Century Liberal.* Westport, Conn.: Greenwood Publishing, 1971. Discusses an editor of the *Chicago Tribune* and owner of the *New York Evening Post* and the *Nation.*

NEVINS, ALLAN, *The Emergence of Modern America, 1865–1878,* A History of American Life, Volume VIII. New York: Macmillan, 1927. A rich social history, whose extensive documentation is accompanied by highly skillful writing.

———, *The Evening Post: A Century of Journalism.* New York: Boni and Liveright, 1922. The Godkin and other eras are presented against a general social and political background.

NYE, RUSSEL B., *Midwestern Progressive Politics; a Historical Study of Its Origins and Development, 1870–1950.* East Lansing: Michigan State College Press, 1951. A comprehensive survey. For more specialized studies, see Solon J. Buck, *The Granger Movement* (Cambridge, Mass.: Harvard University Press, 1913), and John D. Hicks, *The Populist Revolt* (Minneapolis: University of Minnesota Press, 1931).

O'BRIEN, FRANK M., *The Story of The Sun.* New York: Goerge H. Doran Company, 1918. (Revised. New York: Appleton-Century-Crofts, 1928.) One of the most readable histories.

OGDEN, ROLLO, *Life and Letters of Edwin Lawrence Godkin.* New York: Macmillan, 1907. The standard biography.

PAINE, ALBERT BIGELOW, *Th. Nast, His Period and His Pictures.* New York: Macmillan, 1904. Well-illustrated with Nast's famous cartoons.

RHODES, JAMES FORD, *A History of the United States Since the Compromise of 1850.* New York: Macmillan, 1892–1906. A nine-volume political history ending with the turn of the century, written with conspicuous success by a conservative businessman turned scholar.

STAMPP, KENNETH M., *The Era of Reconstruction, 1865–1877.* New York: Knopf, 1965. New points of view admirably presented by consensus school revisionist.

STONE, CANDACE, *Dana and the Sun.* New York: Dodd, Mead, 1938. The top-ranking biography of Dana, critical in tone.

WALL, JOSEPH F., *Henry Watterson: Reconstructed Rebel.* New York: Oxford University Press, 1956. A well-documented study.

WATTERSON, HENRY, *"Marse Henry"; An Autobiography.* New York: George H. Doran Company, 1919. The Louisville editor's own pungent story.

WISH, HARVEY, *Society and Thought in Modern America.* New York: Longmans, Green, 1962. The second volume in Wish's social and intellectual history, beginning with 1865.

WOODWARD, C. VANN, *Origins of the New South, 1877–1913.* Baton Rouge: Louisiana State University Press, 1951. Prize-winning study of the South's emergence from the Civil War.

Periodicals and Monographs

DOWNEY, MATTHEW T., "Horace Greeley and the Politicians," *Journal of American History,* LIII (March 1967), 727. Liberal Republican convention of 1872.

LEITER, KELLY, "U.S. Grant and the *Chicago Tribune,*" *Journalism Quarterly,* XLVII (Spring 1970), 71. Based on his Ph.D. thesis, Southern Illinois University, 1969.

MITCHELL, EDWARD P., "The Newspaperman's Newspaper," *Scribner's,* LXXVI (August 1924), 149. A vivid portrait of Dana and his *Sun* by a longtime *Sun* editor.

MURRAY, RANDALL L., "Edwin Lawrence Godkin: Unbending Editor in Times of Change," *Journalism History,* I (Autumn 1974), 77. Godkin laments late 1880s social change.

NEVINS, ALLAN, "E. L. Godkin: Victorian Liberal," *Nation,* CLXXI (July 22, 1950), 76. An interpretative essay, followed by a study, written by Lewis Gannett, of Oswald Garrison Villard's editorship.

PLUMMER, L. NIEL, "Henry Watterson's Editorial Style: An Interpretative Analysis," *Journalism Quarterly,* XXIII (March 1946), 58.

PRINGLE, HENRY F., "Godkin of 'The Post,'" *Scribner's* XCVI (December 1934), 327. A well-balanced article by a newspaperman turned biographer. Reprinted in Ford and Emery, *Highlights in the History of the American Press.*

———, "Kentucky Bourbon—Marse Henry Watterson," *Scribner's,* XCVII (January 1935), 10. Reprinted in Ford and Emery, *Highlights in the History of the American Press.*

Quarterly of the Oregon Historical Society, XIV, No. 2 (June 1913). An issue devoted to Harvey W. Scott, editor of the *Oregonian.*

THORP, ROBERT K., "'Marse Henry' and the Negro: A New Perspective," *Journalism Quarterly,* XLVI (Autumn 1969), 467. It was not as Marse Henry remembered it; he was scarcely their champion.

TURNBULL, GEORGE, "The Schoolmaster of the Oregon Press," *Journalism Quarterly,* XV (December 1938), 359. A study of the influence of Harvey W. Scott by the author of the *History of Oregon Newspapers* (1939).

WILEY, BONNIE, "History of the Portland *Oregonian,*" Ph.D. thesis, Southern Illinois University, 1965. From Harvey Scott to Samuel Newhouse, 1850 to 1965.

TREFOUSSE, HANS L., *Carl Schurz, A Biography.* Knoxville: University of Tennessee Press, 1982. Fresh biographical study; Schurz viewed as ethnic mediator.

"Shantytown," first halftone published in a U.S. newspaper, 1880 (see page 273).

FRANK LESLIE'S ILLUSTRATED NEWSPAPER

Entered according to Act of Congress in the year 1857, by Frank Leslie, in the Clerk's Office of the District Court for the Southern District of New York. (Copyrighted May 10, 1858.)

No. 128 — Vol. V.] NEW YORK, SATURDAY, MAY 15, 1858. [Price 6 Cents.

OUR EXPOSURE OF THE MILK TRADE OF NEW YORK AND BROOKLYN.

From a hundred sources we are receiving, day by day, thanks for our public spirit and fearless exposure of a nefarious and revolting trade, and good wishes and prayers for the ultimate and speedy success of our undertaking.

We feel sincerely gratified and deeply grateful for the outside encouragement we receive; it will move us to new exerti-ns, for we feel that we have obtained the ear of the public; that its sympathies and hopes are with us, and armed with this assurance we feel our power equal to the emergency. That our blows have been dealt strongly and truly we have ample evidence. Our exposure has not only broken up all the milk routes we have published, but one whose name we were fortunately enabled to give, is selling off his swill milk cows. His stable is broken up, his swill trade gone, and mark the consequence—he has contracted with the country dairies for the milk he requires for his customers. Is not the good work begun? May we not hope for the future?

An early crusade was the 1858 "swill milk" campaign in *Frank Leslie's Illustrated Newspaper.*

15
A Revolution in National Life

The newspaper has a history; but it has, likewise, a natural history. The press, as it exists, is not, as our moralists sometimes seem to assume, the wilful product of any little group of living men. On the contrary, it is the outcome of a historic process. . . .
—Robert E. Park

The journalism of Dana and Godkin was the product of an American society in transition; what was happening to the national life for the first dozen years after the close of the War Between the States could be called a transition. But then, the swelling tide of economic and social change brought not transition but revolution.

In journalism, as in all other aspects of American life, the result was an emergence of new concepts and practices more akin to the twentieth century than to the immediate past. New leaders were to revolutionize the newspaper and the magazine by responding to the abruptly changed environment rather than by clinging to the older patterns. The contrast, by the 1890s, between Dana's cranky, change-resisting journalism and that of the dynamic symbol of the new order—Joseph Pulitzer—was glaring indeed. It was no more glaring, however, than the differences that had developed in literature, in science, in political and economic thought, in business and industry, in the way Americans lived and worked.

AN INDUSTRIAL ECONOMY

What was happening? Industrialization was advancing on a major scale: mechanization of production processes, the rise of the city, vast expansion of communication facilities, the coming of the age of steel, the harnessing of electricity for light and power, and a host of inventions and new businesses.

This was the true nationalization of the United States, the achievement of economic and social interdependence.[1] National growth and increased wealth meant cultural progress in literature, science, and the social sciences. But the wealth was not equally distributed, and there was sharp questioning of the theory of individualism that permitted unrestrained exploitation, enormous concentrations of wealth and economic power, and the many injustices of a materialistic-minded age. Political unrest, the rise of labor unions, and demands for economic and social reform thus were added to the scene.

America was a rich continent for the aggressive and the ingenious to master. Between 1865 and 1880 the national wealth doubled, and by 1900 it had doubled again. The population doubled in those 35 years. The nation's iron ore, its oil, its lumber, and its western agricultural lands were sources of yet untapped wealth. Its people, who by and large admired the successful enterprisers, eagerly provided investment and speculative capital. Only when it became clear that the division of the spoils had been in favor of a few to the detriment of the many did the protests take effect. In the meantime, the patterns had been set. The dynamic capitalism of an expanding America, seizing on unparalleled natural resources and utilizing the new machines of the Industrial Revolution, had transformed the national economy.

Following are some of the figures that show what was happening to the United States. Total manufacturing production increased sevenfold between the end of the Civil War and 1900: Using a base figure of 100 for the years 1909 to 1913, the index figure for 1865 was 8.5; in 1880 it was 27, and by 1900 it was 61.[2] There were 140,000 industries of all types in 1860. By 1880 there were 250,000, and by 1900 the number was over 500,000. The number of persons employed in those industries doubled in each of the 20-year periods. The percentage of the labor force engaged in nonagricultural work was 41 percent in 1860, 50 percent in 1880, and 62 percent in 1900. Estimated national wealth in 1865 was $20 billion. By 1880 it was $43 billion, and by 1900 the figure was $88 billion. Bank deposits tripled between 1865 and 1880, then quadrupled in the next 20 years.

A look at some production figures tells a similar story. The rate of increase was greatest in the 20 years from 1880 to 1900. Coal and pig-iron production quadrupled; copper smelters scored a tenfold increase; steel and cement production increased eight times. Petroleum output more than doubled. Although the production totals continued to climb steadily after 1900, the rate of increase declined, except in the case of petroleum.

CAPTAINS OF BIG BUSINESS

Familiar symbols of this new economic order are John D. Rockefeller and the oil monopoly, and Andrew Carnegie and the steel combine. But similar concentrations of wealth and business control developed throughout American industry and trade. Cornelius Vanderbilt, Jay Gould, and J. Pierpont Morgan in finance, Leland Stanford, Collis P. Huntington, James J. Hill, and George Pullman in railroading; C. C. Washburn and Charles A. Pillsbury in the milling industry that centered in Minneapolis as the great plains opened; Philip D. Armour and Gustavus F. Swift in the meat-packing industry that grew in Chicago and Kansas City as cattle raising became big business; the makers of machine-sewed shoes, ready-made clothes, packaged foods, watches, cameras, farm machinery, and hardware; the timber owners, the mining kings—all rose to dominate the American scene in the late nineteenth century.

The captains of industry and finance obtained power through a variety of means. Some gained control of large segments of natural resources. A few held patents on basic inventions. Others, of whom Rockefeller was the most noted, won supremacy in part through manipulation of transportation rates and ruthless competitive tactics. Some were lucky in the world of financial speculation. Most important, the Rockefellers and the Carnegies usually were successful because they had, or could hire, the brains necessary to create a new manufacturing or financial empire.

But, as usual, there was a flaw in the new order. As the machine revolutionized the American economy, it brought with it the threat of overproduction and disastrous competition among the new producers. The dislocation of labor that resulted and the bankrupting of weaker businesses also promoted economic instability. The captains of industry cast about for ways of avoiding the industrial and financial panics that threatened the strong as well as the weak.

One effort to overcome these dangers took the form of the pool agreement. Direct competitors sought by voluntary secret agreement to limit industrywide production, to allocate production quotas, and to stabilize prices. The trouble was that in times of distress the rule quickly became "every man for himself."

A more successful form of industry control was the trust, developed by the Standard Oil group around 1880. By this method the shareholders in the original companies assigned their capital stock to a board of trustees and received trust certificates in return. The trustees thus obtained legal control of the individual units. They could decide production quotas, set selling prices, and eliminate competition.

Hosts of other industries followed the lead of the oil companies before 1890. Sugar, salt, whiskey, rope, lead, tin plate, crackers, matches, newsprint, fence wire, and many other products fell under near monopolistic control. The number of producing companies declined sharply in such fields as woolen goods, iron and steel, leather, and farm machinery. Congress passed the Sherman Anti-Trust Act of 1890 in an attempt to restore open competition, but the end result was hardly satisfactory to opponents of monopoly. The sugar trust simply became an incorporated company under the laws of New Jersey, and the Standard Oil group developed the holding-company technique. The amalgamation of many businesses now took the form of a single great corporation, whether in manufacturing, in railroading, or in mining and cattle raising.

THE RISE OF THE CITY

The industrial concentration that was maturing between 1880 and 1900 was of vital significance, but it was only a part of the enormous change in American life. Mechanization, industrialization, and urbanization brought swift and extensive social, cultural, and political developments. People were being uprooted physically and mentally by the effects of the economic revolution, and in the new environment no social institution could remain static. Even a brief examination of the character of this new environment will indicate the basic causes of the tremendous changes that developed in the daily newspapers of American cities by the 1880s.

Arthur M. Schlesinger, Sr., chose the phrase "the rise of the city" to characterize the period from 1878 to 1898.[3] Census figures show that the number of American towns and cities of 8000 or more population doubled between 1880 and 1900. The total population of those urban places more than doubled, jumping from some 11 million to 25 million. In 1880 there were 50 million Americans, of whom 22.7 percent were living in towns and cities of more than 8000. By 1900 that figure had risen to 32.9 percent of a total population of 76 million.

The most rapid gain in urbanization occurred during the 10 years between 1880 and 1890, which were the years of greatest ferment in the daily newspaper business. The rise of the city was particularly evident in the Northeastern industrial states, where urban centers now predominated over declining rural areas, and in the older states of the Middle West. New York City jumped in population from a million to a million and a half during the decade. Chicago, the rail and trade center of inland America, doubled its size, passing the million mark in 1890 to become the nation's second city. Next in line were Philadelphia, at a million; Brooklyn, at 800,000; and Boston, Baltimore, and St. Louis, in the half-million class. Altogether there were fifty-eight cities with more than 50,000 population in 1890; 80 percent of them were in the East and Middle West, and 50 percent of them were in the five states of New York, Pennsylvania, Massachusetts, New Jersey, and Ohio.

Into these cities was pouring an ever-rising tide of immigration, which brought new blood and new problems for American society. Again the decade of 1880 to 1890 stands out, since in those 10 years more than 5 million immigrants came to America, double the number for any preceding decade. All told, approximately 9 million foreign-born were added to the population in the 20 years between 1880 and 1900, as many as had come during the 40 years preceding 1880. As a result, the newspapers of New York City in 1890 were serving a population that was 80 percent foreign-born or of foreign parentage, and as might be expected, the character of some of the newspapers changed. Other American cities had from 25 percent to 40 percent foreign-born residents. To the older Irish, British, and German streams of migration were added great numbers of Scandinavians, Poles, French-Canadians, Italians, Russians, and Hungarians. Of these, particularly the Germans and the Scandinavians migrated to the Middle West, while the other groups tended to remain in the Atlantic states.

The rise of the city meant a quickening of material progress, reflected first in the life of the city dweller and transmitted gradually to the rest of the country. The new American cities hastened the installation of water and sewage systems in the years following the Civil War. They paved their streets with asphalt and bricks, and they bridged their rivers with steel structures patterned after the Roeblings' famed Brooklyn Bridge of 1883. A ten-story Chicago building, constructed around a steel and iron skeleton in 1885, heralded the coming of the skyscraper.

Electricity was becoming a great new servant, both as a source of power for industry and transportation and as a source of light. American cities had barely begun to install arc lights in 1879 when Thomas A. Edison invented a practicable incandescent bulb. When the current flowed out from his Pearl Street generating station in 1882 to light the Stock Exchange and the offices of the *New York Times* and *New York Herald,* a new era in living had begun. By 1898 there were nearly 2800 central electric power stations in the country, as businesses and homes were lighted, electric elevators were installed in the new tall buildings, and electric motors became widely used in industry.

THE COMMUNICATIONS NETWORK

America was being tied together by its industrial revolution, and its communications network kept pace with the sense of urgency that was characteristic of the new order. The telephone, invented by Alexander Graham Bell in the 1870s, already had one user for every thousand persons in 1880. By 1900 there was one telephone for each hundred. Intercity lines multiplied during the 1880s, until by 1900 the Bell System covered the country. Western Union quadrupled its telegraph lines between 1880 and 1900. The railroads, with 93,000 miles of track in 1880, reached a near-saturation point of 193,000 miles by 1900. The federal postal service, still the primary means of communication, greatly extended its free carrier service in cities during the two decades and instituted free rural delivery in 1897. Congress, by clearly defining second-class matter in the Postal Act of 1879 and by providing a 1-cent-a-pound rate for newspapers and magazines in 1885, opened the way for low-cost delivery of publications. In business offices the introduction of the typewriter and adding machine speeded the work pace and simplified the handling of increased correspondence and records.

THE EXPANSION OF NEWSPAPERS

The most striking evidence of what was happening to the newspaper is obvious from a bare statistical summary. Between 1870 and 1900, the United States doubled its population and tripled the number of its urban residents. During the same 30 years the number of daily newspapers quadrupled and the number of copies sold each day increased almost sixfold. Both in numbers and in total circulation the daily newspaper was rising even more rapidly than the city that spawned it. The number of English-language, general-circulation dailies increased from 489 in 1870 to 1967 in 1900. Circulation totals for all daily publications rose from 2.6 million copies in 1870 to 15 million in 1900.[4] A similar advance was being made by weekly newspapers, which served mainly the small towns and rural areas, but also the suburbs and sections of the cities. Between 1870 and 1900, the number of weekly publications tripled, increasing from approximately 4000 to more than 12,000. The weeklies, however, still represented personal journalistic ventures, and the revolution in newspaper methods was taking place at the big-city daily level.

There were many less tangible reasons why the newspaper was making such tremendous strides as an American social institution. The forces of social and economic interdependence, products of industrialization and urbanization, played a leading part in the creation of the lusty "new journalism." The peoples of the cities, being molded together as economic and cultural units, increasingly turned to the daily newspapers for the story of their urban life and their common interests. At the same time the country itself was being rapidly unified by the rush toward economic interdependence. Improved communications facilities were a manifestation of this nationalizing influence that pervaded all American life. And again, the daily newspaper was the chronicler of the national scene, the interpreter of the new environment. The city reader, whether seated in new-found comfort on a streetcar or in a better-lighted home, was the eager customer of the publisher who met successfully the new challenge to journalism.

ADVANCES IN EDUCATION

As American social and economic life became more complex and as the national wealth accumulated, many cultural advances were possible that in turn promoted new interest in the newspaper. The cities, with their concentrated populations and earning capacities, naturally led in expansion of social and intellectual activity. But they also set the pace for a nationalized cultural development. The bookstores, libraries, art galleries, museums, theaters, opera houses, churches, retail stores, schools, and newspapers that brought higher standards in the cities stimulated the interests and the desires of the entire country. Progress in education, the result of this general thirst for knowledge and a better life, was particularly important to the expansion of the mass media: newspapers, magazines, books. The percentage of children attending public schools in the United States rose from 57 percent to 72 percent between 1870 and 1900, and illiteracy declined from 20 percent to 10.7 percent of the population. The number of high schools jumped from approximately 100 in 1860 to 800 by 1880, and then skyrocketed to 6000 by 1900.

At higher educational levels, the growth of state universities and private colleges financed by America's newly wealthy resulted in notable advances in the social sciences, as well as progress in the natural and physical sciences and the humanities. Federal land subsidies provided by the Morrill Act of 1862 encouraged the founding and expansion of state universities, particularly in the Middle West and West, where such state-supported universities as Wisconsin, California, Minnesota, and Illinois began to flourish. The private colleges and universities gained in numbers and influence with the founding of Cornell University in 1865 by Ezra Cornell, whose millions came from the electric telegraph; of Johns Hopkins University in 1876 by a Baltimore merchant; of Leland Stanford University in 1885 by a California railroad and business man; of the University of Chicago in 1892 by John D. Rockefeller's benefaction. Johns Hopkins, by emphasizing the role of research in higher education, and Harvard, by giving its students an elective choice of courses, set new patterns for the universities. And university presidents such as Charles W. Eliot of Harvard, Daniel Coit Gilman of Johns Hopkins, and Andrew D. White of Cornell gave effective leadership. No longer was it necessary for Americans interested in scholarly pursuits to go abroad, and the number of graduate students in the United States increased from 400 in 1880 to some 5600 in 1900. Nor were women ignored in the new spread of education. The state universities became coeducational institutions; Smith College was founded in 1875, and was soon followed by Bryn Mawr and Radcliffe, fruits of the women's suffrage movement.

NEW SOCIOECONOMIC PHILOSOPHIES

The scholars of the universities and other men and women whose intellectual and cultural achievements were supported by the new wealth of the nation made great advances in the years between 1880 and 1900. Most importantly, they challenged the socioeconomic philosophies that had developed in nineteenth-century society and suggested new concepts better fitted to the revolutionized character of American life. They organized areas of knowledge needed if the country was to understand its problems and cope with them, and in doing so they laid the groundwork for the vast growth of research and interpretation in the twentieth century.[5]

A socioeconomic theory of individualism had been well developed by 1880 to bolster the argument that government should not interfere in economic affairs. The individual, this school of thought declared, supplies the enterprise that makes possible industrial progress, wealth, and national power. Therefore government should do nothing that would adversely affect individual economic enterprise. Government's function, ran the argument, is to provide an orderly society in which the individual is protected as he or she fulfills his or her destiny.

Powerful support for the theory of individualism was drawn from the work of the English scientist Charles Darwin, who published his *Origin of Species* in 1859 and his *The Descent of Man* in 1871. Darwin's emphasis on the struggle for individual existence in the process of evolution fitted nicely into the pattern. Another major influence on American thinking came from the writings of the English philosopher, Herbert Spencer. The Spencerian doctrine declared that the ultimate achievement of a perfect society would be the result of a natural process—an inevitable development that people themselves should not attempt to hasten or to alter. In the United States, sociologist William Graham Sumner, historian John Fiske, and political scientist John W. Burgess shaped their teaching and writing to conform with Social Darwinism and Spencer's ideas of individualism. The influence of this socioeconomic doctrine became so strong, particularly in the rendering of Supreme Court decisions nullifying reform legislation, that Justice Oliver Wendell Holmes was led to protest that Spencer's *Social Statics* was not part of the Constitution.[6]

Those who decried the negativism of this theory of individualism were being heard by the 1880s. They contended that individuals did have the ability to control their own destinies, and to shape their economic and political actions as the general welfare of society might require. Unrestricted exercise of individual power by some only brings misery and poverty to others, and the outcome is not national strength but national weakness, said this school of thought. True progress, they said, depends on cooperation and the use of government's powers in the common good.

A sociologist, Lester Ward, who published the first volume of his *Dynamic Sociology* in 1883, provided logical arguments for the belief that government should be regarded as a positive force and that it should actively seek ways of achieving social improvement. Economist Richard T. Ely attacked the pat theories of the laissez-faire advocates, theories that he and other economics professors pointed out as not conforming to the facts of industrial life. Ely's *Socialism, Its Nature, Strength and Weakness,* published in 1894, made definite proposals for reasonable reform legislation. Economist Thorstein Veblen compared the theories of economic individualists with the actual practices of industrial capitalism and voiced his bitter protest in 1899 with his *Theory of the Leisure Class.* Henry George assailed the unearned increment of wealth through land ownership in his *Progress and Poverty* (1879), and Henry Demarest Lloyd denounced the oil monopoly in *Wealth against Commonwealth* (1894), an effective plea for socioeconomic cooperation.

Newspaper editors Dana, Godkin, and Reid, as we have observed, were supporters of the theory of individualism and opposed government interference in economic spheres. One might expect, in light of what was happening, that other editors would appear who would support the principles of social cooperation and the use of governmental power to regulate economic life. And, indeed, one of the characteristics of the "new journalism" came to be the expression of editorial-page support for the common people. What publishers and editors like Joseph Pulitzer and E. W. Scripps represented in the field of journalism was only an expression of a larger movement in American thought and life.

ADVANCES IN KNOWLEDGE

Those who thus argued directly with the supporters of individualism were aided by those whose contributions to knowledge widened the country's understanding of its history, its government, and human thought and action. The period of the 1880s and 1890s was one of intense activity in study and publication, and in every field there were major achievements that helped Americans to meet the challenge of economic and social change.

Historians broke new ground by studying and writing about social and economic history, as well as politics. John Bach McMaster pointed the way by using newspapers as source materials for his significantly titled *History of the People of the United States,* begun in 1883. Henry Adams produced his brilliant history of the Jefferson and Madison administrations in 1889, and James Ford Rhodes began publication of his *History of the United States* in 1892. Frederick Jackson Turner's famous essay on the "Significance of the Frontier in American History" appeared in 1893 and fostered a whole new school of historical interpretation. Colonial history was being rewritten by people with an understanding of economic and social conditions of the early American period.

The landmark for this period in the field of government and political science was James Bryce's *American Commonwealth,* in which the talented English writer gave to the United States a description of its new environment. The same year, 1888, Frank W. Taussig wrote his *Tariff History of the United States.* Woodrow Wilson's *Congressional Government* appeared in 1885, and by 1903 Charles E. Merriam had completed his *History of American Political Theories.*

The list of authors and books could be extended: anthropologist Lewis Henry Morgan's *Ancient Society* (1877); philosopher William James' *Principles of Psychology* (1890); philosopher Josiah Royce's *The Spirit of Modern Philosophy* (1892) and *The World and the Individual* (1900); historian Brooks Adams' *The Law of Civilization and Decay* (1895); educator John Dewey's *School and Society* (1899); and Oliver Wendell Holmes' *The Common Law* (1881).

Literature offered Henry James' *Portrait of a Lady* (1881); Samuel Clemens' *Life on the Mississippi* (1883) and *Huckleberry Finn* (1885); and William Dean Howells' *The Rise of Silas Lapham* (1885), an early example of the rise of realism in American literature. In the 1890s, poets Emily Dickinson and Edwin Arlington Robinson and novelists Stephen Crane and Hamlin Garland were making major contributions, while such realistic writers as Theodore Dreiser and Frank Norris were on the verge of fame.

Earlier, women novelists such as Susan B. Warner had discovered a huge audience. Warner's *The Wide, Wide World* paved the way for later best-selling books. *The Curse of Clifton* by Mrs. E. D. E. N. Southworth, *Tempest and Sunshine* by Mary J. Holmes, and *The Lamplighter* by Maria S. Cummins were enormously popular. By the 1880s the domestic novel was in great demand.

Nor was this great cultural stirring and extension of factual information limited to an intellectual class. Millions shared in the new knowledge through the chautauquas and public study courses that became of major importance as means of adult education toward the close of the century. The world fairs and expositions that caught America's fancy in this period were another means of mass education. At the Philadelphia Centennial of 1876 and Chicago's Columbian Exposition of 1893, millions of Americans viewed the material and artistic achievements of their generation. Free public libraries, spreading across the country after 1880, found their great benefactor in Andrew Carnegie. In these libraries were available the literary triumphs and the popular writings of American and British authors.

INFLUENCE OF MAGAZINES

Magazines came to have increasing influence on American life. Earlier ventures like the *North American Review* (1815) and the *Knickerbocker,* a more popular magazine published from 1833 to 1865, had been eclipsed by *Harper's Monthly,* begun in 1850 by the New York book publishing firm. *Harper's* introduced extensive woodcut illustrations, published the writings of leading English and American authors, and ran up a world-record circulation of 200,000 before the Civil War. Two women's magazines, *Godey's Lady's Book* and *Peterson's,* began their careers in 1830 and 1842, respectively, and offered hand-colored engravings of fashions and fiction stories to more than 150,000 readers each by the 1850s.

In 1881, the *Century* joined *Harper's* in the highly literary and artistic class of magazines. *Scribner's* made it a trio in 1886. Unillustrated, but of equal literary quality, was the *Atlantic Monthly,* which was begun in 1857 and specialized in publishing the writings of the New England authors. In the weekly field were two illustrated periodicals, *Frank Leslie's Illustrated Newspaper* (1855) and *Harper's Weekly* (1857). The latter exercised strong influence in public affairs, along with E. L. Godkin's weekly, the *Nation* (1865). In addition, the *Independent* (1848), the *North American Review,* and such newcomers as the *Forum* (1886), the *Arena* (1889), and the *Outlook* (1893) all discussed the new political and social environment. The *Literary Digest* began summarizing contemporary editorial opinion in 1890.

Coming into the field were publications that depended on humor, cartoons, and political satire. *Puck* (1877) featured Joseph Keppler's dynamic color cartoons. The others were *Judge* (1881) and *Life* (1883), famed for its publication of the "Gibson girl" drawings of Charles Dana Gibson. In the children's magazine competition, *Youth's Companion* (1827) was joined by *St. Nicholas* (1873).

Helped by the cheap postage rates established by Congress under its 1879 act, some new leaders struck out in the 1880s for the mass readership that still awaited American magazine publishers. One was Cyrus H. K. Curtis, who founded the *Ladies' Home Journal* in 1883 and, with Edward W. Bok as his editor, soon won a half-million circulation. Curtis bought the *Saturday Evening Post* in 1897 and with editor George Horace Lorimer quickly made it a leader in the low-cost weekly field, which *Collier's* entered in 1888. The older high-quality monthlies found stiff competition from three low-priced popular magazines: *Munsey's,* begun in 1889 by Frank Munsey; *McClure's* started in 1893 by S. S. McClure; and the *Cosmopolitan* (1886). It was these magazines, circulating more extensively than any of their predecessors, that were to open the minds of more readers to social and cultural trends.

THE SOCIETY'S SHORTCOMINGS AND DISCONTENTS

It must be noted, however, that the general level of cultural attainment was still low. Even by 1900 the average American had received only 5 years of schooling in his or her lifetime. If the public bought encyclopedias galore from the book publishers because it wanted to know more, it also bought dime novels by the millions. If the chautauqua was a booming institution, so were horse racing, prizefighting, and baseball. Cultural and business organizations were expanding in number, but growing even faster were fraternal and social groups. In the newspaper world Adolph Ochs would be able to find enough serious readers in the metropolis of New York to support the reborn *New York Times,* but the great mass of readers was attracted by the devices of a journalism that sought a popular level as it both entertained and informed.

It should be noted briefly, too, that not everybody was successful or contented in this new economic and social environment, despite the general blessings that industrialization had bestowed on the country. Sharp divisions began to appear between those who had gained wealth in the process of national economic upheaval, and those who had gained only a crowded room in a city tenement, a poverty-stricken tenant farm in the South, or a precarious existence on the dry plains of the West. Falling farm prices in the 1880s spurred the political activities of the discontented in the South and West. There the Grangers, the Greenbackers, the Farmers' Alliance, and the Populists arose to demand economic equality for agriculture and launched third-party movements that showed real strength. Not until 1896 did one of the major political parties answer the call of the "consistent rebellion"; at that time, the merging of the forces of free silver coinage, paper money, and general political and economic reform under the Democratic banner of William Jennings Bryan provided America with the greatest political excitement of a generation. But despite the bitter experience of the depression of 1893, the advocates of William McKinley and political and economic conservatism won the decision.

In the cities the rise of the labor movement on a nationally organized scale provided a much sharper clash than that between business and agriculture. Some craft unions, such as those of the bricklayers, railroad engineers, and printers, had become established before the Civil War, and a National Labor Union of some stature was organized in 1866, only to disintegrate during the depression of 1873. The Knights of Labor, carrying on the "one big union" plan under the leadership of Terence V. Powderly, reached a peak membership of 700,000 during the 2 years of industrial turbulence that followed the panic of 1884. Powderly advocated moderate cooperative action by all working people to better their pay and working conditions and the use of the strike weapon when necessary. Unfortunately for the Knights of Labor, their aggressive action was discredited in 1886 following the Haymarket Square riot in Chicago, where a rally in support of the 8-hour day organized by a small group of agitators, some of them anarchists, was disrupted by police. A bomb exploded, touching off violence which killed eleven persons, including seven police officers. Although the prosecution lacked sufficient evidence, eight anarchists were convicted of the bomb throwing and four of them were hanged. Even though the trial was unjust, adversaries of the labor movement used the incident to attack the Knights of Labor. In the wake of this criticism the American Federation of Labor, built in 1881 as a national organization of the various craft unions, became the principal voice of the labor movement with Samuel Gompers as its newly elected president. A series of strikes in 1886 led to a reduction of the work day to 8 or 9 hours for some 200,000 of the 350,000 workers involved.

The reaction in many industries was the formation of employers' associations that raised defense funds to fight the carefully planned demands and strikes of the individual craft unions. Although most of the strikes of the 1880s and 1890s were peaceful, several were extensive and led to great violence. National guard troops were used to quell disturbances at Henry C. Frick's Homestead, Pennsylvania, steel plant in July, 1892, and at the Coeur d'Alene, Idaho, mines in that same month, following pitched battles between private guards and workers. A strike at the Chicago railways yards in May, 1894, by the American Railway Union against the Pullman Company led to violence in numerous states, as had happened during the widespread railway strike of 1877. During one of many coal-mine strikes deputies killed eighteen miners in Pennsylvania in 1897. A decade of mining wars erupted in Colorado in 1894, and teamsters and waterfront workers were met with resistance when they began organizing in a number of cities.

A NEW JOURNALISM EMERGING

In such a swiftly changing and exciting environment, then, the daily newspaper was coming of age. From 850 English-language, general-circulation dailies in 1880 to 1967 in 1900; from 10 percent of adults as subscribers to 26 percent—these were the statistical evidences of the newspaper's arrival as a major business. The enormous success of Joseph Pulitzer's *New York World,* which between 1883 and 1887 broke every publishing record in America, was evidence that a "new journalism" had been created that would change the character and the appearance of the daily newspaper and enormously increase its mass influence.

But before focusing attention on the *New York World,* whose triumphs caught the attention of even the most unobservant in the newspaper business, we should briefly examine the changes that were occurring in other cities. Certainly Henry W. Grady in Atlanta, Edward W. Scripps in Cleveland and Cincinatti, Melville E. Stone and Victor Lawson in Chicago, and William Rockhill Nelson in Kansas City were also engaged in the creation of the "new journalism" in the same years that Joseph Pulitzer was exhibiting his skill, first in St. Louis and then in New York. And in many another city, newspapers were being challenged by bright-faced newcomers that, in some cases, were destined to take their places among America's best. The new papers were low priced, aggressive, and easily read. They believed in the news function as the primary obligation of the press; they exhibited independence of editorial opinion; they crusaded actively in the community interest; they appealed to the mass audience through improved writing, better makeup, use of headlines and illustrations, and a popularization of their contents. These were the general characteristics of the "new journalism"; the individual newspapers, of course, exhibited them in varying degrees.

The rise of evening newspapers was a feature of this growth of the daily. The evening field claimed seven-eighths of the increase in numbers of daily newspapers between 1880 and 1900, and by 1890 two out of three papers were evening editions. The swing toward evening publication was due in part to the changed reading habits of the city populations, and it was strengthened by the discovery that the women readers to whom retail-store advertising was directed favored afternoon-delivered newspapers. Mechanical and news-gathering innovations permitted the evening papers to carry "today's news today," particularly in the Middle West and West, where time differentials aided inclusion of news from the East and from Europe on the same day events occurred. Some morning papers found an answer by publishing afternoon editions under the same nameplate, while others established separate evening papers.

JOURNALISM OF THE EAST

New York remained primarily a morning-paper city, with only the *Evening Post* achieving distinction as an afternoon paper before the Pulitzer invasion. Two additions to the field in 1867 were the *Evening Telegram,* begun by James Gordon Bennett as the afternoon edition of the *Herald,* and the *Evening Mail.* The *Mail* was merged with the older *Express* in 1882 to form the *Mail and Express.* The circulation winner of the period was the *Daily News,* a 1-cent evening paper dating back to 1855. The *Daily News,* cheap in content as well as in price, circulated in the tenement districts so widely that it challenged the *Sun* and *Herald* throughout the 1870s, and its success suggested to other publishers new ways of reaching the immigrant-crowded tenement sections of the city.

In Philadelphia, two newcomers in the 1870s were the *Record* and the *Times.* The *Record,* begun in 1870, was taken over in 1877 by William M. Singerly, a millionaire railroad builder who cut the paper's price to 1 cent, brightened its makeup and writing, and engaged in popular crusades against local abuses. By the early 1880s the *Record* was outselling its famous competitor in the morning field, the *Public Ledger,* which had been purchased from the Swain family in 1864 by the able George W. Childs. The *Times* (1875), published by reform-conscious Alexander K. McClure, also pushed into the top circulation bracket, along with the *Evening Item* (1847), which hit its stride in the 1880s as a crusading penny paper, and the *Press* (1857). The *Evening Bulletin* (1847) and the *Inquirer* (1829), ultimately the two survivors in the Philadelphia field, trailed the *Public Ledger* in prestige and the other papers in circulation.

Boston's quiet journalism was upset by the appearance of the *Globe.* Founded in 1872, it had only 8000 circulation when General Charles H. Taylor became publisher in 1873. Taylor established an evening edition, cut the price to 2 cents, ran big headlines, emphasized local news, and gave editorial support to the Democratic party. By 1890 the *Globe,* with combined morning and evening circulation of 150,000, ranked among the top ten papers in the country. The staid *Herald* (1846) and the sensationalized *Journal* (1833) kept pace by establishing evening editions. But the morning *Advertiser* (1813) and *Post* (1831), and evening *Transcript* (1830) and *Traveller* (1825), contented themselves with limited circulations. The *Advertiser* did establish an evening edition, the *Record,* in 1884.

The trend was similar in other Eastern cities. Baltimore's new entry was the *Evening News* (1872), which in the 1890s, under fighting editor Charles H. Grasty, rose to challenge the famous *Sun.* The *Evening Penny Press* of Pittsburgh appeared in 1884 as the forerunner of the *Pittsburgh Press* and promptly undertook civic improvement campaigns. The Butler family's *Buffalo News* dates from 1880, and it immediately asserted leadership in the newspaper field as an aggressively run evening paper. Another influential leader in the 1880s was the evening *Brooklyn Eagle,* begun in 1841. In Providence, the *Journal* (1829) saw the trend early and established the *Evening Bulletin* in 1863. The Noyes and Kauffmann families gave Washington a local evening paper in 1852, and by 1890 their *Evening Star* had as its only competitor the morning *Post* (1877).[7]

THE SOUTH: HENRY W. GRADY OF ATLANTA

In the South, Henry Watterson's well-established *Louisville Courier-Journal* started the *Times* as an evening edition in 1884 and soon saw it outsell the parent morning paper. New Orleans' morning leader, the *Picayune* (1837), found new competition from two evening papers, the *Item* (1877) and the *States* (1879). Two other New Orleans morning papers, the *Times* (1863) and the *Democrat* (1875), found the going more difficult and merged in 1881. A famous editor appeared in Raleigh, North Carolina, in 1885 when Josephus Daniels took over the *State Chronicle,* which he soon merged into the *News and Observer,* thereby establishing what became a great Daniels family newspaper.

Most brilliant of the Southern newspaper makers of the period was Henry W. Grady, who in his brief 39 years demonstrated the qualities of a great reporter and managing editor. Grady's talents were widely exhibited in the dozen years before 1880, when he became managing editor of the *Atlanta Constitution*. Indeed, when Grady became editor and one-third owner of the

Henry W. Grady.

Atlanta Herald in 1872, he nearly put the *Constitution,* founded 4 years before, out of business. But the *Herald,* for all its journalistic superiority, fell victim to the financial depression of 1873 after a 4-year struggle. Grady then became a freelance correspondent for such enterprising newspapers as the *Constitution,* the *New York Herald,* the *Louisville Courier-Journal,* the *Philadelphia Times,* and the *Detroit Free Press,* distinguishing himself for his coverage of politics and for his use of the interview technique in reporting and interpreting the news. He traveled widely and his grasp of events and his acquaintanceships increased accordingly.

When the *Constitution,* published by Evan P. Howell after 1876, obtained Grady as a part owner and managing editor, things began to hum. A network of correspondents was built up, and Grady spent lavishly to get all the news coverage possible in every field from politics to baseball. Grady continued to report major news events and political affairs himself. His brilliant story of the Charleston earthquake of 1886 won him national attention as a reporter. The same year his address entitled "The New South," which advocated industrial advancement of the South as a means of reestablishing national solidarity, won him national fame as a spokesperson for his area. As a consequence Grady devoted increased attention to the editorial page of the *Constitution* until his death in 1889, and his influence furthered the paper's sharing Southern leadership with the *Louisville Courier-Journal.*[8]

With Grady's death, Clark Howell, Sr., son of the publisher, became managing editor of the *Constitution.* The other event of the 1880s in Atlanta journalism was the founding, in 1883, of the *Journal,* an evening paper that was destined to outmaneuver the Howells' *Constitution* by the 1950s.

NEW DAILIES IN THE WEST

To the West, the newspaper that is now the *Dallas News* was established in 1885, and its future publisher, George B. Dealey, appeared in Dallas that year. The *Los Angeles Times,* begun in 1881, saw Harrison Gray Otis assume its leadership in 1882. In San Francisco, the major event of the period was the sale of the *Examiner* (1865) to George Hearst in 1880 and the turning over of the paper to young William Randolph Hearst in 1887. San Francisco journalism had been lively even before the Hearst entry, with the morning *Chronicle* (1865) leading in civic campaigns and political clean-up movements. Its publisher, Michel H. de Young, one of two brothers who founded the paper, remained in control of the *Chronicle* for 60 years.

A REVOLUTION IN THE MIDWEST: E.W. SCRIPPS

What has been described thus far would suffice to prove the point that things were happening to the nation's journalism everywhere. Singerly's *Philadelphia Record,* Taylor's *Boston Globe,* Grady's *Atlanta Herald* and *Constitution* exhibited the major characteristics of the "new journalism." The appearance of the Butler family in Buffalo, of the Noyes family in Washington, of Josephus Daniels in Raleigh, of the Howell family in Atlanta, and of Harrison Gray Otis in Los Angeles meant in each case the beginning of the building of a noted American newspaper. But it was in the Midwest of the 1870s and 1880s that the biggest revolution in newspapering was brewing: Detroit, Cleveland, Cincinnati, Chicago, Kansas City, Milwaukee, St. Louis.

The name Scripps is written boldly into the story of Midwestern newspaper making in the 1870s and early 1880s. James E. Scripps, elder half-brother of the famed Edward Wyllis Scripps, started the family on its journalistic mission when, after working on newspapers in Chicago and Detroit, he founded the *Detroit Evening News* in 1873. By the end of 1880, the Scripps family had fostered newspapers in Cleveland, Cincinnati, St. Louis, and Buffalo. The story of the rise of the Scripps newspaper chain belongs later, but the story of the early successes is a part of the general pattern of the rise of the "new journalism." Scripps' newspapers were low-priced evening publications; small in size, but well written and tightly edited; hard-hitting in both news and editorial-page coverage of the local scene. Above all, they were distinguished for their devotion to the interests of working people.

When James Scripps needed help to keep his *Detroit News* afloat, he called on his brother George and sister Ellen, and eventually on young Edward, who was the thirteenth child of a thrice-married Englishman who had settled on an Illinois farm. Edward helped to build circulation routes for the *News* and reported for it while the struggle to win advertising support was in progress. Detroit had well-established papers, such as the morning *Free Press* (1831), but by the 1880s the *News* emerged as a leading evening paper known for its business operation as well as for its qualities as a newspaper.

Scripps money went into four 1-cent evening papers: the short-lived *Buffalo Evening Telegraph,* the ill-fated *St. Louis Chronicle,* and the famous *Cleveland Press* and *Cincinnati Post.* These two latter papers became the products of Edward Wyllis Scripps' own publishing genius and the parent papers of his eventual chain.

Cleveland of 1878 had three going newspapers: the *Leader* (1854), the *Herald* (1835), and the *Plain Dealer* (1842). When the *Penny Press* appeared as a four-page, five-column evening paper, it looked no more permanent than the alley shack in which it was published. But the editor, Edward Wyllis Scripps, paid the top salary to his advertising solicitor and put his own tremendous energy into the venture in a fashion that drove the circulation to 10,000 within a few months and foreshadowed the rise of the Scripps publishing empire. Its name became the *Press.*

What happened to Cleveland journalism as a result of the rapid growth of the new *Press* can be told briefly. In 1885 one of the first acts of a new owner, L. E. Holden, was to shift the emphasis of the *Plain Dealer* from the evening to the morning field. Holden bought the plant and morning edition of the *Herald;* the evening editions of the *Leader* and the *Herald* were combined as the *News and Herald.* But the *Press* continued to harass its evening competitors, and in

1905 the other afternoon dailies were combined into a new paper, the *Cleveland News.*

The Scripps opposition in Cincinnati was more formidable. In 1880 the evening *Times* (1840) and *Star* (1872) were merged by Charles P. Taft (half-brother of the later president, William Howard Taft). The *Times-Star* was a 2-cent, conservative Republican paper; the Scripps entry that year was 1 cent and Democratic. But in the morning field were the *Enquirer* (1841), published by John R. McLean as a Democratic paper noted for its adoption of the techniques of sensationalism, and the *Commercial Gazette,* edited by the distinguished liberal Republican supporter, Murat Halstead.[9] The Scripps paper, which became the *Cincinnati Post* after Edward Wyllis Scripps took control in 1883, nevertheless soon gained circulation leadership as the *Press* was doing in Cleveland.

STONE'S *CHICAGO DAILY NEWS*

Another star that was rising in the Midwest was that of the *Chicago Daily News.* Together with another newcomer, the *Herald,* the *Daily News* quickly won equal prominence with older Chicago papers. With Joseph Medill as controlling owner and editor after 1874, the *Tribune* (1847), was continuing its development as a substantially edited, alert newspaper leader. The *Inter Ocean* (successor to the *Republican* founded in 1865 with Charles A. Dana as first editor) became widely known for its enterprise in news gathering and in adopting new journalistic and printing techniques. But the circulation went to the newcomers, the *Daily News* and the *Herald.*

Melville E. Stone, the founder of the *Daily News,* was a product both of Chicago journalism and of the new national newspaper environment. Stone became managing editor of the *Republican* in 1872, as an inexperienced young man of 24, and ended up as city editor when the paper became the *Inter Ocean* later that year. In the fall he went on tour for the paper, studying conditions in the South. He records in his autobiography an association with Henry W. Grady and his *Atlanta Herald* partners: "They spent almost every evening with me talking over the profession of journalism. In these discussions we all learned much."[10] On the same trip, Stone studied New Orleans and St. Louis papers, and in St. Louis he met a talented young reporter, Eugene Field.

When Stone returned to Chicago he became managing editor of the *Post and Mail,* but almost immediately he left for Washington to serve as correspondent for his and other papers. In his autobiography, Stone also records another major influence: He was watching the successful 1-cent *New York Daily News* and was deciding that he would try the same price formula in Chicago. He experimented briefly in 1873, returned to Washington for more seasoning as a correspondent, and then laid his plans to leave the *Post and Mail.*

In January, 1876, the *Daily News* appeared as a four-page, five-column sheet with only a few thousand dollars in capital investment. Stone believed that his first responsibility was to print news; his second responsibility was to guide public opinion; and his third, to provide entertainment. The paper did not reject sensational techniques; Stone's personal favorite was the newspaper's detection of criminals. Nor did the *Daily News* fail to entertain. Stone brought Eugene Field to Chicago in 1883 from his earlier St. Louis and Kansas City surroundings; and until his death in 1895 Field conducted the famous "Sharps and Flats" column, in which he commented on politics and people in a witty and highly literary style. But the paper won its place by its style of news presentation, by its determination to remain free of political and outside financial pressures, and by its aggressive editorial-page policies.

The going was difficult at first, however. There was a chronic shortage of pennies in circulation, so Stone had to import pennies for Chicago banks to handle and promoted "99-cent sales" in stores in order to put a sufficient number of pennies in Chicagoans' pockets to sell his papers. In the first year a young Chicago financier, Victor F. Lawson, took over the business managership of the paper and two-thirds of the stock. But by 1878 the *Daily News* had bought out the *Post and Mail,* obtaining its Associated Press news rights. A morning edition, eventually named the *Record,* was begun in 1881, and by 1885 the combined circulation had passed the 100,000 mark. When Stone sold his interest to Lawson in 1888 for $350,000, only Pulitzer's *New York World* had a larger circulation among American newspapers than the *Daily News'* 200,000.

The editorial staff Stone had built was a famous one: Eugene Field as a columnist; Slason Thompson as an editorial writer; George Harvey, George Ade, and Finley Peter Dunne (Mr. Dooley) as young reporters; and literary figures, scientists, and professors such as Chicago's James Laurence Laughlin and Wisconsin's Richard T. Ely as special contributors. Lawson continued the same type of leadership until his death in 1925; Stone comes into the story again as the general manager and builder of the modern Associated Press.

Rivaling the *Daily News* as an exponent of the new order in journalism was the *Herald,* founded by James W. Scott in 1881 as a low-priced, liberal-independent morning paper. Scott had difficulties providing sufficient capitalization for his expanding paper, but it quickly won the runner-up position to the *Daily News* in circulation. The ambitious Scott followed William M. Singerly of the *Philadelphia Record* as the second president of the newly formed American Newspaper Publishers Association, serving from 1889 to 1895. With his business associates, he founded the *Evening Post* in 1890, and in 1895 he consolidated the older *Times* (1854) with the *Herald* as the *Times-Herald.*[11] At this moment of glory, Scott died and his papers passed into less talented hands.

NELSON'S *KANSAS CITY STAR*

Taking his place with Scripps and Stone as one of the great figures in this Midwestern newspaper revolution was William Rockhill Nelson, founder of the *Kansas City Star.* Nelson had been a lawyer and a building contractor before buying into a Fort Wayne, Indiana, newspaper in 1879. But by the time he appeared in Kansas City in the fall of 1880 he was ready to follow the pattern of the times. He and his editors created a small, 2-cent evening newspaper, well

Melville E. Stone.
Chicago Daily News

William Rockhill Nelson.
Kansas City Star

written and filled with entertaining material as well as news, and possessed of the crusading urge. Notably, however, the *Star* shunned sensational treatment of the news in its use of headlines and illustrations.

One other difference stands out strongly. Unlike the other great figures of journalism before him, Nelson was not a writer. He believed that the reporter was the heart of the newspaper and had seven of them on his initial staff. He also sought the best news editors and editorial writers. And he was constantly a part of the news, editorial, and business activities of the *Star,* but only as the publisher who guided the actions and writing of his staff. If he had something to say, as he usually did, he told it to others who put the ideas into the printed page. One of Nelson's biographers ascribes the reasons for the development of the *Star*'s sparkling qualities in this fashion:

> Next to Nelson, but always through Nelson's triumphant spirit, it was the work of Nelson's editors and their staff of inspired reporters and editorial writers. Possibly Nelson's greatest genius lay in his ability to select editorial talent, to exploit it by giving it freedom, and to cherish its flowering, both by positive encouragement to expression and avoidance of negative rules of suppression. . . . By adhering to this policy, Nelson succeeded in exploiting the ablest men and gaining their loyalty despite a salary and wage scale which was niggardly.[12]

Kansas City was a rough, growing town of little beauty when Nelson came in 1880. It was the gateway to the plains and the receiving point of Western cattle. Half-built, cursed with the usual political corruption and vice of the utilitarian America of the 1880s, it offered a great chance for a strong editor. Nelson was that: a big man, with massive face and head, stubborn qualities of independence, and an air of dignity that gave him the title of colonel. William Allen White, writing about Nelson the year he died, commented: "Not that he was ever a colonel of anything; he was just coloneliferous."[13]

Nelson gave Kansas City what he thought it needed through his relentless crusades for big and little things. He fought for low-cost and efficient public transportation, which brought cable cars to the city's hills. He battled against politicians and gamblers. He campaigned for years to establish Kansas City's famous parks and boulevards, then himself built model homes along the boulevards and saw that those who lived in them planted trees and flowers. The *Star* helped to inaugurate the commission form of government in the city and by its espousal of progressive reform in government spread the doctrine throughout its circulation area in the Missouri Valley.

Kansas City and the state of Kansas were captured by 1890, and before Nelson's death in 1915 the *Star*'s circulation hit 170,000. The subscription price was 10 cents a week at the start, but even after a Sunday edition had been added and the morning *Times* (1868) had sold out to Nelson in 1901, the price for morning, evening, and Sunday editions remained at a dime. A weekly edition, selling for 25 cents a year, climbed to 150,000 circulation. The price formula, plus the *Star*'s intensive coverage of its area and its human-interest and literary qualities, made the paper invulnerable to the attacks of competitors who tried to win by using the sensational techniques that Nelson shunned.[14]

OTHER MIDWESTERN CITIES

In other Midwestern cities, changes in newspaper fortunes were in the air. Milwaukee's several dailes greeted a new competitor in 1882, Lucius W. Nieman and his *Milwaukee Journal*, which at once began to show some of the zeal that drove all its competitors, except the morning *Sentinel* (1837), to cover in the next 60 years. In Minneapolis another *Journal* began its career as a leading evening newspaper in 1878, and the morning *Tribune* (1867) was given new life in the 1890s by William J. Murphy. St. Paul's *Pioneer Press* (1849), run by the distinguished team of editor Joseph A. Wheelock and manager Frederick Driscoll, found competition in the evening *Dispatch* (1868). Another aggressive evening newspaper was the *Indianapolis News* (1869).

But it was in St. Louis that the climax was reached. The river city had long been a newspaper center. The *Missouri Republican* (1808), which became the *St. Louis Republic* in 1888, the *Missouri Democrat* (1852), and Carl Schurz's German-language *Westliche Post* (1857) were leading papers. The first shock was the arrival of J. B. McCullagh from Chicago and his consolidation of the newly founded *Morning Globe* with the *Missouri Democrat* to start the *Globe-Democrat* on its way in 1875. The great event was the appearance of Joseph Pulitzer, a penniless immigrant who within 10 years built the *St. Louis Post-Dispatch* and then turned to startle the publishing world with his *New York World*. All around him in

America a new daily newspaper was developing in keeping with the changed character of the national life, but by his spectacular genius Joseph Pulitzer became the recognized leader of the "new journalism." His story becomes the story of the emergence of the modern newspaper.

NOTES

1. Documented in Allan Nevins, *The Emergence of Modern America, 1865–1878* (New York: Macmillan, 1927), and Ida M. Tarbell, *The Nationalizing of Business, 1878–1898* (New York: Macmillan, 1936). David M. Potter, in *People of Plenty* (Chicago: University of Chicago Press, 1954), argued that economic abundance, not activists, provided the touchstone for unified progress.

2. This and following statistical information is from U.S. Department of Commerce, *Historical Statistics of the United States, 1789–1945* (Washington, D.C.: U.S. Government Printing Office, 1949).

3. Schlesinger's *The Rise of the City, 1878–1898* (New York: Macmillan, 1932) is a classic study of the transformation of American life stemming from the economic revolution. See also Blake McKelvey, *The Urbanization of America, 1860–1915* (New Brunswick, N.J.: Rutgers University Press, 1969), and its companion volume, *The Emergence of Metropolitan America, 1915–1966* (1968).

4. The census figures for totals of all types of dailies were 574 in 1870 and 2226 in 1900. The figures used in the text are more comparable to twentieth-century statistics.

5. This topic is well discussed in Henry Steele Commager, *The American Mind* (New Haven: Yale University Press, 1950).

6. The predominant Social Darwinism theory is attacked, but its influence acknowledged, in Richard Hofstadter, *Social Darwinism in American Thought, 1860–1915* (Philadelphia: University of Pennsylvania Press, 1955).

7. Crosby S. Noyes and Samuel H. Kauffmann were leading men in the early years of the *Star;* Noyes' sons, Frank and Theodore, became active before 1890 and guided the *Star* until the 1940s.

8. Raymond B. Nixon, "Henry W. Grady, Reporter: A Reinterpretation," *Journalism Quarterly,* XII (December 1935), 343. The full-length biography is Nixon, *Henry W. Grady, Spokesman of the New South* (New York: Knopf, 1943).

9. The *Commercial Gazette* resulted from an 1883 merger of the *Gazette* (1815) and the *Commercial* (1843), which Halstead had edited since 1865. After Halstead left Cincinnati in 1890 to go to Brooklyn, the *Commercial Gazette* became the *Commercial Tribune* in 1896. It disappeared into the *Enquirer* in 1930.

10. Melville E. Stone, *Fifty Years a Journalist* (Garden City, N.Y.: Doubleday, 1921), p. 44.

11. The *Times,* under editor Wilbur F. Storey, had become known for its shocking sensationalism. Its most famous headline, over an 1875 story of the hanging of four repentent murderers, read "Jerked to Jesus."

12. Charles E. Rogers, "William Rockhill Nelson and His Editors of the *Star,*" *Journalism Quarterly,* XXVI (March 1949), 15. This article is based on *William Rockhill Nelson: Independent Editor and Crusading Liberal* (Ph.D. thesis, University of Minnesota, 1948).

13. William Allen White, "The Man Who Made the Star," *Collier's,* LV (June 26, 1915), 12.

14. Two of the challengers were Scripps with his *Kansas City World* (1897) and the Denver team of Bonfils and Tammen, who operated the *Kansas City Post* from 1909 to 1922. Neither paper survived.

ANNOTATED BIBLIOGRAPHY

Books

Aaron, Daniel, *Men of Good Hope: A Story of American Progressives.* New York: Oxford University Press, 1951. Studies, among others, Henry George, Edward Bellamy, Henry Demarest Lloyd, Thorstein Veblen, William Dean Howells, and Theodore Roosevelt.

Adams, Henry, *The Education of Henry Adams.* Boston: Houghton Mifflin, 1918. A classic personal reaction to a changing society.

Beard, Charles A., and Mary R., *The Rise of American Civilization.* New York: Macmillan, 1930. The chapter in Volume II, "The Second American Revolution," is the best interpretation of the rise of industry in the Civil War and postwar periods.

BOORSTIN, DANIEL J., *The Americans: The Democratic Experience.* New York: Random House, 1973. Prize-winning social history from consensus-theory approach.

BROWN, DEE, *Bury My Heart at Wounded Knee.* New York: Holt, Rinehart & Winston, 1971. The history of the West as finally written by the losers, the American Indians.

BYRNES, GARRETT D., AND CHARLES H. SPILMAN, *The Providence Journal: 150 Years.* Providence, R.I.: Journal Company, 1983. Oldest U.S. paper in continuous circulation as a daily.

CLAYTON, CHARLES G., *Little Mack: Joseph B. McCullagh of the St. Louis Globe-Democrat.* Carbondale: Southern Illinois Press, 1969. Helps to illuminate a great newspaper figure.

COMMAGER, HENRY STEELE, *The American Mind.* New Haven: Yale University Press, 1950. A provocative and sweeping introduction to intellectual and social trends since the 1880s.

CURL, DONALD W., *Murat Halstead and the Cincinnati Commercial.* Gainesville: University Presses of Florida, 1980. Brief conventional biography.

DORFMAN, JOSEPH, *Thorstein Veblen and His America.* New York: Viking, 1934. A study on rebellion against the rugged individualists and their economic thinking.

GOLDMAN, ERIC F., *Rendezvous with Destiny: A History of Modern American Reform.* New York: Knopf, 1952. An interpretative synthesis that traces the tradition of dissent from post-Civil War years to the times of the Fair Deal.

GRAYBAR, LLOYD J., *Albert Shaw of the "Review of Reviews": An Intellectual Biography.* Lexington: University Press of Kentucky, 1974. Account of the birth and death of the *Review of Reviews* and its editor.

HART, JIM ALLEE, *A History of the St. Louis Globe-Democrat.* Columbia: University of Missouri Press, 1961. The story of founder J. B. McCullagh within a social framework.

HARTZ, LOUIS, *The Liberal Tradition in America.* New York: Harcourt Brace Jovanovich, 1955. Major work of the consensus school of historians, based on the theme that the United States was "born free" and had no opposition to liberalism in a land of plenty.

HEUTERMAN, THOMAS H., *Movable Type: Biography of Legh R. Freeman.* Ames: Iowa State University Press, 1979. Skillfully presents the attention-winning editor of the "Press on Wheels" in the post-Civil War West.

HOFSTADTER, RICHARD, *Social Darwinism in American Thought, 1860–1915.* Philadelphia: University of Pennsylvania Press, 1955. A harshly critical study.

JOHNSON, ICIE F., *William Rockhill Nelson and the Kansas City Star.* Kansas City: Burton Publishing, 1935. The best published study of Nelson.

KAROLEVITZ, ROBERT F., *Newspapering in the Old West.* Seattle: Superior Publishing, 1965. Pictorial history of "how it was" on the frontier.

MCJIMSEY, GEORGE T., *Genteel Partisan: Manton Marble, 1834–1917.* Ames: Iowa State Press, 1971. Discusses the editor of *New York World* in the 1860s, and his Spencerian social philosophy.

MCKELVEY, BLAKE, *The Urbanization of America, 1860–1915.* New Brunswick, N.J.: Rutgers University Press, 1969.

———, *The Emergence of Metropolitan America, 1915–1966.* New Brunswick, N.J.: Rutgers University Press, 1968. Two new studies of the trend.

MOTT, FRANK LUTHER. *A History of American Magazines.* Volume II, 1850–1865; Volume III, 1865–1885; Volume IV, 1885–1905. Cambridge, Mass.: Harvard University Press, 1938–57. Volume V, 1905–1930 (1968) of Mott's authoritative study has a cumulative index.

MYERS, JOHN MYERS, *Print in a Wild Land.* Garden City, N.Y.: Doubleday, 1967. Racy account of newspaperin' in the Old West.

NIXON, RAYMOND B., *Henry W. Grady: Spokesman of the New South.* New York: Knopf, 1943. The definitive biography of a leading Southern editor.

NORTH, SIMEON N. D., *History and Present Condition of the Newspaper and Periodical Press of the United States.* Washington, D.C.: U.S. Government Printing Office, 1884. Published as a part of the 1880 census; valuable particularly for its picture of that year.

PAXSON, FREDERIC L., *History of the American Frontier.* Boston: Houghton Mifflin, 1924. Records the passing of the frontier by 1893.

POTTER, DAVID M., *People of Plenty.* Chicago: University of Chicago Press, 1954. American progress has been shaped by the unifying character of economic abundance, not by the efforts of radicals and other advocates of change.

SCHLESINGER, ARTHUR M., *The Rise of the City, 1878–1898,* A History of American Life, Volume X. New York: Macmillan, 1932. A top social history of a crucial period. See later Ida M. Tarbell reference to companion volume.

SHARPE, ERNEST, *G. B. Dealey of the Dallas News.* New York: Holt, Rinehart & Winston, 1955. A favorable biography; covers to 1946.

STONE, MELVILLE E., *Fifty Years a Journalist.* Garden City, N.Y.: Doubleday, 1921. The first portion deals with Stone's Chicago newspaper career, the latter with the Associated Press.

TARBELL, IDA M., *The Nationalizing of Business, 1878–1898.* A History of American Life, Volume IX, New York: Macmillan, 1936.

U.S. DEPARTMENT OF COMMERCE, *Historical Statistics of the United States, 1789–1945.* Washington, D.C.: U.S. Government Printing Office, 1949.

WALSH, JUSTIN E., *To Print the News and Raise Hell.* Chapel Hill: University of North Carolina Press, 1968. Biography of Wilbur F. Storey, controversial editor of the *Chicago Times* in the Civil War period.

WARE, NORMAN J., *The Labor Movement in the United States, 1860–1895.* New York: Appleton-Century-Crofts, 1929. More compact than the massive history of labor by John R. Commons and associates, this book emphasizes the Knights of Labor. See also Lloyd Ulman, *The Rise of the National Trade Union* (Cambridge, Mass.: Harvard University Press, 1955).

WIEBE, ROBERT. *The Search for Order, 1877–1920.* New York: Hill and Wang, 1968. Conservative analysis of American society. See also Robert G. McCloskey, *American Conservatism in the Age of Enterprise, 1865–1910* (New York: Harper & Row, 1971).

YOUNG, JOHN P., *Journalism in California.* San Francisco: Chronicle Publishing, 1913. Principally a history of the *San Francisco Chronicle.*

Periodicals and Monographs

BELMAN, LARY S., "Robert Ezra Park: An Intellectual Portrait of a Journalist and Communication Scholar," *Journalism History,* II (Winter 1975), 116.

"Fifty Years of Harper's Magazine," *Harper's,* C (May 1900), 947.

HALL, MARK W., "The *San Francisco Chronicle:* It's Fight for the 1879 Constitution," *Journalism Quarterly,* XLVI (Autumn 1969), 505. From Master's thesis, University of Missouri, 1967.

HEUTERMAN, THOMAS H., "Assessing the 'Press on Wheels': Individualism in Frontier Journalism," *Journalism Quarterly,* LIII (Autumn 1976), 423. A study of the *Frontier Index* shows that it more accurately reflected its editors than the communities it served.

IRWIN, WILL, "The Power of the Press," *Collier's,* XLVI (January 21, 1911), 15. The first article in Irwin's "The American Newspaper" series, discussing the birth of modern journalism and such publishers as William Rockhill Nelson of the *Kansas City Star* and Harrison Gray Otis of the *Los Angeles Times.*

LENT, JOHN A., "The Press on Wheels: A History of *The Frontier Index,*" *Journal of the West,* X (October 1971), 662.

MANN, RUSSELL A., "Investigative Reporting in the Gilded Age: A Study of the Detective Journalism of Melville E. Stone and the *Chicago Morning News,* 1881–1888," Ph.D. thesis, Southern Illinois University, 1977.

MCCORKLE, WILLIAM L., "Nelson's *Star* and Kansas City, 1880–1898" Ph.D. thesis, University of Texas, 1968. The most recent scholarly study with fresh interpretations.

MOTT, FRANK LUTHER, "Fifty Years of Life: The Story of a Satirical Weekly," *Journalism Quarterly,* XXV (September 1948), 224.

NIXON, RAYMOND B., "Henry W. Grady, Reporter: A Reinterpretation," *Journalism Quarterly,* XII (December 1935), 341. Reprinted in Ford and Emery, *Highlights in the History of the American Press.*

PETERSON, PAUL V., "The *Chicago Daily Herald:* Righting the Historical Record," *Journalism Quarterly,* XLVII (Winter 1970), 697. Melville Stone's early paper appeared in 1873.

ROGERS, CHARLES E., "William Rockhill Nelson and His Editors of the Star," *Journalism Quarterly,* XXVI (March 1949), 15. Based on the author's *William Rockhill Nelson: Independent Editor and Crusading Liberal* (Ph.D. thesis, University of Minnesota, 1948).

STEWART, WALTER H., "The Editorial Paragraph: A Century and More of Development," Ph.D. thesis, Southern Illinois University, 1970. Investigates fourteen newspaper editorialists.

WHITE, WILLIAM ALLEN, "The Man Who Made the Star," *Collier's,* LV (June 26, 1915), 12. A portrait of William Rockhill Nelson by the editor of the *Emporia Gazette.* Reprinted in Ford and Emery, *Highlights in the History of the American Press.*

WHITE, Z. L., "Western Journalism," *Harper's,* LXXVII (October 1888), 678. A contemporary picture of Ohio journalism, including the Scripps enterprises and from farther West.

"KODAK"

Stands for all that is best in Photography.
If it isn't an Eastman, it isn't a Kodak.

EASTMAN KODAK CO.,
Rochester, N. Y.

Kodaks $5.00 to $35.00.
Catalogues at the Dealers or by Mail.

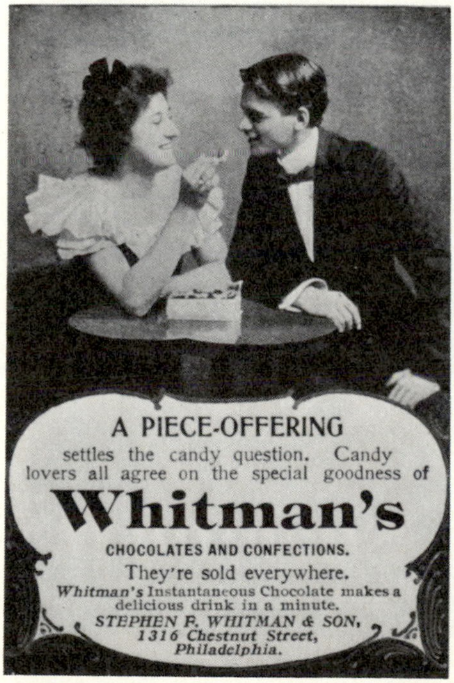

A PIECE-OFFERING
settles the candy question. Candy lovers all agree on the special goodness of
Whitman's
CHOCOLATES AND CONFECTIONS.
They're sold everywhere.
Whitman's Instantaneous Chocolate makes a delicious drink in a minute.
STEPHEN F. WHITMAN & SON,
1316 Chestnut Street,
Philadelphia.

Vartray Ginger Ale
..Is.. Deliciousness Itself.
Vartray Ginger Ale
The highest grade beverage made, and an American product. In competition against 611 other exhibitors at the Paris Exposition of 1900 it was awarded the
Gold Medal,
That being the only and highest award given a Ginger Ale.
On Sale at Clubs, Hotels, Cafes and by Leading Purveyors.
Made by
THE VARTRAY WATER CO.,
Buffalo, N. Y., U. S. A.

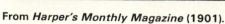

From *Harper's Monthly Magazine* (1901).

Joseph Pulitzer, from the portrait by John S. Sargent.
St. Louis Post-Dispatch

16

The New Journalism

. . . every issue of the paper presents an opportunity and a duty to say something courageous and true; to rise above the mediocre and conventional; to say something that will command the respect of the intelligent, the educated, the independent part of the community; to rise above fear of partisanship and fear of popular prejudice.

—Joseph Pulitzer

Joseph Pulitzer was one of those many immigrants who helped to build the new America of the post-Civil War period. In so doing, he both gave and received: The two great newspapers he established won for him the honor of being named the leading American editor of modern times,[1] and also built for him a fortune appraised at his death at nearly $20 million, one of the largest ever accumulated in the newspaper field.

The story of Joseph Pulitzer's journalistic success climaxes the story of the new national environment. Pulitzer made his own contributions to the creation of the "new journalism," but more important, he achieved his leadership by being receptive to the ideas of others. His immense energy and his highly developed journalistic sense enabled him to adapt and to develop in his own way the publishing concepts and techniques of his time and to satisfy his passionate desire to win unquestioned recognition as the builder of the brilliant staff and the complex mechanism of a great modern newspaper. This was a notable achievement, but it alone was not enough to win Pulitzer his reputation as the most useful and worthy American editor in the estimate of his craft. His true greatness lay in his high-minded conception of a newspaper's role, particularly in his exercising of editorial leadership, and in the way in which he made that conception live in his newspapers.

JOSEPH PULITZER'S EARLY CAREER

Pulitzer was born in Hungary in 1847. His father was Magyar-Jewish, his mother Austro-German. At 17, after receiving a good private-school education, he ran away from home to join an army. But he had weak eyesight and an unmilitary look that brought rejections from the Austrian army and the French Foreign Legion. Less particular, however, was an American agent who was seeking Europeans who would volunteer for the Union Army in that Civil War year of 1864. The agent enlisted Pulitzer, who became a member of the Lincoln cavalry.

When the war ended, without his seeing any real action, Pulitzer found himself in New York, virtually penniless and handicapped by language difficulties. After a series of short-lived, painful job experiences, which included being a waiter in a St. Louis restaurant, his tremendously inquisitive nature and unbounded energy began to lead him forward. In 1867 he became an American citizen and a year later he was hired as a reporter for Carl Schurz's leading German-language daily, the *Westliche Post.* Pulitzer soon surpassed others who laughed at his awkward mannerisms by working endless hours, digging into every type of news.

In rapid order he was elected as a Republican to the Missouri State Assembly from a normally Democratic district, became his paper's legislative correspondent, joined with Schurz in stumping the German-speaking areas of Missouri for Horace Greeley in the 1872 campaign, and became part owner of the *Post.* Planning for his own future, Pulitzer sold his stock in that paper for $30,000 and earned another $20,000 by buying a mediocre St. Louis daily that happened to have a valuable AP membership. He offered this to Joseph B. McCullagh, a Chicago newspaperman who needed the press-association membership to help force a merger between his *Globe* and the rival *Democrat.* Money in his pocket, Pulitzer left St. Louis newspaper work for a few years. He visited Europe four times, was married, and was admitted to the District of Columbia Bar. In the same period he campaigned for Samuel J. Tilden, the 1876 Democratic candidate, and reported for Dana's *New York Sun* on the activities of the electoral commission, which decided that disputed election in favor of Rutherford B. Hayes. By 1878, with a greatly increased knowledge of his adopted country and excellent command of the English language, he returned to St. Louis journalism.

Pulitzer's destiny was now to be fulfilled. The *Dispatch,* founded in 1864, was bankrupt and on the block at a sheriff's sale. Pulitzer won it with a $2500 bid on December 9, 1878, again obtaining as his principal prize an Associated Press membership. Three days later he effected a combination with the *Post,* started by John Dillon in 1875 (Dillon was a partner for only 1 year but remained as a Pulitzer associate).

Thus was born one of the country's greatest newspapers, the *Post-Dispatch.* Within 4 years it was the leading evening paper in St. Louis, netting $45,000 a year and rivaling the morning papers, the influential *Missouri Republican* and McCullagh's powerful *Globe-Democrat.* Behind this achievement lay the talents of the editor-publisher, now in his early 30s. An ambitious and self-contained man, with the artist's love of good music and skilled writing and the scholar's interest in economic, political, and social trends, Pulitzer was driven by his large intellectual capacity and consuming energy.

Pulitzer's flashing eyes expressed his strong will to succeed. Filled with nervous tension, he was not easily approachable, holding even close associates at a distance. But in his own way he showed his appreciation for the work of those who measured up to his exacting standards for newspaper work. Many capable journalists were to serve under the Pulitzer banner in the years ahead, but the most influential was the right-hand man of these early days, John A. Cockerill, who came to the *Post-Dispatch* as managing editor in 1880. A hard-working and pugnacious man capable of carrying out Pulitzer's commands, Cockerill brought with him a keen sense of newspaper methods, which was to serve Pulitzer well for the crucial next 12 years.[2]

But it was Pulitzer who imparted to the *Post-Dispatch* its distinctive spirit. His statement of policies contains memorable words:

> The *Post and Dispatch* will serve no party but the people; be no organ of Republicanism, but the organ of truth; will follow no causes but its conclusions; will not support the "Administration," but criticize it; will oppose all frauds and shams wherever and whatever they are; will advocate principles and ideas rather than prejudices and partisanship.[3]

Even more memorable are the words written by a more mature Pulitzer in 1907, near the end of his career, which have become the *Post-Dispatch* platform, printed on the editorial page:

> I know that my retirement will make no difference in its cardinal principles; that it will always fight for progress and reform, never tolerate injustice or corruption, always fight demagogues of all parties, never belong to any party, always oppose privileged classes and public plunderers, never lack sympathy with the poor, always remain devoted to the public welfare, never be satisfied with merely printing news, always be drastically independent, never be afraid to attack wrong, whether by predatory plutocracy or predatory poverty.

Not content with reporting the surface news, Pulitzer pushed his staff to "Never drop a thing until you have gone to the bottom of it. Continuity! Continuity! Continuity until the subject is really finished."[4] This resulted in determined crusading in the public interest with an intensity heightened by Pulitzer's personal involvement and Cockerill's techniques in writing and news display. Favorite targets were crooked politicians, wealthy tax dodgers, a police-protected gambling ring, and a free-wheeling public utility. Pulitzer's day was a loss if his paper did not have one distinctive feature—a crusade, public service, or big exclusive story.

There were serious blemishes on the Pulitzer record during the early St. Louis years. Cockerill had brought with him a reputation for exploiting stories of murder, sin, and sex, and for sensationalizing accounts of violence, lynchings, public hangings, and dramatic death. Pulitzer found many of these subjects fitting his "apt to be talked about" definition of news. They delighted in printing bits of gossipy scandal about the "best families" of the St. Louis oligarchy under such headlines as "St. Louis Swells," "An Adulterous Pair," "Loved the Cook," and "Does Rev. Mr. Tudor Tipple?" Tales of sex and sin included "Duped and Deserted" and "A Denver Maiden Taken from a Disreputable House." On the day in 1882 when the assassin of President Garfield was executed, Cockerill, who advocated illustrations, ran, on page one, a two-column drawing of a condemned man "as he appeared today on the scaffold"—a technical impossibility. The James Boys, outlaws, gave the *Post-Dispatch* a big circulation lift the same year. In these and many other stories could be found exaggeration, half-truth, and humor at the expense of embarrassed citizens.[5] This was also true, of course, of other papers of the times.

Editorially, Pulitzer's early *Post-Dispatch* hit hard at the wealthy families who monopolized control of the nation's fifth-largest city. The crusades it developed, however, were focused not on the problems of the poor and working classes but on those of the middle class and the small businesspeople with whom the publisher associated.[6] Everyone benefited, of course, from attacks on monopoly, from battles for cleaner living conditions, from crusades against vice. But the focus on the plight of the oppressed poor that was to be a Pulitzer trademark in New York was not yet present. The paper was also developing its coverage of middle-class news interests, such as sports and women's news.

In every field of newspaper publishing, Pulitzer, Cockerill, and their associates on the *Post-Dispatch* were learning the lessons they were soon to apply in New York. There were many mistakes, many stories and editorials falling short of the Pulitzer goals. But there were successes, for as the *World* commented in 1890, "The foundation of the *New York World* was laid in St. Louis. . . . The battle of new ideas and new theories of journalism was fought there under the banner of the *Post-Dispatch.*"[7]

PURCHASE OF THE *NEW YORK WORLD,* 1883

By 1883 Pulitzer was a physical wreck, with his eyesight failing and his nerves badly impaired by incessant work. Matters had not been helped when Cockerill shot and killed a prominent St. Louis attorney whom the *Post-Dispatch* had attacked in its columns. Cockerill was successful in his self-defense plea but a discouraged Pulitzer headed for what he thought would be a long European vacation. Instead, when passing through New York, he heard that the *World,* founded in 1860 as a morning Democratic newspaper, was for sale. Once well-edited by Manton Marble, the paper had fallen into the hands of the unscrupulous financier, Jay Gould, who wanted $346,000.

The situation was not promising, but Pulitzer, perhaps inspired by his brother Albert's success in starting the breezy 1-cent *Morning Journal* the year before with $25,000 capital, closed the deal on May 9. The first installment was paid with profits from the *Post-Dispatch,* but to Gould's surprise, the balance eventually was paid with profits from the *World.*

Pulitzer started with only a 15,000 circulation with his new 2-cent, eight-page paper. Its more powerful Park Row rivals were Bennett's *Herald,* running 12 to 16 pages at 3 cents; Dana's *Sun,* still publishing but four pages at 2 cents;

Whitelaw Reid's *Tribune* and George Jones' *Times,* both selling at 4 cents for eight pages.

Quickly revamping the *World*'s staff and wiring to St. Louis for two good *Post-Dispatch* editors, Pulitzer issued his first edition on May 11. The lead story was an account of a million-dollar storm in New Jersey. Other front-page features were an interview with a condemned slayer, the story of a Wall Street plunger, a Pittsburgh hanging, a riot in Haiti, and the sad story of a wronged servant girl. Ordering a press run of 20,000, Pulitzer was matched only by Bennett in sensational coverage. The next day the *World* was the talk of the town.

Exhibiting another important factor in the Pulitzer success formula—aggressive promotion of the newspaper's qualities—Pulitzer used the page-one area around the nameplate, the "ears," to plug his paper's circulation and exclusives. His first popular cause was to advocate that the new Brooklyn Bridge, hailed as one of the wonders of the world, be a free bridge for the people who would cross it every day on their way to work.

But mixed in with the sensation and promotion was good news coverage and a new editorial policy. A concise ten-point program appeared on the editorial page: Tax luxuries; tax inheritances; tax large incomes; tax monopolies; tax the privileged corporations; institute a tariff for revenue; reform the civil service; punish corrupt officeholders; punish vote buying; punish employers who coerce their employees in elections. "There is room in this great and growing city for a journal that is not only cheap but bright, not only bright but large, not only large but truly Democratic—dedicated to the cause of the people . . . ,"[8] Pulitzer had said in his first issue.

New Yorkers who resented the flaunted wealth of the moneyed class and believed in economic and social reform found the *World* to be delightful reading; those who worshiped successful dollar-chasers found the editorial pages filled with heresy. Pushing harder for the poor and the helpless than he had in St. Louis, the immigrant Pulitzer found New York's mass audience different. Well-developed crusades on behalf of the immigrants, the poor, and the laboring class appeared in his first 2 years at the *World.* In particular, the injustices of the garment district's sweatshops for immigrant women, the lack of school opportunities, and the inequity of the tax burden were subjects of Pulitzer's pressing editorials and news stories. In July, 1883, a heat wave took a terrible toll in the city's teeming slums; the *World* found that of 716 reported deaths the previous week, 392 had been of children under the age of 5 years. Its reporters went to the scenes of death; its headline writers produced "How Babies Are Baked" and "Line of Little Hearses" in an attempt to shock authorities into concern and action. The *World's* crusade for tenement-house reform continued in early 1884 when it covered the efforts of Professor Felix Adler to help the poor. Other stories—similar to those that would be found in the *World* for decades—told of meetings of immigrant societies, violence against immigrants, crowded factory conditions, rights of workers to visit museums and other public buildings on Sunday, and prejudice in political organizations.

The *World*'s liberal political and social stands paid circulation dividends in 1884 when Pulitzer supported Grover Cleveland, the Democratic governor of

The World

VOL. XXIII., NO. 7,947. NEW YORK, THURSDAY, MAY 24, 1883.

BUILDING THE BRIDGE.

INCEPTION AND BIRTH OF THE MAMMOTH ENTERPRISE.

To Whom the Honor is Due—The First Passenger—The Finishing Touches—All in Readiness to Wed the Cities.

NEW YORK JOINS HANDS WITH BROOKLYN.

"NUMBER ONE" UNEARTHED

HE HOLDS A RECEPTION AT HIS HOUSE AND MAKES A STATEMENT.

SHALL BUTLER BE LL.D.?

The Harvard Overseers Get in a Wrangle Over the Question.

A Raid on Philadelphia Gamblers.

NEW YORK, MONDAY, JULY 9, 1883.

LINES OF LITTLE HEARSES.

BURYING THE BABY VICTIMS OF THE HEATED TENEMENTS.

A Cool Wave Strikes the City and Brings Relief to All but the Sorrowing Families.

The expected cool wave struck this city yesterday morning, bringing with it an almost continuous shower of rain. Relief was immediately experienced by everybody, and was not received with more thankfulness by any persons than the poor in the crowded districts, where little children died by scores during the previous day from the effects of the extreme heat.

Two examples of crusades from Joseph Pulitzer's *New York World* of the 1880s.

New York, for the presidency against the conservative Republican champion, James G. Blaine. Some of the gains came from the readership of Dana's *Sun,* which followed an erratic course and endorsed the discredited third-party candidate Benjamin Butler. Pulitzer himself was elected to Congress that year but soon abandoned that career.

Meanwhile, Cockerill had arrived from St. Louis to become managing editor. Ever adept in both playing up human-interest news and maintaining a solid display of significant local, national, and international stories, Cockerill also featured women's and sports news, as he had in St. Louis. Typographically the new *World* was using smaller and lighter type faces than its predecessor, but the words spoke for themselves: "Death Rides the Blast," "Screaming for Mercy," "Little Lotta's Lovers," "Baptized in Blood."[9] Alliteration was frequent; so were sex, conflict, and crime.

Daily circulation at the end of a year was more than 60,000—a fourfold increase that caused other New York papers to cut their prices to meet Pulitzer's threat. The *Herald* even advertised in the *World*'s pages. Four months later the *Sunday World,* effectively using a large number of woodcuts and line drawings,[10] hit the 100,000 mark. Pulitzer's promotion men presented each employee with a tall silk hat and fired 100 cannon shots in City Hall Park by way of celebration. When, in 1887, the 250,000 figure was reached by the *World,* a silver medal was struck off in honor of America's largest newspaper circulation. In addition, by 1884 the *World* had passed the *Herald* in the number of advertising columns printed and had jumped in size to twelve or fourteen pages daily and thirty-six to forty-four pages on Sunday. However, as expenses mounted and advertising rates were raised, the price to the attentive public remained at 2 cents.

REASONS FOR THE *WORLD*'S SUCCESS

What had Pulitzer done? First of all, he had recognized the characteristics of his potential audience. The population of New York City was increasing by 50 percent during the 1880s, and Pulitzer worked to attract the attention of the newcomers to his newspaper. As an immigrant himself, he was alive to the fact that four out of five of the city's residents were either foreign-born or children of foreign-born parents. And as one who was aware of the social and economic trends of his time, he understood the desire of his readers for effective leadership reflecting progressive attitudes, as well as for entertainment.

Therefore he had enlivened the *World's* significant news coverage to satisfy one set of changing conditions and achieved sensationalism both in news content and in newspaper appearance to satisfy another trend. His critics said Pulitzer had done something else that did not reflect to his credit. He had revived, they said, the sensationalism that had marked the first mass newspapers of the penny-press period of the 1830s. Sensationalism was as old as the newspaper press, but no one had depended on its devices so much in recent years as had Pulitzer. His success encouraged imitation, and this was viewed as a disastrous trend in journalism that made Pulitzer's constructive contributions seem not worth the price.

Pulitzer's answer was that human-interest and sensational stories were needed to win a large circulation and that having won the circulation he would create sound public opinion through enticing readers into the editorial columns and news stories about public affairs. He admired the work of the talented Edwin Lawrence Godkin in the *Evening Post,* although he disagreed with Godkin's economic theories, but when he was chided about the contrast between the news policies of the *Post* and the *World* he made his famous retort: "I want to talk to a nation, not a select committee."[11]

Undoubtedly critics were right in accusing Pulitzer of rationalizing when he presented this defense of the *World's* revival of coarse sensationalism. But they were not correct if they wrote Pulitzer off as a cynic. This passage from a letter written by Pulitzer to one of his editors in later life reflects his basic high-mindedness and the spirit that won for him recognition as a courageous, worthy, and effective editor:

> . . . every issue of the paper presents an opportunity and a duty to say something courageous and true; to rise above the mediocre and conventional; to say something that will command the respect of the intelligent, the educated, the independent part of the community; to rise above fear of partisanship and fear of popular prejudice. I would rather have one article a day of this sort; and these ten or twenty lines might readily represent a whole day's hard work in the way of concentrated, intense thinking and revision, polish of style, weighing of words.[12]

On many days Pulitzer's newspapers fell short of attaining this high goal of journalism, but they approached it often enough to stimulate the efforts of other editors and to win their admiration.[13]

Stunts, as distinguished from useful crusades and promotions, were another specialty of the *World.* Most ambitious was the sending of Nellie Bly around the world in 1889 to see if she could beat the time suggested by Jules Verne in his fictional *Around the World in Eighty Days.* Nellie Bly was a byline name for Elizabeth Cochrane, a woman reporter who had brightened the pages of the *World* by inviting the attention of mashers and then exposing them and by feigning insanity in order to write about conditions in the New York asylum. As Nellie traveled around the world by ships, trains, horses, and sampans, the *World* ran a guessing contest that drew nearly a million estimates of her elapsed time. Nellie did not fail her newspaper; a special train brought her from San Francisco to New York with banners flying as the country applauded her time of 72 days.[14]

The expanded size of the *World* permitted its editors to enliven its pages with stunts and features and still maintain coverage of serious and significant news. A large staff of ambitious reporters covered the city in the same manner as Pulitzer had blanketed St. Louis. News editors sought equally hard to get national coverage and cabled news from abroad. Gradually the coarser sensationalism of the first few years of *World* publication under Pulitzer began to disappear, although there was no letup in the demand for well-written human-interest stories and for reader-pulling illustrations. The editorial page continued its political support of the Democratic party, and backed Cleveland in 1888 and 1892. Yet at the same time it exhibited its independence by opposing the local Tammany Hall machine. Labor found the *World* a solid champion in 1892 when several strikers were killed by Pinkerton guards during the bitter Homestead steel strike in Pittsburgh.

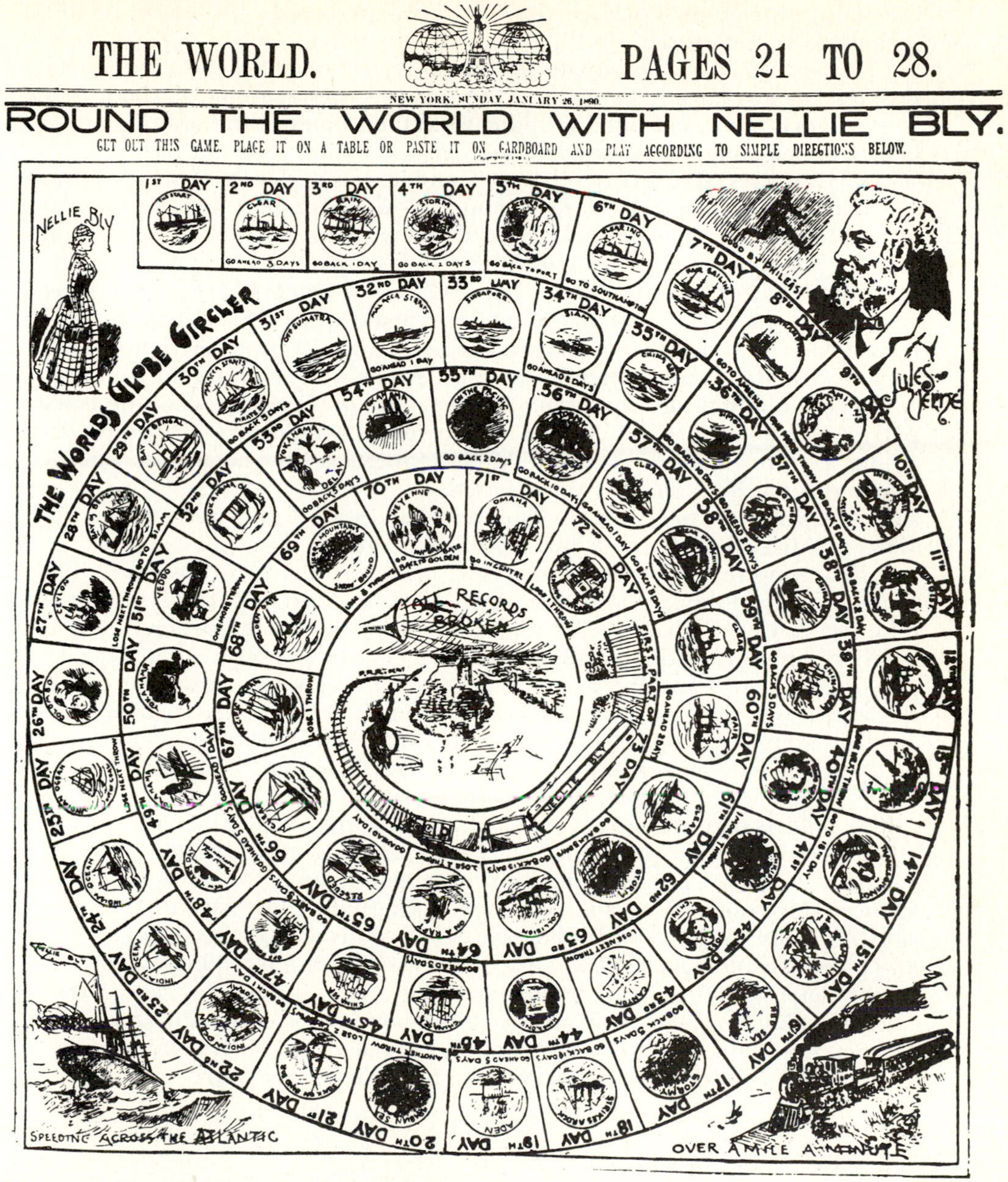

The promotion department offers a Nellie Bly game.
Bettmann Archive

Pulitzer's publishing empire was expanded in 1887 with the establishment of the *Evening World* on the heels of Dana's decision to publish an evening edition of the *Sun.* The evening paper sold for 1 cent and soon outdid the morning edition in popular appeal. It never attained the distinctive character of the morning edition, however, and to newspaperpeople the name *World* still meant the original paper.

A new $2.5 million home for the three *Worlds* was the next order of business. It was an impressive building, among the tallest of its time, topped with a gilded dome and filled with the newest machines of the printing arts. But before the building was finished, tragedy struck. Pulitzer had become completely blind. His nerves were shattered as well, and he was under the care of European specialists. In October, 1890, he announced his retirement from active editorship of his newspapers, and the *Herald,* thinking that it was bidding him goodby, said "We droop our colors to him."

But Pulitzer was not gone. He was to live until 1911, and he was to continue to build his personality into the newspapers. His affliction left him incapable of bearing even the slightest noise, and he went to incredible lengths to isolate himself from tormenting sounds. His associates found him infuriatingly difficult, but they also found him keenly aware of the progress of the newspapers. No matter where the blinded and bearded Pulitzer was—aboard his yacht; at Bar Harbor, Maine; or on the Mediterranean coast—he was constantly in touch with the *World* staff. Copies of each issue were read to him by young male secretaries and streams of instructions and suggestions came to the offices in the *World's* gilded dome by cable, mail, and messenger.

There were important editors and managers there in the *World* offices. Some of them in the late 1880s and early 1890s included Cockerill, who became editor-in-charge; William H. Merrill, who had come from the *Boston Herald* to be chief editorial writer; Ballard Smith, former managing editor of both the *Louisville Courier-Journal* and the *New York Herald,* who served as managing editor; S. S. Carvalho, ex-*Sun* newsman who was city editor of the *Evening World* and later a Pulitzer executive; Colonel Charles H. Jones, a colorful Southerner who served as publisher for Pulitzer in both New York and St. Louis; and George Harvey, later to become an important political figure.

Conflicts between strong-willed rivals for authority and for Pulitzer's favor were inevitable under this policy of assembling many men of high talent under the *World*'s dome. But no editor or manager became too powerful or long ignored the wishes of the absent owner. Cockerill lost his place in 1891 during one of the upheavals by which Pulitzer enforced his will on the staff. Jones, who was given complete editorial control of the *Post-Dispatch* in 1895, was forced out 2 years later when he flouted Pulitzer's wishes. By a constant process of seeking loyal and able assistants from among the country's journalists, Pulitzer was able to keep the *World* steadily progressing in the manner he had conceived, as the leading exponent of what was being called the New Journalism.

THE EDITORIAL STAFF EMERGES

The editorial staff of the metropolitan daily newspaper had taken recognizable modern form by 1890 in numbers and in departmentalized activities. Specialization of duties was necessary as the editing process became more complex and as staffs grew in size. Looking back at the growth of the editorial staff after the founding of the popular press of the 1830s, we can see its evolution from a one-person status to the organization of scores of newspeople who constituted the staff of the *World.*

Regularly employed reporters were rare even after the penny press had become well established in the 1840s. Newspaper editors ran what local news they encountered or had time to cover, used their telegraph news, clipped their exchanges, and printed the contributions of correspondents, such as the group who covered Congress after the mid-1820s. Some owner-editors added chief assistants, notably Horace Greeley, who employed first Henry J. Raymond and then Charles A. Dana to help him handle the news on the *New York Tribune* in the early 1840s. The chief assistants soon became known as managing editors; two of the earliest to hold that title were Dana of the *Tribune* and Frederic Hudson of the *New York Herald.* In the 1850s chief reporters emerged, as forerunners of the city editors. The *Tribune* of 1854 had fourteen reporters and ten editors and had introduced editorial writers, literary editors, and other specialists. But these editorial staff advances were found only on leading newspapers.

Intensified reporting of the Civil War by hundreds of correspondents in the field did much to stimulate the rise of news staffs. Some of the Civil War reporters who thus demonstrated their journalistic skills rose to become editors or owners of newspapers: Murat Halstead, Whitelaw Reid, Henry Villard. Others went on to cover wars in Europe or Indian wars on the western American plains. Killed in Custer's Last Stand on the Little Big Horn in 1876 was *Bismarck Tribune* correspondent Mark Kellogg, who earlier had been a Wisconsin reporter and editor of a Minnesota 1872 Greeley campaign paper.

George W. Smalley was an example of the new type of reporter. A graduate of Yale and of the Harvard Law School, he covered the Civil War for the *Tribune,* then reported the Franco-Prussian War and remained in Europe as London correspondent for the paper. Henry M. Stanley of the *New York Herald* covered the Civil War and the Indian wars, went to Asia and Africa as a *Herald* correspondent, and climaxed his career with his expedition to Africa in 1871 to find the missing missionary, David Livingstone. Jerome B. Stillson, another *Herald* reporter, obtained an exclusive interview with the Indian chief Sitting Bull in 1877 that filled fourteen columns of the paper. John A. Cockerill, Pulitzer's ace reporter and editor, had covered the Russo-Turkish War. Again, these are examples of a limited activity, but they foreshadow the intensified reportorial achievements of the 1890s.

Emphasis increasingly centered on the reporter. Henry Grady, a free-lance correspondent before becoming managing editor of the *Atlanta Constitution,* had advanced the art of interviewing as a means of both gathering and interpreting the news. Dana and Pulitzer prized their reporting staffs because they themselves had handled news, as had Henry Raymond of the *Times* who covered the Austro-Italian War. Some papers, like the *New York Sun,* Chicago's *Inter Ocean,* Nelson's *Kansas City Star,* and Stone's *Chicago Daily News*—in addition to the large New York dailies—became known as training grounds for young reporters who later moved on to other staffs.

The *New York Sun* produced great reporters, among them Julian Ralph, Arthur Brisbane, S. S. Carvalho, Edward W. Townsend, and Richard Harding

Davis. Managing editor Amos J. Cummings, an expert in the human interest story, Chester Lord, managing editor after 1880, and other subeditors molded these careers. Ralph later became a prize Hearst reporter; Brisbane was managing editor of the *Evening Sun* before leaving for a fabulous career with both Pulitzer and Hearst; Carvalho was the *Evening World's* first city editor before he too joined Hearst and ended up a top executive; Davis left the *Sun* for Hearst's lure but achieved greatest fame with the *Herald.* The *Sun* and the *Tribune* shared the reporting career of Jacob A. Riis, who wrote with discernment about conditions in the New York City slums and the tragedies they bred.

The upsurge of circulations and competition brought increased specialization within the newsrooms. By the 1870s, each leading metropolitan daily had a chief editor, a managing editor or night editor in charge of the news, a city editor to direct the staff of perhaps two dozen reporters, a telegraph editor to handle the increasing volume of wire and cable news, a financial editor, a drama critic, a literary editor, and editorial writers. As the years passed and reporting staffs grew, the city editor's role took on more importance.

However, all was not rosy in the cityrooms, where editors often feared for their jobs and many reporters toiled 14 to 16 hours per day to earn perhaps $20 to $30 per week, instead of a regular salary, under a degrading time and space system. Some top reporters had salaries, and by 1890 they were earning from $50 to $100 per week, good pay in 1890 dollars. The managing editor of a large paper might have earned about $125, but many staff members stayed at the same $15 to $25 a week level that had existed for reporters after the Civil War because there was no effective labor organization in the editorial offices as there was in the mechanical departments. Bennett, Pulitzer, and others kept the pressure on the dozens of lower-ranking reporters by forcing keen competition for space, instituting spy systems, and keeping benefits at a minimum. One effect on the news product was the widespread use of combination reporting, in which reporters from competing papers banded together to protect themselves from criticism and to generate enough copy to fill a good deal of valuable space. Another effect was sensationalism, whereby reporters under pressure to come up with exciting stories earned double rates if they reported exclusives. These petty and mean newsroom practices were found even on papers like the *World* that preached different values to the readers. It was years before these practices were minimized.[15]

The newsroom operations became more sophisticated with the use of the telephone, the typewriter, and a rewrite staff. Publishing of an increased number of editions caused pressure for more rapid handling of local news, and the summary lead gained favor as a means of condensing stories. (But the literary stylists and writers of rambling chronological stories were still numerous.) As Sunday papers became common, additional persons were needed to assist the chief editors. Special Sunday staffs were set up, including cartoonists and artists. Along with this attention to regular news, sports news became increasingly important to the mass audience. Pulitzer realized this and arranged the first separate sports department for his *World.* Specialized writers began to appear in each sports field and several columns of sports news were run in big newspapers by 1890. After the turn of the century regular sports pages began to appear.

WOMEN IN JOURNALISM

Another development was the rapid influx of women staff members. The industrial boom and expansion of business opportunities had meant jobs for women, and this included the newspaper business. There had been women journalists of note dating back to the Revolutionary War days. Before the Civil War Margaret Fuller of the *New York Tribune,* for example, and Jane Grey Swisshelm, a Washington correspondent and Minnesota newspaper editor, gained attention. Victoria Woodhull and her sister, Tennessee Claflin, published their weekly in New York in 1870, championing female emancipation, abortion, and free love. Eliza Jane Poitevant Holbrook was literary editor of the *New Orleans Picayune* in the 1860s, married the publisher, and ran the paper after his death. Ellen Scripps worked with her famous brothers when they started their newspapers in the 1870s and 1880s. Nancy Johnson was the *New York Times'* European travel writer in 1857.

Jennie June Croly—who founded America's first women's club, the New York Press Club and Sorosis—began the first fashion column and set up a duplicate exchange service, the forerunner to later syndicated services. Her professional career spanned 40 years, beginning with her work for the *New York Herald* in 1855. Kate Field wrote editorials for the *Times* of London before joining the *New York Herald* staff as a reporter and critic. In 1891 she established "Kate Field's Washington," a weekly review of books, music, and art. Writing women's news for some of the first women's pages in the 1890s were Fanny Fern of the *Philadelphia Ledger* and Grace Greenwood of the *New York Times.* Florence Finch Kelly, who worked on several papers and helped establish the Women's Press Club in New York in 1889, joined the *New York Times* in 1906 for a 30-year stint in the book-review section.

Active writers included Ida M. Tarbell, who was one of the original muckrakers for *McClure's* beginning in 1893; Winifred Black (Annie Laurie), one of Hearst's early stars; Elizabeth Cochrane (Nellie Bly), moral crusader for the *World* who circled the world as a promotional stunt; Nixola Greeley-Smith, the granddaughter of Horace Greeley, who was hired by Pulitzer and spent 20 years as a reporter; Sally Joy (Penelope Penfeather), fashion writer of the *Boston Herald* and first president of the New England Women's Press Association in the 1880s. Jessie White Mario was the *Nation*'s faithful correspondent from Italy from 1866 to 1904, and she provided detailed political news.

Women correspondents in Washington multiplied after Jane Swisshelm took her seat in the Senate press gallery in 1850. Among 166 correspondents the 1879 *Congressional Directory* listed twenty women with gallery privileges. Then women were dropped because each paper was limited to three names on the list, and the women correspondents were not breaking-news reporters. In the years 1866 to 1880, the foremost women Washington correspondents were Mary Clemmer Ames, whose column appeared in the weekly *New York Independent,* and Emily Edson Briggs, columnist for the *Philadelphia Press.* Sara Clarke Lippincott did liberal-oriented columns for the *New York Times* in the 1870s (she was also Grace Greenwood by pen name). Mary Abigail Dodge did conservative articles for the 1877 to 1878 *New York Tribune.*

Carrying on the tradition of many earlier women journalists, Miriam Follin

Leslie edited *Frank Leslie's Illustrated Newspaper* after her husband's death. Anna Benjamin covered the Spanish-American War for that publication, and that same year Marie Manning was hired by Hearst as a reporter and ended up as Beatrice Fairfax, lovelorn writer for the *New York Journal.* Later Dorothy Dix (Elizabeth Meriweather Gilmore) wrote a similar column for the Hearst syndicate. One scholar noted that in 1889 the entire issue of the *Journalist,* a professional periodical, was devoted to profiles of fifty women editors and reporters. Ten of them were black, including Mrs. N. F. Mossell, who edited the women's pages of the *New York Freeman,* and popular columnist Lillian Alberta Lewis, whose pen name was Bert Islew. Her work appeared in the *Boston Advocate* and elsewhere.[16]

ADVANCES IN COOPERATIVE NEWS GATHERING

Pressure for speedier and more comprehensive coverage of the news, which stemmed both from increasing competition among the dailies and from the needs of the new social environment, brought changes in cooperative news gathering. Railroads and telegraph lines that had been part of the race for news in the 1840s spurted ahead to cover the country. Between 1880 and 1900 the number of railroad tracks doubled and those of telegraph lines quadrupled. Bell Telephone lines joined cities in those years; the federal postal service began free rural delivery in 1897, and also improved city carrier service. The Atlantic Cable, which began operating in 1866, linked the United States to London, and another cable stretched eastward to India and the Orient.

The opening of the Atlantic Cable had facilitated reciprocal exchanges of news between the Associated Press of New York (founded by the city's morning papers in 1848) and the press agencies of Europe: Reuters in Britain (1851), Havas in France (1835), Wolff in Germany (1849), and Stefani in Italy (1853). An 1870 agreement between Havas, Reuters, and Wolff allowed those agencies to monopolize the distribution of news by designating parts of the world for exclusive reporting and transmission rights for each organization. Some areas were shared by these major contracting parties or with smaller national news organizations. Reuters, with control of more than half of the world's cable lines, dominated the Ring Combination, as the "grand cartel" was called. In 1893 a merger of the New York Associated Press and the Western Associated Press, which formed the Associated Press of Illinois (API), led in turn to an agreement with the Ring Combination whereby the API was allowed to distribute Reuters in the United States and to share Mexican and Central American news with Reuters and Havas and Canadian and West Indian news with Reuters. The Ring Combination, interrupted by wars and hampered by domestic politics and professional jealousies, lasted until 1934. The Associated Press played a more equal role in the twentieth century.[17]

The AP, controlled by the seven charter-member New York morning newspapers, had formed agreements with the Western Union by which preferred treatment and rates could be offered member papers. Regional and local groups that did become members could restrict membership, and thus prevent new competitors from obtaining the basic coverage afforded by the AP. To discourage press-service competitors, the New York AP forbade those receiving its service to buy the news of any other agency.

Naturally there were many complaints about this news monopoly. The news report favored morning newspapers. Rates to clients were arbitrarily assessed and papers outside of New York felt they were paying too much of the cost and had too little to say about the operations of the service. Despite the fact that in 1880 only half of the morning dailies and a fourth of the evening papers were receiving the service, only the United Press (no relation to the later service of the same name) offered real competition before it was submerged in competition between rival AP factions.[18]

However, some important steps were being taken in cooperative news gathering. A leased wire set up between New York and Washington in 1875 carried up to 20,000 words per day. This improved service reached Chicago in 1884, and by 1900 the AP-leased wires were extended to New Orleans, Denver, and Minneapolis. Smaller dailies were given inexpensive service by the making of thin stereotyped plates that could be set directly into the news columns. The prime distributor of thin plates in the 1880s was the American Press Association, which used AP press reports. Feature stories, illustrations, and entertainment material were also available from these syndicates.[19] In addition, some leading papers syndicated proof slips of their exclusive stories by express service, mail, or telegraph. City news services were formally organized in New York and Chicago in the early 1890s. These agencies for the collection of routine city news had taken form during the Civil War.

The new leaders in journalism were willing to spend money for the gathering of news. To supplement their AP coverage they began to send more correspondents to Congress. At the outbreak of the Civil War forty-five reporters were in the galleries, but by 1870 this number was 130. The famed Washington Gridiron Club was formed in 1885 by Ben Perley Poore of the *Boston Journal*, dean of the capital press corps. There were major problems that money could not solve, however. The AP, by its cooperative nature, depended heavily on the news collected by member papers and the foreign press services. Often this was unsatisfactory and Western Union operators had to be called on to supply the coverage of spot news events that AP members could not provide. Those papers outside the AP fold were forced to struggle along, waiting for the day when other press associations would provide competition to the AP.

THE BUSINESS SIDE: ADVERTISING DEVELOPMENTS

The expansion of the editorial staff and its news-gathering activities, which was thus heralding the arrival of modern journalism, was made possible by tremendous developments in the business and mechanical departments of the metropolitan daily newspapers. But these developments in turn brought an overshadowing of the figures of the old-time editors and a relative lessening of their influence in the new era of corporate journalism. This did not mean that editors and news executives were shunted aside, but they could no longer dominate the scene as in the days when an editor-owner stood in command of a less complex enterprise.

Those larger dailies that had become complex business institutions—headed by the *New York World* with its $10 million valuation and its annual $1 million profit in the mid-1890s—were harassed by a host of new problems. It was they who first reflected the corporate nature of the new journalism, although the pressure of the business problems they faced soon came to be felt by an increasing number of middle-sized dailies and to some degree by all newspapers.

The scramble for advertising and circulation supremacy, widespread mechanical innovations and pyramiding capitalization costs, larger payrolls and more difficult labor-relations problems, increasing concern over newsprint supply for skyrocketing circulations—these and other problems brought the rise of a managerial corps in newspaper publishing, just as was happening with managers as a group in American business generally.

Symbolizing the ascendancy of business problems of the daily newspapers was the establishment of the American Newspaper Publishers Association in 1887 to serve as their trade association. The leaders in the association were representatives of aggressive new papers and of older papers that were alive to the problems of the new journalism. Most of the people taking part in association affairs held managerial posts on their newspapers or were publishers primarily interested in business management.

Two of the early presidents were James W. Scott of the *Chicago Herald* and Charles W. Knapp of the *St. Louis Republic,* both news-trained publishers. But men like Colonel Charles H. Jones, S. S. Carvalho, John Norris, and Don C. Seitz—all of whom contended for managerial-side supremacy on Pulitzer's *World* in the 1890s—were more typical leaders of the ANPA. Seitz, who survived as manager of the *World,* and Norris, who became business manager of the *New York Times,* were particularly important leaders of the Publishers Association after the turn of the century. There they spoke for their absent publishers, Pulitzer and Adolph Ochs.

The ANPA was organized at the call of William H. Brearley, advertising manager of the *Detroit Evening News,* James E. Scripps' successful new paper. There were many state editorial associations—seventeen had been founded between 1853 and 1880—but most of their members published weeklies and small dailies. The National Editorial Association had been organized in 1885, by B. B. Herbert of the *Red Wing Daily Republican* of Minnesota, among the weeklies and smallest dailies.

What Brearley and his associates primarily wanted was a daily newspaper trade association that would help its members with the problem of obtaining national advertising. Although the ANPA soon became deeply involved in problems of labor relations, newsprint supply, government mail rates, and mechanical developments, it centered much of its attention on the field of advertising.

The first advertising agents had appeared in New York and other Eastern cities in the 1840s as links between their advertisers and the newspapers. They purchased space for their clients, receiving discounts of from 15 percent to 30 percent, and sometimes up to 75 percent, on stated advertising rates. This was their profit. Although larger papers were able to obtain ads on a steady basis and

THE CHICAGO TIMES-HERALD, TUESDAY, JULY 12, 1898. 5

ON SCHOOL BOARD

Mayor Appoints Eight New Members and Renames Trude.

HARPER AND CUSACK ARE OUT

EIGHT NEW MEMBERS OF THE BOARD OF EDUCATION

HONORS FOR ILLINOIS.

STATE WINS EDUCATORS' FAVOR.

MISSIONS IN CHINA ATTACKED.

WINNIPEG EXHIBITION OPEN.

TRUSTEES TAKE THE PLANT.

MINISTER CONGER IS RECEIVED.

EXPLANATION BY MR. DE BACA.

DR. CAMILLO VOLINI, WHO "DOWNED" LITTLE JOHNNIE POWERS

LOW EXCURSION RATES

CARSON PIRIE SCOTT & CO.

Our After-Inventory Clearing Sale is now in progress—surplus stocks in all departments are being closed out at the smallest prices. The watchword all along the line is

"SUMMER GOODS MUST GO."

Imported Wash Goods.

Summer Silks.

Extra Special—$1.00 Fancy Silks for 49c.

Season's Greatest Sale Wash Shirt Waists.

Sale Manufacturer's Stock Shirt Waist Ginghams.

Women's Kid Boots, $2.15.

GREAT OXFORD SALE.

$1.15 and $1.65

MARSHALL FIELD & CO.

A prominent manufacturer's surplus stock of

Bureaus, Chiffoniers and Toilet Tables

Reduction of 25%

Women's Tan Kid Shoes $1.45.

Women's Oxfords $1.45.

Men's Shoes, $2.45.

Special Shirt Waists, 75c.

Two still-famous Chicago department stores advertise in an 1898 *Times-Herald.*

to regulate the agents' commissions, smaller papers were sometimes victimized as agents played one publisher against another.

There were many attempts to regulate advertising practices and not all agents operated in this manner. The founding of the respected agencies of George P. Rowell, N. W. Ayer & Son, and Lord and Thomas around 1870 helped. Rowell published his *American Newspaper Directory* in 1869, in an effort to locate all of the newly developed newspapers, and Ayer & Son began its continued annual publication in 1880.[20] But true circulations were hard to determine, and it was not until 1914 that the Audit Bureau of Circulations was established, solving the problem. Identifying trustworthy agencies was another problem and after years of arguments the ANPA headquarters in New York agreed, in 1899, to issue lists of recognized agencies. By common consent the discount figure was determined at 15 percent.

The percentage of newspaper revenue coming from advertising, as compared to circulation income, rose from half in 1880 to 64 percent by 1910. Space given to ads in most dailies rose from 25 percent to a 50-50 ratio with editorial material by World War I. While the amount of advertising was rising, the content was changing. Three pioneers in the department-store business, John Wanamaker of Philadelphia, Marshall Field of Chicago, and A. T. Stewart of New York, gave impetus to retail-store advertising. Ivory soap and Royal baking powder were leaders in national advertising in the 1880s, and in the 1890s many more products appeared—complete with slogans like "It Floats" and "His Master's Voice" for Ivory soap and Victor phonographs, respectively, and others for Eastman Kodak, Wrigley's gum, and foods.

But there was a cloud over the advertising business because the leading clients of newspapers and magazines were the patent medicine makers who pushed Castoria, Scott's Emulsion, and Lydia Pinkham's Female Compound at the unsuspecting public. These misleading, deliberately deceptive, and often outwardly fraudulent advertisements were quickly accepted by most newspaper and magazine representatives because of the great volume of money involved. This practice continued in large scale until Congress began to get involved at the time of World War I. Despite the attempts at governmental regulation, unscrupulous advertisers and dollar-hungry media people continue to the present day to promote useless and sometimes harmful over-the-counter drugs. Television testimonials replaced the crude newspaper pitches, while consumer advocates protested against the overuse of drugs by the American public. The greatest harm came when the cure-alls were accepted for proper medical attention in remote areas and in crowded tenement districts. Many of the drugs were harmless, as some defenders of the practice claimed, but the deception was painful nevertheless, and some of the drugs did contain deadly poisons.[21]

NEW LEADERS FOR MAGAZINES

There were successful new leaders in magazine journalism, just as there were in newspaper making. One was Frank Munsey, a New Englander with a sober and industrious character, who struggled for a decade in the New York magazine-publishing field before achieving success with his *Munsey's,* begun in 1889. Another was S. S. McClure who, after establishing a feature syndicate service for newspapers, brought out his *McClure's* in 1893. A third was *Cosmopolitan,* founded in 1886 and sold to William Randolph Hearst in 1905.

These well-edited, popularized monthly magazines had found the same answer to the problem of obtaining mass circulation that the daily newspapers had found in the past. The secret was cutting the price first to 15 cents, and then to a dime, for magazines that competed with older 35-cent publications. The low 1-cent-a-pound mail rate, in effect from 1885 until zone rates were established during World War I, helped to make this possible. By the turn of the century *Munsey's* had achieved 650,000 circulation to lead by a wide margin, and *McClure's* and *Cosmopolitan* were runners-up. The formula for all three was popular fiction, general articles, and illustrations.

Cyrus H. K. Curtis provided new leadership in the women's magazine field with his *Ladies' Home Journal,* founded in 1883. With Edward W. Bok as editor after 1889, the magazine quickly rose to a half-million circulation at a $1 annual subscription price. In the weekly 5-cent magazine field the *Saturday Evening Post,* bought by Curtis in 1897, and *Collier's,* founded in 1888, pushed to even higher circulations than those of the monthlies.

These new popularly circulated magazines made the biggest inroads on available advertising revenue, arising as they did to public notice at the moment when national advertising was expanding. But the general illustrated monthly magazines of high literary and artistic quality—*Harper's, Century,* and *Scribner's*—continued to have major influence, even though outstripped in circulation. Sharing in the competition for reader attention and revenue too were the illustrated weekly periodicals, *Harper's Weekly* and *Leslie's;* the weeklies depending on humor and cartoons, *Puck, Life,* and *Judge;* and the children's magazines, *Youth's Companion* and *St. Nicholas.*

Taking stock of the amount of advertising revenue gained by magazines, newspaper owners formed two business associations, the International Circulation Managers Association in 1898 and the Newspaper Advertising Executives Association in 1900, as well as regional organizations. Beginning in the late 1870s various representatives and associations worked to promote the newspaper as an advertising medium, and in 1913 the American Newspaper Publishers Association was persuaded to sponsor the founding of the Bureau of Advertising. The Bureau, with a paid staff, did an effective job of arguing the case of newspapers. In 1900 magazines were picking up 60 percent or more of national advertising revenue but by the time of World War I they were sharing the money on an equal basis. Because newspapers had local advertising as well, they received a total of roughly 70 percent of all advertising revenues in the early years of the twentieth century.

A REVOLUTION IN PRINTING: PHOTOGRAPHS

The growth of the modern newspaper thus far described went hand in hand with the development of better printing techniques, improvements in presenting illustrations and eventually photographs, and changing relationships between management and labor brought by unionization and battles over the price of newsprint.

As part of the Industrial Revolution of the late nineteenth century, achievements in printing included the typesetting machine, faster presses, stereotyping, color printing, dry mats, electrotyping, and photoengraving. Ottmar Mergenthaler's Linotype machine first cast a line of type for newspaper use in 1886 in the *New York Tribune* plant. The timesaving performance of the Linotype helped the large evening dailies, which were under pressure to cover more news close to deadline time. Other slugcasting machines were soon developed, and improvements in the type faces themselves began to help readability. The ugly Gothics began to disappear and after 1900 the newly designed Cheltenham family, the graceful Bodoni, and other headline types came into favor. The *New York Tribune* won typographical fame for its early use of the Bodoni upper- and lower-case headlines.

The press of deadlines and the rush for big circulations led to the development of bigger and faster presses. The leader here was R. Hoe & Company, which earlier had converted the presses of leading papers from hand to steam power and from flatbed to rotary before the Civil War. Next came the adaptation of the stereotyped plate to the newspaper press, which allowed the breaking of column rules for illustrations, headlines, and advertising—a practice not practical for users of type-revolving presses. The use of the curved stereotyped plate permitted a speed-up of the hourly rate of printing and extra stereotypes of the same page could be produced for simultaneous use on two or more presses. Other changes allowed the use of a continuous roll of newsprint, printing on both sides of the sheet in one operation, automatic folders, and, in the 1890s, color printing.

By 1890 most of the type-revolving presses had been replaced by presses using stereotyped plates and webs. The finest Hoe press could run off 48,000 twelve-page papers in an hour and owners of the larger papers were making plans for installing banks of presses to keep up with the skyrocketing circulations. Color inserts printed separately had been used earlier, until full-color presses modeled after those being used in Paris were first built for the *Chicago Inter Ocean* by Walter Scott in 1892. Within a year the *New York World* had color presses and soon the Sunday comics were a regular feature of the newspaper.

More than one newspaper owner had sensed the need for better illustrations. The *New York Herald* had stood out for its early use of woodcuts and, beginning about 1870, the *Evening Telegram,* companion paper for the *Herald,* published a daily political cartoon. Of course *Frank Leslie's Illustrated Newspaper, Harper's Weekly,* and later other periodicals did highly artistic work with woodcuts. Women's magazines used engraved-steel fashion plates. But there was a need for something less expensive and faster. In the 1870s Zincographs, line cuts produced by etching on zinc plates, began to appear in United States papers, and illustrators also found that they could print photos directly onto woodblocks or zinc plates, where they would form a guide for the artist or etcher who completed the cut.

A major breakthrough came when *New York World* editors began to publish line drawings of prominent local citizens, beginning in 1884. Within a short time a number of other leading papers were arranging for the work of the artist, Valerian Gribayédoff, who estimated in 1891 that there were about 1000 artists at work supplying illustrations for 5000 newspapers and magazines.[22] An increasing number of papers began to hire their own artists and to install engraving facilities.

Photoengraving was quickly to curtail this boom for the artists, however. The halftone photoengraving process had been developed in England prior to 1860, but the results were unsatisfactory until Frederic E. Ives went to work on the problem of reproducing photographs in the printing process. Ives was made head of the photographic laboratory at Cornell University in 1876, when he was 20. The next year he produced a photoengraving of a pen drawing, which was published in the student paper at Cornell. In 1878 he made his first halftone. Ives saw that the way to break up masses of dark and light was to lay out a series of prominences on a plate that would transfer the ink to paper point by point. If the points were close together, the mass would be dark; and the more widely they were spaced, the lighter the mass would become. Ives moved to Baltimore, and then after 1879 to Philadelphia, and produced commercially used halftones. He perfected his process in 1886.

There still remained, however, the problem of using the halftones on rotary presses. One of the heroes of the struggle to get pictures into the American newspaper was Stephen H. Horgan. Horgan was the art editor of an illustrated paper called the *New York Daily Graphic,* which began in 1873 and battled bravely until 1889 when it succumbed in the big-city competition. It was Horgan who succeeded in publishing in 1880, a newspaper halftone of good quality of a picture called "Shantytown," (see page 225). And it was Horgan who first had the idea of how to run halftones on rotary presses. He was rebuffed by doubting press operators, however, and it was not until 1897 that he perfected the method for the *New York Tribune.* Within a short time other large papers were running halftone reproductions of photographs.

The artists found the news photographers edging into their field in earnest, now that their photos could be reproduced directly. Both groups covered the Spanish-American War. Syndicates quickly added news and feature photographs to their stock in trade, and big-city papers began to employ local photographers who carried their heavy, awkward equipment and their flashlight powder out on assignments. Pictorial journalism was on its way, although its full impact would await the tabloids of the 1920s and the documentary films and *Life* magazine of the 1930s.

The sweep of all of these mechanical developments included labor specialization and larger working forces that in turn brought new labor-relations problems. The American Federation of Labor had organized printers, pressmen, and engravers, who pressed constantly for shorter working hours and higher pay. The danger of plantwide strikes—suspensions of service that could jeopardize the status of newspapers with their advertisers and the public—was reduced when the International Typographical Union split by specialty into four separate unions. Efforts by the labor unions and publishers, led by the American Newspaper Publishers Association, to have local conciliation and arbitration procedures and the right of appeal to a national arbitration board brought comparative peace to the newspaper industry in 1899, during a time of severe labor disturbances in other industries.

The ANPA also took a leadership role in the campaign to bring less expensive newsprint to its members. The Fourdrinier process introduced from Germany in 1867, which allowed low-cost newsprint to be made from wood pulp to which was added a rag content, was a basic factor in the growth of the

American newspaper. Prior to this, an expensive, limited industry produced paper by hand from rag stock. During the Civil War newspaper costs ran to $440 a ton for paper. By the 1890s a chemically produced wood pulp, called sulphite pulp, replaced rag stock as the toughening element in newsprint. Prices tumbled rapidly, reaching $42 a ton in 1899 and remaining there for years, except for periods of paper shortage.[23]

One problem remained, however. Domestic newsprint manufacturers had obtained a good-sized tariff on imported newsprint and had effected a virtual monopolistic control over domestic output and sales prices. The ANPA campaigned for years against the tariff, hoping to free the vast Canadian forest resources for American printing use. Finally, in 1913, Congress carried out the pledge of the Woodrow Wilson administration to lower the tariff, allowing a flood of Canadian newsprint into the country.

It is evident then, from this survey of changing industrial conditions in the daily newspaper and magazine business, that there was a "watershed of the nineties" for the American newspaper. The advance into the modern era had been accomplished and, for better or for worse, the older era of journalism was no more.

NOTES

1. In a poll of American editors conducted by *Editor & Publisher* in 1934.

2. Cockerill's biographer contends that his experience as managing editor of the *Cincinnati Enquirer* in exploiting local news, and his subsequent exposures to national and international news in Washington and Baltimore and as a war correspondent, made Cockerill a definitely superior newsman to Pulitzer. Much of the imaginative handling of the news, and the sensational approach, is credited to Cockerill. See Homer W. King, *Pulitzer's Prize Editor: A Biography of John A. Cockerill, 1845–1896* (Durham, N.C.: Duke University Press, 1965).

3. As quoted in Don C. Seitz, *Joseph Pulitzer: His Life and Letters* (New York: Simon & Schuster, 1924), p. 101. The name of the paper was soon changed to the *Post-Dispatch.*

4. As quoted in *The Story of the St. Louis Post-Dispatch* (St. Louis: Pulitzer Publishing Company, 1949), p. 3.

5. Documented in the chapter, "A Sensational Newspaper," in Julian Rammelkamp, *Pulitzer's Post-Dispatch, 1878–1883* (Princeton, N.J.: Princeton University Press, 1967), pp. 163–206. On the whole Rammelkamp endorses Pulitzer's record.

6. Rammelkamp points out that Pulitzer "mobilized the middle class elements of St. Louis into a dynamic movement of reform" that finally bore fruit early in the twentieth century (ibid., p. 303).

7. As quoted in Willard G. Bleyer, *Main Currents in the History of American Journalism* (Boston: Houghton Mifflin, 1927), p. 325.

8. *New York World,* May 11, 1883.

9. As quoted in Bleyer, *Main Currents in the History of American Journalism,* p. 328.

10. *Journalist,* August 22, 1885.

11. James Creelman, "Joseph Pulitzer—Master Journalist," *Pearson's,* XXI (March 1909), p. 246.

12. As quoted in Seitz, *Joseph Pulitzer,* p. 286.

13. Indicative of that frailty that led to conspicuous failings was Pulitzer's admiration of three publishers in particular whose newspapers utilized sensational techniques but did not measure up to the *World* in high-quality performance. They were William M. Singerly, *Philadelphia Record;* Charles H. Taylor, *Boston Globe;* and the British newspaper popularizer, Alfred Harmsworth, who later became Lord Northcliffe.

14. Three New York newspapers repeated the stunt in 1936. H. R. Ekins of the *World-Telegram* won with a time of 18½ days, defeating Dorothy ("Nellie Bly") Kilgallen of the *Journal* and Leo Kiernan of the *Times.*

15. Ted Curtis Smythe, "The Reporter, 1880–1900," *Journalism History,* VII (Spring 1980), describes in detail the primitive working conditions and their effects on the news products.

16. For a full discussion of these women and dozens

more, see Marion Marzolf, *Up From the Footnote: A History of Women Journalists* (New York: Hastings House, 1977).

17. Robert W. Desmond's books on international communications, particularly pp. 165–68 of *The Information Process* and pp. 384–92 of *Crisis and Conflict,* offer excellent descriptions of the Ring Combination's financial and political dealings.

18. The standard account of this subject is Victor Rosewater, *History of Cooperative News-Gathering in the United States* (New York: Appleton-Century-Crofts, 1930).

19. Alfred M. Lee, *The Daily Newspaper in America* (New York: Macmillan, 1937), p. 511.

20. The detailed story is told in Frank Presbrey, *The History and Development of Advertising* (New York: Doubleday, 1929).

21. William Marz, "Patent Medicine Advertising: Mass Persuasion Techniques and Reform, 1905–1976" (M.A. thesis, California State University at Northridge, 1977).

22. *Cosmopolitan,* XI (August 1891).

23. Lee, *The Daily Newspaper in America,* pp. 743–45.

ANNOTATED BIBLIOGRAPHY

Books

The *Union List of Newspapers,* beginning where Brigham's bibliography leaves off in 1820, is supplemented by directories: *Geo. P. Rowell & Co.'s American Newspaper Directory* (1869) and *N. W. Ayer & Son's American Newspaper Annual* (1880), later called the *Directory of Newspapers & Periodicals.* The *Editor & Publisher International Year Book* dates from 1921.

BARRETT, JAMES W., *Joseph Pulitzer and His World.* New York: Vanguard, 1941. A colorful, rambling story of Pulitzer and the *New York World* by the last city editor of the *World.*

CARNES, CECIL, *Jimmy Hare, News Photographer.* New York: Macmillan, 1940. The biography of one of the early leading press photographers.

DOWNEY, FAIRFAX D., *Richard Harding Davis: His Day.* New York: Scribner's, 1933. Biography of the glamor boy of early modern journalism.

ELLIS, L. ETHAN, *Newsprint: Producers, Publishers, Political Pressures.* New Brunswick, N.J.: Rutgers University Press, 1960. The economics of print paper (includes Ellis' 1948 study, *Print Paper Pendulum*).

EMERY, EDWIN, *History of the American Newspaper Publishers Association.* Minneapolis: University of Minnesota Press, 1950. Covers the activities of the organized daily newspaper publishers in the fields of labor relations, newsprint, advertising, mailing privileges, mechanical research, and legislative lobbying, from 1887 to 1950.

GERNSHEIM, HELMUT, *A Concise History of Photography.* London: Thames and Hudson, 1965. Well illustrated; begins with the 1830s.

HOWER, RALPH M., *The History of an Advertising Agency: N. W. Ayer & Son at Work, 1869–1949.* Cambridge, Mass.: Harvard University Press, 1949.

IRWIN, WILL, *The American Newspaper,* edited by Clifford F. Weigle and David G. Clark. Ames: Iowa State University Press, 1969. Reproductions of the original series in *Collier's* of 1911.

———, *The Making of a Reporter.* New York: G. P. Putnam's Sons, 1942. Autobiography of a discerning newspaperperson who ranked with the best.

JAKES, JOHN, *Great Women Reporters.* New York: G. P. Putnam's Sons, 1969. The stories of dozens who competed with men for news.

JONES, EDGAR R., *Those Were the Good Old Days: A Happy Look at American Advertising, 1880–1930.* New York: Simon & Schuster, 1959. Illustrations of 50 years of advertising from magazines.

JUERGENS, GEORGE, *Joseph Pulitzer and the New York World.* Princeton, N.J.: Princeton University Press, 1966. A detailed, enthusiastic account of Pulitzer's first 4 years at the *World,* 1883 to 1887.

KING, HOMER W., *Pulitzer's Prize Editor: A Biography of John A. Cockerill, 1845–1896.* Durham, N.C.: Duke University Press, 1965. Only detailed study of the managing editor, whose biographer contends he overshadowed Pulitzer in handling news.

KNIGHT, OLIVER A., *Following the Indian Wars: The Story of the Newspaper Correspondents among the Indian Campaigners, 1886–1891.* Norman: University of Oklahoma Press, 1960. Well documented.

LOFT, JACOB, *The Printing Trades.* New York: Holt, Rinehart & Winston, 1944. An inclusive account. See also Elizabeth F. Baker, *Printers and Technology: A History of the International Printing Pressmen and Assistants' Union* (New York: Columbia University Press, 1957).

MARZOLF, MARION, *Up From the Footnote: A History of Women Journalists.* New York: Hastings House, 1977. From colonial days to present, by bibliographer for the area. Also see Marzolf, "The Woman Journalist: Colonial Printer to City Desk," *Journalism History,* I–II (Winter 1974, Spring 1975).

MATHEWS, JOSEPH F., *George Washburn Smalley: Forty Years a Foreign Correspondent.* Chapel Hill: University of North Carolina Press, 1973. Covers the years 1867–1906.

NEWHALL, BEAUMONT, *The History of Photography from 1839 to the Present Day.* New York: Museum of Modern Art, 1964. The standard reference.

POORE, BEN: PERLEY, *Perley's Reminiscences of Sixty Years in the National Metropolis.* Philadelphia: Hubbard, 1886. Two volumes about political, social, and journalistic life in Washington, 1820s to 1880s. Poore was the *Boston Journal's* correspondent.

PRESBREY, FRANK, *The History and Development of Advertising.* New York: Doubleday, 1929. The standard history in its field.

RALPH, JULIAN, *The Making of a Journalist.* New York: Harper & Row, 1903. The autobiography of another top-ranking reporter of the period.

RAMMELKAMP, JULIAN S., *Pulitzer's Post-Dispatch, 1878–1883.* Princeton University Press, 1966. Documented study of the evolving journalistic style of Pulitzer, Cockerill, and others; restrained approval of Pulitzer's social contributions, criticism of his sensationalized news.

ROSEWATER, VICTOR, *History of Cooperative News-Gathering in the United States.* New York: Appleton-Century-Crofts, 1930. The recognized source for the early history of press associations.

ROSS, ISHBEL, *Ladies of the Press.* New York: Harper & Row, 1936. Valuable for stories of early women journalists.

SEITZ, DON C., *Joseph Pulitzer: His Life and Letters.* New York: Simon & Schuster, 1924. The first Pulitzer study; others draw upon it. Written by Pulitzer's onetime business manager.

SWANBERG, W. A., *Pulitzer.* New York: Scribner's, 1967. Latest and best of the studies of the tempestuous editor-publisher.

TURNER, E. S., *The Shocking History of Advertising.* Harmondsworth, Eng.: Penguin Books, 1965. An updated revision of a good history.

WARE, LOUISE, *Jacob A. Riis.* New York: Appleton-Century-Crofts, 1938. Biography of a socially conscious reporter.

WATKINS, JULIAN L., *The 100 Greatest Advertisements,* 2nd ed. New York: Moore Publishing, 1959. Discusses who wrote them and what they did.

WOOD, JAMES PLAYSTED, *The Story of Advertising.* New York: Ronald Press, 1958. Fairly detailed from the 1860s on.

Periodicals and Monographs

The trade journals became available in this period. The leaders were the *Journalist* (1884–1907), the *Fourth Estate* (1894–1927), and *Editor & Publisher* (1901) in the daily newspaper field; the *Publishers' Auxiliary* (1865) in the weekly newspaper field; and *Printers' Ink* (1888) in advertising. The fiftieth anniversary numbers of *Editor & Publisher* (July 21, 1934) and of *Printers' Ink* (July 28, 1938) are particularly valuable sources.

BEASLEY, MAURINE, *The First Women Washington Correspondents.* Washington: GW Washington Studies, No. 4, 1976. Covers six post-Civil War women writers.

BENNION, SHERILYN COX, "A Working List of Women Editors on the 19th Century Frontier," *Journalism History,* VII (Summer 1980), 60.

———, "Fremont Older: Advocate for Women," *Journalism History,* III (Winter 1976–77), 124. San Francisco *Bulletin's* women reporters, editors.

BRIDGES, LAMAR W., "Eliza Jane Nicholson of the 'Picayune'," *Journalism History,* II (Winter 1975), 110. Owner of the New Orleans paper, 1876 to 1896.

BRISBANE, ARTHUR, "Joseph Pulitzer," *Cosmopolitan,* XXXIII (May 1902), 51. An intimate contemporary portrait by an editor who jumped from Pulitzer's *World* to Hearst's *Journal.*

BROD, DONALD F., "John A. Cockerill's St. Louis Years," *Bulletin* of Missouri Historical Society, XXVI (April 1970), 227. Study of a political campaign and Cockerill's shooting of a politician to death.

DANIELS, ELIZABETH A., "Jessie White Mario: 19th Century Correspondent," *Journalism History,* II (Summer 1975), 54. Correspondent in Italy for the *Nation,* 1866 to 1904.

EK, RICHARD A., "Victoria Woodhull and the Pharisees," *Journalism Quarterly,* XLIX (Autumn 1972), 453. Exposure of minister's adultery brings reprisals against editor.

GABLER, WILLIAM G., "The Evolution of American Advertising in the Nineteenth Century," *Journal of Popular Culture,* 11 (Spring 1978), 763.

HART, JACK R., "Horatio Alger in the Newsroom: Social Origins of American Editors," *Journalism Quarterly,* LIII (Spring 1976), 14–20. Shows that editors of 1875 and 1900 are comparable to executives in other major industries.

HUDSON, ROBERT V., "Journeyman Journalist: An Analytical Biography of Will Irwin," Ph.D. thesis, University of Minnesota, 1970. Reportorial career researched in depth.

INGLIS, WILLIAM, "An Intimate View of Joseph Pulitzer," *Harper's Weekly,* LV (November 11, 1911), 7. An article with considerable insight, published at the time of Pulitzer's death.

IRWIN, WILL, "The American Newspaper," *Collier's,* XLVI–XLVII (January 21–July 29, 1911). A series of fifteen articles that constitutes a history of journalism after the Civil War. One article, "The Fourth Current," which traces the rise of yellow journalism, is reprinted in Ford and Emery, *Highlights in the History of the American Press.*

JONES, DOUGLAS C., "Remington Reports from the Badlands: The Artist as War Correspondent," *Journalism Quarterly,* XLVII (Winter 1970), 702. His drawings were in *Harper's Weekly.*

———, "Teresa Dean: Lady Correspondent among the Sioux Indians," *Journalism Quarterly,* XLIX (Winter 1972), 656.

KAHAN, ROBERT S., "The Antecedents of American Photojournalism," Ph.D. thesis, University of Wisconsin, 1969. The artist versus the camera.

KNIGHT, OLIVER A., "Reporting a Gold Rush," *Journalism Quarterly,* XXXVIII (Winter 1961), 43. The story of two young reporters from the *Inter Ocean* and the *New York Herald* in the Black Hills of 1875.

KNIGHTS, PETER R., "The Press Association War of 1866–1867," *Journalism Monographs,* No. 6 (December 1967). An episode in the story of wire services.

MCKERNS, JOSEPH P., "Ben: Perley Poore's Reminiscences: A Reliable Source for Research?" *Journalism History,* II (Winter 1975), 125. Poore was an important Washington correspondent, 1854 to 1887.

———, "Benjamin Perley Poore of the *Boston Journal:* His Life and Times as a Washington Correspondent, 1850–1887." Ph.D. thesis, University of Minnesota, 1979. A well-written, exhaustively researched biography placed in the context of the era.

Outlook, XCIX (November 11, 1911), 603 and 608, contains two estimates of Pulitzer and *The World.*

PIERCE, ROBERT N., "Lord Northcliffe: Trans-Atlantic Influences," *Journalism Monographs,* No. 40 (August 1975).

SAALBERG, HARVEY, "The *Westliche Post* of St. Louis: A Daily Newspaper for German-Americans, 1857–1938," Ph.D. thesis, University of Missouri, 1967. Pulitzer, Schurz, Preetorius figure in the story. See also Saalberg, "The *Westliche Post* of St. Louis: German Language Daily, 1857–1938," *Journalism Quarterly,* XLV (Autumn 1968), 452.

SCHUNEMAN, R. SMITH, "The Photograph in Print: An Examination of New York Daily Newspapers, 1890–1937," Ph.D. thesis, University of Minnesota, 1966. The rise of photojournalism is developed by extensive research.

———, "Art or Photography: A Question for Newspaper Editors of the 1890s," *Journalism*

Quarterly, XLII (Winter 1965), 43. Why the halftone waited until 1897 in big dailies.

SEITZ, DON C., "The Portrait of an Editor," *Atlantic Monthly,* CXXXIV (September 1924), 289. Reprinted in Ford and Emery, *Highlights in the History of the American Press.* Joseph Pulitzer portrayed by biographer.

SMYTHE, TED CURTIS, "The Reporter, 1880–1900: Working Conditions and their Influence on the News," *Journalism History,* VII (Spring 1980), 1.

WARD, HILEY, "A Popular History of the National Newspaper Association," *Publishers' Auxiliary,* CX (July 10, 1975), 14. First of a series extending to 1977, substantially researched. Based on Ph.D. thesis, University of Minnesota, 1977.

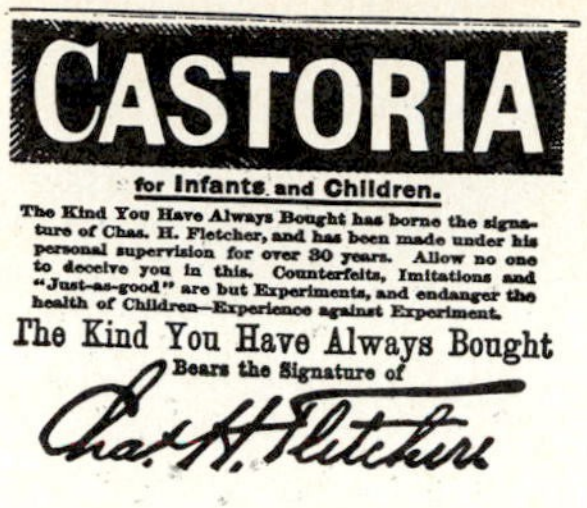
CASTORIA
for Infants and Children.
The Kind You Have Always Bought has borne the signature of Chas. H. Fletcher, and has been made under his personal supervision for over 30 years. Allow no one to deceive you in this. Counterfeits, Imitations and "Just-as-good" are but Experiments, and endanger the health of Children—Experience against Experiment.
The Kind You Have Always Bought
Bears the Signature of
Chas. H. Fletcher

Victor
"HIS MASTER'S VOICE"
REG. U.S. PAT. OFF.

ROYAL
Baking Powder
Is easy to use and makes good things quickly.
ROYAL BAKING POWDER CO., NEW YORK.

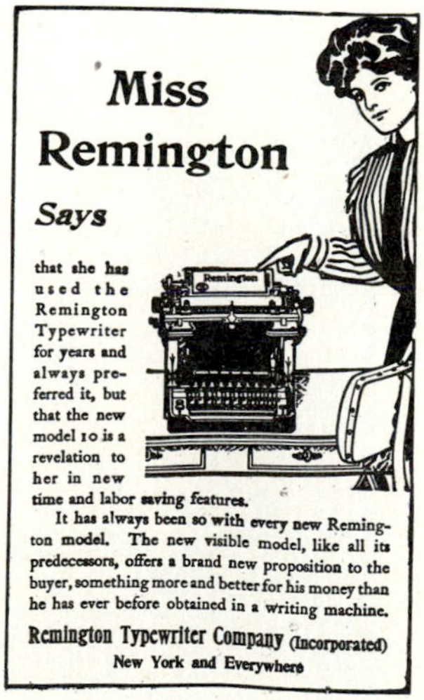
Miss Remington
Says
that she has used the Remington Typewriter for years and always preferred it, but that the new model 10 is a revelation to her in new time and labor saving features.
It has always been so with every new Remington model. The new visible model, like all its predecessors, offers a brand new proposition to the buyer, something more and better for his money than he has ever before obtained in a writing machine.
Remington Typewriter Company (Incorporated)
New York and Everywhere

Old Dutch Cleanser
Chases Dirt
MAKES EVERYTHING "SPICK AND SPAN"

Copyrighted trademarks and brand advertising, 1900 to 1920.

William Randolph Hearst takes a photo from his yacht during the Spanish-American War.

Wide World Photos

Hearst at the peak of his career in the 1930s.

San Francisco Examiner

17
The Age of Yellow Journalism

The reason why such journals lie is that it pays to lie; or, in other words, this is the very reason for which they are silly and scandalous and indecent. They supply a want of a demoralized public.
—E. L. Godkin

The rapidly expanding American newspaper faced sharp challenges during the 1890s, both as a business institution and as an instrument of society. One challenge was to survive the depression of 1893, a major economic crisis that did not relax until the close of the decade. The other was to respond to the country's growing role in world affairs and to a resulting moral crisis stemming from the ascendancy of a spirit of "Manifest Destiny." The story of how the press responded to these crises is not a happy one; the mixed reactions are traced in this and the following chapter.

The financial stability of the new metropolitan dailies always depended on winning more and more readers in order to attract larger advertising revenues. In depression time, there was even greater pressure to appeal to new readers to replace lost ones. Popularizing a product, though inevitable if mass readership were to be achieved, did not need to become mere sensationalizing. Bigger headlines, more readable stories, pictures, and blobs of color could give newspapers new faces, perhaps sometimes even overdoing it, but nevertheless comprising effective, useful, and desirable devices.

By the same token, these new techniques could also be used to emphasize sensationalism at the expense of news. In the mid-1890s some editors proceeded to do just this, as had been done in earlier periods when new audiences were available. But the difference was that now they had better tools with which to make their sensationalism distinctive and seemingly new. The degrading product of this effort became known as *yellow journalism.*

Yellow journalism, at its worst, was the new journalism without a soul. Trumpeting their concern for "the people," yellow journalists at the same time choked up the news channels on which the common people depended with a shrieking, gaudy, sensation-loving, devil-may-care kind of journalism. This turned the high drama of life into a cheap melodrama and led to stories being twisted into the form best suited for sales by the howling newsboy. Worst of all, instead of giving effective leadership, yellow journalism offered a palliative of sin, sex, and violence.

Pulitzer's striking success had demonstrated once again the appeal of the age-old technique of sensation. Other papers, like the *Philadelphia Record* and *Boston Globe,* were playing the same game as the *World.* But it was a mistake to attribute the *World*'s circulation achievements to sensationalism alone, and those who saw the clever promotion and lighter side of the *World* did not see—or disregarded—the solid characteristics of its news coverage and the high qualities of its editorial page. The antics of those who did not make this attempt to balance information and entertainment paid off handsomely in dollars earned. Their competitors were often forced to take on the yellow hue, and although most newspapers eventually recovered from the disease, modern journalism has exhibited some of the effects of this age of yellow journalism ever since.

WILLIAM RANDOLPH HEARST

The man who more than anyone else brought about the era of yellow journalism was watching with sharp interest while Pulitzer was setting New York journalism on its ear in the mid-1880s. He was William Randolph Hearst, who was to become the most controversial figure in modern journalism before his 64-year publishing career was ended. The youthful Hearst was a calculating witness to Pulitzer's climb to glory, and when he eventually invaded New York to challenge the supremacy of the *World,* he came prepared to dazzle the city with a sensationalized and self-promoted kind of journalism that would put Pulitzer to shame. The resulting struggle brought repercussions whose effects are still being felt.

Hearst was a Californian, born in 1863, the son of a successful pioneer who struck it rich in the silver mines of the Comstock Lode and who later won more riches in Anaconda copper and Western and Mexican ranch lands. The only child of George and Phoebe Hearst, he grew up in San Francisco under the guidance of a busy, ambitious father and a schoolteacher mother, who in later years became a noted philanthropist and the able manager of the family fortune.

Having achieved wealth, George Hearst aspired to political power. In 1880 he acquired the *San Francisco Examiner,* a debt-ridden morning paper that lagged behind the *Chronicle,* and converted it into a Democratic party organ. Young Hearst showed an interest in the paper, but his father took a low view of the newspaperpeople who worked for him and packed his heir off to Harvard in 1883.

Hearst's career at Harvard was sensational, if not successful. He was a free-spending Westerner who drank too much beer and listened to too much band music, and who did his best job as business manager of the humor magazine, the *Lampoon.* He was suspended in his sophomore year for celebrating Grover Cleveland's election to the presidency with a noisy fireworks display and was expelled a few months later for perpetrating a practical joke on Harvard's professors. Distinguished faculty members like William James and Josiah Royce could see no humor, it seemed, in finding their likenesses decorating chamber pots.

But the Eastern education had not been entirely wasted. Harvard may not have made its impression on Hearst's mind, but the *Boston Globe* and the *New York World* did. Hearst studied the somewhat sensational techniques of General Charles H. Taylor's successful *Globe* and visited its up-to-date mechanical plant. He was more interested in Pulitzer's *World,* however, and on one of his vacations he worked as a cub reporter for the newspaper he was to battle later. After bowing out at Harvard, Hearst again spent some time in New York studying the *World*'s techniques and then returned to San Francisco.

HEARST'S *SAN FRANCISCO EXAMINER*

William Randolph Hearst assumed the editorship of the *San Francisco Examiner* in 1887 when George Hearst was named Senator from California. He was only 24 but the tall, blue-eyed, shy editor, whose high-pitched voice contrasted with a commanding physical presence, immediately began to staff the paper. Picked as managing editor was Sam S. Chamberlain, who had worked for both Bennett and Pulitzer, edited Bennett's Paris edition of the *Herald,* and in 1884 founded the Paris newspaper *Le Matin.* The brilliant Ambrose Bierce, later famous for his short stories, contributed his "Prattle" column. Star reporters like Edward H. Hamilton signed on, as did Arthur McEwen, an editorial writer who became a key figure in Hearst-style journalism. Homer Davenport began to draw his cartoons, James Swinnerton applied his artist's skill to the new field of comics, and literary flavor was added by Edwin Markham ("The Man With the Hoe," which first appeared in the paper) and E. L. (Phinney) Thayer, whose contribution was "Casey at the Bat."

Chamberlain's grasp of news techniques made him invaluable. He developed the career of Winifred Black—known as "Annie Laurie" to future generations of Hearst readers—who attracted San Francisco women readers with intense stories. Sent to investigate the city hospital's management, Black conveniently fainted on the street, was carried to the hospital, and turned in a story "with a sob for the unfortunate in every line." The *Examiner* was ever experimenting with crusades, stunts, and devices to present the news in a yet more luring manner. A stalwart Democrat, Hearst attacked the Southern Pacific railroad, the bulwark of the Republican state machine, and attempted to present other types of serious stories. But news that was important but dull took a back seat as the paper strove for what McEwen called the "Gee-Whiz" emotion.[1]

Hearst's experiments on the mechanical side were important and constructive contributions to the new journalism. Trying many new patterns of makeup, arranging headlines in symmetrical patterns, and using attractive type faces, Hearst eventually arrived at a distinctive formula that many another paper imitated. Hearst himself often worked on the page forms, but his mechanical genius was George Pancoast, who joined the *Examiner* staff in 1888 and for the next 50 years perfected the electric drive for presses, improved color printing, and designed fourteen printing plants for the Hearst empire.

The *Examiner,* called by the ambitious Hearst "The Monarch of the Dailies," doubled its circulation in the first year, reaching 30,000, and by 1893 had pushed to 72,000. This was more than M. H. de Young's *Chronicle,* the recognized leading daily. Senator Hearst died in 1891 after watching his son turn a losing proposition into a paper averaging a $350,000 to $500,000 yearly profit.[2] And with that success achieved, young Hearst was ready to tackle the challenge he saw in Joseph Pulitzer's city, New York.

HEARST INVADES NEW YORK

The profits from the *Examiner* were now available for an invasion of New York. But Hearst needed more capital, and eventually he persuaded his mother to sell the family holdings in the Anaconda copper mines for $7.5 million and make the cash available for new publishing ventures.[3] Later, when a friend told Mrs. Hearst that she had heard that the *New York Journal* was losing $1 million a year and expressed fear that the family fortune was being thrown away recklessly, Mrs. Hearst replied that, in such an event, her son could hold out for 30 years more.

Somewhat ironically, Hearst entered the New York field by buying the newspaper that Joseph Pulitzer's brother, Albert, had established in 1882. The *Morning Journal* had been a successful 1-cent paper appealing to casual newspaper scanners. In 1894 its price was raised to 2 cents, and circulation fell off. Albert Pulitzer then sold the *Journal* for $1 million to John R. McLean, ambitious publisher of the *Cincinnati Enquirer.* McLean was no stranger to sensational methods of publishing newspapers, but he was unable to break into the highly competitive New York field. In the fall of 1895, Hearst picked up the paper from the defeated McLean for $180,000.

PULITZER'S *SUNDAY WORLD*

Joseph Pulitzer had been busy during the 10 years since Hearst had left New York to launch his career in San Francisco. Particularly he had expanded the mechanical facilities available to his editors, and he had applied the new techniques to the development of the *Sunday World.*

It was Pulitzer who first demonstrated the full potentialities of the Sunday newspaper as a profitable news and entertainment medium. There had been weeklies issued as Sunday papers since 1796. The daily *Boston Globe* put out a Sunday edition briefly in 1833, but James Gordon Bennett's *Herald* was the first daily to print a Sunday edition steadily, starting in 1841. The demand for news during the Civil War stimulated Sunday publication, but even by the time Pulitzer invaded New York in 1883 only about 100 daily newspapers had Sunday editions. Most of them were appearing in Eastern cities and a good share were printed in German and other foreign languages. Some carried a four-page supplement filled with entertaining features, fiction, and trivia.

Pulitzer's new *Sunday World* added many more pages of entertainment to the regular news section. Feature material for women, for young readers, and for sports enthusiasts appeared. Humorous drawings and other illustrations were concentrated in the Sunday pages. The offerings of the literary syndicates, such as that developed by S. S. McClure, added to the Sunday paper's appeal. Circulation of the *Sunday World* passed the 250,000 mark in 1887, and by the early 1890s the paper had reached forty to forty-eight pages in size as retail advertisers realized the extent of its readership by families and by women. Other newspapers were quick to follow suit, and in 1890 there were 250 dailies with Sunday editions, crowding the metropolitan areas and driving the independent Sunday weeklies out of the picture.

Heading the Sunday staff in the early years was Morrill Goddard, a college graduate who as a young city editor had shown ability to spot the feature angle of news events. But in the Sunday section Goddard jazzed up his page spreads, exaggerating the factual information to the point at which serious news sources, particularly people of science and medicine, shied away. The sensationalism and pseudoscientific stories of this era greatly increased the credibility problem of newspapers, but the problem was ignored.

The installation of color presses in 1893 only gave Goddard another medium to exploit. As many as five colors could be used in the Sunday color supplement and included in it were the comic drawings that Goddard knew were most effective in spurring circulation. The *World* had started a regular comic section in 1889 and was the first to use color here (magazines had done so since the 1870s). The most successful of the artists was Richard F. Outcault, whose "Hogan's Alley" depicted life in the tenements. The central figure in each drawing was a toothless, grinning kid attired in a ballooning dress. When the *World*'s printers daubed a blob of yellow on the dress he became the immortal "Yellow Kid."

THE "YELLOW JOURNALISM" WAR

When William Randolph Hearst arrived on the New York scene he immediately set out to buy the men who were making the *Sunday World* a success. Using an office the *Examiner* had rented in the *World* building, he hired away Goddard and most of his staff of writers and artists. Hearst's lavish spending habits made Pulitzer's counteroffers hopeless. Soon even the *World*'s publisher, S. S. Carvalho, was working at the *Journal* building. The battle on, Pulitzer turned to Arthur Brisbane, Socialist Albert Brisbane's brilliant young son who had broken into newspaper work on the *Sun* before joining Pulitzer's staff. As the new Sunday editor, Brisbane drove the circulation to the 600,000 mark, popularizing the news and pushing hard on Pulitzer's social concerns. Goddard had taken Outcault and the "Yellow Kid" with him, but Brisbane used George B. Luks, later a well-known painter, to continue the cartoon.

Circulation people for both papers used posters featuring the happy-go-lucky, grinning kid with his curiously vacant features. To opposition journalists the "Yellow Kid" seemed symbolic of the kind of sensational journalism that was being practiced, and the public agreed. The phase "yellow journalism" soon became widely used and its techniques the object of hard scrutiny. Unfortunately for Pulitzer, Brisbane moved over to the *Evening Journal* as editor in 1897 and Luks also joined Hearst. At this Outcault moaned:

> "When I die don't wear yellow crepe, don't let them put a Yellow Kid on my tombstone and don't let the Yellow Kid himself come to my funeral. Make him stay over on the east side, where he belongs."[4]

Besides raiding Pulitzer's staff, Hearst moved in the best of his San Francisco staffers, including Chamberlain, McEwen, Davenport, and Annie Laurie. Dana's *Sun* lost its star reporters Julian Ralph, Richard Harding Davis, and Edward W. Townsend to Hearst's bankroll. Dorothy Dix joined the women's staff, and writers Stephen Crane, Alfred Henry Lewis, and Rudolph Block (Bruno Lessing) were signed, along with a host of other talented reporters, critics, and artists.

Two other events propelled Hearst into the thick of the fight with Pulitzer. In 1896, when the *Journal* reached the 150,000 mark as a 1-cent paper, Pulitzer cut his price to a penny, gaining circulation but allowing speculation that he was afraid of his challenger. More importantly, Pulitzer, although in sympathy with many of William Jennings Bryan's ideas, could not support his inflationary monetary policies. But Hearst, as a silver-mine owner, had no problem in arguing against the gold standard. Political partisans were attracted by Hearst's stand for Bryan in the conservative East where Bryan was looked upon with horror.

Frankly adopting the sins of yellow journalism, the *Journal* continued its surge in circulation figures. One jump of 125,000 came in a single month in the fall of 1896 when the following headlines were typical: "Real American Monsters and Dragons"—over a story of the discovery of fossil remains by an archaeological expedition; "A Marvellous New Way of Giving Medicine: Wonderful Results from Merely Holding Tubes of Drugs Near Entranced Patients"—a headline that horrified medical researchers; and "Henry James' New Novel of Immorality and Crime; The Surprising Plunge of the Great Novelist in the Field of Sensational Fiction"—the *Journal*'s way of announcing publication of *The Other House.* Other headlines were more routinely sensational: "The Mysterious Murder of Bessie Little," "One Mad Blow Kills Child," "What Made Him a Burglar? A Story of Real Life in New York by Edgar Saltus," "Startling Confession of a Wholesale Murderer Who Begs to Be Hanged." Annie Laurie wrote about "Why Young Girls Kill Themselves" and "Strange Things Women Do for Love."[5]

The *Journal* was crusading, too, but it went beyond other New York newspapers in a manner that enabled it to shout, "While Others Talk the Journal Acts." The paper obtained a court injunction that balked the granting of

The "Yellow Kid," in his nightshirt, was an 1896 smash hit in the *New York World*.

a city franchise to a gas company and, pleased by its success, it took similar actions against alleged abuses in government. Hearst then solicited compliments from civic leaders across the country and printed them under such headings as, "Journalism that Acts; Men of Action in All Walks of Life Heartily Endorse the Journal's Fight in Behalf of the People" and "First Employed by the Journal, the

Novel Concept Seems Likely to Become an Accepted Part of the Function of the Newspapers of This Country."[6]

Before his first year in New York had ended, Hearst had installed large color presses at the *Journal,* added an eight-page colored comic section called *The American Humorist,* and replaced that with a sixteen-page color supplement. *The Sunday American Magazine* (later, with Brisbane as editor, this was to become the famous *American Weekly*). In late 1896 the *Journal*'s daily circulation was 437,000 and on Sunday it was 380,000. Within a year the Sunday figures had reached the *World*'s 600,000. Circulation figures moved up and down, depending on the street sale appeal of the moment: On the day following the McKinley-Bryan election the *World* and *Journal* each sold approximately 1.5 million copies to break all records.

It was in this atmosphere that the leading papers scrambled for news around the nation and the world. And it was under these conditions that American papers approached the events that led to an international crisis and the Spanish-American War.

THE SPIRIT OF "MANIFEST DESTINY"

Of all the wars the United States has fought, the Spanish-American War was the most painless. But the results entirely changed the course of American foreign policy. In fewer than 4 months the Spanish government was forced to request an armistice, at an extraordinarily small cost in American lives, and the American flag floated over an empire stretching from Puerto Rico to the Philippines. Those who have sought to explain the causes of this unwarranted war have often centered the blame on William Randolph Hearst in particular and the newspapers of the country in general. Carefully documented studies made by Marcus M. Wilkerson and Joseph E. Wisan in the early 1930s gave ample proof that Hearst's *Journal,* Pulitzer's *World,* the *Chicago Tribune,* the *New York Sun* and *New York Herald* (and as is usually ignored, many other American papers) so handled the news of events leading up to the crisis of the sinking of the *Maine* that a war psychosis was developed.[7] It must not be forgotten, however, that the newspapers were cultivating public opinion in a favorable atmosphere.

The policies of expansion being advocated were in line with those pursued throughout the nineteenth century. Americans in general subscribed to the belief in "Manifest Destiny" that spurred the westward movement. The War of 1812 was forced on a reluctant New England by Western expansionists who viewed the British in Canada as mortal enemies. The Mexican War and cries of "54–40 or Fight" brought the completion of the continental United States. Americans liked to buy the territory they wanted, but now, as in the past, they were ready to take it by force if necessary.

When viewed in the long perspective, the Spanish-American War was but one in a series of incidents that marked the arrival of the United States as a world and, in particular, a Pacific power. With newly acquired Alaskan territory protecting one flank, Americans moved to gain a foothold in the Samoan Islands. Agitation began in the 1880s for the annexation of Hawaii. Then, with a new modern navy at his disposal, President Grover Cleveland brought his country to the verge of war with Great Britain over a test of the Monroe Doctrine in the Venezuelan crisis of 1895. This was followed by the annexation of Hawaii, the Philippines, Guam, and Puerto Rico, and the building of the Panama Canal. Interest in the Asian mainland brought about John Hay's Open Door Policy in 1899 and President Roosevelt's negotiation of the peace treaty ending the 1904 to 1905 Russo-Japanese War in a little New Hampshire town. Pan-Americanism became open American intervention in the affairs of Central American countries, and Roosevelt took the United States into European affairs as well by participating in the 1905 Moroccan crisis that had been precipitated by German expansionism.

This desire to be a powerful participant in world affairs was not the only driving force behind the American expansion of interest. There was pride felt by many Americans in the addition of new territories and there was keen interest in the expansion of trade and foreign investments. But Americans also felt they had a role to play in promoting the idea of peace and justice in the world. There was widespread sympathy for those Cubans, Armenians, and Greeks who were fighting for their freedoms in the 1890s. Both idealism and national pride came into play during the Spanish-American War. If later the advocates of imperialism and "dollar diplomacy" won out over the idealists, that was but one phase of America's coming of age in international affairs.

Newspapers reflected this conflict in goals, reporting both the atrocities committed by Spanish troops against Cuban insurrectionists and the chance for the new American navy to prove itself against Spain. But mainly there was a strong desire to flex the nation's muscles. As the memory of the Civil War faded, many older Americans wondered if their country's military prowess was still secure. Younger citizens were eager to match the exploits of the boys in Blue and Grey. For them, war, 1898 style, still seemed to be an exciting personal adventure. John D. Hicks, a first-rank American historian who was not unaware of the role of the newspaper as an organ of public opinion, summed up his discussion of the causes of the Spanish-American War by saying:

> Years later, Theodore Roosevelt recaptured the spirit of 1898 when he mourned apologetically, "It wasn't much of a war, but it was the best war we had." America in the spring of 1898 was ripe for any war, and the country's mood was not to be denied.[8]

COVERING CUBAN NEWS, 1895 TO 1898

From March, 1895, when the Cuban insurrection began, until April, 1898, when Spain and the United States went to war, there were fewer than a score of days in which a story about Cuba did not appear in one of the New York newspapers.[9] This was due partly to the aggressive news policies of the big dailies, partly to the manufactured stories by some of the papers (notably the *Journal*), and partly to the increased reader interest in controversial stories. It was also the result of the activities of the Cuban junta that fed information and propaganda to American reporters in New York and at the Florida news bases nearest the island.

A considerable number of Cubans had emigrated to the United States and had settled in New York, Philadelphia, Baltimore, Boston, and several Florida cities. The junta had its headquarters in New York, where a Cuban newspaper was published. Through the Cuban residents in the Eastern cities, a program of mass meetings was established. Money was raised, and several hundred volunteers were obtained in each city for running arms and taking part in filibustering expeditions. Cuban agents funneled information on the progress of the fighting in Cuba to the American newspapers. The work was well under way in 1895, and as the crisis intensified, the activities of the junta reached greater heights. Ministers, educators, civic leaders, and politicians were reached by the junta.

The Spanish decision in 1896 to use strong repressive measures in Cuba brought Captain-General Valeriano Weyler into the news. All loyal Cubans were ordered to congregate in small areas adjoining Spanish bases, and those who did not were considered enemies. But those huddled in the camps quickly fell victim to epidemics and many starved to death when food supplies became disrupted. Much of the newspaper copy centered about the effects of famine and pestilence (approximately 110,000 Cubans died in the 3 years,[10] but newspaper estimates reached 400,000 as part of the exaggeration of these admittedly very serious conditions). Weyler was nicknamed the "Butcher" by American reporters and compared to the "bloodthirsty Cortez and Pizarro" of the days of the Conquistadors.

Competition for news became fierce. The Associated Press provided its own coverage and used information from stories printed by member papers.[11] The *Journal* and *World* led the way as papers with correspondents in Cuba sold their stories to other papers. Papers in competing situations fought to sign up as soon as a rival announced it had obtained *World, Journal, Sun, Herald,* or other "big-league" coverage. Striving to keep ahead in every way was Hearst, who persuaded star reporter James Creelman to stop reporting for the *World* in 1896 and sent Richard Harding Davis and artist Frederic Remington to join him in Cuba. The impact of pictorial journalism increased in 1897 when New York papers began to use halftone photographs that sometimes were accurate portrayals of Cuban misery and sometimes were fakes. It also was during this time that Remington, according to Creelman's 1901 reminiscences, cabled Hearst that there would be no war and that he was coming home. Whereupon Hearst was supposed to have cabled back: "Remington, Havana. Please remain. You furnish the pictures, and I'll furnish the war. W. R. Hearst."[12] There is no evidence that Hearst actually sent this cable, so often quoted as conclusive evidence against him, but in a sense it reflected the situation. Of all the American papers, Hearst's *Journal* worked the hardest to create public sentiment for war. Episodes like this did much to tag him with "Hearst's war."

In the summer of 1897, after open advocacy of war for about a year and the sensationalizing of several minor incidents, the *Journal* built the story of Evangelina Cisneros into a daily chant for intervention. Miss Cisneros, a niece of the Cuban revolutionary president, had been sentenced to 20 years in prison for her rebellious activity. The *Journal* devoted an incredible number of news columns, 375, to the details of her condition and to her "rescue" by *Journal* reporter Karl Decker. Many notables congratulated the *Journal* on this achievement and Miss Cisneros was greeted by President McKinley on the White House lawn. Later it was discovered how other New York papers had treated this exciting but out-of-context story: *World,* twelve and one-half columns; *Times,* ten columns; *Tribune,* three and one-half columns; *Sun,* one column; *Herald,* one column.[13] During the incident, when the *World* published Weyler's account of Miss Cisneros' treatment—which had been exaggerated—the *Journal* accused Pulitzer of unpatriotic motives.

The *Journal*'s most significant "scoop" came on February 9, 1898, when Hearst published a private letter written by Dupuy de Lome, the Spanish ambassador to the United States, to a Spanish newspaper editor visiting in Havana. The letter, stolen in Havana by a Cuban junta member, referred to President McKinley as "weak and catering to the rabble, and besides, a low politician." At the same moment Theodore Roosevelt was commenting that his chief had the backbone of a chocolate eclair, but to have the Spanish ambassador say the same thing, even in a private letter, was a different matter. American opinion of the Spanish government hit a new low and 6 days later the *Maine* blew up in Havana harbor. The impact of the two events proved to be the turning point in the diplomatic crisis.

THE CORRESPONDENTS GO TO WAR

No one has satisfactorily established the cause of the explosion that sank the *Maine,* with the loss of 266 American lives. But some American newspapers set about making it appear that the Spanish were indirectly responsible for the sinking. The *Journal* offered a $50,000 reward for information leading to the arrest and conviction of the criminals, and 3 days later the paper's streamer read "THE WHOLE COUNTRY THRILLS WITH WAR FEVER." Large headlines and striking illustrations became common in big-city papers. Leading the way was Brisbane, who experimented with artist-drawn headlines that virtually filled the front page with two or three words. Later that year Brisbane wrote:

> Before the type size reached its maximum, "War Sure" could be put in one line across a page, and it was put in one line and howled through the streets by patriotic newsboys many and many a time. As war was sure, it did no harm.[14]

Gradually the tide swung toward a declaration of war. Volunteer units such as the Rough Riders were formed, Congress passed a $50 million defense bill for war, and more than once Secretary of State Sherman made statements based on news reports from the *Journal.* In mid-March a leading Republican senator, Proctor of Vermont, made a speech based on his own trip to Cuba. He verified much of what had been published during the previous 3 years about deaths of Cubans, adding to the pressures on President McKinley to come out for war. The *World* at first urged caution in the handling of the *Maine* matter, but on April 10 Pulitzer published a signed editorial calling for a "short and sharp" war. Most of the nation agreed with this sentiment and Congress passed a war resolution on April 18.

The *New York Sun,* which under Dana's cynical editorship had been extremely jingoistic, stood with the *Journal* and *World* in demanding intervention. The *New York Herald,* while keeping up in sensational news coverage, opposed intervention in its editorial stands—an incongruity also true of the *Chicago Times-Herald, Boston Herald, San Francisco Chronicle,* and *Milwaukee Sentinel.* Strongly interventionist were such papers as the *Chicago Tribune, New Orleans Times-Democrat, Atlanta Constitution,* and *Indianapolis Journal.* Keeping calm were such papers as the *New York Tribune, New York Times, Chicago Daily News, Boston Transcript,* and other papers that reflected the thinking of the business community in their editorial columns. In his study of the newspapers for the period, Wilkerson ranks the *Journal* as the leader in excessive journalism, and the *Chicago Tribune* and the *World* next in order. Joseph Medill's *Chicago Tribune,* strongly nationalistic in its editorial columns, did not originate sensational news stories, as did the *Journal* and *World,* but it ran the cream of those collected by both papers.

It should be pointed out that the *World* was not a jingo newspaper. Pulitzer had opposed the annexation of Hawaii and did not support President Cleveland in the 1895 Venezuelan crisis, when most major papers warned that the United States would fight to uphold Venezuela's boundary claims with British Guiana. During the Cuban crisis the *World* did not stand for the annexation of foreign lands and opposed the taking of the Philippine Islands. The *World* based its call for war on the issue of human liberty and in subsequent actions proved it was not merely jingoistic. Pulitzer later regretted the role the *World* played in preparing public opinion for killing and in 1907, when Theodore Roosevelt ordered the American fleet to the Pacific to impress Japan, Pulitzer requested that his editors "show that Spain had granted to Cuba all that we had demanded . . . Give further details of jingoism causing Cuban War after Spain had virtually granted everything."[15]

But in 1898 only Godkin's *Evening Post,* among the New York dailies, held out to the end against yellow journalism and the decision to force Spain from Cuba. Lashing out against Hearst and Pulitzer, he bitterly attacked with statements like this:

> A yellow journal office is probably the nearest approach, in atmosphere, to hell, existing in any Christian state. A better place in which to prepare a young man for eternal damnation than a yellow journal office does not exist.[16]

The newspapers fought the war as determinedly as they had fostered it. Some 500 reporters, artists, and photographers flocked to Florida, where the American army was mobilizing, and to the Cuban and Puerto Rican fronts.[17] Small fleets of press boats accompanied the Navy into action. Correspondents sailed with Dewey to Manila and with Schley to Havana. They covered every battle and skirmish in Cuba and more than once took part in the fighting itself. A *Journal* correspondent lost a leg during one fighting charge. Richard Harding Davis, then reporting for the *New York Herald* and the *Times* of London, led another charge and won the praise of Rough Rider Roosevelt.

Leading the *Journal*'s contingent was the publisher himself, who exuded enthusiasm as he directed the work of his staff of twenty men and women

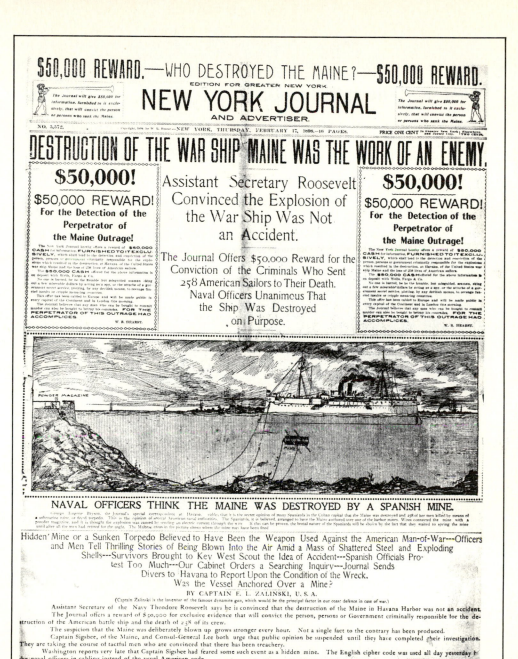

$50,000 REWARD.—WHO DESTROYED THE MAINE?—$50,000 REWARD.

EDITION FOR GREATER NEW YORK

NEW YORK JOURNAL

AND ADVERTISER.

The Journal will give $50,000 for information, furnished to it exclusively, that will convict the person or persons who sank the Maine.

The Journal will give $50,000 for information, furnished to it exclusively, that will convict the person or persons who sank the Maine.

NO. 5,572. Copyright, 1898, by W. R. Hearst.—NEW YORK, THURSDAY, FEBRUARY 17, 1898.—16 PAGES. PRICE ONE CENT In Greater New York and Jersey City. | Elsewhere, TWO CENTS.

DESTRUCTION OF THE WAR SHIP MAINE WAS THE WORK OF AN ENEMY.

$50,000!

$50,000 REWARD!

For the Detection of the Perpetrator of the Maine Outrage!

The New York Journal hereby offers a reward of **$50,000 CASH** for information, **FURNISHED TO IT EXCLUSIVELY**, which shall lead to the detection and conviction of the person, persons or government criminally responsible for the explosions which resulted in the destruction, at Havana, of the United States war ship Maine and the loss of 258 lives of American sailors.

The **$50,000 CASH** offered for the above information is on deposit with Wells, Fargo & Co.

No one is barred, be he the humble but misguided seaman eking out a few miserable dollars by acting as a spy, or the attache of a government secret service, plotting, by any devilish means, to revenge fancied insults or cripple menacing countries.

This offer has been cabled to Europe and will be made public in every capital of the Continent and in London this morning.

The Journal believes that any man who can be bought to commit murder can also be bought to betray his comrades. **FOR THE PERPETRATOR OF THIS OUTRAGE HAD ACCOMPLICES.**

W. R. HEARST.

Assistant Secretary Roosevelt Convinced the Explosion of the War Ship Was Not an Accident.

The Journal Offers $50,000 Reward for the Conviction of the Criminals Who Sent 258 American Sailors to Their Death. Naval Officers Unanimous That the Ship Was Destroyed on Purpose.

$50,000!

$50,000 REWARD!

For the Detection of the Perpetrator of the Maine Outrage!

The New York Journal hereby offers a reward of **$50,000 CASH** for information, **FURNISHED TO IT EXCLUSIVELY**, which shall lead to the detection and conviction of the person, persons or government criminally responsible for the explosions which resulted in the destruction, at Havana, of the United States war ship Maine and the loss of 258 lives of American sailors.

The **$50,000 CASH** offered for the above information is on deposit with Wells, Fargo & Co.

No one is barred, be he the humble but misguided seaman eking out a few miserable dollars by acting as a spy, or the attache of a government secret service, plotting, by any devilish means, to revenge fancied insults or cripple menacing countries.

This offer has been cabled to Europe and will be made public in every capital of the Continent and in London this morning.

The Journal believes that any man who can be bought to commit murder can also be bought to betray his comrades. **FOR THE PERPETRATOR OF THIS OUTRAGE HAD ACCOMPLICES.**

W. R. HEARST.

NAVAL OFFICERS THINK THE MAINE WAS DESTROYED BY A SPANISH MINE.

George Eugene Bryson, the Journal's special correspondent at Havana, cables that it is the secret opinion of many Spaniards in the Cuban capital that the Maine was destroyed and 258 of her men killed by means of a submarine mine, or fixed torpedo. This is the opinion of several American naval authorities. The Spaniards, it is believed, arranged to have the Maine anchored over one of the harbor mines. Wires connected the mine with a powder magazine, and it is thought the explosion was caused by sending an electric current through the wire. If this can be proven, the brutal nature of the Spaniards will be shown by the fact that they waited to spring the mine until after all the men had retired for the night. The Maltese cross in the picture shows where the mine may have been fired.

Hidden Mine or a Sunken Torpedo Believed to Have Been the Weapon Used Against the American Man-of-War---Officers and Men Tell Thrilling Stories of Being Blown Into the Air Amid a Mass of Shattered Steel and Exploding Shells---Survivors Brought to Key West Scout the Idea of Accident---Spanish Officials Protest Too Much---Our Cabinet Orders a Searching Inquiry---Journal Sends Divers to Havana to Report Upon the Condition of the Wreck. Was the Vessel Anchored Over a Mine?

BY CAPTAIN E. L. ZALINSKI, U. S. A.

(Captain Zalinski is the inventor of the famous dynamite gun, which would be the principal factor in our coast defence in case of war.)

Assistant Secretary of the Navy Theodore Roosevelt says he is convinced that the destruction of the Maine in Havana Harbor was not an accident.

The Journal offers a reward of $50,000 for exclusive evidence that will convict the person, persons or Government criminally responsible for the destruction of the American battle ship and the death of 258 of its crew.

The suspicion that the Maine was deliberately blown up grows stronger every hour. Not a single fact to the contrary has been produced.

Captain Sigsbee, of the Maine, and Consul-General Lee both urge that public opinion be suspended until they have completed their investigation. They are taking the course of tactful men who are convinced that there has been treachery.

Washington reports very late that Captain Sigsbee had feared some such event as a hidden mine. The English cipher code was used all day yesterday by the naval officers in cabling instead of the usual American code.

Hearst's *Journal* for February 17. The *Maine* sank the night of February 15.

Weather Indications: FAIR; COLD.

863,956 WORLDS CIRCULATED YESTERDAY

The World.

"Circulation Books Open to All."

VOL. XXXVIII. NO. 13,319. NEW YORK, THURSDAY, FEBRUARY 17, 1898. PRICE ONE CENT in Greater New York and Jersey City. TWO CENTS outside of Greater New York and Jersey City and on trains.

MAINE EXPLOSION CAUSED BY BOMB OR TORPEDO?

Capt. Sigsbee and Consul-General Lee Are in Doubt---The World Has Sent a Special Tug, With Submarine Divers, to Havana to Find Out---Lee Asks for an Immediate Court of Inquiry---260 Men Dead.

IN A SUPPRESSED DESPATCH TO THE STATE DEPARTMENT, THE CAPTAIN SAYS THE ACCIDENT WAS MADE POSSIBLE BY AN ENEMY.

Dr. E. C. Pendleton, Just Arrived from Havana, Says He Overheard Talk There of a Plot to Blow Up the Ship---Capt Zalinski, the Dynamite Expert, and Other Experts Report to The World that the Wreck Was Not Accidental---Washington Officials Ready for Vigorous Action if Spanish Responsibility Can Be Shown---Divers to Be Sent Down to Make Careful Examinations.

DRAWN FROM A DESCRIPTION BY EYE-WITNESSES ON THE STEAMSHIP CITY OF WASHINGTON WHO SAW THE EXPLOSION, FOLLOWED BY "A VOLCANO OF FIRE AND SHOWERS OF BOATS, BODIES, IRON AND GUNS," CABLED TO THE WORLD BY ITS OWN CORRESPONDENT IN HAVANA, SYLVESTER SCOVEL.

THE WHOLE STORY OF THE DISASTER TOLD IN A FEW WORDS.

At the hour of going to press for this edition of The World it is not known whether the explosion which caused the destruction of the battle-ship Maine in the harbor of Havana was an accident or the result of a bomb or torpedo placed with an intent to blow up the vessel.

The consensus of opinion of the naval officers and experts in this country is that the disaster was not accidental. It is believed that the vessel was blown up. This view [illegible] out by Consul-General Lee and Capt. Sigsbee, Commander of the Maine.

In an official cable to the State [illegible] Lee makes the significant request that a court of inquiry be held to ascertain the cause of the explosion.

Capt. Sigsbee officially cabled Secretary Long his conclusion, after a hasty examination, that the disaster was not caused by an accident.

He expressed a belief that whether the explosion originated without or within, it was made possible by an enemy.

Dr. C. E. Pendleton, who has just arrived from Havana, says that he overheard there a conversation in which it was declared that there would shortly come a great sensation; that there were wires all around the Maine and that she could be blown to pieces at a moment's notice.

Capt. [illegible] the foremost living expert upon explosions in warfare, declares that he is almost sure that the Maine was destroyed by a dynamite torpedo or bomb.

A despatch from Washington says that Secretary Long and Assistant Secretary Roosevelt called all [illegible] in consultation yesterday morning [illegible] cause of the Maine's loss [illegible]

Consul-General Lee [illegible] the number of victims is 260. Lieuts. Merritt [illegible]

Another [illegible] United States Govern-

The *World*'s February 17 front page, somewhat more cautious than that of the *Journal*.

reporters, artists, and photographers, including a motion-picture man. Creelman, who was wounded in one battle, records an image of Hearst—wearing a beribboned straw hat on his head and a revolver at his belt—taking the story from his bleeding reporter and then galloping away on horseback to get to a *Journal* press boat.

American correspondents were learning how to use the boats and cables to speed their messages to the news offices. Stories from Cuba had to be brought to Key West for transmission to New York, with leading papers sending several thousand words a day. All this was expensive, but the race for news was an exciting one. The *World* scored the biggest single beat when Edward W. Harden, one of three correspondents to witness Dewey's amazing victory in Manila Bay, got his story off first by paying the "urgent" priority rate of $9.90 a word. Harden's beat arrived in New York too far into the dawn for the *World* to capitalize on it with a full-blown extra, but the *World*'s news client, the *Chicago Tribune,* had time to revamp its final edition and carry the most dramatic story of the war.

While Hearst said he did not care how much all of this cost (his paper spent $500,000 during the 4 months and put out as many as forty extras in one day), Pulitzer began to view the situation with dismay. The *Journal* gleefully asked in its front-page ears, "How do you like the *Journal*'s war?" while Pulitzer began to retreat. In the end, Pulitzer withdrew from the competition in sensationalism at the turn of the century, while Hearst continued to exploit the news in a manner that seriously impeded the effectiveness of his role as a people's champion. By 1900, about one-third of the metropolitan dailies were following the yellow trend, and it was another 10 years before the wave of sensationalism subsided and journalists concentrated on the more intelligent use of headlines, pictures, and color printing.

NOTES

1. Will Irwin, "The Fourth Current," *Collier's,* XLVI (February 18, 1911), 14.

2. Ibid. Estimate by Will Irwin in 1911, for the period up to then.

3. Ferdinand Lundberg, *Imperial Hearst: A Social Biography* (New York: Equinox Cooperative Press, 1936), p. 50. Lundberg presents much information about Hearst's finances but paints the publisher in the blackest possible fashion. For the best balanced accounts see John Tebbel, *The Life and Good Times of William Randolph Hearst* (New York: Dutton, 1952), and W. A. Swanberg, *Citizen Hearst* (New York: Scribner's, 1961).

4. *New York World,* May 1, 1898, p. 7 (supplement).

5. Willard G. Bleyer, *Main Currents in the History of American Journalism* (Boston: Houghton Mifflin, 1927), pp. 357–64. This book documents the case against the *Journal*'s rampant yellow journalism.

6. William Rockhill Nelson, editor of the *Kansas City Star,* had also used his own funds to fight court battles on behalf of the public interest, but not so sensationally.

7. Marcus M. Wilkerson, *Public Opinion and the Spanish-American War* (Baton Rouge: Louisiana State University Press, 1932); Joseph E. Wisan, *The Cuban Crisis as Reflected in the New York Press* (New York: Columbia University Press, 1934).

8. John D. Hicks, *A Short History of American Democracy* (Boston: Houghton Mifflin, 1943), p. 605.

9. Wisan, *The Cuban Crisis,* p. 460.

10. Wilkerson, *Public Opinion and the Spanish-American War,* p. 40.

11. There was competition between the Associated Press and the old United Press until 1897. After that time, all the major New York papers except the *New York Sun* were AP members.

12. James Creelman, *On the Great Highway* (Boston: Lothrop Publishing, 1901), p. 178.

13. Wisan, *The Cuban Crisis,* p. 331.

14. Arthur Brisbane, "The Modern Newspaper in War Time," *Cosmopolitan,* XXV (September, 1898), 541.

15. Don C. Seitz, *Joseph Pulitzer* (New York: Simon & Schuster, 1924), p. 312.

16. Wisan, *The Cuban Crisis,* p. 417.

17. Their story is told by Charles H. Brown in *The Correspondents' War* (New York: Scribner's, 1967).

ANNOTATED BIBLIOGRAPHY

Books

BEISNER, ROBERT L., *Twelve Against Empire: The Anti-Imperialists, 1898–1900.* New York: McGraw-Hill, 1968. Two of the twelve were Godkin and Schurz.

BLEYER, WILLARD G., *Main Currents in the History of American Journalism.* Boston: Houghton Mifflin, 1927. The chapter on Hearst admirably documents charges of sensationalism.

BROWN, CHARLES H., *The Correspondents' War.* New York: Scribner's, 1967. All the details of the press corps for the Spanish-American War.

CARLSON, OLIVER, *Brisbane: A Candid Biography.* New York: Stackpole Sons, 1937. A good critical analysis of the famous Hearst editor.

CARLSON, OLIVER, AND ERNEST SUTHERLAND BATES, *Hearst, Lord of San Simeon.* New York: Viking, 1936. Better than other early biographies by John K. Winkler and Mrs. Fremont Older. Still useful for the early Hearst period, but supplanted by Tebbel and Swanberg (see later reference).

DAVIS, RICHARD HARDING, *Notes of a War Correspondent.* New York: Scribner's, 1910. An American war correspondent in Cuba, Greece, South Africa, and Manchuria, covering four wars.

LUNDBERG, FERDINAND, *Imperial Hearst: A Social Biography.* New York: Equinox Cooperative Press, 1936. A bitter attack on the chain publisher; valuable particularly for financial data.

MERK, FREDERICK, *Manifest Destiny and Mission in American History: A Reinterpretation.* New York: Knopf, 1963. Newspapers document the story of the westward march.

MILLIS, WALTER, *The Martial Spirit; a Study of Our War with Spain.* Boston: Houghton Mifflin, 1931. A readable, critical account.

O'CONNOR, RICHARD, *Pacific Destiny: An Informal History of the U.S. in the Far East.* Boston: Little, Brown, 1969. Thesis is that America moved from Atlantic to Pacific role through deep desires and motives of political, military, and religious leaders at pivotal moments, from Commodore Perry's time to Vietnam. Detailed treatment of Philippine Insurrection.

SWANBERG, W. A., *Citizen Hearst.* New York: Scribner's, 1961. A highly readable study, covering available printed sources in meticulous detail; has some new material.

TEBBEL, JOHN, *The Life and Good Times of William Randolph Hearst.* New York: Dutton, 1952. A well-balanced biography and the best-documented study of the Hearst newspaper empire.

WILKERSON, MARCUS M., *Public Opinion and the Spanish-American War.* Baton Rouge: Louisiana State University Press, 1932. A scholarly study of war propaganda and press influence.

WISAN, JOSEPH E., *The Cuban Crisis as Reflected in the New York Press.* New York: Columbia University Press, 1934. A good specialized study.

Periodicals and Monographs

BERG, MEREDITH AND DAVID, "The Rhetoric of War Preparation: The New York Press in 1898," *Journalism Quarterly,* XLV (Winter 1968), 653. Analysis of New York dailies after the sinking of the *Maine.*

BRISBANE, ARTHUR, "The Modern Newspaper in War Time," *Cosmopolitan,* XXV (September 1898), 541. The *Journal* editor confesses his sins. See also Brisbane, "Yellow Journalism," *Bookman,* XIX (June 1904), 400.

BROWN, CHARLES H., "Press Censorship in the Spanish-American War," *Journalism Quarterly,* XLII (Autumn 1965), 581. It was more extensive and effective than believed.

COMMANDER, LYDIA K., "The Significance of Yellow Journalism," *Arena,* XXXIV (August 1905), 150. A contemporary analysis.

DICKERSON, DONNA, "William Cowper Brann: Nineteenth Century Press Critic," *Journalism History,* V (Summer 1978), 42. Brann published *The Iconoclast* in Waco, Texas, 1895 to 1898, and wrote eighteen essays on the "yellow press."

DONALD, ROBERT, "Sunday Newspapers in the United States," *Universal Review,* VIII (September 1890), 79. A look at a then-new medium.

FRANCKE, WARREN, "An Argument in Defense of Sensationalism," *Journalism History,* V (Autumn 1978), 70. Analyzes differing perceptions of the word *sensationalism* in journalism history.

HACHTEN, WILLIAM A., "The Metropolitan Sunday Newspaper in the United States: A Study of Trends in Content and Practices," Ph.D. thesis, University of Minnesota, 1960 (Ann Arbor: University Microfilms, 1960). The most complete study of the Sunday paper.

IRWIN, WILL, "The American Newspaper," *Collier's,* XLVI (February 18 and March 4, 1911). The sins of yellow journalism described.

MOTT, FRANK L., "The First Sunday Paper: A Footnote to History," *Journalism Quarterly,* XXXV (Fall 1958), 443. The *Boston Globe.*

PETERS, GLEN W., "The *American Weekly,*" *Journalism Quarterly,* XLVIII (Autumn 1971), 466. A review of the Sunday supplements, especially Hearst's.

STEFFENS, LINCOLN, "Hearst, the Man of Mystery," *American Magazine,* LXIII (November 1906), 3. Penetrating study based on interviews of Hearst, rarely obtained.

VANDERBURG, RAY, "The Paradox that Was Arthur Brisbane," *Journalism Quarterly,* XLVII (Summer 1970), 281. Study of the great Hearst editor.

ZOBRIST, BENEDICT KARL, "How Victor Lawson's Newspapers Covered the Cuban War of 1898," *Journalism Quarterly,* XXXVIII (Summer 1961), 323. The nonsensational *Chicago Record* and *Daily News.*

Edward Wyllis Scripps aboard his yacht near the close of his career.

18

The People's Champions

I have only one principle, and that is represented by an effort to make it harder for the rich to grow richer and easier for the poor to keep from growing poorer.

—Edward Wyllis Scripps

The opening of the twentieth century found the United States moving toward a consolidation of its position as an industrial nation. The framework had been completed by 1900: The economic expansion that had begun after the Civil War, the growth in population and the tying together of the country, the rapid development of rich natural resources, the inventive and productive genius, the political and cultural advances—all these factors ensured the future of a new world power.

Vital contests still were in progress, however, that would affect the character of the new America. These contests assumed critical importance at a moment when the economic, political, and social trends of a new era were being shaped. How would the nation conduct itself in the world community? How democratic would it remain? Would there be a balance struck between the advocates of unrestricted economic individualism and the crusaders for social justice? Would the fruits of progress be shared by all the people, in the form of better living conditions, educational and cultural opportunities, higher health standards, and personal security? Would government be responsive to the general welfare? What was to the be the role of the press in advancing or retarding necessary adjustments?

Men and women had struggled to obtain affirmative answers to these questions now confronting America since the Industrial Revolution changed the character of American society. The "consistent rebellion" in the agricultural areas against economic inequities represented one phase of the struggle; the rise of the labor unions in the cities another. The growth of strong political movements that sought to place more power in the hands of the people generally; the efforts of the social scientists to impart knowledge on which wise social and political decisions could be based; the appeals of reformers, agitators, political leaders, and writers for an arousing of the country's social conscience—all these had helped to shape the direction in which the country would turn.

But in the first years of the new century there were major divisions of thought and action that indicated the crucial importance of the struggle to shape public opinion, and to enforce the popular will. Nationalists and internationalists contended in the field of foreign affairs. Economic individualists and social reformers clashed in the domestic arena. The mass media of the times—newspapers, magazines, books—played a most important role in these national debates.

THE TRIUMPH OF "MANIFEST DESTINY"

The generally enthusiastic public response to America's aggressive policy toward Spain in the Caribbean provided the proponents of Manifest Destiny with an excuse for gaining supremacy over as much of Asia as military power could sustain. They included politicians led by Theodore Roosevelt and Henry Cabot Lodge, historian Brooks Adams, evangelist the Reverend Josiah Strong, railroad builder James J. Hill, naval strategist Alfred T. Mahan, entrepreneurs like the American-China Development Company, influential newspaper publishers and editors of rural farm journals, and extremely vocal representatives of the powerful farm bloc, such as Senator William V. Allen of Nebraska.

These leaders, agitating on behalf of Americans of all political faiths, generated the ideas and emotions that resulted in the bloody annexation of the Philippine Islands, the capstone of this nation's relentless drive to be a Pacific rather than an Atlantic power. It also was the propellant for future Asian conflicts. Promises made to insurgent leader Emilio Aguinaldo that American force would guarantee Philippine independence after the overthrow of remaining Spanish troops and friendly Philippine bases would be used for expanded trade with Japan were not kept. Instead, the United States signaled its determination to become a full-fledged colonial power in East Asia, lured on by the mirage of China as a land of vast and lucrative markets where the surplus crops of America's great middlelands could be sold.

This military adventure, which left the United States with an exposed strategic commitment along the axis of Japan's southern expansion, was a colossal blunder that would lead to three more wars in American history. Dewey's victory at Manila had been part of the short but rather exciting 1898 public experience, but the guerrilla war in the Philippines between 1899 and 1902 was, in the words of historian Richard O'Connor, a quickly forgotten "dreary sequel" to the Spanish-American War.[1] At the peak of the fighting approximately 70,000 U.S. troops—fed with notions of racial and religious superiority—were used to brutally crush the insurgency. Horrifying cruelties practiced on Filipino soldiers and massacres of civilians brought the total death count to an estimated 200,000 (American casualties were about 10,000). Fighting against the Moros in the southern Philippines continued until World War I, as America strove to subjugate a determined native population. Ironically, as part of this generally confused foreign policy, the United States sent thousands of volunteers to help reconstruct buildings, teach English, and fight disease.

Half a million Americans joined the Anti-Imperialist League that had been founded in Boston. In actions to be repeated years later in protests against the war in Vietnam, they participated in mass meetings, marches, sit-ins, and teach-ins, all the time pressuring their elected representatives against formal annexation of the islands. A bitter Senate debate featured the elderly George H. Hoar of Massachusetts, who tried to awaken his colleagues by telling of concentration camps, burned villages, and the use of the water-cure torture, against Albert J. Beveridge of Indiana, a leader of the Senate expansionists.

Carl Schurz, who in an 1893 *Harper's* article had insisted that America could obtain economic objectives "without taking those countries into our national household,"[2] was joined in the antiimperialist movement by Jane Addams, Andrew Carnegie, William James, Samuel Gompers, Samuel Clemens, and other influential citizens. Clemens wrote that a new American flag should be designed with the white stripes painted black, and the stars replaced by a skull and crossbones. But much of the dissent was drowned out by the thunder of editors like "Marse" Henry Watterson of the *Louisville Courier-Journal,* who bluntly spoke for many when he said, "We escape the menace and peril of socialism and agrarianism, as England has escaped them, by a policy of colonialism and conquest . . . we risk Caesarism, certainly, but Caesarism is preferable to anarchism."[3] Those were not the only choices, but many Americans pursued this all-or-nothing approach in an effort to become dominant in new market areas.

The end of the major fighting in the Philippines was followed by the Russo-Japanese War in 1904 and more than 100 correspondents—many of them veterans of the Spanish-American War, the Boer War in South Africa, and the Boxer Rebellion—flocked to Japan. Richard Harding Davis, Frederick Palmer, Jack London, and the photographer Jimmy Hare were among those frustrated by the effective Japanese censorship. The Associated Press coverage from St. Petersburg and Tokyo gave the two versions of the fighting at Port Arthur and in Manchuria. At home, most large newspapers editorialized against the corrupt Russian regime, except a number in California who were so affected by their experience wth Oriental immigration that they feared a Japanese victory. Finally, in May 1905, the Czar's fleet was destroyed in battle off the coast of Korea and Japan stood alone in Asia; China had been defeated in 1894. The only possible challengers to Japanese supremacy in the Far East were the Americans in the Philippines, the new arrivals.

Closer to home and part of this hot-blooded American spirit, the Panama Canal had been built in an occupied zone that Columbia complained had been torn from it by an American-backed revolution. This action, and the extension of American military and economic domination in the Central American and Caribbean areas, dissipated hopes for Pan-American understanding. Cuba and Panama virtually became American protectorates under the Platt amendment. The Dominican Republic, Haiti, and Nicaragua in turn were forced to accept United States intervention in their affairs under the Roosevelt corollary to the Monroe

Doctrine, by which the United States undertook to preserve order in those countries and to administer their financial affairs to prevent any possible intervention by European powers. The primary intent was to assure American security in a vital area, but American trade and financial interests followed the flag—and many persons complained that they sometimes preceded it.

At the same time, however, there were powerful forces in operation that sought to commit America to a quite different role in world affairs. Cultural and religious ties were made with China after the Boxer Rebellion. The Philippines were promised their eventual independence after a period of tutelage. Roosevelt himself acted as a mediator in helping to end the Russo-Japanese War and in smoothing relations among Germany, France, and Britain at the Algeciras conference. The United States accepted the idea of an international court of arbitration, advanced at The Hague Peace Conference of 1899, and negotiated several arbitration treaties. Americans played a leading part in the unsuccessful attempt to create an international court of justice during the second conference at The Hague in 1907. Out of these movements came American leadership in proposing the League of Nations and the World Court at the close of World War I—proposals most of the other nations of the world adopted while the United States slumped back into isolationism.

THE CRISIS OF ECONOMIC POWER

Important as was this contest over foreign policy, it was not the major concern of the American people in the years around the turn of the century. Their attention was centered largely on domestic problems created by the Industrial Revolution: the growth of trusts and the centralization of economic power in a few hands; the inadequate incomes of the worker and farmer; corruption and inadequacies in political and business life. To many Americans it seemed that national wealth and strength, while reflecting basic progress for all the people, were actually mainly benefiting a plundering few who were usurping the freedoms of the many.[4]

Concentration of economic power, which had begun to develop rapidly in the 1880s, was greatly accentuated after 1900. A study made in 1904 listed 318 industrial trusts, three-fourths of which had been incorporated since 1898. These 318 trusts, capitalized at $7 billion, represented the merging of 5300 individuals' companies. Six big trusts—in steel, oil, copper, sugar, tobacco, and shipping—that had been organized in those 6 years were capitalized at $2.5 billion. Census figures show that in 1914 one-eighth of American businesses employed more than three-fourths of the wage earners and produced four-fifths of the manufactured products.

The newspaper and magazine editors and the reporters and writers who joined in protesting this economic monopoly were even more concerned with the seemingly insatiable appetite of capitalists for power. Those who won domination in one field promptly reached out into other spheres, until the country's financial power fell largely into the hands of two loosely organized groups, the Morgan and the Rockefeller interests and their satellites. The famous Pujo committee investigation in 1913 reported that four allied financial institutions in New York held 341 directorships in banks, railroads, shipping lines, insurance companies, public utilities, and other businesses with total resources of $22 billion.

Distribution of the wealth being created was heavily one-sided. Two-thirds of the male adult workers failed to earn $600 a year in wages, which was the figure set by sociologists as the minimum needed to maintain decent standards at the current cost of living. There were many material and social advances being made: electricity, gas, and plumbing in homes; better schools and parks; the conveniences of city life; telephones, railroads, and highways. But they did not mean much to the millions in the New York tenements whose plight has been reported on by Jacob Riis.

Labor-union membership increased between 1900 and 1910, jumping from 3.5 percent of all workers to 7 percent. The gains were being made by skilled workers: the railway brotherhoods, building tradespeople, machinists, miners, printing tradespeople, and garment-workers groups. Unskilled workers, women workers, and immigrants remained victims of the economic order. Immigrants were a major factor in creating the social problem. The flood of immigrants during the period 1880 to 1900 was equaled in the single decade 1900 to 1910. The great bulk of the new immigration was from southern and eastern Europe, and a fourth of those arriving were illiterate. By 1910 one-seventh of the United States population was foreign-born, and in the industrial East more than half the population was foreign-born or of foreign-born parentage. These were the "poor and ill-informed" who were to be championed by such newspaper publishers as Edward Wyllis Scripps.

DEMANDS FOR POLITICAL AND ECONOMIC REFORM

Even though these conditions inevitably demanded reform, the "quest for social justice" was slow. Eugene V. Debs did see his Socialist party win nearly a million votes in the presidential election of 1912, and some 300 cities and towns elected Socialist officeholders. In the labor movement William D. Haywood and his Industrial Workers of the World sought a radical approach to the plight of the unskilled laborer. But political leadership remained in the hands of the two major political parties,[5] and most labor followed the moderate program of Samuel Gompers and his American Federation of Labor.

The instruments for political action on the national level were Theodore Roosevelt's "Square Deal" and Woodrow Wilson's "New Freedom." But the decisions these two administrations won in the fields of monetary reform, government regulation of business, welfare legislation, and tariff revision stemmed from the spirit of the times. This spirit was reflected in various forms by the agitation of the Populists, the great crusade headed by William Jennings Bryan in 1896, the governmental reforms being proposed by Robert La Follette and his individualistic Wisconsin progressives, the work of the labor-union leaders, the thinking and writing of the intellectuals, and the demands of the women's movement.

In the Roosevelt years the winning of an antitrust suit against the Northern Securities Company, preventing a monopoly of railroad transportation west of the Mississippi, turned the tide against extreme concentration of economic power. The Hepburn Act brought effective government regulation of transportation rates. And Roosevelt's conservation policies saved a sizable residue of America's natural resources from ruthless exploitation. In the Wilson administration the creation of the Federal Reserve banking system brought a modern currency and credit system to the country for the first time; the Clayton Act struck at the abusive use of court injunctions and contempt citations against striking labor unions; the Federal Trade Commission was given power to regulate unfair business practices; and in other areas government extended its influence to a greater degree than ever before in American history.

But the progress being made, while substantial, was often balked by the supporters of big business. Senators like Nelson Aldrich of Rhode Island were frank spokespeople for the conservative cause and they had great influence. Congressional representatives like George Norris of Nebraska could clip the wings of House Speaker Joe Cannon, a powerful ally of the big-business forces, but they nevertheless lost many battles to their conservative opposition. William Howard Taft, succeeding Roosevelt as president, was unable to cope with the big-business elements of his Republican party, and an irate Roosevelt launched his third-party Progressive movement in 1912. The Bull Moose crusade failed, but it split the Republican party so thoroughly that Woodrow Wilson entered the White House with a minority of the popular vote to inaugurate a Democratic administration.

Many of the gains were made at state and local levels. Popular election of United States Senators, presidential primaries, and adoption of the referendum, initiative, and recall were manifestations of the new trend. State laws protecting working women and children, regulating hours of work, providing for workers' compensation, and advancing social security generally ran the gauntlet of unfavorable court decisions. In the cities, reform movements led by such men as Samuel M. Jones in Toledo, Tom Johnson and Newton D. Baker in Cleveland, Seth Low in New York, and the advocates of commission government in Galveston did yeoman work in restoring governmental decency. Corruption in municipal councils and in state legislatures was a common mark of the times, and newspaper editors who wished to join with the reformers had almost unbelievable instances of bribe taking and graft to expose.

THE WOMEN'S EQUALITY MOVEMENT

Coming to a climax in the first two decades of the twentieth century was the women's equality movement, seeking the rights of women in voting, education, and property holding. The growth of women's colleges in the midnineteenth century and recognition of coeducational status in state universities before the close of the century was matched much more slowly on the voting front. The 1848 women's-rights convention, held in Seneca Falls, New York, led to the founding of *The Lily* (1849 to 1859) by the local temperance society. Its editor was Amelia Bloomer (whose loose-fitting trousers worn in protest of the corset bore her name). Women's-rights leader Elizabeth Cady Stanton worked with Bloomer to make *The Lily* a women's-rights monthly with 6000 subscribers. Most famous of the feminist newspapers was Stanton's *The Revolution* (1868 to 1871), which had Susan B. Anthony as business manager. Advocating a variety of radical causes, it drew only 3000 subscribers. Dismayed by the exclusion of women from the protection of the Fourteenth and Fifteenth amendments, Lucy Stone and other more conservative leaders formed the American Woman Suffrage Association in 1869. Its weekly, *The Woman's Journal,* focused only on the suffrage issue. It was edited by Lucy Stone until 1893, and then by her husband Henry Blackwell and daughter Alice until 1917, by which time it had 6000 readers.

By 1900 the growing entry of women into business and professions had resulted in the forming of some 3300 women's clubs and groups; the *National Business Woman* began in 1919 as their federation's voice. But it was hard for the women's movement to get serious, objective coverage from male newspaper editors. The growth of the suffrage campaign led to front-page coverage of mixed support, like this headline in the *New York Press* in May, 1912: "20,000 Women in Parade for Vote Cheered by Men," followed by a headline deck, "Crowd of a half million lines Fifth Avenue and shouts approval to rich women who tramp with factory workers and shop girls in pageant led by young society women on horseback, many of them riding astride." By 1917 Emma Bugbee and Eleanor Booth Simmons of the *New York Tribune* and Rheta Childe Dorr of the *New York Mail* were covering women's-movement assemblies.[6] Ratification of the Nineteenth amendment in 1920 forbade discrimination in voting based on sex, and the movement subsided without resolution of the property-rights issue.

ALTERNATIVE PRESSES: SOCIALIST

Those who found the country's newspapers too closely conforming in cultural, social, and economic outlooks attempted to publish their own alternative papers, with limited success. The Socialist labor press produced two substantial dailies, the *New York Evening Call* (1908 to 1923) and the *Milwaukee Leader* (1911 to 1942). These founding dates reflect the heyday of the Socialist Party of America in the first two decades of the twentieth century. In 1912, presidential candidate Eugene Debs polled 6 percent of the popular vote and seventy-nine Socialist mayors were elected in twenty-four states. Two million copies of 323 Socialist newspapers were circulated in 1913, by far the largest being the weekly *Appeal to Reason* (1901 to 1922), which distributed 760,000 copies by rail all over the country from its shop in Girard, Kansas. On special occasions, it also sent out bundles of papers numbering into the millions. J. A. Wayland, the founder-editor, devoted only about 20 percent of the space to Socialist theory and party activities, but concentrated instead on protest "muckraking" of the era.[7] The Yiddish-language Socialist paper *Vorwärts* (*Jewish Daily Forward*), founded in 1897 in New York City, had local daily editions in eleven cities by 1923 and reached a 250,000 circulation under editor Abraham Cahan. The Communist *Daily Worker,* founded in 1924, had a 100,000 circulation in the late 1930s.

FOREIGN-LANGUAGE AND LATINO PAPERS

Foreign-language publications, which were nearly all in German or French before the Civil War, numbered 300 in 1860, 800 in 1880, and 1200 in 1910. A peak of 1323 such papers was reached in 1917. The German press, beginning in 1732 in Pennsylvania, peaked at 750 publications in 1890, declined to 627 in 1910, and was cut by the impact of war to 258 by 1920. In 1910 the most numerous papers besides the German ones, by language, were Scandinavian (132), Italian (seventy-three), Spanish (fifty-eight), and Polish (forty-eight).

Foreign-language dailies peaked at 160 in 1914; one-third of them were German (fifty-five). Others were French, Italian, and Polish (twelve each); Yiddish and Japanese (ten each); Spanish and Bohemian (eight each). These dailies circulated a total of 2.6 million copies in 1914, with the German press totaling 823,000 and the Yiddish, 762,000. The largest foreign-language daily was the *New Yorker Staats-Zeitung,* dating from 1845, with a top circulation of 250,000. Its owner, Herman Ridder, was elected a president of the American Newspaper Publishers Association.

While much of the foreign-language press served incoming immigrants in the bigger cities, the Southwestern states developed a distinctive foreign-language press serving the Hispanic or Latino minority population. More than 100 Spanish-language publications appeared in the Southwest in the second half of the nineteenth century. Some, as Spanish sections of Anglo papers, were instruments for social control of a minority; others advocated activism and reflected Hispanic culture (called Chicano in the case of Mexican-American heritage). *El Clamor Público* (1855 to 1859) was outspoken against mob violence in Los Angeles; *La Crónica* continued the fight in the 1870s. *El Fronterizo* of Tucson urged a boycott of hostile merchants in the 1880s. *El Gato* of Santa Fé urged working-class unity against low pay in 1894, and *El Tiempo* of Las Cruces agitated for New Mexican statehood against anti-Hispanic roadblock tactics.[8] There were forty-nine Spanish-language publications in the entire country in 1890, fifty-eight in 1910, and ninety-five in 1920. The eight dailies listed in 1914 had only 28,000 circulation between them. But the impact of such minority presses was strong among readers, and the general press reflected some of their news and views.

THE BLACK PRESS GROWS

One group of Americans who found little to represent their aspirations and interests in the mass media was the black population. Not until the 1950s did the average American newspaper or magazine exhibit an understanding interest in the black 10 percent of citizens, and even then few were sensitive to them as readers. There was a clear need for a black press, but little economic support for it from a black community with few socioeconomic resources. Nevertheless, the black press that began in 1827 survived and gained in stature.*

*See pages 181–84 for a discussion of the founding of the black press.

More than 3000 black newspapers—owned and edited by blacks for black readers—have appeared since *Freedom's Journal* made its 1827 bow. The best historical statistics were gathered by Professor Armistead Scott Pride of Lincoln University for his 1951 doctoral dissertation. Pride's figures showed that 1187 black papers were added during the years 1865 to 1900 to the forty founded before 1865. Another 1500 had been added by 1951, but the survivors numbered only 175. The average life span of a black newspaper, Pride found, was 9 years.[9] Pride gives several reasons for the increase in black papers beginning in the mid-1880s: increased educational opportunitites for blacks, support of black papers by religious and welfare groups working in the South, establishment of political sheets for enfranchised blacks, and growth of urban black communities that could support papers.

Just as the standard daily press grew in numbers, circulation, and stature during the New Journalism era between 1880 and World War I, so did the black press. Among today's leaders that have founding dates in that period are the *Philadelphia Tribune* (1884), Baltimore's *Afro-American* (1892), the *Chicago Defender* (1905), New York's *Amsterdam News* (1909), Norfolk's *Journal and Guide* (1909), and the *Pittsburgh Courier* (1910). Historically important from that period are the *New York Age* (1890), *Boston Guardian* (1901), and *The Crisis* (1910).

Ranking in fame with Frederick Douglass and his *North Star* of 1847 are W. E. B. Du Bois and his *The Crisis* of 1910. Other major figures in black publishers' ranks to 1910 included John H. Murphy, Sr., of the *Afro-American* papers, T. Thomas Fortune of the *New York Age,* William Monroe Trotter of the *Boston Guardian,* Robert S. Abbott of the *Chicago Defender,* and Robert L. Vann of the *Pittsburgh Courier.* Their stories, and those of other major black papers, follow.[10]

The semiweekly *Philadelphia Tribune,* which celebrated its centennial in 1984, is the oldest continuously published black newspaper in the United States. Founded in 1884 by Chris J. Perry, Sr., it became one of the most substantial and best-edited black weeklies. Perry's widow and two daughters continued the *Tribune* after his death in 1921. A son-in-law, E. Washington Rhodes, was publisher and editor until he died in 1970. Criticizing the more affluent blacks for not doing enough to help the poor, the *Tribune* organized charities and scholarship programs as a part of its community responsibility.

The first prominent black woman journalist and editor was Ida B. Wells-Barnett, who during her public career (1887 to 1931) was known as a feminist reformer and race leader, but was essentially a journalist. As co-owner and editor of *Free Speech* in Memphis, she was so determined and aggressive, particularly about the prevalence of lynchings, that the paper was mobbed in 1892. She then worked for the *New York Age* and the weekly *Conservator* in Chicago. She continued to press on racial issues as a journalist and reform leader throughout her career.

John H. Murphy, Sr., is regarded as the founder of the *Afro-American* editions, four regional and one national, centered in Baltimore. Murphy, who did whitewashing for a living, and was superintendent of an African Methodist church Sunday school, began publishing a small paper for the church in his basement. When a Baptist minister, Rev. William M. Alexander, began another religious paper, the *Afro-American,* in 1892, Murphy gained control of it. The paper gained a national reputation before 1920. Murphy wrote a credo that year calling for the *Afro-American* to keep faith with the common people, to fight to get rid of slums and to provide jobs for all, and to "stay out of politics except to expose corruption and condemn injustice, race prejudice and the cowardice of compromise." The credo still appears in his newspapers, which were continued after his death in 1922 by his son, Dr. Carl J. Murphy.

T. Thomas Fortune was one of the best-known black editors at the turn of the century, and his *New York Age* won national attention. Born to slave parents, Fortune ran errands for a Southern newspaper, learned to set type, and entered New York journalism through the back shops. In 1879 a black tabloid named *Rumor* was changed to standard size by George Parker and was renamed the *New York Globe;* Fortune and W. Walter Sampson were the printing crew and became Parker's partners. Within a decade Fortune was the principal figure and the paper had become the *Age.* As its editorial writer, Fortune was quoted by the nation's press and was read by political leaders, including Theodore Roosevelt. Booker T. Washington selected the *Age* as the national voice for the blacks and began to subsidize it. This won the disapproval of W. E. B. Du Bois and other militant black leaders who said that Washington was accepting segregation and subservience to whites. Fortune sold his share of the *Age* in 1907 and in the 1920s supported the back-to-Africa movement of Marcus Garvey, writing for Garvey's widely circulating magazine, *Negro World.* The *Age,* under the editorship of Fred R. Moore, remained a major New York black newspaper until it was sold to the expanding *Defender* group of Chicago in 1952.

William Monroe Trotter, another great black leader at the turn of the century, had a background opposite from Fortune's. His father, a white Union army officer, became interested in racial equality and married a black slave. He then became a merchant in Boston, where the mulatto son won election to Phi Beta Kappa at Harvard and earned a master's degree there. In 1901 with George Forbes, an Amherst graduate, Trotter founded the *Boston Guardian.* It was provocative and militant enough to win the praise of Du Bois. When Booker T. Washington spoke in Boston in 1905 the *Guardian* challenged his conservative leadership, particularly on black education and voting. Trotter later led a protest delegation to the national capital to meet with President Woodrow Wilson and plead the cause of blacks. But in the 1920s his paper languished; Trotter and his wife lost their home and Trotter died in 1934. His sister continued the *Guardian* until her death in 1957.

Robert S. Abbott's *Chicago Defender,* founded in 1905, fared better in the quest for public support than did Trotter's *Guardian.* By 1915 it reached a circulation of 230,000. The figure declined two-thirds by the depression year of 1935, but rose again to 160,000 in postwar 1947. The Chicago paper, with its national edition, then became the cornerstone of the largest American black newspaper group.

Abbott was born of black parents in Georgia in 1868. When his father died, his mother married John H. H. Sengstacke, the son of a German merchant who had married a slave. Abbott learned printing at Hampton Institute, worked on his stepfather's small paper, studied law, and in 1905 founded the *Defender* among Chicago's 40,000 black population. The paper was run on a shoestring from his landlady's house until Abbott developed a familiar black newspaper formula: muckraking on behalf of his race, sensationalizing through "race-angling" of headlines and stories, use of crime and scandal stories, and resolute challenges to the Ku Klux Klan, racial rioting, lynchings, and other threats to black Americans' security. By the 1930s Abbott had moderated the *Defender's* tone and had added much more personal, social, cultural, and fashion news. When he died in 1940 his successor was John H. Sengstacke, a nephew.

Robert L. Vann's *Pittsburgh Courier,* founded in 1910, became the largest in circulation of all black newspapers, approaching 300,000 in the late 1940s. Vann was a lawyer who took over a church-sponsored publishing venture and who struck out to fight against racial discrimination and the Jim Crow tradition. The *Courier* backed black athletes, which helped Jackie Robinson to break the color barrier. Vann developed a circulation in the South and used his influence to attract capable black journalists.

P. Bernard Young, another black publisher who developed a national newspaper, took over the *Journal and Guide* in Norfolk in 1910 and ran it as a moderate, nonsensational weekly until his death in 1962. By contrast, the various publishers of New York's *Amsterdam News* have concentrated on local circulation since its founding by James H. Anderson in 1909, and have only gradually won their way to leadership in the competitive Harlem scene.

W. E. B. DU BOIS AND *THE CRISIS*

W. E. B. Du Bois, the militant apostle of protest in the opening decades of the century, became one of the major folk heroes of the black equality movement of the 1960s. His appeal was strong for the radical left of that movement because late in life he became an advocate of Marxism and went to live in the new African nation of Ghana, where he died in 1963 at 95.

Du Bois was not a newspaperman, although he was a correspondent or columnist for several newspapers. He was primarily a writer and a teacher with a cause to promote—that of rescuing the black race from a crisis that threatened to crush its capability. He is best known for his work between 1910 and 1934 as an executive of the National Association for the Advancement of Colored People and for the founding and editing of its magazine, *The Crisis*. That journal served so well as a combination of a news magazine reporting items of concern to blacks, a journal of editorial opinion, a review of opinion and literature, and a literary magazine that its entire file for the first 50 years has been reproduced as "A Record of the Darker Races."

Born in New England in 1868, Du Bois was raised by his mother in a white society relatively free of discrimination. He himself was of mixed blood. He edited a high-school paper and was correspondent for the *Springfield Republican* and the *New York Age.* At Fisk University he edited the student paper. He studied sociology at Harvard and in Germany and contributed articles to the *Atlantic* and *World's Work.* After attempting two other black journals, he succeeded with *The Crisis.* In it he set out to challenge the whole concept of white supremacy, then nationally accepted, and its counterpart of black inferiority. He said his object

W. E. B. Du Bois

Bettmann Archive

was to "set forth those facts and arguments which show the danger of race prejudice, particularly as manifested today toward colored people. It takes its name from the fact that the editors believe that this is a critical time in the history of the advancement of men."[11]

"Mentally the negro is inferior to the white," said the 1911 *Britannica.* It was this belief Du Bois set out to destroy. His editorials also attacked immediate ills: wartime discrimination against black soldiers, the widespread race riots and lynchings following World War I, the climax of Ku Klux Klan terrorism, continued white refusal to consider black rights in the fields of voting, education, and housing. Circulation of *The Crisis* passed 100,000 in 1918. But dissension within the NAACP and other factors reduced it to fewer than 10,000 when Du Bois retired as editor in 1934 at age 65. Under editor Roy Wilkins until 1949 and then Henry Lee Moon, circulation revived to well above 100,000.

Du Bois became the head of the sociology department at Atlanta University, founded a scholarly journal on world race problems named *Phylon,* and wrote books and countless articles for major publications. Like Frederick Douglass, his writings were being published again in the 1970s as a symbol of achievement by a distinguished member of the black race—and, of course, the human race—who so effectively used the weapon of the journalistic crusade.

"THE PEOPLE'S CHAMPIONS"

The crusading spirit is as old as journalism, but never in American history had there been more opportunity for "the people's champions" than in the years following 1900. Voices of protest were raised in colonial days by people like James Franklin and Samuel Adams, in the early years of the republic by Jeffersonian and Jacksonian editors, by the creators of the first mass press before the Civil War, by the leaders of the "new journalism" before the close of the century. The struggle between big business and workers and farmers was as old as the struggle between the Hamiltonians and the Jeffersonians for control of the government. The battle for the rights of labor and for a more equitable distribution of wealth was a basic issue of similar standing. And warring on corruption in city governments had been a job for conscientious newspaperpeople since the rise of urban life. In the ebb and flow of these contests, however, the years following 1900 became critical ones.

Some newspapers were conspicuous in their response to the challenge. So were some of the new popular magazines, which became important vehicles for those whom Teddy Roosevelt eventually termed the *muckrakers.* And the school of realistic writers that flowered at the turn of the century added important books to the American literature that dealt with life and problems of the day. Joining hands with politicians and labor leaders, reformers and agitators, professors and ministers, social workers and philanthropists, the men and women of journalism and literature helped to shape the course of the great crusade.

PULITZER'S CRUSADES IN THE *WORLD*

Joseph Pulitzer and his *New York World* became increasingly effective as "people's champions" in the years following the Spanish-American War. In foreign affairs the *World* vigorously opposed the annexation of the Philippines and the imperialism of the Caribbean policy. It continued to support the internationalist movement and the policy of peaceful arbitration of the world's problems, which it had espoused during the Venezuelan crisis. In domestic politics, this stand of the *World* on foreign policy led it to support William Jennings Bryan for president in 1900 on an "antiimperialism" platform, while ignoring Bryan's radical monetary policies, which Pulitzer disliked.

The independent qualities and the crusading spirit of the *World* reached new heights, both on local and national issues. This was not a sudden manifestation of interest in crusading, as in the case of some other newspapers of the period, but a flowering of the Pulitzer editorial-page philosophy. Pulitzer, while agreeing that the *World* was Democrat in political sympathy, argued that his newspaper was independent of party and supported only those elements in a political party whose objectives coincided with those of the *World.* In looking at the major political parties of his day, Pulitzer put little trust in a Republican party with strong elements representing the big-business interests of the country, although he admired and supported Republican insurgents who fought to break the power of Speaker Cannon or Republican candidates of the caliber of Governor Charles Evans Hughes of New York. Pulitzer decided that the Democratic party best represented the political philosophy in which he believed and was most likely to act as the defender of individual liberties, grass-roots government, and progressive democracy.

Part of the *World*'s new strength in its editorial columns was the result of a revamping of its editorial-page staff. In 1904 the ailing Pulitzer, tortured by the acute nervous disorders that made the last few years of his life a nightmare, found a brilliant young editor who was destined to become the central force of the *World*'s editorial page. His name was Frank I. Cobb.

Cobb was then 35, a veteran of 15 years' newspaper experience including 4 years as the chief editorial writer for the *Detroit Free Press.* His somewhat limited formal education had been greatly supplemented by his scholarly interest and wide reading in the fields of history, government, and philosophy, and by his experiences as a newspaper reporter and as a political correspondent. Cobb had demonstrated the maturity of his judgment and his great intellectual capacity early, but he also understood human nature and attracted others to him by his friendliness, his eagerness, and his enthusiasm for living.[12] Within a year he had become the recognized chief editorial writer who would succeed to the editorship in 1911 on Pulitzer's death.

The most famous of all the *World*'s crusades began the same year, 1905. A battle had developed for control of the management of the Equitable Life Assurance Society, one of the life-insurance companies that had built up great financial resources as Americans took up the purchase of policies and benefits to provide for their personal and family security. Evidence was presented by two *World* reporters, David Ferguson and Louis Seibold, that officials of the company were using funds paid in by policyholders for their own private investments and thereby were building huge personal fortunes—gambling with the people's money, the *World* said. Other editors, like Ervin Wardman of the *New York Press,* joined in the battle and the spotlight was turned on the Mutual Life and New York Life companies as well.

Demand rose for an investigation by a legislative committee, whose counsel was Charles Evans Hughes, a young and forceful attorney who documented the case against the insurance companies. He also substantiated the *World*'s charges that the company had maintained a large fund of money to bribe legislators. The specter of the "money interests" dominating the life-insurance companies so aroused public opinion that strict regulatory legislation was enacted in New York State. Hughes rode into the governorship in 1906.

One other of the *World*'s crusades deserves mention. Late in 1908, Cobb wrote a lengthy editorial demanding a congressional investigation of what he called "the entire Panama Canal scandal." Cobb's ire had been aroused by "a scandalous personal attack" by President Theodore Roosevelt upon the editor of the *Indianapolis News,* who had raised questions about the Canal. Cobb said Roosevelt had made "deliberate misstatements of fact" and outlined a story of the needless purchase of the rights of the French company which had originally attempted to construct a canal. Roosevelt retaliated with a special message to Congress attacking Pulitzer by name and saying that the government would prosecute him for criminal libel. When the Justice Department sought indictments, they did so in federal court, claiming that newspaper copies had circulated in the West Point federal reservation. Federal judges ruled that the editors could not be forced into federal court in this manner, since the Sixth amendment guarantees the accused the right to trial in the state or district where the crime was allegedly committed. The Supreme Court agreed, and Roosevelt dropped the suit rather than proceed in a state court. Cobb called this a sweeping victory for freedom of the press against an oppressive government. His position proved to be essentially correct. Eventually the Congress compensated Colombia for the loss of the Panama area, and in 1979 the United States returned sovereignty to the Republic of Panama.

Cobb's editorial page represented the realization of Joseph Pulitzer's hopes for the full development of the *New York World.* The editor whom Pulitzer had carefully trained before his own death in 1911 was unexcelled in his forcible expression of logically developed opinions. The *World* commanded deep respect for its intelligent and fair-minded approaches to issues of public importance, for its progressive and hard-hitting crusades that combined the reporting abilities of its news staff and the support of its editorial writers, and for its brilliant, if sometimes erratic, news play. It became one of those favorites of the press world that were called "newspapermen's newspapers."

The *World* helped to "discover" Woodrow Wilson as a presidential candidate, and Cobb and Wilson became close friends. Cobb's often-expressed fear of centralization of authority was in part overcome by his association with Wilson, and the *World* vigorously supported the far-reaching New Freedom program of economic and social reform that gave the federal government vast new powers. Cobb was one of Wilson's advisers at the Versailles peace conference, which encouraged the hopes for international cooperation that the *World* had long held. His battles in the columns of the *World* for American participation in the League of Nations and the World Court were unavailing, but they further established the paper as the leading voice of the Democratic party.

HEARST EXPANDS HIS ROLE

While the *World* was thus rising to greatness, its chief competitor for mass circulation in New York was just as determinedly making a claim to leadership as "the people's champion." William Randolph Hearst, having seen the country start toward annexation of the Philippines and Hawaii, the development of military bases in the Caribbean, and the adoption of other nationalistic policies advocated by the *New York Journal,* turned his attention to domestic affairs. In early 1899 he set forth an editorial platform calling for public ownership of public franchises, the "destruction of criminal trusts," a graduated income tax, election of United States senators by popular vote rather than by state legislatures, and national, state, and local improvement of the public school system. Soon Hearst was urging that the coal mines, railroads, and telegraph lines—the symbols of the new industrial era—all be nationalized. And he gave strong encouragement to labor unions.

One example was the *Journal*'s support of striking miners in the anthracite coal fields of Pennsylvania. In September, 1897, a sheriff's posse near Lattimer fired on a parade of immigrant strikers, killing twenty and wounding scores. The sheriff and sixty-six deputies were charged with murder and were tried in February, 1898. Desperate working conditions in the mines had been worsened by the importation of Eastern European immigrants, often single, who were regarded by the native Americans as a threat both to wage levels and cultural standards. Hearst argued that society would be overturned if justice was not given to the workers. Calling the sheriff and his deputies murderers acting for the mine owners, in twenty-four February issues the *Evening Journal* ran twenty-three news stories, eight editorials, and nine cartoons. Play diminished only after the sinking of the battleship *Maine.* But when the nonimmigrant jury found the defendants innocent, Hearst advised the miners to seek redress without violence. In the bitter anthracite coal-field strikes of 1900 and 1902 the Hearst papers continued their all-out attacks upon the mine owners, and their support of the workers.

Not only was this a more radical program than that of the *World* and other liberal newspapers of the day, but also the impact of Hearst's editorial technique was bitter and extreme. In the presidential campaign of 1900, Homer Davenport's cartoons depicting President McKinley as the stooge of a Mark Hanna wearing a suit made of dollar signs were crude but effective. When President McKinley was fatally wounded by an anarchist with a copy of the *Journal* in his pocket, in September, 1901, the Hearst paper's continual assaults on McKinley were recalled. Hearst found it wise to change the name of his morning New York paper to the *American.* But the incident was to haunt him for the rest of his life.

Hearst now sought to advance his political beliefs by seeking office himself. He served two terms in Congress from a Democratic district in New York City, from 1903 to 1907, but his eye was on the White House. His high point came in 1904 when 204 delegates cast votes for him in the Democratic national convention (Judge Alton B. Parker, the successful nominee, received 658). The next year Hearst ran as an independent candidate for mayor of New York but lost by some 3500 votes as the result of Tammany's counting him out at the ballot boxes.

This was a notable achievement, and Hearst decided to make the race for the New York governorship in 1906 as a stepping-stone to the White House. He won the Democratic nomination in convention but found himself up against Charles Evans Hughes in the November election. Theodore Roosevelt's close associate, Elihu Root, recalled the McKinley assassination episode in a public speech; the *World* and other New York newspapers turned against Hearst, and so did Tammany, which he had challenged the year before. Hughes won by 60,000 votes—the only Republican to be elected that year in the statewide balloting—and Hearst's political star had set.

In his political races and in his newspapers, Hearst was making a heavy play for the support of workers, small businessowners, and other ordinary people. His slashing attacks on the "criminal trusts"—the ice trust, the coal trust, the gas trust—and crooked political bosses found favor with those who had grievances against the established order. His forthright support of the labor unions won him the backing of the American Federation of Labor. And the popularized content of his newspapers appealed to the mass of readers. Emphasis on sensational crime and vice stories, human-interest features, pictures and cartoons, and readable typographical display helped draw crowds of new readers to Hearst papers. But despite the following that Hearst had attracted, there was widespread doubting of his journalistic and political motives by the intellectual leaders of the time.[13]

New publishing ventures brought Hearst to the attention of four more large cities in the first few years of the twentieth century. To his *San Francisco Examiner, New York American,* and *New York Evening Journal,* Hearst added eight more papers, which put him in the business of group publishing. In Chicago, the evening *American* was begun in 1900 and the morning *Examiner,* in 1902. Boston saw the birth of an evening *American* in 1904, to which Hearst added the century-old *Daily Advertiser* in 1917 and the *Record* in 1920. Hearst also bought Atlanta's *Georgian* in 1912 and the *San Francisco Call* in 1913. Los Angeles was invaded in 1903 with the founding of the morning *Examiner.* The Los Angeles entry was welcomed by local labor unions, which were engaged in a bitter fight with the antilabor *Los Angeles Times.* Hearst rode in a parade between two labor leaders to open the head-on contest with the *Times.*

In the first issue of the *Los Angeles Examiner,* the editors advertised their wares. They listed the Hearst writers: Ella Wheeler Wilcox, "world famous poet and essayist"; Mrs. John A. Logan, wife of a General and writer "on behalf of the American home and American womanhood"; Professor Garrett Serviss, noted astronomer; Dorothy Dix, whose name is the first one recognizable eight decades later; Ambrose Bierce, a truly great writer. The editorial page, the ad said, has "thought-stirring editorials which have done so much to mold public thought in this country." Editorial-page cartoonists listed were Opper, Powers, Davenport, and Howarth; comics included the Katzenjammer Kids and Childe Harold. And, said the editors, "There is nothing in the newspaper world like the magazine section of the Hearst newspapers." Within a month the *Examiner* claimed 32,500 readers, and it remained a strong paper for half a century.[14]

E. W. SCRIPPS AND HIS "PEOPLE'S PAPERS"

Another type of "people's paper" was emerging, meanwhile, under the direction of Edward Wyllis Scripps, the Illinois farm boy who had successfully started the first of his many Scripps newspapers by the time he was 24. Scripps got his start in the Middle West at the moment that Pulitzer was achieving his first success in St. Louis, and when Stone was succeeding in Chicago and Nelson in Kansas City. The *Detroit News,* on which Scripps had served his apprenticeship under his brother James, had been one of the early practitioners of the "new journalism." His own first two papers, the *Cleveland Press* and the *Cincinnati Post,* were low-priced afternoon dailies which appealed to the mass of readers.*

But unlike Pulitzer and Hearst, who sought giant circulations in big cities, Scripps set his sights on the working people in the smaller but growing industrial cities of the country. For them he published brightly written, easily read newspapers, small in size but big in heart. Closely edited news, human-interest features, fearless news coverage and local crusades, and hard-fighting independent editorial opinion constituted the Scripps formula.

What made Scripps a distinctive leader as a "people's champion" was his conception of his responsibility to the working people. "The first of my principles," Scripps said, "is that I have constituted myself the advocate of that large majority of people who are not so rich in worldly goods and native intelligence as to make them equal, man for man, in the struggle with individuals of the wealthier and more intellectual class."[15] Scripps viewed his newspapers as the only "schoolroom" the working people had. He believed that nearly all other newspapers were capitalistic and opposed to the working class or else too intellectual in appeal, and he said sadly that the educational system was a failure in its service to his "large majority." So he sought to drive home through his editorial columns the necessity for labor-union organization and collective bargaining as the first prerequisites to a better life for the poor and ill-informed. Scripps was the first to admit that his papers did not always maintain the noble objectives he set for them and that they sometimes made mistakes in "always opposing the rich, always supporting the working man." But Scripps believed that if he kept the focus on such a basic policy he would further the long-range pattern of society that he hoped would emerge.

Above all, the Scripps newspapers reflected a "spirit of protest" that was inherent in the character of their owner-editor. Scripps declared that he protested against everything; his motto was "Whatever is, is wrong." He protested against antiquated governmental systems, against undemocratic political actions, against usurpation of power and prestige by the rich and the intellectuals, against inequality of opportunity, against all sorts of authority in religion and law and politics except those exercised for the benefit of humanity, against corruption, against the power of business interests. He pictured himself as a "damned old crank" who was in rebellion against society. But actually he was seeking to build a progressive democracy, and he was enough of a capitalist to urge the worker to better himself or herself by increasing production and thereby adding to the wealth to be distributed.

*See pages 241–43 for a discussion of Scripps' early career.

Scripps started his newspaper career with an investment of $600 in one share of stock in the *Detroit News.* With the help of his sister Ellen and his brothers James and George, he started the *Cleveland Press* in 1878. In 1883, with an income of $10,000 a year, Scripps turned to Cincinnati and took over management of a struggling penny paper that became the *Post.*

These were the formative years of the Scripps newspaper empire. In Cleveland Scripps found an editor, Robert F. Paine, who for more than 30 years was a leader in editorial policy making. In Cincinnati Scripps found a business manager, Milton A. McRae. In 1889 Scripps and McRae formed the Scripps-McRae League of Newspapers. McRae was to be the speechmaker, the front man, the operations chief. Scripps was to set policy and live as he pleased on a California ranch. And in 1890, at age 36, Scripps did "retire" to a great ranch near San Diego, named Miramar, where he lived a burly life, wearing ranch clothes and cowhide boots, playing poker, drinking whiskey, and smoking innumerable cigars. At Miramar, too, he kept in close touch through correspondence and conferences with his principal editors and managers. There he lived to the age of 71 and built himself a fortune of some $50 million.

The Scripps plan for expansion was simple. He and McRae looked for a growing industrial city, usually fairly small and with stodgy newspaper opposition. They put up a few thousand dollars and sent a young, ambitious editor and a business manager off to start a paper. If the young journalists succeeded, they could obtain as much as 49 percent of the stock; if they faltered, new faces replaced them. If the paper failed to make a profit within 10 years, it was abandoned as a failure. As a result of this policy, Scripps papers had a good many employee-stockholders, but they also paid the usual low journalistic salaries of the times to those who were not so blessed. In this respect, Scripps was typically capitalistic in his publishing behavior.

Since the papers were low-cost afternoon dailies that relied principally on circulation revenue, they had to be edited carefully. Scripps saved newsprint costs by insisting on small headlines and short, concisely edited stories. Saving those extra words so that a Scripps newspaper would be packed with the most news possible became a fine art for Scripps newspeople. Word economy also meant that after the essential news had been told there would be plenty of space for editorial opinion and features.

By 1911 the Scripps-McRae League included eighteen papers in Ohio, Indiana, Tennessee, Iowa, Colorado, Oklahoma, and Texas. Meanwhile, Scripps himself was building his own chain of West Coast newspapers. He started by buying the *San Diego Sun* in 1893, and in the next 15 years opened up shop in ten other West Coast cities. But here, in an only slightly industrialized West, the Scripps record was extremely poor. Only the *San Francisco News* eventually emerged as a strong unit in the Scripps chain. The *Los Angeles Record* and four Pacific Northwest papers seceded from the parent Scripps organization after a quarrel between Scripps and his son James in 1920, and formed the basis for the Scripps League.

Scripps tried another experiment in 1911, when he established in Chicago an adless tabloid named the *Day Book.* Negley D. Cochran was the editor, and poet Carl Sandburg was chief reporter. The little paper, which represented Scripps' fondest dream, reached a circulation of 25,000 and was within $500 a month of breaking even when the rising newsprint costs of the first war year, 1917, caused its suspension. A second adless paper, the *Philadelphia News-Post,* started in 1912 but also failed.

Through the years the Scripps papers continued to fight for the right of workers to organize. They crusaded for public ownership and against utility abuses. They attacked political bossism and corruption. They supported Theodore Roosevelt's reforms and his third-party candidacy. And they backed Woodrow Wilson's "New Freedom" and his reelection campaign. In appearance and in content they were closer to being "labor papers" than any other general-circulation newspapers, yet they also won the support of the intellectual liberals whom Scripps sometimes tried to avoid.

WILLIAM ALLEN WHITE AND THE *EMPORIA GAZETTE*

While publishers like Scripps and Adolph Ochs of the *New York Times* were guiding their newspapers in a relatively impersonal fashion, a small-town Kansas editor was making a highly personal impact on American society. William Allen White was born in Emporia, Kansas, in 1868 and died there in 1944. But between those years he became a citizen of America and a spokesman for its small towns—of which Emporia became the symbol. The editor of the *Emporia Gazette* was anything but a typical representative of his kind of journalism, but nevertheless his newspaper editorship was the foundation for his larger activities, first as a conservative, then as a reformer.

White worked as a printer and reporter while he was at the University of Kansas. At 24, he was an editorial writer for William Rockhill Nelson's *Kansas City Star.* He scraped together $3000 by 1895 and bought the *Emporia Gazette,* a rundown Populist party paper with fewer than 600 subscribers. But William Allen White, age 27, was home in Emporia with his wife, Sallie, to stay.

Kansas had been captured during the 1893 depression by the Populists and the Democrats. White was an active Republican editor and politician: He loved politics all his life and remained a party worker and an intimate of politicians from the time of William McKinley and Theodore Roosevelt to that of Wendell Willkie and Franklin Roosevelt. On August 15, 1896, White exploded with anger at the Populists in an editorial that shot him into national fame. It was "What's the Matter with Kansas?" which White later referred to as representing "conservatism in its full and perfect flower." The editorial cited evidence that Kansas was declining in population and economic standing and placed the blame in a fully unrestrained and effective style on the "shabby, wild-eyed, rattle-brained fanatics" of the reform movement.[16] It was reprinted in virtually every Republican newspaper in the country as ammunition against the Democratic candidate for president, William Jennings Bryan. William McKinley's campaign manager, Mark Hanna, adopted the young editor. But Bryan and the Democrats won the election in Kansas.

White now moved to the national stage. He became the friend of political leaders and came to know the young New York Republican Theodore Roosevelt, to whom he became deeply attached and who was his lifelong political hero. More importantly, he met S. S. McClure and became a member of the circle that

William Allen White.
Emporia Gazette

included Lincoln Steffens, Ray Stannard Baker, John Phillips, and Ida M. Tarbell. His articles and stories about Kansas and politics appeared in several magazines. White was now in tune with the times, hobnobbing with the muckrakers and becoming, with his wife, a frequent visitor at the Oyster Bay home of the Theodore Roosevelts. The *Emporia Gazette* began to demand reforms: conservation of natural resources, railroad rate control, workers' compensation, direct primaries, the initiative and referendum, abolition of child labor.

When Roosevelt split with William Howard Taft in 1912 and the Progressive party was formed, White was the Kansas national committee member for the new third party. He was a supporter of the League of Nations—an internationalist in isolationist territory—and when World War II came, he was a leader in the Committee to Defend America by Aiding the Allies. He admired the social gains of the New Deal, but he preferred the leadership of Theodore Roosevelt to that of Franklin Roosevelt.

Another of America's distinctive small-town editors also lived and worked in Kansas. He was Ed Howe, who, at the age of 22 in 1877, founded the daily *Atchison Globe* with $200 capital. Howe was a superlative reporter. He knew people and how to report their little doings. However, he had none of White's expansiveness and sentimentality but rather he had an amazing ability to make trouble for himself. He told the people of Kansas that religion was all bosh, and he asserted in a time of agitation for women's rights that a woman's place was strictly in the home. His terse, sardonic editorial paragraphs often reflected a keen understanding of human nature, however, and they were widely requoted in the country's newspapers as the work of the "Sage of Potato Hill." His excellent novel, *The Story of a Country Town,* added to his fame.

OTHER NEWSPAPER CRUSADERS

Pulitzer, Hearst, and Scripps were far from being the only champions of the common people among newspaper publishers and editors of the years around the turn of the century. Nor can all those who opposed the business trusts, who fought against onesided public-utilities franchises, who exposed political inadequacy and corruption, be listed. However, some idea of the contributions made by newspaperpeople can be gained by a look across the country.[17]

One battle against a tightly run political machine was that waged by Charles H. Grasty, editor of the *Baltimore Evening News,* and by the *Baltimore Sun.* Grasty had exposed the policy racket in Baltimore despite a criminal libel charge brought by his political opponents. When in 1895 the *Sun* broke with its Democratic party traditions and attacked Senator Arthur P. Gorman's state Democratic machine, Grasty pitched in to help oust the Gorman group. Maryland elected its first Republican adminstration since the Civil War and Gorman lost his Senate seat for one term.

Across the country the spectacular but contradictory career of Fremont Older was being unfolded in San Francisco. Older, a typical roving newspaperperson in his early years, settled down as managing editor of the *Bulletin* in 1895. He built the struggling evening sheet into a fairly substantial paper by his sensational methods and then decided to join the solid civic leader, the *San Francisco Chronicle,* in its fights against city machine politics. The target was a Union-Labor party headed by Mayor Eugene E. Schmitz and a political boss, Abram Ruef. Older stepped out of his role as a newspaperperson to become a civic reform leader, and his dominating personality made him the rallying point for the public-spirited of the city. The reform group brought Schmitz and Ruef to court on indictments for accepting payoffs from houses of prostitution and had Ruef sent to prison. Others involved escaped conviction, despite the work of prosecutors Francis J. Heney (who was shot and critically wounded in the courtroom) and Hiram W. Johnson. Older's last great crusade was in behalf of Tom Mooney, who Older eventually decided had been unjustly convicted of the Preparedness Day bombing in San Francisco in 1916. Breaking with the *Bulletin* management on the Mooney issue, Older joined Hearst's *Call* as editor in 1918, saw it become the *Call-Bulletin* in 1929, and died in 1935 before Mooney won his freedom.

Older had been kidnapped and nearly killed during the height of the San Francisco trials. In South Carolina, an editor was assassinated—N. G. Gonzales of the *Columbia State*—in 1903. Gonzales was one of three brothers who battled against political boss Ben Tillman with their newspaper, founded in 1893. The paper continued to exert leadership, however, calling for compulsory public education and opposing child labor and "lynch law."

A less spectacular, but solid, champion of decency was Josephus Daniels of

North Carolina, who became editor of the *State Chronicle* in Raleigh in 1885. The paper was a weekly, started by Walter Hines Page 2 years before. In his first few years in Raleigh, Daniels campaigned against the Southern Railway and its attempt to extend its control over other lines. He advocated a state public-school fund as a means of equalizing educational opportunity, urged financial support of the state university, supported establishment of teacher-training colleges, and argued for compulsory education as a means of overcoming illiteracy. When the American Tobacco Company was organized by the Duke family in 1890 he began his long campaign against the "tobacco trust."

The established daily in Raleigh was the *News and Observer.* Daniels obtained control of it in 1895 and built it into one of the South's leading newspapers. Daniels was a fervent supporter of the Democratic party; he campaigned for Bryan in his three races for the presidency and supported Woodrow Wilson with full enthusiasm. Wilson made him his Secretary of the Navy in 1913 and the Daniels political career was under way.

In Chicago, the *Tribune* that Joseph Medill had built enjoyed a varied record. In the last years of Medill's editorship, before his death in 1899, the *Tribune* was strongly nationalistic in foreign policy and generally conservative in its outlook. It fought the liberal Illinois governor, John P. Altgeld, and bitterly attacked the Debs-led Chicago labor unions. But the *Tribune* vigorously crusaded against utility and street-railway franchise grabs and used John T. McCutcheon's

Josephus Daniels.
Raleigh News and Observer

Joseph Medill.
Chicago Tribune

front-page cartoons with effectiveness after the artist transferred from the *Record* to the *Tribune* in 1903.

James Keeley, the *Tribune's* outstanding managing editor, helped develop one of the state's biggest exposés in 1910 when the paper published evidence that William Lorimer had won election to the U.S. Senate by bribing state legislators. Despite the evidence Keeley had obtained, it took 2 years of campaigning by the *Tribune* and the *Record-Herald* before Lorimer was ousted from the Senate.

THE MAGAZINES: AN ERA OF MUCKRAKING

Highly important as "people's champions" were the magazines that, in the dozen years after 1900, developed a literature of exposure that Theodore Roosevelt dubbed the work of the "muckrakers." Roosevelt used the expression in a derogatory sense, comparing the more sensational writers to the Man with the Muckrake in *Pilgrim's Progress,* who did not look up to see the celestial crown but continued to rake the filth. The reformers, however, came to accept the designation as a badge of honor, and in the history of American magazines the period is known as "the era of the muckrakers."[18]

When in 1893 three new popular magazines—*McClure's, Cosmopolitan,* and *Munsey's*—cut their prices to a dime, their circulation figures started on an upward climb. After the turn of the century these magazines and such others as the *Ladies' Home Journal, Collier's, Everybody's,* and the *Saturday Evening Post* had circulations running into the hundreds of thousands. Most of them joined with great enthusiasm in the crusade against big business, against corruption, and for social justice. Their writers, who came largely from newspaper ranks, had national audiences for articles that sometimes were original but sometimes were drawn from the stories published by crusading newspapers in various cities. However the articles were obtained, the magazines performed the service of coordinating and interpreting information about social, economic, and political problems for a nationwide audience.

Touching off the muckraking era was S. S. McClure, whose magazine began three significant series of articles in late 1902. McClure, who had founded a newspaper feature syndicate in 1884 and attracted readers and writers to his service, invaded the magazine field in 1893 with a low-priced but unspectacular product filled with interesting and timely articles and literary material. He and his associate editor, John S. Phillips, had selected a staff of talented and responsible writers to handle the nonfiction section of *McClure's.* One was Ida M. Tarbell, whose specialties were biographies and research work. Another was Lincoln Steffens, former reporter for the *Evening Post* and city editor of the *Commercial Advertiser* in New York, who was to become one of the country's most famous crusading liberals. A third was Ray Stannard Baker, who came to *McClure's* from the *Chicago Record* in 1897 and who was later to achieve fame as Woodrow Wilson's biographer. Beginning in late 1902 Tarbell exposed the business practices of John D. Rockefeller and the Standard Oil Company; Steffens opened his attack on corruption in city and state governments; and Baker began discussing the problems of working people. The circulation of

McClure's Magazine

VOL. XX *JANUARY, 1903* NO. 3

THE SHAME OF MINNEAPOLIS

The Rescue and Redemption of a City that was Sold Out

BY LINCOLN STEFFENS

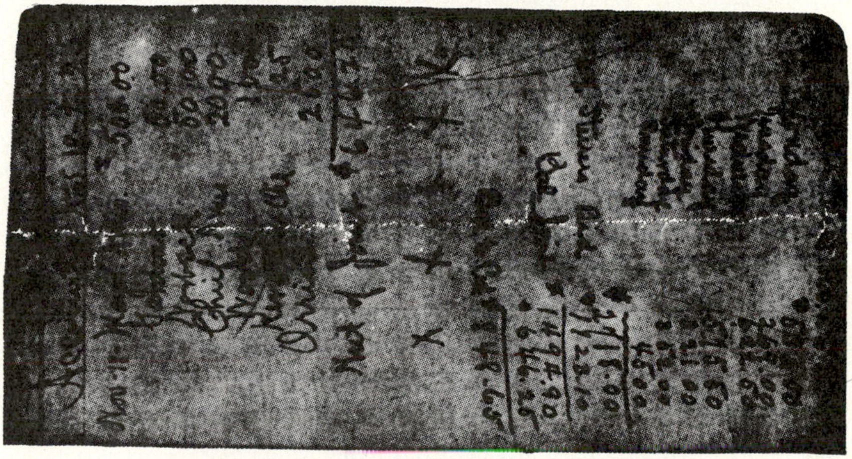

FAC-SIMILE OF THE FIRST PAGE OF "THE BIG MITT LEDGER"

An account kept by a swindler of the dealings of his "Joint" with City Officials, showing first payments made to Mayor Ames, his brother, the Chief of Police and Detectives. This book figured in trials and newspaper reports of the exposure, but was "lost"; and its whereabouts was the mystery of the proceedings. This is the first glimpse that any one, except "Cheerful Charlie' Howard, who kept it, and members of the grand jury, has had of the book

WHENEVER anything extraordinary is done in American municipal politics, whether for good or for evil, you can trace it almost invariably to one man. The people do not do it. Neither do the "gangs," "combines," or political parties. These are but instruments by which bosses (not leaders; we Americans are not led, but driven) rule the people, and commonly sell them out. But there are at least two forms of the autocracy which has supplanted the democracy here as it has everywhere it has been tried. One is that of the organized majority by which, as in Tammany Hall in New York and the Republican machine in Philadelphia, the boss has normal control of more than half the voters. The other is that of the adroitly managed minority. The "good people" are herded into parties and stupefied with convictions and a name, Republican or Democrat; while the "bad people" are so organized or interested by the boss that he can wield their votes to enforce terms with party managers and decide elections. St. Louis is a conspicuous example of this form. Minneapolis is another. Colonel Ed. Butler is the unscrupulous opportunist who handled the non-partisan minority which turned St. Louis into a "boodle town." In Minneapolis "Doc" Ames was the man.

Copyright, 1902, by the S. S. McClure Co. All rights reserved.

One of the articles that made *McClure's* the leading muckraking magazine.

McClure's mounted past the half-million mark and the muckraking trend in magazine editing was in full swing.

What McClure was doing was not entirely new to the magazine field. The older magazines of high quality—*Harper's, Scribner's,* the *Century,* and the *Atlantic Monthly*—had paid some attention to current affairs, although they were primarily literary in tone. There were several journals of opinion that had relatively small but influential audiences: Godkin's *Nation,* Albert Shaw's *Review of Reviews,* Lyman Abbott's *Outlook,* the *North American Review,* the *Forum,* and the *Independent.* In the same class but taking an early leadership in crusading for socioeconomic and political reform was Benjamin O. Flower's *Arena.* These magazines and others were giving attention to the rising business trusts, graft, and political machines, but it was *McClure's* that first made a frontal assault of real magnitude.

Tarbell's "History of the Standard Oil Company" ran in *McClure's* until 1904, and her detailed, thoroughly documented account of the unfair business practices used by the company to squeeze out competitors put Rockefeller on the defensive for many years to come. Steffens began his series on "The Shame of the Cities" by recounting the situation in St. Louis that had first been exposed by the *Post-Dispatch* and followed up with reports on corrupt government in Minneapolis, Pittsburgh, Philadelphia, Chicago, New York, and other cities. George Kibbe Turner, an alumnus of the *Springfield Republican,* continued the city series later in the decade. Baker dealt with labor problems, including child labor and the economic status of the blacks. Other contributors to *McClure's* included Burton J. Hendrick, who wrote about the New York life-insurance companies, and Kansas editor William Allen White. Newspaper reporter Will Irwin served as managing editor and editor for a year in 1906 to 1907.

Cosmopolitan joined the muckrakers when the magazine passed from John Brisben Walker to Hearst by running the series "The Treason of the Senate," which appeared in 1906. The author was David Graham Phillips, one of Pulitzer's editorial writers on the *World* staff who retired from newspaper work to write a series of books examining problems of his time. Phillips denounced a score of conservative Senators—both Republican and Democrat—as spokespeople of "the interests." Among other prominent muckrakers, Alfred Henry Lewis attacked the International Harvester Company in *Cosmopolitan* and followed up with a series examining the careers of America's leading millionaires. Charles Edward Russell, who had been managing editor of the *Minneapolis Journal* at 21 and who had worked for several New York and Chicago newspapers, surveyed the weaknesses of state governments in a 1910 series.

Active in the fray, too, was *Everybody's,* founded in 1899 and edited by John O'Hara Cosgrave. When in 1904 it persuaded a colorful Wall Street financier, Thomas W. Lawson, to write "Frenzied Finance," the public appetite for Lawson's inside information drove the magazine's circulation from 200,000 to 735,000 within a year. Less important, but influential, were *Pearson's, Hampton's* (which built a readership of 440,000 in the years 1907 to 1911), and *La Follette's Weekly,* the voice of the Wisconsin progressives.

Taking the lead from *McClure's* in muckraking after 1905 was *Collier's.* Published by Robert J. Collier and edited by Norman Hapgood, the magazine developed an effective editorial voice in national political affairs. Its articles ranged over many social and economic problems, but it caught popular attention for a series of articles by Samuel Hopkins Adams on the patent-medicine trade. Called "The Great American Fraud," and published in 1905 and 1906, Adams' articles exposed the false claims of many of the popular "cure-alls" and demonstrated that some of the patent medicines contained poisonous ingredients. Equally prominent in the attack on the patent-medicine business was Edward W. Bok, editor of the *Ladies' Home Journal.* It was Bok who shocked his women readers by proving that Lydia E. Pinkham, to whom American women were supposed to write for advice, had been dead for 22 years.

The attack on the patent medicines coincided with a drive against adulterated foods and unsanitary practices in packing plants. Under the leadership of Dr. Harvey H. Wiley, chief chemist of the Department of Agriculture, federal and state officials had proved the widespread adulteration of food and the addition of chemicals and artificial dyes by food manufacturers. But the lid was blown off when Upton Sinclair wrote *The Jungle* in 1906, a novel intended to portray the plight of immigrant workers in Chicago's packinghouses, but which was terrifying in its charges of unsanitary practices.

Passage of the Pure Food and Drugs Act of 1906 was the outcome. This regulated the activities of manufacturers, but the problem of "truth in advertising" remained. Some newspapers had obtained testimonials from readers, extolling the virtues of the medicines, and had run them in their news columns. This use of "readers," as they were called, had also been extended to cover publicity stories paid for by the column inch. As the campaign for "truth in advertising" grew, newspaperpeople cooperated. State laws making untruthful, deceptive, or misleading advertising statements a misdemeanor were adopted after *Printers' Ink* drafted a model statute in 1911, and the federal Newspaper Publicity Law of 1912 required that all matter published for money should be marked "Advertisement."

Other magazines should be noted. One was the *American Magazine,* purchased in 1906 by a group of *McClure's* writers. A disagreement in policy led John S. Phillips, associate editor of *McClure's,* to leave its staff. He took with him Tarbell, Steffens, Baker, William Allen White, and Finley Peter Dunne, America's "Mr. Dooley." These were the leaders of the muckrakers, and for a few years they constituted a distinguished editorial board for the *American.* The high point of muckraking had been reached in 1906, but liberal insurgency continued, climaxed in 1912 by Theodore Roosevelt's third-party candidacy and Woodrow Wilson's election as president. The *New Republic* began its career in 1914 under editor Herbert Croly, whose *The Promise of American Life* (1909) became a creed for Wilsonian liberals. Croly and staff member Walter Lippmann supported Wilson in wartime. *The Masses,* which was edited by Max Eastman and was a brilliant voice of protest from 1911 to 1917 when its pacifist-socialist line led to wartime persecution and demise, did not. Among its contributors were Lippmann, Carl Sandburg, Sherwood Anderson, and cartoonist Art Young.

THE AGE OF REALISM

Playing a role, too, in the quest for social justice were a group of America's writers. William Dean Howells and Henry James had pointed the way toward the realistic novel. Joining them in this movement were novelist Stephen Crane and short-story writers Ambrose Bierce and Hamlin Garland. Of the same school were poets Walt Whitman and Emily Dickinson. From this literary heritage, and from the pressure of the times, came a flowering of realism in literature after 1900.

Californian Frank Norris contributed two volumes of a planned trilogy on the "Epic of Wheat" before his career was cut short by death at 32. His *The Octopus,* which appeared in 1901, told the story of the struggle of California farmers against the power of the Southern Pacific Railroad. His protest against Chicago wheat speculators, *The Pit,* made an equally deep impression. In his stories of adventure and raw, brutal experience another Californian, Jack London, captured a full expression of the rising protest against the capitalistic system. London's *The Iron Heel,* published in 1907, and Upton Sinclair's *The Jungle* were high points in relentless realism. So were Theodore Dreiser's *Sister Carrie,* which was at first suppressed by a frightened publisher, and his later books, *The Financier* and *The Titan.*

More Americans, it is true, were reading historical novels, adventure stories, and popular favorites like *David Harum* and *Mrs. Wiggs of the Cabbage Patch* than were reading the works of Norris, Sinclair, London, and Dreiser. More Americans, too, were reading fiction in *Munsey's* and the *Saturday Evening Post* than were reading the exposés by Lincoln Steffens, Ida M. Tarbell, and Samuel Hopkins Adams. And among newspaper readers, relatively few were absorbing the editorial arguments of Edward Wyllis Scripps, Joseph Pulitzer, and their contemporaries of equal stature. Still, at a critical moment in American history, when an arousing of public opinion was needed to ensure economic and political progress and a more equitable social pattern, journalism and literature played their part and produced effective leaders.

BASTIONS OF NEWS ENTERPRISE

The preceding sections have been concerned with the historical development of patterns of press behavior. A segment of the press was involved successively in important general trends: the rise of the new journalism, the spread of yellow journalism, and service as "people's champions." But it is difficult to fit all newspapers into such patterns, because each newspaper has an individuality born of its publishing environment. In some cases establishment leaders of this period were more noted for news presentation than for editorial passion. One conspicuous example was the *New York Times,* rescued from near oblivion in 1896 to begin a rise to greatness as a journalistic institution. Others were its New York rivals, the *Herald* and the *Sun;* Chicago's *Inter Ocean;* and a future Western leader, the *Los Angeles Times.* Ensuring the growth of the news-enterprise principle was the rise of the modern press associations, the Associated Press and its new rivals, the United Press and International News Service. Each is delineated in turn.

ADOLPH OCHS AND THE *NEW YORK TIMES*

The story of the *New York Times* is the story of the man who rescued it from bankruptcy in 1896 and who guided it until he died in 1935. He was Adolph S. Ochs, a one-time printer's devil from Tennessee, who salvaged the glories of the

Times of Henry J. Raymond's day and set its course as America's leading newspaper. It was the men and women he selected to staff the *Times* who made it an institution.

Ochs, like many another great publisher, struggled up from the ranks to win his place. His parents were German Jews who emigrated to the United States before the Civil War. Adolph, born in 1858 in Cincinnati, was the oldest of six children. The family migrated to Tennessee in a covered wagon, and at 14 Adolph landed a job as printer's devil for the *Knoxville Chronicle.* In 1875 he became assistant composing-room supervisor for the *Louisville Courier-Journal* and did some reporting for Henry Watterson. But he was judged a colorless and awkward writer; his genius lay in his business ability and in his capacity for journalistic leadership.

Back in Knoxville in 1876, Ochs got his chance. The editor of the rival *Tribune,* Colonel John E. MacGowan, wanted to start a newspaper in Chattanooga, a city of 12,000 with no sidewalks, muddy streets, and little interest in newspapers. The city had seen sixteen newspapers come and go in 40 years, including the *Dispatch* that Ochs and MacGowan first published. The only survivor was the *Times,* with a circulation of 250. Ochs got control for the same amount of dollars. It was July, 1878, and he was not yet 21. But he and his 45-year-old editor promised Chattanooga all the local news, the latest news by telegraph, and a strong business and commercial outlook for a booming city. The *Times* boomed with Chattanooga and by 1892 it was clearing $25,000 a year. But Ochs owed money on real-estate ventures that were imperiled by the approaching depression of 1893. What he needed, Ochs decided, was another newspaper and its profits. He searched the country and in March, 1896, he learned that there was a chance to buy the *New York Times.*

Ochs was properly impressed by this opportunity. He knew how respected the *Times* had been since its founding by Henry J. Raymond in 1851. After Raymond's death in 1869, the paper had come under the direction of its business manager, George Jones. Jones, editor Louis J. Jennings, and chief assistant John Foord had helped to smash Boss Tweed in the 1870s. John C. Reid had served well as managing editor from 1872 to 1889 and the paper had maintained its place until the death of Jones in 1891. By then the impact of the "new journalism" was having its effect.

The new guiding spirit on the *Times* became Charles R. Miller, a graduate of Dartmouth and former staff member of the *Springfield Republican,* who assumed the editorship in 1883. In 1893, with associate editor Edward Cary and other staff members, Miller negotiated the purchase of the *Times* from the Jones family heirs for approximately $1 million. But the paper did not prosper. It had the smallest circulation of the city's eight morning dailies, a paltry 9000 paid circulation concealed in a 21,000 press run. This was not far behind the *Tribune*'s 16,000 but was far below the *Sun*'s 70,000 morning circulation, the *Herald*'s 140,000, and the *World*'s 200,000 morning figure.

OCHS BUYS THE *TIMES,* 1896

Ochs did not have the money to save the *Times,* but he convinced Miller that he had the know-how and the vision that would be needed to put the paper in a sound competitive position. An elaborate refinancing plan was advanced that would give Ochs control of the paper within 4 years if he succeeded in revitalizing it. Ochs trudged through the Wall Street district for months persuading financiers, even including J. P. Morgan, to buy bonds in the new enterprise. Finally, in August, 1896, an agreement was completed, with Ochs putting up $75,000 of his own money and risking his Chattanooga paper on the outcome. The 38-year-old Tennessean, with 24 years of experience since his printer's devil days, was now competing with Pulitzer, Hearst, Dana, Reid, and Bennett in the New York field.

The plan of attack Ochs had devised to save the *New York Times* was simple. He would not attempt to match the sensationalism of Hearst and Pulitzer, nor would he popularize the paper's offerings in a halfway effort to keep up with the mass-circulation leaders, as some other New York publishers were attempting to do. Instead he would publish a paper with solid news coverage and editorial opinion that would be designed for readers who did not like overemphasis of entertainment and features. Ochs' declaration of principle contained these lines:

> It will be my earnest aim that the *New York Times* give the news, all the news, in concise and attractive form, in language that is parliamentary in good society, and give it as early, if not earlier, than it can be learned through any other reliable medium; to give the news impartially, without fear or favor, regardless of any party, sect or interest involved; to make the columns of the *New York Times* a forum for the consideration of all questions of public importance, and to that end to invite intelligent discussion from all shades of opinion.[19]

Ochs' first steps were unspectacular, but effective. The *Times* began to publish a guide listing the out-of-town buyers who were in the city. It reported daily real-estate transactions. And it expanded its market reports, adding to the daily coverage a weekly financial review. The business and financial community began to find these *Times* features increasingly valuable. Lawyers were similarly attracted by another column listing court cases and records. The class of readers to which Ochs was appealing also liked the emphasis placed on the reporting of government news. It liked Ochs' Sunday magazine, which featured articles of current news significance rather than entertainment. And it liked the *Times* book-review section.

Ochs determinedly set his face against the popular features of the new journalism, refusing to run "stunt" stories, banning comics from his columns, and giving pictures short shrift. He sniped at the yellow journalists, advertising the *Times* under the slogan "It Does Not Soil the Breakfast Cloth" before choosing the famous front-page ear, "All the News That's Fit to Print." But circulation in 1898 was still at the 25,000 mark. Ochs decided to make one last gamble. The *Times* was selling for 3 cents, the *World* and *Journal* for 2. Why not cut the price of the *Times* to a penny and thus win the circulation needed to ensure solid advertising support?

Once again the old formula of price adjustment was successful. As a penny paper the *Times* jumped to 75,000 circulation in 1899 and passed the 100,000 mark in 1901. Its advertising linage doubled within 2 years. The red ink turned to black and Ochs won majority control of the paper's stock under his purchasing agreement. He promptly went into debt again to build the Times Tower on

Broadway, in what became Times Square, putting $2.5 million into what was in 1904 one of New York's most spectacular buildings. The strategic location of the *Times* plant in what became the city's nighttime heart and the later development of its moving electric news bulletins helped to establish the paper as one of the city's institutions.

CARR VAN ANDA, MANAGING EDITOR

Far more important to the future of the *Times* was another event of 1904, however. That year Carr V. Van Anda, America's foremost managing editor, began his 25-year-career as the guiding genius of the *Times* news staff. To single out Van Anda as America's foremost managing editor perhaps seems extraordinary, for comparisons of the accomplishments of people in different eras and different publishing situations are difficult to make. But it is generally agreed that the chief architect of the superior news department of the *New York Times* was Van Anda, a man who shunned personal publicity so completely that despite his incredible achievements he became almost a legendary figure even to his own craft.[20]

Alexander Woollcott once remarked that Van Anda "loved the editing of a newspaper more than anything in the world." Apparently he was born with this love, for in 1870, as a boy of 6 in an Ohio village, he was pasting clippings on sheets of paper and selling them for 10 cents a copy. At 10 he made a press out of a wooden frame, an ink roller from a cloth-wrapped broom handle, and printed with type salvaged from the village paper. Next he acquired a small press and did job printing, using the profits to finance his study of chemistry and physics. When he entered Ohio University at 16 he specialized in mathematics and science and had not the lure of journalism been so strong he would likely have become a scholar in the realms of astronomy and physics. As it was, he could always keep step with the keen minds in those fields.

Van Anda left college at 18 to become supervisor for his village paper. Next he set type and reported for the *Cleveland Herald* and other Cleveland papers. When he was 22 he applied for work on the *Baltimore Sun* and was selected for the important post of night editor. Two years later, in 1888, he moved to the *New York Sun,* where after 5 years he became night editor. When Ochs decided in 1904 that his first managing editor, Henry Loewenthal, should devote full attention to business news, Van Anda's name was suggested to him. The association was to be an ideal one. Ochs was willing to spend money to get the news; Van Anda was more than willing to spend it for him.

Although he was now a managing editor, Van Anda never stopped serving as night editor. For 20 years his routine at the *Times* never varied. He appeared in the newsroom at 1 P.M., went home at 6 P.M. for dinner and a rest, and returned at 10 P.M. to stay until the last person departed at 5 A.M. Usually he was the last person there. Twelve hours a day, 7 days a week, Van Anda was riding the news, giving as much attention to the flow of stories as to the major news breaks. He loved to match his speed and wits against a deadline. He loved to exploit an important but undeveloped story and give it painstaking coverage and significant play. But he never lost sight of the importance of conscientious and

Adolph S. Ochs, (*above*) rescued the *New York Times* from bankruptcy in 1896 and made it one of the world's great newspapers before he died in 1935. His longtime managing editor, Carr Van Anda (*left*), achieved fame as the man most instrumental in developing the *Times'* superb news coverage. It was Ochs, however, whose leadership made possible the achievements of Van Anda and his staff members.

New York Times

intelligent handling of the bulk of the news, and he transmitted this spirit to his staff. He was not a colorful, dynamic leader; rather he was reserved and cold in appearance and his piercing gaze was called the "Van Anda death ray." But those who worked with him found him a modest, sympathetic chief who backed his workers completely and who never flew into a rage. His secret was in doing his own job so well that the impress was made both on the newspaper and its staff.

There are many stories of Van Anda's almost legendary ability. Soon after he became managing editor of the *Times,* word arrived that the decisive naval battle of the Russo-Japanese War might be at hand. Van Anda recognized the importance of the event and readied himself to handle the story. When the bulletin came, at 4:30 one morning, that the Japanese admiral, Togo, had smashed the Russian fleet, all of Van Anda's elaborate research and preparation went into play. Within 19 minutes the *Times* had put an extra to press with the bulletin and a half-page of war news on page one, running under headlines written by Van Anda as the page was being remade. Inside was more advance material that Van Anda had long before made ready for this moment. Forty thousand copies were run off and the managing editor rode about the city with a fleet of horse-drawn wagons at dawn seeing personally that his news beat was prominently displayed on the newsstands.

Van Anda's classic achievement was his handling of the story of the sinking of the liner *Titanic* in 1912. Here, as in other situations, it was Van Anda's personal ability and the functioning of a well-trained staff of high caliber that combined to produce superior news coverage.

It was 1:20 A.M. Monday, April 15, 1912, when the first Associated Press bulletin reached the *Times* newsroom reporting that the luxury liner *Titanic* had struck an iceberg on its maiden voyage from Britain to America. An SOS had been picked up by the Marconi wireless station in Newfoundland. The *Titanic* was supposedly unsinkable, but Van Anda's rapid calls to *Times* correspondents in Halifax and Montreal and to the offices of the White Star Line told him that the ship's wireless had fallen silent a half-hour after the first call for help and convinced him that the ship must have gone down.

Before 3:30 A.M. Van Anda and his staff had organized the story. Among the more than 2200 aboard were many famous persons. A background story was prepared on the passenger list, and a picture of the *Titanic* was prepared for page one. Two other vessels had reported close scrapes with icebergs in the North Atlantic area; this fitted the pattern of the news available about the *Titanic.* In several columns of type the *Times* reported Monday morning that the ship had sunk, while other papers were handling the story in incomplete and inconclusive form.

Tuesday, Wednesday, and Thursday, the story commanded the world's attention, as the liner *Carpathia* sailed toward New York with survivors. On Tuesday Van Anda hired a floor in a hotel a block from the *Carpathia*'s pier and installed four telephone lines directly connected to the *Times'* city room. The entire staff was mobilized under the direction of Arthur Greaves, city editor, to cover the arrival of the rescue ship Thursday night. Van Anda persuaded Guglielmo Marconi, the wireless inventor, to board the ship to interview the wireless operator—and a *Times* reporter slipped through the police lines with the inventor. He got an exclusive story of the last messages from the *Titanic.*

"All the News That's Fit to Print."

The New York Times.

THE WEATHER.
Unsettled Tuesday; Wednesday, fair, cooler; moderate southerly winds, becoming variable.
For full weather report see Page 23.

VOL. LXI...NO. 19,[illegible] NEW YORK, TUESDAY, APRIL 16, 1912.—TWENTY-FOUR PAGES, ONE CENT In Greater New York, Jersey City, and Newark. | Elsewhere, TWO CENTS.

TITANIC SINKS FOUR HOURS AFTER HITTING ICEBERG; 866 RESCUED BY CARPATHIA, PROBABLY 1250 PERISH; ISMAY SAFE, MRS. ASTOR MAYBE, NOTED NAMES MISSING

Col. Astor and Bride, Isidor Straus and Wife, and Maj. Butt Aboard.

"RULE OF SEA" FOLLOWED

Women and Children Put Over in Lifeboats and Are Supposed to be Safe on Carpathia.

PICKED UP AFTER 8 HOURS

Vincent Astor Calls at White Star Office for News of His Father and Leaves Weeping.

FRANKLIN HOPEFUL ALL DAY

Manager of the Line Insisted Titanic Was Unsinkable Even After She Had Gone Down.

HEAD OF THE LINE ABOARD

J. Bruce Ismay Making First Trip on Gigantic Ship That Was to Surpass All Others.

The admission that the Titanic, the biggest steamship in the world, had been sunk by an iceberg and had gone to the bottom of the Atlantic, probably carrying more than 1,400 of her passengers and crew with her, was made at the White Star Line offices, 9 Broadway, at 8:20 o'clock last night. Then P. A. S. Franklin, Vice President and General Manager of the International Mercantile Marine, conceded that probably only those passengers who were picked up by the Cunarder Carpathia had been saved. Advices received early this morning tended to increase the number of survivors by 200.

The admission followed a day in which the White Star Line officials had been optimistic in the extreme. At no time was the admission made that every one aboard the huge steamer was not safe. The ship itself, it was confidently asserted, was unsinkable, and inquirers were informed that she would reach port, under her own steam probably, but surely with the help of the Allan liner Virginian, which was reported to be towing her.

As the day passed, however, with no new authentic reports from the Titanic or any of the ships which were known to have responded to her wireless call for help, it became apparent that authentic news of the disaster probably could come only from the Titanic's sister ship, the Olympic. The wireless range of the Olympic is 500 miles. That of the Carpathia, the Parisian, and the Virginian is much less, and as they neared the position of the Titanic they drew further and further out of shore range. From the Titanic's position at the time of the disaster it is doubtful if any of the ships except the Olympic could establish communication with shore.

Titanic Sunk at 2:20 A. M. Monday.

In the White Star offices the hope was held out all day that the Parisian and the Virginian had taken off some of the Titanic's passengers, and efforts were made to get into communication with these liners. Until such communication was established the White Star officials refused to recognize the possibility that there were none of the Titanic's passengers aboard them.

But by nightfall came the message from Capt. Haddock of the Olympic to Cape Race, Newfoundland, telling of the foundering of the Titanic and of the rescue of 655 of her passengers by the Cunarder Carpathia, which, the wireless message said, reached the position of the Titanic at daybreak. All they found there, however, was lifeboats and wreckage. The biggest ship in the world had sunk at 2:20 o'clock yesterday morning.

Mr. Franklin admitted late last night that the Parisian and the Virginian, though they were among the first to answer the Titanic's calls for help, could not have reached the scene before 10 o'clock yesterday morning, seven and a half hours after the big Titanic buried her nose beneath the waves and pitched downward out of sight. The Carpathia, so the wireless dispatch from Capt. Haddock to Cape Race announced, reached the scene of the Titanic's foundering at daybreak, several hours before the expected arrival of the Virginian and the Parisian.

The Lost Titanic Being Towed Out of Belfast Harbor.

CAPT. E. J. SMITH,
Commander of the Titanic.

1,655 Lives Lost First Report.

It is unbelievable, so White Star Line officials were compelled to concede finally, that the Carpathia should have failed to pick up every lifeboat which still floated on the waves. If they failed to pick up more than 655 passengers, it was because the others of the ship's complement had gone with her to the bottom.

But it was not until nearly nightfall that the extent of the disaster was realized. Before that the reassuring nature of the bulletins issued by the White Star line was sufficient to quiet the fears of those who had relatives or friends aboard the unfortunate ship and to prevent widespread belief in a serious disaster.

Capt. Haddock's message from the Olympic, which is printed in another column of THE TIMES, strongly indicated that none but the 655 taken from life boats by the Carpathia had been saved. This message was relayed immediately to the White Star offices, but Mr. Franklin positively declined to make the text of the message public. He offered still the hope that passengers were aboard the Parisian and the Virginian, and even when the admission was wrung from him that there seemed little hope of the saving of any others than the 655 aboard the Carpathia, he clung to the hope that in some unexplained way there were other passengers abroad the two Allan liners.

First Reported Titanic in Tow.

Throughout the day there had been reassurances that the Titanic was being towed to port by the Virginian, and when Capt. Haddock's message proved this to be untrue only the admission was made at the White Star offices that the Titanic had sunk. Mr. Franklin said that Capt. Haddock's message was brief and "neglected to say that all the crew had been saved." But the inference was not that all the passengers had been saved. Rather it was that many of them had died, and presently Mr. Franklin admitted the fear that there had been a terrible loss of life on the Titanic.

This version of Capt. Haddock's wireless had been given at the White Star offices:

Capt. Haddock of the Olympic sends a wireless message to the White Star offices here that the steamer Titanic sank at 2:20 A. M., after all the passengers and crew had been lowered to life boats and transferred to the Virginian. The steamship Carpathia, with several hundred passengers of the Titanic, is now en route to New York.

At 9 o'clock, however, he modified this statement, declaring:

As far as we know the situation, there have been rumors from Halifax that three steamers were at the scene of the Titanic's sinking, namely, the Virginian, the Parisian, and the Carpathia. We have heard from Capt. Haddock of the Olympic, who says that the Titanic sank at 2:20 o'clock this morning. Haddock also informs us that the Carpathia has 675 survivors on board. It is very difficult to say whether the Virginian and the Parisian have any survivors on board until we can get a report from those vessels.

Fears Serious Loss of Life.

We have asked for that report from Capt. Haddock, and we are expecting a reply at any time. The Carpathia is proceeding to New York direct. We very much fear that there has been serious loss of life, but it is impossible for us to say definitely concerning this sad part of the situation until we are able to reassure ourselves whether or not any of the Titanic's passengers are aboard the Allan liners.

We are hopeful that the rumors which have reached us by telegraph from Halifax that there are passengers aboard the Virginian and the Parisian will prove to be true, and that these vessels will turn up with some of the passengers. It is the loss of life that makes this thing so awful. We can replace the money loss, but not the lives of those who went down.

Another version of the message from the Olympic was current last night and included the sentence: "Loss likely total 1,800 souls." This sentence was not in the message received by THE TIMES from Cape Race nor in that sent to the White Star line offices.

Continued on Page 3.

THE PROBABLE LOSS.
Number Aboard.

First cabin	325
Second cabin	285
Steerage	710
Crew, (estimated)	800
Total	2,120
Saved.	
By the Carpathia	866
Probably drowned	1,254

POLAND WATER promotes Health. Avoid contagion by drinking purest water in world. Off. 1,180 B'way. Tel. Mad. Sq. 4738.—Adv.

CRETA CREME HAND SOAP. Instantly removes stains. Large Can 15c.—Adv.

GREAT BEAR SPRING WATER. 50c. per case of 6 glass-stoppered bottles.—Adv.

PARTIAL LIST OF THE SAVED.

Includes Bruce Ismay, Mrs. Widener, Mrs. H. B. Harris, and an Incomplete name, suggesting Mrs. Astor's.

Special to The New York Times.

CAPE RACE, N. F., Tuesday, April 16.—Following is a partial list of survivors among the first-class passengers of the Titanic, received by the Marconi wireless station this morning from the Carpathia, via the steapship Olympic:

Mrs. JACOB P. ——— and maid.
Mr. HARRY ANDERSON.
Mrs. ED. W. APPLETON.
Mrs. ROSE ABBOTT.
Miss G. M. BURNS.
Miss D. D. CASSEBERE.
Mrs. WM. M. CLARKE.
Mrs. B. CHIBINACE.
Miss E. G. CROSSBIE.
Miss H. ROSEBIE.
Miss JEAN HIPACK.
Mrs. HY. B. HARRIS.
Mrs. ALEX. HALVERSON.
Miss MARGARET HAYS.
Mr. BRUCE ISMAY.
Mr. and Mrs. ED. KIMBERLEY.
Mr. F. A. KENNYMAN.
Miss EMILE KENCHEN.
Miss G. F. LONGLEY.
Mrs. A. F. LEADER.
Miss BERTHA LAVORY.
Mrs. ERNEST LIVES.
Miss MARY CLINES.
Mrs. SINGRID LINDSTROM.
Mr. GUSTAVE J. LESNEUR.
Miss GIORGETTA A. MADILL.
Mme. MELICARD.
Mrs. TUCKER and maid.
Mrs. J. B. THAYER.
Mr. J. B. THAYER, Jr.
Mr. HENRY WOOLMER.
Miss ANNA WARD.
Mr. RICHARD M. WILLIAMS.
Mrs. F. M. WARNER.
Miss HELEN A. WILSON.
Miss WILLARD.
Miss MARY WICKS.
Mrs. GEO. D. WIDENER and maid.
Mrs. J. STEWART WHITE.
Miss MARIE YOUNG.
Mrs. THOMAS POTTER, Jr.
Mrs. EDNA S. ROBERTS.
Countess of ROTHES.
Mr. C. ROLMANE.
Mrs. SUSAN P. ROGERSON. (Probably Ryerson).
Miss EMILY B. ROGERSON.
Mrs. ARTHUR ROGERSON.
Master ALLISON and nurse.
Miss K. T. ANDREWS.
Miss NINETTE PANHART.
Miss E. W. ALLEN.
Mr. and Mrs. D. BISHOP.
Mr. H. BLANK.
Miss A. BASSINA.
Mrs. JAMES BAXTER.
Mr. GEORGE A. BAYT——.
Miss C. BONNELL.
Mrs. J. M. BROWN.
Miss G. C. BOWEN.
Mr. and Mrs. R. L. BECKW——.
Miss RUTH TAUSSIG.
Miss ELLA THOR.
Mr. and Mrs. E. Z. TAYLOR.
GILBERT M. TUCKER.
Mr. J. B. THAYER.
Mr. JOHN B. ROGERSON.
Mrs. M. ROTHSCHILD.
Miss MADELEINE NEWELL.
Mrs. MARJORIE NEWELL.
HELEN W. NEWSOM.
Mr. FIENNAD OMOND.
Mr. E. C. OSTBY.
Miss HELEN R. OSTBY.
Mrs. MAMAM J. RENAGO.
Mlle. OLIVIA.
Mrs. D. W. MERVIN.
Mr. PHILIP EMOCK.
Mr. JAMES GOOGHT.
Miss RUBERTA MAIMY.
Mr. PIERRE MARECHAL.
Mrs. W. E. MINEHAN.
Miss APPIE RANELT.
Major ARTUR PEUCHEN.
Mrs. KARL H. BEHR.
Miss DESSETTE.
Mrs. WILLIAM BUCKNELL.
Mrs. O. H. BARKWORTH.
Mrs. H. B. STEFFASON.
Mrs. ELSIE BOWERMAN.

The Marconi station reports that it missed the word after "Mrs. Jacob P." In a list received by the Associated Press this morning this name appeared well down, but in THE TIMES list it is first, suggesting that the name of Mrs. John Jacob Astor is intended. This supposition is strengthened by the fact that, except for Mrs. H. J. Allison, Mrs. Astor is the only lady in the "A" column of the ship's passenger list attended by a maid.

NAMES PICKED UP AT BOSTON.

BOSTON, April 15.—Among the names of survivors of the Titanic picked up by wireless from the steamer Carpathia here to-night were the following:

Mr. and Mrs. L. HENRY.
Mrs. W. A. HOOPER.
Mr. MILE.
Mr. J. FLYNN.
Miss ALICE FORTUNE.
Mrs. ROBERT DOUGLAS.
Miss HILDA SLAYTER.
Mrs. P. SMITH.
Mrs. BRAHAM.
Miss LUCILLE CARTER.
Mr. WILLIAM CARTER.
Miss CUMMINGS.
Mrs. FLORENCE MARE.
Miss ALICE PHILLIPS.
Mrs. PAULA MUNGE.
Mrs. JANE ———
Miss PHYLLIS O. ———
HOWARD B. CASE.
Miss MINEHAN.
Miss BERTHA ———

Biggest Liner Plunges to the Bottom at 2:20 A. M.

RESCUERS THERE TOO LATE

Except to Pick Up the Few Hundreds Who Took to the Lifeboats.

WOMEN AND CHILDREN FIRST

Cunarder Carpathia Rushing to New York with the Survivors.

SEA SEARCH FOR OTHERS

The California Stands By on Chance of Picking Up Other Boats or Rafts.

OLYMPIC SENDS THE NEWS

Only Ship to Flash Wireless Messages to Shore After the Disaster.

LATER REPORT SAVES 866.

BOSTON, April 15.—A wireless message picked up late to-night, relayed from the Olympic, says that the Carpathia is on her way to New York with 866 passengers from the steamer Titanic aboard. They are mostly women and children, the message said, and it concluded: "Grave fears are felt for the safety of the balance of the passengers and crew."

Special to The New York Times.

CAPE RACE, N. F., April 15.—The White Star liner Olympic reports by wireless this evening that the Cunarder Carpathia reached, at daybreak this morning, the position from which wireless calls for help were sent out last night by the Titanic after her collision with an iceberg. The Carpathia found only the lifeboats and the wreckage of what had been the biggest steamship afloat.

The Titanic had foundered at about 2:20 A. M., in latitude 41:46 north and longitude 50:14 west. This is about 30 minutes of latitude, or about 34 miles, due south of the position at which she struck the iceberg. All her boats are accounted for and about 655 souls have been saved of the crew and passengers, most of the latter presumably women and children.

There were about 2,100 persons aboard the Titanic.

The Leyland liner California is remaining and searching the position of the disaster, while the Carpathia is returning to New York with the survivors.

It can be positively stated that up to 11 o'clock to-night nothing whatever had been received at or heard by the Marconi station here to the effect that the Parisian, Virginian or any other ships had picked up any survivors, other than those picked up by the Carpathia.

First News of the Disaster.

The first news of the disaster to the Titanic was received by the Marconi wireless station here at 10:25 o'clock last night [as told in yesterday's New York Times.] The Titanic was first heard giving the distress signal "C. Q. D.," which was answered by a number of ships, including the Carpathia,

The *New York Times* handles one of the great news stories of the twentieth century.

Within 3 hours after the arrival of the rescue ship the *Times'* first edition appeared, with fifteen of its twenty-four pages devoted to the story of the loss of 1500 lives in the *Titanic* disaster. In coverage and in organization of a great news story, that edition of the *Times* remains a masterpiece.[21]

Van Anda and Ochs both loved speed in the gathering of the news and this love had led the *Times* to leadership in the use of correspondents and communications facilities in such instances as the *Titanic* sinking. Both men had watched the work of Marconi, the Italian scientist who between the years of 1895 and 1900 devised a practical system of sending telegraphic messages through space by means of electromagnetic waves. Marconi's "wireless" telegraphy was based on the experiments of others, but it was he who obtained the basic patents and formed the first commercial wireless company in London in 1897. Ship-to-shore communication and the use of the wireless by English newspapers and the *New York Herald* to cover sporting events soon followed. In December, 1901, Marconi successfully transmitted signals from England to Newfoundland. But it was not until 1907 that a regular trans-Atlantic service opened.[22]

Ranking above all else in bringing the *Times* to greatness was its coverage of the events of the first World War. It was in this period that the paper began to publish the texts of documents and speeches, a policy that led to its becoming the leading reference newspaper for librarians, scholars, government officials, and other newspaper editors. The compilation of the *New York Times Index* further ensured the paper this position.

Six full pages in an August, 1914, issue of the *Times* presented the British White Paper to American readers. The *Times* had been the first American paper to obtain a copy of the British Foreign Office's correspondence with Germany and Austria and printed it in full. The next day it published the text of the German version of events leading up to the war declaration, brought from Berlin by a *Times* correspondent, for another exclusive.

Meanwhile Van Anda was giving his readers minute coverage of the military news, using press-association accounts, the reports of his own correspondents with the various armies, and stories obtained from the *London Chronicle.* War pictures were carried in a rotogravure section, added by Ochs in 1914 after Van Anda had investigated rotogravure printing in Germany. Political and economic reporting from European capitals was given proper emphasis with the military news. When the United States entered the war the *Times* expanded its coverage, spending $750,000 a year on cabled news.

THE *NEW YORK HERALD,* A LEADER IN NEWS

The *New York Herald,* under the guidance of founder James Gordon Bennett, had achieved leadership in news enterprise. When James Gordon Bennett, Jr., took control in 1872 the *Herald* ranked first in collecting and presenting the news. Its reporters and correspondents were the best and its insistence on the use of the fastest means of communication made it a hard-hitting rival for Pulitzer and Hearst when they invaded New York. Its traditions were still those of its adventurous correspondent of the early 1870s, Henry M. Stanley, who spent 2 years searching in Africa, on an assignment from the younger Bennett, before he found the missing missionary and inquired, "Dr. Livingstone, I presume?" The *Herald* remained a news-enterprise paper in the early twentieth century, contesting vigorously for complete and dramatic coverage of the world's events. It had Joseph L. Stickney with Dewey at Manila; Richard Harding Davis covering the Boer War; Oscar King Davis and W. H. Lewis giving it top coverage of the Russo-Japanese War; Dr. Frederick A. Cook reporting on his trip to the North Pole; and a network of political and war correspondents (supplied in part by the *Paris Herald*) that was the equal of any such group in World War I. Its use of artwork and photographs embellished its crack coverage of such events as the sinking of the *General Slocum* and the *Titanic* disaster.[23]

In the struggle for survival in New York, however, the *Herald* was handicapped by the personality and practices of its owner, the younger Bennett. He was intelligent and alert, and his driving force dominated the paper. He established the Paris edition of the *Herald* in 1887, now the famed *International Herald Tribune.* But in his 45 years as a publisher he proved to be a dictator who put his personal whims first. He lived in Paris most of his life, rarely visiting the *Herald* office, and his royal manner of living drained an estimated $30 million from the profits of his papers.[24] No other publisher, save William Randolph Hearst, equaled Bennett in irresponsible personal control of a journalistic enterprise.

George Jean Nathan has described Bennett as he appeared in 1909, at the age of 67.[25] He was tall, slender, full of nervous energy, but bearing himself with a military erectness accented by steel-gray hair and moustache. Though he lived in Paris, his editors could neither hire nor fire a reporter without his consent. His editorial committee met at a table with an empty chair at the head—that was Bennett. At his place were set fresh copies of the paper each day, as though he might walk in at any moment.

Bennett's connection with the paper was far from being a psychological one, however. Cabled instructions arrived from Paris each day. Frequently department heads were called to Paris for conferences. Bennett kept close watch on the work of each employee and practiced a policy of seeing to it that no individual achieved personal importance. Although he had many good news instincts, he also forced the paper to observe many rules of conduct based on his personal idiosyncrasies and ordered promotion of his personal beliefs. At Bennett's death in 1918, the *Herald* was sold to Frank Munsey, who could not make the leaderless paper profitable and let it disappear into the *Herald Tribune* in 1924. That paper maintained the Bennett news traditions.

THE *NEW YORK SUN* GOES DOWN

The *New York Sun* of the days of editor Charles A. Dana and managing editor Amos J. Cummings had emphasized reporting skill, writing style, and human-interest techniques to a degree worthy of the admiration of the practioners of the "new journalism." It was a city editor of the *Sun,* John B. Bogart, who told a young reporter for the first time: "When a dog bites a man, that is not news; but when a man bites a dog, *that* is news." It was an editorial writer for the *Sun,* Francis P. Church, who in 1897 answered the "Is There a Santa Claus?" inquiry of a little girl named Virginia with an explanation that was reprinted widely for many years. It was a reporter for the *Sun,* Will Irwin, who in 1906 wrote the journalistic masterpiece, "The City That Was," in memory of San Francisco's destruction by earthquake and fire.[26]

Heading the *Sun* news staff from the eighties to the World War I period were managing editor Chester S. Lord and night city editor Selah M. Clarke, called "Boss" by his associates. They helped to train reporters like Irwin, Arthur Brisbane, Julian Ralph, Samuel Hopkins Adams, Richard Harding Davis, and Jacob Riis. From their night desk, too, Carr Van Anda went to his great career on the *Times.* Succeeding Dana as editor was the highly competent and graceful stylist, Edward P. Mitchell. The *Sun* was regarded as a "school of journalism" for young journalists, and its graduates formed an alumni association. They were dismayed when control of the *Sun* passed in 1916 to Frank A. Munsey, a business-minded purchaser of newspapers who understood little of the journalistic traditions of the craft. The famous morning edition of the *Sun* disappeared in 1920 and the evening *Sun,* bearing little resemblance to the paper of old, trudged on toward eventual oblivion.

CHICAGO'S FAMED *INTER OCEAN*

A newspaper in Chicago's past journalism history that for a time attracted a following of reporters was the *Inter Ocean.* It started its career in 1865 as the *Chicago Republican,* edited by Charles A. Dana for the first year. It became the *Inter Ocean* in 1872, a staunch Republican voice owned by William Penn Nixon. Through its reporting enterprise on the frontier, its religious news, and its agricultural news coverage it built up a Midwestern circulation. It also led in introducing mechanical improvements—for example, by installing a color press in 1892 in advance of other American newspapers. During the 1890s the paper lost money and was sold to Charles T. Yerkes, Chicago's traction line boss. Despite its record for conducting crusades in the public interest, the *Inter Ocean* suffered under Yerkes' ownership until he sold it in 1902 to George W. Hinman, who had come from the *New York Sun* to be the *Inter Ocean*'s editor.

Under Hinman the *Inter Ocean* won notice as a training school for newspaperpeople. The paper had been one of those that had catered to the "tramp reporters" of the period and by so doing had obtained the services of many young people with journalistic futures. Belonging to the *Inter Ocean* alumni association were Marquis James, William Cuppy, and Ring Lardner, writers; Walter Howey, later a famous Hearst executive; Richard J. Finnegan, later editor of the *Chicago Times* and *Sun-Times;* and a score of other prominent newspaperpeople. In 1914, however, the *Inter Ocean* fell victim to Chicago's newspaper competition and was added to the list of newspapers that have become reminiscences.[27]

BUILDING THE *LOS ANGELES TIMES*

When local printers in a small town of 12,000 called Los Angeles founded the *Los Angeles Times* in 1881 as a rival to the *Herald* and the *Express,* no one foresaw that both the city and the *Times* would rank in the national forefront a century later. A man who helped build both, Harrison Gray Otis, entered the publishing firm in 1882. He was 45, a Civil War veteran with colonel's rank, and had twice dabbled in newspapering. By 1886 Otis had full control of the 7000-circulation morning daily. A real-estate boom fattened his profits, and by 1900 the *Times,* despite a modest 26,000 circulation, boasted the country's largest advertising linage. Otis began land purchases in California and Mexico that soon totaled a million acres.[28]

Promoted to general when he commanded troops in the Philippines insurrection, he became "General Otis"—a hard-fisted capitalist who relished a brawl and used his paper to make vitriolic denunciations of opponents. He castigated some businesspeople as "robber barons" and supported the 1905 Russian Revolution, but otherwise he garnered a widespread reputation for reactionary thought and action. His biggest troubles began in 1890 when he locked out his printers in a dispute with the International Typographical Union (ITU) over the closed shop and rules for resetting advertising mats. In 1894 he formed an employer's group in Los Angeles to oppose the unions. The ITU brought in William Randolph Hearst in 1903 to found a rival morning paper, the *Examiner,* and attempted a boycott of *Times* advertisers. Resistance to Otis and his conservative stance grew, and by 1910 a Socialist candidate ran first in the primaries for mayor of Los Angeles.

Bombings had been used in recent industrial disputes, but the gutting of the *Times* building on October 1, 1910, caused a sensation. Otis and his son-in-law, Harry Chandler, were absent from the building, escaping death which took twenty of their printers. Detectives traced the bombs to the McNamara brothers, officers of an Indianapolis union. The charges were widely regarded as a frameup engineered by the reactionary Otis, and liberals hired Clarence Darrow to head the defense at the 1911 trial. But one brother confessed and both pleaded guilty. Darrow withdrew from the case, the Socialist lost the mayoral election, and Otis rebuilt his printing plant in a fortresslike atmosphere with an eagle atop the building. In 1914, 3 years before his death, he turned the paper over to Harry and Marian Chandler. Their son Norman and grandson Otis would continue the family role.

RISE OF THE PRESS ASSOCIATIONS

The rise of the American press associations—organizations dedicated to the rapid, thorough, and impartial collection and dissemination of all the news—was an epochal development in the history of journalism. "The right of the people to know" was greatly advanced by the creation of news agencies that utilized journalistic skills and modern communications techniques to find the news, to report it impartially, and to speed it to every corner of the country and every part of the world. Only a few American dailies ever have attempted to maintain staff correspondents in leading news centers of the world, or even of the country, and the press-association logotypes—AP, UP, INS, UPI in the twentieth century—have become the symbols of trustworthy service from outside sources.

The United States has had three major press associations operating on worldwide scales. One is the Associated Press, which arose out of nineteenth-century efforts in cooperative newsgathering. Its twentieth-century competitors

In Two Parts, Complete -28 Pages

Part I—General News Sheet—16 Pages

The Los Angeles Times

Twenty-fifth Year.

PER ANNUM, $9.00 | Per Month, 75 Cents, or 2 1-2 Cents a Copy.

THURSDAY MORNING, APRIL 19, 1906.

On All News Stands, Trains and Streets. | 5 CENTS

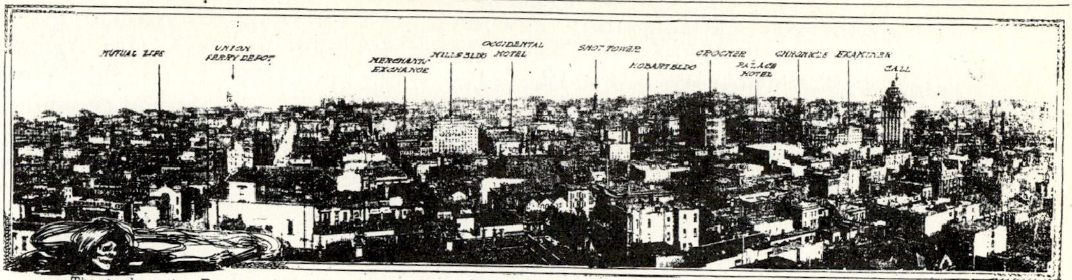

The stricken city. Panorama of San Francisco before the catastrophe, showing principal buildings that are partially or wholly destroyed.

THE WEATHER.

BRIEF REPORT.

YESTERDAY — Maximum temperature, 73 deg.; minimum, 49 deg. Wind 5 a. m., east; velocity, 1 mile; 5 p. m., west; velocity, 7 miles. At midnight the temperature was 60 deg.; clear.

TODAY—At 5 a. m. the temperature was 58 deg.; clear.

POINTS OF THE NEWS

IN TODAY'S ISSUE OF

The Times

INDEX.

SYNOPSIS.

THE CITY. Los Angeles stunned by tidings of sister city's doom, sympathy and money freely offered, nearly $50,000 raised and $100,000 pledged in day; two cities closely connected in business, names of concerns directly affected; panic-stricken crowd besieges telegraph office in vain effort to reach loved ones, and many take trains toward scene of terror; The Times beats all other papers an hour with the news. Horse Show opens brilliantly, with classy equines prancing and society a-sparkle....Mary Powers gets judgment for $500 against man who fell in love with her photograph....Passers of forged checks arrested....City Council places ban on skyscrapers....Maguire defeats Keniston at billiards....Stanford may take Occidental's coach. Quarantine-breaker Kindgren has inning with Health Office....Fund to send Miss Sutton abroad grows....Looloos 3, Seattle 2....Ex-preacher Wylie and Green woman held on ugly charge.

SOUTHERN CALIFORNIA. See page 3, Part I.

CALIFORNIA'S CALAMITY. At 10 o'clock last night fires following earthquake shocks which practically left all San Francisco in ruins were still burning fiercely in that city and the monetary loss at that hour was estimated at $200,000,000....With 500 or more persons killed by falling buildings to accentuate their fears, citizens of the stricken metropolis and surrounding bayside were fleeing to the hills for safety or crowding the ferry-boats, an avenue of escape which, more than once became dangerously congested....Gen. Funston last night telegraphed to the War Department that 100,000 persons are homeless and that thousands of tents and such quantities of provisions as can be taken into the city are urgently needed....Federal troops are aiding the police in maintaining order and several looters have been shot....The area covered in San Francisco alone by flames up to 6 o'clock last night was about eight square miles; insurance companies say they will pay losses in full.. Mayor Schmitz has appointed Committee of Safety composed of prominent citizens. an one of the questions most needing answer is how to supply stricken city with water—In the ruin by earthquake and consequent fire, San Francisco's finest and most noted public buildings and commercial structures went down in destruction, as also hundreds of buildings of an inferior class, taking hundreds of lives—Cities within a radius of many miles of the metropolis were affected by the shocks, and to some of them the blow dealt was terrific, the loss at Salinas alone being $2,500,000—Two hundred patients at Agnews insane asylum perished when the walls of that institution crumbled—All costumes and scenery of Metropolitan Opera Company destroyed—San Maeto water mains broken; Spring Valley flooded—Goldstein, Bowen & Co. offer entire store and contents for use of city—All wharves on San Francisco side of bay have caved in—Twenty persons killed in collapse of Terminal Hotel—Banks, though not fireproof, stand fire well.

HEART IS TORN FROM GREAT CITY.

San Francisco Nearly Destroyed By Earthquakes and Fire—Hundreds of Killed and Injured—Destruction of Other Coast Cities—California's Greatest Horror.

By the Associated Press—P. M.

SAN FRANCISCO, April 19.—It looks now as if the entire city would be burned, following the great quake of yesterday. The government is furnisning tugs to convey news to Oakland, but the confusion is so great that they cannot be relied upon. It will be impcssible to send full details for several days.

The latest reports from Leland Sanford University indicate that the magnicent stone buildings c. that institution have suffered severe damage Many of the buildings were ruined by cracks, which split them from cornice to foundation. The buildings are practically intact. Only a few structures collapsed in Berkeley, the earthquake shock being slight there.

At 10 o'clock at night, the fire was unabated, and thousands of people are fleeing to the hills and clamoring for places on the ferry boats.

The damage is now believed to have reached $200,000,000 and 50,000 people are thought to be homeless.

Under the fierce heat of the sun today, 29 bodies lay in Washington Square, where they were taken at the order of the Mayor when the morgues and Hall of Justice basement held all that could be cared for.

At 10 p. m. last night the newspapers ceased all effort to collect news, and the Associated Press force is compelled to act independently.

THE PRESIDENT'S MESSAGE:

The President sent the following telegram to Gov. Pardee, Sacramento:

"Sir: Rumors of great disaster from an earthquake in San Francisco, but know nothing of the real facts. Call upon me for any assistance I can render.

(Signed) THEODORE ROOSEVELT, Washington, April 18."

The President later sent the following additional telegram to Gov. Pardee:

"It was difficult at first to credit the catastrophe that has befallen San Francisco. I feel the greatest concern and sympathy for you and the people, not only of San Francisco, but of California in the terrible disaster. You will let me know if there is anything that the national government can do.

(Signed) THEODORE ROOSEVELT."

Gov: Pardee sent the following in reply:

"Owing to interruption of telegraphic communication extent of disaster in San Francisco not yet known here, but no doubt calamity is very serious. People of California appreciate your kind inquiry and offer of assistance. State troops doing patrol duty, and if federal assistance is needed will call upon you.

Signed, "GEO. C. PARDEE"

TOSSING SIX HOURS ON SEISMIC WAVES.

SAN FRANCISCO, April 18.—[Special.] During six hours of mortal dread and nameless terror San Francisco was today tossed upon the seismic waves of the most disastrous earthquake known to the history or the traditions of America's west coast. In the mad confusion and helpless horror of this night uncounted bodies of dead men and women are lying in morgues and under unuplifted walls. g through lieved that nearly 1000 lives have been lost. The nuss the wa ers of not fall far short of that, and it may prove to be mudn throug i Fire and flame have added to the destruction, the winds wit i the and despair. The material losses are beyond computation. Wounded and hurt inexpressibly the chief city of the West lies at this hour humbled to the dust, blackened, battered and charred, her glory of yesterday but a hideous dream, and the moans from her stricken heart filling the pitying world.

The first shock came while still the mighty city lay deep in slumber, weary with the revelries and pleasures of the night before. In the quiet homes, in the crowded hotels, men had not yet awakened to the strifes and endeavors of the new-dawned day. The stars had but waned, and the morn was the mists and forough the mists and fogs that hung in gray he wa ers of the placid he waters of the placid bay and over the wait-the Golden Garough the Golden Gate were blowing the greeting ofls with the greeting of the sea to the green-clad heights and flower-strewn fields that skirted the shores and stretched away into the dim distances beyond. The sailors still slept in their hammocks in the harbored ships. A few wan-eyed wanderers of the night were stealing through the streets, a few early toilers were astir. But that was all.

Then came the rumble of deep thunder from the mighty bowels of the startled earth. The city shook like an aspen leaf, and her gray highways suddenly cracked and split as though the batteries of Satan and his America's west coast. In the against them from underneath ror of this night uncounted warped and creaked, and the rakare lying in morgues and u fell like stacks of cards. The lieved that nearly 1000 lives l mont, the Oakland heights and not fall far short of that, and rocked like forests in the wind. Fire and flame have added

The *Los Angeles Times* reports a 1906 disaster.

were the United Press Associations, founded in 1907 by Edward Wyllis Scripps, and the International News Service, begun in 1909 by William Randolph Hearst. The two merged in 1958 to form the United Press International. Abroad, major competitors were Reuters of Great Britain, founded in 1851, and Agence France-Presse, which arose after World War II out of the ruins of the old French Havas agency (1835). By 1920 the three American news agencies had expanded their domestic services and had challenged the European agencies—British, French, German—for international news reporting and sales.

THE ASSOCIATED PRESS: GENESIS

The longest history among the American press associations is that of the Associated Press. The modern cooperative news-gathering association with that name took final form in 1900 after a bitter struggle for control of the press-association facilities of the country. The agreement among New York City's leading newspapers in 1849 that brought about the establishment of the Associated Press of New York set the pattern for similar associations. Midwestern dailies formed the Western Associated Press in 1862, which was followed by the New England Associated Press. Other subsidiary regional groups followed. But always the power of the Associated Press of New York was felt.*

The New York AP had been well guided by its earliest general agents, Dr. Alexander Jones (1849 to 1851), news-gathering pioneer Daniel H. Craig (1851 to 1866), and former Washington correspondent and San Francisco newspaperperson James W. Simonton (1866 to 1882). Ground was given to restive Western AP members when their agent, William Henry Smith, was named general manager (1882 to 1892), and two of five executive committee seats went to Westerners. Despite this, the New York AP faced serious competition from rebels who had tried to form a rival since 1869 and who in 1882 created the United Press (no relation to the present-day UPI). Walter Polk Phillips, its general manager, had strong modernized dailies as members and good foreign news. William M. Laffan, business manager of the *New York Sun,* was a UP leader.

The reaction of the ruling groups within the AP and UP was typical of the times. The two executive committees entered into a secret agreement providing for exchange of news between the two associations and a virtual end to competition. There were financial rewards for insiders. When the deal was uncovered in 1891, a new battle in AP ranks was inevitable.[29] The *New York Sun* and the *Tribune* bolted to the UP in 1892, to be followed the next year by the remaining members of the AP of New York. Taking control of the AP organization was a new corporation, the Associated Press of Illinois, chartered in late 1892.

Melville E. Stone, new AP general manager, obtained exclusive news exchange contracts with Reuters in Britain, Havas in France, and Wolff in Germany. He thus cut the United Press off from the sources of foreign news long enjoyed by its New York members. A 4-year struggle finally ended in early 1897 when all the New York dailies except Dana's *Sun* and Hearst's *Journal* were

*See pages 160–65 and 266–67 for earlier accounts.

admitted to the AP, and the United Press went into bankruptcy. Hearst had never been an AP member; Laffan of the *Sun* stubbornly organized his own Laffan News Bureau, which operated successfully until 1916.

Indirectly Laffan was to cause the AP more trouble before the association's course was finally set. The Chicago *Inter Ocean* went to court in 1898 to prevent the AP from discontinuing service to it as punishment for the *Inter Ocean*'s use of Laffan News Bureau copy. An Illinois court decision, handed down in 1900, found that the incorporation papers of the AP were written so broadly as to make the press association a public utility, bound to provide its service to all newspapers wishing it. For the moment the Illinois ruling seemed to put an end to the exclusive membership character of the AP, but its leaders found a way out. The AP of Illinois was dissolved, and a new AP was formed as a nonprofit membership association under New York State law. Stone continued as general manager of the new AP.

THE NEW ASSOCIATED PRESS OF 1900

The most important fact about the new Associated Press of 1900 was that it was a cooperative. Its members were to supply each other with news originating in individual publication areas. They were to share the cost of this exchange of news, and the cost of maintaining a press-association staff that would direct the flow of news and augment it with other coverage. The staff, headed by the general manager, was to be responsible only to the membership, through its officers and directors. The AP would thus be an agency existing only for the benefit of its member newspapers.

There were some faults, however, in the AP organization. Until 1915 its members could not subscribe to other news services. The original members of 1900 owned bonds that carried additional voting rights, keeping control of the board of directors in the hands of older, larger papers. The smaller dailies were given three seats on a board of eighteen in 1937. Most serious was the problem of protest rights, by which a member could keep a competitor in its city out of the AP. A four-fifths vote of the entire membership was required to override such a veto and was rarely obtained. The only way into AP in larger cities was to buy an existing membership.

Another unhappy situation in which the AP found itself stemmed from the news-exchange contracts it made in 1893 with European news agencies. This meant that news of the United States that was collected by the AP was distributed abroad by foreign news services. Melville E. Stone, as AP general manager, did his best to open news channels in European countries[30] and the AP established some foreign bureaus before World War I to collect its own news. But lacking the right to sell its foreign news abroad, it could not build the kind of foreign service it eventually achieved.

There were many notable names in the AP organization during its formative years under Stone's managership. Charles S. Diehl, a veteran of the Illinois AP regime, became an assistant general manager. So did Jackson S. Elliott, news chief during World War I. Frederick Roy Martin, successful editor of the *Providence Journal,* became assistant general manager in 1912 and succeeded

Stone as manager in 1921. Among the noted bureau chiefs were Salvatore Cortesi in Rome, Seymour B. Conger in Berlin, and Edwin M. Hood in Washington. World War I correspondents included Charles T. Thompson, Frederick Palmer, and DeWitt Mackenzie, later an AP news analyst.

SCRIPPS AND HEARST CHALLENGE THE AP

Rising alongside the Associated Press as aggressive competing press associations were the United Press Associations of Edward Wyllis Scripps and the International News Service of William Randolph Hearst. The new UP and the INS were not cooperatives, as was the AP. They were regular business enterprises that sold their news services to clients on a contract basis. Both arose in answer to the AP's closed-membership policy. The chain newspaper publishers who started the UP and the INS soon found that the news they collected could be sold both at home and abroad to others who could not obtain, or did not wish to have, AP service. Serving a variety of clients, as both the UP and INS soon did, their identification with two strong-minded newspaper publishers became only incidental. Their operating staffs were as anxious to cover all the news thoroughly and impartially, for the benefit of their ultimate readers, as were AP people, or any other newspeople.

Edward Wyllis Scripps once said that he founded the United Press Associations because he was suspicious of his fellow publishers who controlled the AP. He did not take his papers into the AP in 1897, when the old UP folded.

"I knew that at least 90 percent of my fellows in American journalism were capitalistic and conservative," he explained. He went on:

> I knew that, at that time at least, unless I came into the field with a new service, it would be impossible for the people of the United States to get correct news through the medium of the Associated Press. . . . I have made it impossible for the men who control the Associated Press to suppress the truth, or successfully to disseminate falsehood.[31]

The rebellious Scripps was undoubtedly too critical of his fellow publishers, but his concept of competing press associations acting as checks on each other proved to be of inestimable value to American journalism.

Scripps had other reasons for establishing his own news service. The AP was most interested in the news report for its big morning-paper members, and Scripps published evening papers. The closed-membership character of the AP meant that Scripps would have trouble obtaining memberships for the new dailies he was establishing. If he ran his own news service, he could fashion its coverage and writing style to better serve the Scripps type of paper. And finally, he expected to make money running a press association.

THE SECOND UNITED PRESS, 1907, AND ROY HOWARD

After operating two regional news services for his own papers in the Middle West and West for 10 years, Scripps merged them in 1907 with the Publishers' Press Association (begun in 1898 by non-AP Eastern papers) to form the United

Press Associations. A young Scripps newspaperperson named John Vandercook helped create the merger and became head of the United Press, but he died the following year. Succeeding him as general manager was 25-year-old Roy W. Howard, destined to eventually dominate the Scripps publishing empire. Howard had served on the *St. Louis Post-Dispatch* and the Scripps papers in Indianapolis and Cincinnati before getting his big chance with the UP. Scripps described the Roy Howard of this period as

> a striking individual, very small of stature, with a large head and speaking countenance, and eyes that appeared to be windows for a rather unusual intellect. His manner was forceful, and the reverse from modest. Gall was written all over his face. It was in every tone and every word he voiced. There was ambition, self-respect and forcefulness oozing out of every pore of his body.[32]

Howard hustled abroad and established bureaus in the major European capitals. He made connections with leading foreign papers and with commercial news agencies not allied with the AP. Howard's biggest break came when the British cut off the cabling of the German news service to belligerents and neutrals during World War I. Two leading Argentine newspapers, *La Prensa* and *La Nación,* rebelled against receiving only the one-sided reports of the French Havas agency and requested Associated Press service. The AP, under its contract agreements, could not enter the South American area, and Howard rapidly rushed in to give the Argentine papers the type of war-news coverage they wanted. Soon UP was on the way to building up an extensive string of clients in South America and established its own bureaus there.

But Howard and the United Press came a cropper in November, 1918, just when the UP was winning attention. Howard was in American naval headquarters at Brest on November 7 when a message arrived from Paris saying the Armistice had been signed at 11 o'clock that morning. Howard flashed the news to the New York UP office, and by an incredible stroke of bad luck for his news service, the message passed the censors. The UP bulletin set off wild celebrations in the United States—until several hours later the AP broke the news that the UP had cabled a premature report. Although Howard argued that he did what any newsperson would have done when he saw the message at naval headquarters (he decided later that the message had originated with a German secret agent in Paris), some telegraph editors never again fully trusted the UP. Even when, in the 1930s, the AP flashed the wrong verdict on the outcome of the trial of Bruno Richard Hauptmann for the kidnapping and murder of the Lindbergh baby, and when, in 1944, the AP flashed the news of the D-Day landing in France prematurely, oldtime newspersons still recalled how "Roy Howard ended the first World War four days early."[33]

The United Press survived the false Armistice Day report, however. When Howard left it in 1920 to become a partner in the Scripps newspaper chain, the UP had 780 clients and a fairly good news service. Scripps, who held 51 percent of the controlling common stock, estimated that he received $200,000 in dividends during the first 10 years. In the Scripps custom, the remaining 49 percent of the stock went to key United Press people. The intangible "good will" assets were then valued at $2.5 million by Howard.[34]

A common saying among young, low-paid UP reporters was, "They pay you with bylines." Early in its career, the UP began giving enthusiastic young staffers some glory and a chance to develop their own writing styles and news specialties. AP reporters covering World War I were largely anonymous newsgatherers. The UP turned loose young correspondents like Webb Miller, Fred S. Ferguson, William Philip Simms, William G. Shepherd, and Westbrook Pegler. Their vividly written and interpretative copy attracted attention and helped to sell the UP service as a second wire for AP member papers. Miller became European news manager and stayed in command until he was killed in a London blackout early in World War II. Pegler became a widely syndicated columnist, as did three UP Washington staffers of the 1920s: Thomas L. Stokes, Paul Mallon, and Raymond Clapper.

THE INTERNATIONAL NEWS SERVICE, 1909

The third American press association competitor has been the International News Service. Smaller than its rivals and later in establishing itself as a comprehensive news service, the INS nevertheless won prominence for its competitive spirit.

The INS was founded in 1909 as an outgrowth of earlier leased wire facilities of the Hearst newspapers. Richard A. Farrelly was its first manager. By 1918 the INS was serving 400 clients and had a leased wire system approximately half as extensive as those of the AP and UP.

The sparkplug of the INS after 1916 was Barry Faris, editor-in-chief. He established fewer bureaus than the other services, concentrating INS resources on the major news centers. His most successful plan was to offer well-known bylines and special coverage of major news events by talented writers. H. R. Knickerbocker, a Pulitzer Prize winner, and Floyd Gibbons were two longtime INS foreign correspondents. James L. Kilgallen began his roving coverage of major national stories in 1921.

THE FEATURE SYNDICATES: ENTERTAINMENT

The impact of the syndicates on newspaper content was heaviest in the nonnews field. The first to relieve newspaper editors of the necessity of clipping column material, fiction, poetry, and other entertainment features from newspaper and magazine exchanges was Ansel N. Kellogg, the Baraboo, Wisconsin, newsperson who founded a ready-print service in Chicago during the Civil War years. One side of the newsprint sheets was left blank for local news and ads. By 1875 stereotyped plates were being supplied to papers by the American Press Association. The giant of the field became the Western Newspaper Union, founded in Des Moines in 1872 and run by George A. Joslyn after 1890. Joslyn eliminated his rivals by 1917 and refined the "patented insides" business, offering editors alternative preprinted materials. The service, which was supplied to nearly 7000 papers at its peak, gradually declined and was abandoned in 1952.

While the Western Newspaper Union was developing in the weekly field, dailies were being offered syndicated literary material by the feature services of Irving Bacheller (1883), S. S. McClure (1884), and Edward W. Bok (1886). McClure and Bok sensed the public demand for entertaining reading, which led to their own more famous careers as magazine publishers. Hearst joined the syndicate movement in 1895, and in 1914 began his King Features Syndicate. George Matthew Adams entered the field in 1907 and John N. Wheeler in 1913.

The early syndicates featured the writings of Robert Louis Stevenson, Rudyard Kipling, Mark Twain, Bret Harte, Henry James, Alfred Henry Lewis, Jack London, and other literary greats. They also could sample the work of a notable group of poetically inclined columnists and humorous writers, which appeared in newspapers throughout the country. Syndication spread the fame of "M Quad" of the *Detroit Free Press* and *New York Herald;* Bill Nye of Laramie, Wyoming, and the *New York World;* David Ross Locke of the *Toledo Blade,* who created Petroleum V. Nasby; Opie Read of *Arkansaw Traveler* fame; Joel Chandler Harris of the *Atlanta Constitution;* and Finley Peter Dunne, the Chicago newspaperman whose "Mr. Dooley"—a saloon keeper who philosophized on current affairs—became a national institution.

To older newspaperpeople a column was "a little of everything": wit, poetry, sentiment, and comment on personalities and events in the news. One such column conductor was Eugene Field, the St.Louis and Kansas City reporter whom Melville E. Stone brought to the *Chicago Daily News* to write his "Sharps and Flats" before 1900. Another was Bert Leston Taylor, who founded the *Chicago Tribune*'s famed "A Line o' Type or Two" column in 1901. A third was Franklin P. Adams, who wrote for the *Chicago Journal* and *New York Mail* before beginning his "Conning Tower" in the *New York Tribune* in 1914. Don Marquis wrote his "Sun Dial" column, inhabited by "archie," the noncapitalizing cockroach, for the *New York Sun.*

Walter Winchell set the pace for another kind of column. A New Yorker who entered journalism with the racy tabloids of the 1920s, Winchell promoted the "gossip" column as the Broadway reporter of the tabloid *Graphic.* He shifted to the *Mirror* in 1929 and became a star of Hearst's King Features Syndicate. No other columnist ever approached Winchell's sensationalism and intimate coverage of private lives, but such Hollywood columnists as Louella Parsons and Hedda Hopper did their best. Earl Wilson, Leonard Lyons, and Dorothy Kilgallen were other New York scene columnists of the personal type, while O. O. McIntyre and Mark Hellinger wrote about the metropolis in an older literary style.

NOTES

1. Richard O'Connor, *Pacific Destiny* (Boston: Little, Brown, 1969), p. 256.

2. Carl Schurz, "Manifest Destiny," *Harper's* (October 1893), 737–46, as cited by William Appleman Williams in *The Roots of the Modern American Empire* (New York: Random House, 1969), p. 365, as part of Williams' contention that the agricultural majority played the prime role in forcing the war against Spain in order to open more markets. Also see his *The Contours of American History* (Cleveland: World Publishing, 1961, reissued 1973) for an analysis of the effects of Frederick Jackson Turner's frontier theory on U. S. expansion, and the relationship between expansionism and the reform movement.

3. As cited by Leon Wolff in his *Little Brown Brother* (New York: Doubleday, 1961), p. 270.

4. One documented study of the period is Harold U. Faulkner, *The Quest for Social Justice, 1898–1914* (New York: Macmillan, 1931). A full and fascinating account by a journalistic historian is found in the first three volumes of Mark Sullivan, *Our Times* (New York: Scribner's, 1926 ff.). For a revisionist study with a New Left emphasis, see Gabriel Kolko, *The Triumph of Conservatism: A Reinterpretation of American History, 1900–1916* (Chicago: Quadrangle Books, 1967).

5. Louis Hartz in *The Liberal Tradition in America*

(New York: Harcourt Brace Jovanovich, 1955), p. 6, offers this explanation: "It is not accidental that America which has uniquely lacked a feudal tradition has uniquely lacked also a socialist tradition. The hidden origin of socialist thought everywhere in the West is to be found in the feudal ethos."

6. Marion Marzolf, *Up From the Footnote: A History of Women Journalists* (New York: Hastings House, 1977), pp. 219 ff.

7. David Paul Nord, "The *Appeal to Reason* and American Socialism, 1901–1920," *Kansas History*, I (Summer 1978), 75.

8. See Félix Gutiérrez, "Latinos and the Media," in Michael Emery and Ted Curtis Smythe, *Readings in Mass Communication* (Dubuque, Iowa: William C. Brown, 1983), p. 163.

9. Armistead Scott Pride, "Negro Newspapers: Yesterday, Today and Tomorrow," *Journalism Quarterly*, XXVIII (Spring 1951), 179.

10. Substantial accounts of leading black papers can be found in Roland E. Wolseley, *The Black Press, U.S.A.* (Iowa: Iowa State University Press, 1971).

11. Wolsley, *The Black Press*, pp. 136–39, discusses *The Crisis.*

12. For a sketch of Cobb and a collection of his important editorials, see John L. Heaton, *Cobb of "The World"* (New York: Dutton, 1924).

13. W. A. Swanberg, in *Citizen Hearst* (New York: Scribner's, 1961), contends that the Hearst of 1904 presidential ambitions was not a demagogue but sincerely believed he was the best-fitted Democrat to run. For his estimates of Hearst, see pages 208–19 for this period, and the summation, pages 523–27, in which he concludes that Hearst was two men, "a Prospero and a Caliban."

14. *Los Angeles Examiner*, December 12, 1903, p. 4.

15. As quoted in Oliver H. Knight, ed., *I Protest: The Selected Disquisitions of E. W. Scripps* (Madison: University of Wisconsin Press, 1966), p. 270. Knight edited from the Scripps papers a variety of Scripps' personal views that establish the publisher as a thinking observer of American affairs.

16. The editorial is reprinted in *The Autobiography of William Allen White* (New York: Macmillan, 1946), pp. 280–83. It also appears in Allan Nevins, *American Press Opinion* (Boston: Heath, 1928), pp. 419–22.

17. One account, not confined to this period, is Silas Bent, *Newspaper Crusaders* (New York: Whittlesey House, 1939). Another is Jonathan Daniels, *They Will Be Heard: America's Crusading Newspaper Editors* (New York: McGraw-Hill, 1965).

18. The full story was first told in C. C. Regier, *The Era of the Muckrakers* (Chapel Hill: University of North Carolina Press, 1932). However, Regier ignored the contributions of the newspapers in crusading and thus distorts the picture. See the following Bibliography for other references.

19. *New York Times*, August 19, 1896.

20. See Davis, *History of the New York Times* p. 274, and Berger, *The Story of the New York Times*, p. 160, for two estimates of Van Anda's role in building the *Times.* Many tributes to Van Anda from leaders in his profession are found in a short biography: Barnett Fine, *A Giant of the Press* (New York: Editor & Publisher Library, 1933). Berger carries the story of Van Anda's achievements through several chapters.

21. For the full story of the "Titanic" coverage see Berger, *The Story of the New York Times*, pp. 193–201. A contemporary account by Alexander McD. Stoddart appeared in the *Independent*, LXII (May 2, 1912), 945.

22. *New York Times*, October 18, 1907.

23. See, for example, *Herald* pages in Michael C. Emery *et al.*, *America's Front Page News, 1690–1970* (New York: Doubleday, 1970), pp. 83, 104, 109, 124.

24. Don C. Seitz, *The James Gordon Bennetts* (Indianapolis: Bobbs-Merrill, 1928), p. 377.

25. In *Outing*, LIII (March 1909), 690.

26. Some of the color of the *Sun* is found in Frank M. O'Brien, *The Story of The Sun* (New York: George H. Doran Company, 1918). Church's "Is There a Santa Claus?" is reprinted on pp. 409–10.

27. The story of the *Inter Ocean* is told in Walter E. Ewert, "The History of the Chicago *Inter Ocean*, 1872–1914" (Master thesis, Northwestern University, 1940).

28. See Jack R. Hart, *The Information Empire* (Washington, D.C.: University Press of America, 1981).

29. Victor Rosewater, *History of Cooperative News-Gathering in the United States* (New York: Appleton-Century-Crofts, 1930), pp. 182–89.

30. For a description of Stone's activities see *"M.E.S."—His Book* (New York: Harper & Row, 1918).

31. As quoted in Rosewater, *History of Cooperative News-Gathering*, p. 354.

32. As quoted in Charles R. McCabe, ed., *Damned Old Crank* (New York: Harper & Row, 1951), p. 219.

33. Howard gave his explanation in Webb Miller, *I Found No Peace* (New York: Simon & Schuster, 1936), p. 96. The Associated Press blunder on the Hauptmann verdict stemmed from the setting up of a signal system to get the news out of the courtroom. An overanxious AP man got the wrong signal and flashed news of a life sentence when the verdict was death. The premature 1944 D-Day flash by AP was sent by a woman teletype operator who was "practicing," the AP said. The UP was similarly victimized by an employee who flashed the end of the Japanese war prematurely in 1945.

34. McCabe, *Damned Old Crank*, p. 204.

ANNOTATED BIBLIOGRAPHY

For references to the literature about Pulitzer see the Bibliography for Chapter 16; for the Hearst references see Chapter 17. Volume IV of Mott's *History of American Magazines* covers this period (see Chapter 15).

Books: Background History

CORNWELL, ELMER E., JR., *Presidential Leadership of Public Opinion.* Bloomington: Indiana University Press, 1965. The press conference from Theodore Roosevelt to John Kennedy.

DALLEK, ROBERT, *The American Style of Foreign Policy.* New York: Knopf, 1983. A provocative synthesis.

ELLIS, ELMER, *Mr. Dooley's America.* New York: Knopf, 1941. The life and times of Finley Peter Dunne, humorist and reformer.

FAULKNER, HAROLD U., *The Quest for Social Justice, 1898–1914.* A History of American Life, Volume XI. New York: Macmillan, 1931. This volume of the series measures up as a work of social history.

FLEXNER, ELEANOR, *Century of Struggle.* Cambridge, Mass.: Belknap Press, 1959. Leading history of the women's equality movement.

HOFSTADTER, RICHARD, *The Age of Reform.* New York: Knopf, 1955. From Bryan to FDR, the populists, progressives, and liberals wend their way.

JOHNSON, WALTER, *William Allen White's America.* New York: Holt, Rinehart & Winston, 1947. Important as an interpretation of the swiftly changing half-century in which White was a national figure.

KOLKO, GABRIEL, *The Triumph of Conservatism: A Reinterpretation of American History, 1900–1916.* Chicago: Quadrangle, 1967. A revisionist study by a leading New Left historian.

LASCH, CHRISTOPHER, *The New Radicalism in America, 1889–1963.* New York: Knopf, 1965. A New Left historian examines social reform through essays about intellectual writers.

LINK, ARTHUR S., *Woodrow Wilson and the Progressive Era, 1910–1917.* New York: Harper & Row, 1954. A volume in the New American Nation series by the biographer of Wilson.

MAY, HENRY F., *The End of American Innocence.* New York: Knopf, 1969. Intellectual history of the period from 1912 to 1917.

MOWRY, GEORGE E., *Theodore Roosevelt and the Progressive Movement.* Madison: University of Wisconsin Press, 1946. Traces the relationship of Roosevelt to radicalism.

O'CONNOR, RICHARD, *Pacific Destiny: An Informal History of the U.S. in the Far East.* Boston: Little, Brown, 1969. Traces expansionism from 1854 to 1968.

PRINGLE, HENRY F., *Theodore Roosevelt.* New York: Harcourt Brace Jovanovich, 1931. A Pulitzer Prize biography of the key figure of the muckraking era by a former newspaperperson.

REGIER, C. C., *The Era of the Muckrakers.* Chapel Hill: University of North Carolina Press, 1932. An exhaustive study of the crusading magazines and their writers.

SCHALLER, MICHAEL, *The United States and China in the Twentieth Century.* New York: Oxford University Press, 1979. Succinct 200-page account of major events.

SHAPIRO, ROBERT, *A Turning Wheel.* New York: Random House, 1979. Thirty years of Asian revolution, by a *New Yorker* correspondent.

SULLIVAN, MARK, *Our Times.* New York: Scribner's, 1926 ff. Newspaperman Sullivan's six volumes are crowded with the color and the drama of the years 1900 to 1929.

THOMSON, JAMES C., JR., PETER W. STANLEY, AND JOHN CURTIS PERRY, *Sentimental Imperialists: The American Experience in East Asia.* New York: Harper & Row, 1981. Dovish view of Far East mistakes, 1784 to Vietnam, by three Far East scholars.

WELCH, RICHARD E., JR., *Response to Imperialism: The United States and the Philippine-American War, 1899–1902.* Chapel Hill: University of North Carolina Press, 1979. A public-opinion study; the first comprehensive treatment of that war's press coverage.

WILLIAMS, WILLIAM APPLEMAN, *The Roots of the Modern American Empire.* New York: Random House, 1969. A leader of New Left historians dissents from United States foreign policy since the 1890s. See also Williams, *The Contours of American History,* (Cleveland: World Publishing, 1961, reissued 1973).

———, *Empire as a Way of Life.* New York: Oxford University Press, 1980. An essay tracing the theme of imperialism in the United States from colonial times.

Books: Newspapers

BERGER, MEYER, *The Story of the New York Times, 1851–1951.* New York: Simon & Schuster, 1951. Mainly the story of the *Times* after Ochs bought it; other books are better for the pre-Ochs period. But reporter Berger gets many reporters into his story, too rare an event in newspaper history telling, and thus has a lively and interesting book. The *Times* also issued *One Hundred Years of Famous Pages from The New York Times* in its centennial year, and many later reprint volumes.

BOND, F. FRASER, *Mr. Miller of "The Times."* New York: Scribner's, 1931. The biography of *New York Times* editor Charles R. Miller.

BRITT, ALBERT, *Ellen Browning Scripps: Journalist and Idealist.* London: Oxford University Press, 1961. Adds to the early Scripps story when Ellen worked with and advised E. W.

COCHRAN, NEGLEY D., *E. W. Scripps.* New York: Harcourt Brace Jovanovich, 1933. A more factual biography than Gilson Gardner's *Lusty Scripps* (New York: Vanguard, 1932).

DANIELS, JOSEPHUS, *Tar Heel Editor.* Chapel Hill: University of North Carolina Press, 1939. This first volume of the Daniels autobiography deals with his early newspaper career.

DAVIS, ELMER, *History of the New York Times, 1851–1921.* New York: The New York Times, 1921. Still good for its period.

Editorials from the Hearst Newspapers. New York: Albertson Publishing, 1906. Selected reprints of the Hearst editorial-page offerings at the turn of the century.

ELLIS, ELMER, ed., *Mr. Dooley at His Best.* New York: Scribner's, 1938. Writings of Finley Peter Dunne, the famed Chicago columnist.

FINE, BARNETT, *A Giant of the Press.* New York: Editor & Publisher Library, 1933. A short biography of Carr Van Anda, managing editor of the *New York Times.*

HARRISON, JOHN M., *The Man Who Made Nasby, David Ross Locke.* Chapel Hill: University of North Carolina Press, 1969. An excellent biography of the editor of the *Toledo Blade,* who was the creator of Petroleum V. Nasby.

HEATON, JOHN L., *Cobb of "The World."* New York: Dutton, 1924. Includes a sketch of Frank I. Cobb and a collection of his *New York World* editorials.

HOWE, E. W., *Plain People.* New York: Dodd, Mead, 1929. The story of an unusual small-town Kansas editor in the usual small town, and of the *Atchison Globe.*

HUDSON, ROBERT V., *The Writing Game: A Biography of Will Irwin.* Ames: Iowa State University Press, 1982. Definitive study of Irwin's professional work and life.

JOHNSON, GERALD W., *An Honorable Titan.* New York: Harper & Row, 1946. A good, but comparatively uncritical, biographical study of Adolph S. Ochs.

JUERGENS, GEORGE, *News from the White House.* Chicago: University of Chicago Press, 1981. Presidential-press relationships in the Roosevelt and Wilson eras.

KNIGHT, OLIVER H., ed., *I Protest: Selected Disquisitions of E. W. Scripps.* Madison: University of Wisconsin Press, 1966. An admirable, condensed biography is followed by Scripps' private writings as a "thinker." Best book on Scripps.

LINN, JAMES W., *James Keeley, Newspaperman.* Indianapolis: Bobbs-Merrill, 1937. The biography of the *Chicago Tribune*'s crusading managing editor.

LITTLEFIELD, ROY EVERETT, III, *William Randolph Hearst: His Role in American Progressivism.* Lanham, Md.: University Press of America, 1980. Hearst of 1895 to 1920 played a progressive role as reformist, social activist. See Carlisle listing in the Chapter 21 Bibliography.

MCRAE, MILTON A., *Forty Years in Newspaperdom.* New York: Brentano's, 1924. Autobiography of E. W. Scripps' partner and business manager.

MAHIN, HELEN O., ed., *The Editor and His People.* New York: Macmillan, 1924. An excellent collection of William Allen White's editorials.

MARZOLF, MARION, *Up From the Footnote: A History of Women Journalists.* New York: Hastings House, 1977. Includes one chapter on the women's movement.

MITCHELL, EDWARD P., *Memoirs of an Editor.* New York: Scribner's, 1924. By the distinguished editor of the *New York Sun.*

MORRISON, JOSEPH L., *Josephus Daniels Says.*

Chapel Hill: University of North Carolina Press, 1962. Detailed biography of the editor of the Raleigh *News-Observer* from 1894 to 1913; his crusading battles, his white supremacy. See also the political biography, *Josephus Daniels: The-Small-d Democrat* (1966).

NEVINS, ALLAN, *American Press Opinion.* New York: Heath, 1928. Nevins' brilliant interpretative essays and selected editorials continue through this period.

NORD, DAVID PAUL, *Newspapers and New Politics: Midwestern Municipal Reform 1890–1900.* Ann Arbor: UMI Research Press, 1981). Based on a 1979 Ph.D. thesis, University of Wisconsin. Reform succeeds in Chicago, fails in St. Louis. See Nord, "The Politics of Agenda Setting in Late Nineteenth Century Cities," *Journalism Quarterly,* LVIII (Winter 1981), 563.

OLDER, FREMONT, *My Own Story.* New York: Macmillan, 1926. The fighting San Francisco editor tells his piece.

PICKETT, CALDER M., *Ed Howe: Country Town Philosopher.* Lawrence: University Press of Kansas, 1969. Prize-winning biography of the editor of the *Atchison Globe.*

SEITZ, DON C., *The James Gordon Bennetts.* Indianapolis: Bobbs-Merrill, 1928. The younger Bennett brings the *New York Herald* to its downfall.

WHITE, WILLIAM ALLEN, *The Autobiography of William Allen White.* New York: Macmillan, 1946. No one should miss this autobiography, and few do. See also John D. McKee, *William Allen White: Maverick on Main Street.* Westport, Conn.: Greenwood Press, 1975.

Books: Magazines, Muckraking

BAKER, RAY STANNARD, *An American Chronicle.* New York: Scribner's, 1945. The autobiography of one of the *McClure's* writers.

BANNISTER, ROBERT C., *Ray Stannard Baker: The Mind and Thought of a Progressive.* New Haven: Yale University Press, 1966. One of the reporters for *McClure's.*

BOK, EDWARD W., *The Americanization of Edward Bok.* New York: Scribner's, 1920. The famous autobiography of the editor of the *Ladies' Home Journal.*

CHALMERS, DAVID M., *The Social and Political Ideas of the Muckrakers.* New York: The Citadel Press, 1964. A brief analysis of thirteen muckrakers.

FILLER, LOUIS, *Crusaders for American Liberalism.* New York: Harcourt Brace Jovanovich, 1939. A study of the 1902 to 1914 muckrakers based on the politics of the era. Updated to the 1970s in *The Muckrakers* (University Park: Pennsylvania State University Press, 1976).

FORCEY, CHARLES, *The Crossroads of Liberalism.* New York: Oxford University Press, 1961. A case study of Herbert Croly, Walter Weyl, Walter Lippmann, and the 1914 *New Republic.*

HAPGOOD, NORMAN, *The Changing Years.* New York: Holt, Rinehart & Winston, 1930. Reflections of the editor of *Collier's.*

KAPLAN, JUSTIN, *Lincoln Steffens: A Biography.* New York: Simon & Schuster, 1974. Points to discrepancy between Steffens' autobiography and real life.

LYON, PETER, *Success Story: The Life and Times of S. S. McClure.* New York: Scribner's, 1963. His muckraking magazine provides the climax of this prize-winning biography.

MARCOSSON, ISAAC F., *David Graham Phillips and His Times.* New York: Dodd, Mead, 1932. The biography of a muckraker.

MCCLURE, S. S., *My Autobiography.* New York: Frederick A. Stokes & Company, 1914. The story of the magazine publisher.

O'CONNOR, RICHARD, *Jack London.* Boston: Little, Brown, 1964. A popular biography.

PHILLIPS, DAVID GRAHAM, *The Treason of the Senate,* edited by George E. Mowry and Judson A. Grenier. Chicago: Quadrangle, 1964. Excellent discussion by the editors precedes the texts of Phillips' famed articles in *Cosmopolitan.*

SEDGWICK, ELLERY, *The Happy Profession.* Boston: Little, Brown, 1946. Includes a description of the hurly-burly times at *Leslie's,* the *American,* and *McClure's* before Sedgwick became owner and editor of the *Atlantic* in 1909.

STEFFENS, LINCOLN, *The Autobiography of Lincoln Steffens.* New York: Harcourt Brace Jovanovich, 1931. One of the great journalistic autobiographies.

TARBELL, IDA M., *All in the Day's Work.* New York: Macmillan, 1939. The chief woman muckraker reviews her career.

TOMKINS, MARY E., *Ida M. Tarbell.* New York:

Twayne, 1974. Brief but scholarly biography; explains how Tarbell made her mark at a time when newswomen were scarce.

VILLARD, OSWALD GARRISON, *Fighting Years.* New York: Harcourt Brace Jovanovich, 1939. The autobiography of the publisher of the *Nation* and *New York Post.*

WEINBERG, ARTHUR AND LILA, eds., *The Muckrakers.* New York: Simon & Schuster, 1961. A compilation of some of the best magazine articles by the muckrakers.

WILSON, HAROLD S., *McClure's Magazine and the Muckrakers.* Princeton, N.J.: Princeton University Press, 1970. Solid contribution to the subject.

Books: Alternative Press, Minorities, Foreign-Language Press

BACKLUND, JONAS O., *A Century of the Swedish-American Press.* Chicago: Swedish-American Newspaper Co., 1952. Nearly all were rural weeklies.

BULLOCK, PENELOPE L., *The Afro-American Periodical Press, 1839–1909.* Baton Rouge: Louisiana State University Press, 1981. Precedes in time Abby and Roland Johnson, *Propaganda and Aesthetics: The Literary Politics of Afro-American Magazines in the Twentieth Century* (Amherst: University of Massachusetts, 1979).

BUNI, ANDREW, *Robert L. Vann of the Pittsburgh Courier: Politics and Black Journalism.* Pittsburgh: University of Pittsburgh Press, 1974.

CLARKE, JOHN H., ET AL., *Black Titan W. E. B. Du Bois: An Anthology by the Editors of Freedomways.* Boston: Beacon Press, 1970. Writings about Du Bois, first editor of *The Crisis* and legendary black leader.

CONLIN, JOSEPH R., ed., *The American Radical Press, 1880–1960.* Westport, Conn.: Greenwood Press, 1974. Collection of articles; includes *Appeal to Reason.*

DETWEILER, FREDERICK G., *The Negro Press in the United States.* Chicago: University of Chicago Press, 1922. Basic historical study together with Vishnu V. Oak, *The Negro Press* (Yellow Springs, Ohio: Antioch Press, 1948).

DU BOIS, W. E. B., *The Autobiography of W. E. Burghardt Du Bois.* New York: International Publishers, 1968. Written at age 90 by the editor of *The Crisis* as volume three of his autobiography.

FOX, STEPHEN R., *The Guardian of Boston: William Monroe Trotter.* New York: Atheneum, 1971. Trotter's *Guardian* was one of the leading black papers of 1900 to 1920.

MARZOLF, MARION T., *The Danish-Language Press in America.* New York: Arno Press, 1979. Based on Ph.D. thesis, University of Michigan, 1972. Small ethnic press grew from 1872 to 1914.

PARK, ROBERT E., *The Immigrant Press and Its Control.* New York: Harper, 1922. Descriptive and analytical. Finds high point of 1323 papers in the United States in 1917.

PRIDE, ARMISTEAD, *The Black Press: A Bibliography.* Jefferson City, Mo.: Lincoln University Department of Journalism, 1968. Major scholarly effort.

THORNBROUGH, EMMA L., *T. Thomas Fortune: Militant Journalist.* Chicago: University of Chicago Press, 1972. Black editor of the *People's Advocate.*

WELLS-BARNETT, IDA B., *Crusade for Justice.* Chicago: University of Chicago Press, 1970. Writings of a black journalist and reformer, 1887–1931, edited by John Hope Franklin.

WITTKE, CARL F., *The German-Language Press in America.* Lexington: University of Kentucky Press, 1957. A history from 1732 to 1956.

WOLSELEY, ROLAND E., *The Black Press, U.S.A.* Ames: Iowa State University Press, 1971. A comprehensive survey, with substantial historical material for black newspapers, magazines, and broadcasting.

Books: Press Associations, Syndicates

DESMOND, ROBERT W., *The Information Process: World News Reporting to the Twentieth Century.* Iowa City: University of Iowa Press, 1978. Most exhaustive scholarly study of news agencies, leading publications. See also Desmond, *The Press and World Affairs.* (New York: Appleton-Century-Crofts, 1937).

———, *Windows on the World: World News Reporting 1900–1920.* Iowa City: University of Iowa Press, 1980. Includes detailed accounts of the AP, UP, INS, and other news agencies.

MCCABE, CHARLES R., ed., *Damned Old Crank.* New York: Harper & Row, 1951. Contains a chapter in which E. W. Scripps explains why he started the United Press, and gives some financial details.

"M. E. S." His Book. New York: Harper &

Row, 1918. A book commemorating Melville E. Stone's first 25 years as Associated Press general manager. Much of Stone's own writing and his major speeches are included along with other historical materials. See also Stone's autobiography, *Fifty Years a Journalist.*

MORRIS, JOE ALEX, *Deadline Every Minute: The Story of the United Press.* New York: Doubleday, 1957. By a UP staff member, observing the press association's fiftieth anniversary. Highly readable; covers both UP executives and newspeople.

ROSEWATER, VICTOR, *History of Cooperative News-Gathering in the United States.* New York: Appleton-Century-Crofts, 1930. The authoritative source for the rise of the press associations.

WATSON, ELMO SCOTT, *A History of Newspaper Syndicates in the United States, 1865–1935.* Chicago: Publishers' Auxiliary, 1936. Source for the story of the Western Newspaper Union and for the rise of other early syndicates.

Periodicals and Monographs

ABBOT, WILLIS J., "Melville E. Stone's Own Story," *Collier's,* LXV (February 7, 1920), 51. A well-written portrait of the AP general manager.

COOPER, ANNE M., "Suffrage as News: Ten Dailies' coverage of the Nineteenth Amendment," *American Journalism,* I (Summer 1983), 73. Content analysis and evaluation.

DORWART, JEFFERY M., "James Creelman, the New York *World* and the Port Arthur Massacre," *Journalism Quarterly,* L (Winter 1973), 697. Eyewitness report.

ERICKSON, JOHN E., "Newspapers and Social Values: Chicago Journalism, 1890–1910," Ph.D. thesis, University of Illinois, 1973. Press reported and embodied values marking entry into the twentieth century.

EWERT, WALTER E., "The History of the Chicago *Inter Ocean,* 1872–1914," Master's thesis, Northwestern University, 1940. An excellent account of a famous paper.

FINE, BARNETT, "When 'Boss' Lord Ruled 'The Sun,' " *Editor & Publisher,* LXVI (April 22–July 15, 1933). A series of articles about Chester S. Lord, managing editor of the *New York Sun* during 33 of its best years.

FOLKERTS, JEAN LANGE, "William Allen White's Anti-Populist Rhetoric as an Agenda-Setting Technique," *Journalism Quarterly,* LX (Spring 1983), 28. Based on Ph.D. thesis, University of Kansas, 1981 (author, Lange).

FRANCKE, WARREN T., "Investigative Exposure in the Nineteenth Century: The Journalistic Heritage of the Muckrakers," Ph.D. thesis, University of Minnesota, 1974. Muckraking proves to be part of earlier reporting tradition.

GATEWOOD, WILLARD B., JR., "A Negro Editor on Imperialism: John Mitchell, 1898–1901," *Journalism Quarterly,* XLIX (Spring 1972), 43. Mitchell saw the claims of liberating peoples from Spain as a mask for American imperialism.

GRENIER, JUDSON A., "Muckraking and the Muckrakers: An Historical Definition," *Journalism Quarterly,* XXXVII (Autumn 1960), 552. A study of the years 1902 to 1914.

GROSE, CHARLES W., "A Century of Black Newspapers in Texas, 1868–1969," Ph.D. thesis, University of Texas, 1972. Depression broke GOP's hold on them.

HARRISON, JOHN M., "Finley Peter Dunne and the Progressive Movement," *Journalism Quarterly,* XLIV (Autumn 1967), 475. Mr. Dooley's creator was a philosophical anarchist.

HOWE, GENE, "My Father Was the Most Wretchedly Unhappy Man I Ever Knew," *Saturday Evening Post,* October 25, 1941. A dramatic story about E. W. Howe, reprinted in Drewry, *Post Biographies.*

HUDSON, ROBERT V., "Will Irwin's Pioneering Criticism of the Press," *Journalism Quarterly,* XLVII (Summer 1970), 263. Based on his biography of Will Irwin, Ph.D. thesis, University of Minnesota, 1970. Authoritative biographical writing.

IRWIN WILL, "The New York Sun," *American Magazine,* LXVII (January 1909), 301. The story of the *Sun's* school of journalism by one of the pupils.

———, "United Press," *Harper's Weekly,* LVIII (April 25, 1914), 6. An estimate by a top-flight newsman of early UP progress.

KESSLER, LAUREN J., "A Siege of the Citadels: Access of Women Suffrage to the Oregon Press, 1884–1912," Ph.D. thesis, University of Washington, 1980.

KIELBOWICZ, RICHARD B., "The Limits of the Press as an Agent of Reform: Minneapolis

1900–1905," *Journalism Quarterly,* LIX (Spring 1982), 21. Minimizes influence.

KIMBROUGH, MARVIN G., "W. E. B. Du Bois as Editor of the *Crisis,*" Ph.D. thesis, University of Texas, 1974. Study of NAACP's paper from 1910 to 1934.

KNIGHT, OLIVER, "Scripps and His Adless Newspaper, *The Day Book,*" *Journalism Quarterly,* XLI (Winter 1964), 51. Full story of the effort to create an adless daily.

KREILING, ALBERT L., "The Making of Racial Identities in the Black Press: A Cultural Analysis of Race Journalism in Chicago, 1878–1929," Ph.D. thesis, University of Illinois, 1973. Differing cultural groups find expression.

MASEL-WALTERS, LYNNE, " 'Their Rights and Nothing More': A History of *The Revolution,* 1868–70," *Journalism Quarterly,* LIII (Summer 1976), 242–51. Details the beginning of women's political journalism and a short-lived national publication. Also see Masel-Walters, "A Burning Cloud by Day: The History and Content of the 'Woman's Journal,' " *Journalism History,* III (Winter 1976–77), 103. Organ of the feminist movement from 1869 to 1931.

MATHER, ANNE, "A History of Feminist Periodicals," *Journalism History,* I–II (Autumn 1974–Spring 1975). Three-part article.

MCGLASHAN, ZENA BETH, "Club 'Ladies' and Working 'Girls': Rheta Childe Dorr and the *New York Evening Post,*" *Journalism History,* VIII (Spring 1981), 7. Turn of century.

NATHAN, GEORGE JEAN, "James Gordon Bennett, the Monte Cristo of Modern Journalism," *Outing,* LIII (March 1909), 690. The dramatic critic criticizes an erratic publisher.

NORD, DAVID PAUL, "The *Appeal to Reason* and American Socialism, 1901–1920," *Kansas History,* I (Summer 1978), 75. Sixty-issue sampling of leading Socialist weekly.

PRIDE, ARMISTEAD SCOTT, comp., "The Black Press to 1968: A Bibliography," *Journalism History,* IV (Winter 1977–78), 148. Books by subject areas.

———, "Negro Newspapers: Yesterday, Today and Tomorrow," *Journalism Quarterly,* XXVIII (Spring 1951), 179. Report on statistical survey from 1827 to 1951.

PRINGLE, HENRY F., "The Newspaper Man as an Artist," *Scribner's,* XCVII (February 1935), 101. The artist was Frank I. Cobb, editor of the *World.*

SARASOHN, DAVID, "Power Without Glory: Hearst in the Progressive Era," *Journalism Quarterly,* LII (Autumn 1976), 474. Examines Hearst's power and his squandering of political capital.

SIMS, NORMAN H., "The Chicago Style of Journalism," Ph.D. thesis, University of Illinois, 1979. Features Opie Read, George Ade, Ben Hecht, Whitechapel Club.

STARR, LOUIS M., "Joseph Pulitzer and His Most 'Indegoddampendent' Editor," *American Heritage,* XIX (June 1968), 18. The story of Frank Cobb.

STEFFENS, PETE, "The Identity Struggle of Lincoln Steffens—Writer or Reporter?" *Journalism History,* II (Spring 1975), 16. By his son; Lincoln Steffens hesitated to make reporting a career.

STEIN, HARRY H., "American Muckrakers and Muckraking: The 50-Year Scholarship," *Journalism Quarterly,* LVI (Spring 1979), 9. Evaluation of the literature.

STEINER, LINDA, "The Women's Suffrage Press, 1850–1900; A Cultural Analysis," Ph.D. Thesis, University of Illinois, 1979. See also Steiner, "Finding Community in Nineteenth-Century Suffrage Periodicals," *American Journalism,* I (Summer 1983), 1.

STEVENS, GEORGE E., "A History of the Cincinnati *Post,*" Ph.D. thesis, University of Minnesota, 1968. Emphasizes local issues and political coverage of a mainstay Scripps daily. See Stevens, "Scripps' Cincinnati *Post:* Liberalism at Home," *Journalism Quarterly,* XLVIII (Summer 1971), 231.

STOLBERG, BENJAMIN, "The Man Behind 'The Times,' " *Atlantic Monthly,* CXXXVIII (December 1926), 721. A discerning study of Adolph S. Ochs. Reprinted in Ford and Emery, *Highlights in the History of the American Press.*

THORNBROUGH, EMMA LOU, "American Negro Newspapers, 1880–1914," *Business History Review,* XL (Winter 1966), 467. Of hundreds of papers, only a few subsidized ones survived any length of time.

WEIGLE, CLIFFORD F., "The Young Scripps Editor: Keystone of E. W.'s 'System,' " *Journalism Quarterly,* XLI (Summer 1964), 360. A case study of the founding of the *Houston Press.*

WEISSBERGER, S. J., "The Rise and Decline of the Yiddish-American Press," Ph.D. thesis, Syracuse University, 1972. Yiddish papers' fortunes since 1870.

WHITE, W. L., "The Sage of Emporia," *Nieman Reports,* XXIII (March 1969), 23. Human-interest piece by William Allen White's son.

The Associated Press office on Wall Street at century's turn.
Bettmann Archive

"All the News That's Fit to Print."

The New York Times.

THE WEATHER

VOL. LXVIII...NO. 22,206. NEW YORK, MONDAY, NOVEMBER 11, 1918. TWENTY-FOUR PAGES. TWO CENTS

ARMISTICE SIGNED, END OF THE WAR! BERLIN SEIZED BY REVOLUTIONISTS; NEW CHANCELLOR BEGS FOR ORDER; OUSTED KAISER FLEES TO HOLLAND

SON FLEES WITH EX-KAISER

Hindenburg Also Believed to be Among Those in His Party.

ALL ARE HEAVILY ARMED

Automobiles Bristle with Rifles as Fugitives Arrive at Dutch Frontier.

ON THEIR WAY TO DE STEEG

Belgians Yell to Them, "Are You On Your Way to Paris?"

LONDON, Nov. 10.—Both the former German Emperor and his eldest son, Frederick William, crossed the Dutch frontier Sunday morning, according to advices from The Hague. His reported destination is De Steeg, near Utrecht.

The former German Emperor's party, which is believed to include Field Marshal von Hindenburg, arrived at Eysden, [midway between Liége and Maastricht,] on the Dutch frontier, at 7:30 o'clock Sunday morning, according to Daily Mail advices.

Practically the whole German General Staff accompanied the former Emperor, and ten automobiles carried the party. The automobiles were bristling with rifles, and all the fugitives were armed.

The ex-Kaiser was in uniform. He alighted at the Eysden station and paced the platform, smoking a cigarette.

Many photographs were taken by [of?] the members of the Imperial party. On the whole the people were very quiet, but Belgians among them yelled out "En voyage a Paris." (Are you on your way to Paris?)

Chatting with the members of the staff, the former Emperor, the correspondent says, did not look in the least distressed. A few minutes later an imperial train, including restaurant and sleeping cars, ran into the station. Only servants were aboard.

The engine returned to Visé, Belgium, and brought back a second train, in which were a large number of staff officers and others, and also stores of food.

The preparations began for the departure at 10 o'clock this morning, but at 10:40 o'clock the train was still at Eysden. The blinds of the train were all drawn.

The Daily Mail remarks that, if the party arrived in Holland armed, all of them must be interned.

While other dispatches con-

Continued on Page Three.

Kaiser Fought Hindenburg's Call for Abdication; Failed to Get Army's Support in Keeping Throne

By GEORGE RENWICK.

AMSTERDAM, Nov. 10.—I learn on very good authority that the Kaiser made a determined effort to stave off abdication. ...

Kaiser Shivered as He Signed Abdication

GERMAN DYNASTIES BEING WIPED OUT

King of Wuerttemberg Abdicates—Sovereign of Saxony to Follow Suit.

PRINCES MAY BE EXILED

Socialists Are Demanding That Every Sovereign in the Empire Shall be Dethroned.

LONDON, Nov. 10.—A Havas dispatch from Basle says:

"Wilhelm II., the reigning King of the monarchy of Württemberg, abdicated on Friday night."

A Wolff Bureau dispatch from Stuttgart, by way of Amsterdam, says that the King has issued a proclamation saying that his person would never serve to hinder the development of the wishes of the people.

According to a report received from Berne, the German Socialists are demanding that every dynasty in Germany be suppressed and all the Princes exiled. It is reported that the Kings of Bavaria and Saxony intend to abdicate soon.

Continued on Page Two.

MORE WARSHIPS JOIN THE REDS

Four Dreadnoughts in Kiel Harbor Espouse the Revolutionary Cause.

GUARDSHIPS ALSO GO OVER

Those Protecting Mines in the Great Belt and the Baltic Abandon Their Posts.

LONDON, Nov. 10.—The crews of the German dreadnoughts Posen, Ostfriesland, Nassau, and Oldenburg, in Kiel Harbor, have joined the revolution, says a Copenhagen dispatch. Marines occupied the lock gates at Ostmoor and fought down a coast artillery division which offered resistance.

According to the British Wireless Service three German destroyers have anchored outside of Stockholm. All the guardships in the Baltic, it is said, have joined the revolutionary movement.

Six more cruisers flying the red flag arrived at Hamburg last night, says a Wolff News Agency dispatch received in Copenhagen.

An Amsterdam dispatch states that the Berlin Vossische Zeitung and Vorwärts confirm the fact that the inception of the revolution at Kiel was mistaken for the idea that a cruiser had been ordered and that it was intended to give battle to the British fleet.

Up to Friday night the number of persons killed at Kiel was twenty-eight, according to information re-

Continued on Page Three.

BERLIN TROOPS JOIN REVOLT

Reds Shell Building in Which Officers Vainly Resist.

THRONGS DEMAND REPUBLIC

Revolutionary Flag on Royal Palace—Crown Prince's Palace Also Seized.

GENERAL STRIKE IS BEGUN

Burgomaster and Police Submit—War Office Now Under Socialist Control.

LONDON, Nov. 10.—The greater part of Berlin is in control of revolutionists, the former Kaiser has fled to Holland, and Friedrich Ebert, the new Socialist Chancellor, has taken command of the situation. The revolt is spreading throughout Germany with great rapidity.

Dispatches received in London today announce these startling developments. The Workmen's and Soldiers' Council is now administering the municipal government of the German capital.

The War Ministry has submitted, and its acts are valid only when countersigned by a Socialist representative. The official Wolff telegraphic agency has been taken over by the Reds.

The red flag has been hoisted over the royal palace and the Brandenburg Gate. The former Crown Prince's palace is also in possession of the revolutionists.

There was severe fighting in Berlin between 8 and 10 o'clock last night and a violent cannonade was heard from the heart of the city.

Burgomaster and Police Join.

A Copenhagen dispatch states that Dr. Liebknecht, the famous Socialist, who spent many months in prison for antagonizing the German Imperial Government and who was recently released, has issued the following announcement in Berlin in behalf of the Workmen's and Soldiers' Council:

"The Presidency of the police, as well as the Chief Command, is in our hands. Our comrades will be released."

A dispatch from Berne states that the Burgomaster of Berlin has placed himself and his staff at the disposal of the new Government.

Some German newspapers describe the movement as Bolshevism. The people are shouting "Long live the Republic!" and singing the "Marseillaise."

Officers Shelled by Reds.

When revolutionary soldiers attempted to enter a building in Berlin in which they supposed that a number of officers were concealed shots were fired from the windows. The Reds then began shelling the building. Many persons were killed and wounded before the officers surrendered.

When the cannonade began the people thought the Reichsbank was being bombarded, and thousands rushed to the square in front of the Crown Prince's palace. It was later determined that other buildings were under fire. Among those killed in the fighting at the "Cockchafer" Barracks was one of the workmen's leaders known as "Comrade" Haberroth.

Socialist Chancellor Appeals to All Germans To Help Him Save Fatherland from Anarchy

BERNE, Nov. 10, (Associated Press.)—In an address to the people, the new German Chancellor, Friedrich Ebert, says: ...

WAR ENDS AT 6 O'CLOCK THIS MORNING

The State Department in Washington Made the Announcement at 2:45 o'Clock.

ARMISTICE WAS SIGNED IN FRANCE AT MIDNIGHT

Terms Include Withdrawal from Alsace-Lorraine, Disarming and Demobilization of Army and Navy, and Occupation of Strategic Naval and Military Points.

By The Associated Press.

WASHINGTON, Monday, Nov. 11, 2:48 A. M.—The armistice between Germany, on the one hand, and the allied Governments and the United States, on the other, has been signed.

The State Department announced at 2:45 o'clock this morning that Germany had signed.

The department's announcement simply said: "The armistice has been signed."

The world war will end this morning at 6 o'clock, Washington time, 11 o'clock Paris time.

The armistice was signed by the German representatives at midnight.

This announcement was made by the State Department at 2:50 o'clock this morning.

The announcement was made verbally by an officila of the State Department in this form:

"The armistice has been signed. It was signed at 5 o'clock A. M., Paris time, [midnight, New York time,] and hostilities will cease at 11 o'clock this morning, Paris time. [6 o'clock, New York time.]

The terms of the armistice, it was announced, will not be made public until later. Military men here, however, regard it as certain that they include:

Immediate retirement of the German military forces from France, Belgium, and Alsace-Lorraine.

Disarming and demobilization of the German armies.

Occupation by the allied and American forces of such strategic points in Germany as will make impossible a renewal of hostilities.

Delivery of part of the German High Seas Fleet and a certain number of submarines to the allied and American naval forces.

Disarmament of all other German warships

The famous 1918 Armistice Day edition of the *New York Times.*

19
War Comes to America

After the Marne the war grew and spread until it drew in the nations of both hemispheres and entangled them in a pattern of world conflict no peace treaty could dissolve. . . . The nations were caught in a trap, a trap made during the first thirty days out of battles that failed to be decisive, a trap from which there was, and has been, no exit.

—Barbara Tuchman, in *The Guns of August*

The great war that began in Europe in August, 1914, completely altered the pattern of life that a comparatively peaceful nineteenth century had produced. By 1917 it had become a world war, with the embarking of the United States on a "great crusade" to make the world safe for democracy. But people found at war's end they could neither restore the old order nor build a peaceful new one. Political and social disillusionment, economic depression, and the rise of modern dictatorships brought a second great war, and the designations World War I and II came into the language. After that, war and threat of war seemed an unending morass.

In *The Guns of August* Barbara Tuchman agreed with Sir Edward Grey's "The lamps are going out all over Europe; we shall not see them lit again in our lifetime." Tuchman's account began with the pageantry of the funeral procession for King Edward VII in 1910: "the sun of the old world was setting in a dying blaze of splendor never to be seen again." Beside the new king, George V, rode his cousin William II, Emperor of Germany, mounted on a gray horse and wearing the scarlet uniform of a British field marshal. Behind them, among nine kings and fifty more royals, were Albert, King of the Belgians, destined for a hero's role; the Archduke Franz Ferdinand, who would be assassinated at Sarajevo; and former President Theodore Roosevelt, who had projected the United States into world pageantry by sending its "Great White Fleet" around the world.

Many of the beplumed, gold-braided riders represented crowns and empires that would disappear in the coming decade: the Hohenzollerns of Germany, the Hapsburgs of Austria-Hungary, the Romanovs of Russia, the Sultanate of Turkey, the Manchu dynasty of China. But despite the arms rivalries and tensions of the past few years and Kaiser Wilhelm's claim to Germany's "place in the sun," few believed on that 1910 day that so many great dynasties would topple or that the peace of western Europe, unbroken since 1871, would be ruptured. The chancellories of Europe were assuring the world that war was impossible, and their military planners were blueprinting only a short war at most. The failure of the German master battle plan that fateful August, 1914, brought the world into the trap from which there was no exit.

AMERICAN REACTION TO EUROPE'S 1914 WAR

No one could foresee in 1914 the ultimate consequences of Germany's transformation of a "Balkan incident" into a general European war. Even though the United States had entered into the world diplomatic arena after the war with Spain, most Americans probably felt secure behind two oceans and were interested only in preserving peace as far as this country was concerned. No doubt the jesting comment of the *Chicago Herald* summarized this attitude: "Peace-loving citizens of this country will now rise up and tender a hearty vote of thanks to Columbus for having discovered America."[1]

Yet underneath this denial of concern by Americans for what was happening in the Old World lay the first instinctive reactions to the shattering of peace. As Americans read the vivid account by Richard Harding Davis of the entry of the German army into Brussels—"one unbroken steel-gray column . . . twenty-four hours later is still coming . . . not men marching, but a force of nature like a tidal wave, an avalanche"—and as they looked almost unbelievingly at pictures of the sacked city of Louvain, they became increasingly uncomfortable.

It is important to record these first American reactions, since in the depths of later disillusionment, when it was evident that our participation in war had failed to bring a lasting peace, a literature appeared that told a different story.[2] British propagandists, American munitions makers, and cynical politicians had led gullible Americans to an unnecessary slaughter, the theme ran, carrying with it the implication that American newspapers were duped by foreign propagandists and by war-mongering capitalists, and thereby misled their readers. A quite convincing case was built on partial evidence for such a thesis, ignoring or overriding such important factors as these: the impact on American public opinion of crisis events, such as the sinking of the *Lusitania,* which were predominantly unfavorable to the German side; the effects of Allied censorships and control of overseas communications in shaping the available news (as distinct from overt propaganda efforts); the effects of socially important pressure groups in shaping American thought; the natural ties between English-speaking peoples, and the distaste of Americans for German "Kultur"; the legitimate pro-Allied decisions of American officials and diplomats based on German-caused events; the feeling that a strong British navy was less hazardous to American interests than a strong Germany navy; and, most importantly, the basic United States objection to one-nation domination of Europe—an objection that led to two wars with German militarism in defense of the American national interest.[3]

News of military actions was delayed by both sides, and official communiqués often attempted to conceal news of reversals.* Some correspondents managed to obtain beats on news of important battles, but largely as a matter of luck. Front area reporters more often won recognition for their feature stories than for their straight factual accounts, while military analysts in the various European capitals provided the continuing story of the fighting along the sprawling western and eastern fronts. This news, after clearing the military censorships, still had to funnel through the London communications center. This was the result of the British action in cutting the German Atlantic cable on August 5, 1914. Stories written in Berlin, Vienna, and in neutral capitals thereafter had to travel through London to reach the United States.[4]

AMERICA MOVES TOWARD WAR

The course of events was rapidly bolstering pro-Allied sentiment in the United States. The *New York Times* printed the various "white papers" giving each belligerent power's version of the events leading up to the war, but Germany's obvious preparation for war and smashing early victories added reason to believe the Allied versions, imperfectly as they were presented. Natural ties of many Americans to the English traditions, which were particularly strong among social and intellectual leaders, made it fashionable to be pro-British. Yet large segments of the population opposed America's going to war up to the last, for various reasons. The Middle West was more isolationist than the seaboard sections and was suspicious of the pro-Allied Easterners. The Irish, a strong minority, were naturally anti-British because of the Irish civil war, although it should be pointed out that this did not necessarily make them pro-German. The large groups of German-Americans who were, on the whole, loyal to the United States, were at the same time naturally sympathetic with the aims of their Fatherland. They regarded Germany's ambitions as no more dangerous or imperialistic than those of Britain, France, and Russia.

One decisive event was the torpedoing of English Cunard line ship *Lusitania,* then the queen of the Atlantic run. When the *Lusitania* went down off the Irish coast on May 7, 1915, with the loss of 1198 of the 1924 persons aboard—including 114 of 188 American passengers—Germany celebrated the accomplishment of her U-boat captain. But resentment ran high in the United States, particularly when it was remembered that an Imperial Germany Embassy advertisement warning travelers on Allied ships that they did so "at their own risk" had appeared in New York newspapers the morning the *Lusitania* left port.

Even though Germany relaxed its submarine warfare after months of diplomatic note writing by President Wilson, the summer of 1916 was dominated by pro-Allied arguments and by talk of preparedness. Wilson, whose most effective 1916 campaign slogan had been "He kept us out of war," saw his hopes

*British journalist Phillip Knightley, in his *The First Casualty* (New York: Harcourt Brace Jovanovich, 1975) contended (p. 80) that between 1914 and 1918 "More deliberate lies were told than in any other period of history, and the whole apparatus of the state went into action to suppress the truth." His book is a harsh appraisal of war correspondence and government manipulation from the Crimean War to Vietnam.

of the United States serving as a neutral arbiter dashed by two final German actions.

One was resumption of unrestricted submarine warfare by the Germans in February, 1917. This brought a break in diplomatic relations. Clinching the American decision was the Allied interception of German Foreign Minister Zimmermann's note to the Mexican government, offering Mexico the return of Texas, New Mexico, and Arizona after an American defeat, if Mexico would ally itself with Germany. The text of the note, given to the Associated Press unofficially, created a sensation. The sinking in March of three American ships by U-boats brought Wilson's war call on April 2—"The world must be made safe for democracy"—and the declaration of war on April 6. Wilson's masterful phrases played no small part in the determination of the issue. His denunciation of a group of eleven senators, led by Robert La Follette of Wisconsin, as "a little group of willful men" for filibustering against the arming of American merchant ships in early March did much to discredit the opponents of war.

Some periodicals had been pro-Ally almost from the start. Among the most outspoken were the old *Life* magazine, the *New York Herald,* and Henry Watterson's *Louisville Courier-Journal,* whose editor adopted, in October, 1914, the simple but effective battlecry: "To hell with the Hohenzollerns and the Hapsburgs!" The *New York Times* was solidly pro-Ally, along with the *World* and most other New York newspapers. After the sinking of the *Lusitania,* the number of anti-interventionist newspapers dwindled. William Randolph Hearst's chain of papers stood out as bitterly anti-British and was tarred as pro-German because Hearst made special efforts to obtain German-originated news to balance Allied-originated stories. Other holdouts against the war were the *New York Evening Mail* (which had been bought secretly by German agents), *Chicago Tribune, Cincinnati Enquirer, Cleveland Plain Dealer, Washington Post, Milwaukee Sentinel, Los Angeles Times, San Francisco Chronicle,* and *San Francisco Call.*[5] All, of course, supported the war once it was declared. William Jennings Bryan's *Commoner, La Follette's Magazine,* and Oswald G. Villard's *Nation* and *New York Evening Post* were pacifist.

GEORGE CREEL'S COMMITTEE ON PUBLIC INFORMATION

Only a week after the declaration of war, Wilson appointed a Committee on Public Information. Its job was primarily one of disseminating facts about the war. It was also to coordinate government propaganda efforts and to serve as the government's liaison with newspapers. It drew up a voluntary censorship code under which editors would agree to refrain from printing material that might aid the enemy. Before it was through, the committee found itself "mobilizing the mind of the world," and Mark Sullivan characterized it as an American contribution to the science of war. George Creel, the newspaper editor who was named by Wilson to direct the committee's work, explained that "it was a plain publicity proposition, a vast enterprise in salesmanship, the world's greatest adventure in advertising."[6]

The opportunity Wilson gave to Creel was a greater one than any other person had enjoyed in the propaganda arena.[7] Creel was a liberal-minded and

George Creel
Wide World Photos

vigorously competent product of New York, Kansas City, and Denver journalism. He was intensely anxious to achieve every possible task his committee might embrace, and he eventually mobilized 150,000 Americans to carry out its varied and far-flung missions.

Creel first opened up government news channels to the Washington correspondents, and insisted that only news of troop movements, ship sailings, and other events of strictly military character should be withheld. He issued a brief explanatory code calling on the newspapers to censor such news themselves, voluntarily. Throughout the war, newspaper editors generally went beyond Creel's minimum requests in their desire to aid the war effort. In May, 1917, the CPI began publishing an *Official Bulletin* in which releases were reprinted in newspaper form. Before the war was over this publication reached a daily circulation of 118,000. A weekly newspaper editor prepared a digest of the news for rural papers. Still photographs, plates, and mats also were utilized.

An historian who studied the accuracy of CPI news releases years later came to this conclusion: "One of the most remarkable things about the charges against the CPI is that, of the more than 6,000 news stories it issued, so few were called into question at all. It may be doubted that the CPI's record for honesty will ever be equalled in the official war news of a major power."[8]

Creel asked major advertisers and the publications themselves to donate space for various government campaigns, the Red Cross, and other war-related activities. The advertising agencies were organized, and their copy writers and artists were used to create newspaper and magazine advertising, streetcar placards, and outdoor posters. The artists in the CPI's division of pictorial publicity, headed by Charles Dana Gibson, contributed stirring posters. The infant motion-picture industry produced films of a patriotic and instructive nature. Its stars, including Douglas Fairbanks and Mary Pickford, sparked Liberty bond sales. The college professors served in a division of pamphleteering. It produced a *War Cyclopedia* and 75 million pieces of printed matter. Historian Guy Stanton Ford of the University of Minnesota headed the division, which numbered among its scholars such noted historians as Carl Becker of Cornell University, Evarts B. Greene of the University of Illinois, and Frederic L. Paxson of the University of Wisconsin.[9]

CENSORSHIP OF GERMAN AND SOCIALIST PAPERS

The Espionage Act of June 15, 1917, provided the opening wedge for suppression of those who were considered to be disloyal to the American and Allied war cause. Among the crimes that were punishable by heavy fines and imprisonment that the act defined were the willful making of false reports or false statements with the intent to interfere with the successful operation of the military or naval forces, and willful attempts to promote disloyalty in the armed forces or to obstruct recruitments. A section on use of the mails empowered Postmaster General Albert S. Burleson to declare unmailable all letters, circulars, newspapers, pamphlets, books, and other materials violating provisions of the act.

The axe fell most heavily on Socialist organs and German–language newspapers; a few other pacifist or anti-Ally publications also lost their mail privileges. The *American Socialist* was banned from the mails immediately and was soon followed by *Solidarity,* the journal of the left-wing Industrial Workers of the World—the much-feared anticapitalistic IWW. A vociferous advocate of the Irish independence movement, Jeremiah A. O'Leary, lost mailing privileges for his publication, *Bull,* in July, 1917, for opposing wartime cooperation with the British. The magazine *The Masses,* brilliantly edited by Max Eastman, felt the ban in August for publishing an issue containing four antiwar cartoons and a poem defending radical leaders Emma Goldman and Alexander Berkman. An indictment against the editors under the Espionage Act was dismissed in 1919.

Altogether some seventy-five papers either lost their mailing privileges during the first year of the Espionage Act or retained them only by agreeing to print nothing more concerning the war. The best known were two Socialist dailies, the *New York Call* and Victor Berger's *Milwaukee Leader.* The Austrian-born Berger, in 1910 the first Socialist elected to Congress, was convicted on charges of conspiracy to violate the Espionage Act and was sentenced to 20 years imprisonment. The United States Supreme Court later overturned the decision due to the prejudicial actions of the presiding judge. Twice the House of Representatives denied him the seat to which he had been reelected. For a time during and after the war, all incoming mail was prevented from reaching the *Leader*. The Supreme Court upheld the Post Office ban on the *Leader* in a 1921 decision, and it was not until June, 1921, when Postmaster General Will Hays restored their second-class mailing privileges, that the *Leader* and the *Call* were once again able to reach their numerous out-of-town subscribers. The German-language press likewise was hard hit by mail bans and prosecutions and declined one-half in numbers and in circulation during the war.

Other papers felt the weight of public opinion against those who did not wholeheartedly support the war. The Hearst newspapers, which had bitterly opposed American entry into the war and continued to be clearly anti-Ally even though they supported the American war effort itself, were widely attacked. Hearst was hanged in effigy, his papers were boycotted in some places, and he himself was denounced as disloyal. The Hearst newspapers had vigorously denounced the bringing of charges against Socialist and German-language papers—in contrast to editorial approval of those moves by the *New York Times* and widespread media disinterest in First Amendment implications. Oswald Garrison Villard's pacifist views and defenses of civil liberties brought such a decline in the fortunes of the *New York Evening Post* that he was forced to sell it in 1918, and one issue of the *Nation* was held up in the New York Post Office because it carried an editorial titled "Civil Liberty Dead."

THE SEDITION ACT OF 1918

The powers of the government to control expression of opinion were strengthened by the passage of two other laws. The Trading-with-the-Enemy Act of October, 1917, authorized censorship of all communications moving in or out of the United States and provided that translations of newspaper or magazine articles published in foreign languages could be demanded by the Post Office—a move to keep the German-language papers in line. The Sedition Act of May, 1918, amended and broadened the Espionage Act by making it a crime to write or publish "any disloyal, profane, scurrilous or abusive language about the form of government of the United States or the Constitution, military or naval forces, flag, or the uniform" or to use language intended to bring these ideas and institutions "into contempt, scorn, contumely, or disrepute." The Post Office's application of these broad provisions to ban publications from the mails gave the postmaster general immense powers he hesitated to use. The memory of the blundering Sedition Act of 1798 kept him from using his authority to harass orthodox Republican opponents of the administration, and the brunt of persecution continued to fall on the unpopular radical and pro-German minorities.

Former President Theodore Roosevelt was asking heatedly why the Hearst newspapers had not been denied mail privileges (some Republicans said Hearst escaped because he was a Democrat). Roosevelt also was writing editorials for the *Kansas City Star* criticizing the administration, and he was speaking strongly against what he called its incompetence and softness in dealing with the enemy. Senator Robert La Follette of Wisconsin, who was politically crucified by an error the Associated Press made in reporting one of his speeches,[10] likewise was a possible candidate for prosecution.

The Department of Justice, however, moved against lesser-known persons like the IWW leaders, who were arrested and imprisoned, and like Mrs. Rose Pastor Stokes, who got a 10-year sentence for writing a letter to the *Kansas City Star* saying "No government which is for the profiteers can also be for the people, and I am for the people, while the government is for the profiteers." The verdict against Mrs. Stokes was reversed in 1920. But not so fortunate was the four-time Socialist party presidential candidate, Eugene V. Debs. When he told a Socialist convention in June, 1918, that the Allies were "out for plunder" and defended the Bolshevists in Russia, he was jailed. Debs' conviction for violation of the Espionage and Sedition Acts was upheld unanimously by the Supreme Court. He received the record Socialist party presidential vote total of 920,000 while campaigning in 1920 from a federal prison, however, and was pardoned by President Harding in December, 1921.

The wartime atmosphere was favorable to restriction of civil liberties. Generally adopted state laws contained antipacifist, anti-Red, and criminal syndicalism clauses designed to protect business and industry against radical-inspired strikes and violence. Mobs and citizens' committees took care of unpopular persons, including Americans of German ancestry. Many Americans were persuaded by community pressure to buy more Liberty bonds than they desired to own. Prosecutors, juries, and judges went beyond the words of the Espionage and Sedition Acts, often because of public pressure. Zechariah Chafee, Jr., the distinguished Harvard law professor, documented the damage done to the spirit of the Constitutional guarantee of free speech in his 1920 work, *Freedom of Speech.*[11] In such circumstances the great bulk of the American press was fortunate to escape not only direct and violent censorship but also the harassments visited on its Socialist and German-language fringe.

Censorship of foreign communications sent by cable, telephone, or telegraph, as provided in the Trading-with-the Enemy Act, was carried out by a Censorship Board, which Wilson established in October, 1917, to coordinate control of communications facilities. The board was mainly concerned with outgoing messages and news dispatches. There were few causes for complaint against the board and it received a "job well done" commendation.[12]

LEADING WAR CORRESPONDENTS

Notable among the early war reporters were Richard Harding Davis, whose story of the entry of the German army into Brussels was written for the *New York Tribune* and its syndicate, and Will Irwin, whose beats on the battle of Ypres and the first German use of poison gas were also printed in the *Tribune.* Irwin was one of several correspondents who represented American magazines in Europe; he first wrote for *Collier's* and then for the *Saturday Evening Post.* However, the brunt of the news-coverage responsibility fell on the reporters in the European capital bureaus and those who served as military analysts. Some of the leaders were Karl H. von Wiegand of the United Press, Sigrid Schultz of the *Chicago Tribune,* and Cyril Brown of the *New York Times* in Berlin; Paul Scott Mowrer of the *Chicago Daily News* and Wythe Williams of the *New York Times* in Paris; and Edward Price Bell of the *Chicago Daily News* in London. Frank H. Simonds of the *New York Tribune* did distinguished work as a military critic and Herbert Bayard Swope earned respect for his *New York World* stories.

American war correspondents in France found themselves freer to observe the military actions of the American Expeditionary Force (AEF) than those of the other Allied armies. In General Pershing's area correspondents could go into the front lines without military escorts, they could follow the fighting advances, and they could roam the rear areas, living where they chose. This had not been the case for correspondents with the British, French, and German forces in the early years of the war. But everything the correspondents wrote went through the censorship of the press section of the Military Intelligence Service, headed by Major Frederick Palmer, formerly of the Associated Press. News of general engagements, of casualties suffered, and of troop identifications was releasable only if it had been mentioned in official communiqués. Press officers were also attached to the training camps and cantonments at home.

There were some 500 American correspondents for newspapers, magazines, press associations, and syndicates in Europe by 1915 and the number was augmented when American troops joined the fighting. About forty actually covered the actions of the AEF. Among the best-known byliners was Fred S. Ferguson of the United Press, who beat his competitors in reporting the battle of Saint-Mihiel by writing an advance story, based on the American battle plan, and having it filed section by section as the battle proceeded. Webb Miller of the UP and Henry Wales of the INS also won prominence, along with Edwin L. James of the *New York Times,* Martin Green of the *New York World,* and Junius Wood of the *Chicago Daily News.* Floyd Gibbons of the *Chicago Tribune* was hit by German machine-gun fire and lost an eye.

A soldiers' journalism also sprouted during wartime, the best-known example being the *Stars and Stripes.* The eight-page paper was established in Paris in February, 1918. Harold Ross, later editor of the *New Yorker,* became the chief editor, assisted by such well-known writers as Grantland Rice and Alexander Woollcott. Other overseas units had their publications, as did all of the camps in the United States.

DEFEAT OF THE TREATY AND THE LEAGUE

President Wilson had given the world a blueprint for the postwar settlement in his Fourteen Points speech of January, 1918, and later addresses before Congress, which called for the establishment of an association of nations (named the League of Nations), international political and economic cooperation, and self-determination in realigning Europe's boundaries. With the defeat of Germany imminent, Wilson made the first of a series of blunders that gave his political opponents a chance to defeat his program.

Wilson erred in asking voters to return Democrats to Congress in the November, 1918, election so that he might "be your unembarrassed spokesman at home and abroad." The voters' answer was the election of a Republican majority in both houses. Insensitive to this public reminder that no leader is indispensable, Wilson failed to include any Republican, or any Senator, in the American delegation to the Versailles peace conference, even though the treaty would need a two-thirds vote of the Republican-controlled Senate for ratification. He erred finally in making himself the chief negotiator on a daily basis, thereby losing his flexibility and his earlier role as agenda setter for general policy.[13]

By the time the Versailles treaty was signed in June, 1919, Wilson's agenda was in disarray. The British, French, and Italian leaders had compromised some of the Fourteen Points; nationalistic rivalries had endangered idealistic territorial adjustments; a group of thirty-seven senators had announced they would not vote for a treaty containing a League of Nations, thereby leaving it short of the necessary two-thirds approval. Wilson's answer was to undertake a September cross-country train tour, during which he gave eighteen talks in 22 days. He drew large crowds and friendly audiences, and had a good press for his arguments reaffirming basic principles. But right behind him came such relentless Senate opponents as Hiram W. Johnson of California and William E. Borah of Idaho, who picked holes in particular articles of the treaty, and made rebuttals in the press. On the final day of his tour, Wilson suffered a physical breakdown and retired into the White House, partially paralyzed, to stay for the remainder of his term.

Wilson's illness left the internationalists leaderless. The Republican Senate leader, Henry Cabot Lodge of Massachusetts, offered a group of reservations affecting American participation in the League as the price for ratification. Moderate Democrats wished to accept but Wilson denounced the plan as a betrayal and prevented its passage. Thus the United States Senate failed to ratify the treaty, thereby backing out of the international association Wilson had sponsored. As far as the press was concerned, the League had enjoyed reasonably good support from newspapers and magazines, right up to the end. Republican politics and Wilson's mistakes killed it. Wilson's supporters sought to make the 1920 presidential election a "solemn referendum" but the Republican slogan of a "return to normalcy" swept the ticket of Harding and Coolidge into office.

THE GREAT "RED SCARE"

The other major postwar reaction was the continuation of a gigantic "Red Scare," stimulated in part by the events of the Russian Revolution and also by reaction to the radical IWW labor movement and Socialist party successes. The persecutions and prosecutions made during wartime under the Espionage and Sedition Acts continued unabated; indeed, the "Red Scare" intensified in 1919. Approximately 2000 persons were prosecuted under the two laws, and nearly half were convicted.

The year 1919 was marked by large-scale strikes. These were called by workers whose often meager salaries had been eroded by wartime inflation and the high cost of living (called "HCL" in the headlines). In Boston police officers whose annual salaries were as low as $1100 joined the American Federation of Labor and finally struck. Governor Calvin Coolidge's laconic "There is no right to strike against the public safety by anyone, anytime, anywhere" doomed the now locked-out police and propelled Coolidge into the vice-presidential nomination and eventually into the White House.

The International Workers of the World (IWW), formed in 1905, had won 100,000 members among unorganized timber workers, longshoremen, miners, migratory workers, and immigrant textile workers. Called the "Wobblies" by their opponents, they aroused public fears with revolutionary rhetoric and loose talk of violence. Their antiwar stand of 1917 to 1918 brought federal raids on their headquarters, arrests, and deportations of alien members. When Legionnaires raided their Centralia, Washington, headquarters in December, 1919, and gunfire caused several deaths, the "Red Scare" took over. The IWW movement fell apart, leaving unskilled workers leaderless until the emergence of the CIO in the 1930s. The great steel strike of 1919, in which the AFL sought to unionize the iron and steel industry, succeeded in calling out 340,000 workers in Eastern states. But the strike leader, William Z. Foster, was pilloried as a former Wobblie and a believer in revolutionary programs. His vulnerability aided Elbert H. Gary, president of the U.S. Steel Corporation, in breaking the strike and in preventing unionization of the industry until the 1930s. Foster emerged as a militant Communist national leader.

The "Red Scare" approached a public panic. The display of red flags was forbidden in New York and other states; Attorney General Mitchell Palmer hustled groups of "Reds" to Ellis Island for deportation; the offices of the Socialist daily, the *New York Call,* were raided and wrecked; Socialists were ousted from the New York State legislature and the Congress; several universities and colleges dismissed tenured professors who were pacifists, Socialists, and of German ancestry; local school boards prescribed loyalty oaths for teachers; many states passed "anti-Red" and criminal syndicalism laws; bombings and a dynamite explosion on Wall Street reinforced the fear of violence. The evangelist Billy Sunday summed up the widespread feeling:

> If I had my way with these ornery wild-eyed Socialists and IWW's, I would stand them up before a firing squad and save space on our ships.[14]

Fortunately it was Palmer who was in charge in December, 1919, when a ship dubbed the "Soviet Ark" left New York with 249 Russian aliens aboard, including anarchist leaders Emma Goldman and Alexander Berkman, but mostly ordinary workers who had joined the wrong union.

The climax of the "Red Scare" came with the Sacco-Vanzetti case. In 1920 a Massachusetts factory payroll manager and guard were shot and killed. Sacco, a shoemaker, and Vanzetti, a fish peddler, were arrested and convicted for the shooting. Defenders said they were framed due to their Italian origins, radical anarchist ideas, and pacifism that had led them to escape draft service. Others confessed the killings, but the "law and order Establishment" set its face against a protest by liberals and radicals that reached international proportions. Finally, in 1927, the pair were executed. Upton Sinclair, Maxwell Anderson, John Dos Passos, and James T. Farrell created a literature of protest that made "Sacco-Vanzetti" a symbol of national prejudice and class hatred.

In general, the newspapers failed dismally to defend the civil liberties of

MID-WEEK PICTORIAL

Radical Agitators Under Arrest and at Ellis Island

Types of revolutionists who have been gathered in by the Department of Justice, which has now over 6,000 such in its toils. The foreign aspect of most of the faces is evident. The majority of those arrested are aliens. (© N. Y. H. Service.)

Headings of some of the newspapers which have been the most ardent advocates of "direct action," which when analyzed usually means revolution. Some of their plants have been raided by the Department of Justice and many of their editors and writers are now under arrest. (© Pathe Films.)

Group of radicals, many of whom face deportation, at dinner on Ellis Island. The Island at present is unusually crowded, owing to the unprecedented activity recently shown in rounding up revolutionaries, but the food furnished is good and abundant. (© Pathe Films.)

"Reds" snapshotted at Ellis Island while at meals. A riot took place when the arrested men realized that they were being photographed. A rush was made for the cameras, and some of them were smashed, while the mob tried to "manhandle" the operators. (© Pathe Films.)

***Mid-Week Pictorial,* published by the *New York Times,* portrays "revolutionists" with "foreign faces" during 1919–20 Red Scare.**

those being questionably attacked. The epithet "Reds" was applied to all those caught up in the hunt for disloyal or radical persons. One of the worst offenders on this score was the *New York Times,* whose publisher Adolph Ochs exhibited solid capitalistic preferences and an unreasonable fear of any form of radicalism that might endanger the society in which he had prospered. Walter Lippmann and Charles Merz of the *New York World* editorial-page staff published a documented study, "A Test for the News," as a supplement to the August 4, 1920, issue of the *New Republic,* illustrating the inaccuracy with which the Associated Press and the *New York Times* had reported Russian events during 1917 to 1920 (Merz later became editor of the *Times*). Civil liberties were best defended by the liberal magazines, led by the *Nation* and *New Republic,* and by a handful of newspapers, notably the *St. Louis Post-Dispatch* and the *World* and *Globe* in New York City.

LEGAL CASES: "CLEAR AND PRESENT DANGER"

Out of the prosecutions for political expression arose four landmark cases in the establishment of the First-Amendment rights of freedom of speech and freedom of the press. In them Justice Oliver Wendell Holmes advanced what became known as the "clear-and-present danger" theory to determine protection of

The first case involved Charles T. Schenck, Elizabeth Baer, and other members of the Philadelphia Socialist party who printed and distributed antiwar leaflets urging young draft inductees to join the Socialist party and work for the repeal of the draft law. It also denounced the war as a ruthless adventure serving the interests of Wall Street. In the Supreme Court's 1919 decision upholding the convictions (*Schenck* v. *U.S.*)[15] Holmes wrote:

> But the character of every act depends upon the circumstances in which it is done. . . . The question in every case is whether the words used, are used in such circumstances and are of such a nature as to create a clear and present danger that they will bring about the substantive evils that Congress had a right to prevent. It is a question of proximity and degree.

Holmes and the Court found that there had been such a clear and present danger in the Schenck case. In two other Espionage Act cases decided in 1919, the Supreme Court used the same standard to affirm the convictions of Jacob Frohwerk, a German-language newspaper editor, and Eugene Debs, the leader of the American Socialist party.

The second landmark case, the first Supreme Court test of the Sedition Act, was *Abrams* v. *U.S.*.[16] Abrams and four other New York radicals had been sentenced to 20 years imprisonment for distributing pamphlets condemning American troop intervention in Russia (they also denounced German militarism). The pamphlets urged a general strike to prevent production of munitions; for this, Justice John Clarke wrote for the majority, the clear-and-present danger rule applied to mandate conviction. Holmes and Louis Brandeis dissented, arguing that the best test of truth was by "free trade in ideas" and the "power of the thought to get itself accepted in the competition of the market." Now Holmes wrote:

> Only the emergency that makes it immediately dangerous to leave the correction of evil counsels to time warrants making any exception to the sweeping command, "Congress shall make no law . . . abridging the freedom of speech."

In the 1925 case of Benjamin Gitlow,[17] who was convicted under a New York State criminal anarchy law of issuing Socialist manifestoes, the majority advanced the theory of balancing by the courts of the competing private and public interests represented in First-Amendment cases. Holmes and Brandeis dissented, ridiculing the pamphlet, the *Left Wing Manifesto,* as a dreadfully dull political tract. Once more the defendants had lost, but *Gitlow* contained a vitally important statement by the conservative majority that would buttress later defenses of First-Amendment rights of speech and press. This statement said it was proper for the Court to apply the protections of the First Amendment to the states under the Fourteenth Amendment. Positive application of this landmark theory came 6 years later in *Near* v. *Minnesota* (see Chapter 21), when the defendant won.

In 1927, while concurring in the conviction of Anita Whitney under a California law outlawing the Communist party, Brandeis brilliantly restated the clear-and-present-danger theory[18]—cold comfort, perhaps, to the convicted that progressive legal theory was being advanced. In the 1951 case of Eugene Dennis,[19] who was convicted of conspiracy under the Smith Act, the majority once again used the clear-and-present danger argument to convict Communist party members, citing the world tensions of 1948. Whatever the outcomes, such postpublication trials were preferable to prior restraint mandates, for Schenck and his successors had at least had their say.

LONG-RANGE EFFECTS OF THE "RED SCARE"

The "Red Scare" and the fears the Russian Revolution had generated among most Americans succeeded in confounding the American Socialist party and in ostracizing any political movement farther to its left. Socialism and Marxism became tarred with the brush of Communism and a growing image of an evil regime in the Kremlin that sought world dominance and the destruction of all human values.

Historian David Nord, who studied the Socialist party newspaper, *Appeal to Reason,*[20] points out that the consensus view became that Socialism never had any wide appeal because it stood outside the American liberal tradition. The party's successes at the polls in the 1910s were explained because the Socialists had been perceived as social reformers operating within the standard political system. In the 1960s "New Left" historians argued that there did exist a genuine mass anticapitalist movement in America, which failed because the radicals fell to fighting among themselves and because of the governmental repression in the "Red Scare" years. In 1981 Warren Beatty made the motion picture *Reds,* again bringing to life John Reed, Emma Goldman, and others of the radical movements which were confounded by the impact of events in Russia and the spread of the "Red Scare." Reed, the brilliant young Harvard graduate who wrote *Ten Days That Shook the World* after joining the Revolution in Moscow, mingled, along with his lover and wife, Louise Bryant, with editor Max Eastman of the *Masses,* writers Upton Sinclair and Eugene O'Neill, and other Greenwich Village figures. Goldman, a Lithuanian-born anarchist editor, lecturer, and literary critic, came to the United States in 1885, only to be deported in 1919 to a Russia she did not admire.

The American Socialist party split into "patriot" and "pacifist" factions when the United States entered into the war. The pacifists were left in control of the party. The Russian Bolshevist Revolution divided the weakened Socialists into a left wing, which wished to affiliate with Moscow and establish a "dictatorship of the proletariat," and a more conservative group, which remained loyal to the program of social evolution in a democracy. The left wing divided into as many as sixteen factional organizations espousing Communism in the names of Marx, Lenin, and the opposition leader Trotsky. William Z. Foster, hero of the 1919 steel strike, organized many of these groups into the Workers' party, which ran national tickets in 1924 and 1928. The orthodox Socialists supported the Progressive party candidacy of Robert La Follette in 1924 before finding an eminently respectable, pacifist leader in Norman Thomas by 1928. The party's newspapers disintegrated; the *New York Call* succumbed in 1923 despite the efforts of the garment workers to save it and the installation of Thomas as editor.[21] The *New Masses* replaced the *Masses,* and among dailies only the *Milwaukee Leader* survived into the 1930s, before fading away in 1937.

There were no diplomatic relations with the Soviet Union until Franklin Roosevelt's election, and Russian history books recorded in substantial sections the "American invasion" at the close of World War I. In the United States, there was a consolidation of industrial power generated during the war. The Socialists had a chance to temper the drive of the capitalist-industrialist-monopolist society and to offer the country a socialized democracy. This disappeared during the "Red Scare" and the 1920s saw only hard-fought battles for such innocuous aims as public ownership of utilities. It would take the enormous economic disaster of the Great Depression to bring even such basic social reforms as the right to collective bargaining and a system of social security.

NOTES

1. As quoted in Mark Sullivan, *Our Times,* Volume V (New York: Scribner's, 1933), p. 32. Sullivan's six-volume journalistic coverage of the years 1900 to 1925 reflects both the life and history of America in an engrossing manner.

2. Edwin Costrell, "Newspaper Attitudes Toward War in Maine, 1914–17," *Journalism Quarterly,* XVI (December 1939), 334. This measurement of an immediate anti-German reaction, before the introduction of concerted propaganda by the belligerents and before the cutting of cable communications with Germany, is significant.

3. Among the more responsible books of the era of disillusionment were C. Hartley Grattan's *Why We Fought* (1929), Walter Millis' *Road to War* (1935), and H. C. Peterson's *Propaganda for War* (1939). For criticism of Peterson's attitude toward newspapers, see Ralph D. Casey, "The Press, Propaganda, and Pressure Groups," *The Annals of the American Academy of Political and Social Science,* CCXIX (January 1942), 68.

4. The best-balanced picture of American press difficulties in covering the war is found in Ralph O. Nafziger, *The American Press and Public Opinion During the World War, 1914 to April, 1917* (Ph.D. thesis, University of Wisconsin, 1936). Nafziger ranks overt propaganda efforts as having less effect on American news presentation than (1) rigid war censorships and (2) limited and controlled communications facilities.

5. Frank Luther Mott, *American Journalism* (New York: Macmillan, 1950), p. 616.

6. George Creel, *How We Advertised America* (New York: Harper & Row, 1920), p. 4.

7. See Harold D. Lasswell, *Propaganda Technique in the World War* (New York: Peter Smith, 1927), p. 20.

8. Walton E. Bean, "The Accuracy of Creel Committee News, 1917–1919: An Examination of Cases," *Journalism Quarterly,* XVIII (September 1941), 272. The major study of the CPI is James R. Mock and Cedric Larson, *Words That Won the War* (Princeton: Princeton University Press, 1939).

9. Paxson eventually wrote a three-volume series titled *American Democracy and the World War.* The war itself is covered in detail in the second volume, *America at War, 1917–1918* (Boston: Houghton Mifflin, 1939).

10. The AP committed a familiar journalistic blunder by adding a "no" to a La Follette statement concerning the American declaration of war, making it read "we had no grievance." An unsuccessful move to oust La Follette from the Senate resulted.

11. Enlarged and brought up to date in Chafee, *Free Speech in the United States* (Cambridge, Mass.: Harvard University Press,1941).

12. James R. Mock, *Censorship 1917* (Princeton: Princeton University Press,1941), pp. 81, 93.

13. Mark Sullivan, *Our Times: Over Here, 1914–1918* (New York: Scribner's, 1933). This is a contemporary account by a noted newspaper columnist. See Chapter 27 for a discussion of Wilson's treaty effort.

14. Harvey Wish, *Society and Thought in Modern America* (New York: David McKay, 1962), p. 420.

15. *Schenck* v. *United States,* 249 U.S. 47 (1919).

16. *Abrams* v. *United States,* 250 U.S. 616 (1919).

17. *Gitlow* v. *People of the State of New York,* 268 U.S. 652 (1925).

18. *Whitney* v. *California,* 274 U.S. 357 (1927).

19. *Dennis* v. *United States,* 341 U.S. 494 (1951). A subsequent decision of 1957 in the Yates case narrowed the grounds for Smith Act convictions and freed five defendants.

20. David Nord, "The *Appeal to Reason* and American Socialism, 1901–1920," *Kansas History,* Vol. 1, No. 2, Summer 1978.

21. Alfred McClung Lee. *The Daily Newspaper in America* (New York: Macmillan, 1937), pp. 191–92.

ANNOTATED BIBLIOGRAPHY

Books

CHAFEE, ZECHARIAH, Jr., *Free Speech in the United States,* Cambridge, Mass.: Harvard University Press, 1941. The major study of the problem, by a Harvard law professor.

CREEL, GEORGE, *How We Advertised America.* New York: Harper & Row, 1920. The Chairman of the World War I Committee on Public Information makes his report to the public. See also Creel's autobiography, *Rebel at Large* (New York: G. P. Putnam's Sons, 1947).

CROZIER, EMMET, *American Reporters on the Western Front, 1914–1918.* New York: Oxford University Press, 1959. Much detail about both star reporters and "specials."

FISHBEIN, LESLIE, *Rebels in Bohemia: The Radicals of The Masses, 1911–1917.* Chapel Hill: University of North Carolina Press, 1982. Discusses Max Eastman, editor of *The Masses,* John Reed, Emma Goldman, Floyd Dell, Upton Sinclair, and others.

KNIGHTLEY, PHILLIP, *The First Casualty.* New York: Harcourt Brace Jovanovich, 1975. A critical study of war correspondence from the Crimean War to Vietnam. Holds that most war coverage has been poor.

LASSWELL, HAROLD D., *Propaganda Technique in the World War.* New York: Peter Smith, 1927. A standard source for World War I propaganda efforts in the major belligerent countries.

MOCK, JAMES R., *Censorship 1917.* Princeton: Princeton University Press, 1941. The major work on World War I censorship activities.

MOCK, JAMES R., and CEDRIC LARSON, *Words that Won the War.* Princeton: Princeton University Press, 1939. Best account of the work of the Committee on Public Information during World War I.

MURPHY, PAUL L., *The Meaning of Freedom of Speech.* Westport, Conn.: Greenwood, 1972. Intensive study from Wilson to Roosevelt.

MURRAY, ROBERT K., *Red Scare: A Study in National Hysteria, 1919–1920.* Minneapolis:

University of Minnesota Press, 1955. A well-documented study of a period of violation of civil liberties. Lacks a summary evaluation of newspaper performance.

PALMER, FREDERICK, *With My Own Eyes.* Indianapolis: Bobbs-Merrill, 1933. Biographical account by a leading World War I correspondent who became military field censor.

PAXSON, FREDERIC L., *American Democracy and the World War.* Boston: Houghton Mifflin, 1938 ff. A three-volume study of the 10 years from 1913 to 1923; ranks at the top for its completeness, balance, and perceptiveness.

PEMBER, DON R., *Mass Media Law.* Dubuque, Iowa: Wm. C. Brown, 1981. Good discussion of freedom-of-expression cases of the World War I period.

SALVATORE, NICK, *Eugene V. Debs: Citizen and Socialist.* Urbana: University of Illinois Press, 1983. Debs' Socialist party failed but paved way for 1930s unions.

SCHREINER, GEORGE A., *Cables and Wireless.* Boston: Stratford, 1924. Analyzes the effect of World War I on communications.

SLOSSON, PRESTON W., *The Great Crusade and After, 1914–1928,* A History of American Life, Volume XII. New York: Macmillan, 1930. An excellent social history.

WILLIAMS, WYTHE, *Passed by the Censor.* New York: Dutton, 1916. A World War I correspondent's story. Twenty years later his *Dusk of Empire* pictured the decline of Europe into another war.

WISH, HARVEY, *Society and Thought in Modern America.* New York: David McKay, 1962. Includes a lively discussion of the "Red Scare."

WITTKE, CARL F., *The German-Language Press in America.* Lexington: University of Kentucky Press, 1957. A history from 1732 to 1956; three chapters devoted to World War I.

Periodicals and Monographs

BEAN, WALTON E., "The Accuracy of Creel Committee News, 1917–1919; An Examination of Cases," *Journalism Quarterly,* XVIII (September 1941), 263.

BECK, ELMER A., "Autopsy of a Labor Daily: The Milwaukee Leader," *Journalism Monographs,* No. 16 (August 1970).

BRITTON, JOHN A., "In Defense of Revolution: American Journalists in Mexico, 1920–1929," *Journalism History,* V (Winter 1978–79), 124. Carleton Beals, Ernest Gruening, and Frank Tannenbaum oppose U.S. State Department's concern for property rights and opposition to revolution, in pages of the *Nation* and the *New Republic.*

FOUGHT, JOHN P., "News and Editorial Treatment of Alleged Reds and Radicals by Selected Newspapers and Periodicals During 1918–21," Ph.D. thesis, Southern Illinois University, 1970. *New York Times, New York Tribune* had heavy bias.

LARSON, CEDRIC, "Censorship of Army News During the World War, 1917–1918," *Journalism Quarterly,* XVII (December 1940), 313.

MANDER, MARY SUE, "Pen and Sword: A Cultural History of the American War Correspondent, 1895–1945," Ph.D. thesis, University of Illinois, 1979. Flamboyant correspondents disappeared with the cavalry by 1917.

PICKETT, CALDER M., "A Paper for the Doughboys: *Stars and Stripes* in World War I," *Journalism Quarterly,* XLII (Winter 1965), 60. The flavor of the soldier's paper is captured.

STEVENS, JOHN D., "Press and Community Toleration: Wisconsin in World War I," *Journalism Quarterly,* XLVI (Summer 1969), 255. Based on Ph.D. thesis, University of Wisconsin, 1967.

Charlie Chaplin and Jackie Coogan in *The Kid,* 1921; Graham McNamee broadcasting a Polo Grounds baseball game in 1926 for WEAF, New York.

20

The Twenties: Radio, Movies, Jazz Journalism

Radio broadcasting is an essential part of the modern press. It shares the same functions and encounters the same problems as the older agencies of mass communication. On the other hand, radio exhibits significant differences. Its ability to draw millions of citizens into close and simultaneous contact with leaders and with events of the moment gives it a reach and an influence of peculiar importance in the management of public affairs.

—Commission on Freedom of the Press

The first American radio stations to seek regular public listenership made their bows in 1920. A half century later, there were four to five times as many radio and television stations as there were daily newspapers in the United States. In the interval the scratchy-sounding crystal sets of radio's headphone days had been transformed into FM and stereophonic reception. Network radio and big-screen television offered home audiences on-the-spot journalistic coverage of history in the making as well as entertainment.

If the arrival of radio were not enough competition for the print media, in the 1920s "going to the movies" also become a major activity. During that decade some 20,000 motion-picture theaters opened their doors and cinema attendance reached its all-time high by 1930—90 million customers weekly.

The atmosphere of the 1920s was conducive to entertainment in the newspaper as well. The sensationalized tabloid gave the period its name of "jazz journalism," but all the press emphasized human-interest stories, pictures, comic strips, and other enticing fare. The great crusade of 1917 was over, and Woodrow Wilson's hopes for American leadership in world affairs had dissolved into a "Red Scare" at home and a nationalistic-isolationist outlook toward events abroad. The country's cry was "back to normalcy" insofar as politics were concerned. This did not mean that America wanted to stand still; rather it wanted to forget the troubles of the war years and concentrate on "living."

Political conservatism and laissez-faire policies thus prevailed over rebellious but outvoted progressivism. Occupying the White House were three Republicans: the sincere but scandal-plagued Marion, Ohio, newspaper publisher, Warren G. Harding; the close-mouthed Yankee believer in the status quo, Calvin Coolidge; and the efficient but depression-plagued Quaker, Herbert Hoover. America was a relatively complacent land, and business prosperity and the doings of Wall Street outweighed interest in political and social reform or concern for a depressed farm economy.

The press, preoccupied in many instances with sex, crime, and entertainment, reflected the spirit of the times. The majority of newspapers went with the tide, rather than attempting to give the country leadership either by determined display of significant news or through interpretation. There was good copy in the evidences of political laxity that emerge in all postwar periods, however, and even the tabloids played up the Teapot Dome oil-lease scandal and others that issued from the unhappy Harding administration. Dapper Mayor Jimmy Walker's casual handling of New York City affairs was both entertaining and productive of graft exposés. The hue and cry against corruption were valuable, but sober examination of the country's own economic trend and of the world situation went begging in many papers.

And, after all, the atmosphere of the 1920s made this inevitable. The national experiment called Prohibition brought rumrunners, speakeasy operators, and gangsters into the spotlight, and they were interesting people. Al Capone, Dutch Schultz, Waxey Gordon, Legs Diamond, and their rivals were sensational copy. Socialites caught in a speakeasy raid made good picture subjects.

Tabloid editors feasted, too, on stories about glamorous and sexy Hollywood and its stars: Rudolph Valentino, Fatty Arbuckle, Clara Bow. They gloried in the love affairs of the great and not-so-great: Daddy Browning and his Peaches, Kip Rhinelander, the Prince of Wales. They built sordid murder cases into national sensations: Hall-Mills, Ruth Snyder. They glorified celebrities: Charles A. Lindbergh, Queen Marie of Rumania, Channel swimmer Gertrude Ederle. They promoted the country's sports stars: prizefighter Jack Dempsey, golfer Bobby Jones, tennis champion Bill Tilden, football coach Knute Rockne, and homerun hitter Babe Ruth.

Americans also had an eye for business. Advertising expanded enormously as agency copy writers produced legendary slogans for the marketing of automobiles, cigarettes, and other symbols of the good life. "Blow some my way" said the emancipated woman to her carefully groomed escort in one daring cigarette ad. And the 1920s saw the emergence of the public-relations concept in the business world; it was also a decade for slap-dash press agentry.

EARLY BROADCASTING EXPERIMENTS

When the first commercial American radio stations came on the air in 1920, the experimenters found that they had an audience of some size: Amateur enthusiasts who had built their own receivers and transmitters to become wireless "hams" and crystal set owners who could pick up broadcasts on their headphones. The magic of radio had been made possible by a number of scientific breakthroughs during the previous half-century, notably Alexander Graham Bell's invention of the telephone in 1876 and Guglielmo Marconi's experiments with wireless beginning in the 1890s.

Bell's demonstration of the telephone at the Philadelphia Centennial Exposition made it apparent that the instrument could be used to transmit music or information to an audience. During the next few years there were experiments in the United States and Europe whereby music was played by several persons over the telephone; the sound was made more powerful through the invention of the carbon transmitter. In 1877 music transmitted over the phone from New York City to Sarasota Springs, New York, was accidentally heard in Boston and Providence. This had occurred because electricity leaked to other trunk lines, but also because the waves were inducted through the air.[1] This principle was explained later by the German investigator Heinrich Hertz, who in 1888 proved that sound waves could be set in motion and that they could also be detected or received.

A variety of experiments preceded those of Marconi. In the early 1880s Amos Dolbear of Tufts College used a wireless telephone to send messages about a mile. A few years earlier, Thomas Edison had detected the generating of electric sparks from a distance. John Stone developed the concept of modulating a high-frequency wave with the human voice, and beginning in 1892 he conducted experiments designed to lead to voice transmission. But perhaps the most exciting of the early attempts to produce sounds from coils of wire, batteries, and telephones was the work of Nathan B. Stubblefield. In 1892 this Kentucky melon farmer was credited with talking to a friend some distance away, on his farm, using a wireless telephone. During the next 10 years Stubblefield conducted several other documented experiments, including one near Washington, D.C., where he sent a voice message from a boat to shore. Following this Stubblefield told reporters that eventually his invention "will be used for the general transmission of news of every description."[2]

A telephone system in Budapest, Hungary, allowed listeners to receive up to 12 hours of news and music in 1893. The Chicago Telephone Company delivered local and state election results to an estimated 15,000 persons in 1894. But the highly publicized experiments of Marconi gained the most attention. Using the ideas of Hertz, Marconi successfully transmitted dots and dashes across his family's fields in Italy. In February, 1896, the Marconi family traveled to London where Marconi patented his invention, transmitted up to 9 miles, and tbe following year formed the Wireless Telegraph and Signal Company, Ltd., later to be called Marconi's Wireless Telegraph Company, Ltd. His minute-by-minute wireless account of the Kingstown Regatta for the *Dublin Daily Express* in 1898 brought him world acclaim and an invitation from the *New York Herald* to repeat the experiment at the 1899 America's Cup Race. In 1901 he sent a signal from England to Newfoundland and finally in 1907 he linked Europe and America. The headline in the *New York Times* read: "Wireless Joins Two Worlds. Marconi Trans-Atlantic Service Opened With a Dispatch to the *New York Times.*"[3]

FESSENDEN, HERROLD, AND DE FOREST

Without the pioneering work of three other men, however, radio history would have been different. Reginald A. Fessenden is credited with being the first to use continuous waves—instead of the series of bursts used by Marconi—to carry a voice or music. His 1902 patent was the first in the United States for a radiotelegraph system using Hertzian waves. Then, on Christmas Eve, 1906, Fessenden made what is considered the first broadcast. Ship operators for the United Fruit Company were told to listen for messages coming from Brant Rock, Massachusetts. First came the static and the Morse code. Then operators listening to their headphones heard Fessenden reading from St. Luke's Gospel, playing the violin and a phonograph recording of Handel's "Largo," and wishing them a Merry Christmas. The broadcast was repeated on New Year's Eve and was picked up as far away as the West Indies.[4]

This same month Lee De Forest—called by some "the father of radio"—made improvements in the vacuum tube and was able to transmit voice in his laboratory room. This step, adding an element to the tube that allowed easier reception and more amplification of sound, was the discovery that would push the growth of radio. De Forest's device was called the Audion.

De Forest began a series of experiments in 1907 that would make him a world celebrity. Using records supplied by the Columbia Phonograph Company, he broadcast concerts that were enjoyed by ship operators and other wireless enthusiasts. The next year he and his wife broadcast music from the top of the Eiffel Tower over a distance of 500 miles. Then, in 1910, he broadcast the voice of Enrico Caruso from the stage of the Metropolitan Opera House to a scattered audience in the New York City area.

Meanwhile, in San Jose, California, Charles David "Doc" Herrold was making broadcasting history. Herrold opened a broadcasting school in 1909 and built an antenna on the roof of the Garden City Bank Building that was so large that the wires spread from the seven-story bank building to the tops of several adjoining buildings. Using a primitive microphone, Herrold began a regularly scheduled, weekly half-hour news and music program, which changed to a daily in 1910. Herrold's wife Sybil may have been the first woman to broadcast her own show, a music program for young people. A downtown store placed two receiving sets in a "listening room" and hooked up several dozen telephone receivers so customers could sit in comfortable chairs and hear the music. Sybil Herrold even accepted listeners' requests for songs.

Herrold claimed to have been the first "broadcaster" because he aimed his programs at the widest possible audience, and because he offered the first regular programming.[5] His 15-watt station, with the call letters FN and then SJN, became KQW in 1921 and finally KCBS in San Francisco in 1949. An interruption in service during and immediately after World War I deprived KCBS of the distinction of being the nation's oldest station, however. Among his many achievements was a two-way voice-communication system that Herrold set up with another radio station on the roof of the Fairmont Hotel in San Francisco in 1912. At the 1915 Panama Pacific Exposition in San Francisco Herrold's demonstrations overshadowed those of De Forest.

But the name De Forest ended up having the same relationship to the

Lee De Forest, "The Father of Radio."
Bettmann Archive

history of broadcasting as that of Marconi to wireless telegraphy. Installing a transmitter at the Columbia Gramophone Company, De Forest began daily music broadcasts in 1916. Moving his transmitter to the High Bridge in the Bronx, he broadcast the election returns on November 7, 1916, ending with the estimate that Charles Evans Hughes had defeated Woodrow Wilson. This was in error, of course, but the spectacle of broadcasting such important news was impressive.

All nongovernmental radio operations were shut down following the United States' entry into World War I, but the government continued making enormous strides in broadcast technology. As early as 1904 the Navy had operated twenty wireless stations, closely following the work of Marconi. To preclude the possibility of interference with Navy signals, Congress passed a law in 1912 providing that the Department of Commerce should issue licenses to private broadcasters and should assign them wave lengths that did not conflict with government wave lengths. Then in 1915 the American Telephone & Telegraph Company used a Navy station in Arlington, Virginia, to send signals across the Atlantic, which were also picked up as far away as Honolulu. This kind of experimentation continued throughout the war. Finally, after much debate and planning, private operation of broadcasting facilities was fully restored on March 1, 1920.

THE FIRST RADIO STATIONS

Dr. Frank Conrad, a Westinghouse engineer who had operated experimental station 8XK in Pittsburgh since 1916, got a jump on postwar broadcasting because of his connection with the Navy, for whom he had designed equipment. On October 17, 1919, Conrad began broadcasting phonograph records, and he received so many requests for music that he began broadcasting for 2 hours on Wednesday and Sunday evenings. A local department store began advertising the sale of Westinghouse crystal sets to hear "Dr. Frank Conrad's popular broadcasts." Westinghouse decided that there was a new sales market awaiting it and applied for the first full commercial license for standard broadcasting.[6] Its station, KDKA, began operating on November 2, 1920, with a broadcast of returns from the Harding-Cox presidential election. The *Pittsburgh Post* supplied the election bulletins by telephone and a few thousand persons heard the 18-hour program.

KDKA was not the first station to regularly broadcast news, despite claims that it was. The Herrold contributions in San Jose have been noted. In addition, a Detroit experimental station, 8MK, began daily operations from the *Detroit News* building on August 20, 1920, under the newspaper's sponsorship. A De Forest sales organization—the Radio News and Music Company—had obtained a license for the station and on August 31 it broadcast the results of a Michigan election. From that time it carried music, talks, and news for a part of each day. The *News* obtained its full commercial license for what became station WWJ in October, 1921.

Another pioneer was experimental station 9XM, operated by Professors Earle Terry, Edward Bennett, and others at the University of Wisconsin beginning in 1917. The station was allowed to continue broadcasting throughout World War I, and it aimed its signals to Navy stations in the Great Lakes area. It became WHA in 1922. Although it certainly was the oldest educational station, its claim to be the oldest overall had been muddled by arguments over when it began its daily weather and market reports, whether it had a regular audience, and whether some of its early transmissions were only in Morse code.

Among other active stations in 1920 were KQV in Pittsburgh, WRUC at Union College, 6ADZ in Hollywood, which became KNX, and 4XD in Charlotte, North Carolina.

Radio broadcasting thus began as a means of promoting other enterprises: a department store selling crystal sets, a company wishing to make radios, or a newspaper expanding its domain. Other newspapers followed the *Detroit News* in establishing stations, among them the *Kansas City Star, Milwaukee Journal, Chicago Tribune, Los Angeles Times, Louisville Courier-Journal, Atlanta Journal, Dallas News,* and *Chicago Daily News.*

AT&T, WESTINGHOUSE, AND GE

But the most important elements in the growth of national radio broadcasting were the big companies of the communications and electric manufacturing industries: American Telephone & Telegraph (AT&T), Westinghouse, and Gen-

THE FOUR "R'S"—READING, 'RITING, 'RITHMETIC AND RADIO
Miss Sara Muller, teacher at the South Haven school, L. I., one of the smallest schoolhouses in America, instructing her class in calisthenics with the aid of the radio set on the step.
(Fotograms.)

Some of the Manifold Uses of Radio, Wonder Science of the Century

GOVERNOR DONAHEY OF OHIO
in the studio of The Cleveland Plain Dealer listening to the rest of an evening's program to which he had earlier contributed a speech.
(Times Wide World Photos.)

PRESIDENT'S FATHER LISTENING IN ON "CAL"
Colonel John C. Coolidge at the home of a neighbor at Plymouth, Vt., hearing over the radio the address delivered by President Coolidge at the Associated Press luncheon in New York.
(International.)

DR. MARX, CHANCELLOR OF GERMANY
and head of the German Democratic Party, using the radio to expound his political principles during the recent electoral campaign.
(Times Wide World Photos.)

AN AMBITIOUS PROGRAM
Reginald Gouraud of Paris perfecting a radio telephone transmission set which, he claims, will be strong enough to permit President Coolidge and President Millerand of France to converse with each other.
(Times Wide World Photos.)

SWAYING HIS HIDEOUS HEAD IN HARMONY WITH DULCET STRAINS
The king cobra at the Bronx Zoo, most deadly reptile in the world, charmed by the "concord of sweet sounds" that emanates from the loud speaker of a radio receiving set.
(Times Wide World Photos.)

FASTER THAN ANY PLAYS THEY EVER MADE ON THE DIAMOND
is this radio music transmitted at the rate of 186,000 miles a second to the ears of the Yankee baseball players, Urban, Roettger and Johnson, when rain caused a postponement of the game.
(Times Wide World Photos.)

eral Electric (GE). Radio's growth would mean the expansion of outlets for their products and services.

The pioneer Westinghouse station, KDKA, scored many radio firsts as it pointed the way toward achieving public interest in buying radio sets. During 1921 it broadcast a series of public speeches by national figures, an on-the-spot report of a prizefight, and major league baseball games. Westinghouse also opened stations in New York, Chicago, Philadelphia, and Boston. General Electric built WGY, its powerful Schenectady, New York, station, and American Telephone & Telegraph built WEAF (now WNBC) in New York City.

THE RADIO CORPORATION OF AMERICA

More importantly, the three companies had gone together in 1919 to form the Radio Corporation of America (RCA). At government urging, stimulated by United States Navy officers interested in the new medium, the companies had bought up British-owned Marconi patents on radio equipment, which they pooled with their own patent rights in the new RCA. They thus brought into being the future giant of the radio industry, although at first RCA devoted itself to wireless message service.[7]

In 1922 the big companies began a competitive struggle for control of radio. AT&T held two trump cards. Under the patent-pooling agreements with its competitors, AT&T held considerable power over many stations' rights to charge fees for broadcasting. And the telephone company observed that KDKA had been successful in using telephone lines to bring religious and theater programs into the studio for broadcasting.

So when WEAF went on the air in August, 1922, AT&T announced that it would be an advertising-supported station. Within 7 months it had some two dozen sponsors using air time, and the era of commercialization of radio had dawned.[8] At the same time WEAF was experimenting with the use of telephone lines to air intercity broadcasts—telephone lines that AT&T now withheld from its competitors.

DAVID SARNOFF, RCA, AND NBC

But despite AT&T's advantage and its withdrawal from the RCA consortium, its rivals were not discouraged. Coming to power in RCA was David Sarnoff, the son of a Russian immigrant family who had gotten his start as a Marconi wireless operator. Sarnoff had been an advocate of mass radio broadcasting since 1915 when he predicted that radio could become a major industry.

And indeed it was clear that radio could become a paying proposition for many. The number of stations in the country had increased from thirty in January, 1922, to 556 in March, 1923. The number of receiving sets jumped from some 50,000 in 1921 to more than 600,000 in 1922. Newspapers found the story of radio's growth one of continuing interest: In June, 1922, the *New York Times* was averaging 40 column inches of radio information daily.[9] The public was demonstrating avid interest in radio's newly developing stars: announcers

Graham MacNamee and Milton Cross, the vocal duet of Billy Jones and Ernie Hare, and the performers on the Eveready Hour, sponsored by a radio battery company. There were objections to radio's introduction of direct advertising to pay the costs of programming, but they were to prove unavailing in the onward rush of the new medium.

The problem faced by Sarnoff and other entrepreneurs was to break the hold AT&T had won on big-time radio. One example of this power was AT&T's role in early World Series baseball reporting. The 1921 Giants-Yankees series, the first for Babe Ruth in New York, was reported for Newark station WJZ by Sandy Hunt, sports editor of the New York *Sunday Call.* Hunt telephoned play-by-play accounts to announcer Tommy Cowan in Newark, while KDKA received the information by wire. The following year WJZ joined with WGY in Schnectady and WBZ in Springfield, Massachusetts, and carried the descriptions of Grantland Rice, the legendary sportswriter for the *New York Herald Tribune.* The Giants and Yankees played again and an extensive sales campaign was waged. WJZ was owned by RCA and newspaper readers were offered "Radiola Score Sheets" for following the games on the $25 receiver sets being advertised. But in stepped AT&T, which refused to allow the WJZ network to lease the telephone lines. Inferior telegraph lines not designed for voice transmission had to be used, and caused distortion. By 1923 AT&T had assumed control of baseball coverage. The third Giants-Yankees series was distributed to a network of stations through WEAF, which hired W. O. McGeehan, baseball expert for the *Herald Tribune* and Graham McNamee, as announcers. McNamee became an instant celebrity and reported World Series games, in addition to numerous other events, on WEAF until 1935.[10]

The outlook appeared grim as long as RCA was hampered in accepting advertising fees or in using telephone lines for intercity programming. In early 1924 the Eveready Hour bought time over a dozen stations—the first use of national radio advertising. A year later the chain headed by WEAF had twenty-six outlets, reaching as far west as Kansas City. RCA was stuck with its inferior network headed by WJZ and WGY. At the moment Sarnoff was planning to create an RCA subsidiary that could accept unrestricted advertising, the telephone company, secure with the prospect of mounting revenues from leasing its lines, offered to withdraw from the broadcasting business. WEAF was sold to RCA in 1926 and immediately RCA, GE, and Westinghouse incorporated the National Broadcasting Company as an RCA subsidiary with Merlin H. Aylesworth as president.

NBC made its debut on November 15, 1926, with a spectacular 4½-hour show from the ballroom of the Waldorf-Astoria Hotel in New York and other points around the nation, including Chicago, where Mary Garden sang "Annie Laurie," and Independence, Kansas, where Will Rogers mimicked President Coolidge.[11] It was clear that in the future sponsors would pay for shows featuring big-name bands and singers. By January NBC operated two networks, the Red network with WEAF as the flagship station and the Blue network headed by WJZ.

On January 1, 1927, the two networks joined to produce the first coast-to-coast broadcast, of the Rose Bowl football game with McNamee as announcer. For a year NBC had a third network, the Pacific Coast Network, but this was

David Sarnoff, RCA's head.

William S. Paley of CBS.

eliminated in late 1928 when regular coast-to-coast broadcasts linking fifty-eight stations were initiated. In 1930 a federal antitrust action forced GE and Westinghouse to dispose of their holdings in RCA, and the management headed by Sarnoff became supreme. RCA had acquired the Victor phonograph interests and had established the RCA-Victor manufacturing unit to produce phonographs, radio sets, and tubes. RCA Communications, Inc., operated a worldwide radiotelegraph system. Eventually the Federal Communications Commission forced NBC to sell its Blue network. It was purchased in 1943 by Edward J. Noble, who renamed it the American Broadcasting Company in 1945.

CBS AND PALEY

NBC's first competition came in 1927 when a group of broadcasters trying to syndicate program talent formed the United Independent Broadcasters and allied themselves with a sales company of the Columbia Phonograph Record Company called the Columbia Phonograph Broadcasting System, Inc. United acquired the phonograph company's stock in 1927 and renamed the sales company the Columbia Broadcasting System, Inc. The first network show was on September 18, 1927, when listeners were treated to a variety of music and quite a bit of advertising that one reviewer thought was "aggravating."[12] A year later William S. Paley and his family bought control of United and in 1929 the firm dissolved the sales company and gave the network its name, CBS. Young Paley, who initially had to prove to his father radio's ability to increase the sales of the family cigar company, used his vigor and enterprise to push CBS into a competitive position with NBC in the battle to gain affiliated stations. By 1934 CBS had ninety-four affiliates, compared to the 127 owned by the two NBC networks. Paley was to dominate CBS affairs for 50 years, and his shadow still remained on the network's corporate life into the 1980s.

FEDERAL REGULATION: THE FCC

None of this development of radio would have been possible, however, had not the federal government's power been used to avert chaos on the airwaves. Secretary of Commerce Herbert Hoover had endeavored to regulate the growing number of stations, but he lacked sufficient authority under the 1912 law to prevent one station from interfering with the broadcasts of another. By early 1927, when the number of stations had increased to 733, listeners found stations jumping about on the broadcast band to avoid interference, which in metropolitan areas particularly had reached the point of curtailing sales of radio sets.

National radio conferences held in Washington each year after 1922 urged additional federal regulation of use of the limited number of available broadcast channels, which by common consent were recognized as being in the public domain. Radio manufacturers wanted the government to unscramble the situation. So did the National Association of Broadcasters, which had been formed in 1923. So did the listening public. The American Newspaper Publishers Association, a substantial number of whose members owned stations, also wanted the government to resolve the problem. Walter A. Strong of the *Chicago Daily News* served as chairperson of a coordinating committee that sought passage of a new federal radio act. The bill was approved by Congress in February, 1927.

The Radio Act of 1927 established a five-member Federal Radio Commission empowered to regulate all forms of radio communication. The federal government maintained control over all channels, and the Commission granted licenses for the use of specific channels for 3-year periods. Licenses were to be granted "in the public interest, convenience, or necessity" to provide "fair, efficient, and equitable service" throughout the country.

Under this authority the Federal Radio Commission set about eliminating confusion on the broadcast band. The number of stations fell by approximately 150, and the total remained just above the 600 mark for the next 10 years. The Commission established a group of "clear channels" on which only one station could operate at night. Of the fifty-seven clear channel stations in 1947, designed to give rural areas unimpeded reception of a powerful metropolitan station's programs, fifty-five were owned by or affiliated with the networks. They were the lucrative prizes of radio.[13]

Federal authority was broadened by passage of the Communications Act of 1934, which established the seven-member Federal Communications Commission. This Commission took over not only authority to regulate radio broadcasting but also jurisdiction over all telecommunications. The responsibility of the license holders to operate their radio stations in the public interest was more clearly spelled out, and the Commission had the power to refuse renewal of a license in cases of flagrant disregard of broadcasting responsibility. The law forbade, however, any attempt at censorship by the Commission; no station could be directed to put a particular program on or off the air. The FCC rarely used its power to cancel the licenses of broadcasters; rather it resorted only to indirect pressure in carrying out its supervision of station operations. However, that pressure was to become substantial in later years.

THE CLASH OVER RADIO NEWS

With the development of widespread network broadcasting, and the unscrambling of the airwaves by the exercise of federal authority, radio had come of age. But radio's development ran head-on into the interests of other media, particularly incurring the wrath of the newspaper publishers. The major conflict involved radio's growing income taken from the nation's advertising budget. A second involved radio's broadcasting of the news.

Newspaper reaction to radio in the early days of broadcasting was mixed. Newspapers carried the radio log as a reader service and publicized radio's progress and stars. A report by the American Newspaper Publishers Association's radio committee in 1927 showed that forty-eight newspapers were owners of stations, that sixty-nine sponsored programs on unowned stations, and that ninety-seven gave news programs over the air. More than half of the high-grade stations had some newspaper affiliation. The ANPA's radio committee took the position that radio reporting of news events stimulated newspapers sales—a belief borne out fully by later experience.[14] Some of the most exciting broadcasts were of coverage of the 1924 political conventions; the 1925 Scopes "monkey" trial in Dayton, Tennessee, when listeners of the *Chicago Tribune* station WGN heard the arguments of Clarence Darrow and William Jennings Bryan; Charles Lindbergh's arrival in Washington following his 1927 epic flight to Paris; and the 1927 Jack Dempsey-Gene Tunney prizefight, which was carried over sixty-nine stations, the largest network to that point.

There were some holdouts. The AP, for example, tried to retain its 1924 presidential election returns for newspaper publication only and fined the Portland *Oregonian* $100 for broadcasting them. There was a great amount of criticism of advertising messages. But there was no stopping radio's ability to cover major events. Some 10 million Americans listened in on 3 million receiving sets to hear of Calvin Coolidge's victory. Four years later, in 1928, the NBC and CBS networks could reach 8 million sets. In that bitter campaign both Republican Herbert Hoover and Democrat Alfred E. Smith took to the air, spending $1 million on campaign talks. That year the press associations—the AP, UP, and INS—supplied complete election returns to radio stations, and Ted Husing, the popular sports announcer who doubled as a news announcer when major events occurred, delivered a memorable election broadcast.

Stimulated by public interest in radio's coverage of the election, a few stations began to expand their news operations. In December, 1928, KFAB in Lincoln, Nebraska, employed the city editor of the *Lincoln Star* to run its newscasts. Stations followed suit in other cities. The most elaborate early news effort was made by KMPC in Beverly Hills, California, which put ten reporters onto Los Angeles news runs in 1930.[15] Some newspaper publishers complained, justifiably, that radio was using public interest in newscasts as one selling point in attracting advertising.

POPULAR RADIO ENTERTAINMENT

Music was the most popular fare on radio in the late 1920s, most of it classical or semiclassical on shows like the *Palmolive Hour* and the *Maxwell House Hour.* But dance music was catching the public's fancy and soon band leaders Guy Lombardo, Paul Whiteman, and others were known nationwide. Many a New Year's Eve ended with millions of listeners dancing to "Auld Lang Syne" as played by Lombardo and his Royal Canadians. Singers became celebrities too, with Vaughn de Leath, Elsie Janis, Bing Crosby, and Kate Smith breaking onto the air waves. A study of 1927 broadcasts from New York showed that three-fourths of

Amos 'n' Andy—Freeman Gosden and Charles Correll.
Bettmann Archive

the shows carried music, nearly another 15 percent were religious or educational, and only a few dealt with drama, sports, or information.[16]

The demand for drama began to increase, though, with NBC featuring the *Eveready Hour* and *Real Folks* and CBS promoting shows like *Great Moments in History, Biblical Dramas, Main Street Sketches,* and *True Story.* In August, 1929, one of the most popular comedy shows in broadcasting history made its debut on the NBC network. Freeman Gosden and Charles Correll starred as *Amos 'n' Andy.* Bringing their blackface vaudeville act to radio, they first created *Sam 'n' Henry* for WGN in Chicago. Switching to WMAQ, they changed the name to *Amos 'n' Andy.* By 1928 a syndication handled by the *Chicago Daily News* had lined up thirty stations. The five weekly episodes demonstrated how syndication could be used widely in the future: Listeners were enticed by the continuing story and waited eagerly for the next dilemma with the "fresh-air taxi." They enjoyed the story line and did not identify it as a form of racial stereotyping—just fun to hear.

NBC paid Gosden and Correll $100,000 to join the network. The resulting excitement confirmed what some critics said of radio programming—that its main purpose was to sell radio sets. Sales of radios and supplies increased from $650 million to $842 million between 1928 and 1929.[17] The nation shifted its schedules to fit in the *Amos 'n' Andy* show. Factories closed early and cab drivers refused to pick up passengers between 7 and 7:15 P.M. Eastern Time. Radio was in full force, and the concept of national advertising had been accepted. The 1930s would see spectacular expansion, particularly in news and commentary.

THE RISE OF MOTION PICTURES

"Going to the movies" became a major preoccupation for Americans in the 1920s, even though listening to the radio was also becoming a popular activity. The illusion of movement created by the motion-picture projector, and the sense of reality felt by a viewer of the film, made the new medium a fascinating one. After Peter Mark Roget (of *Thesaurus* fame) advanced his theory of "persistence of vision" in 1824, inventors worked on the motion-picture concept. The human eye, Roget contended, retains an image for a fraction of a second longer than it actually appears. Thus a series of still pictures printed on a ribbon of celluloid film, and projected at sixteen or twenty-four frames per second, will create for a viewer the illusion of continuous motion.

By 1840 the work of Joseph Niepce and Louis Daguerre in France had created a photographic process which Mathew Brady used in the American Civil War. In 1877, utilizing twenty-four cameras, Eadweard Muybridge and John D. Isaacs conducted a famous demonstration of the gait of a galloping horse. "Magic lantern" shows became popular on lecture circuits. In 1888 George Eastman's marketing of his Kodak camera, using a roll of film, marked another step. Finishing his invention of the phonograph the same year, Thomas A. Edison set his assistant to work on what became the Kinetoscope. William Kennedy Laurie Dickson adapted the Eastman film to the camera by devising a sprocket system, and offered a 50-foot "peep show" in the 4-foot Kinetoscope box in 1889. Louis and Auguste Lumière and Charles Pathé in France and

Robert W. Paul and William Friese-Greene in England were simultaneously creating moving pictures. The first public showing in a theater in the United States occurred in 1896, using Edison's improved Vitascope.

Just to see Niagara Falls flowing, or an onrushing train, was exciting to the first audiences. But artistry and skill were needed if the nickelodeons were to survive. Georges Méliès of France, a magician, made 1000 brief films offering ideas for others. But it was Edwin S. Porter's 8-minute 1903 film called *The Great Train Robbery* that first told a unified story, utilizing camera angle shifting, film editing, and parallel development of story themes. Porter also set the pace for untold numbers of Westerns to follow.

Three men, working variously as producer-directors and actors, made major imprints on the film history in the second decade of the twentieth century. One was David Wark Griffith, first an actor and then a director at Biograph, which with Pathé and Vitagraph were leading picture-making companies in New York. In 1915 Griffith completed a twelve-reel picture which took nearly 3 hours to show—the first of the "epics" of American film. It was *The Birth of a Nation,* the story of a victimized Southern family told in a setting of Civil War battles, Sherman's march to the sea, renegade blacks, and Ku Klux Klansmen. Griffith was a son of a Confederate war veteran and produced a picture sympathetic to that cause with inflamatory racist stereotypes that sometimes triggered antiblack rioting. Its excellence as film-making artistry, and its emotional impact, gave the film a permanent place in movie history.

In 1912 Mack Sennett, also a graduate of the Biograph studio, established the Keystone Film Company in Los Angeles. Master of slapstick, he created the Keystone Kops as a long-running institution. Among those playing in Sennett's films were Mabel Normand, first of the cinematic comediennes, frozen-faced

D. W. Griffith directs one of his films.
Bettmann Archive

Buster Keaton, and a young English actor named Charlie Chaplin. Gaining fame with *The Tramp* (1915) and *Shoulder Arms* (1918), Chaplin won a $1 million contract to make his own films. Telling largely in pantomime the story of "the little fellow" who never fitted in, Chaplin captivated his audiences with his tramp's costume and orchestrated mannerisms for *The Kid* (1921), *The Gold Rush* (1925), and *City Lights* (1931). In *Modern Times* (1936) he rebelled against the assembly line and industrial system; in 1940 he stepped out of character to oppose totalitarianism in *The Great Dictator.* But it was the wistful little tramp who set a dinner table for guests who never came, or who shuffled off into the night, that won Chaplin his fame.

In 1919, Griffith, Chaplin, swashbuckling actor Douglas Fairbanks, and "America's sweetheart" Mary Pickford formed the United Artists Corporation so they could control their own careers and earnings. By then Hollywood was producing three-quarters of the world's films. Most of the major film companies were in place by the early 1920s: Fox, Metro-Goldwyn-Mayer, Paramount, Warner Brothers, Universal, Columbia. Each had producers like Sam Goldwyn, Thomas Ince, Louis B. Mayer, Jesse Lasky, or William Fox. Each had its "stars" such as horseman William S. Hart, comedian Harold Lloyd, actress Lillian Gish or Gloria Swanson, and Rudolph Valentino, "The Sheik," whose sudden death in 1926 brought about hysterical mourning. Movie goers lined up at cinema palaces to see such spectaculars as the 1923 pair, *The Covered Wagon* and Cecil B. De Mille's *The Ten Commandments.* More sophisticated was *Flesh and the Devil,* starring Greta Garbo and John Gilbert in 1927. Garbo was part of a foreign influence that enhanced Hollywood in the 1920s. Ernst Lubitsch brought his comedy-making skill from Germany and teamed with singer-actor Maurice Chevalier. Josef von Sternberg directed compatriot Marlene Dietrich. Director Erich von Stroheim made his classic *Greed* in 1924, based on Frank Norris' novel *McTeague,* then portrayed the futility of war in his 1926 film, *What Price Glory*? This was followed by Lewis Milestone's filming of Erich Remarque's German novel *All Quiet on the Western Front* in 1930. Sergei Eisenstein captured the sweep and drama of Russian history in films such as *Potemkin,* his 1925 triumph commemorating the 1905 mutiny aboard that Russian battleship against Czarist misrule.

GOING TO THE MOVIES: THE "TALKIES"

More than 20,000 movie houses were scattered across the country by the mid-1920s. Weekly attendance averaged 46 million persons in 1925 and vaulted to an all-time high of 90 million in 1930. Part of the reason for expanding attendance was the addition of a sound track in 1927. The "talkies" were at first a novelty, then quickly became the standard movies. Sound scores had been run with movies, and Fox Movietone News had shown Charles A. Lindbergh's Paris and New York receptions in sound after his 1927 flight. But when Al Jolson sang "Mammy" in a Broadway premiere of *The Jazz Singer* in October, 1927, the "talking picture" excitement swept the studios. Chaplin could still do *City Lights* in silence in 1931, but other stars whose voices were not congenial retired into the wings.

Going to the movies was a low-priced amusement of the Great Depression years. The movie houses offered double bills, even triple bills, for as little as a quarter, and they were warm places to sit for the underpaid and unemployed. In 1940 weekly attendance still averaged 80 million. Humor was an antidote for the Depression; two stars with unique comic elán were Mae West and W. C. Fields. The Marx Brothers solidified their place in film lore with *Duck Soup* (1933). Comedy with a sophisticated touch and elegant setting was offered by comedienne Carole Lombard, by William Powell and Myrna Loy in the *Thin Man* series, and by director Frank Capra in the 1934 smash hit, *It Happened One Night,* starring Clark Gable and Claudette Colbert. There were lavish musicals like *Top Hat* (1935), which featured the flying feet of Fred Astaire and Ginger Rogers. Prohibition and gangsters provided themes for actors Jimmy Cagney, Edward G. Robinson, and Paul Muni.

The art of animation was revolutionized by Walt Disney, who organized teams of artists in his studio to take full advantage of movement, color, sound, musical synchronization, and vocal effects. Mickey Mouse made his debut in 1928, and by 1931 he and Minnie had appeared in ninety short subjects. "Who's afraid of the big bad wolf?" sang Disney's three little pigs in 1933. His full-length features, *Snow White and the Seven Dwarfs* (1937) and *Fantasia* (1940) foreshadowed later Disney enterprises on television and in Disneylands. The 1930s were also the decade of the child stars, led by Jackie Coogan and Shirley Temple. Coogan had been Chaplin's *Kid* of 1921. Temple danced in *Stand Up and Cheer* in 1934 and then in a succession of heart-warming films. Mickey Rooney and Judy Garland were the greatest child team before Garland reached stardom in the 1939 version of *The Wizard of Oz.*

The decade of the Thirties closed with an epic, *Gone With the Wind,* starring Clark Gable as Rhett Butler and English actress Vivian Leigh as Scarlett O'Hara. The novel had been a bestseller, and its story of the Civil War became an all-time fixture on the list of movie box-office successes in the United States. The 1939 film led that list until 1965, and was reproduced periodically on film and on television for succeeding generations. It still stood thirteenth on the box-office list in 1983.

Hollywood became a symbol of high living, sex, and sin in the early 1920s, as pitiless publicity and fan worship took effect. A sordid rape case ended "Fatty" Arbuckle's career; the unsolved murder of a leading director brought testimony damaging to stars Mabel Normand and Mary Miles Minter; Wallace Reid was revealed to be a drug addict. In 1922 the alarmed studios selected Postmaster General Will H. Hays to be their czar, as head of the Motion Picture Producers and Exhibitors of America. The "Hays Office" exercised informal censorship, made more stringent by its own 1930 production code, city and state censors, and the 1934 Legion of Decency.

JAZZ JOURNALISM: THE TABLOID

A new cycle of sensationalism in journalism began with the close of World War I. Just as in 1833, when the penny press appeared, and in 1897, when the Pulitzer-Hearst duel climaxed the introduction of the new journalism, the times were right for a sensationalized appeal to the people. And there was an untapped audience awaiting such an appeal, just as there had been in 1833 and 1897. In the 7 years between 1919 and 1926 three new papers in New York City found more than a million and a half readers without unduly disturbing the circulation balance of the existing dailies. Their sensationalism was accompanied by the use of two techniques that identify the period: the tabloid-style format and the extensive use of photography. As in earlier periods, the wave of sensationalism had its effect on all of the press before it subsided; and, as before, a more substantial journalism followed the era of sensationalized appeal. The 1920s are known as the decade of "jazz journalism,"[18] and the years that followed were marked by a rapid rise in emphasis on the techniques of interpretative reporting, not only in the newspaper field but also in magazine publishing and broadcasting.

The tabloid format introduced so successfully in New York after 1919 was not a stranger to journalism. Before newsprint became relatively plentiful in the middle of the nineteenth century, small-sized pages were common. The *Daily Graphic,* published in New York between 1873 and 1889 and carrying Stephen H. Horgan's early experimental halftone engravings, had a tabloid format. So did Frank A. Munsey's ill-fated *Daily Continent* of 1891, which like the *Daily Graphic* was heavily illustrated but no more sensationalized than other newspapers. It was not these American efforts that stimulated the tabloid era of the 1920s, however. For better or for worse, America owes its tabloids to the cradle of English-language journalism, Great Britain.

Even though English journalistic preoccupation with crime news and court stories played its part in suggesting the advantages of sensationalism to the first American penny press publishers in 1833, newspapers for the masses lagged in Great Britain because of stamp-tax regulations that did not disappear until 1855. The *Daily Telegraph* then became the first penny paper in England, but its appeal was to the middle classes. Not until after the introduction of compulsory education in England in 1870 was there a market for a truly popularized newspaper. Into that market stepped a discerning young man named Alfred C. Harmsworth, who as Lord Northcliffe was to become one of Britain's great press lords. His first project, in 1883, was a human-interest weekly magazine named *Answers,* which was modeled after George Newnes' *Tidbits* of 1881. Both publications used the contest idea as a means of enticing working class readers, and Harmsworth had 250,000 of them within 10 years.

Meanwhile Harmsworth was watching the progress of Joseph Pulitzer's *New York World* and of James Gordon Bennett, Jr.'s, *Paris Herald* with its short-lived London edition. He first adapted the new American techniques to the *London Evening News,* which he bought in 1894, and then to his far more famous *Daily Mail,* founded in 1896. Soon Pulitzer was taking lessons from Harmsworth, whom the *World*'s publisher admired so greatly that he permitted Harmsworth, as guest publisher, to turn the January 1, 1901, issue of the *World* into a tabloid representing "the newspaper of the twentieth century." New York was unimpressed, however, and it remained for Harmsworth to do the job in England.

The first widely circulated tabloid was the *Daily Mirror,* which Harmsworth began in London in 1903 as a newspaper for women but soon converted into a "half-penny illustrated," small, sensational, and amusing. By 1909, its circulation had reached a million copies, and the *Daily Sketch* and *Daily Graphic* jumped into the tabloid field. Harmsworth had become Lord Northcliffe and a leading figure in English journalism by the time of World War I. He still felt that someone should be publishing a tabloid like his *Daily Mirror* in New York, and when he met an American army officer who was overseas from his newspaper desk, Northcliffe told him how lucrative the tabloid could be.

FOUNDING OF THE *NEW YORK DAILY NEWS*

The army officer was Captain Joseph Medill Patterson, partner with Colonel Robert R. McCormick in the publishing of the *Chicago Tribune* since 1914. The two grandsons of Joseph Medill met later in France and agreed to a plan to start a New York tabloid to be called the *Daily News.* The cousins had other reasons than the arguments Northcliffe had advanced for undertaking the New York venture. Colonel McCormick, as is shown in detail in a later chapter, was a king-sized chip off the conservative Medill block. Captain Patterson was unconventional enough to have written two novels (*A Little Brother of the Rich* and *Rebellion*) that constituted protests against social injustice and economic oppression and was considered socialistic in his thinking by others of his wealthy class. The plan for Patterson to start a tabloid in New York would thus give him an opportunity to reach the many immigrants and least literate native-born, as he wished to do, and at the same time would rid Colonel McCormick of an embarrassing copublisher arrangement in Chicago.

So the *Illustrated Daily News,* as the paper was called the first few months, made its bow in New York on June 26, 1919. Its half-size front page was covered with a picture of the Prince of Wales (later King Edward VIII and Duke of Windsor), whose forthcoming visit to America had already stirred anticipatory feminine heartthrobs. Its promotion gimmick was the sponsoring of its own beauty contest, which was announced to startled readers of the *New York Times* in a full-page ad that read: SEE NEW YORK'S MOST BEAUTIFUL GIRLS EVERY MORNING IN THE ILLUSTRATED DAILY NEWS. New York newspeople of 1919, like those of 1833 who had sniffed at Benjamin Day's newly founded *Sun,* dismissed the tabloid venture without much concern. But one of them, at least, foresaw the effect its sensationalism, its entertainment emphasis, and its reliance on photography would have. He was Carr Van Anda, the astute managing editor of the *Times,* who while hardly in the sensationalized picture paper field himself realized that the *Daily News* would satisfy a widespread postwar public craving and reach a new reading audience. "This paper," he said, "should reach a circulation of 2,000,000."[19] Patterson and his editors did not disappoint Van Anda. In 1924 the *Daily News* circulation of 750,000 was the largest in the country. By 1929 the figure was 1.32 million—thus increased while the combined circulation of the other New York morning papers stood still. And before World War II it had hit the 2 million mark.

The *Daily News* did badly at first. Its initial circulation of 200,000 dropped to 26,000 the second month, and two of its four reporters were fired. But Captain Patterson was discovering that his circulation potential was not among readers of the *Times* but among the immigrant and poorly educated American-born population of New York. The *News* was put on stands where only foreign-language papers had sold before, and its pictures sold the paper. By 1921 it was second in circulation to Hearst's *Evening Journal.* Hearst's morning *American* tried to capture some of the readership going to the *News* by filling its columns with pictures and features but the tabloid won the verdict. The sharp battle between Hearst and McCormick circulation people in Chicago was transferred to New York, with lotteries, coupon prizes, and other inducements for readers. Patterson was the victor again with a limerick contest keyed to the popular taste.

THE *MIRROR* AND THE *GRAPHIC*

Direct competition arrived for the *News* in 1924, the year it became America's most widely circulated newspaper. Hearst had experimented unsuccessfully with the tabloid format in Boston—always a poor town for journalistic innovations—but in despair of the *American*'s ever whipping the *News,* he began his tabloid *Daily Mirror.* Close behind him was Bernarr Macfadden, publisher of *Physical Culture* and *True Story* magazines and a millionaire with a yen to influence the public and hold high office. But as in his successful *True Story* venture, his newspaper aims were unconventional. He wanted a paper, he said, that "will shatter precedent to smithereens."[20] Macfadden selected Emile Gauvreau, up to that time the managing editor of the respectable *Hartford Courant,* as his chief editor, and the two brought out the *Daily Graphic.* The *Mirror* began to challenge the *News* on more or less straight journalistic terms, but the *Graphic* set out to see just how sensational and lurid it could be. The result was the battle of what Oswald Garrison Villard called "gutter journalism."

The *Graphic* quickly became the most notorious of the tabloids. Indeed, Macfadden had no intention of running a newspaper. He did not bother with subscribing to a press-association service and played only the "gigantic" general news. He was trying to build a million-reader audience on newsstand sales of a daily that was to be the *True Confessions* of the newspaper world. Reporters wrote first-person stories to be signed by persons in the news, and editors headlined them "I Know Who Killed My Brother," "He Beat Me—I Love Him," and "For 36 Hours I Lived Another Woman's Love Life." Gauvreau's retort to criticism was that the public wanted "hot news,"[21] and the evidence seemed to be on his side, as newsstand sales of the *Graphic* mounted.

The climax year of the war of the tabloids was 1926. First the Broadway producer, Earl Carroll, gave a party at which a nude dancing girl sat in a bathtub full of champagne. Before the furor had died down, the tabloids discovered a wealthy real-estate man, Edward Browning, and his 15-year-old shopgirl bride. This was "hot" romance indeed and the pair became Daddy and Peaches to all of America. The *Graphic* portrayed them frolicking on a bed with Daddy saying "Woof! Woof! I'm a Goof!" Gauvreau decided to thrill his shopgirl audience with the details of Peaches' intimate diary, but at that point the law stepped in.

Meanwhile the desperate editors of the *Mirror* had dug up a 4-year-old murder story in New Jersey. In 1922 a New Brunswick, New Jersey, minister named Edward Hall and his choir-singer sweetheart, Eleanor Mills, were found dead, apparently suicides. The *Mirror* succeeded in having the minister's widow brought to trial and for months the New Jersey town became one of the most

Average net paid circulation of THE NEWS, Dec., 1927:
Sunday, 1,357,556
Daily, 1,193,297

DAILY NEWS

FINAL EDITION

Copyright, 1928, by News Syndicate Co., Inc. Reg. U. S. Pat. Off. NEW YORK'S PICTURE NEWSPAPER Entered as 2nd class matter Post Office, New York, N. Y.

Vol. 9. No. 174 28 Pages New York, Saturday, January 14, 1928 2 Cents IN CITY LIMITS | 3 CENTS Elsewhere

FUNERALS HELD For Gray, Mrs. Snyder

Story on Page 3

(© 1928 by Pacific & Atlantic Photos)

WHEN RUTH PAID HER DEBT TO THE STATE!—The only unofficial photo ever taken within the death chamber, this most remarkable, exclusive picture shows closeup of Ruth Snyder in death chair at Sing Sing as lethal current surged through her body at 11:06 Thursday night. Its first publication in yesterday's EXTRA edition of THE NEWS was the most talked-of feat in history of journalism. Ruth's body is seen straightened within its confining gyves, her helmeted head, face masked, hands clutching, and electrode strapped to her right leg with stocking down. Autopsy table on which body was removed is beside chair.

—*Story and another electrocution picture ...*

This 1928 front page represented the extreme in New York tabloid sensationalism.

important filing points for press associations and big newspapers in America. One witness became "the pig woman" to the 200 reporters at the trial. Unfortunately for the *Mirror,* Mrs. Hall was acquitted and sued the paper for libel.

A second sensational murder trial was drummed up in the spring of 1927. A corset salesperson named Judd Gray and his sweetheart, Mrs. Ruth Snyder, had collaborated in disposing of the unwanted Mr. Snyder. When it came time for Mrs. Snyder's execution in the electric chair at Sing Sing, the *Graphic* blared to its readers:

> Don't fail to read tomorrow's *Graphic.* An installment that thrills and stuns! A story that fairly pierces the heart and reveals Ruth Snyder's last thoughts on earth; that pulses the blood as it discloses her final letters. Think of it! A woman's final thoughts just before she is clutched in the deadly snare that sears and burns and FRIES AND KILLS! Her very last words! Exclusively in tomorrow's *Graphic.*[22]

It was the photography-minded *News* that had the last word, however. The *Graphic* might have its "confession" but the *News* proposed to take its readers inside the execution chamber. Pictures were forbidden, but a photographer, Tom Howard, strapped a tiny camera to his ankle and took his picture just after the current was turned on. The *News* put a touched-up shot on its front page, sold 250,000 extra papers, and then had to run off 750,000 additional copies of the front page later.

PATTERSON'S NEWS VALUES CHANGE

Patterson's news and photo enterprise went beyond shocking people. When the steamer *Vestris* sank off the Atlantic coast, with the loss of several hundred lives, Patterson sent all his staffers to interview the survivors on the chance that one of them had taken a picture. One had, and for $1200 the *News* bought one of the greatest action news pictures ever taken, showing the tilted ship's deck and recording the expressions of the victims as they prepared to jump into the water or go down with the ship. Patterson put $750,000 into Associated Press Wirephoto in the early 1930s, when other publishers were balking, and for a while had exclusive New York use of Wirephoto. The *News* developed its own staff of crack photographers and in addition welcomed shots taken by freelancers in the vast New York area. The payoff was consistent.

With 1929 came the Wall Street crash, depression, and deepening years of unemployment. Patterson, with his finger on the pulse of the people, told his editors and reporters that the depression and its effects on the lives of all Americans was now the big story. Not that the *News* and other papers stopped playing crime and sex news and features. But they also gave great space to the serious news of a people in trouble. Patterson's *Daily News* became a firm supporter of Roosevelt's New Deal through the 1930s, to the disgust of the fiercely anti-New Deal Colonel McCormick in the *Chicago Tribune* tower.

The *Daily News* still wisecracked in its editorial columns and still produced its headlines with a twist that caught any reader's eye. But after 1939 it had no more greetings for the man in the White House. It broke with Roosevelt over involvement in World War II and became bitterly isolationist. Patterson's distrust of the president's foreign policy then led him to fight the administration all

Readers expected to see the faces of personalities. Senator Gerald P. Nye and John D. Rockefeller, surrounded by photographers in 1923.

down the line. After his death in 1946, the *News* was under the control of Colonel McCormick, although its operations were directed by Patterson's former executives. Despite this political break with the Democratic party the *News* remained a "people's paper," climbing to peak circulations of 2.4 million daily and 4.5 million Sunday in 1947, before it felt the effects of a general slackening of metropolitan newspaper circulations and a sharp drop in sales of entertainment-centered papers vulnerable to television's inroads. It remained a paper still sharp enough to produce this 1976 headline on the President's response to the bankrupt city's plea for aid: "FORD TO CITY: DROP DEAD."[23]

THE END OF THE TABLOID ERA

Things did not go so well with the *Mirror* and *Graphic.* Hearst sold the *Mirror* in 1928, had to take it back in 1930, and then bolstered it by stealing columnist Walter Winchell from the *Graphic* and sending Arthur Brisbane in as editor. But the *Mirror* never became a profitable Hearst property and was closed in 1963. The *Graphic* never won any advertising support and died unmourned in 1932, after losing millions of dollars for Macfadden.

Two points should be made clear: Very few of the other newspapers that adopted the tabloid format were of the racy character of the New York tabs; and the quest for sensational news did not die with the passing of the *Graphic* and the semitransformation of the *Daily News.* One hopeful tabloid publisher was Cornelius Vanderbilt, Jr., who started crusading, nonsalacious picture papers in Los Angeles, San Francisco, and Miami in the early 1920s. Vanderbilt won good-sized circulations for his papers, but failed to build up advertiser support, and the chain soon withered. The *Los Angeles Daily News* passed to liberal-minded Manchester Boddy, who built it into a pro-New Deal paper much like orthodox dailies except for a freewheeling style of writing. The *Chicago Times,* founded in 1929, was likewise a liberal, tersely written paper. When Marshall Field combined his *Chicago Sun* with the *Times* in 1947 he kept the tabloid format. The *Daily News* and *Post* in New York and *Newsday* on Long Island were other tabloid leaders. In addition there were the supermarket-circulated tabloids, led by the *National Enquirer* and the *Star,* which focused on scandals, conspiracies, and celebrities. So did the *New York Post,* which in 1982 ran this giant headline on the naming of Yuri Andropov as Soviet premier: "Sinister KGB Biggie Gets Brez' Job."

Although the newspapers of the 1930s devoted far more space to stories about political and economic events and foreign affairs than those of the 1920s, they did not lose the "big story" complex that characterized postwar journalism. The trial of Bruno Hauptmann in 1934 for the kidnapping and murder of the Lindbergh baby drew more than 300 reporters, who wired more than 11 million words in 28 days. The publicity-seeking judge turned the trial into a news reporter's paradise and there was much criticism of "trial by newspaper."

THE *DENVER POST'S* "BUCKET OF BLOOD" DAYS

No account of American journalism history is complete without a mention of the *Denver Post* of the days of Harry H. Tammen and Fred G. Bonfils. With its giant bannerlines printed in red ink, its startling and helter-skelter makeup, and its highly sensationalized news play, the *Post* won fame as a dynamic but irresponsible paper. Its owners won fame, too, as ruthless operators of a journalistic gold mine. Tammen, a onetime bartender, and Bonfils, who had come West to make money in real estate and the lottery business, joined forces in 1895 to buy the *Post.* Their yellow-journalism tactics succeeded in the rough-and-tumble newspaper warfare of Denver and at the height of their fortunes in the 1920s the paper was making more than $1 million a year.

The *Post* was filled with features and sensational stories, but it also engaged in stunts and crusades that spread its fame in the Rocky Mountain area, where it advertised itself as "Your Big Brother." The partners operated from an office with red-painted walls, which Denver promptly called "The Bucket of Blood." Victims of the *Post's* crusades and exposés filed libel suits against Tammen and Bonfils and accusations of blackmailing were leveled against the owners. No such charges were ever proved in court, however, and the *Post* continued in its proclaimed role as "the people's champion."

After Tammen's death in 1924, the *Post's* luck began to change. The conduct of the paper in withholding news of illegal oil leases at Teapot Dome, until Bonfils was in a position to force the lessees to make a contract by which the *Post* would profit by half a million dollars, led the committee on ethics of the American Society of Newspaper Editors to recommend that Bonfils be expelled from membership. Instead, however, he was allowed to resign. His reputation was further darkened just before his death in 1933 when he sued the rival *Rocky Mountain News* for libel and then lost interest when the *News* undertook to document many of the stories about the partners.

Still the *Post* roared on, while the stories about life on Denver newspapers multiplied. Entry of the Scripps-Howard chain into intensified competition with the *Post* in 1926 through purchase of the morning *Rocky Mountain News,* and of the evening *Times* for merger with the Scripps-owned *Express,* brought about one of the country's greatest competitive struggles. No holds were barred by city desks and circulation departments for the next 2 years, and Denver gorged itself on sensational news and free premium offers. In 1928 a truce was arranged by which the *Times* was killed, leaving the *Post* alone in the evening field, and the *News* in the morning. The journalistic habits of the days when anything went continued to haunt Denver, however, for another two decades, until a change in management at the *Post* brought new policies that pushed memories of the Tammen-Bonfils era into the background.

THE WORLD OF COMICS

Highly lucrative for the Sunday papers was the distribution of the drawings of a special set of artists—the comic-strip and humorous-panel originators. The battle between Pulitzer and Hearst for possession of Richard F. Outcault's "Yellow Kid" in 1896 set off a fierce competition in Sunday color comic sections and gave the name to yellow journalism. Early favorites like "Foxy Grandpa," "Buster Brown," and "Little Nemo" tickled newspaper readers with portrayals of humorous episodes centering about the same set of characters, but not relating a continuing story. Charles E. Schultze's grandfather, who played tricks on boys, and Winsor McKay's childish wonderland of Little Nemo both appeared in the *New York Herald* at the turn of the century. But Schultze soon deserted to Hearst's *American.* There "Foxy Grandpa" joined Outcault's "Buster Brown" and other Hearst comics in the same vein.

One was Rudolph Dirks' "Katzenjammer Kids," longest-lived of all American comics. Dirks began drawing Hans, Fritz, Mama, and the Captain in an 1897 color comic. When he transferred to the *World* in 1912, Hearst successfully sued to retain rights to the title and King Features continued the strip into the 1980s. So did Dirks and his son, for United Features, using the name "The Captain and the Kids."

Other Hearst comic successes before 1910 were James Swinnerton's "Little Jimmy," Frederick Burr Opper's "Alphonse and Gaston" and "Happy Hooligan," and George Herriman's "Krazy Kat." In the *World* were "The Newlyweds," drawn by George McManus of later Jiggs and Maggie fame. The doings of the "Toonerville Folks" were first portrayed by Fontaine Fox in the *Chicago Post* of 1908. H. C. (Bud) Fisher's "Mutt and Jeff" was the first regular daily cartoon strip, appearing in the *San Francisco Chronicle* in 1907. When John N. Wheeler organized the Bell Syndicate he obtained Fox and Fisher as two of his major drawing cards.

Arising as major competitors in the comic-strip business by the end of World War I were the Hearst-owned King Features Syndicate and the *Chicago*

Rudolph Dirks' Katzenjammer Kids look down upon their successors: George McManus' Jiggs, 1926; Frank King's Gasoline Alley, 1923, with Walt adopting Skeezix; Harold Gray's Little Orphan Annie and Sandy, 1936; Chic Young's Blondie and Dagwood, 1936; Milton Caniff's Steve Canyon, 1939, in "Terry and the Pirates"; Chester Gould's Dick Tracy as he began in 1931 and again in 1956; and Charlie Brown, Lucy, and Snoopy in 1956 "Peanuts" strip by Charles M. Schulz (with © permissions for years indicated from United Feature, King Features, and Chicago Tribune-New York Daily News Syndicates).

Tribune-New York Daily News combine, whose comics were masterminded by Captain Joseph M. Patterson and Colonel Robert R. McCormick. Some of the long-time Hearst favorites, distributed in *Puck* as a Sunday comic section to millions of Hearst readers and also sold separately, were George McManus' "Bringing Up Father," dating from 1912; Cliff Sterrett's "Polly and Her Pals," 1912; James E. Murphy's "Toots and Casper," 1918; Billy De Beck's "Barney Google," 1919; Elzie C. Segar's "Thimble Theatre" featuring Olive Oyl and Popeye, 1919; Russ Westover's "Tillie the Toiler," 1921; Rube Goldberg's "Boob McNutt," 1924; and the most popular of all American comics, Chic Young's "Blondie," 1930. Winning millions of readers, too, for the *Chicago Tribune-New York Daily News* group have been Sidney Smith's "Andy Gump," 1917 (drawn after Smith's death in 1935 by Gus Edson); Frank King's "Gasoline Alley," 1919; Carl Ed's "Harold Teen," 1919; Martin Branner's "Winnie Winkle," 1920; Frank Willard's "Moon Mullins," 1923; and Harold Gray's "Little Orphan Annie," 1924.

People still called the comic strips "the funny papers" in this period. But two developments were under way that would change the character of the comics. One was the continuing story strip which originated with "Andy Gump" in 1917. Some adults of the 1980s still remember how baby Skeezix was abandoned on Uncle Walt's doorstep in the "Gasoline Alley" of 1921 to begin a chronicle of family life now in a fourth generation. Far less satisfying was the continuity of "Little Orphan Annie," whose waif has been lost from Daddy Warbucks every little while and has never finished school. King died in 1969 and Gray in 1968, but Skeezix and Annie lived on.

The other development was the action story, which entered the comic pages with United Features' "Tarzan" in 1929 and soon extended through countless strips involving detectives, cowboys, adventurers, gangsters, and finally supermen and superwomen. The greatest detective of the comic-strip world has been operating in Chester Gould's "Dick Tracy" strip since 1931. Swashbuckling adventure has been most cleverly portrayed by Milton Caniff in "Terry and the Pirates," a 1934 gold mine, and his 1947 "Steve Canyon." Ham Fisher's "Joe Palooka" began fighting in 1931. The first of the superhumans was Buck Rogers, whose twenty-fifth-century era began in 1929. Superman himself, drawn by Jerry Siegel and Joe Schuster, caught on in 1939.

There was still some humor left in the comic pages, despite the invasion of crime, tragedy, death, and lurid action in the 1930s. Harry J. Tuthill's "The Bungle Family," begun in the *New York Evening Mail* in 1918, and Sol Hess' "The Nebbs," dating from 1923, were family favorites. So were Cal Alley's "The Ryatts," Carl Grubert's "The Berrys," and "Hi and Lois," a 1954 entry by Mort Walker and Dik Browne. New heroines were "Ella Cinders," drawn by Charlie Plumb and Bill Conselman since 1925, and "Dixie Dugan," created by J. P. McEvoy and John H. Striebel in 1929. Children and their antics were not ignored; some of the favorites were Edwina Dumm's "Cap Stubbs and Tippie," Ernie Bushmiller's "Fritzi Ritz and Nancy," Robert Brinkerhoff's "Little Mary Mixup," Harry Haenigsen's "Penny," and four King Features offerings: Carl Anderson's "Henry," Percy Crosby's "Skippy," Charles H. Kuhn's "Grandma," and Jimmy Hatlo's "Little Iodine."

The best humor has been that of the panel artists. Stars of the 1920s were Clare Briggs of the *New York Tribune,* T. A. (Tad) Dorgan of the *American* and

Journal, and H. T. Webster of the *World* and *Herald Tribune.* Briggs originated "Mr. and Mrs.," a favorite *Herald Tribune* feature. Dorgan's panels were "For Better or Worse" and "Indoor Sports." The master performer was Webster, who invented Caspar Milquetoast for "The Timid Soul" and who drew "The Thrill That Comes Once in a Lifetime," "Life's Darkest Moment," "How to Torture Your Wife," and a humorous series on bridge addicts. Webster's "The Unseen Audience" effectively criticized radio and television until his death in 1952. In a similar tradition were J. R. William's "Out Our Way" and "Born Thirty Years Too Soon," Otto Soglow's "Little King," Clifford McBride's "Napoleon," and Tom Wilson's born loser, "Ziggy."

NEWSPAPER CONSOLIDATIONS, 1910 to 1930

The years 1910 to 1914 mark the high point in numbers of newspapers published in the United States. The census of 1910 reported 2600 daily publications of all types, of which 2200 were English-language newspapers of general circulation. General-circulation weekly newspapers numbered approximately 14,000. The totals hovered at these peaks until the economic pressures of World War I were felt by American newspapers.

Wartime pressures, while of marked effect on publishing, only accented trends that were developing as early as 1890. These trends were toward suspension of some competing newspapers, merger of others with their rivals, concentration of newspaper ownership in many cities and towns, and creation of newspaper chains or groups. Before 1930, each of these trends had been clearly developed, to set the pattern for twentieth-century American journalism.

Statistics can often be confusing, and this is true of those concerned with the number of American newspapers published over the years. For example, it might be assumed that if there were 2200 English-language daily newspapers of general circulation in 1910, and but 1942 in 1930, then 258 newspapers died in those two decades. Actually, 1391 daily newspapers suspended publication or shifted to weekly status in those 20 years, and another 362 were merged with rival papers. In the same two decades, 1495 dailies were being born.[24] The turnover among established dailies was less drastic than these figures might seem to indicate, however, since one-fourth of the newcomers died within the first year of publication, and another one-half eventually joined the suspension list. But some of the newcomers were healthy ventures in the growing small towns and cities of an increasingly urbanized country.

Between 1910 and 1930 the population of the United States increased by 30 million, from 92 to 122 million persons. The number of towns and cities of 8000 or more persons jumped from 768 to 1208. Daily newspaper circulation increased at a faster pace, from 22.5 million copies a day in 1910 to 40 million copies in 1930. Sunday newspaper circulation more than doubled in the two decades, moving from 13 million to 27 million copies. Total newspaper advertising revenue tripled in the years 1915 to 1929, increasing from an estimated $275 million to $800 million.[25]

Yet despite this great growth in advertising revenue, in numbers of readers, and in numbers of urban centers that could support daily newspaper publication, there was a net loss of 258 daily newspapers in the 20 years.

Table 20-1 Growth of One-Daily Cities, 1880–1930

	1880	1900	1910	1920	1930
Number of English-language general-circulation dailies	850	1967	2200	2042	1942
Number of cities with dailies	389	915	1207	1295	1402
Number of one-daily cities	149	353	509	716	1002
Number of one-combination cities	1	3	9	27	112
Number of cities with competing dailies	239	559	689	552	288
Percentage of daily cities with only one daily paper	38.3	38.6	42.2	55.3	71.5
Percentage of daily cities with competing dailies	61.4	61.1	57.1	42.6	20.6
Percentage of all dailies published in one-daily cities	17.5	17.9	23.1	35.1	51.6
Number of one-daily cities above 25,000 population	4	8	25	47	93
Number of one-daily cities above 100,000 population	0	1	1	5	6
Total daily circulation (millions)	3.1	15.1	22.4	27.8	39.6

Sources: Data for 1880 tabulated by Edwin Emery from S.N.D. North, *History and Present Condition of the Newspaper and Periodical Press of the United States* (Washington, D.C.: Government Printing Office, 1884). For 1900 to 1920, W. Carl Masche, "Factors Involved in the Consolidation and Suspension of Daily and Sunday Newspapers in the United States Since 1900: A Statistical Study in Social Change" (Master's thesis, University of Minnesota, 1932), and Morris Ernst, *The First Freedom* (New York: Macmillan, 1946), p. 284. For 1930, Alfred McClung Lee, "The Basic Newspaper Pattern," *The Annals of the American Academy of Political and Social Science,* CCXIX (January 1942), 46, except figures for one-daily cities of specified population, from Masche.

Numbers of English-language general curculation dailies for 1880 tabulated from North; for 1900, from Masche; for 1910, from Royal H. Ray (*see footnote 24*); for 1920 to 1930, *Editor & Publisher International Year Book* figures. The census counts of daily publications, which included foreign-language, religious, trade, and technical dailies, were 971 dailies in 1800, 2226 in 1900, 2600 in 1910, and 2441 in 1920. But those figures do not compare with the *Editor & Publisher Year Book* figures available after 1920. Masche, Ernst, and Ray tabulated their data from Ayer directories; Lee used *Editor & Publisher International Year Book* data.

Reduction of the number of competing dailies in larger cities, elimination of all but one newspaper in smaller towns, and suspension of daily newspaper publishing in some fading communities more than offset the number of new dailies started in growing towns and older publishing centers. The figures given in Table 20-1 illustrate daily newspaper publishing trends from 1880 to 1930, including the steady growth of one-daily cities at all population levels.

Many reasons can be listed for the decline in numbers of newspapers published, for the curtailment of competition in most communities, and for the increasing concentration of ownership. They fall under seven general headings: (1) economic pressures stemming from technological changes in the publishing pattern; (2) pressures resulting from competition for circulation and advertising revenues; (3) standardization of the product, resulting in loss of individuality and reader appeal; (4) lack of economic or social need for some newspapers; (5) managerial faults; (6) effects of wartime inflation and general business depressions; (7) planned consolidation of newspapers for various reasons.

METROPOLITAN DAILIES, 1890 to 1930: MUNSEY, CURTIS, KOHLSAAT

New York City boasted fifteen general-circulation, English-language daily newspapers in 1890. Eight were morning papers and seven were afternoon papers. Twelve owners were represented. By 1932 only three morning papers, four evening papers, and two tabloids remained, representing seven ownerships.

The name of Frank A. Munsey plays a large part in that story. Munsey was a successful New Englander whose career had a Horatio Alger ring. He broke into the New York publishing business with a juvenile magazine, the *Golden Argosy,* then turned to the general magazine field with his *Munsey's.* As a 10-cent monthly, *Munsey's* hit 650,000 circulation by 1900 to lead its competitors by a wide margin. The publisher had $1 million-a-year income by 1905. But he dreamt of a great national chain of newspapers, directed from a central headquarters by the most brilliant of American editors and business managers. To Munsey, the successful businessperson, the newspaper business was a disorderly, if not chaotic, enterprise. He proposed to bring efficiency to the newspaper world and thereby improve the product.

In 1901 Munsey bought the old *New York Daily News* and the *Washington Times* as the nucleus of his chain. In 1902, the *Boston Journal* was added; in 1908 he invaded two more Eastern cities, buying the *Baltimore Evening News* and founding the *Philadelphia Evening Times.* Munsey set about to improve the papers, installing color presses, featurizing Sunday editions, and seeking to break into higher readership groups. But the public failed to respond, and by 1917 all the papers were killed or sold to others.

Munsey still owned one newspaper, the *New York Press,* which he had bought in 1912. The *Press,* under the editorship of Ervin Wardman, had a comfortable circulation. But Munsey eyed the New York field for a newspaper that could be combined with it, and his choice was the *Sun.* The *Sun* was still a proud newspaper, edited after the death of Charles A. Dana in 1897 by Edward P. Mitchell. Munsey paid $2.5 million for the *Sun* and the *Evening Sun* in 1916 and merged the *Press* into the morning edition, making Wardman publisher, Mitchell editor, and the *Press'* renowned Keats Speed managing editor. But wartime publishing difficulties cost Munsey the profit he hoped to make, and in 1920 he looked about for another prospect for consolidation.

Munsey's first move was to buy the *New York Herald,* the *Telegram,* and the Paris edition of the *Herald* for $4 million. The younger Bennett had spent lavishly during his long lifetime, and when he died in 1918 his newspapers were in neither a financial nor competitive position to continue. Munsey merged the morning *Sun* into the *Herald* and gave the historical name *Sun* to the evening edition.

The next victim was the *Globe.* Started in 1904, it was considered a healthy, liberal newspaper when Munsey killed it in 1923 for its AP evening membership. The next year Munsey bought the conservative *Mail,* which had survived since 1867, merging it with the *Telegram.*

Munsey's morning paper, the *Herald,* was not faring well. He turned his eyes toward the *Tribune,* lowest in circulation of the morning dailies. But the *Tribune*'s owners, Ogden Mills Reid and his able wife, Helen Rogers Reid, refused to sell. Munsey, true to his belief that further consolidation was necessary, thereupon sold the *Herald* and its Paris edition to the Reids for $5 million. Happily, the new *Herald Tribune* successfully added the bulk of the old *Herald*'s subscribers to its list and saw its advertising volume expand under the business direction of Mrs. Reid. Of all Munsey's newspaper maneuvering, his part in the creation of the *Herald Tribune* was the happiest, even though it meant the merger of the historic Bennett and Greeley papers.

Death claimed Munsey in 1925. Newspaperpeople generally were bitterly resentful of the cold and businesslike approach Munsey had toward both them and their profession. William Allen White best expressed the rebels' sentiments in his famed terse obituary published in the *Emporia Gazette:*

> Frank A. Munsey contributed to the journalism of his day the talent of a meat-packer, the morals of a money-changer and the manners of an undertaker. He and his kind have about succeeded in transforming a once-noble profession into an eight per cent security. May he rest in trust!

Another magazine publisher played a major role in the consolidation of Philadelphia's newspapers. He was Cyrus H. K. Curtis, who entered the Philadelphia newspaper picture by buying the historic *Public Ledger,* founded by William M. Swain in 1836 in the first wave of penny papers. Ably edited by George W. Childs from 1864 until his death in 1894, the *Public Ledger* had been sold in 1902 to Adolph S. Ochs, who put his brother George in charge. By 1913 Ochs was ready to sell to Curtis at a loss.

Curtis' first move was to give Philadelphia another newspaper, the *Evening Public Ledger,* in 1914. But then, like Munsey, he moved in on the competition. The *Evening Telegraph,* dating back to 1864, was bought for its AP membership in 1918 and killed. The *Press,* founded in 1857, was purchased in 1920 for its newsprint contracts. Newspaperpeople mourned again in 1925 when the *North American,* on the scene since 1839 and with a reputation as a crusading force under editor E. A. Van Valkenberg, was killed. Curtis poured money into his newspapers, building them a $15 million plant and developing a famous foreign-news service that was widely syndicated.

The Curtis newspapers collapsed as the 1929 depression deepened. In a final effort, Curtis bought the rival morning *Inquirer,* but when he died in 1933 the *Public Ledger* was merged into the *Inquirer.* Its evening edition lived until 1942, competing with the *Bulletin* and a tabloid *Daily News* begun in 1925. J. David Stern made the *Record* a liberal morning paper after 1928.

Herman Kohlsaat was the chief figure in Chicago's newspaper consolidations. Enriched by a chain of bakeries and lunch counters and enamored of the newspaper business, Kohlsaat bought into the *Inter Ocean* in 1891. Dissatisfied, he sold out and brought the *Evening Post* and a successful morning Democratic paper, the *Times-Herald.* Kohlsaat was a Republican, and the paper had to compete with the conservative *Tribune.* By 1901 he had to sell out, and the *Times-Herald* disappeared into the *Record,* the morning edition of Victor Lawson's *Daily News.*

Chicago in 1902 thus had four morning papers: the *Tribune, Inter Ocean, Record-Herald,* and William Randolph Hearst's newly established *Examiner.* In the evening field were the *Daily News, Post, Journal,* and Hearst's *American.* The highly successful *Tribune* and *Daily News,* and the well-financed Hearst papers, were to squeeze out their competitors in the next 30 years.

One victim was the well-edited *Record-Herald,* which, when Lawson brought Frank B. Noyes from the *Washington Star* to run it from 1902 to 1910, ranked as one of the country's best. But by 1914 Kohlsaat, back in the picture, was merging the *Record-Herald* and the *Inter Ocean* as the *Herald* with James Keeley as editor. It failed, and in 1918 the Hearst interests established the *Herald & Examiner* as the *Tribune*'s only competitor. Victor Lawson's *Daily News* developed a distinguished foreign service and passed to Colonel Frank Knox's hands in 1931. Its only evening rivals were Hearst's *American* and the liberal tabloid *Times,* founded in 1929.

The sharp reduction in the number of morning dailies in New York, Philadelphia, and Chicago was part of a nationwide trend. Reader and advertiser preference for afternoon papers, and the time advantage these had in publishing European war news, helped to cut the number of morning papers from 500 in 1910 to 388 by 1930. Early in this period such morning papers at the *Atlanta Constitution, Indianapolis Star, Minneapolis Tribune,* and *St. Paul Pioneer Press* were alone in their fields. They were joined in 1915 by the *Detroit Free Press,* with the death of the old *Tribune.* In 1917 Cleveland saw the *Leader* disappear into the *Plain Dealer,* leaving the latter as the only morning paper. Elimination of the *Free Press* in Milwaukee in 1919 left the *Sentinel* without morning competition. The same year the *St. Louis Globe-Democrat* bought its morning rival, the *Republic.* In Buffalo in 1926 the merger of the *Courier* (1831) and the *Express* (1846) ended that city's long morning rivalry. Pittsburgh's morning dailies were reduced to one in 1927, and Kansas City joined the trend in 1928. The *Cincinnati Enquirer* closed out its competition in 1930 by buying the *Commercial Tribune,* successor to Murat Halstead's old *Commercial Gazette.* By 1933 the journalistic historian Willard G. Bleyer could list forty cities of more than 100,000 population that had only one morning daily.[26]

Morning paper mergers were the most spectacular in the first decades after 1900, but overall consolidation of metropolitan newspapers, and concentration of ownership, continued from coast to coast. Entry of the Hearst papers into Detroit through purchase of the *Times* in 1921 prompted the *News* (founded by James E. Scripps) to buy out the *Journal* in 1922. Thus Detroit, with more than a million population, was left with but three newspapers, the morning *Free Press* and the evening *News* and *Times.* In New Orleans, the *Times-Democrat* and the *Picayune* were merged in 1914, leaving the new *Times-Picayune* alone in the morning field for 10 years. The *Times-Picayune,* owned by L. K. Nicholson, bought Colonel Robert Ewing's *States* in 1933 for an evening edition. The other evening paper, the *Item,* published a morning edition, the *Tribune,* from 1924 to 1941.

St. Louis afternoon journalism was dominated by Pulitzer's *Post-Dispatch.* The *Chronicle,* the Scripps-McRae entry of 1880, merged with the *Evening Star* (1878) in 1905. The *Times* (1907) joined forces with the *Star* in 1932 as the *Star-Times,* leaving St. Louis with three ownerships. Kansas City rivals of Nelson's *Star* found the going equally difficult. Nelson bought the morning *Times* in 1901. The Scripps-McRae *World,* founded in 1897, faded from the picture. The evening *Post,* started in 1906 and bought by Bonfils and Tammen of *Denver Post* fame in 1909, was sold in 1922 to the owners of the morning *Journal* (1868), and the two papers became the *Journal-Post* in 1928. Kansas City thus dropped to two ownerships.

HEARST AND SCRIPPS-HOWARD 1920s CONSOLIDATIONS

Activities of the country's two biggest group ownerships—Hearst and Scripps-Howard—and of lesser chain aspirants caused newspaper consolidations in still other cities. The Hearst organization, in a buying splurge concentrated in the years 1918 to 1928, put sixteen newspapers to death as consolidations were carried out to bulwark the positions of Hearst-owned dailies. The Scripps-Howard group was responsible for the closing of fifteen newspapers between 1923 and 1934.

In Boston, where the Hearst-owned evening *American* was founded in 1904, the publisher bought the century-old *Daily Advertiser* in 1917 and the *Record* in 1920. The two papers were juggled in an effort to bring tabloid publication to Boston, with the name *Record* surviving for the morning Hearst paper. Meanwhile the *Boston Herald* was buying the *Traveler* in 1912 for an evening edition and was absorbing the Munsey-owned *Journal* in 1917. Thus Boston, which in 1900 had eleven major newspapers operated by seven ownerships, by 1930 had eight newspapers and five ownerships. The others were Edwin A. Grozier's highly successful morning *Post,* the Taylor family's morning and evening *Globes,* and the limping but traditional *Transcript.*

Washington was one of the few large cities to add newspapers during this period, but Hearst promptly consolidated the ownership of two newcomers. The morning *Post* and the Noyes family's evening *Star* were challenged by the founding of the *Times* in 1894 and the *Herald* in 1906. Munsey bought the *Times* in 1901 and killed its morning edition. When he retired from the Washington field in 1917, the *Times* passed to Arthur Brisbane, who sold it to Hearst 2 years later. The *Herald* was added to the Hearst group in 1922. Scripps-Howard gave Washington a fourth ownership when it established the tabloid *Daily News* in 1921.

Baltimore was less fortunate. The *Sun,* the original penny paper of 1837, took over the *Evening World* in 1910 and made it the *Evening Sun.* The *Herald,* a morning penny paper, died in 1906. The *Evening News,* Grasty's crusading paper that fell into Munsey's control, was consolidated with the *Star* in 1921, and the paper was sold to Hearst in 1922. The *American,* dating from 1799, also passed from Munsey to Hearst and after 1928 was published only as a Sunday paper. A 1922 Scripps-Howard entry, the *Post,* was sold to Hearst in 1934. The Hearst *News-Post* thus opposed the *Sun* papers.

Pittsburgh's newspapers were also shuffled by the Hearst and Scripps-Howard organizations. The Scripps-Howard group bought the well-established *Press* in 1923 for $6 million, under an agreement with the city's other newspaper owners that the *Dispatch* and *Leader* would be bought out and killed. Four years later Hearst and Paul Block, a Hearst associate and newspaper broker, bought the remaining four Pittsburgh dailies. The morning *Sun* and *Chronicle Telegraph* were transformed into the Hearst-owned *Sun-Telegraph;* the evening *Post* and *Gazette Times,* into the Block-owned *Post-Gazette.*

Arthur Brisbane and Hearst teamed up in Milwaukee at the end of World War I, with the result that the *Evening Wisconsin,* the *News,* and the *Telegram* were rolled into the *Wisconsin News,* Hearst-owned after 1919. The morning *Sentinel* joined the Hearst chain in 1924 to give the chain two footholds against the steadily increasing pressure of the *Milwaukee Journal.*[27] Also in the Midwest, the *Omaha News* and *Bee* were bought by Hearst in 1928 and merged as the *News-Bee,* a morning, evening, and Sunday publication.

On the West Coast, Hearst created a strong evening companion for his *San Francisco Examiner* by combining three papers. He bought the *Call* (1855) in 1913 and combined the *Evening Post* with it to obtain an Associated Press membership. In 1929 the *Bulletin* (1856) was absorbed by Hearst to form the *Call-Bulletin.* The mergers left San Francisco with Hearst morning and evening papers, the locally owned morning *Chronicle,* and the Scripps-Howard evening *News.* Across the bay in Oakland the *Post-Enquirer* was formed in a 1922 Hearst double purchase and merger as competition for the Knowland family's *Tribune.*

In Los Angeles, Hearst's morning *Examiner* was augmented in 1922 by the purchase of the evening *Herald.* The *Express,* founded in 1871, was swallowed up by Hearst in 1931 to form the *Herald & Express.* The *Record,* established by Scripps in 1895, died in the 1920s but was replaced by the *Daily News,* a tabloid that Manchester Boddy developed into a pro-New Deal newspaper. Hearst's solid morning competition in Los Angeles was still Harry Chandler's conservative *Times.*[28]

Strengthening the Scripps-Howard properties by eliminating the competitors took place in several cities. Knoxville saw the *News-Sentinel* created by the merger of the *News,* started in 1921, and the *Sentinel,* bought in 1926. The *El Paso Post,* founded in 1922, became the *Herald-Post* with the acquisition of the *Herald* in 1931. The *Akron Press,* begun in 1899 by E. W. Scripps, received a badly needed transfusion in 1925 with the purchase of the *Times,* to form the *Times-Press.* The *Memphis Press,* founded in 1906, became the *Press-Scimitar* by absorbing the *News-Scimitar* in 1926; 10 years later Scripps-Howard added the morning *Memphis Commercial Appeal* to the chain. The *New York Telegram,* bought in 1927, became the *World-Telegram* in 1931 when Howard negotiated the purchase of the famous Pulitzer papers. The *Pittsburgh Press* was acquired in 1923 in a deal that eliminated the *Dispatch* and *Leader.*[29]

THE END OF THE *WORLD*

Tragedy struck the *New York World* in 1923 when editor Frank Cobb died at the height of his powers. Just 8 years later the *World* itself succumbed, and many a sorrowing newspaper reporter muttered, "If only Cobb had lived. . . ." There probably would have been no difference in the fate of the *World* but it was true that after Cobb's death the newspaper lacked the genius of leadership it had enjoyed since its purchase by Joseph Pulitzer in 1883.

During the middle 1920s *The World* seemed to be continuing its powerful position. Cobb had left behind a distinguished editorial-page staff, headed now by Walter Lippmann. Among the editorial writers were Maxwell Anderson and Laurence Stallings—more famous for their play, "What Price Glory"—and Charles Merz, later to become editor of the *New York Times.* Appearing on the *World*'s "op. ed." page were Heywood Broun, the liberal-thinking columnist of

"It Seems to Me" fame, Franklin P. Adams, conductor of the "Conning Tower," and Frank Sullivan, who like Anderson and Stallings moved to other creative fields. In this period Rollin Kirby, the cartoonist, won three Pulitzer Prizes for the *World*.

Despite this brilliance and the distinguished record of the paper, Joseph Pulitzer's creation was losing the battle in New York morning journalism. Pressing it on one side were Ochs' *Times* and the merger-created *Herald Tribune*. Soaking up circulation on the other side were the tabloids that appeared in the early 1920s. The *World* failed to keep pace with its orthodox rivals in complete coverage of the news, even though it sometimes performed brilliantly, and it saw some of its subway-riding readers succumbing to the lure of the tabloids. Of the Pulitzer heirs, Joseph Pulitzer, Jr., had shown the most ability but he had assumed control of the *St. Louis Post-Dispatch*. His brothers, Ralph and Herbert, delegated much authority to Herbert Bayard Swope as executive editor, but Swope left the *World* staff in 1928. The newspaper was already running a deficit, and in the depression year of 1930 Pulitzer losses on the morning, evening, and Sunday editions reached nearly $2 million. Then rumors of an impending sale began to be heard, and staff members made a desperate effort to raise enough cash to buy the *World* themselves. They argued, too, that the Pulitzer will forbade the sale of the paper, but in February, 1931, a New York court approved its purchase by Roy W. Howard for the Scripps-Howard interests. The evening *World* was merged with the *Telegram*. The morning *World*—symbol of Pulitzer's journalistic genius—was dead, and there was scarcely a newspaperperson who did not feel that something peculiarly precious and irreplaceable had been lost to the craft.

There were other newspapers that, like the *World*, were regarded as "newspaperpeople's newspapers." Very few combined a conception of public responsibility and journalistic brilliance to the degree that made the *World* great. But wherever oldtime newspeople gathered in this period there likely would be mentioned the work of those who wrote for and edited the *New York Sun* and *New York Herald*. Quite likely, too, the name of the Chicago *Inter Ocean* would be mentioned. These papers, now dead, are a part of the colorful story of American journalism, and the alumni of their excellent training grounds were legion. They lagged behind in the journalistic advance into the modern era but they and the people who worked for them had proud traditions and moments of glory.

THE *NEW YORK TIMES* to 1935

After 25 years of Adolph Ochs' ownership, the *New York Times* of 1921 had achieved major stature. There was one great reason for this success. The paper had taken in some $100 million in those 25 years and had paid out but 4 percent in dividends. Ochs had poured the millions into the *Times* for buildings and equipment, for staff, and for the tremendous news coverage Van Anda had built. Circulation had reached 330,000 daily and more than 500,000 Sunday, while advertising linage had increased tenfold in the 25 years, passing the 23-million mark. Ochs was a great builder and the *Times* was the symbol of his business success.

Politically the *Times* had been Democratic except during the Bryan campaigns. But it was essentially conservative in tone, particularly in its economic outlook. It was progressive in its social viewpoint but Ochs was not one of the crusaders of the "people's champions" variety. After going down to defeat on the League of Nations issue with the 1920 Democratic ticket of James M. Cox and Franklin D. Roosevelt, the *Times'* favorite Democrat of the early 1920s was John W. Davis, the New York lawyer who was defeated by Calvin Coolidge in the 1924 election. The *Times* supported Alfred E. Smith in 1928 and Franklin D. Roosevelt in 1932 in the final campaigns before Ochs' death.

The 1920s saw one era of *Times* history ending and another beginning. Editor Miller died in 1922 and was succeeded by Rollo Ogden, longtime *New York Post* editor. Van Anda went into semiretirement in 1925 although he continued to hold the title of managing editor until 1932. Frederick T. Birchall, his distinguished associate in the newsroom and also a leading foreign correspondent, continued the Van Anda tradition. Appearing on the staff in the early 1920s were such future *Times* luminaries as Anne O'Hare McCormick, who won a Pulitzer Prize for her reporting from Europe as a leading foreign correspondent; Lester Markel, Sunday editor; and Louis Stark, labor reporter. Following them were Waldemar Kaempffert and William L. Laurence in the field of science and Arthur Krock in the Washington bureau. David H. Joseph became city editor in 1927 for a 21-year term, and Edwin L. James became managing editor in 1932 after his European reporting assignments.

While still active in management, Ochs groomed his son-in-law, Arthur Hays Sulzberger, and his nephew, Julius Ochs Adler, to succeed him. The deaths of Ochs and his business manager, Louis Wiley, in 1935 removed the last of the quartet that had been instrumental in building the *Times.* But the organization they had created continued to carry the paper to new heights in the succeeding years.

MAGAZINES OF OPINION AND INTERPRETATION: MENCKEN'S *MERCURY*

Some of the country's magazines became important factors in the trend toward interpretation and news specialization. There was a new element injected into the magazine world, however. It was increasingly clear that the small-circulation opinion journals were being hurt by constant boosts in postal rates, high printing costs, and changing newsstand practices, and that the "slicks" were becoming dominant.

In the muckraking era, such general magazines as *Collier's, McClure's, Everybody's,* and the *American* served both as entertainment media and as "people's champions," exposing industrial monopolies and political corruption and crusading for a broadening of political and economic democracy. But that phase ended by World War I and the old champions withered. *McClure's* went downhill before 1920 and flickered out in 1933; *Everybody's* died in 1930, and *Collier's* and the *American* in 1956.

Most of the serious magazines that were important as sources of information and as vehicles of opinion before World War I fell by the wayside in the

1920s and 1930s. The *Century* was merged with the *Forum* and then both disappeared into *Current History. World's Work,* one of the best, had to combine with *Review of Reviews,* which in turn was sold to the *Literary Digest.* The *Digest,* founded in 1890 and long a highly popular reporter on American newspaper opinion and current affairs, slumped away before the onslaught of newer-type news magazines and abruptly ended its career by publishing the results of a postcard poll that predicted that Alfred M. Landon would defeat Franklin Roosevelt for the presidency in 1936 (Landon carried two states). Of the distinguished literary magazines, *Scribner's* collapsed in 1939.

Henry Louis Mencken's *American Mercury* was a bright new star of the magazine world in 1924, challenging American complacency, shocking solid citizens, and delighting the young rebels who had already enjoyed the work of Mencken and George Jean Nathan in *Smart Set* since 1914. Mencken was the dominant figure in American criticism in the 1920s, working from his base on the *Baltimore Sun.* He had the air of a disdainful aristocrat, who disliked nearly everything in the country; sometimes he found people or customs distasteful, at other times merely absurd. His particular targets were Puritanism, prohibition, and the Anglo-Saxon tradition in literature. His collection of what he called crack-brained deeds and words appeared in his column "Americana." The college generation, and young journalists, envied his sophisticated air and writing style, imitating both. But the national mood changed with the Great Depression and the *American Mercury* declined after Mencken and his associates let it pass into other hands in 1933.

ROSS AND THE *NEW YORKER*

Possibly the most distinctive of American magazines arrived in 1925 when Harold Ross began publication of his *New Yorker.* Ross was editor of the *Stars and Stripes* in World War I days and met Franklin P. Adams and Alexander Woollcott on that distinguished staff. In New York in 1925 they helped him get his magazine venture under way, with the financial backing of Raoul Fleischmann. The magazine, Ross said, would be a humorous one, reflecting metropolitan life and keeping up with the affairs of the day in a light and satirical vein that would mark it as not "for the old lady in Dubuque." Ross was a demanding, irascible editor who hired and fired about 100 staff members in the first struggling year and a half before he began to find his stars: E. B. White, conductor of "Talk of the Town"; Rea Irvin, art editor who drew Eustace Tilley, the supercilious dandy who is the *New Yorker*'s trademark; writers James Thurber, Ogden Nash, Wolcott Gibbs, S. J. Perelman, A. J. Liebling, and Frank Sullivan; artists Peter Arno, Helen Hokinson, Otto Soglow, Charles Addams, and a host of others who contributed the famous *New Yorker* cartoons.

But the *New Yorker* was more than cartoons, whimsy, and curiously plotless fiction; it had its penetrating "Profiles," its "Reporter at Large," and other incisive commentaries on public affairs. One of the most famed series was "Letter from Paris," signed by "Gênet" but written by Janet Flanner. The first of her more than 700 articles from Paris and other European cities was written in 1925, the last in 1975. Flanner described her work as "foreign correspondence

Harold Ross, the *New Yorker* editor.
Fabian Bachrach

with a critical edge." She was the kind of writing stylist Ross so admired. She was also able to bring to her readers both the feel of French society and penetrating comment on the great events of her era.

When Ross died in 1951, his magazine was a solid success, both in circulation and advertising, and under a new editor, William Shawn, it continued its gains. There was some criticism as bylines inevitably changed (*Time* reported in 1960 that Shawn's *New Yorker* had ninety-seven subscribers in Dubuque, including several old ladies). But the magazine won nearly half a million subscribers, who read many pages of sophisticated advertising, the cartoons, and such newer writing talent as Washington correspondent Richard Rovere, writer John Updike, public affairs reporters Calvin Trillin and Jonathan Schell, columnist Elizabeth Drew, and critics Penelope Gilliatt and Michael Arlen.

WALLACE'S *READER'S DIGEST*

Very likely contributing to the demise of the quality magazines was the spectacular success of the *Reader's Digest,* which in 1922 began to print condensed versions of articles of current interest and entertainment value that had appeared in other magazines. The brainchild of DeWitt Wallace and his wife, Lila Acheson Wallace, the *Reader's Digest* slowly won readers during the 1920s, and then mushroomed to a 1-million circulation by 1935. The pocket-size style of the magazine, its staff's keen judgment of popular tastes, and skillful editing for condensation continued to make it a national best seller as circulation reached 3 million in 1938, 5 million in 1942, and 9 million in 1946. Wallace then began to develop his own articles, partly because some magazines began to refuse him reprint rights and partly to support his personal outlook on life. Gradually, during the 1940s, the magazine, which was supposedly an impartial digest of material in other publications, began to acquire a noticeable and conservative point of view of its own. Critics complained that its "inspirational" tone was unrealistic, if not Pollyanna-like, and offered little help in meeting major national and world problems. Nevertheless the *Reader's Digest* grew in size and influence, reaching a nearly 20-million circulation in the United States and an additional 10 or more million for foreign-language editions in sixty countries. Wallace reversed an old ban and accepted advertising, beginning in 1955, which further added to the *Digest*'s profits.

ADVERTISING: AGENCIES AND COPYWRITERS

Advertising enjoyed a fabulous decade in the 1920s. The advertising agencies expanded and produced legendary managers and copywriters. They in turn created such memorable slogans as "I'd walk a mile for a Camel," "The skin you love to touch" (Palmolive), "Reach for a Lucky instead of a sweet," and "The priceless ingredient" (Squibb). Listeners to Jack Benny's radio comedy hour could chant his sponsor's musical "J-E-L-L-O." And advertising developed research methods to measure radio listenership and the effectiveness of printed messages. The agencies also had art directors who favored Art Deco style.

The men and women of the 1920s and 1930s were building upon a considerable heritage. George P. Rowell's pioneer agency began in 1869, as did N. W. Ayer & Son, still a 1920s leader. So were J. Walter Thompson, founded in 1878, and Lord & Thomas, opened in 1880. Among the first copywriters had been John E. Powers of department-store copy fame, Earnest Elmo Calkins of the agencies, and inspirational writer Bruce Barton, who made the 5-foot shelf of books and correspondence schools vital to intellectual progress. Such phrases as Ivory's "It floats," Victor's "His master's voice," and Kodak's "You press the button, we do the rest" had been written.

A truly legendary ad writer appeared at Lord & Thomas in 1898. He was young Albert Lasker, who was to rise to the agency's presidency and dominate it until 1952. Lord & Thomas boasted copywriters John C. Kennedy and Claude C. Hopkins, who cut a swath through the available advertising accounts. By 1928 the agency attracted the attention of the swashbuckling head of the American Tobacco Company, George Washington Hill, who had contributed "It's toasted" to the Lucky Strike slogans in 1917. According to advertising lore, it was Hill who noticed one woman on a corner eating a candy bar while another more dramatic-looking woman was holding a cigarette. "Reach for a Lucky instead of a sweet" was the message that flashed from Hill to Lasker and his copywriters, and that initiated the relentless campaign which doubled American Tobacco's profits between 1925 and 1931. More intriguing were N. W. Ayer's "The Camels are coming" teaser ads of 1914, the beginning of the first major cigarette ad campaign, which ended with "Camel cigarettes are here." Scarcely believable is the legend that a man walked up to a Camels' advertising poster painter and said, "I'd walk a mile for a Camel." Supposedly the painter relayed the now-famous phrase to the sign company, which then relayed it to the agency. Legend notwithstanding, advertising made Camels, Luckies, and Chesterfields ("Blow some my way," said the woman in their daring 1926 ad) into the "big three" selling cigarettes; between them they comprised 80 percent of the United States cigarette market that year.

Young & Rubicam, destined to lead all American agencies in client billings for the early 1980s, was founded in 1923 by two N. W. Ayer & Son employees, copywriter Raymond Rubicam and account executive John Orr Young. It was Rubicam who gave the agency its tone; he had already created the slogans "The instrument of the immortals" for Steinway pianos and "The priceless ingredient . . ." for Squibb pharmaceuticals. J. Walter Thompson had retired from his agency in 1916, turning over control to Stanley Resor and his wife, Helen Lansdowne, products of agency copywriting disciplines. Both the Thompson agency and Young & Rubicam developed research interests. Daniel Starch & Staff began magazine copy testing in 1923; Young & Rubicam first employed the random-sampling techniques of pollster George Gallup in 1932; and Elmo Roper entered the field in 1933. Market research, circulation studies including split-run techniques, and the employment of consumer panels to test products were emerging areas.

The rapidly expanding automobile industry was crowded with dozens of car makers with such still well-known names as Cadillac, Buick, and Ford, and such once-proud appellations as Pierce-Arrow, Hupmobile, and the Apperson Jackrabbit 8. Theodore F. MacManus wrote a Cadillac ad in 1915 that stands as one of the craft's greatest, a full page of copy under the heading, "The penalty of leadership." Henry Ford, the maverick of American business, wrote his own copy introducing the Model T and, in the 1920s, the Model A. And it was Ned Jordan, a Lord & Thomas copywriter who turned to car manufacturing, who in 1923 wrote and published, in the *Saturday Evening Post,* one of the most intriguing advertisements of the century, "Somewhere West of Laramie." Jordan's ad stimulated the sales of the Jordan Playboy car and drew the admiration of generations of creative advertising men and women.

Among the women copywriters of the era whose work was selected for compilations of "the 100 greatest advertisements" were Lillian Eichler of Ruthrauff & Ryan, Miriam Dewey of Young & Rubicam, and Dorothy Dignam and Frances Gerety of N. W. Ayer. And among the slogans were Ivory's "99 and 44/100 pure", Coca-Cola's "The pause that refreshes," Listerine's "Often a bridesmaid but never a bride," and the U.S. School of Music's "They laughed when I sat down at the piano but when I began to play!—"

All but two of the top-ten advertising agencies of the early 1980s were operating by the 1930s. In addition to Young & Rubicam, J. Walter Thompson, and Lord & Thomas (renamed Foote, Cone & Belding in 1943), there were two major agencies created by 1930 mergers of earlier groups, McCann-Erickson and Batten Barton Durstine & Osborn. Also appearing in the 1930s were the Ted Bates, Leo Burnett, and Compton agencies. Other important firms included D'Arcy, 1906; Campbell-Ewald, 1911; Erwin, Wasey, 1912; Grey Advertising, 1917; Dancer-Fitzgerald-Sample, 1923; and three 1929 entries, Benton & Bowles, Kenyon & Eckhardt, and Needham, Louis & Brorby.

Total expenditures for advertising in the United States were \$1.5 billion during 1918; the figure jumped to \$3 billion by 1920, and to \$3.4 billion in

THE CAMELS
are coming!

Drink
Coca-Cola
Delicious and Refreshing

The
pause that
refreshes

Camels
Tomorrow
there'll be more CAMELS in this town than in all Asia and Africa combined!

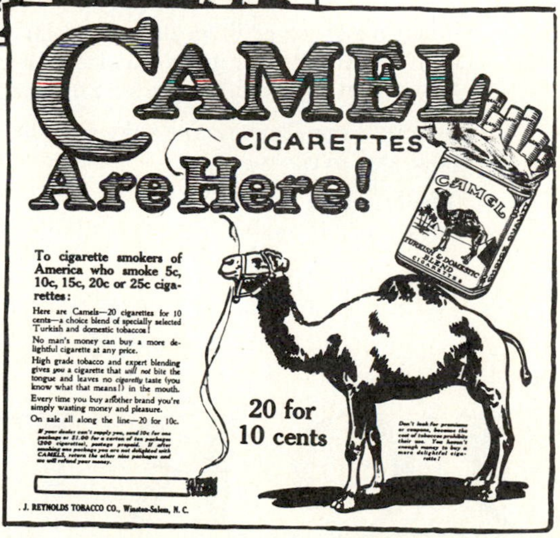
CAMEL
CIGARETTES
Are Here!
To cigarette smokers of America who smoke 5c, 10c, 15c, 20c or 25c cigarettes:
Here are Camels—20 cigarettes for 10 cents—a choice blend of specially selected Turkish and domestic tobaccos!
No man's money can buy a more delightful cigarette at any price.
High grade tobacco and expert blending gives you a cigarette that will not bite the tongue and leaves no cigaretty taste (you know what that means!) in the mouth.
Every time you buy another brand you're simply wasting money and pleasure.
On sale all along the line—20 for 10c.
If your dealer can't supply you, send 10c for one package or $1.00 for a carton of ten packages (200 cigarettes), postage prepaid. If after smoking one package you are not delighted with CAMELS, return the other nine packages and we will refund your money.
20 for 10 cents
Don't look for premiums or coupons, because the cost of tobaccos prohibits their use. You haven't enough money to buy a more delightful cigarette!
CAMEL
TURKISH & DOMESTIC BLEND CIGARETTES
. J. REYNOLDS TOBACCO CO., Winston-Salem, N. C.

"REACH FOR A LUCKY INSTEAD OF A SWEET."

"It's toasted"

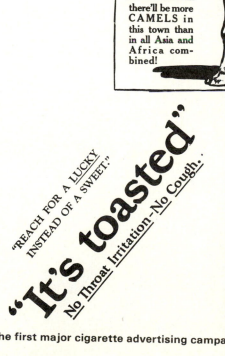

No Throat Irritation-No Cough.

The first major cigarette advertising campaign and two famous slogans.

Somewhere West of Laramie

SOMEWHERE west of Laramie there's a broncho-busting, steer-roping girl who knows what I'm talking about. She can tell what a sassy pony, that's a cross between greased lightning and the place where it hits, can do with eleven hundred pounds of steel and action when he's going high, wide and handsome.

The truth is—the Playboy was built for her.

Built for the lass whose face is brown with the sun when the day is done of revel and romp and race.

She loves the cross of the wild and the tame.

There's a savor of links about that car—of laughter and lilt and light—a hint of old loves—and saddle and quirt. It's a brawny thing—yet a graceful thing for the sweep o' the Avenue.

Step into the Playboy when the hour grows dull with things gone dead and stale.

Then start for the land of real living with the spirit of the lass who rides, lean and rangy, into the red horizon of a Wyoming twilight.

JORDAN

JORDAN MOTOR CAR COMPANY, Inc., Cleveland, Ohio

A legendary feat of copywriting (1923).

1929. Radio's advertising revenue increased from $4 million in 1927 to $40 million in 1929, with the advent of national networks. By 1933 the depression's impact had cut advertising expenditures to $1.3 billion. As the 1930s progressed, advertising began to be the target of consumer groups and social critics. Regulatory efforts had been encouraged by the formation of Better Business Bureaus after 1913, the establishment of the Audit Bureau of Circulations in 1914 to police print-media circulation claims, the founding of the American Association of Advertising Agencies in 1917, and the passage by Congress of an act creating the Federal Trade Commission in 1914. The Wheeler-Lea Act of 1938 gave the FTC added teeth in dealing with advertisements that deceived consumers.

THE ROOTS OF PUBLIC RELATIONS

The roots of the twentieth-century practice of public relations are found in three nineteenth-century developments: the rise of press agentry, the intensification of political campaigning, and the employment by businesses of publicity writers. By the 1920s the image of public relations as an operating concept of management, implemented by a specialized staff function, was beginning to emerge.

Most celebrated of the press agents was Phineas Taylor Barnum, whose skill built his circus into an American institution in post-Civil War years. He and his press agent, Richard F. (Tody) Hamilton, utilized exaggeration, outright fakery, and staged events to obtain reams of stories in the newspapers. They made household names of Tom Thumb, the midget, and Jenny Lind, "the Swedish Nightingale" who made a dazzling American tour. William F. Cody became "Buffalo Bill" through the skills of a half-dozen press agents. And as Will Irwin noted, the successes of theatrical press agents led to the appearance of thousands of publicists in business, politics, and other areas.

American politics had used pamphlets, posters, emblems, and press releases since the Jacksonian era. The focus on the use of the newspaper press became sharper during the 1896 presidential campaign between William Jennings Bryan and William McKinley. Pioneer business publicists like George F. Parker and Ivy Lee cut their teeth in political campaigns. Scott M. Cutlip, a leading public-relations scholar, traces the third strand—business identification with public relations—to pre-1900 events. In 1883 Theodore N. Vail, founding force of AT&T, was mailing sheafs of letters asking for opinions about his American Bell Telephone Company. George Westinghouse hired a personal press representative in 1889. And the Association of American Railroads used the term "public relations" in an 1897 company listing.[30]

The rise of the era of muckraking journalism after 1900, spurred by the political movements led by Presidents Theodore Roosevelt and Woodrow Wilson, brought a new urgency to developments in the publicity field. Roosevelt and Wilson methodically used the press conference and the news release to shape the public image of White House policies. More immediately threatening to business were the muckraking magazines, led by *McClure's,* which published Ida M. Tarbell's 1903 series, "History of the Standard Oil Company." What the methodical Tarbell did in exposing the Rockefeller oil monopoly was matched by the emotion-arousing attack made on the meat packers in 1906 by Upton Sinclair in his book, *The Jungle.* Businesspeople sought defensive publicity, and were in some cases more responsive to the managerial concept of public relations.

George F. Parker and Ivy Lee opened a New York City publicity office in 1904. Parker remained primarily a publicist, but Lee moved into the role of advising companies and industries which were in trouble. One was the anthracite coal industry, embroiled in a 1906 strike; in its behalf Lee issued a declaration to the press that his agency would operate only in the open, using prompt and accurate information. He told the Pennsylvania Railroad it should help reporters cover a train wreck, not hide it. It was harder for Lee to maintain his personal image when he became adviser to John D. Rockefeller, Jr., in 1914, in the wake of vicious strike-breaking activities at the family's Colorado Fuel and Iron Company. Upton Sinclair dubbed Lee "Poison Ivy." Lee's later association with the Guggenheim family brought him more criticism centered on that family's Chilean mining interests. Nevertheless Lee became identified as a founder of public relations; he formed a public-relations firm with T. J. Ross in 1919.

James D. Ellsworth, later an AT&T staff member, formed a Boston publicity bureau in 1906. Pendleton Dudley, another pioneer, opened his New York office in 1909. Henry Ford, who cannily used the press to publicize his Model-T car, founded his internal magazine, *The Ford Times,* in 1908. Theodore Vail, becoming AT&T president in 1907, rapidly expanded the Bell company's programs for customer relations as well as press relations. The American Red Cross and National Tuberculosis Association programs date from 1908. An association of college and university publicists was formed in 1917 and the National Lutheran Council and the Knights of Columbus opened press offices in 1918. Some companies used their advertising agencies, notably N. W. Ayer, for publicity services.

Techniques of publicity, promotion, and propaganda were greatly developed during World War I. President Wilson established the Committee on Public Information (CPI), under the direction of George Creel, to coordinate wartime programs, disseminate information, and stimulate public support of war objectives. Ivy Lee was working for the Red Cross, but two new figures in the public relations area joined the CPI. One, the associate chairperson, was Carl Byoir, later founder of one of the largest counseling firms. The other was Edward L. Bernays, who soon proved to be the most articulate advocate of the public-relations concept. The CPI afforded an opportunity to undertake programs influencing the public mind, and proving the values of publicity campaigns. The lessons were soon used in behalf of products, the corporate image, political candidates, fund-raising drives, and social-work agencies.

Two books of the early 1920s gave direction to the development of the fields of public opinion and public relations. One was Walter Lippmann's 1922 pioneering analysis, *Public Opinion.* Lippmann likened each individual's opinions to "the pictures in our heads" and the pictures acted upon by groups of people as "Public Opinion in capital letters." His book examined how opinions are crystallized into a social purpose or a national will. The next year Bernays published *Crystallizing Public Opinion,* in collaboration with his wife and partner, Doris E. Fleischman. The first sentence read: "In writing this book I have tried

Edward L. Bernays.
Jamie Cope

to set down the broad principles that govern the new profession of public relations counsel."[31] Bernays continued as a leading public-relations counsel, teacher, and writer into the 1980s.

John W. Hill began a public-relations firm in Cleveland in 1927, and later joined with Don Knowlton to form a major counseling firm. Bernays served as counsel to General Electric and Westinghouse during the 1920s. Arthur W. Page became the first public-relations director of AT&T. Corporate public-relations programs utilizing advertising campaigns were begun by Illinois Central, Metropolitan Life, and General Motors between 1920 and 1923. In the prosperous years of the decade the field expanded steadily. General Motors, facing belt-tightening in 1931, named Paul Garrett as the company's first public-relations director. He set a pattern for corporate public relations and continued in office for 25 years.

NOTES

1. Elliot N. Sivowitch, "A Technological Survey of Broadcasting's Prehistory, 1876–1920," *Journal of Broadcasting,* XV (Winter 1970–71), 1–20. This article was reprinted along with a number of other important research articles in Lawrence W. Lichty and Malachi C. Topping, *American Broadcasting: A Source Book on the History of Radio and Television* (New York: Hastings House, 1975).

2. Thomas W. Hoffer, "Nathan B. Stubblefield and His Wireless Telephone," *Journal of Broadcasting,* XV (Summer 1971) 317–29. For details of these early

experiments see also Erik Barnouw, *A Tower in Babel* (New York: Oxford University Press, 1966); Christopher H. Sterling and John M. Kittross, *Stay Tuned: A Concise History of American Broadcasting* (Belmont, Calif.: Wadsworth, 1978); and Sydney W. Head and Christopher Sterling, *Broadcasting in America* (Boston: Houghton Mifflin, 1982).

3. *New York Times,* October 18, 1907.

4. Sterling and Kittross call this the "first publicly announced broadcast of radio telephony," *Stay Tuned,* p. 28. Sivowitch, *Journal of Broadcasting* (Winter 1970–71) offers the most detailed description; see also Barnouw, *A Tower in Babel,* p. 20.

5. This is supported by evidence gathered by Gordon Greb, "The Golden Anniversary of Broadcasting," *Journal of Broadcasting,* III (Winter 1958–59), 3–13, and confirmed by Sterling and Kittross in a lengthy discussion, *Stay Tuned,* p. 40.

6. Head, *Broadcasting in America* (1976 edition), p. 113, cites Department of Commerce records.

7. The full story of RCA's rise and of other concentration of radio control is told in Llewellyn White, *The American Radio* (Chicago: University of Chicago Press, 1947).

8. In 1921 the *Kansas City Star* offered a combination radio-newspaper rate for advertising users of the *Star* and its station WDAF, but there were few immediate takers.

9. From testimony by Ralph D. Casey, director of the University of Minnesota School of Journalism, before the FCC. The testimony was reprinted in part by the Newspaper-Radio Committee in *Freedom of the Press* (booklet, 1942), pp. 5–21.

10. Wayne M. Towers, "World Series Coverage in New York City in the 1920s," *Journalism Monographs,* 73 (August 1981), 5–6.

11. Lichty and Topping, *American Broadcasting,* p. 158, cite an article by Bruce Barton in the *American Magazine,* August 1927, describing his participation at this extravaganza.

12. John Wallace, "What We Thought of the First Columbia Broadcasting Program," *Radio Broadcast* (December 1927), 140–41.

13. White, *The American Radio,* pp. 144–47.

14. The story of the newspaper-radio struggle and ANPA's part in it is told in Edwin Emery, *History of the American Newspaper Publishers Association* (Minneapolis: University of Minnesota Press, 1950), Chapter 13.

15. Mitchell V. Charnley, *News by Radio* (New York: Macmillan, 1948), p. 9.

16. George A. Lundberg, "The Content of Radio Programs," *Social Forces,* 7 (1928), pp. 58–60, cited by Lichty and Topping, *American Broadcasting,* p. 323.

17. Barnouw, *A Tower in Babel,* p. 229.

18. The name comes from the title of a history of the tabloids: Simon M. Bessie, *Jazz Journalism* (New York: Dutton, 1938).

19. As quoted in Bessie, *Jazz Journalism,* p. 82.

20. William H. Taft, "Bernarr Macfadden: One of a Kind," *Journalism Quarterly,* XLV (Winter 1968), 631.

21. Gauvreau used this phrase as the title for a thinly fictionalized account of his editorship of the *Graphic:* Emile Gauvreau, *Hot News* (New York: Macaulay Company, 1931).

22. As quoted in Helen M. Hughes, *News and the Human Interest Story* (Chicago: University of Chicago Press, 1940), p. 235.

23. See Walter E. Schneider, "Fabulous Rise of N.Y. Daily News," *Editor & Publisher,* LXXII (June 24, 1939), 5, for an extensive account of 20 years of the paper's history. Patterson's obituaries appeared in *Editor & Publisher,* LXXIX (June 1, 1946), 9, and in *Time,* LXVII (June 3, 1946), 87.

24. Royal H. Ray, *Concentration of Ownership and Control in the American Daily Newspaper Industry* (Columbia University Microfilms 1951), pp. 401–8. A summary of this Ph.D. dissertation was published in *Journalism Quarterly,* XXIX (Winter 1952), 31.

25. Census population figures and newspaper-circulation totals are conveniently tabulated in the appendices of A. M. Lee, *The Daily Newspaper in America* (New York: Macmillan, 1937). Advertising revenue totals are from figures of the ANPA Bureau of Advertising.

26. Willard G. Bleyer, "Freedom of the Press and the New Deal," *Journalism Quarterly,* XI (March 1934), 29. Those cities with just one morning daily but with two or more evening papers, in addition to the dozen listed in the text were Baltimore, Providence, Rochester, Syracuse, Dayton, Columbus (Ohio), Louisville, Richmond, Memphis, Houston, Dallas, Fort Worth, Oklahoma City, Portland (Oregon), and Seattle. Those cities with just one morning and one evening paper were Hartford, New Haven, Tampa, Chattanooga, Knoxville, Grand Rapids, Tulsa, and Denver. One company owned all the dailies published in six cities: New Bedford and Springfield, Massachusetts, Duluth, Des Moines, Wilmington, Delaware, and Charleston, South Carolina. Springfield, however, had two morning and two evening dailies operating under a single ownership headed by Sherman H. Bowles of the historic *Republican* family.

27. Paul Block leased the *Sentinel* from Hearst and operated it from 1929 to 1937.

28. Among Hearst's other purchases were the *Atlanta Georgian,* 1912; *Detroit Times,* 1921; *Seattle Post-Intelligencer, Rochester Journal,* and *Syracuse Telegram,* 1922: *Albany Times-Union* and *San Antonio Light,* 1924; *Syracuse Journal* (combined with the *Telegram*), 1925.

29. On the loss side, Scripps-Howard sold the *Des Moines News, Sacramento Star,* and *Terre Haute Post* to

competitors during the 1920s, and the *Baltimore Post* to Hearst in 1934. The *Washington Daily News, Fort Worth Press,* and *Birmingham Post* were founded in 1921. Scripps-Howard purchased the *Indianapolis Times* and *Youngstown Telegram* in 1922, the *New Mexico State Tribune* in Albuquerque in 1923, and the *Buffalo Times* in 1929. The *Rocky Mountain News* and *Times* were bought in 1926; the chain consolidated its *Denver Express* and *Times,* then killed the paper in 1928.

30. Cutlip traces the history of public relations in his *Effective Public Relations,* which he coauthored with Allen H. Center (Englewood Cliffs, N.J.: Prentice-Hall, 1978).

31. Eric F. Goldman, *Two-Way Street* (Boston: Bellman Publishing, 1948), tells the story.

ANNOTATED BIBLIOGRAPHY

Books: Background History

ALLEN, FREDERICK LEWIS, *The Big Change.* New York: Harper & Row, 1952. See also Lloyd Morris, *Postscript to Yesterday* (New York: Random House, 1947); Dixon Wecter, *The Age of the Great Depression, 1929–1941.* A History of American Life, Volume XIII (New York: Macmillan, 1948); Harvey Wish, *Contemporary America: The National Scene Since 1900* (New York: Harper & Row, 1966). Excellent social histories.

BARCK, OSCAR T., and NELSON M. BLAKE, *Since 1900.* New York: Macmillan, 1965. See also Arthur S. Link and William B. Catton, *American Epoch* (New York: Knopf, 1963). Twentieth-century histories.

BEARD, CHARLES A., and MARY R. *America in Midpassage.* New York: Macmillan, 1939. Volume III of the *Rise of American Civilization;* surveys the 1920s and 1930s.

MURRAY, ROBERT K., *The Harding Era.* Minneapolis: University of Minnesota Press, 1969. A detailed study of the ill-fated Harding administration.

PERRETT, GEOFFREY, *America in the 20's: A History.* New York: Simon & Schuster, 1982. Detailed study.

TERKEL, STUDS, *Hard Times.* New York: Pantheon, 1970. An oral history of the Great Depression.

Books: Newspapers

BARRETT, JAMES W., *The World, the Flesh, and Messrs. Pulitzer.* New York: Vanguard, 1931. The best story of the sale of the *World* by the paper's last city editor.

BESSIE, SIMON M., *Jazz Journalism.* New York: Dutton, 1938. The best story of of the tabloids, prefaced with a readable account of the rise of sensationalism.

BOYLAN, JAMES, ed., *The World and the Twenties: The Golden Years of New York's Legendary Newspaper.* New York: Dial Press, 1973. Captures the flavor and writing skill.

BRITT, GEORGE, *Forty Years—Forty Millions; The Career of Frank A. Munsey.* New York: Holt, Rinehart & Winston, 1935. A critical biography.

CHAPMAN, JOHN, *Tell It to Sweeney: The Informal History of the New York Daily News.* New York: Doubleday, 1961. Light touch account.

DENNIS, CHARLES H., *Victor Lawson: His Time and His Work.* Chicago: University of Chicago Press, 1935. The authorized story of Lawson and the *Chicago Daily News.*

FOWLER, GENE, *Timber Line.* New York: Covici-Friede, 1933. The colorful story of the Bonfils and Tammen era at the *Denver Post.* No tale was too tall for Denver news writers.

HOSOKAWA, BILL, *Thunder in the Rockies: The Incredible Denver Post.* New York: Morrow, 1976. An update by the executive news editor.

HUGHES, HELEN M., *News and the Human Interest Story.* Chicago: University of Chicago Press, 1940. A sociological study of the feature story and sensationalism, with some discussion of the tabloid era.

HUTCHENS, JOHN K., and GEORGE OPPENHEIMER, eds., *The Best in The World.* New York: Viking Press, 1973. Selections from 1921 to 1928.

PERKIN, ROBERT L., *The First Hundred Years: An Informal History of Denver and the Rocky Mountain News.* New York: Doubleday, 1959. By a staff member of Colorado's first paper.

VILLARD, OSWALD GARRISON, *The Disappearing Daily.* New York: Knopf, 1944. Criticism of the trend toward consolidation and bigness.

———, *Some Newspapers and Newspaper-Men.* New York: Knopf, 1923. Like *The Disappearing Daily,* this book discusses newspapers in major cities as well as major publishers: New York, Boston, Philadelphia, Washington, among others.

Books: Magazines

BAINBRIDGE, JOHN, *Little Wonder.* New York: Reynal & Hitchcock, 1946. A critical study of the *Reader's Digest,* which originally appeared as a *New Yorker* profile.

BAKER, CARLOS, *Ernest Hemingway: A Life Story.* New York: Scribner's, 1969. By far the best biography of Hemingway. See also Scott Donaldson, *By Force of Will* (New York: Viking Press, 1977).

BOK, EDWARD W., *A Man from Maine.* New York: Scribner's, 1923. A life of Cyrus H. K. Curtis by his editor.

FLANNER, JANET, *Janet Flanner's World.* New York: Harcourt Brace Jovanovich, 1979. *Paris Was Yesterday.* New York: Viking, 1972. Her *New Yorker* columns signed Gênet, 1925 to 1939.

FORD, JAMES L. C., *Magzines for Millions.* Carbondale: Southern Illinois University Press, 1969. An account of specialized publications.

HEMINGWAY, ERNEST, *ByLine: Ernest Hemingway,* edited by William White. New York: Scribner's, 1967. His stories in papers and magazines over four decades.

KRAMER, DALE, *Ross and the New Yorker.* Garden City, N.Y.: Doubleday, 1951. See also Brendan Gill, *Here at the New Yorker* (New York: Random House, 1975), and James Thurber, *The Years with Ross* (Boston: Little, Brown, 1957).

Magazine Profiles. Evanston, Ill.: Medill School of Journalism, 1974. Studies by twelve graduate students of nearly fifty then current magazines.

MANCHESTER, WILLIAM, *Disturber of the Peace.* New York: Harper & Row, 1950. Best of the biographies of H. L. Mencken, whose autobiography is titled *The Days of H. L. Mencken* (New York: Knopf, 1947). See also Carl Bode, *Mencken* (Carbondale: Southern Illinois University Press, 1969); George H. Douglas, *H. L. Mencken, Critic of American Life* (Hamden, Conn.: Archon Books, 1978).

MOTT, FRANK LUTHER, *A History of American Magazines.* Volume 5, *Sketches of 21 Magazines, 1905–1930.* Cambridge, Mass.: Harvard University Press, 1968. Contains index for all five volumes.

PETERSON, THEODORE, *Magazines in the Twentieth Century.* Urbana: University of Illinois Press, 1964. A gold mine of interpretation and factual detail about the magazine industry.

SCHREINER, SAMUEL A., JR., *The Condensed World of the Reader's Digest.* New York: Stein and Day, 1977. Highly recommended in reviews.

SOKOLOV, RAYMOND, *Wayward Reporter: The Life of A. J. Liebling.* New York: Harper & Row, 1980. First full-scale biography.

TEBBEL, JOHN W., *The American Magazine: A Compact History.* New York: Hawthorn, 1969. Main threads of the magazine in United States social history.

WOLSELEY, ROLAND E., *The Changing Magazine.* New York: Hastings House, 1973. Trends in readership and management; some individual profiles.

WOOD, JAMES PLAYSTED, *Magazines in the United States.* New York: Ronald Press, 1956. Social background is provided.

———, *Of Lasting Interest: The Story of the Reader's Digest.* Garden City, N.Y.: Doubleday, 1958. Friendly tone.

Books: Comics

BECKER, STEPHEN, *Comic Art in America.* New York: Simon & Schuster, 1959. Surveys comics, political cartoons, magazine humor.

BLACKBEARD, BILL, and MARTIN WILLIAMS, *The Smithsonian Collection of Newspaper Comics.* Washington, D.C.: Smithsonian Institution Press, 1977. Hundred strips, ninety-four color pages, annotated index.

COUPERIE, PIERRE, and MAURICE C. HORN, *A History of the Comic Strip.* New York: Crown, 1968. Covers the comic strip world-wide with emphasis upon American.

PERRY, GEORGE, and ALAN ALDRIDGE, *The Penguin Book of Comics.* Harmondsworth, Eng.: Penguin, 1967. History of comics with copious examples.

ROBINSON, JERRY, *The Comics: An Illustrated History of Comic Strip Art.* New York: Putnam's, 1974. Perhaps the best one-volume overview.

WAUGH, COULTON, *The Comics.* New York: Macmillan, 1947. A first-rate history of the comic pages; detailed but well written and well illustrated.

WEBSTER, H. T., *The Best of H. T. Webster.* New York: Simon & Schuster, 1953. One of the best collections of newspaper humorous drawings.

Books: Broadcasting

BARNOUW, ERIK, *A History of Broadcasting in the United States.* Volume 1, *A Tower in Babel* (to 1933); Volume 2, *The Golden Web* (1933–53); Volume 3, *The Image Empire* (from 1953). New York: The Oxford Press, 1966, 1968, 1970. Best account of radio and television; third volume necessarily becomes less historical in tone.

———, *Tube of Plenty.* New York: Oxford Press, 1975. Condensed updated version of television history.

Broadcasting, Fiftieth Anniversary Issue, October 12, 1981. A 314-page issue including a fifty-seven-page chronology of broadcast history.

CHARNLEY, MITCHELL V., *News by Radio.* New York: Macmillan, 1948. Source for the growth of radio news.

CHASE, FRANCIS, JR., *Sound and Fury.* New York: Harper & Row, 1942. An informal history of radio with much information, but sometimes inaccurate in precise details.

DE FOREST, LEE, *Father of Radio: The Autobiography of Lee De Forest.* Chicago: Wilcox & Follett, 1950. The early years.

DUNNING, JOHN, *Tune In Yesterday: The Ultimate Encyclopedia of Old-Time Radio, 1925–1976.* Englewood Cliffs, N.J.: Prentice-Hall, 1976. Narrative and data listings.

EMERY, WALTER B., *Broadcasting and Government.* East Lansing: Michigan State University Press, rev. ed., 1971. An encyclopedic survey of all aspects of government interest in, and regulation of, U.S. broadcasting.

GROSS, LYNNE SCHAFER, *Telecommunications.* Duque, Ia: Wm. C. Brown, 1983. Historical survey and current status.

HEAD, SYDNEY W., and CHRISTOPHER STERLING, *Broadcasting in America,* 4th ed. Boston: Houghton Mifflin, 1982. Sterling joins Head as coauthor of this classic.

KAHN, FRANK J., ed., *Documents of American Broadcasting,* 4th ed. Englewood Cliffs, N.J.: Prentice-Hall, 1984. The pertinent documents and cases.

KEMPLER, CANDYCE, ed., *The First Fifty Years of Broadcasting.* Washington, D.C.: Broadcasting Publications, 1982. Edited reprint of weekly articles in *Broadcasting* magazine.

LICHTY, LAWRENCE W., and MALACHI C. TOPPING, *American Broadcasting: A Sourcebook on the History of Radio and Television.* New York: Hastings House, 1975. Eight-year editing project yields more than 700 pages of data, chronologies, findings.

MACDONALD, J. FRED, *Don't Touch That Dial!: Radio Programming in American Life from 1920 to 1960.* Chicago: Nelson-Hall, 1979. Radio's varied contributions to U.S. culture.

SARNOFF, DAVID, *Looking Ahead: The Papers of David Sarnoff.* New York: McGraw-Hill, 1968. Papers of the broadcasting pioneer.

SMITH, F. LESLIE, *Perspectives on Radio and Television: An Introduction to Broadcasting in the United States.* New York: Harper & Row, 1979. A good history of broadcasting.

STERLING, CHRISTOPHER H., and JOHN M. KITTROSS, *A Concise History of American Broadcasting.* Belmont, Calif.: Wadsworth, 1978. Leading synthesis; highly usable.

TEBBEL, JOHN W., *David Sarnoff: Putting Electrons to Work.* Chicago: Encyclopaedia Britannica, 1964. A biography of the RCA chairman.

WHITE, LLEWELLYN, *The American Radio.* Chicago: University of Chicago Press, 1947. A publication of the Commission on Freedom of the Press. Best analysis of radio's growth.

Books: Film, Motion Pictures

COOK, DAVID A., *A History of Narrative Film.* New York: Norton, 1981. One of widely used survey texts, along with Gerald Mast, *A Short History of the Movies,* 3rd ed. (Chicago: University of Chicago Press, 1981); John L. Fell, *A History of Films* (New York: Holt, Rinehart & Winston, 1979); Richard Griffith and Arthur Mayer, *The Movies* (New York: Simon & Schuster, 1970); and Paul Rotha,

The Film Till Now: A Survey of World Cinema (London: Spring Books, 1967).

JOWETT, GARTH, *Film: The Democratic Art.* Boston: Little, Brown, 1976. Social impact of the movies and economic, political, cultural adjustments.

KNIGHT, ARTHUR, *The Liveliest Art.* New York: Hastings House, 1978. Particularly good for the period from 1895 to 1930. See also D. J. Wenden, *The Birth of the Movies* (New York: Dutton, 1975).

RHODE, ERIC, *A History of the Cinema from Its Origins to 1970.* New York: Hill and Wang, 1976. Personalized cultural history.

Books: Advertising, Public Relations

BERNAYS, EDWARD L., *Biography of an Idea.* New York: Simon & Schuster, 1965. Memoirs of a pioneer public-relations counselor.

CUTLIP, SCOTT H., and ALLEN H. CENTER, *Effective Public Relations,* 5th ed. Englewood Cliffs, N.J.: Prentice-Hall, 1978. The leading survey, with an extensive historical account.

GUNTHER, JOHN, *Taken at the Flood: The Story of Albert D. Lasker.* New York: Harper & Row, 1960. The career of a famed advertising-agency executive.

HIEBERT, RAY E., *Courtier to the Crowd: The Life Story of Ivy Lee.* Ames: Iowa State University Press, 1966. Pioneer publicist and public-relations practitioner.

HOLME, BRYAN, ed., *Advertising: Reflections of a Century.* New York: Viking, 1982. More than 500 ads, mostly in color, with commentary.

NEWSOME, DOUG, and ALAN SCOTT, *This Is PR: The Realities of Public Relations,* 2nd ed. Belmont, Calif.: Wadsworth, 1981. Widely used survey text.

POPE, DANIEL, *The Making of Modern Advertising.* New York: Basic Books, 1983. A thoughtful, analytic history of advertising to 1920.

PRESBREY, FRANK, *The History and Development of Advertising.* New York: Doubleday, 1929. Long the standard history, still the best source for the early period.

Printers' Ink, 75th Anniversary Edition, "Advertising: Today, Yesterday, Tomorrow," June 14, 1963. A 474-page historical review, compiled by 100 staff members and advertising-industry authorities. Both facts and color.

RAUCHER, ALAN R., *Public Relations and Business, 1900–1929.* Baltimore: Johns Hopkins University Press, 1968. An excellent monograph.

TURNER, E. S., *The Shocking History of Advertising.* Harmondsworth, Eng.: Penguin Books, 1965. An updated reprinting of a good history.

WATKINS, JULIAN L., *The 100 Greatest Advertisements,* 2nd ed. New York: Moore Publishing, 1959. Histories of all the ads, prepared by a veteran copywriter.

WOOD, JAMES PLAYSTED, *The Story of Advertising.* New York: Ronald Press, 1958. Fairly detailed from 1860 on.

WRIGHT, JOHN S., et al., *Advertising.* New York: McGraw-Hill, 1981. A leading text.

WRIGHT, JOHN W., ed., *The Commercial Connection: Advertising and the American Mass Media.* New York: Dell, 1979. Anthology dealing with audiences, content.

Periodicals and Monographs

ALEXANDER, JACK, "Vox Populi," *New Yorker,* XIV (August 6–20, 1938) A profile of Captain Patterson.

BARCUS, FRANCIS E., "A Content Analysis of Trends in Sunday Comics, 1900–1959," *Journalism Quarterly,* XXXVIII (Spring 1961), 171. The first report from a major study of comics at Boston.

BENNION, SHERILYN COX, "Reform Agitation in the American Periodical Press, 1920–29," *Journalism Quarterly,* XLVIII (Winter 1971), 652. General circulation periodicals largely ignored the reform impulse, reflected public opinion.

BERNAYS, EDWARD L., "Emergence of the Public Relations Counsel: Principles and Reflections," *Business History Review,* XLV (Autumn, 1971), 296. Memoir of a pioneer.

BLEYER, WILLARD G., "Freedom of the Press and the New Deal," *Journalism Quarterly,* XI (March 1934), 22. Report on the trend toward newspaper combinations.

BROD, DONALD F., "Church, State, and Press: Twentieth Century Episodes in the United States," Ph.D. thesis, University of Minnesota, 1968. Examines newspaper coverage of the Scopes trial, Vatican relations, and the 1928 and 1960 elections.

DENNIS, EVERETTE, and CHRISTOPHER ALLEN, "*Puck,* the Comic Weekly," *Journalism History,* VI (Spring 1979), 14. Hearst's great comics.

DUFFUS, ROBERT L., "Mr. Munsey," *American Mercury,* II (July 1924); 297. A gently critical rejection of Munsey as a newspaper owner. Reprinted in Ford and Emery, *Highlights in the History of the American Press.*

EVANS, JAMES P., "Clover Leaf: The Good Luck Chain, 1899–1933," *Journalism Quarterly,* XLVI (Autumn 1969), 482. The chain had a *Daily News* in Omaha, St. Paul, and Des Moines and a *Kansas City World.*

FURLONG, WILLIAM B., "The Midwest's Nice Monopolists, John and Mike Cowles," *Harper's,* CCXXVI (June 1963), 64. A sketch of responsible monopoly publishers.

GARVEY, DANIEL E., "Secretary Hoover and the Quest for Broadcast Regulation," *Journalism History,* III (Autumn 1976), 66. Hoover sought stronger regulation than Congress granted.

GODFREY, DONALD G., "The 1927 Radio Act: People and Politics," *Journalism History,* IV (Autumn 1977), 74. Led to FCC.

HYNES, TERRY, "Media Manipulations and Political Campaigns: Bruce Barton and the Presidential Elections of the Jazz Age," *Journalism History,* IV (Autumn 1977), 93. BBDO enters politics.

MARTINSON, DAVID L., "New Images of Presidential Candidates, 1920–24: A Survey of Three Major Newspapers," Ph.D. thesis, University of Minnesota, 1974. Surveys the *Chicago Tribune, St. Louis Post-Dispatch,* and *New York Times.*

MCKERNS, JOSEPH P., "Industry Skeptics and the Radio Act of 1927," *Journalism History,* III (Winter 1976–77), 128.

NELSON, HAROLD L., "The Political Reform Press: A Case Study," *Journalism Quarterly,* XXIX (Summer 1952), 294. An analysis of an almost-successful farmer-labor newspaper, the *Minnesota Daily Star* (1920 to 1924).

NIXON, RAYMOND B., "Trends in U.S. Newspaper Ownership: Concentration with Competition," *Gazette,* XIV (No. 3, 1968), 181. A review with comprehensive data. See also Raymond B. Nixon, and Jean Ward, "Trends in Newspaper Ownership and Inter-Media Competition," *Journalism Quarterly,* XXXVIII (Winter 1961), 3.

SAALBERG, HARVEY, "Don Mellett, Editor of the *Canton News,* Was Slain While Exposing Underworld," *Journalism Quarterly,* LIII (Spring 1976), 88. Details the circumstances surrounding Mellett's attack on crime and his subsequent murder.

SMYTHE, TED C., "A History of the *Minneapolis Journal,* 1878–1939," Ph.D. thesis, University of Minnesota, 1967. Leading Minneapolis afternoon daily.

TAFT, WILLIAM H., "Bernarr Macfadden: One of a Kind," *Journalism Quarterly,* XLV (Winter 1968), 627. Based on extensive research about the publisher.

"The Twenties," articles by Cathy Covert, Garth S. Jowett, James W. Wesolowski, George E. Stevens, Robert V. Hudson, June Adamson, and W. Richard Whitaker, in *Journalism History,* II (Autumn 1975).

WASSMUTH, BIRGIT L. "Art Movements and American Print Advertising: A Study of Advertising Graphics 1915–1935," Ph.D. thesis, University of Minnesota, 1983. Traces uses of art forms, rise of art directors.

WEINFELD, WILLIAM, "The Growth of Daily Newspaper Chains in the United States: 1923, 1926–1935," *Journalism Quarterly,* XIII (December 1936), 357. The first important study of the problem.

WHITAKER, W. RICHARD, "The Night Harding Died," *Journalism History,* I (Spring 1974), 16. Based on "Warren G. Harding and the Press," Ph.D. thesis, Ohio University, 1972.

WILLIAMSON, MARY E., "Judith Cary Waller: Chicago Broadcasting Pioneer," *Journalism History,* III (Winter 1976–77), 111. First station manager of *Daily News'* WMAQ, 1922; 50 years in broadcasting.

Radio came of age during the Roosevelt years.

21

Depression and Reform

Partisanship, in editorial comment which knowingly departs from the truth, does violence to the best spirit of American journalism; in the news columns it is subversive of a fundamental principle of the profession.

—ASNE Canons of Journalism

Criticism of the performance of America's mass media became particularly pointed during the liberal resurgence of the 1930s known as the New Deal. Driven by the impact of the Great Depression, the nation established new patterns of social justice and economic security under the leadership of Franklin D. Roosevelt. In doing so, it vastly expanded governmental participation in socioeconomic affairs. That there was criticism of newspapers during such years of swift change was nothing new; press critics had been having their say since the dawn of newspaper publishing. But whereas much of the earlier criticism had dealt with the cultural and social values of the press, the emphasis in the 1930s was on its political power. Supporters of Franklin Roosevelt and the New Deal charged that much of the press was opposed to socioeconomic reforms, sometimes in ways viewed as bitterly partisan. To the liberals who won sweeping ballot-box victories, it seemed that too often the press was unresponsive to change and democratic decisions. Their wrath particularly centered on a group of publishers dubbed the "press lords."

The prologue for this drama came in 1928. There was a great surge of stock prices on the New York Stock Exchange that carried Radio Corporation of America, for example, from less than $100 a share to $400. "Two chickens in every pot, two cars in every garage" was the slogan of the Republican party, which promised permanent prosperity with the election of Herbert Hoover as president. A "get-rich-quick" mania brought hundreds of thousands of small investors into the market in 1929; many of them put their life savings up as margin for speculative accounts. But permanent prosperity was not to be had. The market wavered in September, plummeted in late October, and on "Black Thursday" crashed an average of forty points. Shoe clerks and stockbrokers were ruined alike, and the boom was over.

The business downturn that ended in the Great Depression was worldwide in character. In the Unted States consumers did not have the money to buy the goods produced by the new industries. Too much wealth had fallen into too few hands. Workers' wages had fallen far behind inflation, and farmers were bankrupted by chronically low crop prices. The stock-market collapse added to the momentum. With unsalable inventories mounting, manufacturers closed plants and laid off workers. In turn, retail stores and businesses failed. More than 1300 banks closed their doors in 1930, and another 3700 in the next 2 years. There was, for the victims of this spreading chaos, no bank-deposit insurance, no unemployment insurance, no help in warding off foreclosures on farms and homes.

By mid-1932, stocks on Wall Street were worth only 11 percent of their 1929 values. Business failures totaled 86,000; unemployment reached 15 million. Those still working earned an average of $16 a week, or $842 a year. A fourth of the population had no income at all. President Hoover, the advocate of rugged individualism, offered constructive financial aid to big businesses, but none to plain people. He ordered General Douglas MacArthur to drive the ragged Bonus Army of war veterans from Washington with gunfire and clubs, a disgraceful episode which was generally condoned by the press and which epitomized capitalist America's lack of feeling for individuals.

Small wonder that Hoover, symbol of the faltering captalist society, would win only six states in the 1932 election, against an opponent offering a "New Deal." The new president, Franklin D. Roosevelt, was equally capitalistic in outlook, but compassionate and flexible in seeking new solutions to the problems of a country with one-third of its people "ill-housed, ill-clad, and ill-nourished." Before he took office on March 4, 1933, most of the country's banks had closed and the economy was at a halt. "The only thing we have to fear is fear itself," Roosevelt said in a reassuring inaugural address. During the "hundred days" which followed Congress rewrote American political history. "I want to talk a few minutes with the people of the United States about banking," Roosevelt said in his first radio network "fireside chat." A complete reorganization of banking and the financial markets followed. A roll call of 1933 to 1935 legislation includes the establishment of the Federal Deposit Insurance Corporation to insure bank deposits; the Works Progress Administration to aid the one-sixth of the population on relief; the National Recovery Administration to stimulate industrial production; the Agricultural Adjustment Administration to stabilize farm prices; and the Securities Exchange Commission to regulate financial markets. The Social Security Act of 1935 and the Wagner Labor Relations Act of 1935 were cornerstones of personal and job security.

There was heavy criticism of the New Deal among conservatives, businesspeople, financiers, and others whose loyalties lay with the Republican party. Roosevelt had the editorial support of only about one-third of the country's dailies in the 1932 and 1936 elections, including few of the influential ones. He was pilloried by some he called the "press lords." The papers were full of complaints as the economy bettered: The Socialist left denounced Roosevelt for propping up capitalism; the Liberty League, founded in 1936 by 2000 of the wealthiest Americans, berated him for imitating Communist Russia. A conservative Supreme Court declared the NRA and AAA unconstitutional. The *Literary Digest* poll based on telephone listings and automobile registrations predicted a 1936 Republican victory (an error that hastened the *Digest*'s demise and sale to *Time*).

Accepting his renomination, Roosevelt said confidently: "There is a mysterious cycle in human events. To some generations much is given. Of other generations much is expected. This generation has a rendezvous with destiny." The tumultuous applause that greeted his campaign speeches forecast the solid vote of those without telephones and cars. "FDR" won all but two states from the hapless Alf Landon as 5 million Republican votes turned Democratic. Flushed with victory, Roosevelt took aim at the Supreme Court. But early in 1937 the Court upheld the Wagner Act and Social Security, taking the steam out of the "Court-packing" plan. The New Deal was coming to a halt, but victory came at last on the labor front. Sitdown strikes in the auto plants were unpopular, but they brought unionization of all except Ford. And John L. Lewis' Congress of Industrial Organization (CIO) won contracts with the steel industry after a bloody massacre of workers by police outside a Chicago plant. Thus the efforts of the IWW, Eugene Debs, and earlier labor leaders bore fruit.

A darkening storm of military adventurism brought about by economic and political crises throughout the world periodically interrupted America's preoccupation with domestic affairs. Soberly the American people read about the new aggressive forces in their newspapers and in newly founded news and picture magazines, listened to radio broadcasts, and watched marching armies in their newsreels, beginning with the Japanese invasion of Manchuria in 1931. Working outside the crumbling League of Nations, the American government attempted to rally world opinion against the Japanese, Italian, and German militarists, but there was no unity of action. Ethiopia fell to Mussolini, the new *Life* magazine pictured a crying Chinese baby in a bomb-destroyed Shanghai railway station, and disturbing headlines recorded Hitler's reoccupation of the Rhineland and *anschluss* with Austria. The disillusionment that had produced the antiwar literature in the 1930s and had set the stage for neutrality legislation was slowly passing. Isolationism died hard, however. In 1935 a Senate committee headed by Gerald P. Nye of North Dakota had advanced the thesis that American munitions makers and bankers were almost solely responsible for the country's entrance into the first World War. The neutrality legislation that followed was designed to prevent American loans or sale of war materials to belligerents, on the theory that such a ban would prevent American involvement in "foreign" wars. Even after Americans heard intensive radio coverage of the Munich crisis of September, 1938, and Hitler's occupation of the remainder of unhappy Czechoslovakia in March, 1939, the isolationists held the upper hand.

THE PRESIDENT AND THE PRESS: FDR

No president had more effective relationships with the press than did Franklin D. Roosevelt. He met the White House correspondents informally, often in his office. He was at ease, communicative, gay, or serious as the news might dictate. Like all presidents he came to be irritated by his critics in the press, once assigning a dunce cap to Robert Post of the conservative *New York Herald Tribune* and another time awarding an iron cross to John O'Donnell of the isolationist *New York Daily News.* But he met the press 998 times during his 12 years in office, an average of eighty-three times a year. He was known for his fireside chats, but in his first term he gave only eight; the same 4 years he communicated with the American people and won forty-six states in the next election by holding 340 press conferences, most of which made solid news. He had one of the most capable press secretaries, Stephen T. Early, and built a tradition of press conferences that would be hard to follow. To look ahead, President Truman dropped the number of press conferences from eighty-three to forty-two; the yearly averages later were Eisenhower twenty-four, Kennedy twenty-two, Johnson twenty-five, Nixon seven, Ford sixteen, Carter twenty-six, and Reagan eight.

As Governor of New York Roosevelt had used radio to make direct appeals to the public. In 1932 he flew to Chicago to give his acceptance speech to the Democratic convention on radio—three unprecedented actions. He pointed out that he was breaking traditions and pledged his party to the task of destroying foolish ones. As a radio president, FDR was able to communicate a sense of comfort and reassurance with his personable radio voice that conveyed sincerity. His fireside chats were truly that.[1]

FDR's warm personality fit the informal lodge atmosphere of the press meetings. He was solicitous of the regulars and was sure to ask if they had comfortable places to stay at Hyde Park or Warm Springs. The President would give out a story, and he would provide the correspondents with several laughs as well as a couple of top-head dispatches in a time-saving 20-minute visit. In fact, the Roosevelt press conferences became the greatest regular show in Washington and FDR knew it, too. Once, he remarked, "Most of the people in the back row are here for curiosity, isn't that right."[2]

Roosevelt had conference rules involving direct quotes (only when stipulated), indirect quotes, and "off the record" material. As many as thirty different background questions might be answered in a longer conference; here FDR could employ his full range of news-management techniques. The conferences were useful to him; he could capture the headlines and the lead stories, whether the publishers wanted him to or not.

CRITICISM OF THE "PRESS LORDS"

Political tension, and accompanying criticism of the newspaper's role in elections, made for extensive public acceptance of a literature of criticism of the press. Upton Sinclair's bitter book, *The Brass Check* (1919), painted a picture of a false, cowardly press dominated by its business offices and its advertisers. Although there were newspaper situations that fitted these patterns, particularly in crowded metropolitan competitive situations where loss of an account could endanger a fourth- or fifth-ranking paper, the issue of advertiser influence was not the most pressing one. It was also one that tended to decline later in the century. The issue which had the most immediate impact was that of the political influence of the press, and particularly the misuse of both news and editorial columns by owners who were called the "press lords" by veteran foreign correspondent and antifascist writer George Seldes.

Caustic surveys of the "press lords" began in earnest with Oswald Garrison Villard's *Some Newspapers and Newspaper-Men* (1923). They flourished in the 1930s, which saw the publication of such books as Seldes' *Lords of the Press* (1938), Harold L. Ickes' *America's House of Lords* (1939), and individual studies such as Ferdinand Lundberg's *Imperial Hearst* (1936). These books were valuable as exposés, but their influence was undue in that they enjoyed wider public circulation than such counterbalancing and constructive discussions as Casper S. Yost's *Principles of Journalism* (1924), Villard's brief *The Press Today* (1930), Herbert Brucker's *The Changing American Newspaper* (1937), Silas Bent's *Newspaper Crusaders* (1939), and such products of the growing journalism schools as Leon N. Flint's *The Conscience of the Newspaper* (1925), Willard G. Bleyer's *Main Currents in the History of American Journalism* (1927), and *Interpretations of Journalism* (1937), edited by Frank L. Mott and Ralph D. Casey.

In any event, the dynamic and intriguing personalities of some of the "press lords" provided more interesting fare for the American reading public than any other material about newspaperpeople and newspaper problems. To understand, therefore, the bitterness and the extent of the criticisms of the press since the 1930s, it is necessary to examine the roles played by the most-often discussed newspaper publishers of the times.

WILLIAM RANDOLPH HEARST

William Randolph Hearst, as has been suggested in previous chapters, is one of the most difficult men of journalism to study and to estimate, considering the complex nature of his personality, the variegated social and political impact of his many ventures, and the length and extent of his career.* Those who wrote about Hearst were never permitted access to the publisher's private papers or the records of the Hearst empire. As a result, the official Hearst biography released by International News Service when the publisher's 64-year newspaper career closed in 1951 noted in its second paragraph: "And as he fashioned his vast enterprises, there grew progressively in the public mind a picture of the builder himself. It was a strange portrait, obscured by myth and legend, confused by controversy and distortion."

When Hearst had lived out his 88 years, the question became: Did he deserve the criticism that had been heaped upon him, more vehemently than on any other publisher? The points most often made in support of a thesis that Hearst made positive contributions to American journalism are these:

*Chapters 17 and 18 deal with Hearst's earlier career. See also pages 401–404 in Chapter 20 for a discussion of the extent of his newspaper operations.

1. Hearst built the world's biggest publishing empire in terms of newspapers and their combined circulations. At the peak, in 1935, Hearst printed twenty-six dailies and seventeen Sunday editions in nineteen cities. The papers had 13.6 percent of the total daily circulation in the country and 24.2 percent of Sunday circulation. In addition, he controlled the King Features Syndicate, largest of its kind; the money-coining *American Weekly;* International News Service, Universal Service, and International News Photos; thirteen magazines, eight radio stations, and two motion-picture companies. This, it is argued, spells a success that must be recognized.
2. Hearst's methods and innovations in newswriting and news handling—particularly in makeup and headline and picture display—and his utilization of new mechanical processes were very important. Hearst newspapers were edited to appeal to the mass of readers and encouraged millions to increase their reading habits. Because of this and because of Hearst's editorial policies and his own political activities, Hearst newspapers exercised a powerful influence in American life that must be recognized.
3. Hearst was in many ways a constructive force: a stalwart in his Americanism; a believer in popular education and in the extension of the power of the people; and, during different phases of his long career, an advocate of many progressive solutions to national problems. These included his early advocacy of the popular election of senators, of the initiative and referendum, of a graduated income tax, of widespread public ownership of utilities, of breaking up of monopolies and trusts, and of the rights of labor unions.

These points, the argument runs, are in the record for all to see. Hearst's critics, and the public record, also provided counterarguments:

1. The Hearst empire, for all its one-time size, was not the roaring success a recital of figures would indicate. Its finances were shaky in the 1920s. The crash came for Hearst in 1937, when he was forced to abdicate temporarily and watch a group of trustees liquidate a portion of his empire. Nine dailies and five Sunday editions were dropped by 1940; Universal Service was consolidated with the INS; movie companies, radio stations, and some magazines were sold. The trustees began liquidating $40 million worth of New York City real estate. Many of the $40 million in art treasures that were Hearst's pride and joy were auctioned off at Gimbels and Macy's. Eventually even many of San Simeon's 275,000 acres were sold to reclaim some of the $36 million spent there.

   Through it all, however, Hearst continued to live in regal style. The man who had bought a castle in Wales, Egyptian mummies, Tibetan yaks, and a Spanish abbey (which was dismantled stone by stone and shipped to a New York warehouse, after which Hearst never saw it again), had a truly precapitalistic attitude toward money as such. His guests at San Simeon, who were legion, continued to dive into an indoor pool from a sixteenth-century Italian marble balcony, to pick flowers in a mile-long pergola stretching along Hearst's private mountain range, and to eat from kingly silver plates. Before World War II had ended, the trimming down of his empire and wartime publishing profits had accomplished the desired miracle, and the Hearst once thought to be broke was back in full command again.

   When death had claimed its founder in 1951, the Hearst organization had sixteen dailies and thirteen Sunday editions appearing in a dozen cities. They had 9.1 percent of the country's total daily circulation and 16.1 percent of the Sunday total, a substantial decline in Hearst influence from the 1935 figures of 13.6 percent daily and 24.2 percent Sunday. The Hearst estate was valued at some $56 million, based on estimated stock values, but the profit margins of the Hearst enterprises were below those of other newspapers of their size for which financial reports are available, forecasting further contraction.

2. Undoubtedly, Hearst drew many new newspaper readers to his fold and held more than 5 million daily and 8 million Sunday to the day of his death. But what was the end result? Pulitzer defended the use of sensationalism in his *World* by arguing that it attracted readers who would then be exposed to the columns of his carefully planned, high-quality editorial page. The same could never be said of a Hearst newspaper. Nor did Hearst ever exercise the powerful influence in American life that his great circulations might indicate. Among the men whom he wanted to see become president of the United States were William Jennings Bryan, Champ Clark, Hiram W. Johnson, William Gibbs McAdoo, John Nance Garner, Alfred M. Landon, General Douglas MacArthur, and William Randolph Hearst. Among the men whom he fought while they were in the White House were William McKinley, Theodore Roosevelt, William Howard Taft, Woodrow Wilson, Herbert Hoover, Franklin D. Roosevelt, and Harry S Truman.
3. What, then, of Hearst as a constructive social force? Certainly he was an advocate of Americanism. But to many his continued espousal of nationalistic policies bordering on jingoism, in a time that demanded American cooperation in international security efforts, was the most distressing feature of his newspapers. And in the 1930s the "Red hunts" his newspapers fostered among the ranks of political leaders, educators, YMCA secretaries, labor leaders, and other citizens were based on the familiar tactics of the demagogue: Those who disagreed with Hearst were "Communists." A nationalist-isolationist to the end, Hearst opposed the basic foreign policy adopted by the American people during and after World War II and distrusted the United Nations as thoroughly as he had distrusted the League of Nations.

In domestic affairs, Hearst newspapers continued to give stalwart support to public education and to the idea of public ownership of utilities. But they backslid during the 1920s and 1930s on many of the other progressive features of the Hearst editorial program as written before World War I. Hearst had helped to elect Franklin Roosevelt and in the spring of 1933 his newspapers applauded vigorously as Roosevelt undertook unemployment relief, suspended exports of gold, and proposed the National Recovery Act—which, a Hearst editorial said, "embodies several basic policies long advocated by the Hearst newspapers."[3] By 1935 the tune had changed. It was the "Raw Deal" and the "National Run Around" in both news and editorial columns. The unanimous Supreme Court decision outlawing the NRA, which the Hearst papers had once proudly claimed for their own, was greeted with an American flag and the headline: "Thank God for the Supreme Court!"

There are other examples in the columns of the Hearst papers of 1935 that illustrate the extent to which the earlier beliefs of Hearst had changed. The publisher who before World War I had been perhaps the most aggressive in supporting the power of labor unions now said "the Wagner Labor Bill . . . is one of the most vicious pieces of class legislation that could be conceived—un-American to the core, violative of every constitutional principle and contrary to the whole spirit of American life. Congress in passing it is betraying the country."[4]

The publisher who had fought so long against monopolies and trusts now said "the Wheeler-Rayburn Bill, decreeing death to the holding companies, is

PURE VENOM distilled by a PERSONAL and MALIGNANT OBSESSION, without a pretense of economic or legal justification."[5]

The publisher who always believed that he understood the common people, and was understood by them, sparked an extensive front-page coverage of WPA activities in 1936 with headlines like this one: "Taxpayers Feed 20,000 Reds on N.Y. Relief Rolls." And his newspapers warned that the Social Security Act was "A Pay Cut for You! . . . Governor Landon, when elected, will repeal this so-called security act."[6]

Hearst newspapers threw every resource of the editorial and news pages into the campaign to elect Governor Alfred M. Landon of Kansas president in 1936. When President Roosevelt was reelected by the greatest majority in history, carrying all the states but two, Hearst's enemies cried for his scalp. But the triumphant liberals overreached themselves in launching the Supreme Court reorganization bill of 1937, which was called the "court-packing bill" by those who defeated it. The New Deal reform period came to an abrupt halt. Just as the Hearst papers weathered their economic difficulties in the next few years, they weathered public attacks against them and moved into a different political climate in which they could once more go on the offensive.

COLONEL McCORMICK AND THE *CHICAGO TRIBUNE*

Second only to Hearst in stirring up the wrath of critics was Colonel Robert R. McCormick, publisher of the *Chicago Tribune.* The quarrel with McCormick was not so much that his *Tribune* clung to an outmoded and dangerous nationalist-isolationist point of view in the face of overwhelming public support of efforts to find peace and security through international cooperation. Nor was it so much that his *Tribune* became the principal voice for the ultraconservative right wing in American politics and rejected a President Eisenhower as violently as it had rejected a President Truman. The real quarrel McCormick's critics had with him was that as he tried so hard to prove that the *Tribune* was right, and most everybody else was wrong, editorial columns became bitter personal proclamations whose prejudiced approaches to matters of public interest spilled over into the news columns. McCormick's answer, until death stilled his voice in 1955, was that his *Tribune* was the "World's Greatest Newspaper."

This claim would have had merit if newspaper greatness were measured only in terms of financial success, circulation, and mechanical excellence. In the mid-1950s the *Tribune* carried as much advertising as its three Chicago rivals combined. Its circulation, while down to 900,000 daily from a 1946 high of 1,075,000, was still the largest of any standard-sized American newspaper and was spread through five states in an area McCormick called "Chicago-land." Its 450-person news staff, operating from the thirty-six-story Tribune Tower, provided blanket coverage of local and area events that was the despair of rival city editors. For a venture that rated as the most-often criticized single American newspaper, the *Tribune* was doing all right, and Colonel McCormick frequently reminded his critics of that fact.

Not all of this success was due to McCormick. The *Tribune* has a long history, beginning in 1847. The builder was Joseph Medill, who from 1855 to 1899 devoted his energies to creating a powerful conservative newspaper. Medill left a financial trust that provided for the families of his two daughters—the McCormicks and the Pattersons. The Robert R. McCormick era began in 1914, the year his brother Medill retired from the paper to become a Senator. Sharing responsibility for the *Tribune* with the future colonel was his cousin, Joseph Medill Patterson, who founded the *New York Daily News* in 1919. The fourth Medill grandchild, Eleanor Medill Patterson, was to become owner of the *Washington Times-Herald.* The young cousins doubled *Tribune* circulation and advertising during the World War I period. Patterson had a particular brilliance for spotting the best comic strips and other features; McCormick proved to be an able business person.

The success of the *New York Daily News,* and the disappearance of Captain Patterson into that venture, further entrenched McCormick's position. The two papers made as much as $13 million a year. The *Tribune-Daily News* feature syndicate, radio station WGN, and Canadian paper and power investments followed. When Captain Paterson died in 1946, McCormick became the head of the *New York Daily News,* although he preferred to exercise influence by remote control. When Eleanor Patterson died in 1948, she willed the *Washington Times-Herald* to seven of her executives, but they sold it to McCormick in 1949 for $4.5 million. The *Tribune* formula did not work in Washington, and in 1954, ill and weary of a paper that was losing $500,000 a year, McCormick sold the *Times-Herald* for $8.5 million to Eugene Meyer's *Washington Post.* But despite this retreat, no one except the Hearst heirs had more readers than McCormick had, with his two big dailies.

The memos signed "R.R.Mc." were law in the *Tribune* empire. The 6-foot 4-inch colonel turned eyes of ice-water blue on all aspects of the business. His private domains were the Tribune Tower and his 1000-acre farm and estate outside Chicago, named Cantigny for the World War I battle in which McCormick participated. McCormick made a deep study of military history, but his opinions about international affairs were based on a belief that foreigners, especially the English, were dangerous. Almost as dangerous, the *Tribune* said, were New York financiers, Eastern internationalists, and educators.

Among those who helped to build the *Tribune* as McCormick's aides were Edward Scott Beck, managing editor from 1910 to 1937; J. Loy Maloney, managing editor from 1939 to 1951, when he became executive editor; W. D. Maxwell, city editor who became managing editor in 1951; and sports editor Arch Ward. Heading the Washington bureau were Arthur Sears Henning and his successor, Walter Trohan, who learned to shape their coverage to back up the Colonel's opinions.

McCormick opposed President Franklin Roosevelt and the domestic policies of the New Deal with every resource. As a result in a 1936 poll of Washington correspondents the *Tribune* was voted as runner-up to the Hearst papers for the title "least fair and reliable." When the World War II crisis began to develop, the *Tribune* bitterly denounced cooperation with Great Britain, the ancient enemy; a typical eight-column banner when the lend-lease bill was under debate read: "HOUSE PASSES DICTATOR BILL." It was this combination of extreme conservatism and nationalism that incited Marshall Field to start the *Chicago Sun* as a rival morning paper (the *Tribune* having inherited the field alone when Hearst retired from it in 1939).

But McCormick's luck held. Three days after the *Sun* appeared, its princi-

Milton J. Pike — Chicago Tribune

Roy W. Howard (left) and Robert R. McCormick, newspaper publishers.

pal issue of isolationism versus interventionism was exploded by the bombs at Pearl Harbor. McCormick supported the American war effort, although the *Tribune* called American entrance an "FDR war plot." The Washington correspondents again estimated the *Tribune's* standing in 1944, voting it "the newspaper . . . most flagrant in angling or weighting the news."[7]

ROY W. HOWARD AND THE SCRIPPS IMAGE

Receiving special attention, too, was Roy W. Howard, the man who by the 1930s had come to dominate the newspapers founded by E. W. Scripps. Howard was held responsible by his critics for a rightward shift in the outlook of the twenty surviving Scripps-Howard dailies, which ranked third behind Hearst and McCormick-Patterson papers in circulation. The complaints were not of the same character as those made against Hearst and McCormick; rather they reflected the disappointment and dismay of the liberals that the "people's papers" of Edward Wyllis Scripps had in many respects become conventionally conservative in tone.*

Robert Paine Scripps, the founder's youngest son, inherited the controlling interest in the newspapers, the United Press, Acme Newsphotos, Newspaper Enterprise Association, and United Feature Syndicate when his father died in 1926. Robert Scripps had been at the editorial helm as family representative since 1918, while Roy Howard, the architect of the United Press, had taken over business management of the newspaper chain in 1922, the year the Scripps-McRae newspapers were renamed Scripps-Howard.

The son was imbued with the philosophy of the father, although his quiet

*See Chapter 18 and pages 403–404 in Chapter 20 for the earlier Scripps story.

and sensitive nature kept him from exercising a firm control over policy. When editor Carl Magee of Albuquerque, New Mexico, was persecuted and driven from business in 1922 because of his efforts to expose the political machine headed by Secretary of the Interior Albert B. Fall (later convicted of bribe taking in the Teapot Dome scandal), Robert Scripps bought the paper, the *Tribune,* and restored Magee to its editorship. In 1924 the Scripps-Howard papers supported Robert M. La Follette, Progressive party candidate for the presidency. The Scripps-Howard editors, called into session periodically to decide matters of national policy, backed Herbert Hoover for the presidency in 1928 but swung back to Franklin D. Roosevelt in 1932 and 1936.

Howard's ascendancy in Scripps-Howard affairs became apparent in 1937, when the chain's papers broke with Roosevelt over the Supreme Court reorganization bill. Lowell Mellett, editor of the *Washington News,* and other old Scripps men left the organization. Robert Paine Scripps, who had been in virtual retirement, died aboard his yacht in 1938. The Scripps wills provided for Howard, William W. Hawkins of the United Press, and George B. Parker, editor-in-chief of the newspapers, to serve as trustees until the sons of Robert Scripps reached the age of 25. Under this regime the Scripps-Howard papers opposed a third term for President Roosevelt in 1940 and supported Republican presidential candidates every 4 years through 1960. Organized labor no longer found the papers to be stalwart champions. They still reflected variety in outlook and reader appeal, however, and won particular recognition in Memphis and Cleveland. After World War II, Scripps heirs inherited the trustee positions, and Charles E. Scripps became chairman. The eventual leadership in editorial matters fell to Edward W. Scripps, II, a Nevadan with traits similar to those of his grandfather.

Howard remained powerful, however, as head of the *New York World-Telegram and Sun* until he died in 1964—just 3 years before his favorite paper succumbed. His son Jack was high in the councils as president and general editorial manager of the Scripps-Howard Newspapers and president of the parent E. W. Scripps Company, in control of far-flung interests in broadcasting, syndicates, and United Press International. In the Far West, the family of James Scripps, eldest son of the founder, who quarreled with his father in 1920, was successfully rebuilding the once nearly defunct Scripps League by developing small daily newspapers in Utah, Idaho, Montana, and Oregon. Another Scripps grandson, John P. Scripps, had built a chain of small California dailies. The name Scripps seemed certain to remain an important one.

LANDMARK LEGAL DECISIONS: THE FIRST AMENDMENT

Significant episodes involving freedom of the press and the right of the people to know became a part of the record beginning in the 1930s. There were landmark cases in which newspapers appealed to the courts to uphold the historic right, under the First Amendment, to freedom of expression without prior restraint and without punitive action by government or courts.

An obscure Minnesota publisher provided a case in which the Supreme Court, in 1931, stated in *Near* v. *Minnesota* a bedrock doctrine defending the

First Amendment rights of the press that was still basic court philosophy a half-century later. It also followed up its doctrine stated in *Gitlow* in 1925, this time holding for the plaintiff as it applied the freedom of the press guarantees of the First Amendment against the states through the due-process clause of the Fourteenth Amendment.

What was known as the Minnesota "gag law" of 1925, permitting the suppression of malicious and scandalous publications, had been applied by a court to the *Saturday Press* of Minneapolis in order to stop its smear attacks on public officials. Calling the law a threat to all newspapers, no matter how unworthy the *Saturday Press* might be, chairman Robert R. McCormick of the ANPA committee on freedom of the press retained counsel to carry the case to the Supreme Court. There Chief Justice Hughes, speaking for the majority in a 5–4 decision, held the Minnesota law unconstitutional because it permitted prior restraint on publication.[8] Suppression, the court said, was a greater danger than an irresponsible attack on public officials, who in any event had proper recourse through libel action.

Huey Long, the Louisiana political boss, provided the next major case in 1934. The Long machine obtained passage by the state legislature of a special 2 percent tax on the gross advertising income of Louisiana papers with a circulation of 20,000 or more. Twelve of the thirteen papers affected were opposed to the Long regime. They appealed to the courts, again with the assistance of Colonel McCormick's ANPA committee, and in 1936 the Supreme Court found the punitive tax unconstitutional. Justice Sutherland wrote a unanimous decision, holding that Long's bill was "a deliberate and calculated device . . . to limit the circulation of information to which the public is entitled by virtue of the constitutional guarantees."[9]

Although the press may not be singled out for discriminatory taxation, it is subject to taxes and other government regulation of general applicability. In *Associated Press* v. *NLRB*[10] the Supreme Court said "the publisher of a newspaper has no special immunity from the application of general laws," thus defining the limits of First Amendment protection the press can expect from government regulation of business.

Newspapers do have latitude in commenting on judges' activities, but they often have had to appeal to higher courts for relief after being held in contempt by lower courts. A landmark case in this area was decided by the Supreme Court in 1941. This was *Bridges* v. *California,*[11] a companion case to another involving the *Los Angeles Times.* Harry Bridges, the longshoreman labor leader, had been cited for contempt because newspapers had published the text of a telegram he had sent the Labor Department threatening to call a strike if a court decision went against him. The *Times* was cited for publishing editorials deemed threatening by a court. The California Bar Association asked the Supreme Court to declare the two contempt citations unconstitutional. The court did this by applying the sanctions of the First Amendment against the state court under the due-process clause of the Fourteenth Amendment and by utilizing the clear-and-present danger test first applied in the Schenck case. In theory newspapers could henceforth comment on a court action not yet closed, without fear of punishment, unless a judge could hold that press comment created so great and immediate a danger that the court could not continue to function. But state courts continued to resist this trend in thinking, and hard battles were fought by the *Miami Herald* and the *Corpus Christi Caller-Times* in 1946 and 1947 to avoid the penalties of contempt charges.[12]

THE RISE OF INTERPRETATIVE REPORTING

The rise of interpretative reporting was the most important development of the 1930s and 1940s. Proper backgrounding of news events and covering of major areas of human activity by specialists were not unknown before that time. But the impact of the political-social-economic revolution of the New Deal years, the rise of modern scientific technology, the increasing interdependence of economic groups at home, and the shrinking of the world into one vast arena for power politics forced a new approach to the handling of news. "Why" became important, along with the traditional "who did what." Coverage of politics, economics and business, foreign affairs, science, labor, agriculture, and social work was improved by reporter-specialists. Editorial pages also became more interpretative. The news magazines and some specialized newspapers and magazines joined in the movement, together with radio commentators. Old-style objectivity, which consisted in sticking to a factual account of what had been said or done, was challenged by a new concept that was based on the belief that the reader needed to have a given event placed in its proper context if truth was really to be served. Old beliefs that difficult subjects like science and economics could not be made interesting to readers were likewise discarded out of sheer necessity. The Washington and foreign correspondents responded with increasing success to the demands thus made on them by the pressure of the news.

Among the specialized newspapers was the *Christian Science Monitor,* established in 1908 by Mary Baker Eddy, founder of the Church of Christ, Scientist. By 1918 the newspaper had 120,000 readers, an excellent foreign staff, and good coverage of cultural news. It was edited by British-trained Frederick Dixon. But an internal battle for control of the paper brought circulation down to 17,500 in 1921. Then Willis J. Abbot became editor during the 1920s and by 1935 the *Monitor* had restored its circulation and its staffing of foreign capitals and leading United States cities. The *Wall Street Journal,* destined to become the country's largest circulation daily by the 1980s, was still being edited as a financial daily like its New York City rival, the *Journal of Commerce,* and had a circulation of 30,000 in the 1930s.

The extreme in interpretation was reached by the New York tabloid, *PM,* founded in 1940 and financed by Marshall Field. Under the editorship of Ralph Ingersoll, *PM* made it a policy to express its liberal point of view in its news columns, to the point at which it became a daily journal of opinion. The paper had a notable staff and contributed a fighting spirit to New York journalism. But its hopes that it could exist on the basis of its intelligent writing, excellent pictures, and interpretative appeal—without solicitation of advertising—had faded by 1946. Even when it accepted advertising, *PM* languished financially. Field sold out in 1948; the paper became the *New York Star* and fought for life under the editorship of Joseph Barnes. It backed President Harry Truman for reelection before suspending publication in 1949.

LABOR NEWS SPECIALISTS

Specialists were required, however, both in Washington and in newspaper offices across the country. The rise of "big labor" to challenge "big business" under the collective-bargaining guarantees of the New Deal brought the labor beat into full prominence. Louis Stark of the *New York Times*, the paper's labor reporter and, with John Leary of the *New York World*, one of the first reporters in the field, transferred his base of operations to Washington in 1933. There Stark became the acknowledged dean of American labor reporters, as writers covered national labor-management bargaining in the steel and coal industries, the activities of the National Labor Relations Board, and legislative contests that culminated in the replacement of the Wagner Act by the Taft-Hartley Law. Coverage of strikes had always been a part of the nation's news report, but fuller interpretation of the problems of labor-management relations now became good reporters' goals. They also sought to increase direct coverage of organized labor's activities and attitudes. Both Washington and local reporting were improved by numerous labor specialists. Stark thought there should be more full-time labor reporters, but he noted with satisfaction that the list had grown considerably over the years to include such reporters as Edwin A. Lahey of the *Chicago Daily News*, Fred Carr of the *Christian Science Monitor*, John Turcott of the *New York Daily News*, John F. Burns of the *Providence Journal*, A. H. Raskin of the *New York Times*, and a score or more of equally competent associates.

SCIENCE AND AGRICULTURE

The worlds of science and medicine were better covered, too, by reporters who repaired the damage done by the sensationalized science stories of the days of yellow journalism. Science Service, directed by Watson Davis, did much to improve the science coverage of its subscribers after 1921. The *New York Times* was again early in the field. Waldemar Kaempffert, an engineer who joined the paper as a science specialist in 1927, was in turn joined by William L. Laurence in 1930. Pulitzer Prizes were given in 1937 to a group of pioneer science writers, including Laurence, David Dietz of the Scripps-Howard newspapers, Howard W. Blakeslee of the Associated Press, John J. O'Neill of the *New York Herald Tribune*, and Gobind Behari Lal of Hearst's Universal Service. The National Association of Science Writers, formed in 1934, had nearly 1000 members four decades later. Top writers included Arthur J. Snider of the *Chicago Daily News*, Victor Cohn of the *Washington Post*, David Perlman of the *San Francisco Chronicle*, Josephine Robertson of the *Cleveland Plain Dealer*, Harry Nelson of the *Los Angeles Times*, Walter Sullivan of the *New York Times*, Christine Russell of the *Washington Star*, John Durham of the *Houston Chronicle*, Earl Ubell of NBC, Delos Smith of UPI, and Alton Blakeslee, Frank J. Carey, and John Barbour of the AP. One of their major concerns was space science.

Federal action to stabilize agricultural prices, provide economic security for farmers, and conserve soil resources became major news with the advent of the Agricultural Adjustment Administration. But the agricultural story had been an important one even before the concerted actions of the New Deal. Alfred D.

Stedman of the *St. Paul Pioneer Press* and *Dispatch* and Theodore C. Alford of the *Kansas City Star* arrived in Washington in 1929 as the first specialists in agricultural news correspondence. The press associations then left even major stories uncovered or undeveloped. Early in the 1930s, however, the Associated Press selected an agricultural expert, Roy F. Hendrickson. Farm editors like the veteran J. S. Russell of the *Des Moines Register* and *Tribune* and Stedman, returned to St. Paul from a long Washington career, kept their own regional coverage at a high pitch.

SPECIAL NEWS SERVICES

Several special news and feature services were established for American newspapers after 1900. The first was the Newspaper Enterprise Association, founded in 1902 by Robert F. Paine, E. W. Scripps' talented editor-in-chief. Although by the 1950s the NEA offered all types of features to newspaper clients, it also had foreign and Washington correspondence, highlighted by the work of prize-winning Peter Edson and Fred Sparks, who transferred from the *Chicago Daily News*. A second Scripps contribution was Science Service, begun in 1921 and directed by Watson Davis as an authoritative science news agency. The Scripps-Howard Newspaper Alliance, developed for the chain's own papers, had its share of Pulitzer Prize winners: science editor David Dietz, Washington correspondents Thomas L. Stokes and Vance Trimble, columnist Ernie Pyle, and foreign correspondent Jim G. Lucas.

A major reorganization of the news syndicates took place in 1930 when the North American Newspaper Alliance was founded by a group of metropolitan newspapers under the managership of John N. Wheeler, head of the Bell Syndicate. NANA and Bell absorbed the Associated Newspaper, Consolidated Press, and McClure services and established NANA as the leading specialized news agency. Among its correspondents was military reporter and analyst Ira Wolfert, 1943 Pulitzer Prize winner.[13]

THE POLITICAL COLUMNISTS

The political column began in the early 1920s with the writings of David Lawrence in his syndicated column and Washington publications, of Mark Sullivan in the *New York Herald Tribune*, and of Frank R. Kent in the *Baltimore Sun*. Walter Lippmann joined this trio as a *Herald Tribune* columnist when his editorship of the *World* ended in 1931. Their columns were concerned with current politics and issues of the day, as contrasted with Arthur Brisbane's philosophical commentary, which began in 1917 and was front-paged by Hearst newspapers for nearly 20 years. But the coming of the New Deal in 1933 and a consequent revolution in Washington coverage brought a new version of the political column to join the syndicated offerings of Lawrence, Sullivan, Kent, and Lippmann.

The four early leaders in political and current-affairs columns were identified as "pundits" who wrote in a sober style and with a serious-minded approach. Sullivan and Kent were masters of the practical political scene of the

1920s, but they were not responsive to the social and economic shifts that brought the widespread increase in governmental activity in the New Deal era. Sullivan, who had been an enthusiastic interpreter of Theodore Roosevelt's progressive program and an intimate of President Herbert Hoover, became far better known for his superb journalistic history of the 1900 to 1925 period, *Our Times,* than for his later columns. Lawrence continued to hold a place as a commentator on national affairs, as did Lippmann in the international field.

A new kind of political column after 1932 was the personalized or "gossip-type" column. The idea stemmed from the successful book, *Washington Merry-Go-Round,* published anonymously in 1931. The authors were soon identified as Drew Pearson of the *Baltimore Sun* and Robert S. Allen of the *Christian Science Monitor.* These two Washington correspondents quickly left their newspapers to coauthor a behind-the-scenes column that Pearson eventually continued alone. Paul Mallon was in the personalized-column competition from the start of the New Deal era; joining in as sympathetic commentators on the New Deal's activities were Ernest K. Lindley, Samuel Grafton, and Joseph and Stewart Alsop, first writing as a team, then separately.

United Features offered a particularly strong and varied group of columnists and commentators in the 1930s. Before his death in a 1944 wartime plane crash, Raymond Clapper was recognized as perhaps the best-balanced interpreter of the Washington scene. Clapper's opinions on national and international problems were widely respected, largely because they were based on his reporting ability and on his long experience as a United Press political writer, as head of the UP Washington bureau, and that of the *Washington Post.* Thomas L. Stokes, a hard-working reporter of the Washington scene for United Press and the Scripps-Howard newspapers, developed a large following for his vigorous and crusading columns. Stokes won a Pulitzer Prize for national reporting and a Clapper memorial award for his column before he died in 1958. Carrying on for United Features were Marquis Childs, distinguished Washington correspondent for the *St. Louis Post-Dispatch* who began his column after Clapper's death, and William S. White, from the *New York Times* Washington staff. Childs won a Pulitzer Prize for his column in 1970, the first given for commentary.

Also in the United Features group of columnists were some commentators of the personal variety. One was Westbrook Pegler, the caustic ex-sports writer and United Press and *Chicago Tribune* writer. Pegler had a distinctive, colorful style and won a 1941 Pulitzer Prize for his exposure-type crusading. Unhappily his work degenerated into monotonous and vicious attacks on three small groups—labor unions, New Dealers, and members of the Franklin D. Roosevelt family—and Pegler switched from Scripps-Howard to Hearst sponsorship in the mid-1940s, becoming known as "the stuck whistle of journalism." Balancing Pegler was the witty, warm personality of Heywood Broun. Best described as "looking like an unmade bed," Broun was a deceptive writer who could switch from light and easy commentary to a hard-hitting defense of liberal traditions whenever his temper was aroused. His "It Seems to Me" ran first in the *New York Tribune,* then in the *World* during the 1920s, and finally in the Scripps-Howard papers. Broun's leading role in the American Newspaper Guild and his liberal line brought a break with Roy Howard and the column was headed for the *New York Post* when Broun died in 1939. Also writing columns for United Features were Mrs. Eleanor Roosevelt, first signed in 1935 in an unprecedented move for

Wide World Photos

Dorothy Thompson and Marquis Childs, distinguished political columnists.

Wide World Photos

Walter Lippmann, dean of the pundits, and Drew Pearson, gossip columnist.

a president's wife, and the lovable Ernie Pyle, whose original cross-country tour columns about little people and things were followed by superb personal glimpses of American fighting men in World World II until he was killed on a Pacific island in 1945.

Well to the right of the United Features columnists in political and social outlooks were the King Features group. Best known were Pegler and the conservative George Sokolsky, both of whom died in the 1960s. Later in the field for King were radio commentator Fulton Lewis, Jr., moral philosopher Bruce Barton, and reporter Jim Bishop.

Women journalists won high honors in column writing. One was Dorothy Thompson, a European correspondent for the *Philadelphia Public Ledger* and the *New Your Post* during the 1920s and early 1930s. Married to Sinclair Lewis,

Thompson returned to the United States and wrote a column on international affairs for the *New York Herald Tribune* until she was dropped for endorsing Franklin Roosevelt for a third term in order to meet the threat of Hilter's regime. Her emotion-charged comments were widely syndicated until her career closed in 1961. Doris Fleeson, who came to the columnist field from the *New York Daily News* to write a smooth political commentary until 1970, in 1954 became the first woman to win the Raymond Clapper award for reporting.

THE EDITORIAL CARTOONISTS

Syndication also affected the profession of editorial cartooning. As in the field of columning, widespread readership offered fame and financial rewards to the talented. But easy access to their proved reader-drawing copy made it less likely that a newspaper would "bring up" its own cartoonist or columnist. Local columnists always had their field, of course, but serious commentary on national and international affairs by a local staff member became scarcer.

The period after the Civil War saw the development of the political cartoon as an editorial device. Until then, the cartoon was more likely to be seen in magazines because of newspaper production difficulties, but the introduction of stereotyping enabled dailies to use illustrations more readily. Thomas Nast, the cartoonist who so savagely attacked the Tweed political ring, drew for the *New York Times* after 1870, as well as for *Harper's Weekly.* In the magazines of the times, Joseph Keppler's work for *Puck* was outstanding. The presidential-campaign cartoons of Homer Davenport, drawn for Hearst's *New York Journal* in 1896, scored a new high point, both in prominence and in bluntness.

The first quarter of the twentieth century was a golden age for cartoonists. The issues were simple enough for easy pictorial interpretation, and they were elemental enough for clever satire. These are the ingredients of the political cartoon. One of the famous cartoonists was John T. McCutcheon, who began drawing for the *Chicago Tribune* in 1903 after serving on the *Chicago Record,* and who won a Pulitzer Prize before he retired in 1946. Clifford K. Berryman, who first appeared in the *Washington Post* as far back as 1889, was closely identified with the *Washington Star* after 1906. He and his son, James T. Berryman, were the only father and son combination to win Pulitzer Prizes for their work, after the younger Berryman succeeded his father in 1949.

Lesser known to the public, but influential among his colleagues, was Arthur Henry Young, who always signed his cartoons "Art Young." He suffered because of his devotion to left-wing causes, especially during the World War I period, but in his day, Young was the cartoonist's cartoonist. He was the first to produce a daily panel, for the Chicago *Inter Ocean,* but the best of his work appeared in *The Masses,* the militantly socialist magazine. Young, unlike earlier cartoonists, strove for simplicity. His technique was to focus attention on a main issue; for example, one of his cartoons showed a ragged child of the slums looking up at the night sky and saying: "Ooh, look at all the stars; they're thick as bedbugs."

Two other great masters of the cartooning art were Rollin Kirby of the *New York World* and Edmund Duffy of the *Baltimore Sun,* both three-time Pulitzer Prize winners. Kirby was a fiercely liberal spirit who began cartooning in 1911 and hit his peak on the old *World* in the 1920s. His "Mr. Dry," a gaunt, black-frocked, blue-nosed caricature of the bigoted prohibitionists, became famous. Duffy exhibited his mastery of satire and caricature for the *Baltimore Sun* for 25 years.

Beginning his work for the *St. Louis Post-Dispatch* in 1913 and continuing until 1958 was Daniel R. ("Fitz") Fitzpatrick, whose devasting cartoon attacks won fame for his paper's editorial page and two Pulitzer Prices for him. Reminiscent of the old school of flowery technique was Jay N. ("Ding") Darling, who began drawing for the *Des Moines Register* in 1906. Darling then joined the *New York Herald Tribune,* and won two Pulitzer Prizes. In this era, too, was Nelson Harding of the *Brooklyn Eagle,* also a two-time Pulitzer award winner.

Rollin Kirby's famous "Two chickens in every garage" barb at Hoover, 1932.

New York World-Telegram

"Halloween 1936"—Jay (Ding) Darling jibed at Wallace, Farley, and FDR.

New York Herald Tribune

"You gambled but I paid"—Daniel Fitzpatrick in a 1947 crusade.

D.R. Fitzpatrick and St. Louis Post-Dispatch

"The outstretched hand"—Edmund Duffy's 1939 Pulitzer Prize cartoon.

Baltimore Sun

THE FOREIGN CORRESPONDENTS

No journalists were more crucial as reporters and news interpreters than the foreign correspondents. Only a few American newspapers have maintained significant numbers of staff correspondents abroad, to augment the reporting of the press-association staffs. In the 1930s four of the leading groups of foreign correspondents were those of the *Chicago Daily News*, the *New York Times*, the *New York Herald Tribune*, and the *Chicago Tribune*.

The *Chicago Daily News* foreign service grew out of the coverage begun in 1898 by Victor Lawson for the *Daily News* and *Record-Herald*. It won wide attention during World War I through the work of Edward Price Bell in London, Paul Scott Mowrer in Paris, and Raymond Gram Swing in Berlin. But it hit its most remarkable peak of performance in the 1930s and early 1940s under publisher Frank Knox and the foreign news director, Carroll Binder, himself a noted correspondent before he became head of the service in 1937.

Pulitzer Prizes were won by Paul Scott Mowrer in 1929 and by Edgar Ansel Mowrer in 1933. Ranking with the Mowrer brothers as among the best of American foreign correspondents of the day were John Gunther in London, William Stoneman in Moscow and London, Wallace Deuel in Rome and Berlin, Helen Kirkpatrick in Paris, and David Nichol in Berlin and Moscow. Other leading *Chicago Daily News* foreign correspondents were Leland Stowe, Robert J. Casey, William McGaffin, Paul Ghali, Ernie Hill, Nat A. Barrows, A. T. Steele, Georgie Anne Geyer, and George Weller, a Pulitzer Prize winner for distinguished reporting. Keyes Beech and Fred Sparks won Pulitzer awards for Korean War coverage. Paul Leach, Edwin A. Lahey, and Peter Lisagor were Washington bureau chiefs. The famed Foreign Service was closed in 1977, a year before the *Daily News* suspended publication.

The New York Times News Service, largest of American news syndicates, was founded in 1917. Three of its staff won Pulitzer Prizes for their European reporting during the 1930s: Walter Duranty, 1932; Anne O'Hare McCormick, 1937; Otto D. Tolischus, 1940. Duranty won honors for his coverage in the Soviet Union during the period of Stalin's rise to power. McCormick won her spurs with a 1921 story that analyzed an unknown Benito Mussolini and predicted that he would master Italy. In 1937 she was made the *Times'* columnist on international affairs and a member of its editorial board. Tolischus was in Berlin at the outbreak of war in 1939 and in Tokyo on Pearl Harbor day. Herbert L. Matthews covered the Ethiopian war for the *Times* and then Germany; active in Europe were Cyrus L. Sulzberger, chief foreign correspondent, Drew Middleton, and Flora Lewis.

The *New York Herald Tribune* foreign service was built on that of the old *Tribune*, which had Frank H. Simonds and Richard Harding Davis as World War I writers. Leland Stowe won a 1930 Pulitzer Prize as a *Herald Tribune* correspondent and Homer Bigart was similarly honored for his World War II work. Other leading *Herald Tribune* correspondents of the war period were Walter Kerr, Joseph Barnes, Major George Fielding Eliot, Russell Hill, Joseph Driscoll, and John O'Reilly. While he was Washington bureau chief, Bert Andrews won the 1948 Pulitzer Prize for national reporting. Jack Steele was a leading Washington staff member in the early 1950s before becoming Scripps-Howard's chief political writer. Bigart and Marguerite Higgins won Pulitzer Prizes as Korean War correspondents. In 1962 columnist Walter Lippmann won the paper's final Pulitzer Prize before its death in 1966.

The *Chicago Tribune* foreign service had as World War I stars Floyd Gibbons, Frazier Hunt, John T. McCutcheon, and Sigrid Schultz. Serving the *Tribune* overseas for varying periods were such well-known journalists as Vincent Sheean, William L. Shirer, George Seldes, Jay Allen, Henry Wales, and Edmond Taylor. Wilfred C. Barber won the *Tribune* news service's first Pulitzer Prize in 1936. In the following years, the leading correspondents of other foreign and Washington services outshone the *Tribune* writers until 1975, when William Mullen, a white reporter, and Ovie Carter, a black photographer, won the Pulitzer Prize for international reporting with a series on famine in Africa and India.

WALTER DURANTY AND THE MOWRER BROTHERS

Of all the foreign correspondents listed in the preceding paragraphs, special attention must be given Walter Duranty of the *New York Times* and the Mowrer brothers of the *Chicago Daily News.* Duranty was a resident correspondent in Russia between 1922 and 1934 and until 1941 he was a special traveling writer, spending an average of 5 months per year studying the land he loved. Even before he began his initial 13-year stint as the leading American reporter in Russia, Duranty had developed a strong philosophy about the rough character

Walter Duranty.

The New York Times

of Communist rule. At the outset he hated and feared the Bolsheviks, but as he told H. R. Knickerbocker of the INS in 1935, he learned to appreciate the Russian position. "I don't see that I have been any less accurate about Russia because I failed to stress casualties so hard as some of my colleagues . . . I am a reporter, not a humanitarian."[14]

It was during the 1930s that Duranty received some bitter criticism for his open assessment of Stalin's ruthlessness and Soviet goals. Heywood Broun said he wrote "editorials disguised as news dispatches" and others claimed he was far too liberal. Stalin began his purge of the Kulaks, the wealthy peasant class, in 1928, and eventually an estimated 10 million persons were killed in the countryside. But on the other hand, Duranty had accepted one of the toughest individual reporting assignments of the twentieth century. His task was to report the unknown. Stalin consented to talk with Duranty only twice, in the fall of 1930 and at Christmas, 1933. Otherwise Duranty depended on his keen knowledge of Russian history and language to overcome physical handicaps. The politically risky business of collectivization was determining many careers within Russia, like that of Leon Trotsky. Duranty sent long interpretative dispatches to the *New York Times* but rarely did these efforts receive prominent display. America was involved with domestic and European problems. During the crucial winter of 1928 to 1929, for example, none of Duranty's nearly 100 stories made page one.[15]

Nevertheless, Duranty's contribution to the field of foreign correspondence was immense. His intellect and analytical ability made him invaluable to the growing *Times'* foreign staff, which at that moment included Wythe Williams in Vienna, Paul Miller in Berlin, Arnaldo Cortesi in Rome, and Allen Raymond in London. Duranty was a confident writer, hardened by scenes of death in World War I. He accepted the brutality of Russian life and wrote from that point. Stalin moved stealthily, the censor was a barrier, the Soviet press did not report internal arguments in any way, official names were rarely mentioned, and travel was restricted. Yet Duranty was able to give detailed and colorful reports of life in that tormented land.

William Henry Chamberlin lived in Russia from 1922 to 1934, writing for the *Manchester Guardian* and then the *Christian Science Monitor* and *Atlantic.* Louis Fischer authored more than forty articles, most of them for the *Nation,* between 1925 and 1932. And world traveler Maurice Hindus wrote a dozen articles and a best-selling book, *Red Bread.* Along with Duranty these men gave a few Americans their only real look at Russia; the bulk of United States newspapers, including those with prominent foreign staffs, carried only casual mention of Russian affairs. Duranty filed the only regularly published newspaper accounts in the late 1920s, and his fair-minded and sometimes sympathetic portrayal of Bolshevik behavior helped restore the faith of some in the *Times,* which during the "Red Scare" period had confused readers about Russian Communists and American Socialists. In fact, a special *New Republic* supplement of August, 1920, edited by Walter Lippmann and Charles Merz, had charged the usually reliable *Times* with irresponsible coverage. Duranty himself had said his paper's early attitude was caused by a fear of the "Red Bogey," which explains why he went to great lengths to provide balanced reports.

Paul Scott Mowrer began his long career in 1905, taking a job with the *Chicago Daily News.* Getting the Midwest out of his system proved to be a problem, as he later admitted.[16] While in Chicago he had shunned Stanley Washburn's dispatches from the Russo-Japanese front. He remembered riding in an elevator with Richard Henry Little, captured by the Japanese at Mukden. But Mowrer cared only for Minnesota, Michigan, and the bustling metropolis, which he considered the heart of journalism. In 1910 he arrived in London, joining men who worked for other papers: Frederic William Wile, Wythe Williams, and a handful of others who knew Europe before war changed the politics and the boundaries. Writers like Will Irwin occasionally sailed to Europe to write for United States magazines, but the years were dull. Earlier, writers had flocked to the Boer War and Boxer Rebellion. The bitter subjugation of the Philippine rebels under Aguinaldo in the 1899 to 1901 period had attracted a host of reporters. That first United States experiment with colonial power at one point involved 70,000 American troops. The Russo-Japanese War of 1904 to 1905, in which Richard Harding Davis, Jack London, Frederick Palmer, and another 100 American and British reporters had fought Japanese censorship, gained considerable attention in the United States press. But things were quiet in Europe, as Paul Scott Mowrer discovered when he showed up as a 22-year-old assistant to Edward Price Bell. At the outbreak of war nearly 4 years later he covered the assassination of French Socialist Jean Jaures and broke in his younger brother, Edgar Ansel Mowrer, who thus began his equally distinguished career. Edgar, who had been contributing to United States and British magazines and studying at the Sorbonne, sneaked through enemy lines for an exclusive story. Then Edgar was allowed to accompany mining engineer Herbert Hoover to Holland, and finally in 1915 he was given the job as Rome correspondent. Paul Scott Mowrer headed for the front and ended up reporting the horrors of Verdun.

Following the war, Paul Scott Mowrer was assigned to direct the *Daily News'* bureau at the Versailles conference. Based in Paris, he filed dispatches during the Moroccan campaign of 1924 to 1925 and in 1934 to 1935 became associate editor and chief editorial writer for his paper. The editorship itself was his between 1935 and 1944, until the last year of World War II, when he accepted a position as European editor for the *New York Post.* Edgar Ansel Mowrer was bureau chief of the *Daily News* in Berlin and Paris during the "between-wars" period. Connected with the Office of War Information after having been forced out of Germany at the start of World War II, he was later a columnist and broadcaster and with his brother contributed several books on foreign affairs.

The Mowrer brothers teamed with many famous byliners—like Dorothy Thompson of the *New York Post,* who covered Vienna, Berlin, Moscow, Budapest, and London, and who was expelled from Germany by Hitler in 1934; Webb Miller of the United Press, who reported the rise of Gandhi in India and the Ethiopian war in between European assignments; Louis P. Lochner of the Associated Press, who recorded daily the rise of Hitler from Berlin; Vincent Sheean, talented author and correspondent for the *Chicago Tribune;* Frederick T. Birchall of the *New York Times;* Reginald Wright Kauffman and Harold Scarborough of the *New York Herald Tribune;* Henry Wales of the *Chicago Tribune,* and the others mentioned earlier—to cover the League of Nations, rise of fascism, and coming of another war. They added color and depth to stories at a time when even familiar European situations were in heavy competition with American domestic conerns for space in newspapers.

RADIO NEWS COMES OF AGE

As the 1930s opened, the only daily news broadcast to reach the growing national audience was one sponsored by the sedate *Literary Digest* and read by the flamboyant Floyd Gibbons, the *Chicago Tribune*'s dashing war correspondent who lost an eye in battle and who wore a white patch as his badge. Positioned in the time period preceding NBC's *Amos 'n' Andy* show, Gibbons delivered the news with breakneck speed. He had originally been signed by NBC to do a weekly half-hour show called *The Headline Hunter,* when he would spin yarns about his foreign adventures. He is also credited with the first remote broadcast, which he accomplished because he was carrying a shortwave transmitter when the German dirigible Graf Zeppelin landed at Lakehurst, New Jersey, in 1929. Two men with him hoisted an antenna that transmitted Gibbons' voice to NBC's facilities for coast-to-coast listening.

Gibbons presented the news in a folksy, rough manner—from the school of Chicago journalism—booming out his "Hello Everybody" and launching into a series of vivid descriptions. In late 1930, when he was earning $10,000 per week, an enormous salary for those Depression era days, he alienated his sponsors with his brusque manner. At that moment William S. Paley decided that CBS should try to convince *Literary Digest* publisher R. J. Cuddihy to switch sponsorship to his network, using another announcer. He had in mind Lowell Thomas, a veteran newsperson whose main claim to fame was his exclusive story of the Arabian campaign in World War I, found in his best-selling book, *With Lawrence in Arabia.*

A test broadcast was arranged; during it, Thomas read the news on CBS ahead of Gibbons' NBC show. Cuddihy listened to both broadcasts. He decided to let Gibbons go and hired Thomas, who made his first broadcast September 29, 1930. The program became the longest running in broadcast history, lasting until May 14, 1976. The first show included Thomas' comments about Adolf Hitler: "There are now two Mussolinis in the world . . . Adolf Hilter has written a book (*Mein Kampf*) in which this belligerent gentleman states that a cardinal policy of his powerful German party is the conquest of Russia. That's a tall assignment, Adolf. You just go ask Napoleon."[17] For 6 months both networks carried the nightly show, NBC in the East and CBS in the West. But Cuddihy finally decided to let NBC have exclusive access to Thomas, who inherited that spot before the *Amos 'n' Andy* show. "Good Evening, Everybody" became a popular phrase in America.

Radio was building audiences in many ways, and coverage of the major news events and personalities of the 1930s helped. Hilter and Mussolini used radio to rally their peoples in the name of patriotism. President Roosevelt was one of the world leaders who realized the potential of radio for achieving national unity; during the depths of the Great Depression and World War II he made twenty-eight "Fireside chats." People were taken with the President's friendly manner and it was said that "Washington was no farther away than the radio receiving sets in their living rooms."[18] The presidential nominating conventions and campaigns provided news bulletins, as did such events as the kidnapping of the Lindbergh baby, the Bonus March in Washington, King Edward VIII's abdication talk, the burning of the German airship *Hindenburg,*

Lowell Thomas
Bettmann Archive

and the outbreak of hostilities in Manchuria, in China, in Ethiopia, and eventually throughout Europe.

ADVERTISING: NEWSPAPERS VERSUS RADIO

In 1929 newspaper fear of radio seemed unjustified. It was true that radio had advanced spectacularly in advertising revenue, from $4 million in 1927 to $40 million in 1929. But that same year newspapers carried a record $800 million worth of advertising, according to the U.S. Census of Manufactures.

Then came the Depression, whose opening phase was recorded with the simplicity that has made *Variety* famous for its headlines: WALL ST. LAYS AN EGG. The financial collapse of October, 1929, brought industrial slowdown, decreasing retail sales, growing unemployment, and, by 1933, a virtual paralysis of business and banking and 15 million unemployed. By 1933 newspaper advertising revenue fell 45 percent from the 1929 peak, and that for magazines was cut in half. But radio advertising revenue doubled in those Depression years. It seemed logical for newspaper publishers to eye radio as a source of trouble.

Actually, however, radio was not taking much advertising away from news-

Table 21-1 Advertising in the Mass Media as a Percentage of Total Advertising Expenditures

YEAR	NEWSPAPERS	MAGAZINES	RADIO	TELEVISION	ALL OTHER
1935	45.2	8.3	6.5		40.0
1940	39.2	9.6	10.5		40.7
1945	32.0	12.5	14.6		40.9
1950	36.5	9.0	10.7	3.0	40.8
1955	34.0	8.0	6.1	11.2	40.7
1960	31.0	7.9	5.8	13.3	42.0
1965	29.4	7.9	5.9	16.5	41.3
1970	29.7	6.7	6.5	18.6	38.5
1975	29.9	5.2	7.0	18.6	39.3
1980	28.5	5.9	5.7	20.7	38.6

Source: McCann-Erickson, Inc., estimates. Current estimates appear in *Advertising Age's* final issue of the year. Originally, they appeared in the now defunct *Printers' Ink*.

papers in those early Depression years. Newspapers' loudest complaints were that national advertising was being lost to radio. But out of the total amount spent by national advertisers each year in just the three major media—newspapers, magazines, radio—how much did each of the media receive? According to ANPA Bureau of Advertising estimates, newspapers got 54 percent in 1929, and still received 50 percent in 1935. Magazines lost some ground, from 42 percent in 1929 to 35.5 percent in 1935. Radio increased from 4 percent to 14.5 percent. By 1939, however, the figures for this three-way split of national advertising showed a different picture: newspapers, 38 percent; magazines, 35 percent; radio, 27 percent. The publishers' fears had been justified.

Another set of figures—estimates of total expenditures for all forms of advertising by both national and local advertisers—is available for the years after 1935. These estimates, made by McCann-Erickson, Inc., an advertising agency, include all types of advertising-connected expenses in addition to the direct revenues of the media. Besides the major media, they include direct mail, business papers, farm papers, outdoor, and a large miscellaneous category. Table 21-1 shows the varying fortunes of newspapers, magazines, radio, and beginning in 1950, television.

Again, what hurt most in the 1930s was that among the mass media only radio was taking in more dollars; newspapers and magazines suffered heavy cuts in actual cash revenue because of declining dollar advertising volume. Some could stand the cuts; some could not. As the Depression deepened, newspaper publishers took out after the well-heeled culprit, radio, with new vengeance.

THE NEWSPAPER-RADIO WAR

The furnishing of 1932 presidential-election returns to the radio networks by the Associated Press, to forestall sale of election coverage by the United Press, precipitated action by the ANPA board of directors in December, 1932. The board recommended that press associations should neither sell nor give away news in advance of its publication in the newspapers. Broadcasting of news should be confined to brief bulletins that would encourage newspaper readership. And radio logs should be treated as paid advertising. There were many qualified observers who felt that radio was too well established as a news medium to be hobbled in this way.[19] But the ANPA recommendations led to a futile 2-year effort to eliminate radio news competition. After a spirited fight, the 1933 AP membership meeting voted not to furnish news to the radio networks and to limit the broadcasting of news by AP members of occasional thirty-five word bulletins. The UP and the INS bowed to their newspaper clients' desires and stopped their sale of news to radio stations. The answer of the radio industry was to undertake the job of gathering news.

The Columbia Broadcasting System set up the leading network news service under the direction of Ed Klauber, a former night city editor of the *New York Times* who was hired by William S. Paley in 1930. Klauber, a strict disciplinarian, quickly rose to second in command of CBS and was instrumental in the network's growth. He served Paley until 1943. Paul White, a former UP reporter, was hired as Klauber's assistant. Together they began staffing bureaus in New York, Washington, Chicago, Los Angeles, and London with other newspaperpeople. CBS built up an extensive system of correspondents and imported the British Exchange Telegraph agency's news report for daily CBS broadcasts. NBC's rival news service was organized by White's counterpart, A. A. Schechter, director of news and special events in the 1930s. Meanwhile, local stations continued to broadcast news regularly by the simple expedient of using the early editions of the newspapers.[20]

The networks found that collecting news was expensive, and the publishers disliked the new competition. So in December, 1933, a solution was proposed. This was the Press-Radio Bureau, which would present two 5-minute unsponsored news broadcasts daily on the networks from news supplied by the press associations. Bulletin coverage of extraordinary events would also be provided. In return, the networks would stop gathering news.

The Press-Radio Bureau began operating in March, 1934, and after a year had 245 subscribers. But it was doomed from the start. Not only was it unrealistic, but it left the door open for the founding of new news-gathering agencies not bound by the agreement. Five news services jumped into the field, led by Herbert Moore's Transradio Press Service, which at its peak in 1937 served 230 radio clients and even signed up several newspapers.

The collapse of the effort to curtail broadcasting came in 1935. The UP and the INS obtained releases from the Press-Radio Bureau agreement so that they could meet Transradio's competition by selling full news reports to stations. The UP began a wire report especially written for broadcasting, which the AP matched after it joined the race for radio clients in 1940. The Press-Radio Bureau suspended in 1940; Transradio slumped away and died in 1951.

MUTUAL NETWORK; *THE MARCH OF TIME*

By 1934 CBS had ninety-seven affiliated stations and the two NBC networks had 127. But there were more than 600 commercial stations and there was room for competition in the news field. That year four independent stations, headed by WOR, New York, and WGN, Chicago, organized the Mutual Broadcasting

System, which primarily served to affiliate smaller stations. WLW, Cincinnati, and WXYZ, Detroit, were the other two founding stations; CKLW, Windsor, Ontario-Detroit, replaced WXYZ in 1935. The first expansion came in 1936 when thirteen New England stations associated with the regional Colonial network and ten in California belonging to the Don Lee network agreed to be Mutual outlets. Adding twenty-three Texas stations in 1938, Mutual grew to a total of 160 outlets by 1940. Of these, twenty-five were also associated with NBC and five with CBS, showing the strong interest in Mutual shows like *Lum 'n' Abner* and *The Lone Ranger.*[21] Networks, radio found, could produce more costly and successful programs because they could draw on the support of national advertisers, and their growth made radio a more formidable competitor for the advertising dollar each year.

Also getting attention in the 1930s was *The March of Time,* which brought radio listeners dramatic reenactments of the week's news. Before its final show in 1945 *The March of Time* had been heard on CBS, both NBC networks, and ABC. The idea for such a show began with Fred Smith, who in 1925 had produced *Musical News* for WLW, Cincinnati, a show during which news items were followed by organ music. Listener response was strong and in 1928 Smith got *Time* magazine to sponsor a weekly news roundup. He joined the *Time* organization later that year, and organized a sixty-station syndication of a daily 10-minute news summary. At the time there was no national newscast. This first show, called *NewsCasting,* was carried over WOR, New York, during the dinner hour. Smith claimed that this was the first use of the word *newscast,* which brought together the concepts of news and broadcasting.[22] Smith believed that the daily news should be dramatized, however, and in 1929 he produced weekly 5-minute recordings of a show called *NewsActing.* More than 100 stations carried it, and it led to the development of *The March of Time* series. Impersonations of famous personalities, including President Roosevelt, were often the highlights of the show. Later in its history the show used actual news updates and remote broadcasts. Ironically, one of the actors in the series was Orson Welles, whose 1938 Mercury Theatre presentation of "War of the Worlds" caused widespread panic on an East coast presumably invaded by Martians. *The March of Time* also had film documentary and television versions.

COMMENTATORS DEBATE THE NATIONAL ISSUES

As Franklin Roosevelt took hold of the Federal machinery and a genuine national debate began over the merits of his New Deal programs, Americans were offered the opinions of a number of highly spirited, controversial broadcasters. The arguments increased in intensity later in the decade when the Roosevelt administration took steps to prepare for World War II. The dean of the commentators was Hans Von Kaltenborn, who quit the newspaper business and joined CBS as a full-time commentator in 1930. A foreign correspondent, managing editor, and associate editor of the *Brooklyn Eagle* in his first journalistic assignments, Kaltenborn had started broadcasting news for a local station in 1922. This dignified, civilized man with clipped, high-pitched, precisely accentuated tones made sense of the turmoil in the world, basing his comments on his own extensive travels and on his own decent instincts.

Kaltenborn's internationalistic outlook was similar to that broadcast by Dorothy Thompson, Edward R. Murrow, Raymond Gram Swing, and later Elmer Davis. Lowell Thomas could be included here, except he was loath to give partisan opinions on the air, but preferred to provide colorful descriptions for the listener. On the conservative side of the ledger were Boake Carter, Upton Close, Fulton Lewis, Jr., and the "Radio Priest," Father Charles Coughlin.

Though not a journalist, Father Coughlin had a tremendous impact on American politics through his Sunday radio show from Royal Oak, Michigan, broadcast nationwide by WJR, Detroit. When he was dropped by CBS in 1931, he set up his own chain of stations. Attacking Socialism, Communism, and capitalism as evil, Coughlin lashed out angrily at international bankers, Presidents Hoover and Roosevelt, Jewish interests, and even Prohibitionists. He bitterly criticized the breaking up of the Bonus Army encampment in Washington, when Hoover ordered General Douglas MacArthur to use force to rout those seeking pension monies. Yet as the years passed, Father Coughlin's broadcasts took on a pro-Nazi stance. An estimated 30 million listeners followed the man who was considered by progressives as a dangerous demagogue. Coughlin's organization, the National Union for Social Justice, was due to one thing: radio.

Boake Carter, a close friend of Father Coughlin, earned his reputation as a CBS reporter while covering the Lindbergh baby kidnapping story. Because he had been born in England, Carter's Americanized accent gave his broadcasts a unique touch. He was immensely popular; his 1936 to 1938 ratings showed him in a virtual tie with NBC's Lowell Thomas. He presented news and commentary each weekday between January, 1933, and August, 1938, when he was dropped by CBS—like Coughlin—for reasons not entirely clear. However, he had been extremely harsh in his attacks against President Roosevelt on radio and in his newspaper column, warning repeatedly that the United States was being dragged into coming wars in Europe and Asia. It is suspected that, like Coughlin, Carter was taken off the air because of the increasing "irrationality" of his comments.[23]

Upton Close broadcast news analyses over NBC stations between 1934 and 1944, when he was droppped following worry within NBC about some of his controversial shows. Over the years Close had become less objective and more reactionary, echoing others in their hatred of the British, Jews, and Russians and in their sympathy for right-wing politics. Fulton Lewis, Jr., who began his commentaries over the Mutual stations in 1937, closely followed partisan Republican party ideas. He became an avid supporter of Charles Lindbergh in 1939 during the debate over Britain's ability to stave off the Nazi threat; this earned the plaudits of conservative listeners.

Dorothy Thompson, Berlin bureau chief for the *Philadelphia Public Ledger* as well as a contributor to other newspapers and magazines while living in Europe between the wars, began delivering commentaries for NBC in 1937. A staunch internationalist, Thompson was widely admired for her interviews with political leaders, and for her role in the women's movement.

Raymond Gram Swing worked for several leading dailies before getting involved with broadcasting. In 1932, during the British elections, he and Cesar Saerchinger of CBS conducted the first trans-Atlantic interview. His regular broadcasts began with Mutual in 1936 and within 2 years he was ranked third to

Kaltenborn and Thomas in a poll of radio editors.[24] Like Thompson and Murrow, Swing detested Hitler, was in full sympathy with Britain, and feared for the Jewish people. Also worried about fascism at home, he wrote and lectured on the subject.

Two other leading commentators whose careers began in this era, among others, were the snappy Walter Winchell and the predictable Gabriel Heatter. Winchell, mainly involved with Hollywood gossip, underworld tips, and scandals, did enlighten Americans about the German menace and provided Roosevelt with strong support during the 1940 campaign. "Good evening, Mr. and Mrs. North America and all the ships at sea. Let's go to press." That was the Winchell opening followed by "Predictions of things to come." Despite his many erroneous predictions, Winchell built a huge audience and was number one in the 1946 ratings, with nearly 19 percent of the audience, ahead of Lowell Thomas, at 11 percent, and a host of other famous names. Before his 40-year career ended in 1969 he had been affiliated with several networks. Heatter, fiercely patriotic and emotional, gained fame by broadcasting the trial of Bruno Hauptmann for the Lindbergh baby murder directly from a New Jersey courtroom. A year later he held the Mutual audience for nearly an hour, ad-libbing while waiting for the news of Hauptmann's execution. More than 50,000 letters poured in following the broadcast and Heatter was given a five-nights-a-week spot for commentary. In his presentations he attempted, for the most part, to comfort the audience rather than take sides in the political battles. He could not be identified as easily as most of the other commentators. At his peak in the postwar years he reached 196 stations and earned $400,000 per year, warming his listeners' hearts with his "There's good news tonight."

THE NETWORKS REACH OVERSEAS

The outbreak of the Spanish Civil War, followed quickly by Hitler's threats first against Austria and then Czechoslovakia, gave radio newspeople an opportunity they fully accepted. The first of a number of memorable broadcasts made between 1936 and the official start of World War II in 1939 was made by Hans Von Kaltenborn. Wearing his dark business suit and trying to act his usual dignified self, Kaltenborn broadcast from a haystack near the French border with Spain where a battle was raging. After a number of interruptions the American audience heard Kaltenborn's voice for 15 minutes, surrounded by the sounds of gunfire and bringing a bit of understanding about the spreading of fascism. The networks did not have foreign staffs at this time, but instead relied on hastily patched-together transmission systems for occasional broadcasts. Often a newspaper reporter was called upon to provide the short description. This changed in early 1938 when Hitler invaded Austria.

Edward R. Murrow, an unknown CBS program arranger who had been named European news chief, was in London when the crisis developed. He had hired as an assistant William L. Shirer, out of a job since the closing of Hearst's Universal Service. The pattern was to do cultural programs and human-interest stories for shortwave broadcasts that were rebroadcast by United States stations. On March 12, 1938, Murrow in Vienna and Shirer in London improvised the first multiple news pickup in history. They quickly asked newspaper reporters Edgar Mowrer, Pierre Huss, and Frank Gervasi to add their impressions from Paris, Berlin, and Rome. Robert Trout was the anchor. The stage was set for radio coverage of the 20 days of crisis in September, beginning with Hitler's demand that the Czechs give him the German-speaking Sudetenland and ending with the signing of the Munich Pact.

At this time more than 91 percent of urban American homes and about 70 percent of rural homes had radios, many because of the Roosevelt administration's programs for rural electrification. In fact, between 1930 and 1938 the number of radio sets had increased more than 100 percent. More homes had radios than telephones.[25] The popular fare, in addition to the many musical programs like *Your Hit Parade,* included *One Man's Family, Gangbusters, Jack Armstrong—The All American Boy, Captain Midnight, The Green Hornet, Baby Snooks,* and *Henry Aldrich.* Jack Benny was the top comedian, Edgar Bergen and his wooden friend Charlie McCarthy had the highest rated show, Kate Smith was the most popular woman singer, and Ted Husing and Clem McCarthy broadcast the

H. V. Kaltenborn, pioneer radio commentator.

biggest sporting events. Other personalties were Bing Crosby, Eddie Cantor, Nelson Eddy, George Burns and Gracie Allen, and Don Ameche. But this lightness and fun was interrupted by the ominous messages from Europe. For those paying attention, World War II was on the horizon and it was only a matter of time when it would break out. Others, of course, did not believe America would or should get involved and were awakened only on December 7, 1941, when Pearl Harbor was bombed.

Listeners heard live broadcasts from fourteen European cities during the Munich crisis period. The voices of Hitler, President Benés of Czechoslovakia, Chamberlain, Goebbels, Litvinoff, Mussolini, and Pope Pius XI came in first-hand. In his "Studio Nine" in New York City, Kaltenborn spent the 3 weeks backstopping the CBS European correspondents who conducted the elaborate hookup system "The European News Roundup," giving hours of analysis and commentary. It was Kaltenborn who translated Hitler's fiery oratory for American listeners and who predicted the diplomatic steps that would follow given events. He was heard eighty-five times during the 3 weeks; between his stints he catnapped on a cot. CBS devoted 471 broadcasts to the crisis, nearly 48 hours of air time; of these 135 were bulletin interruptions, including ninety-eight from European staffers. NBC's two networks logged 443 programs during 59 hours of air time.[26]

NBC's Max Jordan was a worthy competitor for Murrow and Shirer. He had a 46-minute beat on the actual text of the Munich Pact, whereby Britain and France backed down in the face of Nazi bullying and allowed the Germans to regain the Sudetenland section of Czechoslovakia. The Czechs had not been allowed to participate. Broadcasts from Prague were gloomy. While Winston Churchill howled that this was an act of appeasement—it was clear that Hitler was free to take the rest of Czechoslovakia whenever he wished—many persons heaved sighs of relief. London had prepared for air raids, children had been taken to the country, and American listeners hung on every word, wondering if war could be averted. Thomas E. Dewey was making a major political address in which he was accepting the New York GOP's nomination to run for governor when Jordan's broadcast came through. It was one of the few times a major speech had been canceled.

Jordan had a backup crew of top-flight newspaper and press-association correspondents on whom to draw—for example, Walter Kerr of the *New York Herald Tribune,* Karl Von Wiegand of the International News Service, M. W. Fodor of the Chicago Daily News Service, and G. Ward Price of the *London Daily Mail,* who conducted an exclusive interview with Hitler at Cologne during which Hitler gave October 1 as his final deadline. Maurice Hindus, a noted author and international observer, assisted CBS. Mutual had John Steele in London and Louis Huot in Paris. Between September 10, when Czech President Eduard Benés broadcast his nation's desire to resist Hitler, and the final four-power agreement at Munich on the 29th, Americans responded to the tense, colorful broadcasts with a vast and deep interest. The networks had been assisted, of course, by bulletins from the U.P., Transradio, and the Press-Radio Bureau. When World War II came the networks were ready to cover the far-flung action in Asia and Europe.

TELEVISION: THE COMPETITION OF THE 1930S

The development of television in the 1930s was marked by competition between Vladimir K. Zworykin, a Russian scientist working for RCA, and Philo T. Farnsworth, a San Francisco inventor who had obtained private backing for his experiments. Their success had been preceded by numerous tests in Europe, where interest in the transmission of images could be traced to proposals for a facsimile device in the 1840s. Between 1890 and 1920 a number of British, French, American, Russian, and German scientists suggested techniques related to the perfection of the television set.

The first public demonstration of a live television picture was conducted by John L. Baird, a Scottish inventor, on January 26, 1926, in London. Onlookers, including a reporter, substantiated that images were transmitted from one room to another, faint, often blurred, but clear enough to see on a screen of only a few square inches. Two years later Baird televised a woman's image from London to Hartsdale, New York, using a shortwave band, and also sent images to an oceanliner 1000 miles out at sea. In 1932 more than 4000 persons in a London movie house saw Baird's televised pictures of the English Derby on a large screen.[27]

BAIRD, JENKINS, AND IVES: OTHER EXPERIMENTS

Baird, and an American competitor, Charles Francis Jenkins, attempted to develop a "mechanical" system for commerical use that was dependent on a number of moving parts, including scanning drums, to record the minute parts of an image successively and to transmit them in such a way as to give the illusion of motion. Although scanning is the crucial process in the production of television pictures, the "mechanical" system did not offer the clarity—definition—required for wide-scale acceptance. The pictures were dim and the screen size was limited to only a few inches. Later the "electronic" method would allow the various elements of the image to be recorded all at once before being translated into the electrical charges that end up as the picture on the screen.

Jenkins used wireless to send the image of a photograph of President Harding from Washington to Philadelphia in 1923 and transmitted motion pictures (but not live figures) over radio waves in 1925. But after 1930 his company fell into receivership and his patents ended up with RCA. Baird, who had shown the possibility of color television as early as 1923, continued with his experiments for many years, disappointed that the BBC, which used the "mechanical" system when it introduced general telecasting in 1936, switched over to the more comprehensive "electronic" system.

Another vital cog in the early experimentation was Herbert E. Ives, whose work in the Bell Telephone Laboratories on wire-photo transmission led to the sending over wires of Secretary of Commerce Herbert Hoover's image from Washington to New York in 1927. When Hoover's face appeared on a 2-foot screen, his voice was also heard; this generated ideas about the possible future use of the Picturephone. Ives was also instrumental in developing a method for relaying television images by coaxial cable and radio, and in inventing a camera that could be used outdoors. AT&T, however, did not attempt to commercialize its inventions.[28]

SARNOFF, ZWORYKIN, AND FARNSWORTH

David Sarnoff was determined to bring television to the public, however, and his vehicle was Zworykin, who had patented the first electronic television camera tube—the iconoscope—in 1923. In 1926 Zworykin invented the kinescope, a cathode ray tube that would be the core of a receiving unit. Impressed with Zworykin's assessments of television's possibilities, Sarnoff arranged for him to join the Westinghouse research unit in 1929. The following year Zworykin joined the large RCA research team in New Jersey when a court ordered Westinghouse and General Electric to separate from RCA. This remarkable group of scientists had already recorded a number of impressive achievements. In 1928 Ernest F. W. Alexanderson of GE had conducted tests over experimental station W2XAD. The first television drama was telecast, with sound carried by radio station WGY, Schenectady. This was followed by a science-fiction thriller that ended with New York's being destroyed by a guided missile.

Meanwhile Farnsworth had also been building a strong reputation. In 1927 he transmitted his first picture and by the early 1930s he was engaged in the development of a fully electronic system. San Francisco supporters helped him form Television Laboratories, Inc., which kept him in direct competition with the larger research team at RCA. Both groups were able to produce pictures far superior to anything done before. Zworykin's iconoscope had allowed brighter images and a larger screen size. Farnsworth had devised a way to obtain a picture with a 100- to 150-line definition. Earlier experiments had been with a 30- to 50-line definition. By 1931 RCA was able to transmit a 120-line picture and the quality increased steadily.

The resources of RCA proved too much for Farnsworth. In 1932 Sarnoff ordered a television studio to be built in the Empire State Building. RCA's experimental station was 2XBS. Then in 1935, 2 years after Radio City became NBC's home, one of its studios was turned into a large television production area. Sarnoff coordinated every detail. Experimental station W2XF became the center for RCA's tests in 1936; a mobile unit was sent out into New York streets in 1937 and its first live telecast in 1938 was of a fire; Sarnoff gave the first large public demonstration of electronic television at the New York World's Fair in 1939, and Franklin Roosevelt became the first president to appear on television. Sarnoff demonstrated a 441-line system and in 1941 the FCC decided that a 525-line, thirty-frames a second system—still in effect—would be the standard.[29]

RCA also became deeply involved with the development of FM radio, first supporting it and then fighting the man who had invented the system under RCA auspices, Edwin H. Armstrong. The television and FM signals competed for the same upper frequencies and when RCA officers were ready to push into television in the mid-1930s, they set aside their enthusiasm for FM. Armstrong, who had conducted a number of tests demonstrating the clarity of FM sound, removed his equipment from the Empire State Building and fought RCA in court until he died a broken man in 1953. In the course of his career he had become a millionaire and had seen FM accepted, but he had not been given full recognition and royalties by Sarnoff.[30]

Meanwhile, Farnsworth and RCA became entangled in a number of disputes over patents and finally, in 1939, RCA agreed to a complicated set of royalty payments to Farnsworth in return for the use of patents, the first time RCA had ever agreed to such a procedure instead of purchasing patents outright.

Despite the disagreements, television had arrived. Sets were available in department stores in 1938. Models with screens ranging in size from 3 to 12 inches cost from $125 to $600. By the next year more than a dozen manufacturers were involved, which caused the FCC to step in to standardize equipment.[31]

The FCC gave approval for eighteen stations to begin commercial operation beginning July 1, 1941, and the first two, ready that day, were the New York stations of NBC (WNBT) and CBS (WCBW). Within 9 months another eight stations had joined them, serving viewers of an estimated 10,000 to 20,000 sets. The stations were allowed to offer 15 hours of programming per week. WCBW distinguished itself on December 7, 1941, by offering the latest bulletins on the Pearl Harbor attack and by showing its audience of a few thousand some maps of the war zones. A government freeze in May, 1942, halted construction on new stations and most of those in existence drastically cut back on programming. Only six stations were still broadcasting at the war's end in 1945 when the freeze was lifted.

THE NEWSREEL AT THE MOVIES

At most movie houses the standard American newsreel ran for 10 minutes along with other short subjects between showings of the feature film. Five major production companies got out new versions twice weekly, mixing shots of major news events with human interest, sports, and a touch of disaster and crime. The newsreel was in its prime during the 1930s and the war years of the 1940s.

Film historians credit Charles Pathé of France with the first newsreel, the *Pathé Journal* of 1907. In 1911 he also produced the first silent newsreel in the United States, *Pathé's Weekly,* in a New Jersey studio. By 1914 the Pathé Frères company was employing thirty-seven staff camerapeople in North America and had Vitagraph and the Hearst film interests as newsreel competitors.[32]

Fox Movietone News showed the first sound news films in January, 1927, then scored a smash hit with a sound film of Charles Lindbergh's takeoff for Paris in May. The first full-length Fox newsreel, shown in October, entranced viewers with the majesty of Niagara Falls, reviewed the "Romance of the Iron Horse," and covered the Army-Yale football game and a rodeo in New York. Hearst Metrotone News (later renamed *News of the Day*) appeared in sound in 1929. The other major producers were Paramount News ("The Eyes and Ears of the World"), Universal News, and Pathé News. In 1937 Castle's *News Parade* began selling 16 mm. and 8 mm. films for home showing of such subjects as the *Hindenburg* disaster, the life of the Duke of Windsor, and the coronation of Edward VI.

A study of newsreel content from 1938 to 1949 showed that sports took 25 percent of newsreel space during peacetime. World War II took over 50 percent of the time during 1943 to 1944, and foreign shots took 30 percent in postwar years. Government was covered in 5 percent to 10 percent of the film, and disasters and crime never exceeded 4 percent. In a world without television and only recently with picture magazines, the newsreel was an eagerly awaited offering in the movie house, bringing as it did images of the great, the drama of war, and the tragedy of life. But with network television coverage of major news events, the newsreel withered as an institution. In November, 1949, New York's Embassy Newsreel Theater closed after 20 years of showing only newsreels to 11 million customers. The Trans-Lux newsreel theaters were gone by 1950. Newsreels had one last moment of glory when they could show the 1953 coronation of Queen Elizabeth II as rapidly as did television, which did not yet have trans-Atlantic satellite transmission.

The newsreel companies sought television connections, and sold their film libraries. *The March of Time* documentary, a competitor since 1935, transferred to television in 1951. Pathé News closed down in 1956, Paramount in 1957, Fox in 1963, and Hearst and Universal in 1967. The newsreel was no more.

The March of Time, although made in the documentary form, was shown with the newsreels in movie houses monthly for 16 years. An estimated 20 million moviegoers saw it in 9000 theaters in the United States and in others around the world. Produced for Time Inc. by Louis de Rochemont, a journalist and filmmaker, were nearly 300 episodes exploring social issues, many of them controversial. Westbrook Van Voorhis provided the attention-arresting "voice" with a crisis-laden, staccato tone. In reconstructed episodes, and using impersonators at times, *The March of Time* made attacks on Huey Long, Father Coughlin, Gerald L. K. Smith, Hitler, and Mussolini, and deplored the dust bowl, the plight of migratory workers, and the inequalities of wartime. Through film, radio, and television, Americans heard Van Voorhis intone, "Time Marches On!"

HENRY LUCE AND *TIME*

A big new name in magazine journalism was that of Henry R. Luce. He became both extraordinarily successful and a controversial figure. His weekly newsmagazine, *Time,* became dominant in its field, and his picture magazine, *Life,* became a runaway success in circulation and advertising.

The story of Time Inc. began in March, 1923. Luce and a fellow Yale graduate, Briton Hadden, brought out the first issue of *Time* that month. Both had been editors of the *Yale Daily News* and had worked briefly as reporters. The young men looked about them in the era of the 1920s and announced in their prospectus:

> Although daily journalism has been more highly developed in the United States than in any other country in the world—

Magazine founder Henry R. Luce.
Time Inc.—Halsman

> Although foreigners marvel at the excellence of our periodicals, *World's Work, Century, Literary Digest, Outlook,* and the rest—
> People in America are, for the most part, poorly informed.
> This is not the fault of the daily newspapers; they print all the news.
> It is not the fault of the weekly "reviews", they adequately develop and comment on the news.
> To say with the facile cynic that it is the fault of the people themselves is to beg the question.
> People are uninformed because no publication has adapted itself to the time which busy men are able to spend on simply keeping informed.

Time, its editors promised, would organize and departmentalize the news of the week. Its slogan became: "*Time* is written as if by one man for one man." Its coverage of national affairs, foreign news, science, religion, business, education, and other areas was to be written not for people who had expert knowledge of each of the fields, but for *Time's* "busy man." The editors developed the use of the narrative story in telling the news and injected strong elements of human interest. To accumulate myriads of facts that could be woven into each story, *Time* developed an extensive research and library staff as well as a good-sized news-gathering organization of its own to supplement press-association services.

Hadden died in 1929, after seeing *Time* reach a circulation of 200,000, and Luce went on alone. A "March of Time" radio program was begun in 1931 and its motion picture version in 1935. *Fortune,* Luce's lavish magazine for business-people which sold at $1 a copy, was successful even in the first Depression year of 1930. *Life,* hitting the newsstands in 1936, caught the interest of a photography-conscious people and had customers fighting for copies. *Sports Illustrated,* less of a success, was added in 1954. Time Inc. moved to Rockefeller Center in 1938, opened it own forty-eight-story Time & Life building there in 1960, and counted a record-breaking $270 million annual gross. *Time* claimed 3 million circulation for its domestic, Canadian, and three overseas editions in 1962. Luce retired as editor-in-chief in 1964 in favor of Hedley W. Donovan, and died in 1967.

There were many things about *Time* that aroused criticism. Luce and his editors made no pretense of sticking to the usual concepts of journalistic objectivity, which they considered mythical. Nor did *Time* want to be called impartial, it said; rather, "fairness" was *Time*'s goal. In an historic essay published on its twenty-fifth anniversary, *Time* said: "What's the difference between impartiality and fairness? The responsible journalist is 'partial' to that interpretation of the facts which seems to him to fit things as they are. He is fair in not twisting the facts to support his view, in not suppressing the facts that support a different view."[33]

Some critics felt, however, that sometimes *Time* was not fair to its readers since it presented opinion and editorial hypothesis intermingled with the straight news. Later *Newsweek* received the same rebukes. The critics disliked the use of narrative and human-interest techniques. Still, *Time* had widespread influence and it served many readers by summarizing day-by-day news in its weekly digests. Particularly, its specialized departments brought news of science, medicine, religion, business, education, art, radio, the press, and other areas to many who never before had followed happenings in such diverse fields of interest. Its "Essays," begun in the mid-1960s, further enhanced the magazine's appeal for serious readers and its 1976 special Bicentennial editions were outstanding contributions. In that year Time Inc. became the first billion-dollar publishing firm, slightly ahead of the Times Mirror Company of Los Angeles.

NEWSWEEK, U.S. NEWS, BUSINESS WEEK

After *Time* bought the remains of the *Literary Digest* in 1938 its only direct competitor was *Newsweek,* founded in 1933. *Newsweek*'s format was almost identical to that of *Time,* but its early editors injected less opinion into its columns. Financed by the wealth of the Astor and Harriman families and directed by Malcolm Muir after 1937, *Newsweek* grew steadily in influence. By 1961 it had 1.5 million circulation, its own New York headquarters building, two overseas editions, and a network of domestic and foreign news bureaus. That year it was sold to the *Washington Post*'s publisher, Philip L. Graham, for $9 million. Graham then took control of *Newsweek* as chairman of the board but died in 1963 before his plans for the magazine could be fully developed. Katharine Meyer Graham succeeded her husband as head of the *Post* and *Newsweek.*

Devoting itself exclusively to news of national and international importance was *U.S. News & World Report,* a combination of David Lawrence's publishing ventures. Lawrence ran the *United States Daily* in Washington from 1926 to 1933, then changed it to a weekly. In 1946 he launched *World Report,* which he combined with his older journal in 1948. By 1962 the magazine had 1.2 million readers, a large Washington bureau, and several overseas bureaus.

Specializing in news of business and industry was *Business Week,* founded in 1929 by the McGraw-Hill Publishing Company. Along with thirty other McGraw-Hill magazines, it was served by the McGraw-Hill World News Service. *Business Week's* circulation was substantial, reaching 400,000 in 1962.

PHOTOJOURNALISM: *LIFE, LOOK,* AND DOCUMENTARIES

Widespread public interest in the newsreel, in newspaper photos transmitted by wire, and in personal photography led Time Inc. to establish the weekly picture magazine *Life* in November, 1936. People almost fought in the streets to buy copies, and circulation soared. *Life* was patterned after photographic publications in Germany and Britain, but it introduced a disciplined concept of advance research and planning by the editors which guided the photographers. Even such great photographers as its 1936 stars—Margaret Bourke-White, Alfred Eisenstaedt, Peter Stackpole, and Thomas McAvoy—got suggestions from editor Wilson Hicks about how the key shots were to be made when they arrived on the scene. Hicks came from the Associated Press to be picture editor, then executive editor. He built a staff of forty within 3 years and directed it until 1950.

Bourke-White did photographic essays and interpretive picture stories at the close of the Great Depression, captured Gandhi's compelling personality on film in India, and took wartime assignments before illness cut short her career. Robert Capa, W. Eugene Smith, and David Douglas Duncan all recorded the wars, from Capa's great image of a falling Spanish Civil War soldier to Duncan's chilling sequences in Vietnam. Earlier Duncan had also won acclaim for his Korean War photography. Smith's picture essays, including "Spanish Village," "Country Doctor," and "Nurse Midwife," stand as classics. Other noted photojournalists were Gordon Parks, who interpreted the feelings of black America for

Margaret Bourke-White captured this and many other *Life* cover shots.

Wide World Photo

© 1938, Life

Life, Gjon Mili, and Carl Mydans. The managing editors were John Shaw Billings, Edward K. Thompson, George Hunt, and Ralph Graves.

Life's circulation success proved its undoing. The broad approach of television siphoned off some advertisers and readers, and other advertisers diverted contracts from the mass-circulation magazines to those with specialized audiences. Circulation dropped from 8.5 million in 1970 to 5.5 million in 1972 and the revenue flow was not enough to sustain publication. With tears and many a fond remembrance, *Life* staffers headed for other jobs in the media world.[34]

Life's suspension in 1972 had followed on the heels of the death of *Look,* its chief competitor in the world of photojournalism. *Look* was begun by Gardner Cowles in 1937. At first it adopted the rotogravure techniques of the Cowles family newspapers in Des Moines and Minneapolis, but gradually it developed major articles on public affairs. A fortnightly, it reached 2 million circulation in 1945, passed 4 million in 1955, and had touched 8 million when it was suspended in 1971, another victim of inflated costs and deflated advertising revenues. Daniel D. Mich was *Look*'s longtime editor, succeeded by William B. Arthur. Arthur Rothstein came from the Farm Security Administration photojournalism group to be director of photography. Achieving distinction with their cameras were John Vachon, Phillip Harrington, and Paul Fusco. The magazine was a national leader in art direction under art directors Allen Hurlburt and William Hopkins.

Documentary films, recording the lives and social activities of real people, had their beginning in 1922 when a New York fur company commissioned Robert Flaherty to film the life of an Eskimo family. His *Nanook of the North* set a standard for others. John Grierson filmed herring fishermen on the North Sea in 1929 to produce *Drifters,* the first of a series for the British government that he, Paul Rotha, and others continued in the 1930s.

The United States government joined in support of documentary photography through the Farm Security Administration (FSA), which was concerned with soil erosion, dust storms, and their human toll. A team of photo documentarians under the guidance of Roy E. Stryker began touring the Midwest dust bowl in 1935, taking pictures which opened the eyes of the nation to the unchronicled devastation of rural poverty. One of the photographers was Dorothea Lange, whose sensitive images stand as examples of still photography at its finest. Others included Carl Mydans, Walker Evans, and Ben Shahn. The FSA project involved 272,000 negatives and 150,000 prints, now stored at the Library of Congress.

The FSA then commissioned documentary films, produced by Pare Lorentz. His *The Plow That Broke the Plains* (1936) was a graphic documentation of the causes of soil erosion and the dust storms that were turning Great Plains farmers into migrant workers. In 1937 Lorenz completed *The River,* addressed to another major national problem, flooding.

During World War II, Hollywood directors such as John Huston, Frank Capra, William Wyler, and John Ford filmed documentaries on and around battlegrounds, including *San Pietro, Memphis Belle,* and *Battle of Midway* during 1944. The British Ministry of Information did three masterful films: *London Can Take It* (1940), *Target for Tonight* (1941), and *Desert Victory* (1942). Most documentary effort was diverted to television in the 1950s, but the cult of *cinéma vérité,* or spontaneous filmmaking, kept the tradition alive.

BOOK PUBLISHING TURNS THE CORNER

Book publishing, a part of American life since colonial days, reached a turning point about 1915, according to the leading historian of the industry, John Tebbel.[35] A rapidly increasing literacy rate and a mushrooming urbanization meant that more people living in city centers where book stores could prosper wanted to read books. Tebbel also points out the arrival on the publishing scene of a remarkable number of aggressive builders.

Between 1914 and 1926 the newcomers included Alfred A. Knopf, W. W. Norton, and William Morrow, whose publishing houses bore their names; Bennett Cerf and Donald Klopfer of Random House; Harold Guinzburg of Viking Press; and four sets of partners who built illustrious houses: Alfred Harcourt and Donald Brace, Richard Simon and Max Schuster, Albert Boni and Horace Liveright, and John Farrar and Stanley Rinehart.

There were older family names whose publishing companies had already survived for a century, however: John Wiley, 1807; Harper & Bros., 1817; Appleton, 1825; G. P. Putnam, 1836; Dodd of Dodd, Mead, 1839; Scribner's, 1842; A. S. Barnes, 1845; E. P. Dutton, 1852. After the Civil War came a Macmillan branch from England in 1869; Henry Holt & Co., 1871; Funk & Wagnalls and Thomas Y. Crowell, 1876; David McKay, 1882; Frank N. Doubleday's first firm, 1897; the McGraw and Hill firms in 1899 and 1902; and Prentice-Hall, 1913. In Boston, Little, Brown and Houghton Mifflin, dating from 1837 and 1848 respectively, rivaled the dominant New York firms and those in Philadelphia, led by J. P. Lippincott, 1836.

The most exciting publishing house in the 1920s and 1930s was Scribner's. After founder Charles Scribner's death in 1871, the firm became Charles Scribner's Sons, with Charles Scribner, II, serving as president from 1879 to 1928. Among his authors were Edith Wharton, Henry James, and Richard Harding Davis. His more important action, however, was to bring Maxwell Perkins into the offices in 1910. Perkins served as an editor from 1914 until his death in 1947, and with his associates built a remarkable record for literary successes. It was Perkins who worked with F. Scott Fitzgerald to produce his first novel in 1920, *This Side of Paradise;* it was Perkins who answered a tip from Fitzgerald in 1924 that there was a promising young author in Paris named Ernest Hemingway, whose *The Sun Also Rises* came from Scribner's in 1926; it was Perkins who worked endlessly with a young Southern giant named Thomas Wolfe to create in 1929, out of 1100 pages of manuscript, Wolfe's first novel, *Look Homeward, Angel,* and then out of 3000 pages, his second novel, *Of Time and the River.* Meantime, the Scribner's editorial team was producing the *Dictionary of American Biography.*

Cass Canfield arrived at Harper & Bros. in 1924, and served as chief executive officer from 1931 to 1967. An early coup was Wolfe's move from Scribner's to the editorship of Edward Aswell at Harper's in 1937. D. Appleton & Co. celebrated its 100th birthday in 1925 with such authors as Edith Wharton (*The Age of Innocence* was a 1920 event), Edgar Lee Masters, and Vachel Lindsay. Edward P. Dutton, founder of his firm, died in 1923 after 62 years as president; he had on his list Van Wyck Brooks, literary critic; Charles G. Norris, A. A. Milne, and Stewart Edward White. Edward H. Dodd expanded his family's firm in the 1920s by acquiring the lists of five other companies, which included many

English and European authors. At Macmillan, George Brett died in 1936, the same year he published *Gone With the Wind.*

Two of America's leading book clubs, the Book of the Month Club (BOMC) and the Literary Guild, appeared in 1926. The BOMC was begun by Harry Scherman, and had Henry Seidel Canby, founder of the *Saturday Review of Literature,* as its first editor-in-chief. The founder of Viking Press, Harold Guinzburg, also launched the Literary Guild. Books by mail flourished, partly due to the inadequate organization of the book-selling trade. Book trade associations dated from 1900; the American Book Publishers Council (1946) and the American Textbook Publishers Institute (1942) joined forces in 1970 to become the Association of American Publishers. The stores were organized as the American Booksellers Association.

Paperbacks made their start in this period, notably the Boni & Liveright efforts of 1914, the Little Leather Library, and of 1917, the Modern Library. The latter was acquired by Random House in 1925. It was 1939, however, before the promoters of Pocket Books found the right formula and revolutionized the paperback business.

NOTES

1. Betty Houchin Winfield, "Roosevelt and the Press: How Franklin D. Roosevelt Influenced Newsgathering, 1933–1941," Ph.D. thesis, University of Washington, 1978, pp. 46, 200–204.

2. Betty H. Winfield, "Franklin D. Roosevelt's Efforts to Influence the News During His First Term Press Conference," *Presidential Studies Quarterly* (Spring 1981), 192, 196.

3. *San Francisco Examiner,* May 6, 1933.

4. Ibid., May 29, 1935.

5. Ibid., June 21, 1935.

6. Ibid., October 30, 1936.

7. *Time,* XLIX (June 9, 1947), 68. The 1936 survey of Washington correspondents, cited here, was taken by Leo C. Rosten for his book, *The Washington Correspondents* (New York; Harcourt Brace Jovanovich, 1937). Cited most often as "least fair and reliable" by ninety-three correspondents were, in order, the Hearst newspapers, the *Chicago Tribune,* the *Los Angeles Times,* and the Scripps-Howard newspapers. Cited most often as "most fair and reliable" by ninety-nine correspondents were, in order, the *New York Times, Baltimore Sun, Christian Science Monitor,* the Scripps-Howard papers, and the *St. Louis Post-Dispatch.*

8. *Near* v. *Minnesota ex rel. Olson,* 283 U.S. 697 (1931).

9. *Grosiean* v. *American Press Co.,* 297 U.S. 233 (1936). In a 1983 case brought by the *Minneapolis Star and Tribune,* the court voided a Minnesota law imposing a 6 percent tax on newsprint and ink used by larger newspapers, thus extending its doctrine on discriminatory taxation.

10. *Associated Press* v. *NLRB,* 301 U.S. 103 (1937).

11. *Bridges* v. *California,* 314 U.S. 252 (1941).

12. *Pennekamp* v. *Florida,* 328 U.S. 331 (1946); *Craig* v. *Harney,* 331 U.S. 367 (1947).

13. Among other special news agencies were the Dow Jones News Service, with some thirty-five newspaper clients; the Jewish Telegraphic Agency, a world service headquartering in New York, and its Overseas News Agency; the Associated Negro Press, largest for black papers; the Religious News Service, serving 750 clients; and the Copley News Service, specializing in Latin American news.

14. Walter Duranty, *I Write as I Please* (New York: Halcyon House, 1935), pp. 166–67.

15. Michael C. Emery, "The American Mass Media and the Coverage of Five Major Foreign Events, 1900–1950" Ph.D. thesis, University of Minnesota, 1968.

16. Paul Scott Mowrer, *The House of Europe* (Boston: Houghton Mifflin, 1945), p. 70. For his brother's personal account, see Edgar Ansel Mowrer, *Triumph and Tragedy* (New York: Weybright and Talley, 1968).

17. Lowell Thomas, *Good Evening Everybody* (New York: William Morrow, 1976), p. 311.

18. Lawrence W. Lichty and Malachi C. Topping, *American Broadcasting: A Source Book on the History of Radio and Television* (New York: Hastings House, 1975), p. 302.

19. Including *Editor & Publisher,* which expressed skepticism in its issue of December 10, 1932, p. 5.

20. The AP won suits against KSOO, Sioux Falls, South Dakota, and KVOS, Bellingham, Washington, to stop this practice. Eventually the period of time during which there is a protectible property right in news came to be recognized as a minimum of 4 to 6 hours after publication.

21. *Ropert on Chain Boradcasting* (Federal Communications Commission Order No. 37, May 1941), pp. 26–28.

22. Lawrence W. Lichty and Thomas W. Bohn, "Radio's *March of Time:* Dramatized News," *Journalism Quarterly,* LI (Autumn 1973), 458–62.

23. For the best treatment of radio commentators in the 1930s and 1940s see Irving Fang, *Those Radio Commentators!* (Ames: Iowa State University Press, 1977). Other prominent commentators included Frederick William Wile and David Lawrence, who were listed in newspaper columns along with Kaltenborn as commentators prior to 1930; Edwin C. Hill; and John W. Vandercook.

24. Fang, *Those Radio Commentators!,* p. 161.

25. Christopher H. Sterling and John M. Kittross, *Stay Tuned: A Concise History of American Broadcasting* (Belmont, Calif.: Wadsworth, 1978), pp. 182–83.

26. Michael Emery, "The Munich Crisis Broadcasts: Radio News Comes of Age" *Journalism Quarterly,* XLII (Autumn 1965), 576.

27. Sterling and Kittross, *Stay Tuned,* pp. 100–101.

28. For a survey of television experiments dating to 1875, see David T. MacFarland, "Television: The Whirling Beginning" in Lichty and Topping, *American Broadcasting: A Source Book,* pp. 46–52.

29. The story of RCA's dominance of early television is found in Erik Barnouw, *Tube of Plenty: The Evolution of American Television* (New York: Oxford University Press, 1975), and his more detailed studies, *A Tower in Babel* (New York: Oxford University Press, 1966) and *The Golden Web* (New York: Oxford University Press, 1968); and in Sydney W. Head, *Broadcasting in America;* F. Leslie Smith, *Perspectives on Radio and Televison;* Lichty and Topping, *American Broadcasting;* and Sterling and Kittross, *Stay Tuned.*

30. Barnouw, *Tube of Plenty,* pp. 78–83, 143–45.

31. Although RCA dominated the early years, a number of other companies had been active, including CBS, the DuMont Laboratories, Philco Radio and Television Corp., and AT&T. By 1937 there were seventeen experimental stations on the air.

32. See Raymond Fielding, *The American Newsreel, 1911–1967* (Norman: University of Oklahoma Press, 1972), for a definitive history and bibliography. Fielding is also the author of *The March of Time, 1935–1951* (New York: Oxford University Press, 1978), the story of that film documentary.

33. *Time,* LI (March 8, 1948), 66.

34. Chris Welles, "Lessons from *Life,*" *World* (February 13, 1973). *Life* later reappeared, but with a much different format.

35. John Tebbel, *History of Book Publishing in the United States,* is a four-volume effort (see Bibliography for Chapter 2).

ANNOTATED BIBLIOGRAPHY

Books: New Deal, Press Freedom

BEASLEY, MAUREEN, ed. *White House Press Conferences of Eleanor Roosevelt.* New York: Garland Publishing, 1983. Transcripts of 100 women-only press conferences 1933 to 1945.

BRINKLEY, ALAN, *Voices of Protest: Huey Long, Father Coughlin, and the Great Depression.* New York: Knopf, 1982. Pictures them as Populists, reaching masses by radio, rivalling FDR.

CHAFEE, ZECHARIAH, JR., *Government and Mass Communications.* Chicago: University of Chicago Press, 1947. A two-volume scholarly study for the Commission on Freedom of the Press.

CHAMBERLAIN, BILL F., AND CHARLENE J. BROWN, eds., *The First Amendment Reconsidered.* New York: Longman, 1982. Presents six essays by media legal scholars.

CLARK, DAVID G., AND EARL R. HUTCHISON, eds., *Mass Media and the Law: Freedom and Restraint.* New York: Wiley-Interscience, 1970. Good collection of essays in major areas of concern.

CULLEN, MAURICE R., JR., *Mass Media & the First Amendment.* Dubuque, Iowa: Wm. C. Brown, 1981. Introduces media through the First Amendment door.

FRIENDLY, FRED W., *Minnesota Rag.* New York: Random House, 1981. The story of *Near* v. *Minnesota,* the 1931 case which became the First-Amendment bedrock.

GERALD, J. EDWARD, *The Press and the Constitution.* Minneapolis: University of Minnesota

Press, 1948. Freedom of the press cases from 1931 to 1947.

HACHTEN, WILLIAM A., ed., *The Supreme Court on Freedom of the Press: Decisions and Dissents.* Ames: Iowa State University Press, 1968. The main historical story, with commentaries.

HOFSTADTER, RICHARD, *The Age of Reform.* New York: Knopf, 1955. A study of reform leaders, from Bryan to FDR, which won a Pulitzer Prize.

LEUCHTENBERG, WILLIAM E., *Franklin D. Roosevelt and the New Deal.* New York: Harper & Row, 1963. Study of domestic policy.

MANCHESTER, WILLIAM, *The Glory and the Dream.* Boston: Little, Brown, 1973. Narrative history from 1932 to 1972.

PHILLIPS, CABELL, *From the Crash to the Blitz, 1929–1939,* (*New York Times* Chronicle of American Life Series). New York: Macmillan, 1969. A continuation in spirit of Mark Sullivan's *Our Times* series for 1900 to 1929; newspaper-based.

SCHLESINGER, ARTHUR, JR., *The Age of Roosevelt.* Boston: Houghton Mifflin, 1957–60. Volume 1, *The Crisis of the Old Order* (1957), covers 1919 to 1933; Volume 2, *The Coming of the New Deal* (1958), covers 1933 to 1934; Volume 3, *The Politics of Upheaval (1960),* covers 1935 to 1936.

STEVENS, JOHN D., *Shaping the First Amendment: The Development of Free Expression.* Beverly Hills: Sage, 1982. Brief model-based discussion.

WHITE, GRAHAM J., *FDR and the Press.* Chicago: University of Chicago Press, 1979. Examines FDR's good relations with reporters and his dislike of publishers. Finds better support for FDR in press than President pictured.

Books: Newspapers, Correspondents

BRENDON, PIERS, *The Life and Death of the Press Barons.* New York: Atheneum, 1983. The Bennetts, Pulitzer, Hearst, McCormick, Patterson, and in Britain, W.T. Stead, Northcliffe, Beaverbrook, Murdoch, made newspapers a rich variety.

CARLISLE, RODNEY P., *Hearst and the New Deal: The Progressive as Reactionary.* New York: Garland Publishing, 1979. Opposite view to Littlefield (see Chapter 18 Bibliography).

CROWL, JAMES W., *Angels in Stalin's Paradise: Western Reporters in Soviet Russia, 1917 to 1939: A Case Study of Louis Fischer and Walter Duranty.* Washington, D.C.: University Press of America, 1982. How Soviets sought to manipulate key reporters.

DREWRY, JOHN E., ed., *Post Biographies of Famous Journalists.* Athens: University of Georgia Press, 1942. Contains articles about Hearst, Roy Howard, McCormick.

FORD, EDWIN H., AND EDWIN EMERY, eds., *Highlights in the History of the American Press.* Minneapolis: University of Minnesota Press, 1954. Contains articles about Hearst, Scripps-Howard, and McCormick.

GIES, JOSEPH, *The Colonel of Chicago.* New York: Dutton, 1979. A biography of McCormick.

HOHENBERG, JOHN, *Foreign Correspondence: The Great Reporters and Their Times.* New York: Columbia University Press, 1964. Foreign correspondence since the French Revolution; best survey of the reporters and the trends.

KREIGHBAUM, HILLIER, *Science and the Mass Media.* New York: New York University Press, 1967. Impact of science and science reporters since Sputnik.

KROCK, ARTHUR, *Memoirs: Sixty Years on the Firing Line.* New York: Funk & Wagnalls, 1968. By the longtime Washington Chief of the *New York Times.*

LOWITT, RICHARD, AND MAURINE BEASLEY, eds., *One Third of a Nation: Lorena Hickok Reports on the Great Depression.* Urbana: University of Illinois Press, 1981. Hickok was an AP reporter and Eleanor Roosevelt's confidante. See also, Beasley, "Lorena A. Hickok, Woman Journalist," *Journalism History,* VII (Winter 1980), 92.

MILLER, WEBB, *I Found No Peace.* New York: Simon & Schuster, 1936. One of the best of the foreign correspondents' books, by a longtime United Press correspondent.

MOWRER, EDGAR ANSEL, *Triumph and Turmoil: A Personal History of Our Times.* New York: Weybright and Talley, 1968. Autobiography of one of greatest foreign correspondents.

STARTT, JAMES D. *Journalism's Unofficial Ambassador: A Biography of Edward Price Bell, 1869–1943.* Athens: Ohio University Press, 1979. *Chicago Daily News* correspondent.

SULZBERGER, C. L., *A Long Row of Candles.* New York: Macmillan, 1969. Memoirs and diaries of the chief *New York Times* foreign correspondent, 1934–54. His *The Last of the Giants* (1970) carried the story through 1963.

SWANBERG, W. A., *Citizen Hearst.* New York: Scribner's, 1961. Highly readable, detailed.

TEBBEL, JOHN, *An American Dynasty.* New York: Doubleday, 1947. An analysis of the McCormick-Patterson publishing empire.

———, *The Life and Good Times of William Randolph Hearst.* New York: Dutton, 1952. Best single book about both Hearst and his publishing empire.

WALDROPP, FRANK C., *McCormick of Chicago.* Englewood Cliffs, N.J.: Prentice-Hall, 1966. Best biography of the *Chicago Tribune* publisher. See also Jerome E. Edwards, *The Foreign Policy of Col. McCormick's Tribune, 1929–1941* (Reno: University of Nevada Press, 1971), a carefully researched analysis.

Books: Radio, Correspondents

BULMAN, DAVID, ed., *Molders of Opinion.* Milwaukee: Bruce Publishing Company, 1945. Includes chapters on H. V. Kaltenborn, Gabriel Heatter, Fulton Lewis, Jr., and Raymond Gram Swing.

BURLINGAME, ROGER, *Don't Let Them Scare You: The Life and Times of Elmer Davis.* Philadelphia: Lippincott, 1961. A good biography of a top-flight news analyst.

CULBERT, DAVID HOLBROOK, *News for Everyman.* Westport, Conn.: Greenwood Press, 1976. Account of how American radio affected foreign affairs during 1930s.

FANG, IRVING E., *Those Radio Commentators!* Ames: Iowa State University Press, 1977. Study of major commentators of 1930s and 1940s.

KALTENBORN, H. V., *Fifty Fabulous Years, 1900–1950: A Personal Review.* New York: G. P. Putnam's Sons, 1950. Autobiography of a commentator who began on the air in 1922.

SCHECHTER, A. A., WITH EDWARD ANTHONY, *I Live on Air.* New York: Frederick Stokes, 1941. NBC's first director of news and special events.

SHIRER, WILLIAM L., *Berlin Diary.* New York: Knopf, 1941. The years 1934 to 1940 in diary form, by the CBS radio correspondent who covered Hitler's rise to power. Also see his *20th Century Journey.* New York: Simon & Schuster, 1976.

THOMAS, LOWELL, *Good Evening Everybody.* New York: Morrow, 1976. Autobiography of the pioneer CBS radio newscaster, 1930–76.

Books: Columnists

ANDERSON, JACK, WITH JAMES BOYD, *Confessions of a Muckraker.* New York: Random House, 1979. Covers the Pearson-Anderson team years, 1947–69.

CHILDS, MARQUIS, *Witness to Power.* New York: McGraw-Hill, 1975. Autobiography.

CHILDS, MARQUIS, AND JAMES B. RESTON, eds., *Walter Lippmann and His Times.* New York: Harcourt Brace Jovanovich, 1959. Twelve essays by admirers.

CLAPPER, RAYMOND, *Watching the World.* New York: Whittlesey House, 1944. A collection of the writings of a great Washington correspondent and columnist.

DAM, HARI N., *The Intellectual Odyssey of Walter Lippman.* New York: Gordon Press, 1973. The columnist's public philosophy, 1910–60, is analyzed in scholarly, readable style. See also, John Luskin, *Lippmann, Liberty and the Press* (University, Ala.: University of Alabama Press, 1972).

FARR, FINIS, *Fair Enough: The Life of Westbrook Pegler.* New Rochelle, N.Y.: Arlington House, 1975. Favorable biography of the sportswriter and political columnist.

FISHER, CHARLES, *The Columnists.* New York: Howell, Soskin, Publishers, Inc., 1944. A lively study, outdated but still valuable for its time period.

O'CONNOR, RICHARD, *Heywood Broun: A Biography.* New York: G. P. Putnam's Sons, 1975. Newest study; well done. See also Dale Kramer, *Heywood Broun* (New York: A. A. Wyn, 1949).

PILAT, OLIVER, *Drew Pearson: An Unauthorized Biography.* New York: Harper's Magazine Press, 1973. Pearson had questionable newsgathering ethics, but many readers.

SANDERS, MARION K., *Dorothy Thompson: A Legend in Her Time.* Boston: Houghton Mifflin, 1973. Prize-winning biography of outstanding foreign correspondent and columnist.

STEEL, RONALD, *Walter Lippmann and the Ameri-*

can Century. Boston: Atlantic-Little, Brown, 1980. A major effort to place the columnist in perspective.

STOKES, THOMAS L., *Chip Off My Shoulder.* Princeton: Princeton University Press. 1940. Autobiography of a distinguished reporter-columnist.

SULLIVAN, MARK, *The Education of a American.* New York: Doubleday, 1938. The autobiography of one of the first political columnists.

WEINGAST, DAVID E., *Walter Lippmann.* New Brunswick: Rutgers University Press, 1949. An impartial study of the political, social, and economic views of an essentially conservative columnist.

Books: Editorial Cartoonists

HESS, STEPHEN, AND MILTON KAPLAN, *The Ungentlemanly Art: A History of American Political Cartoons.* New York: Macmillan, 1968. A well-done survey from Franklin to Herblock.

JOHNSON, GERALD W., *The Lines Are Drawn.* Philadelphia: Lippincott, 1958. A study of Pulitzer Prize cartoons.

LENDT, DAVID L., *Ding: The Life of Jay Norwood Darling.* Ames: Iowa State University Press, 1979. Cartoonist for *Des Moines Register* and *New York Herald Tribune.* See also John M. Henry, ed., *Ding's Half Century* (New York: Duell, Sloan and Pearce, 1962).

MURRELL, WILLIAM, *A History of American Graphic Humor,* 1865–1938. New York: Macmillan, 1938. The second volume of a work that reproduces many cartoons.

NEVINS, ALLAN, and GEORGE WEITENKAMPF, *A Century of Political Cartoons.* New York: Scribner's, 1944. The cartoons are presented in an historical setting.

PRESS, CHARLES, *The Political Cartoon.* East Brunswick, N.J.: Associated University Presses, 1981. History and analysis, including 250 examples since the seventeenth century.

SPENCER, DICK, III, *Pulitzer Prize Cartoons.* Ames: Iowa State College Press, 1953. A history of the winning cartoons since 1922.

Books: Magazines, Book Publishing

BERG, A. SCOTT, *Maxwell Perkins, Editor of Genius.* New York: Dutton, 1978. Scribner's great editor who worked with Tom Wolfe, Scott Fitzgerald, Ernest Hemingway.

BUSCH, NOEL F., *Briton Hadden.* New York: Farrar, Straus & Giroux, 1949. The biography of the cofounder of *Time.*

DESSAUER, JOHN, *Book Publishing: What It Is, What It Does.* New York: Bowker, 1981. A readable survey.

ELSON, ROBERT T., *Time Inc.: The Intimate History of a Publishing Enterprise, 1923–1941.* New York: Atheneum, 1968. Successfully done first volume of a three-volume project under company auspices. Also *The World of Time, Inc.,* 1973. Covers the 1941 to 1960 period.

HACKETT, ALICE P., and JAMES H. BURKE, *80 Years of Best Sellers, 1895–1975.* New York: Bowker, 1977. Frank Luther Mott's *Golden Multitudes* (1950) is more scholarly.

SWANBERG, W. A., *Luce and His Empire.* New York: Scribner's, 1972. Critical study of Luce and his influence on American life.

TEBBEL, JOHN, *A History of Book Publishing in the United States* (see Chapter 2 listing).

Books: Photojournalism, Documentaries

BARNOUW, ERIK, *Documentary: A History of the Non-Fiction Film.* New York: Oxford University Press, 1974. A leading study, well-integrated analysis.

BOURKE-WHITE, MARGARET, *Portrait of Myself.* New York: Simon & Schuster, 1963. Illustrated autobiography of *Life*'s great photojournalist.

BROWN, THEODORE M., *Margaret Bourke-White: Photojournalist.* Ithaca, N.Y.: Andrew Dickson Museum of Art, 1972. Biography.

CAPA, CORNELL, *Robert Capa.* New York: Grossman, 1974. A collection of Capa's photographic works.

DUNCAN, DAVID DOUGLAS, *Yankee Nomad.* New York: Holt, Rinehart & Winston, 1966. A photographic autobiography by a great photojournalist who won his spurs with *Life.* See also *I Protest!,* Duncan's 1968 collection from Vietnam, and *War Without Heroes* (1970).

EISENSTAEDT, ALFRED, *Witness to Our Times.* New York: Viking, 1966. Photographs over 40 years of one of *Life*'s best.

FABER, JOHN, *Great Moments in News Photography.* New York: Nelson, 1960. Covers from Mathew Brady to Robert Capa in fifty-seven photographs. See also Associated Press, *The Instant It Happened* (New York: Associated Press, 1974).

FIELDING, RAYMOND, *The March of Time, 1935–1951.* New York: Oxford University Press, 1978. The complete story of the film documentary made for the movie houses.

GIDAL, TIM N., *Modern Photojournalism Origin and Evolution, 1910–1933.* New York: Macmillan, 1973. Account of photographers and editors who developed the first picture magazines in Germany between 1928 and 1931.

HAMBLIN, DORA JANE, *That Was the Life.* New York: Norton, 1977. *Life* magazine photographers were gods, their chronicler says. Amusing anecdotes.

JACOBS, LEWIS, ed., *The Documentary Tradition.* New York: Norton, 1979. Updates 1971 book.

JOHNSON, WILLIAM S., ed., *W. Eugene Smith: Master of the Photographic Essay.* Millerton, N.Y.: Aperture, 1982. More than 1800 photographs, all small.

MACDONALD, GUS, *Victorian Eyewitness,* New York: Viking Press, 1979. Classic images from 1826 to 1913.

NEWHALL, BEAUMONT, *The History of Photography from 1839 to the Present Day,* 5th ed. New York: Museum of Modern Art, 1982. The standard account.

NORBACK, CRAIG T., AND MELVIN GRAY, eds., *The World's Great News Photos, 1840–1980.* New York: Crown, 1980. Some 250 photos, many from Bettmann Archive.

OHRN, KARIN BECKER, *Dorothea Lange and the Documentary Tradition.* Baton Rouge: Louisiana State University Press, 1980. Lavishly illustrated, well integrated; based on Ph.D. thesis, Indiana University, 1977. See *Journalism History,* IV (Spring 1977) for a Lange photographic essay on a 1942 Japanese-American internment camp.

PARKS, GORDON, *A Choice of Weapons.* New York: Harper & Row, 1966. By the *Life* photojournalist. See also Leonard Freed, *Black in White America* (New York: Grossman, n.d.).

POLLACK, PETER, *A Picture History of Photography.* New York: Abrams, 1969. Some classics.

ROTHA, PAUL, SINCLAIR ROAD, AND RICHARD GRIFFITH, *The Documentary Film.* London: Faber and Faber, 1966. The standard work.

SCHUNEMAN, R. SMITH ed., *Photographic Communication.* New York: Hastings House, 1972. Trends in photojournalism as seen by its leaders.

Periodicals and Monographs

ALSOP, JOSEPH AND STEWART, "Our Own Inside Story," *Saturday Evening Post,* CCXXXI (November 8–15, 1958). How the columnists operated from 1946 to 1958.

BARTNESS, GAROLD L., "Hearst in Milwaukee," Ph.D. thesis, University of Minnesota, 1968. Study of *Wisconsin News,* "a real Hearst newspaper," from 1918 to 1939.

BLANCHARD, MARGARET A., "Press Criticism and National Reform Movements: The Progressive Era and the New Deal," *Journalism History,* V (Summer 1978), 33. Well documented.

———, "Freedom of the Press and the Newspaper Code: June 1933–February 1934," *Journalism Quarterly,* LIV (Spring 1977), 40. Detailed analysis of NRA code.

CARLISLE, RODNEY P., "William Randolph Hearst: A Fascist Reputation Reconsidered," *Journalism Quarterly,* L (Spring 1973), 125. Hearst supported early New Deal.

"The Chicago Tribune," *Fortune,* IX (May 1934), 101. Detailed study.

CLARK, DAVID G., "The Dean of Commentators: A Biography of H. V. Kaltenborn," Ph.D. thesis, University of Wisconsin, 1965. Written from the Kaltenborn papers.

———, "H. V. Kaltenborn's First Year on the Air," *Journalism Quarterly,* XLII (Summer 1965), 373. The *Brooklyn Eagle* editor takes to the air in 1923 on WEAF for a stormy year.

CRANSTON, PAT, "Political Convention Broadcasts: Their History and Influence," *Journalism Quarterly,* XXXVII (Spring 1960), 186. A survey from 1924 to 1956.

DENNIS, EVERETTE E., and CLAUDE-JEAN BERTRAND, "Seldes at 90: They Don't Give Pulitzers for That Kind of Criticism," *Journalism History,* VII (Autumn/Winter 1980), 81. Interview recalling Seldes' *Tell the Truth and Run* (1953).

EMERY, MICHAEL C., "The American Mass Media and the Coverage of Five Major Foreign Events, 1900–1950: The Russo-Japanese War, Outbreak of World War I, Rise of Stalin, Munich Crisis, Invasion of South Korea," Ph.D. thesis, University of Minnesota, 1968. The press corps and how the media used their coverage.

———, "The Munich Crisis Broadcasts: Radio News Comes of Age," *Journalism Quarterly,* XLII (Autumn 1965), 576. Kaltenborn, Murrow, and Shirer penetrate American minds. Detailed analysis of CBS, NBC, Mutual broadcasts.

GALLAGHER, ROBERT, "Good Evening Everybody," *American Heritage* (August–September 1980), 32. Well-illustrated interview with Lowell Thomas.

GIBBS, WOLCOTT, "Time-Fortune-Life-Luce," *New Yorker,* XII (November 28, 1936), 20. A dissection of the Luce empire.

HIMEBAUGH, GLENN A., "Donald Ring Mellett, Journalist: The Shaping of a Martyr," Ph.D. thesis, Southern Illinois University, 1978. Career of a crusading editor.

JOHNSON, CARL E., "A Twentieth Century Seeker: A Biography of James Vincent Sheean," Ph.D. thesis, University of Wisconsin, 1974. Sheean spent 50 years abroad.

KIRKHORN, MICHAEL J., "The Virtuous Journalist," *The Quill* (February 1982), 9. Well-written exploratory essay focusing on personal characteristics of famous photojournalists.

KROMPACK, FRANK J., "Socio-Economic Influences Affecting Texas Press in the Great Depression," Ph.D. thesis, University of Texas, 1975. Most papers survived declining revenues and circulation by economizing.

———, "A Wider Niche for Westbrook Pegler," *American Journalism,* I (Summer 1983); 31. Emphasis is on Pegler's humor.

LASCH, ROBERT, "PM Post-Mortem" *Atlantic Monthly,* CLXXXII (July 1948), 44. An excellent analysis of the *PM* experiment and the reasons for failure.

LICHTY, LAWRENCE W., and THOMAS W. BOHN, "Radio's *March of Time:* Dramatized News," *Journalism Quarterly,* LI (Autumn 1974), 458. The beginning of this technique.

LIEBLING, A. J., "Publisher," *New Yorker,* XVII (August 2–23, 1941). Critical profile of Roy W. Howard.

MADDUX, THOMAS R., "American News Media and Soviet Diplomacy, 1934–41," *Journalism Quarterly,* LVIII (Spring 1981), 29. Content analysis of editorial opinions in thirty-five dailies.

MARBUT, FREDERICK B., "Congress and the Standing Committee of Correspondents," *Journalism Quarterly,* XXXVIII (Winter 1961), 52. The history of the press gallery rules is traced from 1879.

MEYERS, W. CAMERON, "The Chicago Newspaper Hoax in the '36 Election Campaign," *Journalism Quarterly,* XXXVII (Summer 1960), 356. Criticism of *Chicago Tribune* by the biographer of *Chicago Times* editor Richard J. Finnegan (Ph.D. dissertation, Northwestern University, 1959).

MILLER, MERLE, "Washington, the World and Joseph Alsop," *Harper's,* CCXXXVI (June 1968), 43. The imperious columnist examined.

PARMENTER, WILLIAM, "The News Control Explanation of News Making: The Case of William Randolph Hearst, 1920–1940," Ph.D. thesis, University of Washington, 1979. Finds an overwhelming evidence of control in the Hearst newspapers.

PEARSON, DREW, "Confessions of 'an S.O.B.'," *Saturday Evening Post,* CCXXIX (November 3–24, 1956). Story of an "inside" columnist.

PEER, ELIZABETH, "Walter Lippmann, 1889–1974," *Newsweek,* LXXXIV (December 23, 1974), 40.

PFAFF, DANIEL W., "The Press and the Scottsboro Rape Cases, 1931–32," *Journalism History,* I (Autumn 1974), 72. Newspaper news and editorial coverage.

STROUT, RICHARD L., "Tom Stokes: What He Was Like," *Nieman Reports,* XIII (July 1959), 9. A portrait of a great Washington reporter.

TAYLOR, FRANK J., "The Incredible House That Hearst Built," *Saturday Evening Post,* CCXXXII (May 9, 1959), 38. Hearst's San Simeon estate becomes a California Historical Monument.

TAYLOR, SALLY, "The Life, Work and Times of Walter Duranty, Moscow Correspondent for the *New York Times,* 1921–1941," Ph.D. thesis, Southern Illinois University, 1979. Says his influence waned with inadequate reporting of the Ukrainian famine.

TOBIAS, ANDREW, "The Hottest Newsweekly in Town," *New York,* VIII (April 21, 1975), 57. Depth study of McGraw-Hill's *Business Week.*

"The Story of an Experiment," *Time,* LI (March 8, 1948), 55. *Time* evaluates itself after 25 years.

WINFIELD, BETTY HOUCHIN, "Roosevelt and the Press: How Franklin D. Roosevelt Influenced Newsgathering 1933–41," Ph.D. thesis, University of Washington, 1978. A well-crafted and meticulously researched analysis of FDR's press conferences, relations.

———, "FDR's Pictorial Image: Rules and Boundaries," *Journalism History,* V (Winter 1978–79), 110. A seldom-discussed problem.

———, "Franklin D. Roosevelt's Efforts to Influence the News During His First Term Press Conference," *Presidential Studies Quarterly* (Spring 1981), 192.

———, "Mrs. Roosevelt's Press Conference Association," *Journalism History,* VIII (Summer 1981), 54. Eleanor shines a light on herself.

EXTRA!

San Francisco Chronicle

THE CITY'S ONLY HOME-OWNED NEWSPAPER

COMPARATIVE TEMPERATURES	High	Low		High	Low
San Francisco	60	50	Denver	60	25
San Jose	61	39	New York	56	44
Los Angeles	79	56	Chicago	35	26
Seattle	--	--	New Orleans	61	52
Honolulu	77	70	Salt Lake	44	30

Local Forecast: Fair

FOUNDED 1865—VOL. CLIII, NO. 146 CCCC** SAN FRANCISCO, MONDAY, DECEMBER 8, 1941 DAILY 5 CENTS, SUNDAY 10 CENTS

U.S. AT WAR!

Japan Bombs Hawaii, Manila, Invades Thailand, Malaya; 2 U.S. Battleships Claimed Sunk; FDR Talks to Congress Today!

THIS WORLD TODAY

By ROYCE BRIER

NOW let us look at history, and let us look at it calmly, for we are the greatest people in history, and that imposes upon us a great responsibility.

And let us look at history in its wide and true sense in our time, as the chronicle of mankind. We need not as a people worry unduly about the Japanese. We will take care of these upstarts in a little while and when we have they will be back in the murky feudalism from which they emerged 89 years ago.

But the chronicle of mankind is something else, a deep and mighty river forever flowing toward an unseen sea.

So in the beginning there lived not long ago in the great gray city of Vienna, a man, a John Wilkes Booth kind of crazy man, but not too crazy, brooding and hating in an apparently fathomless anonymity. Yet this man was a true son of our history.

In him, in his hate, his madness, his inborn treachery and tigerish bent, the history of our days strained convulsively, like the white-hot core of a volcano. For he was a revolutionary and an unexampled revolution was burning in many men, and after a certain number of years had passed in turmoil and confusion, then lo! the revolutionary and the revolution were one.

They were one by inner preordination from the beginning, but in the reaches of the deep and mighty river they did not find each other at first. When they did, most of us did not know it, and far across the earth millions upon millions of the unknowing were pitched abruptly into the abyss.

"And the war came - - -"

As in Abraham Lincoln's day, it came slowly and blunderingly and in false-face. But instead of striding across a continent it strode across a world. It moved a little east and a little west, a little north and a little south, this revolutionary war which was in motion through time as well as space. It struck and recoiled, struck and recoiled, but always it engulfed a little more time and a little more space, for this is the way of revolutions.

It did not want to show its face until it had to, for this is the way of revolutions, too, especially is it

Continued on Page 2, Col. 1

LLOYD GEORGE ACCEPTS BRITISH PREMIERSHIP . . . CONVICT WALKS OUT AT SAN QUENTIN . . . SEA-TO-SEA STEAMER LINE FINANCED TO CURB RATES . . . STREET CARS HERE CARRY MORE PASSENGERS THAN IN L. A.

• • •

HERE'S EVERYDAY TOP-HEAD NEWS! *More Robt. Burns Panatelas de luxe have been smoked than all other high-grade panatelas combined.* And more and more young men are finding in this smooth smoking, smooth looking favorite just the combination of suave distinction and sheer smoking pleasure that they seek.

Try a Robt. Burns Panatela de Luxe today. Judge it by appearance . . . judge it by smoking satisfaction . . . and you'll discover why it is the world's leading panatela.

Robt. Burns features four shapely up-to-date cigars: Panatela de Luxe, Corona, and Perfecto Grande, 10¢ each — and Queens, 2 for 25¢. All are invariably 100% clear Havana filler cigars.

Robt. Burns Panatela de Luxe 10¢

The Sophistocrat of Cigars

America at War!

EDITORIAL

By the act of Japan, America is at war. The time for debate has passed and the time for action has come. That action must be united and unanimous. "Politics is adjourned," whether between parties, factions or economic groups. From now on America is an army with every man, woman and child a soldier in it, all joined to the one end of victory.

If war had to come, it is perhaps well that it came this way, wanton, unwarned, in fraud and bad faith, virtually under a flag of truce. For in war there can be only one side in action, and now there is only one side in thought or feeling. Its slogan is, "Americans unite, for victory and freedom."

We can not know how long this war will last, how wide it will range, nor what it will cost us, in toil, in sacrifice and in treasure. We do know that whatever the cost, we will pay it, and that our reward will be to hand down to our children the free America which our fathers bequeathed to us.

Americans, unite!

U. S. Faces War: Losses May Be Heavy, Nation Warned

WASHINGTON, Dec. 8 (Monday) (AP)—Bombs from Japan made war on the United States today and as death tolls mounted President Roosevelt announced he would deliver in person today a special message to Congress.

In the background as the Commander-in-Chief went before the joint session of the House and Senate was a Government report of "heavy" naval and [illegible] losses to the Army. [illegible]

Whether Mr. Roosevelt will ask for a formal declaration of war by this country [illegible] action taken in Tokyo [illegible] after a hurriedly summoned meeting of his Cabinet and congressional leaders of both parties tonight at the White House. Also uncertain was whether that declaration might extend to Japan's Axis allies, Germany and Italy.

It was clear from a statement made by the participants, however, that Congress would be requested to adopt a resolution of some nature and equally clear that it would quickly give its approval. A request for governmental power equivalent to that under a war declaration was expected as a minimum.

WAR CAME WHILE TALKS WERE CONTINUING

War came suddenly to the United States early yesterday afternoon. Without warning, and while Japanese diplomats were still conducting negotiations for peace, the Japanese Air Force struck at Honolulu, Pearl Harbor and Hickham Field, all in the Hawaiian islands. Soon afterward, Japanese bombs were raining upon Guam and, later, portions of the Philippines were attacked.

As quickly as word of the first bursting bomb was received, the President as commander-in-chief called upon the army and navy to repel the attack. Far in advance of any action which Congress may take today, the United States was fighting an attack.

Tokyo later announced its declaration of war on this country, and Great Britain as well. As was the case here, the British Parliament was called into special session for this afternoon to take action.

Quickly many of the discordant elements which have been bickering over foreign policy for months,

Continued on Page 6, Col. 1

Chronicle News Conference Off Air for Duration

The Chronicle News Conference heard over KGO at 6:15 each evening Monday through Friday, is canceled for the duration of the war. Every energy of The Chronicle staff through every 24-hour period will need to be devoted to the job of editing the paper. When better days come the staff of The Chronicle News Conference hopes to greet again its friends of the airlanes. Thank you all for the interest you have displayed in the program and for your substantial evidence of appreciation.

Without Warning, Bombs Break the Peace

350 Slain--Then Tokyo Declares War on U. S., Britain
Pacific Coast, Electrified, Springs to Wartime Alert

Air Raid Precautions Taken; Military Leaves Cancelled; Coastal Guns Manned

The West Coast, from San Diego to the Canadian line, and the entire Western Continental United States were swinging to a wartime basis within a few hours of the air attack on Hawaii by Japan.

Air raid listening devices went into action. The fastest pursuit ships and bombers of the Army Air Corps were poised for any sign of raid by land, sea or air.

Leaves and furloughs of all officers and enlisted men of the 11th, 12th and 13th Naval districts were canceled and the men ordered back to their ships.

FACTORIES TIGHTEN WATCH FOR SABOTEURS

The outposts of the Nation's far-flung Pacific Coast defenses at Alaska and the Panama Canal were blacked out last night.

Leaves of all soldiers in the 9th Corps Area — California, Nevada, Utah, Idaho, Montana, Washington and Oregon—were summarily canceled by the War Department and all men were ordered to their posts.

The United States Coast Guard ordered all Pacific Coast craft into port, and the Customs Department canceled all departure permits. Movements of craft in harbors was restricted.

All enlisted men of Class M-2 Naval Reserve [illegible]

[illegible]

of the 9th Corps Area, closed all entrances to all army posts to civilians excepting those on official business.

"WE'RE READY," SAYS MARE ISLAND OFFICER

[illegible]

of cargo ships are on the ways of shipbuilding plants armed guards were called into immediate service to augment the patrols which have been on the alert against sabotage for months.

Officials of the Pacific Telephone and Telegraph Company and the Pacific Gas and Electric Company announced their properties were under strict guard and that only persons holding passes

Continued on Page H, Col. 5

INSIDE

You'll find full war coverage—news, background and pictures: See Pages A, B, C, D, E, F, G, H, 4, 5 and 6.

Hoover: Our Decision's Clear

By Associated Press

Former President Herbert Hoover last night called for an all-out fight against the Japanese, saying, "American soil has been treacherously attacked by Japan. Our decision is clear."

Wendell Willkie, Republican standard bearer in 1940, said: "I have not the slightest doubt as to what a united America should and will do."

FDR on Air

Network radio stations will carry President Roosevelt's address to the joint session of Congress this morning. Among them will be stations KGO, KPO and KSFO in San Francisco. Time here will be 9:30 a. m.

Raids Took a Heavy Toll, Hawaii Says

(This is the last uncensored Associated Press dispatch from Honolulu in the new war. Soon after this dispatch was telephoned a heavy censorship was imposed on dispatches from the Hawaiian islands. In Washington, some hours later, the War Department gave the White House a preliminary estimate that 104 were dead and more than 300 wounded in the army forces alone by the bombing.)

HONOLULU, Dec. 7 (AP)—War struck suddenly and without warning from the sky and sea today at the Hawaiian islands, and Japanese bombs took a heavy toll in American lives.

[illegible] indicated a naval engagement in progress.

Wave after wave of planes streamed over Oahu in an attack which the army said started at 8:10 a. m., Honolulu time, and which ended at around 9:25 an hour and 15 minutes later.

[illegible]

Continued on Page C, Col. 7

Canada, Dutch Indies, Costa Rica Declare War on Japan; Wake Is Reported Taken

By the Associated Press

Japan assaulted every main United States and British possession in the central and western Pacific and invaded Thailand today (Monday) in a hasty but evidently shrewdly-planned prosecution of a war she began Sunday without warning.

Her formal declaration of war against both the United States and Britain came two hours and 55 minutes after Japanese planes spread death and terrific destruction in Honolulu and Pearl Harbor at 7:35 a. m., Hawaiian time (10:05 a. m., San Francisco) Sunday.

FDR Talks to Nation

Today at 9:30 a. m. San Francisco time, President Roosevelt will address a joint session of Congress and a declaration of war by the United States against Japan is expected. The speech will be carried on all major radio networks.

The claimed successes for this fell swoop include sinking of the U. S. battleship West Virginia and setting afire of the battleship Oklahoma.

From that moment, each tense tick of the clock brought new and flaming accounts of Japanese aggression in her secretly launched war of conquest or death for the land of the rising sun.

Japanese Surprise Attacks

As compiled from official and unofficial accounts from all affected countries, the record ran like this:

Honolulu bombed a second time.

Lumber-laden U. S. Army transport torpedoed 1300 miles west of San Francisco and another transport in distress.

Sinking of the transport Hugh L. Scott 1800 miles from Manila.

Seizure or sinking of another U. S. transport, the former President Harrison.

Shanghai's International Settlement seized; U. S. gunboat Wake captured there and British gunboat Petrel destroyed.

Capture of the U. S. island of Wake.

Bombing of the U. S. island of Guam, which was reported by Tokyo to be surrounded by Japanese naval ships.

Bombing of many points throughout the Philippine islands.

Invasion of Northern Malaya and bombing of Singapore.

Invasion of Thailand (Siam) and bombing of Bangkok.

The first U. S. official casualty report listed 104 dead and more than 300 injured in the army at Hickam Field, alone, near

Continued on Page 11, Col. 1

Big type announced Pearl Harbor and the coming of World War II to America.

22
A World at War

This is a people's war, and to win it the people should know as much about it as they can.

—Elmer Davis

The diplomatic bombshell that signaled the opening of World War II was the signing of the German-Russian neutrality pact on August 23, 1939. This sinister deal between dictators Hitler and Stalin gave the Germans freedom to march against Poland and later their neighbors to the west without fear of Russian intervention. Russia, in return, would annex eastern Poland. The German *blitzkrieg* opened September 1 and the British and French, who had failed repeatedly to stand up against Hitler and Mussolini, responded with declarations of war on September 3. They did not, however, launch offensives.

President Roosevelt immediately increased his efforts to assist the Allies; the Neutrality Act was revised in November, the first step toward reversal of the isolationist trend. Congress repealed the embargo on arms' sales and authorized a cash-and-carry trade with those resisting aggression. This was met with bitter resentment from the anti-Roosevelt segment of the news media led by the McCormick-Patterson *Chicago Tribune* and *New York Daily News* and radio commentators Fulton Lewis, Jr., Upton Close, and Father Charles Coughlin.

The full nature of Hitler's designs—and the danger to the security of the United States—was revealed in the spring of 1940, when Nazi armies first invaded Denmark and Norway and then launched a gigantic offensive against Holland, Belgium, and France on May 10. The shock of the British evacuation of

Dunkerque, the fall of France, and the opening of the Nazi air blitz against Britain in August produced strong pro-Allied sentiment in the United States.

AMERICANS LEARN OF EUROPE'S WAR

Bill Henry of CBS and Arthur Mann of Mutual had been the first front-line radio reporters in 1939, William L. Shirer of CBS and William C. Kerker of NBC had seen Hitler strutting before accepting the French surrender at the railroad car at Compiègne, and night after night in late 1940 Edward R. Murrow told CBS listeners of the Nazi air attacks against London. The greatest impact on American minds was made by the "This is London" broadcasts—the graphic reporting of the Battle of Britain. Murrow's quiet but compelling voice brought images of a bomb-torn and burning London that did much to awaken the still-neutral United States to the nature of the war. Later the poet Archibald MacLeish would say of Murrow's broadcasts: "You burned the city of London in our houses and we felt the flames that burned it."[1]

One of the early standouts among newspaper correspondents was the veteran Leland Stowe of the *Chicago Daily News,* who reported the Russo-Finnish War and the Nazi invasion of Norway, and who in 1941 became the first American to reach the Nazi-Soviet front lines after Hitler's invasion of Russia. Webb Miller of the United Press covered his eleventh war in Finland, then returned to London to be killed in a blackout accident. Frazier Hunt of the INS and M. W. Fodor of the *Chicago Daily News* filed notable accounts of the French retreat in 1940; on the other side, with Hitler's triumphant army, were Louis Lochner of the Associated Press, Pierre J. Huss of the International News Service, and Frederick C. Oechsner of the United Press.

In September, 1940, the Selective Service Act was passed and Roosevelt announced the trade of fifty destroyers to Britain in return for leases on air-sea bases in the Western Hemisphere. Many American newspapers supported both actions and Henry Luce's *Time* magazine agreed with them.

ROOSEVELT'S THIRD-TERM CAMPAIGN

Roosevelt was in the middle of his campaign for an unprecedented third term. His opponent, the enthusiastic Wendell Willkie from Indiana, supported aid for Britain, the draft, and the destroyer deal—although he fairly criticized Roosevelt for not including Congress in the decision. Willkie was in turn called a "me-too" candidate by the Republican "Old Guard." The Republican National Committee went much further than its candidate, issuing radio messages saying "When your boy is dying on some battlefield in Europe . . . and he's crying out 'Mother! Mother!'—don't blame Franklin D. Roosevelt because he sent your boy to war—blame yourself because you sent Franklin D. Roosevelt to the White House!"[2]

The lines were formed between the isolationists and the interventionists. On one side was the America First Committee, headed by General Robert E. Wood and championed by Colonel Charles A. Lindbergh. Senators Gerald P. Nye and Burton K. Wheeler were America Firsters. Unfortunately for them, their side drew such assorted rabble rousers as Father Coughlin, Gerald L. K.

Smith, William Dudley Pelley of the Silver Shirts, Fritz Kuhn of the German-American Bund, and Communists William Z. Foster and Earl Browder. On the other side was the Committee to Defend America by Aiding the Allies, headed by Kansas editor William Allen White, a distinguished leader in journalism. The White group attracted many influential writers and editors and carried out a newspaper-advertisement campaign that resulted in the formation of hundreds of local committees. Among these journalistic leaders were columnist Joseph Alsop, radio commentator Elmer Davis, and playwright Robert E. Sherwood.

The voters decided not to change leadership in the midst of crisis and gave Roosevelt 27 million popular votes to 22 million for Willkie. John L. Lewis of the United Mine Workers urged Roosevelt's defeat, but Roosevelt held the majority of his coalition together. In November, 1940, a Gallup poll showed that 50 percent of the Americans favored helping England, even at the risk of intervention in Europe; by December that total would mount to 60 percent.

THE ARSENAL OF DEMOCRACY

In December, 1940, President Roosevelt called on the nation to become "the great arsenal of democracy." He told a worldwide radio audience that if Britain were defeated the Axis powers would "control the continents of Europe, Asia, Africa, Australasia, and the high seas." He continued, "It is no exaggeration to say that all of us in the Americas would be living at the point of a gun—a gun loaded with explosive bullets, economic as well as military."[3] But, he predicted, the Axis nations would not win the war if America would speed up its arms' production. Earlier that year Winston Churchill, who had emerged from political exile to become Britain's Prime Minister, had thrilled the free nations with his "blood and tears, toil and sweat" speech, also heard on radio.

The Lend-Lease Act of 1941, which empowered the President to provide goods and services to those nations whose defense he deemed vital to the defense of the United States, represented a victory for the pro-Allied group. It also served to make America a nonbelligerent ally of the British, to the disgust of Senators Taft and Vandenberg, Joseph P. Kennedy, and John Foster Dulles. Ironically, it was Taft who also noted Roosevelt's unhappiness with Japanese aggression in Southeast Asia. Taft said that no American mother was ready to have a son die "for some place with an unpronounceable name in Indo-china."[4]

In May, 1941, Roosevelt proclaimed an unlimited state of national emergency to facilitate the American mobilization program. In August he and Churchill met on the high seas and announced their peace aims in the Atlantic Charter. The isolationists were far from beaten, however; that same month the House of Representatives continued the military draft by the narrow margin of one vote.

WAR BREAKS IN THE PACIFIC

Unity for war was achieved on December 7, 1941, when radio brought the astounding news that Japanese planes had bombed the U.S. Pacific Fleet at their Pearl Harbor base in the Hawaiian Islands. Len Sterling, an announcer for

Mutual, broke into the broadcast of a professional football game coming from the Polo Grounds in New York. At 2:22 P.M. the press associations had flashed the White House announcement of the attack—"White House says Japs attack Pearl Harbor"—and were relaying news from correspondents in Honolulu. The United Press provided the first direct account of the attack before military censors cut off communications from Hawaii.

Mrs. Frank Tremaine, wife of the UP's Hawaiian manager, made the call to San Francisco, repeating information from her husband and other staffers. One of those reporters was Francis McCarthy, whose byline appeared over this story:

> **Honolulu, Dec. 7 (UP)—War broke with lightning suddenness in the Pacific today, when waves of Japanese bombers assailed Hawaii and the United States Fleet struck back with a thunder of big naval rifles.[5]**

It was afternoon on the East Coast and a few minutes after the Mutual break-in. John Daly of CBS came on the air at 2:31 P.M. with: "The Japanese have attacked Pearl Harbor, Hawaii, by air, President Roosevelt has just announced. The attack was also made on naval and military activities on the principal island of Oahu."[6] The incredible announcement was repeated by NBC announcers and during the rest of the day the radio carried bulletins—and some commentary based on rumor as much as fact. The following day a record 79 percent of American homes listened to Roosevelt's speech before Congress, when he asked for a declaration of war by beginning, "Yesterday, December 7, 1941, a date which will live in infamy . . ."

All of the grim facts of America's humiliating losses at Pearl Harbor and the disgraceful lack of preparation were not immediately known. In all, 2403 Americans died and another 1178 were wounded. The battleship *Arizona* sank at its berth and seventeen other ships were sunk or damaged, along with more than 200 planes destroyed or damaged. But on that first day it was clear that this had been a great defeat. That evening Eric Sevareid, who had joined Murrow's staff in Europe in 1939, broadcast from the White House press room: " . . . there is one report that I must give you that is not all confirmed—a report which is rather widely believed here and which has just come in. And that is that the destruction at Hawaii was indeed very heavy, more heavy than we really had anticipated."[7]

Although the Pacific war opened with the "sneak attack," it can be argued that war between the United States and Japan had been inevitable because of America's presence in the Philippines since 1898, Japan's desire to spread its Greater East Asia Co-Prosperity Sphere without Western interference, longstanding grudges against America because of discrimination against immigrants, and finally, American insistence that Japan abandon its attempts to occupy Manchuria and China. A final straw had been the American embargo on scrap iron and steel shipments to Japan in September, 1940, which made the Japanese warlords more fearful of United States intentions. In their minds the large U.S. Pacific Fleet was a threat to their nation's Pacific destiny. In fact, the Japanese newspaper *Yomiuri* had stated this position at the time of the embargo: "Britain, the United States, and France must be forced out of the Far East. Asia is the territory of the Asians."[8] The *New York Herald Tribune* understood this too, saying after the attack, "Since the clash now seems to have been inevitable, its occurrence brings with it a sense of relief." While many other papers vented their anger and frustration in bitter denunciations of the "Japs" and vowed that the Japanese homeland would be destroyed, the *Herald Tribune* calmly stated, "The air is clearer. Americans can get down to their task with old controversies forgotten."[9]

Hitler made Roosevelt's task easier on December 11 when, against the advice of many of his military chiefs, he declared war against the United States. Now there could be no argument against fighting on the European front. The President's isolationist foes were shocked into silence.

CENSORSHIP AND PROPAGANDA RENEWED

With organization of the country for war, newspaperpeople recalled that the Espionage Act and Trading-with-the Enemy Act of 1917 were still on the statute books. The more sweeping generalities of the Sedition Act had been repealed in 1921, however. Use of these acts to bar publications from the mails and to suppress free speech was more sharply limited than during World War I and mainly affected pro-Fascist and subversive propaganda sheets. The greatest invasion of civil liberties took place during the early years of the war when Japanese living in the United States, including many American citizens of Japanese ancestry, were rounded up and kept in what amounted to protective custody in isolated camps.

Byron Price, executive news editor of the Associated Press, was named director of the Office of Censorship. Probably no other person could have held the respect and confidence of newspaperpeople everywhere better than Price, who was temperamentally and intellectually equipped to handle the most difficult part of his job—the direction of the voluntary press censorship. He brought into his organization a score of seasoned newspaperpeople—headed by John H. Sorrells, executive editor of the Scripps-Howard newspapers, and Nat. R. Howard, editor of the *Cleveland News*—to handle press relationships.[10]

A *Code of Wartime Practices for the American Press* was issued on January 15, 1942. It carefully outlined to those who published newspapers, magazines, books, and other printed materials what would constitute improper handling of news having to do with troops, planes, ships, war production, armaments, military installations, and weather. Similar instructions were given to radio stations. The code became a Bible for American newspeople, who usually erred in the direction of oversuppression of news possibly harmful to the war effort.

Most of the 14,462 persons in the Office of Censorship were engaged in the mandatory censorship of mail, cables, and radio communications between the United States and other countries. Price's Office of Censorship in World War II thus combined the World War I operations of the Censorship Board and the voluntary press-censorship portion of George Creel's work. Price, however, had nothing to do with originating the news or with the government's propaganda effort. Those aspects of the work of the World War I Committee on Public Information were handled during World War II by a separate agency.

This was the Office of War Information (OWI) established by an executive

Elmer Davis, head of the OWI.

order of the president in June, 1942, to supersede four earlier government agencies. Roosevelt made a wise choice in the person of Elmer Davis as director. Davis had served on the *New York Times* staff for 10 years and had been a news analyst and commentator for the Columbia Broadcasting System. "It is the job of OWI," Davis said, "not only to tell the American people how the war is going, but where it is going and where it came from—its nature and origins, how our government is conducting it, and what (besides national survival) our government hopes to get out of victory."[11] This concept of the total function of OWI was also applied to its work abroad.

One function of the OWI was to act as a city desk for the nation's war news. Government departments and war agencies continued to handle approximately 40 percent of government publicity stories without reference to the OWI. But those news releases relating significantly to the war effort or dealing with activities affecting more than one government agency had to pass through the OWI News Bureau. The OWI cooperated with the War and Navy Departments in handling military news, and the Army and Navy were required to consult with Davis about withholding specific military information. The services, however, retained final authority over such withholding of news and Davis did not often win arguments with them. As a result, Davis took a steady drumming of criticism from those suspicious of any information agency.

The News Bureau operated on $1 million annual budget with 250 regular employees. Three hundred reporters and correspondents used its facilities, including some fifty reporters working full time in the OWI pressroom. Copy flowed from the general news desk, where policy decisions were made, to the domestic and foreign news desks, the radio news desk, the picture desk, and the feature desk. Cartoons, pictures, features, weekly digests, and fillers became a part of the OWI offering. Background information concerning desired propaganda and informational objectives of the government was given to editorial writers, cartoonists and columnists.

In all of this work the OWI had the cooperation of the War Advertising Council and the nation's publishers. The government paid for recruiting advertising, but all other war-related newspaper, magazine, radio, and billboard advertising space was donated by the media or by national and local advertisers.

Overseas operations of the OWI were directed by Robert E. Sherwood. Joseph Barnes, foreign editor of the *New York Herald Tribune,* was deputy director for the important Atlantic area. The overseas news and propaganda programs of the OWI were far more extensive than Creel's work in World War I, particularly because of the availability of radio communication for what became known as the Voice of America. OWI cooperation with the military in the development of psychological-warfare techniques was also an advance over World War I methods.

The overseas section received up to 30,000 words a day of teletyped news from the domestic OWI News Bureau. The overseas offices in New York and San Francisco used also the news reports of the press associations, radio networks, and OWI's own regional offices. At its height of activity in 1943, the overseas news and features bureau, headed by Edward Barrett, cabled 65,000 words daily to all parts of the world, mailed hundreds of thousands of words of feature material, and airmailed or radioed 2500 pictures.[12] OWI was given a $36 million budget in 1943, of which $27 million was allotted for overseas operations. Two-thirds of that sum went for radio operations, mainly the Voice of America.

MILITARY CENSORSHIP

Military censorship for World War II picked up where it had left off at the end of World War I, with the added problem of controlling radio broadcasts. In the early months of the war British censorship was blundering and severe, and it remained tight even after the Ministry of Information became better organized. Nazi Germany was not so badly handicapped by Allied control of cables during World War II, since wireless and radio facilities were available. The Nazis did not censor foreign correspondents before publication, but if they sent stories that Dr. Joseph Goebbels' Ministry of Propaganda did not like, they were subject to expulsion from Germany. Two victims of this policy in the first few months of World War II were Beach Conger of the *New York Herald Tribune* and Otto D. Tolischus of the *New York Times.* Edgar Ansel Mowrer of the *Chicago Daily News* was compelled to leave by reason of threats against his person. Joseph W. Grigg of the UP, the only American reporter to cover the first day and the last day of World War II in Berlin, spent 5 months in internment after being arrested by the Nazis in 1941.

As the war developed, newspeople found the British Admiralty and the U.S. Navy Department most prone to suppressing news of war actions. The American Navy withheld details of the Pearl Harbor disaster, and of the sinkings of ships in the Pacific, for long periods of time on the plea that the Japanese should not be given vital information on a confirmed basis. Reporters grumbled, however, that evidence of inefficient naval operations also was being kept back.

The *Chicago Tribune* was involved in two major incidents in which vital information was disclosed to the enemy. While announcing victory at the Battle of Midway in June, 1942, the paper also carried a story telling, indirectly, that military intelligence had broken the secret Japanese code. The *Tribune* gave full attention to how American commanders knew the position of the oncoming Japanese carriers. In this case the government considered prosecution, but dropped the matter after considerable publicity. Several days prior to Pearl Harbor the *Tribune* published the Roosevelt administration's contingency "war plans." This publication, which showed that American officials felt that only an American expeditionary force could help save the British and Russians, and that the war should be fought in Europe first while the Japanese were held in check in the Pacific, infuriated Roosevelt. But the *Tribune*'s McCormick was robbed of a chance to exploit the matter when the Japanese bombed Pearl Harbor.[13]

On the other hand, the British censorship in Egypt, conflicting British and American censorships in the India-Burma theater, the Chinese censorship in Chungking, and General Douglas MacArthur's censorship in the Pacific also drew heavy fire from correspondents and editors. Many newspeople said that MacArthur's information officers insisted unduly on personal glorification of the commander.

Techniques used by General Dwight D. Eisenhower in Europe were considered generally satisfactory. However, the coverage of the German surrender in Europe ended with arguments over censorship and the confusing case of Edward Kennedy. Kennedy, the AP chief on the Western front, was one of sixteen Allied correspondents taken to the military headquarters in Reims to witness the German surrender. All were pledged not to release their stories until an officially prescribed time. Kennedy, angered by the news that the German radio was announcing the surrender in advance of the time set by American, British, and Russian political leaders, made an unauthorized telephone call to London and dictated part of his story for transmission. The AP thus had the official story of the German surrender a day in advance of V-E day. But Kennedy's fifty-four colleagues in Paris charged him with committing "the most disgraceful, deliberate, and unethical double cross in the history of journalism." Kennedy defended his action as necessary to counteract a needless political censorship and won reinstatement as a war correspondent a year after his suspension. But the AP disassociated itself from its stormy petrel, and he left in 1946.

PRESS AND RADIO COVER THE WAR

Coverage of World War II by the American press and radio was considered by most observers to be the best and fullest the world had ever seen. A great share of the credit for this achievement went to the overseas and war-front correspondents for press associations, newspapers, magazines, and radio. As many as 500 full-time American correspondents were abroad at one time. Altogether the United States armed forces accredited 1646 different persons. The biggest staffs were those of the press associations and radio networks; the *Times* and *Herald Tribune* in New York; the *Daily News, Tribune,* and *Sun* in Chicago; the *Christian Science Monitor, Baltimore Sun,* and *Time, Life,* and *Newsweek.* Of the thirty-seven

American newspeople who lost their lives during the war, eleven were press-association correspondents, ten were representatives of individual newspapers, nine were magazine correspondents, four were photographers, two were syndicated writers, and one was a radio correspondent.

There were many distinguished examples of war correspondence and many personal stories of performance in the face of danger by reporters. Pulitzer Prizes went to Larry Allen of the AP for his exploits with the British Mediterranean fleet; to Hal Boyle and Daniel De Luce of the AP European staff; to military analyst Hanson W. Baldwin of the *New York Times* and Ira Wolfert of the North American Newspaper Alliance; to Mark S. Watson of the *Baltimore Sun* and Homer Bigart of the *New York Herald Tribune;* to AP war photographers Frank Noel, Frank Filan, and Joe Rosenthal; and to Ernie Pyle of the Scripps-Howard Newspaper Alliance. Clark Lee of the AP and Melville Jacoby of *Time* were among the newspeople who shared the dangers of the Bataan evacuation; Jacoby died later in a plane crash but Lee survived to become an INS byline writer. Among other leading war reporters were Vern Haugland and Wes Gallagher of the AP, Quentin Reynolds of *Collier's,* Edward W. Beattie and Henry T. Gorrell of the UP, James Kilgallen and Richard Tregaskis of INS, Drew Middleton of the *New York Times,* and Russell Hill of the *Herald Tribune.*

World War II also had women correspondents. The INS sent its featured writer, Inez Robb, to North Africa and Europe. Three other INS women war correspondents were Lee Carson with the U.S. First Army, Dixie Tighe with the British, and Rita Hume in Italy. Among the UP women correspondents were Eleanor Packard and Dudley Anne Harmon; the AP correspondents were Ruth Cowan and Bonnie Wiley in the field. Other correspondents were Helen Kirkpatrick, *Chicago Daily News;* Peggy Hull (Mrs. Harvey Deuel) of the *Cleveland Plain Dealer,* who served in World War I; Margaret Bourke-White, photographer for *Time* and *Life;* Iris Carpenter, *Boston Globe;* Marguerite Higgins, *New York Herald Tribune,* who became Berlin bureau chief; and Leah Burdette of *PM,* who lost her life in Iran.

The development of mobile units and the use of tape recordings soon brought greatly increased radio coverage. Direct reports came from battlefields, from bombers flying over Berlin and Tokyo, and from other action centers. Some of them were especially memorable: Cecil Brown of CBS describing the fall of Singapore; Edward R. Murrow riding a plane in the great 1943 air raid on Berlin and living to broadcast about it; George Hicks of ABC winning D-Day honors by broadcasting from a landing barge under German fire. Wright Bryan of the *Atlanta Journal* gave NBC and CBS the first eye-witness account from the cross-channel front by flying over it with a planeload of paratroopers.

Perhaps the best-known reporter of the second World War was the columnist friend of the G.I., Ernest Taylor Pyle. Pyle had won attention before the war for his personal notes on life in the United States, as observed in his wanderings across the country. In 1940 he told his readers what the people of Britain felt as they resisted the Nazi air blitz. Then he attached himself to the American army, writing in a hometown style of the intimate daily life of the G.I. in Ireland, North Africa, Sicily, Italy, and France. His column for Scripps-Howard and his *Here Is Your War* and *Brave Men* won him a national reputation and a Pulitzer Prize. Pyle left Europe in 1944, but after a rest he flew out to cover the final stages of the

Ernie Pyle.
Editor & Publisher

Pacific war. When a Japanese sniper killed Ernie Pyle on Ie Shima during the Okinawa campaign of April, 1945, the saga of a great American war correspondent came to a close.

There was a soldiers' journalism again in World War II. The *Stars and Stripes* reappeared as the leading G.I. newspaper in 1942 and eventually had European and Pacific editions. *Yank,* a magazine with twenty-two editions, gained a circulation of 2.5 million. The resentments of the enlisted man were portrayed in *Stars and Stripes* by cartoonist Bill Mauldin, and Sgt. George Baker's "Sad Sack" and Milton Caniff's sexy "Male Call" ran in both publications. Almost every major unit and camp had its own publication. And unlike during World War I, the services developed extensive public-relations units, of which combat correspondents of the Marine Corps were most effective. Sergeant Jim G. Lucas of the Marines, formerly of the *Tulsa Tribune* staff, wrote one of the outstanding eyewitness stories of the war from a beach at Tarawa, the location of the most bloody of all American invasions.

GOOD NEWS FROM THE FRONT

The turning points in the battles against the Axis powers came in 1942, in the Pacific, Russia, and North Africa. Americans had been treated to gloomy news, except for General Jimmy Doolittle's surprise raid on Tokyo in early 1942. In

May, American forces defeated a Japanese task force in the Battle of the Coral Sea, checking the enemy's southward expansion near New Guinea and northern Australia. This was followed quickly by the major naval victory of the Pacific war, the smashing of the Japanese fleet and air forces at the Battle of Midway in June.

Had Admiral Yamamoto's forces won, the Japanese would have been free to cut the lifeline between Australia and the United States, isolating General Douglas MacArthur's forces there, to attack Hawaii, and eventually to launch raids on the American West Coast. But instead the Americans under Admiral Chester Nimitz, having cracked the secret Japanese code, were able to locate the oncoming Japanese carriers and destroy four of them, along with 332 planes. A series of fierce air battles decided the outcome, with Japanese planes caught on the deck refueling at a crucial moment. In August, Americans invaded Guadalcanal as a first step back toward the conquered Philippines.

Despite this success in the Pacific, the news from Russia and Africa remained bad. Newsreels and news magazines showed dramatic pictures of German tanks under General Rommel sweeping toward Egypt. In Russia, Hitler's forces were poised outside of Stalingrad. Then the tide changed. The British, led by General Montgomery, stopped Rommel at El Alamein following massive tank battles in the African desert. The Americans invaded North Africa in November, joining the British and setting the stage for the invasion, the next year, of Sicily and Italy, which surrendered in September, 1943.

The Russians held Stalingrad and encircled 300,000 Nazi troops in November, 1942, taking the offensive for the rest of the war. By the start of 1944 the Allies held air superiority and were preparing for the invasion of Western Europe from England.

THE PRESS ASSOCIATIONS FLASH VICTORY, FDR'S DEATH AT WARM SPRINGS

Wes Gallagher of the Associated Press, who had covered every aspect of the European fighting, was fully prepared for the Allied invasion on June 6, 1944. He pounded out a 1700-word story, sweeping the play across the United States. This was his lead:

> **SUPREME HEADQUARTERS, ALLIED EXPEDITIONARY FORCE, June 6—American, British and Canadian troops landed in northern France this morning, launching the greatest overseas military operation in history with word from their supreme commander, Gen. Dwight D. Eisenhower, that "We will accept nothing except full victory" over the German masters of the continent.**[14]

As General Patton's Third Army stormed across the Rhine River on its way toward Berlin, and the Russians moved in from the east, Hitler's days were numbered. Meanwhile, in the Pacific, American forces triumphed in the Solomon Islands, and New Guinea, and then moved into the Philippine Islands, where General MacArthur gained immense publicity by dramatically wading ashore. In early 1945 U.S. Marines were ready to assault yet another small Pacific Island, Iwo Jima, the tiny strip of land memorialized by AP photographer

Joe Rosenthal's photograph of six Marines planting the Stars and Stripes atop Mt. Suribachi.

The United Press bureau in San Francisco, receiving the communique from the Pacific military radio, flashed the news of the landing ahead of the AP. The lead of the first story reads:

> **GUAM, Feb. 19 (U.P.)—American Marines, protected by a great sea and air bombardment, have invaded the eight-square-mile island of Iwo Jima. This amphibious assault carried the United States Pacific offensive within 750 miles of bomb-blasted Tokyo.**[15]

Victory was at hand—the only question was when the Germans and Japanese would finally quit.

President Roosevelt was serving his fourth term, after conducting an exhausting campaign against Thomas E. Dewey, which he won by the most narrow of his four margins: 54 percent of the popular vote. He had the editorial support of only 22 percent of those dailies endorsing candidates, compared to as much as 38 percent in 1932. It had been an increasingly bitter campaign, marked by Dewey's charges of Communist influence in America and Roosevelt's derisive speeches about GOP tactics. Seriously ill and preoccupied with postwar contingencies, Roosevelt went to his Warm Springs, Georgia, retreat for a 2-week rest. It was there, on April 12, 1945, that he suffered a massive cerebral hemorrhage and died at age 63, having served as President longer than any other American.

In Washington the three press-association offices were not as busy as usual because the President was away. Arthur Hermann of the INS, Joe Myler of the UP, and Gardner Bridge of the AP all lifted their phones when notified by their switchboards of an urgent conference call coming through. The caller was Steve Early, Roosevelt's press secretary, who said, "I have a flash for you. The President died suddenly this afternoon. . . ." Hermann bellowed instinctively to his wire operator, "Flash! FDR Dead!" Thirty seconds later the UP followed with its flash, and the AP was right behind.[16] The news circuits were flooded within minutes and the shock hit around the world, particularly overseas where American soldiers were told their Commander-in-Chief was gone.

In Warm Springs the UP's Merriman Smith, who 18 years later would win a Pulitzer Prize for his coverage of President John Kennedy's assassination, hurried to the cottage of the President's secretary, William Hassett. Harold Oliver of the AP and Bob Nixon of the INS were with him. As Hassett told them the sad news, they jumped for available phones and began dictating. This story appeared under Smith's byline:

> **WARM SPRINGS, (GA) April 12 (U.P.)—Franklin D. Roosevelt, President for 12 of the most momentous years in this country's history, died at 3:35 p.m. C.W.T. today in a small room in the "Little White House" here.**[17]

TRUMAN AND THE ATOMIC BOMB; THE COLD WAR BEGINS

Harry Truman was sworn in less than 3 hours later, setting in motion the final drama of World War II, the decision to use the atomic bomb. The Germans surrendered to the Allies on May 7. Japan was being bombed unmercifully, but there was no sign of its surrender. American officials had a choice, to launch a massive invasion of the Japanese mainland or to use the secret weapon that had been developed during the war. Truman, under extraordinary pressure, made the decision to use the bomb.

On August 6, 1945, three giant Superforts took off from the island base of Tinian, rendezvoused over Iwo Jima, and sped toward Japan. The strike plane, the *Enola Gay,* approached Hiroshima, and at 9:15 A.M. a bomb with power equivalent to 20,000 tons of TNT slipped into the morning air. Sixty seconds later it exploded, opening the Atomic Age. In the city below several square miles disappeared. More than 60,000 persons were killed. Correspondents on Tinian, unaware of the bombing, were told the planes were returning. They were overcome with feeling when told in the press hut that an incredible new weapon had been used. In Washington, President Truman was telling the world of the event, while other officials revealed details of the test conducted in New Mexico several weeks earlier, on July 16.

Three days later William L. Laurence of the *New York Times* rode in one of the planes that flew to Nagasaki to drop the second atomic bomb. Within seconds there was a blinding flash brighter than the midday sun and a massive cloud boiled 45,000 feet into the sky. Laurence, the only reporter to witness the New Mexico test, had been promised a "front-row" seat in return for secrecy about his knowledge of the Manhattan Project. The *New York Times* of September 9 carried his eye-witness description, including these words:

> **. . . the pillar of purple fire had reached the level of our altitude. Only about forty-five seconds had passed. Awe-struck, we watched it shoot upward like a meteor coming in from the earth instead of from outer space, becoming more alive as it climbed skyward through the white clouds. It was no longer smoke, or dust, or even a cloud of fire. It was a living thing, a new species of being, born right before our incredulous eyes.**[18]

Laurence, a science expert who had won a Pulitzer Prize in 1937, won a second one for this article and a series of ten others that followed.

World War II officially ended September 2, 1945, when the Japanese signed surrender documents on the battleship *Missouri* in Tokyo Bay, with General MacArthur presiding. Wirephotos of that solemn ceremony filled front pages nationwide. But the joyous occasion was accompanied by doubts and fears about the intentions of the Russians. One reason for dropping the atomic bomb quickly was to end the war before the Russians advanced too far into Asia. They already occupied all of Eastern Europe and there were arguments over the control of Berlin. President Truman decided that Stalin could not be trusted and an uneasy peace fell across the world.

Not only had the Cold War begun, but questions were soon raised about Roosevelt's agreements with Stalin at the Yalta conference in early 1945, when the future of Eastern Europe was discussed. The use of the atomic bomb frightened many and the moral question was debated, particularly in intellectual magazines. A 1946 issue of the *New Yorker* carrying John Hershey's *Hiroshima* awakened many consciences. Postwar publication of fuller details of the Holocaust, the killing of 6 million Jewish persons by the Nazis, raised queries as to how much Allied officials had known—and when—about the extent of the wholesale slaughter. These arguments have not yet been settled. The most senseless rumor—spread by various books—was that Roosevelt knew that the Japanese fleet was headed for Pearl Harbor and that he let the tragedy occur. Thus did the postwar period begin, with the seeds of recrimination that would multiply in the next few years.

POSTWAR ADJUSTMENTS AT HOME AND ABROAD

President Truman moved the nation into the postwar period with a steady hand. Brisk and sober-minded, Truman provided a sharp contrast to the jovial, witty Roosevelt. He had his own brand of humor, directly related to the ordinary citizen. He earned the respect of Democratic party leaders and some of his Republican opponents with his bluntness and honesty; he spoke with rare candor. He also needed all of the support that he could get because he was faced with a series of labor disputes and foreign crises as he finished Roosevelt's term.

On the domestic front, Truman was challenged by the leader of the United Mine Workers, John L. Lewis, who ordered a strike of 400,000 coal miners in 1946, about the same time a railroad strike threatened to paralyze the transportation industry. Truman forced a settlement of the railroad dispute by seizing control of the lines and he got Lewis to call his miners back to work. Accused of being antilabor in these actions, Truman attempted to take a middle course: He vetoed the Taft-Hartley Act of 1947, a Republican-sponsored law that tightened regulations governing strikes at companies engaged in interstate commerce. One of the most controversial provisions outlawed the closed shop and set up election procedures for union shops. Amidst a great furor, Congress passed the law over Truman's veto. Over time the President was seen as a champion of labor workers, but a foe of anyone whom he suspected of acting against the public interest.

While he battled the Congress and tried to push for his Fair Deal—laws dealing with employment practices, social-security benefits, public housing, price and rent controls, and other social actions stemming from the New Deal days—Truman was forced to cope with increasing pressure from the Russians. In May of 1946 a strong protest from the United States had forced the Soviets to remove troops from Iran, where they attempted to detach one province and threatened to swallow the entire country.

The fear of international Communism, coupled with the disclosure of Soviet spy activity in the United States and the relentless attacks of the House Un-American Activities Committee (HUAC), filled the nation's press and airwaves with charges and countercharges. Fear replaced logic, as it had in the "Red Scare" of 1918 to 1920.

Winston Churchill, who had maintained the traditional British opposition to the Soviet Union throughout the war, traveled to the United States in 1946. Appearing with Truman in Fulton, Missouri, he coined the phrase "Iron Curtain," saying "From Stettin in the Baltic to Trieste in the Adriatic an iron curtain has descended across the Continent." The Cold War rhetoric increased in intensity. In later years historians criticized Truman and other Allied leaders for not presenting a more compromising program to the Soviets, but instead triggering their fears that a hostile Anglo-American alliance was being set up to thwart their natural interests, as it had been following World War I.

On the other hand, the Soviet occupation of Eastern Europe, arguments over the reunification of Germany, and a generally belligerent Russian attitude did little to reassure Americans about Stalin's motives. Truman feared Communist expansion into southern Europe and acted quickly in 1947 to promise economic aid to Greece and Turkey. These acts were part of the Truman Doctrine—the beginning of America's "containment policy." This included the Marshall Plan for the redevelopment of Western Europe in 1947, the airlifting of supplies to break a Soviet blockade of Berlin in 1948, the Point Four Program for underdeveloped nations in 1949, and the creation of the North Atlantic Treaty Organization (NATO), also in 1949. These constituted a mixture of humanitarian and military programs, meshing together as elements of the "Cold War."

Europe was made secure against the perceived Communist threat there, but the President and his advisers could do little about the spread of Communism in Asia. Despite sizable American assistance, the Nationalist forces of warlord Chiang Kai-shek were losing the struggle with the People's Liberation Army under Mao Tse-tung. The Truman administration sent General George C. Marshall on a futile mission to attempt a coalition of the Nationalist and Communist regimes, in the wake of a disastrous effort by the nearly senile American ambassador, General Patrick Hurley, to have Chiang and Mao meet. Hurley resigned, and blamed the State Department China experts and embassy staff for losing China, a theme picked up in the McCarthy era by the entire right wing of American thought. China scholars in universities and journalists in China were likewise harassed. Theodore White and Annalee Jacoby of Time-Life found themselves denounced by conservative newspapers and politicians following the 1946 publication of their best-selling book, *Thunder Out of China.* They and John Hershey testified that their copy was altered by *Time* foreign-news editor Whittaker Chambers.[19]

Edgar Snow, newspaper correspondent and author, went to China in the late 1920s, and scored a journalistic beat by reaching Yenan in 1936 to interview the veterans of the Long March, led by Mao and Chou En-lai. Snow's *Red Star Over China* and his friendships with the Communist leaders brought such McCarthy-era reprisals that he fled to Switzerland. Rivaling Snow as leading journalists in China during the 1940s and authorities on the Communist-led revolution were Anna Louise Strong and Agnes Smedley, correspondents and authors whose radical beliefs made them most popular in the *New Masses.* Tilliman Durdin, Walter Sullivan, and Henry Lieberman of the *New York Times,* A. T. Steele of the *Chicago Daily News* and *New York Herald Tribune,* and Jack Belden and Albert Ravenholt of the UP were among the other reporters who tried to tell the China story. They found their efforts disregarded. The Luce publications, the Scripps-Howard newspapers, and others built up Chiang's reputation, despite well-documented evidence of his regime's corruptness and unpopularity with the people. American public opinion rejected Mao, Chou En-lai, and other Communist leaders as "Red bandits." Julian Schuman of the AP and ABC and John and Sylvia Powell of the *China Weekly Review* were indicted for treason, and won freedom only after 7 years of charges and trials. Later Schuman became editor of the English-language *China Daily* in Beijing, where Israel Epstein of the UP had remained to edit a glossy magazine, *China Reconstructs.*

When Mao's army entered the Chinese capital in 1949, and Chiang fled to

Formosa (later called Taiwan), American diplomatic and journalistic ties with the new People's Republic of China ceased. Snow, who left in 1949, returned in 1960 to Beijing and for a decade was the only American correspondent there. In 1970 he was saluted alongside Mao at Tien An Men square. He died just before President Nixon's arrival in China, an event foreshadowing the rehabilitation of the China diplomats, scholars, and correspondents of the 1940s.

But in 1949 these Chinese supporters suffered the wrath of those who felt the United States' postwar role was to be the world's policeman. The right wing's anger was only increased by the news that the nationalist-Marxist forces of Ho Chi Minh in Indochina were slowly winning their war against the American-supported French army. Truman was ardently anti-Communist—as demonstrated by his tough actions in Europe—and he gave American aid during these Asian civil wars, but he argued strongly against all-out intervention.

NEW YORK DAILIES REACH THEIR PEAK

The flourishing of newspapers in the immediate postwar years was best illustrated in New York, where the nine major dailies boasted a daily circulation of slightly more than 6 million, nearly double the 1983 total for the three major dailies. Every Sunday readers bought 10.1 million copies of the six available newspapers, including 4.7 million copies of the *Daily News,* which reached its all-time circulation peak in 1947, selling 2.4 million copies of its daily morning edition.

Hearst's *Journal-American* sold nearly 1.3 million copies on Sunday and about 700,000 every evening and his *Mirror* topped that, with 2.2 million in Sunday sales and slightly more than 1 million on weekday mornings. The *Times* had reached the million mark in Sunday sales the previous year and had morning sales of about 545,000. The *Herald Tribune* sold 680,000 copies on Sunday and 320,000 each morning. Another 300,000 persons bought the Sunday edition of *PM,* which was nearing the end of its publishing life as a daily journal of opinion and interpretation.

The Hearst and McCormick-Patterson companies greatly outsold their more moderate rivals, the *Times* and the *Herald Tribune,* at the time that President Truman and the Democrats began to look ahead to the 1948 campaign.

TRUMAN'S ELECTION: THE MIRACLE OF 1948

Facing an election in 1948, Truman was not given much of a chance of continuing in office. Southern Democrats, led by Strom Thurmond of South Carolina, bolted from the party and founded the Dixiecrats. The loss of the Democratic party's traditional hold on the "Solid South" was compounded when former Vice President Henry Wallace challenged Truman under the banner of the Progressives and stole some liberal support. Sensing an easy victory, Republicans nominated the popular governor of New York, Thomas E. Dewey, who had lost to Roosevelt in 1944.

Throughout the summer the nation's leading editorial writers and political

Prime evidence of Republican overconfidence—one of the most quoted headlines in history.

columnists described Dewey's strength and Truman's inability to forge a winning coalition. Walter Lippmann, Drew Pearson, Joseph and Stewart Alsop, Marquis Childs, and others wrote of the coming disaster to the Democratic party. But that fall the determined President retaliated by taking his case to the people in the most dramatic "Whistlestop" campaign of the twentieth century. In town after town Truman pulled no punches, attacking the Republican Eightieth Congress and relating to problems in that particular locality. Republicans pounded away on the issue of "Communist subversion." But as the campaign drew to a close, Truman's crowds grew in size and enthusiasm. Although this was noted by some of the traveling reporters, others dismissed the change in atmosphere. By November 1 Truman had caught Dewey, but the Gallup Poll, as reported that morning by the *Washington Post,* predicted Dewey's win: "Gallup Gives Dewey 49.5%, Truman 44.5% of Popular Vote."[20] The November 1 *Life* magazine included a photo of Dewey, with the caption: "The next President travels by ferry boat over the broad waters of San Francisco Bay."[21]

An early edition of the *Chicago Tribune* was handed to Truman when the White House-bound presidential train reached St. Louis on November 3, the day after the election. The unforgettable headline blared "Dewey Defeats Truman," and the *Tribune* never lived it down. During the previous evening NBC commentator Hans Von Kaltenborn had been telling his listeners that the early Truman lead in popular vote could not hold up. But it did, providing an enormous excitement over Truman's achievement. The *Washington Post* of November 4 paid the ultimate tribute, running on page one a copy of a telegram sent to Truman inviting him to a "crow banquet" to which "this newspaper proposes to invite newspaper editorial writers, political reporters and editors, including our own, along with pollsters, radio commentators and columnists for the purpose of providing a repast appropriate to the appetite created by the late elections."[22] Truman not only upset Dewey; he conquered the Republican campaign of fear and carried a Democratic Congress into office with him, despite having the support of only 15 percent of the dailies endorsing a candidate that year.

TRUMAN AND THE PRESS CONFERENCE

The relationship of the president and the news media underwent drastic changes during Truman's nearly 8 years in office. The Truman style, the complexity of events after World War II, and the growth of the news-gathering apparatus—particularly broadcasting—during and after the war contributed to the metamorphosis.

Although Truman and the newspeople around him enjoyed a cordial personal relationship—they generally liked each other—professionally, they remained sharp adversaries throughout his 93 months in office. As president, he held 324 news conferences, averaging three to four a month. This was half of Roosevelt's annual total, but nearly twice as many as any of his successors. The President's abrupt and sometimes unpredictable comments at these sessions often appeared strangely contradictory to a period dominated by the realities of atomic energy and cold-war politics.

If reporters relished the Truman news conferences for the possibility of an unexpected and sensational utterance, they also came to realize that the structure of the conferences was changing to give the administration more control over them. Truman began meeting with press secretary Charles G. Ross and others of his staff for preconference briefings and greatly increased the use of carefully prepared opening statements to which he would refer a questioning reporter when he chose not to elaborate on a matter.

In the spring of 1950, the location of presidential news conferences was moved from the intimate atmosphere of the Oval Room of the White House to a 230-seat room in the Executive Office Building. Though the change was brought about because of the growth in the number of Washington correspondents, its effect was to further formalize the presidential press conference. The move also ushered in the use of microphones and, by 1951, presidential authorization to use excerpts of recordings for broadcast news programs. As news conferences thereby became increasingly public during the Truman years, the President was obliged to exercise greater control over them, to come to them better prepared, and to respond during them with greater care. Truman's tendency to speak his mind, or "shoot from the hip" as some critics termed it, was not obscured entirely by the new overlay of safeguards. Salty, sometimes embarrassing slips continued despite preparation to prevent them. But the groundwork of control was laid for his successors.

Apart from the news conference, another effort to control information created a furor among publishers and correspondents during the Korean War. Convinced that magazines and newspapers were guilty of leaking most of America's military secrets, Truman ordered all government agencies handling military information to classify it at their discretion and to restrict its use by the media. Despite a wave of criticism, the order stood.

Truman responded to harsh and continuing criticism of himself and his administration by the news media with strong denunciations of the media. After his stunning election in 1948 the President lashed out at "the kept press and the paid radio." He attacked what he called the "confusion of fact with mere speculation by which readers and listeners were undoubtedly misguided and intentionally deceived."

Only when he prepared to leave office in January, 1953, did some media opponents relent. Some even saluted him affectionately. It was an unexpected pleasure for the retiring Truman, who later recalled that "some editors ate crow and left the feathers on."[23]

THE WAR IN KOREA, 1950 to 1953

The news of the Communist North Korean attack on the Republic of South Korea on June 25, 1950, was first flashed to the world by Jack James of the UP. Headed for a Sunday morning picnic, James stumbled onto the invasion story at the U.S. embassy in Seoul and after confirming it got off his bulletin, which beat the ambassador's cable to Washington by 20 minutes.

Korea had been divided at the thirty-eighth parallel for occupation purposes in 1945. Russian troops left North Korea after the establishment of a government there in 1948, and Americans left South Korea, save for a small advisory force, early in 1949. No one expected an attack in Korea; State Department representative John Foster Dulles had been in Seoul a week before and had left reassured of the area's stability. The bad news that James and others sent by wireless brought a decision by Secretary of State Dean Acheson and President Truman to seek a United Nations armed intervention, which was voted by the Security Council June 28 after Truman had ordered General Douglas MacArthur to force the North Koreans back.

Walter Simmons of the *Chicago Tribune,* who had traveled to Seoul with Dulles, had stayed on and filed the first action story by a newspaper correspondent. The press associations rushed in Peter Kalischer and Rutherford Poats, UP; O. H. P. King and photographer Charles P. Gorry, AP; and Ray Richards, INS. Richards was the first to fly over the battle area; caught with a lost battalion at Chonan, he was killed 10 days after his arrival. Eleven American correspondents were killed before the war was over, among a total of eighteen from all nations.[24]

Two of the toughest and most outspoken stars of the Korean news brigade

THE WEATHER

NEW YORK Herald Tribune

A European Edition Is Published Daily in Paris

Late City Edition

VOL. CX No. 37,850 — MONDAY, JULY 3, 1950 — FIVE CENTS

U. S. Troops Face Battle in Korea Today; 4 Red Columns Breach Han River Line

Ships Collide At Night; 35 Saved in Bay

11,000-Ton Collier Rams Sand Dredge

Latter Goes Down in 10 Minutes; Crew Rescued in Spite of Heavy Tide

By Earl Mazo

A Spinster's Counsel to Wives: Get a Job, Help Support Family

Dr. Scott Says Husbands Die Early by Overwork for Economic Parasites

By Richard K. Winslow

Dr. K. Frances Scott

U.S. Warships Sink Korean Navy Vessels

British Help to Bag Five Torpedo Boats

U.S. Troops Deploying to Front; MacArthur Puts Gen. Dean in Command

By Homer Bigart

First American Infantry in Korea

Ground troops manning a machine gun atop a truck moving up to the front in South Korea

Felled Plane Has Russian Red Insigne

4 Others in Battle Carry Soviets' Star

Red Tank Columns Sweep Past Suwon; Situation Is 'Seriously Worsened'

By Marguerite Higgins

'Free Europe' To Broadcast to Red Satellites

Radio at Undisclosed Spot to Supplement Messages of the Voice of America

By Edwin Hartrich

Moscow Protest On Potato Bugs Alarms Berlin

West Suspects Blockade May Be Revived to Divert Resources From Korea

By Joseph Newman

Union Rejects U.S. War Plea to End Rail Strike

Switchmen Offer to Help Move 'Essential' Goods; 'Impractical,' Roads Say

First American Casualty List

His 1897 Baseball At Hand, Man Dies

Gas Kills Old-Time Pitcher Who Saved Trophy

First Partial Mobilization Step In U.S. May Be Taken This Week

Move Envisaged as Preparation for Any Soviet Action; Call for Volunteer Reserves Possible

By David Lawrence

In and Out of the City on the Holiday Week End

Troop Planes Circle 6 Hours Over Korea

The Korean War opens for U.S. troops; Marguerite Higgins and Homer Bigart report.

flew to Seoul June 27 from Tokyo under fighter escort. They were Marguerite Higgins of the *New York Herald Tribune* and Keyes Beech of the *Chicago Daily News.*[25] Landing with them at Kimpo airfield were Burton Crane of the *New York Times* and Frank Gibney of *Time.* They were routed from the city during the night as Seoul fell; the men missed death by 25 yards at the River Han and Higgins flew back to Tokyo to file her story. She returned June 29 with General MacArthur on his first visit to the front and got an exclusive interview on the return trip. The next day she, Beech, Tom Lambert of the AP, and Gordon Walker of the *Christian Science Monitor* were at the fall of Suwon airfield. With Carl Mydans of *Life* and the bureau chief of Reuters, Ray McCartney, Higgins saw the first U.S. soldier killed in action July 5. David Douglas Duncan of *Life*

Marguerite Higgins.
Editor & Publisher

was taking the first of his great Korean war photographs and *Life*'s July 10 issue brought home the war to a country not yet linked by television.

The South Koreans and their American reinforcements were being forced back on the beachhead port of Pusan. Its outer defense, Taejon, fell in late July and General William P. Dean was captured. By now many more reporters were risking their lives in the foxholes, rice paddies, and back roads. The *Herald Tribune* sent Homer Bigart to relieve Higgins but she refused to leave Korea and engaged in a give-and-take duel with Bigart for front-page play. The AP sent Relman Morin, Don Whitehead, and Hal Boyle, all veteran war reporters. Fred Sparks came to work with Keyes Beech for the *Chicago Daily News.* When the Pulitzer Prize committee met the following April they honored the *Herald Tribune,* the *Daily News,* and the AP by giving six awards to Bigart and Higgins, Beech and Sparks, Morin and Whitehead. (At that point in time, no one from the UP or the INS had ever won a Pulitzer Prize.) Behind the correspondents at the front were the bureau chiefs in Tokyo, Earnest Hoberecht of the UP, Russell Brines of the AP, Howard Handleman of the INS, and William H. Lawrence coordinating for the *New York Times.* Edward R. Murrow came to tie CBS coverage together; broadcast coverage was essentially by radio, with film being shot for television and newsreels.

Instead of being driven off the Korean beachhead, MacArthur mounted a brilliant amphibious landing with troops from Japan at Inchon on September 15, and he recaptured Seoul on September 26, thus cutting off the North Koreans to the south. One of the correspondents present was Jim G. Lucas, the chronicler of Tarawa, now reporting for Scripps-Howard. Lucas was to win a 1954 Pulitzer Prize for his stories of "Porkchop Hill" during the long stalemate. Another Pulitzer award went to Max Desfor, AP photographer.

MACARTHUR AND THE PRESS; CENSORSHIP IMPOSED

General MacArthur, as United Nations commander in Korea, at first left correspondents to their own devices, refusing to institute the field censorship that had prevailed during both World Wars I and II. In the confused situation of the first months of the fighting, the traditional-minded "team member" reporters found themselves on their own in the thick of battle. Ironically, they also found themselves subject to harsh criticism from MacArthur's staff for stories filed without receiving minimum military assistance. Lambert of the AP and Kalischer of the UP temporarily lost their accreditations on charges of giving aid and comfort to the enemy. Relations between Colonel Marion P. Echols, MacArthur's press officer, and the correspondents became even more strained than they had been during the years of the occupation of Japan, when dissenting reporters had found their accreditations endangered.

The September, 1950, victories following MacArthur's Inchon landing brought an easing of the correspondents' problems. Their interviews with critical and despondent soldiers, which had aroused MacArthur's ire earlier in the summer, were at an end. Nearly 300 correspondents from nineteen countries were reporting the controversial advance of United Nations troops toward the Yalu. Then came the entry of the Chinese Communist army into the war and a disastrous retreat of the UN's units, best pictured by *Life*'s Duncan, with the Marines at Chosin reservoir. Seoul fell to the Chinese in January but was regained 2 months later as the UN forces stabilized a line near the thirty-eighth parallel. Keyes Beech had reported that at the height of the retreat panic MacArthur had recommended withdrawal from Korea, and other correspondents had criticized MacArthur's tactics in splitting the commands of his forces in northern Korea. The general's answer was the institution of a full and formal censorship, which he claimed had been recommended by the country's top newspaper executives.[26]

Stringent regulations imposed in January, 1951, went further, however, than any reporters would have desired.[27] These regulations covered not only censorship of military information but also all statements that would injure the morale of UN forces or that would embarrass the United States, its allies, or neutral countries. Correspondents complained that use of the word *retreat* was interpreted by the censors as being embarrassing, and they contended that MacArthur had brought about a political and psychological censorship, as well as a military one. The most dangerous provision of the new censorship was one making correspondents subject to trial by court martial for serious violations of the rules.

TRUMAN FIRES MACARTHUR: A PRESIDENTIAL CRISIS

President Truman and his commander in the field were at odds throughout the war. MacArthur had received high marks for his handling of Japan's postwar problems—and in fact he was later called the "father of modern Japan" because of his keen understanding of sensitive issues—but he was also giving the impression that he intended to make American foreign policy. In July, 1950, his visit to Formosa was seen at home as a new step in United States-Nationalist relations, despite State Department and White House misgivings about Chiang Kai-shek. The General also ignored Pentagon and White House instructions on the issue of public statements, particularly after disagreements arose on how to conduct the war.

Of concern in Washington was MacArthur's desire to use Chiang's troops against mainland China. In this plan he was supported by Senator Robert A. Taft of Ohio and other Republican conservatives who had been sniping at Truman for "losing China to the Communists." Civilian control of the military was at stake. Truman and MacArthur met on Wake Island in October, 1950, and appeared to reach some sort of understanding, but MacArthur persisted in pushing his ideas through friendly members of Congress. This greatly irritated Truman, who became enraged on April 5, 1951, when Joseph Martin, the House minority leader, released a letter from MacArthur in which the General complained about White House restrictions on his battle plans. One idea was to use Allied planes to bomb across the Yalu River, the dividing line between North Korea and Chinese-held Manchuria. The use of the atomic bomb against the Chinese was fully contemplated, and was encouraged by MacArthur's supporters.

The *New York Times* told of MacArthur's plans for a second front and greatly expanded war: "M'Arthur Wants Chiang Army Used on China Mainland."[28] This was followed by a week of intense controversy in American and European newspapers. Senator Joseph McCarthy of Wisconsin called it "high treason" to refuse MacArthur permission to use Chiang's troops. Others protested MacArthur's disdain of Truman and the United Nations, under whose command he was to serve. Then on April 11 Truman acted, removing MacArthur from all responsibility.

"Impeach Truman" cried the *Chicago Tribune* in a page-one editorial. "President Truman must be impeached and convicted. His hasty and vindictive removal of Gen. MacArthur is the culmination of a series of acts which have shown he is unfit, morally and mentally, for the office."[29] Truman defended his decision in a nationwide broadcast in which he said that MacArthur's actions had threatened a general war—in effect, World War III. The *New York Times, St. Louis Post-Dispatch,* and a number of other major newspapers fully supported Truman, while the Gallup Poll showed that nearly 70 percent of the people were caught up in the enthusiasm for MacArthur. Millions watched MacArthur's speech to a joint session of Congress and showered him with affection during tickertape parades in major cities, beginning in San Francisco. Paying tribute to a military hero of gigantic proportions, the crowds were giving belated thanks for MacArthur's World War II service as much as certifying his Korean record.

A new offensive in Korea and the passing of time took the edge off the story, however, and the General soon passed into private life. As he had told Congress, " . . . old generals never die, they just fade away." Seen in a different light, years later, Truman's action appeared vindicated because of MacArthur's reckless handling of his forces when Communist China entered the war in October, 1950, and his deliberate attempts to disobey orders. In addition to the conventional criticism of MacArthur's attitude and handling of his command, alternative journalists I. F. Stone and James Aronson added their interpretations. In his *The Hidden History of the Korean War* written in 1952, Stone offered evidence that MacArthur forced the Chinese into combat by probing dangerously close to the Yalu River, ignoring a buffer zone. He also strongly suggested that American fears of a Communist Chinese presence in the United Nations ruined chances for an early armistice, despite Russian attempts to bring the fighting to a halt.[30]

A TRUCE IN KOREA

The removal of MacArthur for insubordination brought another easing of the censorship situation, although his chief intelligence officer, Major General C. A. Willoughby, continued to attack such respected reporters as Hal Boyle, Hanson W. Baldwin, Homer Bigart, and Joseph Alsop as "inaccurate, biased, and petulant." When truce negotiations began in Korea in July, 1951, the United Nations Command insisted that reporters be permitted to cover the truce site. Reporting of the war during the prolonged negotiations became a routine affair, punctuated by excitement over the status of prisoners of war. The Defense Department issued new field-censorship instructions in December, 1952, which transferred censorship duties from intelligence officers to public-relations officers, and put the Army, Navy, and Air Force under a uniform plan. Censorship for reasons other than those involving security was forbidden, but as usual the disagreement between newspeople and censors about a definition of "security" continued to the end.

The signing of a truce at Panmunjom in July, 1953, brought an end to the fighting phase of the Korean War. The repatriated prisoners, whose fate had been such an issue, reappeared at the "Bridge of No Return." In the 1980s the UN Command, through U.S. troops, still stood guard at Panmunjom. No peace had yet been signed. The war cost 33,629 United States dead, 1263 other UN allied dead, some 2 million Korean casualties, and several hundred thousand Chinese losses. The principle involved, that the will of the United Nations could not be openly flaunted, had been defended. But one view held that it had been defended by the first recapture of Seoul and that MacArthur's advance to the Yalu River boundary of Communist China had changed the character of the war and had polarized Chinese-American relations for two decades.

The Korean fighting soon merged in the minds of Americans with other events, but future generations would learn of the tragedy, irony, and humor of those days through the television show *M*A*S*H.* The partisanship by those in the field questioning about the purpose of the war, and commenting about people's taking sides at home, became part of television history.

NOTES

1. Erik Barnouw, *The Golden Web* (New York: Oxford University Press, 1968), p. 151.

2. William Manchester, *The Glory and the Dream* (Boston: Little, Brown, 1973), p. 273.

3. *Atlanta Constitution,* December 30, 1940, p. 1.

4. Manchester, *The Glory and the Dream,* p. 267.

5. United Press, December 7, 1941.

6. Christopher H. Sterling and John M. Kitross, *Stay Tuned: A Concise History of American Broadcasting* (Belmont, Calif.: Wadsworth, 1978), p. 203.

7. Ernest D. Rose, "How the U.S. Heard about Pearl Harbor," *Journal of Broadcasting,* V (Fall 1961), 285–98.

8. Gordon W. Prague, *At Dawn We Slept* (New York: McGraw-Hill, 1981), p. 5.

9. Ibid., p. 583.

10. The activities of the Office of Censorship and the work of other individuals are described by Theodore F. Koop, an AP man and assistant to Price, in *Weapon of Silence* (Chicago: University of Chicago Press, 1946). Sorrells, Howard, managing editor Jack Lockhart of the *Memphis Commercial Appeal,* and Koop were successive heads of the voluntary press-censorship division. J. Howard Ryan directed the radio division.

11. Elmer Davis, "OWI Has a Job," *Public Opinion Quarterly,* VII (Spring 1943), 8. For Davis' account of his stewardship, see "Report to the President," *Journalism Monographs,* No. 7 (August 1968), edited by Ronald T. Farrar. See also Robert L. Bishop and LaMar S. Mackay, "Government Information in World War II," *Journalism Monographs,* No. 19 (May 1971).

12. OWI operated everywhere abroad except in Latin America, where Nelson Rockefeller's Office of the Coordinator of Inter-American Affairs held jurisdiction.

13. Jerome E. Edwards, *The Foreign Policy of Col. McCormick's Tribune, 1929–1941* (Reno: University of Nevada Press, 1971), pp. 176–179, 209.

14. *St. Joseph's Gazette,* June 6, 1944, p. 1, a typical front page that day.

15. *San Francisco Chronicle,* February 19, 1945, p. 1.

16. For the full story, see Bernard Asbell, *When F.D.R. Died* (New York: Holt, Rinehart & Winston, 1961).

17. *New York Herald Tribune,* April 13, 1945, p. 1.

18. *New York Times,* September 9, 1945, p. 1.

19. See Theodore White, *In Search of History* (New York: Harper & Row, 1978), pp. 254–58; James C. Thomson, Jr., and Walter Sullivan, "China Reporting Revisited . . . The Crucial 1940's," *Nieman Reports,* XXXVII (Spring 1983), 30–34, a report on a 1982 reunion of surviving U.S. correspondents; and Lois Wheeler Snow, *Edgar Snow's China* (New York: Random House, 1981), an assembling of Snow's writings and photos by his wife.

20. *Washington Post,* November 1, 1948, p. 1.

21. *Life,* November 1, 1948, closing page.

22. *Washington Post,* November 4, 1948, p. 1.

23. See Randall L. Murray, "Harry S. Truman and Press Opinion, 1945–53," Ph.D. thesis, University of Minnesota, 1973.

24. Four of the dead were from INS: Ray Richards and Frank Emery, correspondents, and Charles D. Rosecrans, Jr., and Ken Inouye, photographers. Nine of the total of eighteen died in front-line fighting; nine in air crashes. Among them were Wilson Fielder, *Time-Life;* Charles O. Supple, *Chicago Sun-Times;* Albert Hinton, *Norfolk Journal and Guide,* first black correspondent to lose his life covering a U.S. war; and Ernie Peeler, *Pacific Stars and Stripes.*

25. For an evaluation and account of the early weeks of the war coverage, see Michael Emery, "The American Mass Media and the Coverage of Five Major Foreign Events, 1900–1950" (Ph.D. thesis, University of Minnesota, 1968), pp. 316–72.

26. In a letter to *Editor & Publisher,* LXXXIV (January 20, 1951), 7.

27. The text of the censorship code was carried in *Editor & Publisher,* LXXXIV (January 13, 1951), 8.

28. *New York Times,* April 6, 1951, p. 1.

29. *Chicago Tribune,* April 12, 1951, p. 1.

30. I. F. Stone, *The Hidden History of the Korean War* (New York: Monthly Review Press, 1952). See Chapter 18, "First Warnings," and Chapter 38, "Every Time Stalin Smiles."

ANNOTATED BIBLIOGRAPHY

Books

BLUM, JOHN, *V Was For Victory: Politics and American Culture During World War II.* New York: Harcourt Brace Jovanovich, 1976. Scholarly history, including material on propaganda.

CARROLL, WALLACE, *Persuade or Perish.* Boston: Houghton Mifflin, 1948. An excellent account of the World War II propaganda effort.

DONOVAN, ROBERT J., *Conflict and Crisis: The Presidency of Harry S. Truman, 1945–48.* New York: Norton, 1977. See also Donovan, *Tumultuous Years, 1949–53* (1982). Well-balanced accounts.

FARRAR, RONALD T., *The Reluctant Servant: The Story of Charles G. Ross.* Columbia: University of Missouri Press, 1969. Ross was a longtime *St. Louis Post-Dispatch* star before serving as President Truman's press secretary from 1945 to 1950.

FEIS, HERBERT, *From Trust to Terror: The Onset of the Cold War, 1945–1950.* New York: Norton, 1970. A scholarly examination of six fateful years.

GOLDMAN, ERIC F., *The Crucial Decade: America, 1945–1955.* New York: Knopf, 1956. A sequel to *Rendezvous with Destiny.* See also Joseph C. Goulden, *The Best Years: 1945–50* (New York: Atheneum, 1976); Peter Joseph, *Good Times: An Oral History of America in the Nineteen Sixties* (New York: Charterhouse, 1973). Cover from the postwar years to the changes of the 1960s.

IRONS, PETER, *Justice at War: The Story of the Japanese American Internment Cases.* New York: Oxford University Press, 1983. Liberals failed to defend civil rights principles.

KOOP, THEODORE F., *Weapon of Silence.* Chicago: University of Chicago Press, 1946. The story of the World War II Office of Censorship by one of its principal executives.

LANGER, WILLIAM L., and S. EVERETT GLEASON, *The Challenge to Isolation, 1937–1940;* and *The Undeclared War, 1940–1941.* New York: Harper & Row, 1952–53. An exhaustive, well-documented analysis in two volumes, published for The Council on Foreign Relations under the joint title, "World Crisis and American Foreign Policy." It fairly and objectively traces the story of American entrance into World War II.

LERNER, DANIEL, ed., *Propaganda in War and Crisis.* New York: George W. Stewart, 1951. A collection of writings in the field of psychological warfare, giving the background of twentieth-century war propaganda efforts.

MEYER, ROBERT, Jr., *The "Stars and Stripes" Story of World War II.* New York: McKay, 1960. Anthology of stories, with background.

MIDDLETON, DREW, *Where Has Last July Gone? Memoirs.* New York: Quadrangle, 1973. Details his career as a *New York Times* correspondent, with focus on World War II.

MILLER, LEE G. *The Story of Ernie Pyle.* New York: Viking, 1950. Biography of the famed World War II columnist.

MILLER, MERLE, *Plain Speaking.* New York: G. P. Putnam's Sons, 1973. An oral biography of Harry S. Truman that gives, among many other opinions, the ex-President's views on the press.

MILLER, WEBB, *I Found No Peace.* New York: Simon & Schuster, 1936. One of the best of the foreign correspondents' books by a longtime UP correspondent.

POLLARD, JAMES E., *The Presidents and the Press: Truman to Johnson.* Washington, D.C.: Public Affairs Press, 1964. Continues his earlier study.

PYLE, ERNEST TAYLOR, *Here Is Your War.* New York: Holt, Rinehart & Winston, 1943. A compilation of Pyle's columns.

RAUCH, BASIL, *Roosevelt from Munich to Pearl Harbor.* New York: Creative Age Press, 1950. An able and spirited answer to the isolationist argument.

SHERWOOD, ROBERT E., *Roosevelt and Hopkins.* New York: Harper & Row, 1948. An intimate history of the wartime partnership by the writer-confidant of FDR.

SNOW, LOIS WHEELER, *Edgar Snow's China.* New York: Random House, 1981. His wife covers Snow's reporting career, from 1928 to 1949, using his writing and photos. Snow foresaw Mao's victory.

SNYDER, LOUIS L., ed., *Masterpieces of War Reporting.* New York: Julian Messner, 1962. Great moments of World War II.

SORENSEN, THOMAS C., *The World War: The Story of American Propaganda.* New York: Harper & Row, 1968. Focuses on USIA in postwar crises.

STEIN, M. L., *Under Fire: The Story of American War Correspondents.* New York: Julian Messner, 1968. Good popularly written history.

THOMSON, CHARLES A. H., *Overseas Information*

Service of the United States Government. Washington: Brookings Institution, 1948. Authoritative account.

TOLAND, JOHN, *The Rising Sun: The Decline and Fall of the Japanese Empire, 1936–1945,* 2 vols. New York: Random House, 1970. A comprehensive account of war in the Pacific.

WINKLER, ALLAN M., *The Politics of Propaganda: The Office of War Information, 1942–1945.* New Haven; Yale University Press, 1978. Favorable detailed account.

Periodicals and Monographs

The files of the *Journalism Quarterly* and *Public Opinion Quarterly* contain many important articles published about World War II censorship and propaganda activities. See particularly the Spring 1943 issue of *Public Opinion Quarterly* and *Journalism Quarterly* from 1942 to 1944. Other important articles include the following:

BISHOP, ROBERT L., and LAMAR S. MACKAY, "Mysterious Silence, Lyrical Scream: Government Information in World War II," *Journalism Monographs,* No. 19 (May 1971). The OWI.

BROWNE, DONALD R., "The Voice of America: Policies and Problems," *Journalism Monographs,* No. 43 (February 1976). A comprehensive account.

DAVIS, ELMER, "Report to the President," edited by Ronald T. Farrar, *Journalism Monographs,* No. 7 (August 1968). On his OWI stewardship.

FARRAR, RONALD, "Harry Truman and the Press: A View From Inside," *Journalism History,* VIII (Summer 1981), 56. Based on research in the Truman Library.

FITZPATRICK, DICK, "America's Campaign of Truth Throughout the World," *Journalism Quarterly,* XXVIII (Winter 1951), 3.

LARSON, CEDRIC, "OWI's Domestic News Bureau: An Account and Appraisal," *Journalism Quarterly,* XXVI (March 1949), 3.

MILLER, ROBERT C., "Censorship in Korea," *Nieman Reports,* VI (July 1952), 3.

MURRAY, RANDALL L., "Harry S. Truman and Press Opinion: 1945–1953," Ph.D. thesis, University of Minnesota, 1973. Documented analysis of the influence of press opinion on the President; also excellent for details of Truman's press relations.

STEVENS, JOHN D., "From the Back of the Foxhole: Black Correspondents in World War II," *Journalism Monographs,* No. 27 (February 1973).

THOMSON, JAMES C., JR., and WALTER SULLIVAN, "China Reporting Revisited . . . The Crucial 1940's," *Nieman Reports,* XXXVII (Spring 1983), 30. The survivors of the U.S. press corps in China during the 1940s reassemble.

An RCA television assembly line, 1950.
Bettmann Archive

23

Television Takes Center Stage

It is much easier to report a battle or a bombing than it is to do an honest and intelligible job on the Marshall Plan, the Taft-Hartley Law or the Atlantic Pact.

—Edward R. Murrow

The decade of the 1950s is best remembered for Lucille Ball, Ed Sullivan, and Edward R. Murrow on television, Dwight Eisenhower, Adlai Stevenson, and Joseph McCarthy in politics, the New York Yankees, Elvis Presley, Madison Avenue, Hula-Hoops, drive-in movies, suburban tract homes, interstate highways, and jet airplanes. Later portrayed in the television show *Happy Days* and the motion picture *American Graffiti* as a tranquil, rather uneventful time, the period was actually filled with moments of grave consequence for Americans, as the nation moved toward the explosions of the 1960s and early 1970s.

While America struggled with the problems of postwar adjustment—labor strife, a faltering economy, housing shortages—seeds were sown for future confrontations. The "containment policy" of Truman became the "brinksmanship policy" of Eisenhower and his Secretary of State, John Foster Dulles. A decision was made to ignore the victory of Communist guerrillas in Indochina and to assume the French role there by aiding a weak government in Saigon. This fear of international Communism and internal subversion turned neighbor against neighbor as Senator McCarthy, Richard Nixon, and others skillfully exploited the situation.

Long-suffering blacks in Montgomery boycotted the local bus company and a dispute over the integration of a Little Rock high school became a nationwide controversy. Martin Luther King, Jr.'s, name appeared in the *New*

York Times for the first time. A Supreme Court ruling that the "separate but equal" doctrine for the nation's schools was unconstitutional gave blacks hope that other doors would soon be opened.

Little was said about damage to the environment, abuses by law-enforcement officials, or the need for greater consumer protection, except in alternative publications or in an occasional news story or broadcast documentary. Yet those problems existed while the powerful business and industrial community consolidated its hold on the nation's political, economic and social life during the 1950s.

Instead, the entertainment media—television, radio, movies, magazines, books—aimed to treat the American viewer and reader in an unprecedented way. "See the USA, in a Chevrolet, America's the greatest land of all," crooned Dinah Shore. Such messages struck a common nerve. Americans were ready for fun and excitement after a number of tough years. They were upset that the Korean War had broken out. The Russians and Chinese ruled a good share of the globe, Communist spies had stolen atomic secrets, and the good life was still around the corner. But this was their chance to strive for the American dream, as presented to them daily through mass-media advertising and certified by public relations.

Newspapers, the press associations, news magazines, and radio and television news departments also began to change, faced with the task of interpreting the meaning of those days, when the simplicity of American life began to get confusingly complex.

TELEVISION SHAPES THE 1952 CAMPAIGN

Television became the dominant force in the American political process during the 1952 presidential campaign between General of the Army Dwight D. Eisenhower, the candidate of a frustrated Republican party, and Illinois Governor Adlai E. Stevenson, the choice of Democratic leaders hoping for another 4 years of power. For the first time the public was exposed to commercials, documentaries, and election-night specials, all planned by political consultants and paid for by campaign boosters. The excitement began with Eisenhower's televised announcement that he would challenge Senator Robert A. Taft for his party's nomination, and grew as the conventions of summer 1952 drew near.[1]

The audience not only recognized the familiar faces of political heroes, but also saw new heroes created. The manipulations of rival groups were clear to all, particularly during the Republican convention when Eisenhower forces—pleading for "fair play"—broke Taft's hold on the convention by challenging the accreditation of delegates from several states. Another high point came when Everett Dirksen of Illinois, a candidate for a United States Senate seat, pointed at Thomas E. Dewey and cried, "We followed you before and you took us down the path to defeat."[2]

The mistake of Taft managers in banning television cameras from credentials hearings gave Eisenhower forces more ammunition for their appeal to the delegates for fairness. The home audience was given the impression that Taft was associated with backroom politics, while "Ike" was above such shady dealings. Actually both men had reasonable claims to the disputed delegates. Finally Eisenhower floor managers convinced delegates to defeat a Taft-sponsored amendment dealing with the credentials fight. The momentum switched to Eisenhower, who came within a few votes of victory at the end of the first ballot. Television cameras picked up the waving Minnesota standard and the official switch of that state's votes, which gave Eisenhower the nomination.

Appearing on television screens during the bitterly contested fight had been Senator Joseph McCarthy of Wisconsin, who scornfully referred to Secretary of State Dean Acheson as "the Red Dean" and Democrats in general as "Commie loving." Richard Nixon, selected by Eisenhower to be his running mate, joined in the denunciation of the "whining, whimpering, groveling" Democrats, as did John Foster Dulles. During lulls a young actress named Betty Furness became famous by opening and shutting the doors of Westinghouse refrigerators for the estimated 50 million persons who tuned in for at least one of the sessions.

When the Democrats met to find a replacement for President Truman, who had decided not to run again, they settled on Stevenson and Senator Estes Kefauver of Tennessee, who had gained fame with televised hearings of organized-crime operations. Kefauver had started a fad by wearing a Davy Crockett coonskin cap. He led Stevenson on the first two ballots, but saw the nomination slip away. Stevenson began the campaign with a remarkable speech, saying that the nation was "on the eve of great decisions" and reminding Americans that they lived "in an hour of history haunted with those gaunt, grim specters of strife, dissension and materialism at home, and ruthless, inscrutable, and hostile power abroad."

As the campaign developed, television gave the public a chance to learn about the liberal, idealistic Stevenson, the articulate and witty public servant who built a cadre of devoted followers from the progressive wing of the Democratic party. While listening to his polished speeches, they also saw his flaws, however, and many of them came to agree with the disparaging comment made by columnist Stewart Alsop and popularized by others that Stevenson was an "egghead." Republicans used this in their anti-Communist crusade, implying that intellectuals "lost China" and "sold out" Eastern Europe.

While Stevenson was presenting himself as a gentleman and a scholar, as well as a man of high integrity, Eisenhower's advertising experts took advantage of his sweeping arm waves to crowds and his infectious hearty grin to portray him as a strong leader, a "man of peace." Whereas Eisenhower's 30-minute television shows contained several minutes of opening and closing scenes, Stevenson often had problems fitting his speeches into the half-hour format and audiences saw him still speaking as the shows were cut off the air.

The campaign intensified in September when the Republicans used the slogan "Korea, Crime, Communism, Corruption" to refer to the Roosevelt-Truman years. Nixon, who had become famous during his investigation of the discredited State Department official Alger Hiss, used the name of the convicted perjurer to unfairly link Stevenson to the stealing of secret documents by Russian agents. Newspapers, greatly favoring Eisenhower—only 14.5 percent endorsed Stevenson—freely carried this kind of charge, later causing Stevenson to issue a complaint against a "one party press in a two-party country."

Finally it was Nixon himself in the glare of unfavorable publicity. The *New York Post* broke the story that Nixon's supporters had maintained a "secret slush fund" to help defray campaign expenses. Pressure grew for Nixon to explain in full and for Eisenhower to drop the Californian from the campaign, which had been built on the image of high-level integrity. The Republican National Committee arranged for a nationwide hookup of sixty-four NBC television stations, 194 CBS radio stations, and the Mutual Radio Network, then 560 stations. Speaking with great emotion from a Los Angeles studio, Nixon won back Eisenhower's confidence and that of many Republican voters by offering precise details of his personal expenses, and referring to his wife Pat's cloth coat and his daughters' dog Checkers. The speech became known in broadcast history as the "Checkers speech."[3]

Eisenhower's smashing victory in November ended 20 years of Democratic rule. He had made a pledge during the campaign to "go to Korea" and that December he visited the troops there, with television cameras recording his every move.

EISENHOWER AND THE PRESS

President Eisenhower was not comfortable with television, nor was he able to relax much with reporters. Like other presidents, he had his favorites, but overall he was a private man more familiar with the military life than with the public requirements of his new office. Because of this, he depended on the services of a talented press secretary, James C. Hagerty, who held office for Eisenhower's two terms and who was tauntingly called by some of the newspeople he bested in professional duels "the best Republican president who was never elected." This was unfair to Hagerty, who prided himself on knowing how best to use the press to serve his boss. Eisenhower, in turn, maintained a presidential reserve and dignity in his relations with others, even though they called him Ike.

Eisenhower continued the large formal news conferences that had begun with Truman, having 250 correspondents at his first session and 309 at his final one, 8 years and 190 press conferences later. He permitted direct quotations and taping for later television release, new gains for the press corps. Hagerty, however, had to check the material. Eisenhower made many slips of the tongue, thought faster than he talked, and skipped parts of sentences so that press-conference transcripts had to be reworded to be intelligible. A penetrating personal question might bring a display of the famed Eisenhower controlled anger. But generally he was not too concerned with the press. He told one conference that he went over the important sections of the Sunday papers that reviewed world events and studied them carefully—"but the kind of things you talk of, cartoons and unfriendly quips, I just can't be bothered with."[4] The President had a few bad incidents: Hagerty was mobbed by left-wing demonstrators at the Tokyo airport, forcing cancellation of a presidential visit, and the U-2 spy-plane controversy in 1960 brought about a debacle at the Paris Summit conference.

President Eisenhower and James Hagerty.
UPI

It was the U-2 spy-plane incident that triggered the start of what journalists later called "the credibility gap" between the White House, the press, and the public. When pilot Gary Powers was shot down over Russia the American government issued a statement that he had been flying a weather-surveillance plane which had accidentally strayed off course. But when the Russians produced Powers, a confessed CIA agent, an embarrassed Eisenhower was forced to admit that his administration had lied. The public shock was reflected in the nation's news media. It was one thing to conduct secret operations; it certainly was another thing to lie about it. And Eisenhower, of all persons, was held to be above such conduct. During the next two decades the credibility gap widened considerably and historians pointed to the U-2 story as one glaring starting point for the unfortunate turn of events.

As the first president to travel extensively by jet plane, Eisenhower produced some exciting television coverage of overseas trips. Robert J. Donovan of the *New York Herald Tribune* speculated that the "arrival of the jets . . . changed the presidency more than people realized. There was Eisenhower's great trip to India in 1959—which I covered and which I think was the great spectacle of my life."[5]

EXPANSION OF THE NETWORKS: TV'S GOLDEN AGE

Television had gained a significant place in the American market by 1952. More than 34 percent of the homes—15 million—had television sets. By the end of the decade this figure was 86 percent. NBC and CBS were battling to increase their number of affiliated stations; NBC led sixty-four to thirty-one, with the upstart ABC network trailing with fifteen. DuMont attempted to form a fourth network but dropped from competition in 1955. Regular network service was under way with shows like Milton Berle's *Texaco Star Theatre* and Ed Sullivan's *Toast of the Town.*

In all, there were 108 stations on the air, the number allocated by the FCC when it "froze" the television industry in 1948 to allow for study of a number of issues, particularly for debates over color television and the number of channels needed to meet future demand.[6] In 1952 the FCC provided for VHF (very-high-frequency) television to include channels 2 to 13 and UHF (ultra-high-frequency) stations to range to channel 83. Regarding color, in 1950 the FCC approved a CBS system after acrimonious hearings, but RCA had the support of major manufacturing firms such as DuMont and Philco. CBS was unable to progress and in 1953 the FCC switched, approving RCA's compatible color system, which enables either color or black-and-white sets to receive a show.

The FCC determined that the number of stations would be decided on a city-by-city basis, which permitted more than 2000 channel assignments to 1300 communities, including 242 UHF channels to be set aside for noncommercial educational stations. By 1959 there were 510 stations; of these 485 were affiliated with networks.

Coast-to-coast broadcasting was made possible with the development of coaxial cable. The first lines had been laid by 1946 between New York, Philadelphia, and Washington, and by 1947 to Boston. By 1948 the Midwest was included so that network shows were received simultaneously in the middle and eastern parts of the nation. Finally, in 1951, AT&T completed a microwave relay system to the West Coast, in time for President Truman to address the San Francisco peace conference that officially ended the Pacific war in September. That speech was carried by ninety-four stations. Regular network broadcasting followed, and one of the first shows to be aired was Edward R. Murrow's *See It Now.*

In these formative years the bulk of network programming was arranged in New York by imaginative people like Sylvester L. "Pat" Weaver of NBC, who conceived the *Today* and *Tonight* shows. Beginning in 1952 many Americans awakened to the voice of Dave Garroway, the first host of the *Today* show, which came on the air at 7 A.M. Eastern time. Steve Allen was the host of the first *Tonight* show in 1954, and was followed over the years by Jack Parr and then Johnny Carson.

Television was live in the early days.[7] Milton Berle was called "Mr. Television." Sid Caesar and Imogene Coca starred on *Your Show of Shows,* Ed Sullivan's *Toast of the Town* became the *The Ed Sullivan Show,* Arthur Godfrey and Ted Mack brought their talent-scout shows from radio, and a half-dozen dramatic programs such as *Kraft Television Theatre* and *Studio One* carried the works of leading authors and playwrights into the living room. Comedy shows featured Jimmy

Durante, Bob Hope, Jack Benny and Mary Livingstone, George Burns and Gracie Allen, Edgar Bergen, and Red Skelton. The learned Bishop Fulton J. Sheen used his chalkboard to lecture on the evils of Communism, glibly telling the audience that his "guardian angel" had erased the board. Bing Crosby, Perry Como, and the singers on *Your Hit Parade* offered light fare. Soap operas also made their way from radio to television.

Youngsters who talked their teachers into letting their classes watch the World Series saw games played at Yankee Stadium, Ebbets Field, and the Polo Grounds, as sporting events became regular features on television. Other radio shows coming to television were Eve Arden's *Our Miss Brooks, The Goldbergs, The Life of Riley, The Adventures of Ozzie and Harriet* and *Amos 'n' Andy.* Children watched *Howdy Doody* and *Kukla, Fran and Ollie,* appealing shows with puppets, and *Ding Dong School* with Miss Frances. *Mama,* starring Peggy Wood, was a favorite family show.

The most spectacular audience during television's golden years was recorded in January, 1953, when 72 percent of the nation's 21 million television homes tuned in to see the *I Love Lucy* show during which Lucille Ball, pregnant in real life, gave birth to a son.

Program content began to change in the middle 1950s, however, when most production activities were switched to the Hollywood studios. A half-dozen Westerns were put on the air, led by the popular *Gunsmoke.* An actor named Ronald Reagan was host of *Death Valley Days.* By 1959, when *Bonanza,* another long-running show, appeared, there were thirty regular Western shows. Among a long line of popular detective shows at that time were *Perry Mason* and *Dragnet.*

Television suffered a setback in the late 1950s when it was learned that some of the quiz shows were rehearsed. The CBS show *$64,000 Dollar Question* was television's highest rated show in 1955. But by 1958 it was determined that there had been a wholesale cheating of the public and twenty quiz shows were taken off the air. A New York grand jury investigation in 1959 brought out all of the details. Television's credibility had been hurt, but only temporarily.

MURROW AND McCARTHY: THE DEBATE OVER "DISLOYALTY AND DISSENT"

At no time in the 1950s was the marriage between the emerging television system and partisan politics so clearly displayed than during the encounters of broadcaster Edward R. Murrow and Senator Joseph R. McCarthy of Wisconsin, men who had built their careers in the public eye and who saw the problems of international Communism and internal security—and journalism—quite differently.

Murrow remains the conscience of responsible broadcast journalists because of his relentless pursuit of the truth, his fondness for the English language, and his deep affection for the best in America's heritage. This, of course, includes the First Amendment guarantees to free and vigorous debate, open assemblies, independent gathering of the news, and critical commentaries about public affairs. This sophisticated man's devotion to hard work and his feeling for the common people's rights were developed by his own tireless Quaker parents

Edward R. Murrow, great CBS commentator.
CBS

who moved from their native North Carolina to the farms and logging mills of Washington when Murrow was a boy.

The 1948 political conventions brought Murrow to the television audience, but it was on November 18, 1951, that he made a full introduction of his style and personality. That first *See It Now* show featured Murrow sitting before two monitors, one showing the Golden Gate Bridge and the San Francisco skyline, and the other the Brooklyn Bridge set into New York's profile. During those 30 minutes the cameras showed Murrow in New York and Eric Sevareid in Washington talking about the Korean War, and Howard K. Smith in Paris during a prefilmed telephone conversation with Murrow. Murrow and Fred W. Friendly, his coproducer of radio and television documentaries for the next 10 years, were bringing their *Hear It Now* radio show to the new medium.

For the next 7 years *See It Now* broke the trail, bringing Americans many moments of hard journalism. Murrow believed that the message was more vital than the medium, and his zeal for fine writing and carefully edited film was contagious. This was the time of live television, and Murrow was able to transmit his sense of honesty and accuracy into the nation's living rooms. His familiar deep voice, rich with conviction, added to the impact of the shows, as did his solemn face and dignified manner.

Gradually the *See It Now* show moved from three or four brief looks at various subjects to occasional longer presentations. One milestone was achieved in late 1952 when Murrow took a large reporting and film crew to Korea for *See It Now's* first full-hour show, the highly acclaimed "Christmas in Korea." It was television's first full-length combat report and it drove home the fact that this war was stalemated.

Then in October, 1953, Murrow moved into the most controversial issue of those years, McCarthyism. The tension at CBS was at a peak as Murrow and Friendly prepared the story of a young Air Force reserve officer, Milo Radulovich, who had been classified as a security risk because his father and sister read "subversive" newspapers. The frequent abrasive nature of Murrow's previous shows had caused problems within CBS, and this time the network refused to advertise *See It Now.* Instead Murrow and Friendly paid $1500 of their own funds to buy a *New York Times* advertisement, while CBS felt strong pressure against the show from its own corporate advertisers.

Murrow and his cameras probed into the Dexter, Michigan, community of the Radulovichs and showed that the paper the father read was a Serbian-language one that supported Marshall Tito in Yugoslavia, 5 years after Tito had broken from Russian control. Murrow's final words included an offer to the Air Force for a reply and then this:

> Whatever happens in this whole area of the relationship between the individual and the state, we will do ourselves; it cannot be blamed upon Malenkov, Mao Tse-tung or even our allies. It seems to us—that is, to Fred Friendly and myself—that this is a subject that should be argued about endlessly. . . .[8]

Lieutenant Radulovich was cleared of being a security risk and the Murrow-Friendly team moved deeper into the emotion of the day. Within a month they produced "An Argument in Indianapolis," which dealt with the local American Legion unit's using its influence to stop a newly formed American Civil Liberties Union group from hiring a hall. CBS cameras filmed the Legion and ACLU meetings being held at different locations on the same evening, and the viewer was allowed to judge which speakers were following the dictates of the Constitution.

It also was in 1953 that Murrow began his famed interview show, *Person to Person.* Murrow's distaste for the show-business aspects of television had already caused disagreements between him and CBS executives and had strained his longtime relations with CBS president Frank Stanton. But after a shaky start Murrow grew to like the more informal style in which he was able to sit in the studio and discuss the lighter side of life with America's personalities.[9]

The *Person to Person* show ran through 500 guests until it ended on June 26, 1959. It was in the "top ten" in the ratings and brought many a thoughtful moment as Murrow, cigarette in hand, quietly probed and tried to make his famous guests at ease. But he reserved his loyalty for *See It Now.*

The March 9, 1954, broadcast of *See It Now* was one of the most controversial in broadcast history. Fully disgusted with the tactics employed by Senator McCarthy in charging numerous Americans with subversive activities, Murrow pulled out all stops. In his broadcast that night, while showing films of McCarthy in action, Murrow said:

> As a nation we have come into our full inheritance at a tender age. We proclaim ourselves—as indeed we are—the defenders of freedom abroad, what's left of it, but we cannot defend freedom abroad by deserting it at home. The actions of the junior Senator from Wisconsin have caused alarm and dismay amongst our allies abroad and given considerable comfort to our enemies, and whose fault is that? Not really his. He didn't create this situation of fear; he merely exploited it, and rather successfully. Cassius was right: "The fault, dear Brutus, is not in our stars but in ourselves" . . . Good night, and good luck.[10]

Later that spring the public got another chance to see Senator McCarthy in action during the sensational Army-McCarthy hearings, an investigation of alleged pro-Communist activities within the U.S. Army itself. Bitter arguments and legal maneuvering produced a huge daytime audience. But McCarthy was wearing thin and in August a Gallup Poll showed that only 36 percent of the public felt "favorable" toward him. Censured by Senate colleagues for his bullying tactics, McCarthy left center stage. He died in 1957.

Murrow had tried to educate the public about the difference between disloyalty and dissent. But the strain of unending work and dissatisfaction with trends in television were taking their toll. Board chairman William S. Paley decided to discontinue *See It Now,* and the last show ran on July 9, 1958.* Throughout this period Murrow had continued his nightly radio news show and had often appeared on television twice a week. He also continued his earlier association with *CBS Reports,* as part of which he narrated *Harvest of Shame,* which showed the plight of the migrant worker, in 1960. Then in 1961, greatly disappointed about the commercial nature of television and signs that television news itself would become locked into the ratings scramble, Murrow resigned to take charge of the U.S. Information Agency. Illness forced his retirement in December, 1963.

When Murrow died from cancer in April, 1965, 2 days after his fifty-seventh birthday, Eric Sevareid said of his mentor—whose skill and imagination set future standards for news and documentary broadcasting—"He was a shooting star. We shall live in his afterglow a very long time . . . we shall not see his like again."[11] Ironically, while Murrow argued for public understanding of the dangers of McCarthyism, there were many within the broadcasting, film, and advertising industries who bowed to pressure and agreed to the "blacklisting" of certain writers, actors, producers, and directors because of allegations that they were somehow linked to Communism. Indeed, in June, 1950, a blacklisting group issued *Red Channels: The Report of Communist Influence in Radio and Television.* The monograph listed more than 150 broadcast employees, and suggested that they should not be trusted as loyal Americans. The FBI hounded the New York City Photo League into dissolution. Loyalty oaths were the order of the day, even in universities, as blacklisting became a common practice because of fear and cowardice. It was in this grim atmosphere that Murrow, Friendly, and other courageous journalists worked.

Powerful publications like Henry Luce's *Time* and *Life,* McCormick's *Chicago Tribune,* and the Hearst newspapers, joined by many other newspapers across the land, added to the sensationalizing of the "Red" issue. Sickened by this trend, the alternative journalist I. F. Stone cried out in his July 19, 1954, issue of *I. F. Stone's Weekly:* "The Time to Save America from Fascism Is Now." He told of the House Un-American Activities Committee bill requiring all "subversive"

*John Crosby, television critic for the *New York Herald Tribune,* wrote, "*See It Now* . . . is by every criterion television's most brilliant, most decorated, most imaginative, most courageous and most important program. The fact that CBS cannot afford it but can afford *Beat the Clock* is shocking." Cited by Erik Barnouw, *The Image Empire* (New York: Oxford University Press, 1970), p. 116. For a critical look at the world of William S. Paley, Frank Stanton, and CBS News from the Murrow years through Cronkite, see David Halberstam, *The Powers That Be* (New York: Knopf, 1979).

organizations to register their printing facilities, even their mimeograph machines, "so fearful are we becoming of the printed word."[12]

NBC NEWS: HUNTLEY AND BRINKLEY

For 14 long years, from the 1956 political conventions to the unrest of 1970, the unusual team of Chet Huntley—the deep-voiced, rough-hewn Montanan—and David Brinkley—the dry, cynically whimsical reporter from North Carolina—formed an unlikely match that made millions for NBC.

The Huntley-Brinkley team was conceived for the 1956 conventions by Robert Kintner, then president of NBC News, who brought a surge of excitement to the division. The CBS team of Murrow and Walter Cronkite had outclassed NBC in 1952. At one point, to the sheer frustration of NBC and ABC executives, Richard Nixon used the headset of a CBS floor reporter to give Cronkite and Murrow an exclusive statement on his nomination as Eisenhower's running mate.[13] But it was a different story in 1956, with Huntley and Brinkley working perfectly together, playing to each other's words, while Cronkite and Murrow fared poorly.

NBC first paired Huntley and Brinkley on its evening news show, called *The Huntley/Brinkley Report,* on October 29, 1956, and by 1960 they had overtaken CBS in the ratings' chase. NBC's rise to the top of the televsion news business in the 1950s began with John Cameron Swayze's show of 1949 to 1956, *The Camel News Caravan,* a 15-minute show during which Swayze narrated newsreel clips. CBS had initiated the concept the previous year with *Douglas Edwards With the News.*

The team lasted until 1970, when Huntley retired. When he died of cancer in 1974, Brinkley told the television audience of the many times he and his partner had been told by young persons, "I grew up with you guys." Indeed, many Americans did grow to adulthood with Huntley reading the news from New York and Brinkley adding his part from Washington, each time signing off with the somewhat silly and often imitated exchange: "Goodnight, Chet." "Goodnight, David, and goodnight for NBC News." The NBC news division recorded many triumphs, with the *Today* show, well-edited instant specials on days of unusual news significance, live coverage of historic moments. But it was clear that the hub of the success was the attention gained by Huntley and Brinkley, whose familiar faces and voices dominated political conventions until 1968, when CBS began to gain ground. CBS regained the ratings lead in the 1969 to 1970 season.

Although the industrious *Huntley/Brinkley Report* added much to America's knowledge of itself, the two men were not that close. Huntley was more conservative in outlook, a businessman by nature who retired to his $20 million Big Sky resort complex, defended himself against the protests of conservationists, and did commercials for American Airlines. His many admirers praised his warmth, courage, and strong patriotism. No less patriotic, Brinkley, on the other hand, reflected more of the Washington viewpoint. As early as July, 1967, he publicly criticized the American involvement in Vietnam and said that the air war over North Vietnam should be stopped.[14]

Following Huntley's retirement, Brinkley temporarily found himself in an awkward "troika" arrangement with John Chancellor and Frank McGee. He separated from this to do *David Brinkley's Journal,* a nightly commentary. Chancellor emerged as the sole anchorperson and McGee took over the popular *Today* show. Then in 1976 Brinkley returned to coanchor the evening news when NBC executives decided to intensify the attack against CBS's hold on the ratings. The result was that NBC brought the numbers almost even. Brinkley later joined ABC.

RADIO ADJUSTS TO TELEVISION

Television had written radio's obituary, many observers said. But time proved that there was room for both. Network radio withered, as its established stars moved (with the advertising budgets) to network television. The value of time sales for national radio networks was $40 million in 1935, rose to a high of $133 million in 1948, then dropped back to $35 million in 1960. But the time sales for all of radio increased virtually every year. The "music, news, and sports" pattern proved successful for the spreading number of smaller stations. Incessant newscasts, rather than longer and more meaningful ones, proved annoying, but radio still produced many excellent network and local news and public-affairs broadcasts.

The networks, with the exception of the loosely organized Mutual, moved into television, but they also stayed in radio. The American Broadcasting Company (the NBC Blue network until 1943) merged with Paramount Theatres in 1953 in a mutual defense pact against television. ABC had 1348 radio station affiliates in 1975 in four subnetworks; CBS had 258, and NBC had 232. Mutual, serving 560 stations, went into bankruptcy in 1959 but was successfully reorganized. The number of regional radio networks increased to eighty-one by 1961.

FM (frequency modulation) radio—given its first public demonstration by Edwin Armstrong in 1935—made a bid against the normal AM (amplitude modulation) radio in the 1940s, as Table 23-1 shows. FM radio was looked on as the means of providing smaller towns with thousands of radio stations, since FM covers a smaller area with better reception. But only a few hundred FM stations survived in the 1950s, primarily as "better-listening" stations, because transistor radio sets produced by mass methods did not tune in FM channels until the mid-1960s. From then on, FM became one of the fastest growing elements in American broadcasting. At the decade year of 1960 there were 688 FM stations; in 1965 there were 1270; in 1982, the total was 4492, including 3380 commercial stations. There were several reasons for this mushrooming of FM broadcasting: (1) a better chance of investors for success than in the network-dominated television area and the badly overcrowded AM station fields; (2) an increased interest in cultural affairs and classical music; (3) the arrival of stereo and the high-fidelity industry, coinciding with this interest in better music; (4) various FCC decisions that helped give FM a separate identity from AM, its longtime subsidizer; (5) the driving away by television and radio of some of the audience by poor programming; (6) the increasing use of FM by advertisers as the quality and quantity of its audience became known; (7) the mushrooming sales of FM

Table 23-1 Numbers of Radio and Television Stations and Sets in Use

YEAR	AM STATIONS	FM STATIONS (on the air)	TV STATIONS	RADIO SETS (millions)	TV SETS
1930	612			13	
1935	605			30	
1940	814			51	
1945	943	53	9	60	(8000)
1950	2086	733	97	80	6
1955	2669	552	439	115	33
1960	3398	688	573	156	55
1965	4009	1270	586	228	61
1970	4269	2476	872	303	84
1975	4463	3571	962	413	120
1980	4575	4350	1020	456	150

Source: Broadcasting Yearbooks. Radios were in 96 percent of all households in the United States in 1950, 98.6 percent in 1970. Television household figures were 13 percent in 1950, 68 percent in 1955, 98 percent in 1980. Of the 456 million radio sets in 1980, 333 million were in homes, and 123 million were out of homes.

sets, from 2 million a year in 1960 to 21 million in 1968. By the 1970s combined AM-FM sets were commonplace.

Appearing on the scene with FM was facsimile broadcasting, also limited in scope of reception. Facsimile broadcasting, begun on a daily basis by KSD, St. Louis, in 1938, was viewed as a possible way of delivering printed newspapers into the home. But the innovation failed to reach mass-production use.

THE PRESS ASSOCIATIONS: THE AP'S KENT COOPER

The name of Kent Cooper came to dominate the history of the Associated Press in the 1920s, and his long shadow remained over that news organization through the 1950s. An Indianan, Cooper had started reporting for his local paper at 14. His college education was interrupted by the death of his father, and he left school to join the *Indianapolis Press.* From there he went to the Scripps-McRae news service, and he became head of the Indianapolis bureau of what was to become the AP's major rival. There Cooper got the idea that out-of-the-way papers could be better served by a system of telephoning the news report than by telegraphing it. In 1910 he went to General Manager Stone of the AP and so impressed Stone with his knowledge of news-communications methods that he was made AP traffic chief. He became an assistant general manager in 1920 and then took office as general manager in 1925. Through his subsequent career Cooper demonstrated his strong administrative qualities, but he was never a "newspaperman's newspaperman."

Cooper had plans for improving the efficiency and quality of the AP service, and many changes came with his rise to control. The number of bureaus was increased and staffs were expanded. Human-interest stories, long frowned on by the AP, gained favor. The transition was marked by the AP's first Pulitzer Prize, won by Kirke L. Simpson in 1922 for a series on the burial of the

Unknown Soldier in Arlington Cemetery. State services, permitting exchange of regional news on telephone wires subsidiary to the main AP trunk wires, were expanded. A news photo service was established in 1927, and after a sharp clash between picture-minded publishers and their more conservative colleagues, the AP Wirephoto system was approved in 1935. Automatic news printers, called teletypes, were first used in 1913 and gradually replaced Morse operators.

The pressures of competition from other news services and of World War II coverage requirements brought further advances. In 1934 the AP management had finally brought an end to the restrictive arrangements with European news agencies that prevented sale of AP news abroad and an AP World Service was begun in 1946. The AP had leased cable and radio-teletype circuits across the North Atlantic, European-leased land circuits, and an overseas radiophoto network. The character of the news report was subjected to increasingly intensive review by members of the Associated Press Managing Editors Association, a group formed in 1931. The managing editors of member papers criticized the AP news coverage and writing style orally until 1947, when the reports of a Continuing Study Committee were put into printed form annually. State memberships began similar analyses of their wires. The AP management hired readability expert Rudolph Flesch to advise its staff, and correspondents like James Marlow of the Washington bureau did excellent work in pointing the way to better writing techniques.

One change came involuntarily. This was in the membership-protest right, by which an AP member could blackball a new applicant in his own city. It took a four-fifths vote of the entire membership to override a blackball, a vote rarely obtained. This restriction was challenged by the *Chicago Sun,* which was founded by Marshall Field in 1941 as a morning competitor to the *Tribune.* Court action was begun in 1942, and in 1945 the U.S. Supreme Court held that the AP bylaws concerning protest rights constituted unfair restriction of competition. The AP thereupon amended its membership rules and elected several newspapers previously denied admission. On another front, and after a bitter battle, the AP began to sell its news report to radio stations in 1940, 5 years later than the UP and INS. Radio stations were granted associate membership, without voting rights, in 1946. The Associated Press Radio-Television Association was formed in 1954. And, in 1977, three seats were added to the board of directors for the stations, making twenty-one.

New faces appeared in the AP management. Two of the men most respected by their colleagues for their capabilities as journalists were Byron Price and Paul Miller. Both served as chiefs of the Washington bureau. Price became the AP's first executive news editor in 1936, before retiring from the news service to become director of the Office of Censorship during World War II and later assistant Secretary General of the United Nations. Miller, after being named an assistant general manager, quit the AP to become an executive of the Gannett newspapers. Their departures left Frank J. Starzel as the logical successor to Cooper when he retired in 1948. Starzel, a traditional newsman, had joined the AP in 1929. Alan J. Gould, sports editor since 1932, served as executive editor from 1941 to 1963. Lloyd Stratton directed the AP service abroad until Stanley Swinton was named director of the World Service in 1960, to serve until 1982.

Wes Gallagher, the AP's leading World War II war correspondent and

Associated Press

Associated Press

Kent Cooper (*left*) and Wes Gallagher, general managers of the Associated Press.

postwar foreign-bureau chief, returned to the New York office in 1954 to be groomed as Starzel's 1962 successor. Gallagher, an aggressive AP spokesperson, instituted "task-force" reporting by a ten-person team based in Washington, opened AP reporting ranks to younger men and also to women, and presided over a massive reorganization of the transmission wires.

The names of the AP staff should not be ignored. Serving in Washington were such newspeople as David Lawrence, who left the AP to become a columnist and news magazine publisher, and Stephen T. Early, who became President Franklin D. Roosevelt's press secretary. Pulitzer Prize winners of the 1930s were Francis A. Jamieson, who covered the Lindbergh baby kidnapping story, Howard W. Blakeslee, AP science editor, and Louis P. Lochner, Berlin bureau chief. Among other noted byliners were Edward J. Neil, killed during the Spanish Civil War; Hal Boyle, whose featurized stories were religiously run as columns by small, rank-and-file dailies; the tenaciously hard-working Marvin Arrowsmith, whose fate was to duel with the UP's flamboyant Merriman Smith on the White House beat during the 1950s before becoming Washington bureau chief; longtime European correspondent Eddy Gilmore; and special correspondent Saul Pett. Other major AP figures through the 1950s included general news editors Paul Mickelson and Samuel G. Blackman, foreign editor Ben Bassett, political writer Jack Bell, and news analyst John Hightower.[15]

THE UP AND INS BECOME UPI

The United Press and International News Service established themselves as competitive news agencies during the 1920s and 1930s. They expanded rapidly in response to the pressures of World War II and the growth of the mass media in the postwar years, and then in 1958 combined their forces as the United Press International—a news organization which competed on equal terms with the Associated Press for another two decades.

The UP jumped into several fields ahead of the AP, just as it did in developing its foreign news service. Acme Newspictures began operating in 1925, 2 years earlier than the AP picture service was established. The UP pioneered in supplying news to radio stations and, with the INS, was first into the television news field in 1951. Acme became United Press Newspictures in 1952 and handled UP Telephoto, rival to AP Wirephoto. In 1954 both services began supplying pictures by facsimile, over the UP Unifax and AP Photofax networks. The teletypesetter, producing a tape that automatically runs a typesetting machine, arrived in 1951 and both UP and AP set up teletypesetter circuits for smaller papers, sports, and financial services.

Roy Howard's successors as president of the United Press all came up through the ranks. His assistant, William W. Hawkins, held the post from 1920 to 1923. Then a second strong man of the UP, Karl A. Bickel, moved into the top command. Bickel became a leader in furthering the freedom of international news coverage, and he did much to advance the UP's own position in worldwide service.

Hugh Baillie, who succeeded Bickel in 1935, loved nothing better than to whip his competitors with an exclusive story, preferably a vivid one. He traveled extensively, impressing his own competitive drive for news on his staff and keeping in touch by covering some of the big stories personally. He was succeeded as president in 1955 by Frank H. Bartholemew, who presided over the 1958 merger of the UP and the INS. Mims Thomason became UPI president in 1962.

Earl J. Johnson became the working head of the UP news operation in 1935 and retired as editor in 1965, widely praised for his energetic leadership. Teamed with him was Roger Tatarian, an outstanding European news chief in the 1950s who succeeded Johnson as editor. Tatarian became known thoughout the news world before a heart attack forced his early retirement to a professorship.

United Press spawned some legendary newspeople. One was Merriman Smith, who spent 30 years covering six presidents and intoning the traditional "Thank you, Mr. President" as senior White House correspondent. Another was Henry Shapiro, who arrived in Moscow in the 1930s and served as bureau chief until the 1970s, dominating Moscow coverage of the Stalin, Khrushchev, and Brezhnev eras. Winning wide respect for their work were Lyle Wilson, Washington bureau chief; Harrison Salisbury, wartime foreign-news editor who won fame with the *New York Times;* Walter Cronkite, who was a wartime London correspondent before he joined CBS; diplomatic reporters Stewart Hensley in Washington and K. C. Thaler in London; Supreme Court reporter Charlotte Moulton; European news chiefs Virgil Pinkley and Daniel Gilmore; and foreign editors Joe Alex Morris and Phil Newsome. Russell Jones won a 1957 Pulitzer Prize for covering the Budapest uprising. Reynolds and Eleanor Packard were a colorful overseas reporting team.[16]

Editor-in-chief Barry Faris of the International News Service developed full 24-hour operations for his agency by 1928. Added as talented featured writers

UPI

INS

Hugh Baillie, UP, and Barry Faris, INS.

were Bob Considine and Inez Robb, joining the team of Floyd Gibbons, James L. Kilgallen, and H. R. Knickerbocker. Kilgallen's daughter Dorothy became a noted byliner. Other glamor names on the INS wire were Quentin Reynolds, Frank Gervasi, Paul Gallico, Damon Runyon, Arthur "Bugs" Baer, Louella Parsons, and Edwin C. Hill. The Hearst organization killed its morning-paper news agency, Universal News Service, in 1937, and gave business control of INS first to Joseph V. Connolly and, after 1945, to Seymour Berkson.

The INS foreign service developed stature by the 1930s. Among its leaders were J. C. Oestreicher, foreign editor, Pierre J. Huss, Berlin bureau chief, and J. Kingsbury Smith, who became European general manager. Top World War II correspondents were Howard Handleman, Kenneth Downs, Merrill Mueller, George Lait, Graham Hovey, Frank Conniff, Richard Tregaskis, Lee Van Atta, and Clarke Lee. In Washington were George R. Holmes, William K. Hutchinson, George E. Durno, and Robert G. Nixon. Among the INS women correspondents, Rose McKee achieved prominence for political reporting. In a final burst of glory, the 1956 Pulitzer Prize for international reporting was won for the INS and the Hearst newspapers by William Randolph Hearst, Jr., Kingsbury Smith, and Frank Conniff, who conducted interviews with Communist political leaders behind the Iron Curtain.

There were lumps in many throats when the hard-hitting INS staff of 450 saw their agency merged with the UP in May, 1958. William Randolph Hearst, Jr., and two of his associates took minority seats on the board of directors of the new United Press International, and some INS staffers joined UPI. A few of the brightest INS stars went to work for the newly formed Hearst Headline Service. Otherwise INS was no more.

THE USIA AND THE VOICE OF AMERICA

The creation of an autonomous United States Information Agency in 1953 gave stability to a program established in 1945 when tension and uncertainty was felt in the postwar world and American officials decided that the wartime work of the Office of War Information should be continued in peacetime. That first operation was the Office of International Information and Cultural Affairs, established within the State Department.

In 1948, under the Smith-Mundt Act, the functions were split into an Office of International Information and an Office of Cultural Exchange, with a small annual budget of $12 million, about one-third that of OWI.

As the Soviet Union consolidated its grip on the satellite states of Eastern Europe and attempted the 1948 Berlin blockade, and with the opening of the Korean War in 1950, Congressional appropriations rose swiftly. By 1952 the revamped International Information Administration had $87 million, 25 percent of which was for the Voice of America. The annual budget for the USIA was maintained after 1953 at well over $100 million adjusted for inflation. By 1970 the Voice of America was being heard in forty languages over ninety-two transmitters by an estimated audience of 43 million. The overseas United States Information Service was operating information libraries and reading rooms in seventy countries, and was distributing news services, motion pictures, magazines, and pamphlets. The policy and planning and the research and assessment sections were involved in the country's foreign-policy making, but not enough to satisfy many of the staff.

During the 1950s and 1960s there was a running duel between the professionals who viewed the USIA and the Voice of America as agencies for "tell it like it is" journalism, properly interpreting United States involvement in news events, and officials who wished the agencies to reflect their image of how the world should respond to current U.S. policy and who wished to minimize news of conflict with such a image. Increasing White House concern with the war in Indochina polarized the debate after 1965.[17]

In 1977 President Carter announced a reorganization plan that would combine the USIA and the State Department's educational and cultural-affairs activities in a new International Communication Agency. The Voice of America and overseas USIS would operate as before, and the broadcasters would be assured of freedom of action. But by 1982 the familiar USIA symbol was again in use. The Reagan administration tinkered with the agency's structure, and caused controversy by renewing the 1950s debate over content of programming by the Voice of America. A brief attempt to harden a propaganda line died in the face of staff resistance. The budget was very modest, however, for the obligations placed upon the agency.

ADVERTISING: MADISON AVENUE, U.S.A.

Martin Mayer's 1958 book about the advertising agencies, *Madison Avenue, U.S.A.,* helped popularize the image of the man in the gray flannel suit who contributed to what E. S. Turner called *The Shocking History of Advertising* in a constructively critical 1953 study. Advertising was in full stride, with total expenditures' volume doubling in the first decade of network television, and Madison Avenue was the symbol of its success.

In the World War II years, with consumer products in short supply, advertising made points by being both institutional and patriotic. Lucky Strike cigarettes had been packaged in green, with a red bull's-eye in the center. When the armed forces needed green dye, Luckies switched to a white package with the same red center spot and launched a full-scale campaign, "Lucky Strike green has gone to war." The company donated thousands of cartons to service-people overseas and watched its sales curve mount upward (women, it seemed, also preferred the new white packaging). Ford, producing solely for the military like other auto companies, dinned the slogan, "There's a Ford in your future" so successfully that the company led postwar sales. One of the most famed of the institutional advertisements was the New Haven Railroad's 1942 page, "The Kid in Upper 4," reprinted countless times. A wartime Advertising Council was created by the agencies, the media, and the advertisers to promote sales of war bonds, blood donation, rationing, and the like; after the war the Council continued to sponsor some two dozen public-service campaigns annually.

Television advertising by large companies began for the few thousand set owners of 1944 with commercials for clothing makers and Lifebuoy soap, which joined those of *Reader's Digest* and oil and utility companies. The 30-second television commercials invented for network broadcasts were relentlessly repetitious, but they sold goods. Programs sponsored by Alcoa, Du Pont, General Electric, and other great corporations sold images. By 1957 advertisers were spending more than $1.5 billion for television time, talent, and production costs to reach 37 million set owners.

The criticisms of advertising made in the 1930s were renewed in earnest in the late 1950s and early 1960s, leading to a deeper questioning of the "cult of consumerism" which advertising fosters. Vance Packard's bestselling *The Hidden Persuaders* (1956) attacked advertising for using the techniques of depth psychology to raise "subliminal anxieties" and manipulate desires for alcohol, cigarettes, and other consumer goods. In *The Affluent Society* (1958) John Kenneth Galbraith pointed out that advertising was encouraging wasteful consumption of scarce resources by a small portion of the world's people, to the detriment of both human beings and their environment. In *The One-Dimensional Man* (1964) Herbert Marcuse explained advertising as the means by which technology reached into an individual's consciousness and destroyed his or her freedom. Sloan Wilson's *The Man in the Gray Flannel Suit* (1967) was far more critical than the books of the 1950s.

The techniques of some advertising people aroused criticisms. Ted Bates & Company originated the manipulative technique of the "unique selling proposition" (usp) to up the sales of mass-produced products which in reality differed little from rival brands ("Cleans your breath while it cleans your teeth" for Colgate, and "Washed with live steam" for Schlitz to win finicky beer-bottle

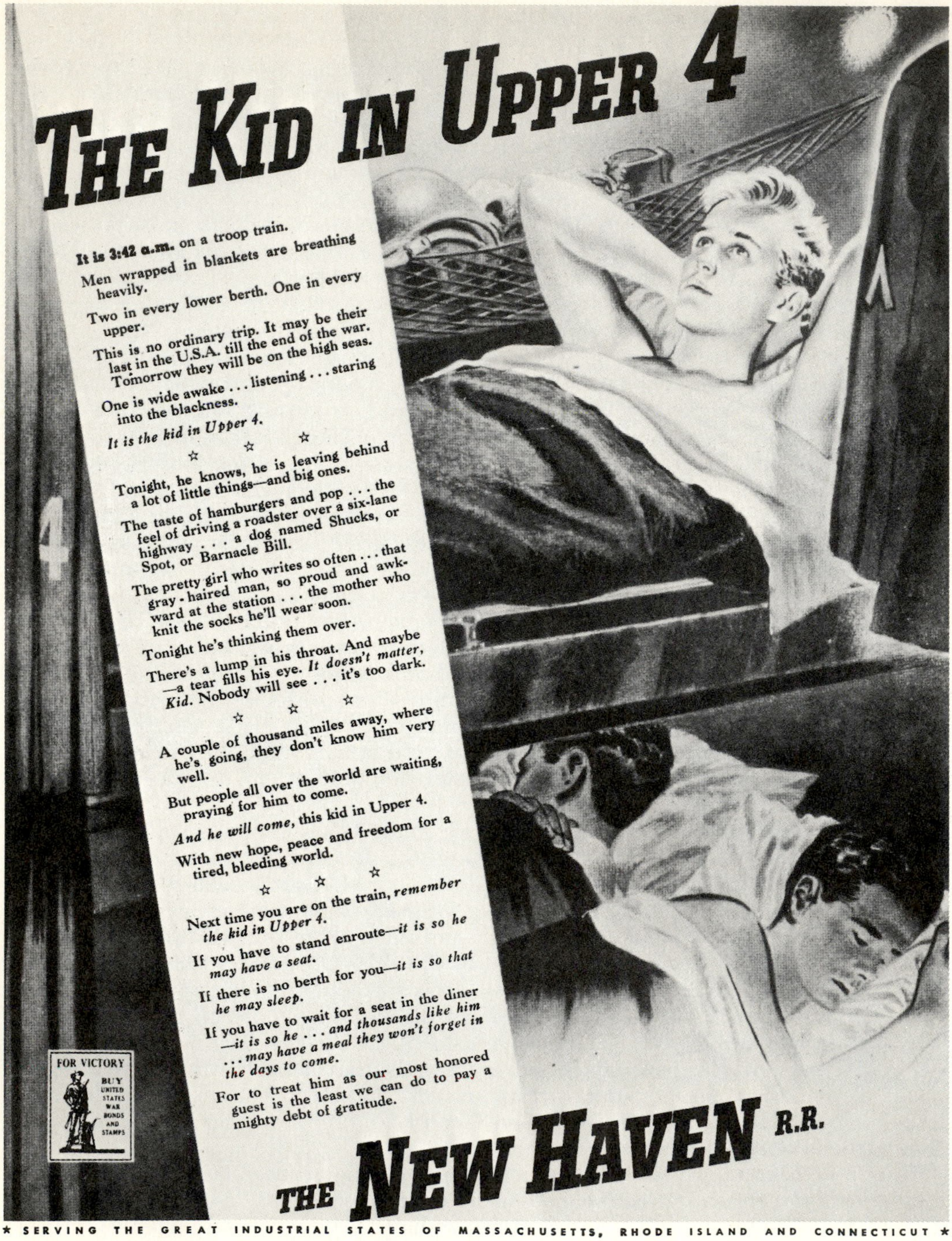

A famous 1942 institutional advertisement.

users). Ernest Dichter's motivational research was used by Chrysler to suggest to men with secret desires to have mistresses that their hardtop convertibles combined feelings of sinning with assurances of safety. There was also considerable discussion of subliminal advertising, by which momentary stimulations were said to trigger responses. One example of such advertising was to project flickering messages that said "Coke" or "pop corn" to stimulate movie-house sales of those products. College students found the research theory's possibilities intriguing.

On another research front, C. E. Hooper made his first television-audience study in 1948 and Dr. Claude Robinson and Dr. George Gallup formed a service to measure the effectiveness of advertising. In 1950 A. C. Nielsen took over the Hooper television-rating service and soon extended it to radio.

The first serious attempt at self-regulation of advertising occurred in 1952 when the National Association of Broadcasters (NAB), nudged by the FCC, established extensive sets of guidelines for both programs and advertising. An NAB code authority professional staff began clearing commercials prior to their airing; each network also reviewed the commercials for truth, taste, and fairness.

Two new advertising-agency leaders appeared: Ogilvy & Mather in 1948 and Doyle Dane Bernbach in 1949. David Ogilvy, an Englishman, emphasized brand image in his advertising campaigns, thus creating distinction for the product on the basis of "snob appeal." In his Hathaway shirt ads, which first appeared in 1951, the shirts were modeled by Russian nobles who wore black eyepatches and had the air of upper-class taste and distinction. This image would transfer to the buyer of a Hathaway shirt, the argument ran; during an 8-year campaign Hathaway's sales increased 250 percent. Schweppes, another Ogilvy account, had a bearded English commander for its image. William Bernbach, creative leader of Doyle Dane Bernbach for its first three decades, offered an opposite style: low-key, ironic, and endearing. His slogan for Avis Rent-a-Car swept the country: "We try harder. We're only Number 2." His long advertising campaign for the Volkswagen beetle ran against American buying habits—"Think small"—but it made Volkswagen the first successful automobile import. Bernbach's New York City billboard campaign, begun in 1963, relaxed ethnic tensions when it showed a smiling young black boy with the slogan, "You don't have to be Jewish to love Levy's real Jewish rye."

When *Printers' Ink* published its seventy-fifth anniversary issue in 1963, it found that it could run pictures of five women vice-presidents of major advertising agencies. Three had come up through the creative side: Jean Brown of Benton & Bowles, Jean Wade Rindlaub of Batten, Barton, Durstine & Osborn, and Margot Sherman of McCann-Erickson. Genevieve Hazzard of Campbell-Ewald had been account executive for Chevrolet; Nancy Stephenson of J. Walter Thompson focused on copywriting. A New York advertising leader was Bernice Fitz-Gibbon, who wrote the slogan "It's smart to be thrifty" for Macy's, then moved to Gimbel's and wrote "Nobody but nobody undersells Gimbel's" before opening her own agency in 1954.

Stanley Resor spent 40 years as J. Walter Thompson's president, 1916 to 1955. Bruce Barton, Ben Duffy, and Charles H. Brower were BBDO presidents. Also notable were Fairfax M. Cone, partner and creative director for Foote, Cone & Belding and a leading industry spokesperson; George Gribbin, copy

The man in the Hathaway shirt

David Ogilvy's best "brand image" ad.

chief and then president of Young & Rubicam; and Marion Harper, Jr., who became president of McCann-Erickson at the age of 32, revolutionizing that agency's activities.

In 1962 the largest agencies, by client billings, were J. Walter Thompson, Young & Rubicam, BBDO, McCann-Erickson, Leo Burnett, Ted Bates, N. W. Ayer, Foote, Cone & Belding, and Benton & Bowles. The leaders had made notable expansions in foreign accounts in the postwar years, particularly J.

Walter Thompson and McCann-Erickson. By the early 1960s, twelve of the twenty largest U.S. agencies had overseas subsidiaries. Young & Rubicam, Ted Bates, Foote, Cone & Belding, Dancer-Fitzgerald-Sample, Grant Advertising, and Erwin Wasey, Ruthrauff & Ryan were other agencies working to expand overseas activities.

Advertising volume as a percentage of all consumer expenditures peaked at 4.7 percent in 1922. It plummeted during the Depression years, then reached a plateau of 3.5 percent throughout the 1950s. Total advertising volume was $2 billion in 1940, $6 billion in 1950, $10 billion in 1955, and $12 billion in 1960.

THE EXPANSION OF CORPORATE PUBLIC RELATIONS

The 1950s were marked by a rapid advance in the field of corporate public relations. Individual firms opened new public-relations departments or expanded older ones. Recognition of public relations as a management concept increased, and the numbers of public-relations counsels retained by businesses and groups was enlarged. *Public Relations News,* the leading journal of the field, defined public relations as "the management function which evaluates public attitudes, identifies the policies and procedures of an individual or an organization with the public interest, and executes a program of action to earn public understanding and acceptance." The development of modern public-opinion and marketing-survey techniques beginning in the 1930s, by George Gallup, Elmo Roper, Claude Robinson, and others, provided a tool by which public-relations counselors could evaluate public attitudes quantitatively and could therefore obtain more objective measurements than their personal estimates of public opinion.

Sales booms in many manufacturing fields and businesses following the end of World War II benefited the public-relations field. By 1950 there were an estimated 17,000 men and 2000 women employed as experienced practitioners in public relations and publicity. In 1960 the census counted 23,870 men and 7271 women; others estimated a 35,000 total. The largest numbers were in manufacturing, business services, finance and insurance, religious and nonprofit groups, public administration, and communications. J. A. R. Pimlott, a British scholar, wrote in 1951, "Public relations is not a peculiarly American phenomenon, but it has nowhere flourished as in the United States. Nowhere else is it so widely practiced, so lucrative, so pretentious, so respectable and disreputable, so widely suspected and so extravagantly extolled."[18]

Detailed descriptions of the public-relations departments of major companies were given in published proceedings of forums sponsored by the Minnesota chapter of the Public Relations Society of America (PRSA) in the early 1950s.[19] The PRSA had been formed in 1948 from earlier organizations, and offered the forums at the University of Minnesota as a showcase. General Mills, which had a staff of three in its Department of Public Services in 1945, reported a professional staff of nearly twenty by 1952, and an outside public-relations consultant of national reputation. The milling firm had offices for press relations, internal communications, stockholder communications, consumer services, rural services, special services and contributions, nutrition education, and economic education. It published an employee newspaper monthly and a stockholder report quarterly, and it made a 16 mm. color newsreel for employee viewing. Betty Crocker was still the company's most famous symbol, however.

The Aluminum Company of America in 1953 had a vice president serving as director of public relations and advertising, with an assistant public-relations director and an advertising manager. Departments included community relations, employee publications, the news bureau, trade-press relations, product publicity, motion pictures and exhibits, and industrial economics (speech writing and educational relations). The company published the *Alcoa News* for employees and twenty additional plant publications. Its most prestigious effort was its sponsoring of Edward R. Murrow's *See It Now* program.

Standard Oil Company of Indiana in 1955 dealt with six defined areas or publics: employees, stockholders, dealers, suppliers, customers, and special publics. Its public-relations director gave a sampling of statistics for 1954 activity: 900 company speakers made 3528 speeches to 435,000 persons; 120,000 stockholders received the annual report and two management letters; 30,000 employees received the company magazine and four management letters; 50,000 persons made plant tours; and the company gave $2 million in philanthropic contributions. In contrast, only 113 general press releases were issued. Thus had public relations advanced from press-agent days.

In the early 1960s the largest public-relations counseling firms were Carl Byoir & Associates, Hill & Knowlton, and Ruder & Finn. Advertising agencies leading in public-relations services were N. W. Ayer, J. Walter Thompson, and Young & Rubicam. Some of the most extensive public-relations departments were found at General Motors, AT&T, United States Steel, and Du Pont.

MAGAZINES OF THE 1950S: THE END OF THE *POST*

The most popular magazines of the 1950s, in addition to the *Reader's Digest,* were *Life, Look, Collier's,* and the *Saturday Evening Post,* all similar to television and the movies in their general appeal. Only *Reader's Digest* survived the fierce competition for the advertising dollar, partly because of a decision in 1955 to accept advertising in the publication's thirty-third year. DeWitt and Lila Wallace stuck to the basic format, condensing articles from leading periodicals that dealt with informative subjects and ideas of value. Often attacked for its conservative, progovernment and business approach, the *Reader's Digest* outlasted many of its critics.

Henry Luce expanded his Time-Life empire in 1954 by establishing *Sports Illustrated,* a flashy magazine that coincided with the expansion of major-league sports in the late 1950s and early 1960s. Luce continued to use his prime publications—*Time, Life,* and *Fortune*—to further his goal of playing an important role in American life. The friend of presidents and prime ministers, he pushed hard during the anti-Communist crusade, attacking President Truman, Secretary of State Dean Acheson, and Adlai Stevenson. Day by day *Time* maintained its circulation lead over rivals *Newsweek* and *U.S. News and World Report. Life* was in a class by itself, with its glossy stock and letterpress printing, as compared with *Look's* rotogravure.

The *Saturday Evening Post* was special, in that its short stories and articles continued to feature America's well-known authors and journalists. Under editor George Horace Lorimer, the *Post* had become the reflection of traditional middle-class America, with inspirational biographies and business success articles interspersed with Clarence Buddington Kelland and other homey writers. After Lorimer's retirement in 1937, the *Post* had a shakedown under editor Ben Hibbs, was modernized, and reached 6.5 million circulation before Hibbs passed the editorship to Robert Fuoss in 1961. Suddenly the *Post's* profits translated into heavy losses, as television competition took its toll, and a succession of editors compounded its difficulties with poor judgments that alienated readers and lost a major libel suit. Seventy-two years after it had been purchased by Cyrus H. K. Curtis, the *Post* ceased publishing in 1969, joining its rival *Collier's* which had closed down in 1956 after 68 years. It was the last of its kind.*

HARPER'S, ATLANTIC, SATURDAY REVIEW

Harper's, once a leading literary journal, became primarily a public-affairs magazine after the mid-1920s and reached its hundredth anniversary in 1950 under the editorship of contemporary historian Frederick Lewis Allen. John Fischer succeeded Allen as editor in 1953 and furthered *Harper's* position among high-grade magazines. His reading audience, he once said, was 85 percent college graduates; more than half had taken some graduate work and had traveled abroad within the calendar year surveyed. But only 6 percent read the more literary-based *Atlantic.* It was this audience that in 1965 attracted John Cowles, Jr., a Harvard graduate who was president of the Minneapolis Star and Tribune Company, to buy a half-interest from Harper & Row, successor to the House of Harper dating from 1817.

Willie Morris, a liberal young writer who had achieved notice for his muckraking articles for the *Texas Observer,* joined the *Harper's* staff in 1963, and was Cowles' choice, at the age of 32, to succeed Fischer in 1967 as *Harper's* eighth editor in 117 years. Morris built a freewheeling staff of Midge Decter, executive editor; Robert Kotlowitz, managing editor; contributing editors David Halberstam, Larry L. King, John Corry, and Marshall Frady. The magazine became unpredictable, imaginative, and a vehicle for personal journalism of social and political concern. Morris ran huge excerpts of William Styron's *The Confessions of Nat Turner* and Norman Mailer's *The Armies of the Night.* But a storm broke at *Harper's* in March, 1971, when Mailer's earthy essay on the women's liberation movement, "The Prisoner of Sex," appeared in an effort to bolster declining circulation. When the uproar was over, Cowles had made Robert Shnayerson the ninth editor of *Harper's;* most of the new staff had resigned along with author Mailer.

Things were quieter at the 120-year-old *Atlantic.* It also had shifted toward public-affairs articles, but to a lesser degree, after Edward A. Weeks replaced longtime editor Ellery Sedgwick in 1938. But the pages that once carried the

*A revival of the *Post* as a quarterly, using its old-time flavor and material, appeared on newsstands in 1971; this was succeeded by a monthly version in 1977.

contributions of Emerson, Thoreau, and Longfellow continued to present the literary great: Ernest Hemingway, Edwin O'Connor, Saul Bellow, and Lillian Hellman. Public-affairs articles gained ground with the 1964 appointment of Robert Manning as executive editor. Manning was an experienced newspaperperson and Assistant Secretary of State for Public Affairs in the Kennedy and Johnson administrations. He became the *Atlantic's* tenth editor-in-chief in 1966, with Michael Janeway as managing editor. Elizabeth Drew wrote the Washington commentary.

The *Saturday Review of Literature* had expanded its interests to include music, science, education, communications, and travel. In 1952 it shortened its name to the *Saturday Review.* Founded in 1924 by Henry Seidel Canby, the first editor-in-chief of the Book-of-the-Month Club, the *Saturday Review* began to grow steadily after Norman Cousins assumed the editorship in 1942. With circulation mounting to 265,000, the magazine put its business affairs in the hands of the *McCall's* publishing corporation in 1961. Cousins advocated restraint in circulation seeking, yet the *Saturday Review* had 615,000 by 1970. Ownership changed in 1971 to Nicolas H. Charney and John J. Veronis, who moved the magazine to San Francisco and transformed it into four rotating weeklies. Cousins quit, but 2 years later he reacquired ownership when the new owners went bankrupt. In 1977 the *Saturday Review,* with 520,000 circulation, was sold to a group headed by Carll Tucker, a 25-year-old writer. Cousins remained as columnist, and in 1980, Robert Weingarten, publisher of *Financial World,* assumed ownership.

THE LIBERAL LEFT AND RELIGION

Among the struggling opinion magazines operating at the liberal left during the reactionary 1950s were the *Nation* (founded in 1865) and the *New Republic* (founded in 1914). E. L. Godkin's *Nation* was owned by the Villard family from 1881 to 1934 and followed Oswald Garrison Villard's liberal, pacifist course. Freda Kirchwey became editor in 1937, and Carey McWilliams in 1955, as the magazine passed through financial crises and intrastaff dissensions over policy toward the Soviet Union. A vigorous liberalism prevailed and by the mid-1960s the *Nation* made perhaps the most passionate attacks on the intensified war in Vietnam. McWilliams and Washington correspondent Robert Sherrill were writers of columns of incisive, fact-supported editorials that accompanied the magazine's articles and sections on books and the arts. Advertising was meager and the unreported circulation was scant, perhaps 25,000. McWilliams retired in 1976 and Blair Clark became editor.

The *New Republic,* founded with money from the Willard D. Straight family in 1914, exerted influence during the Wilsonian era with the writings of editor Herbert Croly and Walter Lippmann. It again had force in the 1930s under editor Bruce Bliven. When Michael Straight took over its direction in 1946 he appointed Henry A. Wallace editor. Circulation touched 100,000, but Wallace's involvement in the ultraliberal Progressive party as its 1948 presidential candidate brought his resignation. Sales slumped but were restored after 1956 by editor Gilbert A. Harrison. One bright feature was a column of hard-hitting comment from Washington, begun in 1943 and signed merely "TRB," which was eventually identified as the moonlighting activity of Richard L. Strout, mild-mannered *Christian Science Monitor* staff writer. Strout continued his column until 1983 when he was succeeded by Michael Kinsley.

Not as fortunate was the *Reporter,* launched in 1949 by Max Ascoli as a fortnightly. It won widespread praise from its liberal and academic audience for its high-grade research articles and sharply pointed opinion pieces, but audience enthusiasm waned when Ascoli supported the escalated war in Vietnam. Despite 200,000 circulation, the disappointed Ascoli sold out in 1968 to *Harper's,* which discontinued it. Douglass Cater had been its star Washington correspondent.

Other opinion magazines with smaller circulations were also being published. The *Progressive,* founded in 1909 by the La Follette family in Wisconsin, continued its excellent work under the editorship of Morris H. Rubin. The *New Leader,* Socialist but strongly anti-Communist in its origins, appeared in 1924 as a tabloid and adopted magazine format in 1950. Samuel M. (Sol) Levitas made it a stronghold of intellectual thought and writing from 1930 until his death in 1961. The *Commonweal,* founded in 1924 by a group of Catholics but not connected with the church, won wide respect under the editorship of Edward Skillin. Another leading religious publication was the *Christian Century,* a nondenominational Protestant organ, dating from 1884, that was given stature by editor Charles Clayton Morrison between 1908 and 1947. Morrison's successors were Dr. Paul Hutchison and Harold E. Fey. A rebellious weekly newspaper owned and edited by Catholic laypeople made its appearance in Kansas City in 1964; edited by Robert Hoyt until he was forced out in 1971, the *National Catholic Reporter* brought strong support to reform elements within the church, but by 1972 it had greatly lost circulation and influence. Traditional forces dominated, led by the National Catholic News Service and two chains of diocesan newspapers run by *Our Sunday Visitor* and *The Register.* There were other religious publications, such as *Christianity in Crisis* and *Christianity Today,* which appeared as public interest in religion grew steadily during the 1960s, but unfortunately they received little subscriber support and like most other magazines were imperiled by the spiraling printing costs of inflation years.

BUCKLEY'S *NATIONAL REVIEW*

The strongest and most intelligent voice of the far right in American political opinion was that of the *National Review.* Founded in 1955 by William F. Buckley, Jr., it had 32,000 readers and an $860,000 deficit by 1960. Buckley and the leaders of political conservatism persisted and by 1977 circulation was 110,000. The 1970 election of William's brother James, Conservative party candidate, to a United States Senate seat for New York stimulated the Buckley family and its publishing enterprise. The editor's sister, Priscilla, was managing editor. Other key staff editors included James Burnham and Russell Kirk. James Jackson Kilpatrick and Ralph de Toledano were contributing editors. Also reaching the American right was *The Alternative,* edited in Bloomington, Indiana, by R. Emmett Tyrrell, Jr., who started it as a campus paper in 1966 and began nationwide distribution in 1970. William Buckley, Irving Kristol, Sidney Hook, and Senator Daniel Patrick Moynihan were among an impressive list of article and review contributors.

PHOTOJOURNALISM: *EBONY, NATIONAL GEOGRAPHIC, SMITHSONIAN*

John H. Johnson started *Ebony,* imitating the format of *Life,* in 1945 with a press run of 50,000. A friend of Henry Luce, Johnson previously had published *Negro Digest. Ebony* became "a pictorial Who's Who in Black America," a high-quality magazine aiming at middle-class leadership but dealing with all aspects of poverty and success.[20] In the late 1960s it became more activist. Johnson later published *Jet, Tan Confessions, Ebony Jr.* for children, and *Black Stars.* With other big picture magazines, *Life* and *Look,* gone by the early 1970s, *Ebony* was left alone in this category of magazine and was eminently successful.

The demise of *Life* and *Look* left a void for outstanding photographers and a number of them joined the venerable *National Geographic,* a one-time travelogue journal begun in 1888. By the 1950s it was an old favorite, but it shot upward in circulation and moved into the general-interest level as other magazines closed their doors. It became a center of photojournalism progress as well,

Magazine owner John H. Johnson.
Ebony

with Robert E. Gilka as director of photography. Gilbert Grosvenor was editor when the *National Geographic* passed the 9 million mark in circulation by 1977.

Among the refugees from *Life* was Edward K. Thompson, who turned *Smithsonian* into a superb example of photojournalism. Founded in 1970 by that Society in Washington, *Smithsonian* filled its pages with color photography, became fat with advertising, and ran its circulation to 1.5 million monthly by the late 1970s.

BOOK PUBLISHING: THE OLD HOUSES LEAD A POSTWAR BOOM; THE PAPERBACK EXPLOSION

It became obvious in the first years after World War II that the major publishing houses and the new paperback producers would give the reading public a greater choice than ever before. The old firms led the way, developing new authors and expanding into uncharted areas. The largest firm was Doubleday & Co., developed by Frank Nelson Doubleday and his son Nelson Doubleday, heralded as two of the greatest booksellers of the twentieth century.[21] Doubleday opened the 1950s with *The Caine Mutiny* by Herman Wouk, who later authored *The Winds of War.* Following in the tradition of *Crusade in Europe*—Doubleday's 1948 publication of Dwight Eisenhower's wartime memoirs—the firm released Harry Truman's *Years of Decision* in 1955. The former president sat in a Kansas City hotel and autographed nearly 4000 books on one day, setting some sort of record. Doubleday survived as the last of the major independent publishing houses.

The energy at Random House came from Bennett Cerf, known better, perhaps, for a number of humor books, but known in the trade as a strong leader who brought into his line the works of Truman Capote, Irwin Shaw, John O'Hara, and Moss Hart. *Witness,* the story of Whittaker Chambers, the man who accused Alger Hiss of treason, became a best seller, as did Don Whitehead's *The FBI Story.* Macmillan also used the 1950s to move ahead; its president George P. Brett, Jr., introduced Arthur Koestler, Mary Ellen Chase, and poet Marianne Moore. Walter Lippmann was a Macmillan author. The firm suffered one setback when it became involved with the Crowell-Collier Publishing Co. and was forced to close *Woman's Home Companion, Collier's,* and the *American,* once all prosperous enterprises.

Alfred A. Knopf, who loved history, fashioned a distinguished list of authors for his business. *The Prophet,* by the mystical Lebanese poet Kahlil Gibran, had been an enormous success, and Knopf was attracted to international literature. That firm was purchased by Random House in 1960, and later—an example of the spread of conglomerate power—both were bought by RCA.

Cass Canfield dominated Harper & Bros.; as his first contribution he brought in Robert Sherwood's *Roosevelt and Hopkins.* Deeply interested in politics, he used his connections to obtain John Kennedy's *Profiles in Courage.* The firm became Harper & Row in 1962 after it acquired Row, Peterson & Co.. In 1966 Canfield was the center of a bitter controversy over William Manchester's *Death of a President,* parts of which were offensive to the Kennedy family.

Gore Vidal, Anaïs Nin, Mickey Spillane, and Françoise Sagan became best sellers with E. P. Dutton & Co. When Elliott Macrae assumed his father's position there, he added a number of exciting works, such as *Annapurna,* Maurice Herzog's story of the conquest of Mount Everest.

The Henry Holt house boasted an impressive list of authors during World War II years, including Ernie Pyle's books and Bill Mauldin's collection of cartoons, but it was in need of stronger leadership by the 1950s even though books of the stature of Norman Mailer's *The Naked and the Dead* had been listed. Texas oil millionaire Clinton Murchison became involved, purchasing 40 percent of Holt stock; his friend Edgar Rigg became president. The firm added *Field and Stream* to its successful magazine list and dramatically built its textbook sales so that by the end of the 1950s it was outsold only by McGraw-Hill and Prentice-Hall. Then in 1959 Rigg acquired Rinehart & Co. and the John C. Winston Co., giving the company its present name, Holt, Rinehart & Winston. CBS took control in 1967, with executives William S. Paley and Frank Stanton taking seats as directors. This followed the pattern of many conglomerate takeovers in which, in the words of historian John Tebbel, publishing houses would be "run by executives who were not bookpeople and who assumed that these houses could be run like any other business."[22]

William Jovanovich was elected president of Harcourt, Brace & Co. in 1955. He soon added his name to the title, as he quickly aimed his firm in the direction of highly diversified activities. Among other things, he was the first modern publisher to arrange for "copublishing," a technique whereby outstanding editors published with him under a joint agreement.

Other major houses were Viking, which in 1975 added Penguin Publishing Ltd. to form Viking Penguin; Simon & Schuster, part of Marshall Field's enterprises for 13 years until it broke loose in 1957; G. P. Putnam's Sons, which took on Mailer's *The Deer Park* and then caused a sensation by publishing Vladimir Nabokov's *Lolita;* Houghton Mifflin, a traditional Boston firm which gave the public Rachel Carson's warnings about the environment, *Silent Spring;* and Little, Brown, another Boston house that became part of the Luce empire in 1968 and later published such notable authors as Frances FitzGerald (*Fire in the Lake,* a distinguished book on Vietnam) and William Manchester (*American Caesar,* the life of Douglas MacArthur).

A major development in 1957 was the establishment of the Atheneum house by the three publishing leaders. Simon Michael Bessie, a senior editor at Harper & Bros., was joined by Hiram Haydn, editor-in-chief at Random House, and Alfred Knopf, Jr., vice president of his father's house. The firm got off to a good start with Jan de Hartog's *The Inspector,* and in 1961 jumped to success by publishing Theodore H. White's *The Making of the President,* which won the Pulitzer Prize for nonfiction. Frederick A. Praeger founded his firm in 1950, starting from scratch and working into the field with books like Hugh Seton-Watson's *From Lenin to Malenkov.* The company became the leading publisher of books about the Cold War; in 1957 it released ex-Communist Howard Fast's repudiation of Communism, *The Naked God*, and Milovan Djilas' *The New Class*, a book written by a Yugoslavian who had split with Marshall Tito.

In the paperback field, the Pocket Books company introduced low-cost books to the public in 1939,* following the ideas of Robert de Graff and Leon

*The first soft cover books appeared in 1842. During the period from 1870 to 1890 there was great interest in dime novels and other paperbacks. The third wave of interest came with Pocket Books.

Shimkin. De Graff had been involved with selling inexpensive reprints for years, and Shimkin was a partner with Richard Simon and Max Schuster. De Graff was backed by the major house and was given 51 percent control. Within 3 years 23 million of the 25-cent Pocket Books had been sold and by the 1950s the company was turning out 180 million books annually.

Bantam Books entered the pocket book field in 1945. It later became a leader in the field by publishing topical books soon after major events, rushing into print with Bantam Extras. Fawcett Publications, with *True Confessions, Woman's Day, Mechanix Illustrated,* and other magazines, had been developed by the family of Wilford H. Fawcett. It joined the paperback competition in 1950 with Gold Medal books. This led to the development of Crest Books, which issued the first paperback to break the $1 price, William L. Shirer's *The Rise and Fall of the Third Reich,* which sold for $1.65. Shirer was paid $400,000 for rights to the book, a then unheard of amount.

Dell began issuing its small-sized books in 1942 as an outgrowth of George T. Delacorte's massive publishing business, which turned out 160 million magazines and comic books per year, including *Walt Disney's Comics* and *Looney Tunes.* It was estimated that in 50 years, Dell published between 600 and 700 magazines and that Delacorte himself had owned, at one time or another, more than 200 of them. A number had press runs of more that 1 million copies. Much of the success was due to the shrewd marketing techniques of Helen Meyer, who finally became president of the firm after working with Delacorte from the opening of the business in 1921.

A quality line of paperbacks was published by New American Library (NAL) founded in 1948 by Kurt Enoch and Victor Weybright, who developed the Signet and Mentor lines for their company. Introducing the "king-size" paperback and better printing, New American Library offered Theodore Dreiser's *An American Tragedy*, Erskine Caldwell's *God's Little Acre,* and similar works. NAL set the standard for the future distribution of literature in paperback form. After spectacular success, it was purchased by the Times Mirror Co. in 1966.

Following the rush of paperback publishing in the 1940s and 1950s, publishing leaders began to develop marketing strategies that would allow systematic distribution of first hard cover and then soft cover editions of popular books. Later lucrative tie-ins to motion pictures and television productions were engineered, adding yet another dimension to the growing publishing field.

THE MOVIES FACE TV'S CHALLENGE

In the late 1940s the movies were still prosperous. Television was not yet a dangerous rival. Hollywood had a huge worldwide market for more than 400 films yearly. The studios turned out major dramatic films, using the actors they had under contract, and they also made a steady run of low-budget B films. Five of the eight big studios owned chains of theaters which had first pick of the new releases, although they, and the independent theaters, had to take movies sight-unseen under the block-booking system. There were still nearly 20,000 movie houses, and attendance was good, although down one-third in 1950 from an estimated 90 million weekly high.

But Hollywood was soon staggering under three blows. The first was an unexpectedly rapid growth of television, whose nationwide transmission networks were completed by 1951. Mass sales of sets for entertainment at home cut into the number of trips to the neighborhood movie houses for millions of families. The second blow came from a series of consent decrees ordered by the federal courts to break up the practice of block-booking and to force the major producing companies to sell their strings of movie houses. Coming between 1946 and 1948, these decrees hastened the end of the low-budget films, brought a sharp decline in the contract player system, and reduced the number of movies made annually by nearly half. Within another decade the number of movie houses would be reduced one-fourth. The third blow, more psychological than economic, resulted from a series of investigations of the film-making industry by the House Un-American Activities Committee (HUAC). Beginning in 1947 the HUAC subjected hundreds of "suspect" liberal writers and directors to cross-examinations, jailed ten as unfriendly witnesses, and condemned many others to an informal "blacklisting" ordered by the frightened industry leaders. Jack Warner renounced his wartime film, *Mission to Moscow,* even though it had merely recounted that wartime alliance, and the studios ground out movies extolling the FBI and the anti-Communist crusade.

One reponse by Hollywood to television was the introduction of the wide screen. Since the pictures on early television sets were very small, the massive scope of the wide screen could hopefully be used to lure audiences back into the movie houses. The standard screen shape since the Kinetoscope had been a rectangle 20 feet wide and 15 feet high, representing a ratio of 1.33 to 1. The new screens were almost twice as wide as they were high; the most successful, Cinemascope, had a proportion of 2.55 to 1. Twentieth Century-Fox released the first wide-screen film, *The Robe,* in 1953.

The new screen permitted further experimentation in visual composition and other movie-making techniques. There had been significant advances during the 1940s, notably by director-actor Orson Welles. His 1941 film, *Citizen Kane*, reflected exciting experimentation, particularly in the technique of narration. The story of an immensely wealthy and domineering businessman, it was clearly identified as a psychological study of publisher William Randolph Hearst. As the decades passed, students of the film ranked it among the top pictures ever made. Director John Ford's production of John Steinbeck's *The Grapes of Wrath* in 1939 had set another standard for the examination of significant social issues. The best of the Hollywood wartime films, produced in 1942, was *Casablanca,* directed by Michael Curtiz and starring Humphrey Bogart and Ingrid Bergman. Katharine Hepburn offered sophisticated comedy, in 1940 with Cary Grant in *The Philadelphia Story* and in 1942 with Spencer Tracy in *Woman of the Year*—the first of eight films for that pair. Bette Davis specialized in melodramas, notably *Jezebel* (1938) and *Little Foxes* (1942); Joan Crawford did the same in *Mildred Pierce* (1945). William Wyler's *Best Years of Our Lives* was a 1946 postwar hit—but was soon condemned by the HUAC as unpatriotic.

Aside from Orson Welles' work, the most significant 1940s films came from abroad. Roberto Rosellini's *Open City* ushered in neorealism in 1945. It was followed by fellow Italian Vittorio de Sica's *The Bicycle Thief* (1947). These war-related films gave way to another theme in Federico Fellini's *La Dolce Vita* (1960). The French "new wave" of 1958 to 1964 took the camera into the streets for imaginative, unstructured story telling best done by François Truffaut and Jean-Luc Godard. British contributions to realism included Tony Richardson's *Room at the Top* (1958), an examination of social mobility, and *A Taste of Honey* (1961). The feelings of a young Russian couple under wartime stress offered reality to viewers of *The Cranes Are Flying* (1957).

Some of these films were breaking down the strictures of the industry production code. In 1956, revisions in the code permitted the depiction of drug addiction, kidnapping, prostitution, and abortion. The 1953 movie *The Moon Is Blue* had depicted adultery. Otto Preminger's *The Man With the Golden Arm* opened up the subject of drugs in 1956. Prostitution was the subject of two 1960 films, *Butterfield 8* and *Girl of the Night.* All were released bearing the Motion Picture Seal of Approval.

There were more conventional films that won critical attention: George Stevens' *Shane,* a 1953 Western; Marlon Brando in *On the Waterfront* (1954); Elizabeth Taylor in *Suddenly Last Summer* (1959), directed by Joseph Mankiewicz. Alfred Hitchcock came to the United States in 1940 after making *The 39 Steps* (1935) in England, in which he used new sound-montage techniques like merging a woman's scream into a train whistle. Hitchcock communicated obsessive or compulsive behavior with maximum intensity in his thrillers *Rear Window* (1954), *Vertigo* (1958), and *Psycho* (1960). David Lean produced notable epics: *Bridge on*

Director Orson Welles, when he won attention with his "War of the Worlds" broadcast.

Vice President Richard Nixon and Soviet Premier Nikita Khrushchev engaged in a spontaneous debate while visiting the kitchen area of a United States exhibit in Moscow. The July, 1959, encounter heightened Nixon's reputation and was called the "Kitchen Debate." On Nixon's right is Leonid Brezhnev, who later assumed power.
AP

the River Kwai (1957), *Lawrence of Arabia* (1962), and *Dr. Zhivago* (1965). The older era of Hollywood film making and "going to the movies" ended on the high note of a new alltime box-office champion in 1965—*Sound of Music* with Julie Andrews, which depicted a joyful outwitting of the Nazis.

Weekly movie attendance had dropped to 40 million by 1960. Movie houses with no more than 500 seats were built at shopping centers, and drive-ins dotted the landscape. The big studios began selling their old films to television beginning in 1955, soon peddling a total of 9000 pre-1948 movies. CBS paid MGM $25 million for rights to *Gone with the Wind.* The cooperative venture of televising the annual Academy Awards shows helped the movies maintain their image. Still, by 1965 more than 6000 movie houses had shut down. RKO, Republic, and Monogram were gone and the remaining studios were issuing scarcely 200 films a year.

A SERIES OF ALARMS

As the decade of the 1950s ended it appeared that America's problems tended to multiply rather than be solved. President Eisenhower had been reelected in 1956 by an overwhelming margin, over Adlai Stevenson, by stressing his attempts to keep peace in the world. There had been a brief thaw in United States-Soviet relations, highlighted by Nikita Khrushchev's "secret" anti-Stalin speech in February, 1956, but this came to an end just before the presidential election, when Russian tanks crushed a revolt in Hungary that had won the sympathy of the world but not its active support. At the same time the Soviets gained new stature in the Middle East through their support of Egypt's Gamal Nasser, who had seized the Suez Canal, the lifeline to the Persian Gulf oil fields. Israel, Britain, and France attempted to regain the canal, but were forced to withdraw after a strong American protest. Following this attempt to act as peace maker, the Eisenhower administration fashioned the "Eisenhower Doctrine": a pledge that the United States would assume responsibility to defend the territory and resources of the Middle East, including Turkey, Iran, Iraq, and Pakistan. Israel, however, was not promised direct assistance because of a fear that this would further alienate the Arab states.

In Asia there was continued controversy over Quemoy and Matsu, two small islands in the Formosa Straits close to the Chinese mainland. The Communist shelling of the islands, which were held by Chiang Kai-shek's Nationalists, had caused angry outbursts in Congress about the need to punish "Red China." Communist control of Indochina's northern area was considered a threat to the American-backed Saigon government, and the general American response to Asian Communism had been the formation of the Southeast Asian Treaty Organization (SEATO), the counterpart to Europe's NATO (where tension also increased in 1958 to 1959 during another crisis over Berlin's status). In fact, between 1947 and 1961 the United States had entered into mutual defense agreements with every major friendly nation in the world.

There was trouble on the horizon in Africa, where the force of nationalism would sweep nearly every nation in the 1960s, and in Cuba, where Fidel Castro was soon to win and become a declared enemy of the United States. In India, Prime Minister Jawaharlal Nehru was irritating American policy makers by attempting to be neutral in world affairs and by dealing with China.

Domestically, there was increased racial tension in the South. The wide-scale civil-rights movement was close at hand. The Russian success with Sputnik had activated American scientists and the "space race" was under way. And another presidential campaign was in the making, with a number of Democrats seeking their party's nomination and Vice-President Richard M. Nixon the apparent choice of Republicans.

In December, 1959, Americans indicated that newspapers were slightly more believable than television news reports, 32 percent to 29 percent, followed by other media. Within 2 years this would switch to television's favor, 39 percent to 24 percent. But when asked which medium of communication they would retain if allowed to keep only one, 42 percent said television, 32 percent newspapers, and 19 percent radio.[23] Television's impact—as an entertainment medium as well as a distributor of vital news—would be felt even more strongly in the 1960s.

NOTES

1. Sig Mickelson, *The Electric Mirror: Politics in an Age of Television* (New York: Dodd, Mead, 1972), offers an analysis of television's changing role in the campaigns of the 1950s and 1960s. As president of CBS News, Mickelson was involved with many of the decisions.

2. William Manchester, *The Glory and the Dream* (Boston: Little, Brown, 1973), gives a colorful description of the 1952 conventions and campaign in Chapter 19, "Right Turn." Television's first wide-scale convention coverage is also discussed in a number of broadcasting histories.

3. Erik Barnouw, *The Tube of Plenty* (New York: Oxford, 1977), pp. 137–39, includes quotations from the speech.

4. *New York Herald Tribune,* May 12, 1960, as quoted in James E. Pollard, *The Presidents and the Press: Truman to Johnson* (Washington, D.C.: Public Affairs Press, 1964).

5. See Godfrey Sperling, Jr.'s, interview with Donovan, *Christian Science Monitor,* September 15, 1982, and Donovan's second volume on the Truman presidency, *Tumultuous Years* (New York: Norton, 1982). Donovan covered Washington for more than 20 years.

6. For a complete description of the historic "freeze" and the FCC's comprehensive report, see Sydney W. Head, *Broadcasting in America* (Boston: Houghton Mifflin, 1976), pp. 162–69.

7. The best descriptions of the golden age of programming are found in Christopher H. Sterling and John M. Kittross, *Stay Tuned: A Concise History of American Broadcasting* (Belmont, Calif.: Wadsworth, 1978); Erik Barnouw, *The Tube of Plenty, The Golden Web* (New York: Oxford, 1968), and *The Image Empire* (New York: Oxford, 1970); and Lawrence W. Lichty and Malachi C. Topping, *American Broadcasting: A Source Book on the History of Radio and Television* (New York: Hastings House, 1975).

8. "The Case Against Milo Radulovich, A0589839," *See It Now,* CBS News, October 20, 1953.

9. Alexander Kendrick who for 20 years worked with Murrow, provides the full story of Murrow's life, including his many battles with CBS, in *Prime Time* (Boston: Little, Brown, 1969).

10. "Senator Joseph R. McCarthy," *See It Now,* CBS News, March 9, 1954.

11. For a poignant remembrance of Murrow, see Edward Bliss, Jr., "Remembering Edward R. Murrow," *Saturday Review* (May 31, 1975), 17.

12. *I. F. Stone's Weekly,* July 19, 1954, p. 1.

13. David Halberstam, *The Powers That Be* (New York: Knopf, 1979), p. 422. In addition to the Kintner story, of interest is the role played at CBS by producer Don Hewitt, who was instrumental at the conventions, with the *See It Now* series and later with *60 Minutes.*

14. *TV Guide,* July 1, 1967, as cited by Erik Barnouw, *The Image Empire,* p. 301.

15. Other major AP figures have included general news editor Rene Cappon, foreign editor Nate Polowetsky, Washington bureau chief William L. Beale, Jr., White House correspondents Ernest B. Vaccaro and Frank Cormier, political writers Douglas Cornell and Relman Morin, news analysts J. M. Roberts, Jr. and William L. Ryan, special correspondent George Cornell, and court trial specialist Linda Deutsch. Some noted byliners were Brian Bell, Larry Allen, Daniel De Luce, Lloyd Lehrbas, Don Whitehead, Edward Kennedy, C. Yates McDaniel, Malcolm Browne, and Peter Arnett. Overseas correspondents have been W. F. Caldwell, Richard O'Regan, Henry Bradsher, Richard K. O'Malley, and David Mason in Europe; Lynn Heinzerling and son Larry Heinzerling in Africa; Nick Ludington in the Middle East, Myron Belkind in India, and George Esper in Asia.

16. Other major UP figures were Frank Tremaine, war correspondent and longtime executive; Washington bureau chiefs Julius Fransden and Grant Dillman; political writers Raymond Lahr and Richard Growald; women's editor Gay Pauley; and European news chiefs Harry Ferguson and Julius B. Humi. Reporting abroad in the 1940s were Frederick C. Oechsner, Ralph Heinzen, Phillip H. Ault, Edward W. Beattie, M. S. Handler, William F. Tyree, William B. Dickinson, and H. D. Quigg. Byliners abroad in the 1950s and 1960s included Joseph W. Grigg, Norman Montellier, Frederick Kuh, A. L. Bradford, W. R. Higginbotham, Joseph W. Morgan, H. R. Ekins, Henry Gorrell, Robert Musel, and Jack Fox.

17. For an account of USIA from 1948 to 1960, see Wilson P. Dizard, *The Strategy of Truth* (Washington, D.C.: Public Affairs Press, 1960). Analysis of the ups and downs is given by Ronald I. Rubin, *The Objectives of the U.S. Information Agency: Controversies and Analysis* (New York: Praeger, 1968).

18. J. A. R. Pimlott, *Public Relations and American Democracy* (Princeton, N.J.: Princeton University Press, 1951), p. 3.

19. *Proceedings of Minnesota Public Relations Forum* (Minneapolis: Public Relations Society and participating company, 1952–1955).

20. William H. Taft, *American Magazines in the 1980s* (New York: Hastings House, 1982), p. 242. This work deals with more than 650 magazines, offering historical background on all leading magazines as well as advertising trends.

21. John Tebbel, *A History of Book Publishing in the United States,* Volume IV (New York: R. R. Bowker Company, 1981), p. 109. This volume covers the 1940 to 1980 period, part of two decades of research leading to this monumental set of books.

22. Tebbel, *A History of Book Publishing in the United States,* Volume IV, p. 165.

23. *A Ten-Year View of Public Attitudes Toward Television and Other Mass Media 1959–68,* a report by Roper Research Associates, pp. 4–5.

ANNOTATED BIBLIOGRAPHY

Books: Background History, Newspapers

BAYLEY, EDWIN R., *Joe McCarthy and the Press.* Madison: University of Wisconsin Press, 1981. Won a national research award. See also an excellent biography, Thomas C. Reeves, *The Life and Times of Joe McCarthy* (New York: Stein & Day, 1982).

BLUMBERG, NATHAN B., *One Party Press?* Lincoln: University of Nebraska Press, 1954. How thirty-five large dailies covered the 1952 campaign; news columns found to be essentially fair.

HALBERSTAM, DAVID, *The Powers That Be.* New York: Knopf, 1979. Examines in detail the influence of the *Washington Post, Los Angeles Times,* Time Inc., CBS, and owners.

HOFSTADTER RICHARD, *Anit-Intellectualism in American Life.* New York: Knopf, 1963. A Pulitzer Prize-winning study of the antiintellectual climate of the 1950s, with historical antecedents.

KUTLER, STANLEY J., *The American Inquisition: Justice and Injustice in the Cold War.* New York: Farrar, Straus & Giroux, 1983. Scholarly analysis of specific cases.

Books: Broadcasting

BERGREEN, LAURENCE, *Look Now, Pay Later: The Rise of Network Broadcasting.* Garden City, N.Y.: Doubleday, 1980. Best to date.

BLUEM, A. WILLIAM, *The Documentary in American Television.* New York: Hastings House, 1965. Includes historical development and 100 pages of photographs.

COMSTOCK, GEORGE, *Television in America.* Beverly Hills: Sage, 1980. Synthesis of published research on the impact of television on society.

FEDERAL COMMUNICATIONS COMMISSION, *Annual Report for Fiscal Year 1964.* Washington, D.C.: Government Printing Office, 1964. Summarizes, as thirtieth-anniversary issue, communication developments since 1934.

FRIENDLY, FRED W., *Due to Circumstances Beyond Our Control . . .* New York: Random House, 1967. The story of life with Edward R. Murrow, of their controversial CBS documentaries, and of Friendly's break with CBS.

KENDRICK, ALEXANDER, *Prime Time: The Life of Edward R. Murrow.* Boston: Little, Brown, 1969. Biography of the great commentator; thorough but misses catching drama of the great events in which Murrow participated.

METZ, ROBERT, *CBS: Reflections in a Bloodshot Eye.* Chicago: Playboy Press, 1975. CBS viewed this critical study with silence. Also, "The Biggest Man in Broadcasting," *New York,* VIII (July 21, 1975), 43. William S. Paley's career.

MURROW, EDWARD R., *In Search of Light: The Broadcasts of Edward R. Murrow, 1938–1961.* New York: Knopf, 1967. Broadcast history through memorable scripts.

PALEY, WILLIAM S., *As It Happened.* Garden City, N.Y.: Doubleday, 1979. Story of CBS.

QUINLAN, STERLING, *Inside ABC: American Broadcasting Company's Rise to Power.* New York: Hastings House, 1979. By an ABC executive.

SEVAREID, ERIC, *This Is Eric Sevareid.* New York: McGraw-Hill, 1964. The CBS commentator's thoughts between 1955 and 1964.

SHIERS, GEORGE, ed., *Technical Development of Television.* New York: Arno Press, 1977. Thirty articles surveying progress from the 1870s to 1975.

Books: Press Associations

BAILLIE, HUGH, *High Tension.* New York: Harper & Row, 1959. Readable autobiography of the former UP president. See also Joe Alex Morris, *Deadline Every Minute: The Story of the United Press.* (Garden City, N.Y.: Doubleday, 1957).

CONSIDINE, BOB, *It's All News to Me.* New York: Meredith, 1967. Autobiography of a great press-association reporter, for the INS, and Hearst star.

COOPER, KENT, *Kent Cooper and the Associated Press.* New York: Random House, 1959. Autobiography of the former general manager. For the story of the AP's restrictive news-exchange agreements, see his *Barriers Down* (New York: Holt, Rinehart & Winston, 1942).

GRAMLING, OLIVER, *AP: The Story of News.* New York: Holt, Rinehart & Winston, 1940. Unreliable in its survey of early period of AP history, on which Rosewater is the authority, the book contains valuable details for the modern era.

ISRAEL, LEE, *Kilgallen.* New York: Delacorte, 1979. Story of Dorothy of the INS.

SMITH, MERRIMAN, *A White House Memoir.* New York: Norton, 1972. How the UPI's great White House correspondent covered the period from FDR to Nixon.

Books: Magazines, Book Publishing

BONN, THOMAS L., *Under Cover: An Illustrated History of American Mass Market Paperbacks.* New York: Penguin, 1982. A short, illustrated history.

COUSINS, NORMAN, *Present Tense: An American Editor's Odyssey.* New York: McGraw-Hill, 1967. The history of the *Saturday Review* at age 25 by its editor.

FRIEDRICH, OTTO, *Decline and Fall.* New York: Harper & Row, 1970. About the death of the *Saturday Evening Post.* See also Joseph C. Goulden, *The Curtis Caper* (New York: G. P. Putnam's Sons, 1965).

MARTY, MARTIN E., JOHN G. DEEDY, JR., AND DAVID W. SILBERMAN, *The Religious Press in America.* New York: Holt, Rinehart & Winston, 1963. Protestant, Catholic and Jewish editors combine to analyze their subject.

PETERSON, THEODORE, *Magazines in the Twentieth Century.* Urbana: University of Illinois Press, rev. ed. 1964. The most comprehensive discussion of magazine-industry economics.

TEBBEL, JOHN W., *George Horace Lorimer and The Saturday Evening Post.* Garden City, N.Y.: Doubleday, 1948. Lorimer edited the *Post* from 1899 to 1937.

WAGNER, PHYLLIS CERF, AND ALBERT ERSKINE, *At Random: The Reminiscences of Bennett Cerf.* New York: Random House, 1977. Based on twenty-one tape-recorded interviews.

Books: Advertising, Public Relations

BARTOS, RENA, AND ARTHUR S. PEARSON, *The Founding Fathers of Advertising Research.* New York: Advertising Research Foundation, 1977. Brief paper account of Ernest Dichter (motivation), George Gallup (polling), Alfred Polits (sampling), Henry Brenner (entrepreneur), Hans Ziesel (sociologist), Frank Stanton (audience), and Archibald Crossley and A. C. Nielson, Sr. (ratings).

BERNAYS, EDWARD L., *Public Relations.* Norman: University of Oklahoma Press, 1979. A case-history type of discussion of the field by one of its founders.

CONE, FAIRFAX M., *With All Its Faults: A Candid Account of Forty Years in Advertising.* Boston: Little, Brown, 1969. By the head of famed Foote, Cone & Belding agency.

GOLDEN, L.L.L., *Only by Public Consent.* New York: 1968. Story of Paul W. Garrett and General Motor's public-relations program.

HILL, JOHN W., *The Making of a Public Relations Man.* New York: McKay, 1963. Counsel.

LESLY, PHILIP, ed., *Public Relations Handbook.* Englewood Cliffs, N.J.: Prentice-Hall, 1978. PR professionals contributed chapters.

MAYER, MARTIN, *Madison Avenue, U.S.A.* New York: Harper, 1958. A picture of advertising in the 1950s. See also Sloan Wilson, *The Man in the Gray Flannel Suit* (New York: Pocket Books, 1967).

OGILVY, DAVID, *Confessions of an Advertising Man.* New York: Atheneum, 1964. Fascinating account of advertising work by a founder of leading agency.

ROSS, IRWIN, *The Image Merchants.* Garden City, N.Y.: Doubleday, 1959. New York public-relations practitioners of the era described.

Periodicals and Monographs

ATWATER, TONY, "Editorial Policy of *Ebony* Before and After Civil Rights Act of 1964," *Journalism Quarterly,* LIX (Spring 1982), 87. Photo-editorial coverage increased.

BENÉT, STEPHEN VINCENT, "The United Press," *Fortune,* VII (May 1933), 67. A compact treatment of UP history and its 1933 status.

BENNION, SHERILYN COX, "*Saturday Review:* From Literature to Life," Ph.D. thesis, Syracuse University, 1968. Reviews *SR's* history.

BETHUNE, BEVERLY M., "The New York City Photo League: A Political History," Ph.D. thesis, University of Minnesota, 1979. Persecution in 1940s Red Scare. See also "A Case of Overkill: The FBI and the N.Y. City Photo League," *Journalism History,* VII (Autumn-Winter 1980), 87.

BOGART, LEO, "Magazines Since the Rise of Television," *Journalism Quarterly,* XXXIII (Spring 1956), 153. A study of magazine readership and economics from 1946 to 1955.

BLISS, EDWARD, JR., "Remembering Edward R. Murrow," *Saturday Review* (May 31, 1975), 17. CBS radio journalist recalls Murrow's courage and skill.

"Broadcasting at 50," *Broadcasting,* LXXIX (November 2, 1970). A special issue, including a year-by-year review of major events from 1931 to 1970.

"CBS: The First Five Decades," *Broadcasting,* XCIII (September 19, 1977), 45–116. Extensive survey.

GOEBBEL, ALFRED R., "*The Christian Century:* Its Editorial Policy and Positions, 1908–1966," Ph.D. thesis, University of Illinois, 1967. Descriptive study.

HARRISON, RICHARD EDES, "AP," *Fortune,* XV (February 1937), 89. The rise of the AP and a contemporary picture of its operations.

"How They Do It," *Newsweek,* LXXIII (December 1, 1969), 56. Story of the Huntley-Brinkley broadcast. See also "First Team," *Newsweek,* LVII (March 13, 1961), 53.

LEAMING, DERYL RAY, "A Biography of Ben Hibbs," Ph.D. thesis, Syracuse University, 1969. Discusses the editor of the *Saturday Evening Post.*

LITTLE, STUART, "What Happened at *Harper's,*" *Saturday Review,* LIV (April 10, 1971), 43. The dismissal of Willie Morris as editor.

MANAGO, B. R., "The *Saturday Evening Post* Under Ben Hibbs, 1942–1961," Ph.D. thesis, Northwestern University, 1968. Decline began in 1950s.

MCKERNS, JOSEPH P., "Television Docudrama: The Image as History," *Journalism History,* VII (Spring 1980), 24. A study of documentaries.

MCWHORTER, DIANE, "The Atlantic: In Search of a Role," *New York Times Magazine* (February 14, 1982), 20. News-making stories give hope for survival.

MURRAY, MICHAEL D., "Television's Desperate Moment: A Conversation with Fred W. Friendly," *Journalism History,* I (Autumn 1974), 68. Interview about Senator Joseph McCarthy and the media.

PFAFF, DANIEL W., "Joseph Pulitzer II and Advertising Censorship, 1929–1939," *Journalism Monographs,* No. 77 (July 1982). Reform at the *Post-Dispatch.*

ROWSE, ARTHUR E., *Slanted News.* Boston: Beacon Press, 1957. Analysis of how thirty-one large dailies reported the "Nixon fund" episode in 1952.

SCHWARZLOSE, RICHARD A., "The American Wire Services: A Study of Their Development as a Social Institution," Ph.D. thesis, University of Illinois, 1965. By a leading student of the press associations.

———, "Trends in U.S. Newspapers' Wire Service Resources, 1934–66," *Journalism Quarterly,* XLIII (Winter 1966), 627. A lessening of competitive service appears in these detailed figures.

SHAPLEN, ROBERT, "A Farewell to Personal History," *Saturday Review,* XLIII (December 1, 1960), 46. Summarizes radio and television network coverage abroad in the 1950s.

SWINDLER WILLIAM F., "The AP Antitrust Case in Historical Perspective," *Journalism Quarterly,* XXIII (March 1946), 40. Scholarly analysis.

WERTENBAKER, CHARLES, "Profiles," *New Yorker,* XXIX (December 26, 1953), 28. An excellent profile of Edward R. Murrow.

CBS

Walter Cronkite of CBS excelled in reporting the first manned space flights. Below, the NBC team of Chet Huntley and David Brinkley led in election-night coverage during the 1960s.

NBC

24
Challenge and Dissent

The United States might leave Vietnam, but the Vietnam War would now never leave the United States.
—Frances FitzGerald in *Fire in the Lake.*

If in later years some Americans harked back to the 1950s, trying to regain a lost sense of security and discipline, others recalled with mixed feelings the traumas and satisfactions of the 1960s when the nation was swept along the gamut of emotions. Shocking news bulletins telling of assassinations, race riots, and escalations of the Vietnam War produced reactions of anger, fear, sadness, and sheer bewilderment. But contentment was felt by those supporting the enforcement of new civil-rights laws and the expansion of political participation. And there was a swelling of pride throughout the land in July, 1969, when Americans stood on the moon.

The images of the decade, captured by print and broadcast journalists, are unforgettable. A panorama of scenes would show President Kennedy fending off tough questions with wit and charm at one of his televised news conferences, Attorney General Robert Kennedy on the phone planning strategy during a civil-rights confrontation in the South, Mrs. Kennedy taking a television crew on a White House tour, and the same Mrs. Kennedy stepping off Air Force One with her husband's coffin in view behind her. There would be Martin Luther King, Jr., giving his "I Have a Dream" speech in Washington, Lyndon Johnson and his advisers pondering the next step during the war, antiwar demonstrators being clubbed by Chicago police, Richard Nixon on the campaign trail again, women parading for equality, and national guardsmen riding through city streets brandishing machine guns. It all began in the spring of 1960 when John Fitzgerald Kennedy entered the presidential primaries, declaring that it was time for a new generation to hold power.

NIXON VS. KENNEDY: "THE GREAT DEBATES"

In late June, 1960, Congress suspended Section 315 of the Communications Act of 1934, the so-called "equal-time" rule requiring broadcasters to offer equal time to candidates of every party seeking a political office. This allowed the campaign managers for Nixon and Kennedy to begin negotiations leading to four televised debates in September and October. Kennedy had won the Democratic nomination with primary-election victories over Hubert H. Humphrey in Wisconsin and West Virginia and through a demonstration of power at the Los Angeles convention after delegates and supporters of Adlai E. Stevenson erupted into a frenzied, memorable demonstration that momentarily threatened to halt the Kennedy surge. Nixon had bested New York Governor Nelson Rockefeller to win the Republican nomination during a Chicago convention at which many of the charges of the 1950s about China, Korea, and internal security were repeated.

More than 85 million Americans tuned in to at least one of the Kennedy-Nixon debates. But the first debate, moderated by CBS news correspondent Howard K. Smith and carried on the three major networks, provided the crucial moment of the campaign. It was that evening in Chicago, September 26, that the less well-known Kennedy showed that he was an even match for the Vice President.[1]

As the two men traded comments about America's economic health and their own qualifications, Kennedy looked poised and fit, while Nixon seemed weary and somewhat gray. Occasionally the camera showed a worried Nixon listening to Kennedy, while a few minutes later a confident Kennedy was shown listening to one of Nixon's countercharges. From this point on Kennedy would be free of being called immature.

Kennedy's November victory by the margin of only 118,550 votes was attributed to his favorable television image. At age 43 he was the youngest man, and the first Roman Catholic, to assume the presidency.

KENNEDY AND THE PRESS: LIVE NEWS CONFERENCES

Kennedy introduced the live televising and broadcasting of presidential press conferences, an innovation with mixed blessings. The White House correspondents found that their home offices heard and saw the presidential responses long before the news stories clattered into their news desks. The mystique of the White House press conference in the oval room was gone. A skillful president could use the correspondents as foils or actors, and a few correspondents became actors by choice. On the positive side, millions of Americans could see the press conferences for themselves, live at the moment or digested in the evening news. Most of Kennedy's press conferences were in the afternoons, in

THE CHRISTIAN SCIENCE MONITOR

Registered in U. S. Patent Office
AN INTERNATIONAL DAILY NEWSPAPER

VOLUME 52 NO. 257 | BOSTON, TUESDAY, SEPTEMBER 27, 1960 | • ATLANTIC EDITION | TWO SECTIONS | BEYOND 30 MILES TEN CENTS | SEVEN CENTS

© 1960, THE CHRISTIAN SCIENCE PUBLISHING SOCIETY All Rights Reserved

Threat to UN Eases; Peking Casts Shadow

By the Associated Press

New York

President Eisenhower and British Prime Minister Harold Macmillan agreed Sept. 27 to give "full support" to United Nations Secretary-General Dag Hammarskjold in his tasks. Mr. Hammarskjold has been a target of Soviet Premier Nikita S. Khrushchev.

By Joseph C. Harsch
Special Correspondent of The Christian Science Monitor

United Nations, N.Y.

The delicate composure of Indian Prime Minister Jawaharlal Nehru and the phlegmatic urbanity of British Prime Minister Harold Macmillan flowed over the United Nations scene as its General Assembly went into the second week of its extraordinary session here in New York.

The effect was steadying on all—with, of course, the exception of Premier Fidel Castro of Cuba, who embarrassed his supposed friends and bored the rest of his audience with his inability to distinguish interminable rhetoric from logic.

The importance of Soviet Premier Nikita S. Khrushchev's role has visibly diminished as the awareness spreads that he has neither wrecked the UN nor possesses the capacity to do so. Dag Hammarskjold is still Secretary-General and will continue to be so.

A count of hands shows that Mr. Khrushchev could barely get 15 votes for his proposals which sounded so ominous a few days before, and the conviction grew that he had launched his assault on the UN—not for an instant expecting to get anywhere with it, but primarily as a talking point for his running argument with the Chinese Communists, with some incidental possible bargaining value here.

It is conceivable that he might at some point withdraw his threats against the UN in return for some benefit in future negotiations with the West, but his real purpose, it was agreed among Western diplomats, had been to forge a weapon he could use in the murky waters of Communist-bloc politics.

Mr. Nehru and Mr. Macmillan arrived on the scene not overexcited by the superficial discussions on disarmament which reflected the theoretical purpose of this gathering and not unduly disturbed by the flurry over the future of the UN which struck both of the new arrivals as equally unrealistic. Mr. Khrushchev had produced massive sound and fury which on examination proved to be nothing but froth.

Nehru's Concern

What concerned Mr. Nehru the most was not Dr. Castro's display of vulgar histrionics, but the flexing muscles of the Chinese giant across his northern frontier. And what was reportedly uppermost in Mr. Macmillan's thinking was the long-term implication of the Soviet-managed operation of recent weeks in the Congo.

The real dangers, as these men see them, and as their Washington colleagues agreed, are not immediate nor here in the UN, but in the fact that Moscow was able to deploy hundreds of "technicians" in the Congo on the first visible sign of an opportunity to make a new conquest for communism there, and of the even more disturbing implication that this abrupt action reflected a level of willingness in Moscow to take long and dangerous risks with the peace under the steady jabs of Peking incitement to violence which is the brand of Communist bloc behavior this year.

Key Question Cited

The visitors from London have been sobered by the Congo operation and while Mr. Macmillan himself can still see much theoretical merit in reviving easier personal relations with Mr. Khrushchev, he and his associates have faced the fact that Moscow proved in the Congo both its possession of a highly trained apparatus for suddenly exploiting an opportunity for conquest far beyond its frontiers and the cynical willingness to use it.

The visitors from India have been sobered by their own experiences under the shadow of Chinese expansionism and the many current indications that the dragon is still hungry and is still pushing with increasing insistence against the walls around it.

The real question which the Western statesmen talked about off the UN stage in the hotel rooms was the long-term problem of how to persuade, some would say help, Mr. Khrushchev to resist the arguments which have for months been beating upon him from Peking to resort to ever greater violence and revolution in a major Communist attack.

Soviet Tack?

The most significant event at this session may well prove to be the meeting between Mr. Nehru and Mr. Khrushchev, although it will certainly be years, if ever, before the real essence of this encounter will be spread on the public record.

It is perfectly obvious that Mr. Nehru called on Mr. Khrushchev to discover as best he could whether Mr. Khrushchev either willingly or under pressures which he thinks he can no longer resist is committed to the Chinese dictated course. Mr. Nehru is far too responsible a statesman to disclose what, if anything, he learned.

The dominant fact overshadowing this meeting is that Mr. Khrushchev, while clinging to his theories of the noninevitability of war and "peaceful coexistence," has done in the Congo precisely the sort of thing which Peking has been urging.

Is he committed permanently down this line, or is he treading it to build strength within the Communist bloc for a showdown with Peking which some Western experts increasingly suspect may be the greatest struggle looming on the world's horizon today?

Meeting Unlikely

Communist bloc leadership is bidden to assemble in Moscow in early November. Every Communist move here is quite probably shaped to that gathering of the clan where the issues outstanding between Moscow and Peking must be handled one way or another whether China is represented or stays away.

Under these circumstances it may now be assumed that the idea of any major effort to bring Mr. Eisenhower and Mr. Khrushchev together has been all but eliminated. Conceivably Mr. Khrushchev might change his tone and strategy before he leaves here sufficiently to permit a personal reconciliation. The likelihood is negligible.

If, as is now widely believed, he came here not to seek reconciliation but to build a record for use in his impending great struggle with Communist China, then there is no possibility of any news here of a surprise meeting between the two men who estranged each other in Paris last May.

The most alarming possibility is that the failure of the Congo venture and the impending failure here to stampede the new African countries into the Communist fold can goad Mr. Khrushchev not toward moderation but toward even more dangerous ventures.

In the meantime, though, the excitement is diminishing here and the British intend to express their views on all this by sending both their Prime Minister and their Foreign Minister back to London come next weekend.

Associated Press Wirephoto

U.S. and U.A.R. Presidents Meet

President Eisenhower (left) and United Arab Republic President Nasser had a show of hands as they met at President Eisenhower's hotel suite in New York Sept. 26. Mr. Eisenhower arrived from Washington earlier and held talks with various foreign dignitaries in New York for the 15th UN General Assembly. President Nasser is reported to have invited Mr. Eisenhower to pay a visit to the U.A.R. as Mr. Nasser's guest of honor.

Eisenhower's busy New York day: Page 3

MDC Probe Hears Political Echoes

By Albert D. Hughes
Staff Writer of The Christian Science Monitor

Political overtones today were injected into the special Massachusetts Senate committee investigation of the Metropolitan District Commission.

Senator John E. Powers (D) of Boston implied that the administration of Gov. Christian A. Herter and MDC commissioner Charles W. Greenough called off the Pleasure Bay project in South Boston for political reasons. The project was an enclosed area along a Boston harbor which would be free of tides and available throughout most of the day as a bathing beach.

Associate Commissioner Greenough, who was on the witness stand, suggested that the project was large and had been politically controversial. He furthermore asserted "I was not ordered to call it off."

Start Recalled

The associate commissioned testified that the Pleasure Bay project originated in a telephone call between himself and Senator Powers while he was on a vacation in Maine. Upon his return the then Commissioner said he sat down with Senator Powers and talked over the project.

Mr. Greenough further asserted that the Herter administration had expressed itself as strongly opposed to the project. Earlier in his testimony Senator Powers interupted Mr. Greenough to ask him what steps he had taken to reorganize the MDC after he became Commissioner.

Mr. Grennough displayed copies of bills which he had placed in the Legislature to put the executive and administration of the MDC under the Commissioner rather than the Board of Commissioners.

Bill Quoted

Senator Powers took a copy of the bill and stated that nowhere in it was there any indication that an MDC official was interested in the legislation, even though it concerned the MDC.

Resentment of key career employees over politics and waste in the operations of the Metropolitan District Commission was illustrated in testimony of Benjamin W. Fink, of Newton, chief engineer in the MDC Parks Division, before the special Senate committee investigating the MDC yesterday.

A career employee with the MDC for 36 years and for 12 years head of its Parks Division, Mr. Fink charged that the MDC is wasting half of the millions it spends on consultants' fees.

The special inquiry is expected to conclude today with testimony from MDC Commissioner John E. Maloney and Associate Commissioners Charles W. Greenough and John Hill.

Already, disclosures at the hearings have promoted one reform and other changes are in stores for the MDC. At its regular meeting last week on Tues- voted to review all new under-$1,000 contracts.

On the subject of these contracts, which it is charged were split to evade requirements for public bidding, Mr. Fink said political overtones were responsible for "poor supervision" of such contracts.

Mr. Fink testified he was forced to rely on subordinates for checking the under-$1,000 contracts and stated that it was a "physical impossibility" for him to oversee this work personally, though it carried his approving signature.

The MDC engineer also testified that members of his staff asked him to relay their complaints over the under-$1,000 "political contracts" to the hearings.

The Newton engineer also said that he has stopped all payment of under-$1,000 contracts, since the investigations began, except for emergency work.

Resignations Sought

Mr. Fink also testified to proposing that qualified steel inspectors be engaged when the Longfellow Bridge contract was begun and of being turned down by the commission. He said the MDC had five inspectors on the Longfellow Bridge job but none of them were qualified steel inspectors.

The disclosures brought from George A. McLaughlin, chief counsel, a statement that "we are going to ask, in our final report, that the Legislature establish one construction division to build all state roads, bridges, buildings, both for the state and the MDC, and that it be properly staffed with a central engineering division, and that it pay these engineers the going rates."

Senator Francis X. McCann (D), of Cambridge, committee member, also remarked "I think resignations are in order."

The Cambridge legislator made this statement after listening to testimony of William A. Meagher, of Wakefield, administrative assistant to Commissioner Maloney.

Pictures: Page 2

Associated Press Wirephoto

John F. Kennedy
Resolved . . .

Debate Winner? Voters of Nation

By Godfrey Sperling, Jr.
Chief of the Central News Bureau of The Christian Science Monitor

Chicago

The focal point of some 130,000,000 eyes, the presidential candidates squared off in the first of four unprecedented joint appearances before a vast TV audience.

The winner? The American public was the winner.

The silent Chicago streets, the cavernous ball park, the almost empty theaters. All this attested to the public's intense interest in the two candidates and a clash that centered on the farm, the aged, the schools, the economic growth rate, the lowering of the national debt, the relative maturity and experience of the two men. But the impact naturally spilled over into America's posture in the world today, and who was best qualified to provide leadership for the next four or eight years.

For reporters who have been following the candidates around the United States, there was little that was new in what the two men said. Senator John F. Kennedy, again, was saying that America's performance, vis-a-vis the Soviet Union, was not good enough. Vice-President Richard M. Nixon was saying it had, indeed, been good enough. And both were agreeing that there must be a step up for the future—militarily, scientifically, educationally, economically.

In the main, the verbal exchanges here showed that the objectives of the two candidates are quite similar. The difference lies in the means—and the cost of the means.

Mr. Nixon said, as he has said before, that he has tabulated the Democratic program and thinks it will cost $13,200,000,000 to perhaps $18,000,000,000 while, he said, his own program would cost some $4,000,000,000 to $4,900,000,000.

First, the Costs

Senator Kennedy later countered by asserting that the revenue for his program would come readily from the expanded growth that would accompany this program.

Even this was not a narrowing or sharpening of issues. It had all been said before as the presidential campaign jets moved back and forth across the country.

But here, for the first time, all these little speeches on all these different issues were being wrapped up into one easily understood package. And the pulling together of all this information was of inestimable value to a public intent on learning more about the candidates and getting a better grasp of the issues.

The men as TV performers? Both were superb. But was this a display of outstanding mental capacity or was this, at least in part, the expression of countless little memorized speeches? The limitations of TV could not answer this with a certainty, although the viewers—and particularly those who had already chosen up sides—probably resolved this question to their own satisfaction.

Actually, the question-from-panel format is not one that brings about a true clash of the "debaters." There was really little opportunity for either of the candidates to probe the other's mind—or to pressure the other with an incisive query.

Text of Statements In TV Debate: Page 16

Production Figures

It was Mr. Nixon, the man of experience under fire, the man of the kitchen debates with Soviet Premier Nikita S. Khrushchev, who looked strained in the early minutes of the discussion. He rallied well, but Kennedy had probably made a point. His consistent poise no doubt helped to put the immaturity charge to rest—for the evening, and, perhaps, for the entire campaign.

In the exchange of figures on economic growth, Mr. Nixon finally said that the Soviet production was 44 per cent that of the United States—the same that it was 20 years ago.

Senator Kennedy seemed to accept this figure but said it was important that the Soviets' production did not rise to 60 or 90 per cent in the next few years.

Earlier, Mr. Nixon had said that the Soviet's economic growth rate had been good in late years only because it was measured against a very low base.

Had Mr. Nixon nailed Senator Kennedy on this acceptance of a production figure, an acceptance that current production was not as bad as he had pictured? Perhaps so, but then, again, maybe only in the minds of Mr. Nixon's partisans.

Public the Critic

Actually, this was a strange occasion, where the press was not reporting anything that the public was not, itself, seeing—and analyzing for itself. And even a reportorial critique seems inconsequential. For the viewers are the critics.

Was Senator Kennedy or Mr. Nixon more persuasive than the other? How many votes were changed or won? The real critiques will be coming in on Nov. 8, in terms of votes for the new President of the United States.

Associated Press Wirephoto

Richard M. Nixon
Resolved . . .

Not One Slip On Banana Peel!

By Richard L. Strout
Staff Correspondent of The Christian Science Monitor

Washington

The first reception of the unprecedented Nixon-Knnedey debate in millions of homes was a gasp of surprise. For all that had been written about it in advance, most viewers were not prepared for the bare, bleak, brutal stage, utterly devoid of any distracting background or decoration, like two men sent flying in space for 65 million to watch.

As the ordeal continued, many viewers must have had a sense of sympathy for either candidate, whatever their political affiliation, at the terrible strain to which they were subjected. Any slip might have speiled ruin for either candidate and his party's hopes. The bare stage was actually strewn with invisible banana peels, and it was hard for the viewer not to feel a sense of admiration for the sure-footed young men, each of whom, in the opinion of many, displayed a quite astonishing grasp of detail and facility for quick mobilization of ideas.

Rise to Challenge

The cameras showed close-ups of the listening candidate's face while the other talked—Senator John F. Kennedy, his chin raised in a Roosevelt tilt with clean profile and lips slightly moving; Vice-President Richard M. Nixon, in turn, looking to many weary from endless campaigning, with chin perspiring under the hot TV lamps. Both men moistened their lips in the tropical glare. No other candidates in American presidential history went through such an ordeal, which seemed at times almost cruel in its revealing details.

The candidates rose to the challenge, however, and after a preliminary period of rigidity seemed to relax in the hour-long interrogation and reply which is the first of four such performances.

By the toss of a coin Mr. Kennedy not merely spoke first but had the last word, an advantage which Mr. Nixon will have at later meetings. Some observers felt that Senator Kennedy was strongest in his opening statement, which was composed of fragments of campaign speeches which he has by heart. In turn, Mr. Nixon seemed to gather strength as the proceedings continued as he threw constantly increasing objections in the path of Mr. Kennedy's sweeping proposals.

To some Senator Kennedy seemed to have a second preliminary advantage in that he was making the attack on the Eisenhower-Republican policies, while Mr. Nixon, at first, was in the position of a defender. As interrogations continued, however, Mr. Nixon in turn took the offensive when he charged that the cost of the Kennedy legislative proposals would be "13.2 to 18 billion dollars" compared with the "4 to 4.9 billion dollar" price tag which he placed on the Republican program.

Politeness Prevails

This confrontation was no exception to the rule that when candidates meet, there is a degree of politeness that hardly obtains when they speak apart. It was evident that neither man dared risk the danger of a breach of decorum with the vast unseen audience. The adept Mr. Nixon managed one ad hominem argument when he obliquely pointed up Mr. Kennedy's wealthy background by saying he was sure of the latter's sincerity and adding for himself, "I know what it means to be poor. . . . I know Senator Kennedy feels as deeply about these problems as I do. . . ."

Both men cited statistics of national "growth" which must have thoroughly confused unseen viewers because they were based on different and irreconcilable years of comparison. Senator Kennedy cited his familiar charges of a low growth rate under President Eisenhower; Mr. Nixon replied by taking Truman versus Eisenhower years.

Public Gains Insight

Millions of American families snapped off the TV to debate, "who won?"

One answer was that everybody won.

Beyond question the uniquely dramatic personal confrontation quickened political interest over the country six weeks before election. For the first time, many people became aware of the rival approaches to minimum wage, school aid, health aid for the aged, and the like, as well as of the contrasting personalities of the two men.

An argument could be made that either candidate benefited.

Senator Kennedy gained, in the opinion of many, because he had the more to win by making his personality known. He is the less familiar figure and has a certain amount of lag to make up by appearing on terms of equality with the Vice-President—a national celebrity for eight years.

Vice-President Nixon benefited for different reasons, it is argued. What the Republicans needed was a stir of excitement to get their supporters to register, to overcome the advantage Democrats are felt to have by their affiliation with nationally organized trade unions. This the Nixon-Kennedy clash has done.

State of the Nations

Who Pays for Reform?

By William H. Stringer
Chief, Washington News Bureau, The Christian Science Monitor

Washington

The first Nixon-Kennedy televised debate points up a consideration which the voters will have to resolve for themselves, and it is this:

Quite evidently, Senator John F. Kennedy would proceed more vigorously—or drastically—using more costly programs than would Vice-President Richard M. Nixon, in his efforts to handle the problems of aid to education, minimum wage, federal power, medical care for the elderly, perhaps defense. The question then is not merely that raised by Mr. Nixon, which is whether Congress would approve the 90 days of vigorous legislation which a President Kennedy in the White House would launch.

The question is also whether the business and industrial community of the United States would take this added burden, which almost certainly would mean an additional tax burden, in stride. Or would such a program disturb and unsettle the free enterprise system which lays the "golden eggs" of national wealth so that business would not respond, would not boost "national growth" levels, and we would be again in the doldrums of the 1930's.

* * *

Not until World War II came along was President Roosevelt able really to terminate the nation's business slump and get full production rolling after the great depression. Necessary reforms, pump priming for business, exhortations and denunciations had little effect. A climate of business opportunity had not been created by Washington, and so business did not boom. Would a President Kennedy encounter a like resistance, a similar failure to go forward?

The answer is partly psychological. If a new administration comes in on a big national tide of endorsement—if the nation has concluded that only vigorous measures will suffice to build educational standards higher, clear out the slums and big-city rot, take care of the elderly and raise the minimum wage—then a national climate will have been created to which the business community will perforce accommodate itself.

If this means added taxation—and there are indications that it must somewhere along the line—then industry will buckle too, and pay the taxes, in response to patriotic purpose. But if there is no evident national resolve that heroic measures are vital now, then a drastic Kennedy program could meet serious resistance and discourage good behavior in the business community.

* * *

The Kennedy brain trusters say that the whole round of additional government enterprise, defense spending, and management of debt and interest rates would be so engineered as to produce a burgeoning economy with high economic growth and that this would develop sufficient taxable wealth so that deficit financing and seriously unbalanced budgets could be avoided.

This may be so, but it would require a ratification by the business world of the proposition that the Kennedy program was either unavoidably crucial or designed to create a favorable business climate, to cause all this to work together for prosperity.

Per Jacobsson, the able and well-traveled Swede who heads the International Monetary Fund, observed last week that one main reason for today's rolling readjustment or lack of boom in business is that the American economy is getting used to moving along without inflation. This is a novel atmosphere; creeping inflation has been here for years, but now it seems to have been halted.

Mr. Jacobsson further reports that as Europeans survey the American economy and consider the possibility of a Kennedy victory, they wonder if this is going to touch off a new round of inflation. They note hopefully that Democrats talk of a national sales tax that could produce perhaps $8,000,000,000 to pay for all of Senator Kennedy's "new frontier" legislation.

If Senator Kennedy should be elected, would Congress pass such a tax? Would the United States's businessmen glance at the Soviet Union's strides and say, "We must sustain whatever burden is necessary to boost production and advance our social progress"? Or would the proposals be deemed too zealous, too drastic, and would business, disturbed or apprehensive, simply not undertake the sufficient investment in new plant, equipment, and enterprise necessary for really massive national growth?

* * *

Certainly Senator Kennedy must make an effective case for the urgencies of larger-scale government intervention, if such a program as he proposes were to be financed without slump, inflation, or seriously unbalanced budgets.

Goldfine Case To Open in Boston

The World's Day

Reg. U.S. Pat. Off.

New England: Tax-Evasion Trial Set for Oct. 3

The $800,000 tax-evasion case of industrialist Bernard Goldfine will open Monday, Oct. 3, in United States District Court, Boston. Mr. Goldfine, currently in the Federal Correctional Institution in Danbury, Conn., on a contempt-of-court sentence ending Monday, will be brought to Charles Street Jail this weekend. United States Attorney Elliot L. Richardson will prosecute the case.

National: Candidates Back on Campaign Trail

Following the "great debate" Vice-President Richard M. Nixon headed south for campaign activities in Tennessee and Arkansas. Senator John F. Kennedy flew to Ohio for a one-day political swing.

The father of U-2 pilot Francis Gary Powers, who failed in attempts to see Soviet Premier Nikita S. Khrushchev on behalf of his son, appealed to the Kremlin leader through the Dave Garroway "Today" show on NBC television.

Asia: South Korea Plans to Grant Pardons

Premier John M. Chang's South Korean Government decided to grant pardons or reduction of sentences to nearly 15,000 prisoners Oct. 1 in celebration of the founding of the Second Republic. Meanwhile, the government prosecution demanded capital punishment for four top-ranking police officials charged with rigging national elections last March.

Weather: Cloudy Tonight and Wednesday [Page 2]
Arts, Music, Theater: Page 7. Radio, TV, FM: Page 6

Inside Reading

Associated Press Wirephoto

Just Before the Opening Gavel

Presidential candidates Nixon and Kennedy trade grins

The crucial first "Great Debate" on television decided the 1960 presidential race.

time for Walter Cronkite and Huntley-Brinkley to feature their highlights. Kennedy handled the star role far better than any of the presidents of his period; he was young, charming, stylish, and as disarmingly humorous or severely grave as circumstances dictated. In short, he put on a good show.

Behind this Kennedy the public knew was a president who was anxious for his administration's image, who gave frequent individual interviews and had correspondents as personal friends, who read a half-dozen leading papers daily and resented their criticisms so much that he once banned the *Herald Tribune* temporarily. His press secretary, Pierre Salinger, took a hard line with the correspondents, as did Pentagon spokesperson Arthur Sylvester, who uttered the ill-fated comment about "the government's inherent right to lie" in cases in which government officials claim that the national security is at stake.

The press was upset in April, 1961, by clouded information given it about the Bay of Pigs, the futile attempt by the Kennedy administration to support a CIA-planned invasion of Castro's Cuba by a small army of exiles. The expedition, planned by the Eisenhower administration and agreed to by Kennedy upon advice by CIA officials, was a disaster. Kennedy accepted full responsibility and angrily dismissed CIA head Allen W. Dulles.

The Kennedy administration unified its news sources, sought to manage the contacts between officials and the press, and was accused of seeking to manage the news itself. During the Cuban Missile Crisis of 1962, when Kennedy grimly told the nation that Russian missiles in Cuba were a threat to the United States and could lead to nuclear war, the administration insisted that the crisis was so severe as to require press self-control and privately suggested possible censorship of the press in the event of actual hostilities. Publication of the Pentagon Papers in 1971 proved a far deeper involvement in Vietnam affairs by 1963 than the Kennedy administration ever acknowledged, including a share of responsibility for the assassination of President Diem, and showed that the Saigon press corps had been essentially correct in vainly protesting the deepening involvement in a "quagmire." While public opinion supported the President, there was enough doubt to indicate that a credibility gap existed.

Following the tradition of previous Democratic presidents, Kennedy had received marginal support from newspapers during his campaign, getting only 16 percent of the endorsements. The *New York Times,* however, had swung behind him after supporting Eisenhower twice, and his friend Philip L. Graham headed the *Washington Post.* But after receiving careful treatment from old family friend Henry Luce during the campaign—until the end when Nixon received the coveted endorsement—Kennedy fell into disfavor with *Time* and *Life* and continued to irritate conservative publishers.[2]

Kennedy was hardly "soft on Communism," however, as some publishers and columnists suggested. The Soviets repeatedly put him to test, first in August, 1961, when they built the Berlin Wall. During the Cuban Missile Crisis in October, 1962, Nikita Khrushchev played brinksmanship to the hilt, forcing Kennedy to declare a blockade of Cuba and to threaten the use of arms if the Soviets persisted in setting up missile bases. On October 22 Kennedy made an historic 17-minute address, informing frightened Americans of his ultimatum. Khrushchev backed down, in return for a pledge that the United States would not attack Cuba in the future. Later Kennedy visited Berlin and home viewers saw him honored by millions of West Germans as he spoke in German, "I am a Berliner." Meanwhile, on the domestic front, the Kennedy brothers used the federal government to protect the civil rights of Southern blacks. Robert Kennedy put Teamsters President James Hoffa in prison, and the President made headlines by attacking the steel industry when leaders attempted to obtain a price hike. During his "1000 days" in office Kennedy was an exciting personality. The Washington press corps responded with uncounted stories about the Kennedy "clan," as well as stories about traditional topics. Because of this general fondness for Kennedy he was spared hard looks into his personal life that might have revealed romantic interests capable of destroying his presidency. He was especially appreciated by television news executives who liked his manner and the drama surrounding him.

THE KENNEDY ASSASSINATION: THE END OF THE "1000 DAYS"

There were many reasons in November, 1963, why a group of conspirators—or a lone deranged killer—would have wished John Fitzgerald Kennedy dead. First there was the "Cuban problem." The island remained in Castro's hands, despite a CIA vendetta against him that was disclosed later. Organized crime leaders were furious over the loss of hundreds of millions of dollars in gambling and prostitution revenues. Ex-CIA officials and veterans of the Bay of Pigs failure were embittered over JFK's decision not to use American forces in 1961 and during the crisis of 1962. Mob leaders worried how far Robert Kennedy might go in his racket-busting campaign, already having obtained a conviction of Teamsters boss James Hoffa. Kennedy had signed a nuclear test-ban treaty with Russia in June, 1963, and finally, in August, he issued a strong statement of support after Martin Luther King, Jr., and other black leaders led the largest civil-rights rally in the nation's history, 200,000 strong, at the Lincoln Memorial.

Looking ahead to the 1964 campaign, Kennedy agreed to travel to Texas in November. Vice President Lyndon Johnson wanted Kennedy to help mend some political fences. It was a bright, sunny day, November 22, when the President's motorcade headed through downtown Dallas on its way to the Trade Mart, where Kennedy was to address a luncheon audience. Merriman Smith of United Press International was in the front seat of a "pool" car—next to a telephone—and three other reporters were in the back seat. Without warning, as the Kennedy car slowly turned a corner at the end of the parade route, shots were fired. It was 12:30 P.M.

The President's limousine and its police and Secret Service escorts roared off at high speed. Smith wrote later: "Our car stood still for probably only a few seconds, but it seemed like a lifetime. One sees history explode before one's eyes and for even the most trained observer, there is a limit to what one can comprehend."[3] As the pool car careened along the freeway, Smith dialed the Dallas UPI number and reached William Payette, the Southwestern division manager. At 12:34 P.M. the UPI "A" wire carried these words:

DALLAS, NOV. 22 (UPI)—THREE SHOTS WERE FIRED AT PRESIDENT KENNEDY'S MOTORCADE TODAY IN DOWNTOWN DALLAS. JT1234PCS

President Kennedy and Merriman Smith.
UPI

The New York UPI office broke in with "Dallas it's yours" meaning that all other bureaus should refrain from transmitting. The wire was kept open. In the pool car Smith held onto the phone, while Jack Bell of the AP pounded him on the back, yelling "Smitty, give me the phone." When the car reached Parkland Hospital Smith threw Bell the phone and rushed to the Kennedy car. He saw both the President and Texas Governor John B. Connolly cradled in their wives' arms. Smith asked about the President and heard Secret Service agent Clint Hill say, "He's dead." With that Smith ran into the hospital and the midst of hysteria. He managed to reach the Dallas bureau and began to dictate what would become a Pulitzer Prize winning story. Smith's "flash" and story were jammed onto the wire. The unusually long "flash" was jumbled. Official style was lost for a few seconds.

FLASH
FLASH
KENNEDY SERIOUSLY WOUNDED. PERHAPS SERIOUSLY
PERHAPS FATALLY BY ASSASSIN'S BULLETS

UPI9N BULLETIN 1ST LEAD SHOOTING
PRESIDENT KENNEDY AND GOV. JOHN B. CONNOLLY OF TEXAS WERE CUT DOWN BY ASSASSIN'S BULLETS AS THEY TOURED DOWNTOWN DALLAS IN AN OPEN AUTOMOBILE TODAY.
More JT1241PCS

Jack Fallon took charge of the writing within the bureau and was later credited with the smooth flow of the copy. The story was rushed onto the UPI broadcast wire and within minutes AP wires were confirming the horrible news. Then at 1:32 P.M. the AP flashed, "TWO PRIESTS SAY KENNEDY DEAD." By this time, television sets around the nation had been switched on. In New York City the audience jumped from 30 percent to 70 percent. At CBS Cronkite had rushed into the newsroom to begin broadcasting the first details. Now he and his counterparts at the other networks had the AP flash. CBS radio, through the reporting of Dan Rather in Texas, had already announced the President's death. Then came the confirmation of the AP report. At 1:35 UPI said "FLASH. PRESIDENT DEAD." Tears welled in Cronkite's eyes, and in millions of others.

There was no other news that day. The press associations used every available wire to pump the Dallas news and reaction stories to their media outlets. Regular television programming was cancelled. Radio stations played somber music. Then came the news that Lee Harvey Oswald, a member of the left-wing Fair Play for Cuba Committee, had been arrested and charged with the assassination.

Later it was said the days November 22 to 25 were the finest in television history. Calm, comprehensive coverage of the news from Dallas and Washington—the transition from Kennedy to Lyndon Johnson—gave the nation a sense of security. On the evening of November 22, Air Force One returned to Washington. The public saw Jacqueline Kennedy, still wearing her blood-stained pink suit, accompanying her husband's body and being comforted by Robert Kennedy and other family members. Lyndon Johnson made a brief statement from the airport. Smith and Charles Roberts of *Newsweek* were the pool reporters on that historic flight. Meanwhile, major news organizations sent additional reporters, photographers, and television crews to Dallas to assist the exhausted members of the White House press corps.

On Sunday, November 24, television cameras were focused on the scene in the Capitol rotunda, where President Kennedy's body had rested overnight. Leaders of the free world were headed to Washington for Monday's funeral. Sunday was a day of eulogies and pleas for an end to violence and hatred. Shortly after 12:30 P.M. Oswald was being transferred from the Dallas police station to the county jail. The scene was picked up on monitors in the three network control rooms in New York. NBC made the decision to switch to Dallas immediately, while CBS and ABC stayed with the pictures from the Capitol, where Mrs. Kennedy and her children stood near the coffin.

Tom Pettit of NBC was only a few feet from Oswald when the suspect was led through the basement door and into an underground parking garage in Dallas. As Pettit began to describe the scene a burly man shoved his way through the edge of the crowd of police, reporters, and photographers. Jack Ruby, handgun extended, fired one shot into Oswald's body. The shot was plainly heard. It was television's first live murder. CBS and ABC videotaped the scene

WEATHER

Today: Sunny and cool.
Tomorrow: Cloudy, milder.
TEMPERATURE RANGE
Yesterday 41-53; Today 32-45.
HUMIDITY
Yesterday 3 p. m. 34%; Today 40-45.
Reports and Maps—Page 26

NEW YORK
Herald Tribune

THE CITY

Established 123 Years Ago. A European Edition Is Published Daily in Paris

VOL. CXXIII No. 42,613 — 230 West 41st Street, New York 10036, N. Y. Telephone PEnnsylvania 6-4000 — MONDAY, NOVEMBER 25, 1963 — © 1963, New York Herald Tribune Inc. — TEN CENTS

A Nation Appalled

Monday, Nov. 25, 1963

IN THE NEWS THIS MORNING

[FROM THE HERALD TRIBUNE'S WORLD-WIDE SOURCES.]

TOPIC A—

The body of John Fitzgerald Kennedy was borne from the White House to the Capitol Rotunda yesterday. An estimated 300,000 watched the mournful procession along Pennsylvania Avenue when the flag-covered coffin was lifted from the black caisson and placed inside the Rotunda, Mrs. Jacqueline Kennedy, dressed in black and wearing a black veil, knelt and kissed it. In a brief ceremony, government leaders mixed their eulogies with pleas for an end to bitterness, violence and hatred in the land. And then the people began to file past. [Page 1]

IN DALLAS—

In the same Dallas Hospital under the hands of the same doctors who had labored to save President Kennedy, Lee Harvey Oswald, the accused assassin, died at 1:07 p. m. One bullet fired point-blank from the nickel-plated revolver of nightclub owner Jack (Ruby) Rubenstein cut down Oswald as an army of Dallas detectives ushered him out of City Hall jail for transfer to County Jail. Within an hour, Rubenstein was charged with Oswald's murder and Dallas homicide chief Will Fritz said the case of the assassination of the 35th President was "closed." [Page 1]

Rubenstein was not regarded as a criminal type although he was arrester six times for minor incidents. Un-married, he lived with a roommate who said he showed "a terrible grievance" over the President's assassination and lamented: "That poor family." He was a physical-fitness enthusiast reportedly well acquainted with Dallas police and newspapermen. [Page 2]

IN WASHINGTON—

Fresh from the melancholy experience of the cortege, President Johnson turned immediately to the country's No. 1 foreign policy problem—the shooting war in Viet Nam. In a conference with top security officials and Henry Cabot Lodge, his Ambassador in Saigon, President Johnson heard a "hopeful" report on a bold Communist move against a training center 20 miles from Saigon. [Stories on Page 5]

The late President's widow and two young children followed directly behind the horse-drawn caisson that brought Mr. Kennedy's flag-draped coffin from the White House to the Capitol. Caroline, nearly six, occasionally looked up at her mother's tear-stained face as if to comfort her. John jr., who will be three today, waved a small American flag. Other members of the Kennedy family followed. The President's father, Joseph, was unable to travel to Washington because of illness. [Full story, Page 9]

Leaders from all parts of the world began to assemble in Washington to pay last respects to the late President Kennedy. Sixty-seven nations indicated they were sending representatives. The U. S. told foreign governments the presence of regular envoys would suffice, did not encourage the mass influx of heads of state. President Johnson will receive heads of state and other dignitaries at 5:30 p. m. today on the eighth floor of the State Department Building. [Reports on Page 7]

IN THE NATION—

The single shot that cracked in the basement of the Dallas City Hall yesterday closed forever the story of the man who the police believe committed one of the century's most incredible crimes. His motives, his preparations, his reasoning will never be known exactly. The bizarre shooting bewildered and angered people across the nation. [Story on Page 4]

Unprecedented radio and television coverage of the events in Dallas and Washington continued into a third day. It appeared there would be no return to normal broadcasting schedules until tomorrow morning. While millions of Americans considered the coverage the medium's finest hour, both the White House and the networks reported receiving calls from people around the country annoyed that their favorite programs had been deleted. [Page 13]

Of the problems suddenly placed on Lyndon Johnson's shoulders, one of the first he must deal with will be the threatened national rail strike. Tomorrow, a board set up by Congress to avoid the strike by compulsory arbitration of two key issues will deliver its decision to the new President. [Details, Page 20]

IN THE CITY—

Clergymen of all faiths eulogized the late President Kennedy, and church attendance increased throughout the city yesterday. A typical response: the Rev. Peter Chase, canon pastor of the Cathedral of St. John the Divine, told his congregation: "This is a great country with a great mission to lead us on." [Story on Page 13]

TODAY IN THE HERALD TRIBUNE

UPI telephoto by BOB JACKSON, copyright, 1963 The Dallas Times-Herald

BULLET STRIKES VITALS of accused assassin Lee Oswald as night club owner Jack Ruby pulls the trigger, detective recoils, in crowded corridor of city hall basement.

Nightclub Owner Silences Assassin

By Maurice C. Carroll
Of The Herald Tribune Staff

DALLAS.

Lee Harvey Oswald met an assassin's death yesterday just 48 hours and seven minutes after the bullets he was accused of firing killed the President of the United States. With much of the nation watching on television, Oswald was shot down amid a crowd of reporters, photographers and policemen as he was to be taken from the Dallas police station to the county jail. He was rushed to Parkland Hospital and gasped out his final breath in the same emergency ward, just 10 feet from the room where John F. Kennedy died Friday.

At the Dallas police station, detectives were mounting guard again over their newest killer, nightclub owner Jack Rubinstein, alias Jack Ruby. Dallas District Attorney Henry Wade, who had vowed to seek the death penalty for Oswald, said he would seek it for Oswald's killer.

Last night police barricaded parts of downtown Dallas to help control the crowds which have been increasing at the scene of the President's assassination and the Oswald shooting.

The chief of the Texas Highway Patrol ordered 20 extra men into Dallas to guard Gov. John Connally, still recuperating in Parkland Hospital after being wounded in the fusillade that killed Mr. Kennedy.

"We have complete respect for the Dallas Police Department and we do not mean to imply that we do not," said Col. Homer Garrison jr., head of the State Department of Public Safety.

The 20 troopers were brought in from Tyler, 98 miles east of Dallas. Col. Garrison refused to say whether more had been ordered in from other areas of the state.

Dallas was increasingly tense as wild rumors of telephone threats of new shootings floated through the city. Dallas and Texas as a whole have free-and-easy laws concerning the possession of firearms, and many citizens apparently feel that the violence of the last three days has disgraced the city's good name. No one is sure the violence is over yet.

Oswald died without ever having changed his statements that he was innocent of the murder of President Kennedy. Authorities had said that they had an overwhelming case prepared against him.

The bullet that killed the admitted Communist sympathizer pierced Oswald's spleen, pancreas, aorta, kidney and liver.

The same physicians who had treated President Kennedy at Parkland were unable to save Oswald, even though they administered repeated transfusions and used an electronic Pacemaker to attempt to bring his heart back into action.

He died in Emergency Room Two, the same room where physicians had worked over his second victim, Texas Gov. John Connally, who is recovering from his wounds. The room is across the corridor from the room where President Kennedy died.

The shooting was witnessed by millions of Americans on all three television networks which had set up cameras to view the President's accused assassin as he was transferred from the police station to the county jail.

This reporter was within eight feet of Oswald when he was shot. I may have shouted the last words he was ever to hear.

The prisoner, hands cuffed in front of him, was led into the cavernous garage under the station. Seconds before

More on MILLIONS—P 2

Associated Press wirephoto

ON THE WHITE HOUSE STEPS, the woman the slain assassin widowed, Jacqueline Kennedy, appears with her children, John jr. and Caroline, to escort the President's body to the Capitol where it lay in state in the Rotunda.

MOURNING IN CAPITAL

By David Wise
Washington Bureau Chief

WASHINGTON.

Under an Amercan flag and a bright autumn sun, to the roll of muffled drums, the body of John F. Kennedy, 35th President of the United States, was borne along Pennsylvania Ave. to the Capitol rotunda yesterday, and rested there overnight. Pleas for an end to bitterness, violence and hatred in the land were voiced in eulogies.

In an unforgettable scene, Mrs. Jacqueline Kennedy, in black and veiled, stood in the rotunda in sorrowful dignity, holding the hands of her two children, Caroline and John jr. Then she and her daughter knelt and Mrs, Kennedy kissed the flag-draped casket.

At the very moment that Sen. Mike Mansfield, the Democratic leader of the Senate, stood at the bier and decried "the hatred, prejudice and the arrogance which converged in that moment of horror to strike him down," there was new horror in Dallas, Texas. At 2:07 p. m., as Sen. Mansfield spoke, Lee Harvey Oswald, accused of assassinating the President, died in an emergency room of Parkland Hospital in Dallas.

He had been shot with a single bullet fired point-blank by a man police identified as Jack Ruby, the owner of a dance hall and a strip-tease club.

All day and into the night, thousands of people filed past the bier of the dead President as the nation and the world paid tribute to his passing. Today, he will be buried in Arlington National Cemetery after a requiem mass.

The leaders of the world converged on Washington to attend the funeral today.

President Lyndon B. Johnson rode in the cortage from the White House to the Capitol, but then sped back to the Executive Office Building to deal with a new crisis in Viet Nam.

Thousands of spectators, many wiping tears from their eyes, watched as seven white horses carried the body of the President to the Capitol on the same caisson that once bore the body of President Franklin D. Roosevelt 18 years ago.

The rain that had poured for hours in Washington Saturday was gone. Yesterday dawned bright, cloudless and crisp. The sun glinted off the black wooden wheels of the caisson, accompanied by a military honor guard, as it moved slowly to the capitol, to the mournful rhythm of the muffled drums. The procession took just 40 minutes.

As it began, word spread among the throngs that the man charged with the assassination of President Kennedy had been killed. It added a new nightmarish twist to the horror of the past 48 hours.

In the brief, moving ceremony in the rotunda, pleas for unity and an end to violence were voiced by Sen.

More on MOURNING—P 6

The great *New York Herald Tribune* records history with superb journalistic skill.

and the three networks showed it repeatedly throughout the rest of the day and evening.*

Oswald died 1 hour later, 10 feet from where Kennedy had died. Americans sat stunned in their living rooms, speculating about the bizarre turn of the events. The next day they watched the funeral. Television cameras were stationed at every major Washington intersection and correspondents sometimes failed to hold back their emotions as the casket passed and the bands played sad hymns. The nation fell silent as the final words were said at Arlington National Cemetery and military planes roared over, with one plane missing from the formation as a symbol of loss.

President Johnson ordered a complete investigation of Kennedy's killing and a commission was established under the leadership of Chief Justice Earl Warren. In 1964 the Warren Commission issued its findings: that Oswald had acted alone, and that he had fired three shots, killing Kennedy with the third shot, which hit the President in the head. There was instant rebuttal of these findings and critics like Mark Lane, author of *Rush to Judgment,* used a homemade movie taken by Abraham Zapruder of Dallas to make their case. A frame-by-frame analysis showed that Oswald had 4.6 seconds to fire the second and third shots. The Warren Commission thesis rested on the statement that there were *three* shots. If so, the first shot had to have hit both Kennedy and Connolly, because the second shot missed and the third shot clearly hit the President in the head. During the next decade a plethora of books and films attempted to prove that a conspiracy existed.

Among news organizations, *Life* offered the best examination of the evidence, partially because the magazine had purchased Zapruder's film. In October, 1964, *Life* said of the report, "The major significance . . . is that it lays to rest the lurid rumors and wild speculations."[4] But in November, 1966, *Life,* relying on Connolly's testimony that he had not been hit by the same bullet as Kennedy, demanded that the case be reopened. A year later *Life* offered unpublished photos by onlookers that suggested the possibility of a conspiracy but fell short of proving it. In December, 1967, *Saturday Evening Post* claimed that Kennedy was killed by three assassins who fired from different angles.

Major papers shied from the conspiracy story, out of disbelief and also because such an investigation would require an enormous amount of time and money. In 1966 the *New York Times* finally decided to go ahead with an investigation, with Harrison Salisbury as the reporter, but he was granted his visa to visit Hanoi at that time and the project was dropped. CBS News, with Rather the reporter, did a documentary and decided that there was little, if any, evidence of a conspiracy. Prior to his death in 1972, however, former President Johnson told Cronkite that he had never believed the Warren Commission report. The comment was part of taped interview but Johnson refused to permit its broadcast, despite Cronkite's pleadings.

Several young reporters established their reputations on the day of Kennedy's assassination. Rather distinguished himself and afterwards was named

*The video tape recorder, produced by Ampex in 1956, was first used that year by Huntley and Brinkley, who played back President Eisenhower's inauguration speech. CBS developed the sports "instant replay" in 1963.

White House correspondent. CBS felt that Rather, a Texan, might gain some advantage with Johnson. Tom Wicker of the *New York Times* also produced an amazingly comprehensive story, by running from one location to another throughout the day.

THE PROTEST MOVEMENTS FIGHT RACISM, SEXISM, IMPERIALISM

The powerful antiestablishment movements of the 1960s were the culmination of many previous efforts to change laws discriminating against minorities and women and to halt imperialistic adventures that depleted the nation's treasure. Much of the activity can be traced to student movements of the late 1950s at Berkeley, Chicago, Columbia, Michigan, and Oberlin. When young blacks staged a sit-in at a F. W. Woolworth store in Greensboro, North Carolina, in February, 1960, they triggered a nationwide reaction. College students in other states began picketing Woolworth stores, which eventually led to the desegregation of public facilities. Also in 1960, a number of Berkeley students protesting a House Un-American Activities Committee session in San Francisco were beaten by police and arrested.

The first Freedom Riders made their way into the South in May, 1961, continuing the sit-ins, and demanding an end to restrictions in voting laws. Television news teams soon spread images of angry whites and defiant Southern authorities. Ku Klux Klansmen organized opposition to the Freedom Riders and on several occasions buses were burned and the riders severely beaten. During the early 1960s several civil-rights workers were murdered. Paving the way for other protesters were members of CORE (the Congress of Racial Equality), led by James Farmer, and SNCC (the Student Nonviolent Coordinating Committee).

Attorney General Robert Kennedy petitioned the Interstate Commerce Commission to desegregate all airport terminals and railroad depots. The "white" and "colored" signs were taken down by the end of 1961. That year the Kennedys also used federal power to force the University of Mississippi to register James Meredith, an Air Force veteran. Dozens of federal marshals were injured, some of them by snipers' bullets, and two persons were killed when a large mob attacked those protecting Meredith. Regular U.S. Army troops were used to quell the bloody rioting.

The Bay of Pigs disaster of 1961 and the terrible fear of nuclear war brought more campus protests. The Students for a Democratic Society (SDS) issued their Port Huron Statement in 1962, denouncing domestic racism and overseas imperialism. Then, in 1963, the civil-rights movement hit full stride, as did its media coverage. Martin Luther King, Jr., declared war on Birmingham, Alabama, which he considered the citadel of racism. The police chief there, T. Eugene "Bull" Connor, became a symbol of Southern resistance. While King led a series of sit-ins and marches, the Kennedys were determined to integrate the University of Alabama in a showdown with the rebellious Governor George C. Wallace.

Wallace did stand in the doorway of a University building, reading for the television cameras a proclamation forbidding the intrusion of the federal government. But Vivian J. Malone and Jimmy A. Hood were registered at the University, one more step in ending segregation in universities. Meanwhile, Birmingham blacks had taken to the streets in protest of the vicious use of police dogs against demonstrators. Pictures of police using dogs and fire hoses against defenseless blacks circulated the world, creating an embarrassing image for the United States.

The first of the long hot summers began in 1964, in Harlem, where blacks went on a rampage after a police officer shot a 15-year-old boy. Waves of hostility long kept under control burst loose. The next summer riots broke out in the Watts area of Los Angeles. More than 20,000 National Guardsmen and local authorities were called into a 50-square-mile riot area. After 6 days of burning and fighting, thirty-four persons were dead and another 1000 injured. A split occurred in the black leadership in 1966 when Stokely Carmichael took over SNCC and Floyd McKissick replaced Farmer at CORE. Carmichael and McKissick urged strong action, but King, the NAACP, and Urban League stuck to the nonviolent course. "Black power" inevitably became the byword for thousands of angry young blacks, some of them devoted to the dissident Muslim leader Malcolm X. In 1966, for a great variety of reasons, there were several dozen racial outbreaks in the United States. In 1967 there was major fighting in Newark, Detroit, and Cambridge, Maryland; in Detroit alone forty-one persons were killed. Following the April 4, 1968 assassination of Martin Luther King in Memphis, while he was urging restraint during a sanitation worker's strike, rioting broke out again in many cities, with much violence in Washington, D.C., and Chicago. Television brought nightly scenes of anger in the streets.

Running parallel to the civil-rights strike were the "free-speech," antiwar, and women's movements. The so-called free-speech movement began on the University of California Berkeley campus in 1964 when Mario Savio and other students protested an administration decision banning on-campus rallies in support of off-campus demonstrations. Police arrested hundreds of students in the first of the student–administration battles that spread to many other campuses during the decade. By 1965 there were anti-Vietnam rallies at Berkeley and the University of Michigan. Radical students were sometimes opposed by Young Americans for Freedom, a conservative organization built by followers of Senator Barry Goldwater of Arizona.

Leading the drive for sexual equality was the National Organization for Women (NOW), founded at the University of Wisconsin in 1966. Other pioneers were the Women's Equity Action League (WEAL) and Federally Employed Women (FEW). Much of the legal planning and leadership was provided by the American Civil Liberties Union's Women's Rights Project. The first female picket line organized by NOW was set up in 1967 to protest the Equal Economic Opportunities Commission's wording of want ads. NOW members had gained experience in the civil–rights movement and union activities and their leaders urged parades and picketing to protest discrimination in employment and sexist portrayals of women in the mass media. Because some of the leaders were skilled at public relations, the movement gained much public attention.

But a younger branch of the movement gradually turned to small-scale

DEPARTMENTAL INDEX
Amuse Sec. 2, P. 6-8 Marine Sec. 2, P 15
Bridge Sec. 3, P 4 Oil News Sec. 3, P 11
Classified S. 3, P 12-25 Police Sec. 3, P 25
Comics Sec. 3, P 11 Radio-TV Sec. 2, P 4
Editorials Sec. 1, P 10 Society Sec. 3, P 2-11
Finance S. 2, P 26-28 Sports Sec. 2, P 9-15

The Times-Picayune

Serving America's International Gateway Since 1837

PARTLY CLOUDY
and turning cooler and north winds, 10-20 miles an hour, is the U.S. Weather Bureau forecast. High expected Friday, 64-68; low, 50-54. High Thursday, 77; low, 67. Weather map, details, Sec. 3, Page 10.

132nd YEAR, NO. 72 — Full Associated Press (AP), National News and Chicago News Wires and AP WIREPHOTO. — NEW ORLEANS, FRIDAY MORNING, APRIL 5, 1968 — Second-Class Postage Paid at New Orleans, La. — SINGLE COPY 10 CENTS

DR. KING FATALLY SHOT BY ASSASSIN IN MEMPHIS

VENUE CHANGE MOTION DENIED BY COURT HERE

Judge States Shaw Can Get Fair Trial

Criminal District Judge Edward A. Haggerty Jr., denied a defense change of venue motion Thursday and ruled that Clay L. Shaw can receive a fair trial in New Orleans.

Shaw is accused of participating in a plot to kill President John F. Kennedy. His attorneys immediately announced they will file a bill of exceptions to the decision and will apply for writs to the Louisiana Supreme Court.

They asked for 30 days in which to ask the state's highest court to review the decision, but Judge Haggerty said this is excessive and gave them 15 days. The judge said:

"I want the record to show that there is nothing the court is doing to delay this case. I would urge the district attorney's office to set this case for trial as soon as possible. Also, the defense could file a motion asking for a speedy trial."

Asst. district attorney James L. Alcock said, "We can't set this case for trial until the application for a writ is disposed of."

Judge Haggerty concluded his eight-page written opinion by saying, "I do not believe that the state of the public mind of the citizens of New Orleans is against the defendant, and I further believe he can receive a fair trial in this jurisdiction."

PUBLICITY HIT

Defense attorneys F. Irvin Dymond and William and Edward Wegmann claimed that publicity given to the assassination probe would prevent a fair trial for Shaw.

Judge Haggerty said that senior Criminal District Judge Bernard J. Bagert, at the preliminary hearing, "took all precautions that he could in keeping and protecting the rights of the defendant . . ."

The judge further commented, reading his entire opinion in court:

"Because of the national and probably the international publicity given to the Warren Report and the death of our beloved President, John F. Kennedy, there is no question that probably everyone over the age of seven years throughout the State of Louisiana has probably heard or read or spoken about those particular matters, the Warren Commission and the assassination of Mr. Kennedy."

It is argued, he said, that "press publications create prejudice and thus jeopardize the right to trial before an impartial jury:

"A—when the press reports specific items of news that either do not make their way into evidence at the trial or that come to the attention of jurors before the trial, unconfronted and unexamined, and

"B—when the amount and intensity of general press coverage of a case become so significant and so partisan that the whole community atmosphere is permeated with passion sufficient to preclude a fair, de-

Cont. in Sec. 1, Page 16, Col. 3

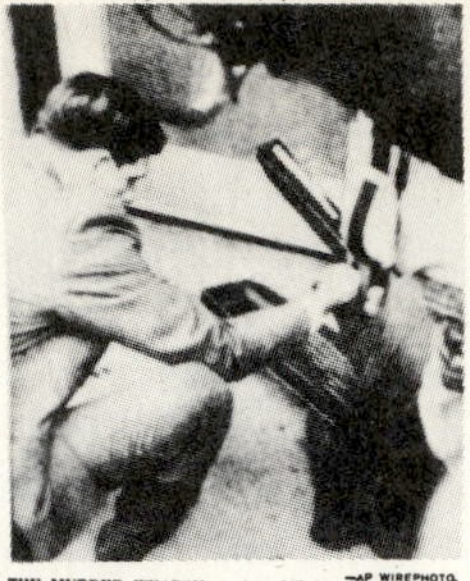

THE MURDER WEAPON used to kill Dr. Martin Luther King is examined by a Memphis detective shortly after King's death Thursday night. The gun is in a fiber box and is partially obscured by the detective's arm. —AP WIREPHOTO.

McKeithen Considering Running with Humphrey

Says He Talked with V-P About Politics

By LYN DYSART

Gov. John J. McKeithen disclosed Thursday that he would consider running as vice-president with Hubert H. Humphrey on a Democratic presidential ticket.

In a news conference after a "Louisiana Made" luncheon in the Royal Orleans Hotel, McKeithen said he discussed politics with Humphrey in a 30-minute telephone call Wednesday. However, the governor refused to reveal details of the conversation. He said it is "up to the vice-president to make any kind of public statement about the discussion."

McKeithen said that he called Humphrey to discuss plans for his visit to Baton Rouge Thursday to address an AFL-CIO meeting.

The governor added that he would have to confer with a presidential candidate to see "if I can run with him and he can run with me. There would have to be a reconciliation of views as Mr. Humphrey and I differ on certain issues.

"The vice-president is more liberal on domestic issues. I don't know if he's as firm as I am on riots," McKeithen said.

Asked if he would discuss running as vice-president with Sen. Robert F. Kennedy, McKeithen said he has no type of private talks planned with the senator during his visit to Louisiana "unless Sen. Kennedy indicates it."

McKeithen emphasized that he is not running as a candidate for vice-president because "the job seeks the man, the man doesn't seek the job.

"I will confess that this will be the time for the South moving into a position of leader-

Cont. in Sec. 1, Page 16, Col. 2

BOMBING PAUSE SEEMS BROADER

No Strikes Near Limit for More Than Day

By EDWIN Q. WHITE

SAIGON (AP) — American sources said Friday no U.S. air strikes had been reported near the 20th parallel in North Vietnam for more than 24 hours, prompting speculation that President Johnson may be further curtailing the bombing of the North.

On the ground, the relief of the Marine combat base at Khe Sanh, in South Vietnam's northwest corner, appeared imminent. Lead elements were reported within half a mile of the beleaguered base's perimeter Thursday night.

The U.S. Command said only 17 Americans had been killed and 159 wounded in the first four days of the Khe Sanh relief drive, which began Monday. A North Vietnamese broadcast monitored in Tokyo claimed 400 of the Americans were killed in fighting Thursday.

The U.S. Command declined comment on missions flown Friday over North Vietnam, leaving unconfirmed the speculation about new bombing curbs near the 20th parallel, set by President Johnson as the northern limit for U.S. raids under his order announced Sunday to de-escalate the air war.

In its morning communique Friday, U.S. headquarters mentioned a strike 225 miles north of the demilitarized zone and less than one mile south of the 20th parallel during the early morning hours Thursday.

Operation Pegasus, the drive to open Khe Sanh, reported meeting only light opposition from artillery and mortar fire since jumping off from Ca Lu, 12 miles away. Soviet reports in London said Thursday that the North Vietnamese were beginning to withdraw as a good-will gesture, but there was no confirmation from Hanoi.

Another reason advanced for the lack of sizeable opposition

Cont. in Sec. 1, Page 7, Col. 1

U.S. Shocked, Saddened by Slaying, Johnson Says

Message Is Given Nation After Assassination

WASHINGTON (AP) — President Johnson spoke Thursday night of an "America shocked and saddened" by the assassination of Dr. Martin Luther King as he condemned violence, lawlessness and divisiveness.

In a brief message to the nation via television and radio, Johnson disclosed that he is postponing a trip to Hawaii for a Vietnam strategy conference. He had been scheduled to leave around midnight. He said he will leave sometime Friday.

The President appeared in the doorway of the White House offices, stern-faced and spoke on all television and radio networks.

"I ask every American citizen," he said, "to reject the blind violence that has struck down Dr. King, who lived by nonviolence."

The President urged prayers for peace and understanding in the land and said:

"We can achieve nothing by lawlessness and divisiveness among the American people."

He said he hopes all Americans will search their hearts.

At that point he said he was cancelling all plans for the evening and postponing until Friday his planned take-off for Hawaii and conferences there on problems of war and peace in Vietnam.

DINNER PLANNNED

He was to have attended a Democratic fund-raising dinner at a Washington Hotel Thursday night and was only minutes from leaving the White House when the tragic news came from Memphis.

The White House said Johnson had telephoned Mrs. King at her home in Atlanta and expressed his sympathy. Johnson was in his office talking with his Ambassador to Moscow, Llewellyn Thompson, when word of King's death reached him.

The text of President Johnson's statement:

"America is shocked and saddened by the brutal slaying tonight of Dr. Martin Luther King.

"I ask every citizen to reject the blind violence that has struck Dr. King who lived by nonviolence.

"I pray that his family can find comfort in the memory of all he tried to do for the land he loved so well. I have just conveyed the sympathy of Mrs. Johnson and myself to his widow, Mrs. King.

"I know that every American of good will joins me in mourning the death of this outstanding leader and in praying for peace and understanding throughout this land.

"We can achieve nothing by lawlessness and divisiveness among the American people. It is only by joining together and only by working together can we continue to move toward equality and fulfillment for all of our people.

"I hope that all Americans tonight will search their hearts as they ponder this most tragic incident.

"I have canceled my plans for

Cont. in Sec. 1, Page 17, Col. 3

ANGUISH VOICED BY U.S. LEADERS

Shock, Grief, Is Reaction; Violence Feared

NEW YORK (AP) — The nation's civil rights and political leaders reacted with anguish, shock and grief Thursday night at the slaying of the Rev. Dr. Martin Luther King Jr. in Memphis.

There also was fear that the slaying could lead to more violence.

"We have been saddened," President Johnson told the nation on radio and television. "I ask every citizen to reject the blind violence that has struck Dr. King who lived in nonviolence."

TRIP PUT OFF

The President said he was postponing his trip to Hawaii, for a Vietnam strategy conference, until Friday. He had been scheduled to leave about midnight Thursday.

Vice President Hubert H. Humphrey said the slaying "brings shame to our country. An apostle of nonviolence has been the victim of violence."

The vice-president said, however, that his death will bring new strength to the cause he fought for.

A spokesman for the National Association for the Advancement of Colored People said, "I am shocked and grieved by this wanton murder of a peace-loving man, a dedicated, courageous man. This murder certainly does not solve anything and it will be deeply resented by Negroes through the country and by other people who believe in nonviolent protest."

NIXON TELEGRAM

Former Vice President Richard M. Nixon sent a telegram to Mrs. King which said: "Dr. King's death is a great personal tragedy for everyone who knew him and a great tragedy for the nation. Mrs. Nixon joins me in sympathy and prayers for you and your family in this terrible ordeal."

New York Mayor John V. Lindsay: "The people of our city of every race, I am sure, will join hands in paying tribute to him. Our greatest tribute to him will be to bear ourselves as he would want us to—with dignity and prayer."

Sen. Wayne Morse, D-Ore., said Dr. King's death is "one of the saddest tragedies to befall the nation" and warned that the shooting will add to "a very serious domestic crisis. It's going to increase marching across our country."

Fred Meely, a spokesman for the militant Student Non-Violent Coordinating Committee, said "There is no real comment that we can make. Everybody knows what happened and everybody knows why it happened and the black people in this country know what they have to do about it. That's all I have to say."

SESSION ADJOURNED

The Michigan House of Representatives adjourned its session

Cont. in Sec. 1, Page 4, Col. 3

DR. MARTIN LUTHER KING —AP WIREPHOTO.
Rifle Bullet Fells Rights Crusader

Dies Hour After Injury; Troops Recalled

By DOUG STONE

MEMPHIS, Tenn. (AP)—Nobel Laureate Martin Luther King Jr., father of non-violence in the American civil rights movement, was killed by an assassin's bullet Thursday night.

King, 39, was hit in the neck by a bullet as he stood on the balcony of a motel here. He died less than an hour later in St. Joseph Hospital.

Gov. Buford Ellington immediately ordered 4,000 National Guard troops back into the city. A curfew, which was clamped on Memphis after a King-led march turned into a riot a week ago, was reimposed.

Police said incidents of violence, including several fire bombings were reported following King's death.

The 1964 Nobel Peace Prize winner was standing on the balcony of his motel here, where he had come to lead protests in behalf of the city's 1,300 striking garbage workers, most of them Negroes, when he was shot.

PAIR ARRESTED

Two unidentified men who were arrested were released several hours later.

As word of King's death spread through the stunned city, Negroes in scattered areas also looted stores, stoned police and fire trucks and tossed several fire bombs. Two policemen were injured, mainly by flying glass when a shotgun blast broke their windshield.

Four hours after King died, the city was quieting some but police still reported sporadic outbreaks.

Police also said they found a .30-.06 rifle on Main Street about one block from the motel, but it was not confirmed whether this was the weapon that killed King.

An aide who was standing nearby said the shot hit King in the neck and lower right part of his face.

"Martin Luther King is dead," said Asst. Police Chief Henry Lux, the first word of the death.

Asst. Hospital Administrator Paul Hess confirmed later that King died at 7 p.m. of a bullet wound in the neck.

The Rev. Jesse Jackson said he and others in the King party were getting ready to go to dinner when the shooting occurred.

"King was on the second floor balcony of the motel," Jackson said. "He had just bent over. If he had been

Cont. in Sec. 1, Page 3, Col. 1

King: Been to Mountaintop No Matter What Happens

Non-Violence Advocate Dead Day Later

By JAY BOWLES

MEMPHIS, Tenn. (AP)—"It really doesn't matter what happens now. I've been to the mountaintop."

The speaker was Martin Luther King Jr. His audience was a cheering crowd of some 2,000 supporters. It was Wednesday night.

Less than 24 hours later, the nation's foremost apostle of non-violence was dead—the victim of an assassin's bullet—as he stood on the threshold of the biggest test of the theories he espoused.

King said Wednesday night that he was aware the threats had been made on his life. But he said he had seen the fulfillment of his goals of

Cont. in Sec. 1, Page 9, Col. 6

NEGROES SMASH AUTO WINDOWS

Jackson Scene of Disorder at News of Death

JACKSON, Miss. (AP) — Young Negroes smashed car windows and burned a newsman's car in the Jackson State College area Thursday night after learning of the assassination of Dr. Martin Luther King.

Charles Evers, state field secretary of the National Association for the Advancement of Colored People, and Negro ministers sought to calm the Negro community at a rally at the Negro Masonic Temple while other Negroes milled about the area.

Associated Press newsman John Pearce of Jackson, at the Masonic Temple, said he watched through a window of the building as a group overturned his car and burned it.

Police set up barricades at the perimeter of the Jackson State area and Jackson State campus police sealed off Lynch st., a main thoroughfare, through the campus area.

WINDOWS BROKEN

Bricks and bottles were thrown at the cars of white persons seeking to drive on Lynch st., a main artery between U.S. 80 and downtown Jackson. Windows were broken out of several cars.

Newsmen at the Masonic Temple, two blocks down four-lane Lynch st. from the campus, reported several Negroes had ad-

Cont. in Sec. 1, Page 3, Col. 4

Let's Not Burn America, Plea

ATLANTA, Ga. (AP)—Hosea Williams, one of Dr. Martin Luther King's top aides who was standing beneath the balcony on which King was shot to death Thursday, called immediately for continued non-violence. "Let's not burn America down," he said.

Williams, an executive in the Southern Christian Leadership Conference, telephoned his plea to the Atlanta Constitution from Memphis, where King died.

"We must—we must—maintain and advocate and promote the philosophy of non-violence," he said.

King Shot from Adjacent Hotel

ARROW MARKS window from which the shot that killed Dr. Martin Luther King was fired early Thursday night in Memphis, Tenn. In identifying the open window as belonging to the killer's lair, Memphis police said the building is an old hotel which overlooks the Lorraine Motel where King was staying. —AP WIREPHOTO

Gist of the News

—Friday Morning, April 5, 1968—

International Affairs

Trudeau builds lead as Canada Liberal party opens balloting to name Pearson successor. —Sec. 1, Page 13

President Johnson and U Thant hold 'strictly private' talk on peace prospects in Vietnam. —Sec. 1, Page 17

Louisiana trade mission in Rio de Janeiro on final leg of South American journey. —Sec. 2, Page 16

National Affairs

PAR spokesman disputes need for junior colleges in Louisiana. Sec. 1, Page 4

Governor may ask Legislature for auto license tag hike without constitutional amendment. —Sec. 1, Page 14

Humphrey all but announces candidacy in speech before roaring AFL-CIO convention —Sec. 1, Page 15

House passes bill to tax international air tickets, cut duty-free customs allowance. —Sec. 3, Page 25

Local Affairs

Six members of Algiers family tied up while burglars crack safes, steal property. —Sec. 1, Page 5

Winners in 4-H contests tour points in New Orleans on prize trip sponsored by Chamber of Commerce. —Sec. 1, Page 8

City Council approves 26 of 28 persons appointed by mayor as members of Human Relations Committee. —Sec. 1, Page 18

Action on new health permit fees ordinance postponed by City Council until May 16. —Sec. 2, Page 2

Jefferson property owners oppose project to raise lakefront levees four feet because of "ups" and "downs". —Sec. 2, Page 4

N.O. Notaries' Association okays commission to work with bar in drafting uniform examinations. —Sec. 2, Page 5

Grand Isle folk vote Saturday in Demo[illegible]mary election to select town officials. Sec. 2, Page 16

Robert L. Simpson re-elected president of Southern Eye Bank board of trustees at annual meeting. —Sec. 3, Page 5

Eventual elimination of malaria in the United States is predicted by government entomologist. —Sec. 3, Page 7

CALL EARLY
to place your weekend classified ad
Miss Want-Ad is on duty as early as 8 a.m. Remember, we must receive your ad completely by 3 p.m. Friday (absolute deadline) for Saturday or by 5 p. m. Friday (absolute deadline) for Sunday.

Miss Want-Ad
The Most Popular Miss in Louisiana
821-1455
Just say "Charge it"

To call all other departments of The Times-Picayune or States-Item—dial 821-1411

Kennedy Cancels Louisiana Talks Out of Respect for Slain Leader

Crowley Judge Edmund Reggie, head of Sen. Robert F. Kennedy's Louisiana campaign said shortly after midnight Friday that Kennedy has cancelled his Louisiana visit.

"Due to the tragic assassination of Dr. Martin Luther King, Sen. Robert F. Kennedy has called off his appearances in Louisiana, as he is canceling all other public meetings for the weekend "out of respect for this slain leader and his family."

"I am deeply appreciative of all the courtesies and assistance so enthusiastically given to the senator's visit," Reggie added, "and I look forward to a make-up visit by Sen. and Mrs. Kennedy in the not-too-distant future.

"The senator himself expressed his desire to reschedule the Louisiana visit and I am confident it will come at first opportunity.

"I offer particular thanks to Dominican College, Loyola, Xavier and Tulane University, Louisiana State University in New Orleans and the University of Southwestern Louisiana, as well as the hundreds of volunteers who did so much to insure that, had the senator been able to make his visit here, it would have been the most memorable one of his campaign.

The killing of Martin Luther King added to the nation's shame.

activities as more effective ways of raising the consciousness of America. By the 1970s there was a cohesive women's movement, based on the concept that consciousness raising (studying the gamut of women's lives) would keep women from becoming involved in single-issue campaigns and would eventually gain the movement more popular support.[5] Among the encouraged consciousness raising activities were the establishment of women's centers, abortion counseling, film and tape production, research, and the publication of feminist newspapers and magazines.

But before that happened the "Women's Liberation Movement" took hold with street demonstrations. In the late 1960s thousands of women marched in Chicago, New York, Boston, and other cities. Gloria Steinem, Betty Friedan, and others addressed rallies and conventions. The movement tackled the problems faced by the growing women's labor force and later affected the whole of male-female relationships, including family life and the educational process. One major goal was not realized, however. That was passage of the Equal Rights Amendment (ERA), the proposed Twenty-seventh Amendment to the Constitution. Approved by the U.S. Congress in 1972, the ERA had early successes, then ran into heavy opposition in male-dominated state legislatures. Conservative women's organizations led by Phyllis Schlafly lobbied against the measure, helping to ensure that it fell slightly short of gaining the approval of three fourths of the legislatures, which is necessary for passage.

Of all the demonstrations of the 1960s, the three most spectacular in size and media impact were King's march on Washington in 1963, the battles between antiwar demonstrators and police at the 1968 Chicago Democratic National Convention, and the 1969 antiwar marches in Washington, D.C.

TELEVISION NEWS: CRONKITE AND CBS

Walter Cronkite, an amiable native of St. Joseph, Missouri, with the stamina of a workhorse, became the leading CBS News personality in the 1960s. By the mid-1970s he was hailed as one of the most admired people in America, after having anchored dozens of CBS specials on presidential elections, the Vietnam agony, racial conflicts, assassinations, Watergate, and the many space flights.

Unlike others within CBS News, Cronkite was not one of Edward R. Murrow's protégés, although Murrow had tried to hire him away from the UP during World War II and eventually did hire him in 1950. Instead of reporting from Korea as planned, Cronkite ended up earning a reputation at CBS's Washington, D.C., station, WTOP-TV. He did not present CBS executives with the outwardly intellectual image of Eric Sevareid or Charles Collingwood but was noted for his devotion to the hard news story. Coming out of the press-association tradition, Cronkite went for the bulletin lead or the exclusive interview. But over the years he also became the star of many CBS documentary shows, including *Eyewitness to History, Twentieth Century,* and *CBS Reports,* and was heard regularly on a CBS radio show.

Cronkite's straight delivery of the news, with a heavy note of seriousness, earned him the evening newscaster spot in 1962. He replaced Douglas Edwards, who had been hired in 1948 to begin a news show. It had been Edwards' fate to be pitted against the popular John Cameron Swayze's *Camel News Caravan* on NBC and later the Huntley-Brinkley team. Cronkite's job was to push CBS up in the ratings.

On Labor Day, 1963, Cronkite and the CBS crew, which included the reliable Sevareid in Washington, inaugurated the first 30-minute network news show. That morning, Cronkite interviewed President Kennedy at Hyannisport and asked JFK about the growing war in Vietnam, where forty-seven Americans had been killed. A young field reporter, Dan Rather, bluntly described a confrontation between police and blacks in the South, and the veteran Peter Kalischer was in Tokyo. During the next few years, with Cronkite serving as managing editor of the evening news show, CBS' reputation as a no-nonsense news organization grew steadily.

Cronkite suffered a personal setback before the 1964 Democratic National Convention when CBS executives replaced him with veteran Bob Trout and a young reporter named Roger Mudd. Cronkite had been the regular convention anchor since 1952 and he was the backbone of the CBS team originally put together by news chief Sig Mickelson and later Richard Salant. But the Huntley-Brinkley team had run away with the ratings. Trout and Mudd did not fare better, however, and Cronkite was given priority from there on.

During the American involvement in Vietnam, Cronkite, like most journalists, did not seriously question the nature of the United States commitment until the late 1960s. In 1965 he rode in a Canberra jet that divebombed the jungle near Danang, just as he had flown in a bomber over Germany in 1943. But in 1968, after visiting Vietnam for a special on the Tet offensive, Cronkite was sufficiently convinced of the futility of the war to end his broadcast with "to say we are mired in stalemate seems the only realistic, yet unsatisfactory conclusion . . . the only rational way out . . . will be to negotiate [and] not as victors."[6] That was the turning point, and in following years the CBS coverage contained more criticism of American tactics.

The CBS team suffered the wrath of Mayor Richard Daley during the riotous 1968 Democratic National Convention, when Cronkite, watching Rather being slugged by a so-called security guard, called the guards "thugs." With typical fairness, however, he granted Daley a long interview the next day and passed up the chance to criticize Chicago's boss for the tactics used by police on journalists and innocent bystanders. Cronkite in turn was criticized for such politeness, but he continually stressed the need for news credibility and insisted that the cameras spoke for themselves.

Although Lyndon Johnson constantly complained to Cronkite following evening news broadcasts, he had respect for Cronkite's sense of fairness. But the White House of Richard Nixon thought of CBS as a prime enemy. And although television journalists in general did a poor job of analyzing the Watergate-related events in 1972 and 1973—before the open revelations of scandal—Cronkite was credited with the best performance. One study showed that between September 14, 1972, and election day, CBS devoted twice as much air time to the Watergate story as either NBC or ABC.[7]

The tough CBS approach to news and Sevareid's voice of reason earned CBS the top spot in the ratings by 1969 to 1970. Another reason for the upsurge was Cronkite's ability as a space reporter. Throughout the 1960s he covered the

The Weather

Today—Showers, thunderstorms, high in 80s. Tuesday—Fair, less humid. Chance of rain, 20% tonight. Winds variable, 10-15 m.p.h. Temperature range: Today, 72-88; Yesterday, 76-88. Details, Page D3.

The Washington Post

Times Herald

Index — 56 Pages, 4 Sections

92d Year ··· No. 228 — © 1969, The Washington Post Co. — MONDAY, JULY 21, 1969 — Phone 223-6000 Circulation 223-6100 Classified 223-6200 — 10c

'The Eagle Has Landed'—Two Men Walk on the Moon

Neil Armstrong and Edwin Aldrin plant the American flag on the surface of the moon. The flag is kept "flying" on the airless moon by a spring device.

'One Small Step For Man . . . Giant Leap for Mankind'

By Thomas O'Toole
Washington Post Staff Writer

HOUSTON, July 20—Man stepped out onto the moon tonight for the first time in his two-million-year history.

"That's one small step for man," declared pioneer astronaut Neil Armstrong at 10:56 p.m. EDT, "one giant leap for mankind."

Just after that historic moment in man's quest for his origins, Armstrong walked on the dead satellite and found the surface very powdery, littered with fine grains of black dust.

A few minutes later, Edwin (Buzz) Aldrin joined Armstrong on the lunar surface and in less than an hour they put on a show that will long be remembered by the worldwide television audience.

American Flag Planted

The two men walked easily, talked easily, even ran and jumped happily so it seemed. They picked up rocks, talked at length of what they saw, planted an American flag, saluted it, and talked by radiophone with the President in the White House, and then faced the camera and saluted Mr. Nixon.

"For every American, this has to be the proudest day of our lives," the President told the astronauts. "For one priceless moment in the whole history of man, all the people on this earth are truly one."

At 1:10 a.m.—2 hours and 14 minutes after Armstrong first stepped upon the lunar surface—the astronauts were back in their moon craft and the hatch was closed.

In describing the moon, Armstrong told Houston that it was "fine and powdery. I can kick it up loosely with my toe.

"It adheres like powdered charcoal to the boot," he went on, "but I only go in a small fraction of an inch. I can see my footprint in the moon like fine grainy particles."

Armstrong found he had such little trouble walking on the moon that he began talking almost as if he didn't want to leave it.

"It has a stark beauty all its own," Armstrong said. "It's like the desert in the Southwestern United States. "It's very pretty out here."

Amazingly Clear Picture

Armstrong shared his first incredible moments on the moon with the whole world, as a television camera on the outside of the wingless Eagle landing craft sent back an amazingly clear picture of his first steps on the moon.

Armstrong seemed like he was swimming along, taking big and easy steps on the airless moon despite the cumbersome white pressure-suit he wore.

"There seems to be no difficulty walking around," he said. "As we suspected, it's even easier than the one-sixth G that we did in simulations on the ground."

One of the first things he did was to scoop up a small sample of the moon with a long-handled spoon with a bag on its end like a small butterfly net.

"Looks like it's easy," Aldrin said, looking down from the Lem.

"It is," Armstrong told him. "I'm sure I could push it in farther but I can't bend down that far."

Guides Aldrin Down Ladder

At 11:11 p.m., Aldrin started down the landing craft's ten-foot ladder to join Armstrong.

Backing down the nine-step ladder, Aldrin was guided the entire way by Armstrong, who stood at the foot of the ladder looking up at him.

"Okay," Armstrong said, "watch your 'pliss' (PLSS, for portable life support system) from underneath. Drop your pliss down. You're clear. About an inch clear on your pliss."

"Okay," Aldrin said. "You need a little arching of the back to come down."

When he stepped onto the first rung of the ladder, Aldrin went back up to the Lem's "front porch" to partially close the Lem's hatch.

"Making sure not to lock it on my way out," he said in comic fashion. "That's our home for the next couple of hours and I want to make sure we can get back in."

Aldrin reported it was a "very simple matter to hop down from one step to the next." To make the last and longest step, he said he put both hands on the fourth rung up and leaned back with his left foot first.

"Beautiful," said Aldrin when he met Armstrong on the lunar surface.

"Isn't that something," said Armstrong. "It's a magnificent sight out here."

See APOLLO, A9, Col. 1

Moon Walk Yields Data for Science

By Victor Cohn
Washington Post Staff Writer

HOUSTON, July 20—They landed, eyes open for science, and within minutes became lunar explorers.

Edwin (Buzz) Aldrin was soon making man's first on-the-spot report from another planetary body.

From the spacecraft he saw a rock collection around the lunar lander of "every shape, regularity, irregularity, every variety you'd find." And "quite a few interesting colors."

This promptly led Dr. Harold Masursky, chief of astrogeology for the U.S. Geological Survey — working in one of the science support rooms here — to comment:

"They've hit a good spot to do collecting."

Then Neil Armstrong left the craft for the lunar surface. Fit, eager, apparently healthy — no moon illness on madness — he began the first scientific traverse on earth's oldest satellite.

The mere fact that he did it and did it well immediately answered a vital question: Man can function on the moon.

One of the first things he reported was: "The MESA came down all right."

That was the "modularized equipment stowage assembly" — a trunk in the skin of the Lem — that held both a television camera and scientific equipment.

He was quickly giving scientists more information about the nature of the lunar surface than they have gained in all their recent years of poking at it with unmanned probes.

"The Lem footpads are only depressed in the surface about one inch or two inches and I only go in a fraction of an inch"—the surface was remarkably firm.

"The surface appears to be very fine ground as you get close to it. It's almost a powder, very fine . . . fine and powdery"—probably because of the constant "gardening" by meteorite borne bombardment over the ages.

See SCIENCE, A10, Col. 4

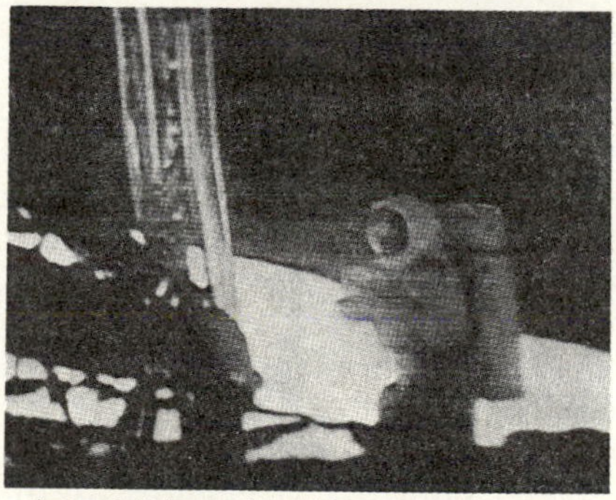

Armstrong takes his first steps on the moon. At left is the Eagle, the lunar landing craft.

'Squared Away and in Good Shape . . .'

The following is a condensed transcript, prepared by UPI, of the conversation during man's first walk on the moon, among astronauts Neil A. Armstrong, Edwin E. (Buzz) Aldrin and Michael Collins; ground communicator Bruce McCandless and Mission Control spokesman John McLeaish:

Armstrong — That's one small step for man, one giant leap for mankind.

[Armstr]ong—The descent [illegible] not [illegible] [illegible] [illegible] [illegible] clearance on the ground. I can see some evidence of rays emanating from the descent engine, but a very insignificant amount.

Armstrong—OK, Buzz, ready to bring down the camera.

Aldrin—All ready. It looks like I'm all squared away and in good shape.

Armstrong—It's quite dark in the shadow and a little hard for me to see but I have good footing. I'll work my way to the sunlight here without looking directly into the sun.

McLeaish—Unofficial time on first step 109:24:20.

Armstrong — Looking at the Lem. I'm standing directly in the shadow now, looking up at Buzz in the windows—and I can see everything quite clearly. The light is sufficiently backlighted in the front of the Lem so that everything is clearly visible.

Aldrin—OK, I'm going to be changing . . .

Armstrong—OK.

McLeaish — The surgeon says the crew is doing well. Data is good, the crew is doing well, 35 and a half minutes of PLSS time expended now.

Armstrong—Right.

McCandless — OK, that's good.

Armstrong — It's very interesting. It's a very soft surface but here and there where I plug with the contingency sampler I run into a very hard surface . . .

Aldrin—OK, the handle is off. It pushes about six or eight inches in the surface. It pushes very easy.

See TRANSCRIPT, A11, Col. 1

Apollo Liftoff Schedule

Apollo 11's key activities slated for today:

1:55 p.m.—Lunar module's ascent engine fires, lifting the module's ascent stage off the moon and leaving the descent stage behind.

5:32 p.m.—Lunar module and command ship dock.

9:25 p.m.—Lunar module is jettisoned.

No live television is scheduled until 9:02 p.m. Tuesday. By this time the Apollo's main engine will have been fire[illegible] it out of lunar orbit.

Millions Follow Moon Landing Around the World, Except in China

By Robert C. Jensen
Washington Post Staff Writer

Man's first journey to the moon was hailed in nearly every part of the world yesterday. The exception was China, where one-fifth of the world's people live.

The Communist rulers in Peking decided to withhold the news that the American astronauts Neil Armstrong and Edwin Aldrin had safely landed on the moon.

The Yugoslav news agency said in a dispatch from Peking that no word of the landing or any part of the Apollo mission was mentioned in China.

In Russia, the news agency Tass announced the moon landing in a 52-word dispatch. And the reports were carried routinely in Soviet television and radio broadcasts. But the Associated Press reported that individual citizens in Moscow cheered and congratulated Americans. "It's a great day," one shouted.

Much the same reaction was voiced by former Vice President Humphrey, who beamed: "What a day to be in Moscow!" Humphrey had returned from a hunting trip with Gen. Sergei L. Sokolov, first deputy defense minister. Humphrey brought back a boar he had shot in a forest near Moscow.

See REACT, A8, Col. 4

Newspapers reproduced television's historic news beats on their front pages.

Mercury and Apollo programs with an interest dating to his World War II UP stories about the German rocket attacks on London. Finally, on July 20, 1969 the normally reserved Cronkite shared his feelings about America's incredible achievement. As the Eagle descended to the moon, Cronkite murmured, "Boy, what a day." Then as former astronaut Walter Shirra, sitting with Cronkite, exclaimed "We're home," Cronkite said, "Man on the moon . . . Oh, Boy! . . . Whew! Boy!. . . Boy! There they sit on the moon!. . . on green with the flight plan, all the way down. Man finally is standing on the surface of the moon. My golly!"[8]

When President Carter held his unprecedented radio talk show with the public in 1977, it was Walter Cronkite who sat in the Oval Office as moderator—the same "Uncle Walter" who babysat Americans through the killing and funeral of John Kennedy, the dangerous reentry periods of the space missions, and the anxiety of the Watergate crisis. He was counted on to hold the fort, and he did until one evening when he intoned: "And that's the way it is, Friday, March 6, 1981. I'll be away on assignment and Dan Rather will be sitting in here for the next few years. Goodnight." Cronkite became a special correspondent, doing depth features.

Sevareid, the acknowledged dean of the television news analysts who had logged 38 years with CBS, including fifteen political conventions, had announced his retirement in 1977. Beginning his CBS career as part of Murrow's *World News Roundup* team, he covered various aspects of World War II from Paris, London, Washington, the China-Burma theater, and finally Europe again. He spent almost all of the postwar years in the Washington bureau—with the exception of 1959 to 1961 when he was a roving correspondent in Europe—from where he delivered regular evening commentaries once CBS moved to a 30-minute format.

The CBS team was a formidable unit. Mudd had become well established as a political reporter, Fred P. Graham offered excellent reports on legal affairs, Charles Kuralt was a favorite for his "On the Road" segments, Bernard and Marvin Kalb covered the State Department with thoroughness, and Lesley Stahl was a leading correspondent on her way to a White House assignment.[9] The documentary show *60 Minutes* became television's top-ranked program, the first time a news show had made the top ten in the ratings. Rather, Mike Wallace, and Morley Safer brought the program into the limelight and later Ed Bradley and Harry Reasoner appeared. (Reasoner began his career with CBS and transferred to ABC for a number of years.) Mayra McLaughlin was CBS' first woman reporter in 1965; longtime correspondent Daniel Schorr was forced from his job in 1976 after he gave a controversial report on the CIA to the *Village Voice* and was threatened with contempt of Congress in a much-debated episode.

NBC: CHANCELLOR AND MCGEE

John Chancellor, one of the most thoughtful and conscientious broadcasters to address the public, assumed the NBC anchor spot in 1970 and temporarily found himself in an awkward "troika" arrangement with Brinkley and Frank McGee. Brinkley left to do a nightly commentary, *David Brinkley's Journal,* and McGee went on to the *Today* show. This left Chancellor to guide his viewers through the maze of the last stages of the Vietnam War, Watergate, and the Ford, Carter, and Reagan years, although Brinkley did return to coanchor in 1976 in an effort to close the gap with CBS.

That year, with the nature of television news being discussed in dozens of periodicals, Chancellor offered this simple explanation of his confident performance:

> What you do is say, "I got up at 10 o'clock this morning, and I worked all day, and read all the wires, and called up a lot of people. Now over there is the news. Let's look at it together. I'll be your guide."[10]

Chancellor began his NBC career in 1950, was a floor reporter at a number of political conventions along with Sander Vanocur, Edwin Newman, and McGee, and headed several NBC foreign bureaus. He took one break in service to briefly run the Voice of America for Lyndon Johnson.

NBC had always fielded a strong lineup of reporters. McGee was one of the most perceptive persons in the business. As early as December 20, 1965, in an NBC special on the war, he concluded that if the United States government could not make a compelling argument why an independent South Vietnam was so vital to American national interests that "it transcends doubts about the legality and morality of the war" then the United States should withdraw.[11] Later he narrated the sensitive "Same Mud, Same Blood" documentary about black and white soldiers surviving or dying together. McGee also covered the South for NBC during the civil-rights battles, anchored many broadcasts of space flights, and anchored the desk for 12 hours on the day of John Kennedy's assassination. He died of cancer in April, 1974, at the age of 52.

In addition to excellent field reporting, NBC compiled an impressive list of documentaries, headed by the *NBC White Paper* and the 2-hour *First Tuesday.* Chemical and biological warfare, Army intelligence units spying on civilians, migrant labor problems, and the nation's pension plans were among the controversial topics covered. In early 1976 NBC cancelled an entire evening of prime time—something that would have made Edward R. Murrow happy—and offered a 3-hour analysis of foreign-policy problems. Later a magazine-type show was instituted, *NBC Magazine,* to compete with *60 Minutes,* but despite some successes, the ratings did not show much public support.

Among women working for NBC were Pauline Frederick, who in 1948 was the first woman to cover a political convention for a network and who stayed until 1974 as UN correspondent; Barbara Walters of *Today* show fame, an expert interviewer for NBC before she left for ABC; Marilyn Berger, who was appointed White House correspondent to replace Tom Brokaw; and Catherine Mackin, a high-ranking political correspondent and commentator.[12] Jessica Savitch and Connie Chung emerged as leading NBC anchorpersons.

ABC NEWS: WALTERS AND REYNOLDS

The television news world awoke one morning in 1976 to discover that Barbara Jill Walters, the star of NBC's *Today* show, would be joining ABC with a 5-year contract calling for $5 million. But the biggest news was that the highest-paid news personality would be coanchoring the evening news with veteran Harry

CBS

CBS

Eric Sevareid, long a CBS commentator, and Lesley Stahl, correspondent.

NBC

NBC

John Chancellor and Connie Chung, NBC anchors.

Steve Fenn/ABC News

ABC

Frank Reynolds, ABC anchor, and Barbara Walters, ABC interviewer.

Reasoner, who immediately began to pout. Cronkite at CBS and Chancellor at NBC were shocked, and critics immediately castigated ABC for its show-business approach to the news. ABC executives came to the defense, though, and pointed out Walters' long record as a writer and interviewer of leading personalities.

It was not the first time that ABC had been criticized for its news tactics. The network had been playing catch-up in the ratings race since 1953, when John Daly was the first in a long line of anchors. Daly lasted until 1960, when John Cameron Swayze had a brief stint. He was followed by Ron Cochran (1963 to 1965), Peter Jennings (1965 to 1968), Bob Young (1968), and Howard K. Smith and Frank Reynolds (1968 to 1970). Smith and Reasoner began a partnership in 1970, but Smith eventually fell into a commentator's slot, leaving Reasoner alone, or so he thought.

In addition to hiring Walters in an effort to put life into the ratings, ABC began experimenting with the heavy use of feature material. The ABC system's encouragement of the so-called "happy talk" format for its local stations in the early 1970s brought strong criticism from traditionalists, who found the joking and exchanges of light comments out of line.

ABC heavily promoted the "marriage" of Walters and Reasoner, but from the beginning there was doubt whether, as one critic put it, "the mix of Manhattan moxie and Iowa wry will chemically click."[13] In addition to the evening news, Walters was scheduled to host a number of special interview shows. Her producer was Lucy Jarvis, who as the first American to receive an invitation from the People's Republic of China to film a news documentary, produced "The Forbidden City" for NBC in January, 1973.

The Walters-Reasoner experiment failed, and Walters left the anchor post to devote herself exclusively to interviews. She recorded a number of notable exchanges with President Anwar Sadat of Egypt and other international figures, as well as with political and show-business personalities. Her yearly salary was more than $1.3 million, topped only by Rather's $1.6 million.[14] Reasoner left ABC in time to rejoin CBS for the 1978 to 1979 season, taking a spot with the top-ranked *60 Minutes* show.

Roone Arledge brought ABC Sports into first place with *Wide World of Sports, Monday Night Football,* and spectacular Olympic coverage—particularly of the 1972 games in Munich when Howard Cosell and other sportscasters helped describe the massacre of Israeli athletes by terrorists. Becoming head of ABC News in 1977, a controversial switch debated in the industry, Arledge instituted the "roving-anchor" concept the following year, with Walters in New York, Frank Reynolds in Washington, Peter Jennings in London, and Max Robinson in Chicago. Later, with Walters out of the daily picture, Reynolds assumed a more prominent role on ABC's *World News Tonight.*

Nancy Dickerson and Lisa Howard, until her death, were among the first women reporters. A number of other women were involved, including Ann Compton, the first woman assigned by a network to cover the White House. Marlene Sanders, a Vietnam correspondent who became a vice president and director of documentaries, was one the the leaders in that field. In fact, Sanders had anchored the network evening news as a substitute in 1964, when a strike intervened; she later anchored the weekend news for several months in 1971.*

*Dorothy Fuldheim of WEWS-TV, Cleveland, became the first woman to anchor a news show when that station hired her in 1947. In the late 1970s, in her 80's she was still delivering commentary.

In 1977 her main project was the prestigious *ABC Closeups* series, with Smith as the main narrator. Reasoner had also been involved with a number of those shows, as well as *ABC News Reports,* the network's principal documentary efforts outside of special reports. One of Sanders' major productions was "Women's Health: A Question of Survival" in 1976. She was a strong advocate of young women broadcasters and gave much time to that cause. ABC, like the other networks, also had talented women at key network stations.[15]

THE QUAGMIRE IN VIETNAM

Robert Capa, the Hungarian-born photographer who was world-renowned for his graphic pictures of the Spanish Civil War and the Normandy invasion beaches, was the first American journalist to die in Vietnam. He stepped on a land mine while photographing for Magnum in 1954, the year the French extricated themselves from the Indochina quagmire by surrendering at Dienbienphu. The French watched as the Americans then took their places in the quagmire that swallowed up one president and was linked to the resignation of another.[16]

The American phase of the 30-year struggle in Indochina—in Vietnam, in Cambodia, and in Laos—became perhaps the most thoroughly covered war in history. Certainly it caused more moral searching than ever before, and by the time of United States withdrawal in 1975, it seemed possible that it represented a revulsion against the Cold War mentality and an ebbing of the spirit of manifest destiny. Much credit should accrue to the print and broadcast correspondents and photographers covering the war, including the more than fifty who died, as well as those few who clarified the issues through their dissent at home.

Vietnam's national hero, Ho Chi Minh, proclaimed a Democratic Republic of Vietnam at Hanoi in 1945, in the wake of the Japanese surrender. But by 1946 the French who had returned to Saigon were engaged in hostilities with Ho's Viet Minh. Ex-emperor Bao Dai was installed in 1948 as chief of state in Saigon by the French, who then obtained financial aid from the United States in 1950 at the time of the Korean crisis. The United States carried up to 80 percent of the cost, but the French were humiliated at Dienbienphu. The Geneva agreements of 1954 ending hostilities provided for the partitioning of Vietnam at the seventeenth parallel and reunification through national elections in 1956. The Bao Dai government did not sign the agreement or honor it; the United States created the SEATO alliance and included South Vietnam in the protected areas. Premier Ngo Dinh Diem ousted Bao Dai, refused to allow the elections, and obtained the help of the U.S. Military Assistance Advisory Group to train his army beginning in 1955. Diem's opposition in South Vietnam formed the National Liberation Front and its guerrilla force, called the Viet Cong by South Vietnamese and Americans.

By 1960 there were 686 United States military advisers, a figure raised to 3200 at the close of President Kennedy's first year in office (1961) as insurgency grew. Diem, his sister-in-law Mme. Nhu, and the ruling Catholic party became increasingly oppressive. The Buddhist uprisings of 1963 in Saigon and Hue, and countryside insurgency, brought a November coup and the death of Diem. The American supporters, now transformed into a U.S. Military Assistance Command with 16,300 men, took over military affairs as ten Saigon governments came and went in the next 18 months. A new president was also entering the White House 3 weeks after the Saigon coup.

THE SAIGON PRESS CORPS FORMS

The Saigon press corps had already distinguished itself by the time of Diem's downfall. Three who became the leaders in pointing out the quagmire's dangers were Malcolm Browne, who came to Vietnam in November, 1961, for the Associated Press; Neil Sheehan, who came in April, 1962, for the United Press International; and David Halberstam, who joined them in May for the *New York Times.* François Sully, the French reporter who had covered Dienbienphu and who stayed on to interpret the war for *Newsweek* and others until he died in Cambodia in 1971, was expelled by Diem in 1962 and could not return until Diem's overthrow. Among others who appeared in 1962 were Horst Faas, photographer, and Peter Arnett, correspondent, for the AP; Homer Bigart, now with the *New York Times;* Peter Kalischer, now with CBS; Charles Mohr, *Time;* and Beverly Deepe, *Newsweek,* a freelancer who took Sully's place and who later joined the *Christian Science Monitor.*

These and other correspondents had bad news to report about the progress of the war, about the weaknesses of the Diem government, about the very ability of anyone to achieve what the United States government had set out to do in Vietnam. But the spirit of the military command and of the civilians in the embassy and aid missions was most often one of "we have a policy and it has to work if we just try hard enough." Anyone reporting facts that pointed in a contradictory direction was labeled noncooperative. When Sheehan and Halberstam viewed a military debacle at Ap Bac in January, 1963, which proved that the United States military advisers had a long way to go to infuse a winning spirit in their allies, they reported the failure of South Vietnamese arms. The U.S. command described this as a victory, and the undermining of the journalistic reputations of the Saigon press corps had begun.[17]

THE SAIGON PRESS CORPS UNDER ATTACK

As Buddhists set themselves afire and the pressures against the Diem dictatorship increased, the Saigon press corps also found conflict within its own ranks. Coming to Saigon for varying amounts of time were Joseph Alsop, the columnist; Marguerite Higgins of the *New York Herald Tribune* and Keyes Beech of the *Chicago Daily News,* veterans of World War II and Korean press corps; and Jim Lucas, Scripps-Howard, who was to win the 1964 Ernie Pyle award for his coverage in Vietnam. These correspondents were typified by Lucas: hard-nosed, ready to fight any attempt at censorship, but more or less ready to accept war as a necessary fact of life, and not activist in probing into the humaneness of the military tactics. Indeed, correspondent Higgins was an avowed "hawk" who

New York Times Associated Press

Saigon press-corps leaders Neil Sheehan (*left*), UPI, and Malcolm Browne, AP.

New York Times New York Times

***New York Times* Vietnam correspondents David Halberstam (*left*) and Harrison Salisbury.**

advocated the use of the atomic bomb if needed to repel the Communists wherever they were; tragically, Higgins fell victim to an Asiatic infection on a 1965 trip and died a lingering death in 1966. The criticism by Alsop, Higgins, Beech, and Lucas of the reporting and interpretation given by Browne, Sheehan, Halberstam, and Kalischer left the established Saigon press corps vulnerable to attack by outsiders.

Those attacks mounted in 1963. The correspondents had fought off a State Department "press guidance" issued in 1962 by Carl T. Rowan saying "newsmen should be advised that trifling or thoughtless criticism of the Diem government would make it difficult to maintain proper cooperation between the United

States and Diem," only to find in 1963 that Diem's police would beat them over the head and smash their cameras.[18] The pot boiled over in September, 1963, when *Time* attacked the Saigon press corps as propagandists plotting to overthrow the Diem government and, through distorted reporting, "helping to compound the very confusion that it should be untangling for its readers at home."[19] *Time* correspondents Charles Mohr and Mert Perry resigned in outraged protest; Mohr joined the *New York Times* and Perry *Newsweek* to stay in Saigon. Mme. Nhu castigated the AP, UPI, *New York Times, Washington Post,* and *Newsweek* as enemies of her brother-in-law, Diem. *Time,* unrepentant, continued to doubt the analyses of the Saigon correspondents until long after their definition of a quagmire had been accepted by all disinterested observers of the Vietnam War.

The attacks on the integrity of the press led Halberstam, Sheehan, Browne, and later others to undertake activist roles in writing books and lecturing at home about the nature of the Vietnamese conflict and the danger to the United States national interest of a "win at any cost" policy there. Halberstam and Browne shared the 1964 Pulitzer Prize for international reporting. Sheehan joined the *New York Times* staff in 1964 and in 1971 was instrumental in the *Times*' publishing of the "Pentagon Papers," taken from a secret analysis by Pentagon researchers and validating the 1961 to 1965 reporting of the Saigon press corps. The furor over this, and the problem of the "credibility gap," which came to affect the mass media as well as Presidents Johnson and Nixon, was a polarizing problem affecting all aspects of American life.

In Vietnam the central problem was not only that the military deliberately falsified information, but also that it more often withheld information detrimental to continued belief in the eventual success of U.S. policies and established elaborate statistical counts to justify the policies of the White House and the Pentagon. General William Westmoreland became the American commander in Saigon in 1964 and remained until Paris peace talks were begun in 1968; it was through him that the twin "search and destroy" and "bomb the North" policies were instituted. The first employed the famed "body-count" statistics used by Defense Secretary Robert McNamara to prove that the enemy was being exhausted. The second utilized minute reports of "precision bombing" of enemy convoys, roads, factories, and troop concentrations at an unprecedented saturation level. At the daily briefing in Saigon, dubbed "The Five O'Clock Follies" by the correspondents, communiqués on the previous day's action were read; it was folly to attend, the press corps said, because the briefing officer only knew what was in his communiqué. Critics of the press contended that the correspondents nevertheless filed stories filled with body-count reports they doubted, as major news events, and created an illusion of conventional battle warfare when none really existed except in calculated situations.

JOHNSON AND THE PRESS: THE WAR ESCALATES

No president worked harder in trying to make himself available to the White House "regulars" than Lyndon Johnson. He did not care to undertake immediately the televised conferences so expertly run by Kennedy, so he called the two dozen or so regular correspondents into his office, plied them with food, and answered their questions. He took them with him to the LBJ ranch and held barbeques; he argued with them on walks in the White House rose garden; he swam with them in the pool; he even subjected himself to 135 regular press conferences, a slightly better average than Eisenhower or Kennedy. In 1964 Johnson was elected president in his own right with a record popular majority and the support of all but a dozen of the country's major newspapers. The next year his Great Society legislation consolidated the gains the country wanted to make in civil rights, aid to education, medical aid, and other social gains. Yet, for all this, the credibility gap grew as the war in Vietnam grew.

The decision to make the war in Indochina a major United States war came in August, 1964, when the administration asserted that two American destroyers on patrol in the Gulf of Tonkin had been attacked by North Vietnamese PT boats. Although it developed later that there was common doubt about the incident, President Johnson requested, and Congress quickly approved, a resolution giving him power to repel attacks and to prevent further aggression. It was the contention of Secretary of State Dean Rusk that an aggression from the North was in progress; others contended that the war in Vietnam was a civil war, particularly the actions involving the Viet Cong, the guerrilla arm of the South Vietnamese National Liberation Front. The incident of the Gulf of Tonkin seemed to foreclose the issue. Bombings of North Vietnam, secretly planned since the previous August, began in earnest in February, 1965, and U.S. advisers went into combat in June, 23,000 strong. By the end of 1965 there were 160,000 more American men in Vietnam. Intensified bombing of the Hanoi-Haiphong area was carried out during 1966. U.S. troops carried out search-and-destroy missions and supported the pacification program aimed at regaining control of the villages.

At the same time President Johnson's 1965 decision to intervene in a Dominican Republic dispute and to send in U.S. Marines caused 160 journalists to flock to the scene. First to arrive was an old Latin American hand, Jules Dubois of the *Chicago Tribune.* Offering heavy interpretation on the United States role were Bernard Collier of the *New York Herald Tribune,* Dan Kurzman of the *Washington Post,* Ted Szulc of the *New York Times,* and Ruben Salazar of the *Los Angeles Times.* CBS's Bert Quint drove to the rebels' section and later reported first-hand observations. The crisis ended quickly and Vietnam was back in the headlines.

Two major controversies developed in this period, not between the correspondents and the military, but between the correspondents and the public. In August, 1965, Morley Safer of CBS News and two Vietnamese photographers shot "The Burning of the Village of Cam Ne." U.S. Marines had been fired on in the village area and in retaliation (after the Viet Cong had slipped away) leveled the 150-home village. "This is what the war in Viet Nam is all about," Safer narrated as he stood in front of the burning huts, "The Viet Cong were long gone . . . the action wounded three women, killed one baby, wounded one Marine and netted four old men as prisoners."[20] Walter Cronkite used the film; a storm broke. The film was too realistic, its critics contended; American soldiers should not be criticized; the presentation was one-sided and negative. Safer, who had thought to show the inhumanity of war, nearly lost his job.

But a greater sensation came in December, 1966, when the respected Harrison Salisbury, a senior editor-correspondent of the *New York Times,* began

Warmer

Tonight — Clear, low in 30s. **Thursday** — Sunny, high upper 60s. **Friday** — Sunny, mild. **Chances of rain:** Less than 10 per cent.

Map and chart on Page 41.

CHICAGO DAILY NEWS

©1966 by Field Enterprises Inc.

Final Markets
RED STREAK
Stocks Up

91st Year, Number 252 8 Sections Wednesday, October 26, 1966 10 Cents Phone 321-2000

Secret 2½-Hour Visit

LBJ Goes to Viet Nam

"I came here today for one good reason: simply because I could not come to this part of the world and not come to see you.

"I came here today for one good purpose, to tell you and through you to tell every soldier, sailor, airman and marine in Viet Nam how proud we are of what you are doing and how proud we are of the way you are doing it.

"I came here today with only one regret: that I could not begin to personally thank every man in Viet Nam for what he is doing."

43 Yanks Die in Fire On Carrier

Daily News Wire Services

SAIGON — A searing fire touched off by an explosion of photo flares raged through five decks of the U.S. Aircraft Carrier Oriskany off the coast of North Viet Nam. The blaze killed 43 men and injured 16.

Some men were trapped below decks and died in their bunks. It was the worst naval tragedy of the Viet Nam war.

Firemen, damage control and demolition experts darted into thick, choking smoke and flames so hot it melted steel girders to drag out bombs, rockets and planes.

Other sailors wheeled fighter-bombers out of danger and still other dived into a nearby officers' quarters and dragged out pilots overcome by heat and smoke.

They were too late for some of the other fliers who had flown through enemy fire over North Viet Nam just a few hours before and died in bed.

THE FIRE broke out shortly after dawn in a locker containing flares on the hangar deck, just below the flight deck, and then spread rapidly to envelop five decks, the Navy said.

Two helicopters were destroyed by the blaze and an undisclosed number of A-4E

Turn to Page 2, Column 1

Closeup Look

President Johnson leans from a jeep to shake hands with servicemen at the U.S. base at Cam Ranh Bay, South Viet Nam. Gen. William Westmoreland, U.S. commander in South Viet Nam, is at his side. (AP)

President Visits GIs At Big Base

By Peter Lisagor
Our Washington Bureau Chief

CAM RANH BAY, South Viet Nam—President Johnson flew to Viet Nam Wednesday for a dramatic 2½-hour visit with American troops and told U.S. commanders to "come home with that coonskin on the wall."

Dressed in light suntan jacket and trousers, with a Presidential seal on the right breast of his jacket, Mr. Johnson stood on a hastily built platform on the airstrip and declared to several hundred troops:

Text of President's talk to troops is on Page 2.

Full page of pictures on Back Page.

"I give you my pledge: We shall never let you down, nor your fighting comrades, nor the 15,000,000 Vietnamese, nor the hundreds of millions of Asians who are counting on us to show here in Viet Nam that aggression doesn't pay and that aggression cannot succeed."

THE PRESIDENT toured the vast base in a jeep with Gen. William C. Westmoreland, com... of U.S. troops in ... visited

A confident President exhorted, "Come home with that coonskin on the wall."

filing stories from Hanoi. He had been granted a visa since North Vietnam did not consider itself at war with the United States. Salisbury's series of stories, filled with detailed observations, directly contradicted much of the claimed success of the U.S. bombing program. The bombing had not been pinpointed on military targets; many smaller towns had been reduced to ghostly ruins; bombs had been dumped indiscriminately by fliers who needed to lose their payloads; and, worst of all, the unprecedented bombing attack had scarcely made a dent in the transportation and war-supplies capability of the North Vietnamese. Angry attacks were made on Salisbury and the *Times;* he was denied a Pulitzer Prize voted him by a judging committee for what most newspeople conceded was the outstanding news beat of 1966. In some sectors of the American public, the credibility of the press suffered (it should not run material favoring the enemy and derogatory to the armed forces); but in more sectors the credibility of the Pentagon suffered a severe blow. For there were also pictures to back up Salisbury's detailed reporting.

Generals Thieu and Ky were elected president and vice president of South Vietnam in 1967; the next year the runner-up was sentenced to 5 years in prison for aiding the enemy. United States troop strength jumped to 485,000 by the close of the year and the number of American dead passed the 15,000 mark. The administration claimed it was grinding out a victory and Secretary McNamara could see "a light at the end of the tunnel," a phrase that became a bitter joke for cartoonists. President Johnson, visiting Camranh Bay in late 1966, had urged his soldiers to "come home with that coonskin on the wall,"[21] and his commanders were trying to oblige. Some journalists, including columnists Joseph Alsop and Hanson W. Baldwin, were assessing the North Vietnamese as badly hurt and incapable of winning. But more were foreboding. Peter Arnett of the AP, whose tireless reporting had won him the 1966 Pulitzer Prize, said that Westmoreland was "in a critical position." Ward Just, *Washington Post* correspondent, said that all the statistics reported by the government gave a false picture of conditions; the country was not pacified when you could not travel on the roads. R. W. Apple, Jr., of the *New York Times* said: "Victory is not close at hand. It may be beyond reach." Robert Shaplen, the *New Yorker* magazine's talented correspondent, and Denis Warner of the *Reporter* magazine added their realistic estimates of a stalled effort in Vietnam.[22]

Those who read and believed these leading members of the Saigon press corps were not as badly surprised as most of the public, the U.S. Command in Saigon, and official Washington by the fury of the Tet offensive of late January, 1968. The National Liberation Front forces assaulted Saigon and put the U.S. Embassy under siege, held Hue for 25 days, and wiped out most of the pacification program in the countryside. General Westmoreland asked President Johnson for another 206,000 troops. The answer was a topping off at a total of 538,900, and a reassessment of the Vietnam War policy.

By that time Senator Eugene McCarthy's antiwar movement was sweeping Johnson out of the presidential race. On March 31—facing a defeat in the Wisconsin primary—the President stunned a vast television audience by withdrawing. He sharply limited the bombing of North Vietnam and initiated plans for preliminary peace talks in Paris that got under way in May. But a combination of public disbelief, disillusionment, and distaste for violence led to a stalemate in public opinion. The assassination of Senator Robert Kennedy in June, minutes after he had defeated McCarthy in the California primary, tore the heart out of the Democratic political campaign and opened the way for a fatal compromise in the welter of Chicago's street demonstrations and riots.

The Administration's candidate was Vice President Hubert H. Humphrey, who despite his liberal domestic achievements, had inherited Johnson's war mantle. He was challenged by his old Minnesota colleague McCarthy and Senator George McGovern of South Dakota, who had picked up some of Robert Kennedy's support. An emotional attempt to recruit Senator Edward Kennedy failed. Faced with the prospect of a continuation of Johnson's war policies—and ignoring the possibility that Richard M. Nixon might be worse for their long-range goals—thousands of demonstrators expressed their disappointment and anger.

CHICAGO 1968 AND THE WALKER REPORT

Late in 1968, after the Humphrey presidential hopes had been wrecked by the image created during the turbulent Democratic convention in Chicago, a study of that convention, known as the Walker Report, was issued. Chicago attorney

Daniel Walker made the report for the National Commission on the Causes and Prevention of Violence. His staff took statements from 1410 eyewitnesses and participants and had access to over 2000 interviews conducted by the FBI. The Walker Report, referring to "a police riot," said that conditions were worse than the media had described them. Following is a quote from that summary:

> During the week of the Democratic National Convention, the Chicago police were the targets of mounting provocation by both word and act. It took the form of obscene epithets, and of rocks, sticks, bathroom tiles and even human feces hurled at police by demonstrators. Some of the acts had been planned; others were spontaneous or were themselves provoked by police action. Furthermore, the police had been put on edge by widely-published threats of attempts to disrupt both the city and the Convention.
>
> That was the nature of the provocation. The nature of the response was unrestrained and indiscriminate police violence on many occasions, particularly at night.
>
> That violence was made all the more shocking by the fact that it was often inflicted upon persons who had broken no law, disobeyed no order, made no threat. These included peaceful demonstrators, onlookers, and large numbers of residents who were simply passing through, or happened to live in, the areas where confrontations were occurring.
>
> Newsmen and photographers were singled out for assault, and their equipment deliberately damaged. Fundamental police training was ignored; and officers, when on the scene, were often unable to control their men. As one police officer put it: "What happened didn't have anything to do with police work."[23]

The final report of the commission, made in December, 1969, said that in Chicago police used "excessive force not only against the provocateurs but also against the peaceful demonstrators and passive bystanders. Their conduct, while it won the support of the majority, polarized substantial and previously neutral segments of the population against the authorities and in favor of the demonstrators."

If these were the documented conclusions of a distinguished national commission appointed by President Johnson—the man against whom much of the bitterness at Chicago 1968 was directed—how did the media come out with tarnished public images?

Here best operated William Small's warning: the public, rather than accept reality, will prefer "to kill a messenger." The messenger was primarily television. CBS anchor Walter Cronkite found himself exploding with wrath when he saw (as did the audience) a floor guard slug CBS correspondent Dan Rather senselessly, but Cronkite later found himself meekly interviewing Chicago's political boss, Mayor Richard J. Daley, on whom primary responsibility for using "law and order" to create disorder rested. NBC correspondent Sander Vanocur never recovered professionally from the public disfavor he incurred while covering the convention and retired from NBC in 1971. The flow of antimedia letters was so intense that the Federal Communications Commission felt compelled to conduct an investigation of the news coverage of the affair by the networks. The networks agreed to cooperate, reluctantly; in September, 1969, the FCC reported that the networks had been fair.

Most Americans saw a 17-minute television sequence reporting the police-crowd confrontation on Wednesday night of convention week in front of the Conrad Hilton Hotel. There, and on the side streets, police brutality reached its peak, the Walker Report said. What most viewers would scarcely believe is the fact that those 17 minutes comprised half of the time CBS used to cover the demonstrations—32 minutes out of 38 hours of network time devoted to covering the week's activities. NBC devoted 36 minutes to violence on the floor out of 35 hours of coverage, 28 minutes to demonstrations outside the hall. ABC devoted 14 minutes to the disorders. Thus only a little more than 1 percent of network time was devoted to violence during the turbulent week, 99 percent to events on the floor, discussions, and the boredom of political-convention coverage.[24]

The public, however, criticized the media for paying too much attention to the demonstrators and for reporting too much violence. A study reported by *Broadcasting* magazine put the Wednesday night audience at 90 million, of whom 21.3 percent thought the police used excessive force and 56.8 percent thought they did not. Only 13 percent thought the tight security measures on the convention floor were unjustified—even though one critic commented that Humphrey was nominated "in a stockade."

In Chicago that week Del Hall of CBS News was clubbed from behind as he filmed. Jim Strickland of NBC News was clubbed in the mouth when he tried to assist Hall. Claude Lewis of the *Philadelphia Bulletin* was clubbed when he refused to give his notebook to a police officer. Jim Jones of *Newsweek* was kicked in the ribs and clubbed over the head while trying to show his press credentials. Robert Jackson of the *Chicago American* suffered the same fate. Altogether the news media suffered some seventy injuries at the hands of the police, equally divided between the electronic and print media.

But scant attention was paid to them. Eric Sevareid summed up the dilemma:

> The explanation seems obvious. Over the years the pressure of public resentment against screaming militants, foul mouthed demonstrators, arsonists, and looters had built up in the national boiler. With Chicago it exploded. The feelings that millions of people released were formed long before Chicago. Enough was enough: the police *must* be right. Therefore, the reporting *must* be wrong.[25]

It was sobering experience for the media. It was a disastrous week for the Democratic party and Hubert Humphrey, whose campaign fell apart fatally in Chicago. The image of violence and radicalism projected from Chicago alienated one group of voters; Humphrey's defense of the Vietnamese war turned off the liberal left that once had supported him. Republican Richard Nixon adroitly used telecasts, and won, by a hairline decision, despite Humphrey's valiant closing rush, the White House that had eluded him in 1960. The public, already recoiling from rioting and racial violence in the cities, rejected violence on its campuses and in its politics. It also rejected the free-speech movement with its four-letter words. Nixon and Spiro T. Agnew were a calm refuge for just enough voters to give them victory.

THE NEW JOURNALISTS

It was in the early 1960s that the term *New Journalism* again came into use. Used during the days of Pulitzer and Hearst, the term referred to a fresh approach to news gathering.[26] Then in the age of disillusionment, writers like Tom Wolfe,

JIMMY BRESLIN

Kids Take A Pounding—From Police, Delegates

By Jimmy Breslin

He was running with his body too far over and he had no control of himself, so he kept stumbling into the cops in the street and the cops chopped down on his head with their clubs.

Here was this young kid running with his legs out of control and his eyes closing and hair flying each time a club came onto his head—all the way from the front entrance of the Conrad Hilton Hotel to the corner. Running, stumbling, running, staggering and then going down on his face in the middle of Michigan Av. in the city of Chicago.

The cops ran up and kicked him. A few steps away, in the gutter under the streetlight, doctors leaned over somebody who seemed badly hurt.

Lines of policemen are strung across Michigan Av. outside the Conrad Hilton Hotel to block demonstrators trying to reach the International Amphitheatre. (Sun-Times Photo by Tom Kneebone)

The crowd in the street stood with handkerchiefs over faces in the tear gas and they screamed at the cops.

The police gathered into groups and then ran into the kids and swung their clubs, cops in blue helmets and short-sleeve blue shirts. Cops with bare arms swinging in the television lights while they went for the head with their clubs, or for any place below the belt they could reach. Chicago cops who had been misdirected all day and now were completely without supervision. They were running into young kids and beating them.

They gather in groups under the lights.

"Get these bastards over there," one of them says.

"Let's get 'em."

"No, no, now wait a minute, wait a minute. Over there. There."

The Worst In 20 Years

And they ran with their clubs into the kids who are unarmed and had, for hours, infuriated the cops with their youth and their dress and their manner of talking.

In 20 years of being policemen, having policemen in the family, riding with policemen in cars, drinking with them, watching them work in demonstrations and crowds in cities all over the world, the performance of the police of Chicago on Michigan Av. last night was the one worst I ever have seen.

"My head, my head, my head, my head," a girl in a gray sweater keeps saying as she falls against the building. Her hands go to her brown head of hair, where she has just been hit by a cop.

"Get out of here," the cop shouts. He aims his clu for below your midsection. He misses, changes direction and goes for somebody else.

The tear gas was everywhere and people ran into buildings with their hands over their mouths. An Ohio delegate came out of his hotel to ride to the convention and the gas hit him. He stumbled into an office building with tears streaming. The tear gas went up, and it got through the open windows of Hubert Humphrey suite.

It began in the afternoon when the kids sat on the grass in the park across the street from the hotel.

"It was a very together thing last night," a kid was saying. "We had an apartment set up and we brought in anybody who got zonked with tear gas."

A girl was on her back, blowing smoke up. "I'd tell you my name," she said. "But I can't give it. Like my parents."

Machineguns At The Ready

The National Guard had machineguns up on the bridges that cross the railroad tracks that run through the park—machineguns, machineguns on tripods. One on each sidewalk of the bridge. The cops had the kids blocked off in the park where they had gone into them with tear gas and clubs earlier.

Now the kids sat on the grass and waited for word from their leader, Sidney Peck, the professor from Case-Western Reserve who is in the militant peace movment with such people as Dave Dellinger.

As Peck is far superior to the police at the simple art of crowd movements, he waited while his kids taunted the National Guardsmen.

"Wouldn't you rather hold a girl than a rifle?" a kid said, his arms around a girl who stood inches away from the line of rifles pointed at them.

Then Peck got on the loud-speaker and told the crowd of perhaps 4,000 to break up into small groups and just walk out of the park. And the kids broke up and walked away from the police and the National Guard. Walked away and left the police and National Guard motionless. And the kids went into Michigan Av. and captured the whole street and began shouting slogans at the hotel.

To the police, however, a kid shouting a political slogan is a thing to be feared and beaten. There was no way to control them. The police of Chicago have been out of hand since April, when Mayor Daley said they should shoot young looters. Daley went over the head of his police chief when he did this. When you deal with the intelligence of the average policeman you must be very careful. Mayor Daley was not.

Voice At Convention Headquarters

So Wednesday night, rather than watch the nomination of a candidate for the office of the President of the United States, you came, crying and choking and burning from tear gas, into the lobby of the Conrad Hilton Hotel, the headquarters for the convention, and the hotel speaker called out," all guests of the hotel please go to your room immediately and stay there." And out in the street, moving through the lights, national guardsmen in gas masks pointed rifles and moved at the crowd.

There were only 4,000 kids in the streets and the treatment given them by police created a national scandal, the effect of which will be felt through the days and the weeks that they try to conduct a campaign for the Presidency. For 4,000 kids is a very small number, compared to what surely will

Turn to Page 22

The *Chicago Sun-Times* covers the climactic "police riot" in picture and story.

Jimmy Breslin, Gay Talese, Truman Capote, and Norman Mailer began to experiment with what was later called new nonfiction reportage. This took on different forms, but generally it meant using perception and interviewing techniques to obtain a view of a happening from inside the source, instead of relying on the standard information-gathering, stock-question approach. It meant focusing on writing style and on the quality of description.

The bulk of the so-called New Journalists were newspaper reporters who spent much of their spare time and a good deal of company time trying to sell articles to magazines like *Esquire, New York,* and the *New Yorker.* Wolfe had worked for the *Washington Post* before joining the *New York Herald Tribune* staff, where Breslin was already a newsroom curiosity. Talese wrote for the *New York Times.* It was natural that these writers would approach *Esquire* with their off-beat portraits of people and life styles. For years Arnold Gingrich, who founded *Esquire* in 1933, had been running the top bylines in American writing, while at the same time dropping away from his habit of filling pages with sexy material. Hemingway, Faulkner, and Steinbeck had preceded the New Journalists. Harold T. P. Hayes and Don Erickson were top editors in the 1960s and Garry Wills and Robert Sherrill were among the contributing editors.

The most spectacular magazine success in the 1960s was that of *New York.* More than a typical city magazine such as those that appeared in other metropolitan centers, *New York* was a continuation of the magazine supplement of the *Herald Tribune.* Editor Clay Felker had developed a style there, printing such new journalism writers as Wolfe, Breslin, and Peter Maas. In 1967 Felker obtained the right to the name and recruited enough support to launch the magazine in April, 1968. He aimed it at the young city dwellers and was rewarded with some 150,000 readers within a year, including a 25,000 newsstand sale that exceeded that of the proud *New Yorker.* Felker's business associate was publisher George Hirsch. Wolfe, Breslin, and Maas continued as contributing editors, along with Judith Crist and George J. W. Goodman ("Adam Smith"). The star writer was Gloria Steinem, whose articles had appeared in other magazines. *New York* did some muckraking, but more often carried articles, departments, and tips to better living that served its city audience. It also interested out-of-towners, who upped circulation to 375,000.

Felker moved on to assume editorial control of the *Village Voice* and then created the splashy *New West,* copying the cover and internal design of *New York.* His empire collapsed in early 1977, however, when Australian press lord Rupert Murdoch outbid Katharine Graham of the *Washington Post* and gained control of three publications by paying $9 million to Felker's fellow stockholders.

Among other city magazines—some of which resembled Chamber of Commerce sheets—*Philadelphia* magazine was twice honored with National Magazine Awards for its tough reporting. In 1970 the magazine exposed a scandal in the Pearl S. Buck Foundation, and in 1972 it examined the management of the Delaware Port Authority, a case not covered by other media. *Los Angeles* magazine gained attention for its life-style coverage and tremendous advertising volume.

Using sights, sounds, and inner thoughts, the New Journalists tackled a wide variety of subjects with their individual styles. In the June, 1966, *Atlantic,* writer Dan Wakefield credited Wolfe's *The Kandy-Kolored Tangerine-Flake Stream-*

line Baby and Capote's *In Cold Blood* with causing the literary world to consider New Journalism as a serious art form. Dozens of articles and several books appeared on the subject but no single definition was agreed upon.[27] But whether New Journalism was merely a concentrated use of old feature-writing techniques or a genuine breakthrough in gaining "the truth," these journalists made a mark. As early as 1952 Lillian Ross of the *New Yorker* contributed *The Picture,* a factual report of a movie company done in novel form. Later Breslin's looks at the little people were found in *The World of Jimmy Breslin* (1968), Mailer poured out his experiences on a march against the Pentagon in his *Armies of the Night* (1968), Wolfe described the age of drugs in his *Electric Kool-Aid Acid Test* (1969), and Talese tattled on his former bosses at the *Times* with marvelous detail in his *The Kingdom and the Power* (1969).

Although examples of new nonfiction reportage appeared in various magazines and books, the writing movement did not spread to newspapers. Of the major writers, only Breslin continued to turn out newspaper columns while doing other forms of writing. Most editors frowned on New Journalism techniques and mistakenly linked them with "advocacy" or "activist" reporting. In addition to this confusion, another group claimed that it had the answer to reporting problems: those advocating the use of social-science survey techniques in reporting. Called *precision journalists,* they learned from the example of Philip Meyer, who covered Washington for the Knight newspapers and authored the book *Precision Journalism.* Of note was his study, *Return to 12th Street,* in which a reporting team examined the Detroit riot of 1967 through interviews with hundreds of black residents. Haynes Johnson and a *Washington Post* team used similar tactics in covering national politics. The object was to gather news data that could be used to interpret trends or describe conditions under which people were living.

THE UNDERGROUND PRESS

The roots of the "underground press" movement that swelled to prominence in the mid-1960s can be found in the words of all the radicals of American journalism, starting with James Franklin and including more recently the radical *Guardian,* founded in New York City in 1948, and *I. F. Stone's Weekly.* The inspiration for the movement came from men like Allan Ginsberg, Bob Dylan, Jack Kerouac, Lenny Bruce, and Norman Mailer. The immediate stimuli were the four-letter word movement, the sex revolution, the generation and credibility gaps that created the anti-Establishment era, and, above all, the bitter antiwar protest typified by the March on the Pentagon.

Underground papers were printed cheaply by offset, free-swinging in style and content, uninhibited in graphic design, unrestricted in viewpoint, and in many cases, also unprofitable. They reflected a rebellion not only against the national Establishment but also against its conventional mass media. The best of the underground papers did a capable job of criticizing both and of breathing new life into the dead-center American social and political scene of the 1960s. By the mid-1970s much of the spark had left the movement.

One historian of the underground papers, Robert Glessing, listed 457 titles of papers in his 1970 book,[28] and commented that they were coming and going almost too rapidly to list. Included in his total were fifty-five military papers and campus, black, and Chicano publications. He estimated that there were 3000 underground high-school papers.

First of the underground papers was the *Village Voice,* a sensational weekly when it was founded in Greenwich Village in 1955. Its creators were Daniel Wolf, a free-lance writer who became editor; Edward Fancher, a psychologist who became publisher; and novelist Norman Mailer. Its political line was anti-Establishment Democrat, it exhibited the Village interest in books and the arts, and its great coup was to break the four-letter word barrier. It started cartoonist Jules Feiffer on his way, helped Jack Newfield upward, and ran contributions from most of the writers who also appeared in the new-journalism columns of *Esquire, New York,* and *Harper's.* It became a fat forty-eight pages, with top "underground" circulation of 150,000, in the 1970s.

Most successful of the really radical underground publishers of the 1960s was former machinist Art Kunkin, who used $15 to start his *Los Angeles Free Press* in 1964. By 1970 his estimated circulation was 95,000, and Kunkin had not missed a week with his antipolice cartoons, his swinging classified ads, and his put-downs of politicians and society leaders. His paper gained additional attention through serious comment on both national and local issues, however startling the language. A 4-year battle between Kunkin and the Los Angeles police over his right to a press pass ended in March, 1971, when the Supreme Court refused to hear the *Free Press'* appeal of an appellate-court decision holding that the weekly paper did not automatically qualify for a press pass under the First Amendment. In New York a media council granted press passes to underground papers, but Los Angeles police were adamant about Kunkin, who had published a list of names of narcotics undercover agents in one defiant episode. He lost financial control of the paper late in 1971 and became a free-lance writer and journalism professor.

Best known and most successful of campus-related papers was the *Berkeley Barb,* born in the summer of 1965 out of the students' passionate dislike for the University of California administration and the excitement of the Berkeley free-speech movement. Its founder, Max Scherr, was in his 50s but was still in touch with the alienated people of the streets. The *Barb* produced major Bay-area exposés, led the disruptive student protests that split the campus apart, advanced to the sex revolution's frontiers, and grew fat on profits from suggestive classified ads and circulation. In 1969 Scherr and some of his staff split, and the dissidents produced the *Tribe.* The resulting controversies diminished the influence of the *Barb.*

There were other important underground papers of the mid-1960s: Detroit's *Fifth Estate* of 1965, the *Washington Free Press* of 1966, and three products of the climactic year of 1967, *Seed* in Chicago, *Kaleidoscope* in Milwaukee, and *Distant Drummer* in Philadelphia. Praised for their graphic effects were Boston's *Avatar* of 1967 and the *San Francisco Oracle,* a 1966 sensation for its psychedelic effect. Closely connected to rock music were John Bryan's *Open City* of 1967 to 1969 in Los Angeles and San Francisco's later *Rolling Stone.* Breaking down the barriers the *Village Voice* had not tested in New York City were Paul Krassner's *Realist,* founded in 1958, and the *East Village Other,* a 1965 protest journal with

Wide World Photos *Marquette University Archives*

I.F. Stone and Dorothy Day, alternative journalists.

innovative art forms that grew in influence. New York's radical political paper, the *Guardian,* became underground in outlook by 1970. The dismal wind-down of the Vietnam War proved I. F. Stone and his *Weekly* to have been right as well as cantankerous.

ALTERNATIVE JOURNALISTS

The incomparable I. F. Stone—working only with his wife and an occasional research assistant—began publishing his *I. F. Stone's Weekly* in 1953, biting at the proponents of McCarthyism. He continued the newsletter until 1971, writing of controversies caused by the Korean War, the problems of the blacks, the early days of Vietnam, and the steady encroachment on private rights in the anti-Vietnam War demonstration days.[29] Stone's documented exposés, often taken from the printed records of the government, fed many other writers and activists with ammunition. Stone emerged as one of America's most distinguished and consistent journalists, along with Carey McWilliams of the *Nation* and Dorothy Day of the *Catholic Worker.* All had to be content with small circulations, but had the satisfaction of knowing that their dedicated readers included some activists and policy makers who eventually made inroads against the status quo in the 1970s. Stone retired from active combat to become a contributing editor for the *New York Review of Books,* where he continued his critical writing.

Carey McWilliams came to the editor's chair of the *Nation* in 1955, succeeding Freda Kirchwey, who had steered the magazine through money shortages and staff crises involving the policy line toward the Soviet Union. McWilliams maintained a vigorous liberalism and by the *Nation*'s 100th anniversary in 1965 it was making the most incisive, fact-supported editorial attacks on the Vietnam War found in American publications. McWilliams continued his investigative journalism during the Watergate period, again putting the *Nation* in the forefront of aggressive attack.

Like Stone, Dorothy Day exhibited a compelling, tenacious, and consistent journalistic purpose. Her impact reached far beyond the circulation of her *Catholic Worker,* a monthly paper that cost but a single penny, and that was graced by the wood engravings of Fritz Eichenberg and the writings of Jacques Maritain, J. F. Powers, Michael Harrington, and others. The Catholic worker movement the paper nurtured acted as a leaven on American social consciences, and its soup kitchens and residences for the poor spread across a recession-hit America in the 1980s, just as they had in the Depression. The *Catholic Worker* publication has surpassed all others by maintaining a consistent editorial line for half a century: an advocacy of personal activism ("personalism") to achieve nonviolent social justice, a rigid devotion to pacifism, and a philosophy of communitarian Christianity.[30] Until her death in 1980, Dorothy Day was clearly the linchpin of the enterprise.

Born into a newspaper family, Day left college at 18 to become an activist reporter for the *Socialist Call* and the *Liberator,* hobnobbing in Greenwich Village with young writers like Eugene O'Neill and Hart Crane, writing for the *Masses,* and picketing the White House for women's suffrage. Converted to Catholicsm in 1927, she started the paper in 1933 with a French Catholic philosopher, Peter Maurin, and saw its circulation reach 190,000 by 1938. Steadfastly pacifist, Day ran counter to majority American Catholic support of Franco in the Spanish Civil War and for American military action in World War II. *Catholic Worker* circulation fell as low as 50,000; George Schuster's *Commonweal* lost one-fourth of its circulation over the Spanish Civil War issue and Schuster was forced out as editor. Day never broke with the Catholic Church; she only sought to reform it. Indeed, the left attacked her for her opposition to the revolutionary class struggle as determinedly as the right shunned her pacifism and concern for the poor. The *Catholic Worker* opposed the 1940 draft, Father Coughlin's anti-Semitism, Japanese internment in California, the atomic bomb, the 1948 peacetime draft, the Korean War, and the Rosenberg executions. Keeping alive the peace movement in the 1950s meant Day's going to jail four times for opposing mandatory civil-defense drills as militarist devices.

Catholic Worker circulation, which rebounded as pacifism became popular again in the Vietnam War era, eventually reached 100,000. The *Catholic Worker* supported draft-card burning but not sabotaging the draft-board offices, which Day believed could spark violence. Day's antiwar stand coincided with that of Pope Paul VI; she was in the company of Thomas Merton, Father Robert Drinan, the Berrigans, *Commonweal* (now edited by John Deedy), *Jubilee, Ave Maria, Critic,* and the *National Catholic Reporter,* of the liberal church press. At 75, Day was arrested while picketing with Cesar Chavez in California. Before she died, Notre Dame University honored her for her influence upon both her country and her church.

Joining in the alternative-journalism category as journals of tough-minded criticism in the 1960s were the *Bay Guardian, Cervi's Rocky Mountain Journal,* and the *Texas Observer.* Each attacked the established press in its area, as well as the political and social establishments, in the best tradition of crusading journalism. The *Bay Guardian*'s editor, Bruce Brugmann, ended up suing the San Francisco dailies for abridging freedom of the press through their joint publishing agreement and won awards for his paper's reporting.

Behind the underground-press revolution were its press associations. One, the Liberation News Service, was founded in 1967 during the march on Washington by two graduate students who had been editors of their college papers, Ray Mungo and Marshall Bloom. The Underground Press Syndicate, organized in 1966 and developed by Tom Forcade, became a trade-association clearing house and advertising representative for the papers. Forcade later argued for and won the right to cover Congress.

While a number of underground and alternative publications either died or slipped in influence in the 1970s, one early leader became a huge financial success: *Rolling Stone.* Jann Wenner was 21 when his first issue rolled off the presses in 1967, and 10 years later he headed a $10-million-a-year enterprise with circulation approaching 500,000. *Rolling Stone* contributors ranged from the sophisticated Tom Wolfe to the eccentric Hunter Thompson, the proponent of "Gonzo" journalism. By moving his headquarters from San Francisco to New York, Wenner confirmed *Rolling Stone*'s place in the Establishment world. The main focus remained music, although tough stands had been taken during the Vietnam War and political and social commentary continued to be part of the attractive package.

Of the many women's magazines—traditional and feminist—that were born in the 1960s and 1970s the most successful and influential was *Ms.,* edited by Gloria Steinem. Letty Pogrebin, Patricia Carbine, and a dozen other active writers assisted with the editing chores in this unusually democratic group effort. *Ms.* not only attacked the white male Establishment but also offered a wide range of views on financial, sexual, psychological, and family matters. *Ms.* reached a circulation of 500,000 by 1983 with Carbine as publisher, doubling its 1972 initial run.

Remaining active in the area of staunch liberal journalism were the *Jewish Daily Forward* (1898), the last Yiddish-language daily in North America, and the *Partisan Review* (1937). Under editor Abraham Cahan, the *Forward* carried analyses and reviews with a Socialist orientation, but mellowed with its readership in later years. Writer Isaac Bashevis Singer joined the staff in 1935 and editor Simon Weber in 1940; they became survivors of economic hardship that saw circulation drop from a peak of 220,000 in 1924 to 35,000 in 1982.

One of *Partisan Review*'s founding editors, William Phillips, remained at his desk, editing the anti-Soviet prose and poetry. His cofounder, Philip Rahv, died in 1974. While its heyday was in the 1940s and 1950s, the *Partisan Review* remained true to its original goal, publishing pieces praising the Polish Solidarity campaign of the 1980s and opposing secret-police tactics.

The Communist party's *Daily Worker,* founded in 1924, had 100,000 circulation in the late 1930s, but only 5600 when it dropped to weekly status in 1958.

INVESTIGATIVE REPORTING

Digging into the activities of the Pentagon, Central Intelligence Agency, Federal Bureau of Investigation, Teamsters' Union, organized crime syndicates, and corrupt politicians were the so-called investigative journalists of the 1960s and 1970s. Investigative reporting meant developing sufficient sources and documents over a long period of time to offer the public a strong interpretation of the event's meaning. The term *investigative* became extremely popular after Seymour Hersh uncovered the story of the My Lai massacre in Vietnam and joined the *New York Times* staff in time to look into the CIA. Jack Nelson of the *Los Angeles Times* helped demythologize FBI Director J. Edgar Hoover, and Bob Woodward and Carl Bernstein of the *Washington Post* became national heroes. But by its very nature, true investigative reporting could be conducted by only the most wealthy and influential newspapers and hardly at all by the television networks, with the exception of occasional in-depth "Specials" by all three networks and one regular program, CBS News' fine *60 Minutes* show.

Investigative journalism did not begin with the 1960s, however. It was a continuation of the muckraking tradition, which never really died. From the 1920s to the present day, small circulation magazines like the *Nation* and the *New Republic* kept reform ideas alive. Heywood Broun, McAlister Coleman, Lewis Gannett, and Louis Adamic wrote for their pages in earlier days. Matthew Josephson attacked large-scale arms spending in the *Nation* in 1956, the same year Fred J. Cook wrote his "The Shame of New York." Editor Carey McWilliams developed special issues on the FBI in 1958 and the CIA in 1962. Ralph Nader's first series, including his "The Safe Car You Can't Buy," appeared in the *Nation* in 1959, and as early as 1953 McWilliams was linking cigarettes and lung cancer.

In addition to magazines, major contributions came from the authors of books. John Steinbeck's *The Grapes of Wrath* and *Factories in the Field* brought the plight of the migrant worker to America's attention in the 1930s. Later, writers like Michael Harrington, Dwight MacDonald, and Herman Miller helped discover the forgotten poor. In the Vietnam and Watergate era a spate of books uncovered governmental deception, white collar and organized crime, and a general neglect of the quality of life. In the broadcasting field CBS led the way, first with Edward R. Murrow's documentaries, and then with *Hunger in America* and *The Selling of the Pentagon.* All three networks and public television looked at the problems of drugs, crime, excessive wealth, and corruption, but for the most part, investigative journalism remained television news' biggest weakness.

Others who made strong efforts in the field of investigative reporting included syndicated columnist Jack Anderson, Denny Walsh, Robert Sherrill, Sanford Watzman, Nick Kotz, Tom Whiteside, Les Whitten, Joseph Goulden, Robert Scheer, George Reasons, and Bob Greene. The controversial Anderson won the 1972 Pulitzer Prize for his exposure of the Nixon administration's deception during the India-Pakistan war; Greene headed a special investigative team at *Newsday* that turned out several important stories, including one of Nixon's Florida connections; and Reasons led the *Los Angeles Times* group that won a Pulitzer Prize for finding corruption in that city's harbor commission.

Walsh won a Pulitzer Prize for his *Life* magazine exposé on organized crime. *Life* and *Look* made a number of attempts to investigate problems in America before they fell victim to economic and management problems. Scheer edited *Ramparts,* a leftist magazine in the 1960s, which among other things exposed the CIA's infiltration of the international student movement. After writing one of the first critical books of the war, *How the U.S. Got Into Vietnam,* he became a free-lance writer and later reported for the *Los Angeles Times.*

Despite these investigative efforts, the record showed that a number of stories were poorly covered. Blind acceptance of governmental statements led to future public cynicism when the facts of the John Kennedy and Martin Luther King, Jr., assassinations were contradicted. The killing of Dr. King caused riots and later, when it was revealed that J. Edgar Hoover had conducted a personal vendetta against Dr. King, the public was doubtful that James Earl Ray was singly involved. Other stories that did not receive adequate investigation included the role of major oil companies during energy crises, white-collar crime in general, the backgrounds of persons appointed to public office or regulatory commissions on all levels, bribery involving arms sales to both sides in international conflicts, and other subjects involving power and money.

URBAN AND ENVIRONMENT WRITERS

An Urban Writers' Society was formed in 1968, reflecting the concern of Americans about urban society and the environment. Outstanding among the urban specialists were Ada Louise Huxtable, architecture critic of the *New York Times* since 1963 and winner of the 1970 Pulitzer Prize for criticism; Wolf Von Eckardt, urban and architecture specialist for the *Washington Post* since 1964; George McCue, art and urban-design critic for the *St. Louis Post-Dispatch;* and Allan Temko, the *San Francisco Chronicle*'s urban columnist. When in 1970 *Editor & Publisher* asked the nation's dailies to send in the names of their writers specializing in environmental news coverage on the ecology beat, 100 did.[31]

Environmental concerns became paramount in the late 1970s and reporters struggled to explain such things as environmental impact reports, nuclear power plants, liquified natural gas, water projects, zoning regulations, and, of course, the economic implications of all this to the tax-paying public. Among the environment and ecology specialists were Gladwin Hill of the *New York Times,* Margaret Freivogel of the *St. Louis Post-Dispatch,* Steve Wynkoop of the *Denver Post,* David Ross Stevens of the *Louisville Courier-Journal,* and Paul Hayes of the *Milwaukee Journal.*

The need for alternative energy sources and conservation of water became acute in 1976 to 1977 when a terrible drought struck the western half of the nation while the eastern half was hit by an unusually severe winter that nearly exhausted fuel supplies. The nation's newspapers and broadcast stations carried the running story with good detail, and the better ones, as usual, offered background stories and editorialized for stringent regulations prohibiting unsafe and wasteful practices. Changing weather patterns were also examined by reporters, who interpreted the divergent viewpoints of leading scientists.

THE BLACK PRESS SURVIVES

At the close of World War II the "big three" of the black newspapers—the *Chicago Defender* (1905), the *Pittsburgh Courier* (1910), and the *Afro-American* of Baltimore (1892)—could be purchased as easily in Mississippi or in Florida as in their hometowns. Gunnar Myrdal's classic study of 1945, *An American Dilemma,* reported that "The Negro press . . . is rightly characterized as the single greatest power in the Negro race."[32] The *Defender* boasted a circulation of 257,000, the *Courier* 202,000, and the *Afro-American* 137,000. The impact of two world wars and heavy black migration to Northern industrial cities brought this peak of circulation influence. But within a few years a general decline began, and nationally circulating papers lost ground to community-based ones, leaving small stable papers as the survivors during the civil-rights battles of the 1960s.

For the most part the older, somewhat conservative black papers were left behind by the rush of events and black militancy in the 1960s. In many cities small organizational newspapers were published to offer a point of view not found in the established white or black press. In Chicago, for example, *Black Truth, Black Liberator,* and *Black Women's Committee News* were among a number of newspapers challenging the *Defender.* The black press concentrated on the routine coverage of the community and was ambivalent to the cries of young blacks for direct action. Fear of losing newly-gained white advertising accounts held back some black papers from joining more vigorously in the black revolution. It was not until the Black Panthers party was ruthlessly treated by law-enforcement agencies that some black papers questioned the role of whites in dealing with the militant group, particularly after the killing of Panther leader Fred Hampton in a 1969 raid on his Chicago apartment.

Nevertheless, the black press survived the economic hardships and the community political pressures. By 1970 the circulation of the *Defender* had dropped to 33,000 and that of the *Pittsburgh Courier* to 20,000. The circulation leader was the nationally distributed *Muhammad Speaks,* the voice of the Black Muslim movement founded by Malcolm X in 1961, with an estimated 700,000. Copies were sold on street corners, proclaiming the programs of Elijah Muhammad and condemning the Vietnam War. Also prominent was *The Black Panther,* founded in 1966 by San Francisco blacks who led the fight against alleged police abuse of minorities. Circulation ran around 100,000 during the late 1960s and the paper was available in major cities. *The Voice* in Jamaica, New York, boasted a circulation of 90,000, and the *Sentinel-Bulletin* of Tampa had 75,000.

Although the bulk of the papers resisted pressure to take up the slogans of black militants, editors did keep an eye on problems with local law-enforcement officials. Another theme was news of federal-government programs and there was considerable criticism during the Nixon years of Washington's attitude. This was repeated later during the Reagan administration's attempts to trim community-assistance programs and health benefits.

Other black papers prominent in the 1960s were the *Atlanta World* (1928), *Los Angeles Sentinel* (1934), Detroit's *Michigan Chronicle* (1936), and the *Philadelphia Tribune* (1884).

BLACK PRESS LEADERS

John H. Sengstacke, editor and publisher of the *Chicago Daily Defender* and head of the Sengstacke Newspapers group, was elected to the board of directors of the American Society of Newspaper Editors in 1970. He was the first black editor to be so honored. This personal recognition also reflected the status of the *Defender* group as the largest in black newspaper publishing, with community and national circulation claims totaling 100,000 in 1983. The *Chicago Defender* had 15,000 daily circulation and 21,000 for its national weekly edition. Largest in the Sengstacke group was the *Michigan Chronicle,* founded in 1936 in Detroit, with 31,000 circulation. The *New Pittsburgh Courier,* purchased in 1966 by Sengstacke along with the *Courier* group, had 10,000.

The *Afro-American* group, headed by John H. Murphy, III, had some 50,000 combined circulation in 1983. Its biggest unit was the semiweekly Baltimore edition, with 20,000 circulation. It also published in Richmond, Washington, and New Jersey, and had a national weekly edition. Mrs. Elizabeth Murphy Moss, vice president of the group, was a leading reporter and war correspondent. So was Ethel L. Payne, Washington correspondent for the Sengstacke papers and only black newswoman to cover the Vietnam war.

The *Amsterdam News,* the largest circulating of the standard black community papers, was purchased by Dr. C. B. Powell in 1936 and was controlled by him until 1971 when ownership passed to Clarence B. Jones. This paper concentrated on local items and sensationalized crime and sex news to combat its competition in Harlem from Congressman Adam Clayton Powell's *People's Voice* and the old *New York Age.* Like the *Afro-American* and *Defender* papers, it became moderate in tone, heavily local in news coverage, strong in sports and women's news, and occasionally crusading. Its 1983 circulation was 43,000.

John H. Sengstacke, head of the *Defender* newspaper group.
Chicago Defender

Out of forty-five efforts to publish black dailies in the United States, as reported by Pride, only two prevailed. One was the *Chicago Daily Defender,* with daily status since 1956. The other was the *Atlanta Daily World,* founded as a weekly in 1928 and a daily since 1932. Its founder, William A. Scott, was assassinated in 1934; his successor, Cornelius A. Scott, edited a consistently conservative paper in news content, typographical appearance, and editorial direction. World news coverage was good. It supported the Republican party politically and opposed such militant black action as economic boycotts of white merchants who discriminated in hiring blacks. Its 1983 circulation was 18,000.

The *Los Angeles Sentinel,* owned and edited by Ruth Washington, was founded in 1934. Its 31,000 circulation made it the most important black publication in Los Angeles, where it displayed a mildly sensational front page and a liberal-moderate editorial page. Other noteworthy black papers were the *Philadelphia Tribune, Cleveland Call and Post, Atlanta Inquirer,* Norfolk's *Journal and Guide,* the semiweekly *Tampa Sentinel-Bulletin,* the *Kansas City Call,* founded in 1919, and the *Louisiana Weekly.* There were large free-circulation shopping papers like the Wave Publications in Los Angeles with a distribution of 230,000, and the Berkeley Post Group, 70,000.

Like the regular weeklies, the black weeklies usually appeared on Thursdays. Advertising occupied about one-third of the total space, with two-thirds or more of that local in origin, but national advertising was increasing in larger black papers beginning in the 1960s. Most of the national black papers and largest weeklies subscribed to the United Press International for their state, regional, national, and international news. The best known of the specialized press services was the Associated Negro Press (ANP), founded in 1919 by Claude A. Barnett. It peaked in 1945 with 112 American subscribers. Barnett made many trips to Africa after World War II and added 100 subscribers there as well as developing African news. But by 1966 ANP had so much competition in the coverage of black news events that it went out of business.[33] The National Negro Press Association, with Louis Lautier as Washington correspondent, operated between 1947 and 1960 with the support of the larger black papers, and it began service again in 1974 with John W. Lewis, Jr. as correspondent.

The number of black papers dropped from 213 to 165 between 1974 and 1979, according to Henry G. LaBrie, III, noted for his research in the area. In earlier studies LaBrie discovered that fewer than forty papers had their own printing facilities and that only a small number had circulations verified by ABC audit.[34] In the face of this decline, at its 1981 convention the National Newspapers Publishers Association endorsed the concept of a single editorial voice for its 115 members. Taking charge and making the proposal was John L. Procope, the publisher of New York's *Amsterdam News.* Procope and others suggested that the black press as a whole should rid itself of complacency and offer its readership a more aggressive editorial stand regarding problems with the criminal-justice system, housing, voting registration, and education. A national editorial board was to coordinate the program, which black publishers thought more necessary than before because of economic cutbacks suggested by the Reagan administration. The editorial change was accompanied by a push to develop more national advertising revenues.[35]

Black papers traditionally have been weeklies or semiweeklies. In the early

Thieves slay blind man

(see page 3)

SENGSTACKE Newspaper

Chicago Defender

CHICAGO'S DAILY PICTURE NEWSPAPER

WEATHER

Today will be partly sunny, high in upper 70s.

VOL. LXXI - NO. 111 | WEDNESDAY, OCTOBER 8, 1975 | 15¢ 20¢ Outside Of Chicago

Islamic groups unite in fete

(see page 4)

HEW tells board end teacher bias

(see page 3)

At showdown...

Dr. James G. Haughton (left photo), director of Cook County Hospital, warned the hospital's 548 doctors and interns yesterday that if their dispute is not settled soon, they could face "maximum discipline," including being fired. Some of the dissatisfied doctors and interns (right) appear bored as they listen to Haughton's recommendations. Members of house staff have said they are prepared to lose their jobs if it will improve patient care and overall working conditions. Dr. Haughton says that many of the criticisms about the care of patients are unfounded. (Defender photos by Phyllis Doering).

She wants cash for 'lemon'

(see page 3)

A front page of a leading black paper.

1980s the only papers publishing more frequently were the *Atlanta Daily World, Chicago Daily Defender,* and New York's new *Daily Challenge.* The only papers distributed nationally were the *Bilalian News,* the Islamic publication that was formerly *Muhammad Speaks,* and a 1982 entry, the *National Leader,* a Philadelphia-based tabloid with reporters in twenty-eight cities and 100,000 circulation, edited by Claude Lewis. The total circulation of all black papers was estimated at 3 million, a drop of about one-third from the 1974 figure of 4.4 million.

THE BLACK MAGAZINES

John Johnson's *Ebony* reached a circulation of 1.3 million in the early 1980s, appealing mainly to urban, middle-class blacks. Founding *Ebony* in 1945, Johnson quickly discovered that sensationalism did not pay, but quality photographs and a serious presentation of black life did. During the turmoil of the 1960s *Ebony* became more concerned with black problems and ran extensive articles on these subjects in addition to pictures and cartoons. Johnson's other main publication, *Jet,* had a circulation of 750,000. It was started as a pocket-sized news weekly to carry material that would not fit into *Ebony.*

The leading publication for black women was *Essence,* begun in 1970. Its circulation climbed to more than 650,000. For its first 10 years *Essence* was edited by Marcia Ann Gillespie, who kept the magazine tied to its roots in the black-power movement of the 1960s. The goal was to relate to the lives of black women and to create awareness among advertisers to the potential of the black women audience. Black businessmen and women read *Black Enterprise* (1970); civil-rights and race-relations advocates were devoted to *Crisis* (1910); college students could buy the *Black Collegian* (1970); and college-educated black men were attracted to *Main Man* (1980). Among other noteworthy black magazines were *Black Scholar, Negro History Bulletin, Journal of Negro History, Black Law Journal,* and *View South.*

THE LATINO MEDIA

The rising consciousness of Latinos in the 1960s, sparked by the leadership of Cesar Chavez, led to the founding of several dozen newspapers dedicated to the organization of Latinos as sensitive, progressive communities. Chavez led his United Farm Workers union against the powerful California grape growers in the San Joaquin Valley and *El Malcriado,* published from a shack in Delano, became the official union voice in 1964. The movement spread from the fields to the cities and in 1967 *La Raza* appeared in Los Angeles, speaking loudly for improvement in educational opportunities, better housing, and an end to what young Chicanos called police harassment. The protests followed in the tradition of earlier Mexican newspapers.

The United Farm Workers succeeded in improving the working conditions of migrant workers in California and Chavez attempted to bring pressure on growers in Texas and Florida, where discrimination was rampant. California had a long history of racist attacks against those who did the necessary inexpensive labor. Indians, Chinese, and Japanese took their turn doing hard labor and picking the crops, ruthlessly victimized by violence and discriminatory laws. The Indians were driven to the mountain areas, the Chinese and Japanese were excluded by immigration laws, and from the 1920s on the fields were worked by

Mexicans and, to a lesser but significant degree, Filipinos. Carey McWilliams summed up the long-standing grievances of the farm workers in his *Factories in the Field.* There were many strikes along the West Coast in the twentieth century, but little support from organized labor until the 1960s. Gompers of the AFL had laid down the rules in the early 1900s—no Mexican or Oriental could share a union with whites—but later auto workers, longshoremen, and AFL-CIO workers around the nation supported Chavez.

Other events in the 1960s caused a number of papers to appear. *El Rebozo,* published by women in San Antonio, was among five Texas papers; other papers were *El Gallo* in Denver, *La Guardia* in Milwaukee, *Adelante* in Kansas City, and *Lado* in Chicago.

By the 1980s Latinos were the fastest growing minority group in the United States, with an estimated population of 21 to 23 million, adding 6 to 8 million undocumented migrants to the official population of 15 million. Latinos were dispersed across the nation, mainly in urban areas. Nearly 80 percent listed themselves as bilingual in Spanish and English. However, as a group Latinos experienced a continuation of past educational, health, and employment problems, some of them due to unequal political representation.

The national media's discovery of the previously invisible Chicanos in the 1960s was attributed by researcher Félix Gutiérrez to the "virtually nonexistent" coverage of Chicanos and other Latinos in the first 70 years of the twentieth century. Studies of both national and local coverage show a pattern similar to that experienced by blacks: " . . . When Mexican labor or immigration impacted national policy or when Latinos were involved in civil strife"—such as the Pauhuco race riots in Los Angeles in the early 1940s or the attempts to seal off the Mexican border to stop immigration—the headlines appeared.[36]

Several newspapers, appreciating the advertising potentiality, began to address their Latino populations in a positive way. The *Miami Herald* introduced a Spanish-language section in 1976, and was followed in this effort in 1981 by the *Chicago Sun-Times* and *Arizona Republic.* The Gannett Corporation bought New York's Spanish-language daily, *El Diario-La Prensa,* in 1981, after completing an extensive study of Latino media habits and attitudes. Several NBC television stations in New York, Chicago, and Los Angeles began simulcasts of evening news broadcasts on local Spanish-language radio stations. There were other positive Anglo responses. The *New York Times* won a Pulitzer Prize for John Crewdon's examination of immigration and the *Los Angeles Herald-Examiner* was widely praised for Merle Wolin's series on the Los Angeles garment district. Reporter Wolin posed as an undocumented worker, in the spirit of Annie Laurie of Hearst's day. A *Los Angeles Times* series by Chicano reporters was notable.

Latinos found it difficult to enter the Anglo reporting and editing ranks, however, just as blacks and other minorities did. The situation was slightly better in broadcasting, because of federal regulations and the pressure of a 1977 federal study, "Window Dressing on the Set," that pointed out gross inequities in the hiring and promoting of minorities.

By 1983 there were nine Spanish-language dailies, led by *El Diario-La Prensa* in New York with 69,000 circulation, *Diario de las Americas* in Miami with 62,000, *La Opinion* of Los Angeles with 51,000, and the *Laredo Times* of Texas with 20,000. More than 600 radio stations aired Spanish programs, about 120 of them as their main format. The New York-based magazine *Nuestro,* an English-language magazine for Latinos, appeared in 1977. Other English or bilingual magazines were New York's *Latin NY* and Washington's *Agenda.* The Spanish International Network (SIN) had an audience of 12 million Latinos in sixty-two American cities. Latinos no longer were invisible. They were becoming increasingly involved with the media to protect their culture and to share more equally in American life.

NATIVE AMERICAN NEWSPAPERS

The Native American press of the 1980s was almost entirely printed in English, although some papers were used to teach tribal languages. There were 325 newspapers listed by the American Indian Press Association in thirty-four states; more than fifty school and college papers; fifteen prison culture-group publications; eight major magazines, four news services, and seven Indian printing firms.[37]

The *Cherokee Phoenix,* the first Native American paper, appeared in Georgia from 1828 to 1832. Other early papers were the *Cherokee Advocate,* the Sioux-language *Shawnee Sun* (*Siwinowe Kesibwi*), and the *Cherokee Rose Bud,* founded in 1848 by Indian women seminary students in present-day Oklahoma.

Front page of *Wassaja* (left); New York's leading Latino daily, a Gannett paper (right).

Wassaja

"Let My People Know"

A National Newspaper of Indian America

Two Indians Die in Ghetto Fire

Urban Poverty Blamed as Search Continues for Bodies

Western Tribes Form Energy Enclave

Ghetto conditions

Wassaja: The Newspaper Most Indians Read

George Shultz suspende su viaje a El Salvador y Brasil

Condena mundial por el atentado terrorista en El Líbano

el diario/la prensa

146 marines, 27 franceses muertos:

MASACRE EN BEIRUT

Página 3

Grupo islámico se atribuye el mortal ataque Pág.3

"Es un acto despreciable" dice Reagan y afirma que las tropas de EU seguirán allí Pág.5

Two 1980s national newspapers were *Akwesasne Notes,* a forty-eight-page tabloid published five times annually as the militant publication of the Mohawk nation, and *Wassaja,* a bimonthly of twenty-four to thirty-two pages sponsored by the American Indian Historical Society and devoted to Indian self-determination and education. Both papers claimed more than 80,000 circulation.

Indian papers suffered from limited funding and editorial inexperience. But they were cause-oriented, promoted the welfare and self-pride of Native Americans, preserved and restored the Indian heritage, and functioned as mirrors of their communities and readerships by presenting their points of view.

NOTES

1. The most descriptive account of the Kennedy-Nixon encounters is found in Theodore H. White, *The Making of the President 1960* (New York: Atheneum, 1961). See also Sig Mickelson, *The Electric Mirror: Politics in an Age of Television* (New York: Dodd, Mead, 1972), for an explanation of Nixon's poor performance and of various camera and lighting techniques agreed to by the two sides.

2. W. A. Swanberg, *Luce and his Empire* (New York: Scribner's, 1972), pp. 412–16. The influence of Joseph Kennedy, Sr., is clearly demonstrated.

3. Merriman Smith, United Press International, November 23, 1963.

4. *Life,* October 2, 1964, p. 41. See also *Life,* November 25, 1966, p. 53, and November 24, 1967, pp. 87–95, and *Saturday Evening Post,* December 2, 1967, p. 27.

5. For a complete analysis of the social movements of the 1960s, see Mayer N. Zald and John D. McCarthy, *The Dynamics of Social Movements* (Cambridge: Winthrop, 1979). The role of NOW is discussed on pp. 176–82.

6. See Leonard Zeidenberg, "Lessons of a Living Room War," *Broadcasting* (May 19, 1975), for an analysis of reporting achievements.

7. This study was conducted by Edwin Diamond, then codirector of the Network News Study Group at the Massachusetts Institute of Technology, and students in 1973.

8. CBS News, July 20, 1969.

9. Other CBS reporters included Bob Schieffer, Bill Henry, Robert Pierpoint, Martin Agronsky, Winston Burdett, Morton Dean, Phil Jones, Michelle Clark, Sylvia Chase, Ed Rabel, Richard Threlkeld, Joe Benti, Susan Peterson, Sharon Lovejoy, Heywood Hale Broun, Renee Poussaint, and Connie Chung.

10. For a long interview with Chancellor, see Philip Noble, "The Cool and Confident Anchorman," *MORE* (May 1976), 7. Also see Barbara Matusow, "Intrigue at NBC," Washington Journalism Review (July–August, 1983), pp. 50–62.

11. NBC News, December 20, 1965. McGee, along with CBS' Morley Safer, was one of the first broadcasters to openly question the United States role. Jerry Jacobs produced the Vietnam segments and wrote much of the script. The program was aired after discussion within NBC News about the conclusion.

12. Other NBC radio and television reporters and commentators were Edwin Newman, the veteran who anchored many NBC specials; Joseph C. Harsch, Irving R. Levine, Elie Abel, Hugh Downs, Ray Scherer, Herbert Kaplow, Tom Pettit, Robert Goralski, Peter Hackes, Clifton Utley, Morgan Beatty, Merrill Mueller, and Garrick Utley. Also prominent were Richard Valeriani, Bob Jamieson, Ford Rowan, John Hart, David Burrington, Floyd Kalber, Don Oliver, Jack Reynolds, John Dancy, Douglas Kiker, Richard Hunt, and Frank Blair.

13. "The New Look of TV News," *Newsweek* (October 11, 1976), 76.

14. *Forbes,* December 7, 1981, p. 133.

15. Other leading correspondents on the team originally built by James C. Hagerty and later Elmer Lower and William Sheehan included Edward P. Morgan, William H. Lawrence, John Scali, Robert Clark, White House reporter Tom Jarriel, Peter Jennings, Peter Clapper, Aline Saarinen and Esther Tufty, both on the air early, Judy Woodruff, Linda Ellerbee, Carole Simpson, and Betty Rollins.

16. *The Making of a Quagmire,* by David Halberstam (New York: Random House, 1965), sets this tone. Halberstam, the Pulitzer Prize-winning correspondent of the *New York Times* in Vietnam, forecast the tragedy.

17. Dale Minor, *The Information War* (New York: Hawthorn Books and Tower Publications, 1970), pp. 29–34. Minor, who finds both heroes and villains in the Saigon press corps, dismisses the war correspondents of earlier wars as "team players" who accepted the official "line" and the necessity of the war itself. His analysis of the conflict between press and govern-

ment in Vietnam, and between moral philosophies and concerns for humanity, is perceptive.

18. *Newsweek,* October 7, 1963, pp. 98–99; Malcolm W. Browne, "Viet Nam Reporting: Three Years of Crisis," *Columbia Journalism Review,* III (Fall 1964), 4.

19. *Time,* September 20, 1963, p. 62, and October 11, 1963, p. 55.

20. *Time,* October 14, 1966, p. 58.

21. As reported in the *Chicago Daily News,* October 26, 1966, p. 1. For a series of front pages depicting the Indochina war, see Michael C. Emery, et al., *America's Front Page News, 1690–1970* (New York: Doubleday, 1970).

22. Minor, *The Information War,* pp. 95–100; *Newsweek,* November 13, 1967, pp. 68–69.

23. As quoted in William Small, *To Kill a Messenger* (New York: Hastings House, 1970), p. 211.

24. Ibid., p. 214.

25. Ibid, p. 216.

26. An early use of the term was in Matthew Arnold's attack against a plan for Irish home rule and the British journalists who supported it, found in his "Up to Easter," *Nineteenth Century* (May 1887), 638–39.

27. See Tom Wolfe, "The Birth of 'The New Journalism'; Eyewitness Report by Tom Wolfe," *New York* (February 14, 1972). For a breakdown of different types of New Journalism writing and a discussion of leading proponents, see also Everette Dennis and William Rivers, *Other Voices: The New Journalism in America* (San Francisco: Canfield, 1974).

28. Robert Glessing, *The Underground Press in America* (Bloomington, Ind.: Indiana University Press, 1970).

29. In addition to numerous articles and books by Stone and Carey McWilliams, see Leonard Downie, *The New Muckrakers* (Washington, D.C.: New Republic, 1977), which examines their work and that of other leading investigative reporters.

30. Nancy L. Roberts, "Dorothy Day and *The Catholic Worker,* 1933–1982" (Ph.D. thesis, University of Minnesota, 1982).

31. *Editor & Publisher,* August 8, 1970, p. 45.

32. As quoted by L. F. Palmer, Jr., "The Black Press in Transition," in Michael Emery and Ted C. Smythe, *Readings in Mass Communication* (Dubuque: William C. Brown, 1972), p. 226.

33. Richard L. Beard and Cyril E. Zoerner II, "Associated Negro Press: Its Founding, Ascendency and Demise," *Journalism Quarterly* XLVI (Spring 1969), 47.

34. See Henry G. LaBrie, III, "A Survey of Black Newspapers in America," *presstime* (October 1980), 54. See also *Perspectives on the Black Press 1974* (Kennebunkport, Maine: Mercer House Press, 1974), and *The Black Press: A Guide* (Iowa City: University of Iowa Press, 1970).

35. Margaret Genovese, "Black Press Seeks Return to Advocacy," *presstime* (September 1981).

36. Félix Gutiérrez, "Latinos and the Media," in Emery and Smythe, *Readings in Mass Communication.* This article is a complete description of the history and current status of Latino media, based on the author's extensive research.

37. James E. and Sharon Murphy, *Let My People Know: American Indian Journalism 1828–1978* (Norman: University of Oklahoma Press, 1981). The first comprehensive synthesis.

ANNOTATED BIBLIOGRAPHY

Books: Background History

Arlen, Michael J., *Living-Room War.* New York: Viking, 1969. Collection of articles from the *New Yorker,* many of television coverage of the Vietnam War.

Associated Press, *Triumph and Tragedy: The Story of the Kennedys.* New York: William Morrow, 1968. Discusses the assassinations of JFK and RFK. See also United Press International, *Assassination: Robert F. Kennedy* (New York: Cowles, 1968).

Braestrup, Peter, *Big Story: How the American Press and Television Reported and Interpreted the Crisis of Tet 1968 in Vietnam and Washington.* Boulder, Colo.: Western Press, 1977. A 1500-page, two-volume analysis by the Saigon bureau chief of the *Washington Post.*

Browne, Malcolm W., *The New Face of War.* Indianapolis: Bobbs-Merrill, 1968. By AP's Pulitzer Prize winner in Vietnam.

Caputo, Philip, *A Rumor of War.* New York: Holt, Rinehart & Winston, 1977. The ugliness of the Vietnam experience is described by a former Marine officer who became a newspaper reporter.

Emerson, Gloria, *Winners and Losers.* New York: Random House, 1977. A former *New York Times* reporter wrote this so Americans would not forget Vietnam.

FALL, BERNARD B., *The Two Viet-Nams: A Political and Military Analysis,* 2nd rev. ed. New York: Praeger, 1967. The most important study of the historical background and changing nature of the Vietnam War.

FITZGERALD, FRANCES, *Fire in the Lake.* Boston: Little, Brown, 1972. The story of the people of Vietnam by an acclaimed magazine journalist. Hailed as one of the best books on the consequences of the war.

GITLIN, TODD, *The Whole World Is Watching.* Berkeley: University of California Press, 1980. This study by a onetime SDS president shows that the demonstrations of the 1960s were played out in the media spotlight, treating the antiwar movement as an oddity or crime, and making celebrities of New Left leaders.

HALBERSTAM, DAVID, *The Making of a Quagmire.* New York: Random House, 1965. By the *New York Times*' Pulitzer Prize winner in Vietnam. See also *The Best and the Brightest* (New York: Random House, 1972). A thoroughly researched analysis of the Ivy Leaguers and Cold-War warriors who created the Vietnam strategies.

KALB, MARVIN, AND ELIE ABEL, *Roots of Involvement.* New York: Norton, 1971. Two distinguished journalists analyze America's role in the Pacific and the beginnings of the Vietnam conflict.

KARNOW, STANLEY, *Vietnam: A History.* New York: Viking, 1983. Companion to PBS television series.

KEARNS, DORIS, *Lyndon Johnson and the American Dream.* New York: Harper & Row, 1976. The best study of LBJ, by a scholar and confidante; portrays his strengths and weaknesses. For his early career, see Robert A. Caro, *The Years of Lyndon Johnson: The Path to Power* (New York: Knopf, 1982), and Ronnie Dugger, *The Politician,* (Volume 1 of *The Life and Times of Lyndon Johnson.* (New York: Norton, 1982). Both are critical.

LUCAS, JIM, *Dateline: Vietnam.* New York: Award Books, 1967. A personal account.

MACLEAR, MICHAEL, *The Ten Thousand Day War: Vietnam 1945–1975.* New York: St. Martin's Press, 1982. Short but comprehensive history. See also George C. Herring, *America's Longest War* (New York: Wiley, 1979).

MANNING, ROBERT, et al., *The Vietnam Experience: America Takes Over.* Boston: Boston Publishing Company, 1983. Fourth in a projected fourteen-volume series, covering 1965.

MINOR, DALE, *The Information War.* New York: Hawthorn, 1970. Perceptive analysis of press-government conflict in Vietnam.

O'CONNOR, RICHARD, *Pacific Destiny: An Informal History of the U.S. in the Far East.* Boston: Little, Brown, 1969. An excellent account.

Report of the National Advisory Commission on Civil Disorders. New York: Bantam Books, 1968. Chapter 15 discusses the mass media.

SALISBURY, HARRISON, *Behind the Lines.* New York: Harper & Row, 1967. The *New York Times* editor's trip to Hanoi opened many eyes to the conduct of the Vietnamese war; almost won him a Pulitzer Prize.

SHEEHAN, NEIL, et al., *The Pentagon Papers.* New York: Quadrangle Books, 1971. The documents showing America's early involvement in Vietnamese affairs, and plans for expansion of this role.

SMALL, WILLIAM, *To Kill A Messenger.* New York: Hastings House, 1970. A prize-winning study of "television news and the real world" by the CBS Washington news manager; excellent coverage of the crises of the 1960s.

SORENSEN, THEODORE C., *Kennedy.* New York: Harper & Row, 1965. One of the best of the studies of President John F. Kennedy and his administration.

UNITED PRESS INTERNATIONAL, *Four Days: The Historical Record of the Death of President Kennedy.* New York: Simon & Schuster, 1964. An *American Heritage* volume, includes journalistic coverage. See also The Associated Press, *The Torch Is Passed* (New York: The Associated Press, 1964).

WHITE, THEODORE H., *The Making of the President—1960.—1964.—1968.—1972.* New York: Atheneum, 1961, 1965, 1969, 1973. The campaigns and their journalistic developments. For a revised version of 1972, see his *Breach of Faith: The Fall of Richard Nixon* (New York: Atheneum, 1975).

Books: Investigative Reporting, New Journalism, Radical and Underground Press

AARON, DANIEL, *Writers on the Left: Episodes in American Literary Communism.* New York: Harcourt Brace Jovanovich, 1961. Left-wing writers from 1912 to 1940s in *The Masses, Liberator, New Masses, Daily Worker, Partisan Review.*

ARMSTRONG, DAVID, *A Trumpet to Arms: Alternative Media in America.* Los Angeles: J. P. Tarcher, 1981. Covers a wide variety of alternative media, including "underground."

BELFRAGE, CEDRIC, AND JAMES ARONSON, *Something to Guard: The Stormy Life of the National Guardian, 1948–1967.* New York: Columbia University Press, 1978. By the editors of the non-Communist, radical paper.

CHRISTMAN, HENRY M., ed., *One Hundred Years of the "Nation."* New York: Macmillan, 1965. An anthology.

CONLIN, JOSEPH R., ed., *The American Radical Press 1880–1960,* 2 volumes. Westport, Conn.: Greenwood Press, 1974. Fifty-eight authors detail left-wing writing.

DENNIS, EVERETTE E., AND WILLIAM L. RIVERS, *Other Voices: The New Journalism in America.* San Francisco: Canfield, 1974. Identifies types of New Journalism and leading personalities.

DOWNIE, LEONARD, *The New Muckrakers.* Washington, D.C.: New Republic, 1977. Profiles of Stone, Woodward, Bernstein, Anderson, Hersh, McWilliams, others.

HARRISON, JOHN M., AND HARRY H. STEIN, eds., *Muckraking—Past, Present and Future.* University Park, Pa.: Pennsylvania State University Press, 1973. A smorgasbord of inquiries into muckraking, investigative reporting, advocacy journalism, the reform tradition, and sensationalism.

KESSLER, LAUREN, *Against the Grain: The Dissident Press in America.* Beverly Hills: Sage, 1984. Examines the journalistic tradition of "other voices" over two centuries, including those of war resisters, radicals, feminists, utopians, immigrants, and blacks.

LEAMER, LAURENCE, *The Paper Revolutionaries: The Rise of the Underground Press.* New York: Simon & Schuster, 1972. History of the 1960s with many reproductions. See also Robert J. Glessing, *The Underground Press in America* (Bloomington: Indiana University Press, 1970).

MCAULIFFE, KEVIN MICHAEL, *The Great American Newspaper: The Rise and Fall of the Village Voice.* New York: Scribner's, 1978. One of first underground papers goes above ground.

MILLER, WILLIAM D., *Dorothy Day: A Biography.* New York: Harper & Row, 1982. The famous radical editor. See also Mel Piehl, *Breaking Bread: The Catholic Worker and the Origin of Catholic Radicalism in America* (Philadelphia: Temple University Press, 1983).

The Nation, special issue on the editorship of Carey McWilliams, December 2, 1978.

OLSON, MCKINLEY C., ed., *J. W. Gitt's Sweet Land of Liberty.* New York: Jerome S. Ozer, 1975. The writings of the editor-publisher of *The Gazette and Daily* of York, Pennsylvania, who crusaded for justice from 1915 to 1970. A small-town I. F. Stone.

ROBERTS, NANCY L., *Dorothy Day and the Catholic Worker.* Albany: State University of New York Press, 1984. Best Study of Day's journalistic influence.

SHORE, ELLIOTT, PATRICIA J. CASE AND LAURA DALY, eds., *Alternative Papers.* Philadelphia: Temple University Press, 1982. Selections from the alternative press, 1979 to 1980.

STEINEM, GLORIA, *Outrageous Acts and Everyday Rebellions.* New York: Holt, Rinehart & Winston, 1983. Autobiography of *Ms.* founder.

STONE, I. F., *Polemics and Prophecies 1967–1970.* New York: Random House, 1970. A collection of some of Stone's significant writings.

———, *In A Time of Torment.* New York: Vintage, 1964. Collections of the writings of the distinguished independent journalist.

WOLFE, TOM, *The New Journalism.* New York: Harper & Row, 1973. Defends the genre, traces the history, and reprints examples.

Books: Magazines

DOUDNA, MARTIN K., *Concerned About the Planet: The Reporter Magazine and American Liberalism, 1949–1968.* Westport, Conn.: Greenwood Press, 1977. Relates the magazine to the environment.

GINGRICH, ARNOLD, *Nothing but People: The Early Days at Esquire.* New York: Crown Publishers, 1971. The founder's account of *Esquire*'s pioneering graphics and literary strengths.

OSMER, HAROLD H., *U.S. Religious Journalism and the Korean War.* Washington, D.C.: University Press of America, 1980. Follows Martin Marty's *The Religious Press in America* (1963).

ROSS, ROBERT W., *So It Was True: The American Protestant Press and the Persecution of the Jews.* Minneapolis: University of Minnesota Press, 1980. A scholarly study.

Books: Minorities' Media

DANIEL, WALTER C., ed., *Black Journals of the United States.* Westport, Conn.: Greenwood Press, 1982. Contains narrative histories, bibliographical references.

FINKLE, LEE, *Forum for Protest: The Black Press During World War II.* Cranbury, N.J.: Fairleigh Dickinson University Press, 1975. Study of editorial policies and campaigns of the major black newspapers in the war years.

LA BRIE, HENRY G., III, *A Survey of Black Newspapers in America.* Kennebunkport, Maine: Mercer House Press, 1979. A seventy-two page listing, updating La Brie, *The Black Press in America: A Guide* (1970). Shows declines in both numbers of papers and circulations.

———, ed., *Perspectives of the Black Press: 1974.* Kennebunkport, Maine: Mercer House Press, 1974. Current summary of La Brie's research and a collection of significant thoughts of black editors.

MURPHY, JAMES E., AND SHARON M. MURPHY, *Let My People Know: American Indian Journalism 1828–1978.* Norman: University of Oklahoma Press, 1981. First comprehensive synthesis.

MURPHY, SHARON, *Other Voices: Black, Chicano, and American Indian Press.* Dayton, Ohio: Pflaum/Standard, 1974. A monograph using survey findings.

Periodicals and Monographs

ARONSON, JAMES, "A Radical Journalist in the 1950's," *Nieman Reports,* XXIX (Spring and Summer 1975), 34, 16. Two-part recollection of his 19 years with the radical *National Guardian.*

BAILEY, GEORGE A., AND LAWRENCE W. LICHTY, "Rough Justice on a Saigon Street: A Gatekeeper Study of NBC's Tet Execution Film," *Journalism Quarterly,* XLIX (Summer 1972), p. 221. Step-by-step on decision to use execution episode.

BECKER, ROBERT, et al., "The Charge of the Right Brigade," *Washington Journalism Review* (November 1981), 21. Graduate students survey New Right press.

BRAESTRUP, PETER, "Covering the Vietnam War," *Nieman Reports,* XXIII (December 1969), 8. By a Vietnam correspondent for the *New York Times* and the *Washington Post.*

BROWNE, MALCOLM W., "Viet Nam Reporting: Three Years of Crisis," *Columbia Journalism Review,* III (Fall 1964), 4. By the AP senior correspondent in Saigon.

BURD, GENE, "Urban Magazine Journalism Thrives During City Crises," *Journalism Quarterly,* L (Spring 1973), 77. Muckraking spirit reborn in 1960s urban magazines. See also Ben L. Moon, "City Magazines, Past and Present," *Journalism Quarterly,* XLVII (Winter 1970).

CLICK, J. W., "Comparison of Editorial Content of Ebony Magazine, 1967 and 1974," *Journalism Quarterly,* LII (Winter 1975), 716. Significant editorial content is down.

COLUMBIA JOURNALISM REVIEW, "Campaign Coverage: An Appraisal of 1960—and Implications for 1964," *Columbia Journalism Review* (Fall 1961), 6. A fourteen-page report on twenty-five metropolitan areas.

CORNWELL, ELMER E., JR., "The Johnson Press Relations Style," *Journalism Quarterly,* XLIII (Spring 1966), 3. The press got much attention from LBJ.

DANIELSON, WAYNE A., AND JOHN B. ADAMS, "Completeness of Press Coverage of the 1960 Campaign," *Journalism Quarterly,* XXXVIII (Autumn 1961), 441. A report on a sample of ninety dailies; based on completeness of coverage of twenty-three campaign events.

FERRETTI, FRED, "The White Captivity of Black Radio," *Columbia Journalism Review,* IX (Summer 1970), 35. Of 310 radio stations serving blacks at least in part, only sixteen were owned by blacks—and no TV licenses.

FLANERY, JAMES A., "Chicago Newspapers' Coverage of the City's Major Civil Disorders of 1968," Ph.D. thesis, Northwestern University, 1971. Violence by police minimized in stories.

GARLAND, PHYL, "The Black Press: Down but Not Out," *Columbia Journalism Review* (September/October 1982), 43. A black journalist/ professor is optimistic.

GRABER, DORIS A., "Press Coverage and Voter Reaction in the 1968 Presidential Election," *Political Science Quarterly,* LXXXIX (March 1974), 68. A major study of sixteen dailies found candidates' personalities covered more than issues, and that voters ignored data.

GUTIÉRREZ, FÉLIX F., "Spanish-Language Radio and Chicano Internal Colonialism," Ph.D. thesis, Stanford University, 1976. Non-Chicanos largely in charge.

———, ed., "Spanish-Language Media Issue," *Journalism History,* IV (Summer 1977).

HAUSMAN, LINDA WEINER, "Criticism of the Press in U.S. Periodicals, 1900–1939: An Annotated Bibliography," *Journalism Monographs,* No. 4, August 1967. What the magazines said about newspapers.

HIRSCH, PAUL M., "An Analysis of *Ebony:* The Magazine and Its Readers," *Journalism Quarterly,* XLV (Summer 1968), 261. Covers 1945 to 1966.

HUTCHISON, EARL R., "Kennedy and the Press: The First Six Months," *Journalism Quarterly,* XXXVIII (Autumn 1961), 453.

———, "John H. Johnson of Ebony," *Nation's Business,* LXII (April 1974), 45.

KOPKIND, ANDREW, "The Importance of Being Izzy," *Ramparts,* XII (May 1974), 39. I. F. Stone's *Weekly* (from 1953 to 1971) celebrated.

LA BRIE, HENRY G., III, "A Profile of the Black Newspaper Old Guard," Ph.D. thesis, University of Iowa, 1972. Based on ninety-three interviews.

LA BRIE, HENRY G., III, AND WILLIAM J. ZIMA, "Directional Quandaries of the Black Press in the United States," *Journalism Quarterly,* XLVIII (Winter 1971), 640. Black editors reexamine the function of their press in depth survey.

MCNULTY, THOMAS M., "Network Television Documentary Treatment of the Vietnam War, 1965 to 1969," Ph.D. thesis, Indiana University, 1974. Reaction to spot news, not preconceived notions, determined content.

MCWILLIAMS, CAREY, "One Hundred Years of *The Nation,*" *Journalism Quarterly,* XLII (Spring 1965), 189. By the then-current editor.

MORRIS, JOHN G., "This We Remember," *Harper's,* 245 (September 1972), 72. The pictures that make Vietnam unforgettable, and portraits of photographers.

MURPHY, JAMES E., "The New Journalism: A Critical Perspective," *Journalism Monographs,* No. 34 (May 1974). A careful attempt to define this approach to journalistic writing.

PALMER, L. F., JR., "The Black Press in Transition," *Columbia Journalism Review,* IX (Spring 1970), 31. A survey from 1945 to 1970.

PAYNE, DARWIN, "The Press Corps and the Kennedy Assassination," *Journalism Monographs,* No. 15 (February 1970). Newspaper and broadcast performance at Dallas.

"The Press and Chicago," a group of articles on the 1968 Democratic convention, by Jules Witcover; the metropolitan Chicago press and the *Chicago Journalism Review,* by Edwin Diamond; and the Chicago suburbs by Gene Gilmore and David Beal, in *Columbia Journalism Review,* VII (Fall 1968), 5.

REICHLEY, A. JAMES, "How John Johnson Made It," *Fortune,* LXXVIII (January 1968), 152. Profile of the black publisher.

REILLY, TOM, ed., "American Indians and the Media," *Journalism History,* VI (Summer 1979). A special issue. See also "The Roots of Black Journalism," *Journalism History,* IV (Winter 1977–78), another special issue.

RILEY, SAM G., "*Indian Journal,* Voice of Creek Tribe, Now Oklahoma's Oldest Newspaper," *Journalism Quarterly,* LIX (Spring 1982), 46.

ROBERTS, NANCY L., "Dorothy Day and *The Catholic Worker,* 1933–1982," Ph.D. thesis, University of Minnesota, 1982. A well-written, scholarly study. For a summary, see Roberts, "Building a New Earth: Dorothy Day and the *Catholic Worker,*" *Christian Century,* December 10, 1980.

SCHWARTZ, TONY, "Tom Wolfe: The Great Gadfly," *New York Times Magazine* (December 20, 1981), 46. Still controversial at age 50.

"The Spanish-Language Media," a special report in the *Washington Journalism Review* (November 1980), 21. Three articles on television and newspapers.

SPAULDING, NORMAN W., "History of Black-Oriented Radio in Chicago 1929–1963," Ph.D. thesis, University of Illinois, 1981. Black radio is a cultural common denominator.

STEMPEL, GUIDO H., III, "The Prestige Press in Two Presidential Elections," *Journalism Quarterly,* XLII (Winter 1965), 15. Study of fifteen leading papers' news coverage in 1960 and 1964.

———, "The Prestige Press Meets the Third-Party Challenge," *Journalism Quarterly,* XLVI (Winter 1969), 685. Coverage of 1968 campaign by fifteen major dailies.

"Tracing the Roots of the New Journalism," a symposium by Warren T. Francke, Jay Jensen, Joseph M. Webb, and Frederick D. Buchstein, in *Journalism History* I (Summer 1974).

VAN DYNE, LARRY, "Carey McWilliams: Western-Style Radical," *Chronicle of Higher Education* (November 13, 1978), R3. Interview traces career of *Nation*'s editor.

"Vietnam: What Lessons?" A symposium by Jules Witcover, Fred W. Friendly, Robert Shaplen, James McCartney, Edwin Diamond, Don Stillman, and Nathan Blumberg, in *Columbia Journalism Review,* IX (Winter 1970–71). Media plusses and minuses.

WILSON, NOEL AVON, "The *Kansas City Call:* An Inside View of the Negro Market," Ph.D. thesis, University of Illinois, 1968. History and influence of the *Call.*

Viet Nam evacuation... the complete story

From Da Nang: Exclusive photos

The first pictures from Da Nang to be released by a Western journalist since the Viet Cong took over the city are on page 8. They are by Abbas, a Iranian photojournalist who was accredited after several hundred photographers were refused entry.

Indochina chronology

The 35-year history of the bloody Indochinese conflict, starting with the Japanese occupancy in 1940, is detailed on page 6. Maps showing the Communist expansion and photographs from the battle areas accompany the year-by-year report.

The longest war for U. S.

It cost this country nearly 57,000 lives, 303,659 wounded, and $140 billion. And when it was all over, the other side had won. The war was the longest in the history of the United States. An account of its cost and photographs are on page 7.

Chicago Tribune

THE WORLD'S GREATEST NEWSPAPER

Sports ★★★★ Final

Wednesday, April 30, 1975

128th Year—No. 120 © 1975 Chicago Tribune

7 Sections 15¢

Saigon surrenders

UPI Telephoto

Americans being evacuated from U. S. Embassy compound in Saigon climb ladder to waiting helicopter.

S. Viet leader gives up 'to avoid bloodshed'

From Tribune Wire Services

SAIGON—The Saigon government surrendered unconditionally to the Viet Cong Wednesday, ending 30 years of warfare.

Columns of South Vietnamese troops pulled out of their defensive positions in the city and marched to central points to turn in their weapons.

President Duong Van [Big] Minh spoke to the nation only hours after an armada of United States Marine helicopters had completed an emergency evacuation of nearly 900 Americans and thousands of Vietnamese from the besieged capital.

WITHIN TWO hours of Minh's broadcast, North Vietnamese and Viet Cong troops began moving into downtown Saigon in tanks and jeeps.

A jeep flying the Viet Cong flag drove along the street a block from the abandoned U. S. Embassy. The eight cheering men in the vehicle were in civilian clothes but carried weapons, including Communist AK47 rifles.

Some Western newsmen and young missionaries decide to stay in South Viet Nam and take their chances. Tribune reporters Ronald Yates and Philip Caputo are yet to be heard from. Page 10.

One of the men was sitting on the fender holding the flag. He beckoned to an American newsman and said in English, "Go home, go home."

THE TANKS and jeeps were greeted by cheering crowds as they pulled into the grounds of Saigon's presidential palace.

People reportedly thronged the streets cheering the green-uniformed troops. The grinning Viet Cong soldiers waved gaily back.

Earlier, the tanks had fired salvos and flares into the air in apparent jubilation.

THE VIET CONG'S mission to Paris, meanwhile, waited for the fulfillment of one remaining demand before accepting the surrender. That is the withdrawal of American ships waiting off the South Vietnamese coast for flights of refugees.

Minh, a retired general and neutralist, was named president Monday in a desperate and unsuccessful attempt to negotiate a peace with the Communist leaders.

In a five-minute radio address, Minh said, "The Republic of Viet Nam policy is the policy of peace and reconciliation, aimed at saving the blood of our people. I ask all servicemen to stop firing and stay where you are. I also demand that soldiers of the Provisional Revolutionary Government [Viet Cong] stop firing and stay in place.

"WE ARE HERE WAITING for the Provisional Revolution-

Continued on page 9, col. 4

Pained Kissinger turns cautious on nation's future commitments

By Bill Neikirk

Chicago Tribune Press Service

WASHINGTON—With the pain of the Viet Nam disaster showing in his face, Secretary of State Henry Kissinger said Tuesday America must now be more careful about its future commitments and more determined to honor them.

"Obviously this has been a very painful experience," said the man who had seen the triumph of his Paris peace agreement crumble away to a tragic defeat for South Viet Nam.

A somber Kissinger said time is needed to heal the wounds of America's role in Viet Nam and "to concentrate on the problems of the future."

Americans should avoid recriminations about the past and look ahead to new goals, President Ford says in statement on Viet Nam. Page 5.

HE SPOKE with more than usual bluntness at a news conference called after the White House announced the last American had been evacuated from Saigon.

If there is any lesson to be learned, he said, it is that the United States "should be careful about the commitments we make and determined to follow those we do make."

Kissinger said that Viet Nam will mean a more mature America when it comes to foreign connections. Now, he said, the nation knows that if foreign policy is going to be effective, it will "have to be sustained over decades."

There was no bitterness in Kissinger's voice as he detailed the last hours of the nation's role in Viet Nam. He refused, however, to give a long analysis of what the war means for the nation and why it was lost.

"I THINK IT will be a long time before anyone will be able to write about it with dispassion," he said. Later, he said this was not the time "to make an assessment of a dec-

Continued on page 2, col. 3

Marines in like heroes, out like foes

EDITORS NOTE—The writer of this dispatch, winner of a Pulitzer Prize for dispatches from Viet Nam, was there when American soldiers first came in force to Indochina. He was there Tuesday when the Americans left, one of several American reporters who elected to remain in Saigon after the evacuation.

By Peter Arnett

SAIGON [AP] — Ten years ago I watched the first United States Marines arrive to help South Viet Nam. They were greeted on the beaches by pretty Vietnamese girls in white silken robes who draped flower leis around their necks.

A decade has passed.

And on Tuesday I watched U. S. Marines, shepherding the last Americans out of South Viet Nam. They were the same, cleancut-looking young men of a decade ago.

But the Vietnamese were different.

Those who didn't have a place on the last helicopters out of Saigon—and there were thousands of them left behind—hooted, booed, and scuffled with the Marines guarding the landing zones.

SOME VIETNAMESE threw themselves over walls and wire fences, only to be thrown back by the Marines.

Bloodshed was avoided seemingly only by good luck and bad aim on the part of some angry Vietnamese soldiers who shot at a few buses and departing helicopters.

But the entire, frantic dash from Saigon by the Americans—and the bitter resentment of the thousands of Vietnamese who couldn't go—seemed a sad but accurate reflection of what relations between Americans and Vietnamese had come to in the 10 years since these flowers were gladly given to the Marines.

Americans and the South Vietnamese used to get along pretty well. That was in the days when the U. S. Marines first arrived in Viet Nam imbued with a determination to see the war thru.

THE SOUTH Vietnamese army, dispirited then, watched with wonder as first the Marines and then the paratroopers and the American infantry came to steaming hot Viet Nam to trudge the coastal plains and mountain valleys in a punishing, unfamiliar environment.

Vietnamese officers began aping the American way. The Americans seemed always to have better pressed uniforms and more detailed maps and diagrams.

Nearly 20,000 Vietnamese officers flew to the United States for education or advanced training, and they returned

Continued on page 19, col. 4

Weather

CHICAGO AND VICINITY: Partly cloudy, Wednesday; high, around 70; southwest to west winds 10 to 20 m. p. h.; low, in upper 40s. Thursday: Mostly cloudy, high, in low to mid 60s. Tuesday's high temperature of 76 degrees at Midway Airport gave Chicago its warmest reading of the year. For map and other reports, see page 13. Sec. 4.

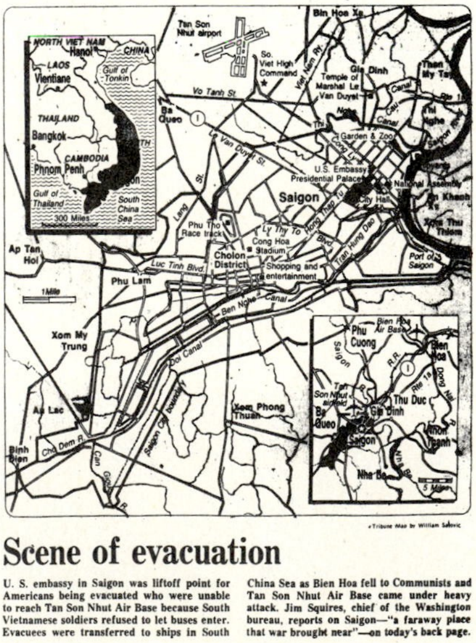

Tribune Map by William Sabovic

Scene of evacuation

U. S. embassy in Saigon was liftoff point for Americans being evacuated who were unable to reach Tan Son Nhut Air Base because South Vietnamese soldiers refused to let buses enter. Evacuees were transferred to ships in South China Sea as Bien Hoa fell to Communists and Tan Son Nhut Air Base came under heavy attack. Jim Squires, chief of the Washington bureau, reports on Saigon—"a faraway place that war brought near"—on today's back page.

America's Vietnam nightmare ends with dramatic suddenness.

© 1975, Chicago Tribune

25
A Crisis of Credibility

The press was to serve the governed, not the governors.
—Justice Hugo L. Black

The credibility gap as an institution became painfully apparent in American life by 1970. There were gaps between president and people, president and press, press and people. To these were added gaps between old and young, black and white, intellectuals and silent majority.

One reason for the difficulties of the presidents was the growth of a cult of disbelief. At his height. Senator Joseph McCarthy had half of the American people believing in him, which meant they believed their government was a combination of Communism and corruption—even the Army harbored treason, McCarthy said. The Senator was unable to bring down war hero Eisenhower, who was less affected than were his successors by the credibility gap. John F. Kennedy inherited a Cuban crisis; news was managed, and many disbelieved their government's explanations. The Warren Commission hearings failed to keep Americans from doubting accounts of President Kennedy's assassination; that doubt increased over the years. Senator Barry Goldwater could offer rueful testimony about the depth of disbelief he encountered in his disastrous 1964 presidential campaign. Senator Eugene McCarthy found in the winter of 1967 to 1968 that President Johnson's public support was a hollow shell; his "children's crusade" and the reality of the Tet attacks in Vietnam shattered belief in the war effort there. The credibility gap that had been attributed to the Lyndon Johnson personality persisted for Richard Nixon as his problems multiplied, partially for the same reason but also because it was a part of the American way of life.

Another reason for the difficulties of both presidents and press was the steady diet of bad news that characterized the 1950s and 1960s, despite many years of prosperity and notable accomplishments. Americans did not want to hear that they had to settle for a stalemate in Korea—"Communism, Corruption, and Korea" was a 1952 election slogan to explain the bad news, not the hard facts of a capable Chinese army opponent. A recession in the late 1950s; antagonistic receptions abroad of Vice President Nixon and even President Eisenhower; and a challenge to American prestige by Charles de Gaulle were all unwanted subjects. They piled up in the 1960s and early 1970s: the Bay of Pigs, the Berlin Wall, the assassination of a president, the Vietnam War, racial riots in big cities, college-campus riots, the assassinations of Senator Kennedy and Martin Luther King, the collapse of the promise of victory in Vietnam, long hair, sex and four-letter words in the open, drug addiction, Kent State, My Lai, a near-depression, and Watergate. Traditionally a president pays politically for adverse news, particularly of an economic nature. But as William Small of CBS put it in a book title, the public seemed willing like the kings of old "to kill a messenger"—in this case, CBS and other networks, the *Washington Post* and other liberal newspapers, even the objectivity-seeking press associations that brought them the bad news.

The situation was ripe for demagogues. There was much bad news people did not want to believe, much reality they did not want to have exist. One group did not believe the president; another did not believe the press. And both president and press encouraged people not to believe the other. It was easy to argue, then, that reporting bad news was unpatriotic; to say that those who made bad news—as at Kent State or in the streets of Chicago—were un-American and deserving of their fates. The only solace defenders of freedom had was that such credibility gaps had existed before in history and that with determination this one also could be overcome. However, it still existed in the mid-1980s.

In seeking to understand the development of this era of the credibility gap, one continues with the record of the relationships between the presidents and the press, examines the overt attacks on the press, estimates the extent of the gap between the press and the people, and also records the frictions between government and press that resulted in legislation and court decisions involving freedom of the press (see Chapter 27).

NIXON AND AGNEW

Richard Nixon had spent years studying his mistakes in the 1960 presidential race, with its "great debates" on television, and in his 1962 failure in California, which ended with an ill-tempered attack on the press. In 1968 he used television skillfully, appearing before controlled audiences with filtered questions rather than giving set speeches. But he held standard press conferences only rarely, at one-third the rate of recent presidents. Instead he relied on a technique Johnson had developed when he had dramatic news from the war to announce: request prime-time network television for a brief appearance. He did this thirty-seven

Chicago Tribune

THE WORLD'S GREATEST NEWSPAPER

SPORTS ★★★★ FINAL

Friday, July 16, 1971

Nixon to Visit China

President Nixon

He Will . . .

Chou En-lai

. . . Visit Him

Kissinger, Chou Hold Secret Talks

BY ALDO BECKMAN

[Chicago Tribune Press Service]

SAN CLEMENTE, Cal., July 15—President Nixon will visit mainland China sometime before next May, he told the nation tonight in a live television and radio broadcast.

The groundwork for the historic meeting was laid by Henry Kissinger, Nixon's assistant for national security, when he met secretly with Chinese Premier Chou En-lai from July 9 to July 11, Nixon said. At that time, it was announced that Kissinger was in Asia to visit Saigon, Pakistan, and India.

Chou extended the invitation for the Nixon visit during his talks with Kissinger, Nixon said. A statement that Nixon read and which was released simultaneously in Peking, said:

"President Nixon has accepted this invitation with pleasure.

"The meeting between the leaders of China and the United States is to seek the normalization of relations between the two countries and also to exchange views on questions of concern to the two sides."

Acts to Mute Criticism

Nixon emphasized, in an obvious effort to mute criticism from supporters of Nationalist China and Chiang Kai-shek, that "our action in seeking a new relationship with the People's Republic of China will not be at the expense of our old friends.

"It is not directed against any other nation. We seek friendly relations with all nations. Any nation can be our friend without being any other nation's friend."

White House officials explained that Nixon was trying to indicate that America's old friendships and alliances will not be discarded because of the new friendlier relations with China.

The President, without giving any hint about when before May he will make the trip, said that he will undertake it "deeply [hoping] that it will become a journey for peace, not just for our generation but for future generations on this earth we share together."

As Nixon began his three-minute statement, he noted that he had pointed out on a number of occasions that "no stable and enduring peace [is possible] without the participation of the People's Republic of China and its 750 million people."

Kissinger Secret Well Kept

Then, he revealed Kissinger's visit, which was one of the best kept secrets in the history of international diplomacy.

Midway during Kissinger's journey, it was announced that he had departed from his prepared itinerary because of an upset stomach. That, apparently, was when he flew to Peking for his meeting with Chou En-lai.

Text of Speech on Page 2

Nixon said he decided to accept the visit to China "because of my profound conviction that all nations will gain from a reduction of tensions and a better relationship between the United States and the People's Republic of China."

Calls Security Council

Several hours before his statement, the Western White House announced that Nixon had called a meeting of the National Security Council for tomorrow. At that time, there was no agenda given for the session.

Kissinger returned from his nine-day trip, which included a stop in Paris to meet with American peace negotiators, on Tuesday, and has spent most of the time since then meeting with Nixon and Secretary of State William Rogers at the Western White House.

While it was assumed that their talks revolved around the Viet Nam War, White House officials said repeatedly that the discussions covered a wide range of foreign policy matters.

Ford Sees Indochina Peace Talks Resulting from Visit

[From Tribune Wire Services]

WASHINGTON, July 15—Republican House Leader Gerald R. Ford said tonight President Nixon's impending visit to mainland China could lead toward the convening of an Indochina peace conference.

"I would expect . . . that one subject that the President and Premier Chou En-lai would discuss would be the convening of an Indochina peace conference," the Michigan congressman and close supporter of Nixon said.

Sen. Hubert Humphrey . . . could be of "immense importance in bringing about a speedy end to war."

Mansfield Delighted

Democratic congressional leaders also reacted positively to Nixon's announcement on a brief televised address that he had been invited to visit China. Senate Democratic leader Mike Mansfield said he was "flabbergasted" and "delighted."

Sen. Hubert H. Humphrey [D., Minn.] said he thought such a journey could be of "immense importance in bringing about a speedy end to the war."

But Ford's remark was considered particularly significant because of his close working relationship with Nixon.

Australian political leader Gough Whitlam said yesterday in Hong Kong after returning from Peking that Premier Chou had told him China was willing to attend a revived Geneva conference on Indochina.

Thant Welcomes Action

United Nations Secretary General U Thant said arrangements for President Nixon to visit China "has opened a new chapter in the history of international relations."

"The Secretary General warmly welcomes Nixon's announcement of his acceptance of Premier Chou En-lai's invitation to visit the People's Republic of China in the course of the next few months," Thant's spokesmen said.

"This development has opened a new chapter in the history of international relations and it augurs well not only for relations between two great countries, but also for the future of the United Nations."

McGovern Applauds Nixon

Sen. George McGovern [D., S. D.] commented: "I applaud the President's imagination and judgment in accepting this opportunity to open up more normal relations with the people of China."

He said he hopes Nixon's announcement that Premier Chou had invited him to visit Peking and the President had accepted would "mark the end of a long period of nonsense in our relations with China and the beginning of a new era of common sense."

Sen. Harold Hughes [D., Ia.] who only 12 hours earlier had ruled himself out of the 1972 Democratic Presidential sweepstakes, said he, too, was delighted. He said he saw in the move a chance to wind down the Viet Nam war at a faster pace.

Senate Republican leader Hugh Scott of Pennsylvania said Nixon's decision "is bound to have worldwide impact and is an extremely important step in producing world peace."

"I join with all Americans in wishing the President Godspeed and good fortune in his journey for peace."

Already a Swinger

Kissinger Sure to Be a Legend

[Chicago Tribune Press Service]

SAN CLEMENTE, Cal., July 15 — Henry Kissinger's secret trip behind the Bamboo Curtain to Peking is certain to make a living legend of the man already romanticized as the swinger of the Nixon administration.

Kissinger, the former Harvard professor who was foreign policy adviser to Gov. Nelson Rockefeller when Rockefeller was running for President, is a divorced father of two who delights in being seen with beautiful women, such as movie star Jill St. John. During his recent stop in Paris, Kissinger was seen leaving a night spot with a pretty girl who turned out to be a CBS television producer.

A German Jew who was driven out of Germany with his parents in the late 1930s, Kissinger still has a heavy German accent, a sharp wit, and is a favorite among White House reporters.

His own accent and his well-publicized foreign policy briefings, complete with ground rules which forbid quoting him or even using his name, are favorite targets of his wit.

The President obviously has great trust in Kissinger's intellect, and White House observers smiled knowingly when Sen. Stuart Symington [D., Mo.] recently said publicly what most people have been saying privately for months—that Kissinger has more influence with Nixon than does Secretary of State William Rogers.

Kissinger's role as a chief architect of the Nixon administration's plan to withdraw from Viet Nam has cost him numer-

[Continued on page 2, col. 5]

Formosa Protests, Others Approve Visit

[From Tribune Wire Services]

Nationalist China announced today in Taipei that it has lodged a strong protest with Washington over President Nixon's projected visit to mainland China.

Formosa was electrified by the joint statement by Nixon and officials in Peking and observers saw the visit as one of the biggest blows to Generalissimo Chiang Kai-shek since the Communists took over the mainland in 1949.

One Sentence Comment

Government spokesman James Wei had only a one-sentence comment to newsmen who surrounded him here.

"The Chinese government has lodged a strong protest with the U. S. government," he announced.

He made the statement after being summoned by Nationalist Premier C. K. Yen this morning.

The foreign ministry was holding an emergency meeting, apparently studying the implications of Nixon's projected visit.

Another, more detailed statement was expected later today.

Formosa has lodged several protests with Washington in recent months, mainly over the Nixon administration's easing of trade and travel restrictions involving China.

There was a tense atmosphere in government circles and some officials appeared visibly perturbed by the announcement.

In Manila earlier, Formosan Foreign Minister Chow Shu-kai commented when asked about the announcement of the visit, "If it is true then it will be part of their [China's] psychological warfare."

The surprise announcement also jolted other officials of America's Asian allies attending the Asia and Pacific Council [ASPA] ministerial meeting in Manila.

Vincente Singian, secretary general of the organization said he would announce the visit to

[Continued on page 2, col. 1]

Why? He Likes the Food

LOS ANGELES, July 15 [Reuters]—President Nixon said tonight after the announcement of his planned visit to the People's Republic of China that his reasons for going were purely gastronomic.

In his only reference to the trip when he spoke to reporters after his television broadcast, he quipped, "I like the food."

What China Visit Means

BY FRANK STARR

[Washington Bureau Chief]

[Chicago Tribune Press Service]

News Analysis

WASHINGTON, July 15 — President Nixon's bombshell announcement that he would visit Peking within the next 10 months carried with it an implicit recognition of China as the third corner in a new triangle of superpowers.

Despite his assurance that "it is not directed against any other nation," this dramatic development was certain to cause a deep reassessment of foreign policy within a Kremlin already actively seeking to mend its Western fences for reasons among which concern over China must be one.

The announcement also represented a personal victory of colossal proportions for the foreign policy of a President who deliberately set out to reverse what has been a firm policy not only of his nation but of his party for more than 21 years.

Blow to Nationalists

Also implicit in the announcement is the severe blow to the Nationalist Chinese government of Generalissimo Chiang Kai-shek, which, since the Communist takeover of the mainland in 1949, had been the beneficiary of such a policy.

Less clear but certainly at issue is the strengthening of the U. S. hand in newly developing war talks with the Communist Vietnamese, whose unqualified support from Red China until recently has included Peking's uncompromising rejection in public pronouncements of everything American.

Among the areas of speculation that were raised by the development was the possibility that China could play a new role in the efforts to reach an Indochina settlement thru multilateral negotiation.

Interest in Conference

Yesterday it was reported by an Australian diplomat in Hong Kong that China had expressed an interest in participating in a new Geneva conference on Indochina, an idea Nixon embraced months ago.

That report, as surprising as it was, nonetheless fit into a pattern of emerging participation in world diplomacy by the Communist Chinese that goes back about two years when Chinese diplomats, recalled from their foreign posts during the turmoil of the Cultural Revolution, gradually began reappearing at international functions in the world's major capitals.

The pattern really began to develop, however, with the positive response of Nixon, who unilaterally took several steps, beginning in July, 1969, to ease the isolation the United States had imposed on the mainland.

One of the most important elements of these efforts to the Chinese, if not apparent to the American people, was the public use for the first time by an American President of Red

[Continued on page 2, col. 3]

How Kissinger's Peking Parley Was Kept Secret

A visit to Red China by Henry A. Kissinger earlier this month to lay the groundwork for President Nixon's impending visit to that country was shrouded in such secrecy the world press never suspected what was going on.

Kissinger, the President's special adviser on foreign affairs, left July 3 for Saigon on what ostensibly was to be a fact-finding trip to form the basis of a major review of the Viet Nam conflict by Nixon.

Spent Time in Viet Nam

Kissinger, indeed, arrived in Viet Nam and talked for several days with officials there, but until last night, nobody except a small group of high-echelon government officials knew Kissinger was also visiting Red China during his trip.

Last night, during his dramatic televised announcement to the nation of his upcoming trip to Communist China, Nixon said Kissinger had made the arrangements in Peking. The President said Kissinger spent three days, from July 9 thru 11, in the Chinese capital talking with Premier Chou En-lai.

Kissinger's mission to mainland China was masterfully hidden from the press.

On the days he was talking to Chinese officials, the government was releasing stories to the press placing him thousands of miles away, in Pakistan, India, and Paris.

Reported 'Indisposed'

On July 9, apparently the day the Presidential advisor made his trip into China, stories datelined from Islamabad, Pakistan, placed him as arriving that day in that country from India.

A story from Pakistan by United Press International said Kissinger had arrived to take "a working holiday" today in

[Continued on page 2, col. 1]

Features

Weather

FRIDAY, JULY 16, 1971

CHICAGO AND VICINITY: Mostly sunny and pleasant today; high, in lower 80s; partly cloudy tonight with chance of thundershowers; low, in lower 60s; west to northwest winds 8 to 15 m. p. h. Tomorrow: Fair with little temperature change; high, in lower 80s. Map and other reports on page 12.

President Nixon announced his 1972 trip to Peking on prime-time television.

© 1971, Chicago Tribune

Cartoonist Paul Conrad expresses American disillusionment with the Vietnam War.

Paul Conrad, © 1971 Los Angeles Times, with permission of the Register and Tribune Syndicate.

times while in office, at a higher frequency than any other president. Nixon averaged eleven regular press conferences a year his first 2 years in the White House but then trailed off and ended with a total of thirty-eight. A committee of the Associated Press Managing Editors, made up of executives of three conservative papers that had supported Nixon (the *Christian Science Monitor, Washington Star,* and *Philadelphia Bulletin*), criticized him for using press conferences to "raise questions about the credibility of the press."

Agnew aroused a stormy debate late in 1969 when, in speeches in Des Moines and later, he declared that the networks and newspapers with multiple media holdings (his favorite targets were the *Washington Post, Newsweek,* and Mrs. Graham's TV stations) exercised such powerful influence over public opinion that they should vigorously endeavor to be impartial and fair in reporting and commenting on national affairs. Specifically, Agnew criticized network managements for using commentators with a preponderant "Eastern Establishment bias" and for failing to provide a "wall of separation" between news and comment.

Also dominated by the "Establishment," he said, were such antiwar papers as the *Washington Post* and *New York Times* (others equally well staffed from similar social backgrounds, but conservative in tone, went unmentioned). Agnew made specific references to the dependence of broadcasting stations on licenses, and no amount of disclaimer by him or the administration that he was threatening a censorship could calm those who assumed they would be the victims. It was indisputably true that never before had such a high federal official made such direct attacks on those reporting and commenting on the news. Their defenders contended that the mere making of the statements by Agnew inhibited the freedom of the broadcasters suffering tongue lashes. A research study comparing random samples of newscast items reporting administration activities for 1-week periods in 1969 and 1970 bore out the contention that the Agnew-generated criticism had significantly affected the newscasts in the direction of "safe" handling.[1]

The Vice President went into eclipse after the Republican setbacks in the 1970 congressional elections, but CBS gave him another opening when it screened "The Selling of the Pentagon" early in 1971. A congressional committee attempted to subpoena all records and unused film CBS had filed in making the Pentagon film; Representative Harley O. Staggers, West Virginia Democrat, obtained the support of the Commerce Committee in requesting the House of Representatives to try CBS and CBS President Frank Stanton on charges of contempt of Congress. This the House refused to do, voting 226 to 181 in July, 1971, to return the request to the committee. The refusal, while encouraging to free-press advocates, was more politically shocking (such turndowns by the House have been rare) than legally reassuring.

Nixon's major accomplishment during this period was helping to part the bamboo curtain. In 1971 an American ping-pong team was invited to play in Peking. China-watcher correspondents routinely asked to accompany them and were astounded to be admitted in some cases. John Roderick of the AP visited China again after an absence of 23 years. So did veterans John Rich of NBC and Tillman Durdin of the *New York Times.* A large contingent traveled with Nixon on his trip in 1972 and the networks broadcast many of the proceedings live, using satellite transmissions. America's age-old love affair with China was resumed but suspicions remained on both sides because of the Taiwan problem, which occasionally flared into the headlines.

PRIOR RESTRAINT: THE PENTAGON PAPERS CASE

In June, 1971, the United States government attempted to impose prior restraint on American newspapers. And for 15 days it successfully stopped one of the country's most influential dailies from publishing a vital news story. For those 15 days the clock was turned back to the time of Henry VIII, who in 1534 imposed prior restraint on the English press. Prior restraint ended in England in 1694 and in the colonies in 1721, to be temporarily revived exactly 250 years later.

That the Supreme Court came to the rescue of press freedom and the First-Amendment guarantee on June 30, by vacating its own temporary stay order of June 25 and earlier lower-court orders, afforded some reassurance. But the fact that President Nixon had ever instructed Attorney General John Mitchell to go to court to seek imposition of a prior restraint on publication did great damage to the concept of liberty of the press so painstakingly developed through historical evolution and legal decisions since 1694. In the history of the Republic, no other president had so acted.

In the judgment of legal scholars, the Pentagon Papers case left little legal residue and will be remembered far longer for its political implications than for its legal stature.[2] In that respect it perhaps paralleled the Zenger case of 1735; there was no guarantee after Zenger's acquittal that another editor would not be charged in another government effort to muzzle the press, but it never seemed politically feasible for colonial administrators to try in the same manner. Possibly the next president faced with circumstances similar to those involved in the Pentagon Papers case will seek a postpublication criminal prosecution, if one seems warranted, rather than attempt again to impose prior restraint on publication. In that sense, the case is worth detailed examination.

Sometime in March, 1971, the *New York Times* came into possession of a forty-seven-volume study entitled "History of the U.S. Decision-Making Process on Vietnam Policy," compiled for the Pentagon at the order of former Secretary McNamara. Many copies of the study were circulating. Its contents were historical and nonmilitary in character but highly explosive in terms of political and diplomatic interest. All documents were classified "Top Secret" under a 1953 executive order. *Times* correspondent Neil Sheehan, who had represented UPI in the original Saigon press corps and who in 1971 covered the Pentagon, was a key figure in the development of the Pentagon Papers series for the paper. Managing editor Abe Rosenthal assigned several leading *Times* staffers to weeks of painstaking work in a hotel room hideaway. On June 13 the *Times* printed the first installment.

Attorney General Mitchell asked the *Times* to stop the series; it refused. The government then went to a federal district judge just appointed by President Nixon and serving the first day on his new bench with its unprecedented prior restraint order request. Judge Murray Gurfein issued a temporary restraining order June 15, forcing the *Times* to stop after the third installment. On June 19 Judge Gurfein refused to grant a permanent restraining order, saying that the government had failed to prove its case other than to plead a "general framework of embarrassment." But he let the temporary order stand. On June 23 the U.S. Court of Appeals in New York reversed Gurfein's decision. In the meantime, the *Washington Post* had started a series of its own and had won a clear-cut victory when Judge Gerhard A. Gesell ruled that the government could not "impose a prior restraint on essentially historical data." The U.S. Court of Appeals for the District of Columbia upheld Gesell and the two cases reached the U.S. Supreme Court on June 25. There, with Justices Black, Douglas, Brennan, and Marshall dissenting, the court voted 5–4 to hear testimony and continue the temporary order of prior restraint.

At this point the case collapsed as a legal landmark. The newspaper attorneys, shaken by the adverse 5–4 vote of the Supreme Court continuing a temporary prior restraint, refused to gamble on a plea that the First Amendment prohibited prior restraint under any and all circumstances. Instead, they preferred to win the immediate case on the grounds that the government could not prove that national security was involved. This they did, on a 6–3 *per curiam* decision.[3] It was based on *Near* v. *Minnesota* and two more recent press-freedom decisions. There were then nine individual decisions, with Justices Black and Douglas, both of whom have since left the Court, arguing that freedom of the press is absolute; Justices Brennan and Stewart declaring that the government had not proved its case; Justice Marshall rejecting the contention that the president had inherent power to declare a document nonpublishable in the national interest; Justice White joining the majority but inviting a criminal prosecution of the newspaperpeople; Chief Justice Burger and Justice Blackmun objecting to the haste shown in the case and requesting an exhaustive review of the documents; and Justice Harlan indicating that he believed the president should have the power to foreclose publication of any document whose disclosure would in his judgment be harmful.

"All the News That's Fit to Print"

The New York Times

CITY EDITION

Weather: Chance of showers today, tonight. Partly sunny tomorrow. Temp. range: today 74-94; Wed. 72-91. Temp. Hum. Index yesterday 82. Full U.S. report on Page 94.

VOL. CXX....No. 41,431 — © 1971 The New York Times Company — NEW YORK, THURSDAY, JULY 1, 1971 — Higher newsstand price in air delivery cities — 15 CENTS

SUPREME COURT, 6-3, UPHOLDS NEWSPAPERS ON PUBLICATION OF THE PENTAGON REPORT; TIMES RESUMES ITS SERIES, HALTED 15 DAYS

Nixon Says Turks Agree To Ban the Opium Poppy

By JOHN HERBERS
Special to The New York Times

WASHINGTON, June 30—President Nixon announced today that Turkey had agreed to eliminate within a year her production of opium poppies, which account for about two-thirds of the illegal heroin reaching the United States.

Mr. Nixon, in a brief announcement delivered in the White House press room, said that as a result of negotiations between the United States and Turkish Governments, Premier Nihat Erim had agreed to ban altogether the cultivation of opium poppies by June, 1972.

He said the joint announcement, made simultaneously in Washington and Ankara, "represents by far the most significant breakthrough that has been achieved in stopping the source of supply of heroin in our world-wide offensive against dangerous drugs."

Two weeks ago, Mr. Nixon sent a message to William J. Handley, the United States Ambassador in Turkey, saying that the time for talk had passed and the United States must have action by the Turkish Government in ending poppy cultivation.

Today, the President praised Premier Erim for "courageous, statesmanlike action" and said the United States would provide money and technical assistance in helping Turkish farmers shift to other crops.

Officials would not say how much American money would be involved, but the United States has made a $3-million commitment to Turkey on the heroin problem.

Secretary of State William P. Rogers, who helped work

Continued on Page 22, Column 1

Soviet Starts an Inquiry Into 3 Astronauts' Deaths

By BERNARD GWERTZMAN
Special to The New York Times

MOSCOW, June 30—The Soviet authorities appointed a special commission tonight to investigate the deaths of their three astronauts who perished this morning when their Soyuz II craft was returning to earth after the longest manned space flight in history.

News of the astronauts' deaths shocked many Soviet people. And Western specialists predicted that their deaths would retard development of the Salyut space station program. The three astronauts had spent more than three weeks working and exercising aboard the Salyut craft, described as the world's first space laboratory.

[...] ican officials said the Soviet space disaster had probably been caused by a failure in the oxygen supply. They also said the accident should not delay United States space flights. Articles on Page 30.]

Tonight, the Soviet people seemed caught up in the human aspects of the disaster and the mystery of what caused the deaths of Lieut. Col. Georgi T. Dobrovolsky, the flight commander; Vladislav N. Volkov, the flight engineer, and Viktor I. Patsayev, the test engineer.

Were their deaths caused by the weakened state of their bodies after nearly 24 days of weightlessness? Were they

PRESIDENT CALLS STEEL AND LABOR TO WHITE HOUSE

He Asks Both Sides to Meet With Him Tuesday Before Contract Talks Start

By PHILIP SHABECOFF
Special to The New York Times

WASHINGTON, June 30 — President Nixon has called negotiators of the steel companies and steelworkers union to meet with him next Tuesday before they sit down to begin contract negotiations, a White House spokesman announced today.

It will be the first time that the President will have met with labor and management in any industry prior to nation-wide contract negotiations, according to Ronald L. Ziegler, the White House press secretary.

Discussion Issues Listed

Mr. Ziegler said that the President had called the meeting to discuss general economic developments and trends in the world steel markets.

Earlier today, the chairman of the Federal Reserve Board, Arthur F. Burns, told a Congressional committee that the "first priority" should be given to a new Government move to try to moderate price and wage increases and expressed his concern over the spread of "inflationary psychology" in this country.

The Administration has repeatedly warned that excessive increases in steel wages and prices would severely retard efforts to control inflation. Hints have been dropped that import quotas that protect domestic steel from foreign competition will be eased or lifted if prices go too high.

President Nixon has been in-

Pentagon Papers: Study Reports Kennedy Made 'Gamble' Into a 'Broad Commitment'

By HEDRICK SMITH

The Pentagon's study of the Vietnam war concludes that President John F. Kennedy transformed the "limited-risk gamble" of the Eisenhower Administration into a "broad commitment" to prevent Communist domination of South Vietnam.

Although Mr. Kennedy resisted pressures for putting American ground-combat units into South Vietnam, the Pentagon analysts say, he took a series of actions that significantly expanded the American military and political involvement in Vietnam but nonetheless left President Lyndon B. Johnson with as bad a situation as Mr. Kennedy inherited.

"The dilemma of the U.S. involvement dating from the Kennedy era," the Pentagon study observes, was to use "only limited means to achieve excessive ends."

Moreover, according to the study, prepared in 1967-68 by Government analysts, the Kennedy tactics deepened the American involvement in Vietnam piecemeal, with each step minimizing public recognition that the American role was growing.

The expansion of that role, over three decades, is traced in the 3,000 pages of the Pentagon's study, which is accompanied by 4,000 pages of documents on the Vietnam era. Previous articles in The Times's presentation of this material have recounted President Johnson's movement to war in 1964 and 1965.

President Kennedy made his first fresh commitments to Vietnam secretly. The Pentagon study discloses that in the spring of 1961 the President ordered 400 Special Forces troops and 100 other American military advisers sent to South Vietnam. No publicity was given to either move.

Small as the numbers seem in retrospect, the Pentagon study comments that even the first such expansion "signaled a willingness to go beyond the 685-man limit on the size of the U.S. [military] mission in Saigon, which, if it were done openly, would be the first formal breach of the Geneva agreement." Under the interpretation of that agreement in effect since 1956, the United States was limited to 685 military advisers in Vietnam. Washington, while it did not sign the accord, pledged not to undermine it.

On May 11, 1961, the day on which President Kennedy decided to send the Special Forces, he also ordered the start of a campaign of clandestine warfare against North Vietnam, to be conducted by South Vietnamese agents directed and trained by the Central Intelligence Agency and some American Special Forces troops. [See text, action memorandum, May 11, 1961, Page 3.]

The President's instructions, as quoted in the documents, were, "In North Vietnam . . . [to] form networks of resistance, covert bases and teams for

Continued on Page 6, Column I

> The Times today resumes its series of articles on the Pentagon's secret study of the Vietnam war. The study was obtained through the investigative reporting of Neil Sheehan, and the articles were researched and written over three months by Mr. Sheehan and other staff members. The fourth and fifth articles, both by Hedrick Smith, are published today and form an account of decisions in the Kennedy Administration.
>
> Three pages of documentary material covering the Kennedy policy begin on Page 3, and documents on the 1963 coup begin on Page 9. A summary of the three earlier articles, covering the Johnson Administration, appears on Page 15.

U.S. and Diem's Overthrow: Step by Step

The Pentagon's secret study of the Vietnam war discloses that President Kennedy knew and approved of plans for the military coup d'état that overthrew President Ngo Dinh Diem in 1963.

"Our complicity in his overthrow heightened our responsibilities and our commitment" in Vietnam, the study finds.

In August and October of 1963, the narrative recounts, the United States gave its support to a cabal of army generals bent on removing the controversial leader, whose rise to power Mr. Kennedy had backed in speeches in the middle nineteen-fifties and who had been the anchor of American policy in Vietnam for nine years.

[...] coup, one of the most dramatic [...]es in the history of the American [...]ement in Vietnam, was a water[...] As the Pentagon study observes, [...] a time when Washington—with [...]iem regime gone—could have re[...]ered its entire commitment to Vietnam and decided to disengage. [...] least two Administration officials [...]ated disengagement but, according [...]e Pentagon study, it "was never seriously considered a policy alternative because of the assumption that an independent, non-Communist SVN was too important a strategic interest to abandon."

The effect, according to this account, was that the United States, discovering after the coup that the war against the Vietcong had been going much worse than officials previously thought, felt compelled to do more—rather than less—for Saigon. By supporting the anti-Diem coup, the analyst asserts, "the U.S. inadvertently deepened its involvement. The inadvertence is the key factor."

According to the Pentagon account of the 1963 events in Saigon, Washington did not originate the anti-Diem coup, nor did American forces intervene in any way, even to try to prevent the assassinations of Mr. Diem and his brother Ngo Dinh Nhu, who, as the chief Diem political adviser, had accumulated immense power. Popular discontent with the Diem regime focused on Mr. Nhu and his wife.

But for weeks—and with the White House informed every step of the way—the American mission in Saigon maintained secret contacts with the plotting generals through one of the Central Intelligence Agency's most experienced and versatile operatives, an Indochina veteran, Lieut. Col. Lucien Conein. The colonel, who is now in retirement, first landed in Vietnam in 1944 by parachute for the Office of Strategic Services, the wartime forerunner of the C.I.A.

So trusted by the Vietnamese generals was Colonel Conein that he was in their midst at Vietnamese General Staff headquarters as they launched the coup. Indeed, on Oct. 25, a week earlier, in a cable to McGeorge Bundy, the President's special assistant for national security, Ambassador Lodge had occasion to describe Colonel Conein of the C.I.A.—referring to the agency, in code terminology, as C.A.S.—as the indispensable man:

"C.A.S. has been punctilious in carrying out my instructions. I have personally approved each meeting between General Don [one of three main plotters] and Conein who has carried out my

Continued on Page 12, Column I

BURGER DISSENTS

First Amendment Rule Held to Block Most Prior Restraints

Decision, concurring opinions, dissents start on Page 17.

By FRED P. GRAHAM
Special to The New York Times

WASHINGTON, June 30 — The Supreme Court freed The New York Times and The Washington Post today to resume immediate publication of articles based on the secret Pentagon papers on the origins of the Vietnam war.

By a vote of 6 to 3 the Court held that any attempt by the Government to block news articles prior to publication bears "a heavy burden of presumption against its constitutionality."

In a historic test of that principle — the first effort by the Government to enjoin publication on the ground of national security — the Court declared that "the Government has not met that burden."

The brief judgment was read to a hushed courtroom by Chief Justice Warren E. Burger at 2:30 P.M. at a special session called three hours before.

Old Tradition Observed

The Chief Justice was one of the three dissenters, along with Associate Justices Harry A. Blackmun and John M. Harlan, but because the decision was rendered in an unsigned opinion, the Chief Justice read it in court in accordance with a long-standing custom.

In New York, Arthur Ochs Sulzberger, president and publisher of The Times, was asked at a news conference whether he thought the motto of The Times—"All the News That's Fit to Print"—had been upheld. "I think it was very much upheld," he said.

The case had been expected to produce a landmark ruling on the circumstances under which prior restraint could be imposed upon the press, but because no opinion by a single Justice commanded the support of a majority, only the unsigned decision will serve as precedent.

Uncertainty Over Outcome

Because it came on the 15th day after The Times had been restrained from publishing further articles in its series mined from the 7,000 pages of material—the first such restraint in the name of "national security" in the history of the United States—there was some uncertainty whether the press had scored a strong victory or whether a precedent for some degree of restraint had been set.

Alexander M. Bickel, the Yale law professor who had argued for The Times in the case, said in a telephone interview that the ruling placed the press in a "stronger position." He maintained that no Federal District Judge would henceforth temporarily restrain a newspaper on the Justice Department's complaint that "this is what they have printed and we don't like it" and that a direct threat of irreparable harm would have to be alleged.

However, the United States Solicitor General, Erwin N. Griswold, turned to another lawyer shortly after the Justices filed from the courtroom

Continued on Page 15, Column 1

STATES RATIFY [...]LL VOTE AT 18

Conferees Cut Military Pay Rise As Authority to Draft Runs Out

By DAVID E. ROSENBAUM
Special to The New York Times

[...]HINGTON, June 30 — [...]xon Administration won [...]r budgetary victory to- [...] the House-Senate con- [...] on the draft extension [...]

[...] conference agreement [...]peared to represent a [...] for supporters of an [...]nteer Army, who had [...] larger pay increases [...]ose cleared by the con- [...]

[...] conferees accepted a fig- [...] military pay and allow- [...]hat was more than $900- [...] below what both the [...] and House had ap- [...] The raises voted by the [...]s would cost about [...]ion in the fiscal year [...] tomorrow and would [...] effect Oct. 1.

[...] figure approved by the [...]nce was still $800-mil- [...]bove what President [...]ought in his budget, but [...]ouse and Senate had [...] increases of about $1.7- [...] over the budget.

[...]ixon Administration had [...] that so large an increase [...] force severe and pos- [...]angerous reductions in [...] parts of the defense [...]

[...] Government's basic au- [...] to draft men into the military expires at midnight tonight.

The conferees completed action on all provisions of the draft bill today except the Senate-passed amendment that calls for the withdrawal of United States troops from Indochina within nine months if prisoners of war are first

Continued on Page 29, Column 1

False Advertising Laid to H&R Block

By JOHN D. MORRIS
Special to The New York Times

WASHINGTON, June 30—H & R Block, Inc., which says it prepares income tax returns for eight million American annually, was accused by the Federal Trade Commission today of false advertising and illegally using confidential information supplied by customers.

The commission published similar but separate citations against H & R Block and the Beneficial Corporation, which offers income tax services on a smaller scale through a subsidiary, the Beneficial Management Corporation. In radio and television advertisements, the name

Continued on Page 57, Column 2

ACTION BY GRAVEL VEXES SENATORS

But No Disciplinary Action Against Him Is Expected

By JOHN W. FINNEY
Special to The New York Times

WASHINGTON, June 30—Many Senators privately expressed dismay, shock and chagrin today at Senator Mike Gravel's release of parts of the Pentagon's secret study of the Vietnam war. But it appeared that no disciplinary action would be taken against the Alaska Democrat.

Last night Senator Gravel tried to read the documents to the Senate in an all-night speech and, when he was blocked for lack of a quorum, proceeded to call an impromptu meeting of his Senate Public Works subcommittee. He read from the study for three and one-half hours, with his voice sometimes breaking into sobs, and tears occasionally rolling down his face.

His action incurred the displeasure of many of his colleagues, who felt that it reflected on the dignity and composure of the Senate. But in the clublike atmosphere of the Senate, there was a widespread reluctance, extending down from the leadership, to take any formal disciplinary

Continued on Page 10, Column 2

Broadcasting

July 19, 1971; Vol. 81, No. 3

Staggers headed off at the pass

Broadcasting wins apparent First Amendment victory as congressional leadership avoids showdown on CBS citation

A landmark case over broadcasters' rights under freedom of the press vs. Congress's right to legislative inquiry was sidelined last Tuesday (July 13) as the House voted 226-to-181 to recommit to the Commerce Committee a proposed contempt citation against CBS and its president, Frank Stanton. Winnerwise, it was CBS's day. Confrontationwise, it was less a bang than a whimper.

The Commerce Committee, under Chairman Harley O. Staggers (D-W. Va.), had voted two weeks earlier to recommend the citation to the House, based on the network's refusal to supply subpoenaed outtakes and other materials from *The Selling of the Pentagon* documentary (BROADCASTING, July 5).

It was the first time in memory that the House had refused to back a committee on a contempt citation. And it was the first time that a committee had tried to cite a broadcaster who, on First Amendment grounds, refused to comply with an order.

In a statement issued after the vote, Dr. Stanton said: "We are very pleased by the decisive House vote to recommit the proposed contempt citation to the Commerce Committee. As responsible journalists, we shall continue to do our best to report on public events in a fair and objective manner."

According to House Speaker Carl Albert (D-Okla.), the issue will remain privileged for the remainder of the 92d Congress. That is, it could be bro[...] to the floor again. However, Chai[...]n Staggers said that would not happen.

Dramatis personnae *in last week's House of Representatives drama concerning the threatened citation of CBS for contempt of Congress: onstage—Harley O. Staggers (D-W. Va.) (below), whose hope it was to force the contempt citation to a successful vote, and (picture at lower right) House Speaker*

Carl Albert (D-Okla.)(r), whose corridor conference here with Parliamentarian Lewis Deschler was one of several steps along the road to maneuvering the matter back to the Commerce Committee and apparent oblivion; offstage—Frank Stanton (top right), president of CBS, who, with his news department and an important part of the future of broadcast journalism, was the object of it all.

The *New York Times* reports its victory; inset, Frank Stanton and CBS avoid censure.

© 1971, New York Times

The anonymous writer of the *per curiam* decision did cite *Near* v. *Minnesota,* the landmark case of 1931 defending liberty of the press and extending the protection of the First Amendment against acts of Congress to include a ban on state action. Also cited were two quotations:

> Any system of prior restraints of expression comes to this court bearing a heavy presumption against its constitutional validity.[4]
>
> The Government thus carries a heavy burden of showing justification for the enforcement of such a restraint.[5]

The first of these quotations indicates strongly that the Supreme Court's majority stood by the landmark case of *Near* v. *Minnesota* and its basic concepts. The second reminds society that there is a loophole in the legal concept of liberty of the press—a loophole that at least Justice Harlan would have allowed the president to use unrestrainedly.

Chief Justice Hughes, in giving the 5–4 verdict in the 1931 *Near* case, had quoted from Blackstone on prior restraint and postpublication punishment:

> The liberty of the press is indeed essential to the nature of a free state; but this consists in laying no *previous* restraints upon publications, and not in freedom from censure for criminal matter when published. Every freeman has an undoubted right to lay what sentiments he pleases before the public; to forbid this is to destroy the freedom of the press; but if he publishes what is improper, mischievous or illegal, he must take the consequences of his own temerity.

Hughes went on to include a dicta, or observation, that weakened the case for absolute protection against prior restraint:

> The objection has also been made that the principle as to immunity from previous restraint is stated too broadly, if every such restraint is deemed to be prohibited. That is undoubtedly true; the protection even as to previous restraint is not absolutely unlimited. But the limitation has been recognized only in exceptional cases.[6]

The Chief Justice then cited examples of military secrets, overthrow of the government, and obscenity as areas in which prior restraint might apply. But he drew the line, in the following passage from *Near,* on the kind of situation the Pentagon Papers case represented—disclosure of activities of public officers deemed by many citizens to be censurable:

> The exceptional nature of its limitations places in a strong light the general conception that liberty of the press, historically considered and taken up in the Federal Constitution, has meant, principally although not exclusively, immunity from previous restraints or censorship. The conception of the liberty of the press in this country had broadened with the exigencies of the colonial period and with the efforts to secure freedom from oppressive administration. That liberty was especially cherished for the immunity it afforded from previous restraint of the publication of censure of public officers and charges of official misconduct.[7]

The question of postpublication punishment was raised in the Pentagon Papers case by Justice White and also by Chief Justice Burger, who chastised the

Times and *Post* for not turning over the papers to the government. Here the freedom of speech cases would apply, involving the concept of clear-and-present danger evolved by Justices Holmes and Brandeis and the opposing balancing theory. The landmark cases include four stemming from the World War I Red Scare period and one from the post-World War II anti-Communist period.

Prior restraint was imposed again in 1979 when the government obtained a restraining order that temporarily stopped the *Progressive* magazine from publishing an article telling how to build a hydrogen bomb, even though the author had obtained his information from public sources. The magazine had voluntarily submitted the detailed story to the government for examination. The *Progressive* appealed a lower-court ban to the Supreme Court, but the government withdrew its charges when the *Madison Press Connection* went ahead and published nearly identical information. The likely outcome of such cases would be more self-censorship, it was feared, in the face of government harassment.

THE WATERGATE STORY

The most widespread political corruption in the nation's history, more than a dozen major events conveniently listed under the headline word *Watergate,* forced the resignation of Richard Nixon and deepened the cynicism of a public already battered by the endless Vietnam fighting, partisan politics, and economic chaos. The scope and magnitude of the illegal activities and deceptions revealed during Nixon's desperate fight to save his presidency between 1972 and 1974 shocked Republicans and Democrats alike, most of whom were loath to believe that men who had entered the White House on a strict "law and order" platform had misused their power, money, and public trust.

Watergate was not an aberration. As previously discussed, its roots lay deep in the misdeeds of other administrations. But these events were unprecedented because of the scope and magnitude of the totalitarian methods used by Nixon and his closest advisers to discredit their foes and maintain their long-sought control over America's destiny.

Crucial to the following developments was Nixon's decision to begin a secret bombing campaign against neutral Cambodia in March, 1969. Enmity and distrust between the White House and Congress grew when the Senate twice rejected Nixon's nominations to the Supreme Court. Then came massive public demonstrations against an open invasion of Cambodia and the killing of four Kent State University students. The White House atmosphere became one of tenseness, and a number of news leaks added to the pressure.

In June, 1970, Nixon agreed to a plan advanced by White House aide Tom Huston that called for a domestic security group to be formed from representatives of the White House, FBI, CIA, and other government agencies. It was to be authorized to wiretap, commit burglary, and violate other laws, if necessary, in the interest of providing intelligence information on persons disloyal to the administration. FBI Director J. Edgar Hoover, jealously protecting his hold over domestic intelligence gathering, refused to cooperate. Nixon then recalled his memos to the other organizations. The White House learned a lesson here. In the future, if sensitive missions needed to be carried out, they would have to be conducted by persons not connected to any official agency.

Bob Woodward and Carl Bernstein.
Newsweek

In the absence of any such secret group, however, Nixon authorized FBI wiretaps on four newsmen and thirteen government officials between May, 1969, and February, 1971. Secretary of State Henry Kissinger, fearful of possible leaks from members of his staff, encouraged some of the wiretaps. A turning point came in June, 1971, with the publication of the Pentagon Papers. Worried that his own secret foreign maneuverings, including the Cambodian bombing,* might be revealed, Nixon authorized the establishment of a White House surveillance team—later to be called the "Plumbers." Their chief assignment was to plug leaks of classified information. On September 3, 1971, several of the unit's members broke into the office of Daniel Ellsberg's psychiatrist in an effort to find personal information that might discredit the man who brought the Pentagon Papers to the *New York Times.*

That same week White House aide Charles Colson, one of Nixon's closest personal confidants, gave John Dean, the President's counsel, a "priority list" of twenty "political enemies." The list, later expanded, contained the names of journalists, politicians, movie stars, and other prominent Americans. From this time until June, 1972, operatives hired by persons with White House contacts attempted to disrupt the campaigns of Democratic candidates, especially the acknowledged frontrunner, Senator Edmund Muskie. Their object was to de-

*The recipient of one news leak was William Beecher of the *New York Times,* who reported on May 9, 1969, that secret B-52 raids were being conducted in Cambodia. The full story did not emerge until 1973. See the journalism review MORE (October 1973, p. 17). Beecher's "offhand disclosure" may have been meant to help Nixon signal a new get-tough policy; if so, he went too far. First his phone was one of those tapped; then, after being judged loyal, he was named Deputy Assistant Secretary of Defense for Public Affairs. Other reporters claimed that they knew of the Cambodian bombings but did not consider them major news. After the one story in the *New York Times,* only *Newsweek,* once in its news-brief section, mentioned the bombing during the 14-month period.

IN CAMBODIA—American soldiers try to spot enemy through rubber trees in the Fishhook region.

IN KENT, OHIO—National guardsmen advance during clash in which four students were killed. (AP Wirephotos)

Los Angeles Times

LARGEST CIRCULATION IN THE WEST, 982,075 DAILY, 1,317,220 SUNDAY.

VOL. LXXXIX | SEVEN PARTS—PART ONE | CC F | TUESDAY MORNING, MAY 5, 1970 | 110 PAGES | Copyright © 1970 Los Angeles Times | DAILY 10c

DEATH ON THE CAMPUS—A girl screams over the body of a student shot at Kent State University. (AP Wirephoto)

Troops Kill Four Students in Antiwar Riot at Ohio College

Large S. Viet-U.S. Force Opens Third Cambodia Offensive

SAIGON (AP)—Thousands of American and South Vietnamese troops launched a third offensive into northeast Cambodia today, seeking to smash more North Vietnamese base camps and sanctuaries, the U.S. command announced.

The American command said the operation was kicked off early this afternoon in the Se San base area, about 50 miles west of Pleiku, in the Central Highlands.

A spokesman said troops of the U.S. 4th Infantry Division and the South Vietnamese 22nd Infantry Division were participating in the operation.

(Their target is a highlands bivouac area that long has served as an entry point for the Ho Chi Minh Trail into Vietnam, United Press International said: It lies just south of the point where the borders of Laos, Cambodia and South Vietnam meet.

(Communist troops operating from this area have besieged several border Green Beret camps in the course of the war.

Defense Secretary Melvin R. Laird said in Washington Saturday that all North Vietnamese and Viet Cong sanctuaries along the full length of the border would be attacked by the allies.

There are numerous enemy base camp areas in Cambodia from the western Mekong Delta to the area north of Saigon which are outside the areas attacked last week by allied troops.

The two earlier allied drives, one into an area known as the Parrot's Beak and the other into an area called the Fishhook, have accounted for 2,171 North Vietnamese and Viet Cong killed. U.S. losses were given as 16 killed and South Vietnamese deaths were put at 151.

WAR SITUATION AT A GLANCE

The stock market took a heavy beating Monday, reacting to concern over U.S. action in Cambodia. The Dow Jones industrial average dropped 19.07. Part 3, Page 9.

The Vietnam peace talks in Paris hung in the balance as the result of the U.S. Cambodia action. Page 18.

The Senate Foreign Relations Committee said the Cambodian invasion was "constitutionally unauthorized." Page 11.

U.S. troops swept through Cambodia's Fishhook toward what was believed to be a major Communist headquarters base. Page 22.

Soviet Premier Alexei N. Kosygin called for "vigorous measures" to get the U.S. out of Indochina. Page 19.

Official Washington, however, noted that Kosygin gave no indication of any Russian action to counter the United States. Page 19.

For Red China, U.S. action was "frantic provocation." Page 16.

Guards' Gunfire Wounds 11 at Kent University

KENT, Ohio (UPI)—Four students were shot to death on the Kent State University campus Monday when national guardsmen, believing a sniper had attacked them, fired into a crowd of rioting antiwar protesters.

At least 11 persons were wounded, three critically, before order was restored. The university was shut down for at least a week.

The town of 18,000 was sealed off and a judge ordered the university's

California student protesters disrupt campuses. See Page 3, Part 1.

20,000 students to leave the campus by noon Tuesday.

By late Monday night only 300 students, most of them foreign students, remained as 800 guardsmen patrolled in convoys of jeeps and personnel carriers armed with .50-caliber machine guns.

Students and National Guard officials gave different versions of what triggered the gunfire, but the guard admitted no warning was given that the troops would begin firing their M-1 semiautomatic rifles.

The battle was the most violent campus confrontation since the antiwar movement began. The trouble started when about 1,000 demonstrators, defying an order not to assemble, rallied on the commons at the center of the tree-lined campus. Guardsmen moved in and fired tear gas grenades at the mob, which broke and ran.

The protesters then regrouped and confronted about 300 guardsmen on a practice football field. The students, now numbering 1,500, charged down a hill and pelted the troops with rocks. Guardsmen exhausted their supply of tear gas. Students, who tossed back the canisters, surrounded the troops on three sides.

Believes Sniper Fired

Then, according to S. T. Del Corso, state adjutant general, "a sniper opened fire against the guardsmen from a nearby rooftop."

Del Corso, who was in Columbus, the state capital, maintained contact with the troops through Brig. Gen. Robert Canterbury, who commanded the guard force on campus. Canterbury said the students were given no warning before the shooting started.

Student eyewitnesses said they did not hear any gunfire before the guardsmen began shooting.

"All of a sudden," said one male student," some of them turned

Please Turn to Page 6, Col. 1

ALABAMA ELECTION

Wallace's Drive for Presidency at Stake Today

BY KENNETH REICH
Times Staff Writer

MONTGOMERY, Ala. — In the 1968 presidential election, George C. Wallace received 65% of the Alabama vote.

In 1966, his late wife Lurleen—a political amateur running in his stead for governor because he could not legally succeed himself—drew 54% of the vote in the Democratic primary and became the nominee without a runoff.

In today's primary election, if there is agreement on anything among the political factions in this state, it is that Wallace won't do as well as his wife did in 1966.

Wallace may still win this election. If he does, victory will likely come after a runoff against his long-time protege, incumbent Gov. Albert P. Brewer. (There are five minor candidates in today's race.)

But Wallace's basic strength in the state he claimed to personify so long has seemingly eroded.

A charismatic man whose political fortune was bred on crisis, he may be in trouble in today's election because Alabama is not in the midst of crisis.

He may be in trouble because at least the state's mind, if not its heart, has changed on the vital racial issue.

He has certainly found trouble, because his tactics in challenging Brewer left a bad taste in many people's mouths and some of them had previously been strong supporters.

"Albert doesn't deserve Wallace opposition," was the way one man put it in Birmingham. And in Mont-

Please Turn to Page 12, Col. 1

Hopes Rise for Teacher Strike Settlement by End of the Week

BY HARRY BERNSTEIN
Times Labor Writer

The Los Angeles teachers' strike started its fourth week Monday amid rising hopes that the walkout will be over by this weekend.

A possible delaying effect on the hoped-for settlement was avoided Monday when Superior Judge Stevens Fargo agreed with another Superior Court judge that the strike is illegal and issued a preliminary injunction to that effect, but delayed action at least until May 18 on contempt of court charges against strike leaders.

This means United Teachers of Los Angeles President Robert Ransom, Vice President Larry Sibelman, Executive Secretary Don Baer and Assistant Executive Secretary Roger Segure can devote full time to seeking a settlement instead of to the court proceedings.

A UTLA spokesman said the preliminary injunction issued Monday against the strike will be appealed on constitutional grounds.

The hopes for a quick end to the strike are based on the belief that UCLA law Prof. Benjamin Aaron will come up Thursday with a contract proposal acceptable both to the striking teachers and the Board of Education.

Neither side is obligated to accept his recommendations, but public pressure for both to do so will be great.

Some of the more militant teachers are unhappy about the procedure proposed by Aaron and accepted by both sides because they feel it means, in effect, that the outcome of the entire strike rests on one man.

If Aaron recommends any significant concessions to the teachers, it will be difficult for the strike to continue because the already divided teachers will be further divided on their next move.

Equally heavy pressure will be felt by the Board of Education to accept the recommendations even if Aaron makes concessions to the teachers that the board majority would not have approved before the strike.

Please Turn to Page 26, Col. 1

My Lai Disclosure Wins Pulitzer Prize

BY RICHARD DOUGHERTY
Times Staff Writer

NEW YORK—Seymour M. Hersh, the reporter who broke the story of the alleged My Lai massacre in Vietnam, won the 1970 Pulitzer Prize for international reporting Monday.

President Andrew W. Cordier of Columbia University announced the award on behalf of Columbia's trustees who make the annual selections for excellence in journalism and letters under terms of the will of the late Publisher Joseph Pulitzer.

Recognition of the 33-year-old Hersh's expose of the alleged killing of nearly all the residents of a Vietnamese hamlet—including women and children—was not unexpected. The story was written by Hersh for Dispatch News Service. It was syndicated in 36 papers in this country

Please Turn to Page 10, Col. 1

New U.S. Air Raids Halted Over North, but Option Remains

BY TED SELL
Times Staff Writer

WASHINGTON—A new bombing campaign against North Vietnam was publicly declared ended Monday but defense sources said privately that a new policy giving field commanders increased authority on launching air strikes remained in effect.

The formal announcement, by Daniel Z. Henkin, assistant secretary of defense for public affairs, was that three heavy strikes against Communist supply areas just north of the border with South Vietnam were "all that were planned." Henkin said that with the strong attacks, the operation had "terminated."

Henkin, chief spokesman for the Defense Department, said there had been no change in the U.S. policy of protecting American reconnaissance flights.

But on Sunday, equally well-informed Pentagon officials said the policy had in fact been changed, permitting far more massive retaliatory bombing of North Vietnam.

Under the old policy, fighter escorts could attack only whatever single antiaircraft positions fired on reconnaissance planes.

It was made clear over the weekend, in connection with the expansion of the raids, that that policy no longer held. If antiaircraft positions in any military base area fired, escorts could attack both that position and any military targets associated with it.

That expansion of authority, Pentagon sources said Monday, has not been revoked. White House officials,

Please Turn to Page 15, Col. 1

Index to The Times

THE WEATHER

U.S. Weather Bureau forecast: Night and morning low clouds with local drizzles but hazy afternoon sunshine today and Wednesday. High today, 70. High Monday, 80; low, 55.

Smog report and complete weather information in Part 2, Page 4.

The *Los Angeles Times* draws a parallel between Cambodia and Kent State in 1970.

stroy Muskie's candidacy in the hopes that a more vulnerable candidate, Senator George McGovern, might emerge as Nixon's opponent in the 1972 elections. Nixon's White House chief of staff, H. R. ("Bob") Haldeman, was kept advised of these activities, known later as the "dirty tricks" campaign.

It was the White House "Plumbers" who on June 17, 1972, entered the Washington headquarters of the Democratic National Committee, located in the Watergate apartment complex. Washington police caught five men redhanded, planting listening devices in the office of Lawrence F. O'Brien, chairperson of the Democratic party. It was later determined that this break-in was part of a large-scale plan to spy on Democratic leaders* and was financed by contributions (some of them illegal) to the Committee to Re-elect the President, called CREEP.

The *Washington Post* ran as its second lead on June 18 an 83-inch story that linked Watergate burglar James McCord to the CIA. The *New York Times* ran a 13-inch story on an inside page, as did most newspapers. Since this broke as a local story, the *Post* assigned several metropolitan reporters to it, including Bob Woodward and Carl Bernstein. It was Woodward who traced the name of E. Howard Hunt, found in one burglar's address book, to a White House office.

The pattern of media coverage quickly developed. As the *Post* pushed onward with its stories by Woodward and Bernstein, assisted by the mysterious contact "Deep Throat," White House spokespeople branded them as being false or misleading. These official rebuttals received more attention than the original stories. On June 19 Ronald Ziegler, Nixon's press secretary, called Watergate a "third-rate burglary attempt" and said "certain elements" would attempt to blow the event out of proportion.

A few papers were disturbed, such as the *St. Louis Post-Dispatch,* which said, "the whole episode has a distasteful aura which cannot be dispelled by bland and unelaborated disclaimers from top Republican strategists."[8] But majority sentiment was reflected in this *Chicago Tribune* editorial: "It is hard to believe that it had the participation, approval, or knowledge of any official Republican organization, let alone the White House . . . it is Mr. O'Brien who is guilty of gutter politics and of sharing guilt by association."[9]

In an impromptu news conference on June 22, Nixon denied White House involvement in any break-in and said that attempted surveillance "has no place in our electoral process or in our governmental process."[10] But the very next day Haldeman brought Nixon up to date on a plan to sidetrack any FBI investigation of the break-in, by telling the FBI that certain CIA operations in Mexico would be endangered. The cover-up was underway and had been since the morning of June 17. The White House knew that the Watergate burglars and their chiefs, E. Howard Hunt and G. Gordon Liddy, had knowledge of other break-ins. If Hunt and Liddy were caught, the entire "dirty tricks" campaign, wiretapping, and other scandals might come to light.[11]

The *Post's* team of Woodward and Bernstein came up with a major breakthrough in an August 1 story that claimed that a $25,000 check deposited in the

*O'Brien was a likely target because of his friendship with Edward Kennedy, his demands for investigation of the ITT case, and his possible knowledge of a $100,000 contribution given to Nixon's friend Charles ("Bebe") Rebozo by billionaire Howard Hughes that was not passed on to CREEP.

account of Watergate burglar Bernard L. Barker had been written by Kenneth H. Dahlberg, Nixon's Midwest finance chairperson, and given to Maurice Stans, in charge of finances for the Republican campaign. Senator McGovern and O'Brien pressed their attack against the Nixon White House, but Republican National Chairman Robert Dole and other GOP spokespeople continued to receive good coverage of their countercharges.

On August 29, Nixon said at a news conference that the FBI, Department of Justice, and General Accounting Office had, at his direction, been given total cooperation by the White House staff. On October 5 he said, "The FBI assigned 133 agents to this investigation. It followed out 1800 leads. It conducted 1500 interviews. . . . I wanted to make sure that no member of the White House staff and no man or woman in a position of major responsibility in the Committee for Re-election had anything to do with this reprehensible activity." Eventually eighteen of those persons pleaded guilty or were convicted despite such efforts to shield them.

The *Post* struck again in October. Courageous decisions by Katharine Graham, the publisher, and Benjamin Bradlee, executive editor, allowed Woodward and Bernstein to publish on October 10 that Watergate had been only part of a White House plan for massive spying and political espionage. But the next time they came out with a major story, they almost made a fatal error. On October 25 they wrote that Hugh Sloan, White House aide, had testified before a Washington grand jury that Haldeman was one of the individuals authorized to disburse payments from a secret cash fund used for political intelligence. Sloan immediately denied that exact testimony, and the *Post* reeled from attacks by Republicans and other newspapers. Ziegler called it the "shoddiest type of journalism," and the *New York Times* gave the rebuttals strong coverage. Even when the *Post* was awarded the gold Pulitzer Prize medal for meritorious public service in 1973, Senators William Proxmire, Mike Mansfield, Hugh Scott, and others continued to denounce the paper for printing what they called "rumor and innuendo."

As with the great bulk of the early accusations, this one also proved to be essentially correct. Six months later it was learned that Sloan had said that if he had been asked by the grand jury about Haldeman, he would have testified to that effect. That same month intensive lobbying by Republicans, including Rep. Gerald R. Ford, kept the House Banking Committee of Rep. Wright Patman from opening its own investigation.

Studies of press performance during the fall of 1972 revealed that for the most part the Watergate story got little attention. The *Post* had been the leader, and the *New York Times* had tried to keep up. In August, *Time* magazine had broken a major story identifying the "Plumbers" as a group run from the White House by Hunt and Liddy. Leads like that were not followed up, however. One press critic calculated that of 433 Washington-based reporters who could in theory have been assigned to the Watergate story, only fifteen actually were. Of some 500 political columns written by Washington pundits between June and election day, fewer than two dozen concerned Watergate.

Regarding television coverage, it was discovered that during the 7-week period beginning September 14, the networks treated the story in a routine way. CBS devoted almost twice as many air time minutes (71) as did NBC and ABC

"I KNOW WHAT IS BEST FOR VIETNAM... I HAVE MORE FACTS."
"I KNOW WHAT IS BEST FOR THE ECONOMY... I HAVE MORE FACTS."
"I KNOW WHAT IS BEST TO STOP INFLATION... I HAVE MORE FACTS."
"I KNOW WHAT IS BEST FOR CAMBODIA... I HAVE MORE FACTS."
"I KNOW WHAT IS BEST FOR AMERICA... I HAVE MORE FACTS."
"HOW COULD I HAVE KNOWN ABOUT WATERGATE?.. I'M JUST THE PRESIDENT!"
CONRAD

In 1973, cartoonist Conrad points to the logical chief Watergate conspirator.

Paul Conrad, © 1973 Los Angeles Times,
with permission of the Register and Tribune Syndicate.

(42 and 41). More than one-third of NBC's coverage came in two broadcasts, the September 15 news of the indictments of the Watergate burglars and the October 10 sabotage story broken by the *Post.* Many of the stories were less than a minute in length. CBS made its strongest efforts with two special reports, 15 and 8 minutes in length, the week preceding the election.[12] It was no wonder that an October Gallup Poll showed that only 52 percent of Americans recognized the word Watergate. McGovern's charges of the worst corruption in American history were openly scoffed at.

It was in this atmosphere that Nixon was reelected. While the *Washington Post, New York Times, Louisville Courier-Journal, St. Louis Post-Dispatch,* and *Minneapolis Tribune* clamored against Nixon's policies, the bulk of the press gave him its blessing, including the *Los Angeles Times,* which lived to regret its decision.

Watergate became the biggest story in 1973 but not merely because of investigative reporting. The trial of the burglars began in Judge John T. Sirica's courtroom in January, and in February the Senate Select Committee on Presidential Campaign Activities, headed by Senator Sam J. Ervin, Jr., of North Carolina, began hearing testimony. The American public began hundreds of hours of television viewing. But behind all of this was a growing revolt against Nixon by persons in the FBI and Department of Justice and finally by Republican congressmen and papers that had endorsed him.

The lid could not be kept on the cover-up. In March, McCord wrote Judge Sirica a letter charging that he and other defendants were under pressure to plead guilty and remain silent, that perjury had been committed at their trial, and that higher-ups were involved. Nixon's response to the allegations was to accept responsibility for Watergate, along with the resignations of top aides H. R. Haldeman and John Erlichman. But in a televised speech the President denied any personal knowledge of the break-in or any cover-up. Nixon also fired White House counsel John Dean, who later provided damaging testimony against the President.

Media pressure intensified. The *New York Times* put its top investigative reporter, Seymour Hersh, onto the story. Jack Nelson of the *Los Angeles Times* and other writers began to dig. *Time* and *Newsweek* ran numerous stories containing serious allegations. CBS's Dan Rather and Nixon engaged in combat at several news conferences. Then came perhaps the most startling discovery of all. On July 16 a presidential aide, Alexander Butterfield, testified before the Senate committee that since 1970 Nixon had secretly taped all conversations in his offices, in the Lincoln Room, and at Camp David.

From this point until July 24, 1974, the President and his lawyers dueled the Senate committee, special prosecutors Archibald Cox and Leon Jaworski, and the local grand jury for possession of the tapes. The issue was decided on that day by an 8–0 vote of the Supreme Court, which held that Nixon had to turn over to Judge Sirica sixty-four recordings that might contain evidence of wrongdoing by his aides. Otherwise, it was clear, the President would be openly guilty of obstruction of justice.

Throughout this same period Nixon suffered a series of other defeats but remained on the defensive in claiming no knowledge of a cover-up. On October 1, 1973, the transcript of a Los Angeles grand jury investigating the Ellsberg break-in revealed Erlichman's testimony that Nixon had supervised the "Plumbers" unit. On October 10 Vice President Agnew resigned, after pleading no contest on charges of income-tax evasion. Nixon picked Gerald Ford to replace him. And on October 20 Nixon fired the original special prosecutor, Cox, in a dispute over subpoenas of the tape recordings. Attorney General Elliot Richardson and his deputy, William Ruckelshaus, resigned in protest of what was immediately called "the Saturday night massacre." Within days, calls for impeachment were heard that would not be quieted.

Nixon raged at an October 26, 1973, televised news conference that he had never seen such "outrageous, vicious, distorted . . . frantic, hysterical reporting." A few days later he felt compelled to tell an Associated Press Managing Editors convention, "I am not a crook." But in early 1974 the dam broke. A panel of experts appointed by Judge Sirica ruled that a strange 18.5-minute gap

The Weather
Today—Rain, high in the low to mid 80s, low in the mid to upper 60s. Chance of rain is 60 per cent today, 40 per cent tonight. Saturday — Cloudy, high around 80. Yesterday's temp. range, 77-68. Details, Page D19.

The Washington Post

Index — 112 Pages, 4 Sections

Amusements	D 1	Metro	D13
Classified	C14	Obituaries	D19
Comics	D20	Outdoors	C 8
Editorials	A30	Sports	C 1
Fed. Diary	D21	Style	D 1
Financial	C 9	TV-Radio	D 8

97th Year ··· No. 247 · © 1974, The Washington Post Co. FRIDAY, AUGUST 9, 1974 Phone (202) 223-6000 Classified 223-6200 Circulation 223-6100 20c Beyond Washington, Maryland and Virginia 15c

Nixon Resigns

By Carroll Kilpatrick
Washington Post Staff Writer

Richard Milhous Nixon announced last night that he will resign as the 37th President of the United States at noon today.

Vice President Gerald R. Ford of Michigan will take the oath as the new President at noon to complete the remaining 2½ years of Mr. Nixon's term.

After two years of bitter public debate over the Watergate scandals, President Nixon bowed to pressures from the public and leaders of his party to become the first President in American history to resign.

"By taking this action," he said in a subdued yet dramatic television address from the Oval Office, "I hope that I will have hastened the start of the process of healing which is so desperately needed in America."

Vice President Ford, who spoke a short time later in front of his Alexandria home, announced that Secretary of State Henry A. Kissinger will remain in his Cabinet.

The President-to-be praised Mr. Nixon's sacrifice for the country and called it "one of the very saddest incidents that I've ever witnessed."

Mr. Nixon said he decided he must resign when he concluded that he no longer had "a strong enough political base in the Congress" to make it possible for him to complete his term of office.

Declaring that he has never been a quitter, Mr. Nixon said that to leave office before the end of his term "is abhorrent to every instinct in my body."

But "as President, I must put the interests of America first," he said.

While the President acknowledged that some of his judgments "were wrong," he made no confession of the "high crimes and misdemeanors" with which the House Judiciary Committee charged him in its bill of impeachment.

Specifically, he did not refer to Judiciary Committee charges that in the cover-up of Watergate crimes he misused government agencies such as the FBI, the Central Intelligence Agency and the Internal Revenue Service.

After the President's address, Special Prosecutor Leon Jaworski issued a statement declaring that "there has been no agreement or understanding of any sort between the President or his representatives and the special prosecutor relating in any way to the President's resignation."

Jaworski said that his office "was not asked for any such agreement or understanding and offered none."

His office was informed yesterday afternoon of the President's decision, Jaworski said, but "my office did not participate in any way in the President's decision to resign."

Mr. Nixon's brief speech was delivered in firm tones and he appeared to be in complete control of his emotions. The absence of rancor contrasted sharply with the "farewell" he delivered in 1962 after being defeated for the governorship of California.

An hour before the speech, however, the President broke down during a meeting with old congressional friends and had to leave the room.

He had invited 20 senators and 26 representatives for a farewell meeting in the Cabinet room. Later, Sen. Barry M. Goldwater (R-Ariz.), one of those present, said Mr. Nixon said to them very much what he said in his speech.

"He just told us that the country couldn't operate with a half-time President," Goldwater reported. "Then he broke down and cried and he had to leave the room. Then the rest of us broke down and cried."

In his televised resignation, after thanking his friends for their support, the President concluded by saying he was leaving office "with this prayer: may God's grace be with you in all the days ahead."

As for his sharpest critics, the President said, "I leave with no bitterness toward those who have opposed me." He called on all Americans to "join together . . . in helping our new President succeed."

The President said he had thought it was his duty to persevere in office in face of the Watergate charges and to complete his term.

"I the past days, however, it has become evident to me that I no longer have a strong enough political base in the Congress to justify continuing that effort," Mr. Nixon said.

His family "unanimously urged" him to stay in office and fight the charges against him, he said. But he came to realize that he would not have the support needed to carry out the duties of his office in difficult times.

"America needs a full-time President and a full-time Congress," Mr. Nixon said. The resignation came with "a great sadness that I will not be here in this office" to complete work on the programs started, he said.

But praising Vice President Ford, Mr. Nixon said that "the leadership of America will be in good hands."

In his admission of error, the outgoing President said: "I deeply regret any injuries that may have been done in the course of the events that led to this decision."

He emphasized that world peace had been the overriding concern of his years in the White House.

When he first took the oath, he said, he made a "sacred commitment" to "consecrate my office and wisdom to the cause of peace among nations."

"I have done my very best in all the days since to be true to that pledge," he said, adding that he is now confident that the world is a safer place for all peoples.

"This more than anything is what I hoped to achieve when I sought the presidency," Mr. Nixon said. "This more than anything is what I hope will be my legacy to you, to our country, as I leave the presidency."

Noting that he had lived through a turbulent period, he recalled a statement of Theodore Roosevelt about the man "in the arena whose face is marred by dust and sweat and blood" and who, if he fails "at least fails while daring greatly."

Mr. Nixon placed great emphasis on his successes in foreign affairs. He said his administration had "unlocked the doors that for a quarter of a century stood between the United States and the People's Republic of China."

In the Mideast, he said, the United States must begin to build on the peace in that area. And with the Soviet Union, he said, the administration had begun the process of ending the nuclear arms race. The goal now, he said, is to reduce and finally destroy those arms "so that the threat of nuclear war will no longer hang over the world." The two countries, he added, "must live together in cooperation rather than in confrontation."

Mr. Nixon has served 2,026 days as the 37th President of the United States. He leaves office with 2½ years of his second term remaining to be carried out by the man he nominated to be Vice President last year.

Yesterday morning, the President conferred with his successor. He spent much of the day in his Executive Office Building hideaway working on his speech and attending to last-minute business.

At 7:30 p.m., Mr. Nixon again left the White House for the short walk to the Executive Office Building. The crowd outside the gates waved U.S. flags and sang "America" as he walked slowly up the steps, his head bowed, alone.

At the EOB, Mr. Nixon met for a little over 20 minutes with the leaders of Congress—James O. Eastland (D-Miss.), president pro tem to the Senate: Mike Mansfield (D-Mont.) Senate majority leader: Hugh Scott (R-Pa.), Senate minor-

See RESIGN, A7, Col. 1

Ford Assumes Presidency Today

By Jules Witcover
Washington Post Staff Writer

Gerald Rudolph Ford Jr., a Grand Rapids, Mich., lawyer who never aspired to national office but had it thrust upon him as a result of two of the greatest political scandals in American history, will become the 38th President of the United States at noon today.

He will be the first American President not elected to national office by the people, having been nominated Vice President by President Nixon last Oct. 12 under provisions of the new 25th Amendment to the Constitution.

Last night, immediately after watching Mr. Nixon's televised announcement that he is resigning, Ford walked onto the lawn of his Alexandria home, praised the President for deciding to step aside and pledged to continue Mr. Nixon's foreign policy "that has achieved peace and built the future blocks for peace."

Ford announced that he had asked Secretary of State Henry A. Kissinger, whom he called "a very great man," to stay on in the new administration and that Kissinger had accepted. "He and I will be working together in the pursuit of peace in the future, as we have achieved it in the past," he said.

Ford is expected to keep on and have the support of the entire Nixon Cabinet, which promises to give him an initial period of stability. But even before he is sworn in, he faces some squabbling within his own party over the question of the Vice President he will choose. Some conservatives were openly advocating yesterday that former New York Gov. Nelson A. Rockefeller be dropped from consideration.

Ford, speaking calmly before a battery of microphones and under hot TV lights in the summer night, also pledged to address himself to domestic problems by working in a "spirit of cooperation" with Congress, where he served in the House for 25 years.

"I've been very fortunate in my lifetime in public office to have a good many adversaries in the political arena in Congress," he said, "but I don't think I have a single enemy in the Congress. And the net result is that I think tomorrow I can start out working with Democrats and Republicans, in the House as well as in the Senate, to work on the problems, serious ones, which we have at home."

The Vice President called the turn of events that has brought him to the presidency "one of the most difficult and very saddest periods, and one of the very saddest incidents, that I've ever witnessed."

He said President Nixon "has made one of the greatest personal sacrifices for the country, and one of the finest personal decisions on behalf of all of us as Americans, by his decision to resign as President of the United States."

"I pledge to you tonight," he concluded, "as I will pledge tomorrow and in the future, my best efforts and cooperation and leadership and dedication to do what's good for America and good for the world."

The swearing in of the new President is to take place at noon at the White House. The ceremony will be held in the Rose Garden if the weather is good, and in the East Room if it is not. The U.S. Weather Service said last night there was a 60 per cent chance of rain today.

Ford is to speak briefly to the nationwide television audience after being sworn in, and according to congres-

See FORD, A12, Col. 1

Official White House Photo

President Nixon and daughter Julie embracing Wednesday after the President's decision to resign.

Era of Good Feeling

Congress Expects Harmony

By Spencer Rich and Richard L. Lyons
Washington Post Staff Writers

From one end of Capitol Hill to the other, members of Congress predicted last night that the presidency of Gerald R. Ford will start with a new era of good feeling between Congress and the White House, helping to heal the deep and wrenching blows the nation's government has suffered in the past two years.

The tone was set by the Democratic leaders of the House and the Senate, both of whom have served with Ford on terms of close cooperation during his 25 years in Congress before he became Vice President.

"Jerry Ford is a personal friend," said House Speaker Carl Albert (D-Okla.). "I am sure our relationship will be good."

Senate Majority Leader Mike Mansfield (D-Mont.) said, "He's a decent man. He's conservative but you know where he stands. He'd give consideration to congressional views. He would get exceptional cooperation."

The predominant reaction to President Nixon's resignation was enormous relief that Congress and the nation have been spared the agony of a House vote and Senate trial that would force each member to be counted and divide the nation.

House leaders of both parties said the tone of the President's resignation speech satisfied them and they didn't see any need to go ahead with a floor vote on impeachment. Albert said, "The manner of his leaving was, I think, one of his best efforts. I believe that bitterness was averted by the tone of his speech . . . he went out not trying to say he was framed."

See CONGRESS, A9, Col. 1

The Washington Post THE NIXON YEARS

A 24-page special section on the Nixon presidency—inside today.

A Solemn Change

Power Is Passed Quietly

By Richard Harwood and Haynes Johnson
Washington Post Staff Writers

When the day finally came, the anger and tensions and recriminations that had so enveloped this capital for weeks had been subdued in the solemnity of change. A sense of calm and a tenuous spirit of conciliation began to emerge.

There was no chorus of jubilation in Washington and no cries for vengeance or retribution. There was an absence of turmoil, mobs, violence, massive protests.

The crowds that began gathering at the White House on Tuesday remained quiet, solemn and patient. They were witnesses to history, yes, and someday they would tell their grandchildren about it. But now on this Thursday, Aug. 8, 1974, they seemed more preoccupied by personal feelings of sorrow and sadness.

"Think of it," said a tourist from Wheaton, Ill. "The most beautiful building in the country, right across the street, and the man that lives there, that has worked all his life to get there, has to give it up. . . . It's a sad terrible thing, but he brought it all on himself. But it makes me sad that he has to be humiliated like this."

Another visitor who had driven up from Myrtle Beach, S.C., was philosophical: "Our country will survive. In a way, this is like the Kennedy assassination. It is a sad time for everyone but we'll pull through."

By nightfall, the crowd had swelled to large proportions, blocking traffic on historic Pennsylvania Avenue, filling up beautiful Lafayette Park with its flower beds, benches and statues.

See DAY, A7, Col. 1

The climax of 2 years of persistent investigative reporting.

© 1974, Washington Post

in a tape recording of a June 20, 1972, Nixon–Haldeman talk (released earlier by the President) was caused by manual erasure. The House voted 410–4 to begin impeachment hearings. Nixon attempted to stem the tide on April 30 by releasing edited transcripts of some White House conversations, but he refused to give up other tapes demanded by Jaworski. The plan failed. The language used and behavior described in the widely published transcripts only caused more of his former supporters, notably the *Chicago Tribune* and *Los Angeles Times,* to call for his impeachment. In June the *Los Angeles Times* reported that Nixon, saved from formal indictment only because of his office, was named an "unindicted coconspirator" by a 19–0 vote of the Washington grand jury, which indicted Attorney General John Mitchell, Haldeman, and Erlichman (all later convicted and sent to prison).

The bipartisan House Judiciary Committee voted three articles of impeachment in late July, charging the President with obstruction of justice, abuse of power, and contempt of Congress for failure to turn over the tapes. Several hold-out Republicans on the Judiciary Committee dropped their staunch support on August 5 when Nixon, complying with the Supreme Court order, released the transcript of his June 23, 1972, talk with Haldeman. It was the "smoking gun" that proved that Nixon had been lying for 2 years to the public, his supporters, and even his lawyers about his lack of knowledge of the break-in.

The end came on the evening of August 8 when Nixon, defending his overall record as he had on so many other occasions during the 26-month ordeal, told a stunned nation he would resign effective the following noon. The next morning he gathered his cabinet and staff for an emotional farewell, which was also televised. A few minutes later Gerald Ford took the oath of office and attempted to reassure the country, saying "Our long national nightmare is over. Our Constitution works."

NIXON AND THE WAR

President Nixon announced a "Vietnamization" policy in November, 1969, under which defense of South Vietnam would be turned over to South Vietnamese troops. As U.S. troops were gradually withdrawn, the command ceased placing troops in exposed positions, as had occurred at Con Thien in 1967 and at Khesanh in 1968, in order to draw the enemy out.

One of the biggest stories of the war in Vietnam escaped the Saigon press corps at about the same time. This was the story of the massacre of civilians by U.S. troops at My Lai, for which Lt. William Calley was convicted of murder in 1971. Even though military pictures were taken at the massacre scene and floating stories existed of the "Pinkville" affair, the story did not break until October, 1969, when a free-lance writer in Washington was tipped to Calley's interrogation. The writer, former AP Pentagon reporter Seymour M. Hersh, won the 1970 Pulitzer Prize for international reporting for a story he had to market through the unknown Dispatch News Service. It was only then that major media outlets began to pick up the story. My Lai was a story Americans did not want to read, just as they had not wanted to hear Morley Safer's anguished broadcast in 1965.

Earlier that year Nixon began planning his secret bombing campaign against neutral Cambodia. For 14 months, beginning in March, 1969, American B-52s pulverized the Cambodian countryside with more than 3600 sorties and 100,000 tons of bombs. Records of the raids were falsified with the knowledge of the President and high military officers. When the story emerged in July, 1973, through the Congressional testimony of an Air Force officer—not from the news media—there was cynical speculation that Nixon's 1968 campaign pledge to use a "secret peace plan" to end the war actually masked a scheme to bomb the opposition into submission. There also were secret bombings in Laos prior to a 1971 American-South Vietnamese invasion that was a complete failure.

Thus the nation was unaware of the full scope of the Asian war when the President appeared on nationwide television on April 30, 1970, to announce the ground invasion of Cambodia. Nixon claimed that American policy since the Geneva Agreement of 1954 had been to "scrupulously respect the neutrality of the Cambodian people," but that North Vietnamese troops were using Cambodian sanctuaries to attack South Vietnam. News reports of the war's expansion triggered shock and anger throughout the nation. Protests, some violent, broke out on college campuses and there were clashes between students and local police. Peaceful marches were held in many communities. But at Kent State University in Ohio, tired and edgy National Guardsmen fired on a crowd of demonstrating students, killing four persons in the area, one walking to class. Anguish and more anger was the result; some newspapers and broadcast stations supported Nixon's criticism of ". . . these bums . . . blowing up the campuses."[13]

Journalist J. Anthony Lukas later wrote that the Cambodian and Kent State experiences, coupled with Senate setbacks, marked a turn as Nixon moved toward a policy of "positive polarization." This meant punishing his enemies and trying to capture the votes of the so-called "silent majority."[14]

In July, 1973, Murrey Marder, diplomatic correspondent for the *Washington Post,* added another dimension with his analysis that the Nixon group fought the 1971 disclosure of the Pentagon Papers—and created the "Plumbers" unit as part of a system of illegal wiretapping and break-ins—because of the risk of exposure of its Cambodian bombing campaign and other sensitive plans of the President and Secretary of State Henry Kissinger. "Facts now available not only overturn the official version of how the United States entered the Cambodian war," Marder wrote, "they illuminate the kind of thinking that led to Watergate."[15]

THE PRESS CORPS: PRIZES AND CASUALTIES

The large number of correspondents who covered a part of the Vietnam story makes it impossible to describe the accomplishments of more than a few. Heading any list, if for no other reason than seniority, would be reporters like Keyes Beech and Peter Arnett. The majority of the journalists, even some of the most well known, had relatively short stints.[16] Malcolm Browne shifted to ABC News in 1965, and later joined the *New York Times* staff. Sheehan also joined the *New York Times.* David Halberstam served briefly as a contributing editor for *Harper's* and then devoted his time to books and articles.

Among photographers who won Pulitzer Prizes for their work in Vietnam was the German-born Horst Faas, 1965 winner, who sparked the AP coverage from the beginning, was wounded in 1967, and met the Tet crisis while still convalescing. Kyoichi Sawada of UPI was the 1966 Pulitzer winner for a picture of a Vietnamese family swimming together in a river current, children's heads bobbing. Sawada won many other prizes, then was killed in 1970 in Cambodia. Toshio Sakai reported for UPI in 1968. Edward T. Adams of the AP swept all 1969 competition with his photo of the Saigon police chief executing a Viet Cong during the Tet offensive. David Douglas Duncan of *Life* won the 1967 Robert Capa Award, and Catherine Leroy, a free lancer for AP, an Overseas Press Club award.

Death struck heavily in the ranks of photographers. Besides Sawada, two other prize winners died: Larry Burrows of *Life,* in Vietnam since 1962 and twice a Capa award winner, and Henri Huet, who had worked for both UPI and AP and had won a Capa award. They died together covering the 1971 Laos invasion. UPI lost three other staff men: Hiromichi Mine, Kent Potter, and Charles Eggleston. Bernard J. Kolenberg of the AP and Dickey Chapelle of the *National Observer* died in 1965. Robert J. Ellison of Empire/Black Star was killed at Khesanh. Paul Schutzer of *Life* won a 1965 Capa award in Vietnam, then died in the 1967 Israeli war.

Bernard Fall, the distinguished historian of the Indochina war, was a 1967 casualty. *Look* editor Sam Castan was killed in 1966. Among the dead and missing in the Cambodian invasion were Frank Frosch of UPI, George Syvertsen and Gerald Miller of CBS, and Welles Hangen of NBC.

MILITARY CENSORSHIP IN VIETNAM

To the credit of the U.S. military command in Saigon, only a minimum of censorship was imposed on the Saigon press corps; its principal troubles were with the South Vietnamese government and critics at home. When bombings of North Vietnam were stepped up in 1965, and troop ships flooded in, some correspondents among the 150 Americans and 400 or more other newspeople ran afoul of military police. As casualties mounted, exact numbers were discontinued in daily briefings in favor of weekly totals, another minor complaint. After Tet, and the limiting of United States military actions, a simple field censorship was imposed that correspondents readily accepted. Major complaints were heard during news blackouts preceding the Cambodian and Laos invasions of 1970 and 1971. In the latter, restrictions on the use of helicopters by photographers cost the lives of four in the crash of a Vietnamese substitute craft. Among correspondents, François Sully had been an early victim of expulsion by the Vietnamese; Homer Bigart narrowly missed the same fate, as did Everett Martin of *Newsweek.* Jack Foisie, *Los Angeles Times;* George Esper, AP; and John Carroll, *Baltimore Sun,* had their credentials temporarily suspended by the U.S. Command for reporting military actions prematurely.

Major censorship in Vietnam affected the newspaper of the GI, the *Stars and Stripes,* and the Armed Forces Vietnam Network, supplying radio programs and news to the troops. The Armed Forces Network, particularly, fell under the heavy hand of the U.S. Command's Office of Information, which endeavored to eliminate stories that would embarrass the South Vietnamese government or adversely affect morale. The result was a rebellion of staffpeople, amid charges that the Saigon Command was violating Defense Department regulations and policy. The controversy simmered down with the censors still in control. *Stars and Stripes* weathered charges that it was undermining morale by reporting life in Vietnam "like it is." The most sharply censored press in Vietnam was, of course, the local one in Saigon, whose ranks were thinned periodically of political dissenters by charges of aid to the enemy.

DEFEAT AND SURRENDER

The end to 30 years of war came quickly when it finally came. On April 30, 1975, a handful of reporters stood on the roof of the famed Caravelle Hotel in downtown Saigon and watched helicopters carry away the last evacuees from the roof of the American Embassy. They reported that the "Stars and Stripes" no longer flew over the embattled city and that Saigon had surrendered. The final stage of the long battle for national unification was over and the vast American military machine had fallen victim to the persistence of Ho Chi Minh's followers, as had the French 21 years earlier. A demoralized South Vietnamese army, denied further U.S. aid, in turn fell victim to its own corruption, inefficiency, and poor training. The Communists unleashed full-scale attacks in January and when Danang fell on March 29 a horrified American television audience saw South Vietnamese troops fighting civilians to board transports leaving the city.

The "peace with honor" that President Nixon and Secretary of State Kissinger had proclaimed in January, 1973, was forgotten. So were the formal agreements signed in Paris by the United States, North and South Vietnam, and the Viet Cong. Pressures for negotiations had mounted after the United States mined Haiphong harbor in May, 1972 and unloaded the heaviest bombing of the entire war at Christmas time of that year. The last American combat troops had departed in August, along with a good number of journalists who moved on to other breaking stories. In March, 1973, the nation watched with mixed emotions the return of American prisoners of war, but the issue of men missing in action added to the debate over how the war should be ended and if America should pay to reconstruct the land it helped destroy. That debate continued in the 1976 election campaign.

More than 55,000 Americans died in combat in Vietnam and several hundred thousand others suffered wounds. There was no estimate of how many millions of Vietnamese, Cambodians, and Laotians were killed or wounded in the 1961 to 1975 period. There seemed to be a consensus that for the most part American journalists had brought the Vietnam dilemma home to the public, but there was continued concern over the failures of the Saigon and Washington press corps to press quickly on stories that would have given some of the fragments greater meaning, such as the Tonkin Gulf incident, My Lai, Cambodian and Laotian bombings and raids, and the truth about the bombing of North Vietnam.

It has been noted that most American journalists—with the exception of those writers and editors for alternative and underground publications—were very slow to truly understand the futility of the Vietnam experience. So were most citizens, and Congress lagged even further behind. The most severe criticism of the news media, however, might be its failure to put the war into an historical perspective. With the exception of an occasional "blockbuster" interpretative article or a television documentary, American journalists reported everything about the war except the essence of why it was being fought. David Halberstam had strong feelings about this and undoubtedly spoke for the handful of journalists who tried to explain it in the 1950s and early 1960s:

> The problem was trying to cover something every day as news when in fact the real key was that it was all derivative of the French Indo-China war, which is history. So you really should have had a third paragraph in each story which would have said, ". . . none of this means anything because we are in the same footsteps as the French and we are prisoners of their experience," but given the rules of newspaper reporting you can't really do that. That is not usually such a problem for a reporter, but to an incredible degree in Vietnam I think we were haunted and indeed imprisoned by the past.[17]

VIETNAM RECONSIDERED; LESSONS OF THE WAR

Eight years after Saigon's surrender an unlikely mix of former Vietnam correspondents, antiwar activists, spies, generals, government press spokespeople, veterans, and Vietnamese—all participants in America's Asian nightmare—met in Los Angeles to discuss the lessons of Vietnam. There were disagreements over the causes and strategies of the War, but it was clear that deep wounds had not healed and that Vietnam had indeed become a myth destined to influence the actions of future generations.[18]

Harrison Salisbury warned against accepting a "revisionist" view that the War had been lost because of "liberal" reporting and not because of blind, imperialistic motives. Salisbury described Vietnam as an "anomaly" and said that Americans should not take it for granted that their government would allow open criticism of its actions in a future conflict. He said the "Vietnam model" was there for all to see, including those who do not respect press freedoms.

Joining in the defense of critical coverage were David Halberstam, Morley Safer, John Laurence, Peter Arnett, and Garrick Utley. Adding their poignant memories were Gloria Emerson, Frances FitzGerald, and Jack Langguth, who had written a bitter denunciation of United States policy for the *New York Times Magazine* after returning home in 1965 following a tour as Saigon bureau chief.

Halberstam said that in retrospect he wished that the press corps had been much more critical during the War's opening days, from 1962 to 1964. Salisbury agreed, noting how the correspondents had been caught in the middle, pleasing neither side at home. The purge of progressives from the State Department in the late 1940s and 1950s, Halberstam said, denied Saigon reporters the kind of open-minded sources within the embassy staff that could have produced more analytical, truthful stories. On the other hand, he said, reporters did find such sources within the United States adviser groups, but generally not within higher commands. Similarities were noted in dealing with State Department officials in

Central America, where in the early 1980s, some of the same military and diplomatic planners were involved, repeating tactics that had failed in Vietnam.

Peter Braestrup's thesis, found in *Big Story,* that Saigon reporters had misrepresented the 1968 Tet offensive and had helped cause the downfall of the United States mission, was angrily refuted by Laurence and Arnett.[19] Michael Arlen, who coined the phrase "living room war" with his book, warned against continued parochialism in American reporting, characterized by only defining events in terms of U.S. interests, as in Vietnam. Film maker Peter Davis noted that after a long, articulate report viewers often knew more about the star television reporter than about the Vietnamese family being filmed, a criticism that held true later. The oldest Asian veteran, Keyes Beech, lamented the loss of Vietnam to the Communists and said that in general the coverage had been "lopsided" against United States efforts to stabilize the area.

It became clear that the intramural press war of the early 1960s had not ended and that the victims of the war—the Vietnamese and the veterans—had been ignored by the nation as a whole. While Vietnamese refugees became part of America's urban poor, thousands of angry veterans demanded recognition in the form of better hospital treatment and benefits. Lyndon Johnson's press secretary, George Reedy, and playwright Arthur Miller argued that Americans shared a collective guilt for Vietnam and that images of the War will continue to pose problems until political leaders and educators come to grips with this reality. President Reagan's claim that Vietnam had been a "noble cause," made when he visited the new Vietnam Memorial in Washington, was ridiculed. Instead, Seymour Hersh angrily said that the War had been "racist" and in this he was joined by others.

In the fall of 1983 Americans intently watched a thirteen-part documentary, "Vietnam: A Television History," on Public Broadcasting Service stations. It was the most ambitious PBS project ever undertaken, requiring nearly $5 million and six years to complete. Critics hailed it as a stunning achievement and the best film chronology of a war ever assembled. Richard Ellison was executive producer and longtime Vietnam War correspondent Stanley Karnow was chief correspondent. A ten-person team scoured film archives around the world, integrating selected historical footage with interviews of 100 Vietnamese obtained in 1981 by a PBS camera crew and interviews of 200 Americans ranging from soldiers to politicians. PBS was aided by the National Endowment for the Humanities, ABC, private foundations, and British and French networks which helped produce six of the programs. The series thus created presented dramatic but documentary accounts, challenging viewers to seek the "why?" of the American war in Vietnam and to reshape their perceptions. Earlier viewers had seen a Canadian-produced series, "Vietnam: The 10,000 Days War," also an excellent effort.

In the mid-1980s a new Vietnam scholarship was in evidence at major universities: comprehensive study of the causes and effects of the nation's unresolved experience that had left so much divisiveness. Included would be the viewing of some of the 10,000 pieces of film shown on evening news shows between 1965 and 1975. When shown along with David Douglas Duncan's haunting black-and-white photographs, the myth of Vietnam intensified with a hold hard to shake.

FORD ATTEMPTS TO RESTORE CREDIBILITY

President Ford has been the only person in United States history to serve either as vice president or as president without being elected by the people. A friendly, down-to-earth man, Ford quickly earned the praise of a press corps tired of the daily battles with the administration. He had inherited the disengagement from Vietnam, a high inflation rate, and a higher degree of public cynicism about politicians. But Ford's honeymoon ended only a month after it began, at the moment he appeared on television, September 8, 1974, to announce that he was giving Richard Nixon a full presidential pardon for any offenses he may have committed, before all investigations had been completed. J. F. terHorst, Ford's press secretary, resigned in protest and the President was subjected to criticism from all quarters. Former NBC newsman Ron Nessen was named press secretary and served with mixed success, frequently butting heads with a press corps whose skepticism had been quickly revived. It was during Ford's tenure that the nation's institutions, including the news media, would undergo a wholesale reappraisal of basic values. In this post-Watergate era, Ford was credited with bringing to the White House a humility it had lacked for some time.

Ford held thirty-nine regular press conferences during his busy 2½ years in office: five in the balance of 1974, nineteen in 1975, and fifteen more in 1976. A stubborn man, he spoke bluntly and plainly, maintaining his conservative credentials. The Nixon pardon hurt his credibility, as did his link to the Nixon years in general. His selection of Nelson A. Rockefeller as Vice President was one move toward unity in his party and the nation, and Ford gave the country some reassurance in that respect.

The 1976 campaign began in August with President Ford thirteen points behind in his bid for his own term. It ended with Georgia's former governor Jimmy Carter's winning the presidency by two poll points and 297 electoral votes, a squeak-through majority. Carter was hurt by media overexposure and repeated charges that he was "fuzzy" on the main issues, despite his issuance of dozens of position papers by his staff. He was also attacked for granting a candid interview with *Playboy* magazine. Ford was belittled for a generally dull performance, and the "trivialization of the news" included accounts of his hitting his head on plane doors and slipping several times. Also hurtful was his association with Earl Butz, the Secretary of Agriculture, whose antiblack comment was reported by former Nixon aide John Dean in *Rolling Stone* and explained more fully by *New Times.* Media critics said events like this distracted from major foreign-policy and domestic issues that needed further amplification.[20]

Three nationally televised debates between Carter and Ford, and one between vice presidential candidates Walter Mondale and Robert Dole, gave millions of Americans the chance to judge the candidates for themselves. Sponsored by the League of Women Voters, the debates (called press conferences by critics who wanted point-by-point challenges by the men) allowed Carter the opportunity to demonstrate his knowledge of foreign-policy issues and his capacity to handle himself under pressure against the more experienced Ford. After a shaky start in the first debate, Carter came on strong in the final two and headed into election day with a slight buildup in poll points, which he held.

"THE BOYS ON THE BUS": PRESIDENTIAL CAMPAIGNS

The long, grueling presidential contests of the 1970s were marred by the lavish spending of advertising monies designed to package the candidates for television and the preoccupation of many press-corps members with the contenders' personal styles rather than the substance of ideas. At times the storytellers became the story, as hordes of tired journalists chased the equally exhausted politicians from dawn to midnight, through state after state.

The tendency of the journalists to report basically the same things gave rise to the terms "pack" and "herd" journalism, while the soft content of much of the reporting led to comments about "news trivia" and "junk news." Coverage devoted to the latest public-opinion poll was called "horserace" reporting. Feeding the American public a steady diet of news were the well-known national political reporters and columnists who joined the circuit for the pivotal moments; the regular reporters for prestige newspapers and magazines and a few smaller papers; the network television and radio correspondents; and the handful of press-association reporters.

It was clear that the whistle-stop technique was still a basic part of political campaigning even if candidate appearances were arranged in part to entice coverage by the ever-present network television cameras. Although research indicated that most voters cast their ballots following traditional lines and did not make up or change their minds during actual campaigns, the number of close elections (1948, 1960, 1968, 1976) showed media influences to be crucially important.

The newspaper reporter with the most personal influence on the coverage by the traveling press corps was R. W. ("Johnny") Apple, Jr., of the *New York Times,* who had been with the paper since 1963. Because the *Times* was the only paper regularly available on many stops, Apple's stories provided continuity for the group. An industrious, aggressive man, Apple worked around the clock to provide the *Times* with updated information and fresh insights. Key press association correspondents were Walter Mears of the AP and Arnold Sawislak of UPI.

Pounding out their columns and background pieces were David Broder of the *Washington Post,* considered by many the most influential political columnist; Peter Lisagor of the *Chicago Daily News;* Rowland Evans and Robert Novak of the *Chicago Sun-Times,* whose column was syndicated in hundreds of papers; the syndicated George Will, a relative newcomer hailed for his fresh writing style and balanced thought; and Robert Donovan of the *Los Angeles Times,* another veteran of the Truman days, a distinguished political writer. Some of the most astute commentaries were by the *New Yorker*'s Elizabeth Drew, who turned her diaries into a book.

"The Boys on the Bus," as they were called by Timothy Crouse in his classic description of the 1972 campaign,[21] received a great amount of criticism after both elections. They were accused of following the lead of a Johnny Apple or a Walter Means and of not developing their own story angles, partly because of laziness and partly because their editors also followed what the *New York Times,* AP or UPI said. Some writers were said to be partial to a particular candidate; some were said to be rude, arrogant, and too ambitious; others were

CBS

Pauline Frederick *(left)*, at PBS after an NBC career, and Elizabeth Drew, *New Yorker* political writer, were two of the panelists at the Ford-Carter debates.

said to be easily manipulated by candidates or their campaign aides. Suggestions were made for more pool reporting and less emphasis on routine speeches.

The 1972 campaign was marked by rough attacks on Senator Edmund Muskie in New Hampshire (later attributed in part to the White House dirty-tricks campaign); Senator George McGovern's fumbles near the end of an otherwise well-organized campaign, including his agony in dropping Senator Thomas Eagleton as his running mate after Eagleton's previous history of nervous disorder was revealed; McGovern's charges, largely ignored, that Nixon's White House was the most corrupt in the nation's history; Nixon's skillful use of the media in an effort to avoid public contact; Nixon's massive war chest of political contributions.

In 1976 Jimmy Carter had an advantage. Not only had he and his staff read Crouse's book, but they had also begun their campaign early, as had McGovern. As early as October, 1975, Apple of the *New York Times* was writing that Carter had a chance. The snowball grew (some cynics said because the news media have a way of making predictions come true), and Carter entered every one of twenty-six statewide Democratic primaries, the most ever held. However, the campaign coverage was criticized as much as before. "Never was so much that meant so little presented in such technologically perfect fashion to such a widely yawning public," one critic wrote.[22]

Four years later and deeply involved with the Iranian crisis, Carter conducted a "Rose Garden" campaign, fully aware that a nontraveling incumbent could obtain as much television coverage as the opponent. Nixon and Ford had limited their traveling time in 1972 and 1976. During the 1980 struggle it became apparent that candidates Carter, Reagan, and Anderson did not worry about access to print reporters, but instead spent every spare minute hurrying from one media market to the next. One reporter calculated that during a 7-day trip to nine states, Reagan spent only 170 minutes speaking in public. Carter spent more time in public, perhaps 3 hours per day, but only a few minutes were devoted to answering reporters' questions. Everything was for the camera.[23]

Veteran print reporters spent much less time on the campaign trail and television network reporters switched off, instead of sticking with one candidate. The preoccupation with television meant that syndicated columnists and political writers had to resort to specially arranged interviews. At times these "exclusives" given to selected writers served the same purpose as full press conferences, but they could also be part of the candidate's control of the news flow.

The 1984 campaign began shortly after Reagan took office, with Democratic candidates making full use of television appearances in order to drum up support for the long presidential primary season. A weary and cynical public braced for another round of television and politics, while the press corps prepared for both the challenge and the frustration that accompanies an American presidential race.

THE CARTER YEARS: THE IRANIAN CRISIS

Carter's close victory brought a new style to the White House. Publicly dedicating himself to total honesty with the public, the religious-minded Carter lost no time in trying to continue where Ford left off in encouraging faith in the nation's cherished institutions. He began holding regular news conferences every 2 weeks trying to avoid frequent charges of the campaign days that he was less than precise in his answers. As a further step in communicating with the public, in March of 1977 he conducted a 2-hour "phone-in" from the Oval Office. Persons lucky enough to have their calls get through the jammed circuits found themselves talking first to Walter Cronkite and then to the President.

Carter's years in office were marked by patient attempts to convince the American people to believe in themselves and in his programs. With longtime aide Jody Powell serving as press secretary, Carter made an attempt to be open to the press. He held up well despite the growing inquisitorial nature of the televised news conferences. His major accomplishments came in the field of foreign affairs: In 1978 he successfully negotiated the gradual return of the Panama Canal to Panama, earning the respect of the peoples of Central and Latin America. Full diplomatic relations were opened with the People's Republic of China that year. It was Carter's persistence that allowed President Anwar Sadat of Egypt and Prime Minister Menachem Begin of Israel to finally agree on peace terms during talks at Camp David in 1979. But the President's first national address on the energy crisis failed when his emotional claim that his program was "the moral equivalent of war" fell on deaf ears. Carter's image also sagged whenever the antics of his troublesome brother Billy became news. Later Billy Carter's financial dealings were categorized by the news media as "Billygate."

Public confidence in Carter dropped further in November, 1979, when the American Embassy in Tehran was seized by supporters of the Ayatollah Khomeini and its American occupants were held captive. The humiliating event found the United States powerless to act. The President had bungled his way into the

The Winchester Sun
Hostages freed
Reagan becomes president

The Evening Gazette
Reagan Takes the Oath As the Hostages Are Freed
New Leader Heralds 'Era Of Renewal'
Freedom Jet Heads On Flight to Algie
Proposition 2½

Charleston Daily Mail
They're Coming Home!
Inauguration Crowns Reagan's Long Quest

Roanoke Times & World-News
Ex-hostages arrive in Germany
Reagan vows 'national renewa

Richmond Times-Dispatch
Hostages Set Free After 444 Days; Reagan Is Sworn In, Sees New Day
Domestic Issues Are Uppermost
Release Follows Inauguration
Carter Will Fly Today To Greet Returnees

The Morning Union
THE ORDEAL ENDS, A NEW ERA BEGINS
Reagan promises 'renewal'
Hostages arrive in Germany
Hostages freed

The Milwaukee Journal
The waiting is over
52 Americans flown out of Tehran after 444 days of captivity
Americans prepare a festive welcome
Spare parts for military are in deal
Reagan sworn in as 40

The Evening Bulletin
Hostages fly to freedom
The hostage ordeal ends as Ronald Reagan's presidency begins
A nation celebrates
Reagan signs U.S. hiring freeze after inauguration

The Birmingham News
It's over: Hostages fly out of Tehran, ending 444 days of captivity
Reagan takes oath, promises era of renewal

The Montgomery Advertiser
Reagan takes presidential mantle
Carter returns to Plains
Hostage release 'makes day perfect'
Carter departs Oval Office with greetings

How Some Newspapers Played It

The twin events of Ronald Reagan's inauguration and the release by Iran of the American hostages caused a dilemma for many newspaper editors: Which story was more important? In the montage above, we show various ways a number of papers played the story.

The two stories produced an emotional outburst of headlines and color displays rarely seen in journalism.

Some newspapers used "yellow ribbon" graphics carrying out the symbol that had been adopted by many Americans to show their concern for the hostages during the long ordeal. The symbol was borrowed from the popular song, "Tie a Yellow Ribbon 'Round the Old Oak Tree."

AP Log

disaster, failing to either defend the Embassy or remove its occupants after pondering the likelihood of a takeover. In April, 1980, an attempt at a dramatic helicopter rescue ended in disaster in the Iranian desert when the mechanical failure of three of eight helicopters forced Carter to abort the mission. Eight Americans died when two helicopters collided in the confusion of fleeing the area. Carter was also severely criticized for not attempting to support the Shah of Iran prior to Khomeini's seizure of power. That criticism came from Nixon, Kissinger, and others who had formed close friendships with the Shah and tolerated his secret police tactics at a time when the United States had few friends in that part of the world and supposed the Shah was a military bulwark.

Edward Kennedy challenged Carter for the Democratic nomination in 1980, causing great anger in the White House. During this time of enormous pressure, with Carter monitoring the Iranian situation daily, he was obliged to combat the Kennedy threat. Exhibiting a toughness that some characterized as "mean," Carter triumphed over Kennedy, who could not shed the image of Chappaquiddick. A damaging blow had been struck to Kennedy in November, 1979, during a CBS interview with Roger Mudd, when he failed to answer basic questions about that 1969 tragedy and about why he was better qualified than Carter for the presidency. The poor television performance, in contrast to his public speeches, haunted Kennedy during the campaign. Carter triumphed at the convention, but the party was split and lacked enthusiasm for his reelection.

Facing Ronald Reagan in the fall campaign, Carter attempted to portray Reagan as a dangerous man who would lead the nation to the brink of war. He said that Reagan would divide the nation along religious and racial lines. But the strategy backfired, as Reagan came across on television as pleasant and open. Finally, on October 28, Reagan and Carter met in a debate from which independent candidate John Anderson had been excluded. While Carter tried to draw a clear distinction between himself and the former California governor on such issues as nuclear proliferation and social security, Reagan was able to reduce the entire campaign to a final series of questions: "Are you better off than you were four years ago . . . Is America as respected throughout the world as it was? Do you feel that our security is safe, that we're as strong as we were four years ago?" (It was later revealed that the Reagan camp had had access to Carter's position papers prior to the debate.)

The voters, asked in television advertisements to choose on this basis, decided that Ronald Reagan would be the next president. In a final dramatic irony, the Iranians punished Carter by not releasing the fifty-two hostages until the moment that Reagan was being sworn into office on January 20, 1981. Carter had urged patience despite nightly television scenes of anti-American hatred, and he had suffered through 444 days of waiting. For weeks there had been rumors of an imminent release of the hostages. Only 33 minutes after Reagan took the oath of office, the flight to freedom began, with excited reporters breaking into the inauguration coverage to give the latest details. The next morning many of the nation's newspapers carried huge two-line headlines and two photos, balancing the competing stories. The *New York Times* summed it up: "Reagan Takes Oath as 40th President; Promises an 'Era of National Renewal'; Minutes Later, 52 Hostages in Iran Fly to Freedom After 444-Day Ordeal."[24]

THE MIDDLE EAST AND CENTRAL AMERICA

War correspondents rushed to the Middle East in 1956 when Israel, threatened since it became an independent state in 1948, attacked Egypt by land while Britain and France sought to occupy the Suez Canal. Eisenhower and State Secretary Dulles refused to support their allies and forced a UN peacekeeping arrangement. The debacle brought down the government of Anthony Eden and hastened the crisis in France over Algerian independence and the rise of General De Gaulle to power in 1958.

The war that broke out in the African Congo in 1960 was covered by a small band of newsmen. Two, Henry N. Taylor of Scripps-Howard and George Clay of NBC, were shot and killed; Sanche de Gramont of the *New York Herald Tribune* was injured. Lynn Heinzerling of the Associated Press won a Pulitzer Prize for his reporting. Ray Wilson of NBC had to eat his UN press pass to appease some Congolese soldiers.

The focus swung back to the Middle East as the standoff between Israel and Egypt resulted in the six-day war of 1967, won by Israeli planes and tanks before correspondents could catch their breaths. Ted Yates, an NBC producer, and Paul Schutzer, *Life* photographer, were U.S. casualties in the blitz war. Egypt and Syria launched a surprise attack in 1973, temporarily pushing the Israelis back and causing concern about that tiny nation's ability to defend itself. The threat of major war was present but Israel regained the lost territory and eventually a United Nations cease-fire agreement was signed. The American audience became used to seeing television scenes from the Suez Canal or Golan Heights areas, as reporters tried to give some meaning to the fast-moving story. The most shocking story broadcast was from Munich during the 1972 Olympic Games when terrorists murdered Israeli athletes in the Olympic village. That plus other raids by various Palestinian guerrilla groups and Israeli retaliation attacks in neighboring countries kept the Middle East in a state of high tension.

Occupation of northern Lebanon by Syria and creation of a Palestine Liberation Organization governmental headquarters in Beirut led to a 1982 Israeli decision to oust the PLO army from Lebanon. The Israelis overran southern Lebanon and captured Beirut in heavy fighting. A brutal massacre of refugee Palestinians in a Beirut camp by anti-PLO militia led to the sending of an international peacekeeping force including U.S. Marines. Loren Jenkins of the *Washington Post,* and Thomas Friedman of the *New York Times* shared the 1983 Pulitzer international reporting award for their stories of the fighting. AP photographer Bill Foley won for his pictures of the massacre camp. Walter Wisniewski and Jack Redden of UPI received the Overseas Press Club award for their massacre coverage.

American interventions in the Caribbean and Central American areas have occurred steadily during the twentieth century, often in support of U.S. corporate investments and trade profits. Most recently, the CIA sent men to Guatemala in 1954 to overthrow a democratically-elected liberal president; the ill-fated U.S.-sponsored "Bay of Pigs" invasion of Cuba failed to upset Fidel Castro in 1961; and troops were sent to the Dominican Republic in 1965 to bolster a right wing dictatorship there. The CIA was involved in the overthrow of the democratically-elected leftist government of Chile in 1973. And U.S. support was given to dictatorships in Nicaragua, El Salvador, and Honduras. In one brighter moment, President Carter negotiated Senate approval of a treaty restoring sovereignty over the Panama Canal to Panama, winning that country's friendship.

In 1979 American attention was focused on Nicaragua and the impending overthrow of the corrupt Somoza dictatorship, which U.S. policy had maintained in control of a country dominated by American military thinking since U.S. Marines searched for the "bandit" Sandino in the 1920s. The deliberate murder of ABC correspondent Bill Stewart by Nicaraguan soldiers as he walked toward a checkpoint furnished an on-camera killing for U.S. television audiences.

With the establishment of the Sandinista junta government in Nicaragua, attention shifted to the chaotic civil war in El Salvador. There in 1980 an inept government, a merciless military force, and a lawless rightwing "death squad" operation brought death to thousands of civilians, including democratic-minded intellectuals, newspapermen, rebellious peasants, and Catholic priests including Archbishop Oscar Romero. Out of the events emerged a familiar pattern of U.S. thinking: The dissenting intellectuals, churchmen, and peasants were perceived as a "left" tainted with "Marxist" thinking and Cuban-Soviet support which endangered hemispheric stability as it sought to rid itself of the dominant "right" composed of wealthy land owners, the military, and rightwing radicals. The Reagan administration steadily increased its support of the "right" and raised alarms over the Sandinistas in Nicaragua and the revolutionists in El Salvador as it increased the number of American military advisers involved. The murders of four American women, including three nuns, and two U.S. agricultural aid workers aroused strong opposition to U.S. military involvement, particularly in Roman Catholic church circles, where the problems of peasant poverty and oppression were recognized as the primary ones.

The number of foreign correspondents in El Salvador grew steadily during 1981 and 1982. During national balloting in March 1982 a peak of nearly 800 was reached, 450 from the U.S. ABC had a team of fifty, led by correspondent Richard Threlkeld and analyst James Wooten. CBS had thirty-six, led by Diane Sawyer and Bill Moyers; NBC thirty-six, headed by Tom Brokaw. PBS sent Hodding Carter and Cable News Network the veteran Peter Arnett.

Women correspondents provided some of the most graphic descriptions of the bloody killings of civilians. Among them were Shirley Christian of the *Miami Herald,* 1981 Pulitzer prize winner; Beth Nissen of *Newsweek;* Joanne Omang of the *Washington Post;* Laurie Becklund of the *Los Angeles Times;* Lynda Schuster of the *Wall Street Journal;* Anne Nelson, freelancer and *Nation* writer; Geri Smith and Cindy Karp of UPI, Hilary Brown of ABC News, Zoe Trujillo of Cable News Service, and once-wounded Susan Meiselas, Magnum photographer. Karen DeYoung, *Washington Post* Latin-American correspondent and later foreign editor, narrowly escaped death in a 1983 Nicaraguan ambush.

Among other El Salvador correspondents winning attention were Raymond Bonner of the *New York Times,* Loren Jenkins of the *Washington Post,* and James Dickman of the *Dallas Times Herald,* who won the 1983 Pulitzer prize for feature photography with a special report on that country's dilemma. Nine foreign correspondents, including a Dutch television crew of four ambushed by government troops, had died by 1983 in El Salvador. Killed on the Honduran-

Nicaraguan border in June 1983 were Dial Torgerson, longtime and trusted *Los Angeles Times* Latin-American correspondent, and freelance photographer Richard Cross.

REAGAN AND THE MEDIA: THE STRUGGLE FOR ACCESS

Ronald Reagan was granted a long and fairly happy honeymoon by the Washington press corps. The President's easy manner and ready smile made him a likable figure, and the excitement of a change in administrations was a welcome relief from the tenseness of the final Carter years. The honeymoon was extended by the attempt on Reagan's life March 30, 1981, when the President was shot outside of a Washington hotel. The President's recovery period, marked by his concern for the seriously injured press secretary James Brady, was relatively free of criticism. White House regulars even agreed to raise their hands instead of jumping up to ask questions at press conferences. But by October, after 8 months in office, it had become apparent that Reagan was the most inaccessible of the modern presidents, with the exception of Nixon during the Watergate period. At that point he had held only three press conferences, while Carter had held fourteen and Ford twelve. Reagan was to average about eight per year.

One reason for Reagan's unfavorable press-conference record was his knowledge that he often fared poorly at them. Unlike Carter, who showed up with facts and figures, Reagan tried to handle questions that he seemed unprepared to answer. On several occasions he made historical errors: He once said, for example, that President Kennedy had sent combat troops to Vietnam when he meant President Johnson. Reagan's aides tried to protect him from meeting with reporters at airports or prior to public appearances because his off-the-cuff comments often made embarrassing headlines. In turn, Reagan complained about the coverage of his administration, particularly by television. He once asked, "Is it news that some fellow out in South Succotash has just been laid off . . .?" The comment was in reference to frequent television interviews with unemployed workers and charts showing rising unemployment figures. The *Los Angeles Times* replied: "The answer is, it is news. It is news in Los Angeles, Detroit, New York and, yes, South Succotash. Unemployment is news." The editorial was headlined "Let Them Eat Succotash," and an adjoining cartoon by Paul Conrad, captioned "Reagan Country", showed a sign reading "Welcome to South Succotash, Population: 9,000,000 Unemployed."[25]

Such editorial barbs increased from 1981 on as Reagan seemed to lose control of events. The recession worsened, before leveling off into a period of uncertainty. Numerous leaks from within the Reagan administration—many of them from the White House itself—brought consternation.

A candid *Atlantic Monthly* interview with David Stockman, the President's budget director, brought deep embarrassment because the piece detailed Stockman's pessimistic views of Reagan's much-heralded economic planning from the supply-side, known widely as Reaganomics. Although the President became angry over these events in private, he tried to maintain an optimistic outlook with the press. He often used homilies and simple examples to get his points across. During nationwide addresses he used maps and charts to explain his plans. Critics said that Reagan's simple view of life and good feelings about himself, dating from his Hollywood days and his switch from progressive Democrat to conservative Republican, prevented him from seeing failures in his own programs and in relationships with overseas allies.

The President's disregard for the press and the public's right to learn about its government was shown in a number of directives that raised serious questions about Reagan's basic attitudes. One new order protecting classified materials said that government employees suspected of leaking classified materials could be required to take lie-detector tests. Those refusing could be demoted or fired. The order also gave federal agencies the power to review and approve articles, books, and speeches by employees or former employees. Thousands of federal employees would be required to sign such secrecy agreements.

Earlier Reagan had launched attacks against the Freedom of Information Act (FOIA), increasing the authority of federal agencies to exclude materials from the FOIA provisions and encouraging agencies to charge fees for information sought. In its 1982 Freedom of Information report card, the Society of Professional Journalists, Sigma Delta Chi, gave the President an "F." The nation's largest journalistic society noted that the Reagan administration gained passage of a bill providing harsh penalties for anyone reporting the name of a past or present CIA agent, regardless of whether the information was already in the public domain or had little value.

As Reagan's formal meetings with the White House correspondents lessened, they met with Larry Speakes, the deputy press secretary (Brady kept his title but was not able to work because of his severe head injuries), who tried to explain the President's reactions to events. This was a thankless job, with ABC's Sam Donaldson, UPI's Helen Thomas, and others complaining about the lack of presidential exposure. It was noted, however, that the press did a poor job of explaining the President's remoteness to the public.[26]

Reagan won the presidency by pledging to end the New Deal legacy of his former hero, Franklin D. Roosevelt, and to replace it with his brand of economic theology. However, as historian Henry Steele Commanger noted, Reagan's ideas were rooted in Herbert Spencer's nineteenth-century concepts and Social Darwinism: "the application of the theory of the survival of the fittest to society and the economy. In the realm of economics, this principle requires that government keep 'hands off' and give free rein to the competitive instinct nourished by individualism."[27] The result was a strong public feeling that Reagan favored the rich at the expense of the poor, despite his stated concerns for the less fortunate.

Reagan struggled not to deeply offend the right-wing of the Republican party, led by North Carolina Senator Jesse Helms. He made pleas for decency in movies, prayer in public schools, an end to most abortions, and vigorous opposition to guerrilla activity in Central America that threatened American financial interests. But his rigidity—particularly in the area of arms control—alienated many moderate Republicans. Reagan officials said that they believed that the Soviet Union was developing a "first-strike capability", that it was building its defenses so Russia could attack the United States without fear of being completely destroyed in the inevitable counterattack. Reagan strategists indicated that they believed that the United States could survive such an attack and that there could be a "winner" in a nuclear exchange. Thus, the United States could begin planning for a "first-strike capability", something foreign to the thinking of past defense planners who advocated "détente" instead of nuclear brinksmanship. *Los Angeles Times* reporter Robert Scheer produced notes and tapes from numerous interviews with Reagan, Vice President George Bush, and others, proving that the nation's top leaders were thinking "the unthinkable."[28]

Reagan's public statements were marked by the increased use of strong anti-Communist rhetoric. The President's adviser on national security matters, William Clark, encouraged the view that the struggle with the Communists was "essentially a struggle between right and wrong, good and evil"—a throwback to the 1950s. Arguing against a freeze on the construction of nuclear weapons, Reagan said the *Bible* called on people to oppose "sin," in this case the actions of the Soviet Union. Opponents said that this all-or-nothing approach would drive the Soviets away from any meaningful chance of compromise in the nuclear arms race.

Meanwhile, another old California friend, Attorney General William French Smith, was instrumental in the Reagan administration's methodical closing off of information sources and attacks on media outlets supporting such activities as the nuclear freeze. As the question of the President's effectiveness and credibility became an open concern, it was apparent that Reagan, his closest advisers, and influential campaign supporters had a "persistent distaste for the raucous, untidy, rambunctious aspects of democracy,"[29] including the American news media system that reported disturbing and unwelcome news.

THE PUBLIC PERCEPTION OF MEDIA CREDIBILITY

According to a 1983 Roper Organization poll, the public considered television the most-relied-upon medium for news: Television was named by 41 percent of the respondents as the prime source of news; 21 percent named newspapers. The number ranking television as the most believable rose to 53 percent, while those so ranking newspapers stayed at 22 percent. Television was found to be the main source for national and state political news, but newspapers regained the lead in the local political category. The Roper polls, which began in 1959, showed that television ousted newspapers as the prime news source in 1963. Other polls showed the news media's ranking ahead of other institutions—schools, local government, police, business, organized religion—in public esteem, despite a disenchantment with the news media.

News media ethics became a popular discussion topic, not only in journalism classrooms but on television and in the movies. Viewers of the *Lou Grant* show were educated about serious ethical considerations in the newspaper business. The film *Absence of Malice* also spurred comment about the supposed motives of reporters and editors. *Network* was a scathing attack on television practices. Newspapers suffered the most, however, following a number of embarrassing disclosures. In 1981 *Washington Post* reporter Janet Cooke was forced to return her Pulitzer Prize after it was learned that she had fabricated her story about an 8-year-old heroin addict. A *New York Daily News* columnist was fired after he made up a story about British troops fighting Irish youths in Belfast during the height of anti-British feeling. News of the newspaper mishaps was, of course, spread by television.

Norman E. Isaacs, the able editor of the *Louisville Courier-Journal* who later became director of the National News Council, summed up his disenchantment with the news media after nearly 9 years with the Council. Nearly 7000 complaints had been received and more than 800 were either settled through Council mediation or dealt with in open meetings. Isaacs said in 1982 that the great majority of journalists involved resisted being told of complaints. A large number of editors allowed reporters to grant confidentialty to sources without serious reason, he said, adding to the credibility problem. Worse, he said, there appeared to be an insatiable desire to gain scoops at the expense of careful journalism.[30] The pressure to win prizes had led to the Janet Cooke fiasco at the *Washington Post* and mistakes at other papers that were quickly perceived by readers.

The push for ratings in television news was commonly criticized, to little avail. Instead station managers persisted in advertising their anchorpersons in local newspapers and television supplements, often making them more important than the news being covered. Television news was the most believable medium, but the audience did not have a great deal of respect for the methods of presentation, particularly the so-called "top-forty" approach to news in which plenty of action film was strung together with short bits of factual information.

Poor practices in some quarters hurt the efforts of responsible journalists to discuss public issues with authority and credibility. Knowledgeable politicians exploited the public's general lack of confidence in the media. But at the same time government leaders themselves were having a difficult time gaining the admiration of the public. The great importance of a period of "crisis of credibility," no matter how painful or embarrassing, is that people learn anew the lesson that all freedoms are dependent on freedom of speech and press.

TELEVISION: CRITICISM AND AUDIENCES

The emotions of the 1960s brought the first strong criticisms of television. Southerners charged that network film crews had distorted the racial picture during the Freedom Rides; blacks and whites alike were angered by coverage of the urban riots; doves and hawks both thought the Vietnam news to be slanted; some veteran broadcasters, like Fred W. Friendly, thought their bosses sought ratings at the expense of public service; conservatives led by former Vice President Agnew thundered against the perceived "liberal bias" of the commentators and reporters covering the Nixon administration. The criticism of general programming, given impetus by FCC Chairman Newton Minow's "vast wasteland" speech in 1961, soon spread to every area of the system.

But in the 1970s, the criticisms began to focus on the very essence of television news, the variables that make it what it is. Edith Efron had written *The News Twisters* in 1971 as an attempt to discredit the major networks, but in 1973 media critic Edward J. Epstein published his scholarly *News From Nowhere,* which simply showed how economic and logistical factors as much as subjective judgments severely hampered the scope and quality of television news.[31] Then followed a rash of criticism in popular publications of the so-called "happy-talk" format devised by ABC for its stations; the hiring of nonjournalistic consultants to advise on the hiring of anchorpersons, the designing of fancy sets, and the length of story and film segments (the "top-forty" concept); the overuse of "pretty faces"; the team approach in which several persons sit around a table; and the extensive use of feature material in a magazine format.[32]

Leading newscasters like Cronkite and Brinkley readily admitted the weaknesses of the existing system; Cronkite severely criticized the "pretty faces" on local television shows and pushed for a 1-hour evening news show in an effort to avoid some of the superficiality. That extra half-hour would have come from local station time, however, and plans for 1-hour news shows were shelved by all three networks in 1977. To the consternation of traditionalists, the major gains in ratings were made by those local stations that pushed ahead with the lighter approach to news; specialists lined up to report on health tips, consumer news, and legal aid, as well as "people in the news." At the network level the major victim was the documentary of the Murrow-Friendly type.

The economic power of television was startling. So was its coverage of public events. Television had recorded massive audiences for news events since the 1950s. Some 60 million Americans saw President Eisenhower inaugurated in 1953. At least 85 million saw one of the "Great Debates" between John Kennedy and Richard Nixon in 1960. John Glenn's first manned orbital flight drew 135 million persons to the edge of their chairs in 1962. When news of President Kennedy's assassination in 1963 became known, the New York City television audience jumped from 30 percent to 70 percent and rose to 93 percent during the funeral service when for a few moments the nation fell silent.

When men first walked on the moon in 1969 and live television pictures were transmitted to Earth, some 125 million Americans saw the climactic broadcast, and a satellite network carried the pictures to an eventual world audience estimated at 500 million. Satellite coverage of World Cup matches in 1970 brought soccer to an estimated 900 million persons. President Nixon's China trip in 1972, the Olympic tragedy in Munich that same year, the signing of the 1973 Vietnam peace accords in Paris, and other international events continued to produce giant audiences. In the United States, 130 million persons watched some part of Nixon's resignation in 1974. The attempt on President Reagan's life on March 31, 1981, exposed a huge audience to the inevitable problems of covering fast-breaking confusing stories. There was much misinformation, including the false report of press secretary James Brady's death. It was first reported that the President had not been struck, and later there were conflicting stories about the extent of his injuries. An equally confused White House staff shared the blame. The wounding of Pope John Paul II in Rome and the killing of Egyptian President Anwar Sadat near Cairo also produced massive worldwide audiences, as did coverage of the battle between Britain and Argentina over the Falkland Islands, the Israeli invasion of Lebanon, and the guerrilla war in Central America.

In the non news field, 110 million persons saw a return of *Gone with the Wind* in 1976; the following year *Roots,* the tracing of black history, set a number of records for that period. During the eight consecutive nights that it was aired it was seen by an estimated 130 million persons. ABC repeated its success in 1983 with a week-long showing of *The Winds of War,* which attracted the second largest miniseries audience ever recorded: 54 percent of television sets tuned on, compared to 66 percent for *Roots.* But because there were 83.3 million television households in 1983, compared with 71.2 million in 1977, more persons saw at least part of one segment of *The Winds of War,* about 140 million.

The highest rated single program in television history was the 2½-hour final episode of CBS' 11-year series *M*A*S*H,* shown February 28, 1983, to 77 percent of all U.S. homes watching television that evening.[33] More than 125 million persons saw some part of the program, more than had watched any World Series game, Super Bowl, or other athletic contest. The show also set advertising records; a 30-second commercial cost $450,000. *M*A*S*H,* the story of the Korean War exploits of the 4077th Mobile Army Surgical Hospital team, starred Alan Alda and brought home with unusual perception and candor the tragedy, humor, and, above all, poignance of wartime experiences. It was the survivor of a number of relevant 1970s shows, including *Archie Bunker, Maude,* and *The Mary Tyler Moore Show.*

The previous record for a single program was held by the 1981 segment of the *Dallas* series during which the villain, J. R., was shot by an unknown person. Like *M*A*S*H,* there was a long advertising build-up for that show, which received a 76 share. However, the "rating" for *M*A*S*H* (the measurement of all television sets as compared with the "share" of those sets turned on) was 60.3 and for *Dallas* 53.3. Ranking behind *Dallas* were the last episode of *Roots* and the first two parts of *The Winds of War.*[34]

Technically, however, the all-time record for a single program belonged to a January, 1953, segment of the *I Love Lucy* show during which Lucille Ball, pregnant in real life, gave birth to a son. The rating was 71.8 and the share was 92 percent. However, there were only 21.2 million television homes at the time.[35]

CBS NEWS

Dan Rather inherited Cronkite's anchor chair at *The CBS Evening News* after signing an $8 million 5-year contract, and he immediately felt the tremendous pressure of trying to maintain the CBS lead in the ratings. Getting off to a slow start, with the audience taking time to get used to Rather's quick delivery, CBS slipped behind briefly before Rather's show picked up steam. Plugging in longer stories, some 5 minutes in length, the CBS team of 125 writers, reporters, producers, executives, and researchers soon opened up a healthy lead over ABC, with NBC falling into third place. Rather had clearly become more comfortable with his nightly audience. His trademarks were his smile and his pullover sweaters.

In effect, however, the three evening news shows were similar in content, quality, and personalities. The networks began to raid each other, breaking up some old reporting teams. Familiar faces from one network would suddenly appear on another, reflecting the higher salaries being offered.

One of those wooed to CBS twice was Bill Moyers, a former press secretary

Dan Rather.
CBS

Diane Sawyer.
CBS

to Lyndon Johnson who became alienated by the Vietnam War and accepted the publisher's chair at *Newsday.* From there Moyers went to public television, where his sharp intellect produced some moving looks at world events. He briefly became involved with *CBS Reports* before returning to public television for the production of *Bill Moyers' Journal,* a long-running series dealing with current events and the human condition. Later his seventeen-part *Creativity* series traced the achievements of productive people. Finally he was back with CBS, this time giving nightly news commentaries, in Sevareid's old spot, planning documentaries, and hosting *Our Times.* His frank approach to life, keen perception, and Texas populism combined to make him one of the most respected of television's observers. In his warm, soft style, he likened television to a "national campfire" around which the nation sits listening. But the minister's son could be severe with those who pushed for a war in Central America or who threatened the health of the nation's poor. On those occasions he spoke in the tradition of Murrow, informing the people of their history and their responsibility.

Diane Sawyer, one of several CBS reporters targeted for success, became well known on the network's morning news show. Facing intense competition, the network continued to steep its younger reporters with the legacies of Murrow and Cronkite. At the same time CBS was not reluctant to make changes. The Sunday news-interview show *Face the Nation,* dating to November 7, 1954, was replaced in 1983 by a new Sunday news program anchored by Lesley Stahl, a veteran political and White House correspondent. And CBS found room on its morning news show for Jane Bryant Quinn, freelance columnist for the *Washington Post, Newsweek,* and *Woman's Day.*

In September, 1982, William S. Paley stepped down after 54 years of running CBS, announcing that he would relinquish his post as board chairman of the communications conglomerate that was doing $4 billion in annual business. He owned $90 million worth of CBS stock, a far cry from 1928 when he paid $500,000 for the controlling interest of the firm that became CBS.

Throughout the years Paley had kept his keen eyes on the news department, working first with Ed Klauber and Paul White and later with Frank Stanton to develop top-rated news teams. He was not without faults; he argued with Ed Murrow and Fred Friendly about their shows and during the Vietnam-Watergate years he was regarded as being too friendly to the Johnson-Nixon point of view. But, overall, Paley was a strong leader who helped his CBS News employees develop standards for others to follow.

The CBS tradition included getting into disputes over its documentaries and the *60 Minutes* show. This, of course, had been the case since Murrow's *See It Now* series and later his *Harvest of Shame* and *Hunger in America.* But in 1982 former General William Westmoreland filed a $120 million lawsuit, claiming that he had been defamed by CBS' *The Uncounted Enemy: A Vietnam Deception.* CBS claimed that the general and others conspired to alter the estimates of enemy troop strength during the war. The network issued an unprecedented lengthy defense, admitting some errors in judgment but sticking with the essence of the story.

In April, 1982, the White House attacked a *CBS Reports* show, narrated by Bill Moyers, called *People Like Us,* which was a look at America's poor and the effects of administration cutbacks in aid. One of the show's sponsors, Holiday Inn, refused to pay for a commercial aired that evening, claiming that the show was an example of one-sided journalism. The *60 Minutes* show was attacked frequently and was also the subject of several lawsuits. In a celebrated Los Angeles case, Dan Rather's testimony helped convince a jury that CBS had not recklessly reported fraud at a health clinic. Despite its high rating, its credibility had slipped, even with its strongest boosters. Producer Don Hewitt, a veteran of the first Murrow show in 1951, built the successful reporting teams and maintained the show's fast pace.

NBC NEWS

Tom Brokaw, a former White House correspondent who had dueled with Rather for scoops before becoming host of the *Today* show in the early 1970s, was named sole anchor of *The NBC Nightly News* in July, 1983, after briefly sharing the anchor responsibilities with former CBS reporter Roger Mudd. Mudd became NBC's chief Congressional correspondent and host of the network's *White Paper* series. The Brokaw-Mudd team was formed in 1982 in an effort to take advantage of Cronkite's departure and Rather's perceived vulnerability.

Although they did not catch CBS in the ratings chase, a factor in Mudd's transfer, Brokaw and Mudd maintained NBC's high credibility, despite complaints that Brokaw in particular was too critical of the Reagan administration. On one occasion Reagan singled out Rather and Brokaw as examples of powerful broadcasters who were giving the public a poor impression of his programs.

Judy Woodruff led NBC White House coverage. Connie Chung became anchor of the early morning news show in 1983 and seemed destined for a higher post.

John Chancellor left his anchor position with hopes that network news would expand to an hour format. He expressed regrets over what he termed a

Tom Brokaw.
NBC News

Ted Koppel.
ABC News

lack of sophistication in television's ability to select stories and to deliver enough important facts to help the viewer understand the stories. "We could have a three-hour program every day and not be able to cover adequately some of the elements of the news which I regard as important. However big the vessel is, it just is not designed to provide a full service."[36]

Chancellor called himself and others who selected, edited, and delivered the news to a captive audience the "telegogues" of the age, and urged viewers to read newspapers to obtain more of the stories. As a commentator for NBC Chancellor suddenly became controversial during the 1982 Israeli invasion of Lebanon when he questioned Israel's bombing tactics and referred to "imperial Israel." While professional journalists praised his commentary as courageous, in light of network television's tradition of supporting Israel almost without question, NBC News president Reuven Frank had to defend the program. It apparently was one of the programs that triggered the anger of Israeli Prime Minister Menachem Begin, who charged that American news teams were biased against Israel.

Like CBS, NBC had its traditions to maintain. Its *Meet the Press* continued as television's longest-running program. It began on November 6, 1947, and outlasted its competitors. Gone from the scene, though, were David Sarnoff and his son, Robert, of NBC, builders of the vast empire.

ABC NEWS

Frank Reynolds took charge of ABC news during such events as the assassination attempt on President Reagan's life. Sam Donaldson offered strong White House coverage. But despite the flexibility and a strong use of flashy graphics, ABC remained behind CBS in the ratings. The outcome of ABC's experiment was made more uncertain by the sudden death of Reynolds in July, 1983, at age 59. He had spent half of his 35 years in broadcast news as a hard-driving reporter and anchorperson for ABC News. The next month ABC opted for the single-anchor solution, selecting Peter Jennings, who had held the post at age 26 from 1964 to 1968. Jennings then reported extensively from abroad, particularly the key London post, from where he joined Reynolds and Max Robinson in the 1978 three-anchor format.

The most exciting ABC personality during the early 1980s was Ted Koppel, an English-born journalist who in 1963, at age 23, became the youngest network correspondent in television history. After covering Vietnam and the State Department during the Nixon and Ford years, Koppel emerged as the no-nonsense host of *Nightline,* a show that ran from 11:30 to midnight Eastern time in competition with NBC's Johnny Carson show. Beginning as a 15-minute update of the Iranian crisis in March, 1980, the show evolved into nightly looks at one of the events or personalities currently in the news, often related to that day's leading news story. Live interviews were the main feature, with Koppel's asking questions back and forth to guests of opposing views. On one occasion, a November, 1980 postelection analysis, ABC allowed Koppel's discussion with Moral Majority leader the Reverend Jerry Falwell and several defeated Democratic senators (George McGovern, Frank Church, and Birch Bayh) to run 43 minutes over schedule because of the powerful nature of the program.

In the morning, ABC's *Good Morning America* held a strong lead over its competitors, the *Today* show and the *CBS Morning News* presentation. The ABC show was launched in 1975, with the seemingly impossible task of overtaking the *Today* show. It was suggested that one of the reasons for success was that the show was run by ABC's entertainment division with actor David Hartman the host: NBC and CBS considered their shows to be news-oriented, despite the many fluffy features on both.

With less money, ABC kept pace over the years by offering as news commentators Howard K. Smith, known for his blunt, crisp phrases, Quincy Howe of World War II fame, and Reynolds, also one of ABC's top political reporters.

Another ABC news show was *20-20,* which was designed to compete with CBS' *60 Minutes.* It often matched its opponent in controversy—the accuracy of the documentaries was increasingly challenged—but it lagged behind in the ratings. The network also created *Viewpoint,* a novel show on which correspondents, news subjects, and members of a studio audience discussed the responsibilities and tastes of the broadcasters. The ABC *Issues and Answers* news-interview show, a fixture since 1961, was replaced by *This Week with David Brinkley* in 1981.

THE KERNER REPORT; HIRING OF MINORITIES

Part of the angry public reaction to violence on television screens undoubtedly stemmed from reporting on news and public-affairs shows of turbulence in cities and on campuses, of disorders and riots in black communities, and of the tragedies of assassination. Following the scenes of destruction in Newark and Detroit President Johnson appointed the National Advisory Commission on

Robert C. Maynard.

Oakland Tribune

Civil Disorders with Governor Otto Kerner of Illinois as chairperson. Chapter 15 of its March, 1968, report dealt with the mass media and the President's question, "What effect do the mass media have on the riots?"[37] The answers offered lessons for the future.

The Kerner Commission said that on the whole the media had tried hard to give a balanced factual account of the 1967 disorders. There had been some evidence of sensationalism, distortion, and inaccuracy: Most of the shooting had been done by the National Guards and police officers, not by blacks; there was no organized conspiracy spurring the rioting, but mainly hostile young ghetto blacks; property damage was exaggerated, by as much as ten times by one AP dispatch from Detroit. In many cases of error, the media had relied on police authorities for their information. This observation by the Commission was graphically reinforced in 1971 when false official statements were made that the prison guards who died at Attica in New York state had had their throats slashed. In reality they had been shot by their would-be rescuers. A courageous coroner and determined media reporters forced a prompt retraction of the false statements in fairness to the black convicts.

Television fared well in its riot coverage. When the Commission staff looked at 955 sequences of news it classified 494 as "calm" treatment and 262 as "emotional." Moderate black leaders were shown three times as often as militants. Because the soldiers and police were white, television scenes of actual rioting tended to make viewers think they were witnessing a black-white confrontation; actually the riots were in black slum areas. Overall, both network and local television coverage was cautious and restrained, the Kerner report said.

But the Commission had a ringing indictment of the mass media, which was also an indictment of American society because the performance of the media largely reflected the public attitude of the times. The communications media, the Commission said,

> have not communicated to the majority of their audience—which is white—a sense of the degradation, misery, and hopelessness of living in the ghetto. They have not

> communicated to whites a feeling for the difficulties and frustrations of being a Negro in the United States. They have not shown understanding or appreciation of—and thus have not communicated—a sense of Negro culture, thought, or history . . . When the white press does refer to Negroes and Negro problems it frequently does so as if Negroes were not part of the audience . . . such attitudes, in an area as sensitive and inflammatory as this, feed Negro alienation and intensify white prejudices.[38]

There has been no serious reporting of the black community, the Commission said; there are few black reporters and fewer race experts. "Tokenism—the hiring of one Negro reporter, or even two or three—is no longer enough. Negro reporters are essential, but so are Negro editors, writers, and commentators," the report declared.

The Commission also recognized the problem conscientious journalists face when it commented:

> Events of these past few years—the Watts riot, other disorders, and the growing momentum of the civil rights movement—conditioned the responses of readers and viewers and heightened their reactions. What the public saw and read last summer thus produced emotional reactions and left vivid impressions not wholly attributable to the material itself.[39]

A CBS News survey in 1968 pointed up this public fear: 70 percent of whites responding thought the police should have been tougher in putting down riots.[40] In the case of Watts, the white community later denied that the area badly needed hospital facilities, even though the *Los Angeles Times* had won a Pulitzer Prize for its analysis of the Watts problem—after the riot was over.

Other studies bore out the Kerner Commission's statements about lack of black participation in the mass media. A 1969 study covering thirty-two of forty-eight major newspapers in sixteen of the twenty largest cities showed that of 4095 news executives, deskpersons, reporters, and photographers, 108, or 2.6 percent, were black, including only one news executive and six on desks.[41] A 1970 survey by *Time* listed the *Washington Post* as the most integrated newspaper, with nineteen black editorial staffers, or 8.5 percent. In 1977 the *Post* reported thirty-four black professionals, or 10 percent. A 1977 ASNE survey obtained responses from 28 percent of dailies with 16,000 employees; they reported 563 black newsroom employees, or 3.5 percent.[42] Among them were Carl T. Rowan, syndicated columnist; William Raspberry, *Washington Post* columnist; Charlayne Hunter, *New York Times;* L. F. Palmer, Jr., *Chicago Daily News* columnist; and William A. Hilliard, appointed city editor of the *Oregonian* in Portland.

Five years later the ASNE reported that 5.5 percent of daily newspaper professionals were nonwhite and that only 106 blacks were classified as part of management. At the *Los Angeles Times,* for example, the highest-ranking black was an assistant city editor of a regional edition. Many large dailies did not have a minority person as an editorial writer or senior editor and the ASNE reported that the rate of integration dropped during those 5 years. About 40 percent of newspaper staffs were integrated.[43]

The most prominent black print journalist was Robert C. Maynard, who became editor, publisher, and owner of the *Oakland Tribune,* across the bay from

San Francisco, in 1983. Maynard was the first black to direct a general circulation metropolitan daily. Self-educated, he got a job on the *York Gazette* in Pennsylvania, won a 1965 Nieman Fellowship to Harvard, reported for the *Washington Post,* and directed media minorities programs at Columbia and Berkeley before becoming editor in heavily-black-populated Oakland in 1979, for the Gannett group, which then sold the paper to Maynard and others.

Minorities were more conspicuous on television, with ABC's Max Robinson and NBC's Bryant Gumbel holding anchor spots. Many local stations had at least one minority person at an anchor position. A continuing problem for minorities in radio and television was in the writing and producing area, where it was difficult for them to obtain decision-making jobs. One criticism was that minorities were being "used' on camera but were not allowed to shape the coverage of the community.

THE EFFECTS OF PROGRAMMED VIOLENCE ON TV

Violence has been a central theme of countless plays, novels, movies, comic books, and television scripts, from the times of the Greek dramatists to those of Matt Dillon. Television, which in the 1960s had a full quota of real violence to report from battlefields and urban riots, also loaded its programming with fantasy violence. The assassinations of John and Robert Kennedy and Martin Luther King, coupled with urban rioting and campus disorders, gave the opponents of programmed violence an opportunity.

They had the statistics in abundance. *The Christian Science Monitor* had counted 210 violent incidents and eighty-one killings in 78 hours of 1967 prime time; a year later the counts for 75 hours were 254 incidents and seventy-one killings despite network promises of reduced violence in the wake of the shootings of Robert Kennedy and Dr. King. The National Commission on the Causes and Prevention of Violence, appointed following those assassinations, logged violent incidents an average of every 15 minutes on NBC and every 10 minutes on ABC. The latter network had some incident of violence in 91 percent of its evening programming in 1968. The Saturday morning children's cartoons had a violent incident every 3.5 minutes.[44]

Senator Thomas Dodd's Juvenile Delinquency Subcommittee focused on television throughout the 1960s as a contributor to increased crime among the young. It pointed out that an impression was created that violence is a satisfying outlet for frustrations, that the fist and the gun are both manly and romantic. Most authorities agreed that seeing violence on the screen rarely caused criminal behavior directly, but they pointed out that it was a needless and dehumanizing experience to watch endless destruction of human life on television. At least at the children's level, marked improvement had occurred by 1971, with the success of such educational fare as *Sesame Street* encouraging the major networks to program similar material and markedly reduce violence.

By contrast, a study of print media in the early 1960s showed a lower percentage of content portraying sex and violence than readers might suppose. An analysis of the stories in fifty-five newsstand magazines (family, intellectual, detective, men's, romance) showed an average of forty-six incidents of violence per issue and twenty-three incidents dealing with sexual themes. The family magazines carried only twelve violence items and four involving sex. A study of ten metropolitan newspapers showed 5 percent of the total news space devoted to violence, less than 1 percent to sex (except for the *New York Daily News,* which devoted a third of its space to news of violence and 3 percent to sex).[45] Violence was defined as news of crime, war, accidents. It is apparent that prominent display of stories of sex and violence in newspapers distorts the public image of the volume of such material. The data also show why the spotlight of public concern shifted to television during the 1960s: It had loaded its entertainment time with common-denominator material—violence spiced with sex. These programs drew good ratings, but the Violence Commission reported that a 1968 Harris poll showed that 63 percent of women and 59 percent of men felt that there was too much violence on television.

The biggest problem for television was that more of its audience was becoming increasingly uncomfortable with the violence, sex, semi-nudity, vulgarity, smoking, and drinking heard and seen on prime-time television shows. In 1975 the FCC encouraged the networks and National Association of Broadcasters to adopt a "family viewing time," known later as the "family hour." The idea was to keep shows with high amounts of sex and violence, like *Kojak, Hawaii Five-O,* and *Charlie's Angels,* off the air until young children were in bed.

Writers and directors guilds immediately challenged the broadcasters' action and charged that FCC pressure was involved in a violation of their First Amendment rights. The National Citizens Committee for Broadcasting (NCCB), led by former FCC commissioner Nicholas Johnson, joined the fight against the networks. The public was not in sympathy, though. The specter of murders and beatings led to increased talk in Congress of revamping the FCC Act of 1934. From the White House, President Carter joined in the criticism, saying, "I think the President has the right or obligation to express to the public displeasure or criticism of programming content."[46]

Coupled with the high degree of violence was the increasing abandonment of entertainment taboos, as demonstrated by the hit of 1975 to 1976, *Mary Hartman, Mary Hartman.* Public awareness of the problem was heightened by the movie *Network,* the Academy Award winner of 1977 that bitterly satirized the ratings system.

Johnson's NCCB group encouraged a boycott of the advertisers of the highest-rated violent shows, claiming that the real power was in the hands of the consumer audience. Other changes were effected by Action for Children's Television (ACT), formed by a Newton, Massachusetts, housewife, Peggy Charren, who was perturbed about programming and advertisements shown to children. In 1975, following a number of improvements, Senator Frank Moss said:

> ACT represents the most significant grass roots effort at consumer protection that exists today . . . ACT was born out of the great promise of television that has been perverted into mind-rotting commercial exploitation of our nation's children.[47]

Then, in 1976, the American Medical Association, the American Psychiatric Association, and the national Parent-Teacher Association pushed national campaigns against televised violence. The J. Walter Thompson and other advertising companies started to disassociate themselves from violent programming, but the battle was far from over.[48]

Coming to the defense of the American television system, while citing its fine achievements and acknowledging its faults, was CBS News commentator Eric Sevareid. Noting the adversary relationship between print and electronic journalism, Sevareid challenged print journalists who criticize television to look at their own products:

> Don't publish lofty editorials and critiques berating the culturally low common denominator of TV entertainment programming and then feature on the cover of your weekly TV supplements, most weeks of the year, the latest TV rock star or gang-buster character. Or be honest enough to admit that you do this, that you play to mass tastes for the same reason the networks do—because it is profitable. Don't lecture the networks for the excess of violence—and it is excessive—on the screen and then publish huge ads for the most violent motion pictures in town, ads for the most pornographic films and plays, as broadcasting does not.[49]

Nevertheless, in the mid-1980s, strong objections continued to be raised about televised violence. Adding his voice was the Reverend Jerry Falwell, leader of the Moral Majority organization. Leading researchers, including George Comstock and George Gerbner, agreed that television is a main agent for socialization, because it brings into the often-unsupervised home "information and portrayals not duplicated or readily testable in their real-life environment . . . viewing of violence increases the likelihood of aggressive behavior on the part of the young."[50] But it was also stressed that the influence of parents, teachers, and religious persons modified the effects of television.

A summary of research studies bearing on the effects of television indicated that the presence of television in the home changed family life, including the use of leisure time and parent-child relationships. Television was a national experience, causing a homogenization of mainly middle-class values. This, scholars contend, led to less toleration of deviance from those norms. Persons in lower classes, including minorities, tended to use television as a primary source of learning how to deal with society.

There was little doubt about television's reshaping of American political campaigns. It also was clear that many breaking news stories, particularly those involving protests against the status-quo, were planned with an eye to media response. Major questions in the mid-1980s revolved around the use of new technology to bring news events into the home with more speed and impact than before: Portable minicameras were common and more news channels were planned for 24-hour satellite delivery. High-definition pictures added to the effect. Debates over content included a concern with the distribution of X-rated, sexually explicit, and excessively violent films over cable systems. Such materials were available through store sales of casettes for use on home video tape-recording (VTR) units.

There seemed to be a consensus that broadcasting content was a legitimate subject for public and governmental concern. The type of action to be taken, however, was not clear. Some groups advocated direct government intervention, while others were wary, expressing fears that First-Amendment rights would be abused and that censorship of broadcasting might lead to excesses in other areas.

THE FCC AND THE BROADCASTERS: LICENSING

Radio and television were still under public regulation, through the Federal Communications Commission. The FCC held license control over stations and limited holding of multiple licenses. No person or group could own more than seven television stations (only five of them VHF) plus seven FM and seven AM stations. No one could own more than one radio and one television station in the same city.

For years the FCC looked askance at ownership of broadcast stations by newspaper publishers, whether or not in the same city. In 1944 the FCC commented that licenses would be granted on the merit of individual applications, under the guiding rule of as much diversification of ownership as possible. But in 1970 the FCC began to get deeply involved in cross-channel ownerships. First it voted to prohibit future acquisitions by anyone of both a VHF television station and a radio station in the same market. Then, after a series of hearings and arguments, in 1975 the FCC banned new joint-ownership arrangements in the same city but said that old ones could stand. However, a federal appeals court decision in 1977 struck this down and appeared to outlaw most of the joint-ownership arrangements that had existed since radio began more than 50 years earlier. It was predicted that the case could affect at least eighty television-newspaper ownership combinations in seventy-five cities and perhaps 400 radio-newspaper combinations in about 200 cities.[51]

Two groups appealed the FCC's 1970 decision to the appeals court: newspaper owners and broadcasters upset about the loss of future combinations, and the National Citizens Committee for Broadcasting, led by former FCC commissioner Nicholas Johnson, who was angered that old relationships were allowed to stand. One easy alternative, of course, was for the newspaper owners, with their deeper community roots, to trade their broadcasting stocks to each other, whenever possible, to avoid multiple ownerships in the same cities. It was expected to take years to iron out the legal arguments. The FCC was also expected to begin examining ownership patterns affecting broadcast stations and cable stations.

Existing owners were further disturbed by a federal appeals-court ruling in mid-1971 that the FCC was still giving too much preference to license holders in renewal hearings required every 3 years. The court sought to open the door for the serious consideration of license challenges by minority groups and for the shifting of licenses on FCC findings of inferior performance by stations. Such challenges were in progress in various metropolitan areas, so far unsuccessfully.

Television found itself subjected to other regulations in the 1970s. For health reasons, Congress passed legislation banning cigarette advertising from the screens beginning in 1971 (magazine cigarette advertising promptly doubled and that in newspapers also increased). The immediate loss to the broadcast industry was $225 million in advertising revenues, unless the time was sold to other advertisers. And the FCC voted to limit network-television affiliate stations in the top fifty markets to 3 hours of network programming in prime time (this prime-time access rule forced the stations to scramble around for 30 minutes of fill-in each evening between 7:30 to 8 p.m.).

By the mid-1980s the FCC was engaged in a policy of deregulation, following the general philosophy set by the Reagan administration in 1981. The

FCC approved the licensing of 125 new AM radio stations, increasing competition in that area and then set the deregulation of television in motion. As an initial action it approved the construction of up to 3000 low-power television stations, which, if built, could be used to provide access to minorities and other segments of society not well served. The FCC gave its blessing to teletext operations and, importantly, to direct broadcasting from satellite to home. There also were proposals that the FCC reverse its rule barring the three major networks from owning and syndicating programs made by studios and independent producers. Congressional opponents of deregulation argued against this and the elimination of the "prime-time access rule."

The major concern with deregulation, articulated by noted television critic Les Brown and others, was that the networks and individual stations could exploit the situation and not adhere to the concept of fairness. Concern was heightened when FCC Chairperson Mark Fowler advocated "No renewal filings, no ascertainment exercises, no content regulation, no ownership restrictions beyond those that apply to media generally, free resale of properties, no petitions to deny, no brownie points for doing this right, no finger-wagging for doing that wrong." Brown replied, "Television without referees is a commercial free-for-all, a sport for scoundrels."[52]

In addition to the possibility of local stations' being purchased and quickly resold for massive profits at the expense of quality programming, there was also worry over who might control the low-power community stations. The monopoly of conglomerates could continue, critics said, if local newspapers purchased low-power stations for teletext operations and denied access to community organizations. Another fear was that without regulation rich lobbying groups could set up their own television and computer networks. Among those interested were the Chamber of Commerce, the AFL-CIO, and major religious organizations. The FCC's role in determining which segments of American society would have access to television—and who would own news systems—was yet to be determined.

THE FCC FAIRNESS DOCTRINE

The problems of editorializing on the air and fairness in presenting all sides of public issues were others involving the stations and the FCC over many decades. In a 1941 ruling, called the "Mayflower decision" because it involved renewal of a Boston station license held by the Mayflower Broadcasting Corporation, the FCC said, "The broadcaster cannot be an advocate." Radio supporters presented arguments against this policy, and in 1949 the FCC decided broadcasters could—and should—"editorialize with fairness." Station owners were cautious in taking up the invitation, but by 1967 a survey showed that 57 percent of radio and television stations were presenting editorial opinion, one-third of them either daily or weekly, the rest occasionally. This figure steadily increased. Some problems of covering politics were removed in 1959 when bona fide newscasts and news programs were exempted from the FCC's "equal-time" rule, but the basic problem of obtaining "fairness" in access to the air and in presenting all sides of controversial issues remained.

The requirement to be "fair" was based on two arguments: The airwaves are public property, by act of Congress, and the FCC was given power to license broadcasters in the "public interest, convenience, and necessity." The public interest is served, FCC held, if the airwaves are made accessible to many differing viewpoints.

Broadcasters said that it was hard to define the "public interest" legally. They also said such extreme efforts to balance editorial comment and interpretative documentaries mitigated against broadcasters covering important social issues. If, as the FCC implied, a station had to go out and look for at least one other side to any issue it discussed, in order to be fair, it would not go out at all (CBS looking for the other side to the migrant labor problem, or the other side of military propaganda, for example). And if the "other side" came in with program demands by any number of offended or interested groups (as in the case of the Vietnam War and activist resistance to war), the station's time would be filled with programming of little interest to the majority of viewers (any newspaper editor knows that a large percentage of citizens is not interested in a given social or political issue, a fact confirmed by opinion polls). In a 1969 decision the Supreme Court did not agree to all this.

Specifically, the Court upheld FCC rules requiring that notice be given to any person subjected to "personal attack" in an editorial or program, or to candidates for office opposing one endorsed, with right of similar reply. But the decision ranged more widely in the "fairness doctrine" issue, noting "it is the right of the viewers and listeners, not the right of the broadcasters, which is paramount." If broadcasters were not willing to present representative community views on controversial issues, Justice Byron White wrote, the granting or renewal of a license might be challenged within the spirit of the Constitution.[53] Promptly dubbed the *Red Lion* doctrine, this decision created excitement. But when in 1970 Dr. Frank Stanton of CBS decided to afford the Democratic party time to answer President Nixon's unprecedented number of prime-time requisitionings to give arguments concerning his foreign policy and the Vietnam War, the FCC emasculated its new power. Yes, it said, CBS was correct in giving the right of reply, but it also had to let the Republican party answer the Democrats, and, presumably, so on and on in an endless circle. CBS cancelled the public discussion it wanted to have and appealed to the courts for relief. The incident served to prove that it is very difficult to legislate "fairness."

In another decision affecting access to the airwaves and public discussion, the FCC reversed a policy that had encouraged antismoking, environmentalist, and other groups to seek access. The FCC narrowed previous rulings that held that all broadcast advertising was subject to the "fairness doctrine" and had to be balanced with "counter-advertising" whenever controversies were involved. The new ruling was that ads designed merely to sell products did not have to be balanced with opposing viewpoints, but that advertisements dealing with issues were still subject to the provisions calling for balance. However, the FCC and Supreme Court ruled that broadcasters could not be required to sell advertising space to anyone who had the money and were only expected to make a "good faith effort" to ensure balance in their overall programming, as opposed to any one program. The inquiry was intended to settle questions that had arisen during license disputes and was considered to be different from "right-of-reply" and "equal-time" problems.

In an extension of regulations governing advertising, in 1978 the Supreme Court ruled that the Federal Trade Commission (FTC) had the authority to enforce corrective advertising. Advertisers found guilty of using false advertising were required to devote a certain percentage of future advertising to acknowledging previous falsehoods. The FTC had decided that advertising for Listerine, which for 100 years had claimed that the product helped cure colds and sore throats, needed correcting. The Supreme Court agreed to this concept of fairness in advertising.

By the mid-1980s there was a rising cry against the fairness doctrine itself, however. As could be expected, broadcast executives were opposed to its continuation. They argued that the networks should be free to cover controversial issues without the fear of government intervention. Cynics suspected that some executives also wanted to be free of pressure from minorities, women, senior citizens, and others demanding balanced coverage. But leading journalists, including many sympathetic to those often denied access, joined in the arguments for the abolition of the fairness doctrine. Both Walter Cronkite and Eric Sevareid said that there were so many ways for the average citizen to gain different viewpoints that there was no reason to assume that the television networks held as much power as in the days when broadcasting frequencies were limited.

On the other hand, advocates for minority causes worried that without the FCC, as ineffective as it had often been in dealing with license disputes and access, their positions would be severely weakened. And they were not alone in their desire to see the rules kept intact. Big business, which had long felt discriminated against by network news departments—particularly during the so-called post-Watergate period—was using its highly talented public-relations staffs to battle back.

Large corporations like Mobil Oil and Kaiser Aluminum began to mount media campaigns against television news and documentary shows, particularly *60 Minutes* and *20/20,* trying to show that the fairness doctrine was being violated. NBC was not immune, running into problems with several documentaries including one that exposed the inadequacy of many pension plans. These corporations placed advertisements in newspapers, sent out mailings to media outlets, and made their own films for distribution to community organizations and schools.

Some called these activities a form of intimidation, while others said careless handling of public issues deserved to be treated harshly. Mobil became known for its Op-Ed page pronouncements, in the *New York Times* and other leading papers, which often discussed media-related topics. The National News Council became involved in a number of these disputes.

A long-promised revision of the Federal Communications Act could lead to drastic changes. First Congress would have to agree, and lobbyists for all groups affected by television would have to be part of the negotiating process before any final decisions could be made. A few persons have suggested abolition of the FCC itself, arguing that any disputes could be settled in court, with the exception of frequency violations, which could be monitored by a small technical staff with federal authority to cite offenders. Such a move would have to be accompanied by other deregulatory maneuvers within the federal government and would depend on the amount of public support for such strong action.

PUBLIC BROADCASTING

A long effort to establish public broadcasting in the United States at the level at which it exists in other countries was given stability in 1967 by the Congress. The Corporation for Public Broadcasting (CPB) was chartered that year to dispense funds for a unified system of national and local programming. Much of the original programming was done by the well-established National Educational Television (NET). After 1970, the country's noncommercial and educational television stations were connected through the Public Broadcasting Service, which hopefully called itself "the fourth network." In radio, many of these stations were linked by the National Public Radio (NPR) system. The future of public financing remained to be determined; the Ford Foundation had given the stations some $200 million, and in 1976 President Ford signed a bill that assured substantial federal funding up to 1981. President Carter then projected $1 billion of support over 5 years beginning in 1981, still far from enough to assure excellence.

However, budget cutbacks ordered by the Reagan administration and internal financial disputes threatened the viability of public broadcasting. In addition to the crisis for television outlets, NPR stations were put under extreme pressure to raise monies to supplement their meager incomes. There was considerable discussion whether public stations should accept advertising. Proponents pointed at the longtime underwriting of major shows by corporate grants; opponents said that the purity of public broadcasting should not be violated, and the question of advertising remained.

For a few years the CPB, which channels the federal funds, and the PBS, which represents the stations and distributes the programs, fought bitterly. CPB complaints, encouraged by the Nixon White House, centered around the alleged Eastern bias of those producing the shows to be distributed. By the late 1970s, a calm was noticeable, but the CPB was still accused of bureaucratic interference in the development of public broadcasting's true potential as an imaginative, alternative source of ideas.

Public television's best-known success was *Sesame Street,* which captured the imaginations of the moppets and, aided by the Action for Children's Television group, brought about some reform in children's shows by the commercial networks, which substituted educational fare for violence part of the time. Its successor was *The Electric Company,* for third to fifth graders. Kenneth Clark's series called *Civilisation* was another high-level success; so were *The Forsythe Saga, The First Churchills,* and *The Great American Dream Machine.* There were such innovative programs as the production of an actual courtroom trial and "The Global Village, a shared electronic experience." Two educational stations pioneering in such efforts were WGBH, Boston, and KQED, San Francisco. NET had other staple programs, such as another delightful children's hour, *Mister Roger's Neighborhood, NET Playhouse, Nova,* and *NET Festival.* KCET, Los Angeles, was another leader.

The programming, supplemented by the best in British television, continued to improve. Other hit shows included *Upstairs, Downstairs, Shoulder to Shoulder, Monty Python, The Adams Chronicles,* and *The Incredible Machine.* Public television provided gavel-to-gavel coverage of the Watergate hearings, and a number

Jim Lehrer and Robert MacNeil.
PBS

Alistair Cooke.
PBS, © Ben Swartz

Charlayne Hunter.
PBS

of candid documentaries appeared; including a major effort in 1983, Vietnam: A Television History.

Alistair Cooke's presentations of *Masterpiece Theatre* comprised another viewer favorite, as the former newspaperman Cooke probed into the manners and mores of different time periods with the precision of an investigative reporter. News buffs relied on NPR's *All Things Considered* for interpretations of the day's events, as well as on the television shows the *MacNeil-Lehrer NewsHour* and *Washington Week in Review.*

Robert MacNeil and Jim Lehrer had brought their expertise to public television in the form of a 30-minute show focusing on one major topic. In 1983 the report was expanded to an hour format, 9 years after MacNeil and Lehrer gained attention by anchoring the Watergate hearings. The chief correspondent for the show was Charlayne Hunter-Gault. The program, underwritten by CPB, the member stations of PBS, AT&T, and Exxon, was considered to be a pacesetter in television news and won numerous awards. The hour format was envied by news executives at the major networks who hoped for similar changes.

NOTES

1. Dennis T. Lowry, "Agnew and the Network TV News; A Before/After Content Analysis," *Journalism Quarterly,* XLVIII (Summer 1971), 205.

2. See Don R. Pember, "The 'Pentagon Papers' Decision: More Questions Than Answers," *Journalism Quarterly,* XLVIII (Autumn 1971), 403, whose conclusions were endorsed by other mass-communications law scholars.

3. *The New York Times Company* v. *United States* and *United States* v. *The Washington Post Company,* 403 U.S. 713 (1971). The government soon admitted its error by selling forty-three volumes of the Pentagon Papers from the Printing Office to all comers.

4. *Bantam Books Inc.* v. *Sullivan,* 372 U.S. 58 (1963).

5. *Organization for a Better Austin* v. *Keefe,* 402 U.S. 215 (1971).

6. *Near* v. *Minnesota,* 283 U.S. 697 (1931).

7. Ibid.

8. *St. Louis Post-Dispatch,* June 20, 1972.

9. *Chicago Tribune,* June 22, 1972.

10. The public record is found in *Watergate: The Chronology of a Crisis* (Washington, D.C.: Congressional Quarterly, 1975), a documentary review of the impartial and authoritative research organization.

11. For background on the Nixon years, see the Bibliographies at the end of this chapter. In particular, see David Wise, *The Politics of Lying,* for a detailed examination of wide-scale government deceit over two decades.

12. Edwin Diamond's 1973 study was part of an effort by the Network News Study Group at MIT, of which he was codirector. See also Edward J. Epstein, "How the Press Handled the Watergate Scandal," *Los Angeles Times,* September 14, 1973.

13. Dan Rather and Gary Paul Gates, *The Palace Guard* (New York: Harper & Row, 1974), pp. 182–83. Rather, the former CBS White House correspondent, takes a critical look at the inner workings of Nixon's operations.

14. J. Anthony Lukas, *Nightmare: The Underside of the Nixon Years* (New York: Viking Press, 1976), p. 3. Lukas, whose remarkable Watergate account filled an entire *New York Times Magazine* issue in July, 1973, comprehensively documents all of the Watergate-related incidents and the fear that radicals might disclose some "really damaging secrets" or pass them to the Soviets (p. 71).

15. *Los Angeles Times,* July 29, 1973, p. 1, Opinion section. The story originally appeared in the *Washington Post* and was distributed to United States and foreign clients by the *Los Angeles Times-Washington Post* News Service.

16. The UPI team included Bryce Miller, Alvin Webb, and Dan Southerland. William Tuohy won a Pulitzer Prize for his reporting for the *Los Angeles Times.* Sydney Schanberg of the *New York Times* won the Pulitzer Prize for his coverage of the surrender in Cambodia. Peter Braestrup divided 4 years between the *New York Times* and *Washington Post.* Charles Mohr of the *New York Times* won high praise. Richard Critchfield won distinction for the *Washington Star.* CBS reporters producing field reports and documentaries included Peter Kalischer, Morley Safer, John Laurence, Don Webster, Dan Rather, and Murray Fromson. Among others reporting for NBC were Frank McGee, Ron Nessen, Kenley Jones, and Howard Truckner, for ABC, Dan North, Roger Peterson. In Cambodia were Laurence Stern, *Washington Post;* Henry Kamm, *New York Times;* Raymond Coffey, *Chicago Daily News;* the indefatigable Arnett of AP; and two who were captured and released, Richard Dudman, *St. Louis Post-Dispatch,* and Elizabeth Pond, *Christian Science Monitor.* There were other women correspondents, including the *New York Times'* Gloria Emerson, magazine journalist Frances FitzGerald, ABC's Marlene Sanders, and Betty Halstead and Kate Webb of UPI. Webb and Michele Ray, a French freelancer, were both captured and released.

17. As quoted by Phillip Knightley in *The First Casualty,* (New York: Harcourt Brace Jovanovich, 1975), p. 423.

18. The conference, the only such gathering held in the post-Vietnam era, was held at the University of Southern California. The proceedings were videotaped for later release. Many of the eighty-five participants were journalists. See Fox Butterfield, "The New Vietnam Scholarship," *New York Times Magazine,* February 13, 1983.

19. Peter Braestrup, *Big Story* (New Haven: Yale University Press, 1977). Braestrup claimed that shocked Saigon reporters overreacted to the Communist attack and that some confused Saigon and Washington officials added to a distortion of reality. See also Braestrup's letter to the editor, *ASNE Bulletin,* April 1978, p. 20, defending his work.

20. Roger Morris, "Foreign Policy Reporting: Quarantined for the Campaign," *Columbia Journalism Review* (November-December 1976), 19.

21. Timothy Crouse, *The Boys on the Bus* (New York: Random House, 1973). Other regulars included Jules Witcover who left the *Los Angeles Times* to join the *Washington Post,* a veteran of more than 25 years; Haynes Johnson of the *Washington Post,* a leader in reporting voter preferences; Jack Germond, another 25-year veteran who headed Gannett's coverage before becoming chief political writer for the *Washington Star;* the old reliable of the *Baltimore Sun,* Phil Potter; James McCartney of the Knight newspapers; Curtis Wilkie, who made his mark in 1972 with Wilmington's *News Journal* and later became the *Boston Globe's* White House correspondent; Kenneth Reich of the *Los Angeles Times,* who gained attention during the

1976 campaign; and Jim Perry of the *National Observer.* Eleanor Randolph of the *Chicago Tribune* and Roger Simon of the *Chicago Sun-Times* were cited for 1976 stories.

Dozens of correspondents reported for the press associations and television networks. Walter Mears, Saul Pett, and Karl Leubsdorf of the AP and Arnold Sawislak, Clay Richards, and Steve Gerstel of United Press International had leading bylines. On television in 1976, CBS' Ed Bradley, ABC's Sam Donaldson, and NBC's Judy Woodruff and Don Oliver led in covering Carter. Tom Jarriel, ABC, Phil Jones, CBS, and Bob Jamieson, NBC, followed Ford. Cassie Mackin, NBC, Ann Compton, ABC, and Sharon Lovejoy, CBS, were active on camera.

22. See the *Columbia Journalism Review* special report, "Reporting the 1976 Campaign" (January-February 1977), with articles by Sanford J. Ungar, Walter Mears, James McCartney, Philip Meyer, and others.

23. This is well explained by Joel Swerdlow in "The Decline of the Boys on the Bus," *Washington Journalism Review* (January/February 1981).

24. *New York Times,* January 21, 1981, p. 1.

25. *Los Angeles Times,* March 19, 1982, p. 10.

26. *Editor & Publisher,* October 9, 1982, reported that that *New York Times* had not been granted a one-on-one interview even though such access had been given to the *Washington Times,* the paper owned by the "Moonies." Ranking reporters were quoted on the access problem. See also *Editor & Publisher,* April 9, 1983.

27. *Los Angeles Times,* January 24, 1982, Opinion Section, p. 2.

28. Robert Scheer, *With Enough Shovels: Reagan, Bush & Nuclear War* (New York: Random House, 1982).

29. Phil Kerby, "When Reagan Chides the Press, There's a Difference," *Los Angeles Times,* April 14, 1983, Part II, p. 1.

30. Norman E. Isaacs, address before California Editors Conference, Palo Alto, June 4, 1982.

31. Edith Efron, *The News Twisters* (Los Angeles: Nash, 1971), and Edward J. Epstein, *News from Nowhere* (New York: Random House, 1973).

32. Eric Sevareid, in his "What's Right with Sight-and-Sound Journalism," *Saturday Review* (October 10, 1976), defended television news from print critics who often wrote for publications that were inferior products.

33. *Broadcasting,* March 7, 1983, p. 35.

34. *Broadcasting,* February 14, 1983, p. 38.

35. *Broadcasting,* March 7, 1983, p. 35.

36. *Christian Science Monitor,* November 18, 1982, magazine section. For a detailed examination of news values, see Herbert J. Gans, *Deciding the News: A Study of CBS Evening News, NBC Nightly News, Newsweek and Time* (New York: Vintage, 1979).

37. *Report of the National Advisory Commission on Civil Disorders* (New York: Bantam Books, 1968).

38. Ibid., p. 383.

39. Ibid., p. 365.

40. William Small, *To Kill a Messenger* (New York: Hastings House, 1970), p. 60.

41. Edward J. Trayes, "The Negro in Journalism," *Journalism Quarterly,* XLVI (Spring 1969), 5.

42. *Time,* April 6, 1970, p. 89; *ASNE Bulletin,* November 1977, p. 18. Of the minorities employed, thirty-eight persons were serving in news-executive positions, 130 as deskpersons.

43. Austin Scott, "The Media's Treatment of Blacks: A Story of Distortion," *Los Angeles Times,* September 5, 1982, Opinion Section. Scott, a *Times* reporter, quoted the 1982 ASNE report. The article was spurred by controversy over a *Times* story headlined "Marauders From Inner City Prey on L.A.'s Suburbs." Blacks were not involved in assisting with the story, which took 6 months to develop. The *Times* won a SPJ/SDX public-service award, even though the National Association of Black Journalists voted it the "most objectionable" news story of 1981. See also continuing studies and comments about minority hiring in *Columbia Journalism Review* and *ASNE Bulletin.*

44. Small, *To Kill a Messenger,* pp. 80–81.

45. Herbert A. Otto, "Sex and Violence on the American Newsstand," *Journalism Quarterly,* XLVI (Spring 1969), 5.

46. "Television: A Gold Mine That's Coming Under Heavy Attack," *U.S. News and World Report* (February 7, 1977), 29.

47. Cited by Donald P. Ranly in "Action for Children's Television," *Freedom of Information Center Report,* No. 364 (December 1976), 10.

48. See George Comstock, "The Role of Social and Behavioral Science in Policymaking for Television," The Rand Corporation (January 1977).

49. Eric Sevareid, "What's Right with Sight-and-Sound Journalism," *Saturday Review* (October 10, 1976), 19.

50. George Comstock, "The Impact of Television on American Institutions," in Michael C. Emery and Ted C. Smythe, *Readings in Mass Communication* (Dubuque: Wm. C. Brown, 1983), p. 232. See also, in that edition, George Gerbner and Kathleen Connolly, "Television as New Religion," an examination of violence on television.

51. *Advertising Age,* March 7, 1977, p. 1.

52. *Channels* (March–April, 1983), 27. See *Broadcasting,* March 2, 1981, for discussion of the Reagan administration's plans, radio deregulation, and low-power television stations.

53. *Red Lion Broadcasting Co., Inc.,* v. *Federal Communications Commission,* 394 U.S. (1969).

ANNOTATED BIBLIOGRAPHY

Books: Background History

BARRETT, MARVIN, ed., *The Politics of Broadcasting.* New York: Thomas Y. Crowell, 1973. This fourth duPont-Columbia University survey finds that Nixon intimidated the press.

———, ed., *Moments of Truth.* New York: Thomas Y. Crowell, 1975. Fifth duPont-Columbia survey of broadcast journalism compresses the story of the 1973 to 1975 confrontation.

BERNSTEIN, CARL, AND BOB WOODWARD, *All the President's Men.* New York: Simon & Schuster, 1974. The *Washington Post's* reporters tell how they laid the groundwork for toppling Nixon; transformed into top-ranking motion picture. See also Bob Woodward and Carl Bernstein, *The Final Days* (New York: Simon & Schuster, 1976).

BRESLIN, JIMMY, *How the Good Guys Finally Won.* New York: Viking, 1975. A great reporter produces one of the best step-by-step accounts of the Nixon impeachment.

CARTER, JIMMY, *Keeping Faith.* New York: Bantam Books, 1982. Presidential memoirs. See also Hamilton Jordan, *Crisis: The Last Year of the Carter Presidency* (New York: Putnam's, 1982). The Iran hostage negotiations from the inside.

DIDION, JOAN, *Salvador.* New York: Simon & Schuster, 1983. A brief analysis.

DREW, ELIZABETH, *Washington Journal: The Events of 1973–1974.* New York: Random House, 1975. *The New Yorker's* political writer details the final year of Watergate.

LANG, GLADYS ENGEL, AND KURT LANG, *The Battle for Public Opinion: The President, the Press, and the Polls during Watergate.* New York: Columbia University Press, 1983. An excellent survey of the role of the media and public reaction.

LUKAS, J. ANTHONY, *Nightmare: The Underside of the Nixon Years.* New York: Viking, 1976. Comprehensive analysis.

New York Times, The End of a Presidency. New York: Bantam Books, 1974. Day-by-day listing of Watergate-related events, with documents.

The Pentagon Papers. New York: Bantam, 1971. Publication in paperback of the decisions and documents, edited by the *New York Times.*

PORTER, WILLIAM E., *Assault on the Media: The Nixon Years.* Ann Arbor: University of Michigan Press, 1976. Penetrating analysis of the 1969 to 1972 Nixon-Agnew assault on media.

Watergate: Chronology of a Crisis. Washington: Congressional Quarterly, 1975. A thousand-page documentary study of 1972 to 1974 events on a week-by-week basis; factual presentation but draws conclusions from evidence in documents, hearings, tapes, press.

WISE, DAVID, *The Politics of Lying.* New York: Vintage Books, 1973. A veteran journalist traces the credibility gap, from the U-2 to Watergate.

WITCOVER, JULES, *Marathon: The Pursuit of the Presidency, 1972–1976.* New York: The Viking Press, 1977. Detailed report of events by a Washington *Post* reporter.

Books: Washington Reporting, Media Overviews

CROUSE, TIMOTHY, *The Boys on the Bus: Riding with the Campaign Press Corps.* New York: Random House, 1973. The reporters' wolf-pack and their presidential quarries. See also Hunter S. Thompson, *Fear and Loathing: On the Campaign Trail* '72 (San Francisco: Straight Arrow Books, 1973). By the national-affairs editor of *Rolling Stone.*

GANS, HERBERT J., *Deciding What's News: A Study of CBS Evening News, NBC Nightly News, Newsweek & Time.* New York: Pantheon, 1979. Content analysis.

HALBERSTAM, DAVID. *The Powers That Be.* New York: Knopf, 1979. Lengthy accounts of CBS News and William Paley, *Time* and Henry Luce, the *Washington Post* and the Grahams, the *Los Angeles Times* and the Chandlers.

HESS, STEPHEN, *The Washington Reporters.* Washington, D.C.: Brookings Institution, 1981. A critical, factually detailed analysis. See also Michael B. Grossman and Martha J. Kumar, *Portraying the President: The White House and the News Media* (Baltimore: Johns Hopkins University Press, 1981). Institutional analysis.

HULTENG, JOHN L., *The Messenger's Motives.* Englewood Cliffs, N.J.: Prentice-Hall, 1976.

Criticisms of the mass media are summarized and evaluated.

McCLENDON, SARAH, *My Eight Presidents.* New York: Wyden Books, 1978. View from the lady with the embarrassing questions at presidential press conferences.

RIVERS, WILLIAM L., *The Other Government: Power and the Washington Media.* New York: Universe, 1982. Updating of his studies of the capital press corps.

WOODRUFF, JUDY, WITH KATHLEEN MAXA, *This Is Judy Woodruff at the White House.* Reading, Mass.: Addison-Wesley, 1982. NBC correspondent. See also Robert Pierpoint, *At The White House* (New York: Putnam's, 1981). From Ike to Carter with CBS.

Books: Broadcasting

ARLEN, MICHAEL, *The Camera Age.* New York: Penguin, 1981. Essays from *New Yorker.*

BARRETT, MARVIN, AND OTHERS, eds., *Broadcast Journalism, 1979–1981: The Eighth Alfred I. du Pont/Columbia University Survey.* New York: Everest House, 1982. The first survey was published in 1968; issued every 2 years.

BLAKELY, ROBERT J., *The People's Instrument.* Washington, D.C.: The Public Affairs Press, 1971. Philosophical view of the role public television can play.

EPSTEIN, EDWARD J., *News from Nowhere: Television and the News.* New York: Random House, 1973. The organization and economics of television news.

FRIENDLY, FRED W., *The Good Guys, The Bad Guys and the First Amendment.* New York: Random House, 1975, 1976. Attack on the "fairness doctrine" as it has been applied.

GATES, GARY PAUL, *Air Time: The Inside Story of CBS News.* New York: Harper & Row, 1978. How the operation runs, with critical comment.

GELFMAN, JUDITH S., *Women in Television News.* New York: Columbia University Press, 1976. Interviews wtih thirty newswomen including Barbara Walters, Pauline Frederick, Lesley Stahl.

GERBNER, GEORGE, ET AL., *Violence Profile No. 7: Trends in Network Drama and Viewer Conceptions of Social Reality, 1967–1975.* Philadelphia: Annenberg School of Communication, 1976. Violence diminished little, "family hour" proved ineffective.

HAMMOND, CHARLES M., JR., *The Image Decade: Television Documentary, 1965–1975.* New York: Hastings House, 1981. Updates Bluem's study.

HOFSTETTER, C. RICHARD, *Bias in the News: Network Television Coverage of the 1972 Election Campaign.* Columbus: Ohio State University Press, 1976. This detailed 213-page study involving a 17-week content analysis finds no bias in a political way.

LEDUC, DON L., *Cable Television and the FCC: A Crisis in Media Control.* Philadelphia: Temple University Press, 1973. Details the history of cable regulation and brings to light various FCC shortcomings.

MATUSOW, BARBARA, *The Evening Stars.* Boston: Houghton Mifflin, 1983. Lively portraits of anchor persons.

POWERS, RON, *The Newscasters.* New York: St. Martin's Press, 1977. TV critic presents news business as show business.

RATHER, DAN, WITH MICKEY HERSKOWITZ, *The Camera Never Blinks.* New York: William Morrow and Company, 1977. The candid autobiography of this CBS reporter who covered the major stories of the 1960s and early 1970s.

SAVITCH, JESSICA, *Anchorwoman.* New York: Putnam's, 1982. By an NBC commentator.

SCHORR, DANIEL, *Clearing the Air.* Boston: Houghton Mifflin, 1982. CBS stormy petrel tells his side of controversies, reviews his career.

SKORNIA, HARRY J., AND JACK W. KITSON, eds., *Problems and Controversies in Television and Radio.* Palo Alto, Calif.: Pacific Books, 1968. Basic readings for the 1960s.

SMYTHE, TED C., AND GEORGE A. MASTROIANNI, eds., *Issues in Broadcasting: Radio, Television and Cable.* Palo Alto, Calif.: Mayfield Publishing, 1975. Readings.

WESTIN, AV, *Newswatch.* New York: Simon & Schuster, 1982. Television executive examines the networks and their news programming.

Periodicals and Monographs

BATTIATA, MARY, "Lesley Stahl," *Washington Journalism Review* (October 1982), 43. Discusses the CBS White House correspondent who joined the network in 1972.

"The Broadcast Media and the Political Process: 1976," *Broadcasting,* XCII (Jan. 3, 1977), 33–76. A special issue on all aspects of the Ford-Carter campaign.

DIAMOND, EDWIN, "How the White House

Keeps Its Eye on the Network News Shows," *New York,* IV (May 10, 1971), 45. President Nixon had television monitors, 7 A.M. to midnight.

DORMAN, WILLIAM A., AND EHSAN OMEED-, "Reporting Iran the Shah's Way," *Columbia Journalism Review* (January/February 1979), 27. Authors predicted that covering Iran in a manner reflecting Washington policies would lead to a quagmire crisis, which it did.

ELLIOTT, OSBORN, "And That's the Way It Is," *Columbia Journalism Review* (May/June 1980), 50. An interview with the retiring Walter Cronkite.

EMERY, MICHAEL, AND SUZANNE STEINER EMERY, "Reporting Proposition 13: Business as Usual," *Columbia Journalism Review* (November/December 1978), 31. California papers were not much help to voters in pointing out the pitfalls.

EMERY, WALTER B., "Nervous Tremors in the Broadcast Industry," *Educational Broadcasting Review,* III (June 1969), 43. A review of FCC rulings and actions affecting license holders.

EPHRON, NORA, "The War Followers," *New York,* XVI (November 12, 1973), 49. A report on some of the correspondents covering the Arab–Israeli fighting.

ERLICK, JUNE CAROLYN, "Women as the New War Correspondents," *Washington Journalism Review* (June 1982), 42. Detailed report by an El Salvador correspondent on women there. See also Joanne Omang, "How the Fourth Estate Invaded the Third World," *Washington Journalism Review* (June 1982), 45. By a correspondent.

EVARTS, DRU, AND GUIDO H. STEMPEL, III, "Coverage of the 1972 Campaign by TV, News Magazines and Major Newspapers," *Journalism Quarterly,* LI (Winter 1974), 645. The study indicates that in the 1972 campaign the media generally showed no news bias.

"The First Amendment on Trial," a special issue containing thirteen articles on the Pentagon Papers case, *Columbia Journalism Review,* (September–October 1971).

FURLONG, WILLIAM B., "Dan ('Killer') Schorr, The Great Abrasive," *New York,* VIII (June 16, 1975), 41. How the controversial CBS correspondent faced his critics.

GRANATO, LEONARD A., "Prior Restraint: Resurgent Enemy of Freedom of Expression," Ph.D. thesis, Southern Illinois University, 1973. From fourteenth-century England to now.

GUNN, HARTFORD N., JR., "United States Public Broadcasting Goes to Satellite," *European Broadcasting Union Review,* March 1977. An update on PBS' plans for simultaneous broadcasting.

HALBERSTAM, DAVID, "Press and Prejudice," *Esquire,* LXXXI (April 1974), 109. Subtitle: "How our last three Presidents got the newsmen they deserved," by one of them.

HANSON, C. T., "Gunsmoke and Sleeping Dogs," *Columbia Journalism Review* (May 1983), 27. Reagan and the press at midterm.

"Journalism and the Kerner Report," a special section in *Columbia Journalism Review* (Fall 1968), 42. An analysis of the report's Chapter 15.

KNIGHTLEY, PHILLIP, "The Falklands: How Britannica Ruled the News," *Columbia Journalism Review* (September/October 1982), 51. A classic case of news management.

KOPKIND, ANDREW, "MacNeil/Lehrer's Class Act," *Columbia Journalism Review* (September/October 1979), 31. PBS news program acclaimed.

———, "The Return of Cold War Liberalism," *Nation,* April 23, 1983, p. 495. Red-Scare tactics of 1950s again in vogue.

KWONG, CHAN YING, AND KENNETH STARCK, "*The New York Times* Stance on Nixon and Public Opinion," *Journalism Quarterly,* LIII (Winter 1976), 723. The paper was ahead of the public.

LATHAM, AARON, "The Reporter the President Hates," *New York,* VII (Jan. 21, 1974), 34. The Nixon duel with Dan Rather, CBS White House correspondent. See also Philip Nobile, "Dan Rather Is Going Fishing," *Esquire,* LXXXI (April 1974), 106.

LEAMER, LAWRENCE, "The Sunset Ride of a TV Reformer," *Harper's* CCXLVII (December 1973), 22. Personal history of Nicholas Johnson is really a picture of the FCC.

LEWIN, LEONARD C., "Public TV's Corporate Angels," *Nation,* CCXXI (November 22, 1975), 520. Growing corporate influence in public television.

LOWER, ELMER W., "American Television News—Rounding Out a Quarter Century," *European Broadcasting Union Review,* XXVI (May 1975), 49. ABC news chief.

LOWRY, DENNIS T., "Agnew and the Network

TV News: A Before/After Content Analysis," *Journalism Quarterly,* XLVIII (Summer 1971), 205. Networks played it somewhat safer post-Agnew.

———, "Measures of Network News Bias in the 1972 Presidential Campaign," *Journal of Broadcasting,* XVIII (Fall 1975), 387. Content analysis shows anti-GOP.

MARTINSON, DAVID L., "Coverage of La Follette Offers Insights for 1972 Campaign," *Journalism Quarterly,* LII (Autumn 1975), 539. How the press stereotypes in campaigns.

MASLOW, JONATHAN EVAN, AND AVA ARANS, "Operation San Salvador," *Columbia Journalism Review* (May/June 1981), 52. U.S. press falls in line with Reagan policy.

MASSING, MICHAEL, "Reshuffling the White House Pack," *Columbia Journalism Review* (March/April 1981), 36. Has the beat lost its glamour?

———, "Central America: A Tale of Three Countries," *Columbia Journalism Review* (July/August 1982), 47. El Salvador, Nicaragua, Guatemala press conditions.

MEADOW, ROBERT G., "Cross-Media Comparison of Coverage of the 1972 Presidential Campaign," *Journalism Quarterly,* L (Autumn 1973), 482. Uniform coverage in the media.

MORRIS, ROGER, "Beirut and the Press—Under Siege," *Columbia Journalism Review* (November/December 1982), 23. Charges the media were anti-Israeli.

NELSON, ANNE, "Remembering the Dutchmen: One Way to Kill the Story," *Nation* (July 24–31, 1982), 75. El Salvador correspondent reports on slain TV newsmen.

NOBILE, PHILIP, "What Makes the Apple Machine Run?," *More,* VI (July–August 1976), 23. Interview with R. W. Apple of the *New York Times,* rated the ablest of the 1976 boys-on-bus.

"NBC: 50th Anniversary; Spearhead of Broadcast Industry Marks Beginning." *Television/Radio Age,* XXIV (June 21, 1976), special issue. Also, *Broadcasting,* XCI (June 21, 1976).

PEER, ELIZABETH, "Barbara Walters—Star of the Morning," *Newsweek,* LXXXIII (May 6, 1974), 56. Cover story on Today show's co-host. Also see "TV News—The New Look" *Newsweek,* LXXXVIII (October 11, 1976).

PEMBER, DON R., "The 'Pentagon Papers' Decision: More Questions than Answers," *Journalism Quarterly,* XLVIII (Autumn 1971), 403. A scholarly analysis.

PIANTADOSI, ROGER, "Ted Koppel," *Washington Journalism Review* (March 1981), 22. ABC's *Nightline* show anchor.

"The Press in the 1972 Campaign," *Nieman Reports,* XXVII (Autumn 1973), 3. Report of a Harvard conference on campaign decision-making.

RANLY, DONALD P., "The Challengers: Social Pressures on the Press, 1965–75," Ph.D. thesis, University of Missouri, 1975. Exhaustive history of non-governmental pressures brought by individuals, groups, various forms of media review.

"Reporting the 1976 Campaign," *Columbia Journalism Review* (January/February 1977), Articles by participants and observers of the Carter-Ford campaign.

SAID, EDWARD W., "Iran and the Press," *Columbia Journalism Review* (March/April 1980), 23. American press went to war with Islam and Iran, scholar says. See also "Iran and the Press in Retrospect," a special report on media coverage of the hostage crisis in *Washington Journalism Review* (May 1981).

SEVAREID, ERIC, "What's Right with Sight-and-Sound Journalism," *Saturday Review* (October 10, 1976).

SWAIN, BRUCE M., "The *Progressive,* the Bomb and the Papers," *Journalism Monographs,* No. 76 (May 1982). A U.S. government effort at prior restraint fails.

SWERDLOW, JOEL, "The Decline of the Boys on the Bus," *Washington Journalism Review* (January/February 1981), 15. Print reporters shoved to back of bus by TV correspondents.

The Last Edition

Chicago Daily News

SATURDAY, MARCH 4, 1978 35¢

©1978 BY FIELD ENTERPRISES

So long, Chicago

Daily News Photo/Fredric Stein

It took 102 years to finish, and these are the final pages of The Chicago Daily News.

By M. W. Newman

The Chicago Daily News, the writers' newspaper, ends as it began—a momentous Book of Life. It took 102 years to finish, and these are the final pages.

But the story isn't over—just The Daily News' part of it. A newspaper dies, but newspapering goes on. Life goes on. Tomorrow is the sequel, and all the tomorrows after that.

We die knowing we did our job to the utmost and to the very end. To today, in fact, precisely 102 years, 2 months and 12 days after founder Melville E. Stone ran off the first issue on a rickety press rented for $12 a week.

Stone's Daily News burst out of the gaslight age, when Ulysses S. Grant was brooding in the White House and Lincoln was dead just 10 years. It dies in the

Turn to Page 3

The News inside:

A truly great newspaper: Why couldn't it make it?

By Mike Royko

About the only good thing that can be said for working on a newspaper that folds is that it is sort of like reading your own obit.

Since the official announcement was made on Feb. 22 that The Chicago Daily News would cease publication on March 4, the nation's press has been lamenting our demise.

We've been reading about how we were one of America's oldest papers (102 years), rich in tradition and boasting of great staffs, past and present.

Most of the obits point out that The Daily News had the nation's first foreign service. It was a great one. Over the years, it included such star reporters as John Gunther, Edgar Ansel Mowrer, Paul Scott Mowrer, Keyes Beech, George Weller and Bill Stoneman.

This was the paper that once employed Carl Sandburg as a silent movie critic. Ben Hecht worked here and gathered the material for "Front Page," his classic play about the roughhouse days of Chicago journalism. The Daily News invented the daily columnist.

Our 15 Pulitzer Prizes and countless other awards put us right up there with the best of papers.

The Daily News was doing investigative reporting and sending politicians to jail when Woodward and Bernstein were toddlers.

Our Washington bureau, while not big in number, was always respected. The late Ed Lahey was a living Washington legend.

Bureau Chief Peter Lisagor, who died in 1976, was often described by his peers as the best reporter in the capital.

The recent staff was as good as its ancestors. Pulitzers were owned by cartoonist John Fischetti, associate editor Lois Wille and Beech, lately of the Washington staff. More than 50 books have been written by recent Daily News writers.

Well, you read enough glowing obits about yourself, and you can be pardoned for thinking: "Boy, we were really pretty good."

But then comes the inevitable question: "Yeah? If we were that good, how come we didn't make it?"

And that is the toughest part of being on a 102-year-old, tradition-laden newspaper that goes under. If it had been a cheap rag, its death would have been easier to take. But The Daily News, while it had some bad days, was still one of the best papers in this country.

The very day publisher Marshall Field stood on a desk in the city room to break the bad news, the paper was notified that Lois Wille had won the William Allen White award, the nation's top honor for excellence in editorial writing.

In recent months it had dominated the city's news coverage, with spectacular front-page exposes of political scandals. The talk in the news room was about which story

Turn to Page 2

A statement from the publisher

With this edition The Chicago Daily News ceases publication. I am saddened that it must be so, for the loss of any great newspaper is a tragedy for the community, its employes, readers and advertisers.

The Daily News has been a Chicago institution for more than a century, and as a winner of 15 Pulitzer Prizes it has been respected throughout the country and the world. The men and women who have worked over the years on this newspaper can be proud of their achievements and the level of excellence attained. I am grateful to them for their talent and devotion and to our readers and advertisers.

Despite all our efforts, the economics of publishing, reader habits and life-styles have changed dramatically in the last two decades, making it impossible for The Daily News to earn the revenues needed for any healthy, sound business operation.

As the publisher and man responsible for The Daily News, I feel this loss very deeply. I feel I owe you, the reader, a personal thank you for your loyalty.

The Chicago Sun-Times, which has been growing steadily, will be expanded greatly and will serve an ever increasing number of readers with vigor and dedication.

Your favorite Daily News columnists, writers and editors will be waiting for you in the new Sun-Times. Now 10 Pulitzer Prize winners on the same team will bring you the finest news coverage. The Chicago Sun-Times can be delivered to your home in the morning or picked up at your newsstand every afternoon—with the latest stock market reports.

I believe you will enjoy this exciting newspaper, and I pledge our continued commitment to journalistic excellence.

Marshall Field
Publisher

The final edition of a great newspaper.

26
The Surviving Newspaper Press

. . . it is as difficult to apply objective standards to newspapers as it is to people, and the greatest newspaper is as difficult to identify as the greatest man. It all depends upon what you require.

—Gerald W. Johnson

The obligations of any newspaper to its community are to strive for honest and comprehensive coverage of the news and for courageous expression of editorial opinion in support of basic principles of human liberty and social progress. Those newspapers that have been most consistent in fulfilling these obligations have been rewarded with public and professional acclaim. Other factors that have operated to give some newspapers greater professional recognition are the brilliance of individual leadership on the staff and the maintenance of a steady and sound publishing tradition. No one, however, can with any certainty rank America's leading papers in numerical order.

At least a half-dozen opinion polls have been taken since 1960 in a effort to determine rankings. While it can be argued that at best these polls determine a newspaper's popularity more than anything else, the results of a 1982 polling of newspaper publishers, editors, and journalism professors do offer some interesting comparisons with the previous polls.

There were 610 responses to the survey,[1] the largest number recorded for any such tabulation, and the *New York Times* was the clear choice for the top spot. The *Wall Street Journal* was second, edging the *Washington Post*. The *Los Angeles Times* was a clear fourth. Fifth was the *Chicago Tribune* and sixth the *Christian Science Monitor.*

Respondents were asked to give their choices for a top ten list (unranked), a top five list (ranked) and a top five regional list (ranked). An overall ranking then was determined. The *New York Times,* the leader in all such polls, was listed as being in the top ten by 95 percent of the respondents and in the top five by 89 percent. Next was the *Wall Street Journal,* with figures of 90 percent and 76 percent.

The *Washington Post* was third, with 87.5 percent and 75 percent to the *Los Angeles Times'* 84.5 percent and 68.5 percent. The *Chicago Tribune,* fifth, had 79 percent and 36.5 percent.

The *New York Times* was listed as the best newspaper in the top five rankings by 368 of the 610 respondents, or 60 percent. The *Wall Street Journal* received 111 first places, the *Washington Post* 35, *Los Angeles Times* 15, and *Chicago Tribune* 6.

A breakdown of the top five rankings by regions (using *Editor & Publisher*'s map showing nine newspaper regions) demonstrated a consistency across the nation. The *New York Times* was first in all nine areas, the *Wall Street Journal* and *Washington Post* battled for positions two and three eight times, and the *Los Angeles Times* was listed fourth in eight of the nine regions.

A number of papers were closely bunched in the rounding out of the top fifteen. In the next group, not ranked, were the *Philadelphia Inquirer, Boston Globe,* and *Miami Herald.* The following papers, in no particular order, completed the list: *Louisville Courier-Journal, Newsday, St. Petersburg Times, Atlanta Constitution, Milwaukee Journal* and *St. Louis Post-Dispatch.*

The poll showed growing enthusiasm for the *Wall Street Journal, Chicago Tribune, Philadelphia Inquirer,* and *Boston Globe.*

Others not listed in the top fifteen but showing high regional recognition were: the *Dallas Morning News, Seattle Times, Kansas City Times, San Francisco Chronicle, Chicago Sun-Times, Minneapolis Star and Tribune, Detroit Free Press, Des Moines Register, Charlotte Observer,* and *Baltimore Sun.*

Three polls in 1960 and 1961 (of 335 editors, 311 publishers, and 125 journalism professors) determined that the following papers were in the top six in all three tabulations: The *New York Times, Christian Science Monitor, St. Louis Post-Dispatch, Washington Post,* and *Milwaukee Journal.* In 1970 a poll taken of 130 publishers by public-opinion expert Edward L. Bernays confirmed most of the previous selections. However the *Los Angeles Times* was a clear second, and the *Louisville Courier-Journal, St. Louis Post-Dispatch,* and *Washington Post* were clustered at the next position. The *Miami Herald* was included for the first time. The *Wall Street Journal* and *Chicago Tribune* were ninth and tenth, destined to move up.

Time's unsystematic listing brought the *Boston Globe* and *Newsday* into the top ten in 1974, and *Adweek*'s 1981 survey of journalists, editors, and journalism school deans added the *Philadelphia Inquirer.*

A 1983 poll by *Advertising Age* of 107 journalism professors showed the *New York Times, Washington Post, Los Angeles Times,* and *Wall Street Journal* leading the field. Tightly bunched—within a few ballots—were the *Boston Globe, Chicago Tribune, Miami Herald, Philadelphia Inquirer, Louisville Courier-Journal* and *Christian Science Monitor. USA Today* was ranked thirteenth and the rest of the top twenty-five were the same as those papers mentioned in the Media Research Institute survey.

THE *NEW YORK TIMES*

The *New York Times* ranked first in all the polls, continuing to hold its place in the forefront of American journalism by maintaining the tradition of telling the news with completeness and integrity. Arthur Hays Sulzberger, who became publisher when his father-in-law, Adolph S. Ochs, died in 1935, lived up to his responsibilities as the head of the country's "newspaper of record." Throughout the 1930s and 1940s, the news staff was led by the team of Edwin L. James, managing editor, and David H. Joseph, city editor. Responsibility for the editorial page, which rested briefly with John H. Finley after the death of Rollo Ogden in 1937, passed in 1938 to Charles Merz. Merz had been managing editor of *Harper's Weekly* and an associate editor of the *New York World.*

Turner Catledge, well-tested as a Washington correspondent, became managing editor in 1951, the *Times'* centennial year. Catledge named two *Times* veterans, Theodore Bernstein and Robert E. Garst, as assistant managing editors with responsibility for enlivening the paper's writing and ensuring its grammatical integrity. Frank S. Adams became city editor, presiding over a block-long city room in the $18-million Times building down 43rd Street from the old Times Square location (the Times Tower was sold in 1961). Major changes came in 1961 when Sulzberger turned over the publisher's chair to his son-in-law, Orvil E. Dryfoos, and Merz retired as editorial page chief in favor of John B. Oakes (a nephew of Adolph Ochs), who had won distinction as an editorial writer. Lester Markel remained as editor of the Sunday edition, a post he had held for 40 years. In 1962 the *Times* began a Western edition printed in Los Angeles but lost heavily and killed it in 1964.

The management struggle described by Gay Talese in *The Kingdom and the Power* began with the sudden death of Dryfoos in June, 1963. The family turned to Arthur Ochs (Punch) Sulzberger, 37, as publisher. Strong man Amory Bradford, chief negotiator for the publishers in the disastrous 1963 New York strike, quit as business manager. In September young Sulzberger named Turner Catledge executive editor for both the daily and Sunday editions, relegating Markel to retirement. Clifton Daniel was named managing editor and Tom Wicker replaced columnist James B. Reston as head of the Washington bureau.

A crisis arose over control of the Washington bureau early in 1968 when a non-*Times* man, James L. Greenfield, was nominated to head it. Wicker and Reston reversed the decision, and the struggle undermined Catledge, who was soon moved up to a vice-presidency in favor of Reston as executive editor. The elder Sulzberger died at the close of 1968, and his son then took full command. Reston was made a vice president in August, 1969, and returned to column writing in Washington, where Wicker was also a columnist and Max Frankel the bureau chief. Clifton Daniel was shunted to control of the New York Times Service and Abe Rosenthal, a loser in the 1968 crisis, became Sulzberger's managing editor. He brought Greenfield to the staff as foreign editor.

Sulzberger soon promoted Rosenthal to executive editor and replaced John Oakes with Max Frankel as editorial page chief. Frankel shrank the fourteen-member editorial board, to the dismay of some of its senior members. Faced with a deterioration of its advertising revenues and readership appeal, the *Times* brightened its typographical appearance, took aim at younger readers with

"Weekend" and "Living" sections like other major dailies, and generally streamlined its operation under Rosenthal's strong guidance. The revised editorial leadership continued with little change into the 1980s, with Rosenthal's personality dominating the newsroom. Associate editors were Tom Wicker, and Charlotte Curtis, who edited the "Op-Ed" page. Seymour Topping was managing editor, and Arthur Gelb metropolitan editor. Hedrick Smith, winner of a Pulitzer Prize covering Moscow, headed the Washington bureau, while Craig Whitney and Warren Hoge served as foreign editors. In 1980 the *Times* launched a national edition, printed by satellite transmission in Chicago, Florida, and California. By 1983 it was circulating 100,000 daily and 200,000 Sunday, 20 percent of which were home-delivered.

Editorially the *Times* was staunchly internationalist in world outlook, progressive-conservative in domestic affairs. It supported Democrat Franklin D. Rooosevelt in 1936 and 1944 and backed Republicans Wendell Willkie in 1940, Thomas E. Dewey in 1948, and Dwight D. Eisenhower in 1952 and 1956. Beginning in 1960, it supported Democrats in six consecutive elections. Like other responsible papers it vigorously defended individual freedoms against reactionary attacks and illegal use of power. For both its editorial opinion and its comprehensive news coverage, the *Times* was sought out in all parts of the world. It and its staff had won a record fifty-three Pulitzer Prizes by 1983.

THE *WALL STREET JOURNAL*

The *Wall Street Journal* was a solidly edited financial daily like its New York competitor, the *Journal of Commerce,* until Bernard Kilgore became its managing editor in 1940. It had been founded in 1889 by Charles H. Dow as the voice of the Dow Jones and Company financial news service. Clarence W. Barron became owner in 1902. Circulation was at a post-Depression level of 30,000 daily when Kilgore took charge. He broadened the paper's coverage to include lucidly written summaries of important national and world news and comprehensive stories interpreting trends in industry. Circulation jumped to 65,000 in 1950, hit 360,000 in 1955, then leaped past 700,000 by 1960 as the *Journal* expanded to eight printing plants across the country, connected to the New York office by electronic typesetting devices. By 1976 the circulation was 1,450,000, second only to the *New York Daily News.*

When Kilgore died in late 1967 he was company president, and a group of former managing editors of the paper, including William F. Kerby, Buren H. McCormack, and Warren H. Phillips, were serving in key positions. Pulitzer Prize winner Edward R. Cony became executive editor in 1970. Editors William H. Grimes and Vermont C. Royster both won Pulitzer Prizes for editorial writing. Louis Kohlmeier, Stanley Penn, and Monroe Karmin all won Pulitzer Prizes for national reporting in the 1960s and Peter Kann won the international award in 1972. Dow Jones launched a general weekly, the *National Observer,* in 1962 and gained more than a half-million circulation but closed the paper in 1977 for lack of sufficient advertising. William Giles, Don Carter, and Henry Gemmill served as editors.

After 1976 the *Wall Street Journal* used satellite transmissions of its pages made up in New York; by 1983 it was producing four essentially similar editions

New York Times

Don Rice

Arthur Hays Sulzberger, *New York Times;* Mrs. Helen Rogers Reid, the *Herald Tribune.*

Washington Post

Los Angeles Times

Katharine Graham, *Washington Post;* Otis Chandler, *Los Angeles Times* and *Newsday.*

Louisville Courier-Journal

St. Louis Post-Dispatch

Barry Bingham, *Louisville Courier-Journal;* Joseph Pulitzer, III, the *Post-Dispatch.*

in seventeen U.S. printing plants, plus editions in Asia and Europe. It had passed the *Daily News* in circulation by 1980 and in 1983 reached the 2 million mark. Warren Phillips was board chairperson for Dow Jones, with onetime reporter Peter Kann serving as associate publisher and heir apparent to Phillips. Robert L. Bartley, 1980 Pulitzer Prize winner for editorial writing, was editor, and the newest managing editor was Norman Pearlstine, previously editor of the new Asian and European editions. Kann and Pearlstine began a daily "Leisure & Arts" page in late 1983 and added to their largely male staff *Washington Post* "Style" editor Lee Lescaze, *Harper's* managing editor Helen Rogan, and *Los Angeles Times* congressional correspondent Ellen Hume.

The paper had twenty-five news bureaus, eleven abroad. Its Washington bureau, second only to that of the *New York Times,* had as top correspondents James M. Perry and Albert R. Hunt in politics and Karen Elliott House in foreign affairs. Manuela Hoelterhoff won the 1983 Pulitzer award for writing criticisms of the arts, in contrast. The *Asian Wall Street Journal* began publishing in 1976 and in 1983 the *Wall Street Journal/Europe* entered the international competition. The AP-Dow Jones News Service covered forty countries with economic news reporting.

THE *WASHINGTON POST*

Other than the *Los Angeles Times,* no American newspaper rose more rapidly in esteem in recent decades than did the *Washington Post* after Eugene Meyer, a civic-minded financier, rescued it from a receivership in 1933. Meyer's object in buying the *Post* from the McLean family heirs was to give Washington a newspaper with a sound and intelligent editorial page. This he achieved with two editors who won Pulitzer Prizes for editorial writing: Felix Morley, editor until 1940, and Herbert Elliston, who served until 1953. Robert H. Estabrook then became editor of the editorial page. Giving the page added distinction were the cartoons of Herbert L. Block, better known as Herblock. Through its editorial page and its interpretative coverage of national news, the *Post* won recognition as the most independent paper in the capital. It also carried a large volume of foreign news.

When Meyer became president of the International Bank in 1946, he named Philip L. Graham, his son-in-law, as publisher, but he and his wife, Agnes E. Meyer, remained influential in the newspaper's continued progress. Purchase of the *Post*'s morning competition, the *Times-Herald,* in 1954, ensured the *Post*'s economic stability. With James Russell Wiggins as editor and Alfred Friendly as managing editor, the paper had effective news-side leaders. They joined Graham in raising voices in behalf of improved journalistic practices and in defense of fundamental press freedoms. Editorially the *Post* avoided direct endorsements, but if favored the Dewey, Eisenhower, and Kennedy candidacies. It was strongly internationalist in outlook and became known for its outspoken and early criticism of Wisconsin Senator Joseph R. McCarthy. Herblock, who had won a 1942 Pulitzer Prize, repeated in 1954 with his dramatically liberal cartoons, which had McCarthy as a particular target. Another was Vice President Nixon, whom the *Post* continued to oppose in future years.

Graham's tragic suicide in 1963 brought his wife Katharine to control of the Washington Post Company, including its television stations and *Newsweek,* purchased in 1961. Mrs. Graham was a friend of both Presidents Kennedy and Johnson and a firm supporter of their reform policies. In 1965 she moved Benjamin C. Bradlee to the *Post* from *Newsweek* and made him managing editor in 1966. Friendly became a roving reporter and won the Pulitzer Prize for covering the war in Israel. Wiggins retired to become UN ambassador in 1968. Bradlee, then 47, became executive editor and Howard Simons managing editor.

The *Post* vigorously favored Hubert Humphrey in 1968, sympathized with dissent movements, and supported the black population of its area, employing more blacks than any other American paper. When activist-philanthropist Agnes Meyer died in 1970, she had seen her daughter's paper pass the half-million mark in circulation and take a position as one of the most influential of the country's liberal-intellectual newspapers.

During the 1970s the *Washington Post* took center stage in the Watergate crisis through the courage of its publisher and chief editors in supporting the investigative reporting of Carl Bernstein and Bob Woodward, despite reprisal threats from the Nixon administration. The paper won a Pulitzer gold medal and much prestige. Editorial-page editor Philip Geyelin, himself a Pulitzer Prize winner, and his associate, Meg Greenfield, also played roles. Columnist David Broder won the 1973 award for commentary; other columnists included Nicholas Von Hoffman, Hobart Rowen on economics, and William Raspberry. Charles B. Seib served as ombudsman.

Donald Graham, the 34-year-old son of the Grahams, was named publisher of the *Post* in 1979, while his mother continued to head the company operations and served as the first woman president of the American Newspaper Publishers Association. Graham learned about his city by serving two years on its police force after returning from Vietnam. Graham replaced Geyelin with Greenfield as editorial-page editor. She, too, had won the Pulitzer editorial-writing prize. Karen DeYoung, prize-winning Latin American correspondent, became foreign editor. The *Post*'s handling of a 1981 episode involving a Pulitzer Prize article which proved fictitious, and its loss of a major libel suit, drew criticism in media circles. But the *Post* recouped with two 1983 Pulitzer awards. It had 60 percent daily and 70 percent Sunday penetration in its circulation area, a top figure in the country. To enhance its national prestige, it launched a tabloid weekly in late 1983 with a goal of 30,000 readers.

THE *LOS ANGELES TIMES*

Bursting out almost as dramatically as California's population in the 1960s, the *Los Angeles Times* became a major force in national and international journalism. It had led the nation's dailies in total advertising linage by a wide margin; it also led in space allocated to editorial material. In the 1970s the *Times* reached the million mark in circulation. It had become something far more than the fat, dullish product the *New York Times* had challenged on its home grounds in the early 1960s.

The heritage of the *Los Angeles Times* was strictly conservative. Harrison Gray Otis assumed control in 1882 and became a civic booster and Republican stalwart. When his plant was dynamited in 1910 by union radicals, his support of antiunion forces in the city was intensified. His son-in-law, Harry Chandler, was an equally conservative publisher engaged in a circulation struggle with the Hearst papers in Los Angeles. The *Times'* political editor, Kyle Palmer, so slanted his news stories that in 1937 the Washington correspondents voted the paper next to Hearst and McCormick papers as "least fair and reliable." Norman Chandler, publisher from 1944 to 1960, was more middle-of-the-road, but the paper lacked drive. It did win Pulitzer Prizes for public service, for fighting a contempt of court charge to the Supreme Court in 1942, and for an exposure of narcotics traffic in 1960.

Changes in the *Times* were being planned even before Norman Chandler's retirement. His wife, Dorothy, and son, Otis, were working with Nick B. Williams, appointed editor in 1958, to revitalize the paper. Otis Chandler, 32 when he became publisher, proved to be one of the most effective American publishers of his time. Two new Sunday sections were created, "Opinion" and "Outlook," and two Sunday magazines, *Home* and *Calendar.* Acres of local and regional news releases were replaced with significant national and foreign news. Otis Chandler struck a bargain with youthful Philip L. Graham of the *Washington Post* to form the Los Angeles Times-Washington Post News Service. By the early 1980s this was the largest supplementary news service in the world, with about 500 newspaper, magazine, and broadcasting clients.

The *Times* had seven national bureaus and twenty foreign bureaus of its own as well as the resources of the *Washington Post.* The *Times'* feature syndicate was one of the fastest growing, with more than 1300 clients. In California the paper had five state bureaus, issued separate editions in San Diego and Orange County, and expanded its suburban "zone" coverage by building an elaborate printing facility at Northridge in the San Fernando Valley.

Despite its advertising power, the paper faced stiff competition from the *Register* in Orange County and, to a lesser extent, from the *Daily News*—a *Chicago Tribune* owned paper in the San Fernando Valley—and a dozen other daily community papers with loyal readers. Within the city limits, an area serving 3 million of Los Angeles County's 7 million persons, the *Times* ran into severe criticism for not paying appropriate attention to the blacks of South Central Los Angeles and the burgeoning Latino population, centered mainly in East Los Angeles but rapidly spreading to other areas. (It was estimated that by 1990 the city's population would be heavily Latino.) However, the paper's obvious advertising strength was in the affluent suburban areas,naturally a decision was made to compete more strongly with papers serving those areas. The only metropolitan competition was the faltering *Herald-Examiner,* once a threat but reduced to a shadow of its former self.

The *Times* moved further onto the national stage through Chandler's 1970 purchase of both *Newsday* and the *Dallas Times Herald.* Later the *Denver Post* and *Hartford Courant* were added. William F. Thomas replaced Williams as editor in 1971. A major change occurred in 1977 when Tom Johnson, the youthful publisher of the *Times Herald,* was brought to the *Times* as president and chief operating officer. Three years later he became the first nonfamily member to assume the publisher's chair, as Chandler moved into the position of editor-in-chief of the entire Times Mirror Corporation. Donald F. Wright then moved from the publisher's job at *Newsday* to the *Times* presidency.

The huge news staff was headed by Thomas, managing editor George Cotliar, and national editor Dennis Britton. Pulitzer Prize winner Jack Nelson ran the Washington bureau, one of the largest, and Anthony Day was in charge of the skillfully edited editorial pages. Jean Sharley Taylor was associate editor. Reporters were given time to develop lengthy, in-depth investigative stories and features that sometimes filled several pages. Some critics wondered about the need for such unusual length, while others praised the paper as being a haven for writers. Another asset was the "View" section, which carried articles on city life, personalities, changing values, health, and consumer issues, some quite interpretative. The paper's syndicated sports columnist, Jim Murray, won the top sports-writing award numerous times.

Richard Nixon noted the *Times'* changing outlook during his ill-fated gubernatiorial campaign in 1962, attacking the paper, among others, in his postelection "blowup." In 1964 the *Times* backed Nelson Rockefeller for the Republican nomination but, failing, endorsed Goldwater for election. That year Paul Conrad joined the paper as editorial cartoonist, and his liberal line drawings won Pulitzer Prizes in 1964 and 1971. The paper also won the 1966 local-coverage award for reporting the Watts riot, and the 1969 international reporting and public-service awards, the latter for an exposure in city government. It won additional awards in 1976 for editorial writing, in 1978 for national reporting, and in 1982 for music criticism. The *Times* bitterly fought the extremist Mayor Sam Yorty and joined in a successful coalition that elected his black opponent, Tom Bradley. Early in 1971 it called on President Nixon for an immediate withdrawal of troops from Vietnam. Lacking faith in George McGovern's foreign and domestic plans, and hesitant to join the *Washington Post* in declining to endorse, the *Times* supported reelection of Nixon in 1972. Embarrassed by this sad decision, the *Times* initiated a policy of not endorsing for the presidency and other high offices. It printed Nelson's Watergate exposure stories, denounced Nixon in 1974, and continued to develop a tradition of strong interpretative reporting. In the early 1980s its foreign correspondents produced a number of notable stories from the Middle East and Central America.

The *Times'* forthright, thoughtful editorials—with some exceptions, particularly in the area of press freedom—seemed to some to lack passion, in keeping with the generally cautious attitude of the paper's management. The paper itself was also never considered "exciting" in design or presentation. Still, the *Times* clearly had moved from a staunch Republican position into one of open-mindedness and independence. In 1982 the paper endorsed far more Democrats for office than Republicans.

The problem facing the *Times* for the future was how to improve its product, given its enormous success. There were suggestions that instead of trying to increase its prestige by buying newspapers, the ambitious *Times* could look South and West, giving even more attention to neighboring Mexico, Latin America, and the Asian/Pacific nations, to eventually become known in those capitals as the leading American daily covering their affairs.

Chicago Tribune

Milwaukee Journal

James Squires, *Chicago Tribune;* Richard H. Leonard, *Milwaukee Journal.*

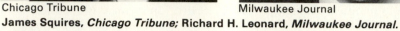

The New York Times

Los Angeles Times

A.M. Rosenthal, *New York Times;* William F. Thomas, *Los Angeles Times.*

Washington Post

Philadelphia Inquirer

Benjamin C. Bradlee, *Washington Post;* Eugene L. Roberts, *Philadelphia Inquirer.*

THE *CHICAGO TRIBUNE*

During the long regime of Colonel Robert R. McCormick as publisher of the *Chicago Tribune,* the paper was known for its ultraconservative, isolationist views and was widely criticized for its violations of journalists' ethical standards.* When McCormick died in 1955, key executives took over his *Tribune* in the absence of direct family heirs, and unswervingly continued its policies for more than a decade. The *Chicago American,* purchased from Hearst in 1956 and renamed *Chicago Today,* was the afternoon rival for the *Daily News.* Under editor W. D. Maxwell the *Tribune* viewed the social and racial crises of the 1960s with uncompromising law-and-order stances that perpetuated the image of the doughty Colonel. As a result, its circulation lead was eroded by its morning rival, the *Sun-Times.*

The *Tribune*'s turning point came with the assumption of the editorship by Clayton Kirkpatrick in 1969. He had the necessary credentials of one who had been a part of the McCormick era, so he was able to achieve changes any less-established editor would have found impossible. The slogan "The American paper for Americans" was dropped, editorializing in the news columns was curbed, and the strident editorial voice was restrained. As the older generation of *Tribune* editors and policy makers retired, Kirkpatrick gave increasing authority to younger minds. The paper's news staff was expanded. And from 1971 to 1976 the *Tribune* won three Pulitzer Prizes for local investigative reporting and an international award. Some of the paper's most unrelenting critics of the past began to talk about the "new *Chicago Tribune.*" Its managing editor was former *Today* editor Maxwell McCrohon, whose paper had been closed down by the *Tribune* in 1974 to consolidate circulation in one paper. The *Sun-Times* had come within 100,000 copies of the *Tribune* in 1974, but 2 years later the gap was 180,000 when the *Tribune* leveled off at 750,000. As 1977 opened the *Tribune* dropped the Colonel's slogan, "World's Greatest Newspaper."

The competition between the *Tribune* and the *Sun-Times* proved fatal for the *Daily News,* also the victim of declining afternoon readership. Its 1978 demise resulted in a 100,000 circulation gap once more, but in 1983 the *Sun-Times* was put up for sale. Kirkpatrick retired in 1981 and McCrohon left to become editor-in-chief of the UPI. James D. Squires, editor of the company's *Orlando Sentinel,* became *Tribune* editor; Stanton R. Cook was publisher and board chairperson. The company also owned an expanding *Daily News* in the San Fernando Valley area of Los Angeles, retained its ownership of the faltering *New York Daily News* after vainly trying to sell it in 1982, and bought the Chicago Cubs baseball team. In 1982 the *Tribune* opened a "state of the art" printing center that transformed the paper's appearance with the lavish use of color.

THE *CHRISTIAN SCIENCE MONITOR*

The *Christian Science Monitor* established itself as one of a handful of nationally read dailies and as one of two specialized newspapers of interpretation. The other was the *Wall Street Journal.* Of the regular dailies, only the *New York Times*

*See pages 430–32 in Chapter 21.

achieved a fully national circulation. However, the Gannett Company's *USA Today* laid down a strong bid for top ranking in readership as the 1980s unfolded.

The *Monitor* was begun in 1908 by Mary Baker Eddy, founder of the Church of Christ, Scientist, in protest against the sensationalism of other dailies and their emphasis on news of crimes and disasters. It was not intended to be, and did not become, a religious propaganda organ, but rather a serious-minded afternoon daily. Since by Christian Science tenets it avoided or minimized stories involving disasters, crime, or death, it had space in which to develop Washington and foreign correspondence, significant regional stories from around the country, and features dealing with literature, music, and art. Eventually it became noted for its ability to sit back periodically and take a long-view look at major news developments.

In its first 10 years the *Monitor* gained 120,000 readers under the editorship of Frederick Dixon, then was temporarily disrupted by a dispute over its management. Editor Willis J. Abbot helped to restore its prestige in the 1920s. But the *Monitor's* outstanding editor was Erwin D. Canham, who joined the staff in 1925 and served as a Washington and foreign correspondent before becoming managing editor in 1940 and editor in 1945. Canham's voice was often raised in discussions of journalistic problems and his professional associates soon came to regard him as an influential editor of a great newspaper. Paul S. Deland and Saville R. Davis followed Canham as managing editors. In 1964 Canham went into semiretirement and DeWitt John, a former *Monitor* foreign correspondent, was named editor to help reverse a circulation slump that had touched 185,000. The *Monitor* adopted a five-column front-page makeup, larger type, splashy art work, and more sparkling writing. Before 1970 the staff had won two national reporting Pulitzer Prizes, by Howard James and Robert Cahn, and the international award, by R. John Hughes in Tokyo. In 1970 Hughes succeeded John as editor. During the next decade the *Monitor*'s quality improved but circulation fluctuated from 260,000 to 150,000. Earl W. Froell was named editor in 1979 and editor-in-chief in 1983. Katherine W. Fanning, who had been editor and publisher of the *Anchorage Daily News* in Alaska, joined the *Monitor* as editor. Richard Newneman was managing editor and Charlotte Saikowski edited a superior editorial page. Godfrey Sperling headed Washington coverage, long famed for the reporting of Richard L. Strout. Among foreign correspondents were Elizabeth Pond in Moscow, where Edmund Stevens had won a Pulitzer Prize earlier, Takashi Oka in London, Henry Hayward in Africa, and Daniel Southerland in Asia. Published in Boston and distributed through several regional printing plants, the *Monitor* also printed a weekly U.S. edition and an international edition.

THE *PHILADELPHIA INQUIRER*

Coming to the front in the Knight-Ridder newspaper group in the past decade, as a rival to the *Miami Herald* and *Detroit Free Press,* has been the *Philadelphia Inquirer,* described before its 1970 purchase by John S. Knight as an "unqualifiedly awful paper." Knight brought Eugene L. Roberts, Jr., the 40-year-old

Harris & Ewing

Wall Street Journal

National newspapers were edited by Erwin D. Canham *(left)* and Bernard Kilgore.

national editor of the *New York Times,* to Philadelphia and gave him free rein as executive editor to compete with the *Bulletin,* long advertised as the paper nearly everybody read. Beginning in 1975 the *Inquirer* staff, under Roberts' prodding, won six consecutive Pulitzer prizes. One was the 1978 gold medal for reporting on police abuse in the city, another pair for national and international reporting, and two for local reporting including the 1980 story of the Three Mile Island crisis. Cartoonist Tony Auth won in 1976.

When the *Bulletin,* faced with mounting deficits, suspended publication in 1982, Roberts persuaded the Knight-Ridder management to give him eighty new reporters and editors, five overseas news bureaus, ten new national and foreign correspondents, a new Sunday book-review section, a 20 percent larger news hole, the UPI news wire, five more photographers, and thirteen new comic strips. Before the end of the year, daily circulation had increased 30 percent and the Sunday paper became the fifth largest in the country. Principal competition was the *Inquirer*'s companion paper, the afternoon *Daily News.* Roberts, known as "the Frog" to his staff and competitors, had made his soft-spoken Southern presence known on the national scene, along with his paper.

THE *BOSTON GLOBE*

Coming into contention for top national ranking in the 1970s was the *Boston Globe,* founded in 1872 and published by four generations of the Taylor family since 1873. The morning and evening *Globes,* which dominated Boston newspapering since the 1960s, won national attention by joining the *New York Times* and the *Washington Post* in publishing the Pentagon Papers until stopped by court order. Under publisher Davis Taylor and editor Thomas Winship in May, 1967, the *Globe* had becme the second major United States paper to oppose the Vietnam War; it also editorialized against the Nixon presidential candidacies in 1968 and 1972. In October, 1973, it became the first major daily to call for his impeachment.

Such a record gave the *Globe* liberal credentials, which it furthered through the reporting of Washington bureau chief Martin Nolan, the cartoons of Paul Szep, and the winning of the 1975 Pulitzer gold medal for its coverage of the Boston school controversy and antibusing riots. In 1980 the paper was awarded a nearly unprecedented three Pulitzer prizes when its local reporting group, called the Spotlight Team, columnist Ellen Goodman, and critic William A. Henry, III, all won. In 1983 the *Globe* once more won a Pulitzer Prize, for a 56-page report on the nuclear arms race.

General Charles H. Taylor took over the *Globe* as publisher in 1873 and as editor after 1880, making it a sensationalized New Journalism product catching the eye of Joseph Pulitzer. The first William O. Taylor held both posts until 1955, when Davis Taylor became publisher and Laurence Winship, managing editor since 1937, took over as editor. Thomas Winship, Laurence's son, became editor in 1965 and was instrumental in giving the *Globe* its "new look." Winning national attention, Winship was elected ASNE president in 1980. The second William O. Taylor became publisher in 1978. The two *Globes* were merged into an all-day paper in 1979.

THE *MIAMI HERALD*

A progressive leader in the South, which won its way to a top place nationally by 1970, was the *Miami Herald,* a member of the Knight-Ridder newspaper group. In 1980 it was the eighteenth largest American daily in circulation and the third in advertising volume, despite Miami's rank in city size: forty-first by population, twenty-first by market area.

John S. Knight began his career in the 1920s on the family's *Akron Beacon-Journal.* Their first expansion outside Ohio was to the *Miami Herald* in 1937. Purchase of the *Detroit Free Press* in 1940 gave the Knights a major group, to which they added the Charlotte and Macon newspapers and the *Philadelphia Inquirer* and *Daily News.* James L. Knight, a brother, concentrated his interest on the Miami and Charlotte operations, while John Knight focused on Detroit. But the management was integrated. In 1974 the Knights merged their sixteen-daily group with Ridder Publications, which owned or had a substantial interest in nineteen dailies. The new Knight-Ridder had the largest combined circulation of all United States groups. Added were such major Ridder papers as the *St. Paul Dispatch and Pioneer Press* and *San Jose Mercury and News.*

Lee Hills joined the *Miami Herald* in 1942, coming from the Scripps-Howard papers. As managing editor, he built up the *Herald*'s Latin American coverage and began an international air-express edition. In 1951 the *Herald* won a Pulitzer public-service award for a drive on organized crime. The same year Hills was named executive editor of the *Detroit Free Press,* where he won a 1955 Pulitzer Prize for spot news. He became executive editor of all Knight newspapers in 1959. Directing the *Herald*'s news operations and helping win a 1976 Pulitzer Prize for local reporting were George Beebe, associate publisher, and Don Shoemaker, editor. John McMullan became executive editor in the 1970s. He expanded the *Herald*'s foreign and domestic bureaus and saw the paper win three more Pulitzer Prizes before retiring in 1983.

John S. Knight had written his famed column, "The Editor's Notebook," for 32 years before he won the Pulitzer Prize for editorial writing in 1968. Both he and Hills served as president of the American Society of Newspaper Editors, Knight twice. Knight helped found and was president of the Inter American Press Association, which Hills later headed. Among American publishers of the 1970s, Knight was one of the most outspoken. Against participation in the Indochina war since 1954, he had a loud and clear position on that issue. Knight and his group of papers generally supported Republicans for the presidency but deserted Senator Goldwater in 1964.

Hills stepped down as Knight-Ridder board chairperson in 1979 but remained as editorial chairperson. Bernard H. Ridder, Jr., succeeded him. Knight died in 1981. The same year Shirley Christian gave his *Herald* another Pulitzer Prize, for international reporting from Central America. The *Herald* published a Spanish-language edition circulating to thirty-one countries.

THE *LOUISVILLE COURIER-JOURNAL*

The South, with a more slowly developing industrial economy, smaller population, and fewer major cities, did not match the East and Midwest in producing newspapers that could win the highest possible rankings in the estimate of the craft. But as early as the 1950s at least one—the *Louisville Courier-Journal* from the border state of Kentucky—became a newspaper that ranked among the nation's best.

The retirement in 1919 of Henry Watterson, editor of the *Courier-Journal* since 1868, brought the Bingham family to the fore. Judge Robert Worth Bingham bought the *Courier-Journal* and the afternoon *Times* in 1917. Before he died in 1937 he saw his son, Barry Bingham, well established as directing owner of the newspapers. At his right hand was Mark Ethridge, former associate editor of the *Washington Post* and publisher of the *Richmond Times-Dispatch,* who came to Louisville as general manager in 1936 and became publisher in 1942. Bingham took the title and writing responsibilities, of editor of the *Courier-Journal.*

Events moved rapidly in Louisville under the Bingham-Ethridge regime. James S. Pope became executive editor of the two papers. Norman E. Isaacs, managing editor of the *St. Louis Star-Times* when it closed down in 1951, came to Louisville as managing editor of the *Times.* Bingham, Ethridge, Pope, and Isaacs all were recognized as vocal, intelligent leaders in the journalistic profession.

Steadily Democratic in its political preferences, the *Courier-Journal* exerted a strong influence as a progressive, fair-minded newspaper dedicated to defending basic democratic principles. In news play, it excelled in international and national coverage, but it also paid close attention to Louisville, where it did effective work in behalf of blacks, union labor, education, music, and art.

The deaths of two of Bingham's sons in accidents left Barry Bingham, Jr., who preferred a broadcasting career, with the family newspaper responsibility. He became editor and publisher in 1971, while his father remained as board chairperson. Ethridge and Pope had retired; Isaacs left the executive editorship in 1970 to teach at Columbia University. Robert P. Clark succeeded him. Carol Sutton, who became managing editor in 1974, was the first woman to hold that post on a major daily. Two years later she was named assistant to young Bingham.

When the *Courier-Journal* won the 1967 Pulitzer Prize for public service, the judges cited a successful campaign to control the Kentucky strip-mining industry and thus preserve the environment. It also won the 1978 local-reporting award and the 1980 international award.

NEWSDAY

Long Island's *Newsday,* founded by Alicia Patterson in 1940 and controlled by her until she died in 1963, won its spurs as one of the top evening papers by combining local area coverage with substantial national and world news. It won the Pulitzer Prize for public service in 1964 and 1970 for uncovering Long Island governmental scandals, and it won another prize in 1974. Tom Darcy won the 1970 award for cartooning.

Alicia Patterson and her husband, Harry F. Guggenheim, differed on politics, he being the more conservative. In presidential races the paper supported Democrats in 1956, 1960, and 1964 and Republicans in 1952 and 1968. The switch to Nixon in 1968 came after Guggenheim took control in 1963. His editors were Mark Ethridge, from Louisville, followed by Bill D. Moyers, President Johnson's press secretary in 1966. Guggenheim apparently intended to put Moyers in control of *Newsday* but became fearful of his policies and in 1970 sold his 51 percent stock interest to Otis Chandler of the *Los Angeles Times.* Moyers resigned and William Attwood came from the Cowles magazines to head *Newsday* as publisher. David Laventhol was executive editor.

Under Otis Chandler's guidance, by the early 1980s *Newsday* was the second largest circulation evening daily. Donald Wright, chief operating officer after 1977, became the president and chief operating officer of the parent *Los Angeles Times* in 1982. Lou Schwartz succeeded Laventhol as executive editor in 1981.

THE *ST. PETERSBURG TIMES*

Nelson Poynter was a fiercely independent newspaperperson who in 1947 imposed upon himself "fifteen standards of ownership" which he published in his *St. Petersburg Times.* His dedication to high journalistic principles and basic liberalism helped him bring his paper into the top ranks of American dailies before his death in 1978.

The *Times* was founded in 1884 and came into Poynter family control in 1912. Nelson assumed direction in 1938. He and his wife Henrietta founded the objective research organization, *Congressional Quarterly,* in Washington, and bought control of their local competition in St. Petersburg, the *Evening Independent,* in 1962. Publishing an aggressive daily in a sleepy Florida city whose population was 30 percent senior citizens was no mean feat, but the Poynters succeeded.

Poynter selected Eugene C. Patterson, who had left the *Atlanta Constitution* editorship in a 1968 dispute, to succeed him. Patterson came in 1972 and was in full control after 1978. The *Times* won the 1964 Pulitzer gold medal, a 1980 Pulitzer Prize for national reporting, and national acclaim for its graphics and spectacular color printing. Its stock was owned by the Modern Media Institute, a writing-coaching school which Poynter created to further journalistic standards, and which under Roy Peter Clark won a national reputation.

THE *ATLANTA CONSTITUTION*

Atlanta gave the South two strong newspapers, the *Constitution* and the *Journal.* Clark Howell, Sr., who succeeded Henry Grady at the *Constitution* in 1889, became the paper's owner and served as editor until 1936. His son, Clark Howell, Jr., named Ralph McGill as editor in 1938. McGill opposed the Ku Klux Klan and the Talmadge political machine in Georgia and won a Pulitzer Prize for editorial writing in 1959.

James M. Cox, owner of the *Journal,* obtained control of the *Constitution* in 1950, but the papers continued to have separate editorial policies. When McGill became a syndicated columnist and publisher of the *Constitution* in 1960, Eugene C. Patterson was named editor. He won the Pulitzer Prize in 1967 for his daily column and editorials attacking racism and political demagoguery. Then, declaring that he lacked support by his management, he left, taking control of the *St. Petersburg Times.* In the early 1980s, Thomas H. Wood headed the publishing company, Harold Gulliver was editor of the *Constitution,* and Jim Minter was executive editor. Anne Cox Chambers, the daughter of the owner, became important in the company after his death.

THE *MILWAUKEE JOURNAL*

The *Milwaukee Journal* stood in the uppermost level of the country's newspapers as a conscientiously edited, well-written, community-conscious daily blessed with one of the nation's largest volumes of advertising and space for comprehensive news coverage. Its editorial page ranked in stature with those of the *St. Louis Post-Dispatch* and other leading progressive dailies.

The *Journal,* founded in 1882, faced strong competition through all its early years. Publisher Lucius W. Nieman set the trend for its community leadership. Under Nieman's guidance the *Journal* developed an international outlook, supporting the League of Nations and the United Nations. The paper clashed with the isolationist-minded La Follette family and Milwaukee's Socialist leader, Victor Berger, on foreign policy. But as a middle-of-the-road, independent paper it tended to support progressive-minded politicians of whatever party. Nationally, it supported Roosevelt in 1932, 1936, and mildly in 1944; Willkie in 1940; Dewey in 1948; and then the Stevenson candidacies. Its fiercest battle was with Senator Joseph R. McCarthy on his home ground; when McCarthy won reelection in 1952 he failed to carry Milwaukee. It refused to support either Nixon or Goldwater in the 1960s, endorsing Kennedy, Johnson, Humphrey, and Carter.

A dominant personality appeared on the *Journal* staff in 1916 when Harry J. Grant became business manager. Grant acquired 20 percent of the stock and the title of publisher in 1919. He imported Marvin H. Creager from the *Kansas City Star,* and Creager, as managing editor and later as editor and company president, reinforced the *Journal's* local coverage and writing qualities with an insistence born of his *Star* experience.

Nieman died in 1935 and his wife in 1936. Part of the Nieman fortune was left to Harvard University, which used it to establish the Nieman Fellowships for newspaperpeople. The Nieman stock holdings in the paper were up for sale, but Grant saved the situation by organizing an employee-ownership plan similar to that of the *Star* in Kansas City. Grant, as board chairperson and a substantial stockholder, remained in firm control. J. Donald Ferguson succeeded Creager as editor in 1943, and Lindsay Hoben followed Ferguson in 1961.

Richard H. Leonard became managing editor in 1962 and moved up to the editorship in 1967, with the death of Hoben. John Reddin and Sig Gissler edited the editorial pages and Joseph M. Shoquist became managing editor. The *Journal* won the 1967 Pulitzer Prize for public service, repeating its 1918 award, and the 1977 local-reporting prize. Its employees owned 80 percent of the stock in the Journal Company, which also owned the *Milwaukee Sentinel* and the city's major television station.

THE *ST. LOUIS POST-DISPATCH*

The revolution of the 1870s and 1880s known as the New Journalism gave the Midwest nationally known newspapers that continued to demonstrate their leadership in the 1980s. None was more consistently in the foremost rank of American newspapers than the *St. Louis Post-Dispatch,* founded in 1878 by the first Joseph Pulitzer, edited from 1911 to 1955 by the second Joseph Pulitzer, and since then by the third of the line, Joseph Pulitzer, III, who began assuming authority in the late 1940s.

Continuity, both of Pulitzer family ownership and the *Post-Dispatch* editorial policies, proved to be the key to greatness. Hammering away consistently to make the editorial page an independent, liberal voice were six editorial page editors: George S. Johns, who served from 1897 to 1928, Clark McAdams, Charles G. Ross, Ralph Coghlan, Irving Dilliard, and Robert Lasch. Daniel R. Fitzpatrick's incisive cartoons dramatized *Post-Dispatch* crusades from 1913 until 1958.

O. K. Bovard, one of America's great newspeople, provided the necessary complement of leadership during his 30 years as *Post-Dispatch* managing editor, from 1908 to 1938. Under his tutelage, such brilliant reporters as Paul Y. Anderson, Charles G. Ross, Marquis Childs, and Raymond P. Brandt advanced from St. Louis to the Washington scene to help win a national reputation for the paper. Anderson proved to be the mainspring of Bovard's effort after World War I to expand *Post-Dispatch* coverage of the national scene. Through his efforts the paper successfully led a campaign in 1923 to obtain the release of fifty-two Americans still imprisoned 5 years after the war's end for expressing radical antiwar opinion. Anderson and his paper were the first to realize the significance of the Teapot Dome scandal. And as a Washington correspondent,

Anderson aided in the impeachment, for improper conduct, of federal judge George W. English of East St. Louis in 1926. English resigned before his impeachment trial.

What *Post-Dispatch* personnel called the "dignity page"—the opening page of the editorial section—was developed by Bovard to carry special articles on political, economic, scientific, and cultural subjects. When Bovard resigned in 1938 after differences with his publisher, Benjamin H. Reese became managing editor. Raymond L. Crowley succeeded Reese in 1951.

During the 15 years beginning in 1937 the *Post-Dispatch* won five Pulitzer Prize gold medals for meritorious public service. Politically, *Post-Dispatch* support had usually been given to Democratic presidential candidates, although it deserted Roosevelt once, in 1936, and supported Dewey in 1948. It opposed Richard Nixon in his three presidential races, and supported George McGovern in 1972.

Crowley's retirement in 1962 brought Arthur R. Bertelson to the managing editorship; when he advanced to executive editor, Evarts A. Graham, Jr. succeeded him. Raymond P. Brandt retired in 1967 after 44 years in the Washington bureau. Marquis Childs, his successor as bureau chief, won the 1970 Pulitzer Prize for commentary before he retired. Richard Dudman, who replaced Childs, became another outstanding Washington bureau chief for the *Post-Dispatch.* William F. Woo was editorial page chief and Thomas Engelhardt cartoonist. Circulation had declined sharply by the early 1980s, like that of other afternoon dailies, but the *Post-Dispatch* still won the plaudits of a *Wall Street Journal* reporter for having the spirit "to say what it thinks" in traditional liberal stance.

THE *INTERNATIONAL HERALD TRIBUNE*

After 1966 the legend *"Herald Tribune"* could be found only on a paper circulating in the world's capitals: "The *International Herald Tribune*. Published with the New York Times and the Washington Post." For reasons of both quality and tradition, the paper should be included among the surviving greats.

The *New York Herald Tribune* was for 42 years a distinguished morning rival of the *Times.* Ogden M. Reid and his wife, Helen Rogers Reid, succeeded to control of the *Tribune* when editor Whitelaw Reid died in 1912. With the purchase of *The Herald* from Frank Munsey in 1924, and the creation of the *Herald Tribune,* a distinctive newspaper emerged. Ogden Reid was content to have his wife assume the major responsibilities of the publisher's office.

Like the *Times,* the *Herald Tribune* became known for its foreign and Washington correspondence and for its coverage of cultural news. Its syndicated columnists included Mark Sullivan, Walter Lippmann, Joseph Alsop, and Roscoe Drummond. Geoffrey Parsons, a Pulitzer Prize winner, served as chief editorial writer from 1924 to 1952. Stanley Walker became one of New York's best-known city editors, and assistant editor Wilbur Forrest was an important journalistic figure. When Ogden Reid died in 1947 his sons, another Whitelaw Reid and Ogden R. Reid, joined their mother in directing the paper's affairs. But difficulties piled up, and in 1958 the Reids reluctantly sold the the *Herald Tribune* to millionaire John Hay Whitney.

The paper adopted a magazine-style format under editors John Denson and James G. Bellows. Crippled by a 114-day strike in 1963, the "Trib" still presented some of the best-designed front pages and the most literate writing in American journalism. But most New York newspapers were losing money, and in early 1966 Whitney, the Hearst group, and Scripps-Howard planned a merger in which the *Herald Tribune* would become the morning edition of a World Journal Tribune Company. The final edition of the *Herald Tribune* appeared on April 24; agreement could not be reached with the printing unions and Whitney announced its death August 15. A *World Journal Tribune* appeared evenings and Sundays from September, 1966, to May, 1967. Mrs. Helen Rogers Reid died in 1970, and an era was no more.

Consistently conservative in its outlook, the old *Herald Tribune* won wide respect for fairness and for high-quality interpretative writing. It supported the internationalist wing of the Republican party and early promoted the presidential bids of Willkie and Eisenhower, and not that of Senator Robert A. Taft. In its final campaign in New York the *Herald Tribune* rejected Barry Goldwater for Lyndon Johnson.

Left from the wreckage was the *International Herald Tribune,* successor to the Bennetts' old *Paris Herald.* In 1967 the *New York Times* gave up its European edition; Whitney, Katharine Graham of the *Washington Post,* and Sulzberger became joint owners of the Paris-based "Trib," which ran editorials from all three ownership sources. The paper increased its circulation throughout the 1970s as it won extensive European readership as well as that of American tourists. Whitney died in 1982 and was succeeded by Walter N. Thayer as head of the paper. Satellite transmission enabled the *International Herald Tribune* to print in Asian plants as circulation reached 150,000. Of this, 100,000 was in Europe, compared to an expected 25,000 for the *Wall Street Journal/Europe* and 33,000 readers on the continent for the *Financial Times* of London.

OTHER EASTERN LEADERS

Among other leading newspapers of the East was the *New York Post,* which completed 175 years of continuous daily publication in 1976, a record for currently published American dailies. The *Post* entered a new phase when Dorothy Schiff bought it in 1939. With editor Ted O. Thackrey, she made the paper a streamlined tabloid, departmentalized the news, and added feature content. Its columnists, led by Max Lerner, were prominently displayed. James W. Wechsler, from the staff of *PM,* became editor in 1949. The *Post* was the only New York City daily supporting Democratic candidate Adlai Stevenson in 1952 and 1956, and it backed Democrats continuously thereafter. When metropolitan New York journalism collapsed in the mid-1960s, the *Post* emerged as the only afternoon daily and increased its circulation by two-thirds. Still, publisher Schiff found the struggle hard and sold the *Post* in 1977 to the newest press lord, Australian Rupert Murdoch. The *Post* was sensationalized in the Murdoch manner, so much so that the *New York Daily News* attempted to publish an intellectual evening rival, *Tonight.* It failed, and the recession of the early 1980s brought the *Daily News* to its knees as well. Its Chicago Tribune Company owners could not sell it, and the *Post* and *Daily News* continued a strenuous rivalry reminiscent of the 1920s tabloid era. By 1983 the *Post* had caught up with the *Times* in daily sales and increased its advertising, while the *Daily News* had stabilized through economies.

John S. Knight's *Detroit Free Press,* survivor with the *News* in that city's circulation battle, won the Pulitzer Prize for public service in 1945, and editor Royce Howes won for editorial writing in 1955. The prize for local reporting followed in 1968. But the *Free Press* and rival *News* were crippled by long strikes and major racial disturbances in the 1960s. The *Free Press* responded to Watergate scandals and Detroit's financial dilemmas by endorsing Jimmy Carter in 1976. Large-scale unemployment in Detroit put both newspapers in the red by the early 1980s. The *Free Press,* with veteran Knight-Ridder executive Lee Hills as publisher, came close to passing the *News* in circulation. David Lawrence, Jr. was its executive editor. His rival at the locally owned *News,* William Giles, resigned in 1983 and was succeeded by Lionel Linder. Both papers won Pulitzer Prizes for reporting in the 1980s rivalry.

In Ohio, publisher Paul Block, Jr.'s *Toledo Blade* advanced steadily after 1950 in comprehensive news coverage, community leadership, and independence of opinion. With its morning edition, the *Times,* it was allied in ownership with the *Pittsburgh Post-Gazette,* published by William Block.

Long vying with the *Washington Post* and the *New York Times* for position on important Washington breakfast tables was the *Baltimore Sun.* The *Sun,* giving special attention to Washington coverage since its founding in 1837, had developed one of the strongest capital bureaus as well as a notable foreign service. Rejuvenated in the decade preceding World War I by Charles H. Grasty and Van-Lear Black, the *Sun* prospered under the effective leadership of Paul C. Patterson, publisher from 1918 to 1950. Hamilton Owens directed an aggressive editorial page. Washington columnist Frank R. Kent, H. L. Mencken, and Gerald W. Johnson were well-known staff members, followed by four Pulitzer Prize winners of the 1940s: Dewey L. Fleming, Paul W. Ward, Mark S. Watson, and Price Day. Philip Potter continued the *Sun* tradition of excellence in foreign and Washington correspondence. Reg Murphy was publisher in the 1980s.

MIDWEST JOURNALISTIC LEADERS

When journalism educators were asked in a 1961 poll to select the best combinations of morning and evening newspapers published by the same organization, they placed the Cowles-owned *Minneapolis Star* and *Tribune* and *Des Moines Register* and *Tribune* second and third, close behind the *Louisville Courier-Journal* and *Times.* Of the four papers owned by John and Gardner Cowles, the *Minneapolis Tribune* ranked highest as an individual daily.

Under publisher John Cowles the morning *Tribune* and evening *Star* developed wide upper Midwest circulations from their Minneapolis base. After a successful career with the Associated Press, Gideon Seymour joined the papers in 1939 and was named executive editor in 1944. Carroll Binder, *Chicago Daily News* foreign editor, became editorial page editor of the *Tribune* in 1945.

Cowles, Seymour, and Binder teamed together to give the papers broadened news coverage, strong interpretative qualities, and independent-minded editorial pages strongly internationalist in outlook. Seymour died in 1954 and Binder in 1956. William P. Steven became executive editor, and Wilbur E. Elston editorial-pages editor. Both left when John Cowles, Jr. took direct control of the news and editorial pages after 1960. Republican in national politics through 1960, the papers endorsed Democrats thereafter and were vigorously opposed to the Vietnam War early. Poor editing decisions, staff dissensions, and the adverse climate for afternoon dailies brought a merger in 1982 in Minneapolis: The paper became the morning *Star and Tribune.* In Des Moines the evening *Tribune* was killed. Early in 1983 a revolt by family members, led by cousin David Kruidenier of Des Moines, forced John Cowles, Jr. to resign his executive posts. The two were grandsons of Gardner Cowles, Sr.

In Des Moines, editorial editors W. W. Waymack, Forrest W. Seymour, and Lauren K. Soth all won Pulitzer Prizes for editorial writing. The Cowles Washington bureau won four Pulitzer awards for national reporting; the 1976 and 1979 national-reporting awards went to James Risser of Des Moines. Kenneth MacDonald became chief operating officer for Gardner Cowles.

While other leading dailies were expanding staff reporting of national news, the *Kansas City Star* was sticking principally to the local and regional area coverage William Rockhill Nelson had emphasized from the time he founded the *Star* in 1880 until his death in 1915. Fine writing of news and features, and vigorous crusading in the community interest, were special ingredients that kept the *Star* high in newspaper ratings. Continuity was ensured when the staff bought stock control in 1926 for $11 million.

Bulky, jovial Roy A. Roberts dominated Kansas City journalism for nearly 40 years. He became the *Star's* managing editor in 1928 after 15 years as Washington correspondent, and was elected president of the *Star* and its evening edition, the *Times,* in 1947. Roberts loved politics and became an important, if unofficial, figure in Republican party affairs. He retired in 1965. In 1977 the employees sold their stock to Capital City Communications, a small publishing group, for $125 million, a move which made some twenty of them millionaires. The *Star* and *Times* shared the 1982 Pulitzer Prize for the local reporting of a hotel collapse disaster and the *Times* won the 1982 national award. Observers were rating the *Times* ahead of its more famous rival.

The morning *St. Louis Globe-Democrat* was the *Post-Dispatch*'s only rival after the closing of the *Star-Times* in 1951. The *Globe-Democrat,* built to prominence by Joseph B. McCullagh before 1900, also worked vigorously for civic progress, although less dramatically and in a conservative political atmosphere. E. Lansing Ray was publisher from 1925 to 1955, when the paper was sold to Samuel I. Newhouse. Editorial editor Louis LaCoss won the Pulitzer Prize for editorial writing in 1952, the paper's centennial year.

OTHER TOP PAPERS OF THE SOUTH

Affiliated with the *Miami Herald* through the Knight newspapers group, the *Charlotte Observer* rose to prominence in Southern journalism during the 1960s. Purchased by the Knight family in 1954, it was given the personal attention of James L. Knight, who became publisher. Named editor in 1955 was C. A. (Pete)

McKnight, who had been editor of the small evening *News* (later bought by Knight). McKnight had just served as editor of the *Southern School News,* an objective reporter of school-desegregation developments, and took the *Observer* along a conciliatory road on civil rights. Cartoonist Eugene Payne won a 1968 Pulitzer Prize and the *Observer* won the 1981 gold medal.

Long known for its liberalism and stubborn fight against the conservative *Nashville Banner,* the paper developed by Silliman Evans, the *Nashville Tennessean,* also won respect for its civil-rights attitudes. The paper's fortunes declined after Evans' death in 1955, but they rose again when his younger son Amon Carter Evans became publisher in 1962, at age 29. With liberal John Seigenthaler as editor, the *Tennessean* supported the Kennedy-Johnson-Humphrey program for domestic reform. It also resumed the local crusading for which the elder Evans was famous. In Memphis, the Scripps-Howard group had one of its best representatives in the *Commercial Appeal,* which developed its coverage and influence across state lines.

There were other famous names in Southern journalism. Josephus Daniels continued his interest in the *Raleigh News and Observer* until his death in 1948, and he passed on his editorship to his son, Jonathan, who also exerted influence in community and political affairs. Editor Virginius Dabney of the *Richmond Times-Dispatch* eyed traditional attitudes skeptically and jarred complacent conservatives with his editorials from 1928 into the 1960s. He won a Pulitzer Prize in 1948. Dr. Douglas Southall Freeman, editor of the *Richmond News Leader* from 1915 to 1949, won Pulitzer Prizes for his biographies of Robert E. Lee and George Washington. In Little Rock, J. N. Heiskell completed 60 years as editor of the respected *Arkansas Gazette* in 1961. His paper won the Pulitzer Prize for public service, and executive editor Harry S. Ashmore won the award for editorial writing, for leadership during the 1957 school-desegregation crisis in Little Rock. The stand cost the paper some of its public support, and Ashmore left to join the Ford Foundation.

Rapidly growing Texas fostered a journalism in keeping with the state's free-enterprise economic atmosphere. Vigorous competition existed in many cities but among dailies essentially conservative in their editorial outlooks. The *Dallas News,* inherited by E. M. (Ted) Dealey in 1946 from his father, George, became an archconservative voice in Republican-voting Dallas. Houston's two largest papers, the morning *Post* and evening *Chronicle,* were carefully conservative. The *Post* was built into prominence by William P. Hobby and his editor-wife, Oveta Culp Hobby. The *Chronicle,* owned by financier Jesse Jones until his death in 1956, obtained William P. Steven as editor in 1960 but discharged him in 1965 for moving too rapidly. Another financier, Amon G. Carter, and his son firmly established the *Fort Worth Star-Telegram* as a leading Texas daily. Noteworthy for taking a strong liberal stand on the integration issue were the *San Antonio Express* and *News.*

Dallas became a competitive city in 1970 when the *Los Angeles Times* bought the *Times Herald.* In 1975 Times Mirror brought Kenneth Johnson from the *Washington Post* to be executive editor, and gave him 100 new staff members in 3 years. The *News* countered in 1980 by making Burl Osborne, the AP's managing editor, its executive editor and sharply upgrading its Washington bureau. Both papers widened their coverage of national and international news in what was called the "Shootout in the Big D."

STRONG VOICES OF THE WEST

Palmer Hoyt's entry into Denver journalism as publisher of the *Post* signaled a definite end of the Tammen-Bonfils type of newspapering. Hoyt gradually modified the *Post*'s gaudy makeup, increased its interpretative news coverage, and gave the paper a better editorial balance. The *Post* developed a strong internationalist point of view and an independent editorial page that swung the usually Republican paper to the Kennedy camp in 1960. It continued to support Democratic candidates Johnson, Humphrey, and Carter. Hoyt retired in 1970. The rival *Rocky Mountain News,* edited for Scripps-Howard by Michael B. Howard, grandson of Roy Howard, caught up with the *Post* in circulation by 1980. Then young Howard suddenly resigned; he later told in the columns of the *Post* his story of a drug addiction. In December, 1980, Times Mirror added the *Post* to its newspaper holdings and brought in recruits from Los Angeles and Dallas, headed by editor Will Jarrett. In 1982 the *Post* switched from afternoon to morning publication for a head-on battle with the *Rocky Mountain News,* which was edited by Ralph Looney with Jean Otto as editorial-page editor. Otto had been the first woman president of the Society of Professional Journalists while she was a *Milwaukee Journal* editor.

The *Seattle Times,* founded in 1896 and long controlled by the Blethen family, held a wide circulation lead over the rival *Post-Intelligencer* of the Hearst group, and in 1983 was seeking permission for a joint printing arrangement to ensure continued competition. It was ranked second only to the *Los Angeles Times* among Western papers. J. A. Blethen was publisher. The paper won the 1982 Pulitzer Prize for local reporting.

The *San Francisco Chronicle* was famed under publisher George T. Cameron, editor Chester Rowell, and general manager Paul C. Smith in the 1930s and 1940s for its comprehensive national- and foreign-news coverage. But in the 1950s, under new direction, the *Chronicle* turned heavily toward features, columnists, and circulation-getting news. It passed the Hearst-owned *Examiner* in readers, but the *Examiner* surpassed it in solid news. The *Chronicle* was always an interesting paper, however, under the editorship of Scott Newhall, who resigned in 1971 to protest what he felt was an increasing managerial conservatism in sociopolitical outlook. Charles deYoung Thieriot long carried the paper's historic family names and the titles of editor and publisher; he was succeeded by Richard Thieriot in the 1980s.

In Portland, the long-respected *Oregonian* ran into difficulties. Its famous editor, Harvey W. Scott, died in 1910, and manager Henry L. Pittock in 1919. Their heirs found a strong editor in Palmer Hoyt, from 1933 until he left to become publisher of the *Denver Post* in 1946. Control of the *Oregonian* passed to Samuel Newhouse in 1950, as did ownership of the rival *Oregon Journal* in 1961. The papers were badly hurt by a prolonged strike, beginning in 1959, that sharply reduced their staff morale. The problem was apparently solved in 1982 when the evening *Journal* was absorbed into the morning *Oregonian.* J. Richard Nokes was editor.

The McClatchy-owned *Bee* newspapers in California, published in Sacramento, Fresno, and Modesto, won reputations as fiercely independent dailies. The *Sacramento Bee,* founded in 1857, became well known under its publisher-editor, C. K. McClatchy, who served from 1883 to 1936. The *Bee* crusaded for public power, spoke out for individual liberties, and won a Pulitzer Prize for public service in 1935 for exposing political corruption. Eleanor McClatchy succeeded her father as publisher and kept to his usually pro-Democratic political beliefs. Another C. K. McClatchy was publisher and editor beginning in the 1970s.

When Helen Copley inherited James S. Copley's newspaper empire in 1973, she became one of the most powerful women in publishing. The paper she knew best was the *San Diego Union,* whose stolid conservatism discouraged newcomers to the booming city. With editor Gerald L. Warren, she shook up the staff, encouraged aggressive reporting, and brought the *Union* toward a more conventional conservative position. The *Santa Barbara News-Press,* long owned by Thomas M. Storke, was another noteworthy Western paper. It won the 1962 Pulitzer Prize for editorial writing by exposing the character of the John Birch Society.

STABILIZING THE DAILIES, 1930–1980s

What were the effects on newspapers of intermedia advertising competition and the ups and downs of the economy from 1930 to the 1980s? In broad strokes, the number of dailies decreased, then stabilized near the 1750 figure; ownership concentration increased as the number of competitive dailies declined; circulation steadily increased; and while financial problems were many, the newspaper publishing economy tended to stabilize comfortably.

The sharp drop in advertising revenue in the early 1930s wiped out many newspaper profit margins despite cutbacks in salaries, production costs, and newsprint prices, which fell as low as $40 a ton. There were 145 suspensions of dailies during 1931 to 1933, and seventy-seven more in the recovery years of 1934 to 1936, mainly in larger cities and industrial areas. Then came the business recession of 1937; advertising revenues dropped at this time, when labor and production costs had mounted to substantially higher post-Depression levels. Some newspaper managements, hit by these new disasters after surviving the Great Depression, were too tired to struggle any longer. Daily newspaper suspensions and mergers accelerated, totaling 165 in the years 1937 to 1939. In many respects these were the blackest years in the history of American newspapers; one-third of salaried employees in the newspaper industry lost their jobs, according to census statistics. The war years of 1940 to 1944 brought another 197 newspaper deaths, mostly small dailies pinched by production problems. With 584 suspensions and 386 new starts of dailies since 1931, the number of English-language general-circulation daily newspapers dropped from 1942 in 1930 to a twentieth-century low of 1744 in 1945.

Postwar expansion brought an excess of new starts over suspensions in the daily field. The mid-1940s and mid-1950s were profitable years for newspapers in general. Despite the loss of 350 dailies between 1945 and 1960, their number rose to 1786 in 1952, then settled back to 1763 in 1961. Inflation and recession took a slight toll in the number, to 1745, by 1981. Consolidations of morning and evening editions and continuing shortfalls in advertising volume brought a new low figure of 1711 dailies in 1983, but they had an all-time high circulation of 62,487,000 copies. Morning dailies led evening papers for the first time, 33 million to 29 million, in circulation.

Circulation of dailies was approximately 40 million copies in 1930 for a population of 122 million; by 1980 it was 62 million for a population of 226 million. The number of papers for each household decreased from 1.32 in 1930 to 1.16 in 1960, an even 1.0 in 1970, and .79 in 1980. Only seven out of ten adults were reading a daily newspaper every day; nine out of ten, a newspaper at least once a week. In the twenty largest cities, newspaper circulation dropped by 21 percent between 1970 and 1980, while population only fell by 6 percent.[2] It was in those metropolitan areas that the losses of dailies were heaviest, and circulation declines there kept the national circulation total on a static plane.

Table 26-1 shows the extent of the decline in competition in cities having daily newspapers, since 1940. The number of one-daily cities steadily increased, and there were more one-combination cities (one owner of two papers) until the 1960s. Joint-printing cities are those in which two owners have merged their printing and business operations and thus are not fully competitive.

Only New York City had three daily newspapers with three different owners in 1983. Among the cities ranking in the top twenty-five in size, Baltimore, San Antonio, and San Diego had three dailies with two owners; no other United States cities of any size had more than two dailies. Twelve of the top twenty-five had two dailies with two owners: Los Angeles, Chicago, Boston, Washington, Houston, Dallas, Detroit, Honolulu, Denver, Seattle, San Francisco, and Columbus (Ohio). Six had two dailies published by the same ownership: Philadelphia, Milwaukee, Indianapolis, Jacksonville, Phoenix, and San Jose. Three had been reduced to single-daily status: Cleveland, where the old flagship paper of the Scripps-Howard group, the *Cleveland Press,* closed down in 1982; New Orleans, where the evening *States-Item* was merged into the morning *Times-Picayune* in 1980; and Memphis, where Scripps-Howard killed the evening *Press-Scimitar* in 1983.

Table 26-1 Competition in Daily Newspaper Cities, 1940–1981

	1940	1945	1954	1961	1971	1976	1981
Number of general circulation dailies	1878	1744	1785	1763	1748	1756	1745
Number of cities with dailies	1426	1396	1448	1461	1511	1550	1559
Number of one-daily cities	1092	1107	1188	1222	1312	1369	1404
Number of one-combination cities	149	161	154	160	141	122	103
Number of joint-printing cities	4	11	19	18	21	20	22
Number of cities with competing dailies	181	117	87	61	37	39	30
Percentage of cities with competing dailies	12.7	8.4	6.0	4.2	2.4	2.5	1.9
Total daily circulation (millions)	41.1	45.9	54.5	58.9	62.1	60.6	61.4

Sources: For number of dailies and circulation, *Editor & Publisher International Year Books.* For other data, Raymond B. Nixon and Jean Ward, "Trends in Newspaper Ownership and Inter-Media Competition," *Journalism Quarterly,* XXXVIII (Winter 1961), 3. For 1971, compiled from 1971 *Year Book* data by Nixon; for 1976, compiled from 1976 *Year Book* data by Judith Sobel. See *Journalism Quarterly's* Spring 1978 volume for an article with more detailed data by Sobel and Emery. For 1981, compiled from 1982 *Year Book* data and from Leo Bogart, "Newspapers in Transition," *Wilson Quarterly* (Special Issue 1982).

Twenty-five major metropolitan dailies were suspended between 1950 and 1978 and eight others were sold to competitors. The effects of the 1980s recession killed four more major dailies in 1982: the *Washington Star,* the *Philadelphia Bulletin,* the *Buffalo Courier-Express,* and the *Cleveland Press.* More alarming was a widespread move to merge evening dailies into their morning affiliates, often to become all-day papers. Between 1978 and 1983 there were thirty-two such mergers among all dailies, and thirteen in large metropolitan areas: Boston, Minneapolis, Des Moines, New Orleans, Austin, Wichita, Topeka, Long Beach, Oakland, Duluth, Tampa, Sarasota, and Portland, Oregon.[3] The number of one-combination cities in 1983 was down to 95, and of cities with competing dailies to 29.

Newspaper managements could cite several reasons for these contractions and the continued concern over newspaper financial stability: a steady increase in the price of newsprint, which after leveling off at $135 a ton in the years 1957 to 1966 jumped to $300 a ton by 1976 and to $500 a ton before again leveling off at $470 in 1983; increasing supply costs; rising wages and salaries; losses of national advertising to television and a recession-caused slump in all advertising, especially classified. Advertising still filled 62 percent of daily newspapers' columns in 1982, however, according to Media Records. Many dailies increased their prices to 25 cents. *Editor & Publisher* surveys of profits each spring showed that smaller dailies, and noncompetitive larger ones, were likely to be making better profit margins than the big-city dailies—up to 10 percent of gross profits.

Circulation gains were going to the mid- and smaller-sized dailies, especially in the suburbs. The tabloid *New York Daily News* was still the second largest United States daily but had lost 2,180,000 Sunday circulation and 735,000 daily since 1950, a reflection, in part, of the inroads of television and other entertainment-oriented media.[4] The *Chicago Tribune* lost 385,000 Sunday and 170,000 daily readers before changing its appeal. The biggest gainer was the country's largest daily, the *Wall Street Journal,* whose nationwide circulation was 2,036,000 in 1983 compared to 153,000 in 1950. Other major gains since 1950 were by the *Los Angeles Times,* 665,000, and the *New York Times,* 460,000.*

The suburbs offered opportunity for new papers, both daily and weekly. In 1983 there were some 2000 suburban papers, including 300 dailies, and as many more big-city neighborhood sheets. Major centers for this growing journalism were Los Angeles, Chicago, New York, Philadelphia, and Detroit. The most conspicuous suburban success was *Newsday,* founded in 1940, which reached 500,000 circulation by 1983. Other suburban ventures attracting attention were the Paddock publications in Chicago; the Gannett group's *Today,* in the Cape Kennedy area of Florida; and the *Los Angeles Times'* satellite paper, the *Orange Coast Daily Pilot.* The growth of these suburban dailies contributed to big-city journalism's decline.

*The largest daily circulations in 1983 were the *Wall Street Journal,* 2,036,789; *New York Daily News,* 1,513,941; *Los Angeles Times,* 1,060,588; *New York Times,* 963,443; *New York Post,* 961,044; *Chicago Tribune,* 756,877; *Washington Post,* 747,676; *Chicago Sun-Times,* 654,957; *Detroit News,* 651,763; *Detroit Free Press,* 635,740; *Philadelphia Inquirer,* 544,777; *San Francisco Chronicle,* 535,050; (Long Island) *Newsday,* 525,217; *Boston Globe,* 507,791. Top Sunday circulations were the *New York Daily News,* 2,004,835; *New York Times,* 1,563,531; *Los Angeles Times,* 1,342,720; *Chicago Tribune,* 1,127,778; Philadelphia Inquirer, 1,036,717; *Washington Post,* 1,005,468. Figures are March 31, 1983, ABC reports. Leaders in advertising linage included the *Los Angeles Times, Houston Chronicle, Miami Herald,* and *Washington Post. USA Today* was not included in the report.

CHANGES IN MAJOR CITIES

The most grievous journalistic loss of the period was in 1978—that of the *Chicago Daily News,* whose disappearance climaxed 40 years of changes in the city's journalism. After Hearst killed his *Herald & Examiner* in 1939 in the wake of a Newspaper Guild strike, Marshall Field launched the *Sun* in 1941 to do battle with McCormick's *Tribune* in the morning field. Finding the going rough, he bought the *Times* in 1947 and made the merged *Sun-Times* a tabloid. The *Tribune* purchased Hearst's *American* as an evening affiliate in 1956 and later renamed it *Chicago Today,* turning it into a tabloid. The *Sun-Times* countered by buying the *Daily News* from John S. Knight in a record $24-million transaction in 1959. *Chicago Today,* and the ghosts of the legendary newspeople of "The Front Page," disappeared in 1974.

The *Daily News* had retained a high place among newspaper leaders despite a series of ownership changes after the deaths of owners Victor F. Lawson in 1925 and Walter A. Strong in 1931. Colonel Frank Knox, former general manager of the Hearst newspapers and a leading Republican political figure, then became publisher. Knox kept the *Daily News* operating in its old traditions until his death in 1944. Its famous foreign and Washington news service reached brilliant heights. Henry Justin Smith, a news executive from 1901 to 1936, ran a "school for reporters."

Sale of the *Daily News* to Knight in 1944 brought in Basil L. Walters as executive editor. Walters introduced new typographical and readership techniques he had learned while with the Cowles newspapers in Des Moines and Minneapolis. The paper emphasized local news and developed crusades on local issues. As a result, the *Daily News* printed the stories of its own foreign staff in less depth, although the service remained a strong one. The paper won two Pulitzer Prizes for public service, in 1950 and 1957, and gained in circulation and financial position.

Chicago newspaper ownership was streamlined in 1959, when Knight sold the *Daily News* to Marshall Field, IV, owner of the *Sun-Times.* The *Daily News* became the evening affiliate of the *Sun-Times* in Chicago's circulation battle, and Field named himself its editor when Walters retired in 1961. His death at 49 in 1965 left control to Field Enterprises executives until Marshall Field, V was ready to assume command in 1969, at age 28. He eventually designated James F. Hoge as editor-in-chief of the papers, with Daryle M. Feldmeir as editor of the *News* and Ralph Otwell as managing editor of the *Sun-Times.*

The *Daily News* won a Pulitzer Prize for public service once again in 1963. Reporter William J. Eaton received the 1970 national reporting prize for exposing the inadequacies of Supreme Court nominee Clement Haynsworth after his paper had endorsed President Nixon's selection. Cartoonist John Fischetti won a Pulitzer Prize in 1969, and columnist Mike Royko one in 1972. Both Field papers usually endorsed Republican presidential candidates but backed Jimmy Carter in 1976. Both were internationalist in outlook.

When the *Daily News* said "So Long, Chicago" in its final edition, its accomplishments became traditions. Some of the *Daily News* staff, including popular columnist Mike Royko, moved to the *Sun-Times.* In 1983 Field Enterprises announced that some Field heirs wanted to cash their holdings, and that the *Sun-Times* was for sale. Rupert Murdoch bought it for $90 million.

New York suffered the most severe losses of any American metropolis, dropping from eight dailies in 1950 to three in 1967. The losses were the *Sun,* 1950; Hearst's tabloid *Mirror,* 1963; the *Herald Tribune,* 1966; and Hearst's *Journal-American* and Scripps-Howard's *World-Telegram and Sun,* which were merged into the *World Journal Tribune* in 1966. When that paper died in 1967, with it went the shades of Pulitzer, Greeley, Bennett, Dana, Scripps, Howard, Hearst, and a dash of Munsey.

The *Washington Star,* solid if unspectacular, celebrated its centennial in 1952, still in the possession of the Noyes and Kauffmann families who took control of it in 1867. Its editors had been Crosby Noyes, 1867 to 1908; Theodore Noyes, to 1946; an outsider, Benjamin McKelway, to 1963; and then Newbold Noyes. Frank B. Noyes, longtime AP president, was president of the *Star* from 1909 to 1948. Samuel H. Kauffmann followed him to 1963 and was succeeded by his son, John. But during the 1960s the *Star's* fortunes dwindled. It vainly bought out the rival *News* to bolster itself and in 1974 was sold to Joe L. Allbritton of Texas. He installed James G. Bellows as editor, and circulation was held even by a rejuvenated staff including three Pulitzer Prize winners: columnist Mary McGrory, reporter James R. Polk, and cartoonist Patrick Oliphant. Bellows resigned and Time Inc. bought the *Star* in 1978. After 4 years and an investment of $85 million, Time Inc. found that the *Post* still held three-quarters of the advertising revenues of the two papers, and killed the *Star.* In its wake, the *Washington Times* appeared, with James R. Whelan as editor. Its financial backing was from the right wing Unification Church of Korean evangelist Sun Myung Moon. Despite this, the new morning daily gained strength and survived its first year.

In Philadelphia, the solid *Bulletin* was being published by William L. McLean, III, grandson of the founder, when it succumbed to Knight-Ridder aggressiveness in 1982. Boston lost three historic newspapers: the 111-year-old staid *Transcript* in 1941, the 125-year-old *Post* in 1956, and the 125-year-old *Traveler* (merged in 1967 as the *Herald Traveler*) in 1972. Two Hearst tabloids were combined as the *Record American* in 1961 (renamed the *Herald American*). The Hearst group sold out to Rupert Murdoch's expanding News America in 1982, and the paper was renamed the *Herald.*

Los Angeles, the third largest city, dropped to two dailies. The Chandler family's *Times* began the tabloid *Mirror* in 1948 to give it a breezier afternoon entry against two Hearst papers, the morning *Examiner* and evening *Herald-Express.* The competition was fatal for a fifth paper, the liberal tabloid *Daily News,* which was suspended in 1954. The *Mirror,* edited drably after a 1957 management shakeup, faltered and was suspended in January, 1962. At the same time the Hearst group elected to kill the *Examiner,* naming their evening paper the *Herald-Examiner.*

In San Francisco, the Hearst and Scripps-Howard evening papers had been combined into the jointly owned *News-Call Bulletin* in 1959; Scripps-Howard bowed out in 1962 and the paper succumbed in 1965 as Hearst's morning *Examiner* moved to the evening field in a joint-business arrangement with the *Chronicle* that saw rivals sharing a Sunday edition.

THE GROWTH OF NEWSPAPER GROUPS

The daily newspaper followed the American business trend in the twentieth century and increasingly became a group-owned enterprise. In 1900 there were only eight groups of dailies, controlling twenty-seven papers (1.3 percent of the total) and 10 percent of the total circulation.[5] By 1935, sixty-three groups were counted, with 328 papers (17 percent of the total) and 41 percent of the total circulation.[6] In 1960 the figures were 109 groups with 560 papers (30 percent) and 46 percent of the circulation. By 1982 there were 155 groups listed (down from a peak of 167 in 1978), with 1136 papers (65 percent of all dailies), and 72 percent of total daily circulation.[7]

The five largest 1982 groups controlled 25 percent of daily newspaper circulation in the country. But the two largest, Gannett and Knight-Ridder, had only 6 percent of the circulation each. By contrast, in 1935 William Randolph Hearst alone controlled 13.6 percent of daily circulation and 24.2 percent of Sunday. In short, the groups were collectively a problem of media effectiveness, but no one group was a threatening factor in the ability to exercise influence. The 155 groups of 1982 averaged 7.4 dailies each. Only sixteen had group-circulation totals exceeding 750,000. Nearly half the groups had only two or three dailies each.*

The most spectacular event in group publishing was the launching of the national daily, *USA Today*, by the Gannett Company in 1982. Printed in scores of regional plants through satellite transmission of images from editorial centers, *USA Today* almost miraculously appeared in news boxes each weekday morning under an expansion program that was to cover thirty-two states by the close of 1983. Allen Neuharth, head of Gannett, claimed 1.1 million daily sales in mid-1983 and projected 2.4 million by 1987. The paper's bright blue trademark, effective use of color and graphics, and focus on such areas as weather and sports for travelers made it the talk of newspaperdom. John C. Quinn was editor.

*From data supplied by *Editor & Publisher Yearbook* and media analyses. Figures for leading groups in 1982 are as follows (in thousands):

GROUP	TOTAL CIRCULATION	PERCENT OF DAILY CIRCULATION	NUMBER DAILIES	NUMBER SUNDAYS
Gannett	3776	6.0	87	57
Knight-Ridder	3709	6.0	31	22
S. I. Newhouse	3154	5.0	27	21
Chicago Tribune Co.	2928	4.7	8	6
Dow Jones	2522	4.0	22	7
Times Mirror	2394	3.8	8	5
Scripps-Howard	1545	2.5	16	6
New York Times Co.	1427	2.3	21	8
Hearst	1320	2.1	14	8
Cox	1204	1.9	17	11
Thomson	1167	1.8	81	34

GANNETT — THE NATION'S NEWSPAPER — 25 CENTS

TUESDAY, JULY 5, 1983

NEWSLINE

A QUICK READ ON THE TOP NEWS OF THE DAY

WEATHER: **Thunderstorms stretch across the** Northeast today with cool air right behind. Midwest and Plains will have highs in the 70s and 80s and low humidity. Sunny skies cover most of the western third of the USA; highs reach the 90s and 100s in the Southwest, the 70s and 80s elsewhere. Full color page. 10A.

NO-HITTER: **Dave Righetti, left, pitches first Yankee** no-hitter since '56, first in majors since '81. 1C. AL 4C. NL 5C.

RIGHETTI: Pitches Yankee no-hitter.

■ **Golf: Mark McCumber tops** Watson, wins Western Open. 1C.

■ **Hockey: NHL top draft choice** Brian Lawton named to Olympic feeder Team USA. 6C.

■ **Auto racing: Buddy Baker** coasts to Firecracker 400 win. 1C.

ANDROPOV ILL?: **Soviet** leader cancels two meetings with West German Chancellor Kohl, sparking more gossip about his possible illness. 7A.

MIDDLE EAST: **Secretary of State Shultz arrives in** Saudi Arabia for peace talks, plans visit to Syria; Damascus calls trip "an impossible mission." 7A.

■ **Arafat negotiates with rebels, offers to withdraw** troops from Bekaa Valley; rebel leader declines.

NATION: **Death row population is largest ever,** increase to continue; Mississippi execution stayed. 3A.

■ **Poll of Evangelical Christians shows they favor a** nuclear freeze but support Reagan, strong defense. 3A.

■ **Theft of $500,000 in gold from New Mexican town** called inside job; residents eyeing each other. 3A.

WASHINGTON: **FBI set to question White House** chief of staff, other Reagan aides about briefing book. 7A.

■ **Supreme Court: In session full of bombshells, yet to** come is ruling on home video versus copyright laws. 7A.

ABROAD: **Lech Walesa takes unauthorized vacation** from Gdansk shipyard; threatened with firing. 7A.

TODAY'S DEBATE: **Tuition tax credits. In USA** TODAY's opinion, Congress, state legislatures must reject efforts to devise a tuition tax credits system. 8A.

■ **Private school parents have been paying double, says** the Rev. William J. Fitzgerald. 8A.

■ **Inquiry: One of the last ramparts of truly free speech** in the world is the stage, says actress Colleen Dewhurst. 9A.

MONEY: **Despite record losses, steel makers expand** by leasing large equipment from lender groups. 1B.

■ **Houseboat sales spurt due to better economy. 1B.**

■ **Southland Corp., owner of 7-Eleven stores, agrees to** buy Citgo Petroleum, market its own cigarettes. 1B.

■ **Number of ways to gamble on the stock market** continues to grow, overcoming opposition by industry. 1B.

■ **Public makes transition from conservative invest**ments to stock market; attendance at seminars grows. 1B.

■ **Future of salmon fishing in Pacific Northwest doubtful** as fish become scarcer, competition tougher. 3B.

SPORTS: **With NFL camps soon to convene, USFL** nears end of first season with three-game playoff. 7C.

■ **John McEnroe's Wimbledon win proves he can play** tennis without tantrums; few can beat him. 3C.

LIFE: **Passion for quilting stays strong though country** fad has passed; collectors pay homage to the art. 4D.

■ **Two-thirds of sports injuries to children can be pre**vented; parents should check play area, equipment. 1D.

■ **Majority of married women are dissatisfied with their** sex lives, survey shows; 40 percent have had affairs. 1D.

Compiled by Tara Connell

Inside USA TODAY

COPYRIGHT 1983 USA TODAY, a division of Gannett Co., Inc.

USA SNAPSHOTS

A look at statistics that shape the nation

Living with children

Of the 62.4 million USA children under 18 — a drop of 10 percent from the 69.2 million in 1970 — three-quarters live with both parents.

Live with:	1982	1970
Both parents	46,797,000 (75%)	58,939,000 (85%)
One parent	13,701,000 (22%)	8,199,000 (12%)
Mother	12,512,000 (20%)	7,451,000 (11%)
Father	1,189,000 (2%)	748,000 (1%)
Other relatives	1,556,000 (2.5%)	1,547,000 (2%)
Non-relatives	352,000 (0.6%)	477,000 (0.7%)

Source: U.S. Census Bureau, 1983

By Julie Stacey, USA TODAY

USA TODAY

VIA SATELLITE

A happy birthday blast heard all across the USA

By Jackie Greene, USA TODAY

CAPITAL SHOW: Crowds estimated at more than 300,000 cheered spectacular Fourth of July fireworks display, set off by lightning flashes, on Washington Monument grounds Monday night.

From sea to sea, we mark 207

Special for USA TODAY

The USA celebrated its 207th birthday Monday with parties, concerts, fireworks, 300,000 balloons and dollar bills dropping from the sky.

■ **St. Louis:** Claimed the biggest party — 4 million attended the Veiled Prophet Fair over the three-day holiday.

■ **Atlantic City:** More than 200,000 packed an Atlantic City beach to hear the Beach Boys — who were not appearing in Washington after Interior Secretary James Watt said they attracted "the wrong element." Police said: "Great bunch."

■ **Washington, D.C.:** 300,000-plus gathered around the Mall heard Beach Boys replacement, entertainer Wayne Newton, and watched fireworks.

■ **Hurricane, W.Va.:** Retired businessman Calvin Jones dropped 1,000 $1 bills from a helicopter. "Maybe, money falling from the sky will give (youngsters) an idea of what this country means," he said.

■ **Itasca, Ill.:** 300,000 red, white and blue balloons are "gone with the wind;" gusts foiled a 1,400-person effort to make the largest flag ever.

■ **Atlanta, Ga.:** 28,000 runners turned out for the annual 6.2-mile Peachtree Road Race.

■ **New York City:** Emil Gomez, 25, of The Bronx, won a hot dog-eating contest on Coney Island. In 10 minutes, the 210-pound accountant ate 10½ hot dogs — with rolls. How did he feel? "Full," he said.

■ **San Francisco:** 300,000 turned out for a weekend celebration at Moffett Naval Air Station, including airplane acrobatics and a balloon race.

■ **Lebanon:** 1,200 U.S. Marine peacekeepers enjoyed hot dogs, beer and sport events.

■ Marine 4th in Lebanon, 7A
■ Willie Nelson concert, 2D

By Barbara J. Ries, USA TODAY

FROM KOREA: Tonya Ann Williams, with adoptive father, Kenneth Williams of Christiansburg, Va., at naturalization ceremony.

COVER STORY

A special 4th for our new Americans

FROM AFGHANISTAN: Assad Ansari of Charlottesville, Va., sworn in.

By Rich Scheinin
USA TODAY

When it was over, the Charlottesville Municipal Band played the National Anthem, the Pham family went home to a picnic of Vietnamese style duckling, Coca Cola, and chips, and Tonya Ann Williams, 4½, shook all the judges' hands.

In the blistering heat Monday, 99 people from 28 countries — including Tonya of Korea who was adopted two years ago, and Chau and Ngamy Pham — were sworn in as new citizens of the USA at Monticello, Thomas Jefferson's Virginia estate.

They included Juana Stitt, a legal secretary from Cuba; Brian Thomas George Robertson, an electrical engineer from Scotland; and Dung Ly Stowe, a sociologist from Sai-

Please see COVER STORY next page ▶

Baseball surprise

Texas, Toronto lead at All-Star break
Sports section, 4C

Abby and Ann at 65

Birthday twins
Life section, 1D

Jennifer

Summer's big no-name success
Life section, 1D

By Herb Ritts, Visages

JENNIFER BEALS: Films stake all on unknowns.

Reagan vs. teachers

Boos, F-plus yesterday, new pitch for his plan today

By Barbara Zigli
USA TODAY

LOS ANGELES — President Reagan, on the eve of a speech here today, got boos and an "F-plus" grade at the annual American Federation of Teachers convention.

Reagan is expected to promote several controversial programs — including merit pay for teachers, tuition tax credits and return to "basics."

AFT leader Albert Shanker said Monday he gave Reagan the "plus" because the president's recent call for better USA schools has focused public attention on education.

Shanker slammed Reagan's call for tuition credits and a Supreme Court ruling last week upholding a Minnesota tax deduction for parents with children in private schools.

But as delegates booed Reagan's name, Shanker offered advice for today's visit: "No, don't do that ... unless you want him re-elected.

"You do that tomorrow and ... everybody's going to say, 'Look how the poor president was treated, these people aren't fit to teach our kids'."

Shanker also slammed the larger, rival NEA for its unyielding opposition to merit pay for outstanding teachers.

But on Monday NEA president-elect Mary Futrell said delegates to its annual meeting in Philadelphia — while not abandoning opposition — have given NEA leaders flexibility to "hear what the other side has to say" about merit pay.

Reagan's appearance today is seen as his latest step in an effort to place the NEA on the defensive — and divide teachers, who traditionally are a key Democratic constituency.

■ Mondale and the NEA, 7A
■ Shanker on schools, 8A

Groceries: Biggest dip in 2 years

Special for USA TODAY

Helped by the falling price of meat, grocery bills across the USA dropped in June by an average 1.2 percent, biggest drop since May 1981, an Associated Press survey showed.

Prices decreased overall by 0.9 percent for the first six months of this year.

Pork prices have been dropping "especially the last couple of weeks," Nancy Ternes of King Soopers grocery in Fort Collins, Colo., said Monday.

For pork, Leland Southard of the Department of Agriculture predicts "roughly the same prices for the third quarter, then a dropoff for the fourth quarter." That will probably force beef prices down because of competition, he said.

The survey showed:

■ All-beef frankfurter prices declined in eight cities.

■ Pork chops decreased in seven cities.

■ Detroit showed the biggest overall drop in food prices — 7.9 percent.

■ Miami's food prices rose the most — 5 percent.

Other cities surveyed: Albuquerque, N.M.; Atlanta; Boston; Chicago; Dallas; Los Angeles; New York; Philadelphia; Providence, R.I.; Salt Lake City and Seattle.

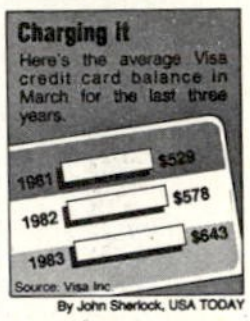
Charging it
Here's the average Visa credit card balance in March for the last three years.
1981 $529
1982 $578
1983 $643
Source: Visa Inc

By John Sherlock, USA TODAY

Credit card use, debt on the rise

By Wayne Beissert
USA TODAY

We'll charge an average 25 percent more on our credit cards this year than we did in 1982.

An average of $1,445 per card was charged last year and we'll top $2,000 this year, publisher Spencer Nilson of the Los Angeles-based Nilson Report said in a weekend interview.

He said there are 68.4 million of us with 103 million credit cards.

Companies report:

■ Average balances on Visa cards are up 21 percent over two years to an average $643.

■ Average balance on Mastercards was $602 at the end of 1982, a 22 percent increase in two years.

American Express had 11.1 million card users in the USA in 1982, up 11 percent from 1981.

Nilson said the average person uses each card 32 times per year for purchases averaging $46 apiece.

We charged $208 billion last year, including $60.4 billion on bankcards and the rest on cards issued by retailers.

Sears reports an all-time high 56 percent of sales were made on credit last year. And the use of credit is growing.

Since October, there has been a very strong recovery in sales of durables — major appliances — which are usually sold on credit, Sears says.

Solo sailor's back in USA

By Blake Sell, UPI

A FIRST: Mark Schrader of Stanwood, Wash., became the first American to solo-circumnavigate the world via the southern route Monday when he sailed his 40-foot sailboat 'Resourceful' into Shilshole Bay, Seattle, Wash., after a 204-day, 27,300-mile voyage.

TOMORROW IN USA TODAY: THE FAULTS IN NO-FAULT DIVORCE

The nation's largest circulation general newspaper, distributed by satellite.

Its circulation clearly would keep Gannett first in that category, as well as first in total dailies. Based in Rochester, New York, the company expanded by buying other groups: Westchester Rockland in 1964; Federated in 1971; the *Honolulu Star-Bulletin* and its satellites in 1971; and in a $173-million stock transaction in 1976, the Speidel western group. Gannett had dailies in twenty-eight states. Allen Neuharth succeeded Paul Miller, the onetime AP executive, as the operating head of Gannett in 1970. Gannett broke other new ground by buying the New York City Spanish-language tabloid, *El Diario—La Prensa,* in 1981. Of its eighty-seven publishers in 1983, eleven were women.

The 1974 merger of the Knight and Ridder newspaper groups created a powerful national organization with several outstanding dailies, including two in the top-ten listings. John S. Knight, starting with the *Akron Beacon-Journal,* bought the *Miami Herald* in 1937 and with Lee Hills as the chief editorial force made it one of the country's top papers. Knight's other major acquisitions were the *Detroit Free Press,* the *Charlotte Observer* and *News,* and the *Philadelphia Inquirer* and *News.* The Ridder group brought to the merger eleven Midwestern dailies led by the *St. Paul Dispatch* and *Pioneer Press* and six California dailies including the *San Jose Mercury* and *News* and the Long Beach and Pasadena papers. Bernard H. Ridder, Jr., represented his family's interests in the new organization.[8]

Samuel Newhouse reached out for major metropolitan dailies, buying the *Oregonian* in Portland in 1950 and the *Oregon Journal* in 1961; the *Birmingham News* and *St. Louis Globe-Democrat* in 1955; the *New Orleans Times-Picayune* and *States-Item* in 1962; and the *Cleveland Plain Dealer* in 1967. His total costs were $125 million. By 1983 he operated the only dailies in Portland, New Orleans, and Cleveland, and conducted joint-printing operations for his Birmingham and St. Louis rivials. In a bidding content for the Booth newspaper group in 1976, Newhouse spent an estimated $300 million to win control of eight strong Michigan dailies. Newhouse's reputation was that of a successful businessperson who permitted local editorial autonomy.

The Times Mirror Company joined the largest groups when the youthful publisher of the *Los Angeles Times,* Otis Chandler, bought the *Dallas Times Herald* and the Long Island tabloid, *Newsday,* in 1970 transactions involving $125 million. Chandler followed by buying the *Hartford Courant* and two other Connecticut dailies and the *Denver Post.* Again, Times Mirror represented a quality group. A long-established group with few papers but major size was the Tribune Company, owner of the *Chicago Tribune, New York Daily News,* the advertising-rich *Orlando Sentinel, Fort Lauderdale News* and *Sun-Sentinel* in Florida, and the *Daily News* (in Los Angeles' San Fernando Valley).

The runner-up in the number of dailies was the Thomson Newspapers group, part of a worldwide enterprise built by Lord Thomson of Fleet, a Canadian. His papers were predominantly small. At his death in 1976 his son Kenneth assumed the title and control. A flamboyant Australian, Rupert Murdoch, put his News America subsidiary on the map by buying the *New York Post, Village Voice,* and *New York* and *New West* magazines in 1977 after founding the *National Star* in 1974 and buying the *San Antonio News* and *Express* in 1975. Murdoch bought the prestigious *Times* of London in 1980 from Lord Thomson and the *Boston Herald American* and *Chicago Sun-Times* by 1983.

The oldtime group newspaper leaders, Hearst and Scripps-Howard, were well down the list. The Scripps-Howard group stayed in a carefully managed but

Newhouse Newspapers

Gannett Newspapers

Group owners Samuel I. Newhouse (*left*); Allen Neuharth, head of Gannett.

Jean Raeburn

New York Post

John S. Knight (*left*); Rupert Murdoch, News America.

San Francisco Examiner

Milton J. Pike

Newspaper owners William Randolph Hearst, Jr. (*left*); Edward W. Scripps, II.

static condition with fifteen dailies. Charles E. Scripps and Edward W. Scripps, II represented the family interests, while B. J. Cutler became editor-in-chief in 1980. William Randolph Hearst, Jr., one of five sons of the founder, took the lead as editor-in-chief in 1955. The original Hearst empire dwindled to eight dailies and seven Sunday editions by 1977, then was bolstered with the purchase of seven small dailies in California, Texas, and Michigan, and twenty-eight Los Angeles suburban weeklies. Major Hearst interests were in cable, magazines, and books.

The Hearst name stayed in the news when granddaughter Patricia (daughter of Randolph, publisher of the *San Francisco Examiner*), was kidnapped by radical terrorists, emerged herself as the radical "Tania," and was convicted of bank robbery after a sensational trial. Fabulous San Simeon became a California Historical Monument in 1958, open to bus loads of tourists. Hearst, Jr. had one major triumph: in 1956 the Pulitzer Prize for international reporting went to him, J. Kingsbury Smith, and Frank Conniff for stories from the Soviet Union. "I have a feeling that Pop and Joe Pulitzer are getting almost as big a kick out of it as we are," he told his readers.

WEEKLIES AND SPECIALIZED PAPERS

Weekly newspapers followed the same general trends. In 1930 only 13.5 percent of weekly towns had competing newspapers. By 1960 the figure was 5.2 percent, which closely paralleled the number of competitive daily cities. The number of weeklies of all types stood at 14,000 in 1910, at 10,000 in 1940, and at 9400 in 1970, according to the *Ayer Directory.* The National Newspaper Association (NNA), the trade group for the weeklies, put the 1970 number at 7610, with the difference depending on its narrower definition of a general-interest newspaper. The NNA's total for 1981 was 7666, with an average circulation per paper of 5875. Total circulation was at 45 million, compared to 21 million in 1960. Larger county-seat weeklies and the fast-growing suburban papers were more profitable—some of the suburban press groups were major businesses.

Another specialized-newspaper publishing field, the foreign-language press, steadily declined during the twentieth century. In 1914, the peak year for foreign-language newspapers, there were approximately 1000 papers, of which 140 were dailies. By 1983 there were fewer than forty dailies and perhaps 200 other papers in some two dozen languages. Chinese, Spanish, Polish, Japanese, German, Russian, Yiddish, Italian, and Lithuanian papers were most numerous.

COLUMNISTS, CARTOONISTS, AND COMICS

The 1970s and 1980s offered many opportunities for commentaries on the political and social scenes, whether by a William Safire or a Mary McGrory with a typewriter, a Bill Mauldin or a Paul Conrad with a cartoonist's brush, or a Garry Trudeau with a comically drawn satire that captured a nation's fancy.

Joseph Kraft was one of a number of liberal-oriented columnists who emerged from the era of Kennedy politics. A speech writer for John Kennedy, he

Joseph Kraft *(left)* and Mary McGrory, political experts in Washington.

William Safire and Art Buchwald, successful columnists of the 1980s.

began a political commentary for *Harper's* in 1965 and became one of those syndicated columnists filling the void when Walter Lippmann retired in 1967. A hard-hitting team that gained increasing favor after its 1963 start was that of Rowland Evans and Robert Novak, who had been Washington reporters for the *New York Herald Tribune* and *Wall Street Journal.* Their "Inside Report" became the top political-exposure column of the 1970s. Joining the competition in 1977 were Jack W. Germond and Jules Witcover, seasoned Washington newspeople who focused on reporting the political activities of the Carter administration. The country's leading black journalist, Carl T. Rowan, signed with the *Chicago Daily News* after a government career. He was joined as a columnist by William Raspberry of the *Washington Post.*

Jack Anderson, who became prominent in the field after his mentor Drew Pearson's death in 1969, uncovered a number of major stories during the "Nixon years." However, Anderson did not escape criticism and his zealousness for the exclusive backfired in 1972 when he mishandled facts about Senator Thomas Eagleton's personal life while Senator George McGovern dropped Eagleton as his running mate. Taking command in the 1970s as a Pulitzer Prize-winning general political columnist was Mary McGrory of the *Washington Star.* Sylvia Porter became the leading business columnist of the country. Betty Beale, Marianne Means, and Virginia Payette were other syndicated women columnists.

William F. Buckley, Jr., of the conservative *National Review,* was one of the intellectual conservatives who gained favor in the late 1960s and the 1970s. Two others were the former Southern newspaper editor, James Jackson Kilpatrick of the *Washington Star* Syndicate, and the young writer for *Esquire* and the *National Review,* Garry Wills. But the most successful conservative writer was William Safire. Safire joined the *New York Times* in 1973 as a columnist, coming directly from being a White House speech writer for Richard Nixon and from creating such phrases as "nattering nabobs of negativism" for Spiro T. Agnew. Ten years later his column had more than 500 daily newspaper takers; he was respected as a master of both puckish wit and mock-macho indignation; he also had a reputation as a literary stylist. In the era of Ronald Reagan and resurgent conservatism, Safire was a columnist with both contacts and a discerning approach.

The *New York Times* contributed other political columnists, its serious-minded James Reston and Tom Wicker, and its Washington "funny man," Russell Baker. Baker and Art Buchwald of the Los Angeles Times Syndicate used satire to make their political and social points during a period of national frustration that called for such relief. Wills, Safire, Baker, and Buchwald all won Pulitzer prizes for commentary.

When the great *St. Louis Post-Dispatch* cartoonist Daniel Fitzpatrick retired in 1958, he was succeeded by Bill Mauldin, of Willie and Joe fame in *Stars and Stripes.* Mauldin quickly won his second Pulitzer Prize in 1959, and then in 1962 he became the syndicated cartoonist of the *Chicago Sun-Times,* which also had the liberal Pulitzer award winner Jacob Burck drawing for its editorial page. Mauldin drew his most famous cartoon in 1963 to honor John Kennedy.

"Fire!"—Herbert L. Block, in the *Washington Post,* defended freedom during the Joseph McCarthy era.

Herblock Book (© 1952 Beacon Press)

Bill Mauldin's famous drawing expressing a nation's grief at John Kennedy's death.

© 1963 Chicago Sun-Times; courtesy Wil-Jo Associates and Bill Mauldin

'YOU WILL FIND THE BABE WRAPPED IN SWADDLING CLOTHS, LYING IN A MANGER.'
ST. LUKE CH. 2, V. 12
CONRAD

Paul Conrad selected this drawing as symbolic of his concern for civil rights and the economic plight of minorities.

Paul Conrad, © Los Angeles Times, with permission of The Register and Tribune Syndicate

The signature "Herblock" became famed in the 1950s and continued to be a solid favorite in the 1980s. Herbert L. Block of the *Washington Post* was widely known through syndication for his distinctive style and extremely effective liberal comment. He won Pulitzer Prizes in 1942, 1954, and 1979. He was challenged by several other Pulitzer winners who attracted attention for their incisive, independent commentary. Becoming equally popular was Paul Conrad, 1964 and 1971 award winner, who started at the *Denver Post* and became the *Los Angeles Times'* editorial cartoonist in 1964. His successor at the *Denver Post,* the Australian-born satirist Patrick Oliphant, was 1967 winner; Don Wright, *Miami News,* won in 1966 and 1980. John Fischetti, 1969 Pulitzer Prize artist for the *Chicago Daily News,* offered a popular new style, as did young Thomas F. Darcy, 1970 winner from *Newsday,* and Paul Szep, the *Boston Globe's* prize artist, a winner in 1974 and 1977.

Garry Trudeau won in 1975 for his "Doonesbury" strip. Vietnam, Nixon, and Watergate gave such cartoonists a field day; other aspects of the era favored the more conservative Jeff MacNelly, 1972 and 1978 Pulitzer Prize winner from the *Richmond News Leader;* Tony Auth, 1976 winner from the *Philadelphia Inquirer;* and the *Chicago Tribune*'s 1983 winner, Richard Locher.

Award-winning cartoonists of conventional outlook who won syndication were Vaughan Shoemaker of the *Chicago Daily News,* Frank Miller of the *Des Moines Register,* Reg Manning of the *Arizona Republic,* and the hard-nosed C. D. Batchelor of the *New York Daily News.*

When Garry Trudeau began drawing his "Doonesbury" comic strip in 1970, he had just twenty-eight clients. When he temporarily retired at the start of 1983 he had 700 newspapers using his strip and millions of readers whose mornings would not be quite the same without Joanie Caucus, B. D., Mark, Duke, Zonker, and Michael J. Doonesbury. Trudeau put Richard Nixon, Henry Kissinger, Jimmy Carter, and Ronald Reagan into his comic strip as he satirized politics—but he also satirized women's liberation, rock, and drugs. Universal Press Syndicate expected a refreshed Trudeau back at the drawing board by 1984.

"Mightier Than the Sword"—Patrick Oliphant celebrated the defeat of Attorney General John Mitchell in the 1971 Pentagon Papers case.

Patrick Oliphant © 1971 Denver Post

The *Richmond News Leader's* syndicated cartoonist comments on President Jimmy Carter's human-rights crusade, which irritated the Kremlin leaders.

Jeffrey K. MacNelly, © 1977 Chicago Tribune

Another artist who gave up an audience was *Richmond News Leader* editorial cartoonist Jeff MacNelly. He turned his *Chicago Tribune* Syndicate slot over to Jack Ohman, youthful *Columbus* (Ohio) *Dispatch* cartoonist, in 1981 so that he could devote more time to his highly successful comic strip "Shoe," in which a wise old owl edits a newspaper. With "Doonesbury" temporarily unavailable, many papers turned to Berke Breathed's "Bloom County" for satire, along with "Shoe."

Also gone from the boards after 1977 was Al Capp's "Li'l Abner." Capp began his work for United Features in 1935, and by the time Li'l Abner finally married Daisy Mae in 1952 the event was featured as a news item in many papers. Capp's strip sometimes had a social message for its readers which went beyond the doings in Dogpatch. Considerably more sutble in its satire was Walt Kelly's "Pogo" sequence dealing with animal characters.

A 1983 poll of teenagers and the paperback best-seller lists both confirmed the popularity of "Garfield" the cat. Jim Davis' 5-year-old strip was appearing in 1400 newspapers, at least temporarily surpassing the little folk of "Peanuts" in

The *Chicago Tribune's* Dick Locher pokes fun at the impasse between President Reagan and the Democratic House.

Richard Locher, © 1983 Chicago Tribune

popularity. But Charlie Brown, Lucy, Linus, and Snoopy were durable characters from the drawing board of Charles M. Schulz, whose tenure with United Features made him the wealthiest contemporary cartoonist.

The impact of the comics is enormous. Chic Young's "Blondie," consistently first in reader-preference surveys, runs in 1600 papers. It and other strips claim from 40 to 80 million readers in up to fifty countries. Mort Walker's "Beetle Bailey" caricature of Army life swept into 1300 papers in a few years. And the first successful daily comic strip, Bud Fisher's "Mutt and Jeff" of 1907, was still around to celebrate its seventy-fifth anniversary in 1982.

THE PRESS IN PRESIDENTIAL ELECTIONS

Criticism of newspapers since the 1930s centered about, more than anything else, their editorial positions in political campaigns. Historically, a small but definite majority of daily newspapers giving editorial-page support to a presidential candidate was to be found on the side of the Republican party. As Franklin Roosevelt entered the first of his four presidential campaigns in 1932, he had the support of 38 percent of the nation's dailies, compared to 55 percent for President Hoover. In 1936, Roosevelt was backed by 34 percent of the dailies, Republican Alfred M. Landon by 60 percent. These figures are approximations gathered by *Editor & Publisher* when it launched, beginning in 1940, a comprehensive preelection poll of dailies concerning editorial-page support. Approximately three-fourths of all dailies, with 90 percent of total daily newspaper circulation, responded to the polls until the 1960s, when the character of the contests caused the responses to drop to 60 percent of the dailies with 80 percent of total circulation. Table 26-2 shows the percentages of the responding newspapers giving editorial-page support to the Republican or Democratic candidate each 4 years and the percentages of circulation they represented.

Table 26-2 Editorial-Page Support of Presidential Candidates

	REPUBLICAN		DEMOCRATIC		UNCOMMITTED	
Year	*Percent of Dailies*	*Percent of Circulation*	*Percent of Dailies*	*Percent of Circulation*	*Percent of Dailies*	*Percent of Circulation*
1940	63.9	69.2	22.7	25.2	13.4	5.6
1944	60.1	68.5	22.0	17.7	17.9	13.8
1948	65.1	78.5	15.3	10.0	15.6	10.0
1952	67.3	80.2	14.5	10.8	18.2	9.0
1956	62.3	72.3	15.1	12.8	22.6	14.9
1960	57.7	70.9	16.4	15.8	25.9	13.3
1964	35.1	21.5	42.3	61.5	22.6	17.0
1968	60.8	69.9	14.0	19.3	24.0	10.5
1972	71.4	77.4	5.3	7.7	23.3	14.9
1976	62.3	62.2	12.1	22.8	25.6	15.0
1980	42.5	48.6	12.9	21.5	40.7	25.5

Source: Editor & Publisher polls. In 1948, Progressive party candidate Henry A. Wallace had the support of 4 percent of the dailies with 1.5 percent of circulation. *See Editor & Publisher,* XCIII (November 5, 1960), 9. In 1968, American Independent party candidate George C. Wallace had the support of twelve dailies (1.2 percent) with 159,000 circulation (0.3 percent). In 1980 independent candidate John Anderson had the support of forty-three dailies (3.9 percent) with 4.4 percent of the circulation. See *Editor & Publisher* (November 1 and 8, 1980), 9.

The figures show that the number of dailies supporting Roosevelt declined for his 1940 and 1944 races with Wendell Willkie and Thomas E. Dewey, as did the circulation they represented. Harry S. Truman reached a low point of support in his successful 1948 contest with Dewey. Dwight D. Eisenhower enjoyed the most support in 1952, for his first race against Adlai E. Stevenson. John F. Kennedy's position was improved as he defeated Richard M. Nixon in 1960. Kennedy was endorsed by twenty-two dailies above 100,000 circulation, while twelve endorsed no candidate. This represented more large pro-Democratic papers, with a better geographic spread, than at any time since 1944.[9]

Then came political upheaval stemming from the assassination of President Kennedy. His successor, Lyndon Johnson of Texas, became the first Southerner to win the Democratic nomination in modern times. His opponent, Senator Barry M. Goldwater, represented the frustrated right wing of the Republican party. Given such a choice, newspaper publishers and editors chose to endorse President Johnson for reelection. The scales were essentially turned. Among dailies over 100,000 in circulation, Nixon had enjoyed the support of eighty-seven to twenty-two for Kennedy in 1960. Johnson won eighty-two to his side 4 years later, and Goldwater only twelve.[10]

Four years later came more upheaval—the assassination of Senator Robert Kennedy, the forced withdrawal of President Johnson from the Democratic race by the Eugene McCarthy crusade—and the nominations in vacuums of Hubert Humphrey and Richard M. Nixon. The scales tilted back, and the big dailies divided seventy-eight for Nixon and twenty-eight for Humphrey. Humphrey's percentage of the reporting circulation was better than any since Roosevelt's in 1940 on the Democratic side, save for the 1964 aberration.[11]

In 1972 it was the Democrats' turn to nominate a candidate from an extreme wing of their party, Senator George McGovern, who won only one state. Dailies representing only two-thirds of the total circulation responded to the poll, and the big dailies split sixty-six for President Nixon and nine for McGovern, with forty uncommitted or unreported.[12]

Participation in the poll was even more dispirited in 1976, with dailies representing only 55 percent of the total circulation responding. Among 114 dailies with more than 100,000 circulation, fifty backed President Gerald Ford, twenty-one backed Democratic candidate Jimmy Carter of Georgia, and forty-three were blank.[13] The *Los Angeles Times, Philadelphia Bulletin, Washington Star,* and *Kansas City Star* were among normally Republican papers avoiding an endorsement in the wake of the forced resignations of President Nixon and Vice President Agnew. The Hearst newspapers also did not endorse. Carter bettered Humphrey's 1968 performance in attracting press support, after McGovern's all-time low.

In the 1980 poll, the percentage of dailies reporting as uncommitted reached an all-time high of 40.7. Responding to the poll were papers representing 58 percent of the circulation. Among the 100 largest papers, thirty-three endorsed Ronald Reagan, twenty backed Carter, three were for independent John Anderson, and forty-four did not respond. Reagan had the support of 460 dailies, Carter 140, and Anderson forty-three.[14]

OTHER OPINION-MAKING FORCES

Adlai Stevenson called it "a one-party press in a two-party country." But partisan critics did not acknowledge the impact day-by-day coverage of the news has on voter decisions, and available studies of campaign news coverage indicate that at least larger dailies were essentially fair in their news columns. Research shows, too, that voters are often strongly affected by social pressures, group associations, and "opinion leaders." Radio and television can become highly important factors.[15]

A classic study of how news came to Paducah, Kentucky, made by *Fortune* magazine (August, 1947), also illustrates that it is impossible for a single newspaper to exercise a monopoly in the realm of opinion making. Paducah's one daily newspaper had a circulation of 12,000 copies within the city. There was also a small weekly, and the city had two radio stations, one owned by the daily paper. Outside publications came into Paducah in the following numbers: *Louisville Courier-Journal,* 1400 copies daily and 2400 on Sunday; New York, Chicago, St. Louis, and Memphis newspapers, 428 daily and 2770 Sunday; weekly news magazines, 429 copies; picture weeklies, 1968 copies; other general weeklies, 1769 copies; monthly magazines, 13,037 copies. The public library had 110 magazines on file and circulated about 10,000 books a month. Motion pictures, public meetings, and club and luncheon gatherings also brought information to Paducah's 33,000 citizens.

MEDIA RESPONSES TO CRITICISMS

Through all the years of external criticism of the media, which increased in the 1930s and escalated in the 1960s and 1970s, those within the profession were responding to pressures for improvement of the press and broadcasting. They also were creating some pressures of their own.

Those responses took the forms of improving professional working conditions, establishing effective media associations, writing voluntary codes of conduct, developing professional organizations devoted to the highest purposes of journalism, encouraging education for journalism, supporting studies of the press, sponsoring press councils and journalism reviews, and taking advantage of improvements in technology.

In the crisis year of 1933, gaining adequate income and job security for newspaper men and women was the first prerequisite. While other workers in newspaper plants had long since unionized, the editorial employees remained unorganized and relatively underpaid. Section 7-a of the National Industrial Recovery Act of (NRA) of 1933 offered them their chance, since it guaranteed the right of collective bargaining. The NRA also contained licensing provisions that alienated conservative leaders of the American Newspaper Publishers Association. This made the writing of a daily newspaper code under the "Blue Eagle" provisions a grueling duel. It provided for a 40-hour week in bigger cities, minimum salaries, and carried an open-shop provision.

Newspaperpeople received the wage and hour provisions of the daily newspaper code with little enthusiasm. The $11 to $15 weekly salary minimums did nothing to further the professional status of journalism or the economic security of its workers—an obvious conclusion to which thoughtful leaders of the profession agreed. The code provisions were far from the $40 a week minimum for those with 2 years or more experience, which New York reporters considered equitable at the time.

THE NEWSPAPER GUILD

Reporters and desk workers around the country began talking about forming collective bargaining units in the summer of 1933 when the trend of the code negotiations became apparent. Heywood Broun, the liberal and combative columnist for the *New York World-Telegram,* sounded a call for action in his syndicated column for August 7, 1933, which sparked the translation of talk into deeds. Broun deftly chastised his fellow newspaper workers for not having formed a union like those of the better-paid printers and gently chided those who feared "the romance of the game" would be lost if they organized. Then in typical Broun style he concluded:

> But the fact that newspaper editors and owners are genial folk should hardly stand in the way of the organization of a newspaper writers' union. There should be one. Beginning at nine o'clock in the morning of October 1, I am going to do the best I can in helping get one up. I think I could die happy on the opening day of the general strike if I had the privilege of watching Walter Lippmann heave a brick through a *Tribune* window at a nonunion operative who had been called in to write the current "Today and Tomorrow" column on the gold standard.[16]

The cautious Lippmann ignored Broun's call to arms, but the newspaper people across the country who read his column did not, nor did they wait until

Heywood Broun.

October 1. Cleveland's reporters were the first to respond, forming what became the first local of the Newspaper Guild on August 20. The Twin Cities, Minneapolis and St. Paul, were second in line. New York, Rockford, Newark, Akron, Duluth—Superior, Cincinnati, Philadelphia, and Youngstown locals followed in rapid order. There had been newswriters' locals chartered by the American Federation of Labor and its affiliated International Typographical Union as early as the 1890s, but few had lived for any length of time. Broun himself had headed a New York effort in 1923.[17]

New York newspeople, headed by Broun, issued the first number of the *Guild Reporter* on November 23, 1933, and called for a national convention to be held in Washington, D.C., on December 15. Delegates from thirty cities responded. Broun was elected president, a post he held until his death in 1939, and Jonathan Eddy became the first executive secretary. The newspapermen and women were seeking, they said, "to preserve the vocational interests of the members and to improve the conditions under which they work by collective bargaining, and to raise the standards of journalism."

By the time the first annual convention met in St. Paul in June, 1934, the Guild had 8000 members. But only one of its local units had a contract with a publisher. The 1934 Guild convention called for more contracts covering minimum wages and maximum hours, paid holidays and vacations, overtime pay, sick leave, severance pay, and other usual trade-union contract provisions—goals that remained to be gained by the average newspaper staff. Publishers who disliked seeing the Guild take on the form of a trade-union organization were further antagonized when the convention approved a code of ethics that listed what the Guild regarded to be harmful practices of newspapers. The Guild, rebuffed in its effort "to raise the standards of journalism" on a philosophical plane and realizing that it faced a hard fight to win union contracts, thereafter stuck closely to problems of salaries and working conditions when dealing with employers. Local units sponsored Guild discussions and competitions designed to improve journalistic practices.

Head-on clashes became unavoidable. The Guild did not shrink from using the strike and picket line and was involved in twenty strikes during its first 5 years. Bitterest was a 508-day strike against Hearst newspapers in Chicago; the longest in Guild history was the strike called in 1967 against Hearst's *Los Angeles Herald-Examiner* that eventually led 15 years later to non-Guild agreements. But in the main the Guild negotiated peacefully. It developed Guild shop provisions to ensure 80 percent membership, joined the CIO in 1937, and broadened the membership base to office employees. All this aroused controversy, but by 1938 the Guild had seventy-five newspaper contracts and its first with a press association, the United Press.[18]

But the biggest early Guild victory was gained in a court case involving one AP staff member, Morris Watson. Watson, who had been discharged by the AP in 1935, asserted that he had been dismissed for Guild activities. He appealed to the National Labor Relations Board for an order compelling his reinstatement under the provisions of the Wagner Labor Relations Act of 1935, whose collective bargaining guarantees had replaced those of the NRA codes outlawed by the Supreme Court that year. When the NLRB ruled in favor of Watson in 1936, the AP carried the case to the Supreme Court, contending that the Wagner Act was unconstitutional and that in any event it did not apply to newspapers or press associations.

The Supreme Court, which had ruled adversely on key New Deal legislation in 1935 and 1936, announced a series of decisions in April, 1937, upholding the constitutionality of the Wagner Act. Among the cases decided was that of Morris Watson. Justices Hughes and Roberts swung to the liberal side to join Justices Brandeis, Stone, and Cardozo in ordering the AP to reinstate Watson in his job. The five justices ruled that Watson had been illegally discharged for union activity, and it was on that point that the case turned.[19] But the majority also observed that "the publisher of a newspaper has no special immunity from the application of general laws."

The upholding of the Wagner Act was a great Guild victory. It assured the Guild a permanent place in newspaper life. Gradually contracts were won in larger cities, including one with the *New York Times,* whose staff had long been skeptical of the Guild. But the road was still a rocky one. The recession years of 1937 to 1939 brought widespread newspaper closings and staff prunings that left thousands of newspapermen and women unemployed and made contract negotiation difficult.

After the tragic death of Heywood Broun from pneumonia at age 51, the Guild became engaged in a bitter fight between conservative or "pro-Guild" members and left-wing elements who were strongest in the New York City locals. Forcing an election of officers by nationwide referendum, however, brought victory to the "pro-Guild" group whose anti-Communist slate was managed by Wilbur Bade, early editor of the *Guild Reporter.* The Guild was the first CIO union to throw out its pro-Communist national officers. New York's locals did the same in 1947. Under the leadership of presidents Milton M. Murray and Harry Martin, and executive vice presidents Sam Eubanks and Ralph B. Novak, the Guild remained vigorously liberal but continued its anti-Communist policy in following years to include material and moral aid to journalists' groups in other countries.[20]

World War II brought a general "freezing" of labor-relations activities. As the war ended, the Guild's goal was a $65 a week top minimum for all contracts. Then in 1946 the goal was set at a seemingly impossible $100 level. When it was reached with ease by 1954, new goals were set. Founders would have been amazed by the breaking of the $500 a week level at the *Washington Post* in 1977 and an average top reporter salary nationally above $450 by 1983. The average starting salary for reporters in Guild shops reached the $275 a week level. The Guild's Associated Press contract called for a $618 top in 1985. Membership, concentrated in larger dailies and press associations, passed 33,000. Guild leaders since 1950 have included Joseph F. Collis, Arthur Rosenstock, William J. Farson, and Charles A. Perlik, Jr.

Although its original hopes for influencing journalistic standards had been shelved, the Guild revived such interests in the 1960s. It established the Mellett Fund for a Free and Responsible Press to finance press councils in local communities. It encouraged establishment of critical media reviews, and Guild members cautiously sought more voice in advising newspaper management on institutional policy. Race discrimination, reporters' privilege, restrictions on the press, and physical harassment of reporters were other issues occupying Guild attention. Remembering their founder, in 1941 the Guild established an annual award for newspaper work "in the spirit of Heywood Broun."

THE AMERICAN NEWSPAPER PUBLISHERS ASSOCIATION

The American Newspaper Publishers Association (ANPA), founded in 1887 as the trade association of the dailies, had grown to 850 members by the 1930s. In contrast to its position on the Guild, the ANPA had sponsored an imaginative policy of voluntary arbitration with the printing unions after 1900. Its Bureau of Advertising was involved in the *Continuing Study of Newspaper Reading.* It had sponsored research in printing processes and had defended newspaper owners' interests in newsprint tariffs and postage rates.

But in the 1930s its leadership proved unresponsive to changing social and economic conditions. Its manager, Lincoln B. Palmer, and counsel, Elisha Hanson, put the ANPA in full opposition to the major legislation of the New Deal. Exemptions for the newspaper business were asked when reform legislation was before the Congress. After Cranston Williams became general manager in 1939, the uncompromising conservative stance was altered. By the time Stanford Smith took charge in 1960, the ANPA was a typical trade association with a progressive flair. Membership rose to 1200 dailies.

The publishers had long supported a mechanical department devoted to the study of improvements in the printing processes. After World War II they felt the growing pressures of a "cold-type revolution" brought about by the introduction of the photographic process into printing. In 1947 a research director was named and funds were voted to establish a research center in Easton, Pennsylvania, which formally opened in 1951. It was incorporated as the ANPA Research Institute in 1954, with its own board of publisher-directors. A

1958 evaluation by a six-member committee headed by Otto A. Silha of the *Minneapolis Star* and *Tribune* gave the Institute new direction, toward experimental work in utilizing the fruits of technological innovations in printing newspapers. An annual mechanical conference for members emphasized photocomposition, offset printing, run-of-paper color printing, computerized typesetting and editing, and other advances.

The establishment of a Newspaper Information Service in 1960 was another step forward. Through it ANPA headquarters could work with educators, students, other media, and the public. Objectives included promoting journalism as a career; giving awards to college and high school newspaper staffs; publishing newsletters, brochures, and booklets; and interpreting the newspaper industry. The ANPA had already worked with other media organizations to support accreditation of journalism schools and departments.

The ANPA's biggest legislative victory was the passage of the Newspaper Preservation Act, after 3 years of debate in the Congress. The act exempted from antitrust suits the joint-printing operations of forty-four newspapers in twenty-two cities and overturned a Supreme Court decision dissolving a pooled business operation in Tucson. Opponents said the new law, signed by President Nixon in 1970, would perpetuate the status quo.

ASNE, NAB, AND CODES OF CONDUCT

The American Society of Newspaper Editors (ASNE) was organized in 1922, under the leadership of Casper S. Yost of the *St. Louis Globe-Democrat,* to fill a long-felt need. As the group's constitution pointed out, "Although the art of journalism has flourished in America for more than two hundred years, the editors of the greater American newspapers have not hitherto banded themselves together in association for the consideration of their common problems and the promotion of their professional ideals." State and regional newspaper associations had considered news and editorial problems, but the American Newspaper Publishers Association had virtually excluded all but business topics from its agendas.

Membership in the ASNE was limited to editors-in-chief, editorial-page editors, and managing editors of dailies published in cities of more than 100,000 population, a figure soon reduced to 50,000. Limited numbers of editors of smaller dailies were admitted to membership in later years.

Early meetings of the society were enlivened by a bitter dispute over the power of the group to expel a member, Fred G. Bonfils of the *Denver Post,* who stood accused of blackmailing oil millionaire Harry Sinclair in connection with the Teapot Dome scandal. At one point a vote of expulsion was taken, but the action was rescinded and the Denver editor was permitted to resign. Later the ASNE clarified its power to expel a member for due cause, but the Bonfils incident made it clear that the group did not propose to serve as a policing organization. Willis J. Abbot of the *Christian Science Monitor* and Tom Wallace of the *Louisville Times* were leaders in the fight for a stern policy, but Yost and others held to a middle course.

A code of ethics, called the "Canons of Journalism," was presented to the first annual meeting in 1923. Chief author was H. J. Wright, founder of the *New York Globe.* Some of the key paragraphs read as follows:

> The right of a newspaper to attract and hold readers is restricted by nothing but considerations of public welfare. The use a newspaper makes of the share of public attention it gains serves to determine its sense of responsibility, which it shares with every member of its staff. A journalist who uses his power for any selfish or otherwise unworthy purpose is faithless to a high trust.
>
> Freedom of the press is to be guarded as a vital right of mankind. It is the unquestionable right to discuss whatever is not explicitly forbidden by law, including the wisdom of any restrictive statute.
>
> Freedom from all obligations except that of fidelity to the public interest is vital.
>
> Partisanship, in editorial comment which knowingly departs from the truth, does violence to the best spirit of American journalism; in the news columns it is subversive of a fundamental principle in the profession.[21]

Annual meetings of the ASNE are held each April, usually in Washington. Proceedings are reported in a series of books, dating from 1923, titled *Problems of Journalism,* which offer in their pages some significant discussions of professional matters.[22] Lively debate is found in the monthly *ASNE Bulletin.*

Codes of conduct for the broadcasting industry were developed by its trade association, the National Association of Broadcasters (NAB). The NAB was founded in 1923 during a skirmish between the radio station owners and ASCAP over fees the latter insisted be paid for broadcasting music of ASCAP members. Paul Klugh was first NAB managing director. The role of the trade association expanded to include relationships with advertising and then, increasingly, its relationships with the Federal Communications Commission.

The NAB Code of Ethics and the NAB Standards of Commercial Practice were adopted in March, 1929, as the first voluntarily imposed regulations on broadcasters. More detailed documents, the NAB Radio Code and the NAB Television Code, were added. About half of all commercial radio and television stations subscribed to the codes. There were other major codes and statements, particularly those of the Radio-Television News Directors Association and the programming standards of the networks and many individual stations.

Headquarters of the NAB are in Washington, with a large staff for administration, legal problems, station services, broadcast management, government affairs, public relations, and research. The NAB Code Authority staff hears complaints concerning violations by those subscribing to the codes. There are also review boards for the Television Code and Radio Code.

NCEW, APME, AND RTNDA

Editorial-page editors and editorial writers who wanted a smaller and more vigorous "working" organization than the 450-member ASNE formed the National Conference of Editorial Writers (NCEW) in 1947. The idea came from a group attending an American Press Institute session at Columbia University[23] and was promoted by Leslie Moore of the *Worcester Telegram* and *Gazette,* Ralph

Coghlan of the *St. Louis Post-Dispatch,* John H. Cline of the *Washington Star,* Robert H. Estabrook of the *Washington Post,* and Forrest W. Seymour of the *Des Moines Register* and *Tribune,* among others. Beginning in 1947 annual sessions were held that featured small-group critique panels in which members appraised the editorial-page efforts of their colleagues. A quarterly magazine, the *Masthead,* and convention proceedings were published. A code of principles was adopted in 1949 "to stimulate the conscience and the quality of the American editorial page."[24]

Another important national group, the Associated Press Managing Editors Association (APME), was formed in 1931 by news executives who found the annual meetings of the ANPA and the AP too little concerned with improving the news columns' content. The organizers in this case included Oliver O. Kuhn of the *Washington Star,* Roy Roberts of the *Kansas City Star,* Sevellon Brown of the *Providence Journal* and *Bulletin,* W. C. Stouffer of the *Roanoke World-News,* and Roy Dunlap of the *St. Paul Pioneer Press* and *Dispatch.* The AP news report was analyzed and criticized orally in annual meetings until 1947 when a printed report was prepared by a Continuing Study Committee. Although the studies of the different portions of the AP news report were penetrating enough to arouse replies from the AP management, they were made public as the *APME Red Book* beginning in 1948.[25] Setting the pattern for the Continuing Study reports were the first chairpeople, William P. Steven of the *Minneapolis Tribune* and Lee Hills of the *Miami Herald.*

The equivalent organization in broadcasting is the Radio-Television News Directors Association (RTNDA), which was founded in 1946 as the National Association of Radio News Directors. Its first leaders were John Hogan, WCSH, Portland, Maine; John Murphy, WCKY, Cincinnati; Sig Mickelson, WCCO, Minneapolis; Jack Shelley, WHO, Des Moines; and Edward Wallace, WTAM, Cleveland. Its publication is the *RTNDA Bulletin.* The group set broadcast news standards and worked closely with journalism schools.

OTHER PROFESSIONAL GROUPS

Other professional groups were concerned with varying aspects of journalistic problems: the National Newspaper Association, representing weeklies and some smaller dailies; the Magazine Publishers Association; the National Association of Educational Broadcasters; the National Press Photographers Association; the United Press International editors; and many regional organizations. Some schools of journalism joined with newspeople in sponsoring various professional conferences dealing with journalistic problems. Awards for outstanding achievement were inaugurated by Sigma Delta Chi, the professional journalism society begun in 1909 at DePauw University and expanded to include professional chapters and both men and women, under the name Society of Professional Journalists. Research about journalism was encouraged by annual awards by both Sigma Delta Chi and Kappa Tau Alpha, a journalism scholastic society founded in 1910 at the University of Missouri. Theta Sigma Phi, a women's journalism society founded in 1909 at the University of Washington, stimulated interest through its annual Matrix table gatherings; it became Women in Communications, Inc.

EDUCATION FOR JOURNALISM BEGINS

The ties between campus and city room were strengthened greatly in the second quarter of the twentieth century. The famous cartoon showing a city editor asking a young hopeful, "And what, may I ask, is a school of journalism?" no longer held true. It was likely that the city editor was a journalism school graduate also—or at least a college graduate with an appreciation of the necessity for sound educational training for newspeople.

Talk about education for journalism began seriously after the Civil War, but little action resulted until the turn of the century. General Robert E. Lee, president of Washington College (later Washington and Lee University), attempted to establish training in printing in 1869, but the program languished, as did another effort at Cornell University in 1875. Kansas State College instruction in printing dates from 1873, and courses in history and materials of journalism were given at the University of Missouri from 1878 to 1884. The first definitely organized curriculum in journalism was offered at the University of Pennsylvania from 1893 to 1901 by Joseph French Johnson, a former financial editor of the *Chicago Tribune.* The University of Illinois organized the first 4-year curriculum in journalism in 1904 under the direction of Frank W. Scott. The first separate school of journalism, with newspaperman Walter Williams as dean, opened in 1908 at the University of Missouri.[26]

In this first period of journalism education, emphasis was placed on establishing technical courses. But journalism teachers, often getting their starts in English departments, had to win academic recognition as well as the confidence of the newspaper profession. Their most successful early leader in this regard was Willard G. Bleyer, who began teaching journalism at the University of Wisconsin in 1904. Bleyer advocated integrating journalism education with the social sciences and, through his development of this concept and his own journalism history research, he established Wisconsin as a center for graduate study by future journalism teachers. Other early leaders were Eric W. Allen of the University of Oregon, H. F. Harrington of Northwestern University, Leon N. Flint of the University of Kansas, Arthur L. Stone of Montana State University, J. W. Piercy of Indiana University, Merle H. Thorpe of the University of Washington, Everett W. Smith of Stanford University, and Talcott Williams and John W. Cunliffe of Columbia University, the first two men to head the Pulitzer School of Journalism, opened in 1912 with a $2 million endowment from the *New York World* publisher.

JOURNALISM AS A SOCIAL INSTITUTION

During the second phase of journalism education emphasis was placed on the study of journalism history and of the press as a social institution, and instruction was widened to areas other than that of the daily and weekly newspapers. Pioneer textbooks had been written by Bleyer, Harrington, James Melvin Lee of New York University, Grant M. Hyde of Wisconsin, and M. Lyle Spencer of Syracuse. In the early 1920s the books of Bleyer in journalism history and of Flint and Nelson Antrim Crawford of Kansas State College in newspaper ethics pointed the way toward integration of technical training with analysis of the social responsibilities of the journalist. Coming into importance were the American Association of Teachers of Journalism, founded in 1912, and the American Association of Schools and Departments of Journalism, established in 1917.

Other publishers than Pulitzer aided in the establishment of journalism schools. Second in size to the Pulitzer gift to Columbia University was the endowment fund provided in 1918, by William J. Murphy, publisher of the *Minneapolis Tribune,* for journalism education at the University of Minnesota. The fund's value by the 1970s was $800,000* The owners of the *Chicago Tribune* established the Medill School of Journalism at Northwestern University in 1921 and continued to assist the school financially in subsequent years. State press associations and individuals played parts in establishing other schools and departments of journalism.

The 1920s saw the founding of the *Journalism Quarterly,* devoted to research studies in the field of mass communications. It began as the *Journalism Bulletin* in 1924, taking the title *Quarterly* in 1930 with Frank Luther Mott of the University of Iowa (later Missouri) as editor. His successors were Ralph D. Casey, Raymond B. Nixon, and Edwin Emery of the University of Minnesota, and Guido H. Stempel, III, of Ohio University. The educators successively founded *Journalism Educator, Journalism Monographs, Journalism Abstracts,* and *Journalism History.* Other research journals included the *Journal of Broadcasting* and the *Journal of Communication.*

JOURNALISM AS A SOCIAL SCIENCE

A third phase of journalism education was developing by the 1930s. Fuller integration of journalism education with the social sciences was the goal, and the leading schools and departments undertook research and teaching in the field of communications as a whole. Journalism students, it was recognized, should receive broad liberal-arts educations, sound journalistic technical training, and understanding of the social implications of their chosen profession. Northwestern University developed a 5-year plan for professional training in 1938; the Pulitzer School at Columbia in 1935 had restricted its year's course to holders of bachelor's degrees. Graduate-level instruction was expanded at other institutions, along with research in mass communications. In 1944 the Minnesota School of Journalism set up a journalism research division, the first of its kind. Among early leaders in mass-communications research based on the social and behavioral sciences were Chilton R. Bush of Stanford University, Ralph O. Nafziger of Minnesota (later at Wisconsin), Wilbur Schramm of Iowa (later at Illinois and Stanford), Paul F. Lazarsfeld of Columbia University's Bureau of Applied Social Research, and Douglas Waples of the University of Chicago.

MEDIA SUPPORT FOR EDUCATION

Closer ties between newspaperpeople and schools were established during the 1930s. The idea of a joint committee that would include representatives of the

*In 1977 John Cowles of the *Minneapolis Star* and *Tribune* established a $2 million endowment for journalism education at the University of Minnesota.

principal newspaper associations and the schools and departments of journalism was suggested by Fred Fuller Shedd, editor of the *Philadelphia Bulletin* who had been instrumental in the founding of the department at Pennsylvania State College (later University). Journalism educators, led by Bleyer of Wisconsin, Allen of Oregon, and Frank L. Martin of Missouri, joined in the plan in 1931. The project lapsed during the Depression years but was brought into full operation in 1939 through the efforts of Kenneth E. Olson of Northwestern University. The American Council on Education for Journalism (ACEJ) was formed by journalism educators and five major newspaper organizations: the American Society of Newspaper Editors, the American Newspaper Publishers Association, the National Newspaper Association, the Inland Daily Press Association, and the Southern Newspaper Publishers Association. The professional associations in broadcasting, magazine publishing, advertising, business communication, and public relations later joined those and other newspaper groups in the Council's work. The ACEJ established an accrediting program and approved studies in one or more areas of journalism at forty schools and departments in the late 1940s. The number of accredited institutions increased to eighty-two.

In 1949 the American Association of Teachers of Journalism reorganized as the Association for Education in Journalism (AEJ). Accepting coordinate roles within the AEJ structure were the American Association of Schools and Departments of Journalism (now composed of the accredited schools) and the American Society of Journalism School Administrators, founded in 1944. In the 1980s the name became Association for Education in Journalism and Mass Communication (AEJMC).

Journalism schools in the 1980s were thus well established in the fields of teaching, research, and service. They had close ties with the profession and their scope of interests included daily and weekly newspapers, magazines, radio and television, photojournalism, advertising, the graphic arts, industrial editing, and public relations. A doctorate in mass communications was offered at more than a dozen universities in the fields of communication theory, mass-communications history, law and social institutions, and international communication.

A million-dollar endowment left to Harvard University in 1936 by the widow of Lucius W. Nieman, founder of the *Milwaukee Journal,* was used for a different type of educational opportunity. The Nieman Foundation, beginning in 1937, annually selected a dozen highly qualified working newspaperpeople for a year of study at Harvard as Nieman Fellows, on leave from their newspapers or press associations. Louis M. Lyons, first curator of the foundation, established a thoughtful quarterly magazine, *Nieman Reports,* in 1947.

EFFORTS TO IMPROVE: STUDIES OF THE PRESS

Other attempts to study the responsibilities and the character of the American press were made in the years after World War II. Magazine publisher Henry R. Luce financed an important private study by the Commission on Freedom of the Press. The commission was headed by Chancellor Robert M. Hutchins of the University of Chicago and was composed chiefly of social-science professors outside the field of journalism. Its summary report, *A Free and Responsible Press*

(1947), covered newspapers, radio, motion pictures, magazines, and books, and consisted of a general statement of principles. The commission itself conducted only a limited research program in the making of its report, but it sponsored the publication of a number of books, including Zechariah Chafee, Jr.'s *Government and Mass Communications,* William E. Hocking's *Freedom of the Press,* and Llewellyn White's *The American Radio.*

The presidential elections of 1948 and 1952 brought flurries of activity in the analysis of press behavior in relation to public questions. *Editor & Publisher,* the trade journal for the daily newspapers, sponsored a meeting in March, 1949, of a panel on the press, composed of ten newspaperpeople and educators. The panel suggested studies for press self-improvement, but an ASNE committee appointed to consider the problem came to no specific conclusions. Before the 1956 election journalism educators and Sigma Delta Chi urged a major study of press election coverage, but a group of hesitant publishers and editors vetoed action. However, effective voices were raised within the profession and among educators in analysis of media performance, and major research studies resulted.

EFFORTS TO IMPROVE: PRESS COUNCILS

The example of the successful British Press Council, established in 1953 to hear complaints against newspapers under rules carefully drawn to protect the rights of both editors and citizens, led to movements to create press councils in the United States. The first to appear were local press councils organized in the late 1960s under the auspices of the Newspaper Guild's Mellett Fund.

One effort was made on the West Coast under the direction of William L. Rivers and his associates from Stanford University; another in Sparta and Cairo, Illinois, by Kenneth Starck and others from Southern Illinois University. A media-black council, to develop a better understanding between media executives and the black community, was directed by Lawrence Schneider of the University of Washington in Seattle for 19 months. In 1971, the first statewide press council was established in Minnesota, through the efforts of the Minnesota Newspaper Association, the Newspaper Guild, Sigma Delta Chi, other media leaders, and public officials. The council membership was divided between representatives of the media and the public, under the direction of a state supreme-court judge. Hawaii's council was formed the same year. The two state councils and local ones in Littleton, Colorado, and Peoria, Illinois, survived.

Efforts to establish a national press council bore fruit in 1973 with the establishment of the National News Council. A task force supported by the Twentieth Century Fund set as its goals "to examine and report on complaints concerning the accuracy and fairness of news reporting in the United States, as well as to initiate studies and report on issues involving the freedom of the press." At first shunned by major media leaders, the National News Council gained support through its handling of issues presented to it for consideration by ten public members and eight professional members. William B. Arthur was exeuctive director, and Norman E. Isaacs chairman, followed by Richard Salant. Beginning in 1977 its reports were printed first in the *Columbia Journalism Review* and later in *Quill.*

EFFORTS TO IMPROVE: JOURNALISM REVIEWS

Another phenomenon was the journalism review. Prior to 1968 only three existed: the *Montana Journalism Review* (1958), *Columbia Journalism Review* (1961), and *Seminar,* a review of sorts published by Copley Newspapers (1966). The *Chicago Journalism Review* (1968 to 1975) inspired a number of local and journalism department reviews but of the approximately forty established between 1968 and 1976, fewer than a dozen survived in 1977, including the Columbia and Montana reviews; *MORE,* a national review published in New York: *Accuracy in Media* (AIM), a conservative newsletter; *Media Report to Women; feed/back,* published in San Francisco; the *St. Louis Journalism Review;* the *Twin Cities Journalism Review; Pretentious Idea* in Tucson; and *Lexington Media Review* (Kentucky).[27] *Washington Journalism Review* appeared in 1977.

The *Chicago Journalism Review* appeared in the wake of the riots at the time of the 1968 Democratic convention. Edited by Ron Dorfman, the monthly afforded an aggressive criticism of the city's press and a forum for issues of press criticism and self-improvement among young news reporters. It inspired not only local imitators but also the springing up of informal "reporter-power" groups in city rooms, where young staff members met to seek improvements in their professional contributions. In some cities regular meetings of journalists and management resulted.

THE INTERNATIONAL FLOW OF THE NEWS

In the years after World War II it became clear that there was an international flow of the news, made increasingly immediate, if not instantaneous, by the miracles of media technology. It was also clear that there was a need for better collection, writing, and distribution of news and information so that they served people more evenly on a worldwide basis, recognizing both their interests and their needs.

There were barriers to such communication improvements. One was the long Cold War between the United States and its Western allies and the USSR and its Eastern bloc. Between stood what became known as the Non-Aligned Countries, which evolved a New World Information Order envisioning the full participation of the Third World in the exchange of news and information. With the support of UNESCO, the large Non-Aligned group brought about a full debate of the issue, and increased activity on the part of the West to improve its news and information systems.

A literature also developed which examined the role of the American media in the cultural and political development of the rest of the world. Some viewed the United States media as an arm of American economic and military imperialism, distorting, on one hand, the images the American public received about events abroad and policies of foreign powers, and attempting to "sell," on the other hand, the advantages of American social and political beliefs to those living abroad. Wherever the balance of truth was to be found, it was clear that the American news media—particularly its press associations, news magazines, and broadcast programs—had major influence in all parts of the world. So, increasingly, were the media of other nations coming to the attention of media personnel, political and educational leaders, and informed audiences in the United States.

U.S. NEWS AGENCIES: AP, UPI

The AP and UPI intensified their competition in the wake of the merger of the United Press and International News Service. By the late 1970s, both had 400,000 miles of leased telephone wires in the United States for transmission of news and pictures. Both used satellite channels, radio teleprinters, and underwater cables to carry their news reports to more than 100 countries in the world. Both had teletype circuits covering more than 20,000 miles in Europe, where their news reports were translated and fed into national wires, and both transmitted pictures worldwide. Both had automated their transmission facilities, using video display terminals and computers to perfect information storage and retrieval systems. The domestic news wire could deliver copy to news offices at 1200 words a minute, ten times earlier speeds. A news report could be flashed around the world, using the automatic editing system, within a single minute.

The systems still worked, as the 1980s began, but the UPI found great difficulties in coping with sharp inflation of costs and the effects of a worldwide recession which intensified at home. Its parent E. W. Scripps Company reported losses running into the millions after 1980. They sought to sell shares in UPI to media using its services, negotiated with the British news agency Reuters about a possible merger, and finally negotiated a sale in June, 1982, to Media News Corporation, a group of American newspaper, cable, and television station owners. Douglas F. Ruhe became the managing director of the new organization. UPI President Robert W. Beaton retired a few months later and was succeeded by William J. Small, a former executive of both CBS News and NBC News. Maxwell McCrohon, *Chicago Tribune* news executive, became editor-in-chief. UPI's key news operations were shifted from New York to Washington.

In 1976, the AP served 1181 U.S. newspapers and the UPI, 823. By late 1982 the AP reported 1325 U.S. members and counted 639 U.S. dailies receiving UPI. The erosion of American newspaper support of the UPI effort played a substantial part in its financial difficulties. Service to broadcast stations remained substantially equal and the UPI competed strongly in television news and photo services, as well as abroad. Much depended, however, on the new UPI management's ability to balance its operating income and expenses and the early return of a more favorable general economic climate. UPI bravely observed the seventy-fifth anniversary of the founding of the UP in 1907, negotiated fresh support from some major newspapers, and promoted new services to broadcasters and non-media users. Both AP and UPI reported in 1983 that only half their income now came from American dailies. UPI now claimed 818 U.S. newspaper clients and forecast a 1984 profit. AP had revenues totaling $188 million and a $2.5 million surplus. Both were delivering news by satellite to virtually all U.S. users.

H. L. Stevenson became executive vice president/editorial of UPI in 1983 although many others of its management retired or resigned, including general manager Robert F. Page and senior executive Frank Tremaine. Perhaps UPI's

Helen Thomas, UPI's White House correspondent.

United Press International

greatest asset was its White House correspondent, Helen Thomas, who succeeded the legendary Merriman Smith upon his death in 1970. Thomas became the head of the White House Correspondents Association and was showered with honors. Arnold Sawislak, dean of the House of Representatives correspondents and 1980 presidential campaign coordinator, was another major capitol figure. In the 1970s, UPI byliners abroad included Peter Uebersex, Arthur Higbee, Wellington Long, and Gerard Loughran in Europe, and Leon Daniel, Alan Dawson, and Joseph Galloway in Asia. Lucinda Franks and Thomas Powers won the 1971 national news Pulitzer Prize.

Keith Fuller replaced Wes Gallagher as president and general manager of the AP at the close of 1976. Louis D. Boccardi was executive editor and Robert H. Johnson the managing editor. Star of AP political reporting was Walter Mears. Stanley Swinton, head of the AP World News Service since its inception, died in 1982 and was succeeded by Larry Heinzerling in 1983. Such veterans of the overseas service as Richard K. O'Malley in Europe, Nick Ludington in the Middle East, Myron Belkind in India, and George Esper in Asia continued to serve.

UNITED STATES NEWS SERVICES ABROAD

Only a handful of United States dailies had their own correspondents abroad to supplement the AP and UPI services (a fact held up by Third-World critics of American coverage). Joining the press-association and newspaper reporters abroad were those for the broadcast media, magazine groups, and news magazines. A 1975 study for the Overseas Press Club of America painted a depressing picture of American news enterprise abroad. All together, the United States media had only 676 full-time staff abroad, a 28 percent decline since a 1969 study. Of these, 429 were American citizens, a 23 percent drop. Fifty percent were in Europe, 25 percent in Asia, 15 percent in the western hemisphere, 8 percent in the troubled Middle East, and 2 percent in Africa. Of the United States nationals abroad, 8 percent were women.[28] Later estimates showed some increase in the staffing of overseas news bureaus by American newspapers, but the 1975 picture remained substantially correct.

One leader of the newspaper syndicates was the New York Times News Service. Founded in 1917, it was claiming more than 500 users in fifty-four countries. Its leased wire carried its news reports to subscribers from thirty foreign correspondents, forty Washington bureau staffers, and the city room. The *Times* had won fifty-three Pulitzer Prizes in 65 years, sixteen of them for foreign correspondence. The best-known winners were Walter Duranty, 1932; Anne O'Hare McCormick, 1937; Otto D. Tolischus, 1940; Hanson W. Baldwin, 1943; Harrison E. Salisbury, 1955; A. M. Rosenthal, 1960; David Halberstam, 1964, from Vietnam; Max Frankel, 1973, from Peking; Hedrick Smith, 1974, from Moscow; and Sydney Schanberg, 1976, reporting the fall of Cambodia. Arthur Krock and James B. Reston were double winners from the Washington bureau, also represented by Louis Stark and Anthony Lewis. Among other foreign byliners were C. L. Sulzberger, Herbert L. Matthews, Drew Middleton, Flora Lewis, and Malcolm Browne.

New on the scene was the Los Angeles Times-Washington Post News Service, begun in 1962 by publishers Otis Chandler and Philip L. Graham. Twenty years later it claimed more than 500 clients in fifty-six countries, who were served by thirty foreign bureaus of the *Times* and the *Post,* their Washington bureaus and local staffs, their other United States bureaus, and the news services of Agence France-Presse and the *Guardian* of London and Manchester.

Listed among the *Times* foreign correspondents were Robert S. Elegant, Jacques Leslie, and George McArthur in Asia; Jack Foisie and David Lamb in Africa; Sharon Rosenhause in India; Tom Lambert, Stanley Meisler, Donald Cook, William Tuohy, and Joe Alex Morris, Jr., in Europe. Among *Post* byliners were Bernard Nossiter in London, John Goshko in Bonn, Don Oberdorfer in Tokyo, and Joanne Omang in Buenos Aires. Pulitzer Prize winners of the two papers covering Washington were Jack Nelson, Haynes Johnson, Carl Bernstein and Bob Woodward, and David Broder. This was indeed rich fare for the subscribers.

A 1981 survey showed 235 U.S. subscribers to the Los Angeles Times-Washington Post News Service; 202 full-service and 106 partial-service subscribers to the New York Times News Service; 130 subscribers to the newly developed Field News Service, called Independent Press; and 122 clients for the Knight News Tribune (KNT) wire, including forty papers belonging to the Knight-Ridder, *New York Daily News,* and *Chicago Tribune* organizations sponsoring it.[29]

Independent Press grew out of the Field News Service, and included in 1983 Washington and foreign coverage of the *Baltimore Sun, Boston Globe, Chicago Sun-Times, Dallas Morning News,* and a linkage with the Newhouse News Service. With Dean Schoelkopf as its editor, KNT had access to the news filed by more than twenty foreign correspondents and eight United States news bureaus of the participating newspapers. The *Chicago Tribune* added bureaus in Tel Aviv, Bonn, and Nairobi to its London and Moscow offices. Various Knight-Ridder newspapers, led by the *Miami Herald* and *Philadelphia Inquirer,* began sending correspon-

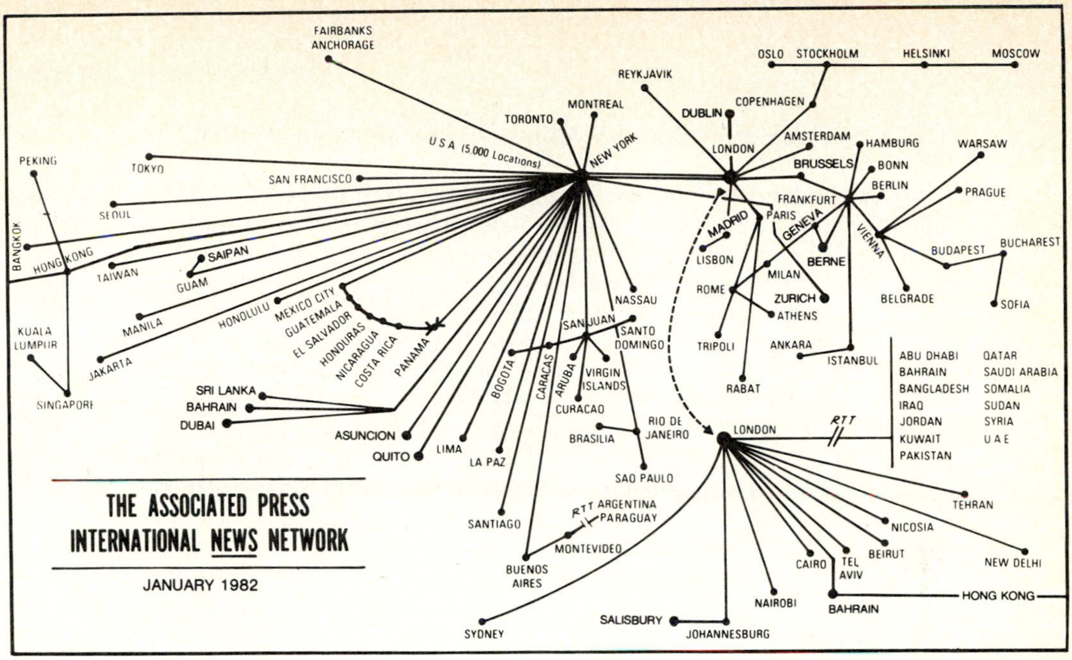

THE ASSOCIATED PRESS
INTERNATIONAL NEWS NETWORK
JANUARY 1982

dents abroad; in the early 1980s correspondents covered London, Rome, Paris, Tokyo, Jerusalem, Bangkok, Beijing, Toronto, and Central America. Two Pulitzer Prize winners working for KNT abroad were Richard Ben Kramer, based in Rome, and Shirley Christian, covering El Salvador.

Other important supplementary news services used by American media were the Dow-Jones News Service, specializing in economic news; the Copley News Service, focusing on Latin America; and Reuters from Great Britain, which had a North American organization and some fourty-six U.S. newspaper subscribers.

WORLD NEWS AGENCIES AND INTERCHANGE

The four major Western news agencies were the Associated Press and the United Press International, Reuters of Britain, and Agence France-Presse, founded in 1946 on the ruins of the old Havas agency. Two others operating on an international scope were TASS of the Soviet Union, founded in 1925 as the official news agency of the USSR, and Xinhua, founded in 1931 and serving as the official news agency of the People's Republic of China in Beijing (also called the New China News Agency).

Other important national news agencies have been the Press Association and Exchange Telegraph of Britain, Germany's Deutsche Press Agentur (DPA), Japan's Kyodo, Italy's old Stefani (now ASNA), Yugoslavia's Tanjug, and Spain's EFE. Organizing in Third World areas were Inter Press Service, founded in 1964 by journalists to provide news services supporting political and social reform in Latin America but now also functioning in Africa, Asia, and Europe; the Caribbean News Agency, the Middle East News Agency, the Pan-African News Agency, and the Asia-Pacific News Network spreading from Turkey to

Japan but centering on the Southeast Asian countries. The Pool of News Agencies of Non-Aligned Countries was established in 1975 under the aegis of Tanjug, the Yugoslav agency, and involving about fifty countries. The Aga Kahn began organizing a Third World News agency in Luxembourg in 1982, with former UPI executives as consultants. Organized by Americans to better cover Third World news were Pacific News Service, founded in 1970 and used by 100 dailies, and Interlink, U.S. affiliate of Inter Press Service.

If the American news media were infiltrating minds abroad, newspapers, magazines, and broadcasting from abroad also had influence in the United States. Newspapers like the *New York Times, Washington Post, Wall Street Journal, Christian Science Monitor, Miami Herald,* and *Los Angeles Times* were circulating abroad, most heavily in the order named. But equally scrutinized in all parts of the world were such international newspapers as *The Times* and *The Guardian* of Britain, *Le Monde* of France, *Frankfurter Allgemeine* of Germany, *Izvestia* and *Pravda* of the USSR, *Asahi Shimbun* of Japan, *The Times of India,* the *Peoples' Daily* and its English affiliate, *China Daily,* of Beijing, Australia's *Sydney Morning Herald, La Prensa* of Argentina, *Excelsior* of Mexico, and Canada's "paper of record," the *Globe and Mail* of Toronto.

Time, Newsweek, and *Reader's Digest* compete with *L'Express* of France and *Der Spiegel* of Germany, leading European news magazines, and *The Economist* of Britain. The *Digest* also owns *Asiaweek,* which competes with the *Far Eastern Economic Review* from their Hong Kong bases. The *International Herald Tribune* and Asian and European editions of the *Wall Street Journal* lock horns with the *Financial Times* of London and the American magazine *Business Week* in Europe and Asia. Britain's *Economist* has more than 75,000 weekly circulation in the United States, the *Guardian* sells a weekly airmail edition, and Reuters news agency expanded its American bureau network in the 1980s to supplement its worldwide service. Reuters Monitor, a specialized financial report, impinged on Dow Jones territory.

THE NEW WORLD INFORMATION ORDER

The flow of news between nations became an increasingly sensitive international issue in the 1970s as Third World leaders spoke out loudly and clearly about the urgent need to reorder the traditional international communication system in order to achieve a better balance of information. By the mid-1980s the Western countries had a better grasp of Third World concerns, if not a willingness to adopt what was being called the New World Information Order.

Among the world's many press associations or news agencies, the four Western transnationals—the Associated Press, United Press International, Reuters, and Agence France-Presse—along with TASS of the Soviet Union, provided more than 90 percent of the daily international news fare. Western powers also were the most advanced in the use of telecommunications channels, including satellites; in 1982 developing nations representing 70 percent of the world's population had only 5 percent of the television transmitters and 12 percent of television receivers. The nonaligned and some other nations viewed this dominance of communication channels as a vestige of colonialism that inhibited them culturally, politically, and economically. Their goal of a New International

Economic Order, proclaimed in 1973, could not be achieved without a new information or communication order, they said.

There were efforts to address the problem as early as the 1953 flow-of-news study by the International Press Institute, whose data showed the one-way flow. IPI was dedicated to the Western-style free press system, but also worked to develop the press in Asia and Africa. So did the Thomson Foundation in Britain, which since 1963 has provided practical training for Third World journalists. UNESCO in 1960 undertook a worldwide survey of press, radio, film, and television, providing data illuminating the problem. It also encouraged the development of national and regional news agencies in Asia, Africa, and Latin America. By 1972 UNESCO had developed a declaration of guiding principles on the use of satellite broadcasting for the free flow of information.

But all this did not satisfy the Third World. The 1970 UNESCO General Assembly asked its Director General to examine communication policies, and began a discussion of the phrase "Right to Communicate." The issue exploded in 1973 at the fourth conference of Heads of State of Non-Aligned Countries, held in Algeria. They called for "reorganization of existing communication channels which are the legacy of the colonial past" and which hampered inter-communication among developing countries, for cheaper press cable rates, and for collective ownership of communications satellites. They also began planning the Non-Aligned News Pool which began operating in 1975 under the guidance of the Yugoslav agency, Tanjug.

The issues were sharpened in an escalating series of meetings in Paris, Tunis, New Delhi, New York, and San José, Costa Rica. The last named meeting, in July 1976, introduced the phrase "free and balanced flow" of the news. The Tunisian foreign minister, Mustapha Masmoudi, earlier had contributed a detailed document of complaint, and the Soviet Union put even more drastic proposals to the 1976 General Assembly of UNESCO at Nairobi in October, 1976. Among the proposals were:

- Establishing independence and equity in access to global communication resources in order that their own views, values, and developmental efforts might be reported more fully.
- Substantial help from the West to speed their own communication development.
- Support of the Pool of News Agencies of Non-Aligned Countries.
- Legitimizing the right of governments to limit access to news sources and the right to censor or restrict the flow of information across national borders.
- The adoption by UNESCO of resolutions proclaiming the right of governments to become involved in the licensing of journalists in order to "protect" them, and in the adoption of an international code of ethics and an international right of reply.
- Establishment of a supranational tribunal by UNESCO to monitor media behavior throughout the world.

A breakdown between the Western bloc and the Soviet-supported Non-Aligned group was avoided when the Assembly agreed to a two-year delay and the appointment of a sixteen-person International Commission for the Study of Communication Problems, under the chairmanship of Sean MacBride of Ireland, recipient of both the Lenin and Nobel Peace Prizes.

At its 1978 General Assembly, UNESCO dropped the "free and balanced flow" concept, using the phrase "a free flow and a wider and better balanced dissemination of information." In return for this concession, the Western group admitted that it was "necessary to correct the inequalities in the flow of information to and from developing countries, and between those countries." The 1980 final report of the MacBride Commission rejected proposals for licensing of journalists or affording them "special protections" beyond those of all citizens; condemned censorship, and argued for right of access to private as well as public sources of information. It failed to put private ownership of news media and communications facilities on the same plane as public control, and in the view of Western press leaders left the transnational agencies open to pressure to transmit stories promoting government-set economic and political goals, regardless of newsworthiness or propaganda content.

The 1980 General Assembly in Belgrade did not vote on the MacBride report, but did adopt a resolution containing many of its principles. UNESCO began a lengthy series of regional meetings on the issues of the New World Information Order and the concept of the "Right to Communicate." Western press leaders, particularly the American-sponsored World Press Freedom Committee, raised more than a million dollars for training programs and equipment shipments to three continents. Third World journalists were invited to internship experiences, and the U.S. government provided free transponder time on Intelsat to the developing world.

But the Third World's basic political objections were not yet met. UNESCO's 1984–1985 discussion program still talked of state-run news agencies, codes of conduct for journalists, and the removal of obstacles to the flow of news from the developing countries to the developed areas of the world—with the Third World definition of what is important news obtaining. Like the New International Economic Order, the New World Information Order was beset with difficulites stemming from basic North-South economic and East-West political confrontations.

NOTES

1. See *Editor & Publisher,* June 11, 1983, p. 11. The poll was conducted by the Media Research Institute, in the Department of Journalism, California State University, Northridge, and was tabulated by graduate students in the Seminar in Media Criticism: Katherine Arai, Mark Bennett, Susan Berryhill, Batel Libes, David Myers, Barbara Ross, Suzanne Roth, Ann Schafer, Esther Schwartz-Uren, Marilyn Tjanjadi, and Nancy Ward. As noted, regional strengths were determined along with votes for national recognition. In any event, the subjective nature of responses makes a listing uncertain after the consensus on the top half-dozen leaders.

2. New York City offers a prime example of changes in center-city newspapers:

YEAR	MAJOR DAILIES	TOTAL CIRCULATION	SUNDAY EDITIONS	TOTAL CIRCULATION
1947	9	6,084,000	6	10,130,000
1959	7	5,164,000	6	7,408,000
1965	6	4,283,000	5	5,811,000
1967	3	3,580,000	2	4,598,000
1982	3	3,409,000	2	3,484,000

3. Well-known dailies which disappeared and were not mentioned in the text included: the *Louisville Herald-Post,* 1936; *Providence Tribune,* 1938; *Kansas City Journal-Post,* 1942; *Brooklyn Citizen,* 1947; *Seattle Star,* 1947; *San Diego Journal,* 1948; *Brooklyn Eagle,* 1955; *Cleveland News,* 1960; Hearst's *Detroit Times* and *Pittsburgh Sun-Telegraph,* 1960; Scripps-Howard's *Houston Press,* 1964, and *Fort Worth Press,* and *Indianapolis Times,* 1965; *Newark News,* 1972; *Hartford Times,* 1976; *Long Island Press,* 1977; the *Portland Journal, Des Moines Tribune,* and *Minneapolis Star,* 1982; and the *Macon News* and *Memphis Press-Scimitar,* 1983.

4. The *Daily News* reached 2,007,000 circulation in 1941 and a peak 2,402,000 circulation daily in 1947 (along with 4,717,000 on Sundays). It stayed at the 2-million level for the next 40 years, quite a record.

5. Frank Luther Mott, *American Journalism* (New York: Macmillan, 1950), p. 648.

6. William Weinfeld, "The Growth of Daily Newspaper Chains in the United States: 1923, 1926–1935," *Journalism Quarterly,* XIII (December 1936), 357.

7. A listing of "Groups of Daily Newspapers under Common Ownership" is published annually in *Editor & Publisher International Year Book,* as compiled and updated by Paul Jess, University of Kansas. Papers in each group are identified, and owners named.

8. The Ridder family founder, Herman Ridder, published the *Staats-Zeitung* in New York City, where his three sons—Bernard H., Joseph E., and Victor F. Ridder—bought the *Journal of Commerce* in 1926. Bernard made the St. Paul papers his center in 1927 and invaded California in 1952. His son Bernard H., Jr. became publisher in St. Paul and Duluth. His other three sons became publishers in California—Joseph B. in San Jose and Herman H. and Daniel as copublishers in Long Beach. Joseph E. Ridder centered his attention on the *Journal of Commerce,* of which one of his sons, Eric, became publisher. The other Bernard J., published the Pasadena newspapers. Victor F. Ridder's son Walter headed the Ridders' Washington bureau, son Robert the family's radio-TV interests. Grandsons later became active.

9. Among major dailies supporting Kennedy in 1960 outside the South were the *New York Times, St. Louis Post-Dispatch, Milwaukee Journal, Louisville Courier-Journal, New York Post, Newsday, Long Island Press, Pittsburgh Post-Gazette, Toledo Blade, Hartford Times, Denver Post,* and *Sacramento Bee.* The *Washington Post* did not endorse, but favored, Kennedy.

10. The twelve major dailies supporting Goldwater in 1964 were the *Chicago Tribune* and *American, Los Angeles Times, Oakland Tribune, Cincinnati Enquirer, Columbus Dispatch, Milwaukee Sentinel, Richmond Times-Dispatch* and *News Leader, Nashville Banner, Tulsa World,* and *Birmingham News.*

11. Nine major dailies that had supported Nixon in 1960 swung to Humphrey: Hearst's *San Francisco Examiner* and *Boston Record-American,* the Cowles' *Minneapolis Star* and *Tribune* and *Des Moines Register* and *Tribune,* the Ridders' *St. Paul Dispatch* and *Pioneer Press,* and Newhouse's *Newark Star-Ledger.* Four that had backed Kennedy in 1960 now endorsed Nixon: *Newsday,* the *Toledo Blade,* Gannett's *Hartford Times,* and the Ridders' *Long Beach Press-Telegram.*

12. The nine major dailies supporting McGovern in 1972 were the *New York Times, New York Post, Louisville Courier-Journal, Minneapolis Tribune, St. Louis Post-Dispatch, Portland Oregon Journal, Arkansas Gazette, Bergen County* (N.J.) *Record,* and *St. Petersburg Independent.*

13. Switching to the Democrats with Carter were the *Chicago Sun-Times* and *Daily News* and the *Detroit Free Press.* Although he carried virtually the entire South, Carter had the backing of only six major Southern dailies: *Atlanta Journal* and *Constitution, Charlotte Observer, St. Petersburg Independent, Nashville Tennessean,* and Little Rock's *Arkansas Gazette.* Other Carter supporters, in addition to McGovern's 1972 list, included the *Des Moines Register, Denver Post, Dayton News, Long Island Press, Milwaukee Journal,* and *Minneapolis Star.*

14. In 1980 Carter retained all of the papers of McGovern's 1972 list except the *New York Post* (which had been sold). His other major endorsements were from the *Philadelphia Inquirer, Detroit Free Press, Chicago Sun-Times, Milwaukee Journal, Kansas City Star, Baltimore Sun* and *News-American, Dayton News, Atlanta Constitution, St. Petersburg Times, Raleigh News and Observer,* and the *Sacramento Bee.*

15. See Bernard Berelson, Paul F. Lazarsfeld, and William N. McPhee, *Voting* (Chicago: University of Chicago Press, 1954). For studies of campaign news coverage in large cities, see the Bibliography for this chapter. In his three studies of the news coverage of the presidential campaigns of the 1960s in fifteen "prestige papers," as selected by the nation's editors and educators (see pages 000 for the polls), Guido H. Stempel found that only one deviated by more than 5 percent from fifty-fifty division of space in both the 1960 and 1964 campaigns. That was the *Chicago Tribune,* whose news of the campaigns was 59.2 percent Republican in 1960 and 65.6 in 1964. But in 1972, a follow-up study showed, of six papers analyzed, all favoring McGovern, the *Tribune* was most favorable to the Democrats in news coverage (62.9 percent).

16. Broun's column is reprinted in the *Guild Reporter,* XVI (December 9, 1949), which contains several pages reviewing early Guild history and Broun's career. The early years of the Guild are examined in Daniel J. Leab, *A Union of Individuals: The Formation of the American Newspaper Guild 1933–1936* (New York: Columbia University Press, 1970).

17. The early AFL efforts are summarized in National Labor Relations Board, *Collective Bargaining in the Newspaper Industry* (Washington, D.C.: Government Printing Office, 1939), and in Alfred McClung Lee, *The Daily Newspaper in America* (New York: Macmillan,

1937). The most successful locals were in Scranton, Milwaukee, Boston, New York, Philadelphia, and Columbus, Ohio.

18. The details can be followed in the *Guild Reporter* and *Editor & Publisher,* and are summarized in the NLRB's *Collective Bargaining in the Newspaper Industry* and in the special issue of the *Guild Reporter,* XVI (December 9, 1949).

19. *Associated Press* v. *NLRB,* 301 U.S. 103 (1937).

20. This subject is explored in detail in Sam Kuczun, "History of the American Newspaper Guild" (Ph.D. thesis, University of Minnesota, 1970). Some other data in this account are taken from Kuczun's research in Guild archives and other documentary sources.

21. Found in *Problems of Journalism,* published annually by ASNE.

22. The proceedings of the twenty-fifth annual ASNE meeting, in 1947, contain on pages 39–53 historical reminiscences of three early members, Grove Patterson of the *Toledo Blade,* Marvin H. Creager of the *Milwaukee Journal,* and Donald J. Sterling of the *Oregon Journal.*

23. The American Press Institute was founded in 1946 through the efforts of Sevellon Brown of the *Providence Journal* and *Bulletin.*

24. The NCEW code of principles appears in *Editor & Publisher,* LXXXII (October 29, 1949), 7.

25. The *APME Red Book* for 1948 opens with a history of the organization and its Continuing Study activities to that time.

26. See Albert A. Sutton, *Education for Journalism in the United States* (Evanston: Northwestern University Press, 1945), for an historical treatment. For a current picture, see Warren K. Agee, Phillip H. Ault, and Edwin Emery, *Introduction to Mass Communications* (New York: Harper & Row, 1982).

27. This was the unpublished report of Claude-Jean Bertrand, University of Paris—Nanterre, studying American media from 1976 to 1977.

28. Ralph E. Kliesch, "A Vanishing Species: The American Newsman Abroad," *1975 Directory of the Overseas Press Club of America* (New York: Overseas Press Club, 1975), pp. 18ff.

29. Thomas B. Littlewood and Raymond DeLong, "Supplemental News Services," *Newspaper Research Journal,* 2:4 (July 1981), 9.

ANNOTATED BIBLIOGRAPHY

Discussions involving media problems are to be found in the American Society of Newspaper Editors' *Problems of Journalism* series, in the Associated Press Managing Editors' *APME Red Book* series, and in the periodicals *Journalism Quarterly, Journal of Broadcasting, Columbia Journalism Review, Washington Journalism Review, Nieman Reports, Masthead, Quill, Matrix, Grassroots Editor, feed/back, Editor & Publisher, Broadcasting, Advertising Age, Publishers' Auxiliary, Public Relations Journal, Publishers' Weekly, ASNE Bulletin, RTNDA Bulletin,* and ANPA's *presstime.*

Books: Newspapers

ANGELO, FRANK, *On Guard: A History of the Detroit Free Press.* Detroit: The Free Press, 1981. A 150-year review by a *Free Press* editor.

BECKER, STEPHEN, *Marshall Field III: A Biography.* New York: Simon & Schuster, 1964. Good portrait of the founder of *PM* and the *Chicago Sun.*

BERGER, MEYER, *The Story of The New York Times, 1851–1951.* New York: Simon & Schuster 1951. The best history of the *Times.*

BRADDON, RUSSELL, *Roy Thomson of Fleet Street.* London: Collins, 1965. A detailed and favorable portrait of a world press lord.

BRAY, HOWARD, *The Pillars of the Post.* New York: W. W. Norton, 1980. Emphasis is on personalities, office problems at the *Washington Post.*

CANHAM, ERWIN D., *Commitment to Freedom: The Story of The Christian Science Monitor.* Boston: Houghton Mifflin, 1958. By the editor of the *Monitor.*

CATLEDGE, TURNER, *My Life and The Times.* New York: Harper & Row, 1971. A readable autobiography of a capable newspaperman, reaching a climax with the struggle for "the kingdom and the power." Candid evidence given.

CHANEY, LINDSAY, AND MICHAEL CIEPLY, *The Hearsts: Family and Empire—The Later Years.* New York: Simon & Schuster, 1981. Hearst empire since his 1951 death.

COLLINS, JEAN E., *She Was There: Stories of Pioneering Women Journalists.* New York: Julian Messner, 1980. Fifteen twentieth-century newswomen; high-school level.

CONRAD, WILL C., KATHLEEN F. WILSON, AND DALE WILSON, *The Milwaukee Journal: The First Eighty Years.* Madison: Univerity of Wisconsin Press, 1964. A good newspaper history of a great daily.

COONEY, JOHN, *The Annenbergs: The Salvation of a Tainted Dynasty.* New York: Simon & Schuster, 1982. Moses and his son Walter *(TV Guide, Seventeen).*

DAVIS, DEBORAH, *Katharine the Great: Katharine Graham and the Washington Post.* New York: Harcourt Brace Jovanovich, 1979. Treats both the woman and publisher.

DRYFOOS, SUSAN W., *Iphigene: Memoirs of Iphigene Ochs Sulzberger of the New York Times Family.* New York: Dodd, Mead, 1981. Frank comments by the daughter, widow, and mother of three *Times* publishers, edited by a granddaughter.

EAGLES, CHARLES W., *Jonathan Daniels and Race Relations.* Knoxville: University of Tennessee Press, 1983. Evolution of a Southern liberal, at Raleigh.

EMERY, MICHAEL, *America's Leading Daily Newspapers: A Media Research Institute Survey.* Indianapolis: R.J. Berg & Co., 1983. Depth report of a major poll and profiles of fifteen top-ranking papers.

The Front Page, 1887–1980. New York: Arno Press, 1981. Reproduces 129 front pages of the old *Paris Herald* and the *International Herald Tribune.*

GHIGLIONE, LOREN, ed., *Gentlemen of the Press.* Indianapolis: News & Features Press, 1983. Editors' profiles drawn from pages of the *ASNE Bulletin.*

GOTTLIEB, ROBERT, AND IRENE WOLT, *Thinking Big: The Story of the Los Angeles Times, Its Publishers and Their Influence on Southern California.* New York: Putnam's, 1977. Unauthorized work; relates development of the paper and city; takes a critical look at General Harrison Gray Otis, Chandlers.

GRIFFIN, DICK, AND ROB WARDEN, eds., *Done in a Day: 100 Years of Great Writing from the Chicago Daily News.* Chicago: Swallow Press, 1977.

HART, JACK R., *The Information Empire: The Rise of the Los Angeles Times and the Times Mirror Corporation.* Washington, D.C.: University Press of America, 1981. A first-rate account, based on Ph.D. thesis, University of Wisconsin, 1975.

HART, JIM ALLEE, *A History of the St. Louis Globe-Democrat.* Columbia: University of Missouri Press, 1961. Tells the story of St. Louis' "other paper" in a social and political framework.

HOHENBERG, JOHN, *The Pulitzer Prizes.* New York: Columbia University Press, 1974. A meticulous accounting of the first 714 awards. See also *The Pulitzer Prize Story, II* (1980), supplement covering years 1959 to 1980.

JOHNSON, GERALD W., et al., *The Sunpapers of Baltimore.* New York: Knopf, 1937. An outstanding newspaper history over a 100-year span.

KERBY, WILLIAM F., *A Proud Profession.* Homewood, Ill.: Dow Jones-Irwin, 1981. By a leading editor of the *Wall Street Journal.*

KOBRE, SIDNEY, *Development of American Journalism.* Dubuque: Wm. C. Brown, 1969. Traces in detail the twentieth-century histories of many leading newspapers.

LENT, JOHN A., *Newhouse, Newspapers, Nuisances.* New York: Exposition Press, 1966. Story of the building of a media empire, with business details.

LYLE, JACK, *The News in Megalopolis.* San Francisco: Chandler, 1967. Los Angeles area news media analyzed.

LYONS, LOUIS M., *Newspaper Story: One Hundred Years of the Boston Globe.* Cambridge, Mass.: Harvard University Press, 1971. Much internal detail.

MARKHAM, JAMES W., *Bovard of the Post-Dispatch.* Baton Rouge: Louisiana State University Press, 1954. A discerning biography.

MARTIN, RALPH G., *Cissy: The Extraordinary Life of Eleanor Medill Patterson.* New York: Simon & Schuster, 1979. Falls short in analyzing her journalistic role.

MCNULTY, JOHN B., *Older than the Nation.* Stonington, Conn.: Pequot Press, 1964. A well-presented, scholarly history of the *Hartford Courant* on its 200th birthday.

MEEKER, RICHARD H., *Newspaperman: S.I. Newhouse and the Business of News.* New York: Ticknor & Fields, 1983. Newspaper and magazine groups owner.

MILLER, ALAN ROBERT, *The History of Current Maine Newspapers.* Lisbon Falls, Maine: Eastland Press, 1978. Excellent state history.

POUND, REGINALD, AND GEOFFREY HARMSWORTH, *Northcliffe.* London: Cassell, 1959. Based on family papers, most definitive of fifteen biographies.

PRICE, WARREN C., *The Eugene Register-Guard.* Portland, Ore.: Binford & Mort, 1976. A leading journalism scholar tells the story of a distinguished smaller daily as a citizen of its community and state.

PUSEY, MERLO J., *Eugene Meyer.* New York: Knopf, 1974. A prize-winning biography of the *Washington Post* publisher, father of Katharine Graham.

RIVERS, WILLIAM L., AND DAVID M. RUBIN, *A Region's Press: Anatomy of Newspapers in the San Francisco Bay Area.* Berkeley: Institute of Governmental Studies, University of California, 1971. Contemporary study with some historical material.

ROBERTS, CHALMERS M., *The Washington Post: The First 100 Years.* Boston: Houghton Mifflin, 1977. Centennial history by a retired staff member.

ROSENBERG, JERRY MARTIN, *Inside the Wall Street Journal.* New York: Macmillan, 1982. History of the *Journal* and assessment of its influence; some criticism.

RUCKER, BRYCE W., ed., *Twentieth Century Reporting at Its Best.* Ames: Iowa State University Press, 1964. Good collection.

SAGE, JOSEPH, *Three to Zero: The Story of the Birth and Death of the World Journal Tribune.* New York: American Newspaper Publishers Association, 1967. A brief analysis placing most blame for the fiasco on labor unions.

SALISBURY, HARRISON E., *Without Fear or Favor.* New York: Times Books, 1980. A personalized account of recent *Times* history by one of its leading foreign correspondents.

———, *A Journey for Our Times.* New York: Harper & Row, 1983. Memoirs.

SIM, JOHN CAMERON, *The Grass Roots Press: America's Community Newspapers.* Ames: Iowa State University Press, 1969. The most penetrating study of weeklies, rural and suburban, and their community roles.

SLOAN, WM. DAVID, ed., *Pulitzer Prize Editorials: America's Best Editorial Writing, 1917–1979.* Ames: Iowa State University Press, 1980. Reprints and comments on winners.

SNYDER, LOUIS L., AND RICHARD B. MORRIS, *Treasury of Great Reporting.* New York: Simon & Schuster, 1962. Excellent historical work.

STEWART, KENNETH, AND JOHN TEBBEL, *Makers of Modern Journalism.* Englewood Cliffs, N.J.: Prentice-Hall, 1952. Contains extensive comment on many of the newspapers and people covered in this chapter; see index.

TALESE, GAY, *The Kingdom and the Power.* New York: New American Library, 1969. Penetrating, informative recent history of the *New York Times.* Studies its publishers and editors as they struggled for power.

WENDT, LLOYD, *The Wall Street Journal: The Story of Dow Jones & the Nation's Business Newspaper.* Chicago: Rand McNally, 1982. Authorized history of the *Journal,* but written independently by a *Chicago Tribune* staff member and author.

———, *Chicago Tribune: The Rise of a Great American Newspaper.* Chicago: Rand McNally, 1979. An 861-page balanced, comprehensive look at the *Tribune* by a staff member who wrote independently. Best overall account of the long-controversial paper.

WILDS, JOHN, *Afternoon Story: The History of the New Orleans States-Item.* Baton Rouge: Louisiana State University Press, 1976. A popular account of city's journalism.

Books: Role of the Press, Media Organizations

AGEE, WARREN K., ed., *The Press and the Public Interest.* Washington, D.C.: Public Affairs Press, 1968. Collection of eighteen William Allen White lectures at the University of Kansas by leading journalists.

CASEY, RALPH D., ed., *The Press in Perspective.* Baton Rouge: Louisiana State University Press, 1963. Seventeen addresses in critical vein by leading journalists and writers, in Guild Lecture series at University of Minnesota.

COMMISSION ON FREEDOM OF THE PRESS, *A Free and Responsible Press.* Chicago: University of Chicago Press, 1947. A penetrating summary.

ELLIS, L. ETHAN, *Newsprint: Producers, Publishers and Political Pressures.* New Brunswick: Rutgers University Press, 1960. Study of costs from 1940 to 1960.

EMERY, EDWIN, *History of the American Newspaper Publishers Association.* Minneapolis: University of Minnesota Press, 1949. Updated in 1962 in seventy-fifth anniversary booklet (New York: ANPA). ANPA's history covered in detail; ANPA-Guild relationships explored.

HOCKING, WILLIAM E., *Freedom of the Press: A Framework of Principle.* Chicago: University of Chicago Press, 1947. Discusses philosophical problems, written for the Commission on Freedom of the Press.

JOHNSTONE, JOHN W.C., EDWARD J. SLAWSKI, AND WILLIAM W. BOWMAN, *The News People: A Sociological Portrait of American Journalists and Their Work.* Urbana: University of Illinois Press, 1976. Based on 1300 interviews in the 1970s.

LEAB, DANIEL J., *A Union of Individuals: The Formation of the American Newspaper Guild 1933–1936.* New York: Columbia University Press, 1970. Scholarly detail.

LEVY, H. PHILLIP, *The Press Council: History, Procedure and Cases.* London: Macmillan, 1967. The British Press Council examined in detail 1953 to 1967. For U.S. examples, see Kenneth Starck, "What Community Press Councils Talk About," *Journalism Quarterly,* XLVII (Spring 1970), 20; William B. Blankenburg, "Local Press Councils," *Columbia Journalism Review,* VIII (Spring 1969), 14; Lawrence Schneider, "A Media–Black Council: Seattle's 19-Month Experiment," *Journalism Quarterly,* XLVII (Autumn 1970), 439; and Rivers, Bertrand, and Rampal references listed later.

LINDSTROM, CARL E., *The Fading American Newspaper.* New York: Doubleday, 1960. A strong critique of trends and methods by a 40-year newspaperman (*Hartford Times*).

MACDOUGALL, A. KENT, ed., *The Press: A Critical Look from the Inside.* Princeton, N.J.: Dow Jones Books, 1972. Reflections on the press from the columns of the *Wall Street Journal.*

MARTIN, L. JOHN, ed., *Role of the Mass Media in American Politics. Annals* of the American Academy of Political and Social Science, No. 427, September 1976. A special issue with thirteen articles on media coverage, effects, image building, perspectives.

MOTT, FRANK LUTHER, *The News in America.* Cambridge, Mass.: Harvard University Press, 1952. An excellent discussion of news gathering and news distribution and of sociopolitical responsibilities.

MOTT, FRANK LUTHER, AND RALPH D. CASEY, eds., *Interpretations of Journalism.* New York: Appleton-Century-Crofts, 1937. The most important historical collection of statements on press problems.

NATIONAL LABOR RELATIONS BOARD, *Collective Bargaining in the Newspaper Industry.* Washington, D.C.: Government Printing Office, 1938. Studies both the Guild and printing union movements.

PITTS, ALICE FOX, *Read All About It—Fifty Years of the ASNE.* Reston, Va.: American Society of Newspaper Editors, 1974. The ASNE's own story.

RESTON, JAMES B., *The Artillery of the Press.* New York: Harper & Row, 1967. Essays discussing press influence on foreign policy.

RIVERS, WILLIAM L., AND WILBUR SCHRAMM, *Responsibility in Mass Communication.* New York: Harper & Row, 1969. An examination of the social problem, also done by J. Edward Gerald in *The Social Responsibility of the Press* (Minneapolis: University of Minnesota Press, 1963) and by John Hohenberg in *The News Media* (New York: Holt, Rinehart & Winston, 1968).

RIVERS, WILLIAM L., WILLIAM B. BLANKENBURG, KENNETH STARCK, AND EARL REEVES, *Backtalk: Press Councils in America.* San Francisco: Canfield Press, 1971. By men who operated several local press councils.

RUCKER, BRYCE W., *The First Freedom.* Carbondale: Southern Illinois University Press, 1968. Prize-winning analysis of the position of mass media, designed as an updating of Morris Ernst's *The First Freedom* (1946).

Books: Columnists, Cartoonists

ALSOP, JOSEPH AND STEWART, *The Reporter's Trade.* New York: Reynal & Company, 1958. A discussion of Washington reporting and a compilation of the Alsop brothers' columns from 1946 to 1958.

BLOCK, HERBERT L., *The Herblock Gallery.* New York: Simon & Schuster, 1968. One of several collections of the great cartoonist's work; for his anti-Nixon best, see *Herblock Special Report* (New York: W.W. Norton, 1974).

CATER, DOUGLASS, *The Fourth Branch of Government.* Boston: Houghton Mifflin, 1959. Surveys the Washington press corps.

KRAMER, DALE, *Heywood Broun.* New York: A.A. Wyn, 1949. Biography of the Guild's founder, a famous columnist.

RIVERS, WILLIAM L., *The Opinionmakers.* Boston: Beacon Press, 1965. A top-flight study of Washington journalists. See also *The Adversaries* (1970).

Books: World News Agencies, Press Associations

BOYD-BARRETT, OLIVER, *The International News Agencies.* Beverly Hills: Sage, 1980. Includes the AP, UPI, Reuters, AFP, TASS, Non-Aligned News Pool, Inter Press.

DESMOND, ROBERT W., *Windows on the World: World News Reporting 1900–1920.* Iowa City: University of Iowa Press, 1980. *Crisis and Conflict: World News Reporting Between Two Wars 1920–1940* (1982). Volumes 2 and 3 of a five-volume study of prize-winning caliber by leading authority (see Chapter 1 Bibliography).

STOREY, GRAHAM, *Reuters.* New York: Crown, 1951. Standard account to that time.

THOMAS, HELEN, *Dateline: White House.* New York: Macmillan, 1975. UPI's top woman.

UNESCO, *News Agencies: Their Structure and Operations.* New York: Columbia University Press, 1953. Includes discussions of the AP, UP, and INS and examines their roles in world-wide news distribution. Later information is found in Kurian (see later reference).

Books: International News Flow, World Press

ATWOOD, L. ERWIN, STUART J. BULLION, AND SHARON M. MURPHY, eds., *International Perspectives on News.* Carbondale: Southern Illinois University Press, 1982. Research papers on global news flow, media performance, images of America.

BERTRAND, CLAUDE-JEAN, AND MIGUEL URABAYEN, eds., *World Media.* Ames: Iowa State University Press, 1984. Synthesis by two European scholars.

FISCHER, HEINZ-DIETRICH, AND JOHN C. MERRILL, eds., *International and Intercultural Communication.* New York: Hastings House, 1976. Forty-five scholarly articles.

HACHTEN, WILLIAM A., *The World News Prism: Changing Media, Clashing Ideologies.* AMES: Iowa State University Press, 1981. A superb, 133-page introduction to the New World Information Order controversy of the 1970s.

———, *Muffled Drums: The News Media in Africa.* Ames: Iowa State University Press, 1971. Descriptive account by a leading U.S. scholar on the subject.

HAWKINS, JOHN, *Mass Communication in China.* New York: Longman, 1982. A 1979 study.

HOHENBERG, JOHN, *Free Press/Free People—The Best Cause.* New York: Columbia University Press, 1971. A sweeping review of the coverage of major world events with a concentration on the twentieth century.

HOPKINS, MARK W., *Mass Media in the Soviet Union.* New York: Pegasus, 1970. See also International Organization of Journalists, *Mass Media in CMEA Countries* (1976), covering Eastern Europe and the USSR.

KATZ, ELIHU, AND GEORGE WEDELL, *Broadcasting in the Third World: Promise and Performance.* Cambridge, Mass.: Harvard University Press, 1978. Data on ninety-one developing countries including eleven in-depth case studies.

KESTERTON, WILFRED H., *A History of Journalism in Canada.* Toronto: McClelland and Stewart, 1967. The standard account.

KURIAN, GEORGE, ed., *World Press Encyclopedia,* 2 vol. New York: Facts on File, 1982. Profiles of the press for most countries. Updates earlier surveys by UNESCO, *World Communications: A 200-Country Survey of Press, Radio, Television, Film,* 5th ed. (New York: Unipub, 1975), and by John C. Merrill, et al., *The Foreign Press: A Survey of the World's Journalism* (Baton Rouge: Louisiana State University Press, 1970).

LEE, CHIN-CHUAN, *Media Imperialism Reconsidered.* Beverly Hills: Sage, 1980. Focuses on television, using examples of China, Taiwan, Canada.

LENT, JOHN A., ed., *The Asian Newspapers' Reluctant Revolution.* Ames: Iowa State University Press, 1971. Essays on history and current status, by country.

MACBRIDE, SEAN, et al., *Many Voices: One World.* New York: Unipub, 1980. The MacBride Commission report on the proposal for a New World Information Order and increased Third-World participation in news flow. See ten articles on the subject in *Journal of Communication,* XXXI (Autumn 1981), 102–87.

MARTIN, L. JOHN, and ANJU GROVER CHAUDHARY, eds., *Comparative Mass Media Systems.* New York: Longman, 1983. Chapters by eighteen scholars addressing six major aspects of the mass media, from Western, Communist, and Third-World viewpoints in each case.

MERRILL, JOHN C., et al., *Global Journalism.* New York: Longman, 1983. Six coauthors survey the world's mass media.

MERRILL, JOHN C., AND HAROLD A. FISHER, *The World's Great Dailies: Profiles of 50 Newspapers.* New York: Hastings House, 1980. Updates Merrill's *Elite Press* (1968).

OLSON, KENNETH E., *The History Makers.* Baton Rouge: Louisiana State University Press, 1966. A survey of European press history.

PAULU, BURTON, *Television and Radio in the United Kingdom.* Minneapolis: University of Minnesota Press, 1981. An authoritative account. See also Paulu, *Radio and Television Broadcasting on the European Continent* (1967) and *Radio and Television Broadcasting in Eastern Europe* (1974), from the same Press.

READ, WILLIAM H., *America's Mass Media Merchants.* Baltimore: Johns Hopkins University Press, 1977. Examines overseas impact of ten specific media, including the AP, UPI, *Time, Newsweek, Reader's Digest,* and major news syndicates.

RICE, MICHAEL, AND JAMES A. CRONEY, eds., *Reporting U.S.-European Relations.* New York: Pergamon Press, 1982. Aspen Institute comparative study of the *New York Times, Times* of London, *Le Monde,* and *Frankfurter Allgemeine Zeitung.*

RICHSTAD, JIM, AND MICHAEL H. ANDERSON, eds., *Crisis in International News: Policies and Prospects.* New York: Columbia University Press, 1981. Balanced compilation of major scholarly articles dealing with New World Information Order movement.

RIGHTER, ROSEMARY, *Whose News? Politics, the Press, and the Third World.* London: Times Books, 1978. IPI-sponsored, essentially Western press viewpoint.

SCHRAMM, WILBUR, AND L. ERWIN ATWOOD, *Circulation of News in the Third World—A Study of Asia.* Hong Kong: Chinese University Press, 1981. Analyzes flow of agency news to nineteen Asian dailies.

TUNSTALL, JEREMY, *The Media Are American.* New York: Columbia University Press, 1977. An examination of the influence of Anglo-American media in the world.

Periodicals and Monographs

ARMSTRONG, DAVID, "A Thinking Approach to News," *Columbia Journalism Review* (September/October 1978), 61. Pacific News Service operates from California base.

BAGDIKIAN, BEN, "The *Wall Street Journal's* Split Personality," *Washington Journalism Review* (July/August 1981), 35. Front and editorial pages differ.

BERTRAND, CLAUDE-JEAN, "Press Councils: An Evaluation," *Gazette* (Winter 1977), updated in Michael Emery and Ted Smythe, *Readings in Mass Communication,* 5th ed. (Dubuque, Iowa: Wm. C. Brown, 1982), p. 20. Most exhaustive study, lists all councils worldwide.

BOGART, LEO, "Newspapers in Transition," in *Wilson Quarterly,* 1982 Special Issue devoted to the news media.

BROUN, HEYWOOD, "An Army with Banners," *Nation,* CXL (February 13, 1935), 154. The Guild president's own account.

CHU, CHI-YING, "Henry Justin Smith (1875–1936), Managing Editor of the *Chicago Daily News,*" Ph.D. thesis, Southern Illinois University, 1970. A teacher of writing.

CONN, EARL L., "The American Council on Education for Journalism: An Accrediting History," Ed.D. thesis, Indiana University, 1970. Traces the growth of accrediting standards.

COPE, NEIL B., "A History of the *Memphis Commercial Appeal,*" Ph.D. thesis, University of Missouri, 1969. Story of a leading Scripps-Howard paper.

COULSON, DAVID C., "Nelson Poynter: Study of an Independent Publisher and His Standards of Ownership," Ph.D. thesis, University of Minnesota, 1982. Builder of *St. Petersburg Times.*

CUTHBERT, MARLENE, "Reaction to International News Agencies: 1930s and 1970s Compared," *Gazette,* 26:2 (1981), 99. Americans disliked European news cartel in the 1930s; Third World dislikes dominant Western news agencies in the 1970s.

DEMOTT, BENJAMIN, "The Pursuit of Charm," *Nation* (March 27, 1982), 353. An essay on columnist George Will.

DENNIS, EVERETTE E., "The Regeneration of Political Cartooning," *Journalism Quarterly,* LI (Winter 1974), 664. Focuses on "new wave" debate and three current leaders. See also Everette and Melvin Dennis, "100 Years of Political Cartooning," *Journalism History,* I (Spring 1974), 6, comparing caustic Watergate cartoons with Nast era.

DEVOTO, BERNARD, "Always Be Drastically Independent," *Harper's,* CCVII (December 1953), 42. The *St. Louis Post-Dispatch* is nominated as the "finest practitioner of liberal journalism."

DIAMOND, EDWIN, "Rupert Murdoch: Power Without Prestige," *Washington Journalism Re-*

view (June 1980), 21. The Australian publisher's empire.

DUNCAN, CHARLES T., "The *International Herald Tribune:* Unique (World) Newspaper," *Journalism Quarterly,* L (Summer 1973), 348. Contemporary status.

EBERHARD, WILLIAM B., "Clark Howell and the *Atlanta Constitution,*" *Journalism Quarterly* LX (Spring 1983), 118. Career summary.

GOTHBERG, JOHN A., "The Local Influence of J. R. Knowland's Oakland *Tribune,*" *Journalism Quarterly,* XLV (Autumn 1968), 487. Knowland's half-century.

GROTTA, GERALD L., "Changes in the Ownership Structure of Daily Newspapers and Selected Performance Characteristics, 1950–1968," Ph.D. thesis, Southern Illinois University, 1970. Data and analysis.

HENRY, WILLIAM A., III, "The Decline and Fall of the *New York Daily News,*" *Washington Journalism Review* (March 1982), 18. Financial collapse analyzed.

HENSHER, ALAN, "No News Today: How Los Angeles Lost a Daily," *Journalism Quarterly,* XLVII (Winter 1970), 684. Death of the *Daily News* in 1954.

HESTER, ALBERT L., "The Associated Press and News from Latin America: A Gatekeeper and News-Flow Study," Ph.D. thesis, University of Wisconsin, 1972. News becomes more superficial as it flows from Latin America through New York to United States papers.

HOLDER, DENNIS, "The *Los Angeles Times* Reaches for the Top," *Washington Journalism Review* (July/August 1982), 16. Past and present of Times Mirror.

———, "*Chicago Tribune:* Keeping Up with the Cubs," *Washington Journalism Review* (January/February 1983), 39. Chicago's big brother buys its baseball team.

———, "Knight-Ridder: The Chain," *Washington Journalism Review* (April 1981), 24.

HOLDER, DENNIS, AND ELIZABETH FRANKLIN, "Mergers," *Washington Journalism Review* (April 1983), 28. Review of 1982 newspaper consolidations.

HYNDS, ERNEST C., "How Distinctive Are Southern Newspapers Today?" *Newspaper Research Journal,* 3:2 (January 1982), 32. Poll of region's editors.

"Interview with Donald Graham," *Washington Journalism Review* (April/May 1979), 33. The *Washington Post's* new publisher.

KEATING, ISABELLE, "Reporters Become of Age," *Harper's,* CLXX (April 1935), 601. One of the best early articles about the Guild.

KENNEDY, GEORGE, "Up to Date in Kansas City," *Columbia Journalism Review* (March/April 1979), 59. The *Star* and the *Times* adjust to new owners.

KLEINFELD, N.R., "The Great Press Chain," *New York Times Magazine* (April 8, 1979), 41. The Gannett newspaper group. See also David Shaw, "The News Mogul Who Would Be Famous," *Esquire* (September 1979), 63. Dissects Allen Neuharth, Gannett news chief.

KLIESCH, RALPH E., "History and Operations of the McGraw-Hill World News Service," Ph.D. thesis, University of Minnesota, 1968. Describes McGraw-Hill news gathering since the 1880s, and the World News Service from 1945 to 1968.

KUCZUN, SAM, "History of the American Newspaper Guild," Ph.D. thesis, University of Minnesota, 1970. Comprehensive overview based on access to Guild archives.

LANSON, GERALD AND MITCHELL STEPHENS, "Abe Rosenthal: The Man and His *Times.*" *Washington Journalism Review* (July/August 1983), 23. A personality study.

LEE, SANG-CHUL, "The Japanese Image Projected in Four U.S. Dailies (1905–1972)," Ph.D. thesis, University of Minnesota, 1979.

LEUNG, KENNETH WAI YIN, "News Flow Between the United States and Asia," Ph.D. thesis, University of Minnesota, 1979. News files of the AP and UPI are used in the study.

LITTLEWOOD, THOMAS B., AND RAYMOND DE LONG, "Supplemental News Services," *Newspaper Research Journal,* 2:4 (July 1981), 9. Review as of 1981.

MACHALABA, DAVID, "Spirit of St. Louis," *Wall Street Journal* (August 23, 1982), 1. *Post-Dispatch* editorial page found to be still liberal, drawing fire.

NAVASKY, VICTOR, "Safire Appraised," *Esquire* (January 1982), 44. The editor of the *Nation* looks at conservative columnist William Safire.

"Newsroom Salaries," a special issue of *The Bulletin* of the American Society of Newspaper Editors (February 1982). Surveys top editor and reporters' salaries.

NORWOOD, CHRISTOPHER, "The Last Puritans," *New York,* VIII (November 3, 1975),

58. Depth study of *New York Times* editorial board in John Oakes' era.

ODENDAHL, ERIC M., "The Story and Stories of the Copley News Service," Ph.D. thesis, University of Missouri, 1966. History of the service and analysis of its content.

PEER, ELIZABETH, "Fastest Gun in Op-Ed Land," *Newsweek* (April 23, 1979), 87. Safire.

PETERSON, PAUL V., "The Omaha *Daily World* and *World-Herald*, 1885–1964," Ph.D. thesis, University of Minnesota, 1965. Story of a major Midwest daily.

PIANTADOSI, ROGER, "Meg Greenfield," *Washington Journalism Review* (April 1982), 32.

QUIGG, H.D., "UPI . . . As It Was and It Is," *Editor & Publisher* (September 25, 1982), 16. One of several articles in issue observing the UPI's seventy-fifth anniversary and 1982 sale. See also "Goodbye Mr. Scripps" in *feed/back* (Summer 1982).

RADOFF, ANDREW, "32 Dailies Have Merged since 1978," *Editor & Publisher* (September 18, 1982), 12. Lists the twenty-nine cities still having competitive papers in 1982.

RAMPAL, KULDIP, "The Concept of the Press Council," Freedom of Information Center Report No. 350 (March 1976). A review of the importance of press councils.

RASKIN, A.H., "The Once and Future Newspaper Guild," *Columbia Journalism Review* (September/October 1982), 26. Veteran labor writer evaluates 50-year-old Guild.

REINHARDT, RICHARD, "Doesn't *Everybody* Hate the *Chronicle?*" *Columbia Journalism Review* (January/February 1982), 25. History of successful but maligned San Francisco daily.

REISS, BOB, "Helen Thomas," *Washington Journalism Review* (April 1980), 48. UPI.

ROBINSON, JOHN P., "The Press as King-Maker: What Surveys from Last Five Campaigns Show," *Journalism Quarterly*, LI (Winter 1974), 587. Excellent summary from Michigan Survey Center showing a relationship between newspaper endorsements and voters' choices.

ROSENBAUM, LEE, "Charlotte Curtis: Opting for Op-Ed," *Quill*, LXII (February 1974), 22. Woman editor of the *New York Times* opposite-editorials page.

RUPP, CARLA MARIE, "Lee Hills: A Reporter in the Executive Suite," *Editor & Publisher*, CIX (March 13, 1976), 12. Portrait of Knight-Ridder executive.

SAALBERG, HARVEY, "The Canons of Journalism: A 50-Year Perspective," *Journalism Quarterly*, L (Winter 1973), 731. History of the ASNE's code of ethics.

SALISBURY, HARRISON, "Mr. New York Times," *Esquire* (January 1980), 26. Portrait of A. M. Rosenthal, *Times* executive editor.

SCHAFER, ROBERT, "The Minnesota News Council: Developing Standards for Press Ethics," *Journalism Quarterly*, LVIII (Autumn 1981), 355. Leading state council at 10 years.

SEVERIN, WERNER J., "The *Milwaukee Journal:* Employee-Owned Prizewinner," *Journalism Quarterly*, LVI (Winter 1979), 783.

SHANOR, DONALD R., "CDN: What We'll Miss About the *Chicago Daily News*," *Columbia Journalism Review* (May/June 1978), 35. Mourning for famed foreign service.

SHAPIRO, FRED C., "The Life and Death of a Great Newspaper," *American Heritage*, XVIII (October 1967), 97. Extensive portrait of the *New York Tribune* and *Herald Tribune*.

SHEEHY, GAIL, "The Life of the Most Powerful Woman in New York," *New York*, VI (December 10, 1973), 51. Extensive feature on then *New York Post* publisher Dorothy Schiff. See also, Nora Ephron's "Media" column in *Esquire*, LXXXIII (April 1975), 8.

"S. I. Newhouse and Sons: America's Most Profitable Publisher," *Business Week*, XLVIII (January 26, 1976), 56. Major article on multimedia group.

SINGLETARY, MICHAEL W., "Newspaper Use of Supplemental Services: 1960–73," *Journalism Quarterly*, LII (Winter 1975), 748. See also Edward J. Trayes, "News/Feature Services by Circulation Group Use," *Journalism Quarterly*, XLIX (Spring 1972), 133.

SINICHAK, STEVEN, "The Chicago Journalism Review," *Grassroots Editor*, XI (July/August 1970), 10. Story of the journal's first 2 years.

STEMPEL, GUIDO H. III, and JOHN W. WINDHAUSER, "The Prestige Press Revisited: Coverage of the 1980 Presidential Campaign," *Journalism Quarterly LXI* (Spring 1984). Largely for Carter.

STERN, MORT P., "Palmer Hoyt and the *Denver Post*," Ph.D. thesis, University of Denver, 1969. A field study of organizational change.

TAYLOR, PAUL, "Gene Roberts: Down-Home Editor of the *Philadelphia Inquirer*," *Washington Journalism Review* (April 1983), 55. The editor with impact.

TEBBEL, JOHN, "Rating the American Newspaper," *Saturday Review,* XLIV (May 13 and June 10, 1961). Ratings by 125 journalism educators.

UDELL, JON G., "Economic Trends in the Daily Newspaper Business 1946 to 1970," Research report of the Bureau of Business Research and Service, University of Wisconsin, Madison, 1970. Data-laden; sponsored by ANPA.

VIVIAN, JOHN H., "PMs Future in the Shakeout and Reconfiguration of American Newspapers," *Newspaper Research Journal,* 3:3 (April 1982), 69. Traces conversions to AM from PM from 1976 to 1981.

WARD, HILEY H., "Ninety Years of the National Newspaper Association," Ph.D. thesis, University of Minnesota, 1977. The history of the weekly newspaper group.

WERTHEIMER, JERROLD L., "The Community Press of Suburbia," Ph.D. dissertation, Northwestern University, 1960. Chicago case study.

WHITE, RAY, "The *Washington Star,* 1852–1981," *Washington Journalism Review* (September 1981), 11. A farewell to the once-leading capitol daily.

WINTER, WILLIS L., JR., "The Metamorphosis of a Newspaper: The *San Francisco Chronicle, 1935–1965,*" Ph.D. thesis, University of Illinois, 1968. The editorships of Paul C. Smith and Scott Newhall.

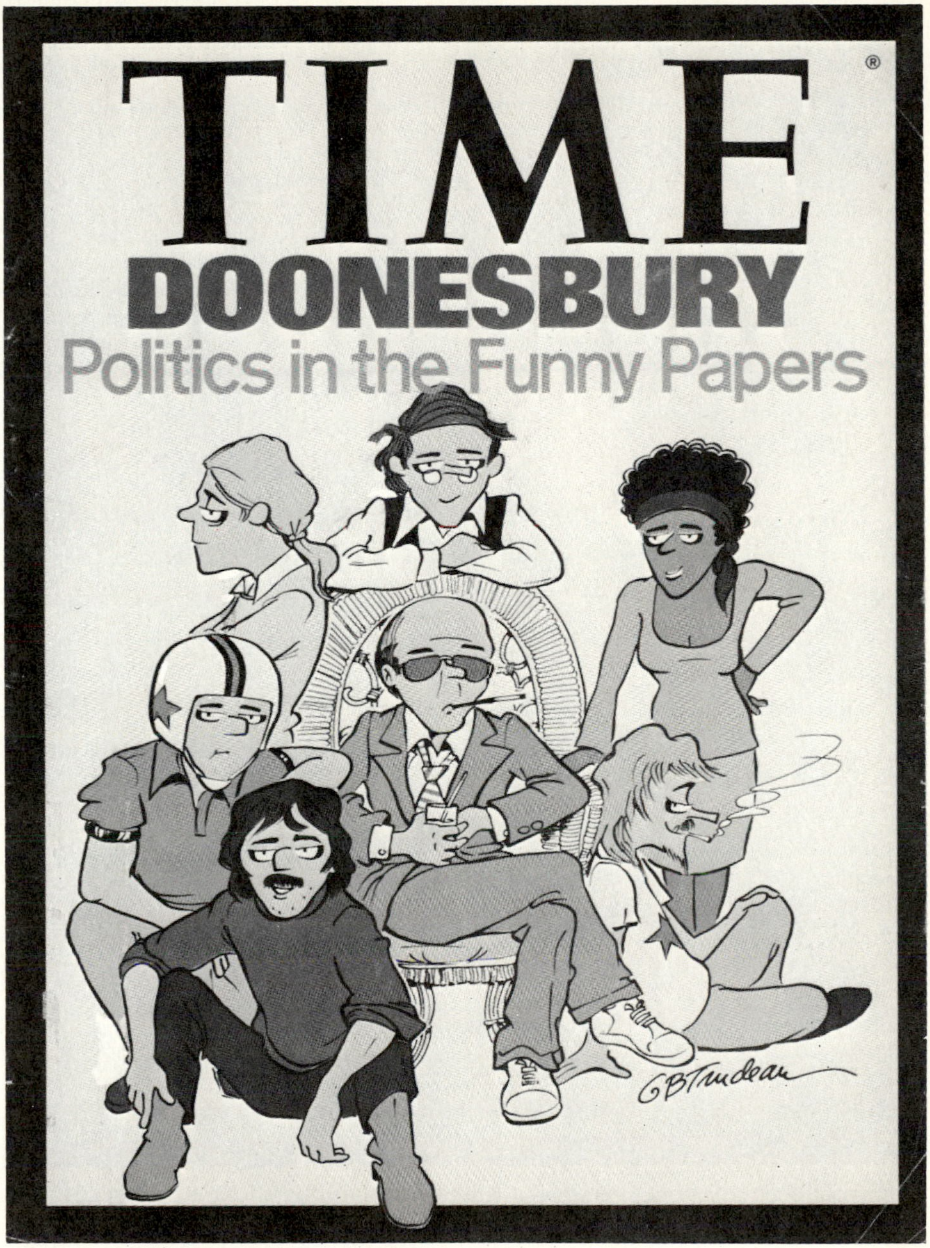

Copyright, 1976, G. B. Trudeau/Distributed by Universal Press Syndicate. Copyright 1976 Time Inc. All rights reserved.

The continued popularity of the comic strips was symbolized by the *Time* cover drawn by Garry Trudeau, the creator of "Doonesbury." From top center, clockwise, are Michael J. Doonesbury, Ginny, Zonker, Duke, Mark, B.D., and Joanie Caucus.

Satellites brought live television from virtually anywhere in the world.

Comsat

27

Media Technology: The Challenge of the 1980s

. . . the main end of science is not to answer questions but to generate new ones; not to relieve curiosity but to enlarge it and ignite it; not to build better machines but to enable people to run them and control them.

—Norman Cousins

The array of electronic equipment used by journalists and marketing specialists during the 1980s gave them access to the fragments of American society, and the future was limited only by the ability of the consumers within these specialized audiences to purchase what manufacturers and advertisers agreed was the next item in an endless list of communication tools. Home earth receivers, decoders, personal computers, low-power television, optic fibres, direct satellite broadcasting, pagination, digital darkrooms, memory clips, high-definition television, video discs, microbooks, teletext, and videotex were only some of the media terms added to the language.

The world's largest corporations took the lead in the developing of the new technology, investing uncounted billions in research and development and racing for patents just as the inventors of radio and television competed fiercely in the early twentieth century and the penny-press leaders raced for news in the previous century. The invention of the semiconductor chip by Jack Kilby and Robert Noyce in 1958 and 1959 was an astounding technological and commercial breakthrough, ranking with the contributions of Bell, Edison, and Ford. The integration of all parts of the electronic circuit—resistors, transistors, capacitors, and diodes—in one tiny piece of material turned the media world upside down.

The age of electronic marvels was also an age of contradiction. While millions could obtain instant world news by satellite and use two-way data-processing systems to produce information on their color television screens, the rate of illiteracy was alarming. In the United States it was estimated that 50 million Americans would have difficulty understanding a basic Medicaid form. There was deep concern that the gap between classes would widen—that the new information machines would not benefit those in the lower segment of society who badly needed help in surviving the severity of everyday life. The moral and legal problems of the computer age were as perplexing as the possibilities for expansion into untapped areas of money making.

PRINT TECHNOLOGY

The revolution in the newspaper, magazine, and book-publishing industries caused by the introduction of the video display terminal (VDT) was accelerated by experiments with pagination—the direct transmission of complete pages from computer memory to printing plates. The entire process of producing the daily newspaper, the weekly news magazine, or a paperback book was computerized. The work on pagination that began with research at Brown University in 1973 to 1975 under the leadership of Dr. Hans Anderseen led to pioneering experiments in 1981 at the Westchester Rockland Newspapers in Harrison, New York.[1]

Using two video display screens that were interactive—information on one screen could be transferred to the other—an editor could move stories into a page layout, write headlines, edit copy to fit, and transfer that image to the production department for the making of the plate. Equipment manufacturers were eager to become involved, as they were in the 1970s and early 1980s when video display terminals replaced typewriters.

The VDT, a television-like screen sitting above a keyboard, allowed a journalist to type a story, edit it, and store it in a central computer. From there it could be retrieved for editing and transferral to an automatic typesetting machine. Press association stories could be "called up" on VDTs.

Publishers watched carefully, too, because of the heavy expenses involved with pagination, but the conversion was inevitable. The ultimate step was to install photo and graphics subsystems so that an entire page could be fed automatically without any delay.

Other major developments, spurred by research sponsored by the American Newspaper Publishers Association, were the introduction of flexographic newspaper presses and anilox inking systems—both designed to give cleaner, brighter images. Flexography was developed to meet the need for more affordable presses and was considered an alternative to the letterpress and offset systems. Weighing half that of a letterpress and less complicated than an offset unit, the flexographic press used water-based inks that did not produce messy ink mists. It was predicted that lightweight newsprint could be used in the future. The anilox inking system and laser beam plate-making devices were part of the drive to develop better printing products.

Previous to these breakthroughs, the major change in print technology came with the introduction of the "cold-type" process, which introduced photography into the printing process. Such machines of the 1950s as the Fotoset-

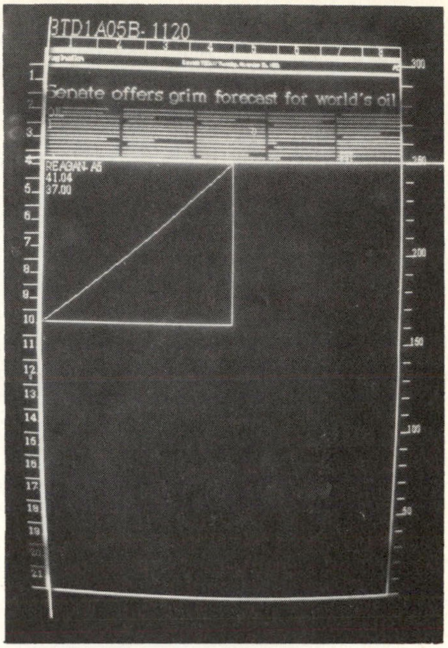

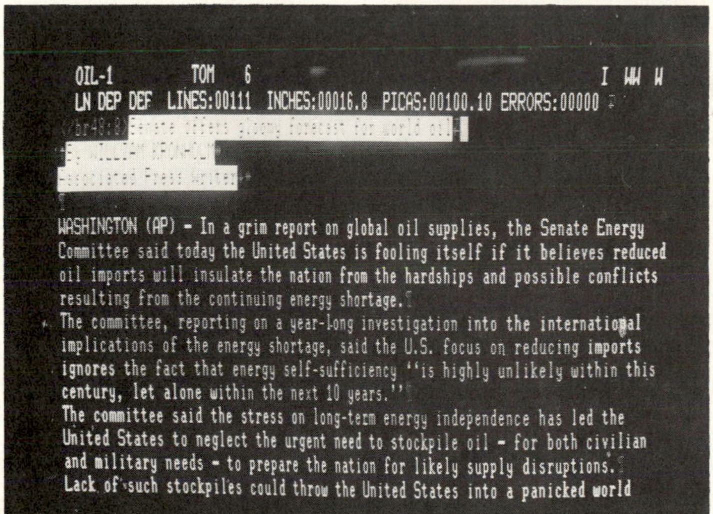

The pagination process permits an editor to plan a page layout on a screen and transfer that image to production for the making of a printing plate. Top left, editor at a VDT–like keyboard; right, enlargement of page layout showing a story spread across the top of the page and a box denoting an illustration. Lower left, the story is on a second screen, ready for editing and transfer. Process illustrated was developed at Westchester Rockland Newspapers in White Plains, New York.

ter, Linofilm, and Photon produced words on film and transferred them directly to a printing plate. Widely used in advertisement composition, they proceeded to make steady inroads on "hot-metal" typesetting.

Offset printing, based on the age-old lithography process, avoids both typesetting and photoengraving by use of pasteups photographed onto flexible printing plates. The *Opelousas Daily World* in Louisiana, begun in 1939, was the first successful daily to print by offset. The Phoenix *Arizona Journal,* founded in 1962 as a rival to the jointly owned *Arizona Republic* and *Gazette,* was the first attempt at producing an offset daily in a metropolitan competitive situation. It died in 1964, but the *Oklahoma Journal* founded that year was still printing by offset against two established rivals in 1980, when economic recession killed it.

The conversion from hot type to photo composition of pages was completed. Figures showed that 99 percent of dailies used photo composition, even though a quarter of all dailies still used the letterpress operation for printing. In fact, those using letterpress accounted for more than half of the daily circulation.[2] The slow process of purchasing new presses and the introduction of flexography would change this figure in the future.

Keeping pace with the developments were the Associated Press and United Press International. Instead of sending stories at the old speed of sixty words per minute on an old-fashioned teletype machine, the press associations used high-speed computers to process stories at 1200 words per minute, with the possibility of even higher speeds in the future. Dish-type antennas were installed at newspapers to receive satellite transmissions. Soon every station and daily newspaper would have this facility. The press associations also became involved with teletext, low-power television stations, and data-retrieval projects, in addition to providing radio and television reports to customers. Pictures flashed to newspaper offices from around the world, with the press associations using satellites and cables, lasers, and electronic darkrooms to bring high-quality photos to editors within minutes. Lightweight portable transmitters, some weighing only 15 pounds, allowed photographers to beam photos to relay points from near the scenes of action, saving precious time.

Reporters equipped with portable video display terminals could go anywhere in the world where there was telephone service and they could send stories to home-based computers. Within minutes stories could be edited and sent into production through the pagination process. The portable units were commonly used at major sporting events and political conventions. The reporter typed the story into the unit, edited it if there was time, and then used an attached telephone to send it to the main office. However, later developments in satellite technology opened the possibility of a reporter's covering a major breaking story by beaming a signal to a satellite, using satellite time purchased or owned by the newspaper, magazine, or press association.

In addition to *USA Today,* the national satellite newspaper, other papers used satellites for delivery. They were the *Wall Street Journal,* the *Christian Science Monitor,* and the *New York Times.* Publishers, too, were considering the distribution of national advertising by satellite, through a facsimile advertising project called SAT-FAX.

Miniature cassette recorders used by reporters were called electronic notebooks. Less than 1-inch thick and weighing only a few ounces, they became tools of the trade. Larger models allowed speeches and interviews to be played back at high speeds without changes in the pitch of the sound; this allowed the reporters to quickly find important quotations.

From the first thoughts of Gutenberg to the computerized newsroom, the implications of printing technology had enormous impact. By the mid-1980s those involved with the distribution of printed information had quickly integrated themselves with the emerging broadcast technology, trying to avoid being swallowed up by the avalanche of new television systems. As they had done with the first radio and television stations, newspaper publishers moved into ownership positions. However there were many questions to resolve regarding the future of the newspaper, magazine, and book industries.

DOMESTIC BROADCAST TECHNOLOGY

It was inevitable that emerging broadcast technologies would end up competing for the same advertising dollars. The development of domestic satellites led to the quick expansion of the cable television system, with entrepreneurs like Ted Turner of Atlanta starting their own news, sports, and religious networks and competing with the three major networks. But before the nation's cable pattern was established, in 1982 the Federal Communications Commission approved rules for direct broadcast satellites (DBS). Rooftop dish antennas were a reality.

Regardless of how the signal eventually reached private homes, consumers were asked to pay for a dizzying number of services. Advertisers were most interested in *teletext,* the printing of messages on television screens, sometimes accompanied by elaborate color graphics. The first American broadcast of commercial teletext was in September, 1981, when Chicago viewers read "pages" of information on their screens. The teletext operation allowed information to stay on the screen for about 20 seconds, before the next appeared. Over a number of years there had been previous experiments in Britain, France, and Japan.[3] In 1983 CBS began plans to introduce teletext messages to those sets equipped with special decoding devices. Immediately manufacturers began plans for making decoders standard equipment on future models of television sets. An important development had been the use of fibre optics to allow a proliferation of cable channels.

There also were experiments in the United States, Europe, and Japan with two-way interactive systems. Causing attention was Warner Cable's QUBE system in Columbus, Ohio, whereby viewers participated in public-opinion polls by punching buttons in their homes.[4] The common name for the interactive systems was *videotex.* However, some referred to them as *viewdata* systems, saying that videotex was a generic term covering all such techniques including teletext. The sending of information to a selective audience was dubbed *narrowcasting.*

The future of teletext and videotex was highly problematical, for it depended on the general economy, the whims of investors, and the desires of advertisers. Neither service posed an immediate threat to newspapers or broadcast news, although there was a great deal of discussion as to whether a newspaper would have to adapt to meet the challenge of a good teletext operation, one updating local news. The greatest danger to newspapers would be if videotex caught on, bringing vast amounts of information to consumers. While teletext provided common information, such as news, weather, traffic updates, and some advertising, the videotex system was potentially more extensive. Viewers could call up library information, airline schedules, insurance-company rates, community-group news, sports schedules, stock-market averages, and many other items. The ultimate would be if viewers conducted their banking, bill paying, and store ordering through videotex. Direct mail and catalog advertisers would issue numbers to be punched into the computer.

The number of homes wired for cable television rapidly reached the point at which advertisers considered the medium a major marketing possibility. By the mid-1980s about one-third of television homes had cable programming. Pay-television subscribers were estimated at about 14 percent, about half of whom were included in the cable figures.[5] Although some parts of the nation accepted cable quickly, and there were fights over the issuing of franchises, other sections were noticeably slow in developing. Unlikely customers were the central-city residents of older regions.

Even though cable television was firmly established in some quarters, because it provided clear reception of regular network programming and a wide variety of services from all parts of the nation, it was vulnerable to the excitement caused by the introduction of direct broadcasting from a satellite (DBS). The FCC originally granted nine firms the right to go ahead with DBS, including RCA, CBS, Comsat, and Western Union. The FCC dismissed complaints from the National Association of Broadcasters that the introduction of DBS into a locality would harm the local broadcasters by decreasing the audience. Instead, in 1982 the FCC ruled in favor of increasing the general television service to any given area.

There was heavy investment in DBS; the United Satellite Communications, Inc. jumped into an agreement with the Prudential Life Insurance Company, its major shareholder, to pay a major manufacturer $600 million in an initial order for Earth stations and decoders.[6] Similar arrangements and orders were made by the other corporations involved with DBS. Stanley S. Hubbard, president of Hubbard Broadcasting of St. Paul, one of the firms involved, claimed that the DBS system would allow a number of independent stations to both produce and disseminate the news, and thus give viewers news programs truly representative of different perspectives on the news from across the nation.[7] There had been talk for many years of a "fourth network" made up of independent stations. The major networking, however, had been accomplished by suppliers to cable companies.

In 1972 the FCC had opened up the nation's skies to all financially responsible firms interested in providing satellite transmission of television, telephone, news, and data services. The first private domestic satellite was Western Union's Westar, launched in April, 1974. Seven others were launched by RCA, Communications Satellite Corporation (called Cosmat), and Western Union in the next 3 years, as satellite communication became less costly than land transmission in some cases.

TIME INC.'S HOME BOX OFFICE

Time Inc. inaugurated the concept of linking satellite programming to cable systems on September 30, 1975 with its showing of the Ali-Frazier prizefight from Manila. Its Home Box Office (HBO) dated to 1972 but it wasn't until 1975 that the satellite was utilized. The financial success of HBO was staggering. In 1980 Time Inc.'s Video Group, headed by HBO and Time's cable company, American Television & Communications, earned more money than the entire NBC network. HBO alone had 11 million subscribers in fifty states.[8]

Time Inc. also became Hollywood's largest financier of movies. HBO needed 200 new films per year for its broadcasting schedule and threatened to become the dominant economic force in the movie business. The six major studios—Columbia, MGM/UA, 20th Century Fox, Paramount, Universal, and Warner Bros.—failed to recognize the growing consumer demand for televised films and their slowness cost them dearly. When a movie was shown in a theater, the studio that distributed it earned about 45 cents per box-office dollar. When HBO distributed the film by satellite to the home, the studio ended up with only 20 cents, with HBO earning the lion's share of the profits.

Independent producers, heavily dependent on the studios in the past, began to look to HBO, while the major studios and HBO's smaller pay-cable competitors, Movie Channel and Showtime, made efforts to form alliances in order to stop HBO from controlling the industry. HBO serviced more than 60 percent of the nation's pay-cable movie-service subscribers.

While HBO planned to remain primarily a financier of movies, with investments of more than $1 billion in future films, it did join with Columbia and CBS to form Tri-Star Pictures. The goal was to become Hollywood's seventh major studio. In addition, HBO money financed two other production companies that in return gave HBO exclusive cable rights to their films. The trend was clear: Americans were spending more money than ever before on home movies ($2.4 billion in 1983), rivaling the amount spent at conventional theaters ($3.5 billion). Unless checked by antitrust laws or aggressive studio actions, HBO was destined to become even more powerful.

TED TURNER'S CABLE NEWS NETWORK

Following on the heels of HBO's experiment vas Ted Turner, owner of a money-losing Atlanta station. In 1976 Turner put his WTBS onto a satellite, offering cable stations sports and reruns of movies. The concept of the "superstation" was born, and New York's station WOR and Chicago's WGN followed suit. Turner capitalized on this success and launched his Cable News Network (CNN), a direct challenge to the established networks, in 1980. The 24-hour service included hourly news summaries, heavy treatment of news, sports, and business in the early evening hours, and lengthy interviews on various subjects throughout the day. The experiment met with mixed reviews; some critics complained about poor visual quality and inexperienced reporters. However, the quick access to world and national news and the direct no-nonsense approach pleased many viewers who were impressed with CNN's overall coverage.[9]

CNN did make its mark with several scoops. Because of its ability to stay on the air after the regular networks resumed programming, CNN was the first to report that President Reagan had not escaped injury during the 1981 assassination attempt. Also, CNN's films of the El Salvador fighting showed an American military adviser carrying a weapon contrary to regulations. This caused a nation-

Ted Turner

wide furor. Demanding to share pool responsibilities at the White House, Turner won a court battle to have his network represented. Former CBS correspondent Daniel Schorr was CNN's commentator and the host of interview shows.

Turner received direct competition when ABC and Westinghouse introduced their Satellite News Channel (SNC) in 1982, which offered news in 18-minute cycles, a faster clip than CNN. Veteran broadcaster Lou Cioffi was Washington bureau chief. He had become the "first satellite reporter" when he gave the first live overseas telecast report over Telstar on July 24, 1962. SNC broadcast from Stamford, Connecticut, using ABC film (but not reporters' faces), a half-dozen reporters, and two remote units to produce the news.

Responding to SNC's challenge, Turner pushed back with his CNN2 network, offering a shorter turnaround on the news cycle. But the operation extended his already-thin news staff and he fell into financial trouble. CNN had reached 13.9 million homes, with 5.8 million watching at least once a week. CNN2 added another 1.5 million homes. Turner kept his news networks alive through huge profits from WTBS, which was piped into more than 20 million homes, or about two-thirds of the potential cable audience. SNC jumped off with 3.5 million homes, but faltered in 1983 and the service was sold to Turner.

The networks saw all of this activity and reacted as well. They started overnight news programs for the millions of night owls who watched television while most persons were sleeping. CBS jumped into the cable business with a cultural network that quickly failed, and ABC started ARTS, another cultural network. NBC offered the music-video format begun on cable by MTV in 1981. Extremely aggressive, ABC joined with the cable sports network ESPN to start a pay-TV sports enterprise, signed an agreement with Cox Cable Communications to develop home banking and shopping, started a movie network called Home View Network, and added a special cable show for women. CBS and NBC were equally interested in sharing cable television's vast potential. They noted the successful religious network of the Reverend Jerry Falwell and other ministers, the sports programming of ESPN, the coverage of the House of Representatives (and possibly later the Senate) by C-SPAN (Cable Satellite Public Affairs Network), MTV's 24-hour rock musical skits, and particularly movie channels (HBO, Showtime, The Movie Channel, and a dozen other top offerings). The networks made arrangements with movie companies to secure films and they signed huge contracts with professional sports leagues to keep coverage with them. Major-league baseball received $1 billion for a 5-year contract. Professional football received $2.1 billion for a 4-year pact. Network officials also realized, however, that their share of the television audience decreased by 3 percent during the 1982 to 1983 season. It was estimated that by 1990 the three major networks' share of viewing in homes with cable would be 55 percent to 60 percent, even though they shared 80 percent of viewing in cable homes in 1982.

Another improvement in communications came with the gradual installation of optical fibre systems between major cities. In early 1983 a 372-mile link between New York and Washington, D.C. carried telephone calls by light instead of by electricity. Two glass fibres, encased in cable and only as thin as a human hair, could carry 1300 simultaneous telephone conversations, compared with twenty-four that conventional copper wires could carry. Using the energy of a laser beam, the entire contents of a Webster's dictionary could be transmitted through a single fibre in only 6 seconds.[10] Again, the speed of installation of such a system would be determined by the state of the economy and the financial benefit to investors.

Rapid changes also occurred in the field of teleconferencing, where professional groups used satellite hookups to gain access to speakers. This became popular during the 1980 political campaign and was later used by President Reagan to reach small, select audiences. It was also a feature at major conventions. The cost of a single transmission was several thousand dollars but this was expected to drop with the expansion of satellite services.

Select audiences also could be reached by low-power television systems. The FCC approved the eventual construction of as many as 4000 stations, but originally gave the go-ahead to 200, and only twenty were operating in 1983. Experiments were conducted with high-density television (HDTV), a system allowing for high-resolution transmission. CBS led a fight in Washington, D.C. to delay DBS so that it could become the medium to carry HDTV to homes before 1990, but DBS operators did not think the plan was financially viable. A 1981 demonstration by CBS showed that HDTV, designed in Japan and using 1125 lines per screen instead of 525, would not only give amazingly clear pictures but that it would also improve the quality of color transmission.[11] The dispute would take years to resolve, as would most problems with domestic broadcast technology.

In television newsrooms Electronic Newsgathering (ENG) was firmly established. Computers and video display terminals were common. Using lightweight cameras, field reporters had the option of reporting live from city council meetings as well as from the scenes of shootouts. Sophisticated videotape recorders allowed instant editing of these transmissions and the days of the motorcycle carrier of film were doomed. Portable videotape recorders and editing machines permitted a field reporter to know at once what the camera had captured, instead of waiting for the film to be developed. How news producers would use the new tool was open to serious question, but the ENG system, developed first by KMOX-TV in St. Louis, was adopted by most other stations.

INTERNATIONAL SATELLITE TECHNOLOGY

The successful launching of AT&T's Telstar on July 10, 1962, permitted the first live transmission of pictures between the United States and Europe. These were staged shows lasting for the few minutes that the signal could be bounced off the moving satellite. RCA's Relay carried pictures to twenty-three nations at the time of President Kennedy's assassination. The effort to develop continuous service by launching a satellite that would achieve a fully synchronous orbit (an orbit and speed that keep the craft directly over one spot on Earth) met success when Howard Hughes launched Syncom III in 1964. Four such satellites, equally spaced around the world, could provide television coverage to all inhabited portions of the planet.

The Communications Satellite Corporation, formed by Congress in 1962 to unify the United States effort and to provide international leadership, carried out technical progress well. Early Bird went into synchronous orbit in 1965, followed by successive Intelsat series. By 1977 the Intelsat IV satellites were carrying 4000 or 6000 voice circuits and two television channels to 150 antennas in eighty countries using the system to receive simultaneous television broadcasts. In May, 1971, a seventy-nine nation Intelsat conference wound up 2 years of work to develop revised rules for the International Telecommunications Satellite Consortium.

Intelsat became responsible for all international nonmilitary satellite communication outside of the Soviet bloc nations. Within that Soviet sphere satellite operations were managed by Intersputnik. More than forty commercial communications satellites were orbiting the Earth at an altitude of 22,300 miles, and more launchings were planned. The satellites generated about $3 billion in revenue per year for the common carriers, the television, telephone, and private companies using them. By the 1990s these revenues were expected to be around $40 billion.[12]

Intelsat brought live television from virtually anywhere in the world. In 1965 only 80 television hours were transmitted; in 1982 the figure was 45,000. In 1981 Intelsat voted to allow member nations or groups of nations to lease full-time channels, which would make possible a regular exchange of programming. Meanwhile the demand for telephone circuits increased. Intelsat V-A was scheduled for 1984 with a capacity for 15,000 voice circuits; Intelsat VI in 1986 would carry 36,000; 1988 and 1989 Intelsats would have ten times that capacity.[13]

In 1982 a developing nation could lease a quarter of a transponder—the unit on the satellite that handles the signal—for $200,000 per year; it took $200

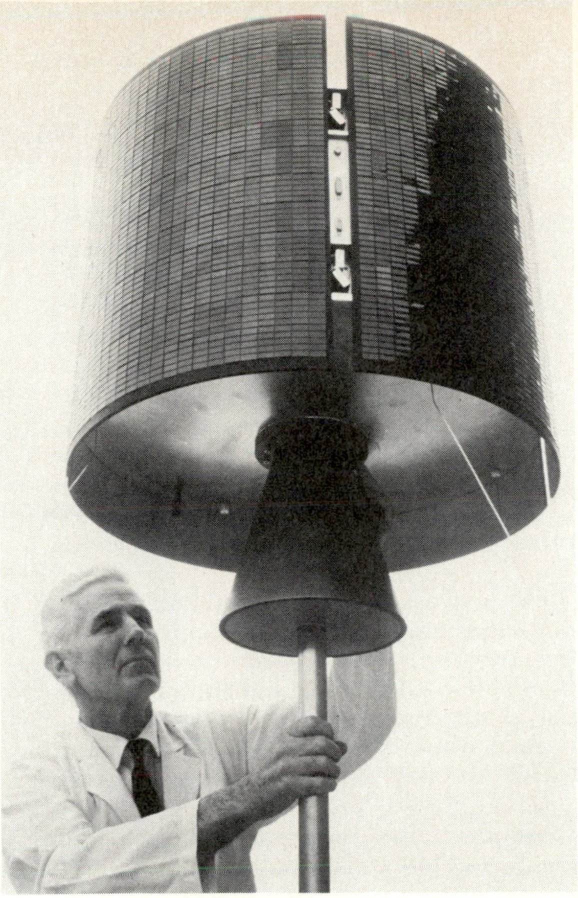

Early Bird satellite being prepared for orbit and the satellite earth station at Andover, Maine.
Comsat

million to establish a satellite system. Thus a small nation could use Intelsat for its domestic needs and be part of the satellite community of nations.

In the United States the FCC decided that Comsat would be entitled to sell its international services to individuals, businesses, and government agencies. Previously Comsat could only sell to other common carriers, such as AT&T, Western Union, and RCA Global Communications, who in turn would sell Comsat's services to other individuals or groups. Comsat controlled 50 percent of all Earth stations and the FCC was considering allowing the other major American common carriers to own Earth stations linked to the international satellite system. Comsat's restructuring was planned, with the possibility of its operating independently of Intelsat and offering pay-television channels and other services directly to home antennas.[14]

AM/FM RADIO

By the mid-1980s, there were nearly 460 million radio sets in the United States; 99 percent of the homes had at least one radio. More than 9000 stations were on the air, including about 4600 AM and 3300 FM commercial stations and another 1100 noncommercial outlets. Locally generated advertising accounted for about 95 percent of radio's annual revenues of $3.5 billion.[15]

In the nation's top three markets—New York, Los Angeles, and Chicago—news and talk shows were the most popular with listeners.[16] There were eight major station groups: CBS, Mutual, NBC, Sheridan Broadcasting, and ABC, which had four, three AM and one FM. The controversial Pacifica Network had five stations. Despite the popularity of radio, total profits were small in comparison with the high revenues. For example, the FCC reported in 1980 that radio accounted for 26.5 percent of all broadcast revenues but ended up with only 8.5 percent of profits. The profit margin in television was much greater.

The FCC was considering licensing up to another 700 AM stations, after allowing 125 new AM stations to be created. The FCC gained spectrum space by ruling that twenty-five superstations with "clear-channel" rights granted in 1928 were no longer entitled to those privileges. The stations appealed the FCC decision.

The satellites brought a new life to network radio. National Public Radio used a satellite to beam its *Morning Edition* program to 230 of the approximately 1050 public stations. The four ABC networks, arranged around different formats, had a total of more than 1700 affiliates. Advertising and special features could be targeted to specific audiences. Future developments in radio's sound could be linked to cable: Radio by cable would mean higher fidelity sound, perhaps over multiple channels. AM stereo already was a reality, inaugurated in 1982 at station KDKA in Pittsburgh.

Meanwhile, the enormous recording industry, with annual revenues of more than $4 billion, gave radio its many options for music. There were 2000 country and western stations on the air, as the Nashville brand of music challenged the traditional Top-Forty concept. Other stations favored "middle-of-the-road" music, classical, soul, hard rock sounds, or just plain "easy listening." Radio had something for everyone, with "music, news, and sports" providing the backbone of the system.

Cellular radio communication was also being discussed by the FCC in another attempt to deregulate broadcasting and maximize the number of audiences. The plan called for a city to be divided up into cells, each equipped with its own transmitter capable of providing a radio frequency for persons with mobile phones. Along this line, technology had advanced to the point at which a person with a portable beeper unit could be reached via satellite. The use of cordless telephones, a radio-transmitted telephone service, also got a boost when the FCC doubled the number of frequencies for cordless-phone use. However, the receiving range of such phones was only 700 feet.[17]

MAGAZINES IN THE 1980s

One of the most influential and successful media groups in the United States remained Time Inc. At *Time* itself, Henry Anatole Grunwald succeeded Hedley Donovan as editor-in-chief. United States circulation exceeded 4.5 million copies weekly; worldwide circulation was 5.8 million in 1982, with advertising revenues of $350 million, making *Time* first among all magazines. Satellite transmissions carried images of *Time* pages to printing plants in the United States, the Netherlands, and Hong Kong. *Time* had twenty-three bureaus abroad and ten at home, with ninety-six correspondents, and 450 staffers in New York. Time Inc. also produced a fluffy weekly started in 1974, *People,* and *Sports Illustrated,* both at the 2.5 million circulation level; a revived monthly edition of *Life* without its famed photojournalism impact, 1.5 million; and *Fortune,* successful as a fortnightly at 650,000 circulation. Time Inc. experimented with several new magazines in the late 1970s and early 1980s. Successful were *Money,* at 1 million copies; *Discover,* a newsmagazine of science, at 825,000; and *TV-Cable Week,* a 1983 entry into the field long dominated by *TV Guide,* which was killed after 5 months and a $47 million loss.

Newsweek, still *Time*'s major rival at 3 million copies weekly, called William Broyles, Jr. from editorships of *Texas Monthly* and *California* to stimulate its staff as editor-in-chief. Kenneth Auchincloss became managing editor, supervising eleven United States and sixteen foreign bureaus. *U.S. News,* at 2.1 million circulation, and *Business Week,* at 775,000, were other major news magazines. The monthly *World Press Review,* founded as *Atlas* in 1961, doubled its circulation between 1976 and 1982, reaching 150,000. Alfred Balk was editor and publisher for the owners, the Stanley Foundation. The world-renowned British weekly, the *Economist,* had 180,000 circulation and 77,500 subscribers to its United States edition. *Paris Match,* the world's leading photojournalism magazine, vainly attempted to resuscitate *Look* and served as a substitute for it and *Life.*

Among the quality and opinion magazines, the *New Yorker* remained a jewel of American journalism. William Shawn, successor to founder Harold Ross as editor in 1951, was contemplating retirement in 1983, when circulation stood at a half-million. *Esquire* had 650,000 readers but its quality declined after founder Arnold Gingrich sold out in 1976. The magazine passed first to Clay Felker and then to Phillip Moffitt. *New York,* coupled in ownership with *New West* and the *Village Voice* by Felker and then bought by Rupert Murdoch in 1977, also lost much of its sophisticated appeal, but retained 430,000 readers.

Smithsonian, strong in photojournalistic skills and travel appeal, sold 2 million copies monthly in 1983 with Don Moser as editor and Ralph Backlund as executive editor. The venerable *Atlantic,* generating front-page newspaper coverage for its startling public-affairs articles, had 365,000 readers. Its staff included William Whitsworth, editor; Louise Desaulniers, managing editor; and James Fallows and Seymour Hersh in Washington. *Harper's* gained a respite under the 18-month editorship of Michael Kinsley after barely escaping a closing in 1981. Kinsley took over the TRB column in the *New Republic* in late 1983 and former editor Lewis Lapham again filled the "Easy Chair" for Harper's. *Saturday Review* closed down in 1982, but was at least temporarily revived in March, 1983, by Jeffrey and Debra Gluck in Columbia, Missouri. They still had longtime editor Norman Cousins as a contributor.

New entries among the activist opinion journals were *Mother Jones* and the *Washington Monthly. Mother Jones,* a cooperative staff effort headed by executive editor Deidre English, appeared in 1976 in San Francisco and had a 220,000 monthly circulation by 1983. Starting in 1969 editor-in-chief Charles Peters put out the sprightly *Washington Monthly* as a keen commentary on the capital. New editor Victor Navasky had 50,000 readers for the *Nation,* compared to 100,000 each for the less radical *New Republic,* owned by Martin Perets, and William Buckley's conservative *National Review.* Erwin Knoll kept the *Progressive* contributing to liberal thought and criticism in Wisconsin. *Ms.,* leading feminist monthly, had half a million circulation under publisher Patricia Carbine.

Revivals were a fad. Nostalgia-type newsstand monthly editions of the *Saturday Evening Post* and the *Country Gentleman* were successfully marketed beginning in 1976 by Beurt and Cory SerVaas of Indianapolis, who also took over *Holiday* and *Jack and Jill* from the defunct Curtis Publishing Company. *Vanity Fair,* lavishly produced by Condé Nast for the reading rich, from 1914 until it succumbed to the Depression in 1936, reappeared in March, 1983, with great promotional fanfare by the Condé Nast magazine group but with mixed reviews.

Reader's Digest remained the largest circulating United States magazine, with 18.1 million copies sold at home and up to 10 million sold in international editions. *TV Guide* had 17 million sales in regional editions. The *National Geographic,* a family favorite, had difficulty producing enough copies as its circulation topped 10 million.*

In all, there were more than 9000 periodicals of all types, but only 600 were considered of general interest. The biggest subfields included specialized business and trade publications, 2500; religious magazines, 1300; and agricultural journals, 700.

In addition to Time Inc., major groups and their leading magazines were: McGraw-Hill (*Business Week* and thirty trade publications); Hearst Magazines (thirteen, including *Good Housekeeping, Redbook, Cosmopolitan, Popular Mechanics, Sports Afield*); Samuel Newhouse (eleven Condé Nast and Street & Smith magazines purchased in 1969, including *Vogue* and *Mademoiselle*); Meredith Publishing Company (*Better Homes and Gardens, Successful Farming*); Walter H. Annenberg's Triangle Publications (*TV Guide* and *Seventeen*), and CBS Publications (nine, including *Woman's Day, Mechanix Illustrated,* and *Field and Stream*).

CROSS-CHANNEL OWNERSHIP; MEDIA WEALTH AND INFLUENCE

The final threat to the diversity of communications ownership was the phenomenon of cross-channel ownership that became pronounced in the 1970s and continued in the 1980s. The Times Mirror Corporation, headed by Otis Chandler, was the only media conglomerate to be significantly involved in as many as five segments, with holdings in newspapers, magazines, broadcasting, cable, and book publishing.[18] The sprawling business giant published telephone directories, road maps and Bibles, owned two Oregon newsprint mills, and was deeply

*Leading circulations in 1983, in round numbers, were *Reader's Digest,* 18.1 million; *TV Guide,* 17 million; *National Geographic,* 10 million; *Better Homes and Gardens,* 8 million; *Woman's Day* and *Family Circle,* supermarket outlet magazines, 7 million; *McCall's,* 6 million; *Good Housekeeping, Ladies' Home Journal,* and *Playboy,* above 5 million; *Time, Penthouse,* and *Redbook,* 4.5 million; *Newsweek* and *Cosmopolitan,* 3 million; and *People, Sports Illustrated, U.S. News, Smithsonian, Glamour, Field and Stream,* and *Popular Science,* between 2.5 and 2 million.

involved in cable television. The Chandler family, owners of about 30 percent of Times Mirror and vast amounts of California real estate, had a net personal worth of from $600 million to $1 billion.

Among the richest of the media families was the Newhouse group that shared twenty-one daily papers, five magazines, more than thirty broadcast properties, and the Random House publishing firm. The magazines included *Vogue, Mademoiselle,* and *Glamour.* Family wealth was estimated at between $1 and $2 billion.

In the same range were the Cox and Hearst families. The Cox family, owners of the ninth largest newspaper chain, which included the *Atlanta Constitution* and *Journal,* also owned the fifth largest cable-television company and an oil refinery. The Hearsts, rapidly advancing in broadcast holdings, owned eight dailies, twenty magazines, including *Cosmopolitan* and *Good Housekeeping,* more than a dozen broadcast properties, two publishing houses, and many real-estate holdings.

The several dozen heirs of E. W. Scripps controlled the Scripps-Howard newspaper chain and 75 percent of Scripps-Howard Broadcasting, for a net worth of from $300 to $600 million. The McCormick-Patterson family, worth from $200 to $300 million, still controlled half of the *Chicago Tribune,* which in turn owned the *New York Daily News,* plus many broadcast holdings and several smaller newspapers.

The Sulzberger family of the *New York Times,* connected to that paper's many subsidiaries, including more than a dozen newspapers, three publishing houses, and several magazines and broadcast stations, was worth from $100 to $200 million. Katharine Graham and her family were in the same category; they owned the majority stock in the Washington Post Company, which included *Newsweek* and valuable broadcast outlets.

The list of wealthy media personalities, compiled by *Quill* in 1982, contained the names of fifty-one families worth at least $100 million.[19] In addition, from abroad came Lord Thomson of Fleet, whose worldwide publishing empire included about 180 newspapers, more than 100 magazines, and a group of broadcast holdings. Lord Thomson owned nearly sixty American enterprises. Rupert Murdoch, the Australian press lord, owned the *Times* of London, the *New York Post,* the *Village Voice,* the *Star, New York* magazine, the *San Antonio Express* and *News,* the *Boston Herald-American,* and a host of properties in Great Britain and Australia.

Among corporations, AT&T was the world's largest company, with an annual payroll of $21 billion. A court-ordered reorganization of AT&T was carried out after a 1982 antitrust suit brought by the Justice Department. AT&T's largest subsidiary had planned to enter the videotex business, aiming to win over the majority of transaction services, such as home banking and shopping, but AT&T was forbidden to enter the electronic publishing business because such an action would result in a conflict of interest.

At the same time, IBM, the world's largest computer manufacturer, was interested in direct-broadcast satellites, laser video discs, and personal computers. A consumer satellite service was being considered. Time Inc., the world's largest magazine publisher, was also the nation's most active cable-system operator. Home Box Office, the leader in the cable movie business, was a Time

Inc. enterprise. Sears Roebuck & Company, one of the nation's leading retailers, planned a coast-to-coast videotex system. ABC, CBS, and NBC were all intensively involved with pay cable, satellites, and other video enterprises, while at the same time earning massive profits through their news and sports divisions. All three (including RCA, owner of NBC) listed a number of subsidiaries, including magazines, book-publishing houses, recording agencies, and nonmedia firms. Warner Amex, the combination of Warner Communications and American Express, owned many of the major cable franchises and the Atari computer operations. The Gannett newspaper chain, headed by Allen H. Neuharth, owned eighty-seven newspapers, seven television stations, thirteen radio stations, and the nation's largest outdoor-advertising company.

Another measurement of personal and organizational power is the interlocking directorate. One study showed that most of the 290 directors of the twenty-five largest newspapers were tied to a number of institutions that their newspapers routinely covered. The directors were overwhelmingly white males (no blacks, fifteen women in 1979). Times Mirror Corp., for example, had more than two dozen "interlocks" with companies listed by *Fortune* magazine as being the nation's leaders. So did Dow Jones, publisher of the *Wall Street Journal,* Field Enterprises (*Chicago Sun-Times*), and the New York Times Company. The Ford Motor Company shared directors with corporations that published the *New York Times,* the *Washington Post,* and the *Los Angeles Times.*[20]

A handful of corporations in each of the communications fields controlled more than 50 percent of each industry. For example, twenty newspaper chains dominated newspaper sales, twenty corporations had the majority of magazine sales, another ten companies claimed half the commercial radio audience, and eleven book firms raked in more than half of total book sales. And, as stated, there were many cross-ownership relationships between these corporations.

INTERMEDIA ADVERTISING COMPETITION

As explained in Chapter 21, only radio made gains in advertising revenue during the 1930s.* During that decade of depression, recovery, and recession, expenditures on radio advertising rose from $40 million in 1929 to $225 million in 1941, the last peacetime year. Newspaper advertising revenue, peaking at $800 million in 1929, fell 45 percent by 1933 and was still down 20 percent in 1941, at $650 million. Magazine advertising revenue followed a similar pattern, being cut in half by 1933 from its $240 million 1929 high and recovering to $210 million by 1941. Then came the general advances in the economy of the war years and corresponding gains in advertising revenues.

The story of competition for advertising among the media after 1945—and of the rise of television—can be told in two statistical tables. Table 27-1 shows the total dollar costs of all advertising expenditures by both national and local advertisers, including advertising-related costs. The percentage figures make it clear that television's inroads were made most heavily against radio, and that magazines took the next heaviest percentage drop. Radio's rather steady dollar

*See pages 447–48.

Table 27-1 Dollar Volumes (in Millions) and Percentages of Total Advertising Expenditures Obtained by the Mass Media

YEAR	NEWSPAPERS		MAGAZINES		RADIO		TELEVISION	
	Dollars	*%*	*Dollars*	*%*	*Dollars*	*%*	*Dollars*	*%*
1945	920	32.0	360	12.5	420	14.6		
1950	2080	36.5	510	9.0	610	10.7	170	3.0
1955	3070	34.0	720	8.0	550	6.1	1010	11.2
1960	3700	31.0	940	7.9	690	5.8	1590	13.3
1965	4435	29.4	1200	7.9	890	5.9	2500	16.5
1970	5850	29.7	1320	6.7	1280	6.5	3660	18.6
1975	8440	29.9	1465	5.2	1980	7.0	5265	18.6
1980	15615	28.5	3225	5.9	3690	5.7	11330	20.7

Source: McCann-Erickson, Inc., estimates. The percentage for all other advertising expenditures was approximately 40 percent for each period.

volume in the 1950s, in contrast to the gains of other media, was due to its substantial cutting of advertising time rates (and parallel cutting of operating costs) and declines in national advertising.

Total advertising expenditures increased from $2.87 billion in 1945 to $54.75 billion, in 1980, according to McCann-Erickson, Inc., estimates. But total disposable income in the country was also increasing greatly, and the amount of advertising expenditures stayed at a range between 2 percent and 3 percent of disposable income. Thus the sizable dollar gains kept the mass media only roughly even in their financial race.

Table 27-2 shows the division among the major mass media of the national and local advertising revenues spent on them alone. In other words, the four major media together were allotted varying amounts of advertising expenditures each year by national and local advertisers. How were these total sums split among the contestants? Table 27-2 shows that television became dominant in this division of national advertising, cutting most sharply into radio but halving newspapers' share and reducing that of magazines (particular victims among the magazines were the large general ones appealing to mass audiences, rather than specialized ones).

The changes in divisions of local advertising were small, with television taking a relatively small amount from newspapers. The percentage of total newspaper advertising revenue coming from local advertisers increased from 70 percent to 85 percent between 1950 and 1980; the percentage of total radio advertising revenue coming from local sources jumped from 41 percent to 74 percent. Television decreased in percentage of local advertising during the same 30 years, from 27 percent to 26 percent, as its volume of national advertising revenue increased so dramatically. Radio thus joined newspapers as primarily a local advertising medium. Magazines have no advertising categorized as local, although by the 1970s they offered split-runs so that the advertisers could buy space in copies being distributed in restricted areas; perhaps 15 percent of advertising revenue is regional in origin.

Table 27-2 Division of Advertising Expenditures Allotted Only to the Mass Media (Percentages)

	NATIONAL ADVERTISING IN				LOCAL ADVERTISING IN		
Year	*Newspapers*	*Magazines*	*Radio*	*Television*	*Newspapers*	*Radio*	*Television*
1948	33.5	37.0	29.5		84.1	15.9	
1950	33.6	32.4	24.8	9.2	82.4	14.6	3.0
1952	28.8	31.5	18.9	20.8	80.6	13.6	5.8
1956	28.6	28.8	8.0	34.6	80.3	11.3	8.4
1960	25.0	28.0	7.9	39.1	80.2	12.0	7.8
1965	19.3	26.7	7.1	46.9	78.4	12.6	9.0
1970	18.1	23.0	7.2	51.7	75.6	13.6	10.8
1975	16.8	20.5	7.4	55.3	71.6	14.8	13.6
1980	15.7	21.7	6.3	56.3	69.9	14.5	15.6

Source: McCann-Erickson, Inc., estimates.

MINORITIES AND WOMEN IN THE MEDIA

Despite the governmental and public pressure of the late 1960s and early 1970s to increase the representation of minorities and women in the media, there was concern in the mid-1980s that far more needed to be done. For example, only 5.5 percent of the daily newspaper reporters and editors were nonwhite. Latinos made up 1 percent. Women fared much better, as 30 percent to 40 percent of newsroom staffs were female. But women held less than 8 percent of senior editing positions on dailies. Minority representation in broadcasting was better, because of federal pressure on the industry, but nevertheless many minorities and women ended up with lower-level positions. The exception got an on-the-air position or worked up to a decision-making job.

The same problems existed in the movie industry. Statistics of the Director's Guild of America showed that of 6220 members, slightly more than 10 percent were women and about 2 percent were black. Less than 2 percent of the Writer's Guild were black.

In broadcasting, while there were worries that major cable companies would ignore minorities, the Black Entertainment Television (BET) began programming in 1980, bringing shows to about 9 million homes. There were nearly 260 black radio stations and 120 Spanish-language radio stations. The Spanish International Network (SIN), largely owned by a Mexican television network, exported programs to be shown on Spanish television stations.

Significant breakthroughs in the print media occurred in 1983, when Robert Maynard became the first black owner of a major metropolitan newspaper, the *Oakland Tribune,* and Katherine Fanning was named editor of the *Christian Science Monitor.* As chronicled in earlier chapters, women had achieved major editorial posts: Mary Anne Dolan, editor of the *Los Angeles Herald Examiner;* Meg Greenfield, editorial page editor of the *Washington Post,* with Charlotte Saikowski in a similar position at the *Christian Science Monitor* and Jean Otto at

Denver's *Rocky Mountain News.* Two leading publisher-owner heads of newspaper groups were Katharine Graham of the Washington Post Company and Helen Copley of the Copley Newspapers in San Diego.

LANDMARK LEGAL CASES: A NEW "PUBLIC LAW OF LIBEL"

The historic law providing citizens recourse against defamation of character in the press always provided for fair comment on, and criticism of, those who were in the public eye when they became involved in the news. But in the 1960s the Supreme Court so clarified and extended the media's protections against libel that a new theory emerged, called the "public law of libel." Under this theory, public officials and public figures cannot recover for libel unless they can prove deliberate lying or extreme recklessness in publishing without ascertaining truth.[21]

The landmark case was *New York Times Co.* v. *Sullivan,* decided in 1964. In 1960 the *Times* had published an advertisement protesting police actions in Montgomery, Alabama, against followers of Rev. Martin Luther King, Jr. Sullivan, a police commissioner, sued for libel and was awarded $500,000 damages in a state court. Reversing the judgment, the Supreme Court held that errors contained in the advertisement were not malicious and that the First Amendment protects "uninhibited, robust and wide-open" debate of public issues without any test of truth.[22]

In 1967 the Supreme Court extended this theory to cover "public figures" as well as "public officials" but drew a line concerning recklessness in not following professional precautions in checking truth when time permits. The Court reversed a $500,000 judgment a right-wing spokesperson, General Edwin A. Walker, had obtained against the Associated Press, ruling that Walker was a public figure subject to criticism. But it upheld a $460,000 judgment given University of Georgia football coach Wallace Butts for a story in the *Saturday Evening Post* accusing Butts of throwing games. The court said handling of the story "involved highly unreasonable conduct constituting an extreme departure from the standards of investigation and reporting ordinarily adhered to by responsible publishers."[23]

In *Time Inc.* v. *Hill* in 1967, the Court restricted the theory of right of privacy in favor of the theory of public law of libel by ruling that newsworthy persons may not seek damages for invasion of privacy without proving deliberately false publication.[24] In a 1974 case the Supreme Court sustained an invasion of privacy judgment against an Ohio newspaper in which the plaintiffs had been placed in a "false light," but in 1975 the Court rejected an invasion of privacy suit against an Atlanta radio station that had broadcast, contrary to state law, the name of a rape victim who had been identified in open court.[25]

And in 1971, the Supreme Court, which had "buried the common law crime of seditious libel" in *Sullivan,* extended its "actual malice" requirement from public officials and public persons to include even private individuals who had been projected into the public-interest area. The case, *Rosenbloom* v. *Metromedia,* involved a broadcaster's references to a book dealer's "obscene" literature.[26]

By a five to four majority in 1974, however, the Court held in *Gertz* v. *Robert Welch, Inc.* that private citizens, even if involved in events of public interest, were entitled to recover damages without having to prove the *New York Times* malice test, but only if they could prove actual damages. The *Times* malice rule still applied to a plaintiff who sought punitive damages. The range of the public law of libel appeared to be lessening. The controlling case in 1983 was still Gertz.*

OBSCENITY AND CENSORSHIP

The Post Office Department, with its power to exclude publications from the mails under certain conditions, has at times also been a threat to freedom of the press. Over the years, court decisions and administrative actions, and during World War I the sweeping use of the postmaster's power to throw Socialist publications out of the mails built up a spirit of censorship in the Post Office. Matters came to a head in 1943 when the Postmaster General proposed to withdraw use of the second-class mailing rate from *Esquire* magazine. The second-class rate, it was contended, was a privilege the government could withdraw if the publication using it was not making a "special contribution to the public welfare." The Post Office thought *Esquire* was not worthy of the use of the second-class rate. The magazine's publishers, who were faced with paying a half-million dollars a year in additional postal charges, carried the case to the Supreme Court. There *Esquire* was upheld, and Justice Douglas commented, "But to withdraw the second-class rate from this publication today because its contents seemed to one official not good for the public would sanction withdrawal of the second-class rate tomorrow from another periodical whose social or economic views seemed harmful to another official."[27] The decision put the Post Office Department back into its normal role of excluding publications for reasons of obscenity.

It was not an easy task to determine what was obscene, however, and society's standards on that subject, as they affected newspapers, magazines, and films, changed dramatically in the 1960s and 1970s. This was particularly true in the areas of four-letter words and nudity. But the Supreme Court was slow to find clear-cut guides. A landmark case came in 1957 with *Roth* v. *United States.* Roth, who sold distasteful material, had been convicted under the federal obscenity statute. The court upheld his conviction but set a new standard for testing obscenity: "Whether to the average person, applying contemporary community standards, the dominant theme of the material taken as a whole appeals to prurient interest."[28] To this the court in later decisions added a test of "redeeming social importance"; if this were present, the law need not apply. Under this interpretation, *Fanny Hill* was cleared. But Ralph Ginzburg, publisher of *Eros,* was not. The court ruled that he had flaunted this test and had exploited erotic materials solely on prurient appeal.[29] How to define these terms remained a puzzle.

**Gertz* v. *Robert Welch, Inc.,* 418 U.S. 323 (1974). In 1976 the court, in *Time Inc.* v. *Firestone,* narrowed its definition of "public figures" to only those who have roles to play in the resolution of public issues, while giving a prominent socialite libel damages against *Time.*

A 5–4 majority of the Supreme Court revised the *Roth* standard in *Miller* v. *California,* a 1973 case.[30] The Court held that to be judged obscene the work must only lack "serious literary, artistic, political or scientific value" and added that the contemporary community standards against which the jury is to measure prurient appeal are to be the standards of the state or local community. This ruling, which left standards of taste to individual communities, posed serious problems for products distributed nationwide for audiences of diverse sophistication, and the courts were left grappling with the problem of how to define these terms. There was no significant change in the *Miller* ruling during the next decade.

PUBLIC ACCESS TO THE MEDIA

The concept of "fairness," involving the right of access to the broadcast media by persons or ideas, has already been discussed in Chapter 25. The theory of a public right of access to the print media was advanced by law professor Jerome A. Barron in a 1967 *Harvard Law Review* article that envisioned a two-dimensional First Amendment that not only forbade the inhibiting of expression by the government, but also, in some circumstances, mandated government affirmative action to provide for public access to the media.[31] Barron later saw the *Red Lion* decision as a media case, not just a broadcast case, and unsuccessfully tried to have a right of access rider attached to the Newspaper Preservation Act.[32]

Barron's concept was unanimously rejected by the Supreme Court in a constitutional test of a 1913 Florida law granting a political candidate the right to equal space by reply to criticism and attacks on his record by a newspaper. Chief Justice Burger ruled for the Court in the 1974 *Tornillo* case that mandatory access was unconstitutional:

> A responsible press is an undoubtedly desirable goal, but press responsibility is not mandated by the Constitution and like many other virtues it cannot be legislated.[33]

Although media spokespeople agree that efforts should be made to open more time and white space to individuals, minority groups, unpopular ideas, and simply nonconsensus thinking, they also quail at the idea of compulsory acceptance of everything offered a station, newspaper, or magazine.

ECONOMIC THREATS TO FREEDOM

Freedom of the press can, of course, be jeopardized by a newspaper publisher. This was found true by the Supreme Court in the case of the *Lorain Journal,* an Ohio daily. When a radio station was established in the nearby town of Elyria in 1948, the *Journal's* management refused to carry the advertising of any merchant who also bought time on the radio station. The radio station obtained an injunction against the newspaper, under the antitrust laws, that the *Journal* insisted was unconstitutional. But the Supreme Court held that the First Amendment was not intended to protect monopolistic practices that would destroy a competing medium and in a unanimous decision forced the *Journal* to recant.[34]

This was a clear-cut case involving the use of boycott to destroy a competitor. Less clear-cut was the government's subsequent contention that the selling of advertising in jointly owned morning and evening papers under a unit-rate plan also constituted an illegal action. A complaint brought by the *New Orleans Item* against the jointly owned *Times-Picayune* and *States* reached the Supreme Court in 1953. The court held, in a 5–4 decision, that the *Times-Picayune* and *States* were not violating the antitrust laws, but the decision was limited to the New Orleans situation alone.[35] The *Item* sold out to its rivals in 1958.

The government's next case was stronger. In 1955 it obtained a jury conviction of the *Kansas City Star* and its advertising manager on charges of monopolizing dissemination of news and advertising in the Kansas City area. The *Star,* together with its morning edition, the *Times,* and its broadcasting stations, WDAF and WDAF-TV, accounted for 85 percent of mass-media advertising income in the metropolitan area. The government charged that forced and tied-in sales of advertising and of newspaper subscriptions had brought about the death of the competing *Journal-Post* in 1942. The Supreme Court declined to review the case in 1957, and the *Star* agreed to end its combination sales and to sell the two stations, which in both instances had been pioneering efforts.[36] The *Wichita Eagle*'s advertising and circulation price policies for morning, evening, and Sunday editions were brought under regulation in a 1959 antitrust suit, but the action did not save the rival *Beacon* from being forced to sell out in 1960.

FREE PRESS, FAIR TRIAL

The weighing of the rights of a free press and its readers against the rights of an accused to a fair trial continued in the 1980s as a major problem. In this case, the courts clearly had their way, and in the end the press generally agreed that the placing of restrictions on reporters, photographers, and broadcasters was warranted—provided that they stemmed from cooperative agreements and not from judicial fiat.

Early action centered about the presence of photographers in the courtroom. The American Society of Newspaper Editors, the National Press Photographers Association, and the National Association of Broadcasters waged a battle through the 1950s to gain access to courtrooms for newspaper and television photographers. Their argument that the photographers need not be interrupting the trials had merit, for pictures could be made without noise or light. But lawyers said the publicity stemming from photographs served to frighten witnesses and accused persons, affected juries, and offended the judicial feeling. In 1959 the American Bar Association did agree to review its Canon 35 regulating such activity in the courtroom. But no action resulted and admission of cameras remained a local decision of a judge or a state decision.

Meanwhile other events vastly broadened the "free press, fair trial" debate. The assassination of President Kennedy and the haphazard conditions surrounding the killing of the accused by Jack Ruby in a press-filled area brought a plea for reform from the Warren Commission. When a Texas judge permitted television cameras into the trial of financier Billy Sol Estes, the Supreme Court reversed his conviction.[37] That 1965 decision was followed by one in 1966 ruling that Dr. Sam Sheppard had been deprived of a fair trial in Cleveland on a charge of murdering his wife because the trial judge failed to protect him from massive prejudicial "trial by newspaper" before and during his prosecution.[38]

The Reardon Report of the American Bar Association came out of the debate. Issued in October, 1966, by a ten-member committee of lawyers and judges headed by Justice Paul C. Reardon of Massachusetts, the report favored putting the responsibility on judges to curtail pretrial publicity generated either by the prosecution or the defense. The commission recommended withholding such information as the prior criminal record of the accused, existence of a confession, names of prospective witnesses, speculation on a possible plea, and interviews or photographs obtained without the consent of the accused. The American Bar Association adopted the Reardon Report in 1968, leaving the spelling out of specific provisions to negotiations with media representatives. By the fall of 1969 the press-bar committees of the Bar and the ASNE had found common ground for the imposition of the "fair-trial" provisions without endangering the "free press." The media, in major trials of the late 1960s and 1970s, resorted to using artists to make sketches of courtroom scenes for both print and television use, thus reverting to the late nineteenth-century practice of using artists' skills to catch the drama of an event.

Reporters were placed in the position of having to either face contempt charges or obey a judicial ruling, even if unconstitutional, after the ruling in a 1972 Louisiana case, *United States* v. *Dickenson.*[39] A judge ordered the press not to report a hearing held in open court, and two reporters who wrote stories despite the warning were then convicted of contempt. The Appeals Court said the order was unconstitutional, but upheld the conviction, saying the reporters should have obeyed the order and appealed it. The Supreme Court declined to review the case, letting the decision stand.

A Nebraska murder trial in 1976 brought another press-bar confrontation when the trial judge entered an order that, as modified by the state supreme court, restrained the news media from reporting (1) the existence of any confession or admissions made by the defendant to law-enforcement officers or third parties, except members of the press; (2) the substance of these confessions or statements; and (3) other facts "strongly implicative" of the defendant. The order, designed to follow *Sheppard* guidelines concerning pretrial publicity, expired when the jury was impaneled.

Chief Justice Burger, speaking for the Supreme Court, struck down this order, commenting that the media can report evidence presented at an open preliminary hearing and also that the prohibition on "implicative" information was "too vague and too broad" to survive scrutiny given restraints on First Amendment rights. The press victory was somewhat diluted, however, in that the Supreme Court denied a motion to expedite the appeal, which was not heard until it was moot. Also, the wording of the opinion did not preclude future "gag" orders.

"We need not rule out the possibility of showing the kind of threat to fair trial rights that would possess the requisite degree of certainty to justify restraint," Burger wrote, but "the barriers to prior restraint remain high and the presumption against its use remains intact."[40]

THE RIGHT TO KNOW

The battles for freedom to print and freedom to criticize, carried on in the courtrooms, were important ones. But just as important were the fights put up for the right to have access to the news—for the right to publish news is worthless if the sources of information have been dried up.

Freedom of information campaigns were carried on beginning in the late 1940s by the American Society of Newspaper Editors (ASNE), the Associated Press Managing Editors Association, the Radio-Television News Directors Association, and the Society of Professional Journalists, Sigma Delta Chi. Through their efforts, and those of others, by 1970 all but five states had some sort of laws requiring open public records and open meetings for conduct of public business. Leaders of the fight included James S. Pope, *Louisville Courier-Journal;* J. R. Wiggins, *Washington Post;* V. M. Newton, Jr., *Tampa Tribune;* and Harold L. Cross, ASNE legal counsel.

The creation of the House Subcommittee on Government Information in 1955, headed by Representative John E. Moss of California, brought a campaign against secrecy at the federal level. In 1958, aided by the news media groups, the Moss committee won revision of the 1789 "housekeeping statute" to stop its use in denying access to records. It also won some ground in opposing the claim of executive privilege by the president and his subordinates and reported success in ninety-five of 173 cases exposing undue federal censorship of information during 1958 to 1960. Controversy between the Kennedy administration and the press flared up during the Cuban crisis and gave impetus to an effort to adopt the Freedom of Information Act, which was passed and signed by President Johnson on July 4, 1966. It provided that after 1 year a citizen could go to court if a federal official arbitrarily withheld information of a public transaction other than in the areas specifically exempted under the law. There were nine such areas, including the all-important "national defense or foreign policy" one. Nevertheless, Representative Moss and others said a victory had been scored. The effect was as much to aid businesspeople seeking information in federal offices as to aid reporters.

In an effort to speed up the search process, the Freedom of Information Act was amended in 1974, requiring each federal agency to promulgate detailed regulations implementing the substance of the amendments and outlining information-request procedures, appeal procedures, and search and duplicating costs. The amendments sought to eliminate agency stalling by shortening the allowable response time by agencies, providing for judicial review of denial decisions, and authorizing fines for officials who arbitrarily refused to release information. The Reagan administration sought to exclude more agencies from the inquiry procedure and institute fee charges for searches, but legislation was stalled.

Another encouraging sign in the battle for the right to know was enactment by Congress of a Government in the Sunshine Law that took effect early in 1977. This law requires open meetings of more than fifty federal boards and agencies with two or more members. The Sunshine Law allows meetings to be closed for certain specified reasons but requires that the reasons for any closed meetings be certified by the chief legal officer or general counsel of the agency.

WORLDWIDE ADVERTISING

Total advertising volume in the United States stood at $57 billion as the 1980s opened, close to 2 percent of total consumer spending. The dollar volume was up with inflation; the percentage of the gross national product was down from the 3.5 level of the 1950s. An estimated million persons worked in the field. There were about 8000 advertising agencies. Four were billing clients more than $2 billion a year in 1982: Young & Rubicam, Ted Bates Worldwide, J. Walter Thompson, and Ogilvy & Mather International. Even so, they were exceeded in billings by a Japanese giant, Dentsu.

Next in size were McCann-Erickson Worldwide, part of the Interpublic, Inc. group formed in 1961; BBDO International, Leo Burnett, Saatchi & Saatchi Compton International, Doyle Dane Bernbach International, and Foote, Cone & Belding. The country's top five advertisers in 1981 were Procter & Gamble, $671 million; Sears, Roebuck, $544 million; and General Foods, Philip Morris, and General Motors, all above $400 million.

Overseas operations were increasingly important for both the advertising agencies and their clients. All the top-ten agencies were involved overseas. McCann-Erickson had seventy offices in forty-seven countries, J. Walter Thompson, sixty in twenty-five countries. With Saatchi & Saatchi Compton, they grossed half the take of the top-ten agencies abroad. For some major companies the international field was vital. IBM earned more than half its corporate income abroad in 1981, and Exxon, Coca-Cola Export, General Motors, and Monsanto were also heavily involved abroad.

The 1970s were marked by consolidations and the creation of new agencies. This brought intensive competition for accounts, as 20 percent of advertisers shift agencies in any given year; an average account stays with an agency 8 to 10 years. One of the new, aggressive New York agencies was Wells, Rich, Greene, founded in 1966 by Mary Wells. Her major client was Braniff, whose president she married to become Mary Wells Lawrence. When Braniff faltered, the agency switched to Continental. Similarly, Doyle Dane Bernbach switched from American Airlines to Pan Am, and Leo Burnett recouped losing Nestlé by getting McDonald's.

One trend in the field was comparative advertising, particularly on television. The Federal Trade Commission encouraged comparative ads, on the theory that consumers would be enlightened; as a result one-fourth of television commercials became comparative by the early 1980s. The public was witness to battles between pizza makers, Jeno's and Totino's; fast-food chains, McDonald's and Burger King; soft drinks, Pepsi and Coke; and video game makers, Atari and Intellivision. Sometimes these battles ended up in court. The rule was that you could disparage your competitor so long as you did not lie or mislead.

Another trend was corporate advertising. GTE and TRW aimed to make the public as conscious of their names as of IBM. Alcoa, Exxon, Ford, Pan Am, and Raytheon were other major corporate advertisers. The big agencies created subsidiaries to handle this special type of business. After the onslaughts of Ralph Nader and the consumer groups of the 1960s, the threats of regulation diminished under the Reagan administration policy of deregulation, which to some extent included the FTC.

In the 1980s Madison Avenue found a new way to approach the public: The Stanford Research Institute created VALS—Values and Life Styles—as a way to divide the total public into clumps, rather than by age groups or occupations. Young & Rubicam, using VALS, was conducting up to 100 consumer interviews lasting more than 7 hours each—one more way of making certain its $2.5 billion in client billings stayed number one in the field.

PUBLIC RELATIONS AS A PROFESSION

By 1980 there were an estimated 100,000 practitioners of public relations and its affiliated functions in the United States. Most of the 100,000 were specialists in some form of communications activity; some were generalists at the executive or managerial level. There were some 1500 public-relations counseling firms, and about one-third of large American companies retained an outside consultant, according to a comprehensive survey by *O'Dwyer's 1980 Directory of Corporate Communications.* Eighty percent of 2675 large companies and trade associations reported an identifiable public-relations activity under such organizatonal titles as public relations, corporate relations, public information, corporate communications, or external relations.

The two largest public-relations counseling agencies, with worldwide offices stretching from New York to Singapore, were Hill & Knowlton and Burson-Marsteller. Each had some 700 employees and more than $22 million in annual income. Next in order were Carl Byoir & Associates, Ruder & Finn, J. Walter Thompson PR, Infoplan International (Interpublic), and Harshe-Rotman & Druck. The public-relations arms of such groups as the American Medical Association, the AFL/CIO, and the National Association of Manufacturers were both large and controversial. Those of leading corporations were involved in both public-relations management decisions and operating functions using communications techniques.

The Public Relations Society of America (PRSA), founded in 1948, had some 9000 members. Fewer than 3000 had won professional accreditation since the group began a stiffly operated accrediting program in 1965. PRSA membership tended to be concentrated among the generalist professionals, while such groups as the International Association of Business Communicators flourished with memberships among publications editors and information specialists. The International Public Relations Association, founded in 1955, had members in fifty countries. There were perhaps two dozen specialized public-relations associations in such fields as finance, agriculture, education, and social work. Whatever the level of operation, those involved tended to strive for acceptable performance standards.

MOTION PICTURES HOLD THEIR PLACE

Buffeted by the competition of television and by the changing entertainment preferences of Americans, the movies sank to an all-time low of 17.7 million weekly attendance in 1970. But by 1975 the figure had rebounded to approximately 20 million and remained there in the early 1980s. Box-office receipts, which dipped below $1 billion in 1963, rose to $3.5 billion by 1983—due in good part, of course, to inflation and rising admission prices. There were still 14,000 movie outlets, 4000 of them drive-ins. Most of the studios had changed hands. MGM auctioned off its props, including Clark Gable's trenchcoat, Ben Hur's chariot, and Judy Garland's red shoes, before the lion stopped roaring in 1973. But at Academy Award time each spring, there was proof that "going to the movies" was still an American habit.

A "new American cinema" appeared in the late 1960s, an extension of the French "new wave." Its guiding light was the magazine *Film Culture,* produced by the Mekas brothers. Jonas Mekas made *The Brig* in 1964 and Kenneth Anger, *Scorpio Rising* in 1966. The high point was reached with Dennis Hopper's *Easy Rider,* a 1969 low-budget film ($370,000) that won widespread audience support. Hopper, Peter Fonda, Jack Nicholson, and Karen Black topped the cast, making a rebellious statement to their youthful audiences. This marked the emergence in the United States of the "auteur theory" of cinema which views the director as the primary creative force.

Warren Beatty and Faye Dunaway exhibited a taste for "violence for violence's sake" in their 1967 *Bonnie and Clyde.* Two films depicting the generation gap were Mike Nichols' *The Graduate* (1967), introducing Dustin Hoffman, and *Goodbye Columbus* (1969). Robert Altman's 1970 movie *M*A*S*H* ushered in a Korean War legacy for television. Francis Ford Coppola directed Marlon Brando in *The Godfather* (1972), the story of the Mafia. In comedy, Paul Newman and Robert Redford won acclaim for *The Sting* (1973) and Woody Allen and Diane Keaton for *Annie Hall* in 1977. Dustin Hoffman and Meryl Streep excelled in *Kramer vs. Kramer* (1979), which examined family relationships. Henry Fonda and Katharine Hepburn won honors along with Henry's daughter Jane in *On Golden Pond* in 1981, a sentimental story of old age with exceptional photography. Warren Beatty, epitomizing the auteur, wrote, directed, and acted in *Reds* in 1981, the story of John Reed and the American radical movement that was confounded by the 1917 Russian Revolution. The epic *Gandhi,* a 1982 effort at portraying an historical event, starred Ben Kingsley as the Mahatma.

On the basis of box–office draw, two fantasies of outer space led the list of American movies in 1983. Both had exceeded the $200 million mark. One was *Star Wars* (1977), the first of George Lucas' three dramatic action films about Luke Skywalker, R2-D2, and the worlds beyond. The other was a human-interest triumph—*E.T. The Extra Terrestrial* (1982)—about a little visitor from outer space and his little friends on Earth. Challenging them for box office supremacy, however, were Lucas' sequels, *The Empire Strikes Back* (1980) and *Return of the Jedi* (1983), rated as certain to surpass all others. High on the box–office champions list were such other special effects triumphs as *Jaws* (1975) and *Raiders of the Lost Ark* (1981).

BOOK PUBLISHING

The United States book-publishing industry, which had net sales exceeding $7 billion annually by the early 1980s, produced more than 1.8 billion books and

40,000 new titles each year from 1750 publishing houses. Trade books, fiction, and nonfiction sold to the reading public earned more than $1 billion in total sales, closely followed by the college-textbooks, public-school books, and professional-books segments of the industry. Mass-media paperbounds totaled $700 million in sales, book clubs and subscription reference books, $500 million each, religious books, $300 million, and the university presses, $75 million.

There were 12,000 book outlets of all kinds, of which half handled new trade books. More than a third of trade and paperback sales were made by two nationwide chains, B. Dalton Booksellers and Waldenbooks, which employed computerized inventory control and ordering systems. Such outlets made *Jane Fonda's Workout Book, What Every Woman Should Know About Men,* and collections of cartoons about Garfield the cat far better sellers than such distinguished biographies as Robert Caro's of Lyndon Johnson, *The Path to Power,* William Manchester's *American Caesar: Douglas MacArthur,* or Justin Kaplan's *Mr. Clemens and Mark Twain.* Bantam Books paid more than $3 million for reprint rights to a Judith Krantz novel, *Princess Daisy,* and Pocket Books paid nearly that much for John Irving's *Hotel New Hampshire* to an ailing Dutton (later sold).

The major publishing houses continued to merge, or change in ownership. Thomas Nelson, the nation's largest Bible publisher, bought the long-established Dodd, Mead and Company. William Morrow was sold to the Hearst Corporation, operator of Avon Books and Arbor House. CBS sold Fawcett Books to Random House and disposed of much of Popular Library. Harper & Row's employees reversed the trend, buying back controlling stock in their 165-year-old house from John Cowles, Jr., and the Minneapolis Star and Tribune Company. In another switch, RCA sold Random House to Newhouse Publications, which owned several dozen newspaper, magazine, and broadcast holdings.

LESSONS FOR THE AGE OF TECHNOLOGY

In this age of power and influence it was incumbent upon the men and women who worked in the rush of technological change not to forget that the freedom to speak and write the truth is never secure, never certain, always capable of being lost. In 1971 the United States government tried to deny its people the right to read a report prepared by their own government about a war in which they had fought and died. At the same time the President and his staff used illegal means to try to intimidate members of the news media and others who opposed his policies. Those crises passed, but others could occur.

Using the sophisticated electronic equipment made available to them, today's reporters and news managers can transmit the sights and sounds of an antinuclear demonstration to the entire nation, bring the funeral of an Anwar Sadat to the entire world, and help the public decide the pressing economic, military, and social issues of the times.

The rights of citizens are only as strong as their will to defend them and their willingness to defend those who bring them this news and opinion with no other interest than their own. From James Franklin the printer to Edward R. Murrow the broadcaster, men and women have so tried.

NOTES

1. See the April, 1981, issue of *presstime* for a description of the pioneering work with pagination.

2. The September 11, 1980, report of the American Newspaper Publishers Association, No. 80–6, said that 24.7 percent of dailies in the United States accounted for 57.8 percent of the daily circulation, or 36.9 million. There were 439 letterpress operations among dailies.

3. See Kenneth Edwards, "Delivering Information to the Home Electronically," in Michael Emery and Ted C. Smythe, *Readings in Mass Communication* (Dubuque: Wm. C. Brown, 1983). Edwards has written extensively on the subject.

4. Ralph Lee Smith, "The Birth of a Wired Nation," *Channels* (April/May 1982).

5. The rating services, Nielsen and Arbitron, varied widely on this. In July, 1982, Nielsen said that the figure was 34 percent and Arbitron, 26 percent. Nielsen's figure would mean that 27.9 million homes had cable. See *Broadcasting,* September 13, 1982.

6. *Broadcasting,* February 7, 1983, p. 31.

7. Stanley S. Hubbard, remarks before the House Subcommittee on Telecommunications, December 15, 1981; see also *Wall Street Journal,* September 22, 1981 for plans to create a new network.

8. *Channels,* December/January 1982, p. 36. See also Robert Lindsey, "Home Box Office Moves In on Hollywood," *New York Times Magazine,* June 12, 1983, p. 31.

9. *Time,* August 9, 1982; *Broadcasting,* September 20, 1982.

10. *New York Times,* February 11, 1983, p. 29.

11. *Broadcasting,* March 2, 1981, p. 35.

12. *Los Angeles Times,* November 8, 1982, p. 3.

13. *Broadcasting,* September 6, 1982, p. 57.

14. *Editor & Publisher,* August 14, 1982, p. 16.

15. *Broadcasting-Cablecasting Yearbook,* 1982.

16. *Broadcasting,* April 11, 1983, p. 38.

17. *Time,* April 11, 1983.

18. Diana Tillinghast, "The *Los Angeles Times,*" paper presented to Association for Education in Journalism, 1981 convention, p. 9.

19. *Quill,* December 1982, p. 7.

20. *Columbia Journalism Review* (November–December 1979), p. 51.

21. See Donald M. Gillmor and Jerome A. Barron, *Mass Communication Law: Cases and Comment* (St. Paul: West Publishing, 1969), 250 ff.

22. *New York Times Co.* v. *Sullivan,* 376 U.S. 245 (1964).

23. *Curtis Publishing Co.* v. *Butts* and *Associated Press* v. *Walker,* 388 U.S. 130 (1967).

24. *Time Inc.* v. *Hill,* 385 U.S. 374 (1967).

25. *Cantrell* v. *Forest City Publishing Co.,* 419 U.S. 245 (1974); *Cox Broadcasting Corp.* v. *Cohn,* 420 U.S. 469 (1975).

26. *Rosenbloom* v. *Metromedia,* 403 U.S. 29 (1971).

27. *Hannegan* v. *Esquire,* 327 U.S. 146 (1946).

28. *Roth* v. *United States,* 354 U.S. 476 (1957).

29. *Ginzburg* v. *United States,* 383 U.S. 463 (1966).

30. *Miller* v. *California,* 413 U.S. 15 (1973).

31. Jerome A. Barron, "Access to the Press—A New First Amendment Right," 80. *Harvard Law Review* 1641 (1967).

32. Jerome A. Barron, *Freedom of the Press for Whom? The Right of Access to Mass Media* (Bloomington: Indiana University Press, 1973). For the *Red Lion* case, see p. 421.

33. *Miami Herald Publishing Co.* v. *Tornillo,* 418 U.S. 241 (1974).

34. *Lorain Journal* v. *United States,* 342 U.S. 143 (1951).

35. *Times-Picayune Publishing Co.* v. *United States,* 345 U.S. 594 (1953).

36. *Kansas City Star Co.* v. *United States; Emil A. Sees* v. *United States* (8th Circuit) 240 Fed. 2d 643 (1957).

37. *Estes* v. *State of Texas,* 381 U.S. 532 (1965).

38. *Sheppard* v. *Maxwell,* 384 U.S. 333 (1966).

39. *United States* v. *Dickenson,* 46496 (5th Cir. 1972).

40. *Nebraska Press Association* v. *Stuart,* 427 U.S. 539 (1976).

ANNOTATED BIBLIOGRAPHY

Books: Media Surveys, Evaluations

AGEE, WARREN K., PHILLIP H. AULT, AND EDWIN EMERY, *Introduction to Mass Communications,* 7th ed. New York: Harper & Row, 1982. Current status of mass media, research.

BAGDIKIAN, BEN H., *Media Monopoly.* Boston: Beacon Press, 1983. Study of corporate influence on publishing, adverse effects of conglomerate ownership.

BARNOUW, ERIK, *The Sponsor: Notes on a Modern Potentate.* New York: Oxford University Press, 1978. Study mainly of indirect influences.

CLABES, JUDITH G., ed., *New Guardians of the Press.* Indianapolis: News & Feature Press, 1983. Profiles of new women editors.

COMPAINE, BENJAMIN M., *The Book Industry in Transition.* White Plains, N.Y.: Knowledge Industry Publications, 1978. Study of distribution and marketing.

———, *Future Directions of the Newspaper Industry: The 1980s and Beyond.* White Plains, N.Y.: Knowledge Industry Publications, 1977. See also Ernest C. Hynds, *American Newspapers in the 1980s.* New York: Hastings House, 1980.

CZITROM, DANIEL J., *Media and the American Mind: From Morse to McLuhan.* Chapel Hill: University of North Carolina Press, 1982. Describes impacts of the telegraph, motion pictures, radio and analyzes theories of audience responses.

EMERY, MICHAEL, AND TED CURTIS SMYTHE, eds., *Readings in Mass Communication: Concepts and Issues in the Mass Media,* 5th ed. Dubuque, Iowa: William C. Brown, 1983. Articles examining principal issues and changing media images.

FORNATELE, PETER, AND JOSHUA MILLS, *Radio in the Television Age.* Woodstock, N.Y.: Overlook Press, 1980. Descriptive account of how radio fared.

ROTZELL, KIM B., JAMES E. HAEFNER, AND CHARLES H. SANDAGE, *Advertising in Contemporary Society.* Columbus, Ohio: Grid, 1976. Excellent structural explanation of how consumer movements waxed and waned. See also John S. Wright and John E. Mertes, *Advertising's Role in Society* (St. Paul: Webb, 1976).

STERLING, CHRISTOPHER H., AND TIMOTHY R. HAIGHT, comp., *The Mass Media: Aspen Institute Guide to Communication Industry Trends.* New York: Praeger, 1978. Contemporary picture. See also William L. Rivers, et al., *The Aspen Handbook on the Media,* 1977–79 ed. (New York: Praeger, 1977). Selective guide to research, organizations, and publications in communications.

TAFT, WILLIAM A., *American Magazines for the 1980s.* New York: Hastings House, 1982. A state-of-the-art summary of the industry.

Books: Media Technology

BAGDIKIAN, BEN H., *The Information Machines.* New York: Harper & Row, 1971. A provocative book based on a RAND Corporation study dealing with news-communication methods for the next three decades; many data.

BALDWIN, THOMAS F., AND D. STEVENS MCVOY, *Cable Communication.* Englewood Cliffs, N.J.: Prentice-Hall, 1983. Broad introduction and survey of cable technology, services, public policy, organization and operations, and future.

BROOKS, JOHN, *Telephone: The First Hundred Years.* New York: Harper & Row, 1976. A popular history of AT&T.

CLARKE, ARTHUR C., *Voice Across the Sea.* New York: Harper & Row, 1974. From the Atlantic Cable to satellites.

DIZARD, WILSON, *The Coming Information Age.* New York: Longman, 1982. Overview of technology, economics, and politics.

NATIONAL ASSOCIATION OF BROADCASTING, *New Technologies Affecting Radio and Television Broadcasting.* Washington, D.C.: NAB Books, 1982. A readable summary.

SMITH, ANTHONY, *Goodbye Gutenberg: The Newspaper Revolution of the 1980s.* New York: Oxford University Press, 1980. A British media critic evaluates the effects of technological change on the appearance and role of the newspaper.

TYDEMAN, JOHN, et al., *Teletext and Videotex in the United States.* New York: McGraw-Hill, 1982. Excellent background information and outlook for the future.

WEAVER, DAVID, *Videotex Journalism: Teletext, Viewdata and the News.* Hillsdale, N.J.: Lawrence Erlbaum Associates, 1982. Emerging systems appear to be adjuncts of existing media.

WILLIAMS, CHRISTIAN, *Lead, Follow or Get Out of the Way: The Story of Ted Turner.* New York: Times Books, 1982. Informal analysis of Atlanta's cable king.

Books: Film

JOWETT, GARTH, *Film: The Democratic Art.* Boston: Little, Brown, 1976. Film's social impact, economic and political adjustments.

JOWETT, GARTH, AND JAMES M. LINTON, *Movies as Mass Communication.* Beverly Hills: Sage, 1980. Research-oriented discussion.

KAEL, PAULINE, *When The Lights Go Down.* New York: Holt, Rinehart & Winston, 1980. *Reeling.* Boston: Little, Brown, 1976. Reviews by the noted film critic.

LEES, DAVID, AND STAN BERKOWITZ, *The Movie Business.* New York: Vintage, 1981. Contemporary picture. See also Michael F. Mayer, *The Film Industry* (New York: Hastings House, 1978).

MCCREADIE, MARSHA, *Women in Film: The Critical Eye.* New York: Praeger, 1983. A discussion of the work of twelve major women film critics.

MONACO, JAMES, *American Film Now.* New York: Oxford University Press, 1980. Films of the 1970s.

Books: Media Law, Freedom of Information

BITTNER, JOHN R., *Broadcast Law and Regulation.* Englewood Cliffs, N.J.: Prentice-Hall, 1982. Leading book in its field.

BRUCKER, HERBERT, *Freedom of Information.* New York: Macmillan, 1949. Able defense of press by *Hartford Courant* editor.

CROSS. HAROLD L., *The People's Right to Know.* New York: Columbia University Press, 1953. Scholarly, detailed study of the problems of access to news.

DEVOL, KENNETH S., ed., *Mass Media and the Supreme Court: The Legacy of the Warren Years,* 3rd ed. New York: Hastings House, 1982. Fifty selected court cases; also interpretative articles and the editor's perceptive comments on trends.

GILLMOR, DONALD M., *Free Press and Fair Trial.* Washington, D.C.: Public Affairs Press, 1966. Scholarly survey and analysis of critical cases, best of the literature. See also John Lofton, *Justice and the Press* (Boston: Beacon Press, 1966).

GILLMOR, DONALD M., AND JEROME A. BARRON, *Mass Communication Law: Cases and Comments,* 4th ed. St. Paul, Minn: West, 1983. Comprehensive casebook, comments.

NELSON, HAROLD L., *Libel in News of Congressional Investigating Committees.* Minneapolis: University of Minnesota Press, 1961. Scholarly study of problems faced in reporting attacks on individuals.

NELSON, HAROLD L., AND DWIGHT L. TEETER, JR., *Law of Mass Communications: Freedom and Control of Print and Broadcast Media,* 4th ed. Mineola, N.Y.: Foundation Press, 1981. Casebook exploring trends in communications law.

PEMBER, DON R., *Mass Media Law,* 2nd ed. Dubuque, Iowa: Wm. C. Brown, 1981. Leading textbook synthesis in media-law area.

SCHMIDT, BENNO C., *Freedom of the Press Versus Public Access.* New York: Praeger, 1975. A comprehensive review of the background and constitutional implications of access.

WHALEN, CHARLES W., JR., *Your Right to Know.* New York: Random House, 1973. A congressional representative argues for shield law by examining cases.

WIGGINS, JAMES RUSSELL, *Freedom or Secrecy.* New York: Oxford University Press, 1964. A summation of access-to-news problems by an ASNE leader.

Periodicals and Monographs

AGEE, WARREN K., "Cross-Channel Ownership of Communication Media," *Journalism Quarterly,* XXVI (Fall 1949), 410. Summary of Master's thesis, 1949, University of Minnesota. First detailed study of the problem.

BLANCHARD, ROBERT O., "Present at the Creation: The Media and the Moss Committee," *Journalism Quarterly,* XLIX (Summer 1972), 271. Story of the information crusade. See also Blanchard, "A Watchdog in Decline," *Columbia Journalism Review,* V (Summer 1966), 17, and "The Freedom of Information Act—Disappointment and Hope," *Columbia Journalism Review,* VI (Fall 1967), 16.

BOTTOROFF, DANA, "Mary Anne Dolan: Woman Editor of the Year," *feed/back* (Spring 1982), 12. First nonowner woman editor of a major daily, the *Los Angeles Herald-Examiner.* See also Dennis Holder, "Mary Anne Dolan," *Washington Journalism Review* (June 1982), 19.

DEARMAN, MARION, AND JOHN HOWELLS, "Computer Technology and the Return of the Printer-Journalist," *Journalism History,* II (Winter 1975), 133. New technology's outcome.

DENNIS, EVERETTE E., "Purloined Information as Property: A New First Amendment Challenge," *Journalism Quarterly,* L (Autumn 1973), 456. Based on his Ph.D. thesis, University of Minnesota, 1974, which covers episodes in 1795, 1848, and 1970s.

DONAGHUE, PETER, "Reconsideration of Mandatory Public Access to the Print Media," 21 *St. Louis University Law Journal,* 91 (1977). Newspapers urged to adopt a voluntary code.

ENDRES, KATHLEEN L., "Capitol Hill Newswomen: A Descriptive Study," *Journalism Quarterly,* LIII (Spring 1976), 132. Background material and current research.

GERALD, J. EDWARD, "Press-Bar Relationships: Progress Since *Sheppard* and Reardon," *Journalism Quarterly,* XLVII (Summer 1970), 223. Outcome of free-press versus fair-trial debate summarized.

GILLMOR, DONALD M., "The Puzzle of Pornography," *Journalism Quarterly,* XLII (Summer 1965), 363. Traces court decisions in the area of obscenity including Roth. For *Ginzburg* case and aftermath, see Kenneth S. Devol, "The Ginzburg Decision: Reactions in California," *Journalism Quarterly,* XLV (Summer 1968), 271.

GORDON, A. DAVID, "Protection of News Sources: The History and Legal Status of the Newsman's Privilege," Ph.D. thesis, University of Wisconsin, 1971. Cases from 1848.

HALL, PETER, "Making Quirkiness Work," *Columbia Journalism Review* (March/April 1982), 51. *The Economist* reaches 70,000 U.S. circulation. See also reminiscence of retiring editor Alastair Burnet in *The Economist* (October 12–26, 1974), 15, "After 10 years."

HOLDER, DENNIS, et al., "Magazines in the 1980s," *Washington Journalism Review* (November 1981), 28. A decade of specialization.

HOWARD, HERBERT H., "Broadcast Station Group Ownership: A 20th Century Phenomenon," *Journalism History,* II (Autumn 1975), 68. Study of the top 100 markets.

———, "Cross-Media Ownership of Newspapers and TV Stations," *Journalism Quarterly,* LI (Winter 1974), 715. Legal status. See also "The Contemporary Status of Television Group Ownership," *Journalism Quarterly,* LIII (Autumn 1976), 399. Background and current data in the top 100 markets.

HUDSON, ROBERT V., "FoI Crusade in Perspective: Three Victories for the Press," *Journalism Quarterly,* L (Spring 1973), 118. Breakthrough in congressional action.

KOEHLER, MARY A., "Facsimile Newspapers: Foolishness or Foresight?," *Journalism Quarterly,* XLVI (Spring 1969), 29. History of a disappointment.

LINDSEY, ROBERT, "Home Box Office Moves In on Hollywood," *New York Times Magazine* (June 12, 1983), 31. Time Inc.'s bold move to dominate moviemaking documented by the *Times'* Los Angeles correspondent.

MCGLASHAN, ZENA BETH, "The Evolving Status of Newspaperwomen," Ph.D. thesis, University of Iowa, 1978. Historical base and case studies of five current women managers.

MINER, MICHAEL, "Maynard of Oakland," *The Quill* (May 1982), 9. Editor of *Oakland Tribune* and highest-ranking black journalist.

MORSE, R. C., "Videotex in America: The Birth of Electronic Newspapering," *Editor & Publisher* (June 26, 1982), 41. A special report. See also "Electronic Newspaper Found Unprofitable," *Editor & Publisher* (Aug. 28. 1982), 7.

PETRICK, MICHAEL J., "Inspection of Public Records in the States: The Law and the News Media," Ph.D. thesis, University of Wisconsin, 1970. Covers the period from 1824 to 1969.

PFAFF, DANIEL W., "The First Amendment and Symbolic Speech: Toward a Rationale of the Public Forum," Ph.D. thesis, University of Minnesota, 1972. Sit-ins, flag burnings.

———, "Race, Libel, and the Supreme Court," *Columbia Journalism Review,* VIII (Summer 1969), 23. Surveys Supreme Court decisions of 1960s in libel area that involved press freedom, points out connection to racial decisions.

"The 'Red Lion' Decision," *Journal of Broadcasting,* XIII (Fall 1969), 145. Text of Supreme Court decision on application of the fairness doctrine.

RUGGLES, ROBERT M., ed., *Newspaper Journalism . . . for Minorities.* Tallahassee, Florida: Department of Journalism, Florida A&M University, 1982. A thirty-six-page pamphlet. See also Jay T. Harris, "Minority Employment in Newspapers: A Statistical Analysis," *ASNE Bulletin* (April 1981).

SCHER, JACOB, "Access to Information: Recent Legal Problems," *Journalism Quarterly,* XXXVII (Winter 1960), 41. An authoritative summary for the 1950s by a Northwestern journalism professor who was special counsel for the Moss committee.

SMITH, EDWARD J., AND GILBERT L. FOWLER, JR., "The Status of Magazine Group Ownership," *Journalism Quarterly,* LVI (Autumn 1979), 572.

STERLING, CHRISTOPHER H., "Newspaper Ownership of Broadcast Stations, 1920–68," *Journalism Quarterly,* XLVI (Summer 1969), 227. Data and discussion of issues.

———, "Decade of Development: FM Radio in the 1960s," *Journalism Quarterly,* XLVIII (Summer 1971), 222. Analysis of reasons for rapid growth.

———, "Trends in Daily Newspaper and Broadcast Ownership, 1922–70," *Journalism Quarterly,* LII (Summer 1975), 247. More concentration.

STONECIPHER, HARRY, AND ROBERT TRAGER, "The Impact of Gertz on the Law of Libel," *Journalism Quarterly,* LIII (Winter 1976), 609. Case of *Gertz* v. *Robert Welch, Inc.*

WATKINS, JOHN J., "Newsgathering and the First Amendment," *Journalism Quarterly,* LIII (Autumn 1976), 406. Right of newsgathering not yet adequately dealt with in courts.

WHITESIDE, THOMAS, "Onward and Upward with the Arts: The Blockbuster Complex," *New Yorker* (September 29, October 6, October 13, 1980). Three-part series on the book-publishing business.

The Global Newspaper Edited in Paris Printed Simultaneously in Paris, London, Zurich, Hong Kong, Singapore and The Hague.

INTERNATIONAL Herald Tribune

Published With The New York Times and The Washington Post

No. 31,324 — PARIS, SATURDAY-SUNDAY, NOVEMBER 5-6, 1983 — ESTABLISHED 1887

Israel Sends Jets Against Syrians After 39 Die in Lebanon Attack

A crane removes rubble from a crater left by the explosion Friday at Israeli military headquarters in the southern Lebanese town of Tyre. At least 39 persons died in the attack.

Burma Says N. Korea Was Behind Blast

Nitze Plan Would Permit Each Side 300 Warheads in Europe, 600 Overall

INSIDE

200 Are Reported Killed In 2 Days of PLO Battles

Reagan Praises Troops Killed in Grenada, Beirut

Under heavy guard, Libyan diplomats and their families arrive at the airport at Point Salines, Grenada, to be taken to Mexico. U.S. aircraft also evacuated Russians, Cubans, East Germans, North Koreans and Bulgarians. Page 2.

Jobless Rate Fell in U.S. In October

In El Salvador, Guerrillas Have Taken Initiative Against a Weak Army, U.S. Advisers Say

The international press corps covered the world's wars and political debates. However, there was a firestorm of protest from all media when the Reagan administration denied reporters access to the invasion of Grenada—the first such censorship of American correspondents.

Index